D0100091

WITHDRAWN

ST/ESA/STAT/SER.S/36

Department of Economic and Social Affairs
Statistics Division

Département des affaires économiques et sociales
Division de statistique

Statistical Yearbook 2017 edition

Sixtieth issue

Annuaire statistique 2017 édition

Soixantième édition

United Nations | Nations Unies
New York, 2017

Department of Economic and Social Affairs

The Department of Economic and Social Affairs of the United Nations Secretariat is a vital interface between global policies in the economic, social and environmental spheres and national action. The Department works in three main interlinked areas: (i) it compiles, generates and analyses a wide range of economic, social and environmental data and information on which Member States of the United Nations draw to review common problems and to take stock of policy options; (ii) it facilitates the negotiations of Member States in many intergovernmental bodies on joint courses of action to address ongoing or emerging global challenges; and (iii) it advises interested Governments on the ways and means of translating policy frameworks developed in United Nations conferences and summits into programmes at the country level and, through technical assistance, helps build national capacities.

Note

The designations employed and the presentation of material in this publication do not imply the expression of any opinion whatsoever on the part of the Secretariat of the United Nations concerning the legal status of any country, territory, city or area; or of its authorities, or concerning the delimitation of its frontiers or boundaries.

In general, statistics contained in the present publication cover a period up to 2017 and as available to the United Nations Secretariat as of 31 July 2017. They reflect the country nomenclature currently in use.

The term "country" as used in the text of this publication also refers, as appropriate, to territories or areas.

The designations "developed" and "developing" which appear in some tables are intended for statistical convenience and do not necessarily express a judgement about the stage reached by a particular country or area in the development process.

Symbols of the United Nations documents are composed of capital letters combined with figures.

ST/ESA/STAT/SER.S/36

UNITED NATIONS PUBLICATION
Sales No. B.17.XVII.1.H

ISBN 978-92-1-061401-6
e-ISBN 978-92-1-362703-7
Print ISSN 0082-8459
Online ISSN 2412-1436

Département des affaires économiques et sociales

Le Département des affaires économiques et sociales du Secrétariat de l'Organisation des Nations Unies assure le lien essentiel entre les politiques adoptées au plan international dans les domaines économique, social et écologique et les mesures prises au plan national. Il mène ses activités dans trois grands domaines interdépendants : i) il compile, produit et analyse une grand variété de données et d'informations économiques, sociales et écologiques dont les États Membres de l'ONU tirent parti pour examiner les problèmes communs et faire le point sur les possibilités d'action; (ii) il facilite les négociations que les États Membres mènent dans un grand nombre d'organes intergouvernementaux sur les moyens d'action à employer conjointement pour faire face aux problèmes mondiaux existants ou naissants; et (iii) il aide les gouvernements intéressés à traduire les orientations politiques établies lors des conférences et sommets de l'ONU en programmes nationaux et contribue à renforcer les capacités des pays en leur apportant une assistance technique.

Note

Les appellations employées dans la présente publication et la présentation de données qui y figurent n'impliquent, de la part du Secrétariat de l'Organisation des Nations Unies, aucune prise de position quant au statut juridique des pays, territoires, villes ou zones, ou de leurs autorités, ni quant au tracé de leurs frontières ou limites.

En règle générale, les statistiques contenues dans la présente publication couvrent pour la période jusqu'en 2017 et sont celles dont disposait le Secrétariat de l'Organisation des Nations Unies au 31 juillet 2017. Elles reflètent donc la nomenclature de pays en vigueur à l'époque.

Le terme « pays », tel qu'il est utilisé dans la présente publication peut également désigner des territoires ou des zones.

Les appellations « développées » et « en développement » qui figurent dans certains tableaux sont employées à des fins exclusivement statistiques et n'expriment pas nécessairement un jugement quant au niveau de développement atteint par tel pays ou telle région.

Les cotes des documents de l'Organisation des Nations Unies se composent de lettres majuscules et de chiffres.

ST/ESA/STAT/SER.S/36

PUBLICATION DES NATIONS UNIES
Numéro de vente: B.17.XVII.1.H

ISBN 978-92-1-061401-6
e-ISBN 978-92-1-362703-7
Print ISSN 0082-8459
Online ISSN 2412-1436

Preface

The 2017 edition of the United Nations *Statistical Yearbook* is the sixtieth issue of the publication, prepared by the Statistics Division of the Department of Economic and Social Affairs. Ever since the compilation of data for the *Statistical Yearbook* series was initiated in 1948, it has consistently provided a wide range of internationally available statistics on social, economic and environmental conditions and activities at the national, regional and world levels.

The contents of the Yearbook continue to be under review and additional tables are expected to be introduced in future editions. Please send any comments or views to our email address, statistics@un.org. The tables include series covering an appropriate historical period, depending upon data availability and space constraints, for as many countries, territories and statistical areas of the world as available. The tables cover a period up to 2017, with some of the data being estimated.

The *Yearbook* tables are based on data which have been compiled by the Statistics Division mainly from official national and international sources as these are more authoritative and comprehensive, more generally available as time series and more comparable among countries than other sources. These sources include the United Nations Statistics Division in the fields of national accounts, industry, energy and international trade, the United Nations Statistics Division and the Population Division in the field of demographic statistics, and over 20 offices of the United Nations system and international organizations in other specialized fields. In some cases, official sources have been supplemented by other sources and estimates, where these have been subjected to professional scrutiny and debate and are consistent with other independent sources.

The United Nations agencies and other international, national and specialized organizations which furnished data are listed under "Source" at the end of each table. Acknowledgement is gratefully made for their generous and valuable cooperation in continually providing data.

After the first table, which presents key world aggregates and totals, the *Yearbook* is organized in three parts as follows; part one, relating to population and social topics; part two, relating to economic activity; and part three relating to energy, environment and infrastructure. The tables in the three parts are presented mainly by countries or areas, and world and regional aggregates are shown where available.

The four annexes contain information on country and area nomenclature (annex I), summary technical notes on statistical definitions, methods and sources for all tables of the *Yearbook* (annex II), the conversion coefficients and factors used in certain tables (annex III), and a list of those tables which were added, omitted or discontinued since the last issue of the *Yearbook* (annex IV).

The *Statistical Yearbook* is prepared by the Statistical Dissemination Section, Statistical Services Branch of the Statistics Division, Department of Economic and Social Affairs of the United Nations Secretariat. The programme manager is Matthias Reister and the chief editor is Ian Rutherford. They are assisted by David Carter, Anuradha Chimata, Mohamed Nabassoua, and Junping Bao. Bogdan Dragovic provided IT support.

Comments on the present *Yearbook* and its future evolution are welcome. They may be sent via e-mail to statistics@un.org or to the United Nations Statistics Division, Statistical Dissemination Section, New York, NY 10017, USA.

Préface

L'Annuaire statistique des Nations Unies 2017 est la cinquante-neuvième édition de cette publication, préparée par la Division de statistique du Département des affaires économiques et sociales. Depuis son instauration en 1948 comme outil de compilation des données statistiques internationales, l'*Annuaire statistique* s'efforce de constamment diffuser un large éventail de statistiques disponibles sur les activités et conditions économiques et sociales, aux niveaux national, régional et mondial.

Le contenu de l'Annuaire est actuellement en cours de révision et des tableaux seront inclus dans les prochaines éditions. Pour tout commentaire, veuillez envoyer un courriel à notre adresse électronique : statistics@un.org. Les tableaux présentent des séries qui couvrent une période historique appropriée, en fonction de la disponibilité des données et des contraintes d'espace, pour autant de pays, territoires et zones statistiques du monde comme disponibles. Les tableaux couvrent généralement la période allant jusqu'en 2017.

Les tableaux de l'*Annuaire* sont construits essentiellement à partir des données compilées par la Division de statistique et provenant de sources officielles, nationales et internationales; c'est en effet la meilleure source si l'on veut des données fiables, complètes et comparables, et si l'on a besoin de séries chronologiques. Ces sources sont: la Division de statistique du Secrétariat de l'Organisation des Nations Unies pour ce qui concerne la comptabilité nationale, l'industrie, l'énergie et le commerce extérieur, la Division de statistique et la Division de la population du Secrétariat de l'Organisation des Nations Unies pour les statistiques démographiques; et plus de 20 bureaux du système des Nations Unies et d'organisations internationales pour les autres domaines spécialisés. Dans quelques cas, les données officielles sont complétées par des informations et des estimations provenant d'autres sources qui ont été examinées par des spécialistes et confirmées par des sources indépendantes.

Les institutions spécialisées des Nations Unies et les autres organisations internationales, nationales et spécialisées qui ont fourni des données sont énumérées dans la "Source" sur chaque tableau. Les auteurs de l'*Annuaire statistique* les remercient de leur précieuse et généreuse collaboration.

Après le premier tableau qui fournit les principaux agrégats et totaux au niveau mondial, l'*Annuaire* est groupés en trois parties. La première partie est consacrée à la population et aux questions sociales, la deuxième est consacrée à l'activité économique, et la dernière est consacrée à l'énergie, environnement et infrastructures. Dans ces trois parties, les tableaux sont généralement présentés par pays ou régions, mais les agrégats mondiaux ou régionaux sont indiqués si disponibles.

Les quatre annexes donnent des renseignements sur la nomenclature des pays et des zones (annexe I), des notes récapitulatives sur les définitions, méthodes statistiques et techniques utilisées dans les sources de chaque tableau de *l'Annuaire* (annexe II), ainsi que sur les coefficients et facteurs de conversion employés dans les différents tableaux (annexe III), enfin une liste de nouveaux tableaux, de tableaux omis ou supprimés depuis la dernière édition est disponible (annexe IV).

L'Annuaire statistique est préparé par la Section de la diffusion statistique, Service des statistiques de services de la Division de statistique, Département des affaires économiques et sociales du Secrétariat de l'Organisation des Nations Unies. La responsable du programme est Matthias Reister, et le rédacteur en chef est Ian Rutherford. Ils sont secondés par David Carter, Anuradha Chimata, Mohamed Nabassoua et Junping Bao. Bogdan Dragovic est responsable du support en informatique.

Les observations sur la présente édition de l'*Annuaire* et les suggestions de modification pour l'avenir seront reçues avec intérêt. Elles peuvent être envoyées par message électronique à statistics@un.org, ou adressées à la Division de statistique des Nations Unies, Section de la diffusion statistique, New York, NY 10017 (États-Unis d'Amérique).

Explanatory notes

Symbols and conventions used in the tables

.	A point is used to indicate decimals.
-	A hyphen between years, for example, 2010-2015, indicates the full period involved, including the beginning and end
/	A slash indicates a financial year, school year or crop year, for example 2014/15.
...	Data are not available or not applicable.
*	Data are provisional, estimated or include a major revision.
#	Marked break in the time series.
~0	Not zero, but less than half of the unit employed.
-~0	Not zero, but negative and less than half of the unit employed.
&	Refers to a footnote shown at the end of the table which applies to the entire column
M/H	Males
F	Females

A space is used as a thousands separator, for example 1 000 is one thousand. Subtotals and percentages in the tables do not necessarily add to totals because of rounding.

Country notes and nomenclature

As a general rule, the data presented in the *Yearbook* relate to a given country or area as described in the complete list of countries and territories, see annex I.

References to statistical sources and methods in tables

For brevity the *Yearbook* omits specific information on the source or methodology for individual data points, and when a data point is estimated no distinction is made between whether the estimation was done by the international or national organization. See the technical notes to the tables in annex II for the primary source which may provide this information.

Units of measurement

The metric system of weights and measures has been employed throughout the *Yearbook*. For conversion coefficients and factors, see annex III.

Notes explicatives

Signes et conventions employés dans les tableaux

. Les décimales sont précédées d'un point.

- Un tiret entre des années, par exemple "2013-2014", indique que la période est embrassée dans sa totalité, y compris la première et la dernière année.

/ Une barre oblique renvoie à un exercice financier, à une année scolaire ou à une campagne agricole, par exemple

... Données non disponibles ou non applicables.

* Données provisoire, estimatif ou avec une révision majeure.

Discontinuité notable dans la série chronologique.

~0 Non nul mais inférieur à la moitié de l'unité employée

-~0 Non nul mais négatif et inférieur à la moitié de l'unité employée

& Fait référence à une note de bas de page présentée à la fin de la table qui s'applique à la colonne entière.

M/H Hommes

F Femmes

Le séparateur utilisé pour les milliers est l'espace : par exemple, 1 000 correspond à un millier. Les chiffres étant arrondis, les sous-totaux ou pourcentages ne correspondent pas toujours à la somme exacte des éléments figurant dans les tableaux.

Notes sur les pays et nomenclature

En règle générale, les données renvoient au pays ou zone en question que décrite dans la liste complète des pays et territoires figure à l'annexe I.

Références à des sources et des méthodes statistiques dans les tableaux

Par souci de brièveté, l'*Annuaire* omet les informations relatives aux sources et méthodologies employées pour les points de données individuels. De plus, quand un point de données est estimé aucune distinction n'est faite entre une estimation provenant d'une organisation internationale ou d'une organisation nationale. Voir les notes techniques relatives aux tableaux dans l'annexe II ou se trouvent les références aux différentes sources contentant ces informations.

Unités de mesure

Le système métrique de poids et mesures a été utilisé dans tout l'*Annuaire*. On trouvera à l'annexe III les coefficients et facteurs de conversion.

Contents

Note: See **Annex IV** for table names presented in previous issues of the *Statistical Yearbook* which are not contained in the present issue.

Table des matières

Voir Annexe IV pour les tableaux publiés dans les éditions précédentes de l'Annuaire statistique mais qui n'ont pas été repris dans la présente edition.

Introduction

The 2017 edition of the United Nations *Statistical Yearbook* is the sixtieth issue of this publication, prepared by the Statistics Division, Department of Economic and Social Affairs, of the United Nations Secretariat. The contents of the *Yearbook* continue to be under review. Please send any comments or views to our email address, statistics@un.org. The tables include series covering an appropriate historical period, depending upon data availability (as of 31 July 2017) and space constraints, for as many countries, territories and statistical areas of the world as available. The tables cover a period up to 2017, with some of the data being estimated.

Objective and content of the Statistical Yearbook

The main purpose of the *Statistical Yearbook* is to provide in a single volume a comprehensive compilation of internationally available statistics on social, economic and environmental conditions and activities, at world, regional and national levels, for an appropriate historical period.

Most of the statistics presented in the *Yearbook* are extracted from more detailed, specialized databases prepared by the Statistics Division and by many other international statistical services. Thus, while the specialized databases concentrate on monitoring topics and trends in particular social, economic and environmental fields, the *Statistical Yearbook* tables aim to provide data for a comprehensive, overall description of social, economic and environmental structures, conditions, changes and activities. The objective has been to collect, systematize, coordinate and present in a consistent way the most essential components of comparable statistical information which can give a broad picture of social, economic and environmental processes.

The content of the *Statistical Yearbook* is planned to serve a general readership. The *Yearbook* endeavours to provide information for various bodies of the United Nations system as well as for other international organizations, governments and non-governmental organizations, national statistical, economic and social policy bodies, scientific and educational institutions, libraries and the public. Data published in the *Statistical Yearbook* may also be of interest to companies and enterprises and to agencies engaged in market research. The *Statistical Yearbook* thus provides information on a wide range of social, economic and environmental issues which are of concern in the United Nations system and among the governments and peoples of the world. A particular value of the *Yearbook* is that it facilitates meaningful analysis of issues by systematizing and coordinating the data across many fields and shedding light on such interrelated issues as:

- General economic growth and related economic conditions;
- Gender equality;
- Population by sex and rate of increase, surface area and density;
- Unemployment, inflation and prices;
- Energy production and consumption;
- Expansion of trade;
- The financial situation of countries;
- Education;
- Improvement in general living conditions;
- Pollution and protection of the environment;
- Assistance provided to developing countries for social, economic and environmental development purposes.

Organization of the Yearbook

After the first table which presents key world aggregates and totals, the tables of the *Yearbook* are grouped into three parts as follows:

- Part One: Population and Social Statistics (chapters II-VI: tables 1-12);
- Part Two: Economic Activity (chapters VII-XI: tables 13-21);
- Part Three: Energy, environment and infrastructure (chapters XII-XVI: tables 22-33).

The first table provides a summary picture of development at the global level. More specific and detailed information for analysis concerning regions, individual countries or areas are presented in the three thematic parts.

Part One, Population and Social Statistics, comprises 11 tables which contain more detailed statistical series on population and migration, gender, education, health and crime.

Part Two, Economic Activity, comprises 9 tables on national accounts, finance, labour market, price and production indices and international merchandise trade.

Part Three, Energy, environment and infrastructure, comprises 12 tables on energy, environment, science and technology, international tourism and transport and development assistance.

Annexes and regional groupings of countries or areas

The annexes to the *Statistical Yearbook*, and the section "Explanatory notes" preceding the Introduction, provide additional essential information on the *Yearbook*'s contents and presentation of data.

Annex I provides information on countries or areas covered in the *Yearbook* tables and on their arrangement in geographical regions and economic or other groupings. The geographical groupings shown in the *Yearbook* are generally based on continental regions unless otherwise indicated. However, strict consistency in this regard is impossible. A wide range of classifications is used for different purposes in the various international agencies and other sources of statistics for the *Yearbook*. These classifications vary in response to administrative and analytical requirements.

Annex II provide brief descriptions of major statistical concepts, definitions and classifications required for interpretation and analysis of the data.

Annex III provides detailed information on conversion coefficients and factors used in various tables, and Annex IV provides a list of tables added, omitted and discontinued in the present edition of the *Yearbook*. Some Tables do not feature in this edition of the *Yearbook* due to space limitations or an insufficient amount of new data being available. Their titles nevertheless are still listed in this Annex since it is planned that they will be published in a later issue as new data are compiled by the collecting agency and where space permits.

Data comparability, quality and relevance

The major challenge continuously facing the *Statistical Yearbook* is to present series which are as comparable across countries as the available statistics permit. Considerable efforts have already been made among the international suppliers of data and by the staff of the *Statistical Yearbook* to ensure the compatibility of various series by aligning time periods, base years, prices chosen for valuation, and so on. This is indispensable in relating various bodies of data to each other and in facilitating analysis across different sectors. In general, the data presented reflect the methodological recommendations of the United Nations Statistical Commission issued in various United Nations publications, and of other international bodies concerned with statistics. The use of international recommendations promotes international comparability of the data and ensures a degree of compatibility regarding the underlying concepts, definitions and classifications relating to different series. However, much work remains to be done in this area and, for this reason, some tables serve only as a first source of data and require further adjustment before being used for more in-depth analytical studies. While on the whole, a significant degree of comparability has been achieved in international statistics, there will remain some limitations, for a variety of reasons.

One common cause of non-comparability of economic data is different valuations of statistical aggregates such as national income, wages and salaries, output of industries and so forth. Conversion of these and similar series originally expressed in national prices into a common currency, for example into United States dollars, through the use of exchange rates, is not always satisfactory owing to frequent wide fluctuations in market rates and differences between official rates and rates which would be indicated by unofficial markets or purchasing power parities. The use of different kinds of sources for obtaining data is another cause of incomparability. This is true, for example, in the case of employment and unemployment, where data are obtained from different sources, namely household and labour force sample surveys, establishment censuses or surveys, official estimates, social insurance statistics and employment office statistics, which are not fully comparable in many cases. Non-comparability of data may also result from differences in the institutional patterns of countries. Certain variations in social, economic and environmental organization and institutions may have an impact on the comparability of the data even if the underlying concepts and definitions are identical. These and other causes of non-comparability of the data are briefly explained in the technical note associated with each table (see Annex II).

A further set of challenges relate to timeliness, quality and relevance of the data contained in the *Yearbook*. Users generally demand the most up-to-date statistics. However, due to the different development stages of statistical capacity in different countries, data for the most recent years may only be available for a small number of countries. For a global print publication, therefore, a balance has to be struck between presenting the most updated information and satisfactory country coverage. Of course the United Nations Statistics Division's website offers greater flexibility in presenting continuously updated information and is therefore a useful complement to the annual print publication. Furthermore, as most of the information presented in this *Yearbook* is collected through specialized United Nations agencies and partners, the timeliness is continuously enhanced by improving the communication and data flow between countries and the specialized agencies on the one hand, and between the United Nations Statistics Division and the specialized agencies on the other. The development of new XML-based data transfer protocols will address this issue and is expected to make international data flows more efficient in the future.

Data quality at the international level is a function of the data quality at the national level. The United Nations Statistics Division in close cooperation with its partners among the UN agencies and the international statistical system continues to support countries' efforts to improve both the coverage and the quality of their data. Metadata, as for example reflected in the footnotes and technical notes of this publication, are an important service to the user to allow an informed assessment of the quality of the data. Given the wide variety of sources for the *Yearbook*, there is of course an equally wide variety of data formats and accompanying metadata. An important challenge for the United Nations Statistics Division and its partners for the future is to work further towards the standardization, or at least harmonization, of metadata.

A crucial challenge is to maintain the relevance of the series included in the *Yearbook*. As new policy concerns enter the developmental debate, the United Nations Statistics Division will need to introduce new series that describe concerns that have gained prominence as well as to prune data as they become outdated and continue to update the recurrent *Yearbook* series that still address those issues which are most pertinent. Often choosing the appropriate moment when the statistical information on new topics has matured sufficiently so as to be able to disseminate meaningful global data can be challenging. Furthermore, a balance has to continuously be found between the ever-increasing amount of information available for dissemination and the space limitations of the print version of the *Statistical Yearbook*. International comparability, data availability, data quality and relevance will remain the key criteria to guide the United Nations Statistics Division in its selection.

Needless to say, more can always be done to improve the *Statistical Yearbook*'s scope, coverage, design, metadata and timeliness. The *Yearbook* team continually strives to improve upon each of these aspects and to make its publication as responsive as possible to its users' needs and expectations, while at the same time focusing on a manageable body of data and metadata. Since data disseminated in digital form have clear advantages over those in print, as much of the *Yearbook* information as possible will continue to be included in the Statistics Division's online databases. Please feel welcome to provide feedback and suggestions to statistics@un.org.

Introduction

L'*Annuaire statistique* des Nations Unies 2017 est la cinquante-neuvième édition de cette publication, établi par la Division de statistique du Département des affaires économiques et sociales du Secrétariat de l'Organisation des Nations Unies. Le contenu de l'*Annuaire* est actuellement en cours de révision. Pour tout commentaire, veuillez envoyer un courriel à notre adresse électronique : statistics@un.org. Les tableaux présentent des séries qui couvrent une période historique appropriée, en fonction de la disponibilité des données (à la date du 31 juillet 2017) et des contraintes d'espace, pour autant de pays, territoires et zones statistiques du monde comme disponibles. Les tableaux couvrent généralement pour la période jusqu'à 2017.

Objectif et contenu de l'Annuaire statistique

Le principal objectif de *l'Annuaire statistique* est de fournir en un seul volume un inventaire complet de statistiques internationales concernant la situation et les activités sociales, économiques et environnementales aux niveaux mondial, régional et national, sur une période adéquate.

La plupart des données qui figurent dans l'*Annuaire statistique* proviennent de bases de données spécialisées davantage détaillées, préparées par la Division de statistique et par bien d'autres services statistiques internationaux. Tandis que les bases de données spécialisées se concentrent sur le suivi de domaines socioéconomiques et environnementaux particuliers, les données de l'*Annuaire* sont présentées de telle sorte qu'elles fournissent une description globale et exhaustive des structures, conditions, transformations et activités socioéconomiques et environnementaux. On a cherché à recueillir, systématiser, coordonner et présenter de manière cohérente les principales informations statistiques comparables, de manière à dresser un tableau général des processus socioéconomiques et environnementaux.

Le contenu de l'*Annuaire statistique* a été élaboré en vue d'un lectorat large. Les renseignements fournis devraient ainsi pouvoir être utilisés par les divers organismes du système des Nations Unies, mais aussi par d'autres organisations internationales, les gouvernements et les organisations non gouvernementales, les organismes nationaux de statistique et de politique économique et sociale, les institutions scientifiques et les établissements d'enseignement, les bibliothèques et les particuliers. Les données publiées dans l'*Annuaire* peuvent également intéresser les sociétés et entreprises, et les organismes spécialisés dans les études de marché. L'*Annuaire* présente des informations sur un large éventail de questions socioéconomiques et environnementales liées aux préoccupations actuelles du système des Nations Unies, des gouvernements et des peuples du monde entier. Une qualité particulière de l'*Annuaire* est de faciliter une analyse approfondie de ces questions en systématisant et en articulant les données d'un domaine/secteur à l'autre, et en apportant un éclairage sur des sujets interdépendants, tels que :

- La croissance économique générale, et les conditions économiques qui lui sont liées;
- La situation de femmes;
- La population, taux d'accroissement, superficie et densité;
- Le chômage, l'inflation et les prix;
- La production et la consommation d'énergie;
- L'expansion des échanges;
- La situation financière des pays;
- L'éducation;
- L'amélioration des conditions de vie;
- La pollution et la protection de l'environnement;
- L'assistance aux pays en développement à des fins socioéconomiques et environnementaux.

Présentation de l'Annuaire

Après le premier tableau qui fournit les principaux agrégats et totaux au niveau mondial, l'Annuaire est groupés en trois parties comme suit:

- Première partie: Statistiques démographiques et sociales (chapitres II à VI, tableaux 1 à 12)
- Deuxième partie: Activité économique (chapitres VII à XI, tableaux 13 à 21)
- Troisième partie: Energie, environnement et infrastructures (chapitres XII à XVI, tableaux 22 à 33)

Le premier tableau donne un aperçu du développement à l'échelon mondial, tandis que les trois autres parties contiennent des renseignements plus précis et détaillés qui se prêtent mieux à une analyse par régions, pays ou par zones. Chacune de ces trois parties est subdivisée en unités thématiques.

La première partie, intitulée "Population et statistiques sociales", comporte 11 tableaux où figurent des séries plus détaillées concernant la population et la migration, la situation des femmes, l'éducation, la santé et la criminalité.

La deuxième partie, intitulée "Activité économique", comporte 9 tableaux qui présentent des statistiques concernant les comptes nationaux, le finances, le marché du travail, les indices des prix et de la production, et au commence international des marchandises. Les tableaux traitant de certains produits de base associent autant que possible les données relatives à la consommation aux valeurs concernant la production.

La troisième partie, intitulée "Energie, environnement et infrastructures", comprend 12 tableaux relatifs à l'énergie, l'environnement, la science et technologie, au tourisme et transport internationaux et à l'aide au développement.

Annexes et groupements régionaux des pays et zones

Les annexes à l'*Annuaire statistique*, et la section intitulée "Notes explicatives" qui précède l'introduction, offrent d'importantes informations complémentaires quant à la teneur et à la présentation des données figurant dans le présent ouvrage.

L'annexe I donne des renseignements sur les pays ou zones couverts par les tableaux de l'*Annuaire* et sur leur regroupement en régions géographiques et groupements économiques ou autres. Sauf indication contraire, les groupements géographiques figurant dans l'*Annuaire* sont généralement fondés sur les régions continentales, mais une présentation absolument systématique est impossible à cet égard car les diverses institutions internationales et autres sources de statistiques employées pour la confection de l'*Annuaire* emploient, selon l'objet de l'exercice, des classifications fort différentes en réponse à diverses exigences d'ordre administratif ou analytique.

L'annexe II contient les notes techniques de chaque chapitre apportent une brève description des principales notions, définitions et classifications statistiques nécessaires pour interpréter et analyser les données.

L'annexe III fournit des renseignements sur les coefficients et facteurs de conversion employés dans les différents tableaux, et l'annexe IV contient la liste de tableaux qui ont été ajoutés omis ou supprimés dans la présente édition de l'*Annuaire*. Certains tableaux ne figurent pas dans cet *Annuaire* en raison du manque d'espace ou de données nouvelles. Comme ils seront repris dans une prochaine édition à mesure que des données nouvelles seront dépouillées par l'office statistique d'origine, ses titres figurent toujours dans la table des matières.

Comparabilité, qualité et pertinence des statistiques

Le défi majeur auquel l'*Annuaire Statistique* fait continuellement face est de présenter des séries aussi comparables entre les pays que la disponibilité des statistiques le permettent. Les sources internationales de données et les auteurs de l'*Annuaire* ont réalisé des efforts considérables pour faire en sorte que diverses séries soient compatibles, en harmonisant les périodes de référence, les années de base, les prix utilisés pour les évaluations, etc. Cette démarche est indispensable si l'on veut rapprocher divers ensembles de données, et faciliter l'analyse intersectorielle de l'économie. De façon générale, les données sont présentées selon les recommandations méthodologiques formulées par la Commission de statistique des Nations Unies, et par les autres entités internationales impliquées dans les statistiques. Le respect des recommandations internationales tend non seulement à promouvoir la comparabilité internationale des données, mais elle assure également une certaine comparabilité entre les concepts, les définitions et classifications utilisés. Mais comme il reste encore beaucoup à faire dans ce domaine, les données présentées dans certains tableaux n'ont qu'une valeur indicative, et nécessiteront des ajustements plus poussés avant de pouvoir servir à des analyses approfondies. Bien que l'on soit parvenu, dans l'ensemble, à un degré de comparabilité appréciable en matière de statistiques internationales, diverses raisons expliquent que subsistent encore de nombreuses limitations.

Une cause commune de non comparabilité des données économiques réside dans la diversité des méthodes d'évaluation employées pour comptabiliser des agrégats tels que le revenu national, les salaires et traitements, la production des différentes branches d'activité industrielle, etc. Il n'est pas toujours satisfaisant de ramener la valeur des séries de ce type—exprimée à l'origine en prix nationaux—à une monnaie commune (par exemple le dollar des États-Unis) car les taux de change du marché connaissent fréquemment de fortes fluctuations, et parce que les taux officiels ne coïncident pas avec ceux des marchés officieux ni avec les parités réelles de pouvoir d'achat. Le recours à des sources diverses pour la collecte des données est un autre facteur qui limite la comparabilité. C'est le cas, par exemple, des données d'emploi et de chômage, obtenues par des moyens aussi peu comparables que les sondages, le dépouillement des registres d'assurances sociales et les enquêtes auprès des entreprises. Dans certains cas, les données ne sont pas comparables en raison de différences entre les structures institutionnelles des pays. Des changements dans l'organisation et les institutions sociales, économiques et environnementales peuvent affecter la comparabilité des données, même si les concepts et définitions sont fondamentalement identiques. Ces causes, et d'autres, de non comparabilité des données sont brièvement expliquées dans les notes techniques associée à chaque tableau (voir annexe II).

Un autre ensemble de défis à relever concerne la fraîcheur, la qualité et la pertinence des données présentées dans l'*Annuaire*. Les utilisateurs exigent généralement des données les plus récentes possibles. Toutefois, selon le niveau de développement de la capacité statistique des pays, les données pour les dernières années peuvent n'être disponibles que pour un nombre limité de pays. Dans le cadre d'une publication mondiale, un équilibre doit être trouvé entre la présentation de l'information la plus récente et une couverture géographique satisfaisante. Bien entendu, le site Internet de la Division de statistique des Nations Unies offre une plus grande flexibilité, puisqu'il propose une information actualisée au fil de l'eau, et constitue ainsi un complément utile à la publication papier annuelle. Par ailleurs, étant donné que la plupart des informations présentées dans cet *Annuaire* sont collectées parmi les agences spécialisées des Nations Unies et autres partenaires, la fraîcheur des données est continuellement améliorée, grâce à une meilleure communication et un meilleur échange de données entre les pays et les agences spécialisées d'une part, et entre la Division de statistique des Nations Unies et les agences spécialisées d'autre part. Le développement de nouveaux protocoles de transfert de données basés sur le langage XML devrait contribuer à rendre, à l'avenir, les échanges de données internationales encore plus efficaces.

La qualité des données au niveau international est fonction de la qualité des données au niveau national. La Division de statistique des Nations Unies, en étroite collaboration avec ses partenaires dans les agences de l'ONU et dans le système statistique international, continue de soutenir les efforts des pays pour améliorer à la fois la couverture et la qualité de leurs données. Des métadonnées, comme l'illustrent les notes de bas de page et les notes techniques de cette publication, constituent un important service fourni à l'utilisateur pour lui permettre d'évaluer de manière avisée la qualité des données. Etant donné la grande variété des sources de l'*Annuaire*, il y a bien entendu une non moins grande variété de formats de données et de métadonnées associées. Un important défi que la Division de statistique des Nations Unies et ses partenaires doivent relever dans le futur est d'aboutir à la standardisation, ou au moins l'harmonisation, des métadonnées.

Le défi majeur reste la constance de la pertinence des séries présentées dans l'*Annuaire*. Au fur et à mesure que de nouvelles préoccupations politiques pénètrent le débat lié au développement, la Division de statistique des Nations Unies doit introduire dans l'*Annuaire* de nouvelles séries qui leur sont liées, et, ce faisant, effectuer une coupe sombre parmi les données qui lui semblent dépassées, tout en s'assurant de continuer à actualiser les séries récurrentes de qui paraissent encore pertinentes. Souvent, choisir le moment idoine auquel les données statistiques sur de nouveaux thèmes sont suffisamment matures pour qu'elles puissent, au niveau mondial, être diffusées sans hésitation, est un défi en soi. Par ailleurs, un équilibre doit continuellement être trouvé entre le volume toujours croissant d'informations disponibles à la diffusion, et les contraintes d'espace de la version papier de l'*Annuaire* statistique. La comparabilité internationale, la disponibilité, la qualité et la pertinence des données devront rester les principaux critères à considérer par la Division de statistique des Nations Unies dans sa sélection.

Inutile de dire qu'il est toujours possible d'améliorer l'*Annuaire* statistique en ce qui concerne son champ, sa couverture, sa conception générale, ses métadonnées et sa mise à jour. L'équipe en charge de l'*Annuaire* s'évertue en permanence à améliorer chacun de ces aspects, et de faire en sorte que cette publication réponde au plus près aux besoins et aux attentes de ses utilisateurs, sans toutefois oublier de mettre l'accent sur un corpus gérable de données et de métadonnées. Puisqu'il est avéré que les données diffusées de manière digitale ont des avantages comparés à celles diffusées sur papier, autant d'informations de l'*Annuaire* que possible continueront d'être inclues dans les bases de données électroniques de la Division de statistique. L'*Annuaire* statistique garde toujours une place de choix parmi les produits de la Division de statistique comme une ressource utile pour une compréhension général de la situation sociale, économique et environnementale globale. N'hésitez pas à nous faire part de vos commentaires et suggestions à statistics@un.org

World statistics: selected series

Population and social statistics, economic activity and energy, environment and infrastructure

Statistiques mondiales : séries principales

Population et statistiques sociales, activité économique et énergie, environnement et infrastructures

Series Séries	Unit or base Unité ou base	2005	2010	2013	2014	2015	2016	2017
Population and Migration • Population et migration								
Population [1]	million	6 542.2	6 958.2	7 213.4	7 298.5	7 383.0	7 467.0	7 550.3
Population density [1] Densité de population [1]	per km² pour km²	50.3	53.5	55.5	56.1	56.8	57.4	58.0
Population, male [1] Population, hommes [1]	million	3 296.1	3 508.2	3 638.0	3 681.2	3 724.1	3 766.7	3 808.9
Population, female [1] Population, femmes [1]	million	3 246.0	3 450.0	3 575.4	3 617.2	3 658.9	3 700.2	3 741.3
Sex ratio [1] Rapport des sexes [1]	males per 100 females hom. p. 100 fem.	101.5	101.7	101.8	101.8	101.8	101.8	101.8
Population age distribution, 0-14 [1] Répartition par âge de la population, 0-14 [1]	percentage of pop. pourcentage de la pop.	28.0	26.8	26.4	26.3	26.1	26.0	25.9
Population age distribution, 60+ [1] Répartition par âge de la population, 60+ [1]	percentage of pop. pourcentage de la pop.	10.3	11.1	11.8	12.0	12.3	12.5	12.7
Population rate of increase [2] Population taux d'accroissement [2]	percentage pourcentage	1.3	1.2	...	...	1.2	...	...
Maternal mortality Mortalité infantile	p. 100 000 live births p. 100 000 naiss. vivan.	288	246	...	...	216	...	...
Infant Mortality rate [2] Taux de mortalité infantile [2]	p. 1 000 live births p. 1 000 naiss. vivan.	49.1	41.3	...	...	35.0	...	...
Total fertility rate [2] Taux de fécondité [2]	live births per woman naiss. vivan. par femme	2.6	2.6	...	...	2.5	...	...
Life expectancy at birth [2] Espérance de vie à la naissance [2]	years année	67.2	69.1	...	...	70.8	...	...
Life expectancy at birth, male [2] Espérance de vie à la naissance, hommes [2]	years année	65.0	66.9	...	...	68.6	...	...
Life expectancy at birth, female [2] Espérance de vie à la naissance, femmes [2]	years année	69.5	71.3	...	...	73.1	...	...
International migrant stock: total Stock de migrants internationaux : total	thousand millier	191 269	221 714	...	...	243 700	...	...
International migrant stock: total Stock de migrants internationaux : total	percentage of pop. pourcentage de la pop.	2.9	3.2	...	...	3.3	...	...
International migrant stock: male Stock de migrants internationaux : hommes	percentage of pop. pourcentage de la pop.	3.0	3.3	...	...	3.4	...	...
International migrant stock : female Stock de migrants internationaux : fémmes	percentage of pop. pourcentage de la pop.	2.9	3.1	...	...	3.2	...	...
Refugees Réfugiés	thousand millier	...	...	...	...	15 098	...	...
Asylum seekers Demandeurs d'asile	thousand millier	...	...	...	...	2 344	...	...
Other of concern to UNHCR Autres personnes relevant de la comp. du HCR	thousand millier	...	...	...	...	40 518	...	...
Total population of concern to UNHCR Population totale de préoccupation pour le HCR	thousand millier	...	...	...	...	57 960	...	...
Gender • Le genre								
Seats held by women in national parliament Pro. de sièges occupés par les fem. au par. nat.	percentage of seats pourcentage du sièges	15.9	19.0	20.8	22.1	22.3	22.7	23.4
Girls to boys in primary education Filles/garçons dans l'enseigne. primaire	ratio rapport	0.95	0.97	0.99	0.99	1.00	...	...
Girls to boys in secondary education Filles/garçons dans l'enseigne. secondaire	ratio rapport	0.95	0.97	0.98	0.99	0.99	...	...
Girls to boys in tertiary education Filles/garçons dans l'enseigne. supérieur	ratio rapport	1.05	1.08	1.10	1.11	1.12	...	...

Series Séries	Unit or base Unité ou base	2005	2010	2013	2014	2015	2016	2017
Education • Enseignement								
Students enrolled in primary education Les étudiants inscrits dans l'enseignement primaire	thousand millier	679 010	697 179	718 801	715 619	724 094	...	...
Gross enrollment ratio - primary, male Taux brut de scolarisation - primaire, hommes	percentage pourcentage	104.6	106.6	106.0	104.4	104.5	...	...
Gross enrollment ratio - primary, female Taux brut de scolarisation - primaire, fémmes	percentage pourcentage	99.7	103.9	105.5	103.9	104.1	...	...
Students enrolled in secondary education Les étudiants inscrits dans l'enseignement second.	thousand millier	508 649	545 119	572 500	578 766	579 207	...	...
Gross enrollment ratio - secondary, male Taux brut de scolarisation - secondaire, hommes	percentage pourcentage	65.5	72.0	75.9	76.9	76.9	...	...
Gross enrollment ratio - secondary, female Taux brut de scolarisation – secondaire, fémmes	percentage pourcentage	62.0	69.5	74.8	76.0	76.0	...	...
Students enrolled in tertiary education Les étudiants inscrits dans l'enseigne. supérieur	thousand millier	139 271	181 425	198 962	210 730	212 670	...	...
Gross enrollment ratio - tertiary, male Taux brut de scolarisation - tertiaire, hommes	percentage pourcentage	23.7	28.3	31.2	33.2	33.8	...	...
Gross enrollment ratio – tertiary, female Taux brut de scolarisation – tertiaire, féminin	percentage pourcentage	24.8	30.4	34.5	36.9	37.7	...	...
Teaching staff at the primary level Personnel enseignant au niveau primaire	thousand millier	26 889	28 643	30 472	30 679	30 897	...	...
Teaching staff at the secondary level Personnel enseignant au niveau secondaire	thousand millier	28 438	32 220	32 353	32 862	33 066	...	...
Teaching staff at the tertiary level Personnel enseignant au niveau supérieur	thousand millier	9 192	11 133	12 167	12 648	12 795	...	...
Pupils to teachers in the primary level Élèves/enseignant dans l'enseigne. primaire	ratio rapport	25.3	24.4	23.6	23.4	23.4	...	...
Pupils to teachers ratio in the secondary level Élèves/enseignant dans l'enseigne. secondaire	ratio rapport	17.9	16.9	17.7	17.6	17.5	...	...
Crime • La criminalité								
Intentional homicide rate [3] Homicides volontaires [3]	per 100,000 population pour 100,000 pop.	...	...	...	...	5.3	...	...
National Accounts • Comptes nationaux								
GDP in current prices PIB aux prix courants	billion US $ milliard $ E.-U.	47 539	65 912	76 831	78 612	74 177	...	...
GDP per capita PIB par habitant	US $ $ E.-U.	7 293	9 514	10 700	10 822	10 095	...	...
GDP in constant 2005 prices PIB aux prix constants	billion US $ milliard $ E.-U.	47 539	53 113	57 109	58 560	60 092	...	...
GDP real rates of growth Taux de croissance	percentage pourcentage	3.6	4.1	2.3	2.5	2.6	...	...
Labour market • Marché du travail								
Labour force - total Force de travail - total	percentage of pop. pourcentage de la pop.	64.7	63.2	62.9	62.9	62.9	62.8	62.8
Labour force - male Force de travail - hommes	percentage of pop. pourcentage de la pop.	77.6	76.5	76.2	76.1	76.1	76.1	76.1
Labour force - female Force de travail - femmes	percentage of pop. pourcentage de la pop.	51.9	50.0	49.6	49.6	49.6	49.5	49.4
Unemployment rate - total Chômage - total	percent. of active pop. pour. de la pop. active	6.2	6.1	5.9	5.8	5.7	5.7	5.8
Unemployment rate - male Chômage - mâle	percent. of active pop. pour. de la pop. active	5.9	5.8	5.6	5.5	5.5	5.5	...
Unemployment rate - female Chômage - feminin	percent. of active pop. pour. de la pop. active	6.8	6.6	6.4	6.1	6.1	6.2	...

Labour market *(continued)* • Marché du travail *(suite)*

Series Séries	Unit or base Unité ou base	2005	2010	2013	2014	2015	2016	2017
Employment in agriculture - total L'emploi dans agriculture - total	percent. of employees pourcent. des employ.	36.0	32.4	30.5	29.8	29.5	29.1	28.8
Employment in agriculture - male L'emploi dans agriculture - hommes	percent. of employees pourcent. des employ.	34.2	31.2	29.3	28.7	29.4	28.0	27.6
Employment in agriculture - female L'emploi dans agriculture - femmes	percent. of employees pourcent. des employ.	38.6	34.2	32.2	31.5	31.2	30.8	30.5
Employment in industry - total L'emploi dans industrie - total	percent. of employees pourcent. des employ.	20.5	21.3	21.5	21.6	21.5	21.5	21.5
Employment in industry - male L'emploi dans industrie - hommes	percent. of employees pourcent. des employ.	24.5	25.9	26.4	26.6	26.6	26.6	26.6
Employment in industry - female L'emploi in industrie - femmes	percent. of employees pourcent. des employ.	14.6	14.3	13.9	13.8	13.7	13.7	13.6
Employment in services - total L'emploi dans services - total	percent. of employees pourcent. des employ.	43.5	46.3	48.0	48.6	48.9	49.4	49.7
Employment in services - male L'emploi dans services - hommes	percent. of employees pourcent. des employ.	41.3	42.9	44.2	44.7	45.0	45.4	45.7
Employment in services - female L'emploi dans services - femmes	percent. of employees pourcent. des employ.	46.7	51.6	53.9	54.7	55.1	55.5	55.9

Price and production indices • Indices de la production

Series Séries	Unit or base Unité ou base	2005	2010	2013	2014	2015	2016	2017
Agriculture (gross) Agriculture (brut)	2004-2006 = 100	100.0	112.9	122.4	123.9	...	...	...
Food (gross) Ailmentaires (brut)	2004-2006 = 100	100.0	113.3	122.9	124.3	...	...	...

International merchandise trade • Commerce international des marchandises

Series Séries	Unit or base Unité ou base	2005	2010	2013	2014	2015	2016	2017
Exports FOB Exportations FOB	billion US $ milliard $ E.-U.	10 373	15 098	18 820	18 812	16 471	15 840	...
Imports CIF Importations CIF	billion US $ milliard $ E.-U.	10 576	15 295	18 746	18 727	16 499	15 932	...
Balance Balance	billion US $ milliard $ E.-U.	-204	-161	73	85	-28	-92	...

Energy • Ènergie

Series Séries	Unit or base Unité ou base	2005	2010	2013	2014	2015	2016	2017
Primary energy production Production d'énergie primaire	petajoules pétajoules	476 824	530 011	560 493	567 417	...	...	...
Net imports Importations nettes	petajoules pétajoules	-14 076	-13 179	-18 269	-16 753	...	...	...
Changes in stocks Variations des stocks	petajoules pétajoules	-302	-2	454	3 131	...	...	...
Total supply Approvisionnement total	petajoules pétajoules	463 050	516 833	541 770	547 533	...	...	...
Supply per capita Approvisionnement par habitant	gigajoules	71	75	75	75	...	...	...

Environment • Environnement

Series Séries	Unit or base Unité ou base	2005	2010	2013	2014	2015	2016	2017
Land area Terres superficie	1,000 hectares	13 011 699	13 009 625	13 009 153	13 009 010			
Arable land Terres arables	000 hectares	1 405 845	1 388 256	1 409 128	1 417 153	...	...	...
Arable land Terres arables	percentage of land pourcent. de la superf.	10.8	10.7	10.8	10.9	...	...	...
Forest cover Superficie forestière	1,000 hectares	4 032 743	4 015 673	4 005 749	4 002 442	...	...	...

Environment *(continued)* • Environnement *(suite)*

Series Séries	Unit or base Unité ou base	2005	2010	2013	2014	2015	2016	2017
Forest cover Superficie forestière	percentage of land pourcent. de la superf.	31.0	30.9	30.8	30.8	...	...	...
Permanent crops Cultures permanentes	1,000 hectares	148 372	159 210	164 644	164 650	...	...	...
Permanent crops Cultures permanentes	percentage of land pourcent. de la superf.	1.1	1.2	1.3	1.3	...	...	...
Sites protected for terrestrial biodiversity Sites pour la bio. terre. dans aires protég	percentage of sites pourcentage du sites	40.7	44.8	46.3	46.5	46.6	46.6	46.6
Emissions Émissions	million metric tons million de tonnes	29 490	33 472	35 838	36 138	...	...	...
Emissions per capita Émissions par habitant	metric ton tonne	4.5	4.8	5.0	5.0	...	...	...
Safely managed drinking water sources, total Ser. d'alimen. en eau potable gérés en toute séc.	percentage of pop. pourcentage de la pop.	66.1	70.8	71.1	71.1	71.2	...	...
Safely managed drinking water sources, rural Ser. d'alimen. en eau potable gérés en toute séc.	percentage of pop. pourcentage de la pop.	48.0	55.5	55.2	55	54.8	...	...
Safely managed drinking water sources, urban Ser. d'alimen. en eau potable gérés en toute séc.	percentage of pop. pourcentage de la pop.	84.9	85.2	85.2	85.2	85.1	...	...
Safely managed sanitation facilities, total Services d'assainissement gérés en toute	percentage of pop. pourcentage de la pop.	31.3	35.5	37.8	38.5	39.3	...	...
Safely managed sanitation facilities, rural Services d'assainissement gérés en toute	percentage of pop. pourcentage de la pop.	27.5	31.2	33.2	33.9	34.6	...	...
Safely managed sanitation facilities, urban Services d'assainissement gérés en toute	percentage of pop. pourcentage de la pop.	35.3	39.5	41.8	42.5	43.2	...	...

Science and technology • Science et technologie

Series Séries	Unit or base Unité ou base	2005	2010	2013	2014	2015	2016	2017
Grant of patents Brevets délivrés	per million population par million d'habitants	633 900	915 700	1 175 400	1 179 800	1 241 100	...	...
Gross domestic expenditure on R & D Dépenses intérieures brutes de R-D	percentage of GDP pourcentage du PIB	1.5	1.6	1.7	1.7	...	...	...

Development assistance • Aide au developpement

Series Séries	Unit or base Unité ou base	2005	2010	2013	2014	2015	2016	2017
Net ODA received: bilateral APD nette reçue : bilatérale	million US $ million $ E.-U.	82 923	94 401	111 431	119 754	117 235	...	...
Net ODA received: multilateral APD nette reçue : multilatérale	million US $ million $ E.-U.	25 620	37 133	39 735	41 952	35 368	...	...
Net ODA received: total APD nette reçue : total	million US $ million $ E.-U.	108 542	131 534	151 165	161 705	152 603	...	...
Net ODA received: total APD nette reçue : total	% of recipients' GNI % du RNB des bénéfic.	1.2	0.7	0.6	0.6	0.7	...	...

Source:
These data are presented in other tables of this Yearbook; please refer to the relevant table for source notes and last access data.

Source:
Ces données sont présentées dans d'autres tableaux du présent Annuaire, veuillez donc vous reporter au tableau correspondant pour les notes de source et la date du dernier accès.

1 Mid-year estimates and projections (medium fertility variant).

2 Data refers to a 5-year period preceding the reference year.

3 Data is for 2015, or latest available data from 2010 onwards.

1 Les estimations et projections approximative (variante moyenne fécondité) au milieu de l'année.

2 Les données se réfèrent a période de 5 ans précédant l'année de référence.

3 Données pour 2015, ou dernières données disponibles à partir de 2010.

Part One

Population and social statistics

Chapter II	Population and migration (tables 2 - 4)
Chapter III	Gender (table 5 and 6)
Chapter IV	Education (tables 7 - 9)
Chapter V	Health (tables 10 and 11)
Chapter VI	Crime (table 12)

Première partie

Population et statistiques sociales

Chapitre II	Population et migration (tableaux 2 - 4)
Chapitre III	La situation des femmes (tableau 5 et 6)
Chapitre IV	Éducation (tableaux 7 - 9)
Chapitre V	Santé (tableaux 10 et 11)
Chapitre VI	Criminalité (tableau 12)

2 Population, surface area and density

Population, superficie et densité

Country or area Pays ou zone	Year Année	Mid-year population estimates and projections (millions) Estimations et projections de population au milieu de l'année (millions) Total	 Male Hommes	 Females Femmes	Sex Ratio (males per 100 females) Rapport des sexes (hommes pour 100 femmes)	Population age distribution (percentage) Répartition par âge de la population (pourcentage) Aged 0 to 14 years old âgée de 0 à 14 ans	 Aged 60+ years old âgée de 60 ans ou plus	Population density (per km²) Densité de population (pour km²)	Surface area Superficie (000 km²)
Total, all countries or areas	**2005**	**6 542.16**	**3 296.12**	**3 246.04**	**101.5**	**28.0**	**10.3**	**50.3**	**...**
Total, tous pays ou zones	**2010**	**6 958.17**	**3 508.24**	**3 449.93**	**101.7**	**26.8**	**11.1**	**53.5**	**...**
	2015	**7 383.01**	**3 724.13**	**3 658.88**	**101.8**	**26.1**	**12.3**	**56.8**	**136 162**
	2017[1]	**7 550.26**	**3 808.93**	**3 741.33**	**101.8**	**25.9**	**12.7**	**58.0**	**...**
Africa	2005	924.76	460.95	463.80	99.4	41.8	5.2	31.2	...
Afrique	2010	1 049.45	523.31	526.14	99.5	41.4	5.2	35.4	...
	2015	1 194.37	596.26	598.11	99.7	41.0	5.4	40.3	30 311
	2017[1]	1 256.27	627.39	628.88	99.8	40.8	5.5	42.4	...
Northern Africa	2005	187.83	94.37	93.47	101.0	33.3	7.0	24.2	...
Afrique septentrionale	2010	204.31	102.50	101.81	100.7	31.9	7.4	26.3	...
	2015	225.14	113.06	112.07	100.9	32.3	8.0	29.0	7 880
	2017[1]	233.60	117.35	116.25	100.9	32.5	8.3	30.1	...
Sub-Saharan Africa	2005	736.93	366.59	370.34	99.0	44.0	4.7	33.7	...
Afrique subsaharienne	2010	845.14	420.80	424.33	99.2	43.7	4.7	38.6	...
	2015	969.23	483.19	486.04	99.4	43.1	4.8	44.3	22 431[2]
	2017[1]	1 022.66	510.04	512.62	99.5	42.7	4.8	46.7	...
Eastern Africa	2005	300.60	148.83	151.77	98.1	45.5	4.5	45.1	...
Afrique orientale	2010	346.99	171.95	175.04	98.2	44.8	4.5	52.0	...
	2015	399.46	198.12	201.33	98.4	43.4	4.6	59.9	7 005
	2017[1]	422.04	209.40	212.64	98.5	42.8	4.7	63.3	...
Middle Africa	2005	111.95	55.56	56.39	98.5	45.6	4.6	17.2	...
Afrique centrale	2010	131.35	65.31	66.04	98.9	45.7	4.5	20.2	...
	2015	153.74	76.56	77.18	99.2	45.7	4.5	23.7	6 613
	2017[1]	163.49	81.46	82.04	99.3	45.5	4.6	25.2	...
Southern Africa	2005	55.76	27.34	28.42	96.2	32.6	6.6	21.0	...
Afrique australe	2010	59.02	28.95	30.07	96.3	31.2	7.0	22.3	...
	2015	63.42	31.11	32.31	96.3	30.1	7.8	23.9	2 675
	2017[1]	65.14	31.95	33.20	96.2	29.8	8.1	24.6	...
Western Africa	2005	268.61	134.86[3]	133.75[3]	100.8[3]	44.0[3]	4.6[3]	44.3	...
Afrique occidentale	2010	307.78	154.59[3]	153.19[3]	100.9[3]	44.1[3]	4.6[3]	50.8	...
	2015	352.61	177.39[3]	175.22[3]	101.2[3]	43.9[3]	4.5[3]	58.1	6 138
	2017[1]	371.99	187.24[3]	184.75[3]	101.3[3]	43.7[3]	4.6[3]	61.3	...
Americas [2]	2005	889.20	439.77	449.43	97.9	26.5	11.8	22.9	...
Amériques [2]	2010	940.50	465.09	475.41	97.8	24.8	13.0	24.2	...
	2015	988.38	488.80	499.58	97.8	23.2	14.6	25.5	42 322
	2017[1]	1 006.80	497.91	508.89	97.8	22.6	15.3	26.0	...
Northern America	2005	327.55	161.70[4]	165.84[4]	97.5[4]	20.6[4]	16.8[4]	17.6	...
Amérique septentrionale	2010	342.94	169.46[4]	173.47[4]	97.7[4]	19.8[4]	18.5[4]	18.4	...
	2015	356.00	176.16[4]	179.84[4]	98.0[4]	18.9[4]	20.7[4]	19.1	21 776
	2017[1]	361.21	178.83[4]	182.38[4]	98.1[4]	18.6[4]	21.7[4]	19.4	...
Latin America & the Caribbean	2005	561.66	278.07	283.59	98.1	29.9	8.8	27.9	...
Amérique latine et Caraïbes	2010	597.56	295.63	301.94	97.9	27.6	9.8	29.7	...
	2015	632.38	312.64	319.74	97.8	25.6	11.2	31.4	20 546
	2017[1]	645.59	319.09	326.51	97.7	24.9	11.8	32.1	...
Caribbean	2005	40.12	19.89[5]	20.23[5]	98.3[5]	28.2[5]	11.1[5]	177.5	...
Caraïbes	2010	41.72	20.67[5]	21.06[5]	98.1[5]	26.5[5]	12.0[5]	184.6	...
	2015	43.31	21.44[5]	21.87[5]	98.0[5]	25.0[5]	13.3[5]	191.6	234
	2017[1]	43.88	21.71[5]	22.17[5]	97.9[5]	24.5[5]	13.8[5]	194.2	...
Central America	2005	148.21	73.52	74.69	98.4	33.6	7.5	60.4	...
Amérique centrale	2010	160.56	79.67	80.89	98.5	31.0	8.2	65.5	...
	2015	172.64	85.68	86.95	98.5	28.6	9.3	70.4	2 480
	2017[1]	177.32	88.01	89.31	98.5	27.7	9.7	72.3	...
South America	2005	373.33	184.66[6]	188.66[6]	97.9[6]	28.6[6]	9.1[6]	21.4	...
Amérique du Sud	2010	395.28	195.29[6]	199.99[6]	97.6[6]	26.4[6]	10.2[6]	22.6	...
	2015	416.44	205.52[6]	210.91[6]	97.4[6]	24.4[6]	11.8[6]	23.8	17 832
	2017[1]	424.39	209.36[6]	215.03[6]	97.4[6]	23.7[6]	12.4[6]	24.3	...

Country or area Pays ou zone	Year Année	Mid-year population estimates and projections (millions) Estimations et projections de population au milieu de l'année (millions) Total	 Male Hommes	 Females Femmes	Sex Ratio (males per 100 females) Rapport des sexes (hommes pour 100 femmes)	Population age distribution (percentage) Répartition par âge de la population (pourcentage) Aged 0 to 14 years old âgée de 0 à 14 ans	 Aged 60+ years old âgée de 60 ans ou plus	Population density (per km²) Densité de population (pour km²)	Surface area Superficie (000 km²)
Asia Asie	2005	3 964.34	2 026.43	1 937.91	104.6	27.4	9.3	127.7	...
	2010	4 194.43	2 145.95	2 048.47	104.8	25.6	10.1	135.2	...
	2015	4 419.90	2 261.59	2 158.31	104.8	24.6	11.6	142.4	31 915
	2017[1]	4 504.43	2 304.73	2 199.70	104.8	24.2	12.2	145.1	...
Central Asia Asie centrale	2005	58.74	28.96	29.77	97.3	31.0	7.3	15.0	...
	2010	63.16	31.19	31.97	97.6	28.7	7.0	16.1	...
	2015	68.71	33.97	34.73	97.8	29.1	7.8	17.5	4 103[2]
	2017[1]	70.84	35.04	35.80	97.9	29.5	8.3	18.0	...
Eastern Asia Asie orientale	2005	1 555.01	794.78	760.23	104.5	19.4	12.4	134.5	...
	2010	1 595.83	816.14	779.69	104.7	17.5	14.1	138.0	...
	2015	1 635.15	836.81	798.34	104.8	17.2	16.8	141.4	11 799
	2017[1]	1 648.16	843.55	804.61	104.8	17.2	17.7	142.6	...
South-central Asia Asie centrale et du Sud	2005	1 641.83	846.20	795.63	106.4	33.3	7.1	159.0	...
	2010	1 768.53	910.40	858.13	106.1	31.4	7.5	171.3	...
	2015	1 892.01	973.04	918.98	105.9	29.5	8.4	183.2	10 791
	2017[1]	1 939.82	997.29	942.53	105.8	28.7	8.8	187.8	...
South-eastern Asia Asie du Sud-Est	2005	561.77	279.94	281.83	99.3	30.0	7.6	129.4	...
	2010	597.33	298.52	298.81	99.9	28.0	8.1	137.6	...
	2015	634.61	317.03	317.58	99.8	26.7	9.3	146.2	4 495
	2017[1]	648.78	323.97	324.81	99.7	26.2	9.9	149.5	...
Southern Asia Asie méridionale	2005	1 583.09	817.24	765.85	106.7	33.4	7.1	247.4	...
	2010	1 705.37	879.21	826.16	106.4	31.5	7.5	266.5	...
	2015	1 823.31	939.06	884.25	106.2	29.5	8.4	284.9	6 688[2]
	2017[1]	1 868.98	962.26	906.73	106.1	28.7	8.8	292.0	...
Western Asia Asie occidentale	2005	205.73	105.50	100.23	105.3	33.4	7.2	42.8	...
	2010	232.74	120.90	111.84	108.1	31.0	7.3	48.4	...
	2015	258.12	134.71	123.41	109.2	29.9	7.9	53.7	4 831
	2017[1]	267.66	139.92	127.74	109.5	29.4	8.3	55.7	...
Europe Europe	2005	730.29	352.16	378.13	93.1	15.9	20.6	33.0	...
	2010	737.16	355.52	381.64	93.2	15.5	22.0	33.3	...
	2015	740.81	357.69	383.12	93.4	15.8	23.9	33.5	23 049
	2017[1]	742.07	358.54	383.53	93.5	15.9	24.7	33.5	...
Eastern Europe Europe orientale	2005	297.51	140.23	157.28	89.2	15.4	18.2	16.5	...
	2010	294.54	138.45	156.09	88.7	14.8	19.3	16.3	...
	2015	293.24	137.96	155.28	88.8	15.9	21.5	16.2	18 814
	2017[1]	292.45	137.62	154.84	88.9	16.4	22.5	16.2	...
Northern Europe Europe septentrionale	2005	96.38	47.16[7]	49.22[7]	95.8[7]	18.0[7]	21.1[7]	56.6	...
	2010	100.31	49.25[7]	51.07[7]	96.4[7]	17.4[7]	22.6[7]	58.9	...
	2015	103.10	50.78[7]	52.32[7]	97.1[7]	17.5[7]	23.7[7]	60.6	1 810
	2017[1]	104.20	51.38[7]	52.82[7]	97.3[7]	17.6[7]	24.2[7]	61.2	...
Southern Europe Europe méridionale	2005	150.39	73.64[8]	76.76[8]	95.9[8]	15.1[8]	22.5[8]	116.1	...
	2010	153.94	75.33[8]	78.61[8]	95.8[8]	14.8[8]	24.1[8]	118.9	...
	2015	152.44	74.43[8]	78.01[8]	95.4[8]	14.6[8]	26.1[8]	117.7	1 317
	2017[1]	151.99	74.23[8]	77.76[8]	95.5[8]	14.3[8]	26.9[8]	117.4	...
Western Europe Europe occidentale	2005	186.01	91.14[9]	94.87[9]	96.1[9]	16.4[9]	22.6[9]	171.5	...
	2010	188.37	92.49[9]	95.88[9]	96.5[9]	15.9[9]	24.3[9]	173.6	...
	2015	192.03	94.52[9]	97.52[9]	96.9[9]	15.5[9]	25.8[9]	177.0	1 108
	2017[1]	193.43	95.31[9]	98.12[9]	97.1[9]	15.4[9]	26.4[9]	178.3	...
Oceania Océanie	2005	33.57	16.80	16.77	100.2	24.9	14.1	4.0	...
	2010	36.64	18.37	18.27	100.5	24.0	15.3	4.3	...
	2015	39.54	19.79	19.76	100.2	23.6	16.5	4.7	8 564
	2017[1]	40.69	20.36	20.33	100.1	23.5	17.0	4.8	...
Australia and New Zealand Australie et Nouvelle-Zélande	2005	24.37	12.13	12.25	99.0	20.1	17.3	3.1	...
	2010	26.49	13.21	13.28	99.4	19.3	18.8	3.3	...
	2015	28.41	14.13	14.28	98.9	19.0	20.3	3.6	8 012
	2017[1]	29.16	14.49	14.66	98.9	19.1	20.9	3.7	...

Country or area Pays ou zone	Year Année	Mid-year population estimates and projections (millions) Estimations et projections de population au milieu de l'année (millions) Total	Male Hommes	Females Femmes	Sex Ratio (males per 100 females) Rapport des sexes (hommes pour 100 femmes)	Population age distribution (percentage) Répartition par âge de la population (pourcentage) Aged 0 to 14 years old âgée de 0 à 14 ans	Aged 60+ years old âgée de 60 ans ou plus	Population density (per km²) Densité de population (pour km²)	Surface area Superficie (000 km²)
Melanesia Mélanésie	2005	8.05	4.09	3.96	103.5	38.1	5.4	15.2	...
	2010	8.98	4.57	4.41	103.5	37.1	5.8	17.0	...
	2015	9.93	5.05	4.88	103.5	35.7	6.4	18.8	541
	2017[1]	10.32	5.25	5.07	103.4	35.1	6.6	19.5	...
Micronesia Micronésie	2005	0.50	0.25[10]	0.25[10]	101.0[10]	33.3[10]	6.5[10]	158.6	...
	2010	0.50	0.25[10]	0.25[10]	101.7[10]	32.1[10]	7.8[10]	158.7	...
	2015	0.52	0.26[10]	0.26[10]	101.6[10]	30.0[10]	9.6[10]	163.7	3
	2017[1]	0.53	0.27[10]	0.26[10]	101.5[10]	29.2[10]	10.4[10]	166.4	...
Polynesia Polynésie	2005	0.64[11]	0.33[12]	0.31[12]	104.7[12]	33.9[12]	7.7[12]	79.4[11]	...
	2010	0.66[11]	0.34[12]	0.32[12]	104.0[12]	31.9[12]	8.4[12]	81.5[11]	...
	2015	0.68[11]	0.34[12]	0.33[12]	103.6[12]	30.6[12]	9.6[12]	83.7[11]	8
	2017[1]	0.69[11]	0.35[12]	0.34[12]	103.4[12]	29.8[12]	10.2[12]	84.8[11]	...
Afghanistan Afghanistan	2005	25.07	12.97	12.10	107.2	47.6	3.6	38.4	...
	2010	28.80	14.80	14.01	105.7	47.8	3.9	44.1	...
	2015	33.74	17.39	16.35	106.4	44.5	4.0	51.7	653
	2017[1]	35.53	18.31	17.22	106.3	43.2	4.1	54.4	...
Albania Albanie	2005	3.08	1.54	1.54	100.6	26.5	12.3	112.4	...
	2010	2.94	1.48	1.47	100.7	22.5	15.0	107.3	...
	2015	2.92	1.48	1.45	102.0	18.0	17.8	106.7	29
	2017[1]	2.93	1.48	1.45	101.9	17.4	19.0	106.9	...
Algeria Algérie	2005	33.29	16.84	16.45	102.3	29.1	7.0	14.0	...
	2010	36.12	18.23	17.89	101.9	27.2	7.8	15.2	...
	2015	39.87	20.13	19.74	102.0	28.7	8.9	16.7	2 382
	2017[1]	41.32	20.87	20.45	102.0	29.3	9.4	17.3	...
American Samoa Samoa américaines	2000	0.06	...	...	104.4[13,14]	38.8[13,14]	5.4[13,14]	287.6	...
	2005	0.06	...	...	...	...	...	295.6	...
	2010	0.06	...	...	103.0[13,14]	35.0[13,14]	6.7[13,14]	278.2	...
	2015	0.06	...	...	...	...	...	277.7	~0
	2016	0.06[1]	...	...	# 103.6	# 33.3	# 9.0	278.0[1]	...
	2017[1]	0.06	...	...	...	...	...	278.2	...
Andorra Andorre	2005	0.08	...	...	109.0[13,15]	15.1[13,15]	16.1[13,15]	167.8	...
	2010	0.08	...	...	108.5[13,15]	14.0[13,15]	18.6[13,15]	179.7	...
	2015	0.08	...	...	101.7[13,15]	...	...	166.0	~0
	2016	0.08[1]	...	...	102.3[13,15]	14.4[13,15]	19.0[13,15]	164.4[1]	...
	2017[1]	0.08	...	...	...	...	...	163.8	...
Angola Angola	2005	19.55	9.56	10.00	95.6	47.2	3.7	15.7	...
	2010	23.37	11.43	11.94	95.8	47.3	3.6	18.7	...
	2015	27.86	13.65	14.21	96.1	47.1	3.9	22.3	1 247
	2017[1]	29.78	14.61	15.18	96.2	46.8	4.0	23.9	...
Anguilla Anguilla	2001	0.01	...	...	97.3	27.7	10.2	126.4	...
	2005	0.01	...	...	...	...	...	140.4	...
	2010	0.01	...	...	...	...	...	153.0	...
	2011	0.01	...	...	* 97.6	* 23.3	* 7.6[16]	155.0	...
	2015	0.01	...	...	...	...	...	162.3	~0
	2017[1]	0.01	...	...	...	...	...	165.7	...
Antigua and Barbuda Antigua-et-Barbuda	2005	0.09	0.04	0.05	92.1	28.4	9.3	202.8	...
	2010	0.09	0.05	0.05	92.0	26.6	8.9	215.1	...
	2015	0.10	0.05	0.05	92.2	24.6	10.1	227.1	~0
	2017[1]	0.10	0.05	0.05	92.3	23.9	10.9	231.8	...
Argentina Argentine	2005	39.15	19.15	20.00	95.8	26.9	13.8	14.3	...
	2010	41.22	20.16	21.06	95.7	25.9	14.4	15.1	...
	2015	43.42	21.25	22.17	95.8	25.2	15.1	15.9	2 780
	2017[1]	44.27	21.67	22.60	95.9	24.9	15.4	16.2	...
Armenia Arménie	2005	2.98	1.40	1.58	88.8	21.5	14.4	104.7	...
	2010	2.88	1.35	1.53	87.9	19.5	14.8	101.1	...
	2015	2.92	1.37	1.55	88.7	19.8	15.8	102.5	30
	2017[1]	2.93	1.38	1.55	88.8	20.0	16.9	102.9	...

Country or area Pays ou zone	Year Année	Mid-year population estimates and projections (millions) Estimations et projections de population au milieu de l'année (millions) Total	 Male Hommes	 Females Femmes	Sex Ratio (males per 100 females) Rapport des sexes (hommes pour 100 femmes)	Population age distribution (percentage) Répartition par âge de la population (pourcentage) Aged 0 to 14 years old âgée de 0 à 14 ans	 Aged 60+ years old âgée de 60 ans ou plus	Population density (per km²) Densité de population (pour km²)	Surface area Superficie (000 km²)
Aruba Aruba	2005	0.10	0.05	0.05	90.7	21.5	12.6	555.7	...
	2010	0.10	0.05	0.05	91.1	20.9	15.5	564.8	...
	2015	0.10	0.05	0.05	90.6	18.7	18.4	579.7	~0
	2017[1]	0.11	0.05	0.06	90.4	17.9	19.7	584.8	...
Australia Australie	2005[17]	20.24	10.10	10.14	99.6	19.8	17.4	2.6	...
	2010[17]	22.12	11.06	11.06	100.0	19.0	18.9	2.9	...
	2015	23.80[17]	11.86[17]	11.94[17]	99.4[17]	18.8[17]	20.4[17]	3.1[17]	7 692[18]
	2017[1,17]	24.45	12.18	12.27	99.3	19.0	21.0	3.2	...
Austria Autriche	2005	8.25	4.01	4.24	94.6	16.0	22.1	100.2	...
	2010	8.41	4.10	4.31	95.1	14.7	23.3	102.1	...
	2015	8.68	4.25	4.43	95.9	14.1	24.3	105.3	84
	2017[1]	8.74	4.28	4.45	96.2	14.1	25.1	106.0	...
Azerbaijan Azerbaïdjan	2005[19]	8.54	4.21	4.33	97.1	26.2	8.5	103.3	...
	2010[19]	9.03	4.48	4.56	98.2	22.8	8.1	109.3	...
	2015	9.62[19]	4.79[19]	4.83[19]	99.1[19]	22.9[19]	9.3[19]	116.4[19]	87
	2017[1,19]	9.83	4.90	4.93	99.3	23.3	10.1	118.9	...
Bahamas Bahamas	2005	0.33	0.16	0.17	95.4	25.6	9.4	32.9	...
	2010	0.36	0.18	0.18	95.6	22.5	10.5	36.0	...
	2015	0.39	0.19	0.20	95.9	20.7	12.6	38.6	14
	2017[1]	0.40	0.19	0.20	95.9	20.5	13.5	39.5	...
Bahrain Bahreïn	2005	0.89	0.53	0.36	150.5	25.7	3.4	1 170.0	...
	2010	1.24	0.77	0.47	165.8	20.3	3.5	1 632.7	...
	2015	1.37	0.85	0.53	161.3	20.8	4.1	1 805.1	1
	2017[1]	1.49	0.94	0.56	168.3	19.7	4.6	1 963.9	...
Bangladesh Bangladesh	2005	143.43	73.05	70.38	103.8	34.4	6.6	1 101.9	...
	2010	152.15	76.94	75.21	102.3	32.1	6.9	1 168.8	...
	2015	161.20	81.34	79.86	101.9	29.4	7.1	1 238.4	148
	2017[1]	164.67	83.04	81.63	101.7	28.4	7.3	1 265.0	...
Barbados Barbade	2005	0.27	0.13	0.14	92.3	20.7	15.5	637.2	...
	2010	0.28	0.13	0.15	92.2	19.9	17.3	650.2	...
	2015	0.28	0.14	0.15	92.0	19.4	19.8	661.0	~0
	2017[1]	0.29	0.14	0.15	91.9	19.1	21.0	664.5	...
Belarus Bélarus	2005	9.62	4.49	5.13	87.5	15.6	18.6	47.4	...
	2010	9.47	4.40	5.07	86.9	14.8	19.1	46.7	...
	2015	9.49	4.41	5.07	87.0	16.1	20.4	46.7	208
	2017[1]	9.47	4.41	5.06	87.0	16.7	21.3	46.7	...
Belgium Belgique	2005	10.55	5.17	5.37	96.3	17.2	22.1	348.3	...
	2010	10.94	5.37	5.57	96.5	16.9	23.2	361.3	...
	2015	11.29	5.55	5.74	96.7	17.0	24.0	372.8	31
	2017[1]	11.43	5.64	5.79	97.3	17.1	24.6	377.5	...
Belize Belize	2005	0.28	0.14	0.14	101.0	39.0	4.7	12.4	...
	2010	0.32	0.16	0.16	100.1	35.7	5.7	14.1	...
	2015	0.36	0.18	0.18	99.4	32.5	5.9	15.8	23
	2017[1]	0.37	0.19	0.19	99.2	31.4	6.2	16.4	...
Benin Bénin	2005	7.98	3.96	4.03	98.2	44.4	5.0	70.8	...
	2010	9.20	4.57	4.63	98.7	43.8	4.9	81.6	...
	2015	10.58	5.27	5.31	99.3	43.0	5.0	93.8	115
	2017[1]	11.18	5.57	5.60	99.5	42.7	5.0	99.1	...
Bermuda Bermudes	2005	0.07	...	...	91.8[13,20]	18.4[13]	16.4[13]	1 302.6	...
	2010	0.06	...	...	92.4[13,21]	17.4[13]	18.7[13]	1 279.1	...
	2015	0.06	...	...	91.4[13,21]	15.3[13,21]	23.4[13,21]	1 240.1	~0
	2017	0.06[1]	...	...	91.4[13,21]	14.8[13,21]	24.9[13,21]	1 227.0[1]	...
Bhutan Bhoutan	2005	0.66	0.34	0.31	110.6	34.9	5.7	17.2	...
	2010	0.73	0.39	0.34	112.7	30.6	6.2	19.1	...
	2015	0.79	0.42	0.37	113.4	27.4	6.9	20.7	38
	2017[1]	0.81	0.43	0.38	113.1	26.5	7.3	21.2	...

Country or area Pays ou zone	Year Année	Mid-year population estimates and projections (millions) Estimations et projections de population au milieu de l'année (millions) Total	 Male Hommes	 Females Femmes	Sex Ratio (males per 100 females) Rapport des sexes (hommes pour 100 femmes)	Population age distribution (percentage) Répartition par âge de la population (pourcentage) Aged 0 to 14 years old âgée de 0 à 14 ans	 Aged 60+ years old âgée de 60 ans ou plus	Population density (per km²) Densité de population (pour km²)	Surface area Superficie (000 km²)
Bolivia (Plurin. State of) Bolivie (État plurin. de)	2005	9.13	4.57	4.55	100.5	36.6	7.8	8.4	...
	2010	9.92	4.97	4.95	100.5	34.7	8.3	9.2	...
	2015	10.72	5.37	5.35	100.3	32.4	9.2	9.9	1 099[22]
	2017[1]	11.05	5.53	5.52	100.2	31.6	9.5	10.2	...
Bonaire, St. Eustatius & Saba Bonaire, St-Eustache et Saba	2005	0.01	...	...	...	...	...	43.9	...
	2010	0.02	...	...	...	...	...	63.8	...
	2017[1]	0.03	...	...	...	...	...	77.4	...
Bosnia and Herzegovina Bosnie-Herzégovine	2005	3.78	1.86	1.92	96.6	17.7	17.4	74.1	...
	2010	3.72	1.83	1.89	96.5	15.7	19.2	73.0	...
	2015	3.54	1.74	1.80	96.4	14.5	22.4	69.3	51
	2017[1]	3.51	1.72	1.79	96.4	14.1	23.4	68.8	...
Botswana Botswana	2005	1.86	0.92	0.94	97.5	35.1	5.0	3.3	...
	2010	2.01	1.00	1.02	97.8	33.0	5.3	3.6	...
	2015	2.21	1.09	1.12	97.7	31.8	6.1	3.9	582
	2017[1]	2.29	1.13	1.16	97.7	31.4	6.4	4.0	...
Brazil Brésil	2005	186.92	92.22	94.69	97.4	27.4	8.7	22.4	...
	2010	196.80	96.93	99.86	97.1	24.9	10.0	23.5	...
	2015	205.96	101.28	104.68	96.8	22.5	11.9	24.6	8 516
	2017[1]	209.29	102.86	106.43	96.6	21.7	12.6	25.0	...
British Virgin Islands Îles Vierges britanniques	2001	0.02	...	...	106.1	26.3	7.4	140.6	...
	2005	0.02	...	...	...	...	...	154.5	...
	2010	0.03	...	...	97.1	22.3	9.7	181.5	...
	2015	0.03	...	...	...	...	...	200.8	~0
	2017[1]	0.03	...	...	...	...	...	208.0	...
Brunei Darussalam Brunéi Darussalam	2005	0.37	0.19	0.18	104.3	27.8	4.8	69.3	...
	2010	0.39	0.20	0.19	106.7	26.0	5.4	73.7	...
	2015	0.42	0.22	0.20	106.3	23.7	7.1	79.2	6
	2017[1]	0.43	0.22	0.21	106.0	23.0	8.0	81.3	...
Bulgaria Bulgarie	2005	7.68	3.74	3.94	94.8	13.6	23.1	70.8	...
	2010	7.40	3.61	3.80	94.9	13.3	25.3	68.2	...
	2015	7.18	3.49	3.69	94.7	14.0	27.1	66.1	111
	2017[1]	7.08	3.44	3.64	94.6	14.2	27.7	65.3	...
Burkina Faso Burkina Faso	2005	13.42	6.62	6.80	97.4	46.5	4.1	49.1	...
	2010	15.61	7.74	7.87	98.3	46.2	3.9	57.0	...
	2015	18.11	9.02	9.09	99.2	45.6	3.8	66.2	273
	2017[1]	19.19	9.57	9.62	99.5	45.2	3.9	70.2	...
Burundi Burundi	2005	7.42	3.65	3.77	96.8	45.7	4.2	289.1	...
	2010	8.77	4.31	4.46	96.5	44.1	4.0	341.4	...
	2015	10.20	5.02	5.18	96.7	44.8	4.2	397.2	28
	2017[1]	10.86	5.35	5.52	96.9	45.0	4.4	423.1	...
Cabo Verde Cabo Verde	2005	0.47	0.23	0.24	95.8	38.1	7.2	117.8	...
	2010	0.50	0.25	0.25	98.7	34.0	6.7	124.7	...
	2015	0.53	0.27	0.27	99.2	31.2	6.7	132.2	4
	2017[1]	0.55	0.27	0.27	99.3	30.2	6.9	135.6	...
Cambodia Cambodge	2005	13.27	6.44	6.83	94.3	37.1	5.3	75.2	...
	2010	14.31	6.97	7.34	95.0	33.3	5.9	81.1	...
	2015	15.52	7.57	7.95	95.2	31.6	6.8	87.9	181
	2017[1]	16.01	7.81	8.20	95.3	31.3	7.1	90.7	...
Cameroon Cameroun	2005	17.42	8.70	8.72	99.7	44.0	5.0	36.9	...
	2010	19.97	9.99	9.99	100.0	43.5	4.9	42.2	...
	2015	22.83	11.42	11.41	100.1	43.0	4.8	48.3	476
	2017[1]	24.05	12.04	12.02	100.2	42.7	4.8	50.9	...
Canada Canada	2005	32.29	16.01	16.28	98.3	17.7	17.9	3.6	...
	2010	34.17	16.95	17.22	98.5	16.5	20.0	3.8	...
	2015	35.95	17.83	18.12	98.4	16.0	22.4	4.0	9 985
	2017[1]	36.62	18.17	18.45	98.5	16.0	23.5	4.0	...

Country or area / Pays ou zone	Year / Année	Mid-year population estimates and projections (millions) / Estimations et projections de population au milieu de l'année (millions): Total	Male / Hommes	Females / Femmes	Sex Ratio (males per 100 females) / Rapport des sexes (hommes pour 100 femmes)	Population age distribution (percentage) / Répartition par âge de la population (pourcentage): Aged 0 to 14 years old / âgée de 0 à 14 ans	Aged 60+ years old / âgée de 60 ans ou plus	Population density (per km²) / Densité de population (pour km²)	Surface area / Superficie (000 km²)
Cayman Islands / Îles Caïmanes	2005	0.05	...	...	101.0[13]	...	...	202.6	...
	2010	0.06	...	...	97.8[13,23]	18.1[13,23]	8.6[13,23]	231.3	...
	2015	0.06	...	...	100.4[13]	18.3[13]	6.7[13,16]	249.8	~0
	2017[1]	0.06	...	...	...	...	...	256.5	...
Central African Republic / République centrafricaine	2005	4.13	2.03	2.09	97.2	42.2	5.7	6.6	...
	2010	4.45	2.19	2.25	97.4	42.5	5.5	7.1	...
	2015	4.55	2.24	2.30	97.3	43.7	5.5	7.3	623
	2017[1]	4.66	2.30	2.36	97.3	43.2	5.5	7.5	...
Chad / Tchad	2005	10.07	5.03	5.04	99.7	49.1	4.2	8.0	...
	2010	11.89	5.95	5.94	100.0	48.6	4.0	9.4	...
	2015	14.01	7.01	7.00	100.2	47.6	4.0	11.1	1 284
	2017[1]	14.90	7.46	7.44	100.2	47.1	4.0	11.8	...
Channel Islands [24] / Îles Anglo-Normandes [24]	2005	0.15	0.08	0.08	96.6	16.3	20.4	812.1	...
	2010	0.16	0.08	0.08	98.1	15.3	21.7	839.9	...
	2015	0.16	0.08	0.08	98.3	14.7	23.7	861.9	~0
	2017[1]	0.17	0.08	0.08	98.4	14.5	24.5	870.1	...
Chile / Chili	2005	16.15	7.99	8.16	97.9	24.6	11.8	21.7	...
	2010	16.99	8.41	8.58	98.0	22.5	13.2	22.9	...
	2015	17.76	8.80	8.97	98.1	20.8	15.2	23.9	756
	2017[1]	18.05	8.94	9.11	98.2	20.3	16.0	24.3	...
China / Chine	2005[25]	1 321.62	679.54	642.08	105.8	19.9	11.0	140.8	...
	2010[25]	1 359.76	699.88	659.87	106.1	17.8	12.6	144.8	...
	2015	1 397.03[25]	719.76[25]	677.27[25]	106.3[25]	17.7[25]	15.4[25]	148.8[25]	9 600
	2017[1,25]	1 409.52	726.32	683.20	106.3	17.7	16.2	150.1	...
China, Hong Kong SAR / Chine, Hong Kong RAS	2005	6.83	3.28	3.55	92.2	14.4	15.6	6 502.6	...
	2010	7.03	3.30	3.73	88.4	11.9	18.4	6 690.7	...
	2015	7.25	3.35	3.90	85.9	11.2	21.8	6 900.7	1
	2017[1]	7.36	3.39	3.98	85.1	11.5	23.5	7 014.2	...
China, Macao SAR / Chine, Macao RAS	2005	0.48	0.23	0.25	90.5	16.9	9.6	16 139.1	...
	2010	0.54	0.26	0.28	92.3	12.7	11.0	17 958.8	...
	2015	0.60	0.29	0.31	92.2	12.4	14.4	20 098.4	~0[26]
	2017[1]	0.62	0.30	0.32	92.3	13.3	16.1	20 821.6	...
Colombia / Colombie	2005	43.29	21.38	21.91	97.6	28.9	7.6	39.0	...
	2010	45.92	22.64	23.28	97.3	26.4	9.0	41.4	...
	2015	48.23	23.74	24.49	97.0	24.3	10.8	43.5	1 142
	2017[1]	49.07	24.14	24.93	96.8	23.5	11.6	44.2	...
Comoros / Comores	2005	0.61	0.31	0.30	101.4	42.3	4.6	328.7	...
	2010	0.69	0.35	0.34	101.6	41.0	4.5	370.6	...
	2015	0.78	0.39	0.39	101.7	40.1	4.7	417.7	2
	2017[1]	0.81	0.41	0.40	101.8	39.8	4.9	437.4	...
Congo / Congo	2005	3.72	1.86	1.86	99.9	41.6	5.2	10.9	...
	2010	4.39	2.19	2.19	100.1	41.7	5.0	12.8	...
	2015	5.00	2.50	2.50	100.1	42.4	5.1	14.6	342
	2017[1]	5.26	2.63	2.63	100.1	42.3	5.2	15.4	...
Cook Islands / Îles Cook	2001	0.02	...	...	106.6	30.0	10.6	76.3	...
	2005	0.02	...	...	...	...	...	82.1	...
	2006	0.02	...	...	* 103.1	* 26.1	* 11.9	82.1	...
	2010	0.02	...	...	...	...	...	77.3	...
	2015	0.02	...	...	...	...	...	72.7	~0
	2016	0.02[1]	...	...	# 97.4	# 26.9	# 14.2	72.4[1]	...
	2017[1]	0.02	...	...	...	...	...	72.4	...
Costa Rica / Costa Rica	2005	4.25	2.13	2.12	100.6	27.4	9.4	83.2	...
	2010	4.55	2.28	2.27	100.4	24.6	11.1	89.0	...
	2015	4.81	2.41	2.40	100.1	22.3	12.8	94.2	51
	2017[1]	4.91	2.45	2.45	100.1	21.6	13.6	96.1	...
Côte d'Ivoire / Côte d'Ivoire	2005	18.34	9.40	8.94	105.2	44.1	4.6	57.7	...
	2010	20.40	10.41	9.99	104.2	43.7	4.7	64.2	...
	2015	23.11	11.73	11.38	103.1	42.7	4.7	72.7	322
	2017[1]	24.29	12.31	11.99	102.7	42.4	4.8	76.4	...

Country or area Pays ou zone	Year Année	Mid-year population estimates and projections (millions) Estimations et projections de population au milieu de l'année (millions) Total	 Male Hommes	 Females Femmes	Sex Ratio (males per 100 females) Rapport des sexes (hommes pour 100 femmes)	Population age distribution (percentage) Répartition par âge de la population (pourcentage) Aged 0 to 14 years old âgée de 0 à 14 ans	 Aged 60+ years old âgée de 60 ans ou plus	Population density (per km²) Densité de population (pour km²)	Surface area Superficie (000 km²)
Croatia Croatie	2005	4.38	2.11	2.27	92.9	15.7	21.9	78.2	...
	2010	4.33	2.08	2.24	92.9	15.4	23.8	77.3	...
	2015	4.24	2.04	2.20	93.0	14.8	25.8	75.7	57
	2017[1]	4.19	2.02	2.17	93.1	14.7	26.8	74.9	...
Cuba Cuba	2005	11.28	5.66	5.62	100.7	19.4	15.2	106.0	...
	2010	11.33	5.68	5.66	100.4	17.4	17.0	106.5	...
	2015	11.46	5.74	5.73	100.2	16.3	19.4	107.7	110
	2017[1]	11.48	5.74	5.74	100.1	16.0	20.1	107.9	...
Curaçao Curaçao	2005	0.13	0.06	0.07	88.2	21.1	17.2	291.4	...
	2010	0.15	0.07	0.08	84.8	19.9	18.8	332.5	...
	2015	0.16	0.07	0.09	84.3	18.9	21.9	355.9	~0
	2017[1]	0.16	0.07	0.09	84.6	18.7	22.9	361.6	...
Cyprus Chypre	2005[27]	1.03	0.52	0.51	102.6	20.0	14.9	111.2	...
	2010[27]	1.11	0.56	0.56	99.7	17.8	16.1	120.4	...
	2015	1.16[27]	0.58[27]	0.58[27]	100.3[27]	16.9[27]	17.7[27]	125.6[27]	9
	2017[1,27]	1.18	0.59	0.59	100.2	16.8	18.5	127.7	...
Czechia Tchéquie	2005	10.26	5.00	5.26	95.0	14.7	19.8	132.8	...
	2010	10.54	5.17	5.36	96.4	14.2	22.4	136.4	...
	2015	10.60	5.21	5.39	96.6	15.1	24.9	137.3	79
	2017[1]	10.62	5.22	5.40	96.7	15.4	25.6	137.5	...
Dem. People's Rep. Korea Rép. pop. dém. de Corée	2005	23.90	11.67	12.23	95.4	24.7	11.9	198.5	...
	2010	24.59	12.02	12.58	95.6	22.8	12.9	204.2	...
	2015	25.24	12.35	12.90	95.7	21.1	12.7	209.6	121
	2017[1]	25.49	12.47	13.02	95.7	20.6	13.5	211.7	...
Dem. Rep. of the Congo Rép. dém. du Congo	2005	54.75	27.20	27.55	98.8	45.8	4.7	24.2	...
	2010	64.52	32.12	32.40	99.1	46.1	4.7	28.5	...
	2015	76.20	38.00	38.20	99.5	46.3	4.7	33.6	2 345
	2017[1]	81.34	40.58	40.76	99.6	46.3	4.7	35.9	...
Denmark Danemark	2005	5.42	2.69	2.74	98.1	18.7	21.2	127.8	...
	2010	5.55	2.76	2.80	98.5	17.9	23.3	130.9	...
	2015	5.69	2.83	2.86	98.9	16.8	24.8	134.1	43
	2017[1]	5.73	2.85	2.88	99.0	16.5	25.3	135.1	...
Djibouti Djibouti	2005	0.78	0.39	0.39	101.0	37.9	5.2	33.8	...
	2010	0.85	0.43	0.42	100.9	34.8	5.8	36.7	...
	2015	0.93	0.47	0.46	100.8	32.0	6.2	40.0	23
	2017[1]	0.96	0.48	0.48	100.7	31.1	6.4	41.3	...
Dominica Dominique	2001	0.07	...	...	101.5[28]	29.0[29]	13.2[29]	92.9	...
	2005	0.07	...	...	101.4	...	...	94.2	...
	2006	0.07	...	...	103.7	29.5	13.3	94.4	...
	2010	0.07	...	...	101.4	...	...	95.3	...
	2014	0.07	...	...	103.0	...	...	97.0	1
	2015	0.07	...	...	...	...	...	97.5	1
	2017[1]	0.07	...	...	...	...	...	98.6	...
Dominican Republic République dominicaine	2005	9.24	4.62	4.62	100.0	33.2	8.0	191.2	...
	2010	9.90	4.94	4.96	99.7	31.4	8.7	204.8	...
	2015	10.53	5.25	5.28	99.3	30.0	9.7	217.9	49
	2017[1]	10.77	5.36	5.41	99.2	29.3	10.2	222.8	...
Ecuador Équateur	2005	13.74	6.88	6.86	100.3	32.7	8.0	55.3	...
	2010	14.93	7.47	7.46	100.1	30.7	8.7	60.1	...
	2015	16.14	8.07	8.07	100.0	29.0	9.9	65.0	257
	2017[1]	16.62	8.31	8.32	99.9	28.4	10.5	66.9	...
Egypt Égypte	2005	76.78	38.71	38.07	101.7	33.3	7.1	77.1	...
	2010	84.11	42.47	41.64	102.0	32.1	7.5	84.5	...
	2015	93.78	47.41	46.37	102.2	33.1	7.7	94.2	1 002
	2017[1]	97.55	49.33	48.23	102.3	33.5	7.9	98.0	...
El Salvador El Salvador	2005	6.03	2.88	3.15	91.4	34.8	9.1	291.0	...
	2010	6.16	2.92	3.25	89.9	31.6	10.0	297.5	...
	2015	6.31	2.97	3.34	88.9	28.3	11.1	304.7	21[30]
	2017[1]	6.38	3.00	3.38	88.5	27.4	11.6	307.8	...

Country or area Pays ou zone	Year Année	Mid-year population estimates and projections (millions) Estimations et projections de population au milieu de l'année (millions) Total	 Male Hommes	 Females Femmes	Sex Ratio (males per 100 females) Rapport des sexes (hommes pour 100 femmes)	Population age distribution (percentage) Répartition par âge de la population (pourcentage) Aged 0 to 14 years old âgée de 0 à 14 ans	 Aged 60+ years old âgée de 60 ans ou plus	Population density (per km²) Densité de population (pour km²)	Surface area Superficie (000 km²)
Equatorial Guinea	2005	0.76	0.40	0.36	112.6	39.5	5.3	27.0	...
Guinée équatoriale	2010	0.95	0.52	0.43	118.8	38.4	4.8	33.9	...
	2015	1.18	0.65	0.53	123.0	37.4	4.6	41.9	28
	2017[1]	1.27	0.70	0.57	124.0	37.2	4.4	45.2	...
Eritrea	2005	3.97	1.99	1.98	100.1	41.0	5.5	39.3	...
Érythrée	2010	4.39	2.20	2.19	100.2	41.6	5.5	43.5	...
	2015	4.85	2.43	2.42	100.4	42.3	5.3	48.0	118
	2017[1]	5.07	2.54	2.53	100.4	41.8	5.3	50.2	...
Estonia	2005	1.36	0.63	0.73	86.8	15.2	21.9	32.0	...
Estonie	2010	1.33	0.62	0.71	87.2	15.1	23.2	31.4	...
	2015	1.32	0.62	0.70	87.9	16.1	25.1	31.0	45
	2017[1]	1.31	0.61	0.70	88.2	16.4	25.9	30.9	...
Ethiopia	2005	76.73	38.28	38.45	99.5	46.2	4.9	76.7	...
Éthiopie	2010	87.70	43.77	43.93	99.6	44.5	5.1	87.7	...
	2015	99.87	49.86	50.01	99.7	41.6	5.2	99.9	1 104
	2017[1]	104.96	52.41	52.55	99.7	40.6	5.3	105.0	...
Falkland Islands (Malvinas) [31]	2001	~0.00	...	...	121.5	15.0	12.0	0.2	...
Îles Falkland (Malvinas) [31]	2005	~0.00	...	...	...	...	...	0.2	...
	2006	~0.00	...	...	113.2	15.9	14.0	0.2	...
	2010	~0.00	...	...	...	...	...	0.2	...
	2012	~0.00	...	...	110.5[32]	16.4[32]	15.7[32]	0.2	...
	2015	~0.00	...	...	...	...	...	0.2	12
	2017[1]	~0.00	...	...	...	...	...	0.2	...
Faroe Islands	2005	0.05	...	...	108.0[13]	...	...	34.6	...
Îles Féroé	2008	0.05	...	...	108.1[13]	22.0[13]	19.3[13]	34.7	...
	2010	0.05	...	...	108.0[13]	...	...	34.8	...
	2015	0.05	...	...	107.2[13]	21.0[13]	22.5[13]	35.1	1
	2017[1]	0.05	...	...	...	...	...	35.3	...
Fiji	2005	0.82	0.42	0.40	104.0	30.5	6.9	45.0	...
Fidji	2010	0.86	0.44	0.42	104.2	29.0	7.9	47.1	...
	2015	0.89	0.45	0.44	103.4	28.7	9.3	48.8	18
	2017[1]	0.91	0.46	0.45	103.1	28.5	9.9	49.6	...
Finland [33]	2005	5.26	2.57	2.68	95.9	17.3	21.5	17.3	...
Finlande [33]	2010	5.37	2.63	2.73	96.4	16.5	24.8	17.7	...
	2015	5.48	2.70	2.78	96.9	16.4	27.1	18.0	338
	2017[1]	5.52	2.72	2.80	97.2	16.4	27.8	18.2	...
France	2005	61.23	30.04	31.19	96.3	18.4	20.9	111.8	...
France	2010	63.03	30.93	32.09	96.4	18.4	23.1	115.1	...
	2015	64.46	31.67	32.78	96.6	18.3	25.0	117.7	552
	2017[1]	64.98	31.95	33.03	96.7	18.1	25.7	118.7	...
French Guiana	2005	0.20	0.10	0.10	98.2	36.1	5.7	2.5	...
Guyane française	2010	0.23	0.12	0.12	99.9	35.3	6.5	2.8	...
	2015	0.27	0.13	0.13	100.0	33.9	7.9	3.3	84
	2017[1]	0.28	0.14	0.14	100.0	33.2	8.4	3.4	...
French Polynesia	2005	0.25	0.13	0.12	105.3	27.7	8.0	69.6	...
Polynésie française	2010	0.27	0.14	0.13	104.7	25.2	9.3	73.2	...
	2015	0.28	0.14	0.14	104.0	23.9	11.1	75.9	4
	2017[1]	0.28	0.14	0.14	103.7	23.3	11.9	77.3	...
Gabon	2005	1.40	0.70	0.70	100.3	39.0	7.7	5.4	...
Gabon	2010	1.64	0.84	0.80	104.2	37.0	7.0	6.4	...
	2015	1.93	0.99	0.94	105.7	35.8	6.4	7.5	268
	2017[1]	2.03	1.04	0.98	105.6	35.9	6.4	7.9	...
Gambia	2005	1.44	0.72	0.73	98.4	46.3	4.0	142.7	...
Gambie	2010	1.69	0.84	0.85	98.1	46.3	3.7	167.2	...
	2015	1.98	0.98	1.00	98.0	45.7	3.8	195.4	11
	2017[1]	2.10	1.04	1.06	98.0	45.3	3.8	207.6	...

Country or area Pays ou zone	Year Année	Mid-year population estimates and projections (millions) Estimations et projections de population au milieu de l'année (millions) Total	 Male Hommes	 Females Femmes	Sex Ratio (males per 100 females) Rapport des sexes (hommes pour 100 femmes)	Population age distribution (percentage) Répartition par âge de la population (pourcentage) Aged 0 to 14 years old âgée de 0 à 14 ans	 Aged 60+ years old âgée de 60 ans ou plus	Population density (per km²) Densité de population (pour km²)	Surface area Superficie (000 km²)
Georgia Géorgie	2005[34]	4.49	2.12	2.37	89.5	19.5	18.2	64.6	...
	2010[34]	4.23	2.01	2.22	90.5	18.0	18.8	60.9	...
	2015	3.95[34]	1.89[34]	2.07[34]	91.3[34]	18.7[34]	20.3[34]	56.9[34]	70
	2017[1,34]	3.91	1.87	2.04	91.4	19.2	20.8	56.3	...
Germany Allemagne	2005	81.67	39.91	41.76	95.6	14.4	24.9	234.3	...
	2010	80.89	39.66	41.24	96.2	13.6	26.1	232.1	...
	2015	81.71	40.19	41.52	96.8	13.1	27.3	234.4	357
	2017[1]	82.11	40.43	41.68	97.0	13.1	28.0	235.6	...
Ghana Ghana	2005	21.54	10.76	10.78	99.9	40.6	5.2	94.7	...
	2010	24.51	12.13	12.38	98.0	39.6	5.4	107.7	...
	2015	27.58	13.72	13.86	99.0	38.8	5.2	121.2	239
	2017[1]	28.83	14.37	14.47	99.3	38.5	5.3	126.7	...
Gibraltar Gibraltar	2001	0.03	...	...	98.5[35]	18.4[35]	20.5[35]	3 137.4	...
	2005	0.03	...	...	97.3[36]	...	...	3 208.5	...
	2010	0.03	...	...	99.2[36]	...	...	3 318.9	...
	2012	0.03	...	...	99.6[13,36]	18.1[13,36]	22.4[13,36]	3 362.3	...
	2015	0.03	...	...	101.8[36]	...	...	3 422.8	~0
	2017[1]	0.03	...	...	...	...	...	3 457.1	...
Greece Grèce	2005	11.30	5.60	5.71	98.1	15.1	22.5	87.7	...
	2010	11.45	5.64	5.80	97.2	14.9	24.0	88.8	...
	2015	11.22	5.52	5.69	97.0	14.5	25.7	87.0	132
	2017[1]	11.16	5.49	5.67	96.9	14.2	26.5	86.6	...
Greenland Groenland	2005	0.06	...	...	113.4[13,15]	25.0[13,15]	9.6[13,15]	0.1	...
	2010	0.06	...	...	112.6[13,15]	22.6[13,15]	10.9[13,15]	0.1	...
	2015	0.06	...	...	111.9[13,15]	21.1[13,15]	12.7[13,15]	0.1	2 166
	2016	0.06[1]	...	...	112.1[13,15]	21.0[13,15]	13.2[13,15]	0.1[1]	...
	2017[1]	0.06	...	...	...	...	...	0.1	...
Grenada Grenade	2005	0.10	0.05	0.05	98.8	30.0	9.9	302.8	...
	2010	0.10	0.05	0.05	99.8	27.5	9.6	307.9	...
	2015	0.11	0.05	0.05	100.6	26.5	10.2	314.2	~0
	2017[1]	0.11	0.05	0.05	100.9	26.3	10.5	317.1	...
Guadeloupe Guadeloupe	2005[37]	0.44	0.21	0.23	94.2	23.8	15.6	260.1	...
	2010[37]	0.45	0.21	0.24	87.4	22.0	19.3	266.7	...
	2015	0.45[37]	0.21[37]	0.24[37]	86.6[37]	19.4[37]	22.4[37]	266.5[37]	2
	2017[1,37]	0.45	0.21	0.24	86.4	18.6	23.6	266.0	...
Guam Guam	2005	0.16	0.08	0.08	104.0	29.5	9.2	293.3	...
	2010	0.16	0.08	0.08	103.3	27.5	11.1	295.3	...
	2015	0.16	0.08	0.08	102.7	25.4	13.2	299.6	1
	2017[1]	0.16	0.08	0.08	102.6	24.7	14.0	304.1	...
Guatemala Guatemala	2005	13.10	6.42	6.67	96.2	42.3	5.9	122.2	...
	2010	14.63	7.19	7.44	96.5	39.4	6.1	136.5	...
	2015	16.25	8.00	8.26	96.8	36.2	6.7	151.7	109
	2017[1]	16.91	8.32	8.59	96.9	35.1	6.9	157.8	...
Guinea Guinée	2005	9.68	4.84	4.84	99.9	44.0	5.1	39.4	...
	2010	10.79	5.40	5.39	100.1	43.5	4.9	43.9	...
	2015	12.09	6.06	6.03	100.5	42.7	5.1	49.2	246
	2017[1]	12.72	6.38	6.34	100.6	42.3	5.2	51.8	...
Guinea-Bissau Guinée-Bissau	2005	1.38	0.67	0.71	95.4	43.6	4.5	49.1	...
	2010	1.56	0.76	0.79	96.2	42.3	4.6	55.3	...
	2015	1.77	0.87	0.90	96.7	41.7	4.9	63.0	36
	2017[1]	1.86	0.92	0.95	96.9	41.5	4.9	66.2	...
Guyana Guyana	2005	0.75	0.38	0.37	100.4	36.2	6.0	3.8	...
	2010	0.75	0.37	0.37	100.1	32.7	7.2	3.8	...
	2015	0.77	0.39	0.38	101.5	29.8	8.1	3.9	215
	2017[1]	0.78	0.39	0.39	101.9	29.0	8.6	4.0	...
Haiti Haïti	2005	9.26	4.58	4.69	97.7	38.0	6.4	336.1	...
	2010	10.00	4.94	5.06	97.8	35.9	6.5	362.8	...
	2015	10.71	5.30	5.41	97.9	33.7	7.1	388.6	28
	2017[1]	10.98	5.43	5.55	97.8	33.0	7.3	398.4	...

Country or area Pays ou zone	Year Année	Mid-year population estimates and projections (millions) / Estimations et projections de population au milieu de l'année (millions): Total	Male Hommes	Females Femmes	Sex Ratio (males per 100 females) Rapport des sexes (hommes pour 100 femmes)	Population age distribution (percentage) / Répartition par âge de la population (pourcentage): Aged 0 to 14 years old âgée de 0 à 14 ans	Aged 60+ years old âgée de 60 ans ou plus	Population density (per km²) Densité de population (pour km²)	Surface area Superficie (000 km²)
Holy See Saint-Siège	2000	~0.00	...	...	196.7[15,38]	...	...	1 784.1	...
	2005	~0.00	...	...	...	...	...	1 813.6	...
	2009	~0.00	...	...	219.2	...	...	1 806.8	...
	2010	~0.00	...	...	...	...	...	1 804.5	...
	2015	~0.00	...	...	...	...	...	1 825.0	~0[39]
	2017[1]	~0.00	...	...	...	...	...	1 800.0	...
Honduras Honduras	2005	7.37	3.67	3.70	99.1	39.9	5.5	65.9	...
	2010	8.19	4.08	4.11	99.3	36.6	5.8	73.2	...
	2015	8.96	4.47	4.49	99.4	33.0	6.6	80.1	112
	2017[1]	9.27	4.62	4.65	99.4	31.6	7.0	82.8	...
Hungary Hongrie	2005	10.09	4.79	5.30	90.3	15.5	21.4	111.4	...
	2010	9.93	4.71	5.22	90.3	14.9	22.1	109.7	...
	2015	9.78	4.65	5.13	90.6	14.4	25.0	108.1	93
	2017[1]	9.72	4.62	5.10	90.7	14.3	26.0	107.4	...
Iceland Islande	2005	0.30	0.15	0.15	100.6	22.2	15.8	2.9	...
	2010	0.32	0.16	0.16	101.5	20.8	16.9	3.2	...
	2015	0.33	0.17	0.16	100.7	20.3	19.1	3.3	103
	2017[1]	0.34	0.17	0.17	100.7	20.1	20.1	3.3	...
India Inde	2005	1 144.12	593.06	551.06	107.6	32.8	7.3	384.8	...
	2010	1 230.98	638.47	592.51	107.8	30.9	7.8	414.0	...
	2015	1 309.05	678.56	630.49	107.6	28.7	8.9	440.3	3 287
	2017[1]	1 339.18	693.96	645.22	107.6	27.8	9.4	450.4	...
Indonesia Indonésie	2005	226.71	113.82	112.89	100.8	30.0	7.4	125.1	...
	2010	242.52	122.28	120.25	101.7	29.0	7.4	133.9	...
	2015	258.16	130.04	128.12	101.5	27.9	8.1	142.5	1 911
	2017[1]	263.99	132.90	131.09	101.4	27.4	8.6	145.7	...
Iran (Islamic Republic of) Iran (Rép. islamique d')	2005	70.42	35.96	34.46	104.4	26.1	6.8	43.2	...
	2010	74.57	37.72	36.85	102.3	23.5	7.1	45.8	...
	2015	79.36	39.94	39.42	101.3	23.6	8.2	48.7	1 629[40]
	2017[1]	81.16	40.82	40.35	101.2	23.7	8.8	49.8	...
Iraq Iraq	2005	27.01	13.65	13.36	102.2	42.0	5.1	62.2	...
	2010	30.76	15.55	15.21	102.2	41.7	4.8	70.8	...
	2015	36.12	18.28	17.84	102.4	40.7	5.0	83.2	435
	2017[1]	38.27	19.38	18.90	102.5	40.4	5.0	88.1	...
Ireland Irlande	2005	4.21	2.10	2.11	99.8	20.2	14.8	61.2	...
	2010	4.63	2.31	2.32	99.3	20.7	16.1	67.2	...
	2015	4.70	2.33	2.37	98.4	21.7	18.4	68.2	70
	2017[1]	4.76	2.36	2.40	98.4	21.6	19.1	69.1	...
Isle of Man Île de Man	2005	0.08	...	...	96.9[13]	17.3[13]	22.1[13]	133.5	...
	2009	0.08	...	...	98.4[13]	16.4[13]	24.1[13]	139.2	...
	2010	0.08	...	...	98.6[13]	...	...	140.5	...
	2015	0.08	...	...	99.3[13]	16.3[13]	25.7[13]	145.9	1
	2016	0.08[1]	...	...	98.2[13]	16.0[13]	26.9[13]	146.9[1]	...
	2017[1]	0.08	...	...	...	...	...	147.9	...
Israel Israël	2005	6.60	3.26	3.35	97.4	27.9	13.2	305.1	...
	2010	7.43	3.67	3.76	97.6	27.3	14.9	343.2	...
	2015	8.06	4.00	4.07	98.4	27.9	15.8	372.7	22
	2017[1]	8.32	4.13	4.19	98.7	27.9	16.1	384.5	...
Italy Italie	2005	58.81	28.61	30.20	94.8	14.1	25.1	199.9	...
	2010	59.73	29.02	30.71	94.5	14.0	26.9	203.1	...
	2015	59.50	28.96	30.54	94.8	13.7	28.6	202.3	302
	2017[1]	59.36	28.93	30.43	95.1	13.5	29.4	201.8	...
Jamaica Jamaïque	2005	2.74	1.36	1.39	98.0	30.1	10.8	253.4	...
	2010	2.82	1.40	1.42	98.6	27.0	11.6	260.1	...
	2015	2.87	1.43	1.44	99.0	23.5	13.0	265.2	11
	2017[1]	2.89	1.44	1.45	99.0	22.7	13.6	266.9	...

Country or area Pays ou zone	Year Année	Mid-year population estimates and projections (millions) Estimations et projections de population au milieu de l'année (millions) Total	 Male Hommes	 Females Femmes	Sex Ratio (males per 100 females) Rapport des sexes (hommes pour 100 femmes)	Population age distribution (percentage) Répartition par âge de la population (pourcentage) Aged 0 to 14 years old âgée de 0 à 14 ans	 Aged 60+ years old âgée de 60 ans ou plus	Population density (per km²) Densité de population (pour km²)	Surface area Superficie (000 km²)
Japan	2005	128.34	62.89	65.45	96.1	13.8	26.3	352.0	...
Japon	2007	128.51	62.92	65.58	95.9	13.6	27.9	352.5	378[41]
	2010	128.55	62.88	65.67	95.7	13.4	30.3	352.6	...
	2017[1]	127.48	62.26	65.23	95.4	12.9	33.4	349.7	...
Jordan	2005	5.71	2.95	2.77	106.6	37.8	5.3	64.4	...
Jordanie	2010	7.18	3.66	3.52	104.1	37.0	5.4	80.9	...
	2015	9.16	4.64	4.52	102.7	36.0	5.5	103.2	89
	2017[1]	9.70	4.91	4.79	102.6	35.5	5.7	109.3	...
Kazakhstan	2005	15.54	7.49	8.05	93.0	24.5	10.1	5.8	...
Kazakhstan	2010	16.40	7.93	8.47	93.6	24.0	9.9	6.1	...
	2015	17.75	8.60	9.15	93.9	26.8	10.7	6.6	2 725
	2017[1]	18.20	8.82	9.39	93.9	27.9	11.1	6.7	...
Kenya	2005	36.05	17.91	18.14	98.7	43.8	3.7	63.3	...
Kenya	2010	41.35	20.55	20.80	98.8	43.2	3.8	72.7	...
	2015	47.24	23.48	23.76	98.8	41.3	4.1	83.0	592
	2017[1]	49.70	24.70	25.00	98.8	40.5	4.3	87.3	...
Kiribati	2005	0.09	0.05	0.05	97.1	36.9	5.4	114.0	...
Kiribati	2010	0.10	0.05	0.05	97.0	36.1	5.4	126.7	...
	2015	0.11	0.06	0.06	97.2	34.9	6.1	138.8	1[42]
	2017[1]	0.12	0.06	0.06	97.3	35.0	6.4	143.7	...
Kuwait	2005	2.28	1.34	0.93	144.2	26.0	3.6	127.8	...
Koweït	2010	3.00	1.73	1.26	137.1	23.2	3.4	168.2	...
	2015	3.94	2.26	1.67	135.0	20.9	4.1	220.9	18
	2017[1]	4.14	2.38	1.76	134.9	21.1	4.9	232.1	...
Kyrgyzstan	2005	5.08	2.52	2.56	98.3	31.0	7.1	26.5	...
Kirghizistan	2010	5.42	2.68	2.74	97.7	29.9	6.4	28.3	...
	2015	5.87	2.91	2.96	98.3	31.1	7.2	30.6	200
	2017[1]	6.05	3.00	3.05	98.4	31.8	7.6	31.5	...
Lao People's Dem. Rep.	2005	5.75	2.85	2.90	98.4	40.3	5.5	24.9	...
Rép. dém. populaire lao	2010	6.25	3.11	3.14	99.0	36.3	5.6	27.1	...
	2015	6.66	3.32	3.34	99.4	33.7	6.1	28.9	237
	2017[1]	6.86	3.42	3.44	99.5	32.9	6.3	29.7	...
Latvia	2005	2.25	1.03	1.22	84.7	14.7	22.5	36.2	...
Lettonie	2010	2.12	0.97	1.15	84.5	14.1	23.6	34.1	...
	2015	1.99	0.91	1.08	84.8	15.1	25.4	32.0	65
	2017[1]	1.95	0.90	1.05	84.9	15.4	26.2	31.3	...
Lebanon	2005	3.99	2.03	1.96	103.3	27.9	10.7	389.7	...
Liban	2010	4.34	2.21	2.13	104.1	23.7	11.9	424.0	...
	2015	5.85	2.94	2.91	100.9	24.0	11.5	572.0	10
	2017[1]	6.08	3.05	3.03	100.6	23.1	12.0	594.6	...
Lesotho	2005	1.95	0.94	1.01	93.5	39.4	6.3	64.2	...
Lesotho	2010	2.04	0.99	1.05	93.9	37.3	6.6	67.2	...
	2015	2.17	1.05	1.12	94.2	35.7	6.7	71.6	30
	2017[1]	2.23	1.08	1.15	94.4	35.4	6.7	73.6	...
Liberia	2005	3.26	1.64	1.63	100.6	43.3	4.9	33.9	...
Libéria	2010	3.95	1.99	1.96	101.2	43.3	4.8	41.0	...
	2015	4.50	2.27	2.23	101.7	42.4	4.8	46.7	111
	2017[1]	4.73	2.39	2.34	101.8	41.8	4.9	49.1	...
Libya	2005	5.79	2.99	2.81	106.5	30.1	5.9	3.3	...
Libye	2010	6.17	3.15	3.02	104.3	28.4	6.0	3.5	...
	2015	6.24	3.15	3.09	102.0	28.6	6.5	3.5	1 676
	2017[1]	6.37	3.21	3.16	101.7	28.2	6.6	3.6	...
Liechtenstein	2005	0.03	...	...	97.0[13]	17.5[13]	16.8[13]	217.8	...
Liechtenstein	2010	0.04	...	...	97.9	16.0	20.1	225.0	...
	2015	0.04	...	...	98.4[13]	15.0[13]	22.5[13]	233.8	~0
	2016	0.04[1]	...	...	98.4[13]	14.9[13]	22.7[13]	235.4[1]	...
	2017[1]	0.04	...	...	...	...	...	237.0	...

Country or area Pays ou zone	Year Année	Mid-year population estimates and projections (millions) Estimations et projections de population au milieu de l'année (millions) Total	 Male Hommes	 Females Femmes	Sex Ratio (males per 100 females) Rapport des sexes (hommes pour 100 femmes)	Population age distribution (percentage) Répartition par âge de la population (pourcentage) Aged 0 to 14 years old âgée de 0 à 14 ans	 Aged 60+ years old âgée de 60 ans ou plus	Population density (per km²) Densité de population (pour km²)	Surface area Superficie (000 km²)
Lithuania Lituanie	2005	3.34	1.55	1.79	86.8	16.8	21.1	53.4	...
	2010	3.12	1.44	1.69	85.3	14.8	22.4	49.8	...
	2015	2.93	1.35	1.58	85.4	14.6	24.5	46.8	65
	2017[1]	2.89	1.33	1.56	85.4	14.8	25.3	46.1	...
Luxembourg Luxembourg	2005	0.46	0.23	0.23	97.4	18.6	19.0	176.8	...
	2010	0.51	0.25	0.26	98.7	17.6	19.0	196.1	...
	2015	0.57	0.28	0.28	100.8	16.4	19.1	218.8	3
	2017[1]	0.58	0.29	0.29	101.0	16.4	19.6	225.3	...
Madagascar Madagascar	2005	18.34	9.13	9.21	99.2	44.7	4.4	31.5	...
	2010	21.15	10.54	10.62	99.3	43.5	4.3	36.4	...
	2015	24.23	12.08	12.15	99.4	41.6	4.6	41.7	587
	2017[1]	25.57	12.75	12.82	99.5	41.0	4.8	44.0	...
Malawi Malawi	2005	13.04	6.44	6.60	97.5	46.7	4.4	138.3	...
	2010	15.17	7.50	7.67	97.8	46.2	4.5	160.9	...
	2015	17.57	8.70	8.87	98.1	44.7	4.3	186.4	118
	2017[1]	18.62	9.23	9.40	98.2	44.0	4.3	197.5	...
Malaysia Malaisie	2005[43]	25.66	13.15	12.51	105.1	30.5	7.1	78.1	...
	2010[43]	28.11	14.49	13.62	106.3	27.9	7.9	85.6	...
	2015	30.72[43]	15.88[43]	14.85[43]	106.9[43]	25.0[43]	9.1[43]	93.5[43]	330
	2017[1,43]	31.62	16.33	15.30	106.7	24.3	9.7	96.3	...
Maldives Maldives	2005	0.32	0.17	0.15	111.5	31.6	6.3	1 062.8	...
	2010	0.36	0.20	0.16	121.1	25.5	6.0	1 215.0	...
	2015	0.42	0.24	0.18	130.2	23.4	6.0	1 394.7	~0
	2017[1]	0.44	0.25	0.19	131.8	23.4	6.3	1 454.4	...
Mali Mali	2005	12.80	6.37	6.43	99.1	46.9	4.6	10.5	...
	2010	15.08	7.53	7.54	99.8	47.5	4.2	12.4	...
	2015	17.47	8.74	8.73	100.0	47.9	4.0	14.3	1 240
	2017[1]	18.54	9.28	9.26	100.2	47.7	4.0	15.2	...
Malta Malte	2005	0.41	0.20	0.20	99.1	17.7	18.8	1 271.2	...
	2010	0.42	0.21	0.21	99.1	15.2	22.9	1 300.3	...
	2015	0.43	0.21	0.21	100.6	14.4	25.1	1 336.3	~0
	2017[1]	0.43	0.22	0.21	100.9	14.4	26.1	1 346.4	...
Marshall Islands Îles Marshall	2004	0.05	...	...	104.0[44,45]	40.6[44,45]	3.6[44,45]	289.3	...
	2005	0.05	...	...	...	...	...	289.2	...
	2010	0.05	...	...	105.2[44,45]	40.9[44,45]	4.5[44,45]	291.3	...
	2015	0.05	...	...	...	...	...	294.4	~0
	2016	0.05[1]	...	...	# 104.5	# 39.0	# 5.5	294.8[1]	...
	2017[1]	0.05	...	...	...	...	...	295.2	...
Martinique Martinique	2005	0.40	0.19	0.21	87.3	21.1	18.0	374.6	...
	2010	0.39	0.18	0.21	85.8	19.6	20.6	372.6	...
	2015	0.39	0.18	0.21	83.9	18.4	24.3	364.0	1
	2017[1]	0.38	0.18	0.21	83.5	17.7	25.7	363.1	...
Mauritania Mauritanie	2005	3.13	1.57	1.56	100.4	42.1	4.8	3.0	...
	2010	3.61	1.81	1.80	100.9	41.2	4.8	3.5	...
	2015	4.18	2.11	2.08	101.4	40.2	4.9	4.1	1 031
	2017[1]	4.42	2.23	2.19	101.6	39.9	5.0	4.3	...
Mauritius Maurice	2005[46]	1.22	0.61	0.62	98.3	24.7	9.6	602.0	...
	2010[46]	1.25	0.62	0.63	98.3	21.9	12.1	614.8	...
	2015	1.26[46]	0.62[46]	0.64[46]	98.1[46]	19.4[46]	15.4[46]	620.4[46]	2[47]
	2017[1,46]	1.27	0.63	0.64	97.9	18.4	16.6	623.2	...
Mayotte Mayotte	2005	0.18	0.09	0.09	97.2	42.4	4.8	474.9	...
	2010	0.21	0.10	0.11	95.6	42.9	5.1	556.6	...
	2017[1]	0.25	0.12	0.13	96.7	40.6	5.8	674.8	...
Mexico Mexique	2005	108.47	53.95	54.53	98.9	32.3	7.7	55.8	...
	2010	117.32	58.39	58.93	99.1	29.8	8.4	60.4	...
	2015	125.89	62.68	63.21	99.2	27.5	9.6	64.8	1 964
	2017[1]	129.16	64.31	64.85	99.2	26.7	10.1	66.4	...

Country or area Pays ou zone	Year Année	Mid-year population estimates and projections (millions) Estimations et projections de population au milieu de l'année (millions) Total	 Male Hommes	 Females Femmes	Sex Ratio (males per 100 females) Rapport des sexes (hommes pour 100 femmes)	Population age distribution (percentage) Répartition par âge de la population (pourcentage) Aged 0 to 14 years old âgée de 0 à 14 ans	 Aged 60+ years old âgée de 60 ans ou plus	Population density (per km²) Densité de population (pour km²)	Surface area Superficie (000 km²)
Micronesia (Fed. States of)	2005	0.11	0.05	0.05	103.3	38.8	5.5	151.7	...
Micronésie (États féd. de)	2010	0.10	0.05	0.05	104.3	36.9	6.2	148.0	...
	2015	0.10	0.05	0.05	105.0	34.1	7.5	149.2	1
	2017[1]	0.11	0.05	0.05	105.1	33.1	8.0	150.8	...
Monaco	2000	0.03	...	...	94.3[13]	13.2[13]	28.9[13]	21 531.5	...
Monaco	2005	0.03	...	...	...	...	...	22 679.9	...
	2008	0.04	...	...	94.7[13]	12.7[13]	31.2[13]	24 062.4	...
	2010	0.04	...	...	...	...	...	24 895.3	...
	2015	0.04	...	...	...	...	...	25 709.4	~0
	2017[1]	0.04	...	...	...	...	...	25 969.8	...
Mongolia	2005	2.53	1.26	1.27	99.0	28.9	5.6	1.6	...
Mongolie	2010	2.71	1.35	1.37	98.5	27.0	5.7	1.7	...
	2015	2.98	1.47	1.50	98.1	28.8	6.2	1.9	1 564
	2017[1]	3.08	1.52	1.55	97.9	29.7	6.6	2.0	...
Montenegro	2005	0.62	0.30	0.31	96.6	20.2	17.0	45.8	...
Monténégro	2010	0.62	0.31	0.32	97.1	19.2	17.9	46.4	...
	2015	0.63	0.31	0.32	97.3	18.5	20.4	46.7	14
	2017[1]	0.63	0.31	0.32	97.4	18.1	21.3	46.8	...
Montserrat	2001	~0.00	...	...	116.6	19.3	19.9	45.1	...
Montserrat	2004	~0.00	...	...	112.7	...	...	46.4	...
	2005	~0.00	...	...	...	...	...	47.8	...
	2006	~0.00	...	...	108.7[48]	19.6[48]	19.0[48]	48.5	...
	2010	~0.00	...	...	...	...	...	49.4	...
	2011	0.01	...	...	107.2[13]	19.7[13]	19.6[13]	49.9	...
	2015	0.01	...	...	...	...	...	51.2	~0
	2016	0.01[1]	...	...	106.0	...	...	51.5[1]	...
	2017[1]	0.01	...	...	...	...	...	51.8	...
Morocco	2005	30.52	15.08	15.45	97.6	30.8	8.2	68.4	...
Maroc	2010	32.41	15.97	16.44	97.2	28.5	8.6	72.6	...
	2015	34.80	17.22	17.58	97.9	27.7	10.0	78.0	447
	2017[1]	35.74	17.70	18.04	98.1	27.4	10.7	80.1	...
Mozambique	2005	20.92	10.11	10.82	93.4	45.6	4.8	26.6	...
Mozambique	2010	24.22	11.76	12.46	94.4	45.7	4.8	30.8	...
	2015	28.01	13.66	14.35	95.2	45.2	4.8	35.6	799
	2017[1]	29.67	14.49	15.18	95.5	44.8	4.8	37.7	...
Myanmar	2005	48.48	23.68	24.80	95.5	30.9	7.0	74.2	...
Myanmar	2010	50.16	24.48	25.68	95.3	30.0	7.5	76.8	...
	2015	52.40	25.59	26.81	95.5	27.9	8.9	80.2	677
	2017[1]	53.37	26.07	27.30	95.5	26.8	9.4	81.7	...
Namibia	2005	2.03	0.99	1.04	94.5	39.8	5.0	2.5	...
Namibie	2010	2.17	1.05	1.12	93.9	38.4	5.2	2.6	...
	2015	2.43	1.18	1.25	94.5	37.0	5.4	2.9	824
	2017[1]	2.53	1.23	1.30	94.7	36.7	5.5	3.1	...
Nauru	2002	0.01	...	...	104.2	38.1	2.5	504.0	...
Nauru	2005	0.01	...	...	...	...	...	505.7	...
	2010	0.01	...	...	...	...	...	501.3	...
	2015	0.01	...	...	...	...	...	563.0	~0
	2016	0.01[1]	...	...	# 101.9	# 39.5	# 4.0	567.4[1]	...
	2017[1]	0.01	...	...	...	...	...	568.0	...
Nepal	2005	25.64	12.72	12.92	98.5	39.7	6.7	178.9	...
Népal	2010	27.02	13.18	13.84	95.2	37.0	7.4	188.5	...
	2015	28.66	13.90	14.75	94.2	32.6	8.5	199.9	147
	2017[1]	29.31	14.23	15.08	94.3	30.9	8.8	204.4	...
Netherlands	2005	16.37	8.12	8.25	98.4	18.3	19.3	485.4	...
Pays-Bas	2010	16.68	8.28	8.40	98.6	17.5	22.0	494.7	...
	2015	16.94	8.42	8.52	98.9	16.8	24.1	502.3	42
	2017[1]	17.04	8.48	8.56	99.0	16.4	25.0	505.2	...

Country or area Pays ou zone	Year Année	Mid-year population estimates and projections (millions) Estimations et projections de population au milieu de l'année (millions) Total	 Male Hommes	 Females Femmes	Sex Ratio (males per 100 females) Rapport des sexes (hommes pour 100 femmes)	Population age distribution (percentage) Répartition par âge de la population (pourcentage) Aged 0 to 14 years old âgée de 0 à 14 ans	 Aged 60+ years old âgée de 60 ans ou plus	Population density (per km²) Densité de population (pour km²)	Surface area Superficie (000 km²)
New Caledonia	2005	0.23	0.12	0.12	101.1	27.5	10.3	12.7	...
Nouvelle-Calédonie	2010	0.25	0.13	0.12	102.9	24.1	13.1	13.7	...
	2015	0.27	0.14	0.13	101.9	22.8	13.8	14.7	19
	2017[1]	0.28	0.14	0.14	101.5	22.5	14.2	15.1	...
New Zealand	2005	4.14	2.03	2.11	96.0	21.5	16.4	15.7	...
Nouvelle-Zélande	2010	4.37	2.15	2.22	96.5	20.5	18.4	16.6	...
	2015	4.61	2.27	2.35	96.7	20.0	20.0	17.5	268
	2017[1]	4.71	2.31	2.39	96.7	19.8	20.8	17.9	...
Nicaragua	2005	5.38	2.66	2.72	97.5	36.0	6.1	44.7	...
Nicaragua	2010	5.74	2.83	2.91	97.1	32.8	6.5	47.7	...
	2015	6.08	3.00	3.08	97.2	30.0	7.8	50.5	130
	2017[1]	6.22	3.07	3.15	97.2	29.0	8.4	51.7	...
Niger	2005	13.62	6.78	6.83	99.3	49.2	4.1	10.8	...
Niger	2010	16.43	8.21	8.22	99.9	50.0	4.1	13.0	...
	2015	19.90	9.97	9.93	100.4	50.2	4.1	15.7	1 267
	2017[1]	21.48	10.77	10.71	100.6	50.2	4.2	17.0	...
Nigeria	2005	138.94	70.16	68.78	102.0	43.7	4.6	152.6	...
Nigéria	2010	158.58	80.20	78.37	102.3	44.0	4.5	174.1	...
	2015	181.18	91.77	89.41	102.6	44.1	4.5	198.9	924
	2017[1]	190.89	96.73	94.16	102.7	44.0	4.5	209.6	...
Niue	2005	~0.00	...	...	94.8[13]	26.1[13]	15.1[13]	6.5	...
Nioué	2010	~0.00	...	...	101.9[13]	25.7[13]	16.8[13]	6.3	...
	2015	~0.00	...	...	...	...	...	6.3	~0
	2016	~0.00[1]	...	...	# 100.0	# 22.8	# 20.1	6.2[1]	...
	2017[1]	~0.00	...	...	...	...	...	6.2	...
Northern Mariana Islands	2005	0.06	...	...	83.3[44]	22.9[44,49]	3.7[44,49]	138.6	...
Îles Mariannes du Nord	2010	0.05	...	...	106.2	26.7	5.8	118.3	...
	2015	0.05	...	...	...	...	...	119.2	~0
	2016	0.06[1]	...	...	# 107.1	# 23.5	# 10.0	119.6[1]	...
	2017[1]	0.06	...	...	...	...	...	119.9	...
Norway [50]	2005	4.63	2.30	2.33	98.5	19.6	19.8	12.7	...
Norvège [50]	2010	4.89	2.44	2.44	100.0	18.8	21.0	13.4	...
	2015	5.20	2.62	2.58	101.4	18.0	21.8	14.2	386
	2017[1]	5.31	2.68	2.63	101.8	17.8	22.3	14.5	...
Oman	2005	2.51	1.42	1.09	130.2	32.5	4.1	8.1	...
Oman	2010	3.04	1.83	1.21	152.0	25.7	3.9	9.8	...
	2015	4.20	2.72	1.48	184.4	22.2	3.8	13.6	310
	2017[1]	4.64	3.05	1.58	192.8	21.8	4.0	15.0	...
Other non-specified areas	2005	22.60	11.48	11.12	103.2	19.2	13.1	638.3	...
Autres zones non-spécifiées	2010	23.10	11.63	11.47	101.4	16.1	14.9	652.4	...
	2017[1]	23.63	11.79	11.84	99.6	13.3	20.2	667.2	...
Pakistan	2005	153.91	79.33	74.58	106.4	38.2	6.5	199.7	...
Pakistan	2010	170.56	87.69	82.87	105.8	36.2	6.6	221.3	...
	2015	189.38	97.29	92.09	105.6	35.0	6.6	245.7	796
	2017[1]	197.02	101.20	95.82	105.6	34.8	6.7	255.6	...
Palau	2005	0.02	...	...	116.2[13]	24.1[13]	8.2[13]	43.3	...
Palaos	2010	0.02	...	...	...	...	...	44.5	...
	2015	0.02	...	...	114.6[13]	20.5[13]	12.1[13]	46.3	~0
	2016	0.02[1]	...	...	# 113.3	# 20.3	# 13.1	46.7[1]	...
	2017[1]	0.02	...	...	...	...	...	47.2	...
Panama	2005	3.33	1.68	1.65	101.3	30.4	8.8	44.8	...
Panama	2010	3.64	1.83	1.81	100.9	29.1	9.7	49.0	...
	2015	3.97	1.99	1.98	100.6	27.9	10.8	53.4	75
	2017[1]	4.10	2.05	2.04	100.4	27.4	11.4	55.1	...
Papua New Guinea	2005	6.31	3.21	3.10	103.4	39.1	5.1	13.9	...
Papouasie-Nvl-Guinée	2010	7.11	3.62	3.49	103.5	38.3	5.4	15.7	...
	2015	7.92	4.03	3.89	103.5	36.6	5.9	17.5	463
	2017[1]	8.25	4.20	4.05	103.5	35.9	6.1	18.2	...

Country or area Pays ou zone	Year Année	Mid-year population estimates and projections (millions) Estimations et projections de population au milieu de l'année (millions) Total	 Male Hommes	 Females Femmes	Sex Ratio (males per 100 females) Rapport des sexes (hommes pour 100 femmes)	Population age distribution (percentage) Répartition par âge de la population (pourcentage) Aged 0 to 14 years old âgée de 0 à 14 ans	 Aged 60+ years old âgée de 60 ans ou plus	Population density (per km²) Densité de population (pour km²)	Surface area Superficie (000 km²)
Paraguay	2005	5.80	2.93	2.86	102.6	35.3	7.1	14.6	...
Paraguay	2010	6.21	3.15	3.06	103.0	32.7	7.9	15.6	...
	2015	6.64	3.37	3.27	103.0	30.1	9.0	16.7	407
	2017[1]	6.81	3.45	3.36	102.9	29.4	9.4	17.1	...
Peru	2005	27.61	13.80	13.81	99.9	31.7	8.1	21.6	...
Pérou	2010	29.37	14.68	14.70	99.8	29.4	8.9	22.9	...
	2015	31.38	15.67	15.70	99.8	27.9	10.0	24.5	1 285
	2017[1]	32.17	16.07	16.10	99.8	27.4	10.4	25.1	...
Philippines	2005	86.27	43.36	42.91	101.0	37.1	5.4	289.3	...
Philippines	2010	93.73	47.31	46.42	101.9	33.9	6.5	314.3	...
	2015	101.72	51.24	50.48	101.5	32.2	7.3	341.1	300
	2017[1]	104.92	52.80	52.12	101.3	31.7	7.6	351.9	...
Poland	2005	38.36	18.57	19.79	93.9	16.6	17.0	125.3	...
Pologne	2010	38.32	18.53	19.79	93.6	15.2	19.4	125.1	...
	2015	38.27	18.48	19.78	93.4	14.9	22.6	125.0	313
	2017[1]	38.17	18.43	19.74	93.4	14.8	24.0	124.6	...
Portugal	2005	10.57	5.11	5.46	93.7	15.4	22.5	115.4	...
Portugal	2010	10.65	5.10	5.55	91.9	15.0	24.7	116.3	...
	2015	10.42	4.94	5.48	90.0	14.1	27.0	113.8	92
	2017[1]	10.33	4.89	5.44	89.8	13.6	27.9	112.8	...
Puerto Rico	2005	3.77	1.81	1.96	92.3	22.3	16.7	424.5	...
Porto Rico	2010	3.72	1.79	1.93	92.5	20.6	18.1	419.0	...
	2015	3.67	1.77	1.91	92.5	18.7	19.7	414.2	9
	2017[1]	3.66	1.76	1.90	92.6	17.9	20.4	413.0	...
Qatar	2005	0.86	0.58	0.28	208.4	21.7	2.5	74.5	...
Qatar	2010	1.78	1.35	0.43	313.7	13.1	1.8	153.3	...
	2015	2.48	1.87	0.61	306.6	13.8	2.3	213.7	12
	2017[1]	2.64	1.98	0.66	301.2	13.9	2.8	227.3	...
Republic of Korea	2005	48.71	24.43	24.27	100.7	18.8	12.8	501.0	...
République de Corée	2010	49.55	24.83	24.72	100.4	16.1	15.3	509.6	...
	2015	50.59	25.32	25.27	100.2	13.9	18.4	520.4	100
	2017[1]	50.98	25.51	25.47	100.2	13.5	20.1	524.3	...
Republic of Moldova	2005[51]	4.16	1.99	2.17	91.9	18.5	13.6	126.6	...
République de Moldova	2010[51]	4.08	1.96	2.12	92.6	16.5	14.1	124.3	...
	2015	4.07[51]	1.95[51]	2.11[51]	92.5[51]	15.7[51]	16.5[51]	123.8[51]	34
	2017[1,51]	4.05	1.94	2.11	92.2	15.7	17.6	123.3	...
Réunion	2005	0.79	0.39	0.40	96.4	26.9	10.3	316.6	...
Réunion	2010	0.83	0.40	0.43	93.9	25.4	12.2	332.2	...
	2015	0.86	0.42	0.45	93.9	24.3	15.3	345.3	3
	2017[1]	0.88	0.42	0.45	93.9	23.6	16.4	350.6	...
Romania	2005	21.43	10.45	10.99	95.1	15.9	19.6	93.1	...
Roumanie	2010	20.44	9.92	10.52	94.4	15.8	21.4	88.8	...
	2015	19.88	9.63	10.24	94.0	15.4	23.9	86.4	238
	2017[1]	19.68	9.53	10.14	94.0	15.3	24.9	85.5	...
Russian Federation	2005	143.62	66.83	76.78	87.0	15.2	17.2	8.8	...
Fédération de Russie	2010	143.15	66.39	76.77	86.5	14.9	18.0	8.7	...
	2015	143.89	66.85	77.04	86.8	16.8	20.1	8.8	17 098
	2017[1]	143.99	66.92	77.07	86.8	17.6	21.1	8.8	...
Rwanda	2005	8.99	4.39	4.60	95.6	41.7	4.1	364.5	...
Rwanda	2010	10.25	5.02	5.23	95.9	41.8	4.1	415.4	...
	2015	11.63	5.70	5.93	96.2	40.8	4.6	471.4	26
	2017[1]	12.21	5.99	6.22	96.2	40.1	4.9	494.9	...
Saint Helena [52]	2005	~0.00	...	...	...	...	...	11.0	...
Sainte-Hélène [52]	2010	~0.00	...	...	...	...	...	10.7	...
	2015	~0.00	...	...	...	...	...	10.3	~0
	2017[1]	~0.00	...	...	...	...	...	10.4	...

Country or area Pays ou zone	Year Année	Mid-year population estimates and projections (millions) Estimations et projections de population au milieu de l'année (millions) Total	 Male Hommes	 Females Femmes	Sex Ratio (males per 100 females) Rapport des sexes (hommes pour 100 femmes)	Population age distribution (percentage) Répartition par âge de la population (pourcentage) Aged 0 to 14 years old âgée de 0 à 14 ans	 Aged 60+ years old âgée de 60 ans ou plus	Population density (per km²) Densité de population (pour km²)	Surface area Superficie (000 km²)
Saint Kitts and Nevis Saint-Kitts-et-Nevis	2000	0.05	...	...	101.9	28.0	9.9	174.5	...
	2005	0.05	...	...	* 95.7	...	...	187.0	...
	2010	0.05	...	...	* 95.7	...	...	197.9	...
	2011	0.05	...	...	* 97.0	...	...	200.0	...
	2015	0.05	...	...	...	...	...	208.8	~0
	2017[1]	0.06	...	...	...	...	...	212.9	...
Saint Lucia Sainte-Lucie	2005	0.16	0.08	0.08	95.8	27.7	9.8	268.4	...
	2010	0.17	0.08	0.09	96.4	23.2	12.1	282.9	...
	2015	0.18	0.09	0.09	96.0	19.7	13.1	290.5	1[53]
	2017[1]	0.18	0.09	0.09	95.9	18.9	13.7	293.2	...
Saint Pierre and Miquelon Saint-Pierre-et-Miquelon	2005	0.01	...	...	...	...	...	27.2	...
	2006	0.01	...	...	98.2	19.1	17.8	27.2	...
	2010	0.01	...	...	...	...	...	27.3	...
	2015	0.01	...	...	...	...	...	27.3	~0
	2017[1]	0.01	...	...	...	...	...	27.5	...
Saint Vincent & Grenadines Saint-Vincent-Grenadines	2005	0.11	0.05	0.05	102.0	28.5	9.4	278.8	...
	2010	0.11	0.06	0.05	102.0	26.5	9.5	280.3	...
	2015	0.11	0.06	0.05	101.8	24.5	10.9	280.7	~0
	2017[1]	0.11	0.06	0.05	101.7	23.8	11.7	281.8	...
Samoa Samoa	2005	0.18	0.09	0.09	107.4	39.6	6.9	63.6	...
	2010	0.19	0.10	0.09	106.5	38.3	7.2	65.8	...
	2015	0.19	0.10	0.09	106.6	37.2	8.0	68.5	3
	2017[1]	0.20	0.10	0.10	106.6	36.6	8.5	69.4	...
San Marino Saint-Marin	2004	0.03	...	...	96.2[15]	15.2[15]	21.5[15]	481.1	...
	2005	0.03	...	...	96.1[15]	...	...	487.3	...
	2010	0.03	...	...	* 93.5	* 20.9[54]	* 21.6[55]	518.5	...
	2015	0.03	...	...	94.9[15]	15.0[15]	24.1[15]	549.3	~0
	2017[1]	0.03	...	...	...	...	...	556.7	...
Sao Tome and Principe Sao Tomé-et-Principe	2005	0.16	0.08	0.08	98.8	44.1	5.6	162.1	...
	2010	0.17	0.09	0.09	99.0	44.1	4.7	182.1	...
	2015	0.20	0.10	0.10	99.2	43.4	4.3	203.7	1
	2017[1]	0.20	0.10	0.10	99.2	42.8	4.3	212.8	...
Saudi Arabia Arabie saoudite	2005	23.91	13.31	10.60	125.5	33.8	4.4	11.1	...
	2010	27.43	15.40	12.03	128.1	29.8	4.5	12.8	...
	2015	31.56	17.89	13.66	130.9	26.0	5.2	14.7	2 207
	2017[1]	32.94	18.80	14.14	132.9	25.2	5.6	15.3	...
Senegal Sénégal	2005	11.25	5.52	5.73	96.2	43.7	4.9	58.4	...
	2010	12.92	6.32	6.59	95.9	43.2	4.7	67.1	...
	2015	14.98	7.35	7.63	96.4	43.1	4.7	77.8	197[56]
	2017[1]	15.85	7.79	8.06	96.6	42.9	4.7	82.3	...
Serbia Serbie	2005[57]	9.22	4.50	4.71	95.6	18.6	19.0	105.4	...
	2010[57]	9.03	4.42	4.61	95.7	17.3	21.0	103.2	...
	2015	8.85[57]	4.33[57]	4.53[57]	95.6[57]	16.7[57]	23.8[57]	101.2[57]	88[58]
	2017[1,57]	8.79	4.30	4.50	95.6	16.5	24.5	100.5	...
Seychelles Seychelles	2005	0.09	0.04	0.04	99.9	24.9	9.2	192.9	...
	2010	0.09	0.05	0.04	106.5	22.8	10.0	198.7	...
	2015	0.09	0.05	0.05	98.2	21.7	12.4	203.8	~0
	2017[1]	0.09	0.05	0.05	97.2	22.2	13.3	206.0	...
Sierra Leone Sierra Leone	2005	5.66	2.79	2.87	97.3	44.4	4.1	78.4	...
	2010	6.46	3.19	3.27	97.6	44.0	4.1	89.5	...
	2015	7.24	3.58	3.66	98.0	42.7	4.1	100.3	72
	2017[1]	7.56	3.74	3.81	98.1	42.1	4.2	104.7	...
Singapore Singapour	2005	4.49	2.23	2.26	98.5	19.1	12.6	6 415.8	...
	2010	5.07	2.50	2.57	97.4	17.3	14.1	7 248.9	...
	2015	5.54	2.73	2.80	97.6	15.5	17.9	7 907.5	1[59]
	2017[1]	5.71	2.82	2.89	97.7	15.0	19.5	8 155.5	...

Country or area Pays ou zone	Year Année	Mid-year population estimates and projections (millions) Estimations et projections de population au milieu de l'année (millions) Total	 Male Hommes	 Females Femmes	Sex Ratio (males per 100 females) Rapport des sexes (hommes pour 100 femmes)	Population age distribution (percentage) Répartition par âge de la population (pourcentage) Aged 0 to 14 years old âgée de 0 à 14 ans	 Aged 60+ years old âgée de 60 ans ou plus	Population density (per km²) Densité de population (pour km²)	Surface area Superficie (000 km²)
Sint Maarten (Dutch part)	2005	0.03	...	...	93.9[13]	...	...	956.8	...
St-Martin (partie néerland.)	2010	0.03	...	...	91.0[13]	...	...	974.2	...
	2013	0.04	...	...	95.8[13]	21.0[13]	10.4[13]	1 071.7	~0
	2014	0.04	...	...	95.7[13]	...	...	1 108.7	~0
	2015	0.04	...	...	...	...	...	1 139.7	~0
	2017[1]	0.04	...	...	...	...	...	1 180.0	...
Slovakia	2005	5.40	2.62	2.78	94.1	16.8	16.1	112.3	...
Slovaquie	2010	5.40	2.62	2.78	94.2	15.3	17.8	112.4	...
	2015	5.44	2.64	2.80	94.6	15.3	20.7	113.1	49[60]
	2017[1]	5.45	2.65	2.80	94.6	15.4	21.8	113.3	...
Slovenia	2005	2.00	0.97	1.02	95.4	14.0	20.8	99.1	...
Slovénie	2010	2.05	1.01	1.03	97.9	14.1	22.2	101.5	...
	2015	2.07	1.03	1.05	98.5	14.7	25.1	103.0	20
	2017[1]	2.08	1.03	1.05	98.6	15.0	26.3	103.3	...
Solomon Islands	2005	0.47	0.24	0.23	104.5	41.3	4.8	16.8	...
Îles Salomon	2010	0.53	0.27	0.26	103.3	40.8	5.1	18.9	...
	2015	0.59	0.30	0.29	103.4	39.6	5.2	21.0	29
	2017[1]	0.61	0.31	0.30	103.4	38.8	5.4	21.8	...
Somalia	2005	10.41	5.21	5.20	100.2	47.9	4.3	16.6	...
Somalie	2010	12.05	6.02	6.04	99.7	47.7	4.3	19.2	...
	2015	13.91	6.93	6.98	99.3	46.7	4.3	22.2	638
	2017[1]	14.74	7.34	7.40	99.3	46.4	4.4	23.5	...
South Africa	2005	48.82	23.96	24.86	96.4	31.7	6.7	40.2	...
Afrique du Sud	2010	51.58	25.33	26.26	96.5	30.4	7.2	42.5	...
	2015	55.29	27.15	28.14	96.5	29.3	8.0	45.6	1 221
	2017[1]	56.72	27.84	28.88	96.4	29.0	8.4	46.8	...
South Sudan	2005	8.11	4.05	4.06	99.6	44.3	5.1	13.3	...
Soudan du sud	2010	10.07	5.03	5.03	99.9	43.3	5.3	16.5	...
	2015	11.88	5.95	5.93	100.3	42.1	5.1	19.4	659
	2017[1]	12.58	6.30	6.27	100.4	41.7	5.1	20.6	...
Spain	2005[61]	44.04	21.72	22.32	97.3	14.3	21.6	88.3	...
Espagne	2010[61]	46.79	23.13	23.66	97.8	14.6	22.4	93.8	...
	2015	46.40[61]	22.77[61]	23.63[61]	96.4[61]	14.9[61]	24.4[61]	93.0[61]	506
	2017[1,61]	46.35	22.73	23.62	96.2	14.7	25.3	92.9	...
Sri Lanka	2005	19.52	9.63	9.90	97.2	25.6	10.4	311.3	...
Sri Lanka	2010	20.20	9.83	10.37	94.8	25.4	11.8	322.1	...
	2015	20.71	9.98	10.74	93.0	24.6	13.9	330.3	66
	2017[1]	20.88	10.03	10.84	92.5	24.0	14.9	332.9	...
State of Palestine	2005[62]	3.58	1.81	1.76	102.9	45.6	4.0	594.0	...
État de Palestine	2010[62]	4.07	2.06	2.00	102.9	42.4	4.3	675.6	...
	2015	4.66[62]	2.36[62]	2.30[62]	102.9[62]	40.1[62]	4.5[62]	774.6[62]	6
	2017[1,62]	4.92	2.50	2.43	102.9	39.6	4.6	817.4	...
Sudan	2005	30.91	15.50	15.41	100.6	43.5	4.9	17.5	...
Soudan	2010	34.39	17.15	17.23	99.5	43.0	5.1	19.5	...
	2017[1]	40.53	20.26	20.28	99.9	40.8	5.5	23.0	...
Suriname	2005	0.50	0.25	0.25	101.5	30.8	8.5	3.2	...
Suriname	2010	0.53	0.26	0.26	101.2	28.7	9.1	3.4	...
	2015	0.55	0.28	0.28	100.9	26.9	9.9	3.5	164
	2017[1]	0.56	0.28	0.28	100.7	26.4	10.4	3.6	...
Swaziland	2005	1.11	0.54	0.57	93.8	42.1	4.6	64.3	...
Swaziland	2010	1.20	0.58	0.62	94.2	39.5	4.7	69.9	...
	2015	1.32	0.64	0.68	94.0	37.6	4.8	76.7	17
	2017[1]	1.37	0.66	0.71	93.9	37.2	4.8	79.5	...
Sweden	2005	9.04	4.48	4.56	98.4	17.4	23.5	22.0	...
Suède	2010	9.39	4.68	4.71	99.2	16.5	24.9	22.9	...
	2015	9.76	4.88	4.88	99.9	17.3	25.2	23.8	439
	2017[1]	9.91	4.96	4.95	100.2	17.5	25.5	24.2	...

Country or area Pays ou zone	Year Année	Mid-year population estimates and projections (millions) / Estimations et projections de population au milieu de l'année (millions): Total	Male Hommes	Females Femmes	Sex Ratio (males per 100 females) Rapport des sexes (hommes pour 100 femmes)	Population age distribution (percentage) / Répartition par âge de la population (pourcentage): Aged 0 to 14 years old âgée de 0 à 14 ans	Aged 60+ years old âgée de 60 ans ou plus	Population density (per km²) Densité de population (pour km²)	Surface area Superficie (000 km²)
Switzerland Suisse	2005	7.41	3.63	3.78	95.9	16.3	21.3	187.5	...
	2010	7.83	3.86	3.98	97.0	15.1	22.8	198.2	...
	2015	8.32	4.12	4.20	98.0	14.8	23.5	210.5	41
	2017[1]	8.48	4.20	4.28	98.2	14.9	24.1	214.5	...
Syrian Arab Republic République arabe syrienne	2005	18.29	9.33	8.96	104.2	39.1	4.9	99.6	...
	2010	21.02	10.61	10.41	101.9	36.4	5.1	114.5	...
	2015	18.74	9.48	9.26	102.3	38.1	6.4	102.0	185
	2017[1]	18.27	9.23	9.04	102.1	36.6	6.8	99.5	...
Tajikistan Tadjikistan	2005	6.85	3.45	3.40	101.3	38.1	5.1	49.0	...
	2010	7.64	3.85	3.79	101.6	35.7	4.9	54.6	...
	2015	8.55	4.30	4.25	101.1	35.1	5.5	61.1	143
	2017[1]	8.92	4.48	4.44	100.9	35.3	5.8	63.7	...
Thailand Thaïlande	2005	65.43	32.18	33.25	96.8	21.3	11.1	128.1	...
	2010	67.21	32.94	34.27	96.1	19.2	12.9	131.6	...
	2015	68.66	33.53	35.13	95.4	18.0	15.6	134.4	513
	2017[1]	69.04	33.66	35.37	95.2	17.3	16.9	135.1	...
TFYR of Macedonia ex-R.Y. de Macédoine	2005	2.06	1.03	1.03	99.9	20.2	15.3	81.7	...
	2010	2.07	1.03	1.04	99.8	17.9	16.4	82.1	...
	2015	2.08	1.04	1.04	100.0	16.8	18.6	82.4	26
	2017[1]	2.08	1.04	1.04	100.0	16.7	19.5	82.6	...
Timor-Leste Timor-Leste	2005	1.03	0.52	0.51	102.8	49.2	4.3	69.0	...
	2010	1.11	0.56	0.55	103.2	45.6	5.1	74.6	...
	2015	1.24	0.63	0.61	103.2	44.0	5.4	83.5	15
	2017[1]	1.30	0.66	0.64	103.2	43.6	5.4	87.2	...
Togo Togo	2005	5.68	2.82	2.86	98.7	42.6	4.5	104.5	...
	2010	6.50	3.24	3.27	99.1	42.5	4.4	119.6	...
	2015	7.42	3.70	3.72	99.3	42.0	4.5	136.4	57
	2017[1]	7.80	3.89	3.91	99.4	41.6	4.6	143.4	...
Tokelau Tokélaou	2001	~0.00	...	...	98.1	40.7	9.5	150.3	...
	2005	~0.00	...	...	...	...	...	120.8	...
	2006	~0.00	...	...	102.6	36.6	11.3	116.7	...
	2010	~0.00	...	...	...	...	...	114.0	...
	2015	~0.00	...	...	...	...	...	125.2	~0
	2016	~0.00[1]	...	...	# 100.0	# 28.3	# 12.2	128.2[1]	...
	2017[1]	~0.00	...	...	...	...	...	130.0	...
Tonga Tonga	2005	0.10	0.05	0.05	100.6	38.2	8.3	140.3	...
	2010	0.10	0.05	0.05	100.3	37.4	8.0	144.6	...
	2015	0.11	0.05	0.05	100.6	36.7	8.1	147.7	1
	2017[1]	0.11	0.05	0.05	100.7	35.8	8.5	150.0	...
Trinidad and Tobago Trinité-et-Tobago	2005	1.30	0.64	0.65	98.3	21.8	10.8	252.8	...
	2010	1.33	0.66	0.67	98.0	20.7	12.4	258.9	...
	2015	1.36	0.67	0.69	97.4	20.8	14.2	265.1	5
	2017[1]	1.37	0.67	0.69	97.1	20.7	15.0	266.9	...
Tunisia Tunisie	2005	10.10	5.03	5.07	99.2	25.5	10.0	65.0	...
	2010	10.64	5.28	5.36	98.4	23.3	10.4	68.5	...
	2015	11.27	5.57	5.70	97.7	23.7	11.7	72.6	164
	2017[1]	11.53	5.70	5.84	97.6	24.0	12.3	74.2	...
Turkey Turquie	2005	67.90	33.42	34.48	96.9	28.6	9.6	88.2	...
	2010	72.33	35.56	36.76	96.7	26.9	10.4	94.0	...
	2015	78.27	38.50	39.77	96.8	25.6	11.5	101.7	784
	2017[1]	80.75	39.77	40.98	97.0	25.0	12.0	104.9	...
Turkmenistan Turkménistan	2005	4.75	2.34	2.42	96.8	32.6	6.1	10.1	...
	2010	5.09	2.50	2.58	96.8	29.5	6.1	10.8	...
	2015	5.57	2.74	2.83	97.0	30.4	6.8	11.8	488
	2017[1]	5.76	2.84	2.92	97.0	30.9	7.3	12.3	...

Country or area Pays ou zone	Year Année	Mid-year population estimates and projections (millions) Estimations et projections de population au milieu de l'année (millions) Total	Male Hommes	Females Femmes	Sex Ratio (males per 100 females) Rapport des sexes (hommes pour 100 femmes)	Population age distribution (percentage) Répartition par âge de la population (pourcentage) Aged 0 to 14 years old âgée de 0 à 14 ans	Aged 60+ years old âgée de 60 ans ou plus	Population density (per km²) Densité de population (pour km²)	Surface area Superficie (000 km²)
Turks and Caicos Islands Îles Turques-et-Caïques	2001	0.02	...	...	99.1	28.6	5.2	21.2	...
	2005	0.03	...	...	99.1[13,44]	...	...	27.8	...
	2010	0.03	...	...	106.7[13,44]	...	...	32.6	...
	2015	0.03	...	...	103.8[13,44]	19.8[13,44]	6.9[13,44]	36.1	1[63]
	2017	0.04[1]	...	...	104.1[13,44]	19.2[13,44]	7.6[13,44]	37.3[1]	...
Tuvalu Tuvalu	2002	0.01	...	...	97.9	36.2	8.6	321.2	...
	2005	0.01	...	...	...	...	...	334.2	...
	2010	0.01	...	...	...	...	...	351.0	...
	2015	0.01	...	...	...	...	...	366.7	~0
	2016	0.01[1]	...	...	102.0	31.1	9.9	369.9[1]	...
	2017[1]	0.01	...	...	...	...	...	373.1	...
Uganda Ouganda	2005	28.54	14.13	14.41	98.1	49.8	3.6	142.9	...
	2010	33.92	16.84	17.07	98.6	49.3	3.4	169.7	...
	2015	40.14	19.96	20.18	98.9	48.2	3.3	200.9	242
	2017[1]	42.86	21.32	21.54	99.0	47.7	3.3	214.5	...
Ukraine Ukraine	2005[64]	46.89	21.75	25.14	86.5	14.6	20.4	80.9	...
	2010[64]	45.79	21.14	24.66	85.7	14.1	21.0	79.0	...
	2015	44.66[64]	20.64[64]	24.02[64]	85.9[64]	15.1[64]	22.5[64]	77.1[64]	604
	2017[1,64]	44.22	20.45	23.78	86.0	15.5	23.2	76.3	...
United Arab Emirates Émirats arabes unis	2005	4.58	3.22	1.36	236.2	18.4	1.7	54.8	...
	2010	8.27	6.16	2.11	292.1	13.4	1.5	98.9	...
	2015	9.15	6.69	2.46	272.2	13.8	2.0	109.5	84
	2017[1]	9.40	6.81	2.59	262.4	13.9	2.4	112.4	...
United Kingdom Royaume-Uni	2005	60.29	29.51	30.77	95.9	18.0	21.2	249.2	...
	2010	63.31	31.10	32.21	96.6	17.5	22.7	261.7	...
	2015	65.40	32.23	33.17	97.2	17.6	23.5	270.3	242
	2017[1]	66.18	32.65	33.53	97.4	17.7	23.9	273.6	...
United Rep. of Tanzania Rép.-Unie de Tanzanie	2005[65]	39.41	19.44	19.97	97.3	45.3	4.6	44.5	...
	2010[65]	46.10	22.75	23.35	97.4	45.3	4.7	52.0	...
	2015	53.88[65]	26.63[65]	27.25[65]	97.7[65]	45.2[65]	4.6[65]	60.8[65]	947
	2017[1,65]	57.31	28.34	28.97	97.8	44.9	4.7	64.7	...
United States of America États-Unis d'Amérique	2005	295.13	145.63	149.50	97.4	20.9	16.7	32.3	...
	2010	308.64	152.45	156.19	97.6	20.2	18.4	33.7	...
	2015	319.93	158.27	161.66	97.9	19.2	20.6	35.0	9 834
	2017[1]	324.46	160.59	163.87	98.0	18.9	21.5	35.5	...
United States Virgin Islands Îles Vierges américaines	2005	0.11	0.05	0.06	93.5	22.4	16.6	308.0	...
	2010	0.11	0.05	0.06	91.8	20.8	20.4	303.3	...
	2015	0.11	0.05	0.05	91.2	20.4	24.0	299.9	~0
	2017[1]	0.10	0.05	0.05	91.1	20.1	25.3	299.7	...
Uruguay Uruguay	2005	3.33	1.61	1.72	93.3	23.8	17.9	19.0	...
	2010	3.37	1.63	1.75	93.1	22.5	18.4	19.3	...
	2015	3.43	1.66	1.78	93.3	21.4	19.1	19.6	174
	2017[1]	3.46	1.67	1.79	93.5	21.1	19.5	19.8	...
Uzbekistan Ouzbékistan	2005	26.51	13.17	13.34	98.8	32.6	6.6	62.3	...
	2010	28.61	14.23	14.38	99.0	29.1	6.2	67.2	...
	2015	30.98	15.43	15.54	99.3	28.1	7.1	72.8	449
	2017[1]	31.91	15.91	16.00	99.4	28.0	7.6	75.0	...
Vanuatu Vanuatu	2005	0.21	0.11	0.10	104.1	39.7	5.2	17.2	...
	2010	0.24	0.12	0.12	103.1	38.2	5.7	19.4	...
	2015	0.26	0.13	0.13	102.6	36.5	6.5	21.7	12
	2017[1]	0.28	0.14	0.14	102.4	35.9	6.7	22.7	...
Venezuela (Boliv. Rep. of) Venezuela (Rép. boliv. du)	2005	26.78	13.41	13.38	100.2	31.7	7.4	30.4	...
	2010	29.03	14.49	14.54	99.7	29.8	8.3	32.9	...
	2015	31.16	15.51	15.64	99.2	28.2	9.4	35.3	912
	2017[1]	31.98	15.91	16.07	99.0	27.6	9.9	36.3	...
Viet Nam Viet Nam	2005	84.31	41.52	42.79	97.0	27.2	8.6	271.9	...
	2010	88.47	43.68	44.79	97.5	23.7	8.9	285.3	...
	2015	93.57	46.28	47.29	97.9	23.1	10.3	301.8	331
	2017[1]	95.54	47.28	48.26	98.0	23.1	11.1	308.1	...

Country or area Pays ou zone	Year Année	Mid-year population estimates and projections (millions) Estimations et projections de population au milieu de l'année (millions) Total	Male Hommes	Females Femmes	Sex Ratio (males per 100 females) Rapport des sexes (hommes pour 100 femmes)	Population age distribution (percentage) / Répartition par âge de la population (pourcentage) Aged 0 to 14 years old âgée de 0 à 14 ans	Aged 60+ years old âgée de 60 ans ou plus	Population density (per km²) Densité de population (pour km²)	Surface area Superficie (000 km²)
Wallis and Futuna Islands	2003	0.01	...	...	100.6	...	...	104.7	...
Îles Wallis-et-Futuna	2005	0.01	...	...	...	...	...	104.1	...
	2008	0.01	...	...	98.4	...	...	99.9	...
	2010	0.01	...	...	...	...	...	95.9	...
	2015	0.01	...	...	...	...	...	86.2	~0
	2016	0.01[1]	...	...	# 93.4	25.5	15.4	85.0[1]	...
	2017[1]	0.01	...	...	...	...	...	84.1	...
Western Sahara	2005	0.44	0.23	0.21	111.5	31.5	3.6	1.6	...
Sahara occidental	2010	0.48	0.25	0.23	111.2	29.4	3.8	1.8	...
	2015	0.53	0.28	0.25	110.5	28.5	4.8	2.0	266[66]
	2017[1]	0.55	0.29	0.26	110.1	28.1	5.4	2.1	...
Yemen	2005	20.58	10.40	10.18	102.1	45.7	4.2	39.0	...
Yémen	2010	23.61	11.93	11.68	102.1	42.5	4.4	44.7	...
	2015	26.92	13.60	13.32	102.1	40.6	4.5	51.0	528
	2017[1]	28.25	14.27	13.98	102.1	39.9	4.6	53.5	...
Zambia	2005	12.05	5.97	6.09	98.1	47.0	3.9	16.2	...
Zambie	2010	13.85	6.86	6.99	98.3	46.8	3.8	18.6	...
	2015	16.10	7.99	8.11	98.5	45.4	3.7	21.7	753
	2017[1]	17.09	8.48	8.61	98.5	44.8	3.7	23.0	...
Zimbabwe	2005	12.94	6.31	6.63	95.3	41.8	4.5	33.4	...
Zimbabwe	2010	14.09	6.86	7.23	94.9	41.5	4.3	36.4	...
	2015	15.78	7.68	8.10	94.8	41.5	4.2	40.8	391
	2017[1]	16.53	8.05	8.48	95.0	41.2	4.2	42.7	...

Source:

United Nations Population Division, New York, World Population Prospects: The 2017 Revision, last accessed June 2017.
United Nations Population Division, New York, World Population Prospects: The 2017 Revision; supplemented by data from the United Nations Statistics Division, New York, Demographic Yearbook 2015 and Secretariat for the Pacific Community (SPC) for small countries or areas, last accessed June 2017.

United Nations Statistics Division, New York, "Demographic Yearbook 2015" and the demographic statistics database, last accessed June 2017.

Source:

Organisation des Nations Unies, Division pour la population, New York, Perspectives de la population mondiale: révision de 2017, denier accès juin 2017.
Organisation des Nations Unies, Division pour la population, New York, Perspectives de la population mondiale: révision de 2017; complétées par des données de l'Organisation des Nations Unies, Division de statistique, New York, Annuaire démographique 2015 et Secrétariat de la Communauté du Pacifique (CPS) pour petits pays ou zones, denier accès juin 2017.
Organisation des Nations Unies, Division de statistique, New York, Annuaire démographique 2015, denier accès juin 2017.

1 Projected estimate (medium fertility variant).
2 Calculated by the United Nations Statistics Division.
3 Including Saint Helena.
4 Including Bermuda, Greenland, and Saint Pierre and Miquelon.
5 Including Anguilla, Bonaire, St. Eustatius & Saba, British Virgin Islands, Cayman Islands, Dominica, Montserrat, Saint Kitts and Nevis, Sint Maarten (Dutch part) and Turks and Caicos Islands.
6 Including Falkland Islands (Malvinas).
7 Including the Faroe Islands and the Isle of Man.
8 Including Andorra, Gibraltar, Holy See, and San Marino.
9 Including Liechtenstein, and Monaco.
10 Including Marshall Islands, Nauru, Northern Mariana Islands, and Palau.
11 Including Pitcairn.
12 Including American Samoa, Cook Islands, Niue, Pitcairn, Tokelau, Tuvalu, and Wallis and Futuna Islands.
13 De jure population.
14 Including armed forces stationed in the area.
15 Population statistics are compiled from registers.

1 Projection approximative (variante moyenne fécondité).
2 Calculés par la Division de statistique des Nations Unies.
3 Y compris Sainte-Hélène.
4 Y compris les Bermudes, le Groenland et Saint-Pierre-et-Miquelon.
5 Y compris Anguilla, les îles Vierges britanniques, les îles Bonaire, St-Eustache et Saba, les îles Caïmans, la Dominique, Montserrat, Saint-Kitts-et-Nevis, Saint-Martin (partie Hollandaise) et les îles Turks et Caicos.
6 Y compris iles Falkland (Malvinas)
7 Y compris les îles Féroé et l'île de Man.
8 Y compris Andorre, Gibraltar, Saint-Siège, et Saint-Marin.
9 Y compris le Liechtenstein, et Monaco.
10 Y compris les Îles Marshall, Nauru, les païles Mariannes du Nord, et Palau.
11 Y compris Pitcairn.
12 Y compris les Îles Cook, Nioué, Pitcairn, Tokélaou, Tuvalu, et les Îles Wallis et Fatuna.
13 Population de droit.
14 Y compris les militaires en garnison sur le territoire.
15 Les statistiques de la population sont compilées à partir des registres.

2 Population, surface area and density *(continued)*

Population, superficie et densité *(suite)*

16 Population aged 65 years and over.
17 Including Christmas Island, Cocos (Keeling) Islands and Norfolk Island.
18 Including Norfolk Island.
19 Including Nagorno-Karabakh.
20 Data refer to projections based on the 2000 population census.
21 Data refer to projections based on the 2010 Population Census.
22 Data updated according to "Superintendencia Agraria". Interior waters correspond to natural or artificial bodies of water or snow.
23 Excluding the institutional population.
24 Refers to Guernsey and Jersey.
25 For statistical purposes, the data for China do not include those for the Hong Kong Special Administrative Region (Hong Kong SAR), Macao Special Administrative Region (Macao SAR) and Taiwan Province of China.
26 Inland waters include the reservoirs.
27 Refers to the whole country.
28 Excluding residents of institutions.
29 Data have not been adjusted for underenumeration, estimated at 1.4 per cent.
30 The total surface is 21 040.79 square kilometres, without taking into account the last ruling of The Hague.
31 A dispute exists between the governments of Argentina and the United Kingdom of Great Britain and Northern Ireland concerning sovereignty over the Falkland Islands (Malvinas).
32 Excluding military personnel and their families, visitors and transients.
33 Including Åland Islands.
34 Including Abkhazia and South Ossetia.
35 Excluding families of military personnel, visitors and transients.
36 Excluding military personnel, visitors and transients.
37 Including Saint Barthélemy and Saint Martin (French part).
38 Including nationals outside the country.
39 Surface area is 0.44 Km2.
40 Land area only.
41 Data refer to 1 October.
42 Land area only. Excluding 84 square km of uninhabited islands.
43 Including Sabah and Sarawak.
44 Estimates should be viewed with caution as these are derived from scarce data.
45 Projections are prepared by the Secretariat of the Pacific Community based on 1999 census of population and housing.
46 Including Agalega, Rodrigues and Saint Brandon.
47 Excludes the islands of Saint Brandon and Agalega.
48 Intercensus data.
49 Refers to the island of Saipan.
50 Including Svalbard and Jan Mayen Islands.
51 Including Transnistria.
52 Including Ascension and Tristan da Cunha.
53 Refers to habitable area. Excludes St. Lucia's Forest Reserve.
54 Population aged 0 to 20 years.
55 Population aged 61 years and over.
56 Surface area is based on the 2002 population and housing census.
57 Including Kosovo.
58 Changes in total area per year are the result of new measuring and correcting of the administrative borders between former Yugoslavian countries.
59 The land area of Singapore comprises the mainland and other islands.
60 Excluding inland water.
61 Including Canary Islands, Ceuta and Melilla.
62 Including East Jerusalem.
63 Including low water level for all islands (area to shoreline).

16 Population âgée de 65 ans ou plus.
17 Y compris les îles Christmas, Cocos (Keeling) et Norfolk.
18 Y compris l'île de Norfolk.
19 Y compris le Haut-Karabakh.
20 Les données se réfèrent aux projections basées sur le recensement de la population 2000.
21 Les données se réfèrent aux projections basées sur le recensement de la population de 2010.
22 Données actualisées d'après la « Superintendencia Agraria ». Les eaux intérieures correspondent aux étendues d'eau naturelles ou artificielles et aux étendues neigeuses.
23 Non compris la population dans les institutions.
24 Se rapporte à Guernsey et Jersey.
25 Pour la présentation des statistiques, les données pour la Chine ne comprennent pas la région administrative spéciale de Hong Kong (Hong Kong RAS), la région administrative spéciale de Macao (Macao RAS) et la province chinoise de Taïwan.
26 Les eaux intérieures comprennent les réservoirs.
27 Ensemble du pays.
28 À l'exclusion de personnes en établissements de soins.
29 Les données n'ont pas été ajustées pour le sous-dénombrement, estimé à 1,4 pour cent.
30 La superficie totale est égale à 21 040.79 km2, sans tenir compte de la dernière décision de la Haye.
31 La souveraineté sur les îles Falkland (Malvinas) fait l'objet d'un différend entre le Gouvernement argentin et le Gouvernement du Royaume-Uni de Grande-Bretagne et d'Irlande du Nord.
32 À l'exception des personnels militaires et leurs familles, les personnes de passage et les visiteurs.
33 Y compris les Îles d'Åland.
34 Y compris l'Abkhazie et l'Ossétie du Sud.
35 Non compris les familles des militaires, ni les visiteurs et voyageurs en transit.
36 Non compris les militaires, ni les visiteurs et transients.
37 Y compris Saint-Barthélémy et Saint-Martin (partie français).
38 Y compris les ressortissants étrangers.
39 Superficie: 0,44 Km2
40 La superficie des terres seulement.
41 Les données se réfèrent au 1er octobre.
42 La superficie des terres seulement. Exclut des îles inhabitées d'une superficie de 84 kilomètres carrés.
43 Y compris Sabah et Sarawak.
44 Les montants estimatifs sont à prendre avec prudence, car calculés à partir de données peu nombreuses.
45 Les projections sont préparées par le Secrétariat de la Communauté du Pacifique en fonction du recensement de la population et du logement de 1999.
46 Y compris Agalega, Rodrigues et Saint Brandon.
47 Non compris les îles Saint-Brandon et Agalega.
48 Données intercensitaires.
49 Fait référence seulement à l'île de Saipan.
50 Y compris îles Svalbard et Jan Mayen.
51 Y compris la Transnistrie.
52 Y compris Ascension et Tristan da Cunha.
53 S'applique à la zone habitable. Exclut la réserve forestière de Sainte-Lucie.
54 Population âgée de 0 à 20 ans.
55 Population âgée de 61 ans ou plus.
56 La superficie est fondée sur les données provenant du recensement de la population et du logement de 2002.
57 Y compris Kosovo.
58 Les changements des totaux par année résultent de nouvelles mesures et de corrections des frontières administratives entre pays ex-yougoslaves.
59 La superficie terrestre de Singapour comprend l'île principale et les autres îles.
60 Exception faite des eaux intérieures.
61 Y compris les Iles Canaries, Ceuta et Melilla.
62 Y compris Jérusalem-Est.
63 Incluent le niveau de basses eaux pour toutes les iles.

64 Including Crimea.
65 Including Zanzibar.
66 Comprising the Northern Region (former Saguia el Hamra) and Southern Region (former Rio de Oro).

64 Y compris Crimea
65 Y compris Zanzibar.
66 Comprend la région septentrionale (ancien Saguia el Hamra) et la région méridionale (ancien Rio de Oro).

3 Population growth and indicators of fertility and mortality

Croissance démographique et indicateurs de fécondité et mortalité

Country or area Pays ou zone	Year Année	Population rate of increase (annual %) Population taux d'accroisse-ment (% annuel)	Fertility rate, total (live births per woman) Taux de fécondité (naissances vivantes par femme)	Mortality rates (per live births) Taux de mortalite (pour naissances vivantes) Infant Infantile p. 1 000	Maternal Maternale p. 100 000	Life expectancy at birth (years) Espérance de vie à la naissance (en années) Total Totale	Male Hommes	Females Femmes
Total, all countries or areas	**2005**	**1.3[1]**	**2.6[1]**	**49.1[1]**	**288**	**67.2[1]**	**65.0[1]**	**69.5[1]**
Total, tous pays ou zones	**2010**	**1.2[1]**	**2.6[1]**	**41.3[1]**	**246**	**69.1[1]**	**66.9[1]**	**71.3[1]**
	2015	**1.2[1]**	**2.5[1]**	**35.0[1]**	**216**	**70.8[1]**	**68.6[1]**	**73.1[1]**
Africa [1]	2005	2.5	5.1	80.7	...	53.7	52.2	55.2
Afrique [1]	2010	2.5	4.9	68.1	...	57.0	55.5	58.4
	2015	2.6	4.7	57.2	...	60.2	58.6	61.9
Northern Africa	2005	1.7[1]	3.2[1]	39.3[1]	95[2]	67.9[1]	66.0[1]	69.9[1]
Afrique septentrionale	2010	1.7[1]	3.1[1]	33.3[1]	82[2]	69.6[1]	67.7[1]	71.6[1]
	2015	1.9[1]	3.3[1]	28.1[1]	70[2]	71.1[1]	69.4[1]	72.8[1]
Sub-Saharan Africa	2005	2.7[1]	5.6[1]	87.3[1]	717[3]	50.7[1]	49.3[1]	52.1[1]
Afrique subsaharienne	2010	2.7[1]	5.4[1]	73.7[1]	624[3]	54.3[1]	52.9[1]	55.7[1]
	2015	2.7[1]	5.1[1]	62.1[1]	546[3]	57.9[1]	56.2[1]	59.5[1]
Eastern Africa [1]	2005	2.8	5.8	77.4	...	52.0	50.4	53.5
Afrique orientale [1]	2010	2.9	5.3	62.8	...	57.0	55.5	58.5
	2015	2.8	4.9	52.2	...	61.5	59.5	63.4
Middle Africa [1]	2005	3.1	6.4	100.1	...	50.8	49.3	52.2
Afrique centrale [1]	2010	3.2	6.2	84.6	...	54.4	52.9	55.9
	2015	3.1	5.9	72.2	...	57.4	55.8	59.1
Southern Africa [1]	2005	1.3	2.9	62.4	...	53.2	50.7	55.8
Afrique australe [1]	2010	1.1	2.7	53.7	...	53.0	50.6	55.4
	2015	1.4	2.6	38.0	...	59.3	56.0	62.7
Western Africa [1]	2005	2.6	6.0[4]	95.7[4]	...	49.3[4]	48.4[4]	50.2[4]
Afrique occidentale [1]	2010	2.7	5.8[4]	82.7[4]	...	52.3[4]	51.5[4]	53.2[4]
	2015	2.7	5.5[4]	70.5[4]	...	54.7[4]	53.9[4]	55.6[4]
Northern America [1]	2005	0.9	2.0[5]	6.9[5]	...	77.4[5]	74.8[5]	80.0[5]
Amérique septentrionale [1]	2010	0.9	2.0[5]	6.7[5]	...	78.4[5]	75.9[5]	80.9[5]
	2015	0.7	1.9[5]	5.9[5]	...	79.2[5]	76.8[5]	81.5[5]
Latin America & the	2005	1.3[1]	2.5[1]	25.4[1]	88	72.1[1]	68.8[1]	75.5[1]
Caribbean	2010	1.2[1]	2.3[1]	21.4[1]	81	73.4[1]	70.1[1]	76.8[1]
Amérique latine et Caraïbes	2015	1.1[1]	2.1[1]	18.7[1]	67	74.6[1]	71.4[1]	78.0[1]
Caribbean [1]	2005	0.9	2.5[6]	33.0[6]	...	70.0[6]	67.4[6]	72.6[6]
Caraïbes [1]	2010	0.8	2.4[6]	30.4[6]	...	71.3[6]	68.7[6]	74.0[6]
	2015	0.7	2.3[6]	27.0[6]	...	72.4[6]	69.8[6]	75.2[6]
Central America [1]	2005	1.4	2.8	23.3	...	73.9	71.3	76.5
Amérique centrale [1]	2010	1.6	2.5	21.8	...	74.9	72.3	77.4
	2015	1.5	2.4	20.0	...	75.8	73.2	78.4
South America [1]	2005	1.3	2.4[7]	25.5[7]	...	71.7[7]	68.1[7]	75.5[7]
Amérique du Sud [1]	2010	1.1	2.1[7]	20.3[7]	...	73.2[7]	69.6[7]	76.9[7]
	2015	1.0	2.0[7]	17.1[7]	...	74.5[7]	71.0[7]	78.1[7]
Asia [1]	2005	1.2	2.4	45.6	...	68.6	67.0	70.3
Asie [1]	2010	1.1	2.3	37.2	...	70.3	68.6	72.2
	2015	1.0	2.2	30.5	...	71.8	69.9	73.8
Central Asia [1]	2005	1.1	2.5	48.0	...	65.8	61.7	70.1
Asie centrale [1]	2010	1.5	2.7	38.0	...	67.5	63.5	71.6
	2015	1.7	2.7	28.5	...	69.8	66.3	73.3
Eastern Asia	2005	0.6[1]	1.5[1]	23.2[1]	48[8]	74.2[1]	72.3[1]	76.2[1]
Asie orientale	2010	0.5[1]	1.6[1]	15.7[1]	36[8]	75.7[1]	73.8[1]	77.8[1]
	2015	0.5[1]	1.6[1]	11.0[1]	27[8]	76.8[1]	74.9[1]	78.7[1]
South-central Asia [1]	2005	1.7	3.2	61.0	...	64.1	63.1	65.1
Asie centrale et du Sud [1]	2010	1.5	2.8	51.4	...	66.0	64.9	67.2
	2015	1.4	2.5	43.4	...	67.9	66.5	69.5
South-eastern Asia	2005	1.4[1]	2.5[1]	34.1[1]	166	68.1[1]	65.4[1]	70.9[1]
Asie du Sud-Est	2010	1.2[1]	2.4[1]	28.6[1]	136	69.4[1]	66.5[1]	72.3[1]
	2015	1.2[1]	2.3[1]	24.0[1]	110	70.5[1]	67.7[1]	73.4[1]
Southern Asia	2005	1.7[1]	3.2[1]	61.4[1]	288	64.0[1]	63.1[1]	65.0[1]
Asie méridionale	2010	1.5[1]	2.9[1]	51.9[1]	221	65.9[1]	64.9[1]	67.0[1]
	2015	1.3[1]	2.5[1]	44.1[1]	176	67.9[1]	66.5[1]	69.4[1]

Country or area Pays ou zone	Year Année	Population rate of increase (annual %) Population taux d'accroissement (% annuel)	Fertility rate, total (live births per woman) Taux de fécondité (naissances vivantes par femme)	Mortality rates (per live births) / Taux de mortalite (pour naissances vivantes): Infant Infantile p. 1 000	Maternal Maternale p. 100 000	Life expectancy at birth (years) / Espérance de vie à la naissance (en années): Total Totale	Male Hommes	Females Femmes
Western Asia Asie occidentale	2005	2.1[1]	3.2[1]	30.9[1]	110[9]	70.9[1]	68.4[1]	73.5[1]
	2010	2.5[1]	3.0[1]	25.0[1]	96[9]	72.0[1]	69.5[1]	74.8[1]
	2015	2.1[1]	2.9[1]	22.8[1]	91[9]	72.8[1]	70.1[1]	75.7[1]
Europe [1] Europe [1]	2005	0.1	1.4	8.4	...	73.8	69.6	78.1
	2010	0.2	1.5	6.5	...	75.3	71.3	79.3
	2015	0.1	1.6	5.3	...	77.2	73.7	80.7
Eastern Europe [1] Europe orientale [1]	2005	-0.4	1.3	13.8	...	67.9	62.4	73.8
	2010	-0.2	1.4	9.8	...	69.5	64.1	75.1
	2015	-0.1	1.6	7.6	...	72.2	67.3	77.1
Northern Europe [1] Europe septentrionale [1]	2005	0.4	1.7[10]	5.0[10]	...	77.9[10]	75.2[10]	80.5[10]
	2010	0.8	1.9[10]	4.4[10]	...	79.2[10]	76.6[10]	81.6[10]
	2015	0.5	1.8[10]	3.7[10]	...	80.5[10]	78.3[10]	82.7[10]
Southern Europe [1] Europe méridionale [1]	2005	0.6	1.4[11]	5.8[11]	...	78.8[11]	75.6[11]	81.8[11]
	2010	0.5	1.4[11]	4.7[11]	...	80.0[11]	77.1[11]	82.9[11]
	2015	-0.2	1.4[11]	4.0[11]	...	81.1[11]	78.4[11]	83.7[11]
Western Europe [1] Europe occidentale [1]	2005	0.3	1.6[12]	4.3[12]	...	78.9[12]	75.8[12]	82.0[12]
	2010	0.3	1.6[12]	3.7[12]	...	80.2[12]	77.3[12]	83.0[12]
	2015	0.4	1.7[12]	3.4[12]	...	81.1[12]	78.4[12]	83.7[12]
Oceania [1] Océanie [1]	2005	1.4	2.4	25.2	...	75.7	73.1	78.2
	2010	1.7	2.5	22.4	...	77.0	74.6	79.4
	2015	1.5	2.4	20.8	...	77.9	75.7	80.2
Australia and New Zealand [1] Australie et Nouvelle-Zélande [1]	2005	1.2	1.8	5.0	...	80.1	77.6	82.6
	2010	1.7	2.0	4.5	...	81.3	79.0	83.5
	2015	1.4	1.9	4.0	...	82.1	80.1	84.2
Melanesia [1] Mélanésie [1]	2005	2.2	4.2	51.0	...	63.7	61.4	66.1
	2010	2.2	3.9	47.3	...	65.2	62.9	67.7
	2015	2.0	3.7	44.3	...	66.1	63.8	68.7
Micronesia [1] Micronésie [1]	2005	0.2	3.2[13]	31.0[13]	...	70.9[13]	68.9[13]	73.1[13]
	2010	~0.0	3.0[13]	29.1[13]	...	71.9[13]	69.7[13]	74.3[13]
	2015	0.6	3.0[13]	27.9[13]	...	72.8[13]	70.5[13]	75.3[13]
Polynesia [1] Polynésie [1]	2005	0.9[14]	3.3[15]	19.9[15]	...	71.6[15]	68.9[15]	74.6[15]
	2010	0.5[14]	3.2[15]	17.6[15]	...	73.2[15]	70.6[15]	76.1[15]
	2015	0.5[14]	3.0[15]	15.2[15]	...	74.5[15]	72.0[15]	77.4[15]
Afghanistan Afghanistan	2005	4.4[1]	7.2[1]	89.5[1]	821	56.9[1]	55.8[1]	58.1[1]
	2010	2.8[1]	6.4[1]	76.7[1]	584	60.0[1]	58.9[1]	61.3[1]
	2015	3.2[1]	5.3[1]	68.6[1]	396	62.3[1]	61.1[1]	63.5[1]
Albania Albanie	2005	-0.3[1]	1.9[1]	21.1[1]	30	74.8[1]	72.3[1]	77.8[1]
	2010	-0.9[1]	1.6[1]	16.8[1]	30	75.6[1]	73.2[1]	78.5[1]
	2015	-0.1[1]	1.7[1]	14.6[1]	29	77.7[1]	75.6[1]	79.9[1]
Algeria Algérie	2005	1.3[1]	2.4[1]	37.3[1]	148	71.5[1]	70.1[1]	72.9[1]
	2010	1.6[1]	2.7[1]	32.6[1]	147	73.9[1]	72.6[1]	75.2[1]
	2015	2.0[1]	3.0[1]	27.7[1]	140	75.3[1]	74.1[1]	76.5[1]
American Samoa Samoa américaines	2005[1]	0.5	...	...	...	...	...	...
	2006	...	...	...	...	...	68.5	76.2
	2010[1]	-1.2	...	...	...	...	...	...
	2011	...	...	...	...	...	71.1	77.8
	2012[16]	...	...	9.6	...	...	...	...
	2013	...	2.6	...	...	...	...	...
	2015[1]	-~0.0	...	...	...	...	...	...
Andorra Andorre	2005	3.7[1]	1.2	...	...	...	...	...
	2010	1.4[1]	1.2	...	...	...	...	...
	2012	...	1.2	...	...	...	...	...
	2015[1]	-1.6	...	...	...	...	...	...
Angola Angola	2005	3.5[1]	6.6[1]	108.3[1]	705	50.0[1]	47.5[1]	52.5[1]
	2010	3.6[1]	6.4[1]	83.8[1]	561	55.6[1]	53.0[1]	58.2[1]
	2015	3.5[1]	6.0[1]	65.4[1]	477	60.2[1]	57.4[1]	63.0[1]

3 Population growth and indicators of fertility and mortality *(continued)*

Croissance démographique et indicateurs de fécondité et mortalité *(suite)*

Country or area Pays ou zone	Year Année	Population rate of increase (annual %) Population taux d'accroissement (% annuel)	Fertility rate, total (live births per woman) Taux de fécondité (naissances vivantes par femme)	Mortality rates (per live births) Taux de mortalite (pour naissances vivantes): Infant Infantile p. 1 000	Maternal Maternale p. 100 000	Life expectancy at birth (years) Espérance de vie à la naissance (en années): Total Totale	Male Hommes	Females Femmes
Anguilla	2004	...	2.9	...	...	78.9[17]	76.5[17]	81.1[17]
Anguilla	2005	2.6[1]	1.8	...	...	...	...	...
	2006	...	2.0	...	...	...	...	...
	2010[1]	1.7	...	...	...	...	...	...
	2015[1]	1.2	...	...	...	...	...	...
Antigua and Barbuda [1]	2005	1.3	2.3	12.2	...	74.1	71.5	76.4
Antigua-et-Barbuda [1]	2010	1.2	2.2	10.0	...	75.0	72.6	77.4
	2015	1.1	2.1	9.1	...	75.8	73.3	78.2
Argentina	2005	1.1[1]	2.5[1]	15.0[1]	58	74.3[1]	70.6[1]	78.1[1]
Argentine	2010	1.0[1]	2.4[1]	14.6[1]	58	75.2[1]	71.3[1]	79.0[1]
	2015	1.0[1]	2.3[1]	13.7[1]	52	76.0[1]	72.2[1]	79.8[1]
Armenia	2005	-0.6[1]	1.7[1]	27.0[1]	40	72.4[1]	69.1[1]	75.3[1]
Arménie	2010	-0.7[1]	1.7[1]	21.0[1]	33	72.7[1]	69.4[1]	75.8[1]
	2015	0.3[1]	1.7[1]	13.2[1]	25	74.0[1]	70.6[1]	77.0[1]
Aruba [1]	2005	1.9	1.8	17.8	...	74.0	71.5	76.4
Aruba [1]	2010	0.3	1.8	16.2	...	74.7	72.2	77.1
	2015	0.5	1.8	14.8	...	75.4	72.9	77.8
Australia	2005	1.2[1,18]	1.8[1,18]	4.9[1,18]	7	80.3[1,18]	77.8[1,18]	82.8[1,18]
Australie	2010	1.8[1,18]	2.0[1,18]	4.4[1,18]	6	81.5[1,18]	79.2[1,18]	83.8[1,18]
	2015	1.5[1,18]	1.9[1,18]	3.9[1,18]	6	82.3[1,18]	80.2[1,18]	84.4[1,18]
Austria	2005	0.5[1]	1.4[1]	4.5[1]	5	78.9[1]	75.9[1]	81.7[1]
Autriche	2010	0.4[1]	1.4[1]	3.8[1]	4	80.1[1]	77.3[1]	82.8[1]
	2015	0.6[1]	1.4[1]	3.3[1]	4	81.0[1]	78.4[1]	83.5[1]
Azerbaijan	2005	1.0[1,19]	1.9[1,19]	54.2[1,19]	34	67.4[1,19]	64.6[1,19]	70.3[1,19]
Azerbaïdjan	2010	1.1[1,19]	1.8[1,19]	40.7[1,19]	27	70.1[1,19]	66.9[1,19]	73.4[1,19]
	2015	1.3[1,19]	2.1[1,19]	31.4[1,19]	25	71.6[1,19]	68.6[1,19]	74.6[1,19]
Bahamas	2005	2.0[1]	1.9[1]	11.6[1]	74	73.2[1]	70.0[1]	76.2[1]
Bahamas	2010	1.8[1]	1.9[1]	10.0[1]	85	74.3[1]	71.2[1]	77.3[1]
	2015	1.4[1]	1.8[1]	9.1[1]	80	75.1[1]	72.0[1]	78.1[1]
Bahrain	2005	5.8[1]	2.7[1]	9.8[1]	20	74.9[1]	74.2[1]	75.9[1]
Bahreïn	2010	6.7[1]	2.3[1]	8.0[1]	16	75.7[1]	74.9[1]	76.7[1]
	2015	2.0[1]	2.1[1]	6.9[1]	15	76.4[1]	75.6[1]	77.5[1]
Bangladesh	2005	1.7[1]	2.9[1]	56.0[1]	319	66.7[1]	66.2[1]	67.3[1]
Bangladesh	2010	1.2[1]	2.5[1]	43.3[1]	242	69.0[1]	68.2[1]	70.0[1]
	2015	1.2[1]	2.2[1]	33.3[1]	176	71.2[1]	69.8[1]	72.9[1]
Barbados	2005	0.3[1]	1.8[1]	12.4[1]	40	73.8[1]	71.4[1]	76.0[1]
Barbade	2010	0.4[1]	1.8[1]	11.0[1]	33	74.6[1]	72.1[1]	76.9[1]
	2015	0.3[1]	1.8[1]	9.6[1]	27	75.4[1]	72.9[1]	77.7[1]
Belarus	2005	-0.6[1]	1.3[1]	9.6[1]	13	67.8[1]	62.3[1]	73.7[1]
Bélarus	2010	-0.3[1]	1.4[1]	6.3[1]	5	69.3[1]	63.6[1]	75.2[1]
	2015	~0.0[1]	1.6[1]	3.6[1]	4	72.1[1]	66.5[1]	77.7[1]
Belgium	2005	0.5[1]	1.7[1]	4.2[1]	8	78.4[1]	75.3[1]	81.4[1]
Belgique	2010	0.7[1]	1.8[1]	3.8[1]	8	79.6[1]	76.8[1]	82.3[1]
	2015	0.6[1]	1.8[1]	3.5[1]	7	80.5[1]	78.0[1]	83.0[1]
Belize	2005	2.7[1]	3.4[1]	19.7[1]	52	68.5[1]	65.7[1]	71.6[1]
Belize	2010	2.5[1]	2.8[1]	17.0[1]	37	69.6[1]	67.0[1]	72.4[1]
	2015	2.2[1]	2.6[1]	14.3[1]	28	69.8[1]	67.2[1]	72.7[1]
Benin	2005	3.0[1]	5.8[1]	84.1[1]	502	56.2[1]	54.6[1]	57.7[1]
Bénin	2010	2.8[1]	5.5[1]	74.5[1]	446	58.6[1]	57.1[1]	60.0[1]
	2015	2.8[1]	5.2[1]	67.7[1]	405	59.9[1]	58.5[1]	61.4[1]
Bermuda	2005	0.3[1]	1.8	...	...	...	...	...
Bermudes	2010	-0.4[1]	1.7	...	...	79.3	76.9	82.3
	2015	-0.6[1]	1.5	...	...	...	77.3	84.9
	2016	...	1.5	...	...	...	77.5	85.1
Bhutan	2005	2.7[1]	3.1[1]	51.9[1]	308	62.9[1]	62.7[1]	63.1[1]
Bhoutan	2010	2.1[1]	2.6[1]	39.5[1]	204	66.5[1]	66.3[1]	66.7[1]
	2015	1.6[1]	2.2[1]	30.5[1]	148	68.8[1]	68.6[1]	68.9[1]

Country or area Pays ou zone	Year Année	Population rate of increase (annual %) Population taux d'accroissement (% annuel)	Fertility rate, total (live births per woman) Taux de fécondité (naissances vivantes par femme)	Mortality rates (per live births) / Taux de mortalite (pour naissances vivantes): Infant Infantile p. 1 000	Maternal Maternale p. 100 000	Life expectancy at birth (years) / Espérance de vie à la naissance (en années): Total Totale	Male Hommes	Females Femmes
Bolivia (Plurin. State of)	2005	1.8[1]	3.8[1]	61.2[1]	305	62.1[1]	60.1[1]	64.3[1]
Bolivie (État plurin. de)	2010	1.7[1]	3.4[1]	51.0[1]	253	64.9[1]	62.7[1]	67.3[1]
	2015	1.6[1]	3.0[1]	42.9[1]	206	67.7[1]	65.3[1]	70.2[1]
Bonaire, St. Eustat. & Saba [1]	2005	~0.0	...	...	...	...	...	...
Bonaire, St-Eustache et	2010	7.5	...	...	...	...	...	...
Saba [1]	2015	3.2	...	...	...	...	...	...
Bosnia and Herzegovina	2005	0.1[1]	1.3[1]	9.9[1]	14	74.8[1]	72.0[1]	77.5[1]
Bosnie-Herzégovine	2010	-0.3[1]	1.3[1]	9.0[1]	13	75.5[1]	72.9[1]	78.1[1]
	2015	-1.0[1]	1.3[1]	7.6[1]	11	76.3[1]	73.7[1]	78.8[1]
Botswana	2005	1.4[1]	3.2[1]	65.4[1]	276	49.2[1]	47.3[1]	51.0[1]
Botswana	2010	1.6[1]	2.9[1]	46.5[1]	169	56.5[1]	54.4[1]	58.5[1]
	2015	1.8[1]	2.9[1]	35.2[1]	129	62.9[1]	59.8[1]	66.1[1]
Brazil	2005	1.3[1]	2.1[1]	28.2[1]	67	71.1[1]	67.3[1]	75.0[1]
Brésil	2010	1.0[1]	1.9[1]	20.4[1]	65	72.9[1]	69.2[1]	76.7[1]
	2015	0.9[1]	1.8[1]	15.8[1]	44	74.7[1]	71.0[1]	78.4[1]
British Virgin Islands	2004	...	2.0	...	...	...	69.9	78.5
Îles Vierges britanniques	2005[1]	2.3	...	...	...	...	...	...
	2010[1]	3.2	...	...	...	...	...	...
	2015[1]	2.0	...	...	...	...	...	...
Brunei Darussalam	2005	1.8[1]	2.0[1]	8.2[1]	30	75.7[1]	74.2[1]	77.5[1]
Brunéi Darussalam	2010	1.2[1]	1.8[1]	6.5[1]	27	76.7[1]	75.1[1]	78.4[1]
	2015	1.4[1]	1.9[1]	6.5[1]	23	76.7[1]	75.1[1]	78.4[1]
Bulgaria	2005	-0.8[1]	1.2[1]	12.7[1]	15	72.2[1]	68.8[1]	75.8[1]
Bulgarie	2010	-0.7[1]	1.5[1]	9.5[1]	11	73.1[1]	69.7[1]	76.7[1]
	2015	-0.6[1]	1.5[1]	8.3[1]	11	74.3[1]	70.8[1]	77.8[1]
Burkina Faso	2005	2.9[1]	6.4[1]	90.0[1]	468	51.6[1]	50.5[1]	52.6[1]
Burkina Faso	2010	3.0[1]	6.1[1]	77.6[1]	417	55.3[1]	54.6[1]	55.8[1]
	2015	3.0[1]	5.6[1]	64.8[1]	371	58.7[1]	58.0[1]	59.3[1]
Burundi	2005	3.0[1]	6.9[1]	94.6[1]	863	52.0[1]	50.3[1]	53.7[1]
Burundi	2010	3.3[1]	6.5[1]	86.2[1]	808	53.7[1]	52.0[1]	55.4[1]
	2015	3.0[1]	6.0[1]	77.9[1]	712	56.1[1]	54.2[1]	58.0[1]
Cabo Verde	2005	1.7[1]	3.4[1]	25.0[1]	54	71.3[1]	69.5[1]	72.8[1]
Cabo Verde	2010	1.1[1]	2.9[1]	23.5[1]	51	71.8[1]	69.9[1]	73.4[1]
	2015	1.2[1]	2.5[1]	22.5[1]	42	72.2[1]	70.1[1]	74.0[1]
Cambodia	2005	1.8[1]	3.4[1]	65.9[1]	315	60.8[1]	58.5[1]	63.0[1]
Cambodge	2010	1.5[1]	3.1[1]	45.0[1]	202	65.1[1]	62.7[1]	67.4[1]
	2015	1.6[1]	2.7[1]	29.9[1]	161	67.6[1]	65.5[1]	69.6[1]
Cameroon	2005	2.6[1]	5.5[1]	88.5[1]	729	51.5[1]	50.6[1]	52.3[1]
Cameroun	2010	2.7[1]	5.3[1]	77.2[1]	676	54.4[1]	53.4[1]	55.4[1]
	2015	2.7[1]	5.0[1]	67.5[1]	596	56.4[1]	55.1[1]	57.7[1]
Canada	2005	1.0[1]	1.5[1]	5.3[1]	9	79.7[1]	77.2[1]	82.1[1]
Canada	2010	1.1[1]	1.6[1]	5.1[1]	8	80.8[1]	78.4[1]	83.0[1]
	2015	1.0[1]	1.6[1]	4.7[1]	7	81.8[1]	79.7[1]	83.8[1]
Cayman Islands	2005[1]	3.1	...	...	...	...	...	...
Îles Caïmanes	2006[20]	...	...	...	...	...	76.3	83.8
	2007	...	1.6	...	...	...	...	...
	2010[1]	2.6	...	...	...	...	...	...
	2015[1]	1.5	...	...	...	...	...	...
Central African Republic	2005	1.9[1]	5.5[1]	113.4[1]	1 058	43.7[1]	42.5[1]	44.9[1]
République centrafricaine	2010	1.5[1]	5.3[1]	105.9[1]	909	46.0[1]	44.6[1]	47.4[1]
	2015	0.4[1]	5.1[1]	93.5[1]	882	49.4[1]	47.8[1]	51.0[1]
Chad	2005	3.8[1]	7.2[1]	110.8[1]	1 168	47.7[1]	46.8[1]	48.5[1]
Tchad	2010	3.3[1]	6.9[1]	105.2[1]	1 036	48.9[1]	48.1[1]	49.7[1]
	2015	3.3[1]	6.3[1]	91.2[1]	856	51.7[1]	50.5[1]	52.8[1]
Channel Islands [1,21]	2005	0.7	1.4	10.3	...	78.3	76.0	80.5
Îles Anglo-Normandes [1,21]	2010	0.7	1.4	8.7	...	79.6	77.5	81.7
	2015	0.5	1.5	7.9	...	80.6	78.7	82.4

Country or area Pays ou zone	Year Année	Population rate of increase (annual %) Population taux d'accroissement (% annuel)	Fertility rate, total (live births per woman) Taux de fécondité (naissances vivantes par femme)	Mortality rates (per live births) Taux de mortalite (pour naissances vivantes) Infant Infantile p. 1 000	Maternal Maternale p. 100 000	Life expectancy at birth (years) Espérance de vie à la naissance (en années) Total Totale	Male Hommes	Females Femmes
Chile	2005	1.1[1]	2.0[1]	8.4[1]	27	77.4[1]	74.3[1]	80.3[1]
Chili	2010	1.0[1]	1.9[1]	7.8[1]	26	78.1[1]	75.3[1]	80.8[1]
	2015	0.9[1]	1.8[1]	7.4[1]	22	78.8[1]	76.2[1]	81.3[1]
China	2005	0.6[1,22]	1.6[1,22]	25.3[1,22]	48	73.1[1,22]	71.7[1,22]	74.7[1,22]
Chine	2010	0.6[1,22]	1.6[1,22]	16.7[1,22]	35	74.7[1,22]	73.2[1,22]	76.3[1,22]
	2015	0.5[1,22]	1.6[1,22]	11.6[1,22]	27	75.7[1,22]	74.2[1,22]	77.2[1,22]
China, Hong Kong SAR [1]	2005	0.5	1.0	2.5	...	81.4	78.5	84.5
Chine, Hong Kong RAS [1]	2010	0.6	1.0	1.9	...	82.4	79.5	85.5
	2015	0.6	1.2	1.6	...	83.4	80.5	86.4
China, Macao SAR [1]	2005	2.4	0.8	4.9	...	81.0	78.2	83.6
Chine, Macao RAS [1]	2010	2.1	0.9	3.8	...	82.1	79.1	84.9
	2015	2.3	1.2	3.0	...	83.3	80.3	86.2
Colombia	2005	1.4[1]	2.3[1]	20.5[1]	80	71.7[1]	68.0[1]	75.4[1]
Colombie	2010	1.2[1]	2.1[1]	19.0[1]	72	72.9[1]	69.2[1]	76.6[1]
	2015	1.0[1]	1.9[1]	17.9[1]	64	73.7[1]	70.2[1]	77.4[1]
Comoros	2005	2.4[1]	5.2[1]	72.6[1]	436	59.6[1]	58.0[1]	61.2[1]
Comores	2010	2.4[1]	4.9[1]	66.7[1]	388	60.9[1]	59.3[1]	62.5[1]
	2015	2.4[1]	4.6[1]	58.1[1]	335	62.8[1]	61.2[1]	64.5[1]
Congo	2005	2.8[1]	5.1[1]	81.1[1]	596	52.1[1]	51.1[1]	53.1[1]
Congo	2010	3.3[1]	5.0[1]	61.0[1]	509	58.0[1]	56.7[1]	59.2[1]
	2015	2.6[1]	4.9[1]	46.5[1]	442	62.5[1]	61.0[1]	64.1[1]
Cook Islands	2001	...	...	...	...	...	68.0	74.0
Îles Cook	2005[1]	1.7	...	...	...	...	...	...
	2006	...	...	...	...	...	69.5	76.2
	2010[1]	-1.2	...	...	...	...	...	...
	2011	...	2.6	...	...	...	...	...
	2013[23]	...	...	3.6	...	75.3	# 71.7	# 79.6
	2015[1]	-1.2	...	...	...	...	...	...
Costa Rica	2005	1.6[1]	2.2[1]	10.9[1]	31	77.8[1]	75.5[1]	80.2[1]
Costa Rica	2010	1.4[1]	2.0[1]	10.0[1]	29	78.4[1]	76.1[1]	80.8[1]
	2015	1.1[1]	1.9[1]	9.3[1]	25	79.2[1]	76.7[1]	81.7[1]
Côte d'Ivoire	2005	1.9[1]	5.7[1]	91.6[1]	742	46.7[1]	45.9[1]	47.6[1]
Côte d'Ivoire	2010	2.1[1]	5.4[1]	84.6[1]	717	49.2[1]	48.5[1]	50.0[1]
	2015	2.5[1]	5.1[1]	71.6[1]	645	51.7[1]	50.4[1]	53.2[1]
Croatia	2005	-0.2[1]	1.4[1]	6.5[1]	11	74.9[1]	71.4[1]	78.4[1]
Croatie	2010	-0.2[1]	1.5[1]	5.7[1]	10	76.1[1]	72.6[1]	79.5[1]
	2015	-0.4[1]	1.5[1]	3.9[1]	8	77.0[1]	73.6[1]	80.4[1]
Cuba	2005	0.2[1]	1.6[1]	6.1[1]	41	77.2[1]	75.3[1]	79.1[1]
Cuba	2010	0.1[1]	1.6[1]	5.7[1]	44	78.7[1]	76.7[1]	80.7[1]
	2015	0.2[1]	1.7[1]	5.5[1]	39	79.2[1]	77.1[1]	81.3[1]
Curaçao [1]	2005	-0.4	2.1	14.7	...	75.0	71.2	78.6
Curaçao [1]	2010	2.6	2.0	13.0	...	76.1	72.7	79.4
	2015	1.4	2.1	10.3	...	77.8	74.5	80.7
Cyprus	2005	1.7[1,24]	1.6[1,24]	5.6[1,24]	12	78.3[1,24]	76.3[1,24]	80.5[1,24]
Chypre	2010	1.6[1,24]	1.5[1,24]	4.4[1,24]	8	79.0[1,24]	76.9[1,24]	81.1[1,24]
	2015	0.9[1,24]	1.4[1,24]	4.2[1,24]	7	79.9[1,24]	77.7[1,24]	82.2[1,24]
Czechia	2005	-0.1[1]	1.2[1]	3.9[1]	6	75.5[1]	72.2[1]	78.8[1]
Tchéquie	2010	0.5[1]	1.4[1]	3.1[1]	5	77.0[1]	73.8[1]	80.1[1]
	2015	0.1[1]	1.5[1]	2.5[1]	4	78.2[1]	75.1[1]	81.2[1]
Dem. People's Rep. Korea	2005	0.8[1]	2.0[1]	28.5[1]	105	68.1[1]	64.2[1]	71.5[1]
Rép. pop. dém. de Corée	2010	0.6[1]	2.0[1]	27.3[1]	97	68.4[1]	64.8[1]	71.8[1]
	2015	0.5[1]	2.0[1]	18.5[1]	82	70.8[1]	67.2[1]	74.1[1]
Dem. Rep. of the Congo	2005	3.0[1]	6.7[1]	99.5[1]	787	51.8[1]	50.4[1]	53.3[1]
Rép. dém. du Congo	2010	3.3[1]	6.6[1]	83.9[1]	794	55.5[1]	54.0[1]	56.9[1]
	2015	3.3[1]	6.4[1]	73.2[1]	693	58.1[1]	56.7[1]	59.5[1]
Denmark	2005	0.3[1]	1.8[1]	4.5[1]	8	77.3[1]	75.0[1]	79.6[1]
Danemark	2010	0.5[1]	1.9[1]	3.7[1]	7	78.6[1]	76.4[1]	80.8[1]
	2015	0.5[1]	1.7[1]	3.5[1]	6	80.1[1]	78.1[1]	82.2[1]

3 Population growth and indicators of fertility and mortality *(continued)*

Croissance démographique et indicateurs de fécondité et mortalité *(suite)*

Country or area Pays ou zone	Year Année	Population rate of increase (annual %) Population taux d'accroissement (% annuel)	Fertility rate, total (live births per woman) Taux de fécondité (naissances vivantes par femme)	Mortality rates (per live births) Taux de mortalite (pour naissances vivantes) Infant Infantile p. 1 000	Maternal Maternale p. 100 000	Life expectancy at birth (years) Espérance de vie à la naissance (en années) Total Totale	Male Hommes	Females Femmes
Djibouti Djibouti	2005	1.8[1]	4.2[1]	68.1[1]	341	57.3[1]	55.9[1]	58.8[1]
	2010	1.7[1]	3.6[1]	63.4[1]	275	59.1[1]	57.6[1]	60.5[1]
	2015	1.7[1]	3.1[1]	55.3[1]	229	61.6[1]	60.0[1]	63.2[1]
Dominica Dominique	2001	...	3.0	...	...	...	...	...
	2005[1]	0.3	...	...	...	...	...	...
	2008	...	...	...	...	...	73.8	78.2
	2010[1]	0.2	...	...	...	...	...	...
	2015[1]	0.5	...	...	...	...	...	...
Dominican Republic République dominicaine	2005	1.5[1]	2.8[1]	34.9[1]	64	71.1[1]	68.1[1]	74.4[1]
	2010	1.4[1]	2.7[1]	29.6[1]	75	72.2[1]	69.2[1]	75.5[1]
	2015	1.2[1]	2.5[1]	25.1[1]	92	73.2[1]	70.2[1]	76.5[1]
Ecuador Équateur	2005	1.7[1]	2.9[1]	27.1[1]	74	73.6[1]	70.7[1]	76.8[1]
	2010	1.7[1]	2.7[1]	23.4[1]	75	74.6[1]	71.7[1]	77.5[1]
	2015	1.6[1]	2.6[1]	21.1[1]	64	75.5[1]	72.8[1]	78.4[1]
Egypt Égypte	2005	1.9[1]	3.2[1]	29.4[1]	52	69.0[1]	66.7[1]	71.4[1]
	2010	1.8[1]	3.0[1]	23.5[1]	40	69.9[1]	67.6[1]	72.2[1]
	2015	2.2[1]	3.4[1]	18.9[1]	33	70.8[1]	68.7[1]	73.1[1]
El Salvador El Salvador	2005	0.5[1]	2.7[1]	23.6[1]	68	69.6[1]	65.0[1]	74.1[1]
	2010	0.4[1]	2.4[1]	20.7[1]	59	71.1[1]	66.4[1]	75.6[1]
	2015	0.5[1]	2.2[1]	17.0[1]	54	72.6[1]	67.9[1]	77.1[1]
Equatorial Guinea Guinée équatoriale	2005	4.2[1]	5.7[1]	89.7[1]	483	53.6[1]	52.3[1]	54.9[1]
	2010	4.6[1]	5.4[1]	80.4[1]	379	54.9[1]	53.8[1]	56.2[1]
	2015	4.2[1]	5.0[1]	70.0[1]	342	56.8[1]	55.5[1]	58.4[1]
Eritrea Érythrée	2005	3.1[1]	5.1[1]	59.4[1]	619	56.7[1]	54.7[1]	58.8[1]
	2010	2.0[1]	4.8[1]	51.7[1]	579	60.7[1]	58.7[1]	62.7[1]
	2015	2.0[1]	4.4[1]	45.0[1]	501	63.4[1]	61.4[1]	65.6[1]
Estonia Estonie	2005	-0.6[1]	1.4[1]	7.3[1]	15	71.6[1]	66.0[1]	77.1[1]
	2010	-0.4[1]	1.7[1]	4.7[1]	8	73.8[1]	68.3[1]	79.0[1]
	2015	-0.3[1]	1.6[1]	3.2[1]	9	76.8[1]	71.9[1]	81.2[1]
Ethiopia Éthiopie	2005	2.9[1]	6.1[1]	78.0[1]	743	53.6[1]	52.3[1]	55.0[1]
	2010	2.7[1]	5.3[1]	59.9[1]	523	59.1[1]	57.6[1]	60.6[1]
	2015	2.6[1]	4.6[1]	45.8[1]	353	63.7[1]	61.9[1]	65.5[1]
Falkland Islands (Malvinas) [1] Îles Falkland (Malvinas) [1]	2005	0.4	...	...	...	...	...	...
	2010	-0.6	...	...	...	...	...	...
	2015	0.3	...	...	...	...	...	...
Faroe Islands Îles Féroé	2005	0.4[1]	2.6	...	...	...	...	...
	2008	...	2.6	...	...	...	76.8	82.3
	2010	0.1[1]	2.5	...	...	...	...	...
	2015	0.2[1]	2.4	...	...	...	...	...
	2016[16]	...	...	...	...	...	78.3	84.5
Fiji Fidji	2005	0.3[1]	3.0[1]	19.0[1]	39	68.0[1]	65.5[1]	70.7[1]
	2010	0.9[1]	2.8[1]	17.9[1]	34	68.8[1]	66.1[1]	71.9[1]
	2015	0.7[1]	2.6[1]	16.0[1]	30	69.7[1]	66.9[1]	72.9[1]
Finland Finlande	2005	0.3[1,25]	1.8[1,25]	3.2[1,25]	4	78.4[1,25]	74.9[1,25]	81.7[1,25]
	2010	0.4[1,25]	1.8[1,25]	2.7[1,25]	3	79.5[1,25]	76.1[1,25]	82.9[1,25]
	2015	0.4[1,25]	1.8[1,25]	2.3[1,25]	3	80.7[1,25]	77.7[1,25]	83.7[1,25]
France France	2005	0.5[1]	1.9[1]	4.3[1]	10	79.4[1]	75.8[1]	83.1[1]
	2010	0.6[1]	2.0[1]	3.7[1]	9	80.8[1]	77.4[1]	84.3[1]
	2015	0.4[1]	2.0[1]	3.4[1]	8	81.9[1]	78.8[1]	85.0[1]
French Guiana [1] Guyane française [1]	2005	4.5	3.7	13.6	...	76.1	72.8	80.1
	2010	2.8	3.6	10.6	...	78.0	75.0	81.4
	2015	2.8	3.5	9.3	...	79.2	76.1	82.6
French Polynesia [1] Polynésie française [1]	2005	1.4	2.4	9.4	...	73.2	70.7	76.1
	2010	1.0	2.2	8.8	...	75.0	72.8	77.5
	2015	0.7	2.1	6.9	...	76.1	74.0	78.6
Gabon Gabon	2005	2.6[1]	4.4[1]	58.1[1]	370	59.1[1]	58.3[1]	59.8[1]
	2010	3.1[1]	4.2[1]	49.3[1]	322	61.3[1]	60.8[1]	61.8[1]
	2015	3.3[1]	4.0[1]	40.8[1]	291	64.5[1]	63.1[1]	65.8[1]

Country or area Pays ou zone	Year Année	Population rate of increase (annual %) Population taux d'accroissement (% annuel)	Fertility rate, total (live births per woman) Taux de fécondité (naissances vivantes par femme)	Mortality rates (per live births) Taux de mortalite (pour naissances vivantes): Infant Infantile p. 1 000	Mortality rates: Maternal Maternale p. 100 000	Life expectancy at birth (years) Espérance de vie à la naissance (en années): Total Totale	Male Hommes	Females Femmes
Gambia Gambie	2005	3.2[1]	5.9[1]	59.4[1]	807	56.9[1]	55.9[1]	58.1[1]
	2010	3.2[1]	5.8[1]	52.4[1]	753	58.8[1]	57.6[1]	60.2[1]
	2015	3.1[1]	5.6[1]	49.8[1]	706	60.3[1]	59.1[1]	61.6[1]
Georgia Géorgie	2005	-1.0[1,26]	1.6[1,26]	29.0[1,26]	37	72.6[1,26]	68.9[1,26]	76.1[1,26]
	2010	-1.2[1,26]	1.8[1,26]	20.2[1,26]	40	72.7[1,26]	68.6[1,26]	76.5[1,26]
	2015	-1.4[1,26]	2.0[1,26]	11.2[1,26]	36	72.8[1,26]	68.5[1,26]	77.0[1,26]
Germany Allemagne	2005	~0.0[1]	1.4[1]	4.2[1]	7	78.6[1]	75.6[1]	81.5[1]
	2010	-0.2[1]	1.4[1]	3.7[1]	7	79.7[1]	77.0[1]	82.4[1]
	2015	0.2[1]	1.4[1]	3.4[1]	6	80.4[1]	77.9[1]	82.9[1]
Ghana Ghana	2005	2.6[1]	4.6[1]	60.9[1]	376	57.5[1]	56.7[1]	58.3[1]
	2010	2.6[1]	4.4[1]	55.4[1]	325	60.0[1]	59.2[1]	60.9[1]
	2015	2.4[1]	4.2[1]	46.5[1]	319	61.7[1]	60.7[1]	62.6[1]
Gibraltar Gibraltar	2001	...	...	...	...	...	78.5	83.3
	2005[1]	0.6	...	...	...	...	...	...
	2010[1]	0.7	...	...	...	...	...	...
	2015[1]	0.6	...	...	...	...	...	...
Greece Grèce	2005	0.3[1]	1.3[1]	4.6[1]	3	79.1[1]	76.4[1]	81.9[1]
	2010	0.3[1]	1.5[1]	3.5[1]	3	80.0[1]	77.3[1]	82.8[1]
	2015	-0.4[1]	1.3[1]	3.3[1]	3	80.6[1]	78.0[1]	83.3[1]
Greenland Groenland	2005	0.3[1]	2.3	...	...	...	...	...
	2010	-0.1[1]	2.3	...	...	...	65.7[23]	71.0[23]
	2014	...	2.0	...	...	...	67.8[23]	72.8[23]
	2015	-0.1[1]	...	...	...	...	68.2[23]	72.9[23]
	2016[23]	...	...	...	...	...	68.7	73.5
Grenada Grenade	2005	0.3[1]	2.4[1]	12.0[1]	25	70.9[1]	68.5[1]	73.2[1]
	2010	0.3[1]	2.3[1]	10.2[1]	27	72.0[1]	69.6[1]	74.4[1]
	2015	0.4[1]	2.2[1]	9.6[1]	27	73.2[1]	70.8[1]	75.6[1]
Guadeloupe [1,27] Guadeloupe [1,27]	2005	0.7	2.1	8.7	...	77.9	74.3	81.4
	2010	0.5	2.1	7.0	...	79.3	75.7	82.9
	2015	-~0.0	2.0	5.8	...	80.5	76.8	84.0
Guam [1] Guam [1]	2005	0.4	2.7	13.5	...	75.9	73.6	78.5
	2010	0.1	2.5	11.4	...	77.4	74.7	80.3
	2015	0.3	2.4	9.6	...	78.8	76.4	81.5
Guatemala Guatemala	2005	2.3[1]	4.3[1]	37.3[1]	120	68.9[1]	65.7[1]	72.1[1]
	2010	2.2[1]	3.6[1]	31.3[1]	109	70.5[1]	67.3[1]	73.7[1]
	2015	2.1[1]	3.2[1]	26.9[1]	88	72.4[1]	69.2[1]	75.6[1]
Guinea Guinée	2005	1.9[1]	5.9[1]	95.2[1]	831	51.3[1]	51.3[1]	51.3[1]
	2010	2.2[1]	5.5[1]	77.7[1]	720	55.5[1]	54.5[1]	56.4[1]
	2015	2.3[1]	5.1[1]	65.7[1]	679	57.9[1]	57.5[1]	58.4[1]
Guinea-Bissau Guinée-Bissau	2005	2.1[1]	5.6[1]	101.0[1]	714	52.7[1]	52.0[1]	53.3[1]
	2010	2.4[1]	5.2[1]	91.1[1]	570	54.2[1]	52.8[1]	55.6[1]
	2015	2.6[1]	4.9[1]	80.4[1]	549	56.0[1]	54.3[1]	57.7[1]
Guyana Guyana	2005	-0.1[1]	2.9[1]	36.5[1]	232	65.3[1]	62.6[1]	68.1[1]
	2010	-0.1[1]	2.7[1]	34.4[1]	241	65.8[1]	63.4[1]	68.4[1]
	2015	0.6[1]	2.6[1]	33.2[1]	229	66.3[1]	64.0[1]	68.6[1]
Haiti Haïti	2005	1.6[1]	4.0[1]	56.0[1]	459	58.3[1]	56.5[1]	60.1[1]
	2010	1.5[1]	3.5[1]	52.2[1]	389	60.2[1]	58.2[1]	62.3[1]
	2015	1.4[1]	3.1[1]	46.9[1]	359	62.3[1]	60.2[1]	64.4[1]
Holy See [1] Saint-Siège [1]	2005	0.3	...	...	...	...	...	...
	2010	~0.0	...	...	...	...	...	...
	2015	~0.0	...	...	...	...	...	...
Honduras Honduras	2005	2.4[1]	3.8[1]	31.2[1]	150	71.0[1]	68.6[1]	73.4[1]
	2010	2.1[1]	3.2[1]	29.4[1]	155	72.0[1]	69.6[1]	74.5[1]
	2015	1.8[1]	2.7[1]	27.8[1]	129	72.9[1]	70.4[1]	75.4[1]
Hungary Hongrie	2005	-0.3[1]	1.3[1]	7.4[1]	14	72.5[1]	68.3[1]	76.7[1]
	2010	-0.3[1]	1.3[1]	5.7[1]	15	73.7[1]	69.6[1]	77.8[1]
	2015	-0.3[1]	1.3[1]	4.9[1]	17	75.4[1]	71.7[1]	78.9[1]

Population growth and indicators of fertility and mortality *(continued)*

Croissance démographique et indicateurs de fécondité et mortalité *(suite)*

Country or area Pays ou zone	Year Année	Population rate of increase (annual %) Population taux d'accroissement (% annuel)	Fertility rate, total (live births per woman) Taux de fécondité (naissances vivantes par femme)	Mortality rates (per live births) Taux de mortalite (pour naissances vivantes) Infant Infantile p. 1 000	Maternal Maternale p. 100 000	Life expectancy at birth (years) Espérance de vie à la naissance (en années) Total Totale	Male Hommes	Females Femmes
Iceland Islande	2005	1.0[1]	2.0[1]	2.5[1]	4	80.7[1]	78.8[1]	82.6[1]
	2010	1.6[1]	2.1[1]	2.0[1]	4	81.4[1]	79.6[1]	83.2[1]
	2015	0.6[1]	2.0[1]	1.6[1]	3	82.2[1]	80.6[1]	83.8[1]
India Inde	2005	1.7[1]	3.1[1]	59.9[1]	280	63.5[1]	62.7[1]	64.4[1]
	2010	1.5[1]	2.8[1]	49.8[1]	215	65.6[1]	64.7[1]	66.5[1]
	2015	1.2[1]	2.4[1]	41.3[1]	174	67.6[1]	66.2[1]	69.1[1]
Indonesia Indonésie	2005	1.4[1]	2.5[1]	36.5[1]	212	66.7[1]	64.9[1]	68.5[1]
	2010	1.3[1]	2.5[1]	29.7[1]	165	67.7[1]	65.6[1]	69.8[1]
	2015	1.3[1]	2.5[1]	25.0[1]	126	68.6[1]	66.6[1]	70.7[1]
Iran (Islamic Republic of) Iran (Rép. islamique d')	2005	1.3[1]	2.0[1]	25.0[1]	34	71.1[1]	70.0[1]	72.3[1]
	2010	1.1[1]	1.8[1]	18.9[1]	27	72.7[1]	71.0[1]	74.6[1]
	2015	1.2[1]	1.7[1]	14.8[1]	25	75.1[1]	74.0[1]	76.2[1]
Iraq Iraq	2005	2.7[1]	4.7[1]	34.7[1]	54	68.9[1]	66.9[1]	71.0[1]
	2010	2.6[1]	4.6[1]	33.3[1]	51	68.0[1]	65.1[1]	71.2[1]
	2015	3.2[1]	4.6[1]	32.1[1]	50	69.2[1]	67.0[1]	71.4[1]
Ireland Irlande	2005	1.8[1]	2.0[1]	5.2[1]	8	77.8[1]	75.3[1]	80.4[1]
	2010	1.9[1]	2.0[1]	3.7[1]	7	79.7[1]	77.4[1]	82.0[1]
	2015	0.3[1]	2.0[1]	3.4[1]	8	80.9[1]	78.7[1]	83.0[1]
Isle of Man [1] Île de Man [1]	2005	1.0	...	...	...	...	...	...
	2010	1.0	...	...	...	...	...	...
	2015	0.8	...	...	...	...	...	...
Israel Israël	2005	1.9[1]	2.9[1]	5.0[1]	7	79.6[1]	77.4[1]	81.6[1]
	2010	2.3[1]	2.9[1]	4.0[1]	6	80.9[1]	79.0[1]	82.8[1]
	2015	1.7[1]	3.0[1]	3.4[1]	5	81.9[1]	80.0[1]	83.7[1]
Italy Italie	2005	0.5[1]	1.3[1]	4.1[1]	4	80.3[1]	77.3[1]	83.1[1]
	2010	0.3[1]	1.4[1]	3.4[1]	4	81.5[1]	78.8[1]	84.1[1]
	2015	-0.1[1]	1.4[1]	3.0[1]	4	82.3[1]	79.9[1]	84.7[1]
Jamaica Jamaïque	2005	0.7[1]	2.5[1]	20.0[1]	92	72.8[1]	70.1[1]	75.6[1]
	2010	0.5[1]	2.3[1]	17.9[1]	93	74.2[1]	71.7[1]	76.8[1]
	2015	0.4[1]	2.1[1]	15.0[1]	89	75.5[1]	73.1[1]	77.9[1]
Japan Japon	2005	0.1[1]	1.3[1]	3.0[1]	7	81.8[1]	78.3[1]	85.2[1]
	2010	~0.0[1]	1.3[1]	2.6[1]	6	82.7[1]	79.2[1]	86.0[1]
	2015	-0.1[1]	1.4[1]	2.2[1]	5	83.3[1]	80.0[1]	86.4[1]
Jordan Jordanie	2005	2.3[1]	3.9[1]	22.4[1]	62	72.2[1]	70.8[1]	73.8[1]
	2010	4.6[1]	3.7[1]	19.7[1]	59	73.0[1]	71.5[1]	74.6[1]
	2015	4.9[1]	3.6[1]	17.1[1]	58	73.8[1]	72.2[1]	75.5[1]
Kazakhstan Kazakhstan	2005	0.6[1]	2.0[1]	32.0[1]	44	64.6[1]	59.1[1]	70.4[1]
	2010	1.1[1]	2.5[1]	23.9[1]	20	66.1[1]	60.6[1]	71.9[1]
	2015	1.6[1]	2.7[1]	14.1[1]	12	69.1[1]	64.3[1]	73.9[1]
Kenya Kenya	2005	2.7[1]	5.0[1]	62.2[1]	728	52.7[1]	51.0[1]	54.5[1]
	2010	2.7[1]	4.7[1]	49.4[1]	605	59.7[1]	58.1[1]	61.3[1]
	2015	2.7[1]	4.1[1]	39.4[1]	510	65.4[1]	63.0[1]	67.8[1]
Kiribati Kiribati	2005	1.8[1]	4.0[1]	51.6[1]	135	64.5[1]	61.6[1]	67.5[1]
	2010	2.1[1]	3.9[1]	49.3[1]	109	65.1[1]	62.0[1]	68.1[1]
	2015	1.8[1]	3.8[1]	46.9[1]	90	65.7[1]	62.4[1]	68.9[1]
Kuwait Koweït	2005	2.1[1]	2.6[1]	10.2[1]	6	73.3[1]	72.6[1]	74.4[1]
	2010	5.5[1]	2.4[1]	9.7[1]	5	73.7[1]	73.0[1]	74.8[1]
	2015	5.4[1]	2.1[1]	8.4[1]	4	74.3[1]	73.5[1]	75.5[1]
Kyrgyzstan Kirghizistan	2005	0.6[1]	2.5[1]	37.8[1]	85	66.9[1]	63.0[1]	71.0[1]
	2010	1.3[1]	2.8[1]	30.3[1]	84	67.5[1]	63.5[1]	71.7[1]
	2015	1.6[1]	3.1[1]	19.6[1]	76	70.3[1]	66.4[1]	74.3[1]
Lao People's Dem. Rep. Rép. dém. populaire lao	2005	1.5[1]	3.9[1]	69.2[1]	418	60.3[1]	59.0[1]	61.7[1]
	2010	1.6[1]	3.4[1]	56.7[1]	294	63.2[1]	61.8[1]	64.5[1]
	2015	1.3[1]	2.9[1]	47.3[1]	197	65.4[1]	63.9[1]	66.8[1]
Latvia Lettonie	2005	-1.1[1]	1.3[1]	9.9[1]	22	70.8[1]	65.2[1]	76.2[1]
	2010	-1.2[1]	1.5[1]	7.8[1]	19	71.6[1]	66.0[1]	77.0[1]
	2015	-1.2[1]	1.5[1]	6.5[1]	18	73.9[1]	68.8[1]	78.7[1]

Country or area Pays ou zone	Year Année	Population rate of increase (annual %) Population taux d'accroissement (% annuel)	Fertility rate, total (live births per woman) Taux de fécondité (naissances vivantes par femme)	Mortality rates (per live births) Taux de mortalite (pour naissances vivantes)		Life expectancy at birth (years) Espérance de vie à la naissance (en années)		
				Infant Infantile p. 1 000	Maternal Maternale p. 100 000	Total Totale	Male Hommes	Females Femmes
Lebanon Liban	2005	4.2[1]	2.0[1]	13.8[1]	27	75.6[1]	73.9[1]	77.4[1]
	2010	1.7[1]	1.6[1]	10.6[1]	19	77.7[1]	76.0[1]	79.7[1]
	2015	6.0[1]	1.7[1]	9.2[1]	15	78.9[1]	77.3[1]	80.9[1]
Lesotho Lesotho	2005	0.8[1]	3.8[1]	86.8[1]	746	45.6[1]	44.7[1]	46.4[1]
	2010	0.9[1]	3.4[1]	74.1[1]	587	49.0[1]	47.6[1]	50.2[1]
	2015	1.3[1]	3.3[1]	59.8[1]	487	52.5[1]	50.1[1]	54.7[1]
Liberia Libéria	2005	2.5[1]	5.7[1]	96.9[1]	1 020	52.4[1]	51.6[1]	53.2[1]
	2010	3.8[1]	5.2[1]	71.8[1]	811	58.1[1]	57.2[1]	59.0[1]
	2015	2.6[1]	4.8[1]	59.0[1]	725	60.7[1]	59.8[1]	61.6[1]
Libya Libye	2005	1.6[1]	2.6[1]	27.2[1]	11	70.8[1]	69.1[1]	72.8[1]
	2010	1.3[1]	2.4[1]	24.3[1]	9	71.8[1]	69.5[1]	74.4[1]
	2015	0.2[1]	2.4[1]	24.3[1]	9	71.5[1]	68.8[1]	74.4[1]
Liechtenstein Liechtenstein	2005	0.9[1]	1.5	...	...	...	...	...
	2010	0.7[1]	1.4	...	...	...	...	...
	2012	...	1.5	...	...	...	...	...
	2015[1]	0.8	...	...	...	...	...	...
Lithuania Lituanie	2005	-0.9[1]	1.3[1]	7.7[1]	12	71.6[1]	65.7[1]	77.5[1]
	2010	-1.4[1]	1.4[1]	6.0[1]	9	71.9[1]	66.0[1]	77.8[1]
	2015	-1.3[1]	1.6[1]	4.4[1]	10	74.0[1]	68.5[1]	79.3[1]
Luxembourg Luxembourg	2005	1.0[1]	1.7[1]	5.0[1]	13	78.3[1]	75.1[1]	81.4[1]
	2010	2.1[1]	1.6[1]	2.3[1]	11	79.5[1]	76.7[1]	82.2[1]
	2015	2.2[1]	1.5[1]	3.4[1]	10	81.1[1]	78.8[1]	83.5[1]
Madagascar Madagascar	2005	3.0[1]	5.3[1]	58.0[1]	508	60.0[1]	58.8[1]	61.3[1]
	2010	2.9[1]	4.8[1]	45.5[1]	436	62.2[1]	60.8[1]	63.7[1]
	2015	2.7[1]	4.4[1]	36.8[1]	353	64.5[1]	63.0[1]	66.0[1]
Malawi Malawi	2005	2.7[1]	6.0[1]	99.1[1]	648	47.3[1]	45.7[1]	48.9[1]
	2010	3.0[1]	5.7[1]	79.7[1]	629	53.4[1]	51.5[1]	55.2[1]
	2015	2.9[1]	4.9[1]	66.5[1]	634	60.7[1]	58.2[1]	63.1[1]
Malaysia Malaisie	2005	2.0[1,28]	2.5[1,28]	6.8[1,28]	52	73.2[1,28]	71.2[1,28]	75.4[1,28]
	2010	1.8[1,28]	2.2[1,28]	6.8[1,28]	48	73.7[1,28]	71.6[1,28]	76.1[1,28]
	2015	1.8[1,28]	2.1[1,28]	6.5[1,28]	40	74.7[1,28]	72.6[1,28]	77.1[1,28]
Maldives Maldives	2005	2.6[1]	2.6[1]	26.7[1]	101	72.1[1]	71.1[1]	73.9[1]
	2010	2.7[1]	2.3[1]	14.8[1]	87	75.6[1]	74.6[1]	76.8[1]
	2015	2.8[1]	2.2[1]	9.0[1]	68	76.3[1]	75.4[1]	77.4[1]
Mali Mali	2005	3.1[1]	6.9[1]	106.6[1]	714	50.0[1]	49.3[1]	50.6[1]
	2010	3.3[1]	6.7[1]	89.1[1]	630	54.0[1]	53.4[1]	54.7[1]
	2015	2.9[1]	6.4[1]	78.5[1]	587	56.2[1]	55.6[1]	56.9[1]
Malta Malte	2005	0.5[1]	1.5[1]	6.9[1]	13	78.5[1]	76.8[1]	80.2[1]
	2010	0.5[1]	1.4[1]	5.8[1]	11	79.4[1]	77.7[1]	81.1[1]
	2015	0.5[1]	1.4[1]	4.8[1]	9	80.3[1]	78.6[1]	82.0[1]
Marshall Islands Îles Marshall	2004	...	...	...	...	...	67.0	70.6
	2005[1]	-~0.0	...	...	...	...	...	...
	2010[1]	0.1	...	...	...	...	...	...
	2011	...	4.1	25.4[17]	...	71.8	# 71.3	# 72.5
	2015[1]	0.2	...	...	...	...	...	...
Martinique [1] Martinique [1]	2005	0.5	1.9	8.5	...	78.9	75.5	82.2
	2010	-0.1	2.1	7.6	...	80.1	76.7	83.2
	2015	-0.5	2.0	6.4	...	81.2	77.8	84.4
Mauritania Mauritanie	2005	2.9[1]	5.3[1]	75.6[1]	750	60.3[1]	58.6[1]	61.9[1]
	2010	2.8[1]	5.1[1]	72.4[1]	723	61.3[1]	59.8[1]	62.9[1]
	2015	2.9[1]	4.9[1]	68.0[1]	602	62.6[1]	61.2[1]	64.1[1]
Mauritius Maurice	2005	0.6[1,29]	1.9[1,29]	13.4[1,29]	39	72.1[1,29]	68.9[1,29]	75.5[1,29]
	2010	0.4[1,29]	1.7[1,29]	13.2[1,29]	59	72.8[1,29]	69.4[1,29]	76.3[1,29]
	2015	0.2[1,29]	1.5[1,29]	12.0[1,29]	53	74.1[1,29]	70.7[1,29]	77.7[1,29]
Mayotte [1] Mayotte [1]	2005	3.4	4.8	7.6	...	76.5	73.0	80.6
	2010	3.2	4.6	5.6	...	78.0	74.5	81.9
	2015	2.8	4.1	4.2	...	79.3	76.0	82.9

Country or area Pays ou zone	Year Année	Population rate of increase (annual %) Population taux d'accroissement (% annuel)	Fertility rate, total (live births per woman) Taux de fécondité (naissances vivantes par femme)	Mortality rates (per live births) Taux de mortalite (pour naissances vivantes): Infant Infantile p. 1 000	Mortality rates: Maternal Maternale p. 100 000	Life expectancy at birth (years) Espérance de vie à la naissance (en années): Total Totale	Male Hommes	Females Femmes
Mexico Mexique	2005	1.3[1]	2.6[1]	20.5[1]	54	74.9[1]	72.4[1]	77.4[1]
	2010	1.6[1]	2.4[1]	19.9[1]	45	75.7[1]	73.3[1]	78.1[1]
	2015	1.4[1]	2.3[1]	18.8[1]	38	76.5[1]	74.0[1]	78.9[1]
Micronesia (Fed. States of) Micronésie (États féd. de)	2005	-0.2[1]	4.1[1]	37.9[1]	134	67.6[1]	66.9[1]	68.2[1]
	2010	-0.5[1]	3.6[1]	34.9[1]	115	68.3[1]	67.6[1]	69.1[1]
	2015	0.2[1]	3.3[1]	33.2[1]	100	68.8[1]	67.7[1]	69.9[1]
Monaco [1] Monaco [1]	2005	1.0	...	...	...	...	...	...
	2010	1.9	...	...	...	...	...	...
	2015	0.6	...	...	...	...	...	...
Mongolia Mongolie	2005	1.0[1]	2.1[1]	40.8[1]	95	64.1[1]	60.8[1]	67.7[1]
	2010	1.4[1]	2.4[1]	30.5[1]	63	66.1[1]	62.4[1]	70.3[1]
	2015	1.9[1]	2.8[1]	22.8[1]	44	68.5[1]	64.5[1]	72.7[1]
Montenegro Monténégro	2005	0.1[1]	1.9[1]	11.6[1]	9	73.4[1]	70.6[1]	76.2[1]
	2010	0.3[1]	1.8[1]	10.9[1]	8	74.2[1]	71.9[1]	76.5[1]
	2015	0.1[1]	1.7[1]	4.1[1]	7	76.4[1]	74.0[1]	78.8[1]
Montserrat Montserrat	2004	...	1.7	...	...	...	...	...
	2005[1]	-0.7	...	...	...	...	...	...
	2010[1]	0.7	...	...	...	...	...	...
	2015[1]	0.7	...	...	...	...	...	...
Morocco Maroc	2005	1.1[1]	2.7[1]	36.6[1]	190	70.0[1]	68.5[1]	71.4[1]
	2010	1.2[1]	2.6[1]	33.2[1]	153	72.9[1]	71.3[1]	74.4[1]
	2015	1.4[1]	2.6[1]	28.1[1]	121	74.9[1]	73.7[1]	76.0[1]
Mozambique Mozambique	2005	2.9[1]	5.8[1]	94.3[1]	762	49.6[1]	47.9[1]	51.2[1]
	2010	2.9[1]	5.7[1]	78.1[1]	619	53.2[1]	51.4[1]	55.0[1]
	2015	2.9[1]	5.5[1]	67.3[1]	489	56.1[1]	54.0[1]	58.1[1]
Myanmar Myanmar	2005	1.0[1]	2.9[1]	57.9[1]	248	62.9[1]	60.9[1]	65.0[1]
	2010	0.7[1]	2.6[1]	52.2[1]	205	64.3[1]	62.2[1]	66.3[1]
	2015	0.9[1]	2.3[1]	45.0[1]	178	66.0[1]	63.7[1]	68.3[1]
Namibia Namibie	2005	1.4[1]	3.8[1]	59.4[1]	390	53.8[1]	51.7[1]	55.9[1]
	2010	1.3[1]	3.6[1]	46.6[1]	319	55.0[1]	53.3[1]	56.6[1]
	2015	2.2[1]	3.6[1]	36.4[1]	265	61.7[1]	59.1[1]	64.3[1]
Nauru Nauru	2000	0.1[1]	...	...	...	...	57.0	64.0
	2005[1]	0.1	...	...	...	...	...	...
	2007[30]	...	...	...	...	55.0	52.5	58.2
	2010[1]	-0.2	...	...	...	...	...	...
	2013[17]	...	3.9	18.0	...	# 61.2	# 57.8	# 64.8
	2015[1]	2.3	...	...	...	...	...	...
Nepal Népal	2005	1.5[1]	3.6[1]	52.9[1]	444	64.1[1]	62.9[1]	65.2[1]
	2010	1.1[1]	3.0[1]	41.3[1]	349	66.8[1]	65.5[1]	68.1[1]
	2015	1.2[1]	2.3[1]	32.8[1]	258	68.9[1]	67.4[1]	70.5[1]
Netherlands Pays-Bas	2005	0.5[1]	1.7[1]	4.9[1]	11	78.7[1]	76.2[1]	81.0[1]
	2010	0.4[1]	1.7[1]	4.1[1]	8	80.2[1]	78.0[1]	82.2[1]
	2015	0.3[1]	1.7[1]	3.5[1]	7	81.3[1]	79.4[1]	83.1[1]
New Caledonia [1] Nouvelle-Calédonie [1]	2005	1.8	2.3	17.4	...	74.1	71.3	77.2
	2010	1.5	2.3	15.1	...	75.2	72.4	78.3
	2015	1.4	2.2	13.0	...	76.3	73.7	79.3
New Zealand Nouvelle-Zélande	2005	1.4[1]	1.9[1]	5.4[1]	14	79.1[1]	76.8[1]	81.3[1]
	2010	1.1[1]	2.1[1]	5.0[1]	13	80.3[1]	78.3[1]	82.3[1]
	2015	1.1[1]	2.0[1]	4.4[1]	11	81.3[1]	79.5[1]	83.1[1]
Nicaragua Nicaragua	2005	1.4[1]	2.8[1]	26.4[1]	190	70.9[1]	68.0[1]	73.8[1]
	2010	1.3[1]	2.6[1]	24.0[1]	166	72.8[1]	69.8[1]	75.9[1]
	2015	1.2[1]	2.3[1]	20.0[1]	150	74.5[1]	71.4[1]	77.5[1]
Niger Niger	2005	3.6[1]	7.7[1]	88.1[1]	723	51.4[1]	50.8[1]	52.0[1]
	2010	3.7[1]	7.6[1]	74.8[1]	657	54.9[1]	54.3[1]	55.6[1]
	2015	3.8[1]	7.4[1]	65.8[1]	553	58.5[1]	57.6[1]	59.5[1]
Nigeria Nigéria	2005	2.5[1]	6.1[1]	104.0[1]	946	46.9[1]	46.1[1]	47.8[1]
	2010	2.6[1]	5.9[1]	89.9[1]	867	49.7[1]	49.0[1]	50.5[1]
	2015	2.7[1]	5.7[1]	76.3[1]	814	51.9[1]	51.2[1]	52.6[1]

Country or area Pays ou zone	Year Année	Population rate of increase (annual %) Population taux d'accroissement (% annuel)	Fertility rate, total (live births per woman) Taux de fécondité (naissances vivantes par femme)	Mortality rates (per live births) Taux de mortalite (pour naissances vivantes): Infant Infantile p. 1 000	Maternal Maternale p. 100 000	Life expectancy at birth (years) Espérance de vie à la naissance (en années): Total Totale	Male Hommes	Females Femmes
Niue	2005[1]	-2.4	...	...	...	...	...	...
Nioué	2006	...	...	...	...	...	67.0	76.0
	2010[1]	-0.7	...	...	...	...	...	...
	2011	...	2.6[17]	8.1[23]	...	73.2[23]	# 70.1[23]	# 76.3[23]
	2015[1]	-0.1	...	...	...	...	...	...
Northern Mariana Islands	2000	4.1[1]	1.6	...	...	...	72.5	77.8
Îles Mariannes du Nord	2005	-1.6[1]	1.5	...	...	...	...	...
	2009	...	2.2	...	...	...	74.5	79.9
	2010	-3.2[1]	2.2	...	...	...	...	...
	2012	...	...	6.4	...	76.4	# 74.9	# 77.9
	2013	...	1.6	...	...	...	...	...
	2015[1]	0.1	...	...	...	...	...	...
Norway	2005	0.6[1,31]	1.8[1,31]	3.5[1,31]	7	79.3[1,31]	76.8[1,31]	81.8[1,31]
Norvège	2010	1.1[1,31]	1.9[1,31]	3.0[1,31]	6	80.6[1,31]	78.3[1,31]	82.8[1,31]
	2015	1.2[1,31]	1.8[1,31]	2.4[1,31]	5	81.6[1,31]	79.5[1,31]	83.6[1,31]
Oman	2005	2.0[1]	3.2[1]	14.6[1]	20	73.2[1]	71.4[1]	75.5[1]
Oman	2010	3.8[1]	2.9[1]	9.8[1]	18	75.1[1]	73.2[1]	77.5[1]
	2015	6.5[1]	2.9[1]	9.6[1]	17	76.2[1]	74.5[1]	78.7[1]
Other non-specified areas [1]	2005	0.7	1.3	6.1	...	76.9	74.2	80.0
Autres zones non-spécifiées [1]	2010	0.4	1.1	5.2	...	78.2	75.2	81.5
	2015	0.3	1.1	4.2	...	79.2	76.4	82.3
Pakistan	2005	2.1[1]	4.2[1]	84.0[1]	249	63.3[1]	62.5[1]	64.3[1]
Pakistan	2010	2.1[1]	4.0[1]	76.9[1]	211	64.4[1]	63.5[1]	65.3[1]
	2015	2.1[1]	3.7[1]	69.8[1]	178	65.9[1]	65.0[1]	66.8[1]
Palau	2000	2.1[1]	1.5	...	...	...	66.6	74.5
Palaos	2005	0.8[1]	...	...	...	...	66.3	72.1
	2010[1]	0.6	...	...	...	...	...	...
	2015	0.8[1]	# 2.2[32]	13.3	...	73.0	# 68.1	# 77.8
Panama	2005	1.9[1]	2.7[1]	19.8[1]	87	75.5[1]	73.0[1]	78.2[1]
Panama	2010	1.8[1]	2.6[1]	16.8[1]	101	76.4[1]	73.5[1]	79.4[1]
	2015	1.7[1]	2.6[1]	15.2[1]	94	77.3[1]	74.3[1]	80.5[1]
Papua New Guinea	2005	2.5[1]	4.4[1]	55.5[1]	277	62.6[1]	60.3[1]	65.1[1]
Papouasie-Nvl-Guinée	2010	2.4[1]	4.1[1]	51.9[1]	238	64.2[1]	61.8[1]	66.7[1]
	2015	2.2[1]	3.8[1]	49.0[1]	215	65.0[1]	62.6[1]	67.5[1]
Paraguay	2005	1.8[1]	3.2[1]	35.5[1]	159	70.8[1]	68.7[1]	72.9[1]
Paraguay	2010	1.4[1]	2.9[1]	32.0[1]	139	71.8[1]	69.7[1]	73.9[1]
	2015	1.3[1]	2.6[1]	28.8[1]	132	72.7[1]	70.7[1]	74.9[1]
Peru	2005	1.3[1]	2.8[1]	27.4[1]	114	71.6[1]	69.0[1]	74.3[1]
Pérou	2010	1.2[1]	2.6[1]	21.0[1]	92	73.1[1]	70.5[1]	75.9[1]
	2015	1.3[1]	2.5[1]	18.6[1]	68	74.2[1]	71.5[1]	76.8[1]
Philippines	2005	2.0[1]	3.7[1]	28.1[1]	127	67.5[1]	64.4[1]	70.8[1]
Philippines	2010	1.7[1]	3.3[1]	25.0[1]	129	68.1[1]	64.8[1]	71.5[1]
	2015	1.6[1]	3.1[1]	22.2[1]	114	68.6[1]	65.4[1]	72.1[1]
Poland	2005	-0.1[1]	1.3[1]	7.1[1]	6	74.6[1]	70.4[1]	78.8[1]
Pologne	2010	-~0.0[1]	1.4[1]	5.7[1]	4	75.6[1]	71.3[1]	79.8[1]
	2015	-~0.0[1]	1.3[1]	4.5[1]	3	77.0[1]	72.9[1]	81.0[1]
Portugal	2005	0.4[1]	1.5[1]	4.5[1]	12	77.6[1]	74.1[1]	81.0[1]
Portugal	2010	0.2[1]	1.4[1]	3.3[1]	11	79.3[1]	76.0[1]	82.5[1]
	2015	-0.4[1]	1.3[1]	2.9[1]	10	80.5[1]	77.3[1]	83.5[1]
Puerto Rico	2005	-0.2[1]	1.9[1]	8.0[1]	19	76.8[1]	72.7[1]	80.9[1]
Porto Rico	2010	-0.3[1]	1.7[1]	7.0[1]	16	77.9[1]	73.8[1]	81.8[1]
	2015	-0.2[1]	1.5[1]	6.3[1]	14	79.2[1]	75.2[1]	83.2[1]
Qatar	2005	7.6[1]	3.0[1]	9.4[1]	21	76.6[1]	75.6[1]	78.1[1]
Qatar	2010	14.4[1]	2.2[1]	7.8[1]	16	77.0[1]	75.9[1]	78.6[1]
	2015	6.6[1]	2.0[1]	7.2[1]	13	77.7[1]	76.9[1]	79.4[1]
Republic of Korea	2005	0.6[1]	1.2[1]	5.0[1]	14	77.2[1]	73.6[1]	80.6[1]
République de Corée	2010	0.3[1]	1.2[1]	3.5[1]	15	79.5[1]	76.0[1]	82.7[1]
	2015	0.4[1]	1.2[1]	3.0[1]	11	81.3[1]	77.9[1]	84.4[1]

Country or area Pays ou zone	Year Année	Population rate of increase (annual %) Population taux d'accroissement (% annuel)	Fertility rate, total (live births per woman) Taux de fécondité (naissances vivantes par femme)	Mortality rates (per live births) / Taux de mortalite (pour naissances vivantes): Infant Infantile p. 1 000	Mortality rates: Maternal Maternale p. 100 000	Life expectancy at birth (years) / Espérance de vie à la naissance (en années): Total Totale	Male Hommes	Females Femmes
Republic of Moldova	2005	-0.2[1,33]	1.2[1,33]	18.9[1,33]	39	67.6[1,33]	63.6[1,33]	71.6[1,33]
République de Moldova	2010	-0.4[1,33]	1.3[1,33]	15.5[1,33]	34	68.3[1,33]	64.4[1,33]	72.1[1,33]
	2015	-0.1[1,33]	1.3[1,33]	14.3[1,33]	23	71.0[1,33]	66.7[1,33]	75.2[1,33]
Réunion [1]	2005	1.4	2.4	7.6	...	76.8	73.0	80.6
Réunion [1]	2010	1.0	2.4	5.6	...	78.2	74.5	81.9
	2015	0.8	2.4	4.2	...	79.5	76.0	82.9
Romania	2005	-0.6[1]	1.3[1]	16.9[1]	33	71.5[1]	67.9[1]	75.2[1]
Roumanie	2010	-0.9[1]	1.4[1]	12.0[1]	30	73.1[1]	69.5[1]	76.7[1]
	2015	-0.6[1]	1.5[1]	8.7[1]	31	74.8[1]	71.4[1]	78.4[1]
Russian Federation	2005	-0.4[1]	1.3[1]	16.2[1]	42	64.9[1]	58.6[1]	72.0[1]
Fédération de Russie	2010	-0.1[1]	1.4[1]	10.7[1]	29	67.1[1]	61.0[1]	73.7[1]
	2015	0.1[1]	1.7[1]	8.3[1]	25	70.3[1]	64.7[1]	75.9[1]
Rwanda	2005	2.3[1]	5.4[1]	90.7[1]	567	50.6[1]	49.6[1]	51.5[1]
Rwanda	2010	2.6[1]	4.9[1]	59.8[1]	381	60.1[1]	58.6[1]	61.5[1]
	2015	2.5[1]	4.2[1]	44.0[1]	290	65.2[1]	63.1[1]	67.1[1]
Saint Helena [1,34]	2005	-3.6	...	...	...	...	...	...
Sainte-Hélène [1,34]	2010	-0.5	...	...	...	...	...	...
	2015	-0.7	...	...	...	...	...	...
Saint Kitts and Nevis [1]	2005	1.4	...	...	...	...	...	...
Saint-Kitts-et-Nevis [1]	2010	1.1	...	...	...	...	...	...
	2015	1.1	...	...	...	...	...	...
Saint Lucia	2005	0.8[1]	1.9[1]	14.2[1]	67	72.1[1]	70.1[1]	74.0[1]
Sainte-Lucie	2010	1.1[1]	1.6[1]	11.8[1]	54	74.0[1]	71.4[1]	76.6[1]
	2015	0.5[1]	1.5[1]	10.9[1]	48	74.8[1]	72.2[1]	77.6[1]
Saint Pierre and Miquelon [1]	2005	-~0.0	...	...	...	...	...	...
Saint-Pierre-et-Miquelon [1]	2010	~0.0	...	...	...	...	...	...
	2015	~0.0	...	...	...	...	...	...
Saint Vincent & Grenadines	2005	0.2[1]	2.2[1]	21.2[1]	50	70.7[1]	68.3[1]	73.3[1]
Saint-Vincent-Grenadines	2010	0.1[1]	2.1[1]	18.5[1]	50	71.8[1]	69.8[1]	74.0[1]
	2015	~0.0[1]	2.0[1]	16.5[1]	45	72.7[1]	70.7[1]	74.9[1]
Samoa	2005	0.6[1]	4.4[1]	25.7[1]	77	70.1[1]	67.2[1]	73.6[1]
Samoa	2010	0.7[1]	4.5[1]	21.3[1]	64	72.1[1]	69.1[1]	75.4[1]
	2015	0.8[1]	4.2[1]	18.0[1]	51	74.1[1]	71.1[1]	77.4[1]
San Marino	2000	1.2[1]	1.3	...	...	...	77.4	84.0
Saint-Marin	2004	...	1.3	...	...	...	...	...
	2005[1]	1.3	...	...	...	...	...	...
	2010[1]	1.2	...	...	...	...	...	...
	2013	...	...	...	...	...	81.7	86.4
	2015[1]	1.2	...	...	...	...	...	...
Sao Tome and Principe	2005	2.3[1]	5.1[1]	51.8[1]	181	63.8[1]	62.0[1]	65.6[1]
Sao Tomé-et-Principe	2010	2.3[1]	4.9[1]	46.0[1]	162	65.5[1]	63.6[1]	67.4[1]
	2015	2.2[1]	4.7[1]	43.8[1]	156	66.1[1]	64.1[1]	68.2[1]
Saudi Arabia	2005	2.8[1]	3.7[1]	17.5[1]	18	72.9[1]	71.5[1]	74.6[1]
Arabie saoudite	2010	2.7[1]	3.2[1]	14.7[1]	14	73.2[1]	71.9[1]	74.8[1]
	2015	2.8[1]	2.7[1]	13.0[1]	12	74.0[1]	72.7[1]	75.6[1]
Senegal	2005	2.6[1]	5.3[1]	61.1[1]	427	58.9[1]	57.3[1]	60.6[1]
Sénégal	2010	2.8[1]	5.1[1]	51.1[1]	375	62.4[1]	61.0[1]	63.8[1]
	2015	3.0[1]	5.0[1]	43.9[1]	315	65.7[1]	63.8[1]	67.5[1]
Serbia	2005	-0.6[1,35]	1.7[1,35]	14.1[1,35]	15	72.4[1,35]	69.4[1,35]	75.4[1,35]
Serbie	2010	-0.4[1,35]	1.6[1,35]	12.4[1,35]	16	73.3[1,35]	70.6[1,35]	76.1[1,35]
	2015	-0.4[1,35]	1.6[1,35]	9.8[1,35]	17	74.7[1,35]	71.8[1,35]	77.5[1,35]
Seychelles [1]	2005	1.8	2.2	10.6	...	72.1	67.9	76.8
Seychelles [1]	2010	0.6	2.3	10.2	...	72.4	68.1	77.3
	2015	0.5	2.4	10.2	...	72.9	68.7	77.9
Sierra Leone	2005	4.3[1]	6.1[1]	134.9[1]	1 986	41.3[1]	40.1[1]	42.6[1]
Sierra Leone	2010	2.6[1]	5.6[1]	116.9[1]	1 633	45.9[1]	45.1[1]	46.7[1]
	2015	2.3[1]	4.8[1]	94.4[1]	1 360	50.2[1]	49.7[1]	50.7[1]

Country or area Pays ou zone	Year Année	Population rate of increase (annual %) Population taux d'accroissement (% annuel)	Fertility rate, total (live births per woman) Taux de fécondité (naissances vivantes par femme)	Mortality rates (per live births) Taux de mortalite (pour naissances vivantes) Infant Infantile p. 1 000	Maternal Maternale p. 100 000	Life expectancy at birth (years) Espérance de vie à la naissance (en années) Total Totale	Male Hommes	Females Femmes
Singapore Singapour	2005	2.8[1]	1.3[1]	2.5[1]	16	79.2[1]	76.7[1]	81.8[1]
	2010	2.4[1]	1.3[1]	2.2[1]	11	81.2[1]	78.7[1]	83.7[1]
	2015	1.7[1]	1.2[1]	2.1[1]	10	82.3[1]	80.1[1]	84.5[1]
Sint Maarten (Dutch part) St-Martin (partie néerland.)	2005[1]	0.4	...	...	...	...	...	...
	2010	0.4[1]	...	...	...	...	72.0[17]	77.2[17]
	2013[16]	...	...	...	...	...	69.2	77.1
	2015[1]	3.1	...	...	...	...	...	...
Slovakia Slovaquie	2005	-~0.0[1]	1.2[1]	7.3[1]	7	73.8[1]	69.8[1]	77.8[1]
	2010	~0.0[1]	1.3[1]	6.2[1]	6	74.8[1]	70.8[1]	78.6[1]
	2015	0.1[1]	1.4[1]	5.7[1]	6	76.3[1]	72.7[1]	79.8[1]
Slovenia Slovénie	2005	0.1[1]	1.2[1]	4.0[1]	11	76.7[1]	72.8[1]	80.4[1]
	2010	0.5[1]	1.4[1]	3.2[1]	9	78.6[1]	75.0[1]	82.0[1]
	2015	0.3[1]	1.6[1]	2.5[1]	9	80.3[1]	77.3[1]	83.3[1]
Solomon Islands Îles Salomon	2005	2.6[1]	4.6[1]	49.9[1]	164	64.7[1]	63.5[1]	66.0[1]
	2010	2.3[1]	4.4[1]	38.7[1]	136	67.4[1]	66.1[1]	68.8[1]
	2015	2.1[1]	4.1[1]	30.0[1]	114	69.6[1]	68.3[1]	71.1[1]
Somalia Somalie	2005	2.9[1]	7.5[1]	97.0[1]	939	51.5[1]	50.0[1]	53.1[1]
	2010	2.9[1]	7.1[1]	89.8[1]	820	53.2[1]	51.7[1]	54.8[1]
	2015	2.9[1]	6.6[1]	79.5[1]	732	54.9[1]	53.3[1]	56.5[1]
South Africa Afrique du Sud	2005	1.3[1]	2.8[1]	60.5[1]	112	53.8[1]	51.2[1]	56.7[1]
	2010	1.1[1]	2.6[1]	52.7[1]	154	53.1[1]	50.7[1]	55.6[1]
	2015	1.4[1]	2.6[1]	36.5[1]	138	59.5[1]	56.1[1]	63.0[1]
South Sudan Soudan du sud	2005	3.8[1]	6.0[1]	101.4[1]	1 088	50.2[1]	49.1[1]	51.3[1]
	2010	4.3[1]	5.6[1]	89.1[1]	876	52.3[1]	51.3[1]	53.3[1]
	2015	3.3[1]	5.2[1]	77.7[1]	789	55.1[1]	54.1[1]	56.0[1]
Spain Espagne	2005	1.5[1,36]	1.3[1,36]	4.0[1,36]	5	79.9[1,36]	76.5[1,36]	83.3[1,36]
	2010	1.2[1,36]	1.4[1,36]	3.4[1,36]	5	81.2[1,36]	78.1[1,36]	84.3[1,36]
	2015	-0.2[1,36]	1.3[1,36]	2.9[1,36]	5	82.5[1,36]	79.6[1,36]	85.3[1,36]
Sri Lanka Sri Lanka	2005	0.8[1]	2.3[1]	13.1[1]	43	73.2[1]	69.6[1]	77.1[1]
	2010	0.7[1]	2.3[1]	10.1[1]	35	74.1[1]	70.6[1]	77.7[1]
	2015	0.5[1]	2.1[1]	8.2[1]	30	74.6[1]	71.2[1]	78.0[1]
State of Palestine État de Palestine	2005	2.1[1,37]	5.0[1,37]	24.9[1,37]	62	71.2[1,37]	69.5[1,37]	72.9[1,37]
	2010	2.6[1,37]	4.6[1,37]	22.3[1,37]	54	72.0[1,37]	70.2[1,37]	73.9[1,37]
	2015	2.7[1,37]	4.3[1,37]	20.0[1,37]	45	72.9[1,37]	71.1[1,37]	74.8[1,37]
Sudan Soudan	2005	2.5[1]	5.3[1]	61.8[1]	440	59.4[1]	57.5[1]	61.3[1]
	2010	2.1[1]	5.0[1]	53.7[1]	349	61.5[1]	59.8[1]	63.3[1]
	2015	2.3[1]	4.8[1]	48.7[1]	311	63.6[1]	62.1[1]	65.1[1]
Suriname Suriname	2005	1.1[1]	2.8[1]	24.2[1]	223	68.1[1]	64.8[1]	71.7[1]
	2010	1.1[1]	2.6[1]	22.2[1]	169	69.6[1]	66.4[1]	73.1[1]
	2015	1.0[1]	2.5[1]	17.4[1]	155	70.9[1]	67.8[1]	74.2[1]
Swaziland Swaziland	2005	0.8[1]	4.0[1]	86.6[1]	595	46.0[1]	44.2[1]	47.6[1]
	2010	1.7[1]	3.8[1]	75.8[1]	436	48.4[1]	46.5[1]	50.2[1]
	2015	1.8[1]	3.3[1]	56.3[1]	389	55.0[1]	51.6[1]	58.2[1]
Sweden Suède	2005	0.4[1]	1.7[1]	3.2[1]	5	80.1[1]	77.9[1]	82.3[1]
	2010	0.8[1]	1.9[1]	2.6[1]	4	81.1[1]	79.0[1]	83.1[1]
	2015	0.8[1]	1.9[1]	2.4[1]	4	81.9[1]	80.0[1]	83.7[1]
Switzerland Suisse	2005	0.7[1]	1.4[1]	4.6[1]	7	80.5[1]	77.7[1]	83.1[1]
	2010	1.1[1]	1.5[1]	4.2[1]	6	81.8[1]	79.3[1]	84.1[1]
	2015	1.2[1]	1.5[1]	3.9[1]	5	82.7[1]	80.5[1]	84.8[1]
Syrian Arab Republic République arabe syrienne	2005	2.2[1]	3.8[1]	17.7[1]	58	73.6[1]	71.4[1]	75.9[1]
	2010	2.8[1]	3.4[1]	15.0[1]	49	74.5[1]	72.0[1]	77.3[1]
	2015	-2.3[1]	3.1[1]	17.9[1]	68	69.9[1]	64.4[1]	76.3[1]
Tajikistan Tadjikistan	2005	2.0[1]	3.6[1]	62.9[1]	46	66.5[1]	63.6[1]	69.6[1]
	2010	2.2[1]	3.5[1]	48.9[1]	35	68.7[1]	66.0[1]	71.9[1]
	2015	2.2[1]	3.5[1]	38.9[1]	32	70.4[1]	67.7[1]	73.5[1]
Thailand Thaïlande	2005	0.8[1]	1.6[1]	16.7[1]	26	71.2[1]	67.7[1]	74.9[1]
	2010	0.5[1]	1.6[1]	13.4[1]	23	73.2[1]	69.8[1]	76.6[1]
	2015	0.4[1]	1.5[1]	11.2[1]	20	74.6[1]	70.8[1]	78.4[1]

Country or area Pays ou zone	Year Année	Population rate of increase (annual %) Population taux d'accroissement (% annuel)	Fertility rate, total (live births per woman) Taux de fécondité (naissances vivantes par femme)	Mortality rates (per live births) Taux de mortalite (pour naissances vivantes): Infant Infantile p. 1 000	Maternal Maternale p. 100 000	Life expectancy at birth (years) Espérance de vie à la naissance (en années): Total Totale	Male Hommes	Females Femmes
TFYR of Macedonia	2005	0.2[1]	1.6[1]	12.9[1]	10	73.8[1]	71.3[1]	76.4[1]
ex-R.Y. de Macédoine	2010	0.1[1]	1.5[1]	10.8[1]	8	74.2[1]	72.1[1]	76.3[1]
	2015	0.1[1]	1.5[1]	9.0[1]	8	75.1[1]	73.2[1]	77.2[1]
Timor-Leste	2005	3.3[1]	7.0[1]	64.0[1]	506	61.5[1]	60.0[1]	63.0[1]
Timor-Leste	2010	1.6[1]	6.5[1]	50.2[1]	317	66.4[1]	65.2[1]	67.6[1]
	2015	2.2[1]	5.9[1]	43.9[1]	215	67.7[1]	66.1[1]	69.5[1]
Togo	2005	2.7[1]	5.3[1]	77.3[1]	427	53.9[1]	53.0[1]	54.7[1]
Togo	2010	2.7[1]	5.0[1]	63.2[1]	393	55.8[1]	55.1[1]	56.5[1]
	2015	2.6[1]	4.7[1]	55.7[1]	368	59.1[1]	58.3[1]	59.8[1]
Tokelau	2005[1]	-5.0	...	...	...	...	...	...
Tokélaou	2010[1]	-1.3	...	...	...	...	...	...
	2012	...	2.1	...	...	...	...	...
	2015[1]	1.9	...	...	...	...	...	...
Tonga	2005	0.6[1]	4.2[1]	23.5[1]	114	71.2[1]	68.8[1]	73.5[1]
Tonga	2010	0.6[1]	4.0[1]	22.0[1]	130	71.8[1]	69.1[1]	74.7[1]
	2015	0.4[1]	3.8[1]	20.6[1]	124	72.5[1]	69.6[1]	75.6[1]
Trinidad and Tobago	2005	0.5[1]	1.8[1]	28.9[1]	62	68.7[1]	65.1[1]	72.5[1]
Trinité-et-Tobago	2010	0.5[1]	1.8[1]	26.6[1]	65	69.3[1]	65.9[1]	73.0[1]
	2015	0.5[1]	1.8[1]	24.8[1]	63	70.2[1]	66.9[1]	73.8[1]
Tunisia	2005	0.8[1]	2.0[1]	23.0[1]	74	73.7[1]	71.4[1]	76.3[1]
Tunisie	2010	1.0[1]	2.0[1]	18.7[1]	67	74.6[1]	72.3[1]	77.0[1]
	2015	1.2[1]	2.3[1]	18.5[1]	62	75.0[1]	73.0[1]	77.1[1]
Turkey	2005	1.4[1]	2.4[1]	24.7[1]	57	71.4[1]	68.0[1]	74.9[1]
Turquie	2010	1.3[1]	2.2[1]	16.4[1]	23	73.4[1]	69.9[1]	76.9[1]
	2015	1.6[1]	2.1[1]	12.6[1]	16	74.8[1]	71.5[1]	78.1[1]
Turkmenistan	2005	1.0[1]	2.8[1]	62.1[1]	53	64.2[1]	60.3[1]	68.2[1]
Turkménistan	2010	1.4[1]	2.7[1]	54.2[1]	46	65.9[1]	62.2[1]	69.6[1]
	2015	1.8[1]	3.0[1]	46.9[1]	42	67.3[1]	63.9[1]	70.8[1]
Turks and Caicos Islands	2001	...	...	...	...	77.5	79.0	77.4
Îles Turques-et-Caïques	2002	...	...	...	...	...	75.1	77.3
	2005[1]	6.7	...	...	...	...	...	...
	2010[1]	3.2	...	...	...	...	...	...
	2012	...	...	...	...	...	75.8	77.8
	2015[1]	2.1	...	...	...	...	...	...
Tuvalu	2002	...	3.7	...	...	...	...	...
Tuvalu	2005[1]	1.2	...	...	...	...	...	...
	2010	1.0[1]	...	10.3	...	69.6	67.4	71.9
	#2012	...	3.6	...	...	...	...	...
	2015[1]	0.9	...	...	...	...	...	...
Uganda	2005	3.4[1]	6.7[1]	79.4[1]	504	49.9[1]	47.8[1]	52.1[1]
Ouganda	2010	3.4[1]	6.4[1]	68.2[1]	420	55.2[1]	53.6[1]	56.7[1]
	2015	3.4[1]	5.9[1]	60.2[1]	343	58.6[1]	56.5[1]	60.7[1]
Ukraine	2005	-0.8[1,38]	1.1[1,38]	14.8[1,38]	30	67.5[1,38]	61.9[1,38]	73.4[1,38]
Ukraine	2010	-0.5[1,38]	1.4[1,38]	12.6[1,38]	26	67.9[1,38]	62.3[1,38]	73.8[1,38]
	2015	-0.5[1,38]	1.5[1,38]	8.8[1,38]	24	71.1[1,38]	66.1[1,38]	76.0[1,38]
United Arab Emirates	2005	7.5[1]	2.4[1]	9.2[1]	6	74.8[1]	74.1[1]	76.3[1]
Émirats arabes unis	2010	11.8[1]	2.0[1]	6.9[1]	6	75.9[1]	75.2[1]	77.3[1]
	2015	2.0[1]	1.8[1]	6.2[1]	6	76.7[1]	76.0[1]	78.2[1]
United Kingdom	2005	0.4[1]	1.7[1]	5.3[1]	12	78.4[1]	76.1[1]	80.6[1]
Royaume-Uni	2010	1.0[1]	1.9[1]	4.8[1]	10	79.7[1]	77.5[1]	81.8[1]
	2015	0.7[1]	1.9[1]	4.1[1]	9	81.0[1]	79.0[1]	82.8[1]
United Rep. of Tanzania	2005	2.8[1,39]	5.7[1,39]	67.1[1,39]	687	53.7[1,39]	52.0[1,39]	55.4[1,39]
Rép.-Unie de Tanzanie	2010	3.1[1,39]	5.6[1,39]	52.4[1,39]	514	58.8[1,39]	57.5[1,39]	60.1[1,39]
	2015	3.1[1,39]	5.2[1,39]	44.0[1,39]	398	62.8[1,39]	60.8[1,39]	64.8[1,39]
United States of America	2005	0.9[1]	2.0[1]	7.0[1]	13	77.2[1]	74.5[1]	79.7[1]
États-Unis d'Amérique	2010	0.9[1]	2.1[1]	6.8[1]	14	78.2[1]	75.6[1]	80.6[1]
	2015	0.7[1]	1.9[1]	6.0[1]	14	78.9[1]	76.5[1]	81.3[1]

3 Population growth and indicators of fertility and mortality *(continued)*

Croissance démographique et indicateurs de fécondité et mortalité *(suite)*

Country or area Pays ou zone	Year Année	Population rate of increase (annual %) Population taux d'accroisse-ment (% annuel)	Fertility rate, total (live births per woman) Taux de fécondité (naissances vivantes par femme)	Mortality rates (per live births) / Taux de mortalite (pour naissances vivantes): Infant Infantile p. 1 000	Maternal Maternale p. 100 000	Life expectancy at birth (years) / Espérance de vie à la naissance (en années): Total Totale	Male Hommes	Females Femmes
United States Virgin Islands [1] Îles Vierges américaines [1]	2005	-0.2	2.1	11.6	...	77.1	74.9	79.5
	2010	-0.3	2.4	10.7	...	77.8	75.5	80.3
	2015	-0.2	2.3	9.3	...	79.1	76.7	81.5
Uruguay Uruguay	2005	~0.0[1]	2.2[1]	14.4[1]	26	75.3[1]	71.6[1]	78.9[1]
	2010	0.3[1]	2.1[1]	13.4[1]	19	76.2[1]	72.5[1]	79.7[1]
	2015	0.3[1]	2.0[1]	12.7[1]	15	77.0[1]	73.3[1]	80.4[1]
Uzbekistan Ouzbékistan	2005	1.3[1]	2.5[1]	49.5[1]	42	67.7[1]	64.5[1]	71.0[1]
	2010	1.5[1]	2.5[1]	40.7[1]	39	69.1[1]	66.1[1]	72.2[1]
	2015	1.6[1]	2.4[1]	31.3[1]	36	70.8[1]	68.1[1]	73.5[1]
Vanuatu Vanuatu	2005	2.5[1]	4.1[1]	34.6[1]	116	68.4[1]	66.7[1]	70.3[1]
	2010	2.4[1]	3.6[1]	28.6[1]	94	70.0[1]	68.2[1]	72.1[1]
	2015	2.3[1]	3.4[1]	24.3[1]	78	71.4[1]	69.4[1]	73.6[1]
Venezuela (Boliv. Rep. of) Venezuela (Rép. boliv. du)	2005	1.8[1]	2.7[1]	18.1[1]	93	72.8[1]	68.8[1]	77.2[1]
	2010	1.6[1]	2.5[1]	15.9[1]	99	73.4[1]	69.4[1]	77.7[1]
	2015	1.4[1]	2.4[1]	13.8[1]	95	73.9[1]	69.9[1]	78.2[1]
Viet Nam Viet Nam	2005	1.0[1]	1.9[1]	25.3[1]	61	73.8[1]	68.9[1]	78.7[1]
	2010	1.0[1]	1.9[1]	22.2[1]	58	74.7[1]	69.7[1]	79.7[1]
	2015	1.1[1]	2.0[1]	19.3[1]	54	75.6[1]	70.7[1]	80.3[1]
Wallis and Futuna Islands Îles Wallis-et-Futuna	2003	...	...	...	...	...	73.1	75.5
	2005[1]	0.1	...	...	...	...	...	...
	2008[40]	...	...	5.2	...	...	...	...
	2010[1]	-1.6	...	...	...	...	...	...
	2013	...	2.1	...	...	75.8	# 72.8	# 78.7
	2015[1]	-2.1	...	...	...	...	...	...
Western Sahara [1] Sahara occidental [1]	2005	6.6	2.9	52.9	...	63.9	62.3	65.8
	2010	1.9	2.6	43.1	...	66.2	64.7	68.1
	2015	1.8	2.6	34.1	...	68.4	66.9	70.3
Yemen Yémen	2005	2.8[1]	5.9[1]	67.9[1]	428	61.0[1]	59.7[1]	62.4[1]
	2010	2.7[1]	5.0[1]	53.0[1]	416	62.7[1]	61.4[1]	64.1[1]
	2015	2.6[1]	4.4[1]	47.2[1]	385	64.2[1]	62.8[1]	65.6[1]
Zambia Zambie	2005	2.7[1]	6.0[1]	82.2[1]	372	46.9[1]	45.3[1]	48.5[1]
	2010	2.8[1]	5.6[1]	65.2[1]	262	52.9[1]	51.2[1]	54.7[1]
	2015	3.0[1]	5.2[1]	53.8[1]	224	59.7[1]	57.5[1]	61.9[1]
Zimbabwe Zimbabwe	2005	1.1[1]	4.0[1]	67.2[1]	629	44.1[1]	42.7[1]	45.5[1]
	2010	1.7[1]	4.0[1]	58.3[1]	446	48.4[1]	47.2[1]	49.4[1]
	2015	2.3[1]	4.0[1]	46.5[1]	443	57.6[1]	56.1[1]	59.0[1]

Source:

United Nations Population Division, New York, World Population Prospects: The 2017 Revision, last accessed June 2017.

United Nations Population Division, New York, World Population Prospects: The 2017 Revision; supplemented by data from the United Nations Statistics Division, New York, Demographic Yearbook 2015 and Secretariat for the Pacific Community (SPC) for small countries or areas, last accessed June 2017.

United Nations Statistics Division, New York, "Demographic Yearbook 2015" and the demographic statistics database, last accessed June 2017.
World Health Organization (WHO), the United Nations Children's Fund (UNICEF), the United Nations Population Fund (UNFPA), the World Bank and the United Nations Population Division, "Trends in Maternal Mortality 1990 - 2015."

Source:

Organisation des Nations Unies, Division pour la population, New York, Perspectives de la population mondiale: révision de 2017, denier accès juin 2017.
Organisation des Nations Unies, Division pour la population, New York, Perspectives de la population mondiale: révision de 2017; complétées par des données de l'Organisation des Nations Unies, Division de statistique, New York, Annuaire démographique 2015 et Secrétariat de la Communauté du Pacifique (CPS) pour petits pays ou zones, denier accès juin 2017.
Organisation des Nations Unies, Division de statistique, New York, Annuaire démographique 2015, denier accès juin 2017.
Organisation mondiale de la Santé (OMS), le Fonds des Nations Unies pour l'enfance (UNICEF), le Fonds des Nations Unies pour la population (UNFPA), la Banque mondiale et la Division des Nations Unies pour la population, Les tendances de la mortalité maternelle 1990-2015.

1	Data refers to a 5-year period preceding the reference year.	1	Les données se réfèrent a période de 5 ans précédant l'année de référence.
2	Excluding Sudan.	2	Exclut le Soudan.
3	Including Sudan.	3	Comprend le Soudan.
4	Including Saint Helena.	4	Y compris Sainte-Hélène.
5	Including Bermuda, Greenland, and Saint Pierre and Miquelon.	5	Y compris les Bermudes, le Groenland et Saint-Pierre-et-Miquelon.
6	Including Anguilla, Bonaire, St. Eustatius & Saba, British Virgin Islands, Cayman Islands, Dominica, Montserrat, Saint Kitts and Nevis, Sint Maarten (Dutch part) and Turks and Caicos Islands.	6	Y compris Anguilla, les îles Vierges britanniques, les îles Bonaire, St-Eustache et Saba, les îles Caïmans, la Dominique, Montserrat, Saint-Kitts-et-Nevis, Saint-Martin (partie Hollandaise) et les îles Turks et Caicos.
7	Including Falkland Islands (Malvinas).	7	Y compris iles Falkland (Malvinas)
8	Excludes Japan.	8	Exclut le Japon.
9	Data excludes Armenia, Azerbaijan, Cyprus, Georgia, Israel and Turkey.	9	Les données excluent l'Arménie, l'Azerbaïdjan, Chypre, la Géorgie, l'Israël et la Turquie.
10	Including the Faroe Islands and the Isle of Man.	10	Y compris les îles Féroé et l'île de Man.
11	Including Andorra, Gibraltar, Holy See, and San Marino.	11	Y compris Andorre, Gibraltar, Saint-Siège, et Saint-Marin.
12	Including Liechtenstein, and Monaco.	12	Y compris le Liechtenstein, et Monaco.
13	Including Marshall Islands, Nauru, Northern Mariana Islands, and Palau.	13	Y compris les Îles Marshall, Nauru, les paîles Mariannes du Nord, et Palau.
14	Including Pitcairn.	14	Y compris Pitcairn.
15	Including American Samoa, Cook Islands, Niue, Pitcairn, Tokelau, Tuvalu, and Wallis and Futuna Islands.	15	Y compris les Îles Cook, Nioué, Pitcairn, Tokélaou, Tuvalu, et les Îles Wallis et Fatuna.
16	Data refers to a 2-year period up to and including the reference year.	16	Les données se réfèrent a période de 2 ans jusqu'à et y compris l'année de référence.
17	Data refers to a 3-year period up to and including the reference year.	17	Les données se réfèrent a période de 3 ans jusqu'à et y compris l'année de référence. .
18	Including Christmas Island, Cocos (Keeling) Islands and Norfolk Island.	18	Y compris les îles Christmas, Cocos (Keeling) et Norfolk.
19	Including Nagorno-Karabakh.	19	Y compris le Haut-Karabakh.
20	Data are based on a small number of deaths.	20	Les données sont basées sur un nombre limité de décès.
21	Refers to Guernsey and Jersey.	21	Se rapporte à Guernsey et Jersey.
22	For statistical purposes, the data for China do not include those for the Hong Kong Special Administrative Region (Hong Kong SAR), Macao Special Administrative Region (Macao SAR) and Taiwan Province of China.	22	Pour la présentation des statistiques, les données pour la Chine ne comprennent pas la région administrative spéciale de Hong Kong (Hong Kong RAS), la région administrative spéciale de Macao (Macao RAS) et la province chinoise de Taïwan.
23	Data refers to a 5-year period up to and including the reference year.	23	Les données se réfèrent a période de 5 ans jusqu'à et y compris l'année de référence.
24	Refers to the whole country.	24	Ensemble du pays.
25	Including Åland Islands.	25	Y compris les Îles d'Åland.
26	Including Abkhazia and South Ossetia.	26	Y compris l'Abkhazie et l'Ossétie du Sud.
27	Including Saint Barthélemy and Saint Martin (French part).	27	Y compris Saint-Barthélémy et Saint-Martin (partie français).
28	Including Sabah and Sarawak.	28	Y compris Sabah et Sarawak.
29	Including Agalega, Rodrigues and Saint Brandon.	29	Y compris Agalega, Rodrigues et Saint Brandon.
30	Data refers to a 6-year period up to and including the reference year.	30	Les données se réfèrent a période de 6 ans jusqu'à et y compris l'année de référence.
31	Including Svalbard and Jan Mayen Islands.	31	Y compris îles Svalbard et Jan Mayen.
32	Preliminary census results.	32	Résultats provisoires.
33	Including Transnistria.	33	Y compris la Transnistrie.
34	Including Ascension and Tristan da Cunha.	34	Y compris Ascension et Tristan da Cunha.
35	Including Kosovo.	35	Y compris Kosovo.
36	Including Canary Islands, Ceuta and Melilla.	36	Y compris les Iles Canaries, Ceuta et Melilla.
37	Including East Jerusalem.	37	Y compris Jérusalem-Est.
38	Including Crimea.	38	Y compris Crimea
39	Including Zanzibar.	39	Y compris Zanzibar.
40	Data refers to a 4-year period up to and including the reference year.	40	Les données se réfèrent a période de 4 ans jusqu'à et y compris l'année de référence.

International migrants and refugees

International migrant stock (number and percentage) and refugees and others of concern to UNHCR

Migrants internationaux et réfugiés

Stock de migrants internationaux (nombre et pourcentage) et réfugiés et autres personnes relevant de la compétence du HCR

Region, country or area Région, pays ou zone	Year Année	International Migrant Stock (mid-year) Stock de migrants internationaux (milieu de l'année) Total Total	% of total pop. % de la pop. totale MF/HF	M/H	F	Refugees and others of concern to UNHCR (mid-year) Réfugiés et autres personnes relevant de la compétence du HCR (milieu de l'année) Refugees[&] Réfugiés[&]	Asylum seekers Demandeurs d'asile	Other[&&] Autres[&&]	Total pop. Pop. totale
Total, all countries or areas	**2005**	**191 269 100**	**2.9**	**3.0**	**2.9**	...	...	...	...
Total, tous pays ou zones	**2010**	**221 714 243**	**3.2**	**3.3**	**3.1**	...	...	...	...
	2015	**243 700 236**	**3.3**	**3.4**	**3.2**	**15 097 633**	**2 343 919**	**40 518 150**	**57 959 702**
Africa	2005	15 191 146	1.7	1.8	1.5	...	...	...	...
Afrique	2010	16 840 014	1.6	1.7	1.5	...	...	...	...
	2015	20 649 557	1.7	1.9	1.6	4 493 139	1 044 031	11 530 138	17 067 308
Northern America	2005	45 363 387	13.8	13.9	13.7	...	...	...	...
Amérique septentrionale	2010	51 220 996	14.9	14.7	15.0	...	...	...	...
	2015	54 488 725	15.2	15.0	15.5	416 385	238 989	...	655 374
Latin America & the Caribbean	2005	7 233 098	1.3	1.3	1.3	...	...	...	...
Amérique latine et Caraïbes	2010	8 238 795	1.4	1.4	1.4	...	...	...	...
	2015	9 233 989	1.5	1.5	1.4	336 552	37 378	6 697 290	7 071 220
Asia	2005	53 371 224	1.4	1.5	1.2	...	...	...	...
Asie	2010	65 914 319	1.6	1.8	1.4	...	...	...	...
	2015	75 081 125	1.7	1.9	1.5	8 178 380	320 437	19 921 907	28 420 724
Europe	2005	64 086 824	8.8	8.8	8.8	...	...	...	...
Europe	2010	72 374 755	9.8	9.8	9.9	...	...	...	...
	2015	76 145 954	10.3	10.2	10.4	1 626 214	678 737	2 368 815	4 673 766
Oceania	2005	6 023 421	18.1	17.9	18.2	...	...	...	...
Océanie	2010	7 125 364	19.6	19.4	19.8	...	...	...	...
	2015	8 100 886	20.6	20.3	20.9	46 963	24 347	...	71 310
Afghanistan	2005	87 300	0.4	0.4	0.3	32[1]	14[1]	159 551[1]	159 597[1]
Afghanistan	2010	102 246	0.4	0.4	0.3	6 434[1]	30[1]	1 193 523[1]	1 199 987[1]
	2015	382 365	1.2	1.2	1.2	225 714	101	1 195 604	1 421 419
	2016	...	...	...	...	54 920	97	1 458 057	1 513 074
Albania	2005	64 739	2.1	2.1	2.1	56[1]	35[1]	1[1]	92[1]
Albanie	2010	52 784	1.8	1.8	1.8	76[1]	23[1]	...	99[1]
	2015	57 616	2.0	2.0	1.9	154	501	7 443	8 098
	2016	...	...	...	...	110	1 277	7 439	8 826
Algeria	2005	247 537[2,3]	0.7[2,3]	0.8[2,3]	0.7[2,3]	94 101[1]	306[1]	...	94 407[1]
Algérie	2010	244 964[2,3]	0.7[2,3]	0.7[2,3]	0.6[2,3]	94 144[1]	304[1]	...	94 448[1]
	2015	242 391[2,3]	0.6[2,3]	0.7[2,3]	0.6[2,3]	94 144[4]	5 892	...	100 036
	2016	...	...	...	...	94 219[4]	5 608	...	99 827
American Samoa	2005	24 233	41.0	...	...	...	...	...	...
Samoa américaines	2010	23 555	42.3	...	...	...	...	...	...
	2015	23 216	41.8	...	...	...	...	...	...
Andorra [3]	2005	50 298	61.9	...	...	...	...	...	...
Andorre [3]	2010	52 053	61.7	...	...	...	...	...	...
	2015	42 082	59.7	...	...	...	...	...	...
Angola	2005	61 329[2]	0.3[2]	0.3[2]	0.3[2]	13 984[1]	885[1]	45[1]	14 914[1]
Angola	2010	76 549[2]	0.4[2]	0.4[2]	0.4[2]	15 155[1]	4 241[1]	...	19 396[1]
	2015	106 845[2]	0.4[2]	0.4[2]	0.4[2]	15 572	30 086	2 887	48 545
	2016[5]	...	...	...	...	15 555	30 143	...	45 698
Anguilla	2005	4 684	37.1	...	...	...	...	...	...
Anguilla	2010	5 103	37.1	...	...	...	...	...	...
	2015	5 470	37.4	...	...	...	...	...	...
	2016	...	...	...	...	1	...	...	1
Antigua and Barbuda	2005	24 741	30.0	28.0	31.7	...	...	...	...
Antigua-et-Barbuda	2010	26 412	30.3	28.3	32.1	...	...	...	...
	2015	28 083	30.6	28.5	32.5	...	10	...	10
	2016	...	...	...	...	15	...	...	15
Argentina	2005	1 673 088	4.3	4.0	4.5	3 074[1]	825[1]	2[1]	3 901[1]
Argentine	2010	1 805 957	4.4	4.1	4.6	3 276[1]	947[1]	...	4 223[1]
	2015	2 086 302	4.8	4.5	5.1	3 523	897	...	4 420
	2016	...	...	...	...	3 222	1 764	...	4 986

International migrants and refugees *(continued)*

International migrant stock (number and percentage) and refugees and others of concern to UNHCR

Migrants internationaux et réfugiés *(suite)*

Stock de migrants internationaux (nombre et pourcentage) et réfugiés et autres personnes relevant de la compétence du HCR

Region, country or area Région, pays ou zone	Year Année	International Migrant Stock (mid-year) Stock de migrants internationaux (milieu de l'année) Total Total	% of total pop. % de la pop. totale MF/HF	M/H	F	Refugees and others of concern to UNHCR (mid-year) Réfugiés et autres personnes relevant de la compétence du HCR (milieu de l'année) Refugees& Réfugiés&	Asylum seekers Demandeurs d'asile	Other&& Autres&&	Total pop. Pop. totale
Armenia Arménie	2005	469 119[2]	15.6[2]	12.9[2]	18.1[2]	219 550[1]	70[1]	...	219 620[1]
	2010	221 560[2]	7.5[2]	5.9[2]	9.1[2]	3 296[1]	23[1]	82 525[1]	85 844[1]
	2015	191 199[2]	6.3[2]	5.5[2]	7.0[2]	15 690	114	238	16 042
	2016	...	...	...	...	18 851	54	421	19 326
Aruba Aruba	2005	32 540	32.5	30.6	34.3	...	...	...	...
	2010	34 327	33.8	31.6	35.8	...	1[1]	...	1[1]
	2015	36 114	34.8	32.6	36.7	...	2	...	2
	2016	...	...	...	...	2	4	...	6
Australia Australie	2005	4 878 030[6]	24.1[6]	23.9[6]	24.2[6]	64 964[1]	1 822[1]	8[1]	66 794[1]
	2010	5 882 980[6]	26.5[6]	26.4[6]	26.7[6]	21 805[1]	3 760[1]	15[1]	25 580[1]
	2015	6 763 663[6]	28.2[6]	27.9[6]	28.6[6]	35 582	22 837[7,8]	...	58 419
	2016	...	...	...	...	36 648	21 505[7]	...	58 153
Austria Autriche	2005	1 136 270	13.8	13.6	14.0	21 230[1]	40 710[1]	830[1]	62 770[1]
	2010	1 275 992	15.2	14.9	15.5	42 630[1]	25 625[1]	470[1]	68 725[1]
	2015	1 492 374	17.5	17.1	17.8	60 747[8]	30 900[8]	570[8]	92 217[8]
	2016	...	...	...	...	82 217	83 229	929	166 375
Azerbaijan Azerbaïdjan	2005	302 220[2,9]	3.5[2,9]	3.2[2,9]	3.8[2,9]	3 004[1]	115[1]	581 194[1]	584 313[1]
	2010	276 901[2,9]	3.0[2,9]	2.9[2,9]	3.2[2,9]	1 891[1]	17[1]	594 969[1]	596 877[1]
	2015	264 241[2,9]	2.7[2,9]	2.6[2,9]	2.8[2,9]	1 357	262	626 477	628 096
	2016	...	...	...	...	1 251	259	621 805	623 315
Bahamas Bahamas	2005	45 595	13.8	14.7	13.0	...	...	...	...
	2010	54 736	15.2	15.8	14.6	28[1]	9[1]	...	37[1]
	2015	59 306	15.3	15.8	14.8	7	19	30	56
	2016	...	...	...	...	11	17	97	125
Bahrain Bahreïn	2005	404 018[3]	46.6[3]	55.4[3]	33.3[3]	...	15[1]	...	15[1]
	2010	657 856[3]	52.2[3]	60.5[3]	38.4[3]	165[1]	69[1]	...	234[1]
	2015	704 137[3]	51.1[3]	59.6[3]	37.3[3]	277	78	...	355
	2016	...	...	...	...	271	79	...	350
Bangladesh Bangladesh	2005	1 166 700[2]	0.8[2]	1.4[2]	0.2[2]	21 098[1]	58[1]	250 094[1]	271 250[1]
	2010	1 345 546[2]	0.9[2]	1.5[2]	0.2[2]	229 253[1]	...	...	229 253[1]
	2015	1 422 805[2]	0.9[2]	1.5[2]	0.2[2]	232 975[10]	11	...	232 986
	2016	...	...	...	...	233 019[10]	...	...	233 019
Barbados Barbade	2005	30 624	11.2	10.3	12.0	...	...	...	...
	2010	32 825	11.7	11.0	12.4	...	...	...	...
	2015	34 475	12.1	11.4	12.8	1	...	...	1
Belarus Bélarus	2005	1 106 982	11.5	11.3	11.7	725[1]	56[1]	12 421[1]	13 202[1]
	2010	1 090 378	11.5	11.3	11.6	589[1]	66[1]	7 734[1]	8 389[1]
	2015	1 082 905	11.4	11.2	11.5	1 369	257	6 302	7 928
	2016	...	...	...	...	2 136	136	5 635	7 907
Belgium Belgique	2005	870 862[3]	8.2[3]	8.6[3]	7.9[3]	15 282[1]	18 913[1]	398[1]	34 593[1]
	2010	1 052 844[3]	9.6[3]	10.0[3]	9.3[3]	17 892[1]	18 288[1]	696[1]	36 876[1]
	2015	1 387 940[3]	12.3[3]	12.9[3]	11.7[3]	31 115	9 396	5 267	45 778
	2016	...	...	...	...	33 624	28 156	2 027	63 807
Belize Belize	2005	41 424[2]	14.6[2]	14.8[2]	14.5[2]	624[1]	14[1]	...	638[1]
	2010	46 360[2]	14.4[2]	14.6[2]	14.2[2]	134[1]	30[1]	2[1]	166[1]
	2015	53 860[2]	15.0[2]	15.1[2]	14.9[2]	...	146	...	146
	2016	...	...	...	...	165	2 761	200	3 126
Benin Bénin	2005	171 499[2,3]	2.1[2,3]	2.3[2,3]	1.9[2,3]	30 294[1]	1 695[1]	77[1]	32 066[1]
	2010	209 267[2,3]	2.2[2,3]	2.5[2,3]	1.9[2,3]	7 139[1]	101[1]	47[1]	7 287[1]
	2015	245 399[2,3]	2.3[2,3]	2.5[2,3]	2.0[2,3]	488	84	...	572
	2016	...	...	...	...	647	105	...	752
Bermuda Bermudes	2005	18 276	28.1	...	...	...	...	...	...
	2010	18 884	29.5	...	...	...	...	...	...
	2015	19 126	30.8	...	...	...	...	...	...
Bhutan Bhoutan	2005	40 279	6.2	9.4	2.5	...	...	...	...
	2010	48 420	6.7	10.2	2.7	...	...	...	...
	2015	51 106	6.6	10.0	2.7	...	...	...	...

International migrants and refugees *(continued)*

International migrant stock (number and percentage) and refugees and others of concern to UNHCR

Migrants internationaux et réfugiés *(suite)*

Stock de migrants internationaux (nombre et pourcentage) et réfugiés et autres personnes relevant de la compétence du HCR

		International Migrant Stock (mid-year) Stock de migrants internationaux (milieu de l'année)				Refugees and others of concern to UNHCR (mid-year) Réfugiés et autres personnes relevant de la compétence du HCR (milieu de l'année)			
			% of total pop. % de la pop. totale						
Region, country or area Région, pays ou zone	Year Année	Total Total	MF/HF	M/H	F	Refugees[&] Réfugiés[&]	Asylum seekers Demandeurs d'asile	Other[&&] Autres[&&]	Total pop. Pop. totale
Bolivia (Plurin. State of) Bolivie (État plurin. de)	2005	107 745	1.2	1.2	1.1	535[1]	3[1]	2[1]	540[1]
	2010	122 846	1.2	1.3	1.2	695[1]	41[1]	3[1]	739[1]
	2015	142 989	1.3	1.4	1.3	767	8	...	775
	2016	...	...	...	...	778	2	...	780
Bonaire, St. Eustatius & Saba Bonaire, St-Eustache et Saba	2005[11]	49 105	...	...	...	...	...	...	...
	2010	11 445	54.7	...	...	...	1[1,12]	...	1[1,12]
	2015	13 002	52.3	...	...	...	...	...	...
Bosnia and Herzegovina Bosnie-Herzégovine	2005	* 47 272[2]	* 1.2[2]	* 1.2[2]	* 1.3[2]	10 568[1]	215[1]	188 735[1]	199 518[1]
	2010	* 38 792[2]	* 1.0[2]	* 1.0[2]	* 1.1[2]	7 016[1]	153[1]	171 790[1]	178 959[1]
	2015	* 34 803[2]	* 0.9[2]	* 0.9[2]	* 1.0[2]	6 805	11	137 035	143 851
	2016	...	...	...	...	6 782	12	150 824	157 618
Botswana Botswana	2005	88 829[3]	4.8[3]	5.3[3]	4.2[3]	3 109[1]	47[1]	592[1]	3 748[1]
	2010	120 912[3]	5.9[3]	6.5[3]	5.3[3]	2 986[1]	249[1]	111[1]	3 346[1]
	2015	160 644[3]	7.1[3]	7.8[3]	6.4[3]	2 164	248	...	2 412
	2016	...	...	...	...	2 120	221	504	2 845
Brazil Brésil	2005	638 582	0.3	0.4	0.3	3 458[1]	195[1]	4 093[1]	7 746[1]
	2010	592 568	0.3	0.3	0.3	4 357[1]	872[1]	8[1]	5 237[1]
	2015	713 568	0.3	0.4	0.3	7 762	17 902	40 338	66 002
	2016	...	...	...	...	9 077	25 739	6 268	41 084
British Virgin Islands Îles Vierges britanniques	2005	13 808	59.6	...	...	...	...	...	...
	2010	15 558	57.2	...	...	2[1]	...	...	2[1]
	2015	17 308	57.5	...	...	...	...	...	...
Brunei Darussalam Brunéi Darussalam	2005	98 441	27.2	29.8	24.5	...	...	...	...
	2010	100 587	25.6	27.9	23.1	...	...	20 992[1]	20 992[1]
	2015	102 733	24.3	26.7	21.7	...	...	20 524	20 524
	2016	...	...	...	...	...	...	20 524	20 524
Bulgaria Bulgarie	2005	61 074	0.8	0.7	0.9	4 413[1]	805[1]	...	5 218[1]
	2010	76 287	1.0	0.9	1.1	5 530[1]	1 412[1]	...	6 942[1]
	2015	102 113	1.4	1.4	1.5	11 046[8]	7 840	67	18 953
	2016	...	...	...	...	17 008	16 647	67	33 722
Burkina Faso Burkina Faso	2005	596 972[2]	4.4[2]	4.3[2]	4.6[2]	511[1]	784[1]	7[1]	1 302[1]
	2010	673 904[2]	4.3[2]	4.1[2]	4.5[2]	531[1]	534[1]	9[1]	1 074[1]
	2015	704 676[2]	3.9[2]	3.7[2]	4.0[2]	34 027	180	...	34 207
	2016	...	...	...	...	32 544	138	...	32 682
Burundi Burundi	2005	172 874[2]	2.2[2]	2.2[2]	2.2[2]	20 681[1]	19 900[1]	12 988[1]	53 569[1]
	2010	235 259[2]	2.5[2]	2.5[2]	2.5[2]	29 365[1]	12 062[1]	159 338[1]	200 765[1]
	2015	286 810[2]	2.6[2]	2.6[2]	2.6[2]	54 126	2 733	80 851	137 710
	2016	...	...	...	...	53 465	2 894	46 799	103 158
Cabo Verde Cabo Verde	2005	12 700	2.7	2.8	2.5	...	...	1[1]	1[1]
	2010	14 373	2.9	3.0	2.8	...	...	...	...
	2015	14 924	2.9	2.9	2.8	...	...	115	115
	2016	...	...	...	...	...	...	115	115
Cambodia Cambodge	2005	114 031	0.9	0.9	0.8	127[1]	68[1]	207[1]	402[1]
	2010	81 977	0.6	0.6	0.5	129[1]	51[1]	...	180[1]
	2015	73 963	0.5	0.5	0.4	80	33	131	244
	2016	...	...	...	...	65	200	...	265
Cameroon Cameroun	2005	258 737	1.4	1.6	1.3	52 042[1]	6 766[1]	7 444[1]	66 252[1]
	2010	289 091	1.4	1.6	1.3	104 275[1]	2 383[1]	66[1]	106 724[1]
	2015	381 984	1.6	1.6	1.7	302 293	7 835	81 693	391 821
	2016	...	...	...	...	343 289	2 649	199 007	544 945
Canada Canada	2005	6 078 985	18.8	18.2	19.4	147 171[1]	20 552[1]	12[1]	167 735[1]
	2010	7 011 226	20.5	19.8	21.3	165 549[1]	51 025[1]	7[1]	216 581[1]
	2015	7 835 502	21.8	21.0	22.6	149 163[8]	14 481	...	163 644
	2016	...	...	...	...	135 888[5]	19 951	...	155 839
Cayman Islands Îles Caïmanes	2005[3]	21 655	44.5	...	...	...	...	...	...
	2010	24 057[3]	43.3[3]	...	...	1[1]	4[1]	...	5[1]
	2015	23 726[3]	39.6[3]	...	...	6	1	100	107
	2016	...	...	...	...	13	61	...	74

International migrants and refugees *(continued)*

International migrant stock (number and percentage) and refugees and others of concern to UNHCR

Migrants internationaux et réfugiés *(suite)*

Stock de migrants internationaux (nombre et pourcentage) et réfugiés et autres personnes relevant de la compétence du HCR

		International Migrant Stock (mid-year) Stock de migrants internationaux (milieu de l'année)				Refugees and others of concern to UNHCR (mid-year) Réfugiés et autres personnes relevant de la compétence du HCR (milieu de l'année)			
			% of total pop. % de la pop. totale						
Region, country or area Région, pays ou zone	**Year Année**	**Total Total**	**MF/HF**	**M/H**	**F**	**Refugees& Réfugiés&**	**Asylum seekers Demandeurs d'asile**	**Other&& Autres&&**	**Total pop. Pop. totale**
Central African Republic République centrafricaine	2005	94 449[3]	2.3[3]	2.5[3]	2.1[3]	24 569[1]	1 960[1]	2 167[1]	28 696[1]
	2010	93 466[3]	2.1[3]	2.3[3]	1.9[3]	21 574[1]	1 219[1]	192 531[1]	215 324[1]
	2015	81 598[3]	1.7[3]	1.8[3]	1.5[3]	7 906	394	508 904	517 204
	2016	...	...	...	...	11 473	403	458 590	470 466
Chad Tchad	2005	352 062[2]	3.5[2]	3.2[2]	3.8[2]	275 412[1]	68[1]	...	275 480[1]
	2010	416 924[2]	3.5[2]	3.1[2]	3.9[2]	347 939[1]	110[1]	185 000[1]	533 049[1]
	2015	516 968[2]	3.7[2]	3.4[2]	4.0[2]	420 774	2 749	50 000	473 523
	2016	...	...	...	...	386 050	2 263	124 001	512 314
Channel Islands [13] Îles Anglo-Normandes [13]	2005	70 941	46.0	44.3	47.6	...	...	...	...
	2010	77 581	48.6	46.8	50.4	...	...	...	...
	2015	82 307	50.3	48.5	52.0	...	...	...	...
Chile Chili	2005	273 384	1.7	1.6	1.8	806[1]	107[1]	...	913[1]
	2010	369 436	2.2	2.1	2.3	1 621[1]	274[1]	...	1 895[1]
	2015	469 436	2.6	2.5	2.7	1 798	719	...	2 517
	2016	...	...	...	...	1 890	1 780	...	3 670
China [14] Chine [14]	2005	678 947[3]	0.1[3]	0.1[3]	~0.0[3]	301 041[1]	84[1]	1[1]	301 126[1]
	2010	849 861[3]	0.1[3]	0.1[3]	0.1[3]	300 986[1]	122[1]	...	301 108[1]
	2015	978 046[3]	0.1[3]	0.1[3]	0.1[3]	301 057[15]	564	...	301 621
	2016	...	...	...	...	301 043[15]	654	...	301 697
China, Hong Kong SAR Chine, Hong Kong RAS	2005	2 721 235	39.8	36.2	43.0	1 934[1]	1 097[1]	...	3 031[1]
	2010	2 779 950	39.8	35.0	44.0	154[1]	486[1]	3[1]	643[1]
	2015	2 838 665	38.9	32.7	44.5	151	9 940	1	10 092
	2016	...	...	...	...	140	2 315	1	2 456
China, Macao SAR Chine, Macao RAS	2005	279 308	59.7	58.1	61.1	...	...	...	...
	2010	318 506	59.6	57.1	61.9	...	9[1]	1[1]	10[1]
	2015	342 703	58.3	55.0	61.4	...	6	...	6
	2016	...	...	...	...	...	6	...	6
Colombia Colombie	2005	107 612	0.2	0.3	0.2	155[1]	41[1]	2 000 009[1]	2 000 205[1]
	2010	124 271	0.3	0.3	0.3	212[1]	167[1]	3 672 065[1]	3 672 444[1]
	2015	133 134	0.3	0.3	0.3	219	56	6 520 304	6 520 579
	2016	...	...	...	...	245	266	7 126 459	7 126 970
Comoros Comores	2005	13 209	2.1	2.0	2.3	1[1]	...	...	1[1]
	2010	12 618	1.8	1.7	1.9	...	...	...	...
	2015	12 555	1.6	1.5	1.7	...	...	...	...
Congo Congo	2005	315 238	9.0	9.8	8.2	66 075[1]	3 486[1]	8 079[1]	77 640[1]
	2010	419 649	10.3	11.2	9.4	133 112[1]	5 524[1]	59[1]	138 695[1]
	2015	392 996	8.5	9.3	7.7	61 492	3 248	1 070	65 810
	2016	...	...	...	...	45 361	6 472	3 049	54 882
Cook Islands Îles Cook	2005	3 277	16.9	...	...	...	...	...	...
	2010	3 769	18.6	...	...	...	...	...	...
	2015	4 152	19.9	...	...	...	...	...	...
Costa Rica Costa Rica	2005	358 175[2]	8.4[2]	8.3[2]	8.6[2]	11 253[1]	223[1]	...	11 476[1]
	2010	405 404[2]	8.9[2]	8.6[2]	9.2[2]	19 505[1]	375[1]	40[1]	19 920[1]
	2015	421 697[2]	8.8[2]	8.4[2]	9.1[2]	3 475	1 819	2 613	7 907
	2016	...	...	...	...	3 785	4 605	1 756	10 146
Côte d'Ivoire Côte d'Ivoire	2005	2 010 824[3]	11.1[3]	12.0[3]	10.2[3]	41 627[1]	2 443[1]	71 050[1]	115 120[1]
	2010	2 095 185[3]	10.4[3]	11.3[3]	9.5[3]	26 218[1]	256[1]	538 068[1]	564 542[1]
	2015	2 175 399[3]	9.6[3]	10.4[3]	8.7[3]	1 972	667	724 131	726 770
	2016	...	...	...	...	1 895	627	1 020 489[16]	1 023 011
Croatia Croatie	2005	579 273[2]	13.2[2]	12.9[2]	13.6[2]	2 927[1]	8[1]	7 932[1]	10 867[1]
	2010	573 248[2]	13.3[2]	12.9[2]	13.6[2]	936[1]	81[1]	24 463[1]	25 480[1]
	2015	576 883[2]	13.6[2]	13.2[2]	14.0[2]	710	90	16 684	17 484
	2016	...	...	...	...	442	257	14 752	15 451
Cuba Cuba	2005	17 023	0.2	0.1	0.2	706[1]	32[1]	...	738[1]
	2010	14 818	0.1	0.1	0.1	411[1]	11[1]	1[1]	423[1]
	2015	13 336	0.1	0.1	0.1	313	12	...	325
	2016	...	...	...	...	333	22	...	355

International migrants and refugees *(continued)*

International migrant stock (number and percentage) and refugees and others of concern to UNHCR

Migrants internationaux et réfugiés *(suite)*

Stock de migrants internationaux (nombre et pourcentage) et réfugiés et autres personnes relevant de la compétence du HCR

Region, country or area Région, pays ou zone	Year Année	International Migrant Stock (mid-year) Stock de migrants internationaux (milieu de l'année) Total Total	% of total pop. % de la pop. totale MF/HF	M/H	F	Refugees and others of concern to UNHCR (mid-year) Réfugiés et autres personnes relevant de la compétence du HCR (milieu de l'année) Refugees& Réfugiés&	Asylum seekers Demandeurs d'asile	Other&& Autres&&	Total pop. Pop. totale
Curaçao	2010	34 627	23.5	21.0	25.6	7[1]	2[1]	...	9[1]
Curaçao	2015	37 611	23.9	21.3	26.1	44	41	...	85
	2016	...	...	...	...	47	43	...	90
Cyprus	2005	117 165[17]	11.3[17]	9.7[17]	13.1[17]	701[1]	13 067[1]	1[1]	13 769[1]
Chypre	2010	187 923[17]	17.0[17]	14.6[17]	19.5[17]	3 394[1]	5 396[1]	...	8 790[1]
	2015	196 167[17]	16.8[17]	14.6[17]	19.1[17]	5 763	2 339	6 000	14 102
	2016	...	...	...	...	7 940	2 225	6 000	16 165
Czechia	2005	322 540[3]	3.2[3]	3.6[3]	2.7[3]	1 802[1]	924[1]	...	2 726[1]
Tchéquie	2010	397 785[3]	3.8[3]	4.6[3]	3.0[3]	2 449[1]	1 065[1]	1[1]	3 515[1]
	2015	405 093[3]	3.8[3]	4.5[3]	3.2[3]	3 137[8]	409	1 502	5 048
	2016	...	...	...	...	3 947	582	1 502	6 031
Dem. People's Rep. Korea	*2005	40 097	0.2	0.2	0.2	...	...	...	...
Rép. pop. dém. de Corée	*2010	44 010	0.2	0.2	0.2	...	...	...	...
	*2015	48 458	0.2	0.2	0.2	...	...	...	...
Dem. Rep. of the Congo	2005	622 869[2]	1.1[2]	1.1[2]	1.1[2]	204 341[1]	140[1]	47 435[1]	251 916[1]
Rép. dém. du Congo	2010	588 950[2]	0.9[2]	0.9[2]	0.9[2]	166 336[1]	932[1]	2 196 591[1]	2 363 859[1]
	2015	545 694[2]	0.7[2]	0.7[2]	0.7[2]	* 160 271	1 124	1 839 611	2 001 006
	2016	...	...	...	...	382 561[18]	1 200	1 779 575	2 163 336
Denmark	2005	440 383	8.1	7.9	8.3	44 374[1]	510[1]	573[1]	45 457[1]
Danemark	2010	509 740	9.2	8.9	9.4	17 922[1]	3 363[1]	3 238[1]	24 523[1]
	2015	572 520	10.1	9.8	10.3	17 785[8]	4 566	4 984	27 335
	2016	...	...	...	...	30 699	10 941	6 580	48 220
Djibouti	2005	92 091[2]	11.8[2]	13.1[2]	10.5[2]	10 456[1]	19[1]	7 668[1]	18 143[1]
Djibouti	2010	101 575[2]	12.2[2]	12.8[2]	11.7[2]	15 104[1]	732[1]	7[1]	15 843[1]
	2015	112 351[2]	12.7[2]	13.3[2]	12.1[2]	14 787	2 586	...	17 373
	2016	...	...	...	...	16 696	3 091	106	19 893
Dominica	2005	4 744	6.7	...	...	...	...	...	...
Dominique	2010	5 765	8.1	...	...	...	...	...	...
	2015	6 720	9.2	...	...	...	...	...	...
Dominican Republic	2005	376 001	4.1	4.9	3.2	...	...	...	...
République dominicaine	2010	393 720	4.0	4.8	3.1	599[1]	1 759[1]	...	2 358[1]
	2015	415 564	3.9	4.8	3.1	609[19]	752[19]	133 770[19]	135 131[19]
	2016	...	...	...	...	590	751	...	1 341
Ecuador	2005	187 404[2]	1.4[2]	1.4[2]	1.3[2]	10 063[1]	2 489[1]	250 001[1]	262 553[1]
Équateur	2010	325 366[2]	2.2[2]	2.2[2]	2.1[2]	121 249[1]	49 887[1]	...	171 136[1]
	2015	387 513[2]	2.4[2]	2.5[2]	2.3[2]	121 722[8]	11 583[8]	...	133 305[8]
	2016[5]	...	...	...	...	121 535	11 583	...	133 118
Egypt	2005	274 001[2]	0.4[2]	0.4[2]	0.3[2]	88 946[1]	11 005[1]	203[1]	100 154[1]
Égypte	2010	295 714[2]	0.4[2]	0.4[2]	0.3[2]	95 056[1]	14 303[1]	570[1]	109 929[1]
	2015	491 643[2]	0.5[2]	0.6[2]	0.5[2]	226 344	30 019	21	256 384
	2016	...	...	...	...	210 865	45 643	13	256 521
El Salvador	2005	36 019[2]	0.6[2]	0.6[2]	0.6[2]	49[1]	1[1]	44[1]	94[1]
El Salvador	2010	40 324[2]	0.7[2]	0.7[2]	0.7[2]	38[1]	18[1]	...	56[1]
	2015	42 045[2]	0.7[2]	0.7[2]	0.7[2]	48	...	...	48
	2016	...	...	...	...	44	...	4 700	4 744
Equatorial Guinea [3]	2005	6 588	1.1	1.1	1.0	...	...	...	...
Guinée équatoriale [3]	2010	8 658	1.2	1.3	1.1	...	...	...	...
	2015	10 825	1.3	1.4	1.2	...	...	...	...
Eritrea	2005	* 14 314	* 0.3	* 0.4	* 0.3	4 418[1]	1 591[1]	31[1]	6 040[1]
Érythrée	2010	* 15 676	* 0.3	* 0.4	* 0.3	4 809[1]	137[1]	13[1]	4 959[1]
	2015	* 15 941	* 0.3	* 0.3	* 0.3	2 944	1	22	2 967
	2016	...	...	...	...	2 293	5	6	2 304
Estonia	2005	233 701	17.2	15.0	19.2	7[1]	8[1]	136 000[1]	136 015[1]
Estonie	2010	217 890	16.4	14.1	18.3	39[1]	10[1]	100 983[1]	101 032[1]
	2015	202 348	15.4	13.2	17.3	117	117	86 522[20]	86 756
	2016	...	...	...	...	226	59	83 918[20]	84 203

International migrants and refugees *(continued)*

International migrant stock (number and percentage) and refugees and others of concern to UNHCR

Migrants internationaux et réfugiés *(suite)*

Stock de migrants internationaux (nombre et pourcentage) et réfugiés et autres personnes relevant de la compétence du HCR

Region, country or area Région, pays ou zone	Year Année	International Migrant Stock (mid-year) Stock de migrants internationaux (milieu de l'année) Total Total	% of total pop. % de la pop. totale MF/HF	M/H	F	Refugees and others of concern to UNHCR (mid-year) Réfugiés et autres personnes relevant de la compétence du HCR (milieu de l'année) Refugees& Réfugiés&	Asylum seekers Demandeurs d'asile	Other&& Autres&&	Total pop. Pop. totale
Ethiopia Éthiopie	2005	514 242[2]	0.7[2]	0.7[2]	0.6[2]	100 817[1]	209[1]	4 110[1]	105 136[1]
	2010	567 720[2]	0.6[2]	0.7[2]	0.6[2]	154 295[1]	1 028[1]	47[1]	155 370[1]
	2015	1 072 949[2]	1.1[2]	1.1[2]	1.1[2]	702 467	2 871	348	705 686
	2016	...	...	...	...	742 725	2 290	670	745 685
Falkland Islands (Malvinas) Îles Falkland (Malvinas)	2005	1 166	39.6	...	...	...	...	...	...
	2010	1 436	50.3	...	...	...	...	...	...
	2015	1 571	54.1	...	...	...	...	...	...
Faroe Islands Îles Féroé	2005	4 583	9.5	...	...	...	...	...	...
	2010	5 096	10.5	...	...	...	...	...	...
	2015	5 517	11.4	...	...	...	...	...	...
Fiji Fidji	2005	12 435	1.5	1.6	1.5	...	...	...	...
	2010	13 351	1.6	1.6	1.5	1[1]	6[1]	...	7[1]
	2015	13 751	1.5	1.6	1.4	12	8	...	20
	2016	...	...	...	...	12	2	...	14
Finland Finlande	2005	192 169[21]	3.7[21]	3.8[21]	3.6[21]	11 809[1]	...	849[1]	12 658[1]
	2010	248 135[21]	4.6[21]	4.8[21]	4.5[21]	8 724[1]	2 097[1]	3 133[1]	13 954[1]
	2015	315 881[21]	5.7[21]	5.9[21]	5.6[21]	11 798[8]	2 622	1 928	16 348
	2016	...	...	...	...	15 059	15 074	2 427	32 560
France France	2005	6 737 600	11.0	11.0	11.0	137 316[1]	41 279[1]	946[1]	179 541[1]
	2010	7 196 481	11.4	11.4	11.4	200 687[1]	48 576[1]	1 171[1]	250 434[1]
	2015	7 784 418	12.1	12.1	12.1	264 972	53 827	1 290	320 089
	2016	...	...	...	...	290 178	64 702	1 334	356 214
French Guiana Guyane française	2005	86 468	42.5	42.4	42.6	...	...	...	...
	2010	96 288	41.2	39.9	42.5	...	...	...	...
	2015	106 108	39.5	37.5	41.5	...	...	...	...
French Polynesia Polynésie française	2005	32 286	12.7	14.1	11.2	...	...	...	...
	2010	31 640	11.8	13.1	10.4	...	...	...	...
	2015	30 058	10.6	11.9	9.3	...	...	...	...
Gabon Gabon	2005	214 123[3]	15.5[3]	17.7[3]	13.3[3]	8 545[1]	4 843[1]	291[1]	13 679[1]
	2010	243 992[3]	15.8[3]	17.9[3]	13.7[3]	9 015[1]	4 132[1]	84[1]	13 231[1]
	2015	268 384[3]	15.6[3]	17.6[3]	13.5[3]	1 008	1 886	...	2 894
	2016	...	...	...	...	913	1 980	...	2 893
Gambia Gambie	2005	181 905	12.6	13.5	11.8	7 330[1]	602[1]	42[1]	7 974[1]
	2010	185 763	11.0	11.7	10.3	8 378[1]	74[1]	31[1]	8 483[1]
	2015	192 540	9.7	10.3	9.1	11 773	2	...	11 775
	2016	...	...	...	...	7 890	3	...	7 893
Georgia Géorgie	2005	199 805[22]	4.5[22]	4.1[22]	4.8[22]	2 497[1]	8[1]	236 097[1]	238 602[1]
	2010	182 202[22]	4.3[22]	3.9[22]	4.6[22]	639[1]	44[1]	361 547[1]	362 230[1]
	2015	168 802[22]	4.2[22]	3.8[22]	4.6[22]	1 659	587	266 060	268 306
	2016	...	...	...	...	2 048	644	271 457	274 149
Germany Allemagne	2005	10 299 160	12.7	12.6	12.8	700 016[1]	71 624[1]	12 340[1]	783 980[1]
	2010	11 605 690	14.4	14.0	14.8	594 269[1]	51 991[1]	24 378[1]	670 638[1]
	2015	12 005 690	14.9	14.4	15.3	250 299	311 551	11 978	573 828
	2016	...	...	...	...	478 581	561 159	12 387	1 052 127
Ghana Ghana	2005	304 436	1.4	1.5	1.4	53 537[1]	5 496[1]	1 212[1]	60 245[1]
	2010	337 017	1.4	1.5	1.3	13 828[1]	749[1]	184[1]	14 761[1]
	2015	399 471	1.5	1.6	1.3	18 476	2 855	...	21 331
	2016	...	...	...	...	16 409	2 048	8 871	27 328
Gibraltar Gibraltar	2005	9 211	31.7	...	...	...	...	...	...
	2010	10 369	33.7	...	...	...	...	...	...
	2015	11 065	34.3	...	...	...	...	...	...
Greece Grèce	2005	1 190 707	10.8	10.8	10.7	2 390[1]	8 867[1]	3 000[1]	14 257[1]
	2010	1 269 749	11.4	11.2	11.5	1 444[1]	55 724[1]	260[1]	57 428[1]
	2015	1 242 514	11.3	10.8	11.9	8 231	29 157	214	37 602
	2016	...	...	...	...	66 852	27 778	45	94 675
Greenland Groenland	2005	6 686	11.7	...	...	...	...	...	...
	2010	6 226	11.0	...	...	...	...	...	...
	2015	6 009	10.7	...	...	...	...	...	...

International migrants and refugees *(continued)*
International migrant stock (number and percentage) and refugees and others of concern to UNHCR

Migrants internationaux et réfugiés *(suite)*
Stock de migrants internationaux (nombre et pourcentage) et réfugiés et autres personnes relevant de la compétence du HCR

		International Migrant Stock (mid-year) Stock de migrants internationaux (milieu de l'année)				Refugees and others of concern to UNHCR (mid-year) Réfugiés et autres personnes relevant de la compétence du HCR (milieu de l'année)			
			% of total pop. % de la pop. totale						
Region, country or area Région, pays ou zone	Year Année	Total Total	MF/HF	M/H	F	Refugees& Réfugiés&	Asylum seekers Demandeurs d'asile	Other&& Autres&&	Total pop. Pop. totale
Grenada	2005	6 902	6.7	6.7	6.7	...	...	...	...
Grenade	2010	6 980	6.7	6.6	6.7	...	3[1]	...	3[1]
	2015	7 057	6.6	6.5	6.7	...	...	...	...
	2016	...	...	...	...	1	...	...	1
Guadeloupe [23]	2005	89 065	19.8	19.3	20.1	...	...	...	...
Guadeloupe [23]	2010	94 942	20.8	20.0	21.4	...	...	...	...
	2015	98 507	21.0	20.2	21.7	...	...	...	...
Guam	2005	74 743	47.2	47.8	46.5	...	...	...	...
Guam	2010	75 416	47.3	48.0	46.5	...	...	...	...
	2015	76 089	44.8	45.6	44.0	...	...	...	...
Guatemala	2005	57 252[2]	0.4[2]	0.4[2]	0.5[2]	391[1]	3[1]	...	394[1]
Guatemala	2010	66 384[2]	0.5[2]	0.4[2]	0.5[2]	138[1]	2[1]	...	140[1]
	2015	76 352[2]	0.5[2]	0.5[2]	0.5[2]	202	73	...	275
	2016	...	...	...	...	239	196	1 400	1 835
Guinea	2005	229 611[2,3]	2.4[2,3]	2.3[2,3]	2.4[2,3]	63 525[1]	3 808[1]	29 645[1]	96 978[1]
Guinée	2010	205 111[2,3]	1.9[2,3]	1.8[2,3]	1.9[2,3]	14 113[1]	764[1]	117[1]	14 994[1]
	2015	228 413[2,3]	1.8[2,3]	1.8[2,3]	1.8[2,3]	8 704	293	...	8 997
	2016	...	...	...	...	9 018	198	...	9 216
Guinea-Bissau	2005	20 736[2]	1.4[2]	1.4[2]	1.4[2]	7 616[1]	166[1]	...	7 782[1]
Guinée-Bissau	2010	21 061[2]	1.3[2]	1.3[2]	1.3[2]	7 679[1]	330[1]	5[1]	8 014[1]
	2015	22 333[2]	1.2[2]	1.2[2]	1.2[2]	8 684	123	...	8 807
	2016	...	...	...	...	8 684[8]	123	...	8 807
Guyana	2005	10 868	1.5	1.6	1.3	...	...	...	...
Guyana	2010	13 126	1.7	1.9	1.6	7[1]	...	...	7[1]
	2015	15 384	2.0	2.1	1.9	11	1	...	12
	2016	...	...	...	...	11	...	...	11
Haiti	2005	30 468	0.3	0.4	0.3	...	...	...	...
Haïti	2010	35 104	0.4	0.4	0.3	...	4[1]	...	4[1]
	2015	39 529	0.4	0.4	0.3	5	5	...	10
	2016	...	...	...	...	4	9	1 881[24]	1 894
Holy See	*2005	793	99.4	...	...	...	...	...	...
Saint-Siège	*2010	799	100.0	...	...	...	...	...	...
	*2015	800	100.0	...	...	...	...	...	...
Honduras	2005	27 875[2]	0.4[2]	0.4[2]	0.4[2]	22[1]	50[1]	...	72[1]
Honduras	2010	27 288[2]	0.4[2]	0.4[2]	0.3[2]	14[1]	...	1[1]	15[1]
	2015	28 070[2]	0.3[2]	0.4[2]	0.3[2]	23	19	...	42
	2016	...	...	...	...	23	24	176 200	176 247
Hungary	2005	366 787[2]	3.6[2]	3.6[2]	3.6[2]	8 046[1]	684[1]	192[1]	8 922[1]
Hongrie	2010	436 616[2]	4.4[2]	4.4[2]	4.3[2]	5 414[1]	367[1]	62[1]	5 843[1]
	2015	449 632[2]	4.6[2]	4.7[2]	4.4[2]	4 192	24 431	128	28 751
	2016	...	...	...	...	4 649	9 665	134	14 448
Iceland	2005	25 492	8.6	8.3	8.9	293[1]	29[1]	53[1]	375[1]
Islande	2010	35 091	11.0	11.0	11.1	83[1]	39[1]	113[1]	235[1]
	2015	37 522	11.4	11.0	11.8	104	225	119	448
	2016	...	...	...	...	231	126	131	488
India	2005	5 923 642[2]	0.5[2]	0.5[2]	0.5[2]	139 283[1]	303[1]	2 792[1]	142 378[1]
Inde	2010	5 436 012[2]	0.4[2]	0.4[2]	0.4[2]	184 821[1]	3 746[1]	5 109[1]	193 676[1]
	2015	5 240 960[2]	0.4[2]	0.4[2]	0.4[2]	200 383	5 381	...	205 764
	2016	...	...	...	...	202 185	8 916	...	211 101
Indonesia	2005	289 568[2]	0.1[2]	0.1[2]	0.1[2]	89[1]	58[1]	263[1]	410[1]
Indonésie	2010	305 416[2]	0.1[2]	0.1[2]	0.1[2]	811[1]	2 071[1]	12[1]	2 894[1]
	2015	328 846[2]	0.1[2]	0.1[2]	0.1[2]	5 277	7 911	...	13 188
	2016	...	...	...	...	6 590	7 248	...	13 838
Iran (Islamic Republic of)	2005	2 568 930[2]	3.7[2]	3.9[2]	3.4[2]	974 302[1]	140[1]	344 914[1]	1 319 356[1]
Iran (Rép. islamique d')	2010	2 761 561[2]	3.7[2]	4.2[2]	3.2[2]	1 073 366[1]	1 775[1]	10 168[1]	1 085 309[1]
	2015	2 726 420[2]	3.4[2]	3.6[2]	3.3[2]	979 441	42	8	979 491
	2016	...	...	...	...	978 120	163	5	978 288

International migrants and refugees *(continued)*

International migrant stock (number and percentage) and refugees and others of concern to UNHCR

Migrants internationaux et réfugiés *(suite)*

Stock de migrants internationaux (nombre et pourcentage) et réfugiés et autres personnes relevant de la compétence du HCR

		International Migrant Stock (mid-year) Stock de migrants internationaux (milieu de l'année)	% of total pop. % de la pop. totale			Refugees and others of concern to UNHCR (mid-year) Réfugiés et autres personnes relevant de la compétence du HCR (milieu de l'année)			
Region, country or area Région, pays ou zone	Year Année	Total Total	MF/HF	M/H	F	Refugees[&] Réfugiés[&]	Asylum seekers Demandeurs d'asile	Other[&&] Autres[&&]	Total pop. Pop. totale
Iraq	2005	132 915[2,3]	0.5[2,3]	0.6[2,3]	0.4[2,3]	50 177[1]	1 948[1]	1 526 104[1]	1 578 229[1]
Iraq	2010	117 389[2,3]	0.4[2,3]	0.5[2,3]	0.3[2,3]	34 655[1]	3 073[1]	1 758 603[1]	1 796 331[1]
	2015	353 881[2,3]	1.0[2,3]	1.1[2,3]	0.8[2,3]	288 035	7 420	4 016 205[25]	4 311 660
	2016	...	...	...	...	282 331	7 420	4 446 465[25]	4 736 216
Ireland	2005	589 046	14.0	14.8	13.3	7 113[1]	2 414[1]	4[1]	9 531[1]
Irlande	2010	730 542	15.8	15.7	16.0	9 107[1]	5 129[1]	1[1]	14 237[1]
	2015	746 260	15.9	15.5	16.3	5 853[8]	4 300	99	10 252
	2016	...	...	...	...	6 125[5]	4 267	100	10 492
Isle of Man	2005	41 475	51.6	...	...	...	...	...	...
Île de Man	2010	43 447	51.5	...	...	...	...	...	...
	2015	45 221	51.5	...	...	...	...	...	...
Israel	2005	1 889 503[2]	28.6[2]	26.6[2]	30.5[2]	609[1]	939[1]	...	1 548[1]
Israël	2010	1 950 615[2]	26.3[2]	24.3[2]	28.2[2]	25 471[1]	5 575[1]	9[1]	31 055[1]
	2015	2 011 727[2]	24.9[2]	22.8[2]	27.0[2]	38 500	6 591	88	45 179
	2016	...	...	...	...	32 946	11 677	42	44 665
Italy	2005	3 954 790	6.7	6.4	7.1	20 675[1]	...	940[1]	21 615[1]
Italie	2010	5 787 893	9.7	9.2	10.2	56 397[1]	4 076[1]	858[1]	61 331[1]
	2015	5 788 875	9.7	9.0	10.4	93 715[8]	48 307	606	142 628
	2016	...	...	...	...	131 993	84 034	701	216 728
Jamaica	2005	24 314	0.9	0.9	0.9	...	...	...	...
Jamaïque	2010	23 677	0.9	0.9	0.8	21[1]	...	...	21[1]
	2015	23 167	0.8	0.8	0.8	15	3	...	18
	2016	...	...	...	...	15	10	...	25
Japan	2005	2 012 916[3]	1.6[3]	1.5[3]	1.7[3]	1 941[1]	533[1]	1 770[1]	4 244[1]
Japon	2010	2 134 151[3]	1.7[3]	1.5[3]	1.8[3]	2 586[1]	3 047[1]	1 397[1]	7 030[1]
	2015	2 043 877[3]	1.6[3]	1.5[3]	1.7[3]	* 2 419	* 10 705	* 631	* 13 755
	2016	...	...	...	...	2 462	16 324	603	* 19 389
Jordan	2005	2 325 414[2,3]	43.6[2,3]	42.8[2,3]	44.4[2,3]	965[1]	16 570[1]	329[1]	17 864[1]
Jordanie	2010	2 722 983[2,3]	41.8[2,3]	41.2[2,3]	42.4[2,3]	450 915[1]	2 159[1]	107[1]	453 181[1]
	2015	3 112 026[2,3]	41.0[2,3]	40.3[2,3]	41.7[2,3]	664 102[26]	20 693	...	684 795
	2016	...	...	...	...	691 769[26]	29 660	...	721 429
Kazakhstan	2005	3 102 962	20.1	19.9	20.3	7 265[1]	65[1]	50 598[1]	57 928[1]
Kazakhstan	2010	3 334 623	20.4	20.7	20.2	4 406[1]	314[1]	7 969[1]	12 689[1]
	2015	3 546 778	20.1	20.7	19.6	662	149	7 038	7 849
	2016	...	...	...	...	691	184	8 360	9 235
Kenya	2005	756 894[2]	2.1[2]	2.2[2]	2.1[2]	251 271[1]	16 460[1]	481[1]	268 212[1]
Kenya	2010	926 959[2]	2.3[2]	2.3[2]	2.3[2]	402 905[1]	27 966[1]	320 083[1]	750 954[1]
	2015	1 084 357[2]	2.4[2]	2.4[2]	2.4[2]	552 272	40 341	21 231	613 844
	2016	...	...	...	...	523 498	38 859	20 000	582 357
Kiribati	2005	2 487	2.7	2.9	2.5	...	...	...	...
Kiribati	2010	2 868	2.8	3.0	2.6	...	...	...	...
	2015	3 153	2.8	3.0	2.6	...	...	...	...
Kuwait	2005	1 333 327[2,3]	58.9[2,3]	69.2[2,3]	44.3[2,3]	1 523[1]	203[1]	101 000[1]	102 726[1]
Koweït	2010	1 871 537[2,3]	61.2[2,3]	76.0[2,3]	42.1[2,3]	184[1]	3 275[1]	93 000[1]	96 459[1]
	2015	2 866 136[2,3]	73.6[2,3]	86.4[2,3]	57.3[2,3]	593	1 040	93 000	94 633
	2016	...	...	...	...	807	888	93 000	94 695
Kyrgyzstan	2005	312 897	6.1	5.1	7.1	2 598[1]	498[1]	100 004[1]	103 100[1]
Kirghizistan	2010	231 511	4.2	3.5	5.0	2 458[1]	554[1]	301 164[1]	304 176[1]
	2015	204 382	3.4	2.8	4.1	433	168	13 678	14 279
	2016	...	...	...	...	339	125	7 763	8 227
Lao People's Dem. Rep. [2,3]	2005	20 371	0.4	0.4	0.3	...	...	...	...
Rép. dém. populaire lao [2,3]	2010	21 185	0.3	0.4	0.3	...	...	...	...
	2015	22 244	0.3	0.4	0.3	...	...	...	...
Latvia	2005	376 725	16.9	15.2	18.4	11[1]	9[1]	418 638[1]	418 658[1]
Lettonie	2010	313 786	15.0	13.1	16.7	68[1]	53[1]	326 906[1]	327 027[1]
	2015	263 126	13.4	11.4	15.0	195	171	262 802[27]	263 168
	2016	...	...	...	...	253	143	252 195[27]	252 591

International migrants and refugees *(continued)*

International migrant stock (number and percentage) and refugees and others of concern to UNHCR

Migrants internationaux et réfugiés *(suite)*

Stock de migrants internationaux (nombre et pourcentage) et réfugiés et autres personnes relevant de la compétence du HCR

		International Migrant Stock (mid-year) Stock de migrants internationaux (milieu de l'année)				Refugees and others of concern to UNHCR (mid-year) Réfugiés et autres personnes relevant de la compétence du HCR (milieu de l'année)			
			% of total pop. % de la pop. totale						
Region, country or area Région, pays ou zone	Year Année	Total Total	MF/HF	M/H	F	Refugees[&] Réfugiés[&]	Asylum seekers Demandeurs d'asile	Other[&&] Autres[&&]	Total pop. Pop. totale
Lebanon	2005	756 784[2]	19.0[2]	19.3[2]	18.7[2]	1 078[1]	1 450[1]	451[1]	2 979[1]
Liban	2010	820 655[2]	18.9[2]	19.3[2]	18.5[2]	8 063[1]	1 417[1]	40[1]	9 520[1]
	2015	1 997 776[2]	34.1[2]	32.7[2]	35.6[2]	1 172 388	10 851	5 813	1 189 052
	2016	...	...	...	...	1 035 701	13 711	4 828	1 054 240
Lesotho	2005[2,3]	6 290	0.3	0.4	0.3	...	...	...	...
Lesotho	2010[2,3]	6 414	0.3	0.4	0.3	...	...	...	...
	2015	6 572[2,3]	0.3[2,3]	0.3[2,3]	0.3[2,3]	44	1	...	45
	2016	...	...	...	...	41	2	...	43
Liberia	2005	87 188	2.7	3.1	2.2	10 168[1]	29[1]	498 604[1]	508 801[1]
Libéria	2010	99 129	2.5	2.9	2.1	24 743[1]	28[1]	1 855[1]	26 626[1]
	2015	113 779	2.5	2.9	2.2	38 904	18	1 486	40 408
	2016	...	...	...	...	20 560	24	1 480	22 064
Libya	2005	625 212[3]	10.8[3]	14.9[3]	6.4[3]	12 166[1]	200[1]	35[1]	12 401[1]
Libye	2010	683 998[3]	10.9[3]	15.3[3]	6.4[3]	7 923[1]	3 194[1]	37[1]	11 154[1]
	2015	771 146[3]	12.3[3]	17.4[3]	7.1[3]	27 948	8 904	434 869	471 721
	2016	...	...	...	...	9 300	28 302	434 869	472 471
Liechtenstein	2005	18 898	54.2	...	...	150[1]	60[1]	...	210[1]
Liechtenstein	2010	22 342	61.6	...	...	92[1]	44[1]	6[1]	142[1]
	2015	23 493	62.6	...	...	107	75	2	184
	2016	...	...	...	...	154	100	...	254
Lithuania	2005	201 209	6.0	6.1	6.0	531[1]	55[1]	8 709[1]	9 295[1]
Lituanie	2010	160 772	5.1	4.8	5.4	803[1]	71[1]	3 679[1]	4 553[1]
	2015	136 036	4.7	4.3	5.1	1 055	54	3 583	4 692
	2016	...	...	...	...	1 121	76	3 466	4 663
Luxembourg	2005	150 618	32.9	33.2	32.6	1 822[1]	...	74[1]	1 896[1]
Luxembourg	2010	163 142	32.1	32.3	32.0	3 254[1]	697[1]	173[1]	4 124[1]
	2015	249 325	44.0	44.3	43.6	1 192	831	81	2 104
	2016	...	...	...	...	1 537	2 529	85	4 151
Madagascar	2005[3]	26 058	0.1	0.2	0.1	...	...	...	...
Madagascar	2010	28 905[3]	0.1[3]	0.2[3]	0.1[3]	...	...	1[1]	1[1]
	2015	32 075[3]	0.1[3]	0.2[3]	0.1[3]	10	9	...	19
	2016	...	...	...	...	10	56	...	66
Malawi	2005	221 661[2]	1.7[2]	1.7[2]	1.8[2]	4 240[1]	5 331[1]	49[1]	9 620[1]
Malawi	2010	217 722[2]	1.5[2]	1.4[2]	1.5[2]	5 740[1]	9 362[1]	131[1]	15 233[1]
	2015	215 158[2]	1.2[2]	1.2[2]	1.3[2]	8 963	13 669	...	22 632
	2016	...	...	...	...	8 643	17 054	...	25 697
Malaysia	2005	1 722 344[2,3,28]	6.7[2,3,28]	7.7[2,3,28]	5.7[2,3,28]	33 693[1]	10 838[1]	61 555[1]	106 086[1]
Malaisie	2010	2 406 011[2,3,28]	8.6[2,3,28]	10.3[2,3,28]	6.8[2,3,28]	81 516[1]	11 339[1]	120 015[1]	212 870[1]
	2015	2 514 243[2,3,28]	8.3[2,3,28]	10.2[2,3,28]	6.4[2,3,28]	97 573	54 400	120 000	271 973
	2016	...	...	...	...	92 524	54 450	91 641	238 615
Maldives [2,3]	2005	45 045	14.8	17.7	11.8	...	...	...	...
Maldives [2,3]	2010	73 604	22.1	28.8	15.4	...	...	...	...
	2015	94 086	25.9	36.3	15.4	...	...	...	...
Mali	2005	256 797[2]	2.0[2]	2.0[2]	1.9[2]	11 233[1]	1 833[1]	...	13 066[1]
Mali	2010	336 607[2]	2.2[2]	2.3[2]	2.2[2]	13 558[1]	1 703[1]	...	15 261[1]
	2015	363 145[2]	2.1[2]	2.1[2]	2.0[2]	14 970	386	132 953	148 309
	2016	...	...	...	...	17 923	283	72 556	90 762
Malta	2005	24 560	6.2	6.1	6.3	1 939[1]	149[1]	...	2 088[1]
Malte	2010	33 084	8.0	8.2	7.9	6 136[1]	1 295[1]	...	7 431[1]
	2015	41 442	9.9	10.5	9.3	6 095	425	...	6 520
	2016	...	...	...	...	7 684	442	...	8 126
Marshall Islands	2005	2 417	4.6	...	...	...	...	...	...
Îles Marshall	2010	3 089	5.9	...	...	...	...	...	...
	2015	3 284	6.2	...	...	...	...	...	...
Martinique	2005	57 034	14.4	14.0	14.7	...	...	...	...
Martinique	2010	59 575	15.1	14.4	15.6	...	...	...	...
	2015	61 731	15.6	14.9	16.2	...	...	...	...

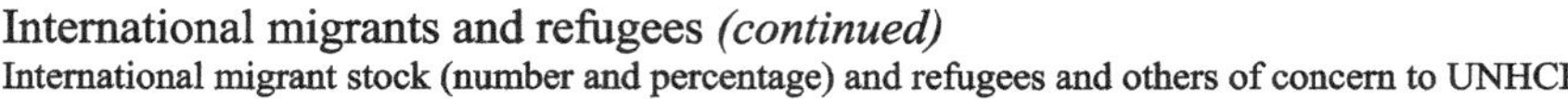

4 International migrants and refugees *(continued)*

International migrant stock (number and percentage) and refugees and others of concern to UNHCR

Migrants internationaux et réfugiés *(suite)*

Stock de migrants internationaux (nombre et pourcentage) et réfugiés et autres personnes relevant de la compétence du HCR

Region, country or area Région, pays ou zone	Year Année	International Migrant Stock (mid-year) Stock de migrants internationaux (milieu de l'année) Total Total	% of total pop. % de la pop. totale MF/HF	M/H	F	Refugees and others of concern to UNHCR (mid-year) Réfugiés et autres personnes relevant de la compétence du HCR (milieu de l'année) Refugees[&] Réfugiés[&]	Asylum seekers Demandeurs d'asile	Other[&&] Autres[&&]	Total pop. Pop. totale
Mauritania Mauritanie	2005	58 119[2,3]	1.8[2,3]	2.1[2,3]	1.6[2,3]	632[1]	92[1]	29 500[1]	30 224[1]
	2010	84 679[2,3]	2.4[2,3]	2.7[2,3]	2.0[2,3]	26 717[1]	241[1]	9[1]	26 967[1]
	2015	138 162[2,3]	3.4[2,3]	3.9[2,3]	2.9[2,3]	76 851	407	...	77 258
	2016	...	...	...	...	68 590	407	...	68 997
Mauritius [3,29] Maurice [3,29]	2005	19 647	1.6	1.5	1.7	...	...	...	...
	2010	24 836	2.0	2.1	1.9	...	...	...	...
	2015	28 585	2.2	2.5	2.0	...	...	...	...
Mayotte Mayotte	2005	63 176	35.5	35.7	35.2	...	...	...	...
	2010	72 757	34.9	33.8	35.9	...	...	...	...
	2015	76 992	32.1	30.2	33.9	...	...	...	...
Mexico Mexique	2005	712 487[2]	0.6[2]	0.7[2]	0.6[2]	3 229[1]	161[1]	...	3 390[1]
	2010	969 538[2]	0.8[2]	0.8[2]	0.8[2]	1 395[1]	172[1]	6[1]	1 573[1]
	2015	1 193 155[2]	0.9[2]	1.0[2]	0.9[2]	2 158	...	68	2 226
	2016	...	...	...	...	4 363	1 514	13	5 890
Micronesia (Fed. States of) Micronésie (États féd. de)	2005	2 905	2.7	2.9	2.6	...	...	...	...
	2010	2 805	2.7	2.8	2.6	...	...	...	...
	2015	2 756	2.6	2.8	2.5	...	34	...	34
	2016	...	...	...	...	3	1	...	4
Monaco Monaco	2005	21 312	63.0	...	...	...	...	...	...
	2010	21 132	57.4	...	...	...	1[1]	...	1[1]
	2015	21 042	55.8	...	...	33	...	...	33
	2016	...	...	...	...	32	...	...	32
Mongolia Mongolie	2005	11 475[3]	0.5[3]	0.6[3]	0.3[3]	...	2[1]	581[1]	583[1]
	2010	16 061[3]	0.6[3]	0.9[3]	0.3[3]	12[1]	1[1]	260[1]	273[1]
	2015	17 620[3]	0.6[3]	0.9[3]	0.3[3]	11	5	16	32
	2016	...	...	...	...	14	1	9	24
Montenegro Monténégro	2010	78 507	12.6	10.3	14.9	16 364[1]	5[1]	1 886[1]	18 255[1]
	2015	82 541	13.2	10.8	15.5	6 203	7	13 602	19 812
	2016	...	...	...	...	1 637	12	14 400	16 049
Montserrat Montserrat	2005	1 244	26.0	...	...	...	...	...	...
	2010	1 277	25.8	...	...	...	14[1]	...	14[1]
	2015	1 351	26.4	...	...	...	...	...	...
Morocco Maroc	2005	54 379[3]	0.2[3]	0.2[3]	0.2[3]	219[1]	1 843[1]	4[1]	2 066[1]
	2010	70 909[3]	0.2[3]	0.2[3]	0.2[3]	792[1]	280[1]	...	1 072[1]
	2015	88 511[3]	0.3[3]	0.3[3]	0.3[3]	2 144	2 216	...	4 360
	2016	...	...	...	...	4 329	2 069	...	6 398
Mozambique Mozambique	2005	204 830[2]	1.0[2]	1.0[2]	0.9[2]	1 954[1]	4 015[1]	40[1]	6 009[1]
	2010	214 612[2]	0.9[2]	0.9[2]	0.9[2]	4 077[1]	5 914[1]	1[1]	9 992[1]
	2015	222 928[2]	0.8[2]	0.8[2]	0.8[2]	4 552	14 257	7	18 816
	2016	...	...	...	...	5 627	18 336	2	23 965
Myanmar Myanmar	2005	83 025[3]	0.2[3]	0.2[3]	0.2[3]	...	...	236 495[1]	236 495[1]
	2010	76 414[3]	0.1[3]	0.2[3]	0.1[3]	...	...	859 403[1]	859 403[1]
	2015	73 308[3]	0.1[3]	0.2[3]	0.1[3]	...	...	1 466 501[30]	1 466 501
	2016	...	...	...	...	...	1	1 392 096[30]	1 392 097
Namibia Namibie	2005	106 274	5.2	5.8	4.7	5 307[1]	1 073[1]	2 752[1]	9 132[1]
	2010	102 405	4.7	5.2	4.2	7 254[1]	1 421[1]	93[1]	8 768[1]
	2015	93 888	3.8	4.2	3.4	1 659	1 100	1 684	4 443
	2016	...	...	...	...	1 776	1 289	1 715	4 780
Nauru Nauru	2005[3]	2 253	22.3	...	...	...	...	...	...
	2010[3]	2 112	21.1	...	...	...	...	...	...
	2015	3 178[3]	31.1[3]	...	...	506	816	...	1 322
	2016	...	...	...	...	506[5]	290	...	796
Nepal Népal	2005	679 457[2]	2.7[2]	1.9[2]	3.5[2]	126 436[1]	1 272[1]	410 929[1]	538 637[1]
	2010	578 657[2]	2.2[2]	1.4[2]	2.8[2]	89 808[1]	938[1]	800 571[1]	891 317[1]
	2015	518 278[2]	1.8[2]	1.2[2]	2.4[2]	36 287	57	409[31]	36 753
	2016	...	...	...	...	30 277	23	351[31]	30 651

International migrants and refugees *(continued)*

International migrant stock (number and percentage) and refugees and others of concern to UNHCR

Migrants internationaux et réfugiés *(suite)*

Stock de migrants internationaux (nombre et pourcentage) et réfugiés et autres personnes relevant de la compétence du HCR

Region, country or area Région, pays ou zone	Year Année	International Migrant Stock (mid-year) Stock de migrants internationaux (milieu de l'année) Total Total	% of total pop. % de la pop. totale MF/HF	M/H	F	Refugees and others of concern to UNHCR (mid-year) Réfugiés et autres personnes relevant de la compétence du HCR (milieu de l'année) Refugees& Réfugiés&	Asylum seekers Demandeurs d'asile	Other&& Autres&&	Total pop. Pop. totale
Netherlands Pays-Bas	2005	1 736 127	10.6	10.4	10.8	118 189[1]	14 664[1]	6 872[1]	139 725[1]
	2010	1 832 510	11.0	10.7	11.3	74 961[1]	13 053[1]	2 095[1]	90 109[1]
	2015	1 979 486	11.7	11.2	12.2	82 494[8]	8 097	1 951	92 542
	2016	...	...	...	...	99 155	15 148	1 951	116 254
New Caledonia Nouvelle-Calédonie	2005	55 405	24.2	26.0	22.4	...	...	...	...
	2010	61 158	24.8	26.3	23.3	...	...	...	...
	2015	64 290	24.4	26.1	22.8	...	...	...	...
New Zealand Nouvelle-Zélande	2005	839 952	20.3	20.1	20.5	5 307[1]	396[1]	6[1]	5 709[1]
	2010	947 443	21.7	21.4	22.0	2 307[1]	216[1]	1[1]	2 524[1]
	2015	1 039 736	23.0	22.7	23.2	1 349[8]	251	...	1 600
	2016	...	...	...	...	1 413	266	...	1 679
Nicaragua Nicaragua	2005	34 918[2]	0.6[2]	0.7[2]	0.6[2]	227[1]	1[1]	...	228[1]
	2010	37 333[2]	0.7[2]	0.7[2]	0.6[2]	64[1]	12[1]	...	76[1]
	2015	40 262[2]	0.7[2]	0.7[2]	0.6[2]	361	25	5	391
	2016	...	...	...	...	331	298	3	632
Niger Niger	2005	124 461[2]	0.9[2]	0.9[2]	1.0[2]	301[1]	48[1]	37[1]	386[1]
	2010	126 464[2]	0.8[2]	0.7[2]	0.8[2]	314[1]	18[1]	5[1]	337[1]
	2015	189 255[2]	1.0[2]	0.9[2]	1.0[2]	82 064	122	120 000	202 186
	2016	...	...	...	...	143 538	62	168 861	312 461
Nigeria Nigéria	2005	648 019[2,3]	0.5[2,3]	0.5[2,3]	0.4[2,3]	9 019[1]	420[1]	3 290[1]	12 729[1]
	2010	920 118[2,3]	0.6[2,3]	0.6[2,3]	0.5[2,3]	8 747[1]	1 815[1]	34[1]	10 596[1]
	2015	1 199 115[2,3]	0.7[2,3]	0.7[2,3]	0.6[2,3]	1 279	909	1 508 017	1 510 205
	2016	...	...	...	...	1 243	469	2 435 781	2 437 493
Niue Nioué	2005	522	31.0	...	...	...	...	...	...
	2010	545	33.6	...	...	...	...	...	...
	2015	557	34.6	...	...	...	...	...	...
Northern Mariana Islands Îles Mariannes du Nord	2005	37 542	58.3	...	...	...	...	...	...
	2010	24 168	44.9	...	...	...	...	...	...
	2015	21 648	39.3	...	...	...	...	...	...
Norway Norvège	2005	361 144[32]	7.8[32]	7.7[32]	7.9[32]	43 034[1]	...	1 143[1]	44 177[1]
	2010	526 799[32]	10.8[32]	11.0[32]	10.6[32]	40 260[1]	12 473[1]	3 150[1]	55 883[1]
	2015	741 813[32]	14.2[32]	14.7[32]	13.7[32]	47 043[8]	5 885	1 997	54 925
	2016	...	...	...	...	53 909	16 765	2 561	73 235
Oman Oman	2005	666 160[3]	26.6[3]	37.7[3]	12.5[3]	7[1]	4[1]	...	11[1]
	2010	816 221[3]	27.7[3]	37.5[3]	13.3[3]	78[1]	13[1]	...	91[1]
	2015	1 844 978[3]	41.1[3]	50.2[3]	23.1[3]	122	268	...	390
	2016	...	...	...	...	321	275	...	596
Pakistan Pakistan	2005	3 171 132[2]	2.1[2]	2.2[2]	2.0[2]	1 084 694[1]	3 426[1]	461 123[1]	1 549 243[1]
	2010	3 941 586[2]	2.3[2]	2.4[2]	2.3[2]	1 900 621[1]	2 095[1]	2 248 308[1]	4 151 024[1]
	2015	3 628 956[2]	1.9[2]	1.9[2]	1.9[2]	1 540 854	6 103	1 893 008	3 439 965
	2016	...	...	...	...	1 576 771	9 250	1 153 341	2 739 362
Palau Palaos	2005	6 043	30.4	...	...	...	...	...	...
	2010	5 787	28.3	...	...	...	...	...	...
	2015	5 664	26.6	...	...	1	...	...	1
	2016	...	...	...	...	...	1	...	1
Panama Panama	2005	117 563	3.5	3.6	3.5	1 730[1]	433[1]	10 273[1]	12 436[1]
	2010	157 309	4.3	4.5	4.2	17 073[1]	479[1]	6[1]	17 558[1]
	2015	184 710	4.7	4.8	4.6	17 303	2 038	2	19 343
	2016	...	...	...	...	17 338	4 200	2	21 540
Papua New Guinea Papouasie-Nvl-Guinée	2005	29 967[2,3]	0.5[2,3]	0.6[2,3]	0.4[2,3]	9 999[1]	4[1]	135[1]	10 138[1]
	2010	25 424[2,3]	0.4[2,3]	0.5[2,3]	0.3[2,3]	9 698[1]	1[1]	...	9 699[1]
	2015	25 782[2,3]	0.3[2,3]	0.4[2,3]	0.2[2,3]	9 510	400	...	9 910
	2016	...	...	...	...	9 652	68	...	9 720
Paraguay Paraguay	2005	168 243	2.9	3.0	2.8	50[1]	8[1]	...	58[1]
	2010	160 299	2.6	2.6	2.5	107[1]	8[1]	...	115[1]
	2015	156 462	2.4	2.4	2.3	161	39	...	200
	2016	...	...	...	...	181	42	...	223

4 International migrants and refugees *(continued)*

International migrant stock (number and percentage) and refugees and others of concern to UNHCR

Migrants internationaux et réfugiés *(suite)*

Stock de migrants internationaux (nombre et pourcentage) et réfugiés et autres personnes relevant de la compétence du HCR

		International Migrant Stock (mid-year) Stock de migrants internationaux (milieu de l'année)				Refugees and others of concern to UNHCR (mid-year) Réfugiés et autres personnes relevant de la compétence du HCR (milieu de l'année)			
			% of total pop. % de la pop. totale						
Region, country or area Région, pays ou zone	**Year Année**	**Total Total**	**MF/HF**	**M/H**	**F**	**Refugees& Réfugiés&**	**Asylum seekers Demandeurs d'asile**	**Other&& Autres&&**	**Total pop. Pop. totale**
Peru Pérou	2005	77 541	0.3	0.3	0.3	848[1]	336[1]	1[1]	1 185[1]
	2010	84 066	0.3	0.3	0.3	1 146[1]	264[1]	1[1]	1 411[1]
	2015	90 881	0.3	0.3	0.3	1 407	366	...	1 773
	2016	...	...	...	...	1 570	909	...	2 479
Philippines Philippines	2005	257 468[2,3]	0.3[2,3]	0.3[2,3]	0.3[2,3]	96[1]	42[1]	775[1]	913[1]
	2010	208 599[2,3]	0.2[2,3]	0.2[2,3]	0.2[2,3]	243[1]	73[1]	139 577[1]	139 893[1]
	2015	211 862[2,3]	0.2[2,3]	0.2[2,3]	0.2[2,3]	254	163	385 746	386 163
	2016	...	...	...	...	356	190	239 624	240 170
Poland Pologne	2005	722 509	1.9	1.6	2.1	4 604[1]	1 627[1]	75[1]	6 306[1]
	2010	642 417	1.7	1.4	1.9	15 555[1]	2 126[1]	763[1]	18 444[1]
	2015	619 403	1.6	1.4	1.8	15 741[8]	2 470	10 825	29 036
	2016	...	...	...	...	12 912	...	10 825	23 737
Portugal Portugal	2005	771 184	7.4	7.4	7.3	363[1]	...	...	363[1]
	2010	762 825	7.2	7.3	7.1	384[1]	72[1]	31[1]	487[1]
	2015	837 257	8.1	7.9	8.2	699[8]	641	14	1 354
	2016	...	...	...	...	1 055	751	14	1 820
Puerto Rico Porto Rico	2005	352 144	9.4	9.2	9.5	...	...	...	...
	2010	304 969	8.2	8.0	8.4	...	...	...	...
	2015	274 972	7.5	7.2	7.7	...	...	...	...
Qatar Qatar	2005	646 026[3]	77.2[3]	89.3[3]	52.9[3]	46[1]	28[1]	...	74[1]
	2010	1 456 413[3]	82.5[3]	90.7[3]	57.4[3]	51[1]	16[1]	1 200[1]	1 267[1]
	2015	1 687 640[3]	75.5[3]	87.2[3]	44.4[3]	133	100	1 200	1 433
	2016	...	...	...	...	148	121	1 200	1 469
Republic of Korea République de Corée	2005	485 546[3]	1.0[3]	1.2[3]	0.8[3]	69[1]	519[1]	...	588[1]
	2010	919 275[3]	1.9[3]	2.1[3]	1.6[3]	358[1]	712[1]	179[1]	1 249[1]
	2015	1 327 324[3]	2.6[3]	3.0[3]	2.3[3]	1 313	5 102	200	6 615
	2016	...	...	...	...	1 532	6 295	197	8 024
Republic of Moldova République de Moldova	2005	173 957[33]	4.2[33]	3.8[33]	4.5[33]	84[1]	148[1]	1 543[1]	1 775[1]
	2010	157 668[33]	3.9[33]	3.1[33]	4.6[33]	148[1]	81[1]	2 032[1]	2 261[1]
	2015	142 904[33]	3.5[33]	2.6[33]	4.4[33]	389	164	6 233	6 786
	2016	...	...	...	...	433	124	4 901	5 458
Réunion Réunion	2005	115 076	14.5	15.2	13.9	...	...	...	...
	2010	123 029	14.8	15.6	14.1	...	...	...	...
	2015	127 209	14.8	15.5	14.1	...	...	...	...
Romania Roumanie	2005	145 162	0.7	0.6	0.7	2 056[1]	264[1]	400[1]	2 720[1]
	2010	155 982	0.8	0.8	0.8	1 021[1]	388[1]	321[1]	1 730[1]
	2015	226 943	1.2	1.3	1.1	2 426	138	294	2 858
	2016	...	...	...	...	2 608	309	251	3 168
Russian Federation Fédération de Russie	2005	11 667 588	8.1	8.7	7.6	1 523[1]	292[1]	481 282[1]	483 097[1]
	2010	11 194 710	7.8	8.3	7.4	4 922[1]	1 463[1]	126 170[1]	132 555[1]
	2015	11 643 276	8.1	8.6	7.7	315 313	2 423	113 474[34]	431 210
	2016	...	...	...	...	314 507	2 088	101 843[34]	418 438
Rwanda Rwanda	2005	432 797[2]	4.8[2]	5.1[2]	4.6[2]	45 206[1]	4 301[1]	14 849[1]	64 356[1]
	2010	436 787[2]	4.2[2]	4.4[2]	4.1[2]	55 398[1]	290[1]	2[1]	55 690[1]
	2015	441 525[2]	3.8[2]	4.0[2]	3.7[2]	132 743	253	2 557	135 553
	2016	...	...	...	...	150 611	430	4 023	155 064
Saint Helena [35] Sainte-Hélène [35]	2005	487	11.4	...	...	...	...	...	...
	2010	569	13.6	...	...	...	...	...	...
	2015	604	15.2	...	...	...	...	...	...
Saint Kitts and Nevis Saint-Kitts-et-Nevis	2005	6 682	13.6	...	...	...	...	...	...
	2010	7 245	13.8	...	...	...	...	...	...
	2015	7 443	13.4	...	...	1	...	...	1
Saint Lucia Sainte-Lucie	2005	11 468	6.9	7.1	6.7	...	...	...	...
	2010	12 100	6.8	7.0	6.6	...	6[1]	1[1]	7[1]
	2015	12 771	6.9	7.1	6.7	2	2	60	64
	2016	...	...	...	...	2	1	...	3
Saint Pierre and Miquelon Saint-Pierre-et-Miquelon	2005	1 147	18.3	...	...	...	...	...	...
	2010	1 017	16.2	...	...	...	...	...	...
	2015	986	15.7	...	...	...	...	...	...

Region, country or area Région, pays ou zone	Year Année	International Migrant Stock (mid-year) Stock de migrants internationaux (milieu de l'année) Total Total	% of total pop. % de la pop. totale MF/HF	M/H	F	Refugees and others of concern to UNHCR (mid-year) Réfugiés et autres personnes relevant de la compétence du HCR (milieu de l'année) Refugees& Réfugiés&	Asylum seekers Demandeurs d'asile	Other&& Autres&&	Total pop. Pop. totale
Saint Vincent & Grenadines	2005	4 395	4.0	3.9	4.2	...	...	...	...
Saint-Vincent-Grenadines	2010	4 485	4.1	4.0	4.2	...	...	...	...
	2015	4 577	4.2	4.1	4.3	...	...	...	...
Samoa	2005	5 746	3.2	3.2	3.2	...	...	...	...
Samoa	2010	5 122	2.8	2.7	2.8	...	...	...	...
	2015	4 929	2.6	2.5	2.6	...	...	...	...
	2016	...	...	...	...	...	3	...	3
San Marino	2005	4 218	14.4	...	...	...	...	...	...
Saint-Marin	2010	4 399	14.3	...	...	...	...	...	...
	2015	4 717	14.8	...	...	...	...	...	...
Sao Tome and Principe [3]	2005	3 433	2.2	2.3	2.2	...	...	...	...
Sao Tomé-et-Principe [3]	2010	2 700	1.6	1.6	1.6	...	...	...	...
	2015	2 394	1.3	1.3	1.3	...	...	...	...
Saudi Arabia	2005	6 501 819[2,3]	26.3[2,3]	32.4[2,3]	18.6[2,3]	240 701[1]	212[1]	70 084[1]	310 997[1]
Arabie saoudite	2010	8 429 956[2,3]	30.0[2,3]	37.5[2,3]	20.3[2,3]	582[1]	87[1]	70 000[1]	70 669[1]
	2015	10 185 945[2,3]	32.3[2,3]	38.9[2,3]	23.7[2,3]	211	93	70 000	70 304
	2016	...	...	...	...	131	34	70 000	70 165
Senegal	2005	238 298[2]	2.1[2]	2.3[2]	2.0[2]	20 712[1]	2 629[1]	12[1]	23 353[1]
Sénégal	2010	256 092[2]	2.0[2]	2.1[2]	1.8[2]	20 672[1]	2 177[1]	1 401[1]	24 250[1]
	2015	263 242[2]	1.7[2]	1.9[2]	1.6[2]	14 304	2 956	...	17 260
	2016	...	...	...	...	14 453	3 161	...	17 614
Serbia	2005[36]	845 120	9.2	8.3	10.0	148 264[1]	33[1]	338 641[1]	486 938[1]
Serbie	2010[36]	826 066	9.1	8.2	10.0	73 608[1]	209[1]	238 810[1]	312 627[1]
	2015[36]	807 441	9.1	8.2	10.0	35 309	464	223 949	259 722
	2016	...	...	...	...	29 493	321	224 251	254 065
Seychelles	2005	8 997	10.1	13.1	7.2	...	...	...	...
Seychelles	2010	11 420	12.3	16.4	7.9	...	...	...	...
	2015	12 791	13.3	18.3	8.1	...	...	...	...
Sierra Leone	2005	149 615[2]	3.0[2]	3.2[2]	2.7[2]	59 965[1]	177[1]	6 202[1]	66 344[1]
Sierra Leone	2010	97 452[2]	1.7[2]	1.9[2]	1.5[2]	8 363[1]	210[1]	38[1]	8 611[1]
	2015	91 213[2]	1.4[2]	1.6[2]	1.3[2]	1 371	16	...	1 387
	2016	...	...	...	...	765	17	...	782
Singapore	2005	1 710 594	38.1	34.0	42.0	3[1]	1[1]	...	4[1]
Singapour	2010	2 164 794	42.6	38.2	47.0	7[1]	...	...	7[1]
	2015	2 543 638	45.4	40.6	50.0	...	...	1	1
	2016	...	...	...	...	...	...	1	1
Sint Maarten (Dutch part)	2005	13 100	40.3	...	...	...	...	...	...
St-Martin (partie néerland.)	2010	26 200	79.1	...	...	1[1]	3[1]	...	4[1]
	2015	27 295	70.4	...	...	3	5	...	8
	2016	...	...	...	...	3	5	...	8
Slovakia	2005	130 491	2.4	2.2	2.6	368[1]	2 707[1]	...	3 075[1]
Slovaquie	2010	146 319	2.7	2.6	2.8	461[1]	267[1]	911[1]	1 639[1]
	2015	177 190	3.3	3.2	3.3	799[8]	61	1 671	2 531
	2016	...	...	...	...	978	23	1 651	2 652
Slovenia	2005	197 276	9.9	11.0	8.8	251[1]	185[1]	715[1]	1 151[1]
Slovénie	2010	253 786	12.4	13.9	10.9	314[1]	121[1]	4 119[1]	4 554[1]
	2015	235 966	11.4	13.1	9.7	283	43	4	330
	2016	...	...	...	...	350	257	4	611
Solomon Islands	2005	3 271	0.7	0.8	0.6	...	...	...	...
Îles Salomon	2010	2 760	0.5	0.6	0.5	...	...	...	...
	2015	2 585	0.4	0.5	0.4	3	...	...	3
	2016	...	...	...	...	3	...	...	3
Somalia	2005	* 20 670[2]	* 0.2[2]	* 0.3[2]	* 0.2[2]	493[1]	98[1]	400 000[1]	400 591[1]
Somalie	2010	* 23 995[2]	* 0.3[2]	* 0.3[2]	* 0.2[2]	1 937[1]	24 111[1]	1 463 780[1]	1 489 828[1]
	2015	* 25 291[2]	* 0.2[2]	* 0.3[2]	* 0.2[2]	3 582	9 320	1 152 073	1 164 975
	2016	...	...	...	...	10 027	11 479	1 146 930	1 168 436

International migrants and refugees *(continued)*
International migrant stock (number and percentage) and refugees and others of concern to UNHCR

Migrants internationaux et réfugiés *(suite)*
Stock de migrants internationaux (nombre et pourcentage) et réfugiés et autres personnes relevant de la compétence du HCR

		International Migrant Stock (mid-year) Stock de migrants internationaux (milieu de l'année)				Refugees and others of concern to UNHCR (mid-year) Réfugiés et autres personnes relevant de la compétence du HCR (milieu de l'année)			
			% of total pop. % de la pop. totale						
Region, country or area Région, pays ou zone	Year Année	Total Total	MF/HF	M/H	F	Refugees[&] Réfugiés[&]	Asylum seekers Demandeurs d'asile	Other[&&] Autres[&&]	Total pop. Pop. totale
South Africa	2005	1 210 936[2]	2.5[2]	3.0[2]	2.0[2]	29 714[1]	140 095[1]	100[1]	169 909[1]
Afrique du Sud	2010	1 943 099[2]	3.8[2]	4.5[2]	3.1[2]	57 899[1]	171 702[1]	134[1]	229 735[1]
	2015	3 142 511[2]	5.8[2]	7.0[2]	4.6[2]	114 512	798 080	...	912 592
	2016	...	...	...	...	122 392	1 079 482[37]	...	1 201 874
South Sudan	2010[2]	257 905	2.6	2.6	2.5	...	...	...	...
Soudan du sud	2015	824 122[2]	6.7[2]	6.8[2]	6.5[2]	265 887	632	1 792 014[38]	2 058 533
	2016	...	...	...	...	263 752	1 230	1 966 244[38]	2 231 226
Spain	2005	4 107 226[39]	9.4[39]	9.9[39]	8.8[39]	5 374[1]	...	27[1]	5 401[1]
Espagne	2010	6 280 065[39]	13.5[39]	14.1[39]	12.9[39]	3 820[1]	2 712[1]	31[1]	6 563[1]
	2015	5 852 953[39]	12.7[39]	12.6[39]	12.8[39]	5 798[8]	11 020	440	17 258
	2016	...	...	...	...	9 510	18 695	609	28 814
Sri Lanka	2005	39 526[2]	0.2[2]	0.2[2]	0.2[2]	106[1]	121[1]	351 884[1]	352 111[1]
Sri Lanka	2010	38 959[2]	0.2[2]	0.2[2]	0.2[2]	223[1]	138[1]	434 903[1]	435 264[1]
	2015	38 706[2]	0.2[2]	0.2[2]	0.2[2]	848	461	50 499[40]	51 808
	2016	...	...	...	...	764	555	42 853[40]	44 172
State of Palestine	2005[41,42]	266 617	7.4	6.6	8.3	...	...	...	...
État de Palestine	2010[41,42]	258 032	6.3	5.6	7.1	...	...	...	...
	2015	255 507[41,42]	5.5[41,42]	4.8[41,42]	6.2[41,42]	...	...	3	3
Sudan	2005	541 994[2,43]	1.7[2,43]	1.7[2,43]	1.7[2,43]	147 256[1]	4 425[1]	878 067[1]	1 029 748[1]
Soudan	2010	578 363[2]	1.6[2]	1.6[2]	1.6[2]	178 308[1]	6 046[1]	1 767 167[1]	1 951 521[1]
	2015	503 477[2]	1.3[2]	1.3[2]	1.2[2]	356 191	11 448	2 400 270[44]	2 767 909
	2016	...	...	...	...	351 450	13 982	3 254 143	3 619 575
Suriname	2005[3]	33 664	6.8	7.4	6.3	...	...	...	...
Suriname	2010	39 713[3]	7.7[3]	8.3[3]	7.0[3]	1[1]	7[1]	...	8[1]
	2015	46 836[3]	8.6[3]	9.4[3]	7.8[3]	1	...	...	1
	2016	...	...	...	...	2	7	...	9
Swaziland	2005	27 097[2]	2.5[2]	2.7[2]	2.2[2]	760[1]	256[1]	...	1 016[1]
Swaziland	2010	30 476[2]	2.6[2]	2.7[2]	2.4[2]	759[1]	...	...	759[1]
	2015	31 579[2]	2.5[2]	2.6[2]	2.3[2]	539	321	4	864
	2016	...	...	...	...	721	332	9	1 062
Sweden	2005	1 125 790	12.5	12.0	12.9	74 915[1]	15 702[1]	5 785[1]	96 402[1]
Suède	2010	1 384 929	14.8	14.4	15.1	82 629[1]	18 635[1]	9 545[1]	110 809[1]
	2015	1 639 771	16.8	16.6	17.0	142 207[8]	56 135	27 167	225 509
	2016	...	...	...	...	186 404	131 073	31 062	348 539
Switzerland	2005	1 805 437	24.4	25.4	23.3	48 030[1]	14 428[1]	990[1]	63 448[1]
Suisse	2010	2 075 182	26.5	24.3	28.6	48 813[1]	12 916[1]	127[1]	61 856[1]
	2015	2 438 702	29.4	29.1	29.7	69 390	17 085	76	86 551
	2016	...	...	...	...	78 041	32 003	73	110 117
Syrian Arab Republic	2005	876 410[2,3]	4.8[2,3]	4.8[2,3]	4.8[2,3]	26 089[1]	1 898[1]	300 001[1]	327 988[1]
République arabe syrienne	2010	1 661 922[2,3]	8.0[2,3]	8.1[2,3]	7.9[2,3]	1 005 472[1]	2 446[1]	300 194[1]	1 308 112[1]
	2015	875 189[2,3]	4.7[2,3]	4.8[2,3]	4.7[2,3]	149 200[45]	4 839	7 792 500	7 946 539
	2016	...	...	...	...	20 323[45]	8 609	6 739 578	6 768 510
Tajikistan	2005	280 444	4.1	3.5	4.7	1 018[1]	22[1]	25[1]	1 065[1]
Tadjikistan	2010	278 152	3.7	3.2	4.2	3 131[1]	1 656[1]	2 338[1]	7 125[1]
	2015	275 059	3.2	2.8	3.7	1 782	79	10 082[46]	11 943
	2016	...	...	...	...	2 485	409	18 883	21 777
Thailand	2005	2 163 447[2]	3.3[2]	3.3[2]	3.2[2]	117 053[1]	32 163[1]	136[1]	149 352[1]
Thaïlande	2010	3 224 131[2]	4.8[2]	4.9[2]	4.7[2]	96 675[1]	10 250[1]	542 505[1]	649 430[1]
	2015	3 913 258[2]	5.8[2]	5.9[2]	5.6[2]	110 372	8 166	506 718[47]	625 256
	2016	...	...	...	...	107 071	7 825	439 164[48]	554 060
TFYR of Macedonia	2005	127 667	6.2	5.2	7.3	1 274[1]	723[1]	2 451[1]	4 448[1]
ex-R.Y. de Macédoine	2010	129 701	6.3	5.3	7.3	1 398[1]	161[1]	1 731[1]	3 290[1]
	2015	130 730	6.3	5.3	7.3	828	43	717	1 588
	2016	...	...	...	...	688	83	640	1 411
Timor-Leste	2005	11 286	1.1	1.1	1.2	3[1]	10[1]	...	13[1]
Timor-Leste	2010	10 983	1.0	1.2	0.9	1[1]	4[1]	...	5[1]
	2015	10 834	0.9	1.1	0.8	...	...	5	5
	2016	...	...	...	...	...	...	6	6

International migrants and refugees *(continued)*

International migrant stock (number and percentage) and refugees and others of concern to UNHCR

Migrants internationaux et réfugiés *(suite)*

Stock de migrants internationaux (nombre et pourcentage) et réfugiés et autres personnes relevant de la compétence du HCR

		International Migrant Stock (mid-year) Stock de migrants internationaux (milieu de l'année)				Refugees and others of concern to UNHCR (mid-year) Réfugiés et autres personnes relevant de la compétence du HCR (milieu de l'année)			
			% of total pop. % de la pop. totale						
Region, country or area Région, pays ou zone	Year Année	Total Total	MF/HF	M/H	F	Refugees& Réfugiés&	Asylum seekers Demandeurs d'asile	Other&& Autres&&	Total pop. Pop. totale
Togo	2005	203 379[2,3]	3.6[2,3]	3.8[2,3]	3.5[2,3]	9 287[1]	420[1]	9 012[1]	18 719[1]
Togo	2010	255 262[2,3]	4.0[2,3]	4.1[2,3]	3.9[2,3]	14 051[1]	151[1]	5[1]	14 207[1]
	2015	276 844[2,3]	3.8[2,3]	3.9[2,3]	3.7[2,3]	21 877	687	...	22 564
	2016	...	...	...	...	13 083	724	5	13 812
Tokelau	2005	258	21.3	...	...	...	...	...	...
Tokélaou	2010	429	37.8	...	...	...	...	...	...
	2015	487	39.0	...	...	...	...	...	...
Tonga	2005	4 301	4.3	4.6	3.9	...	...	...	...
Tonga	2010	5 022	4.8	5.2	4.4	...	3[1]	...	3[1]
	2015	5 731	5.4	5.9	4.9	...	...	...	...
Trinidad and Tobago	2005	44 812	3.5	3.2	3.7	...	...	...	...
Trinité-et-Tobago	2010	48 226	3.6	3.5	3.7	29[1]	102[1]	...	131[1]
	2015	49 883	3.7	3.6	3.7	121	59	...	180
	2016	...	...	...	...	88	110	7	205
Tunisia	2005	35 040[3]	0.3[3]	0.4[3]	0.3[3]	87[1]	26[1]	...	113[1]
Tunisie	2010	43 172[3]	0.4[3]	0.4[3]	0.4[3]	89[1]	23[1]	3[1]	115[1]
	2015	56 701[3]	0.5[3]	0.5[3]	0.5[3]	824	156	3	983
	2016	...	...	...	...	688	38	4	730
Turkey	2005	1 319 236[2]	1.9[2]	1.9[2]	2.0[2]	2 399[1]	4 872[1]	1 434[1]	8 705[1]
Turquie	2010	1 367 034[2]	1.9[2]	1.8[2]	2.0[2]	10 032[1]	6 715[1]	1 086[1]	17 833[1]
	2015	2 964 916[2]	3.8[2]	3.9[2]	3.6[2]	1 838 848[49]	145 335	1 086	1 985 269
	2016	...	...	...	...	2 773 827[49]	231 694	780	3 006 301
Turkmenistan	2005	213 051	4.5	4.0	4.9	11 963[1]	2[1]	45[1]	12 010[1]
Turkménistan	2010	197 979	3.9	3.6	4.2	62[1]	...	20 000[1]	20 062[1]
	2015	196 386	3.7	3.5	3.8	27	...	7 144	7 171
	2016	...	...	...	...	26	...	7 125	7 151
Turks and Caicos Islands	2005	9 945	37.6	...	...	...	...	...	...
Îles Turques-et-Caïques	2010	10 875	35.1	...	...	...	...	...	...
	2015	11 688	34.0	...	...	4	4	...	8
	2016	...	...	...	...	4	...	...	4
Tuvalu [3]	2005	183	1.9	...	...	...	...	...	...
Tuvalu [3]	2010	154	1.6	...	...	...	...	...	...
	2015	141	1.4	...	...	...	...	...	...
Uganda	2005	652 968[2]	2.3[2]	2.3[2]	2.3[2]	257 256[1]	1 809[1]	1 636[1]	260 701[1]
Ouganda	2010	529 160[2]	1.6[2]	1.6[2]	1.6[2]	135 801[1]	20 804[1]	437 775[1]	594 380[1]
	2015	749 471[2]	1.9[2]	1.9[2]	1.9[2]	428 397	38 068	180 000	646 465
	2016	...	...	...	...	512 623	34 440	180 000	727 063
Ukraine	2005	5 050 302	10.8	10.0	11.5	2 346[1]	1 618[1]	72 896[1]	76 860[1]
Ukraine	2010	4 818 767	10.6	9.8	11.2	3 022[1]	2 981[1]	40 357[1]	46 360[1]
	2015	4 834 898	10.8	10.0	11.4	3 232	6 169	1 417 179	1 426 580
	2016	...	...	...	...	3 241	6 424	1 635 171[50]	1 644 836
United Arab Emirates	2005	3 281 036[2,3]	73.2[2,3]	75.0[2,3]	68.9[2,3]	104[1]	79[1]	...	183[1]
Émirats arabes unis	2010	7 316 611[2,3]	87.8[2,3]	87.7[2,3]	88.3[2,3]	538[1]	86[1]	...	624[1]
	2015	8 095 126[2,3]	88.4[2,3]	90.1[2,3]	83.7[2,3]	424	378	...	802
	2016	...	...	...	...	773	492	...	1 265
United Kingdom	2005	5 926 156	9.8	9.6	10.1	303 181[1]	12 500[1]	909[1]	316 590[1]
Royaume-Uni	2010	7 604 583	12.1	11.9	12.3	238 150[1]	14 880[1]	229[1]	253 259[1]
	2015	8 543 120	13.2	12.7	13.7	117 234[8]	37 829	16	155 079
	2016	...	...	...	...	117 176	34 445	60	151 681
United Rep. of Tanzania	2005	770 846[2]	2.0[2]	2.5[2]	1.4[2]	548 824[1]	307[1]	81 519[1]	630 650[1]
Rép.-Unie de Tanzanie	2010	308 600[2]	0.7[2]	0.7[2]	0.7[2]	109 286[1]	1 247[1]	163 269[1]	273 802[1]
	2015	261 222[2]	0.5[2]	0.5[2]	0.5[2]	159 014	1 150	168 019	328 183
	2016	...	...	...	...	230 229	3 223	168 668	402 120
United States of America	2005	39 258 293	13.3	13.4	13.1	379 340[1]	169 743[1]	76[1]	549 159[1]
États-Unis d'Amérique	2010	44 183 643	14.3	14.2	14.4	264 569[1]	6 285[1]	89[1]	270 943[1]
	2015	46 627 102	14.5	14.3	14.7	267 222[8,51]	224 508	...	491 730
	2016	...	...	...	...	272 267[51]	344 211	...	616 478

4 International migrants and refugees *(continued)*

International migrant stock (number and percentage) and refugees and others of concern to UNHCR

Migrants internationaux et réfugiés *(suite)*

Stock de migrants internationaux (nombre et pourcentage) et réfugiés et autres personnes relevant de la compétence du HCR

Region, country or area Région, pays ou zone	Year Année	International Migrant Stock (mid-year) Stock de migrants internationaux (milieu de l'année) Total Total	% of total pop. % de la pop. totale MF/HF	M/H	F	Refugees and others of concern to UNHCR (mid-year) Réfugiés et autres personnes relevant de la compétence du HCR (milieu de l'année) Refugees& Réfugiés&	Asylum seekers Demandeurs d'asile	Other&& Autres&&	Total pop. Pop. totale
United States Virgin Islands Îles Vierges américaines	2005	56 647	52.6	51.8	53.3	...	...	...	...
	2010	56 684	53.3	52.6	53.9	...	...	...	...
	2015	56 721	53.4	52.8	53.9	...	...	...	...
Uruguay Uruguay	2005	82 318	2.5	2.3	2.6	121[1]	9[1]	...	130[1]
	2010	76 263	2.3	2.1	2.4	189[1]	40[1]	...	229[1]
	2015	71 799	2.1	2.0	2.2	289	68	...	357
	2016	...	...	...	...	306	171	...	477
Uzbekistan Ouzbékistan	2005	1 329 345	5.1	4.6	5.6	43 950[1]	587[1]	5[1]	44 542[1]
	2010	1 220 149	4.4	4.1	4.7	311[1]	...	2[1]	313[1]
	2015	1 170 899	3.9	3.7	4.1	118	...	86 703[52]	86 821
	2016	...	...	...	...	28	...	86 705[52]	86 733
Vanuatu Vanuatu	2005	2 800	1.3	1.3	1.4	...	...	...	...
	2010	2 991	1.3	1.2	1.3	4[1]	...	...	4[1]
	2015	3 187	1.2	1.2	1.2	...	1	...	1
Venezuela (Boliv. Rep. of) Venezuela (Rép. boliv. du)	2005	1 070 562	4.0	4.0	4.0	408[1]	5 912[1]	200 001[1]	206 321[1]
	2010	1 331 488	4.6	4.6	4.6	201 547[1]	15 859[1]	...	217 406[1]
	2015	1 404 448	4.5	4.5	4.5	174 191	704	...	174 895
	2016	...	...	...	...	173 999	235	...	174 234
Viet Nam Viet Nam	2005	51 768[2,3]	0.1[2,3]	0.1[2,3]	~0.0[2,3]	2 357[1]	...	15 000[1]	17 357[1]
	2010	61 756[2,3]	0.1[2,3]	0.1[2,3]	0.1[2,3]	1 928[1]	...	10 200[1]	12 128[1]
	2015	72 793[2,3]	0.1[2,3]	0.1[2,3]	0.1[2,3]	...	...	11 000	11 000
	2016	...	...	...	...	...	...	11 000	11 000
Wallis and Futuna Islands Îles Wallis-et-Futuna	2005	2 365	16.6	...	...	...	...	...	...
	2010	2 776	20.5	...	...	...	...	...	...
	2015	2 849	21.7	...	...	...	...	...	...
Western Sahara Sahara occidental	*2005	3 891	0.9	1.0	0.8	...	...	...	...
	*2010	4 493	0.9	1.0	0.8	...	...	...	...
	*2015	5 179	0.9	1.0	0.8	...	...	...	...
Yemen Yémen	2005	171 073[2,3]	0.8[2,3]	1.0[2,3]	0.7[2,3]	81 937[1]	798[1]	48[1]	82 783[1]
	2010	285 837[2,3]	1.2[2,3]	1.3[2,3]	1.1[2,3]	190 092[1]	2 557[1]	315 929[1]	508 578[1]
	2015	344 131[2,3]	1.3[2,3]	1.3[2,3]	1.2[2,3]	263 047	9 902	1 267 590	1 540 539
	2016	...	...	...	...	268 486	10 852	3 092 080	3 371 418
Zambia Zambie	2005	252 749[2]	2.1[2]	2.1[2]	2.1[2]	155 718[1]	146[1]	29 833[1]	185 697[1]
	2010	149 637[2]	1.1[2]	1.1[2]	1.1[2]	47 857[1]	325[1]	9 687[1]	57 869[1]
	2015	127 915[2]	0.8[2]	0.8[2]	0.8[2]	25 737	2 606	23 415	51 758
	2016	...	...	...	...	28 035	2 904	24 374	55 313
Zimbabwe Zimbabwe	2005	392 693[2]	3.0[2]	3.5[2]	2.6[2]	13 850[1]	118[1]	7[1]	13 975[1]
	2010	397 891[2]	2.8[2]	3.3[2]	2.4[2]	4 435[1]	416[1]	...	4 851[1]
	2015	398 866[2]	2.6[2]	3.0[2]	2.2[2]	6 085	123	* 301 883	308 091
	2016	...	...	...	...	6 903	303	* 301 357	308 563

Source:

United Nations Population Division, New York, International migrant stock: The 2015 Revision, last accessed June 2016.

United Nations High Commissioner for Refugees (UNHCR), Geneva, UNHCR Population Statistics Database, last accessed March 2017.

Source:

Organisation des Nations Unies, Division pour la population, New York, Stock de migrants internationaux: La révision 2015, dernièr accéss juin 2016.

L'Office du Haut Commisariat des Nations Unies pour les réfugiés (UNHCR), Genève, base de données d'UNHCR, dernier accès mars 2017.

& Number of refugees or persons in refugee-like situations as reported by the Office of the United Nations High Commissioner for Refugees (UNHCR). && Figure includes sum of returned refugees, internally displaced persons (IDPs) protected/assisted by UNHCR, including people in IDP like situations, returned IDPs, Persons under UNHCR's stateless mandate, and others of concern to UNHCR categories.

&Nombre de réfugiés ou de personnes en situation analogue à celle de réfugiés, tel que donné par le Bureau des Nations Unies. && Les chiffres correspondent au total des réfugiés rapatriés, des personnes déplacées protégées ou assistées par le HCR, notamment celles se trouvant dans une situation analogue à celle des personnes déplacées, des personnes déplacées de retour, des apatrides relevant du mandat du HCR et d'autres catégories de personnes relevant de la compétence du HCR.

4 International migrants and refugees *(continued)*

International migrant stock (number and percentage) and refugees and others of concern to UNHCR

Migrants internationaux et réfugiés *(suite)*

Stock de migrants internationaux (nombre et pourcentage) et réfugiés et autres personnes relevant de la compétence du HCR

1 Data as at the end of December.
2 Including refugees.
3 Refers to foreign citizens.
4 According to the Government of Algeria, there are an estimated 165,000 Sahrawi refugees in the Tindouf camps.
5 Data relates to the end of 2015.
6 Including Christmas Island, Cocos (Keeling) Islands and Norfolk Island.
7 Asylum-seekers are based on the number of applications lodged for protection visas.
8 Data relates to the end of 2014.
9 Including Nagorno-Karabakh.
10 The refugee population includes 200,000 persons originating from Myanmar in a refugee-like situation. The Government of Bangladesh estimates the population to be between 300,000 and 500,000.
11 The estimates for 2005 refer to the former Netherlands Antilles.
12 Bonaire only.
13 Refers to Guernsey and Jersey.
14 For statistical purposes, the data for China do not include those for the Hong Kong Special Administrative Region (Hong Kong SAR), Macao Special Administrative Region (Macao SAR) and Taiwan Province of China.
15 The 300,000 Vietnamese refugees are well integrated and in practice receive protection from the Government of China.
16 The statelessness figure is based on government estimate on individuals who have not established their nationality prior to the nationality law of 1972. The estimate includes denied voter registration cases and naturalised cases mid-2015. The estimate excludes abandoned children.
17 Including northern Cyprus.
18 The figure 245,000 Rwandan refugees was provided by the Government of the Democratic Republic of the Congo.
19 Revised estimate includes only individuals born in the country where both parents were born abroad. This estimate does not include subsequent generations of individuals of foreign descent as such it does not include all persons without nationality.
20 Almost all people recorded as being stateless have permanent residence and enjoy more rights than foreseen in the 1954 Convention relating to the Status of Stateless Persons.
21 Including Åland Islands.
22 Including Abkhazia and South Ossetia.
23 Including Saint Barthélemy and Saint Martin (French part).
24 Figure refers to individuals without a nationality who were born in the Dominican Republic prior to January 2010 and who were identified by UNHCR in Haiti since June 2015.
25 Including an estimate for stateless persons populations in line with Law 26 of 2006, which allows stateless persons to apply for nationality in certain circumstances.
26 Includes Iraqi refugees registered with UNHCR in Jordan. The Government estimated the number of Iraqis at 400,000 individuals at the end of March 2015. This included refugees and other categories of Iraqis.
27 The figure of stateless persons includes persons covered by two separate Laws; Law on Stateless Persons dated 17 February 2004 and the Law on the Status of Those Former USSR Citizens who are not Citizens of Latvia or of Any Other State.
28 Including Sabah and Sarawak.
29 Including Agalega, Rodrigues and Saint Brandon.
30 Stateless persons population refers to persons without citizeship in Rakhine State only.

1 Données à la fin de décembre.
2 Y compris les réfugiés.
3 Se rapportent aux citoyens étrangers.
4 Selon le Gouvernement algérien, les camps de Tindouf accueillent environ 165 000 réfugiés sahraouis.
5 Le nombre se rapporte à fin 2015.
6 Y compris les îles Christmas, Cocos (Keeling) et Norfolk.
7 Les chiffres de l'Australie concernant les demandeurs d'asile sont établis sur la base du nombre de demandes de visa de protection présentées.
8 Le nombre se rapporte à fin 2014.
9 Y compris le Haut-Karabakh.
10 Au nombre des réfugiés figurent 200 000 personnes originaires du Myanmar se trouvant dans une situation analogue à celle des réfugiés. Le Gouvernement bangladais estime que le nombre de réfugiés se situe entre 300 000 et 500 000.
11 Les estimations pour 2005 se rapportent aux Antilles néerlandaises.
12 Bonaire seulement.
13 Se rapporte à Guernsey et Jersey.
14 Pour la présentation des statistiques, les données pour la Chine ne comprennent pas la Région Administrative Spéciale de Hong Kong (Hong Kong RAS), la Région Administrative Spéciale de Macao (Macao RAS) et la province de Taiwan.
15 Les 300 000 réfugiés vietnamiens sont bien intégrés et, dans la pratique, recoivent la protection du Gouvernement chinois.
16 Le chiffre sur l'apatride est basé sur l'estimation par le gouvernement des individus qui n'ont pas établi leur nationalité avant la loi sur la nationalité de 1972. Cette estimation inclut les cas refusés d'inscription des électeurs et les cas de naturalisation de la mi-2015. Cette estimation exclut les enfants abandonnés.
17 Y compris la partie nord de Chypre.
18 Le chiffre 245,000 réfugiés Rwandais a été fourni par le gouvernement de la République démocratique du Congo .
19 Cette réestimation concerne uniquement les personnes nées dans le pays dont les deux parents sont nés à l'étranger. Cette estimation ne comprend pas les générations futures de personnes d'origine étrangère tels que les apatrides.
20 La quasi totalité des personnes enregistrées comme apatrides ont une résidence permanente et jouissent de davantage de droits que ceux prévus par la Convention de 1954 relative au statut des apatrides.
21 Y compris les Îles d'Åland.
22 Y compris l'Abkhazie et l'Ossétie du Sud.
23 Y compris Saint-Barthélémy et Saint-Martin (partie français).
24 Chiffre correspond aux individus sans nationalité qui sont nés en République Dominicaine avant Janvier 2010 et qui ont été identifiés par le HCR en Haïti depuis Juin 2015.
25 Y compris une estimation des populations apatrides conforme à la loi 26 de 2006,qui permet aux apatrides de demander la nationalité dans certaines circonstances.
26 Y compris réfugiés iraquiens enregistrés par le HCR en Jordanie. À la fin de mars 2015, le Gouvernement estimait le nombre d'Iraquiens à 400 000 (réfugiés et autres).
27 Le nombres d'apatrides comprend les personnes couvertes par deux lois distinctes: La loi sur les apatrides du 17 février 2004 et la loi relative au Statut des citoyens de l'ex-URSS qui ne sont pas citoyens de la Lettonie ou d'un autre État.
28 Y compris Sabah et Sarawak.
29 Y compris Agalega, Rodrigues et Saint Brandon.
30 Les apatrides s'entendent des personnes dépourvues de nationalité, dans l'État de Rakhine uniquement.

31 Various studies estimate that a large number of individuals lack citizenship certificates in Nepal. While these individuals are not all necessarily stateless, UNHCR has been working closely with the Government of Nepal and partners to address this situation.
32 Including Svalbard and Jan Mayen Islands.
33 Including Transnistria.
34 Stateless persons refers to census figure from 2010 adjusted to reflect the number of people who acquired nationality since 2011.
35 Including Ascension and Tristan da Cunha.
36 Including Kosovo.
37 Adjustment to 2014 year-end figures for appeal pending asylum applications resulted in higher figure for number of asylum seekers reported in South Africa for 2015. South Africa does not allow withdrawal (whether explicit or implicit) of asylum applications once lodged.
38 Internally displaced persons (IDP) figure in South Sudan includes 105,000 people who are in an IDP-like situation.
39 Including Canary Islands, Ceuta and Melilla.
40 The statistics of the remaining IDPs, while provided by the Government authorities at the district level, are being reviewed by the central authorities. Once this review has been concluded, the statistics will be changed accordingly.
41 Including East Jerusalem.
42 Refugees are not part of the foreign-born migrant stock in the State of Palestine.
43 The estimates for 2005 refer to Sudan and South Sudan.
44 Internally displaced persons (IDP) figure in Sudan includes 77,300 people who are in an IDP-like situation.
45 The figure for Iraqi refugees is a Government estimate.
46 Figure refers to a registration exercise in three regions and 637 persons registered as stateless by the Ministry of Internal Affairs of Tajikistan.
47 Figure of stateless persons in Thailand refers to 2011.
48 Updated statelessness figure from the Royal Thai Government. The decrease includes the grant of Thai nationality to over 23,000 stateless people between the beginning of 2012 and mid-2016.
49 Refugee figure for Syrians in Turkey is a Government estimate.
50 Internally displaced persons (IDP) figure in Ukraine includes 800,000 people who are in an IDP-like situation.
51 This figure is under review.
52 Figure of stateless persons refers to those with permanent residence reported in 2010 by the Government. Information on other categories of stateless persons is not available.

31 Selon différentes études, un grand nombre de personnes ne disposeraient pas de certificat de nationalité au Népal. Elles ne sont pas nécessairement toutes apatrides, mais le HCR travaille en coopération étroite avec les autorités népalaises et des partenaires pour régler la situation.
32 Y compris îles Svalbard et Jan Mayen.
33 Y compris la Transnistrie.
34 Le nombre d'apatrides se rapporte aux données du recensement effectué en 2010, ajustées pour tenir compte du nombre de personnes ayant acquis la nationalité depuis 2011.
35 Y compris Ascension et Tristan da Cunha.
36 Y compris Kosovo.
37 L'ajustement des chiffres de fin d'année 2014 pour les demandes d'asile en attente on aboutit à un chiffre plus élevé pour le nombre de demandeurs d'asile rapporté en Afrique du Sud en 2015. L'Afrique du Sud ne permet pas de retirer (qu'elles soient explicites ou implicites) les demandes d'asile une foi enregistrées.
38 Au nombre des déplacés au Soudan du Sud figurent 105 000 personnes dans une situation analogue à celle des déplacés.
39 Y compris les Iles Canaries, Ceuta et Melilla.
40 Les statistiques relatives au reste des déplacés ont été fournies par les autorités locales au niveau des districts, mais examinées par les autorités centrales, et seront ajustées en fonction des résultats de l'examen.
41 Y compris Jérusalem-Est.
42 Les réfugiés ne sont pas comptabilisés parmi les migrants nés à l'étranger qui se trouvent dans l'État de Palestine.
43 Les estimations de 2005 se rapportent au Soudan et au Soudan du Sud.
44 Au nombre des déplacés au Soudan figurent 77 300 personnes dans une situation analogue à celles des déplacés.
45 Le nombre de réfugiés iraquiens est une estimation du Gouvernement.
46 Les chiffres se rapportent aux enregistrements effectués dans trois régions; 637 personnes ont été enregistrées comme apatrides par le Ministère de l'intérieur tadjik.
47 Les chiffres relatifs au nombre d'apatrides en Thaïlande remontent à 2011.
48 Chiffre actualisé sur l'apatride provenant du gouvernement royal thaï. La baisse inclut l'octroi de la nationalité thaïlandaise à plus de 23000 personnes apatrides entre début 2012 et mi-2016
49 Le nombre de réfugiés syriens en Turquie est une estimation du Gouvernement.
50 Le chiffre sur les personnes déplacées à l'intérieur de leur propre pays (PDI) en Ukraine inclut 800000 personnes qui sont dans une situation similaire aux PDI.
51 Le chiffre est en cours d'étude.
52 Le nombre d'apatrides renvoit au nombre de résidents permanents recensés en 2010 par le Gouvernement. On ne dispose d'aucune information sur d'autres catégories d'apatrides.

Proportion of seats held by women in national parliament

Percentage, as of January/February each year

Proportion de sièges occupés par les femmes au parlement national

Pourcentage, données disponibles en janvier/février de chaque année

Country or area&	Last Election date Dernière date de l'élection	1990	2000	2005	2010	2013	2014	2015	2016	2017	Pays ou zone&
Total, all countries or areas		**...**	**13.3**	**15.9**	**19.0**	**20.8**	**22.1**	**22.3**	**22.7**	**23.4**	**Total, tous pays ou zones**
Northern Africa		...	4.5	8.7	10.9	18.8	24.1	22.0	23.2	23.8	Afrique septentrionale
Sub-Saharan Africa		...	11.5	14.4	18.4	20.8	22.8	22.6	23.3	23.7	Afrique subsaharienne
Eastern Africa		...	11.9	16.6	21.6	25.2	27.3	27.2	28.9	29.7	Afrique orientale
Middle Africa		...	8.6	11.2	13.5	14.7	18.7	18.1	18.1	17.4	Afrique centrale
Southern Africa		...	22.5	24.6	33.4	32.2	33.2	33.4	33.4	33.4	Afrique australe
Western Africa		...	8.2	10.2	11.6	13.6	14.6	14.5	14.0	14.9	Afrique occidentale
Northern America		...	16.3	17.5	19.0	20.6	21.1	21.8	22.3	22.2	Amérique septentrionale
Latin America & Caribbean		...	15.2	19.0	22.7	24.5	25.9	27.4	28.2	29.4	Amérique latine et Caraïbes
Caribbean		...	20.6	26.0	29.4	30.3	32.9	33.1	33.0	33.8	Caraïbes
Central America		...	14.3	17.4	21.6	28.3	29.3	30.1	32.5	33.1	Amérique centrale
South America		...	12.5	15.8	19.2	18.7	19.6	22.2	22.7	24.5	Amérique du Sud
Asia		...	12.1	13.4	16.8	17.4	17.5	17.8	17.9	18.4	Asie
Central Asia		...	7.0	13.4	20.0	21.2	23.2	21.8	21.1	21.3	Asie centrale
Eastern Asia		...	18.2	18.1	18.7	18.5	19.9	20.4	20.4	20.5	Asie orientale
South-eastern Asia		...	12.3	15.5	19.3	18.0	18.4	17.8	18.3	19.3	Asie du Sud-Est
Southern Asia		...	6.8	8.8	18.2	18.5	16.0	17.6	17.7	18.0	Asie méridionale
Western Asia		...	5.2	5.7	9.3	12.7	12.8	12.8	13.2	13.8	Asie occidentale
Europe		...	16.8	20.5	23.2	24.9	26.4	26.7	27.2	28.0	Europe
Eastern Europe		...	9.5	14.1	15.2	16.2	16.3	16.9	17.6	19.4	Europe orientale
Northern Europe		...	27.0	28.0	29.6	30.8	30.9	30.4	32.5	33.3	Europe septentrionale
Southern Europe		...	11.0	17.1	23.0	25.7	29.4	30.0	29.0	29.4	Europe méridionale
Western Europe		...	23.0	25.8	28.4	30.5	32.5	32.0	32.2	32.1	Europe occidentale
Oceania		...	11.3	11.2	13.2	12.7	13.4	13.2	13.4	15.0	Océanie
Australia and New Zealand		...	25.5	26.3	30.1	28.0	29.5	28.8	28.8	31.1	Australie et Nvl-Zélande
Melanesia		...	3.9	3.2	1.4	1.9	1.9	4.2	4.6	4.6	Mélanésie
Micronesia		...	2.5	2.4	2.4	3.9	4.7	4.7	5.5	7.8	Micronésie
Polynesia		...	4.4	3.2	5.2	4.3	4.3	4.4	4.4	7.7	Polynésie
Afghanistan	2010-09	3.7	...	...	27.3	27.7	27.7	27.7	27.7	27.7	Afghanistan
Albania	2013-06	28.8	5.2	6.4	16.4	15.7	20.0	20.7	20.7	22.9	Albanie
Algeria	2012-05	2.4	3.2	6.2	7.7	31.6	31.6	31.6	31.6	31.6	Algérie
Andorra	2015-03	...	7.1	14.3	35.7	50.0	50.0	50.0	39.3	32.1	Andorre
Angola	2012-08	14.5	15.5	15.0	38.6	34.1	36.8	36.8	36.8	38.2	Angola
Antigua and Barbuda	2014-06	0.0	...	10.5	10.5	10.5	10.5	11.1	11.1	11.1	Antigua-et-Barbuda
Argentina	2015-10	6.3	28.0	33.7	38.5	37.4	36.6	36.2	35.8	38.9	Argentine
Armenia	2012-05	35.6	3.1	5.3	9.2	10.7	10.7	10.7	10.7	9.9	Arménie
Australia	2016-07	6.1	22.4	24.7	27.3	24.7	26.0	26.7	26.7	28.7	Australie
Austria	2013-09	11.5	26.8	33.9	27.9	27.9	32.2	30.6	30.6	30.6	Autriche
Azerbaijan	2015-11	...	12.0	10.5	11.4	16.0	15.6	15.6	16.9	16.8	Azerbaïdjan
Bahamas	2012-05	4.1	15.0	20.0	12.2	13.2	13.2	13.2	13.2	13.2	Bahamas
Bahrain	2014-11	...	...	0.0	2.5	10.0	10.0	7.5	7.5	7.5	Bahreïn
Bangladesh	2014-01	10.3	9.1	2.0	18.6	19.7	6.4	20.0	20.0	20.3	Bangladesh
Barbados	2013-02	3.7	10.7	13.3	10.0	10.0	16.7	16.7	16.7	16.7	Barbade
Belarus	2016-09	...	4.5	29.4	31.8	26.6	26.6	27.3	27.3	34.5	Bélarus
Belgium	2014-05	8.5	23.3	34.7	38.0	38.0	41.3	39.3	39.3	38.0	Belgique
Belize	2015-11	0.0	6.9	6.7	0.0	3.1	3.1	3.1	3.1	9.4	Belize
Benin	2015-04	2.9	6.0	7.2	10.8	8.4	8.4	8.4	7.2	7.2	Bénin
Bhutan	2013-07	2.0	2.0	9.3	8.5	8.5	8.5	8.5	8.5	8.5	Bhoutan
Bolivia (Plurin. State of)	2014-10	9.2	11.5	19.2	22.3	25.4	25.4	53.1	53.1	53.1	Bolivie (État plurin. de)
Bosnia and Herzegovina	2014-10	...	28.6	16.7	19.0	21.4	21.4	21.4	21.4	21.4	Bosnie-Herzégovine
Botswana	2014-10	5.0	...	11.1	7.9	7.9	9.5	9.5	9.5	9.5	Botswana
Brazil	2014-10	5.3	5.7	8.6	8.8	8.6	8.6	9.0	9.9	10.7	Brésil
Brunei Darussalam	2017-01	...	...	...	...	...	...	...	...	9.1	Brunéi Darussalam
Bulgaria	2014-10	21.0	10.8	26.3	20.8	22.9	24.6	20.4	20.4	19.2	Bulgarie
Burkina Faso	2015-11	...	8.1	11.7	15.3	15.7	18.9	13.3	9.4	11.0	Burkina Faso
Burundi	2015-06	...	6.0	18.4	31.4	30.5	30.5	30.5	36.4	36.4	Burundi
Cabo Verde	2016-03	12.0	11.1	11.1	18.1	20.8	20.8	20.8	20.8	23.6	Cabo Verde
Cambodia	2013-07	...	8.2	9.8	21.1	20.3	20.3	20.3	20.3	20.3	Cambodge

Proportion of seats held by women in national parliament *(continued)*

Percentage, as of January/February each year

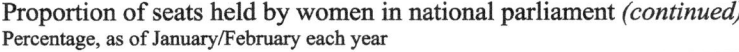

Proportion de sièges occupés par les femmes au parlement national *(suite)*

Pourcentage, données disponibles en janvier/février de chaque année

Country or area&	Last Election date Dernière date de l'élection	1990	2000	2005	2010	2013	2014	2015	2016	2017	Pays ou zone&
Cameroon	2013-09	14.4	5.6	8.9	13.9	13.9	31.1	31.1	31.1	31.1	Cameroun
Canada	2015-10	13.3	20.6	21.1	22.1	24.7	25.1	25.2	26.0	26.3	Canada
Central African Republic	2016-02	3.8	7.3	...	9.6	12.5	...	...	...	8.6	République centrafricaine
Chad	2011-02	...	2.4	6.5	5.2	14.9	14.9	14.9	14.9	12.8	Tchad
Chile	2013-11	...	10.8	12.5	14.2	14.2	15.8	15.8	15.8	15.8	Chili
China	2013-03	21.3	21.8	20.2	21.3	21.3	23.4	23.6	23.6	23.7	Chine
Colombia	2014-03	4.5	11.8	12.0	8.4	12.1	12.1	19.9	19.9	18.7	Colombie
Comoros	2015-01	0.0	...	3.0	3.0	3.0	3.0	...	3.0	6.1	Comores
Congo	2012-07	14.3	12.0	8.5	7.3	7.4	7.4	7.4	7.4	7.4	Congo
Costa Rica	2014-02	10.5	19.3	35.1	36.8	38.6	38.6	33.3	33.3	35.1	Costa Rica
Côte d'Ivoire	2016-12	5.7	...	8.5	8.9	10.4	9.4	9.2	9.2	11.5	Côte d'Ivoire
Croatia	2016-09	...	...	21.7	23.5	23.8	23.8	25.8	15.2	19.9	Croatie
Cuba	2013-02	33.9	27.6	36.0	43.2	45.2	48.9	48.9	48.9	48.9	Cuba
Cyprus	2016-05	1.8	5.4	16.1	12.5	10.7	12.5	12.5	12.5	17.9	Chypre
Czechia	2013-10	...	15.0	17.0	15.5	22.0	19.5	19.0	20.0	20.0	Tchéquie
Dem. People's Rep. Korea	2014-03	21.1	20.1	20.1	15.6	15.6	15.6	16.3	16.3	16.3	Rép. pop. dém. de Corée
Dem. Rep. of the Congo	2011-11	5.4	...	12.0	8.4	8.9	10.6	8.9	8.9	8.9	Rép. dém. du Congo
Denmark	2015-06	30.7	37.4	38.0	38.0	39.1	39.1	38.0	37.4	37.4	Danemark
Djibouti	2013-02	0.0	0.0	10.8	13.8	13.8	12.7	12.7	12.7	10.8	Djibouti
Dominica	2014-12	10.0	9.4	19.4	14.3	12.5	12.9	21.9	21.9	25.0	Dominique
Dominican Republic	2016-05	7.5	16.1	17.3	19.7	20.8	20.8	20.8	20.8	26.8	République dominicaine
Ecuador	2013-02	4.5	17.4	16.0	32.3	32.3	41.6	41.6	41.6	41.6	Équateur
Egypt	2015-10	3.9	2.0	2.9	1.8	2.0	...	...	14.9	14.9	Égypte
El Salvador	2015-03	11.7	16.7	10.7	19.0	26.2	26.2	27.4	32.1	32.1	El Salvador
Equatorial Guinea	2013-05	13.3	5.0	18.0	10.0	10.0	24.0	24.0	24.0	24.0	Guinée équatoriale
Eritrea	1994-02	...	14.7	22.0	22.0	22.0	22.0	22.0	22.0	22.0	Érythrée
Estonia	2015-03	...	17.8	18.8	22.8	20.8	19.0	19.8	23.8	26.7	Estonie
Ethiopia	2015-05	...	2.0	7.7	21.9	27.8	27.8	27.8	38.8	38.8	Éthiopie
Fiji	2014-09	...	11.3	8.5	...	...	...	14.0	16.0	16.0	Fidji
Finland	2015-04	31.5	37.0	37.5	40.0	42.5	42.5	42.5	41.5	42.0	Finlande
France	2012-06	6.9	10.9	12.2	18.9	26.9	26.2	26.2	26.2	25.8	France
Gabon	2011-12	13.3	8.3	9.2	14.7	15.8	15.0	14.2	14.2	17.1	Gabon
Gambia	2012-03	7.8	2.0	13.2	7.5	7.5	9.4	9.4	9.4	9.4	Gambie
Georgia	2016-10	...	7.2	9.4	5.1	12.0	12.0	11.3	11.3	16.0	Géorgie
Germany	2013-09	...	30.9	32.8	32.8	32.9	36.5	36.5	36.5	37.0	Allemagne
Ghana	2016-12	...	9.0	10.9	8.3	10.3	10.9	10.9	10.9	12.7	Ghana
Greece	2015-09	6.7	6.3	14.0	17.3	21.0	21.0	23.0	19.7	18.3	Grèce
Grenada	2013-02	...	...	26.7	13.3	13.3	33.3	33.3	33.3	33.3	Grenade
Guatemala	2015-09	7.0	7.1	8.2	12.0	13.3	13.3	13.3	13.9	12.7	Guatemala
Guinea	2013-09	...	8.8	19.3	...	...	21.9	21.9	21.9	21.9	Guinée
Guinea-Bissau	2014-04	20.0	...	14.0	10.0	14.0	11.0	13.7	13.7	13.7	Guinée-Bissau
Guyana	2015-05	36.9	18.5	30.8	30.0	31.3	31.3	31.3	30.4	31.9	Guyana
Haiti	2015-08	...	3.6	3.6	4.1	4.2	4.2	4.2	0.0	2.6	Haïti
Honduras	2013-11	10.2	9.4	5.5	18.0	19.5	25.8	25.8	25.8	25.8	Honduras
Hungary	2014-04	20.7	8.3	9.1	11.1	8.8	9.4	10.1	10.1	10.1	Hongrie
Iceland	2016-10	20.6	34.9	30.2	42.9	39.7	39.7	41.3	41.3	47.6	Islande
India	2014-04	5.0	9.0	8.3	10.8	11.0	11.4	12.0	12.0	11.8	Inde
Indonesia	2014-04	12.4	...	11.3	18.0	18.6	18.6	17.1	17.1	19.8	Indonésie
Iran (Islamic Republic of)	2016-02	1.5	4.9	4.1	2.8	3.1	3.1	3.1	3.1	5.9	Iran (Rép. islamique d')
Iraq	2014-04	10.8	6.4	...	25.5	25.2	25.2	26.5	26.5	25.3	Iraq
Ireland	2016-02	7.8	12.0	13.3	13.9	15.1	15.7	16.3	16.3	22.2	Irlande
Israel	2015-03	6.7	11.7	15.0	19.2	21.7	22.5	22.5	26.7	27.5	Israël
Italy	2013-02	12.9	11.1	11.5	21.3	21.4	31.4	31.0	31.0	31.0	Italie
Jamaica	2016-02	5.0	13.3	11.7	13.3	12.7	12.7	12.7	12.7	17.5	Jamaïque
Japan	2014-12	1.4	4.6	7.1	11.3	7.9	8.1	9.5	9.5	9.3	Japon
Jordan	2016-09	0.0	0.0	5.5	6.4	12.0	12.0	12.0	12.0	15.4	Jordanie
Kazakhstan	2016-03	...	10.4	10.4	17.8	24.3	25.2	26.2	26.2	27.1	Kazakhstan
Kenya	2013-03	1.1	3.6	7.1	9.8	9.8	19.1	19.7	19.7	19.4	Kenya
Kiribati	2015-12	0.0	4.9	4.8	4.3	8.7	8.7	8.7	6.5	6.5	Kiribati

Proportion of seats held by women in national parliament *(continued)*

Percentage, as of January/February each year

Proportion de sièges occupés par les femmes au parlement national *(suite)*

Pourcentage, données disponibles en janvier/février de chaque année

Country or area&	Last Election date Dernière date de l'élection	1990	2000	2005	2010	2013	2014	2015	2016	2017	Pays ou zone&
Kuwait	2016-11	...	0.0	0.0	7.7	6.2	4.6	1.5	1.5	3.1	Koweït
Kyrgyzstan	2015-10	...	1.4	10.0	25.6	23.3	23.3	23.3	19.2	19.2	Kirghizistan
Lao People's Dem. Rep.	2016-03	6.3	21.2	22.9	25.2	25.0	25.0	25.0	25.0	27.5	Rép. dém. populaire lao
Latvia	2014-10	...	17.0	21.0	22.0	23.0	25.0	18.0	18.0	16.0	Lettonie
Lebanon	2009-06	0.0	2.3	2.3	3.1	3.1	3.1	3.1	3.1	3.1	Liban
Lesotho	2015-02	...	3.8	11.7	24.2	26.7	26.7	26.7	25.0	25.0	Lesotho
Liberia	2011-10	...	...	5.3	12.5	11.0	11.0	11.0	11.0	12.3	Libéria
Libya	2014-06	...	...	...	7.7	16.5	16.5	16.0	16.0	16.0	Libye
Liechtenstein	2013-02	4.0	4.0	12.0	24.0	24.0	20.0	20.0	20.0	12.0	Liechtenstein
Lithuania	2016-10	...	17.5	22.0	19.1	24.5	24.1	23.4	23.4	21.3	Lituanie
Luxembourg	2013-10	13.3	16.7	23.3	20.0	21.7	28.3	28.3	28.3	28.3	Luxembourg
Madagascar	2013-12	6.5	8.0	6.9	...	17.5	23.1	20.5	20.5	19.2	Madagascar
Malawi	2014-05	9.8	8.3	14.0	20.8	22.3	22.3	16.7	16.7	16.7	Malawi
Malaysia	2013-05	5.1	...	9.1	9.9	10.4	10.4	10.4	10.4	10.4	Malaisie
Maldives	2014-03	6.3	...	12.0	6.5	6.5	6.8	5.9	5.9	5.9	Maldives
Mali	2013-11	...	12.2	10.2	10.2	10.2	9.5	9.5	8.8	8.8	Mali
Malta	2013-03	2.9	9.2	9.2	8.7	8.7	14.3	12.9	12.9	12.5	Malte
Marshall Islands	2015-11	...	...	3.0	3.0	3.0	3.0	3.0	9.1	9.1	Îles Marshall
Mauritania	2013-11	...	3.8	3.7	22.1	22.1	25.2	25.2	25.2	25.2	Mauritanie
Mauritius	2014-12	7.1	7.6	5.7	17.1	18.8	18.8	11.6	11.6	11.6	Maurice
Mexico	2015-06	12.0	18.2	22.6	27.6	36.8	37.4	38.0	42.4	42.6	Mexique
Micronesia (Fed. States of)	2015-03	...	0.0	0.0	0.0	0.0	0.0	0.0	0.0	0.0	Micronésie (États féd. de)
Monaco	2013-02	11.1	22.2	20.8	26.1	19.0	20.8	20.8	20.8	20.8	Monaco
Mongolia	2016-06	24.9	7.9	6.8	3.9	14.9	14.9	14.9	14.5	17.1	Mongolie
Montenegro	2016-10	...	...	...	11.1	17.3	14.8	17.3	17.3	23.5	Monténégro
Morocco	2016-10	0.0	0.6	10.8	10.5	17.0	17.0	17.0	17.0	20.5	Maroc
Mozambique	2014-10	15.7	...	34.8	39.2	39.2	39.2	39.6	39.6	39.6	Mozambique
Myanmar	2015-11	...	...	...	...	6.0	5.6	6.2	9.9	10.2	Myanmar
Namibia	2014-11	6.9	22.2	25.0	26.9[1]	24.4	25.6	41.3	41.3	41.3	Namibie
Nauru	2016-07	5.6	0.0	0.0	0.0	0.0	5.3	5.3	5.3	10.5	Nauru
Nepal	2013-11	6.1	5.9	...	33.2	33.2	29.9	29.5	29.5	29.6	Népal
Netherlands	2012-09	21.3	36.0	36.7	42.0	38.7	38.7	37.3	37.3	38.0	Pays-Bas
New Zealand	2014-09	14.4	29.2	28.3	33.6	32.2	33.9	31.4	31.4	34.2	Nouvelle-Zélande
Nicaragua	2016-11	14.8	9.7	20.7	20.7	40.2	40.2	39.1	41.3	45.7	Nicaragua
Niger	2016-02	5.4	1.2	12.4	9.7	13.3	13.3	13.3	13.3	17.0	Niger
Nigeria	2015-03	...	...	4.7	7.0	6.7	6.7	6.7	5.6	5.6	Nigéria
Norway	2013-09	35.8	36.4	38.2	39.6	39.6	39.6	39.6	39.6	39.6	Norvège
Oman	2015-10	...	...	2.4	0.0	1.2	1.2	1.2	1.2	1.2	Oman
Pakistan	2013-05	10.1	...	21.3	22.2	22.5	20.7	20.7	20.6	20.6	Pakistan
Palau	2016-11	...	0.0	0.0	0.0	0.0	0.0	0.0	0.0	12.5	Palaos
Panama	2014-05	7.5	...	16.7	8.5	8.5	8.5	19.3	18.3	18.3	Panama
Papua New Guinea	2012-06	0.0	1.8	0.9	0.9	2.7	2.7	2.7	2.7	2.7	Papouasie-Nvl-Guinée
Paraguay	2013-04	5.6	2.5	10.0	12.5	12.5	15.0	15.0	15.0	13.8	Paraguay
Peru	2016-04	5.6	10.8	18.3	27.5	21.5	22.3	22.3	22.3	27.7	Pérou
Philippines	2016-05	9.1	12.4	15.3	21.0	22.9	27.3	27.2	27.2	29.5	Philippines
Poland	2015-10	13.5	13.0	20.2	20.0	23.7	24.3	24.1	27.4	28.0	Pologne
Portugal	2015-10	7.6	18.7	19.1	27.4	28.7	31.3	31.3	34.8	34.8	Portugal
Qatar	2013-07	...	...	...	0.0	0.0	0.0	0.0	0.0	0.0	Qatar
Republic of Korea	2016-04	2.0	3.7	13.0	14.7	15.7	15.7	16.3	16.3	17.0	République de Corée
Republic of Moldova	2014-11	...	8.9	15.8	23.8	19.8	18.8	20.8	21.8	22.8	République de Moldova
Romania	2016-12	34.4	7.3	11.4	11.4	13.3	13.5	13.7	13.7	20.7	Roumanie
Russian Federation	2016-09	...	7.7	9.8	14.0	13.6	13.6	13.6	13.6	15.8	Fédération de Russie
Rwanda	2013-09	17.1	17.1	48.8	56.3	56.3	63.8	63.8	63.8	61.3	Rwanda
Saint Kitts and Nevis	2015-02	6.7	13.3	0.0	6.7	6.7	6.7	6.7	13.3	13.3	Saint-Kitts-et-Nevis
Saint Lucia	2016-06	0.0	11.1	11.1	11.1	16.7	16.7	16.7	16.7	16.7	Sainte-Lucie
Saint Vincent & Grenadines	2015-12	9.5	4.8	22.7	21.7	17.4	13.0	13.0	13.0	13.0	Saint-Vincent-Grenadines
Samoa	2016-03	0.0	8.2	6.1	8.2	4.1	4.1	6.1	6.1	10.0	Samoa
San Marino	2016-11	11.7	13.3	16.7	16.7	16.7	18.3	16.7	16.7	26.7	Saint-Marin
Sao Tome and Principe	2014-10	11.8	9.1	9.1	7.3	18.2	18.2	18.2	18.2	18.2	Sao Tomé-et-Principe

Proportion of seats held by women in national parliament *(continued)*
Percentage, as of January/February each year

Proportion de sièges occupés par les femmes au parlement national *(suite)*
Pourcentage, données disponibles en janvier/février de chaque année

Country or area&	Last Election date Dernière date de l'élection	1990	2000	2005	2010	2013	2014	2015	2016	2017	Pays ou zone&
Saudi Arabia	2016-12	...	...	0.0	0.0	19.9	19.9	19.9	19.9	19.9	Arabie saoudite
Senegal	2012-07	12.5	12.1	19.2	22.7	42.7	43.3	42.7	42.7	42.7	Sénégal
Serbia	2016-04	...	...	...	21.6	33.2	33.6	34.0	34.0	34.4	Serbie
Serbia and Monten. [former]		...	5.1	7.9	...	...	...	...	...	...	Serbie-et-Monténégro [anc.]
Seychelles	2016-09	16.0	23.5	29.4	23.5	43.8	43.8	43.8	43.8	21.2	Seychelles
Sierra Leone	2012-11	...	8.8	14.5	13.2	12.4	12.1	12.4	12.4	12.4	Sierra Leone
Singapore	2015-09	4.9	4.3	16.0	23.4	24.2	25.3	25.3	23.1	23.8	Singapour
Slovakia	2016-03	...	12.7	16.7	18.0	18.7	18.7	18.7	18.7	20.0	Slovaquie
Slovenia	2014-07	...	7.8	12.2	14.4	32.2	33.3	36.7	36.7	36.7	Slovénie
Solomon Islands	2014-11	0.0	2.0	0.0	0.0	2.0	2.0	2.0	2.0	2.0	Îles Salomon
Somalia	2016-10	4.0	...	...	6.9	13.8	13.8	13.8	13.8	24.2	Somalie
South Africa	2014-05	2.8	30.0	32.8	44.5	42.3	44.8	41.5	42.0	42.2	Afrique du Sud
South Sudan	2016-08	...	...	...	...	26.5	26.5	26.5	26.5	28.5	Soudan du sud
Spain	2016-06	14.6	21.6	36.0	36.6	36.0	39.7	41.1	40.0	39.1	Espagne
Sri Lanka	2015-08	4.9	4.9	4.9	5.8	5.8	5.8	5.8	5.8	5.8	Sri Lanka
Sudan	2015-04	...	...	...	...	24.6	24.3	24.3	30.5	30.5	Soudan
Sudan [former]		...	...	9.7	18.9	...	...	...	...	...	Soudan [anc.]
Suriname	2015-05	7.8	15.7	19.6	25.5	11.8	11.8	11.8	25.5	25.5	Suriname
Swaziland	2013-09	3.6	3.1	10.8	13.6	13.6	6.2	6.2	6.2	6.2	Swaziland
Sweden	2014-09	38.4	42.7	45.3	46.4	44.7	45.0	43.6	43.6	43.6	Suède
Switzerland	2015-10	14.0	22.5	25.0	29.0	29.0	31.0	30.5	32.0	32.5	Suisse
Syrian Arab Republic	2016-04	9.2	10.4	12.0	12.4	12.0	12.0	12.4	12.4	13.2	République arabe syrienne
Tajikistan	2015-03	...	2.8	12.7	17.5	19.0	15.9	16.9	19.0	19.0	Tadjikistan
Thailand	2014-08	2.8	5.6	8.8	13.3	15.8	15.8	6.1	6.1	4.9	Thaïlande
TFYR of Macedonia	2016-12	...	7.5	19.2	32.5	32.5	34.1	33.3	33.3	31.7	ex-R.Y. de Macédoine
Timor-Leste	2012-07	...	...	25.3	29.2	38.5	38.5	38.5	38.5	38.5	Timor-Leste
Togo	2013-07	5.2	...	6.2	11.1	11.1	16.5	17.6	17.6	17.6	Togo
Tonga	2014-11	0.0	...	0.0	3.1	3.6	3.6	0.0	0.0	3.8	Tonga
Trinidad and Tobago	2015-09	16.7	11.1	19.4	26.8	28.6	28.6	28.6	31.0	31.0	Trinité-et-Tobago
Tunisia	2014-10	4.3	11.5	22.8	27.6	26.7	28.1	31.3	31.3	31.3	Tunisie
Turkey	2015-11	1.3	4.2	4.4	9.1	14.2	14.4	14.4	14.9	14.9	Turquie
Turkmenistan	2013-12	26.0	26.0	...	16.8	16.8	26.4	25.8	25.8	25.8	Turkménistan
Tuvalu	2015-03	7.7	0.0	0.0	0.0	6.7	6.7	6.7	6.7	6.7	Tuvalu
Uganda	2016-02	12.2	17.9	23.9	31.5	35.0	35.0	35.0	35.0	34.3	Ouganda
Ukraine	2014-10	...	7.8	5.3	8.0	9.4	9.7	11.8	12.1	12.3	Ukraine
United Arab Emirates	2011-09	0.0	0.0	0.0	22.5	17.5	17.5	17.5	22.5	20.0	Émirats arabes unis
United Kingdom	2015-05	6.3	18.4	18.1	19.5	22.5	22.6	22.8	29.4	30.0	Royaume-Uni
United Rep. of Tanzania	2015-10	...	16.4	21.4	30.7	36.0	36.0	36.0	36.6	36.4	Rép.-Unie de Tanzanie
United States of America	2016-11	6.6	13.3	14.9	16.8	17.8	18.3	19.4	19.4	19.1	États-Unis d'Amérique
Uruguay	2014-10	6.1	12.1	12.1	14.1	12.1	13.1	13.1	16.2	20.2	Uruguay
Uzbekistan	2014-12	...	6.8	17.5	22.0	22.0	22.0	16.0	16.0	16.0	Ouzbékistan
Vanuatu	2016-01	4.3	0.0	3.8	3.8	0.0	0.0	0.0	0.0	0.0	Vanuatu
Venezuela (Boliv. Rep. of)	2015-12	10.0	12.1	9.7	17.5	17.0	17.0	17.0	14.4	22.2	Venezuela (Rép. boliv. du)
Viet Nam	2016-05	17.7	26.0	27.3	25.8	24.4	24.3	24.3	24.3	26.7	Viet Nam
Yemen	2003-04	4.1	0.7	0.3	0.3	0.3	0.3	0.3	0.0	0.0	Yémen
Zambia	2016-08	6.6	10.1	12.0	14.0	11.5	10.8	12.7	12.7	18.0	Zambie
Zimbabwe	2013-07	11.0	14.0	10.0	15.0	15.0	31.5	31.5	31.5	32.6	Zimbabwe

Source:

Inter-Parliamentary Union (IPU), Geneva, Women in National Parliament dataset and the Millennium Development Goals Indicators database, last accessed March 2017.

Source:

Union interparlementaire, Genève, données des femmes dans les parlements et la base de données des Objectifs du Millénaire pour le développement, dernier accès mars 2017.

& The data are as at 1 February for 2013 – 2017, as at 31 January for 2005 and 2010, and as at 25 January for 2000.

& Les données sont au 1er février en 2013 – 2017, au 31 janvier en 2005 et 2010, et au 25 janvier en 2000.

5

Proportion of seats held by women in national parliament *(continued)*
Percentage, as of January/February each year

Proportion de sièges occupés par les femmes au parlement national *(suite)*
Pourcentage, données disponibles en janvier/février de chaque année

1 Figure excludes 11 members yet to be sworn in.

1 Ce chiffre ne tient pas compte de 11 membres qui n'avaient pas encore été assermentés.

Ratio of girls to boys in primary, secondary and tertiary education

Rapport filles/garçons dans l'enseignement primaire, secondaire et supérieur

Region, country or area	1985	1995	2005	2010	2013	2014	2015	Région, pays ou zone
Total, all countries or areas								**Total, tous pays ou zones**
Primary education	**0.85**	**0.90**	**0.95**	**0.97**	**0.99**	**0.99**	**1.00**	**Enseignement primaire**
Secondary education	*** 0.81**	**0.88**	**0.95**	**0.97**	**0.98**	**0.99**	**0.99**	**Enseignement secondaire**
Tertiary education	*** 0.85**	*** 0.95**	**1.05**	**1.08**	**1.10**	**1.11**	**1.12**	**Enseignement supérieur**
Africa								**Afrique**
Primary education	0.81	0.84	0.90	0.93	0.94	0.94	* 0.94	Enseignement primaire
Secondary education	* 0.66	* 0.82	0.85	0.86	* 0.89	* 0.90	* 0.90	Enseignement secondaire
Tertiary education	* 0.55	* 0.67	0.80	0.84	* 0.85	* 0.84	* 0.86	Enseignement supérieur
Northern Africa [1]								**Afrique septentrionale** [1]
Primary education	0.77	0.87	0.94	0.96	0.97	0.98	* 0.97	Enseignement primaire
Secondary education	0.69	0.87	* 0.99	0.99	* 0.98	* 0.99	* 0.99	Enseignement secondaire
Tertiary education	* 0.57	* 0.74	0.95	1.06	1.08	1.08	1.11	Enseignement supérieur
Sub-Saharan Africa [2]								**Afrique subsaharienne** [2]
Primary education	0.81	0.84	0.89	0.93	0.94	0.94	* 0.94	Enseignement primaire
Secondary education	* 0.65	* 0.81	0.79	0.83	* 0.87	* 0.87	* 0.88	Enseignement secondaire
Tertiary education	* 0.54	* 0.62	0.69	0.71	* 0.73	* 0.72	* 0.73	Enseignement supérieur
North America								**Amérique du Nord**
Primary education	0.99	0.98	0.98	0.99	0.99	0.99	0.99	Enseignement primaire
Secondary education	1.00	1.02	1.04	1.04	1.03	1.03	* 1.03	Enseignement secondaire
Tertiary education	1.05	1.23	1.35	1.35	1.32	1.30	1.30	Enseignement supérieur
Latin America & the Caribbean								**Amérique latine et Caraïbes**
Primary education	0.98	* 0.97	0.97	0.97	0.98	0.98	0.98	Enseignement primaire
Secondary education	* 1.03	* 1.08	1.08	1.08	1.07	1.06	1.05	Enseignement secondaire
Tertiary education	* 0.88	* 1.08	1.21	1.30	1.30	1.30	* 1.31	Enseignement supérieur
South America								**Amérique du Sud**
Primary education	* 0.98	* 0.97	0.97	0.96	0.97	0.98	0.98	Enseignement primaire
Secondary education	* 1.06	* 1.09	1.08	1.09	1.07	1.06	1.05	Enseignement secondaire
Tertiary education	* 0.92	* 1.12	1.22	1.33	1.35	1.35	1.38	Enseignement supérieur
Asia								**Asie**
Primary education	0.82	0.89	* 0.97	0.99	1.02	1.02	1.02	Enseignement primaire
Secondary education	* 0.70	0.79	* 0.92	0.96	0.99	1.00	1.00	Enseignement secondaire
Tertiary education	* 0.57	* 0.70	0.86	0.93	1.02	1.05	1.05	Enseignement supérieur
Eastern Asia [3]								**Asie orientale** [3]
Primary education	0.84	0.95	* 1.00	0.99	1.00	1.00	1.00	Enseignement primaire
Secondary education	0.73	0.87	* 0.99	1.00	1.02	1.02	1.02	Enseignement secondaire
Tertiary education	* 0.44	* 0.56	0.86	1.02	1.09	1.12	1.14	Enseignement supérieur
South-eastern Asia								**Asie du Sud-Est**
Primary education	0.95	0.97	0.97	1.00	0.99	0.98	0.98	Enseignement primaire
Secondary education	* 0.87	* 0.92	1.00	1.01	1.00	1.01	* 1.00	Enseignement secondaire
Tertiary education	* 0.87	0.95	* 1.00	1.06	1.15	1.18	1.19	Enseignement supérieur
Southern Asia								**Asie méridionale**
Primary education	0.69	0.81	* 0.95	1.00	1.06	1.06	1.06	Enseignement primaire
Secondary education	* 0.53	0.66	0.85	0.93	0.98	0.99	0.99	Enseignement secondaire
Tertiary education	0.43	0.54	0.74	0.76	0.92	0.96	0.95	Enseignement supérieur
Western Asia [4]								**Asie occidentale** [4]
Primary education	0.84	* 0.86	0.90	0.93	0.93	* 0.93	* 0.93	Enseignement primaire
Secondary education	* 0.61	* 0.71	0.85	0.89	0.92	* 0.91	* 0.91	Enseignement secondaire
Tertiary education	0.52	0.70	0.84	0.91	0.93	0.94	0.95	Enseignement supérieur
Caucasus and Central Asia [5]								**Caucase et Asie centrale** [5]
Primary education	* 0.99	1.00	0.99	0.99	0.99	0.99	0.99	Enseignement primaire
Secondary education	...	* 0.99	0.98	1.00	1.00	1.00	1.00	Enseignement secondaire
Tertiary education	...	* 1.00	1.05	1.04	1.04	1.04	1.04	Enseignement supérieur
Europe								**Europe**
Primary education	* 0.99	0.99	0.99	1.00	1.00	1.00	1.00	Enseignement primaire
Secondary education	* 1.02	1.02	1.00	0.99	1.00	0.99	1.00	Enseignement secondaire
Tertiary education	* 1.08	1.14	1.28	1.29	1.24	1.22	1.22	Enseignement supérieur
Oceania								**Océanie**
Primary education	0.96	0.97	0.98	0.97	0.97	0.97	0.97	Enseignement primaire
Secondary education	* 0.99	0.99	0.97	0.96	0.95	0.95	* 0.94	Enseignement secondaire
Tertiary education	0.92	1.07	1.28	1.37	1.39	1.39	* 1.38	Enseignement supérieur
Afghanistan								**Afghanistan**
Primary education	0.49	0.51	0.59	0.68	0.71	0.70	0.69	Enseignement primaire
Secondary education	0.46	0.37	0.33	0.50	0.56	0.56	0.56	Enseignement secondaire
Tertiary education	...	...	...	...	...	0.28	...	Enseignement supérieur

Ratio of girls to boys in primary, secondary and tertiary education *(continued)*

Rapport filles/garçons dans l'enseignement primaire, secondaire et supérieur *(suite)*

Region, country or area	1985	1995	2005	2010	2013	2014	2015	Région, pays ou zone
Albania								**Albanie**
Primary education	0.98	0.96	0.99	0.97	0.97	0.98	0.97	Enseignement primaire
Secondary education	0.91	0.98	0.95	0.99	0.94	0.93	0.94	Enseignement secondaire
Tertiary education	0.86	1.08	1.43	1.40	1.39	1.41	1.40	Enseignement supérieur
Algeria								**Algérie**
Primary education	0.79	0.88	0.92	0.93	0.94	0.94	0.94	Enseignement primaire
Secondary education	0.73	0.89	1.10	1.03	...	...	...	Enseignement secondaire
Tertiary education	...	...	1.28	1.44	1.50	1.53	1.56	Enseignement supérieur
Angola								**Angola**
Primary education	...	...	...	0.81	...	...	...	Enseignement primaire
Secondary education	...	...	...	0.69	...	...	...	Enseignement secondaire
Tertiary education	...	...	...	...	0.80	...	0.79	Enseignement supérieur
Antigua and Barbuda								**Antigua-et-Barbuda**
Primary education	...	...	...	0.92	...	0.92	0.94	Enseignement primaire
Secondary education	...	...	...	1.01	...	1.01	1.02	Enseignement secondaire
Tertiary education	...	...	...	2.50	...	...	...	Enseignement supérieur
Argentina								**Argentine**
Primary education	1.00	...	0.99	0.99	0.99	1.00	...	Enseignement primaire
Secondary education	1.12	...	1.10	1.10	1.08	1.07	...	Enseignement secondaire
Tertiary education	1.11	...	1.46	1.51	1.61	1.62	...	Enseignement supérieur
Armenia								**Arménie**
Primary education	...	1.02	1.08	...	...	...	1.00	Enseignement primaire
Secondary education	...	...	...	...	...	...	1.01	Enseignement secondaire
Tertiary education	...	...	1.53	1.57	1.31	1.21	1.13	Enseignement supérieur
Aruba								**Aruba**
Primary education	...	...	0.94	0.99	0.98	0.97	...	Enseignement primaire
Secondary education	...	...	1.00	1.05	...	...	...	Enseignement secondaire
Tertiary education	...	...	1.44	1.41	2.20	2.27	2.26	Enseignement supérieur
Australia								**Australie**
Primary education	0.99	1.00	1.02	1.00	0.99	0.99	1.00	Enseignement primaire
Secondary education	...	1.00	0.98	0.97	0.95	0.95	...	Enseignement secondaire
Tertiary education	0.95	1.04	1.26	1.38	1.40	1.41	...	Enseignement supérieur
Austria								**Autriche**
Primary education	0.99	0.99	1.00	0.99	0.99	0.99	0.99	Enseignement primaire
Secondary education	0.93	0.94	0.95	0.96	0.96	0.95	0.95	Enseignement secondaire
Tertiary education	0.84	0.94	1.20	1.17	1.21	1.20	1.20	Enseignement supérieur
Azerbaijan								**Azerbaïdjan**
Primary education	...	1.14	* 0.95	* 0.99	* 0.97	* 0.99	* 0.98	Enseignement primaire
Secondary education	...	1.03	...	...	...	...	...	Enseignement secondaire
Tertiary education	...	0.90	...	* 0.99	* 1.11	* 1.14	* 1.16	Enseignement supérieur
Bahamas								**Bahamas**
Primary education	1.01	1.00	0.99	1.02	...	...	...	Enseignement primaire
Secondary education	1.16	1.00	1.00	1.05	...	...	...	Enseignement secondaire
Tertiary education	...	2.71	...	...	...	...	...	Enseignement supérieur
Bahrain								**Bahreïn**
Primary education	1.00	1.01	1.04	...	1.02	1.02	1.01	Enseignement primaire
Secondary education	0.92	1.04	1.11	1.01	1.01	1.01	1.00	Enseignement secondaire
Tertiary education	1.39	1.62	3.06	...	2.24	1.98	1.92	Enseignement supérieur
Bangladesh								**Bangladesh**
Primary education	0.69	...	1.05	* 1.06	1.04	...	1.08	Enseignement primaire
Secondary education	0.40	...	1.07	1.12	1.08	...	1.13	Enseignement secondaire
Tertiary education	0.24	...	0.52	...	...	0.74	...	Enseignement supérieur
Barbados								**Barbade**
Primary education	0.96	...	1.00	* 1.02	...	1.01	...	Enseignement primaire
Secondary education	1.02	...	0.99	* 1.01	...	1.03	...	Enseignement secondaire
Tertiary education	0.98	...	...	2.18	...	...	...	Enseignement supérieur
Belarus								**Bélarus**
Primary education	...	0.96	0.97	1.00	1.00	1.00	1.00	Enseignement primaire
Secondary education	...	...	...	0.97	0.98	0.98	0.99	Enseignement secondaire
Tertiary education	...	...	1.37	* 1.45	1.35	1.33	1.33	Enseignement supérieur
Belgium								**Belgique**
Primary education	1.01	0.99	1.00	1.00	1.00	1.00	1.00	Enseignement primaire
Secondary education	1.02	1.07	0.97	0.97	1.14	1.13	1.14	Enseignement secondaire
Tertiary education	0.86	1.01	1.23	1.27	1.30	1.31	1.31	Enseignement supérieur

Region, country or area	1985	1995	2005	2010	2013	2014	2015	Région, pays ou zone
Belize								**Belize**
Primary education	...	0.96	0.96	0.96	0.96	0.95	0.95	Enseignement primaire
Secondary education	...	1.03	1.03	1.08	1.04	1.05	1.03	Enseignement secondaire
Tertiary education	...	...	1.58	1.60	1.64	...	1.61	Enseignement supérieur
Benin								**Bénin**
Primary education	0.48	0.55	0.77	0.88	0.90	0.91	0.92	Enseignement primaire
Secondary education	0.40	...	...	...	0.66	0.68	0.70	Enseignement secondaire
Tertiary education	* 0.21	0.20	...	0.35	0.37	...	...	Enseignement supérieur
Bermuda								**Bermudes**
Primary education	1.01	1.00	1.05	...	0.97	0.97	0.98	Enseignement primaire
Secondary education	...	...	1.13	1.18	1.17	1.14	1.12	Enseignement secondaire
Tertiary education	...	...	...	2.11	2.26	1.89	2.32	Enseignement supérieur
Bhutan								**Bhoutan**
Primary education	0.53	0.78	0.98	1.02	1.01	1.01	...	Enseignement primaire
Secondary education	...	...	0.89	1.02	1.07	1.07	...	Enseignement secondaire
Tertiary education	...	...	0.67	0.61	0.74	...	...	Enseignement supérieur
Bolivia (Plurin. State of)								**Bolivie (État plurin. de)**
Primary education	...	0.96	0.99	0.98	0.97	0.97	0.97	Enseignement primaire
Secondary education	...	...	0.94	0.99	0.99	0.99	0.98	Enseignement secondaire
Botswana								**Botswana**
Primary education	1.11	1.01	0.99	...	0.97	0.97	...	Enseignement primaire
Secondary education	1.13	1.10	1.03	...	...	...	...	Enseignement secondaire
Tertiary education	0.82	0.91	0.89	...	...	1.25	1.37	Enseignement supérieur
Brazil								**Brésil**
Primary education	...	...	* 0.94	...	* 0.95	* 0.96	* 0.97	Enseignement primaire
Secondary education	...	...	* 1.10	...	* 1.09	* 1.08	* 1.05	Enseignement secondaire
Tertiary education	...	...	* 1.29	...	* 1.35	* 1.35	* 1.40	Enseignement supérieur
Brunei Darussalam								**Brunéi Darussalam**
Primary education	...	0.97	0.98	1.00	1.00	1.00	1.00	Enseignement primaire
Secondary education	...	...	1.01	1.01	1.02	1.00	1.00	Enseignement secondaire
Tertiary education	...	...	1.98	1.87	1.82	1.69	1.65	Enseignement supérieur
Bulgaria								**Bulgarie**
Primary education	1.00	0.99	0.99	1.00	0.99	0.99	0.99	Enseignement primaire
Secondary education	0.99	1.00	0.96	0.96	0.95	0.97	0.97	Enseignement secondaire
Tertiary education	1.21	1.60	1.16	1.32	1.27	1.25	1.27	Enseignement supérieur
Burkina Faso								**Burkina Faso**
Primary education	0.60	0.66	0.80	0.91	0.96	0.96	0.96	Enseignement primaire
Secondary education	0.55	...	0.71	0.76	0.85	0.87	0.92	Enseignement secondaire
Tertiary education	0.29	0.28	0.45	0.48	0.49	...	...	Enseignement supérieur
Burundi								**Burundi**
Primary education	0.68	0.80	0.84	0.97	1.00	1.01	1.01	Enseignement primaire
Secondary education	0.51	...	* 0.72	0.69	0.78	0.85	0.91	Enseignement secondaire
Tertiary education	* 0.34	...	* 0.38	0.51	0.42	0.31	...	Enseignement supérieur
Cabo Verde								**Cabo Verde**
Primary education	0.97	...	0.96	0.95	0.95	0.95	0.95	Enseignement primaire
Secondary education	...	...	1.13	1.18	1.15	1.14	1.12	Enseignement secondaire
Tertiary education	...	...	1.08	1.27	1.39	1.40	1.39	Enseignement supérieur
Cambodia								**Cambodge**
Primary education	...	0.82	0.93	0.94	0.91	0.95	0.99	Enseignement primaire
Tertiary education	...	0.18	0.46	0.59	...	...	0.82	Enseignement supérieur
Cameroon								**Cameroun**
Primary education	0.84	0.90	* 0.84	0.86	...	0.89	0.90	Enseignement primaire
Secondary education	0.61	0.69	0.79	...	0.86	0.85	0.86	Enseignement secondaire
Tertiary education	...	...	* 0.66	0.81	0.77	0.78	0.77	Enseignement supérieur
Canada								**Canada**
Primary education	0.98	0.99	0.99	1.00	1.01	...	...	Enseignement primaire
Secondary education	1.00	1.00	0.98	0.98	1.00	...	...	Enseignement secondaire
Tertiary education	...	1.17	...	...	...	...	...	Enseignement supérieur
Central African Republic								**République centrafricaine**
Primary education	0.56	...	0.69	0.71	...	...	...	Enseignement primaire
Tertiary education	...	...	...	0.32	...	...	...	Enseignement supérieur
Chad								**Tchad**
Primary education	0.38	0.49	0.68	0.74	0.77	...	...	Enseignement primaire
Secondary education	0.18	0.24	* 0.35	0.42	...	...	...	Enseignement secondaire
Tertiary education	0.09	...	0.06	* 0.17	...	* 0.20	...	Enseignement supérieur

Region, country or area	1985	1995	2005	2010	2013	2014	2015	Région, pays ou zone
Chile								**Chili**
Primary education	0.96	...	0.95	0.97	0.97	0.97	0.97	Enseignement primaire
Secondary education	1.05	...	1.00	1.03	1.02	1.02	1.01	Enseignement secondaire
Tertiary education	0.78	0.85	0.95	1.08	1.13	1.14	1.14	Enseignement supérieur
China [6]								**Chine** [6]
Primary education	0.83	0.95	...	0.99	1.00	1.00	1.00	Enseignement primaire
Secondary education	0.70	0.85	...	1.00	1.02	1.02	1.03	Enseignement secondaire
Tertiary education	...	...	0.91	1.07	1.14	1.16	1.19	Enseignement supérieur
China, Hong Kong SAR								**Chine, Hong Kong RAS**
Secondary education	1.06	...	1.00	0.99	0.97	0.96	0.96	Enseignement secondaire
Tertiary education	...	...	0.98	* 0.99	1.13	1.15	1.16	Enseignement supérieur
China, Macao SAR								**Chine, Macao RAS**
Primary education	...	...	0.94	0.98	0.99	0.99	0.99	Enseignement primaire
Secondary education	...	...	1.03	0.99	0.98	0.98	0.99	Enseignement secondaire
Tertiary education	...	...	0.64	0.97	1.28	1.31	1.33	Enseignement supérieur
Colombia								**Colombie**
Primary education	1.03	0.99	0.98	0.98	0.97	0.97	0.97	Enseignement primaire
Secondary education	1.03	1.16	1.11	1.10	1.08	1.08	1.07	Enseignement secondaire
Tertiary education	0.96	1.05	1.08	1.10	1.15	1.15	1.16	Enseignement supérieur
Comoros								**Comores**
Primary education	0.90	...	...	...	0.94	0.93	...	Enseignement primaire
Secondary education	...	...	...	...	1.04	1.07	...	Enseignement secondaire
Tertiary education	...	...	...	0.74	0.87	0.81	...	Enseignement supérieur
Congo								**Congo**
Primary education	0.96	0.85	0.93	0.94	...	...	...	Enseignement primaire
Secondary education	0.75	...	...	...	...	...	...	Enseignement secondaire
Tertiary education	0.18	...	...	...	0.75	...	...	Enseignement supérieur
Cook Islands								**Îles Cook**
Primary education	...	...	* 1.03	* 0.99	* 0.98	* 0.97	* 0.94	Enseignement primaire
Secondary education	...	...	* 1.13	* 1.09	* 1.16	* 1.10	* 1.09	Enseignement secondaire
Costa Rica								**Costa Rica**
Primary education	0.97	0.99	0.97	0.98	0.99	0.99	0.99	Enseignement primaire
Secondary education	1.09	1.08	1.04	1.04	1.06	1.05	1.04	Enseignement secondaire
Tertiary education	...	...	...	...	1.22	1.24	1.31	Enseignement supérieur
Côte d'Ivoire								**Côte d'Ivoire**
Primary education	0.70	0.73	...	...	0.87	0.87	0.89	Enseignement primaire
Secondary education	...	...	...	...	...	0.71	0.72	Enseignement secondaire
Tertiary education	...	0.33	...	0.52	0.62	0.59	0.66	Enseignement supérieur
Croatia								**Croatie**
Primary education	...	1.00	1.00	1.00	1.00	1.00	1.00	Enseignement primaire
Secondary education	...	1.04	1.03	1.07	1.04	1.04	1.05	Enseignement secondaire
Tertiary education	...	1.01	1.21	1.34	1.35	1.37	1.36	Enseignement supérieur
Cuba								**Cuba**
Primary education	0.94	0.99	0.97	0.99	0.99	0.96	0.95	Enseignement primaire
Secondary education	1.06	1.12	1.02	1.01	1.02	1.03	1.05	Enseignement secondaire
Tertiary education	1.20	1.46	* 1.70	1.66	1.68	...	1.43	Enseignement supérieur
Curaçao								**Curaçao**
Primary education	...	...	...	...	0.96	...	...	Enseignement primaire
Secondary education	...	...	...	...	1.05	...	...	Enseignement secondaire
Tertiary education	...	...	...	...	2.33	...	...	Enseignement supérieur
Cyprus								**Chypre**
Primary education	0.99	* 1.00	* 1.00	* 1.00	* 1.00	* 1.01	* 1.00	Enseignement primaire
Secondary education	1.05	* 1.01	* 1.02	* 1.01	* 1.00	* 1.00	* 0.99	Enseignement secondaire
Tertiary education	0.90	* 1.27	* 1.13	* 0.90	* 1.29	* 1.42	* 1.36	Enseignement supérieur
Czechia								**Tchéquie**
Primary education	0.97	1.00	0.99	1.00	1.00	1.00	1.00	Enseignement primaire
Secondary education	1.07	1.03	1.02	1.01	1.01	1.00	1.01	Enseignement secondaire
Tertiary education	0.74	0.96	1.16	1.40	1.42	1.40	1.41	Enseignement supérieur
Dem. People's Rep. Korea								**Rép. pop. dém. de Corée**
Primary education	...	...	...	...	...	...	1.00	Enseignement primaire
Secondary education	...	...	...	...	...	...	1.01	Enseignement secondaire
Tertiary education	...	...	...	...	...	...	0.55	Enseignement supérieur
Dem. Rep. of the Congo								**Rép. dém. du Congo**
Primary education	0.65	0.69	...	0.87	0.91	0.91	...	Enseignement primaire
Secondary education	0.41	0.61	...	0.58	0.62	0.62	...	Enseignement secondaire
Tertiary education	...	...	...	...	0.46	...	...	Enseignement supérieur

Ratio of girls to boys in primary, secondary and tertiary education *(continued)*

Rapport filles/garçons dans l'enseignement primaire, secondaire et supérieur *(suite)*

Region, country or area	1985	1995	2005	2010	2013	2014	2015	Région, pays ou zone
Denmark								**Danemark**
Primary education	1.00	1.00	1.00	1.00	0.99	0.99	0.98	Enseignement primaire
Secondary education	0.99	1.03	1.04	1.01	1.02	1.04	1.04	Enseignement secondaire
Tertiary education	1.02	1.12	1.38	1.45	1.38	1.40	1.38	Enseignement supérieur
Djibouti								**Djibouti**
Primary education	0.73	0.78	0.82	...	0.88	0.87	0.89	Enseignement primaire
Secondary education	0.61	0.69	0.67	...	0.77	0.81	0.80	Enseignement secondaire
Tertiary education	...	...	0.73	0.69	...	...	...	Enseignement supérieur
Dominica								**Dominique**
Primary education	...	1.14	1.00	0.98	0.98	1.00	0.98	Enseignement primaire
Secondary education	...	...	1.08	1.09	...	...	0.99	Enseignement secondaire
Tertiary education	2.04	...	...	...	...	...	...	Enseignement supérieur
Dominican Republic								**République dominicaine**
Primary education	1.03	...	0.95	0.88	0.91	0.91	0.91	Enseignement primaire
Secondary education	...	...	1.20	1.13	1.12	1.11	1.10	Enseignement secondaire
Tertiary education	...	...	...	...	...	1.62	1.84	Enseignement supérieur
Ecuador								**Équateur**
Primary education	0.99	0.99	1.00	1.00	1.01	1.00	1.00	Enseignement primaire
Secondary education	1.02	...	1.01	1.05	1.05	1.04	1.04	Enseignement secondaire
Egypt								**Égypte**
Primary education	0.79	0.89	0.95	0.97	0.99	1.00	...	Enseignement primaire
Secondary education	0.68	0.88	...	0.97	0.98	0.99	...	Enseignement secondaire
Tertiary education	0.51	...	0.84	0.92	0.89	0.90	0.96	Enseignement supérieur
El Salvador								**El Salvador**
Primary education	...	0.98	0.97	0.95	0.95	0.96	0.96	Enseignement primaire
Secondary education	...	...	1.00	0.99	1.00	1.01	1.01	Enseignement secondaire
Tertiary education	0.73	0.97	1.12	1.10	1.09	1.09	1.10	Enseignement supérieur
Equatorial Guinea								**Guinée équatoriale**
Primary education	...	...	0.96	0.98	...	...	0.98	Enseignement primaire
Secondary education	...	...	0.72	...	...	...	...	Enseignement secondaire
Eritrea								**Érythrée**
Primary education	...	0.81	0.82	0.86	1.05	0.86	0.86	Enseignement primaire
Secondary education	...	0.72	0.60	0.77	0.80	0.82	0.85	Enseignement secondaire
Tertiary education	...	0.15	...	0.38	...	0.50	...	Enseignement supérieur
Estonia								**Estonie**
Primary education	0.98	0.97	0.97	0.98	0.99	1.00	1.00	Enseignement primaire
Secondary education	...	1.12	1.04	1.00	0.99	0.99	0.99	Enseignement secondaire
Tertiary education	...	1.10	1.68	1.66	1.50	1.52	1.53	Enseignement supérieur
Ethiopia								**Éthiopie**
Primary education	0.65	0.60	0.83	0.92	...	0.92	0.91	Enseignement primaire
Secondary education	...	0.79	0.60	0.83	...	...	0.96	Enseignement secondaire
Tertiary education	...	0.26	0.32	0.43	...	0.48	...	Enseignement supérieur
Fiji								**Fidji**
Primary education	0.99	1.00	...	...	1.01	...	0.99	Enseignement primaire
Secondary education	1.03	...	...	...	...	...	...	Enseignement secondaire
Tertiary education	0.61	...	* 1.19	...	...	...	...	Enseignement supérieur
Finland								**Finlande**
Primary education	1.00	1.00	0.99	0.99	1.00	1.00	1.00	Enseignement primaire
Secondary education	1.17	1.15	1.05	1.05	1.09	1.09	1.09	Enseignement secondaire
Tertiary education	0.98	1.17	1.21	1.22	1.21	1.21	1.21	Enseignement supérieur
France								**France**
Primary education	0.98	0.98	0.99	0.99	0.99	0.99	...	Enseignement primaire
Secondary education	1.09	0.99	1.00	1.01	1.01	1.01	...	Enseignement secondaire
Tertiary education	1.03	1.26	1.26	1.26	1.23	1.23	...	Enseignement supérieur
Gabon								**Gabon**
Primary education	0.98	1.00	...	...	...	...	...	Enseignement primaire
Secondary education	0.71	0.84	...	...	...	...	...	Enseignement secondaire
Gambia								**Gambie**
Primary education	0.61	0.75	1.03	1.03	1.04	1.05	1.07	Enseignement primaire
Secondary education	0.41	0.54	...	* 0.95	...	...	...	Enseignement secondaire
Tertiary education	...	0.54	...	0.68	...	...	...	Enseignement supérieur
Georgia								**Géorgie**
Primary education	...	0.98	0.97	1.01	1.01	1.01	1.02	Enseignement primaire
Secondary education	...	0.91	0.97	...	0.99	1.00	1.00	Enseignement secondaire
Tertiary education	...	1.32	1.03	1.26	1.29	1.26	1.22	Enseignement supérieur

Ratio of girls to boys in primary, secondary and tertiary education *(continued)*

Rapport filles/garçons dans l'enseignement primaire, secondaire et supérieur *(suite)*

Region, country or area	1985	1995	2005	2010	2013	2014	2015	Région, pays ou zone
Germany								**Allemagne**
Primary education	...	1.00	1.00	1.00	0.99	0.99	0.99	Enseignement primaire
Secondary education	...	0.97	0.97	0.95	0.95	0.95	0.94	Enseignement secondaire
Tertiary education	...	0.81	...	...	0.92	0.94	0.96	Enseignement supérieur
Ghana								**Ghana**
Primary education	0.80	0.90	0.96	...	1.00	1.00	1.00	Enseignement primaire
Secondary education	0.63	0.72	* 0.83	...	0.91	0.94	0.95	Enseignement secondaire
Tertiary education	...	...	0.53	...	0.63	0.66	0.69	Enseignement supérieur
Greece								**Grèce**
Primary education	1.01	1.03	0.98	0.98	0.99	0.99	...	Enseignement primaire
Secondary education	0.98	1.02	0.96	0.94	0.96	0.94	...	Enseignement secondaire
Tertiary education	1.02	1.06	1.13	1.04	1.00	1.00	...	Enseignement supérieur
Grenada								**Grenade**
Primary education	0.94	0.93	0.97	0.97	0.96	0.98	0.96	Enseignement primaire
Secondary education	1.18	...	* 1.02	1.03	0.98	0.99	1.00	Enseignement secondaire
Tertiary education	...	...	...	...	...	...	1.16	Enseignement supérieur
Guatemala								**Guatemala**
Primary education	0.84	0.86	0.93	0.97	0.96	0.96	0.96	Enseignement primaire
Secondary education	...	...	0.92	0.94	0.93	0.94	0.93	Enseignement secondaire
Tertiary education	...	...	...	...	1.06	...	1.17	Enseignement supérieur
Guinea								**Guinée**
Primary education	0.46	0.51	0.80	0.82	0.85	0.85	...	Enseignement primaire
Secondary education	0.36	...	* 0.50	...	...	0.66	...	Enseignement secondaire
Tertiary education	0.34	...	0.23	0.33	0.44	0.45	...	Enseignement supérieur
Guinea-Bissau								**Guinée-Bissau**
Primary education	0.51	0.58	...	0.93	...	...	...	Enseignement primaire
Secondary education	0.27	...	...	...	...	...	...	Enseignement secondaire
Guyana								**Guyana**
Primary education	0.97	0.95	0.94	0.96	...	...	...	Enseignement primaire
Secondary education	0.95	...	0.95	1.00	...	...	...	Enseignement secondaire
Tertiary education	0.91	0.83	2.03	2.54	...	...	...	Enseignement supérieur
Haiti								**Haïti**
Primary education	0.87	0.95	...	...	...	...	...	Enseignement primaire
Honduras								**Honduras**
Primary education	1.01	1.01	1.00	1.00	0.99	0.98	0.99	Enseignement primaire
Secondary education	...	...	...	1.22	1.21	1.17	1.19	Enseignement secondaire
Tertiary education	...	...	...	1.14	1.36	1.35	1.35	Enseignement supérieur
Hungary								**Hongrie**
Primary education	1.00	0.99	0.98	0.99	0.99	0.99	0.99	Enseignement primaire
Secondary education	1.00	1.04	0.99	0.98	1.00	1.00	1.00	Enseignement secondaire
Tertiary education	1.18	1.13	1.46	1.35	1.28	1.29	1.25	Enseignement supérieur
Iceland								**Islande**
Primary education	...	1.00	0.98	1.01	0.99	...	...	Enseignement primaire
Secondary education	...	0.97	1.02	1.02	1.04	...	...	Enseignement secondaire
Tertiary education	...	1.40	1.91	1.80	1.71	...	...	Enseignement supérieur
India								**Inde**
Primary education	0.70	0.81	...	* 1.02	1.12	1.11	1.12	Enseignement primaire
Secondary education	...	0.64	* 0.82	0.93	1.01	1.01	1.01	Enseignement secondaire
Tertiary education	0.45	0.57	0.70	0.73	0.94	0.98	0.99	Enseignement supérieur
Indonesia								**Indonésie**
Primary education	0.95	0.97	* 0.97	1.03	1.00	0.98	0.97	Enseignement primaire
Secondary education	...	0.86	* 0.99	1.01	0.97	0.99	1.00	Enseignement secondaire
Tertiary education	0.49	0.63	...	0.87	1.11	1.12	1.12	Enseignement supérieur
Iran (Islamic Republic of)								**Iran (Rép. islamique d')**
Primary education	0.79	0.93	0.98	0.99	1.01	1.04	1.05	Enseignement primaire
Secondary education	0.70	0.83	0.96	0.98	0.99	0.99	0.99	Enseignement secondaire
Tertiary education	...	...	1.06	0.99	0.96	0.93	0.89	Enseignement supérieur
Iraq								**Iraq**
Primary education	0.86	...	...	...	...	...	...	Enseignement primaire
Secondary education	0.57	...	...	...	...	...	...	Enseignement secondaire
Tertiary education	0.41	...	* 0.60	...	...	...	...	Enseignement supérieur
Ireland								**Irlande**
Primary education	1.00	1.00	0.99	1.00	1.01	1.01	1.01	Enseignement primaire
Secondary education	1.10	1.06	1.10	1.04	...	1.02	1.03	Enseignement secondaire
Tertiary education	0.79	1.02	1.26	1.12	1.06	1.07	1.09	Enseignement supérieur

Region, country or area	1985	1995	2005	2010	2013	2014	2015	Région, pays ou zone
Israel								**Israël**
Primary education	1.03	...	1.01	1.00	1.00	1.00	1.01	Enseignement primaire
Secondary education	1.07	...	0.99	1.02	1.02	1.02	1.01	Enseignement secondaire
Tertiary education	...	...	1.33	...	1.35	1.34	1.38	Enseignement supérieur
Italy								**Italie**
Primary education	1.00	0.99	0.99	0.99	0.99	0.99	0.99	Enseignement primaire
Secondary education	0.99	1.00	0.99	0.99	0.98	0.98	0.98	Enseignement secondaire
Tertiary education	0.85	1.14	1.37	1.43	1.40	1.38	1.36	Enseignement supérieur
Jamaica								**Jamaïque**
Primary education	1.02	...	...	...	...	...	...	Enseignement primaire
Secondary education	1.09	...	1.06	1.08	1.08	1.08	1.07	Enseignement secondaire
Tertiary education	...	...	...	2.31	2.28	...	1.73	Enseignement supérieur
Japan								**Japon**
Primary education	1.00	1.00	1.00	1.00	1.00	1.00	...	Enseignement primaire
Secondary education	1.02	1.01	1.00	1.00	1.00	1.00	...	Enseignement secondaire
Tertiary education	0.54	0.82	0.89	0.89	0.91	0.93	...	Enseignement supérieur
Jordan								**Jordanie**
Primary education	1.05	1.01	1.01	1.00	1.00	1.01	...	Enseignement primaire
Secondary education	1.04	...	1.03	1.06	1.05	1.06	...	Enseignement secondaire
Tertiary education	0.96	...	1.09	1.15	...	...	1.11	Enseignement supérieur
Kazakhstan								**Kazakhstan**
Primary education	...	1.00	1.00	1.00	1.00	1.00	1.00	Enseignement primaire
Secondary education	...	...	...	1.01	1.02	1.03	1.03	Enseignement secondaire
Tertiary education	...	1.26	...	1.27	1.27	1.26	1.28	Enseignement supérieur
Kenya								**Kenya**
Primary education	0.96	0.98	0.96	...	...	* 1.00	0.99	Enseignement primaire
Secondary education	0.75	...	* 0.95	...	...	...	...	Enseignement secondaire
Tertiary education	0.35	...	* 0.60	...	...	...	...	Enseignement supérieur
Kiribati								**Kiribati**
Primary education	1.00	1.03	1.01	...	...	1.04	1.03	Enseignement primaire
Secondary education	1.01	1.24	1.15	...	...	...	...	Enseignement secondaire
Kuwait								**Koweït**
Primary education	1.00	1.04	0.98	1.04	1.02	1.01	...	Enseignement primaire
Secondary education	0.91	0.97	* 1.14	0.94	1.08	* 1.11	1.16	Enseignement secondaire
Tertiary education	1.20	1.82	...	...	1.62	...	...	Enseignement supérieur
Kyrgyzstan								**Kirghizistan**
Primary education	...	1.01	0.99	0.99	0.99	0.99	0.99	Enseignement primaire
Secondary education	...	...	1.00	1.00	1.01	1.01	1.02	Enseignement secondaire
Tertiary education	...	1.25	1.25	1.30	1.29	1.30	1.31	Enseignement supérieur
Lao People's Dem. Rep.								**Rép. dém. populaire lao**
Primary education	0.79	0.81	0.87	0.92	0.95	0.95	0.96	Enseignement primaire
Secondary education	...	0.66	0.75	0.83	0.89	0.91	0.93	Enseignement secondaire
Tertiary education	0.54	0.41	0.70	0.77	0.88	0.93	0.96	Enseignement supérieur
Latvia								**Lettonie**
Primary education	...	0.97	0.96	0.99	0.99	0.99	0.99	Enseignement primaire
Secondary education	...	1.08	1.00	0.98	0.97	0.98	0.99	Enseignement secondaire
Tertiary education	1.46	...	1.79	1.76	1.51	1.43	...	Enseignement supérieur
Lebanon								**Liban**
Primary education	0.92	0.99	* 0.92	0.91	0.91	0.92	0.91	Enseignement primaire
Secondary education	0.94	1.16	* 1.01	1.02	1.01	1.01	0.99	Enseignement secondaire
Tertiary education	0.60	...	1.05	1.04	1.09	1.16	...	Enseignement supérieur
Lesotho								**Lesotho**
Primary education	1.27	1.15	1.01	0.98	0.98	0.98	0.97	Enseignement primaire
Secondary education	1.48	...	1.30	1.42	* 1.36	1.37	1.36	Enseignement secondaire
Tertiary education	1.01	1.35	1.37	...	1.46	1.45	...	Enseignement supérieur
Liberia								**Libéria**
Primary education	...	...	...	...	...	0.92	0.90	Enseignement primaire
Secondary education	...	...	...	...	...	0.78	0.78	Enseignement secondaire
Tertiary education	...	...	...	0.53	...	...	...	Enseignement supérieur
Libya								**Libye**
Primary education	...	...	0.99	...	...	...	...	Enseignement primaire
Secondary education	...	...	* 1.19	...	...	...	...	Enseignement secondaire
Liechtenstein								**Liechtenstein**
Primary education	...	...	...	* 0.94	...	* 0.99	* 0.98	Enseignement primaire
Secondary education	...	...	...	* 0.85	...	* 0.81	* 0.78	Enseignement secondaire
Tertiary education	...	...	...	* 0.62	...	* 0.48	* 0.49	Enseignement supérieur

Region, country or area	1985	1995	2005	2010	2013	2014	2015	Région, pays ou zone
Lithuania								**Lituanie**
Primary education	...	0.97	0.99	0.99	1.00	1.00	1.00	Enseignement primaire
Secondary education	...	1.05	0.99	0.98	0.96	0.96	0.96	Enseignement secondaire
Tertiary education	...	1.44	1.57	1.50	1.47	1.47	...	Enseignement supérieur
Luxembourg								**Luxembourg**
Primary education	...	...	1.00	1.01	1.01	1.00	...	Enseignement primaire
Secondary education	...	1.01	1.05	1.03	1.03	1.02	...	Enseignement secondaire
Tertiary education	0.52	...	...	1.11	...	...	...	Enseignement supérieur
Madagascar								**Madagascar**
Primary education	0.93	1.04	0.96	0.98	0.99	1.00	1.00	Enseignement primaire
Secondary education	...	...	* 0.96	...	...	0.98	...	Enseignement secondaire
Tertiary education	...	0.83	0.89	0.91	* 0.94	0.92	...	Enseignement supérieur
Malawi								**Malawi**
Primary education	0.81	0.90	1.01	1.02	1.02	1.02	1.02	Enseignement primaire
Secondary education	0.49	0.67	0.80	0.90	0.90	0.91	0.90	Enseignement secondaire
Tertiary education	0.29	0.41	* 0.54	0.61	...	...	...	Enseignement supérieur
Malaysia								**Malaisie**
Primary education	0.99	1.00	1.00	1.01	1.00	1.00	1.00	Enseignement primaire
Secondary education	1.01	1.09	1.10	1.07	1.07	1.08	1.08	Enseignement secondaire
Tertiary education	0.82	...	1.32	1.37	1.40	1.47	1.53	Enseignement supérieur
Maldives								**Maldives**
Primary education	...	0.97	0.97	...	...	...	...	Enseignement primaire
Secondary education	...	1.05	...	...	...	...	...	Enseignement secondaire
Tertiary education	...	...	...	...	...	1.63	...	Enseignement supérieur
Mali								**Mali**
Primary education	0.61	0.69	0.80	0.87	...	0.90	0.91	Enseignement primaire
Secondary education	...	0.50	* 0.63	0.70	0.80	0.76	0.81	Enseignement secondaire
Tertiary education	0.15	0.18	...	0.42	...	...	...	Enseignement supérieur
Malta								**Malte**
Primary education	0.94	0.97	0.98	1.01	1.00	1.02	1.02	Enseignement primaire
Secondary education	0.97	0.93	0.96	0.89	1.04	1.05	1.07	Enseignement secondaire
Tertiary education	0.45	0.99	1.35	1.35	1.34	1.31	1.37	Enseignement supérieur
Marshall Islands								**Îles Marshall**
Primary education	...	...	1.26	...	...	...	1.00	Enseignement primaire
Secondary education	...	...	1.00	...	...	...	1.10	Enseignement secondaire
Mauritania								**Mauritanie**
Primary education	0.69	0.84	1.03	1.04	1.05	1.06	1.05	Enseignement primaire
Secondary education	...	0.58	0.88	* 0.85	0.94	0.91	0.93	Enseignement secondaire
Tertiary education	...	0.21	0.34	0.41	0.44	...	0.50	Enseignement supérieur
Mauritius								**Maurice**
Primary education	0.99	1.00	1.00	1.01	1.02	1.02	1.02	Enseignement primaire
Secondary education	0.91	...	* 0.98	* 1.05	* 1.03	1.02	1.05	Enseignement secondaire
Tertiary education	0.60	1.00	* 1.03	1.21	1.22	1.23	1.31	Enseignement supérieur
Mexico								**Mexique**
Primary education	0.97	0.97	0.98	0.99	0.99	1.00	...	Enseignement primaire
Secondary education	0.90	1.01	1.09	1.09	1.07	1.07	...	Enseignement secondaire
Tertiary education	...	0.88	1.02	1.03	1.01	1.01	...	Enseignement supérieur
Micronesia (Fed. States of)								**Micronésie (États féd. de)**
Primary education	...	...	0.97	...	...	0.99	1.00	Enseignement primaire
Secondary education	...	...	1.08	...	...	...	...	Enseignement secondaire
Mongolia								**Mongolie**
Primary education	0.97	1.03	1.00	0.98	0.97	0.98	0.98	Enseignement primaire
Secondary education	...	1.33	1.11	1.07	...	...	1.02	Enseignement secondaire
Tertiary education	...	...	1.65	1.54	1.42	1.44	1.38	Enseignement supérieur
Montenegro								**Monténégro**
Primary education	...	...	1.00	0.98	...	...	0.98	Enseignement primaire
Secondary education	...	...	1.03	1.01	...	...	1.00	Enseignement secondaire
Tertiary education	...	...	1.58	1.26	...	...	...	Enseignement supérieur
Montserrat								**Montserrat**
Primary education	...	...	* 1.04	...	...	...	...	Enseignement primaire
Secondary education	...	...	* 1.10	...	...	...	...	Enseignement secondaire
Morocco								**Maroc**
Primary education	0.64	0.74	0.91	0.94	0.96	0.96	0.95	Enseignement primaire
Secondary education	0.68	0.74	0.85	0.87	...	...	...	Enseignement secondaire
Tertiary education	...	0.71	0.80	0.90	0.95	0.97	0.96	Enseignement supérieur

Region, country or area	1985	1995	2005	2010	2013	2014	2015	Région, pays ou zone
Mozambique								**Mozambique**
Primary education	0.77	0.71	0.84	0.90	* 0.91	* 0.92	* 0.92	Enseignement primaire
Secondary education	0.45	0.61	0.69	0.82	* 0.90	* 0.91	* 0.92	Enseignement secondaire
Tertiary education	0.29	0.30	0.48	0.65	0.67	0.71	0.73	Enseignement supérieur
Myanmar								**Myanmar**
Primary education	0.91	0.94	1.00	0.99	...	0.97	...	Enseignement primaire
Secondary education	...	...	0.97	1.05	...	1.03	...	Enseignement secondaire
Tertiary education	...	1.58	...	...	...	...	...	Enseignement supérieur
Namibia								**Namibie**
Primary education	...	0.99	1.00	0.98	0.97	...	...	Enseignement primaire
Secondary education	...	1.18	1.12	...	...	...	...	Enseignement secondaire
Tertiary education	...	1.55	0.86	...	...	...	...	Enseignement supérieur
Nauru								**Nauru**
Primary education	...	...	* 1.05	...	...	* 0.92	...	Enseignement primaire
Secondary education	...	...	* 1.13	...	...	* 1.02	...	Enseignement secondaire
Nepal								**Népal**
Primary education	0.45	0.69	0.92	1.07	1.08	1.08	1.08	Enseignement primaire
Secondary education	0.31	0.59	* 0.81	* 0.95	* 1.05	* 1.06	* 1.07	Enseignement secondaire
Tertiary education	...	...	0.53	0.61	0.82	...	1.02	Enseignement supérieur
Netherlands								**Pays-Bas**
Primary education	1.03	0.98	0.98	0.99	* 0.99	0.99	0.99	Enseignement primaire
Secondary education	0.97	0.95	0.98	0.99	...	...	1.01	Enseignement secondaire
Tertiary education	0.73	0.93	1.08	1.12	...	...	...	Enseignement supérieur
New Zealand								**Nouvelle-Zélande**
Primary education	0.98	1.00	0.99	1.00	1.00	1.00	1.00	Enseignement primaire
Secondary education	1.02	0.98	1.06	1.05	1.06	1.06	1.06	Enseignement secondaire
Tertiary education	0.88	1.25	1.45	1.46	1.43	1.38	1.35	Enseignement supérieur
Nicaragua								**Nicaragua**
Primary education	1.11	1.04	0.99	0.99	...	...	...	Enseignement primaire
Secondary education	2.09	...	1.16	1.13	...	...	...	Enseignement secondaire
Tertiary education	1.30	1.05	...	...	...	...	...	Enseignement supérieur
Niger								**Niger**
Primary education	0.59	0.63	0.72	0.82	0.84	0.86	0.86	Enseignement primaire
Secondary education	...	...	0.63	0.67	0.68	0.70	0.71	Enseignement secondaire
Tertiary education	0.17	...	0.34	0.37	...	...	...	Enseignement supérieur
Nigeria								**Nigéria**
Primary education	0.81	0.83	0.85	* 0.92	0.98	...	...	Enseignement primaire
Secondary education	...	...	0.84	0.89	0.93	...	...	Enseignement secondaire
Tertiary education	0.36	...	0.72	0.75	...	...	...	Enseignement supérieur
Niue								**Nioué**
Primary education	...	...	* 0.89	...	...	* 0.98	* 0.82	Enseignement primaire
Secondary education	...	...	* 1.63	...	...	* 1.25	* 1.10	Enseignement secondaire
Norway								**Norvège**
Primary education	1.00	1.00	1.00	1.00	1.00	1.00	1.00	Enseignement primaire
Secondary education	1.06	0.95	1.01	0.99	0.97	0.97	0.97	Enseignement secondaire
Tertiary education	1.05	1.25	1.52	1.61	1.50	1.45	1.46	Enseignement supérieur
Oman								**Oman**
Primary education	0.76	0.99	0.98	...	1.05	1.06	1.03	Enseignement primaire
Secondary education	0.46	0.95	0.95	...	1.09	...	1.07	Enseignement secondaire
Tertiary education	0.73	1.20	...	...	...	...	...	Enseignement supérieur
Pakistan								**Pakistan**
Primary education	0.52	...	0.77	0.85	0.87	0.85	0.85	Enseignement primaire
Secondary education	0.36	...	...	0.77	0.73	0.79	0.79	Enseignement secondaire
Tertiary education	...	...	0.87	...	0.98	1.06	0.87	Enseignement supérieur
Palau								**Palaos**
Primary education	...	...	...	...	* 0.98	* 0.96	...	Enseignement primaire
Secondary education	...	...	...	...	* 1.03	* 1.06	...	Enseignement secondaire
Tertiary education	...	...	...	...	* 1.55	...	...	Enseignement supérieur
Panama								**Panama**
Primary education	0.95	...	0.97	0.96	0.97	0.97	...	Enseignement primaire
Secondary education	1.12	...	1.07	1.06	1.06	1.07	...	Enseignement secondaire
Tertiary education	1.40	...	1.64	1.53	1.49	...	...	Enseignement supérieur
Papua New Guinea								**Papouasie-Nvl-Guinée**
Primary education	...	0.87	0.85	...	...	...	...	Enseignement primaire
Secondary education	...	0.68	...	...	...	...	...	Enseignement secondaire
Tertiary education	0.32	0.47	...	...	...	...	...	Enseignement supérieur

Ratio of girls to boys in primary, secondary and tertiary education *(continued)*

Rapport filles/garçons dans l'enseignement primaire, secondaire et supérieur *(suite)*

Region, country or area	1985	1995	2005	2010	2013	2014	2015	Région, pays ou zone
Paraguay								**Paraguay**
Primary education	0.94	0.97	0.97	0.96	...	...	...	Enseignement primaire
Secondary education	...	1.07	1.03	1.06	...	...	...	Enseignement secondaire
Tertiary education	...	...	1.13	1.42	...	...	...	Enseignement supérieur
Peru								**Pérou**
Primary education	0.96	0.97	1.01	1.01	1.00	1.00	1.00	Enseignement primaire
Secondary education	0.90	0.93	0.98	1.00	1.00	1.00	1.00	Enseignement secondaire
Tertiary education	...	...	1.03	1.10	...	...	...	Enseignement supérieur
Philippines								**Philippines**
Primary education	1.00	0.99	0.99	...	1.00	...	...	Enseignement primaire
Secondary education	1.07	...	1.12	...	1.10	...	...	Enseignement secondaire
Tertiary education	...	1.37	1.23	1.25	1.26	1.28	...	Enseignement supérieur
Poland								**Pologne**
Primary education	...	0.99	0.99	0.99	1.00	1.00	...	Enseignement primaire
Secondary education	...	1.00	0.99	0.99	0.96	0.96	...	Enseignement secondaire
Tertiary education	1.30	1.41	1.41	1.51	1.55	1.52	...	Enseignement supérieur
Portugal								**Portugal**
Primary education	0.95	0.95	0.95	0.97	0.96	0.96	0.96	Enseignement primaire
Secondary education	...	1.08	1.10	1.03	0.98	0.98	0.97	Enseignement secondaire
Tertiary education	1.14	1.34	1.31	1.18	1.15	1.16	1.13	Enseignement supérieur
Puerto Rico								**Porto Rico**
Primary education	...	...	...	1.04	1.02	1.01	...	Enseignement primaire
Secondary education	...	...	...	1.06	1.06	1.06	...	Enseignement secondaire
Tertiary education	...	...	...	1.48	1.43	1.41	...	Enseignement supérieur
Qatar								**Qatar**
Primary education	0.98	1.00	0.97	1.01	1.05	1.03	1.01	Enseignement primaire
Secondary education	0.94	0.97	0.94	1.04	...	1.38	1.26	Enseignement secondaire
Tertiary education	3.08	5.60	* 3.52	5.32	5.94	6.36	6.95	Enseignement supérieur
Republic of Korea								**République de Corée**
Primary education	1.01	1.02	0.99	0.99	0.99	0.99	0.99	Enseignement primaire
Secondary education	0.94	1.00	0.98	0.99	0.99	0.99	0.99	Enseignement secondaire
Tertiary education	0.48	0.58	0.66	0.74	0.75	0.76	0.77	Enseignement supérieur
Republic of Moldova								**République de Moldova**
Primary education	...	0.99	* 0.99	* 1.00	* 1.00	* 1.00	* 0.99	Enseignement primaire
Secondary education	...	1.04	* 1.04	* 1.02	* 1.01	* 1.01	* 1.01	Enseignement secondaire
Tertiary education	...	1.15	* 1.46	* 1.34	* 1.29	* 1.32	* 1.34	Enseignement supérieur
Romania								**Roumanie**
Primary education	...	1.00	0.99	0.98	...	...	0.98	Enseignement primaire
Secondary education	...	1.03	1.02	0.99	0.98	0.99	0.99	Enseignement secondaire
Tertiary education	0.81	0.94	1.27	1.37	1.24	1.24	1.23	Enseignement supérieur
Russian Federation								**Fédération de Russie**
Primary education	...	0.99	1.00	...	1.01	1.01	1.01	Enseignement primaire
Secondary education	...	...	0.99	...	0.99	0.98	0.98	Enseignement secondaire
Tertiary education	...	...	1.37	...	1.24	1.21	1.21	Enseignement supérieur
Rwanda								**Rwanda**
Primary education	0.95	...	1.01	1.03	1.02	1.02	1.01	Enseignement primaire
Secondary education	0.78	...	0.89	0.99	1.07	1.10	1.09	Enseignement secondaire
Tertiary education	0.16	...	...	0.78	0.79	0.83	0.78	Enseignement supérieur
Saint Kitts and Nevis								**Saint-Kitts-et-Nevis**
Primary education	0.86	1.01	1.02	1.00	1.03	1.02	1.02	Enseignement primaire
Secondary education	0.97	...	* 1.07	* 0.99	1.18	1.03	1.06	Enseignement secondaire
Tertiary education	2.67	...	...	...	...	1.02	2.04	Enseignement supérieur
Saint Lucia								**Sainte-Lucie**
Primary education	1.00	...	0.96	...	...	...	...	Enseignement primaire
Secondary education	1.64	...	1.18	0.99	1.00	0.99	0.99	Enseignement secondaire
Tertiary education	0.83	...	2.72	2.58	2.00	2.09	1.90	Enseignement supérieur
Saint Vincent & Grenadines								**Saint-Vincent-Grenadines**
Primary education	...	...	0.91	0.93	0.95	0.97	0.98	Enseignement primaire
Secondary education	1.49	...	1.25	1.02	0.96	0.97	0.97	Enseignement secondaire
Samoa								**Samoa**
Primary education	...	1.03	1.01	0.99	...	1.00	1.00	Enseignement primaire
Secondary education	...	1.12	1.13	1.14	...	1.13	1.11	Enseignement secondaire
San Marino								**Saint-Marin**
Primary education	...	...	...	* 1.13	...	...	...	Enseignement primaire
Secondary education	...	...	...	* 1.02	...	...	...	Enseignement secondaire
Tertiary education	...	...	...	* 1.46	...	...	...	Enseignement supérieur

Ratio of girls to boys in primary, secondary and tertiary education *(continued)*

Rapport filles/garçons dans l'enseignement primaire, secondaire et supérieur *(suite)*

Region, country or area	1985	1995	2005	2010	2013	2014	2015	Région, pays ou zone
Sao Tome and Principe								**Sao Tomé-et-Principe**
Primary education	...	...	0.96	0.99	0.97	0.96	0.96	Enseignement primaire
Secondary education	...	...	1.06	1.02	1.10	* 1.10	1.11	Enseignement secondaire
Tertiary education	...	...	...	0.97	...	0.87	1.03	Enseignement supérieur
Saudi Arabia								**Arabie saoudite**
Primary education	...	...	* 0.99	1.00	0.99	0.99	1.03	Enseignement primaire
Secondary education	...	...	* 0.95	...	* 0.81	* 0.76	...	Enseignement secondaire
Tertiary education	0.66	0.96	1.34	1.18	0.95	0.96	0.96	Enseignement supérieur
Senegal								**Sénégal**
Primary education	0.68	0.77	0.96	1.06	1.12	1.09	1.12	Enseignement primaire
Secondary education	0.50	...	0.75	0.87	...	...	0.98	Enseignement secondaire
Tertiary education	* 0.26	...	...	* 0.59	0.59	0.60	0.60	Enseignement supérieur
Serbia								**Serbie**
Primary education	...	...	* 1.01	* 1.00	* 1.00	* 1.00	* 1.00	Enseignement primaire
Secondary education	...	...	* 1.03	* 1.02	* 1.03	* 1.02	* 1.01	Enseignement secondaire
Tertiary education	...	...	* 1.30	* 1.30	* 1.33	* 1.31	* 1.33	Enseignement supérieur
Seychelles								**Seychelles**
Primary education	1.04	1.02	0.98	1.03	1.02	1.01	1.03	Enseignement primaire
Secondary education	1.02	1.00	1.07	* 1.05	1.09	1.05	1.07	Enseignement secondaire
Tertiary education	...	...	...	...	2.18	2.52	2.11	Enseignement supérieur
Sierra Leone								**Sierra Leone**
Primary education	0.67	...	...	...	1.00	...	1.01	Enseignement primaire
Secondary education	0.47	...	...	...	0.85	...	0.86	Enseignement secondaire
Tertiary education	0.30	...	...	...	...	...	...	Enseignement supérieur
Slovakia								**Slovaquie**
Primary education	...	1.00	0.99	0.99	0.98	0.99	0.99	Enseignement primaire
Secondary education	...	1.05	1.01	1.01	1.02	1.01	1.01	Enseignement secondaire
Tertiary education	...	1.00	1.29	1.55	1.54	1.55	...	Enseignement supérieur
Slovenia								**Slovénie**
Primary education	...	1.00	0.98	0.99	1.00	1.00	...	Enseignement primaire
Secondary education	...	1.03	0.99	0.99	1.00	1.00	...	Enseignement secondaire
Tertiary education	1.06	1.34	1.42	1.50	1.45	1.44	...	Enseignement supérieur
Solomon Islands								**Îles Salomon**
Primary education	...	...	0.94	0.97	0.99	0.97	0.99	Enseignement primaire
Secondary education	...	...	0.83	0.86	...	...	...	Enseignement secondaire
Somalia								**Somalie**
Primary education	0.52	...	...	...	...	...	...	Enseignement primaire
Secondary education	0.55	...	...	...	...	...	...	Enseignement secondaire
South Africa								**Afrique du Sud**
Primary education	...	0.98	1.07	1.06	0.96	0.95	...	Enseignement primaire
Secondary education	...	...	1.11	1.15	...	1.27	...	Enseignement secondaire
Tertiary education	...	...	...	...	1.47	1.48	...	Enseignement supérieur
South Sudan								**Soudan du sud**
Primary education	...	...	...	...	...	...	0.71	Enseignement primaire
Secondary education	...	...	...	...	...	...	0.54	Enseignement secondaire
Spain								**Espagne**
Primary education	0.99	0.98	0.99	1.00	1.01	1.01	1.01	Enseignement primaire
Secondary education	1.05	1.09	1.07	1.02	1.00	1.00	1.00	Enseignement secondaire
Tertiary education	0.96	1.16	1.23	1.24	1.20	1.19	1.18	Enseignement supérieur
Sri Lanka								**Sri Lanka**
Primary education	0.96	0.97	0.99	0.98	0.98	0.98	0.98	Enseignement primaire
Secondary education	1.11	1.08	...	1.01	1.05	...	...	Enseignement secondaire
Tertiary education	0.70	...	...	1.79	1.55	1.29	1.54	Enseignement supérieur
State of Palestine								**État de Palestine**
Primary education	...	0.99	0.99	0.98	1.00	0.99	1.00	Enseignement primaire
Secondary education	...	0.96	1.05	1.08	1.10	1.10	1.10	Enseignement secondaire
Tertiary education	...	...	1.01	1.34	1.50	1.55	1.58	Enseignement supérieur
Sudan								**Soudan**
Primary education	...	...	0.88	0.90	0.90	...	...	Enseignement primaire
Secondary education	...	...	0.93	0.87	0.95	...	...	Enseignement secondaire
Tertiary education	...	...	1.13	1.18	1.12	1.06	...	Enseignement supérieur
Suriname								**Suriname**
Primary education	0.98	...	0.98	0.95	0.96	0.97	0.98	Enseignement primaire
Secondary education	...	...	1.29	1.28	1.32	1.33	1.27	Enseignement secondaire
Tertiary education	1.12	...	...	...	...	...	...	Enseignement supérieur

Ratio of girls to boys in primary, secondary and tertiary education *(continued)*

Rapport filles/garçons dans l'enseignement primaire, secondaire et supérieur *(suite)*

Region, country or area	1985	1995	2005	2010	2013	2014	2015	Région, pays ou zone
Swaziland								**Swaziland**
Primary education	0.98	0.97	0.94	0.92	0.92	0.92	…	Enseignement primaire
Secondary education	…	…	1.02	1.00	0.98	0.99	…	Enseignement secondaire
Tertiary education	…	…	1.07	…	1.05	…	…	Enseignement supérieur
Sweden								**Suède**
Primary education	1.01	1.01	1.00	0.99	1.06	1.06	1.04	Enseignement primaire
Secondary education	1.13	1.15	1.00	0.99	1.13	1.14	1.14	Enseignement secondaire
Tertiary education	1.14	1.26	1.54	1.53	1.56	1.54	1.53	Enseignement supérieur
Switzerland								**Suisse**
Primary education	1.01	1.00	1.00	1.00	1.00	1.00	1.00	Enseignement primaire
Secondary education	0.91	0.94	0.94	0.97	0.98	0.97	0.97	Enseignement secondaire
Tertiary education	0.48	0.60	0.87	0.99	1.01	1.02	1.03	Enseignement supérieur
Syrian Arab Republic								**République arabe syrienne**
Primary education	0.86	0.91	0.97	0.97	0.97	…	…	Enseignement primaire
Secondary education	0.66	0.83	0.96	1.00	1.00	…	…	Enseignement secondaire
Tertiary education	0.52	0.72	0.90	0.86	1.01	1.05	1.14	Enseignement supérieur
Tajikistan								**Tadjikistan**
Primary education	…	0.97	0.97	0.97	0.98	1.00	1.00	Enseignement primaire
Secondary education	…	…	0.83	0.87	0.90	…	…	Enseignement secondaire
Tertiary education	…	…	0.48	0.53	0.56	0.61	0.67	Enseignement supérieur
Thailand								**Thaïlande**
Primary education	…	…	0.97	0.98	0.98	1.01	0.94	Enseignement primaire
Secondary education	…	…	* 1.06	1.06	1.07	1.04	0.94	Enseignement secondaire
Tertiary education	…	…	1.14	1.28	1.34	1.33	1.41	Enseignement supérieur
TFYR of Macedonia								**ex-R.Y. de Macédoine**
Primary education	…	0.99	0.98	0.98	0.99	0.98	0.99	Enseignement primaire
Secondary education	…	0.98	0.97	0.97	0.97	0.96	0.97	Enseignement secondaire
Tertiary education	…	1.22	1.38	1.17	1.26	1.26	1.25	Enseignement supérieur
Timor-Leste								**Timor-Leste**
Primary education	…	…	0.92	0.96	0.97	0.99	0.99	Enseignement primaire
Secondary education	…	…	0.97	1.01	1.06	1.08	1.07	Enseignement secondaire
Tertiary education	…	…	…	0.72	…	…	…	Enseignement supérieur
Togo								**Togo**
Primary education	0.62	0.68	0.85	0.90	0.94	0.94	0.95	Enseignement primaire
Secondary education	0.31	0.35	0.53	…	…	…	…	Enseignement secondaire
Tertiary education	…	0.15	…	…	…	0.42	0.43	Enseignement supérieur
Tonga								**Tonga**
Primary education	0.99	0.99	0.97	0.98	1.00	0.99	…	Enseignement primaire
Secondary education	1.10	…	…	1.07	1.03	1.09	…	Enseignement secondaire
Tertiary education	1.42	…	…	…	…	…	…	Enseignement supérieur
Trinidad and Tobago								**Trinité-et-Tobago**
Primary education	1.02	1.00	* 0.97	0.97	…	…	…	Enseignement primaire
Secondary education	1.02	…	…	…	…	…	…	Enseignement secondaire
Tertiary education	0.61	…	…	…	…	…	…	Enseignement supérieur
Tunisia								**Tunisie**
Primary education	0.82	0.92	0.96	0.97	0.97	0.97	0.97	Enseignement primaire
Secondary education	0.68	0.91	1.08	1.07	…	…	…	Enseignement secondaire
Tertiary education	0.59	0.78	1.23	1.53	1.59	1.64	1.65	Enseignement supérieur
Turkey								**Turquie**
Primary education	0.90	0.92	0.95	0.99	0.99	1.00	0.99	Enseignement primaire
Secondary education	…	0.65	0.83	0.92	0.97	0.97	0.97	Enseignement secondaire
Tertiary education	0.46	0.62	0.73	0.81	0.86	0.87	0.87	Enseignement supérieur
Turkmenistan								**Turkménistan**
Primary education	…	…	…	…	…	0.98	…	Enseignement primaire
Secondary education	…	…	…	…	…	0.96	…	Enseignement secondaire
Tertiary education	…	…	…	…	…	0.64	…	Enseignement supérieur
Tuvalu								**Tuvalu**
Primary education	…	…	* 0.96	…	…	* 1.01	* 1.01	Enseignement primaire
Secondary education	…	…	…	…	…	* 1.25	* 1.28	Enseignement secondaire
Uganda								**Ouganda**
Primary education	0.79	0.84	0.99	1.02	1.02	…	…	Enseignement primaire
Secondary education	…	…	…	…	…	…	0.91	Enseignement secondaire
Tertiary education	0.30	0.48	…	0.79	…	0.78	…	Enseignement supérieur

Ratio of girls to boys in primary, secondary and tertiary education *(continued)*

Rapport filles/garçons dans l'enseignement primaire, secondaire et supérieur *(suite)*

Region, country or area	1985	1995	2005	2010	2013	2014	2015	Région, pays ou zone
Ukraine								**Ukraine**
Primary education	...	...	1.00	1.01	1.02	1.02	...	Enseignement primaire
Secondary education	...	...	* 0.93	* 0.98	0.97	0.98	...	Enseignement secondaire
Tertiary education	...	...	1.24	1.26	1.19	1.16	...	Enseignement supérieur
United Arab Emirates								**Émirats arabes unis**
Primary education	0.98	0.98	0.99	1.03	1.02	1.01	0.99	Enseignement primaire
Secondary education	0.96	1.06	...	...	...	...	...	Enseignement secondaire
Tertiary education	2.11	...	...	...	...	...	...	Enseignement supérieur
United Kingdom								**Royaume-Uni**
Primary education	1.00	...	1.00	1.00	1.00	1.00	...	Enseignement primaire
Secondary education	1.03	0.99	1.03	1.00	1.04	1.04	...	Enseignement secondaire
Tertiary education	0.84	1.06	1.39	1.35	1.31	1.31	...	Enseignement supérieur
United Rep. of Tanzania								**Rép.-Unie de Tanzanie**
Primary education	1.00	0.98	0.95	1.01	1.01	1.02	1.03	Enseignement primaire
Secondary education	0.59	0.80	...	0.79	0.91	...	...	Enseignement secondaire
Tertiary education	0.17	0.19	* 0.47	0.78	0.51	...	...	Enseignement supérieur
United States of America								**États-Unis d'Amérique**
Primary education	1.02	0.99	0.99	0.99	0.99	0.99	1.00	Enseignement primaire
Secondary education	1.02	1.03	1.03	1.02	1.01	1.02	...	Enseignement secondaire
Tertiary education	1.14	1.31	1.42	1.41	1.38	1.37	1.37	Enseignement supérieur
Uruguay								**Uruguay**
Primary education	0.99	0.99	0.97	0.97	0.97	0.98	...	Enseignement primaire
Secondary education	...	1.20	1.15	1.14	...	1.11	...	Enseignement secondaire
Tertiary education	...	...	1.74	1.73	...	...	...	Enseignement supérieur
Uzbekistan								**Ouzbékistan**
Primary education	...	0.96	1.00	0.98	0.98	0.98	0.98	Enseignement primaire
Secondary education	...	...	0.97	1.00	0.99	0.98	0.98	Enseignement secondaire
Tertiary education	...	...	0.68	0.67	0.59	0.61	0.62	Enseignement supérieur
Vanuatu								**Vanuatu**
Primary education	...	...	0.97	0.99	0.98	...	0.98	Enseignement primaire
Secondary education	...	...	...	1.00	...	...	1.06	Enseignement secondaire
Venezuela (Boliv. Rep. of)								**Venezuela (Rép. boliv. du)**
Primary education	0.99	...	0.98	0.97	0.98	0.98	0.97	Enseignement primaire
Secondary education	1.26	...	1.13	1.10	1.09	1.08	1.08	Enseignement secondaire
Viet Nam								**Viet Nam**
Primary education	0.95	0.99	0.95	0.95	0.97	0.99	0.99	Enseignement primaire
Tertiary education	...	...	0.71	1.00	0.90	1.05	1.00	Enseignement supérieur
Yemen								**Yémen**
Primary education	...	...	0.74	0.82	0.84	...	...	Enseignement primaire
Secondary education	...	...	0.49	0.62	0.69	...	...	Enseignement secondaire
Tertiary education	...	...	0.36	0.44	...	...	...	Enseignement supérieur
Zambia								**Zambie**
Primary education	0.90	0.92	0.95	1.01	1.01	...	...	Enseignement primaire
Zimbabwe								**Zimbabwe**
Primary education	0.95	0.97	...	...	0.98	...	...	Enseignement primaire
Secondary education	0.68	0.84	...	...	0.98	...	...	Enseignement secondaire
Tertiary education	...	...	...	0.79	0.84	...	0.90	Enseignement supérieur

Source:

United Nations Educational, Scientific and Cultural Organization (UNESCO) Institute for Statistics, Montreal, the UNESCO Institute for Statistics (UIS) statistics database, last accessed June 2017.

1 Excludes Sudan.
2 Includes Sudan.
3 Excludes Japan.
4 Data excludes Armenia, Azerbaijan, Cyprus, Georgia, Israel and Turkey.
5 Caucasus refers to Armenia, Azerbaijan, Cyprus, Georgia, Israel and Turkey.

Source:

L'Institut de statistique de l'Organisation des Nations Unies pour l'éducation, la science et la culture (UNESCO), Montréal, la base de données de l'institut de statistique de l'UNESCO (ISU), dernier accès juin 2017.

1 Exclut le Soudan.
2 Comprend le Soudan.
3 Exclut le Japon.
4 Les données excluent l'Arménie, l'Azerbaïdjan, Chypre, la Géorgie, l'Israël et la Turquie.
5 Le Caucase se rapportent à l'Arménie, l'Azerbaïdjan, Chypre, la Géorgie, l'Israël et la Turquie.

Ratio of girls to boys in primary, secondary and tertiary education *(continued)*

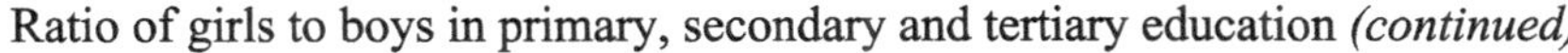

Rapport filles/garçons dans l'enseignement primaire, secondaire et supérieur *(suite)*

6 For statistical purposes, the data for China do not include those for the Hong Kong Special Administrative Region (Hong Kong SAR) and Macao Special Administrative Region (Macao SAR).

6 Pour la présentation des statistiques, les données pour la Chine ne comprennent pas la Région Administrative Spéciale de Hong Kong (Hong Kong RAS) et la Région Administrative Spéciale de Macao (Macao RAS).

7 Enrollment in primary, secondary and tertiary levels

Number of students enrolled (thousands) and gross enrollment ratio by sex

Enseignement primaire, secondaire et supérieur

Nombre d'élèves inscrits (milliers) et taux brut de scolarisation par sexe

Region, country or area Région, pays ou zone	Year & Année &	Primary education Enseignement primaire Total ('000)	Gross enrollment ratio Taux brut de scolarisation M	F	Secondary education Enseignement secondaire Total ('000)	Gross enrollment ratio Taux brut de scolarisation M	F	Tertiary education Enseignement supérieur Total (000)	Gross enrollment ratio Taux brut de scolarisation M	F
Total, all countries or areas	**2005**	**679 010**	**104.6**	**99.7**	**508 649**	**65.5**	**62.0**	**139 271**	**23.7**	**24.8**
Total, tous pays ou zones	**2010**	**697 171**	**106.6**	**103.9**	**545 119**	**72.0**	**69.5**	**181 425**	**28.3**	**30.4**
	2015	**724 094**	**104.5**	**104.1**	**579 207**	**76.9**	**76.0**	**212 670**	**33.8**	**37.7**
Africa	2005	136 433	99.5	89.1	48 941	42.2	35.7	8 622	10.8	8.6
Afrique	2010	159 545	101.3	94.7	62 174	48.4	41.8	11 342	12.4	10.4
	*2015	183 266	102.2	96.5	73 920	50.2	45.2	13 734	13.7	11.8
Northern Africa [1]	2005	19 846	107.1	100.2	* 15 574	* 74.3	* 73.7	4 222	26.2	24.9
Afrique septentrionale [1]	2010	19 609	112.0	107.3	15 697	78.5	77.7	4 989	28.1	30.0
	2015	* 21 235	* 110.3	* 107.5	* 16 451	* 86.8	* 86.3	5 673	33.7	37.4
Sub-Saharan Africa [2]	2005	116 587	98.3	87.4	33 368	35.6	28.2	4 399	7.2	5.0
Afrique subsaharienne [2]	2010	139 937	100.0	93.2	46 477	43.2	35.7	6 353	9.0	6.4
	*2015	162 031	101.3	95.2	57 468	45.0	39.6	8 060	10.2	7.4
North America	2005	52 783	103.9	102.3	43 698	84.7	88.1	22 882	47.8	64.4
Amérique du Nord	2010	53 190	104.9	103.5	45 026	85.6	88.9	27 283	54.6	73.6
	2015	53 100	104.4	103.6	* 46 049	* 89.4	* 92.3	26 770	52.1	67.9
Latin America & the Caribbean	2005	69 074	117.5	114.0	58 892	83.5	90.3	16 129	27.9	33.7
Amérique latine et Caraïbes	2010	67 197	114.1	110.6	61 105	86.2	93.4	21 827	35.4	45.8
	2015	65 581	110.3	108.3	63 090	90.5	95.3	* 25 132	* 40.3	* 53.0
South America	2005	43 072	124.6	120.4	42 233	89.5	97.0	11 813	30.5	37.3
Amérique du Sud	2010	40 572	117.4	112.9	42 888	92.1	100.0	16 336	39.9	53.2
	2015	39 523	111.2	108.9	43 679	96.4	101.2	19 302	47.4	65.1
Asia	2005	* 405 137	* 105.0	* 101.4	305 456	* 62.6	* 57.8	62 579	18.9	16.3
Asie	2010	403 525	108.5	107.3	333 435	71.6	68.8	91 202	24.3	22.5
	2015	405 298	105.2	107.6	354 436	78.5	78.3	121 388	32.6	34.2
Eastern Asia [3]	2005	* 119 129	* 102.7	* 102.3	* 107 731	* 67.5	* 66.7	24 702	23.5	20.2
Asie orientale [3]	2010	106 448	112.6	110.9	106 423	85.7	85.5	35 373	25.8	26.4
	2015	100 645	103.4	103.6	92 378	93.4	95.7	47 710	42.1	48.1
South-eastern Asia	2005	68 322	106.4	103.4	40 744	61.7	61.4	11 145	* 20.7	* 20.7
Asie du Sud-Est	2010	68 466	106.7	107.1	45 500	70.0	70.7	14 451	26.0	27.7
	2015	68 817	109.1	106.6	* 51 251	* 80.0	* 80.2	15 241	25.3	30.2
Southern Asia	2005	* 181 474	* 106.2	* 100.7	120 645	55.3	46.9	16 055	11.8	8.7
Asie méridionale	2010	191 840	107.7	107.2	143 372	62.0	57.4	28 470	19.5	14.9
	2015	197 692	105.0	111.8	170 521	70.1	69.7	41 895	25.5	24.3
Western Asia [4]	2005	22 354	105.7	95.6	17 247	78.3	66.1	4 356	27.1	22.9
Asie occidentale [4]	2010	23 681	105.8	98.1	20 060	78.7	70.1	6 688	35.8	32.7
	2015	* 24 739	* 104.4	* 97.4	* 23 119	* 84.4	* 76.6	10 374	52.6	49.9
Caucasus and Central Asia [5]	2005	5 844	100.2	99.0	10 641	88.8	86.8	1 951	25.8	27.0
Caucase et Asie centrale [5]	2010	5 129	99.4	98.5	10 012	90.9	90.7	1 992	23.4	24.3
	2015	5 806	104.2	103.1	9 162	93.6	93.6	1 895	24.0	25.0
Europe	2005	38 443	102.6	101.9	64 859	97.8	97.3	32 082	55.3	70.9
Europe	2010	36 749	103.4	102.8	58 232	101.5	100.2	33 688	60.1	77.3
	2015	38 561	102.5	102.5	57 631	109.7	109.2	29 726	63.5	77.6
Oceania	2005	3 142	91.9	90.0	3 463	110.2	107.0	1 295	45.6	58.6
Océanie	2010	3 597	101.8	99.1	3 365	102.3	98.2	1 574	48.9	67.1
	2015	4 346	108.2	104.6	* 3 492	* 103.5	* 97.7	* 1 750	* 52.2	* 72.2
Afghanistan	2004	4 430	153.4	66.7	594	30.2	6.3	28	1.9	0.5
Afghanistan	2005	4 319	130.4	76.5	651	29.3	9.6	...	...	...
	2009	4 946	122.3	81.0	1 716	62.4	30.1	95	6.2	1.5
	2010	5 279	124.6	85.3	2 044	70.3	35.1	...	...	...
	2014	6 218	130.7	91.8	2 603	70.7	39.7	263	13.3	3.7
	2015	6 334	131.6	91.1	2 699	70.7	39.7	...	...	...
Albania	2005	238	101.9	101.0	407	78.7	75.0	63	19.1	27.3
Albanie	2010	225	100.2	97.7	356	88.8	88.0	122	37.5	52.4
	2015	188	115.5	111.7	315	98.8	92.5	161	48.7	68.1
Algeria	2005	4 362	111.9	103.4	3 654	75.3	82.5	792	18.3	23.3
Algérie	2010	3 312	119.4	111.3	4 616	95.6	98.9	1 144	24.5	35.3
	2011	3 363	120.8	112.6	4 573	98.1	101.7	1 189	25.5	37.0
	2015	3 925	119.5	112.7	...	...	...	1 289	28.9	45.1

Enrollment in the primary, secondary and tertiary levels *(continued)*
Number of students enrolled (thousands) and gross enrollment ratio by sex

Enseignement primaire, secondaire et supérieur *(suite)*
Nombre d'élèves inscrits (milliers) et taux brut de scolarisation par sexe

Region, country or area Région, pays ou zone	Year & Année &	Primary education Enseignement primaire Total ('000)	Gross enrollment ratio Taux brut de scolarisation M	 F	Secondary education Enseignement secondaire Total ('000)	Gross enrollment ratio Taux brut de scolarisation M	 F	Tertiary education Enseignement supérieur Total (000)	Gross enrollment ratio Taux brut de scolarisation M	 F
American Samoa Samoa américaines	2007	...	...	...	...	...	...	2	...	...
Andorra Andorre	2005	4	...	...	4	...	...	~0	...	...
	2008	4	...	...	4	...	...	~0	...	...
	2010	4	...	...	4	...	...	...	...	...
	2015	4	...	...	4	...	...	1	...	...
Angola Angola	2002	...	...	...	* 462	* 18.4	* 15.2	13	* 1.0	* 0.6
	2005	...	...	...	...	...	...	48	...	...
	2006	...	...	...	...	...	...	49	...	...
	2010	4 273	125.2	101.8	850	34.2	23.4	...	...	...
	2011	5 027	156.9	100.4	885	35.1	22.7	143	10.2	3.8
	2015	...	...	...	...	...	...	221	10.4	8.2
Anguilla Anguilla	2005	1	...	...	1	...	...	~0	...	...
	2008	2	...	...	1	...	...	~0	...	...
	2010	2	...	...	1	...	...	...	...	...
	2011	2	...	...	1	...	...	...	...	...
Antigua and Barbuda Antigua-et-Barbuda	2000	13	...	...	5	* 82.8	* 73.6	...	...	...
	2010	11	107.9	98.8	8	105.7	106.7	1	9.1	22.7
	2012	10	101.3	94.5	8	97.9	112.9	2	15.1	31.1
	2015	10	100.0	94.1	8	101.6	103.8	...	...	...
Argentina Argentine	2005	4 873	117.7	116.6	3 884	89.8	98.4	2 083	52.1	75.8
	2010	4 947	117.5	115.9	4 213	97.1	106.6	2 521	59.1	89.2
	2014	4 780	110.2	109.8	4 451	103.4	110.3	2 869	63.5	102.9
Armenia Arménie	2000	180	98.7	98.3	409	87.0	94.5	93	30.7	38.7
	2005	125	91.0	98.2	370	...	...	115	30.5	46.7
	2009	115	95.8	111.2	313	89.9	105.1	146	39.3	60.7
	2010	102	...	...	306	...	...	146	40.3	63.1
	2015	145	98.5	98.5	240	88.1	89.0	108	41.6	46.9
Aruba Aruba	2005	10	115.0	107.8	7	95.7	96.1	2	25.9	37.3
	2010	10	114.5	113.0	7	93.5	98.3	2	31.1	43.9
	2012	9	102.8	105.4	8	110.3	112.1	3	30.5	45.6
	2014	10	119.1	115.4	...	...	...	1	10.1	23.0
	2015	...	...	...	...	...	...	1	9.4	21.4
Australia Australie	2005	1 935	101.6	103.2	2 497	150.1	146.5	1 025	64.2	80.8
	2010	2 015	105.8	105.6	2 282	134.4	130.3	1 276	68.4	94.5
	2014	2 169	106.4	105.8	2 371	141.3	133.6	1 454	75.4	106.3
	2015	2 141	102.3	102.1	...	...	...	...	...	...
Austria Autriche	2005	363	101.1	100.9	781	102.9	98.0	244	43.5	52.2
	2010	328	100.5	99.1	744	100.8	96.8	350	63.4	74.2
	2015	328	103.7	102.2	691	102.4	97.6	426	74.3	89.2
Azerbaijan Azerbaïdjan	2005	568	* 98.2	* 92.8	...	...	...	...	...	...
	2010	482	* 94.2	* 93.2	...	...	...	181	* 19.4	* 19.2
	2015	551	* 107.4	* 105.6	...	...	...	204	* 23.6	* 27.5
Bahamas Bahamas	2005	37	109.9	108.4	32	89.5	89.1	...	...	...
	2010	34	106.9	108.9	34	90.2	95.1	...	...	...
Bahrain Bahreïn	2005	83	94.1	97.5	72	91.5	101.5	19	13.0	39.9
	2006	90	96.1	101.0	74	92.1	101.1	18	12.2	38.3
	2010	...	...	...	80	92.2	93.5	...	...	...
	2015	108	100.6	101.8	92	102.4	101.9	39	30.9	59.4
Bangladesh Bangladesh	2005	16 219	96.5	100.9	10 109	44.1	47.0	912	8.2	4.2
	2009	* 16 539	* 97.5	* 102.2	10 907	46.7	50.4	1 582	13.1	7.9
	2010	* 16 987	* 99.6	* 105.9	11 334	47.3	53.1	...	...	...
	2014	...	...	...	...	...	...	2 068	15.4	11.4
	2015	19 068	116.0	125.1	14 567	59.8	67.4	...	...	...
Barbados Barbade	2001	24	99.9	98.7	21	103.3	103.7	8	23.1	57.0
	2005	22	96.3	95.9	21	109.1	108.0	...	...	...
	2010	* 23	* 98.9	* 100.6	* 19	* 101.7	* 102.2	13	43.9	95.9
	2011	* 23	* 98.4	* 98.5	20	101.7	105.5	12	40.3	90.6
	2014	21	93.1	94.2	21	107.9	110.7	...	...	...

Enrollment in the primary, secondary and tertiary levels *(continued)*

Number of students enrolled (thousands) and gross enrollment ratio by sex

Enseignement primaire, secondaire et supérieur *(suite)*

Nombre d'élèves inscrits (milliers) et taux brut de scolarisation par sexe

Region, country or area Région, pays ou zone	Year & Année &	Primary education Enseignement primaire			Secondary education Enseignement secondaire			Tertiary education Enseignement supérieur		
			Gross enrollment ratio Taux brut de scolarisation			Gross enrollment ratio Taux brut de scolarisation			Gross enrollment ratio Taux brut de scolarisation	
		Total ('000)	M	F	Total ('000)	M	F	Total (000)	M	F
Belarus Bélarus	2005	380	98.9	95.6	...	...	...	529	56.8	77.8
	2010	358	103.5	103.4	763	108.7	105.3	569	*65.2	*94.4
	2015	387	101.4	101.3	644	107.8	106.4	477	75.9	100.7
Belgium Belgique	2005	739	101.4	101.0	815	110.1	106.5	390	55.2	67.7
	2010	732	103.3	103.2	806	107.3	104.2	445	59.9	75.8
	2015	783	104.2	104.2	1 218	156.4	177.7	505	65.0	85.4
Belize Belize	2005	50	115.8	110.8	29	75.3	77.7	5	12.5	19.7
	2010	53	114.8	110.3	33	72.5	78.2	7	16.8	26.9
	2015	52	115.8	110.4	38	79.8	81.8	9	17.9	28.7
Benin Bénin	2001	1 055	106.3	72.0	*257	*32.1	*14.8	28	*7.3	*1.7
	2004	1 320	116.4	86.7	345	38.9	17.9	41	...	...
	2005	1 318	111.3	85.8	...	...	...	42	...	...
	2010	1 788	123.9	108.6	...	...	...	114	19.6	6.9
	2013	2 064	130.5	118.1	869	65.4	42.9	145	22.4	8.4
	2015	2 238	134.2	123.7	964	66.7	46.8	...	...	...
Bermuda Bermudes	2005	5	96.8	101.5	5	76.0	85.9	...	...	...
	2006	5	93.7	100.7	5	74.4	81.0	1	18.7	41.6
	2010	4	...	...	4	72.3	85.4	1	19.3	40.6
	2015	4	91.3	89.4	4	67.7	75.5	1	14.7	34.1
Bhutan Bhoutan	2005	99	95.7	93.4	42	48.5	43.0	4	5.6	3.7
	2010	110	108.2	110.7	60	65.6	66.7	5	8.6	5.3
	2013	104	104.3	105.4	69	74.6	79.9	9	12.6	9.2
	2014	102	101.4	102.9	74	81.4	87.1	...	...	...
	2016	97	96.6	96.9	...	...	...	...	...	...
Bolivia (Plurin. State of) Bolivie (État plurin. de)	2004	1 504	116.2	114.9	1 010	88.8	82.7	*346	...	...
	2005	1 513	115.5	114.4	1 038	89.6	84.3	...	...	...
	2007	1 512	113.2	112.1	1 052	87.7	84.4	*353	*41.8	*34.9
	2010	1 429	105.7	103.6	1 058	83.6	82.6	...	...	...
	2015	1 344	98.5	95.7	1 153	87.1	85.7	...	...	...
Bosnia and Herzegovina Bosnie-Herzégovine	2005	...	...	...	...	...	...	84	...	...
	2010	175	...	...	323	...	...	105	...	...
	2015	163	...	...	278	...	...	108	...	...
Botswana Botswana	2005	329	107.9	106.5	173	77.3	79.7	20	9.7	8.6
	2006	330	108.7	106.5	177	78.4	82.7	22	11.0	9.0
	2008	327	107.8	105.1	168	73.5	80.3	31	...	...
	2009	331	109.3	105.7	...	...	...	48	...	...
	2010	...	...	...	...	...	...	42	...	...
	2014	341	109.4	105.8	...	...	...	55	22.3	27.8
	2016	...	...	...	...	...	...	52	19.2	27.7
Brazil Brésil	2005	18 661	*137.2	*129.2	24 863	*96.5	*106.2	4 572	*22.8	*29.3
	2009	17 452	*133.9	*128.2	23 617	*91.5	*102.1	6 115	*31.9	*42.2
	2010	16 893	...	...	23 539	...	...	6 553	...	...
	2015	17 036	*116.8	*113.8	23 502	*97.2	*102.2	8 285	*42.4	*59.3
British Virgin Islands Îles Vierges britanniques	2004	3	...	...	2	...	...	1	...	...
	2005	3	...	...	2	...	...	...	...	...
	2009	3	...	...	2	...	...	1	...	...
	2010	3	...	...	2	...	...	...	...	...
	2015	3	...	...	2	...	...	1	...	...
Brunei Darussalam Brunéi Darussalam	2005	46	113.1	111.0	44	97.2	98.0	5	9.9	19.7
	2010	44	107.3	106.9	49	98.9	99.7	6	11.1	20.6
	2015	40	108.1	108.2	47	95.9	96.3	11	23.5	38.6
Bulgaria Bulgarie	2005	290	101.8	100.6	686	92.4	88.4	238	41.1	47.6
	2010	260	103.6	103.7	532	92.4	88.3	287	50.1	66.4
	2015	262	97.7	96.7	501	100.5	97.4	279	65.4	82.9
Burkina Faso Burkina Faso	2005	1 271	64.7	51.8	295	16.7	11.8	28	3.2	1.4
	2010	2 048	81.6	73.9	538	24.8	18.9	51	4.8	2.3
	2015	2 707	89.9	86.1	966	35.1	32.2	...	...	...
	2016	...	...	...	...	...	...	95	7.3	3.8

Enrollment in the primary, secondary and tertiary levels *(continued)*

Number of students enrolled (thousands) and gross enrollment ratio by sex

Enseignement primaire, secondaire et supérieur *(suite)*

Nombre d'élèves inscrits (milliers) et taux brut de scolarisation par sexe

Region, country or area Région, pays ou zone	Year & Année &	Primary education Enseignement primaire Total ('000)	Gross enrollment ratio Taux brut de scolarisation M	F	Secondary education Enseignement secondaire Total ('000)	Gross enrollment ratio Taux brut de scolarisation M	F	Tertiary education Enseignement supérieur Total (000)	Gross enrollment ratio Taux brut de scolarisation M	F
Burundi Burundi	2005	1 037	85.8	72.4	* 171	* 14.8	* 10.7	17	* 3.4	* 1.3
	2010	1 850	133.7	129.2	338	27.2	18.7	29	4.2	2.2
	2014	2 047	126.8	128.4	583	41.1	34.8	51	7.7	2.4
	2015	2 072	123.1	124.5	664	44.5	40.5	...	...	...
Cabo Verde Cabo Verde	2005	83	112.4	108.0	53	64.5	73.0	4	7.2	7.7
	2010	71	114.7	108.6	62	79.5	93.4	10	15.3	19.4
	2015	66	112.8	106.9	59	87.7	98.3	13	18.1	25.2
Cambodia Cambodge	2004	2 763	136.8	125.9	* 630	* 36.6	* 25.6	45	3.9	1.7
	2005	2 695	135.1	125.6	...	...	...	57	4.6	2.1
	2008	2 341	127.2	119.3	* 930	* 48.5	* 41.4	137	12.0	6.2
	2010	2 273	126.9	119.8	...	...	...	195	17.6	10.5
	2015	2 179	117.1	116.2	...	...	...	217	14.3	11.8
Cameroon Cameroun	2005	2 978	* 109.2	* 91.4	784	29.8	23.5	* 100	* 7.0	* 4.6
	2009	3 351	111.3	96.3	1 269	43.2	36.0	174	10.0	7.9
	2010	3 510	113.9	98.4	...	...	...	220	12.2	9.9
	2015	4 370	123.5	110.7	2 108	62.6	53.5	390	19.7	15.2
Canada Canada	2000	2 456	100.3	100.4	2 519	100.6	102.5	1 212	50.5	67.7
	2005	2 321	97.5	96.6	2 602	102.2	99.9	...	...	...
	2010	2 168	98.5	98.9	2 612	103.6	101.1	...	...	...
	2013	2 206	100.1	101.1	2 698	109.8	110.0	...	...	...
Cayman Islands Îles Caïmanes	2003	...	...	...	...	...	...	1	...	...
	2005	3	...	...	3	...	...	...	...	...
	2008	4	...	...	3	...	...	1	...	...
	2013	4	...	...	3	...	...	...	...	...
Central African Republic République centrafricaine	2000	...	...	...	...	...	...	6	3.2	0.6
	*2001	459	92.7	63.3	70	15.6	8.1	...	...	...
	*2002	411	82.4	55.1	72	...	...	...	...	...
	2004	363	70.4	46.7	...	...	...	6	...	...
	2005	412	77.1	53.1	...	...	...	...	...	...
	2009	608	104.1	73.8	93	17.7	9.8	10	3.4	1.5
	2010	637	107.4	76.4	...	...	...	11	3.9	1.2
	2012	662	107.3	79.8	126	23.0	11.8	13	4.1	1.5
Chad Tchad	2005	1 262	85.6	58.0	* 245	* 23.2	* 8.1	12	2.7	0.2
	2010	1 727	95.1	69.9	430	31.8	13.4	* 22	* 3.6	* 0.6
	2012	2 091	106.6	81.2	458	30.7	14.0	...	...	...
	2013	2 331	114.6	88.0	...	...	...	...	...	...
	*2014	...	...	...	...	...	...	42	5.7	1.1
Chile Chili	2005	1 721	112.3	106.6	1 630	97.5	97.8	664	51.3	48.6
	2010	1 547	104.9	101.6	1 518	93.2	96.0	988	67.1	72.3
	2015	1 478	103.3	100.0	1 546	100.0	101.3	1 222	83.0	94.4
China Chine	2003	121 662	113.7	113.2	95 625	63.7	60.7	15 186	17.1	14.1
	2005	...	...	...	...	...	...	20 601	20.3	18.3
	2010	101 019	113.3	111.6	99 218	85.0	84.8	31 047	23.1	24.8
	2015	95 958	104.0	104.3	86 127	93.2	95.6	43 367	39.9	47.3
China, Hong Kong SAR Chine, Hong Kong RAS	2005	451	...	...	498	80.5	80.3	152	32.7	31.9
	2010	349	...	...	508	88.4	87.6	265	* 58.9	* 58.1
	2015	333	...	...	394	102.8	98.8	299	63.5	73.7
China, Macao SAR Chine, Macao RAS	2005	37	107.5	101.4	47	103.8	106.7	23	79.0	50.4
	2010	25	95.3	93.3	38	94.2	93.3	29	62.7	60.9
	2015	24	101.1	99.7	30	97.0	95.9	31	65.2	86.3
Colombia Colombie	2005	5 298	128.7	126.2	4 297	79.3	87.7	1 224	28.0	30.4
	2010	5 085	125.4	123.1	5 080	97.3	106.9	1 674	37.6	41.3
	2015	4 479	115.4	111.6	4 794	94.8	101.5	2 294	51.5	59.9
Comoros Comores	2003	104	120.0	98.8	38	42.8	35.9	2	3.4	2.6
	2004	104	113.7	100.9	43	49.1	37.5	...	...	...
	2008	111	111.6	102.8	...	...	...	...	...	...
	2010	...	...	...	...	...	...	4	6.5	4.9
	2014	120	106.8	99.5	70	58.4	62.4	6	9.8	8.0

Enrollment in the primary, secondary and tertiary levels *(continued)*

Number of students enrolled (thousands) and gross enrollment ratio by sex

Enseignement primaire, secondaire et supérieur *(suite)*

Nombre d'élèves inscrits (milliers) et taux brut de scolarisation par sexe

Region, country or area Région, pays ou zone	Year & Année &	Primary education Enseignement primaire Total ('000)	Gross enrollment ratio Taux brut de scolarisation M	F	Secondary education Enseignement secondaire Total ('000)	Gross enrollment ratio Taux brut de scolarisation M	F	Tertiary education Enseignement supérieur Total (000)	Gross enrollment ratio Taux brut de scolarisation M	F
Congo Congo	2003	510	103.9	97.6	204	47.9	32.9	* 12	* 5.5	* 2.2
	2004	584	116.2	108.9	* 235	* 49.7	* 42.0	...	...	...
	2005	597	115.9	107.8	...	...	...	...	...	...
	2009	672	115.0	107.1	...	...	...	23	10.8	2.3
	2010	705	116.3	109.8	...	...	...	...	...	...
	2012	734	107.0	114.8	339	58.4	50.6	39	12.8	8.0
	2013	...	...	...	...	...	...	37	11.1	8.3
Cook Islands Îles Cook	2005	2	* 110.2	* 113.0	2	* 75.1	* 84.9	...	...	...
	2010	2	* 104.6	* 103.6	2	* 80.7	* 88.1	...	...	...
	2012	2	* 110.4	* 105.3	2	* 92.6	* 99.1	1	* 40.1	* 49.5
	2015	2	* 106.0	* 99.3	2	* 83.0	* 90.1	...	...	...
Costa Rica Costa Rica	2004	558	116.7	114.0	340	80.8	84.3	109	24.5	30.2
	2005	542	114.4	111.5	347	82.6	86.2	...	...	...
	2010	521	118.1	115.8	414	100.1	104.3	...	...	...
	2015	473	110.1	109.5	460	120.7	125.6	218	46.6	60.9
Côte d'Ivoire Côte d'Ivoire	*2003	2 046	80.4	64.4	...	...	...	...	...	...
	2009	2 383	80.3	65.6	...	...	...	* 153	* 11.5	* 6.1
	2010	...	...	...	...	...	...	144	10.6	5.5
	2015	3 371	99.2	88.0	1 587	51.0	36.6	193	11.0	7.3
Croatia Croatie	2005	196	103.3	103.3	400	91.6	94.7	135	40.5	49.2
	2010	167	91.7	91.9	389	97.3	104.2	150	46.8	62.8
	2015	162	97.8	98.1	360	95.9	100.6	162	58.8	79.8
Cuba Cuba	2005	895	100.1	97.5	937	91.8	93.6	472	* 46.8	* 79.6
	2010	853	103.0	101.8	809	91.3	92.5	801	73.5	122.1
	2015	746	100.1	94.9	825	98.2	102.7	261	30.1	43.0
Curaçao Curaçao	2013	21	179.1	171.3	11	86.1	90.6	2	12.2	28.4
Cyprus Chypre	2005	61	* 100.9	* 100.8	64	* 95.7	* 97.5	20	* 31.2	* 35.3
	2010	55	* 101.6	* 101.6	64	* 90.9	* 92.0	32	* 50.9	* 45.6
	2015	54	* 99.3	* 99.3	57	* 100.1	* 99.4	37	* 51.1	* 69.4
Czechia Tchéquie	2005	503	100.1	98.7	975	95.0	96.7	336	44.9	52.1
	2010	463	104.2	103.8	837	94.6	95.1	437	53.7	75.0
	2015	535	99.6	99.9	770	105.1	106.1	396	54.2	76.3
Dem. People's Rep. Korea Rép. pop. dém. de Corée	2009	1 547	99.8	99.8	2 474	102.1	102.0	593	40.8	20.6
	2015	1 358	76.7	76.9	2 148	92.9	93.9	565	36.0	19.8
Dem. Rep. of the Congo Rép. dém. du Congo	2002	5 455	71.6	56.5	...	...	...	...	...	...
	2009	10 244	103.4	88.7	3 399	50.7	28.5	378	9.9	3.1
	2010	10 572	102.3	89.1	3 484	49.9	28.8	...	...	...
	2013	12 601	107.9	97.8	3 996	50.6	31.4	443	9.1	4.2
	2014	13 535	112.0	101.8	4 388	53.6	33.3	...	...	...
Denmark Danemark	2005	414	98.9	98.7	465	122.0	126.5	232	67.7	93.4
	2010	403	99.5	99.7	504	119.0	120.1	241	60.4	87.5
	2015	469	102.3	100.7	553	128.3	133.4	314	69.7	96.3
Djibouti Djibouti	2005	51	47.6	39.2	30	26.9	18.0	2	2.7	2.0
	2009	56	62.8	56.6	44	38.5	28.4	3	4.0	2.8
	2010	...	...	...	...	...	...	3	4.1	2.8
	2011	61	68.6	62.4	51	43.6	35.0	5	5.9	4.0
	2016	62	68.6	60.9	61	52.9	43.5	...	...	...
Dominica Dominique	2005	9	99.4	99.4	7	103.3	111.7	...	...	...
	2010	8	110.0	107.6	7	92.8	101.4	...	...	...
	2015	8	117.2	114.8	6	101.2	99.8	...	...	...
Dominican Republic République dominicaine	2003	1 375	* 112.4	* 113.4	...	...	...	287	25.9	40.7
	2005	1 290	108.6	103.3	808	63.6	76.0	...	...	...
	2010	1 318	114.1	100.5	905	71.5	80.6	...	...	...
	2015	1 307	108.1	98.7	929	74.1	81.7	480	35.4	65.0
Ecuador Équateur	2005	1 998	112.0	111.5	1 053	61.5	62.2	...	...	...
	2008	...	...	...	...	...	...	535	36.0	41.5
	2010	2 099	115.7	116.0	1 571	86.6	91.0	...	...	...
	2012	2 128	117.5	117.6	1 750	95.7	99.8	573	34.6	45.3
	2013	2 089	114.8	115.4	1 823	99.1	103.7	586	...	...
	2016	1 998	107.4	107.9	1 932	105.3	109.2	...	...	...

Enrollment in the primary, secondary and tertiary levels *(continued)*
Number of students enrolled (thousands) and gross enrollment ratio by sex

Enseignement primaire, secondaire et supérieur *(suite)*
Nombre d'élèves inscrits (milliers) et taux brut de scolarisation par sexe

Region, country or area Région, pays ou zone	Year & Année &	Primary education Enseignement primaire Total ('000)	Gross enrollment ratio Taux brut de scolarisation M	F	Secondary education Enseignement secondaire Total ('000)	Gross enrollment ratio Taux brut de scolarisation M	F	Tertiary education Enseignement supérieur Total (000)	Gross enrollment ratio Taux brut de scolarisation M	F
Egypt Égypte	2004	* 7 928	* 101.3	* 98.0	* 8 330	* 82.9	* 78.6	2 261	31.5	25.5
	2005	9 564	102.9	97.5	...	...	...	2 352	32.2	27.1
	2010	10 542	108.6	105.5	6 846	72.5	70.5	2 646	32.2	29.5
	2014	11 128	104.1	103.8	8 208	86.3	85.9	2 544	33.4	29.9
	2015	...	...	...	...	...	...	2 869	36.9	35.6
El Salvador El Salvador	2005	1 045	125.4	121.2	524	68.5	68.5	122	21.7	24.3
	2010	940	123.6	118.0	577	72.3	71.8	150	25.0	27.6
	2015	741	111.4	106.8	600	79.2	79.7	179	27.7	30.5
Equatorial Guinea Guinée équatoriale	2000	73	115.3	94.5	21	42.4	18.7	1	4.4	2.0
	2005	76	98.3	94.0	26	31.8	22.9	...	...	...
	2010	85	82.6	80.6	...	...	...	...	...	...
	2015	93	80.0	78.2	...	...	...	...	...	...
Eritrea Érythrée	2004	375	77.3	62.9	194	32.6	18.7	5	1.8	0.3
	2005	378	77.5	63.6	217	35.4	21.4	...	...	...
	2010	286	52.6	45.1	248	38.4	29.7	12	3.4	1.3
	2014	362	55.1	47.1	270	38.1	31.3	13	3.4	1.7
	2015	362	53.2	45.9	246	32.9	28.1	...	...	...
Estonia Estonie	2005	86	100.2	97.6	124	101.0	104.7	68	50.9	85.8
	2010	73	103.8	102.2	95	105.3	105.3	69	51.6	85.8
	2015	80	98.3	98.5	78	115.6	114.7	55	55.4	84.8
Ethiopia Éthiopie	2005	10 020	86.1	71.9	2 488	30.8	18.6	191	4.2	1.3
	2010	13 635	95.6	88.3	4 207	38.0	31.6	578	10.2	4.4
	2014	15 733	104.3	95.8	...	...	...	757	10.9	5.3
	2015	16 198	106.9	97.2	5 029	35.9	34.4	...	...	...
Fiji Fidji	2004	113	113.4	111.8	102	88.0	93.9	13	14.6	17.4
	*2005	...	...	...	...	...	...	13	14.7	17.6
	2009	101	105.9	104.3	98	83.1	90.9	...	...	...
	2012	103	104.5	105.4	97	84.3	93.4	...	...	...
	2015	109	106.0	105.1	...	...	...	...	...	...
Finland Finlande	2005	382	98.9	98.2	431	109.5	114.5	306	83.4	100.6
	2010	347	99.5	98.8	427	104.9	109.8	304	85.0	103.7
	2015	355	101.7	101.4	540	142.8	156.3	302	79.3	95.6
France France	2005	4 015	109.5	108.2	6 036	112.2	112.4	2 187	49.1	62.0
	2010	4 159	108.9	107.6	5 873	111.0	111.7	2 245	50.6	63.9
	2014	4 189	105.7	105.0	5 947	110.1	111.2	2 389	57.9	71.0
Gabon Gabon	2002	282	142.8	142.1	* 105	...	...	...	...	...
	2003	280	139.3	138.7	...	...	...	10	10.6	6.2
	2011	318	144.0	139.9	...	...	...	...	...	...
Gambia Gambie	2004	205	93.3	94.0	...	...	...	2	1.9	0.4
	2005	205	89.3	92.1	...	...	...	...	...	...
	2010	229	83.2	85.6	* 124	* 58.9	* 56.0	3	2.6	1.8
	2012	244	82.2	85.9	...	...	...	5	3.7	2.5
	2016	309	90.1	96.8	...	...	...	...	...	...
Georgia Géorgie	2005	338	96.5	93.6	316	83.0	80.3	174	45.9	47.2
	2008	311	110.6	109.6	305	92.8	88.5	130	* 31.1	* 37.5
	2009	299	110.5	110.5	342	...	...	95	22.8	28.4
	2010	289	109.3	110.7	...	...	...	106	25.6	32.3
	2015	289	115.5	118.2	278	103.6	103.8	128	39.2	47.8
Germany Allemagne	2005	3 306	104.7	104.7	8 268	103.8	101.1	...	...	...
	2010	3 068	103.8	103.6	7 664	106.6	101.2	...	...	...
	2015	2 879	105.2	104.7	7 113	105.6	99.6	2 978	69.7	66.8
Ghana Ghana	2005	2 930	92.1	88.6	* 1 370	* 44.9	* 37.2	120	7.7	4.1
	2009	3 659	106.5	104.5	1 812	53.0	46.5	203	11.4	6.7
	2015	4 342	109.9	109.9	2 440	63.0	59.8	418	19.1	13.2
	2016	4 358	107.3	108.7	2 512	63.1	61.1	...	...	...
Gibraltar Gibraltar	2001	2	...	...	2	...	...	...	...	...
	2009	3	...	...	2	...	...	...	...	...
Greece Grèce	2005	650	100.3	97.8	716	101.7	97.4	647	81.9	92.7
	2010	643	101.2	99.3	717	108.3	101.5	642	100.6	104.9
	2014	629	98.1	97.1	668	109.5	103.4	677	114.0	113.7

7

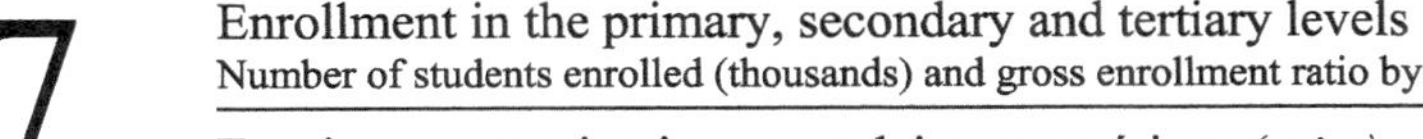

Enrollment in the primary, secondary and tertiary levels *(continued)*
Number of students enrolled (thousands) and gross enrollment ratio by sex

Enseignement primaire, secondaire et supérieur *(suite)*
Nombre d'élèves inscrits (milliers) et taux brut de scolarisation par sexe

Region, country or area Région, pays ou zone	Year & Année &	Primary education Enseignement primaire			Secondary education Enseignement secondaire			Tertiary education Enseignement supérieur		
			Gross enrollment ratio Taux brut de scolarisation			Gross enrollment ratio Taux brut de scolarisation			Gross enrollment ratio Taux brut de scolarisation	
		Total ('000)	M	F	Total ('000)	M	F	Total (000)	M	F
Grenada Grenade	2005	14	98.4	95.5	* 13	* 96.9	* 98.7	...	...	...
	2009	14	107.6	101.5	11	100.7	100.8	7	44.8	60.9
	2010	14	105.1	101.5	12	106.2	109.4	...	...	...
	2015	13	106.8	102.9	9	99.4	99.0	9	84.5	97.9
Guatemala Guatemala	2002	2 076	109.7	100.5	608	45.2	40.4	112	10.2	7.5
	2005	2 345	115.4	107.5	754	51.9	47.6	...	...	...
	2007	2 449	115.6	109.2	864	55.9	52.3	234	16.7	17.1
	2010	2 653	118.7	115.2	1 082	65.2	61.0	...	...	...
	2015	2 382	103.8	99.8	1 221	67.9	63.3	367	20.2	23.5
Guinea Guinée	2005	1 207	87.8	70.4	* 420	* 38.9	* 19.4	24	4.7	1.1
	2008	1 364	90.9	76.2	531	43.1	24.9	80	13.4	4.4
	2010	1 453	92.6	76.4	...	...	...	99	15.4	5.1
	2014	1 730	98.6	83.8	716	46.8	30.7	118	14.9	6.7
Guinea-Bissau Guinée-Bissau	2000	150	86.1	57.6	26	22.3	12.1	...	...	...
	2005	252	...	...	51	...	...	3	...	...
	2006	269	...	...	55	...	...	4	...	...
	2010	279	117.5	109.8	...	...	...	...	...	...
Guyana Guyana	2005	117	102.6	96.1	71	99.3	94.5	7	8.5	17.2
	2010	99	87.0	83.7	81	88.7	88.6	8	7.5	18.9
	2012	94	86.9	83.9	86	89.7	89.0	9	8.2	16.8
Honduras Honduras	2004	1 257	115.0	114.2	...	...	...	* 123	* 14.1	* 20.0
	2005	1 232	111.8	111.4	...	...	...	...	...	...
	2010	1 275	116.8	116.3	655	65.5	80.0	170	19.3	22.0
	2015	1 154	111.3	110.1	638	64.8	77.0	195	18.8	25.4
Hungary Hongrie	2005	431	99.1	97.1	960	96.7	95.7	436	53.1	77.6
	2010	388	102.6	101.6	905	100.7	99.1	389	51.4	69.7
	2015	396	101.9	101.3	827	105.1	105.3	308	45.3	56.7
Iceland Islande	2005	31	99.1	96.7	33	108.0	110.3	15	48.6	92.9
	2010	30	98.4	99.0	36	108.3	110.4	18	56.2	101.3
	2013	30	99.7	98.6	38	116.3	121.0	19	60.2	103.1
India Inde	2003	125 569	104.3	101.5	81 050	55.0	44.2	11 295	12.6	8.5
	2005	...	...	...	89 462	* 59.2	* 48.7	11 777	12.5	8.8
	2010	138 414	* 108.1	* 110.4	107 687	65.5	60.9	20 741	20.6	15.0
	2015	138 518	102.8	115.1	129 542	73.5	74.5	32 107	27.0	26.7
Indonesia Indonésie	2004	29 142	109.6	108.0	16 354	62.1	61.6	3 551	18.5	14.7
	2005	29 150	* 109.4	* 106.1	15 993	* 60.4	* 59.8	* 3 662	...	...
	2010	30 342	106.9	110.5	19 976	76.3	76.8	5 001	25.8	22.6
	2015	29 700	107.2	104.4	23 756	85.7	86.0	5 108	22.9	25.7
Iran (Islamic Republic of) Iran (Rép. islamique d')	2005	6 207	101.3	98.8	9 066	77.2	74.4	2 126	22.2	23.5
	2010	5 630	106.2	105.3	7 347	82.7	81.1	3 791	42.9	42.3
	2015	7 670	106.3	111.7	5 712	89.4	88.9	4 803	75.9	67.7
Iraq Iraq	2004	4 335	113.1	95.2	1 706	56.5	38.2	413	19.8	11.8
	*2005	...	...	...	...	...	...	425	20.0	11.9
	2007	4 864	117.0	98.7	2 038	60.9	45.6	...	...	...
Ireland Irlande	2005	454	107.0	106.3	317	104.6	114.7	187	48.0	60.7
	2010	506	106.6	107.0	336	120.8	126.2	194	59.6	66.5
	2015	545	100.9	102.0	355	125.6	129.4	215	80.1	87.6
Israel Israël	2005	722	103.3	103.8	673	105.0	104.4	311	50.1	66.4
	2009	786	102.6	103.2	694	100.9	103.1	343	54.5	70.7
	2010	807	104.0	104.5	708	100.9	103.3	360	...	...
	2015	884	104.4	105.1	785	102.0	103.0	374	54.6	75.5
Italy Italie	2005	2 771	102.0	100.9	4 507	98.6	97.9	2 015	54.3	74.3
	2010	2 822	102.7	101.6	4 626	102.9	101.5	1 980	54.8	78.1
	2015	2 856	101.4	100.6	4 606	104.1	101.7	1 826	53.2	72.2
Jamaica Jamaïque	2002	330	97.1	96.9	228	84.1	86.9	45	12.0	26.0
	2004	331	97.1	97.4	246	88.9	92.9	52	...	...
	2005	326	...	...	246	87.9	93.4	48	...	...
	2010	294	...	...	260	89.2	96.6	71	16.6	38.3
	2015	258	...	...	215	79.2	85.1	75	20.1	34.6

Enrollment in the primary, secondary and tertiary levels *(continued)*

Number of students enrolled (thousands) and gross enrollment ratio by sex

Enseignement primaire, secondaire et supérieur *(suite)*

Nombre d'élèves inscrits (milliers) et taux brut de scolarisation par sexe

Region, country or area / Région, pays ou zone	Year & / Année &	Primary education / Enseignement primaire: Total ('000)	Gross enrollment ratio Taux brut de scolarisation: M	F	Secondary education / Enseignement secondaire: Total ('000)	Gross enrollment ratio Taux brut de scolarisation: M	F	Tertiary education / Enseignement supérieur: Total (000)	Gross enrollment ratio Taux brut de scolarisation: M	F
Japan	2005	7 232	101.9	101.9	7 710	100.9	101.1	4 038	58.1	51.7
Japon	2010	7 099	102.2	102.2	7 296	101.5	101.7	3 836	61.3	54.7
	2014	6 715	101.3	101.2	7 227	101.6	101.9	3 862	65.7	60.9
Jordan	2005	805	104.8	106.3	626	89.7	92.4	218	37.3	40.6
Jordanie	2010	820	91.1	90.9	710	86.1	91.1	247	37.7	43.5
	2014	980	97.1	97.6	749	80.2	84.8	...	...	...
	2015	...	...	...	...	...	...	313	42.5	47.3
Kazakhstan	2000	1 208	96.1	96.7	1 994	91.5	95.4	418	29.4	34.1
Kazakhstan	2005	1 024	101.8	101.7	...	...	...	...	...	...
	2010	958	107.3	107.9	1 818	97.5	98.0	757	40.5	51.5
	2016	1 274	108.8	109.1	1 713	110.6	113.5	624	41.4	51.3
Kenya	2005	6 076	109.8	105.5	* 2 468	* 49.0	* 46.8	* 114	* 3.7	* 2.2
Kenya	2009	7 150	114.5	112.0	3 204	63.5	57.4	168	4.8	3.3
	2015	8 169	109.3	108.7	...	...	...	...	...	...
Kiribati	2005	16	111.2	112.8	12	83.1	95.3	...	...	...
Kiribati	2008	16	108.4	113.1	12	82.9	91.6	...	...	...
	2009	16	108.0	113.8	...	...	...	...	...	...
	2015	16	102.9	106.1	...	...	...	...	...	...
Kuwait	2004	158	109.2	108.7	267	99.4	111.3	* 37	* 13.6	* 28.1
Koweït	2005	203	109.8	107.6	* 244	* 103.4	* 118.3	...	...	...
	2010	214	100.9	104.9	264	96.5	90.6	...	...	...
	2013	239	103.1	105.3	279	89.2	96.2	72	20.4	33.1
	2014	253	102.4	103.0	* 283	* 88.9	* 98.9	...	...	...
	2015	263	...	...	287	88.2	102.7	...	...	...
Kyrgyzstan	2005	434	98.4	97.0	721	86.2	86.3	220	37.7	47.1
Kirghizistan	2010	391	98.4	97.5	694	86.7	86.5	261	36.6	47.5
	2015	451	107.9	106.8	643	91.4	92.8	265	40.8	53.3
Lao People's Dem. Rep.	2005	891	119.1	104.1	394	49.6	37.4	47	9.2	6.5
Rép. dém. populaire lao	2010	916	127.8	117.9	435	50.4	41.7	118	18.5	14.2
	2015	850	113.5	109.1	640	64.1	59.3	130	17.3	16.5
Latvia	2005	84	95.5	91.7	272	103.9	104.2	131	56.9	101.7
Lettonie	2010	114	106.2	105.4	147	99.2	97.5	113	51.4	90.3
	2014	115	100.8	100.0	122	116.6	114.0	90	55.5	79.2
	2015	117	100.1	99.2	118	119.9	119.1	86	...	...
Lebanon	2005	* 476	* 107.8	* 99.0	* 378	* 80.2	* 80.8	166	43.0	45.2
Liban	2010	462	109.6	100.0	383	74.5	76.1	202	47.4	49.3
	2014	481	98.3	90.0	370	61.5	61.8	229	39.5	45.7
	2015	491	96.6	88.3	382	61.5	61.0	216	...	...
Lesotho	2005	422	116.8	117.5	94	34.5	44.9	8	3.1	4.3
Lesotho	2006	425	117.2	117.7	96	34.6	45.2	9	3.4	4.4
	2010	389	111.5	109.4	126	41.7	59.3	...	...	...
	2014	366	108.3	105.8	131	44.1	60.4	24	8.0	11.7
	2015	362	107.0	104.0	133	45.7	62.0	...	...	...
Liberia	2000	496	129.6	95.4	136	40.7	29.6	52	24.9	13.8
Libéria	2009	605	105.0	94.1	...	...	...	...	...	...
	2010	...	...	...	...	...	...	33	12.1	6.4
	2012	...	...	...	...	...	...	44	14.2	9.0
	2015	684	98.5	89.1	227	41.9	32.5	...	...	...
Libya	2003	739	111.1	107.9	* 798	* 101.7	* 108.4	* 375	* 58.1	* 64.3
Libye	2005	714	108.7	107.6	702	* 86.7	* 103.3	...	...	...
	2006	755	116.8	112.1	733	93.6	109.9	...	...	...
Liechtenstein	2004	2	* 109.9	* 108.5	3	* 117.2	* 103.9	1	* 35.7	* 13.3
Liechtenstein	2005	2	...	...	3	...	...	1	...	...
	2010	2	* 108.6	* 102.3	3	* 117.6	* 100.0	1	* 44.3	* 27.4
	2015	2	* 106.5	* 104.8	3	* 130.7	* 101.7	1	* 44.8	* 21.9
Lithuania	2005	158	94.9	94.4	424	104.6	103.7	195	62.9	98.5
Lituanie	2010	122	100.6	99.5	343	101.9	100.0	201	68.7	103.1
	2014	108	102.3	102.6	277	108.9	104.6	148	55.8	82.0
	2015	108	103.2	103.7	263	110.3	106.1	141	...	...

Enrollment in the primary, secondary and tertiary levels *(continued)*

Number of students enrolled (thousands) and gross enrollment ratio by sex

Enseignement primaire, secondaire et supérieur *(suite)*

Nombre d'élèves inscrits (milliers) et taux brut de scolarisation par sexe

		Primary education Enseignement primaire			Secondary education Enseignement secondaire			Tertiary education Enseignement supérieur		
			Gross enrollment ratio Taux brut de scolarisation			Gross enrollment ratio Taux brut de scolarisation			Gross enrollment ratio Taux brut de scolarisation	
Region, country or area Région, pays ou zone	Year & Année &	Total ('000)	M	F	Total ('000)	M	F	Total (000)	M	F
Luxembourg Luxembourg	2003	34	99.5	99.3	35	93.6	98.7	3	11.1	13.3
	2005	35	100.7	100.9	36	92.9	97.9	...	...	...
	2010	35	97.1	98.1	43	99.9	102.9	5	17.3	19.2
	2012	35	96.9	97.2	44	98.5	102.0	6	18.2	20.7
	2014	35	96.9	97.3	47	101.1	103.5	...	...	...
Madagascar Madagascar	2005	3 598	141.4	135.3	* 621	* 21.6	* 20.7	45	3.0	2.7
	2009	4 324	151.6	148.2	* 1 022	* 31.3	29.4	68	3.6	3.3
	2010	4 242	145.9	143.3	...	...	...	74	3.8	3.4
	2014	4 611	146.9	146.5	1 494	38.8	38.1	113	5.0	4.6
	2015	4 764	148.9	148.9	...	...	...	...	...	...
Malawi Malawi	2005	2 868	126.3	128.0	516	30.3	24.3	6	* 0.6	* 0.3
	2010	3 417	135.1	138.4	692	34.9	31.2	10	0.9	0.5
	2011	3 564	137.1	140.9	736	36.0	32.4	12	1.0	0.6
	2015	4 205	144.0	147.0	1 038	45.8	41.0	...	...	...
Malaysia Malaisie	2005	3 202	101.4	101.4	2 489	65.5	72.1	697	24.1	31.9
	2010	3 234	99.7	100.6	2 616	64.5	69.3	1 061	31.4	43.2
	2015	3 108	101.7	101.9	2 991	74.6	80.7	818	20.8	31.8
Maldives Maldives	2003	66	125.1	122.4	29	66.1	72.9	~0	0.1	0.3
	2004	63	124.1	120.5	* 29	* 65.8	* 74.0	...	...	...
	2005	58	117.6	114.5	...	...	...	...	...	...
	2008	47	107.3	103.2	...	...	...	5	12.0	13.5
	2009	45	104.0	100.8	...	...	...	...	...	...
	2010	42	...	...	...	...	...	...	...	...
	2014	40	...	...	...	...	...	6	12.4	20.3
	2016	44	97.3	98.6	...	...	...	...	...	...
Mali Mali	2002	1 227	74.3	56.7	...	...	...	23	2.7	1.4
	2005	1 506	81.3	64.8	430	* 31.2	* 19.6	...	...	...
	2010	2 019	88.7	77.1	758	45.4	31.9	81	8.4	3.6
	2012	2 114	85.7	75.8	...	...	...	97	9.6	4.1
	2015	2 227	79.3	72.1	945	45.6	36.8	...	...	...
Malta Malte	2005	30	98.0	95.7	40	104.5	100.3	9	27.5	37.3
	2010	25	98.7	99.3	37	109.7	98.0	11	31.6	42.7
	2015	25	102.2	104.7	29	91.7	98.1	13	40.3	55.2
Marshall Islands Îles Marshall	2002	9	124.6	116.1	6	71.7	74.4	1	14.2	18.3
	2005	8	103.0	129.9	5	75.6	75.7	...	...	...
	2009	8	107.4	107.9	5	101.4	104.4	...	...	...
	2012	...	...	...	...	...	...	1	44.6	41.2
	2015	8	93.5	93.3	5	73.1	80.4	...	...	...
Mauritania Mauritanie	2005	444	89.3	92.2	93	23.7	20.8	9	4.3	1.5
	2010	531	94.3	98.4	* 110	* 21.9	* 18.7	15	6.3	2.5
	2015	633	100.0	105.0	188	31.7	29.5	21	7.4	3.7
	2016	...	...	...	...	...	...	20	7.1	3.6
Mauritius Maurice	2005	124	103.3	103.1	* 129	* 89.7	* 87.6	* 21	* 21.0	* 21.7
	2010	117	102.5	103.1	* 127	* 87.2	* 91.3	33	30.5	36.9
	2015	102	102.2	103.9	129	93.6	97.9	38	31.7	41.7
Mexico Mexique	2005	14 700	103.8	102.2	10 564	76.0	82.6	2 385	22.9	23.3
	2010	14 906	104.0	102.8	11 682	79.7	86.8	2 847	25.7	26.6
	2014	14 627	103.6	103.2	12 993	87.7	93.5	3 419	29.9	30.0
Micronesia (Fed. States of) Micronésie (États féd. de)	*2000	...	...	...	...	...	...	2	...	...
	2005	19	112.8	109.8	14	80.1	86.7	...	...	...
	2007	19	110.9	112.4	...	...	...	...	...	...
	2015	14	95.4	95.7	...	...	...	...	...	...
Monaco Monaco	2004	2	...	...	3	...	...	...	...	...
	2010	2	...	...	3	...	...	...	...	...
	2015	2	...	...	3	...	...	...	...	...
Mongolia Mongolie	2005	251	98.0	98.0	339	85.6	95.0	124	33.8	55.9
	2010	274	127.1	124.2	276	88.4	94.8	166	42.5	65.3
	2015	251	101.8	100.0	282	90.5	92.4	180	57.7	79.7
Montenegro Monténégro	2005	38	112.7	112.6	68	93.2	95.8	11	17.2	27.2
	2010	35	107.7	105.8	70	100.1	101.4	24	49.2	61.8
	2015	38	95.2	93.3	61	90.4	90.3	...	...	...

Enrollment in the primary, secondary and tertiary levels *(continued)*
Number of students enrolled (thousands) and gross enrollment ratio by sex

Enseignement primaire, secondaire et supérieur *(suite)*
Nombre d'élèves inscrits (milliers) et taux brut de scolarisation par sexe

Region, country or area / Région, pays ou zone	Year & / Année &	Primary education / Enseignement primaire			Secondary education / Enseignement secondaire			Tertiary education / Enseignement supérieur		
			Gross enrollment ratio Taux brut de scolarisation			Gross enrollment ratio Taux brut de scolarisation			Gross enrollment ratio Taux brut de scolarisation	
		Total ('000)	M	F	Total ('000)	M	F	Total (000)	M	F
Montserrat Montserrat	2005	1	* 114.6	* 118.7	~0	* 111.0	* 122.5	...	...	...
	2007	~0	* 101.2	* 112.9	~0	* 101.1	* 103.2	...	...	...
	2009	~0	...	...	~0	...	...	~0	...	...
	2010	...	...	...	...	...	...	~0	...	...
	2014	~0	...	...	~0	...	...	...	...	...
Morocco Maroc	2005	4 023	110.0	99.8	1 948	53.7	45.8	368	13.0	10.5
	2010	3 945	115.6	108.8	2 393	66.9	58.3	447	15.2	13.7
	2012	4 017	119.2	113.7	2 554	74.4	63.5	606	20.0	18.5
	2015	4 039	117.7	111.6	...	...	...	877	28.7	27.5
Mozambique Mozambique	2005	3 943	104.4	87.8	306	15.5	10.7	28	1.9	0.9
	2010	5 278	114.7	103.0	672	26.6	21.7	104	5.5	3.6
	2015	* 5 902	* 110.4	* 101.2	* 1 073	* 33.8	* 31.1	175	7.4	5.4
Myanmar Myanmar	2001	4 782	98.4	96.3	2 302	38.6	36.2	553	...	...
	2005	4 948	98.2	98.4	2 589	45.0	43.6	...	...	...
	2007	5 014	...	...	2 686	46.3	46.2	508	8.9	12.2
	2010	5 126	97.1	96.3	2 852	47.0	49.3	...	...	...
	2012	...	...	...	...	...	...	634	12.1	14.9
	2014	5 177	101.0	98.3	3 191	50.6	52.0	...	...	...
Namibia Namibie	2005	404	109.2	108.9	148	59.8	67.2	14	7.4	6.3
	2007	410	110.4	108.9	158	60.1	69.6	...	...	...
	2008	407	109.7	107.8	...	...	...	20	8.2	10.4
	2010	407	109.0	106.3	...	...	...	...	...	...
	2013	425	113.3	109.5	...	...	...	...	...	...
Nauru Nauru	2005	2	* 122.3	* 128.5	1	* 44.4	* 50.3	...	...	...
	2008	1	* 90.1	* 96.0	1	* 57.6	* 68.9	...	...	...
	2014	2	* 109.5	* 100.4	1	* 81.9	* 83.4	...	...	...
Nepal Népal	2005	4 030	120.3	110.1	2 054	* 53.9	* 43.6	187	10.6	5.6
	2010	4 901	137.8	147.1	* 2 694	* 60.3	* 57.3	377	18.2	11.1
	2015	4 335	130.2	140.9	* 3 176	* 64.9	* 69.6	445	14.8	15.1
	2016	4 265	130.7	141.2	* 3 277	* 67.1	* 72.2	...	...	...
Netherlands Pays-Bas	2005	1 278	108.2	105.5	1 411	120.5	118.2	565	57.5	62.1
	2010	1 294	109.8	108.5	1 475	124.0	122.2	651	61.6	68.9
	2012	1 277	108.0	107.1	1 550	131.4	128.9	794	74.7	82.5
	2015	1 208	105.0	104.4	1 613	134.7	136.3	843	...	...
Netherlands Antilles [former] Antilles néerlandaises [anc.]	2002	23	...	...	15	...	...	2	...	...
New Zealand Nouvelle-Zélande	2005	353	100.0	99.2	526	116.9	123.4	240	65.8	95.8
	2010	348	100.9	101.3	512	116.3	121.7	266	67.3	98.6
	2015	368	99.6	99.1	487	113.4	119.9	270	71.6	96.7
Nicaragua Nicaragua	2002	923	116.4	116.6	383	55.3	65.8	100	16.8	18.7
	2005	945	121.9	120.2	438	63.7	74.1	...	...	...
	2010	924	123.8	122.7	465	69.8	78.8	...	...	...
Niger Niger	2005	1 064	56.7	40.8	182	12.2	7.7	11	1.8	0.6
	2010	1 726	69.6	56.8	307	16.2	10.9	17	2.2	0.8
	2012	2 051	75.3	63.3	389	18.7	12.5	22	2.6	0.9
	2015	2 445	77.9	66.8	595	24.2	17.2	...	...	...
Nigeria Nigéria	2005	22 115	109.0	92.6	6 398	37.6	31.7	1 392	12.1	8.7
	2010	* 21 558	* 88.3	* 80.9	9 057	46.4	41.2	1 395	10.8	8.1
	2011	23 669	93.0	87.4	9 591	48.3	41.9	1 513	11.8	8.3
	2013	26 168	94.5	92.8	12 533	57.8	53.5	...	...	...
Niue Nioué	2005	~0	* 118.9	* 105.9	~0	* 71.3	* 116.5	...	...	...
	2015	~0	* 147.2	* 120.2	~0	* 104.1	* 114.1	...	...	...
Norway Norvège	2005	430	98.4	98.7	403	113.4	114.4	214	62.5	95.2
	2010	424	98.9	99.1	435	114.0	112.4	225	56.1	90.4
	2015	431	100.5	100.3	437	114.7	111.1	268	62.8	91.5
Oman Oman	2005	312	89.7	87.7	302	91.0	86.0	48	...	...
	2009	302	106.7	100.0	322	107.1	95.3	76	...	...
	2010	...	...	...	...	...	...	78	...	...
	2015	351	107.4	111.2	287	101.0	107.9	127	...	...

Enrollment in the primary, secondary and tertiary levels *(continued)*

Number of students enrolled (thousands) and gross enrollment ratio by sex

Enseignement primaire, secondaire et supérieur *(suite)*

Nombre d'élèves inscrits (milliers) et taux brut de scolarisation par sexe

Region, country or area Région, pays ou zone	Year & Année &	Primary education Enseignement primaire Total ('000)	Gross enrollment ratio Taux brut de scolarisation M	 F	Secondary education Enseignement secondaire Total ('000)	Gross enrollment ratio Taux brut de scolarisation M	 F	Tertiary education Enseignement supérieur Total (000)	Gross enrollment ratio Taux brut de scolarisation M	 F
Pakistan	2005	17 258	99.2	76.3	6 852	...	...	783	5.3	4.6
Pakistan	2009	18 468	101.1	86.3	9 433	39.2	31.1	* 1 226	* 7.5	* 6.3
	2010	18 756	103.1	87.8	9 655	40.3	31.1	...	...	...
	2015	19 847	99.7	85.2	12 078	49.5	39.2	1 872	10.6	9.2
Palau	*2002	...	...	...	...	...	...	~0	25.6	52.3
Palaos	2004	2	* 104.6	* 101.1	2	* 97.7	* 99.9	...	...	...
	2005	2	...	...	2	...	...	...	...	...
	2007	2	...	...	2	...	...	...	...	...
	2013	2	* 115.3	* 113.4	2	* 113.9	* 117.1	1	* 49.1	* 76.1
	2016	1	* 100.3	* 99.0	1	* 96.2	* 95.2	...	...	...
Panama	2005	430	109.1	105.4	256	65.9	70.6	126	32.1	52.5
Panama	2010	440	109.0	104.9	284	69.2	73.5	139	35.2	53.8
	2013	436	106.9	103.7	310	73.2	77.9	124	31.2	46.5
	2014	427	103.5	100.9	312	72.9	78.3	...	...	...
Papua New Guinea	2005	532	62.7	53.3	...	...	...	...	...	...
Papouasie-Nvl-Guinée	2008	601	63.8	56.9	...	...	...	...	...	...
	2012	1 427	119.8	109.3	378	45.8	34.6	...	...	...
Paraguay	2005	934	113.5	110.3	529	66.0	67.8	156	24.3	27.5
Paraguay	2010	839	105.9	101.8	561	66.5	70.2	225	29.1	41.2
	2012	838	107.6	104.3	631	74.2	79.1	...	...	...
Peru	2005	4 077	117.0	118.0	2 470	86.3	84.6	908	32.8	33.6
Pérou	2010	3 763	109.8	111.0	2 675	94.5	94.9	1 151	38.6	42.5
	2015	3 513	101.7	101.7	2 682	95.7	95.8	...	...	...
Philippines	2005	13 084	106.6	105.4	6 352	78.3	87.6	2 403	24.7	30.4
Philippines	2009	13 687	109.1	108.6	6 767	81.0	87.6	2 625	25.7	31.8
	2010	...	...	...	...	...	...	2 774	26.5	33.1
	2013	14 460	116.8	116.9	7 220	84.4	92.7	3 317	29.8	37.6
	2014	...	...	...	...	...	...	3 563	31.4	40.3
Poland	2005	2 724	96.5	96.0	3 445	98.9	98.1	2 118	52.4	74.1
Pologne	2010	2 235	98.9	98.3	2 842	97.2	96.2	2 149	58.6	88.3
	2014	2 153	100.5	100.7	2 641	110.0	106.1	1 763	54.2	82.6
Portugal	2005	753	121.2	115.4	670	93.5	102.8	381	48.2	63.1
Portugal	2010	734	113.6	110.2	721	105.5	108.4	384	60.3	71.2
	2015	657	109.4	105.3	779	121.0	117.3	338	58.0	65.7
Puerto Rico	2010	300	93.2	96.5	291	80.7	85.3	249	69.9	103.2
Porto Rico	2014	259	89.1	90.4	266	78.8	83.9	241	70.1	98.8
Qatar	2005	70	107.1	103.7	56	102.3	96.0	* 10	* 8.8	* 31.1
Qatar	2010	89	104.7	105.9	69	99.2	103.3	14	4.8	25.6
	2015	130	102.4	103.6	96	82.0	103.6	28	6.3	43.9
Republic of Korea	2005	4 032	112.0	111.2	3 796	94.1	92.2	3 210	107.4	71.1
République de Corée	2010	3 306	102.5	101.3	3 959	96.6	95.6	3 270	113.5	83.9
	2015	2 722	99.3	98.7	3 397	99.3	98.4	3 268	104.8	80.2
Republic of Moldova	2005	184	* 98.6	* 97.2	394	* 86.2	* 90.0	130	* 29.5	* 42.9
République de Moldova	2010	141	* 93.7	* 93.3	308	* 87.0	* 89.0	130	* 32.7	* 43.7
	2015	139	* 92.9	* 91.9	233	* 85.8	* 86.5	109	* 35.3	* 47.4
Romania	2005	970	109.4	107.9	2 090	82.9	84.5	739	40.2	51.1
Roumanie	2010	842	98.0	96.5	1 822	100.7	99.8	1 000	57.4	78.9
	2015	947	90.5	89.0	1 563	92.5	92.0	542	47.8	59.0
Russian Federation	2005	5 309	95.2	95.4	12 433	83.4	82.5	9 003	61.3	84.2
Fédération de Russie	2009	5 015	99.0	99.4	9 614	85.6	84.2	9 330	64.3	86.9
	2015	5 983	100.1	100.9	9 385	105.5	103.4	6 592	72.9	88.3
Rwanda	2004	1 753	134.9	133.8	204	15.2	13.8	25	3.5	2.0
Rwanda	2005	1 858	136.1	137.1	219	16.9	15.1	28	...	...
	2010	2 299	140.5	144.1	426	32.9	32.6	63	6.3	4.9
	2015	2 451	131.7	133.4	568	35.2	38.2	80	8.9	6.9
	2016	...	...	...	...	...	...	82	9.1	6.9
Saint Kitts and Nevis	2005	6	98.2	100.1	* 4	* 84.1	* 89.9	...	...	...
Saint-Kitts-et-Nevis	2008	6	95.9	97.3	4	99.5	104.9	1	11.8	24.7
	2010	6	93.4	93.5	* 4	* 97.9	* 97.1	...	...	...
	2015	5	81.7	83.4	4	88.0	92.8	4	52.6	107.2

Enrollment in the primary, secondary and tertiary levels *(continued)*

Number of students enrolled (thousands) and gross enrollment ratio by sex

Enseignement primaire, secondaire et supérieur *(suite)*

Nombre d'élèves inscrits (milliers) et taux brut de scolarisation par sexe

Region, country or area / Région, pays ou zone	Year & / Année &	Primary education / Enseignement primaire: Total ('000)	Gross enrollment ratio / Taux brut de scolarisation: M	F	Secondary education / Enseignement secondaire: Total ('000)	Gross enrollment ratio / Taux brut de scolarisation: M	F	Tertiary education / Enseignement supérieur: Total (000)	Gross enrollment ratio / Taux brut de scolarisation: M	F
Saint Lucia	2005	24	105.4	100.7	14	71.4	84.0	2	7.0	19.0
Sainte-Lucie	2007	22	102.9	97.7	15	83.4	92.7	1	5.2	12.0
	2010	19	...	...	16	95.8	94.7	2	7.0	18.0
	2015	17	...	...	13	85.5	84.8	3	11.6	22.0
Saint Vincent & Grenadines	2005	18	123.9	112.3	10	79.6	99.5	...	...	...
Saint-Vincent-Grenadines	2010	14	108.8	101.2	11	106.3	108.8	...	...	...
	2015	13	105.8	103.2	10	107.9	105.0	...	...	...
Samoa	2000	28	95.9	97.3	22	73.7	83.9	1	7.8	7.2
Samoa	2005	31	109.0	109.8	24	78.2	88.2	...	...	...
	2010	31	111.5	109.9	26	82.3	93.6	...	...	...
	2015	32	106.7	106.7	26	80.7	89.5	...	...	...
San Marino	2000	1	...	...	1	...	...	1	...	...
Saint-Marin	2004	1	...	...	...	...	...	...	...	...
	2010	2	* 88.8	* 100.6	2	* 96.3	* 98.2	1	* 53.0	* 77.3
	2012	2	* 93.9	* 92.6	2	* 93.5	* 95.9	1	* 50.5	* 69.9
Sao Tome and Principe	2005	30	132.3	127.2	8	41.9	44.4	...	...	...
Sao Tomé-et-Principe	2010	34	122.6	121.4	10	52.5	53.4	1	4.4	4.2
	2015	36	116.1	111.1	22	80.7	89.3	2	13.2	13.6
	2016	36	117.7	112.2	23	80.8	91.7	...	...	...
Saudi Arabia	2005	* 3 098	* 93.7	* 92.3	* 2 610	* 88.4	* 83.8	604	25.2	33.9
Arabie saoudite	2009	3 255	98.4	96.2	* 2 997	* 101.8	* 89.4	758	27.1	35.1
	2010	3 321	99.2	99.1	...	...	...	904	33.7	39.6
	2014	3 737	109.2	108.3	* 3 419	* 122.6	* 93.7	1 497	62.4	59.9
	2015	3 845	107.9	111.1	...	...	...	1 528	64.4	61.8
Senegal	2005	1 444	80.2	77.2	406	25.2	18.8	* 59	...	...
Sénégal	2010	1 695	79.7	84.2	725	38.0	33.1	* 92	* 9.3	* 5.5
	2015	1 977	77.6	86.9	1 136	50.2	49.1	145	12.9	7.8
Serbia	2005	325	* 102.5	* 103.0	632	* 87.3	* 90.0	225	* 38.6	* 50.1
Serbie	2010	283	* 96.1	* 95.6	591	* 90.5	* 92.4	227	* 42.8	* 55.6
	2015	279	* 101.5	* 101.2	553	* 96.0	* 97.4	241	* 50.2	* 66.9
Seychelles	2005	9	110.1	108.0	9	79.0	84.8	...	...	...
Seychelles	2010	9	108.9	112.5	8	* 72.4	* 75.9	...	...	...
	2015	9	101.1	103.6	7	78.8	84.5	1	9.3	19.6
Sierra Leone	2001	554	98.3	68.6	156	* 31.8	* 22.5	9	3.2	1.3
Sierra Leone	*2002	...	...	...	...	...	...	9	3.1	1.2
	2015	1 360	127.0	128.2	449	46.5	40.1	...	...	...
Singapore	2009	295	...	...	232	...	...	199	...	...
Singapour	2010	...	...	...	...	...	...	213	...	...
	2013	...	...	...	...	...	...	255	...	...
Sint Maarten (Dutch part)	2014	4	...	...	3	...	...	~0	...	...
St-Martin (partie néerland.)	2015	...	...	...	...	...	...	~0	...	...
Slovakia	2005	242	99.2	98.1	663	93.3	94.2	181	35.4	45.7
Slovaquie	2010	212	102.9	101.8	550	92.2	93.1	235	44.9	69.3
	2014	214	101.6	100.4	465	91.5	92.3	198	41.8	64.6
	2015	216	100.2	99.2	454	92.1	92.8	...	...	...
Slovenia	2005	93	101.0	99.3	181	97.4	96.8	112	65.6	93.4
Slovénie	2010	107	98.5	98.0	138	98.3	97.4	115	71.2	107.0
	2014	112	99.2	99.4	145	110.8	110.5	91	68.2	98.5
Solomon Islands	2005	75	103.6	97.8	22	33.2	27.4	...	...	...
Îles Salomon	2010	95	116.6	113.3	40	52.1	44.9	...	...	...
	2012	98	114.6	111.9	42	49.8	47.0	...	...	...
	2015	104	115.0	113.6	...	...	...	...	...	...
Somalia										
Somalie	2007	457	37.6	20.8	87	10.1	4.6	...	...	...
South Africa	2005	7 314	96.5	103.0	4 658	84.3	93.7	...	...	...
Afrique du Sud	2010	7 024	93.6	99.3	4 690	84.4	96.7	...	...	...
	2014	7 195	102.2	97.3	5 221	88.0	111.5	1 019	15.7	23.3
South Sudan										
Soudan du sud	2015	1 274	74.9	53.1	164	12.3	6.6	...	...	...

Enrollment in the primary, secondary and tertiary levels *(continued)*

Number of students enrolled (thousands) and gross enrollment ratio by sex

Enseignement primaire, secondaire et supérieur *(suite)*

Nombre d'élèves inscrits (milliers) et taux brut de scolarisation par sexe

Region, country or area Région, pays ou zone	Year & Année &	Primary education Enseignement primaire			Secondary education Enseignement secondaire			Tertiary education Enseignement supérieur		
			Gross enrollment ratio Taux brut de scolarisation			Gross enrollment ratio Taux brut de scolarisation			Gross enrollment ratio Taux brut de scolarisation	
		Total ('000)	M	F	Total ('000)	M	F	Total (000)	M	F
Spain Espagne	2005	2 485	103.8	102.4	3 108	113.9	121.3	1 809	60.6	74.4
	2010	2 721	106.0	105.5	3 185	123.0	125.8	1 879	70.5	87.4
	2015	3 010	104.5	105.6	3 313	130.0	129.6	1 964	82.5	97.1
Sri Lanka Sri Lanka	2005	1 611	99.9	99.3	...	...	...	...	...	...
	2010	1 721	101.0	98.4	2 525	96.3	97.5	262	11.7	20.9
	2013	1 767	101.9	99.4	2 606	97.5	102.0	298	14.8	22.9
	2015	1 778	102.7	100.6	...	...	...	308	15.6	24.0
State of Palestine État de Palestine	2005	387	88.5	87.9	657	87.7	91.7	138	40.6	41.2
	2010	403	91.6	89.8	711	82.4	89.0	197	41.1	54.9
	2015	450	94.4	94.3	721	79.2	87.0	221	34.5	54.4
Sudan Soudan	2005	3 177	66.0	57.8	1 344	38.9	36.1	364	11.0	12.4
	2010	4 024	73.6	66.1	1 687	44.1	38.2	523	13.8	16.2
	2013	4 292	74.1	66.6	1 871	43.9	41.5	640	16.0	17.9
	2014	...	...	...	...	...	...	632	15.8	16.8
Sudan [former] Soudan [anc.]	2000	2 567	...	...	980	...	...	* 204	...	...
	2005	3 278	...	...	* 1 370	...	...	...	...	...
	2009	4 744	...	...	1 837	...	...	...	...	...
Suriname Suriname	2002	64	100.7	100.3	42	59.0	81.8	5	9.4	16.1
	2005	66	113.7	111.2	46	59.7	76.9	...	...	...
	2010	71	121.5	115.3	50	69.9	89.2	...	...	...
	2015	72	124.2	121.4	55	71.7	90.9	...	...	...
Swaziland Swaziland	2005	222	106.3	99.9	71	46.2	47.1	6	4.6	4.9
	2006	230	111.8	104.5	77	49.7	51.0	6	4.5	4.4
	2010	241	120.7	110.8	89	58.0	58.0	...	...	...
	2013	239	118.2	108.3	93	63.6	62.4	8	5.2	5.5
	2014	240	117.5	108.0	97	66.2	65.8	...	...	...
Sweden Suède	2005	658	96.0	95.7	735	104.3	103.9	427	64.8	100.0
	2010	576	101.8	101.2	731	98.7	97.7	455	59.3	90.8
	2015	792	120.6	125.6	844	131.5	150.0	429	49.6	75.7
Switzerland Suisse	2005	524	102.2	101.9	575	98.0	92.2	200	49.0	42.4
	2010	493	102.8	102.3	605	97.3	94.4	249	53.1	52.5
	2015	490	104.1	103.8	614	103.0	99.4	294	56.9	58.5
Syrian Arab Republic République arabe syrienne	2005	2 252	123.0	119.5	2 389	71.5	68.4	361	19.2	17.2
	2010	2 429	124.4	120.0	2 732	72.8	72.9	574	27.9	24.1
	2013	1 547	81.4	78.7	1 857	50.5	50.5	660	34.3	34.8
	2015	...	...	...	...	...	...	773	41.3	47.0
Tajikistan Tadjikistan	2005	693	100.6	97.2	984	87.7	72.9	149	28.3	13.5
	2010	682	101.5	98.5	1 032	90.2	78.5	196	29.7	15.6
	2013	665	99.9	98.0	1 063	92.5	83.1	195	28.9	16.2
	2016	718	99.8	101.2	...	...	...	247	33.6	24.0
Thailand Thaïlande	2005	5 975	99.7	96.9	4 533	* 69.6	* 73.6	2 359	41.4	47.2
	2010	5 147	97.1	95.0	4 807	81.2	86.1	2 427	44.1	56.3
	2015	5 081	106.1	99.2	6 757	132.6	125.3	2 235	40.5	57.3
TFYR of Macedonia ex-R.Y. de Macédoine	2005	110	95.2	93.3	214	86.1	83.6	49	24.8	34.1
	2010	111	86.3	84.9	197	84.6	82.4	62	36.2	42.3
	2015	109	93.6	92.8	169	80.3	78.2	64	37.5	46.8
Timor-Leste Timor-Leste	2002	184	...	...	53	...	...	* 6	* 8.3	* 9.5
	2005	178	98.4	90.1	75	54.3	52.8	...	...	...
	2010	230	133.8	128.4	102	67.2	67.7	19	21.1	15.2
	2015	244	137.5	136.2	129	74.1	79.6	...	...	...
Togo Togo	2005	997	121.9	103.5	404	58.9	31.2	...	...	...
	2007	1 022	118.7	102.7	409	* 57.6	* 30.5	33	...	...
	2010	1 287	134.9	121.8	...	...	...	56	...	...
	2011	1 300	131.8	120.0	546	...	...	63	...	...
	2015	1 414	125.1	118.5	...	...	...	71	14.9	6.4
Tokelau Tokélaou	2003	~0	* 101.8	* 132.6	~0	* 83.3	* 75.8	...	...	...
	2016	~0	* 121.0	* 114.3	~0	* 129.1	* 120.7	...	...	...

7

Enrollment in the primary, secondary and tertiary levels *(continued)*

Number of students enrolled (thousands) and gross enrollment ratio by sex

Enseignement primaire, secondaire et supérieur *(suite)*

Nombre d'élèves inscrits (milliers) et taux brut de scolarisation par sexe

Region, country or area Région, pays ou zone	Year & Année &	Primary education Enseignement primaire			Secondary education Enseignement secondaire			Tertiary education Enseignement supérieur		
			Gross enrollment ratio Taux brut de scolarisation			Gross enrollment ratio Taux brut de scolarisation			Gross enrollment ratio Taux brut de scolarisation	
		Total ('000)	M	F	Total ('000)	M	F	Total (000)	M	F
Tonga	2002	17	113.2	108.1	15	105.7	116.6	1	* 4.2	* 7.1
Tonga	2003	18	119.5	113.1	16	...	...	1	4.8	8.0
	2004	17	114.9	109.2	14	...	...	...	...	...
	2005	17	113.6	110.3	...	...	...	...	...	...
	2010	17	109.3	107.2	15	100.9	107.7	...	...	...
	2014	17	108.6	107.5	15	86.4	94.2	...	...	...
Trinidad and Tobago	2004	* 137	* 103.4	* 100.0	* 105	* 82.6	* 88.5	17	10.6	13.4
Trinité-et-Tobago	*2005	130	100.7	97.8	...	...	...	...	...	...
	2010	131	108.0	104.3	...	...	...	...	...	...
Tunisia	2005	1 184	114.0	109.3	1 239	81.4	88.3	327	28.6	35.1
Tunisie	2010	1 030	109.0	105.4	1 164	87.6	93.4	370	27.8	42.6
	2011	1 028	109.4	106.0	1 152	90.0	94.2	362	26.7	43.1
	2015	1 115	115.8	112.5	1 008	...	...	323	26.2	43.3
Turkey	2005	6 678	105.8	100.5	6 345	91.0	75.6	2 106	37.8	27.6
Turquie	2010	6 635	102.3	100.8	7 531	87.8	80.5	3 529	61.7	50.2
	2015	5 434	102.8	102.1	10 969	103.8	101.1	6 063	101.0	88.3
Turkmenistan										
Turkménistan	2014	359	90.1	88.6	651	86.9	83.7	44	9.7	6.2
Turks and Caicos Islands	2005	2	...	...	2	...	...	...	...	...
Îles Turques-et-Caïques	2009	3	...	...	2	...	...	...	...	...
	2010	...	...	...	...	...	...	~0	...	...
	2015	3	...	...	2	...	...	~0	...	...
Tuvalu	2001	1	* 94.9	* 106.9	1	* 67.4	* 74.1	...	...	...
Tuvalu	2005	1	* 101.4	* 97.6	...	...	...	...	...	...
	2006	1	* 102.4	* 97.6	...	...	...	...	...	...
	2015	1	* 103.0	* 104.3	1	* 76.0	* 97.5	...	...	...
Uganda	2004	7 377	130.3	128.4	733	21.5	17.3	88	4.4	2.8
Ouganda	2005	7 224	123.2	122.2	...	...	...	...	...	...
	2007	7 538	119.7	120.2	1 032	26.9	22.1	...	...	...
	2010	8 375	119.3	121.2	...	...	...	121	4.5	3.5
	2013	8 459	108.9	110.9	...	...	...	...	...	...
	2014	...	...	...	...	...	...	165	5.4	4.2
	2015	...	...	...	1 284	24.3	22.1	...	...	...
Ukraine	2005	1 946	106.1	105.7	4 043	* 100.6	* 93.2	2 605	63.8	78.8
Ukraine	2010	1 540	102.4	103.1	3 133	* 96.2	* 93.9	2 635	72.8	91.5
	2014	1 685	102.8	105.1	2 714	100.2	98.2	2 146	76.5	88.4
	2015	1 537	...	...	2 370	...	...	1 776	...	...
United Arab Emirates	2005	263	105.8	105.2	...	...	...	...	...	...
Émirats arabes unis	2010	327	98.1	101.5	...	...	...	102	...	...
	2015	461	116.7	116.0	...	...	...	157	...	...
United Kingdom	2005	4 635	106.3	106.2	5 761	103.9	107.0	2 288	49.5	68.9
Royaume-Uni	2010	4 422	106.1	105.6	5 538	102.1	101.7	2 479	50.4	68.1
	2014	4 737	108.4	108.1	6 557	125.3	130.4	2 353	49.0	64.1
United Rep. of Tanzania	2005	7 541	106.2	101.0	...	...	...	* 52	* 2.0	* 0.9
Rép.-Unie de Tanzanie	2010	8 419	98.6	99.3	1 826	34.8	27.5	85	2.4	1.9
	2013	8 232	86.2	87.4	2 052	33.7	30.8	158	4.9	2.5
	2015	8 298	80.5	82.9	...	...	...	...	...	...
United States of America	2005	24 455	101.1	100.3	24 432	94.4	97.1	17 272	68.2	96.8
États-Unis d'Amérique	2010	24 393	101.0	100.2	24 193	93.5	95.2	20 428	78.6	110.7
	2014	24 538	99.8	99.2	24 230	96.7	98.5	19 700	73.5	100.7
	2015	24 786	100.3	100.0	...	...	...	19 532	72.8	99.6
United States Virgin Islands										
Îles Vierges américaines	2007	...	...	...	...	...	...	2	...	...
Uruguay	2005	366	115.3	112.4	323	94.2	108.5	111	33.2	57.9
Uruguay	2010	342	113.9	110.2	287	84.6	96.2	163	46.5	80.3
	2014	322	109.8	107.3	292	90.3	100.0	148	...	...
	2015	...	...	...	...	...	...	146	...	...
Uzbekistan	2005	2 383	102.7	102.6	4 516	91.2	88.3	266	12.0	8.2
Ouzbékistan	2010	1 971	97.7	95.8	4 449	95.0	94.8	289	11.2	7.6
	2016	2 261	105.6	103.2	3 909	96.8	95.1	266	11.0	7.1

7

Enrollment in the primary, secondary and tertiary levels *(continued)*

Number of students enrolled (thousands) and gross enrollment ratio by sex

Enseignement primaire, secondaire et supérieur *(suite)*

Nombre d'élèves inscrits (milliers) et taux brut de scolarisation par sexe

Region, country or area / Région, pays ou zone	Year & / Année &	Primary education / Enseignement primaire: Total ('000)	Gross enrollment ratio Taux brut de scolarisation: M	F	Secondary education / Enseignement secondaire: Total ('000)	Gross enrollment ratio Taux brut de scolarisation: M	F	Tertiary education / Enseignement supérieur: Total (000)	Gross enrollment ratio Taux brut de scolarisation: M	F
Vanuatu	2004	39	122.4	120.0	14	45.8	39.5	* 1	* 5.9	* 3.5
Vanuatu	2005	39	119.2	116.1	...	...	...	...	...	...
	2010	42	123.0	121.9	20	59.6	59.5	...	...	...
	2015	46	120.6	118.7	21	53.4	56.4	...	...	...
Venezuela (Boliv. Rep. of)	2003	3 450	104.0	101.9	1 866	63.4	72.9	* 983	* 38.4	* 41.2
Venezuela (Rép. boliv. du)	2004	3 453	104.1	101.9	1 954	66.1	75.3	* 1 050	...	...
	2005	3 449	103.8	101.8	2 028	68.6	77.5	...	...	...
	2008	3 439	103.3	100.5	2 224	76.1	83.8	2 109	* 57.8	* 97.7
	2009	3 462	103.6	100.8	2 252	77.4	84.6	2 123	...	...
	2010	3 458	103.1	100.1	2 255	77.3	84.7	...	...	...
	2015	3 476	101.3	98.6	2 523	86.5	93.0	...	...	...
Viet Nam	2005	7 773	99.6	94.6	...	...	...	1 355	18.7	13.3
Viet Nam	2010	6 923	107.7	102.3	...	...	...	2 020	22.7	22.7
	2015	7 544	109.3	108.4	...	...	...	2 467	28.8	28.9
Yemen	2005	3 220	100.7	74.5	1 455	61.0	29.8	200	14.0	5.1
Yémen	2010	3 427	99.8	81.5	1 561	53.3	33.1	272	14.6	6.4
	2011	3 641	104.3	85.1	1 643	55.4	35.1	267	13.7	6.1
	2013	3 875	105.7	88.9	1 768	57.4	39.5	...	...	...
Zambia	2005	2 573	113.1	108.0	...	...	...	...	...	...
Zambie	2010	2 899	106.9	108.3	...	...	...	...	...	...
	2012	3 135	108.7	109.7	...	...	...	57	4.5	3.4
	2013	3 075	103.3	104.0	...	...	...	...	...	...
Zimbabwe	2003	2 362	96.8	95.4	758	39.6	35.6	...	...	...
Zimbabwe	2010	...	...	...	...	...	...	95	6.6	5.2
	2013	2 663	100.8	99.1	957	48.1	47.1	94	6.4	5.4
	2015	...	...	...	...	...	...	136	8.9	8.0

Source:

United Nations Educational, Scientific and Cultural Organization (UNESCO) Institute for Statistics, Montreal, the UNESCO Institute for Statistics (UIS) statistics database, last accessed June 2017.

& Data relate to the calendar year in which the academic year ends.

1 Excluding Sudan.
2 Including Sudan.
3 Excludes Japan.
4 Caucasus refers to Armenia, Azerbaijan, Cyprus, Georgia, Israel and Turkey.
5 Refers to Armenia, Azerbaijan, Cyprus, Georgia, Israel, Turkey and Central Asia.

Source:

L'Institut de statistique de l'Organisation des Nations Unies pour l'éducation, la science et la culture (UNESCO), Montréal, la base de données de l'institut de statistique de l'UNESCO (ISU), dernier accès juin 2017.

& Les données se réfèrent à l'année civile durant laquelle l'année scolaire se termine.

1 Exclut le Soudan.
2 Comprend le Soudan.
3 Exclut le Japon.
4 Le Caucase se rapportent à l'Arménie, l'Azerbaïdjan, Chypre, la Géorgie, l'Israël et la Turquie.
5 Le Caucase se rapportent à l'Arménie, l'Azerbaïdjan, Chypre, la Géorgie, l'Israël, la Turquie et Asie centrale.

Teaching staff at the primary, secondary and tertiary levels

Number of teachers and Pupil teacher ratio

Personnel enseignant au niveau primaire, secondaire et supérieur

Nombre d'enseignants et ratio élèves/enseignant par niveau d'enseignement

Region, country or area Région, pays ou zone	Year & Année &	Primary education / Enseignant primaire: Total Totale ('000)	Primary education / Enseignant primaire: Pupil-teacher ratio Ratio élèves/ enseignant	Secondary education / Enseignant secondaire: Total Totale ('000)	Secondary education / Enseignant secondaire: Pupil-teacher ratio Ratio élèves/ enseignant	Tertiary education / Enseignant supérieur: Total Totale ('000)	Tertiary education / Enseignant supérieur: Pupil-teacher ratio Ratio élèves/ enseignant
Total, all countries or areas	**2005**	*** 26 889**	*** 25.3**	*** 28 438**	*** 17.9**	**9 192**	**...**
Total, tous pays ou zones	**2010**	**28 643**	**24.4**	**32 220**	**16.9**	**11 133**	**...**
	2015	**30 897**	**23.4**	*** 33 066**	*** 17.5**	*** 12 795**	**...**
Africa	2005	3 521	38.8	* 2 161	* 22.7	* 350	...
Afrique	2010	4 116	38.8	* 3 023	* 20.6	* 473	...
	*2015	5 210	35.2	3 773	19.6	604	...
Northern Africa [1]	2005	794	25.0	* 917	* 17.0	* 164	...
Afrique septentrionale [1]	2010	779	25.2	* 1 057	* 14.9	* 198	...
	*2015	930	22.8	1 039	15.8	252	...
Sub-Saharan Africa [2]	2005	2 726	42.8	1 244	26.8	* 186	...
Afrique subsaharienne [2]	2010	3 337	41.9	* 1 966	* 23.6	* 275	...
	*2015	4 280	37.9	2 734	21.0	352	...
North America	2005	2 844	18.6	2 720	16.1	1 792	...
Amérique du Nord	2010	2 967	17.9	2 979	15.1	2 264	...
	*2015	2 926	18.2	3 003	15.3	2 356	...
Latin America & the Caribbean	2005	2 935	23.5	3 479	16.9	* 1 224	...
Amérique latine et Caraïbes	2010	2 913	23.1	3 565	17.1	* 1 662	...
	*2015	3 008	21.8	3 840	16.4	1 765	...
South America	2005	1 956	22.0	2 533	16.7	* 800	...
Amérique du Sud	2010	1 866	21.7	2 483	17.3	* 1 035	...
	*2015	1 917	20.6	2 601	16.8	1 158	...
Asia	2005	* 15 740	* 25.7	* 14 936	* 20.5	3 913	...
Asie	2010	* 16 849	* 23.9	18 089	18.4	4 877	...
	2015	17 964	22.6	18 152	19.5	* 6 257	...
Eastern Asia [3]	2005	* 6 301	* 18.9	* 5 885	* 18.3	1 683	...
Asie orientale [3]	2010	6 257	17.0	6 817	15.6	1 877	...
	2012	6 169	16.9	6 967	14.6	* 1 998	...
	2015	6 155	16.4	6 637	13.9	...	...
South-eastern Asia	2005	2 942	23.2	2 234	18.2	566	...
Asie du Sud-Est	2010	3 252	21.1	* 2 699	* 16.9	* 695	...
	*2015	3 523	19.5	2 695	19.0	701	...
Southern Asia	*2005	4 583	39.6	4 151	29.1	760	...
Asie méridionale	2010	* 5 275	* 36.4	5 699	25.2	* 1 291	...
	2015	6 055	32.6	5 757	29.6	1 865	...
Western Asia [4]	2005	* 1 153	* 19.4	* 1 047	* 16.5	184	...
Asie occidentale [4]	2010	* 1 292	* 18.3	* 1 302	* 15.4	257	...
	*2015	1 415	17.5	1 486	15.6	372	...
Caucasus and Central Asia [5]	2005	318	18.3	* 935	* 11.4	* 171	...
Caucase et Asie centrale [5]	2010	308	16.7	884	11.3	168	...
	2015	333	17.4	895	10.2	172	...
Europe	2005	2 672	14.4	5 873	11.0	2 279	...
Europe	2010	2 673	13.7	* 5 453	* 10.7	* 2 419	...
	2015	* 2 689	* 14.3	5 334	10.8	* 2 348	...
Oceania	*2005	157	20.0	...	...	59	...
Océanie	*2010	172	21.0	...	...	67	...
	2013	* 190	* 22.5	...	...	68	...
	*2014	...	...	...	...	70	...
Afghanistan	2004	...	...	...	...	2	15.5
Afghanistan	2007	110	42.8	33	31.6	...	...
	2009	115	42.8	...	...	3	28.5
	2010	119	44.4	...	...	...	...
	2014	...	...	...	...	11	23.9
	2015	143	44.3	72	37.7	...	...
Albania	2001	13	21.8	22	17.0	3	13.5
Albanie	2003	12	21.5	22	17.7	...	...
	2010	11	19.7	24	14.8	...	...
	2014	10	18.9	23	14.3	7	23.6
	2015	10	18.6	23	13.5	...	...

Teaching staff at the primary, secondary and tertiary levels *(continued)*
Number of teachers and Pupil teacher ratio

Personnel enseignant au niveau primaire, secondaire et supérieur *(suite)*
Nombre d'enseignants et ratio élèves/enseignant par niveau d'enseignement

Region, country or area Région, pays ou zone	Year & Année &	Primary education Enseignant primaire Total Totale ('000)	Primary education Pupil-teacher ratio Ratio élèves/ enseignant	Secondary education Enseignant secondaire Total Totale ('000)	Secondary education Pupil-teacher ratio Ratio élèves/ enseignant	Tertiary education Enseignant supérieur Total Totale ('000)	Tertiary education Pupil-teacher ratio Ratio élèves/ enseignant
Algeria	2005	171	25.4	...	...	28	27.9
Algérie	2010	142	23.3	...	...	40	28.8
	2015	165	23.8	...	...	54	24.0
American Samoa							
Samoa américaines	2007	...	...	...	...	~0	...
Andorra	2004	~0	12.7	~0	7.1	~0	3.9
Andorre	2005	~0	11.5	~0	7.8	...	...
	2008	~0	10.0	...	...	~0	5.3
	2009	~0	10.3	...	...	~0	...
	2010	~0	9.6	...	...	...	...
	2015	~0	9.9	1	8.1	~0	4.6
Angola	*2001	...	...	22	19.0	...	...
Angola	*2002	...	...	...	...	1	9.8
	2006	...	...	...	...	1	37.9
	2010	94	45.6	...	...	...	...
	2011	118	42.5	32	27.4	8	18.2
	2015	...	...	...	...	9	25.5
Anguilla	2005	~0	15.4	* ~0	* 12.5	~0	1.4
Anguilla	2007	~0	16.1	~0	10.4	~0	3.9
	2008	~0	14.1	...	...	~0	3.9
	2010	~0	14.5	...	...	...	...
	2011	~0	14.8	~0	8.5	...	...
Antigua and Barbuda	2000	1	18.7	~0	13.4	...	...
Antigua-et-Barbuda	2010	1	15.1	1	12.2	~0	6.8
	2012	1	13.8	1	11.6	~0	8.2
	2015	1	14.3	1	11.5	...	...
Argentina	2004	274	18.0	254	15.4	142	14.9
Argentine	2005	279	17.4	257	15.1	...	...
	2008	289	17.2	324	12.2	...	...
	2009	...	...	...	...	142	16.8
Armenia	2005	6	21.2	...	...	17	6.8
Arménie	2007	7	19.3	...	...	16	8.3
	2010	...	...	...	...	16	9.2
	2015	...	...	...	...	16	6.9
Aruba	2005	1	18.1	1	14.2	~0	9.2
Aruba	2010	1	16.8	1	13.8	~0	10.4
	2012	1	14.8	1	15.1	~0	9.9
	2015	...	...	...	...	~0	13.6
Australia							
Australie	2013	...	...	...	...	51	27.5
Austria	2003	29	13.2	73	10.5	29	8.0
Autriche	2005	29	12.4	71	11.0	...	...
	2010	30	11.0	75	10.0	47	7.5
	2015	31	10.6	72	9.6	61	7.0
Azerbaijan	2005	42	13.4	...	...	...	...
Azerbaïdjan	2010	44	11.0	...	...	26	7.0
	2015	41	13.5	...	...	21	9.7
Bahamas	*2004	2	16.8	2	14.2	...	...
Bahamas	2005	...	...	2	13.6	...	...
	2010	2	14.1	3	12.1	...	...
Bahrain	2003	...	...	...	...	1	22.3
Bahreïn	*2004	...	...	...	...	1	...
	2015	9	11.7	9	9.9	3	15.4
Bangladesh	2005	345	47.0	423	23.9	52	17.4
Bangladesh	2009	361	* 45.8	387	28.2	59	26.9
	2010	395	* 43.0	400	28.3	...	...
	2013	...	...	378	35.2	...	...
	2014	...	...	...	...	90	22.9
	2015	528	36.1	...	...	...	...

Region, country or area Région, pays ou zone	Year & Année &	Primary education Enseignant primaire Total Totale ('000)	 Pupil-teacher ratio Ratio élèves/ enseignant	Secondary education Enseignant secondaire Total Totale ('000)	 Pupil-teacher ratio Ratio élèves/ enseignant	Tertiary education Enseignant supérieur Total Totale ('000)	 Pupil-teacher ratio Ratio élèves/ enseignant
Barbados	*2001	1	17.0	1	17.2	1	13.5
Barbade	2005	1	15.1	* 1	* 15.9	...	...
	2006	...	...	1	14.6	...	...
	2007	2	14.5	...	...	1	14.5
	*2010	2	13.0	...	...	...	...
	2014	1	18.5	...	...	...	...
Belarus	2005	24	16.0	...	...	42	12.7
Bélarus	2010	24	15.0	...	...	41	14.0
	2015	22	17.6	77	8.4	33	14.6
Belgium	2002	64	11.9	109	10.6	23	15.7
Belgique	2005	64	11.5	...	...	26	15.1
	2010	66	11.0	...	...	29	15.4
	2014	69	11.2	128	9.4	29	17.3
Belize	2005	2	23.6	* 2	* 18.7	...	...
Belize	2010	2	22.2	2	16.8	...	...
	2015	3	20.4	2	16.3	1	14.2
Benin	2001	20	53.5	* 12	* 21.6	* 1	* 29.4
Bénin	2004	26	51.6	* 14	* 23.9	...	...
	2005	28	46.8	...	...	...	...
	2010	39	46.4	...	...	6	17.8
	2011	42	44.2	...	...	6	17.3
	2015	50	45.0	93	10.3	...	...
Bermuda	2005	1	8.3	1	7.0	~0	...
Bermudes	2010	1	7.4	1	5.4	~0	15.3
	2015	~0	10.4	1	6.3	~0	18.7
Bhutan	2005	3	31.1	1	28.1	...	...
Bhoutan	2010	4	25.9	3	21.4	1	6.7
	2012	5	24.0	3	19.9	1	7.7
	2014	4	26.7	5	14.3	...	...
	2016	3	38.0	...	...	...	...
Bolivia (Plurin. State of)	*2004	...	...	...	...	18	19.5
Bolivie (État plurin. de)	2007	...	...	...	...	16	* 22.5
	2015	74	18.1	55	20.8	...	...
Bosnia and Herzegovina	2010	...	...	...	...	8	12.4
Bosnie-Herzégovine	2015	9	17.2	27	10.1	10	11.3
Botswana	2005	13	25.6	13	13.8	...	...
Botswana	2007	13	25.2	13	13.8	...	...
	2009	13	25.5	...	...	...	...
	2013	15	22.6	...	...	...	...
	2016	...	...	...	...	3	20.1
Brazil	2005	887	21.0	1 612	15.4	293	15.6
Brésil	2010	762	22.2	1 413	16.7	345	19.0
	2014	795	20.9	1 451	16.7	426	19.0
British Virgin Islands	2004	~0	13.9	~0	9.3	~0	10.9
Îles Vierges britanniques	2005	~0	14.9	~0	9.3	...	...
	2009	~0	13.5	~0	8.7	~0	11.5
	2010	~0	13.2	~0	8.7	...	...
	2015	~0	11.7	~0	8.1	~0	9.5
Brunei Darussalam	2005	5	10.1	4	10.1	1	8.5
Brunéi Darussalam	2009	4	12.0	5	10.5	1	9.6
	2010	4	11.3	...	...	1	8.3
	2015	4	10.0	5	8.8	1	11.9
Bulgaria	2005	18	16.2	57	12.0	21	11.3
Bulgarie	2010	15	17.5	44	12.1	21	13.8
	2014	15	17.7	39	13.2	23	12.3
Burkina Faso	2003	23	44.7	8	31.3	...	...
Burkina Faso	2005	27	47.2	...	...	2	14.1
	2010	39	52.4	18	30.3	3	17.7
	2015	64	42.2	38	25.2	...	...
	2016	...	...	...	...	6	14.6

Teaching staff at the primary, secondary and tertiary levels *(continued)*
Number of teachers and Pupil teacher ratio

Personnel enseignant au niveau primaire, secondaire et supérieur *(suite)*
Nombre d'enseignants et ratio élèves/enseignant par niveau d'enseignement

Region, country or area Région, pays ou zone	Year & Année &	Primary education Enseignant primaire Total Totale ('000)	Primary education Enseignant primaire Pupil-teacher ratio Ratio élèves/ enseignant	Secondary education Enseignant secondaire Total Totale ('000)	Secondary education Enseignant secondaire Pupil-teacher ratio Ratio élèves/ enseignant	Tertiary education Enseignant supérieur Total Totale ('000)	Tertiary education Enseignant supérieur Pupil-teacher ratio Ratio élèves/ enseignant
Burundi	2005	21	48.7	* 7	* 22.8	1	16.1
Burundi	2010	37	50.6	11	29.9	2	16.4
	2014	47	43.7	16	37.2	2	25.2
	2015	48	43.2	19	35.8	...	...
Cabo Verde	2005	3	26.0	2	23.5	~0	8.1
Cabo Verde	2010	3	23.6	4	17.5	1	11.0
	2015	3	21.9	4	16.4	1	9.2
Cambodia	2003	49	56.2	24	23.6	2	17.4
Cambodge	2005	51	53.2	...	...	2	22.7
	2006	51	50.4	27	30.0	3	29.0
	2007	49	50.9	30	28.9	...	...
	2010	47	48.4	...	...	...	...
	2015	48	45.5	...	...	12	17.7
Cameroon	2005	* 62	* 47.8	* 48	* 16.2	3	* 31.5
Cameroun	2008	70	46.0	43	26.3	4	38.5
	2010	77	45.8	...	...	* 4	* 52.0
	2014	94	44.2	98	20.4	* 7	* 52.3
	2015	105	41.5	106	19.9	...	...
Canada Canada	2000	141	17.4	...	...	133	9.1
Cayman Islands	2001	~0	15.2	* ~0	* 9.8	* ~0	* 18.8
Îles Caïmanes	2005	~0	12.8	* ~0	* 10.3	...	...
	2008	~0	12.1	~0	8.9	~0	26.8
	2012	~0	13.3	1	5.3	...	...
	2013	~0	13.0	...	...	...	...
Central African Republic	2000	...	...	...	...	~0	19.5
République centrafricaine	2005	5	88.6	...	...	...	...
	2009	6	94.6	1	80.1	~0	30.7
	2010	8	84.3	2	...	...	...
	2011	8	81.3	2	66.8	~0	34.6
	2012	8	80.1	2	68.1	...	...
Chad	2005	20	63.2	* 7	* 33.5	1	9.5
Tchad	2009	27	61.0	13	32.3	2	8.6
	2010	28	62.2	13	32.5	...	...
	2011	31	62.6	14	32.0	2	10.9
	2012	34	61.3	15	29.8	...	...
	2013	37	62.4	15	...	...	...
Chile	2005	66	26.1	66	24.8	...	...
Chili	2010	66	23.4	69	21.9	70	14.1
	2013	75	19.5	75	21.0	78	15.0
China [6]	2003	5 779	21.1	5 138	18.6	* 742	* 20.5
Chine [6]	2005	...	...	...	...	1 404	14.7
	2010	5 997	16.8	6 417	15.5	1 557	19.9
	2011	5 939	16.8	6 431	15.2	1 607	19.5
	2015	5 889	16.3	6 234	13.8	...	...
China, Hong Kong SAR	2005	25	18.3	* 28	* 18.1	...	...
Chine, Hong Kong RAS	2010	23	15.2	* 30	* 16.7	...	...
	2015	24	13.7	* 30	* 13.0	...	...
China, Macao SAR	2005	2	23.2	2	22.4	2	15.4
Chine, Macao RAS	2010	2	16.1	2	16.2	2	14.4
	2015	2	14.1	3	11.4	2	15.3
Colombia	2005	187	28.3	164	26.2	94	13.1
Colombie	2009	181	29.3	187	26.7	* 110	* 14.2
	2010	181	28.1	187	27.1	...	...
	2015	188	23.8	187	25.6	149	15.4
Comoros	2003	3	35.9	3	11.3	~0	13.7
Comores	2004	3	35.0	3	13.8	...	...
	2008	4	30.2	...	...	...	...
	2010	...	...	...	...	~0	17.1
	2013	4	27.8	8	8.7	~0	25.7
	2014	...	...	8	8.6	~0	26.3

8 Teaching staff at the primary, secondary and tertiary levels *(continued)*
Number of teachers and Pupil teacher ratio

Personnel enseignant au niveau primaire, secondaire et supérieur *(suite)*
Nombre d'enseignants et ratio élèves/enseignant par niveau d'enseignement

Region, country or area Région, pays ou zone	Year & Année &	Primary education / Enseignant primaire: Total Totale ('000)	Primary education / Enseignant primaire: Pupil-teacher ratio Ratio élèves/ enseignant	Secondary education / Enseignant secondaire: Total Totale ('000)	Secondary education / Enseignant secondaire: Pupil-teacher ratio Ratio élèves/ enseignant	Tertiary education / Enseignant supérieur: Total Totale ('000)	Tertiary education / Enseignant supérieur: Pupil-teacher ratio Ratio élèves/ enseignant
Congo	2003	8	65.2	* 7	* 28.1	* 1	* 13.8
Congo	2004	7	82.8	* 7	* 34.3	...	...
	2009	10	64.4	...	...	1	20.0
	2010	14	49.1	...	...	...	...
	2012	17	44.4	18	18.7	3	11.8
	2013	...	...	...	...	3	12.3
Cook Islands	2005	~0	16.1	~0	15.6	...	...
Îles Cook	2010	~0	15.0	~0	16.2	...	...
	2015	~0	17.2	~0	13.9	~0	...
Costa Rica	2002	24	22.6	15	18.8	...	...
Costa Rica	2005	25	21.3	...	...	...	...
	2010	29	17.9	27	15.5	...	...
	2015	37	12.7	33	14.0	...	...
Côte d'Ivoire	*2003	48	42.4	...	...	...	...
Côte d'Ivoire	2009	57	42.1	...	...	...	...
	2010	...	...	...	...	10	14.2
	2015	80	42.1	60	26.6	19	10.3
Croatia	2005	11	17.5	39	10.1	...	...
Croatie	2010	12	14.3	48	8.1	16	9.5
	2015	12	13.7	51	7.0	16	10.1
Cuba	2005	87	10.3	85	11.1	91	5.2
Cuba	2010	93	9.1	85	9.5	153	5.2
	2015	84	8.9	91	9.0	57	4.6
Cyprus	2005	3	17.7	6	11.3	1	13.8
Chypre	2010	4	13.8	7	9.8	3	12.6
	2015	5	11.9	6	10.4	3	12.7
Czechia	2005	31	16.2	93	10.4	24	13.8
Tchéquie	2006	30	15.7	92	10.5	23	15.0
	2010	25	18.7	76	11.0	...	...
	2013	26	18.9	69	11.5	16	26.0
Dem. People's Rep. Korea	2009	70	22.0	124	20.0	69	8.6
Rép. pop. dém. de Corée	2015	66	20.5	123	17.5	63	9.0
Dem. Rep. of the Congo	2002	159	34.3	...	...	...	...
Rép. dém. du Congo	2009	274	37.3	212	16.0	23	16.4
	2010	286	37.0	218	16.0	...	...
	2013	340	37.1	281	14.2	29	15.3
	2014	383	35.3	301	14.6	...	...
Denmark	2001	40	9.9	44	10.1	...	...
Danemark	2014	44	10.7	49	11.3	28	10.7
	2015	...	...	...	...	37	8.5
Djibouti	2002	...	...	1	31.9	* ~0	* 15.2
Djibouti	2004	1	34.5	...	...	~0	12.3
	2005	...	...	...	...	~0	17.7
	2009	2	34.1	1	29.7	~0	20.1
	2010	...	...	...	...	~0	20.5
	2011	2	35.2	2	27.9	~0	19.2
	2016	2	31.1	3	23.8	...	...
Dominica	2005	1	18.2	~0	15.1	...	...
Dominique	2010	1	16.0	1	13.2	...	...
	2015	1	14.0	1	10.7	...	...
Dominican Republic	2003	...	...	...	...	11	25.8
République dominicaine	2005	53	24.3	31	26.4	...	...
	2010	52	25.5	32	28.2	...	...
	2015	71	18.3	42	22.1	19	25.5
Ecuador	2001	85	23.1	* 69	* 13.6	15	...
Équateur	2005	87	22.9	* 76	* 13.9	...	...
	2008	...	...	...	...	27	19.9
	2010	91	23.1	77	20.4	...	...
	2012	97	21.9	84	20.9	39	14.5
	2014	89	23.3	82	23.0	39	...
	2016	80	25.1	86	22.3	...	...

Teaching staff at the primary, secondary and tertiary levels *(continued)*

Number of teachers and Pupil teacher ratio

Personnel enseignant au niveau primaire, secondaire et supérieur *(suite)*

Nombre d'enseignants et ratio élèves/enseignant par niveau d'enseignement

Region, country or area Région, pays ou zone	Year & Année &	Primary education / Enseignant primaire Total Totale ('000)	Pupil-teacher ratio Ratio élèves/ enseignant	Secondary education / Enseignant secondaire Total Totale ('000)	Pupil-teacher ratio Ratio élèves/ enseignant	Tertiary education / Enseignant supérieur Total Totale ('000)	Pupil-teacher ratio Ratio élèves/ enseignant
Egypt	*2004	363	21.9	488	17.1	81	28.0
Égypte	*2005	373	25.6	...	...	...	...
	2009	382	27.2	549	12.1	...	...
	2010	380	27.7	...	...	...	...
	2014	481	23.1	572	14.4	107	23.9
El Salvador	2005	24	43.2	* 18	* 28.9	8	15.2
El Salvador	2009	31	31.0	23	24.4	9	16.2
	2010	...	...	...	...	9	16.5
	2015	25	29.7	19	30.8	10	18.1
Equatorial Guinea	2000	2	43.4	* 1	* 23.2	~0	4.9
Guinée équatoriale	2003	2	32.0	...	...	...	...
	2005	...	...	1	19.2	...	...
	2010	3	27.2	...	...	...	...
	2015	4	23.2	...	...	...	...
Eritrea	2004	8	46.7	4	47.8	~0	10.8
Érythrée	2005	8	47.5	4	51.3	...	...
	2010	8	38.0	6	38.7	1	19.2
	2014	* 9	* 42.5	* 7	* 40.6	1	20.2
	2015	8	43.3	6	38.9	...	...
Estonia	2001	8	14.1	12	10.1	7	8.8
Estonie	2005	...	...	...	...	6	10.7
	2006	8	10.6	...	...	* 6	* 10.7
	2010	6	11.7	11	8.8	...	...
	2013	7	11.5	10	8.1	...	...
Ethiopia	2000	87	67.3	...	...	2	27.1
Éthiopie	2005	...	...	...	...	5	39.4
	2009	234	57.9	82	47.4	12	34.1
	2010	252	54.1	98	43.1	...	...
	2011	260	55.1	113	40.3	...	...
	*2012	...	...	122	40.4	...	...
	2014	...	...	...	...	24	31.2
Fiji	2004	4	28.2	* 5	* 22.4	...	...
Fidji	2008	4	26.0	5	18.7	...	...
	2012	4	28.0	5	19.3	...	...
Finland	2005	25	15.5	42	10.3	19	16.4
Finlande	2010	25	14.0	43	9.9	15	19.7
	2014	26	13.3	42	12.8	16	19.3
France	2004	203	18.6	511	11.4	136	15.9
France	2005	216	18.6	528	11.4	...	...
	2010	234	17.8	463	12.7	...	...
	2013	229	18.2	457	12.9	110	21.3
Gabon	2003	8	36.0	...	...	...	...
Gabon	2011	13	24.5	...	...	...	...
Gambia	2004	5	38.5	...	...	~0	11.4
Gambie	2005	6	36.6	...	...	...	...
	*2010	6	37.5	...	...	...	...
	2012	7	33.9	...	...	~0	23.2
	2016	7	42.1	...	...	...	...
Georgia	2003	17	14.5	49	9.2	29	5.5
Géorgie	2005	...	...	...	...	29	5.9
	2009	* 34	* 8.9	* 45	* 7.6	12	7.7
	2010	...	...	...	...	13	7.9
	2015	32	9.0	38	7.2	18	7.1
Germany	2002	236	14.3	590	14.3	277	...
Allemagne	2005	234	14.1	596	13.9	...	...
	2010	242	12.7	594	12.9	...	...
	2015	236	12.2	586	12.1	396	7.5
Ghana	2005	89	32.8	* 73	* 18.8	...	...
Ghana	2009	111	33.1	99	18.3	...	...
	*2010	121	...	112	...	...	...
	2015	139	31.3	147	16.6	14	28.9
	2016	143	30.6	148	17.0	...	...

Teaching staff at the primary, secondary and tertiary levels *(continued)*
Number of teachers and Pupil teacher ratio

Personnel enseignant au niveau primaire, secondaire et supérieur *(suite)*
Nombre d'enseignants et ratio élèves/enseignant par niveau d'enseignement

		Primary education Enseignant primaire		Secondary education Enseignant secondaire		Tertiary education Enseignant supérieur	
Region, country or area **Région, pays ou zone**	**Year &** **Année &**	**Total** **Totale ('000)**	**Pupil-teacher ratio** **Ratio élèves/ enseignant**	**Total** **Totale ('000)**	**Pupil-teacher ratio** **Ratio élèves/ enseignant**	**Total** **Totale ('000)**	**Pupil-teacher ratio** **Ratio élèves/ enseignant**
Gibraltar	2001	~0	20.7	~0	11.7	...	...
Gibraltar	2009	~0	16.0	~0	5.9	...	...
Greece	2005	59	11.1	86	8.3	27	23.8
Grèce	2007	62	10.3	87	7.9	29	20.8
	2014	67	9.4	80	8.3	15	44.5
Grenada	2004	1	17.7	* 1	* 20.1	...	...
Grenade	2005	1	18.2	...	...	...	...
	2010	1	16.1	1	15.5	...	...
	2015	1	17.0	1	11.9	2	4.3
Guatemala	2002	69	30.1	44	13.7	4	27.7
Guatemala	*2003	...	...	...	...	4	...
	2005	76	31.1	48	15.8	...	...
	2010	99	26.9	77	14.0	...	...
	2015	117	20.4	111	11.0	...	...
Guinea	2005	27	44.9	12	* 34.4	...	...
Guinée	2008	31	44.1	16	33.3	...	...
	2010	34	42.2	...	...	5	19.1
	2011	35	44.1	19	33.1	6	17.9
	2014	38	45.6	...	...	6	18.7
Guinea-Bissau	2000	3	44.1	* 2	* 15.0	...	...
Guinée-Bissau	2006	4	62.2	1	37.3	~0	147.6
	2010	5	51.9	...	...	...	...
Guyana	2005	4	28.0	* 4	* 18.0	1	12.6
Guyana	2010	4	24.6	4	21.4	1	10.6
	2012	4	23.2	4	20.3	1	13.1
Honduras	2004	38	32.9	17	...	* 7	* 17.1
Honduras	*2005	42	29.1	...	...	...	...
	2009	37	33.9	...	...	...	...
	2010	...	...	...	...	9	19.8
	2015	40	29.1	40	16.1	10	20.0
Hungary	2005	41	10.4	97	9.9	25	17.2
Hongrie	2010	37	10.6	89	10.2	25	15.8
	2015	36	11.0	80	10.3	21	14.6
Iceland	2005	...	...	...	...	2	8.5
Islande	2010	...	...	...	...	2	8.6
	2012	3	9.9	...	...	2	8.7
	2013	3	9.9	...	...	...	...
India	2003	3 038	41.3	2 507	32.3	428	26.4
Inde	2004	...	...	2 586	32.7	539	22.0
	2010	...	...	4 252	25.3	...	...
	2015	4 399	31.5	4 093	31.7	1 322	24.3
Indonesia	2005	1 428	20.4	1 282	12.5	272	* 13.5
Indonésie	2010	1 596	19.0	1 641	12.2	271	18.4
	2014	1 802	16.6	1 460	15.5	258	25.0
Iran (Islamic Republic of)	2005	285	21.7	...	...	115	18.4
Iran (Rép. islamique d')	2009	278	20.5	...	...	164	20.5
	2010	...	...	...	...	174	21.8
	2015	286	26.8	336	17.0	315	15.3
Iraq	2004	211	20.5	91	18.8	19	22.1
Iraq	*2005	...	...	...	...	19	22.1
	2007	287	17.0	148	13.7	...	...
Ireland	2005	25	17.9	...	...	12	16.0
Irlande	2010	32	15.8	...	...	13	15.4
	2012	32	16.1	...	...	...	...
Israel	*2005	55	13.0	68	9.9	...	...
Israël	*2009	60	13.1	71	9.8	...	...
	2010	62	13.1	...	...	...	...
	2014	71	12.1	62	12.4	...	...
Italy	2005	264	10.5	428	10.5	94	21.4
Italie	2007	273	10.3	451	10.1	104	19.5
	2010	...	...	...	...	106	18.7
	2015	237	12.0	408	11.3	90	20.3

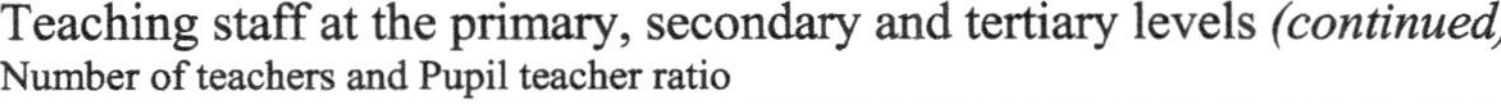

8 Teaching staff at the primary, secondary and tertiary levels *(continued)*

Number of teachers and Pupil teacher ratio

Personnel enseignant au niveau primaire, secondaire et supérieur *(suite)*

Nombre d'enseignants et ratio élèves/enseignant par niveau d'enseignement

Region, country or area Région, pays ou zone	Year & Année &	Primary education Enseignant primaire Total Totale ('000)	Primary education Enseignant primaire Pupil-teacher ratio Ratio élèves/ enseignant	Secondary education Enseignant secondaire Total Totale ('000)	Secondary education Enseignant secondaire Pupil-teacher ratio Ratio élèves/ enseignant	Tertiary education Enseignant supérieur Total Totale ('000)	Tertiary education Enseignant supérieur Pupil-teacher ratio Ratio élèves/ enseignant
Jamaica Jamaïque	2002	...	...	* 12	* 19.3	2	22.8
	2004	12	27.5	13	19.1	...	...
	2010	...	...	18	14.3	...	...
	2015	12	21.9	13	16.4	...	...
Japan Japon	2005	383	18.9	610	12.6	497	8.1
	2010	399	17.8	614	11.9	528	7.3
	2012	405	17.1	624	11.7	537	7.2
	2014	408	16.4	...	...	545	7.1
Jordan Jordanie	2003	* 39	* 19.9	* 34	* 17.9	7	26.8
	2005	...	...	...	...	8	26.4
	2010	...	...	...	...	10	24.6
	2014	58	16.9	51	14.6	...	...
	2015	...	...	...	...	14	22.5
Kazakhstan Kazakhstan	2000	...	...	...	...	31	13.4
	2005	59	17.3	...	...	...	...
	2010	59	16.2	...	...	49	15.5
	2016	69	18.6	252	6.8	38	16.4
Kenya Kenya	*2005	145	42.0	91	27.2	...	...
	*2009	165	43.4	96	33.3	...	...
	*2015	267	30.7	199	...	...	...
Kiribati Kiribati	2005	1	24.7	1	17.0	...	...
	2008	1	25.0	1	17.4	...	...
	2014	1	26.4	...	...	...	...
Kuwait Koweït	2004	12	12.8	25	10.6	* 2	* 17.0
	2005	17	12.1	...	...	...	...
	2009	25	8.6	* 31	* 8.2	...	...
	2010	26	8.4	...	...	...	...
	2015	30	8.8	40	7.2	...	...
Kyrgyzstan Kirghizistan	2005	18	24.5	54	13.4	13	16.5
	2010	16	24.3	48	14.3	17	14.9
	2015	17	26.2	52	12.5	21	12.8
Lao People's Dem. Rep. Rép. dém. populaire lao	2005	28	31.5	16	24.8	2	20.7
	2010	32	28.8	21	20.2	5	22.5
	2015	35	24.2	* 34	* 18.7	12	10.6
Latvia Lettonie	2005	7	12.2	25	10.8	6	20.9
	2010	10	11.9	16	9.0	7	16.3
	2015	11	11.1	15	8.0	7	12.6
Lebanon Liban	2005	* 33	* 14.6	* 42	* 9.0	21	8.0
	2010	33	14.1	43	8.9	25	8.0
	2014	39	12.3	48	7.7	46	5.0
Lesotho Lesotho	2005	10	41.6	3	27.0	1	14.2
	2006	10	40.8	4	25.8	1	13.3
	2010	12	33.8	* 5	* 24.5	...	...
	2014	11	32.8	* 6	* 23.5	1	29.3
	2015	11	33.1	6	24.0	...	...
Liberia Libéria	2000	13	38.3	...	...	1	72.3
	*2001	...	...	...	...	1	...
	2009	22	27.4	...	...	...	...
	2010	...	...	...	...	1	24.4
	2012	...	...	...	...	2	21.6
	2015	22	30.4	12	18.4	...	...
Libya Libye	*2003	...	...	...	...	16	23.9
Liechtenstein Liechtenstein	2005	~0	8.6	~0	9.6	...	...
	2009	~0	6.5	~0	9.3	...	...
	2010	~0	6.1	...	...	...	...
	2015	~0	7.8	~0	9.9	~0	6.3
Lithuania Lituanie	2005	11	14.1	43	9.9	13	14.9
	2010	10	12.8	39	8.8	14	14.3
	2015	8	12.9	33	7.9	13	10.8

Teaching staff at the primary, secondary and tertiary levels *(continued)*
Number of teachers and Pupil teacher ratio

Personnel enseignant au niveau primaire, secondaire et supérieur *(suite)*
Nombre d'enseignants et ratio élèves/enseignant par niveau d'enseignement

Region, country or area Région, pays ou zone	Year & Année &	Primary education / Enseignant primaire: Total Totale ('000)	Primary education / Enseignant primaire: Pupil-teacher ratio Ratio élèves/ enseignant	Secondary education / Enseignant secondaire: Total Totale ('000)	Secondary education / Enseignant secondaire: Pupil-teacher ratio Ratio élèves/ enseignant	Tertiary education / Enseignant supérieur: Total Totale ('000)	Tertiary education / Enseignant supérieur: Pupil-teacher ratio Ratio élèves/ enseignant
Luxembourg	2005	3	11.3	3	10.3	...	...
Luxembourg	2010	4	9.3	5	8.5	1	5.4
	2012	4	8.4	6	7.9	2	3.8
	2014	4	8.2	5	9.1	...	...
Madagascar	2005	67	53.6	* 29	* 21.6	2	25.5
Madagascar	2009	90	47.9	44	* 23.5	4	16.3
	2010	106	40.1	...	...	4	16.6
	2014	111	41.7	65	23.1	6	18.8
	2015	116	41.2	...	...	...	...
Malawi	2005	...	...	...	...	1	7.5
Malawi	2010	* 43	* 79.3	* 16	* 43.2	1	11.6
	2011	* 47	* 76.1	* 17	* 42.1	1	13.6
	*2015	60	69.5	25	40.9	...	...
Malaysia	2005	190	16.9	153	16.3	45	15.4
Malaisie	2010	257	12.6	191	13.7	75	14.2
	2015	270	11.5	249	12.0	80	10.2
Maldives	2003	4	18.2	2	13.7	~0	1.9
Maldives	2005	3	20.1	...	...	...	...
	2010	4	11.7	...	...	...	...
	2016	4	10.3	...	...	...	...
Mali	2000	16	65.3	* 9	* 29.0	* 1	* 20.5
Mali	2005	28	54.4	...	...	...	...
	2009	38	50.1	* 29	* 23.4	...	...
	2010	40	50.4	...	...	...	...
	2012	...	...	...	...	2	52.4
	2015	52	42.7	49	19.2	...	...
Malta	2005	2	18.4	3	11.5	1	11.4
Malte	2008	2	17.5	4	10.6	1	9.8
	2010	2	14.3	...	...	1	9.0
	2015	2	12.2	4	7.5	2	8.0
Marshall Islands	2002	1	16.9	~0	16.7	~0	18.8
Îles Marshall	*2003	...	...	~0	14.9	...	...
	2012	...	...	...	...	~0	19.6
Mauritania	2005	11	40.3	3	31.0	~0	24.6
Mauritanie	2006	11	41.4	* 4	* 26.2	~0	28.8
	2010	14	37.2	...	...	~0	38.4
	2013	16	35.4	...	...	~0	43.0
	2015	18	35.8	6	33.5	...	...
Mauritius	2005	6	22.3	7	* 17.4	...	...
Maurice	2010	5	21.5	8	* 15.3	1	30.4
	2015	5	18.8	10	12.9	...	...
Mexico	2005	519	28.3	593	17.8	251	9.5
Mexique	2010	530	28.1	652	17.9	310	9.2
	2014	534	27.4	806	16.1	349	9.8
Micronesia (Fed. States of)	*2000	...	...	...	...	~0	17.1
Micronésie (États féd. de)	*2015	1	19.7	...	...	...	...
Monaco	2001	~0	22.3	~0	10.8	...	...
Monaco	2004	...	...	~0	11.1	...	...
	2008	...	...	1	5.8	...	...
	2015	~0	12.6	~0	8.1	...	...
Mongolia	2005	7	34.2	15	22.4	8	15.4
Mongolie	2010	9	30.2	19	14.5	9	18.9
	2014	9	27.2	21	...	9	19.7
	2015	9	28.2	...	...	9	20.3
Montserrat	2005	~0	20.4	~0	11.5	...	...
Montserrat	2009	~0	13.1	~0	13.3	...	...
	2014	~0	11.0	~0	12.7	...	...
Morocco	2004	148	27.6	* 100	* 18.7	19	18.5
Maroc	2005	148	27.1	...	...	19	19.0
	2009	145	26.6	...	...	20	21.4
	2010	150	26.2	...	...	...	...
	2015	156	25.9	...	...	...	...

Teaching staff at the primary, secondary and tertiary levels *(continued)*
Number of teachers and Pupil teacher ratio

Personnel enseignant au niveau primaire, secondaire et supérieur *(suite)*
Nombre d'enseignants et ratio élèves/enseignant par niveau d'enseignement

Region, country or area Région, pays ou zone	Year & Année &	Primary education / Enseignant primaire: Total Totale ('000)	Primary: Pupil-teacher ratio Ratio élèves/ enseignant	Secondary education / Enseignant secondaire: Total Totale ('000)	Secondary: Pupil-teacher ratio Ratio élèves/ enseignant	Tertiary education / Enseignant supérieur: Total Totale ('000)	Tertiary: Pupil-teacher ratio Ratio élèves/ enseignant
Mozambique	2005	59	66.3	* 10	* 32.2	3	9.4
Mozambique	2010	90	58.5	* 20	* 34.1	6	16.2
	2014	104	* 54.8	* 26	* 40.0	10	15.2
	2015	108	* 54.7	* 27	* 39.7	...	...
Myanmar	2001	148	32.3	75	30.8	11	52.6
Myanmar	2005	160	30.9	78	33.1	...	...
	2007	172	29.1	82	32.8	11	47.6
	2010	182	28.2	84	34.1	...	...
	2012	...	...	...	...	25	25.3
	2014	188	27.6	100	31.8	...	...
Namibia	2003	13	31.6	6	25.2	1	13.1
Namibie	2005	13	30.8	6	25.1	...	...
	2007	14	29.9	6	24.6	...	...
	2008	14	29.4	...	...	1	16.4
	2010	14	29.8	...	...	...	...
	2014	...	...	...	...	3	...
Nauru	2005	~0	27.9	~0	15.4	...	...
Nauru	2007	~0	19.9	~0	20.9	...	...
	2008	~0	22.4	...	...	...	...
	2014	~0	39.5	~0	22.8	...	...
Nepal	2003	110	35.7	53	34.7	...	...
Népal	2005	101	39.7	...	...	7	27.2
	2007	113	40.0	...	...	10	25.7
	2010	154	31.9	* 84	* 32.0	...	...
	2013	179	25.6	* 107	* 29.2	8	60.0
	2016	190	22.4	* 113	* 28.9	...	...
Netherlands	2005	...	...	107	13.1	45	12.7
Pays-Bas	2010	...	...	107	13.7	52	12.6
	2015	104	11.6	112	14.5	63	13.5
Netherlands Antilles [former] Antilles néerlandaises [anc.]	2002	1	...	1	...	* ~0	...
New Zealand	2005	22	16.3	36	14.7	15	15.9
Nouvelle-Zélande	2010	24	14.5	35	14.5	17	16.0
	2014	25	14.4	35	14.0	15	17.4
Nicaragua	2002	26	35.2	* 11	* 33.9	7	15.3
Nicaragua	2005	28	33.6	13	33.7	...	...
	2010	31	30.2	15	30.8	...	...
Niger	2005	24	43.7	7	27.4	1	14.9
Niger	2010	45	38.6	10	30.8	2	11.3
	2012	53	38.8	...	...	2	12.3
	2015	67	36.6	21	28.0	...	...
Nigeria	2004	598	35.8	155	40.6	37	34.8
Nigéria	2005	599	36.9	159	40.2	...	...
	2010	574	* 37.6	390	23.2	57	24.6
	2011	...	...	...	...	67	22.6
Niue	2004	~0	11.5	~0	8.4	...	...
Nioué	2005	...	...	~0	8.2	...	...
	2015	~0	17.3	~0	7.9	...	...
Norway	2001	...	...	...	...	15	12.3
Norvège	2015	49	8.9	51	8.5	27	9.9
Oman	*2003	16	19.9	16	17.4	...	...
Oman	2005	...	...	...	...	3	16.2
	2010	...	...	...	...	5	16.8
	2015	...	...	...	...	8	16.2
Pakistan	2005	450	38.3	* 295	* 23.3	...	...
Pakistan	2009	465	39.7	...	...	* 63	* 19.3
	2010	464	40.5	...	...	...	...
	2015	428	46.3	* 572	* 21.1	107	17.6
Palau	2000	~0	15.7	~0	15.1	* ~0	* 10.9
Palaos	*2002	...	...	...	...	~0	10.5
	2013	...	...	...	...	~0	8.2
	2016	~0	14.2	~0	18.8	...	...

Region, country or area Région, pays ou zone	Year & Année &	Primary education Enseignant primaire Total Totale ('000)	Pupil-teacher ratio Ratio élèves/ enseignant	Secondary education Enseignant secondaire Total Totale ('000)	Pupil-teacher ratio Ratio élèves/ enseignant	Tertiary education Enseignant supérieur Total Totale ('000)	Pupil-teacher ratio Ratio élèves/ enseignant
Panama	2005	18	24.2	16	15.6	11	11.0
Panama	2010	19	23.5	19	15.3	15	9.2
	2013	20	22.3	20	15.5	11	10.9
	2014	19	22.0	23	13.6	...	...
Papua New Guinea	*2001	14	36.2	...	...	...	...
Papouasie-Nvl-Guinée	2012	32	45.2	14	27.4	...	...
Paraguay	*2004	33	27.8	44	11.8	...	...
Paraguay	2012	35	24.2	34	18.4	...	...
Peru	2002	171	25.1	134	18.9	56	14.8
Pérou	2005	177	23.0	148	16.7	...	...
	2010	191	19.7	167	16.0	...	...
	2015	195	18.0	190	14.1	...	...
Philippines	2005	373	35.1	168	37.9	* 113	* 21.3
Philippines	2009	435	31.4	194	34.8	...	...
	2013	461	31.4	268	27.0	...	...
Poland	2005	236	11.5	296	11.6	95	22.3
Pologne	2010	240	9.3	273	10.4	103	20.9
	2014	211	10.2	279	9.5	100	17.6
	2015	220	...	273	...	97	...
Portugal	2005	72	10.5	94	7.1	37	10.4
Portugal	2010	68	10.8	98	7.3	36	10.6
	2015	49	13.3	78	9.9	32	10.4
Puerto Rico	2010	26	11.7	26	11.1	16	15.4
Porto Rico	2014	19	13.4	15	17.2	16	15.2
Qatar	2005	6	11.1	5	11.6	1	* 14.6
Qatar	2010	7	12.0	7	9.9	2	8.6
	2015	11	11.6	9	10.7	2	12.9
Republic of Korea	2005	144	27.9	210	18.1	191	16.8
République de Corée	2010	158	20.9	225	17.6	223	14.7
	2014	166	16.5	240	14.9	224	14.8
Republic of Moldova	2005	10	18.0	31	12.8	8	16.7
République de Moldova	2010	9	15.4	29	10.5	8	16.8
	2015	8	17.5	25	9.3	7	16.5
Romania	2005	57	17.0	162	12.9	31	23.9
Roumanie	2010	52	16.1	146	12.5	31	32.1
	2015	50	18.9	129	12.1	28	19.5
Russian Federation	2005	* 317	* 16.7	* 1 306	* 9.5	625	14.4
Fédération de Russie	2009	278	18.1	1 136	8.5	670	13.9
	2012	282	19.6	1 046	8.8	554	14.4
	2013	285	19.8	...	...	683	11.0
	2014	289	19.8	...	...	...	...
Rwanda	2005	27	69.0	8	28.7	* 2	* 15.3
Rwanda	2009	33	68.3	15	22.6	3	18.7
	2010	36	64.6	...	...	3	22.2
	2015	42	58.3	30	19.2	3	23.9
	2016	...	...	...	...	3	32.5
Saint Kitts and Nevis	2005	~0	17.6	* ~0	* 9.9	...	...
Saint-Kitts-et-Nevis	2010	~0	14.1	~0	* 9.3	...	...
	2015	~0	15.1	1	8.3	~0	7.6
Saint Lucia	2005	1	22.0	1	16.9	~0	12.6
Sainte-Lucie	2010	1	18.5	* 1	* 15.7	~0	9.3
	2015	1	15.5	1	11.7	~0	10.2
Saint Vincent & Grenadines	*2004	1	17.2	1	18.1	...	...
Saint-Vincent-Grenadines	2010	1	16.3	1	16.8	...	...
	2015	1	14.9	1	15.0	...	...
Samoa	2000	1	24.0	1	21.2	~0	7.8
Samoa	2002	1	27.2	1	21.0	...	...
	2010	1	30.2	1	21.5	...	...
San Marino	2004	~0	6.3	...	...	...	...
Saint-Marin	2010	~0	6.5	~0	14.5	...	...
	2012	~0	6.3	...	...	...	...

Teaching staff at the primary, secondary and tertiary levels *(continued)*

Number of teachers and Pupil teacher ratio

Personnel enseignant au niveau primaire, secondaire et supérieur *(suite)*

Nombre d'enseignants et ratio élèves/enseignant par niveau d'enseignement

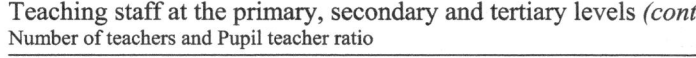

Region, country or area Région, pays ou zone	Year & Année &	Primary education / Enseignant primaire: Total Totale ('000)	Primary: Pupil-teacher ratio Ratio élèves/ enseignant	Secondary education / Enseignant secondaire: Total Totale ('000)	Secondary: Pupil-teacher ratio Ratio élèves/ enseignant	Tertiary education / Enseignant supérieur: Total Totale ('000)	Tertiary: Pupil-teacher ratio Ratio élèves/ enseignant
Sao Tome and Principe	2005	1	30.8	* ~0	* 21.7	...	...
Sao Tomé-et-Principe	2009	1	26.2	...	...	...	...
	2010	...	...	...	...	~0	8.1
	2015	1	38.8	1	20.8	~0	8.0
	2016	1	32.2	1	24.8	...	...
Saudi Arabia	2005	* 273	* 11.3	* 234	* 11.1	27	22.5
Arabie saoudite	2009	* 285	* 11.4	* 264	* 11.3	39	19.2
	2010	298	11.2	...	...	50	18.2
	2014	347	10.8	312	* 11.0	74	20.3
	2015	353	10.9	...	...	77	19.8
Senegal	2005	35	41.7	* 15	* 26.4	...	...
Sénégal	2010	50	33.7	...	...	...	...
	2015	62	32.1	56	20.4	6	25.8
Serbia	2010	17	16.4	62	9.6	15	15.3
Serbie	2015	18	15.2	65	8.5	11	22.5
Seychelles	2005	1	13.7	1	14.4	...	...
Seychelles	2010	1	12.5	1	12.8	...	...
	2015	1	13.7	1	12.0	~0	14.4
Sierra Leone	2001	15	37.3	6	26.6	1	7.7
Sierra Leone	*2002	...	...	...	...	1	7.5
	2015	74	18.4	40	11.2	...	...
Singapore	2009	17	17.4	16	14.9	15	13.1
Singapour	2010	...	...	...	...	15	13.8
	2013	...	...	...	...	19	13.5
Sint Maarten (Dutch part)	2012	~0	11.3	~0	11.8	~0	3.3
St-Martin (partie néerland.)	2014	...	...	~0	7.6	~0	3.6
	2015	...	...	...	...	~0	3.6
Slovakia	2005	14	17.5	51	13.1	13	14.3
Slovaquie	2010	14	15.2	46	12.0	13	17.6
	2014	14	15.2	42	11.1	13	15.5
	2015	14	15.2	41	11.2	13	...
Slovenia	2005	6	15.1	16	11.2	4	25.1
Slovénie	2009	6	17.2	16	9.2	6	18.3
	2010	6	17.0	...	...	7	16.5
	2013	6	16.9	15	10.1	7	13.6
Solomon Islands	*2000	...	...	1	10.1	...	...
Îles Salomon	2010	5	19.9	1	28.1	...	...
	2012	5	19.1	2	25.9	...	...
	2015	4	25.7	2	...	...	...
Somalia Somalie	2007	13	35.5	5	19.3	...	...
South Africa	2005	* 233	* 31.4	142	32.9	...	...
Afrique du Sud	2009	* 212	* 33.6	187	25.0	...	...
	*2010	215	32.7	...	...	...	...
	*2014	214	33.6	...	...	...	...
South Sudan Soudan du sud	*2015	27	46.8	6	27.5	...	...
Spain	2005	181	13.8	280	11.1	145	12.5
Espagne	2010	219	12.4	295	10.8	155	12.1
	2015	228	13.2	276	12.0	157	12.5
Sri Lanka	2005	73	21.9	...	...	...	...
Sri Lanka	2010	72	23.9	...	...	5	49.6
	2011	72	24.1	149	17.3	5	45.2
	2012	72	24.4	150	17.3	...	...
	2015	77	23.2	...	...	...	...
State of Palestine	2005	16	24.5	25	26.6	* 5	* 30.5
État de Palestine	2010	14	27.8	32	22.5	7	27.2
	2015	19	24.0	36	19.9	8	26.1
Sudan Soudan	2014	...	...	...	...	14	46.0

Teaching staff at the primary, secondary and tertiary levels *(continued)*
Number of teachers and Pupil teacher ratio

Personnel enseignant au niveau primaire, secondaire et supérieur *(suite)*
Nombre d'enseignants et ratio élèves/enseignant par niveau d'enseignement

Region, country or area Région, pays ou zone	Year & Année &	Primary education / Enseignant primaire Total Totale ('000)	Primary education / Enseignant primaire Pupil-teacher ratio Ratio élèves/ enseignant	Secondary education / Enseignant secondaire Total Totale ('000)	Secondary education / Enseignant secondaire Pupil-teacher ratio Ratio élèves/ enseignant	Tertiary education / Enseignant supérieur Total Totale ('000)	Tertiary education / Enseignant supérieur Pupil-teacher ratio Ratio élèves/ enseignant
Sudan [former]	*2000	...	...	...	...	4	45.5
Soudan [anc.]	2005	113	29.0	64	* 21.5	...	...
	*2009	124	38.4	83	22.2	...	...
Suriname	2005	4	18.6	3	13.9	...	...
Suriname	2010	5	14.9	4	13.8	...	...
	2015	5	14.3	4	13.2	...	...
Swaziland	2005	7	32.9	4	16.7	~0	13.7
Swaziland	2006	7	33.3	4	19.3	~0	12.3
	2010	7	32.3	5	18.1	...	...
	2013	9	28.1	6	16.0	~0	17.6
	2014	9	28.0	6	15.9	...	...
	2015	...	...	...	...	1	...
Sweden	2005	66	10.1	76	9.7	38	11.3
Suède	2010	60	9.5	75	9.7	29	15.6
	2015	65	12.1	66	12.9	34	12.6
Switzerland	2005	...	...	...	...	34	5.9
Suisse	2010	...	...	...	...	40	6.2
	2012	45	10.8	65	9.3	46	5.8
	2014	48	10.1	...	...	33	8.9
Syrian Arab Republic	2002	115	25.3	65	18.1	...	...
République arabe syrienne	2015	...	...	...	...	12	64.4
Tajikistan	2005	32	21.3	60	16.4	10	14.9
Tadjikistan	2010	27	25.2	60	17.1	13	14.8
	2011	29	23.3	68	15.4	13	14.5
	2016	32	22.2	...	...	14	17.4
Thailand	2002	326	18.6	* 173	* 24.0	64	33.6
Thaïlande	*2003	...	...	...	...	66	33.6
	2008	348	16.0	223	21.2	* 76	* 32.1
	2010	317	16.3	...	...	...	...
	2015	301	16.9	240	28.2	104	21.5
TFYR of Macedonia	2005	6	19.4	15	14.7	3	16.9
ex-R.Y. de Macédoine	2010	7	15.9	17	11.9	3	17.8
	2014	7	15.2	18	9.6	3	18.1
Timor-Leste	2002	4	47.2	2	29.5	* ~0	* 51.6
Timor-Leste	2004	4	50.7	3	27.6	...	...
	2005	...	...	3	23.7	...	...
	2009	7	29.8	...	...	1	14.0
	2010	8	30.2	4	23.0	...	...
	2011	8	31.4	4	24.3	...	...
Togo	2005	30	33.6	13	30.5	~0	...
Togo	2007	26	39.1	* 12	* 35.5	~0	69.2
	2010	32	40.6	...	...	...	...
	2011	32	40.9	21	26.2	...	...
	2015	34	41.7	...	...	3	26.2
Tokelau Tokélaou	2003	~0	5.8	~0	7.1	...	...
Tonga	2000	1	22.1	1	14.6	* ~0	* 5.1
Tonga	2002	1	22.1	1	14.4	...	...
	2005	1	20.3	...	...	...	...
	2010	1	24.9	1	14.9	...	...
	2014	1	21.9	1	13.4	...	...
Trinidad and Tobago	2004	* 8	* 17.5	...	...	2	9.7
Trinité-et-Tobago	*2005	8	16.5	...	...	...	...
	*2009	7	17.6	...	...	...	...
Tunisia	2005	59	20.0	72	17.2	17	19.6
Tunisie	2010	60	17.1	88	13.3	21	17.4
	2011	59	17.4	85	13.6	22	16.8
	2014	66	16.5	...	...	23	14.5
	2015	71	15.8	...	...	...	...
Turkey	2005	...	...	...	...	82	25.7
Turquie	2010	...	...	...	...	105	33.5
	2014	288	19.3	559	19.5	142	38.4

Teaching staff at the primary, secondary and tertiary levels *(continued)*
Number of teachers and Pupil teacher ratio

Personnel enseignant au niveau primaire, secondaire et supérieur *(suite)*
Nombre d'enseignants et ratio élèves/enseignant par niveau d'enseignement

Region, country or area Région, pays ou zone	Year & Année &	Primary education Enseignant primaire Total Totale ('000)	Pupil-teacher ratio Ratio élèves/ enseignant	Secondary education Enseignant secondaire Total Totale ('000)	Pupil-teacher ratio Ratio élèves/ enseignant	Tertiary education Enseignant supérieur Total Totale ('000)	Pupil-teacher ratio Ratio élèves/ enseignant
Turkmenistan Turkménistan	2014	...	...	...	...	8	5.4
Turks and Caicos Islands	2003	~0	15.2	~0	8.7	...	...
Îles Turques-et-Caïques	2014	~0	9.3	~0	8.8	...	...
	2015	...	...	~0	9.6	...	...
Tuvalu	2004	~0	19.2	...	...	...	...
Tuvalu	2015	~0	12.7	~0	6.2	...	...
Uganda	2004	147	50.1	40	18.5	4	21.2
Ouganda	2005	140	51.7	* 40	...	...	...
	2007	152	49.6	56	18.5	...	...
	2010	172	48.6	66	...	5	22.6
	2011	170	47.8	49	...	6	24.5
	2013	186	45.6	67	...	...	...
	2014	191	...	64	...	...	...
	2015	193	...	...	...	...	...
Ukraine	2000	105	19.9	389	13.4	* 146	* 12.4
Ukraine	2005	104	18.7	...	...	187	13.9
	2010	98	15.7	...	...	201	13.1
	2014	100	16.9	...	...	195	11.0
	2015	...	...	340	7.0	169	10.5
United Arab Emirates	2005	17	15.2	...	...	...	...
Émirats arabes unis	2009	20	15.6	...	...	5	18.6
	2010	19	16.8	...	...	...	...
	2015	20	23.6	...	...	9	17.8
United Kingdom	2005	265	17.5	388	14.9	122	18.7
Royaume-Uni	2008	244	18.3	* 375	* 14.3	134	17.4
	2010	252	17.5	...	...	140	17.7
	2014	272	17.4	414	15.8	152	15.5
	2015	...	...	412	...	149	...
United Rep. of Tanzania	2005	135	55.9	...	...	3	* 18.8
Rép.-Unie de Tanzanie	2010	166	50.8	...	...	4	18.9
	2012	181	45.6	80	26.4	5	34.4
	2014	191	43.1	...	...	...	...
United States of America	2005	1 731	14.1	1 635	14.9	1 208	14.3
États-Unis d'Amérique	2010	1 795	13.6	1 758	13.8	1 439	14.2
	2014	1 688	14.5	1 639	14.8	1 581	12.5
United States Virgin Islands Îles Vierges américaines	2007	...	...	...	...	~0	...
Uruguay	2005	18	20.2	22	14.6	12	9.3
Uruguay	2010	25	13.8	25	11.3	17	9.9
	2014	28	11.5	...	...	23	6.4
	2015	...	...	...	...	21	7.1
Uzbekistan	2005	119	19.9	339	13.3	20	13.3
Ouzbékistan	2010	111	17.8	342	13.0	23	12.5
	2016	111	20.4	375	10.4	25	10.7
Vanuatu	2001	2	23.7	1	15.1	~0	25.0
Vanuatu	2002	2	23.2	...	...	* ~0	* 24.9
	2004	2	20.0	...	...	...	...
	2010	2	21.7	...	...	...	...
	2015	2	26.6	1	20.6	...	...
Venezuela (Boliv. Rep. of)	*2004	...	...	...	...	82	12.8
Venezuela (Rép. boliv. du)	*2009	...	...	...	...	165	12.9
Viet Nam	2005	361	21.6	...	...	48	28.4
Viet Nam	2010	348	19.9	...	...	70	29.0
	2015	392	19.2	...	...	91	27.1
Yemen	*2005	...	...	...	...	7	29.2
Yémen	2007	...	...	...	...	7	32.2
	2010	111	30.8	...	...	...	...
	*2012	122	30.3	...	...	...	...
Zambia	*2005	46	56.5	...	...	...	...
Zambie	*2010	55	53.0	...	...	...	...
	*2013	64	47.9	...	...	...	...

8 Teaching staff at the primary, secondary and tertiary levels *(continued)*
Number of teachers and Pupil teacher ratio

Personnel enseignant au niveau primaire, secondaire et supérieur *(suite)*
Nombre d'enseignants et ratio élèves/enseignant par niveau d'enseignement

Region, country or area Région, pays ou zone	Year & Année &	Primary education Enseignant primaire Total Totale ('000)	Primary education Enseignant primaire Pupil-teacher ratio Ratio élèves/ enseignant	Secondary education Enseignant secondaire Total Totale ('000)	Secondary education Enseignant secondaire Pupil-teacher ratio Ratio élèves/ enseignant	Tertiary education Enseignant supérieur Total Totale ('000)	Tertiary education Enseignant supérieur Pupil-teacher ratio Ratio élèves/ enseignant
Zimbabwe	2003	61	38.6	34	22.3	...	...
Zimbabwe	2010	...	...	...	...	4	23.2
	2013	73	36.4	43	22.5	6	17.0
	2015	...	...	...	...	8	17.9

Source:

United Nations Educational, Scientific and Cultural Organization (UNESCO) Institute for Statistics, Montreal, the UNESCO Institute for Statistics (UIS) statistics database, last accessed June 2017.

Source:

L'Institut de statistique de l'Organisation des Nations Unies pour l'éducation, la science et la culture (UNESCO), Montréal, la base de données de l'institut de statistique de l'UNESCO (ISU), dernier accès juin 2017.

& Data relate to the calendar year in which the academic year ends.

& Les données se réfèrent à l'année civile durant laquelle l'année scolaire se termine.

1 Excludes Sudan.
2 Includes Sudan.
3 Excludes Japan.
4 Data excludes Armenia, Azerbaijan, Cyprus, Georgia, Israel and Turkey.
5 Caucasus refers to Armenia, Azerbaijan, Cyprus, Georgia, Israel and Turkey.
6 For statistical purposes, the data for China do not include those for the Hong Kong Special Administrative Region (Hong Kong SAR) and Macao Special Administrative Region (Macao SAR).

1 Exclut le Soudan.
2 Comprend le Soudan.
3 Exclut le Japon.
4 Les données excluent l'Arménie, l'Azerbaïdjan, Chypre, la Géorgie, l'Israël et la Turquie.
5 Le Caucase se rapportent à l'Arménie, l'Azerbaïdjan, Chypre, la Géorgie, l'Israël et la Turquie.
6 Pour la présentation des statistiques, les données pour la Chine ne comprennent pas la Région Administrative Spéciale de Hong Kong (Hong Kong RAS) et la Région Administrative Spéciale de Macao (Macao RAS).

Public expenditure on education

By expenditure type, level of education, total government expenditure and GDP

Dépenses publiques afférentes à l'éducation

Par type de dépenses, niveau de scolarité, dépenses publiques totales et PIB

Country or area Pays ou zone	Year Année	Percentage of total expenditure in public institutions / Pourcentage des dépenses publiques totales en faveur de l'éducation: Current expenditure Dépenses courantes	Staff Compensation Rémunération du personnel	Capital expenditure Dépenses en Capital	Percentage of government expenditure on education by level / Pourcentage des dépenses publiques selon le niveau d'enseignement: Pre-primary Préprimaire	Primary Primaire	Secondary Secondaire	Tertiary Tertiaire	As % of Govt. Expenditure En % des dépenses du gouvt.	As % of GDP En % du PIB
Afghanistan	2010	9.3	72.4	18.3	...	62.1	26.7	9.0	17.1	3.5
Afghanistan	2015	9.0	71.4	19.6	...	56.7	24.4	16.0	12.5	3.3
Albania	2005	...	...	...	...	...	...	...	11.4	3.2
Albanie	2007	...	...	...	...	...	...	...	11.2	3.3
	2013	11.5	79.9	8.6	...	...	19.8	21.9	12.1	3.5
	2015	11.8	77.7	10.5	...	...	...	...	...	...
Algeria Algérie	2008	...	...	...	...	...	...	27.0	11.4	4.4
Andorra	2005	...	...	...	16.9	24.1	20.6	3.9	...	1.6
Andorre	2010	30.9	36.7	1.7	14.6	28.9	20.9	3.9	...	3.1
	2013	59.4	40.0	0.6	18.2	32.1	35.2	4.6	...	2.5
	2015	63.6	...	1.3	13.2	22.1	24.9	5.5	...	3.3
Angola	2005	...	...	...	...	36.5	55.2	8.3	8.0	2.8
Angola	2006	...	...	24.3	13.5	31.4	42.4	8.7	7.5	2.9
	2010	...	...	...	...	...	...	...	8.7	3.5
Anguilla	2005	6.7	80.9	...	1.9	28.5	51.3	18.3	...	...
Anguilla	2008	* 9.8	* 69.4	* 20.8	1.6	39.4	56.1	2.8	...	2.8
Antigua and Barbuda	2002	25.7	...	3.9	2.1	28.6	35.2	6.7	8.9	3.4
Antigua-et-Barbuda	2009	21.6	73.2	5.2	0.3	41.6	48.4	7.4	6.9	2.6
Argentina	2004	11.6	87.6	0.8	8.3	36.7	37.8	17.2	15.2	3.5
Argentine	2005	...	...	...	7.9	34.2	41.7	16.2	15.8	3.8
	2010	9.9	85.9	4.2	7.4	33.1	39.7	19.9	15.8	5.0
	2014	7.8	85.3	7.0	8.1	30.1	41.5	20.4	14.7	5.3
Armenia	2005	...	...	...	...	...	...	...	13.6	2.7
Arménie	2009	...	...	...	11.3	...	...	9.4	13.5	3.8
	2010	...	...	...	...	...	...	11.7	12.4	3.2
	2014	8.5	65.5	26.0	...	...	54.5	13.6	9.4	2.2
	2015	11.6	88.5	...	11.8	19.4	...	12.7	10.7	2.8
Aruba	2005	6.1	90.7	3.2	6.8	26.7	26.8	11.5	18.9	4.7
Aruba	2009	5.7	87.0	...	...	...	...	...	21.5	5.9
	2010	...	...	...	...	...	...	...	22.1	6.7
	2014	6.1	93.9	...	5.8	26.2	34.4	20.0	19.6	6.2
Australia	2000	24.7	68.3	7.0	1.2	34.1	38.6	23.4	13.4	4.9
Australie	2005	...	...	...	1.0	34.6	39.7	22.2	13.6	4.9
	2010	...	...	...	1.2	36.8	36.8	22.3	14.3	5.6
	2014	27.0	64.6	8.4	2.9	32.6	32.4	26.5	13.9	5.2
Austria	2005	23.2	72.1	4.7	7.4	19.0	45.9	27.3	9.9	5.3
Autriche	2010	24.9	70.2	4.9	10.3	17.1	44.4	27.7	10.9	5.7
	2014	26.2	68.9	5.0	8.8	16.3	40.4	32.5	10.5	5.5
Azerbaijan	2005	31.6	66.8	1.6	6.9	...	...	6.9	13.1	3.0
Azerbaïdjan	2010	32.6	64.8	2.5	7.1	...	...	14.0	8.7	2.8
	2011	34.6	62.7	2.8	7.0	...	...	14.6	7.3	2.4
	2014	43.0	53.1	3.9	...	...	...	...	7.4	2.6
Bahamas Bahamas	*2000	...	...	...	...	...	...	...	18.9	2.9
Bahrain	2008	...	...	...	...	...	...	...	10.6	2.5
Bahreïn	2012	13.8	82.3	3.8	...	...	...	...	8.9	2.6
	2015	...	...	...	...	33.0	44.2	...	7.7	2.7
Bangladesh	2004	...	...	...	...	40.0	48.5	11.5	16.0	1.9
Bangladesh	2009	21.2	59.8	19.0	...	44.7	40.2	13.5	14.0	1.9
	*2013	...	...	...	...	...	...	...	13.8	2.0
	2016	71.6	19.2	9.2	...	43.5	35.4	20.0	...	1.9
Barbados	2005	16.2	79.9	4.0	* 6.3	* 27.9	31.7	31.6	15.4	5.6
Barbade	2008	14.5	78.6	6.9	0.4	36.9	29.4	30.1	13.4	5.1
	2010	10.4	83.4	6.2	...	...	29.6	32.5	15.6	5.9
	2014	47.8	48.6	3.6	...	...	22.5	39.3	14.2	6.6

Public expenditure on education *(continued)*
By expenditure type, level of education, total government expenditure and GDP

Dépenses publiques afférentes à l'éducation *(suite)*
Par type de dépenses, niveau de scolarité, dépenses publiques totales et PIB

		Percentage of total expenditure in public institutions Pourcentage des dépenses publiques totales en faveur de l'éducation			Percentage of government expenditure on education by level Pourcentage des dépenses publiques selon le niveau d'enseignement					
Country or area Pays ou zone	**Year Année**	**Current expenditure Dépenses courantes**	**Staff Compensation Rémunération du personnel**	**Capital expenditure Dépenses en Capital**	**Pre-primary Préprimaire**	**Primary Primaire**	**Secondary Secondaire**	**Tertiary Tertiaire**	**As % of Govt. Expenditure En % des dépenses du gouvt.**	**As % of GDP En % du PIB**
Belarus	2005	30.1	65.2	4.8	17.4	...	...	25.5	13.0	5.9
Bélarus	2010	26.5	62.6	10.9	19.0	...	...	17.1	12.9	5.4
	2011	26.8	65.4	7.8	21.0	...	...	17.3	14.0	4.8
	2015	26.4	68.9	4.8	...	...	...	16.8	11.2	4.9
Belgium	2005	11.7	85.5	2.8	9.6	23.6	43.1	21.7	11.2	5.8
Belgique	2010	11.9	84.3	3.8	9.5	23.5	42.5	22.2	12.0	6.4
	2014	13.7	81.5	4.8	10.7	23.2	42.0	22.0	12.0	6.6
Belize	2003	* 18.3	* 62.3	* 19.3	...	...	...	...	16.2	5.2
Belize	2004	...	...	...	0.6	42.6	39.2	10.8	16.8	5.3
	2010	...	...	...	1.5	46.1	41.1	8.7	23.1	6.6
	2013	...	...	...	1.4	40.0	38.1	13.6	23.0	6.2
	2014	...	...	...	...	37.8	39.3	13.0	20.9	6.4
Benin	2001	15.2	56.8	28.0	* 1.2	* 55.4	* 25.1	18.3	15.3	3.2
Bénin	2005	13.3	73.0	13.7	...	* 46.0	* 32.8	21.2	18.8	3.6
	2010	6.2	85.7	8.2	2.6	52.8	28.0	15.6	26.1	5.0
	2015	22.2	69.5	8.3	4.3	49.8	23.7	22.1	17.5	4.4
Bermuda	2005	...	...	...	* 7.0	* 40.7	* 52.3	...	12.1	2.0
Bermudes	2010	...	...	...	8.9	30.8	45.4	13.5	12.9	2.6
	2014	...	...	...	7.5	29.9	44.3	18.2	7.8	1.8
	2015	18.6	79.9	1.5	7.0	30.7	44.3	...	9.0	1.7
Bhutan	2005	...	...	...	...	22.3	50.9	14.1	22.8	7.1
Bhoutan	2010	...	...	...	...	29.9	53.9	15.1	11.8	4.0
	2014	...	...	...	...	32.0	55.7	10.3	17.0	5.9
	2015	50.1	35.9	14.0	...	57.0	41.5	...	25.5	7.4
Bolivia (Plurin. State of)	2000	...	...	14.5	6.3	* 40.5	* 18.5	28.9	18.7	5.5
Bolivie (État plurin. de)	2003	...	...	...	3.3	44.1	24.3	21.6	19.9	6.4
	2009	31.8	68.2	...	2.6	40.5	26.0	29.7	22.6	8.1
	2010	...	...	...	2.8	39.4	26.3	29.9	24.1	7.6
	2014	19.9	63.3	16.8	5.0	41.6	27.1	26.2	16.8	7.3
Botswana	2005	...	...	...	...	30.0	39.6	27.9	25.8	10.7
Botswana	2009	...	...	9.8	...	17.8	32.7	41.5	20.5	9.6
Brazil	2005	23.6	70.3	6.1	8.2	34.0	38.8	19.0	11.3	4.5
Brésil	2010	24.3	68.5	7.2	7.6	31.3	44.7	16.4	14.6	5.6
	2013	24.0	69.7	6.2	10.5	27.4	43.9	18.2	16.0	6.0
British Virgin Islands	*2004	2.3	90.3	7.4	...	...	...	...	...	...
Îles Vierges britanniques	2005	0.7	99.3	...	0.1	33.7	31.2	34.2	...	...
	2007	15.1	77.8	7.1	0.1	28.4	37.7	33.1	...	3.6
	2010	...	...	...	0.1	34.1	34.0	...	...	4.4
	2015	...	...	...	~0.0	16.6	19.0	22.1	...	6.6
Brunei Darussalam	2000	...	...	...	...	...	...	...	8.9	3.7
Brunéi Darussalam	2010	...	...	...	...	28.5	46.8	24.4	5.3	2.0
	2014	...	...	...	...	...	38.7	31.9	10.0	3.4
	2016	30.6	66.2	3.2	0.7	19.5	60.8	18.9	...	4.4
Bulgaria	2005	26.7	63.2	10.1	16.9	20.3	45.9	16.9	12.1	4.1
Bulgarie	2010	28.4	66.6	5.1	22.5	19.6	43.0	14.8	11.2	3.9
	2013	20.9	71.8	7.3	25.3	19.7	38.9	15.9	11.4	4.1
Burkina Faso	2005	...	...	...	0.2	71.2	10.3	9.6	19.5	4.4
Burkina Faso	2007	8.0	56.7	35.3	0.6	67.0	15.7	15.2	17.9	4.6
	2010	...	...	...	...	60.3	18.0	18.8	17.3	3.9
	2015	...	...	...	0.1	57.9	22.1	13.7	18.0	4.1
Burundi	2004	15.7	57.8	26.6	~0.0	50.7	29.5	18.3	13.0	3.7
Burundi	2005	...	...	...	...	51.6	33.1	15.3	13.9	3.6
	2010	23.7	68.5	7.9	~0.0	45.4	27.9	18.0	16.6	6.8
	2012	20.5	77.6	1.9	~0.0	44.0	24.2	20.6	16.4	5.8
	2013	...	...	...	~0.0	45.4	26.8	24.2	17.2	5.4

Public expenditure on education *(continued)*

By expenditure type, level of education, total government expenditure and GDP

Dépenses publiques afférentes à l'éducation *(suite)*

Par type de dépenses, niveau de scolarité, dépenses publiques totales et PIB

Country or area Pays ou zone	Year Année	Percentage of total expenditure in public institutions / Pourcentage des dépenses publiques totales en faveur de l'éducation: Current expenditure Dépenses courantes	Staff Compensation Rémunération du personnel	Capital expenditure Dépenses en Capital	Percentage of government expenditure on education by level / Pourcentage des dépenses publiques selon le niveau d'enseignement: Pre-primary Préprimaire	Primary Primaire	Secondary Secondaire	Tertiary Tertiaire	As % of Govt. Expenditure En % des dépenses du gouvt.	As % of GDP En % du PIB
Cabo Verde Cabo Verde	2002	...	...	...	...	43.8	29.8	17.5	19.8	7.9
	2004	3.3	80.0	16.7	...	...	...	...	20.8	7.5
	*2005	2.1	82.4	16.7	...	...	...	...	...	...
	2008	...	...	15.9	0.3	36.3	36.6	11.3	18.6	5.5
	2009	...	...	...	...	44.1	33.0	14.0	16.2	5.3
	2010	15.6	77.1	7.3	...	...	...	...	14.4	5.6
	2013	...	...	...	0.7	38.4	40.3	15.8	15.0	5.0
Cambodia Cambodge	2001	...	...	...	1.1	74.4	11.2	...	11.4	1.7
	2002	...	...	...	1.0	64.6	...	...	10.1	1.7
	2004	...	...	...	...	...	...	...	12.4	1.7
	2010	...	...	...	1.7	50.0	42.5	5.8	7.7	1.5
	2012	57.3	42.7	...	2.0	49.2	44.1	...	7.5	1.6
	2013	...	...	...	2.7	49.7	41.5	6.1	9.9	2.0
	2014	...	...	0.5	2.6	48.5	44.1	...	9.1	1.9
Cameroon Cameroun	2005	...	...	...	...	35.1	52.0	12.6	21.4	3.1
	2010	6.5	80.2	13.4	3.9	34.2	52.7	9.0	18.8	3.3
	2012	...	...	...	3.5	36.2	52.6	7.8	15.2	3.0
	2013	10.7	75.7	13.6	4.0	33.9	...	10.2	13.8	3.0
Canada Canada	2000	25.9	70.5	3.6	3.9	...	...	...	13.0	5.5
	2005	25.4	70.0	4.6	...	...	...	...	12.2	4.8
	2010	24.5	65.8	9.7	...	...	...	35.4	12.3	5.4
	2011	24.1	65.5	10.4	...	...	26.4	35.6	12.2	5.3
	2013	23.4	68.8	7.8	...	...	...	...	...	...
Cayman Islands Îles Caïmanes	2005	...	...	...	1.2	49.3	49.5	...	...	...
	2006	2.4	97.6	...	...	46.0	54.0	...	...	...
Central African Republic République centrafricaine	2005	...	79.2	2.2	...	...	...	...	9.7	1.6
	2008	13.5	84.2	2.3	...	...	25.9	17.5	7.9	1.3
	2010	...	...	1.1	2.3	53.3	24.0	20.5	6.5	1.2
	2011	...	...	...	...	...	...	27.3	7.8	1.2
Chad Tchad	2005	...	...	...	...	45.8	35.5	18.7	14.7	1.7
	2010	...	...	31.3	0.4	51.6	27.4	19.8	8.1	2.0
	2011	...	...	20.8	0.3	40.7	34.9	16.3	10.1	2.3
	2012	2.6	75.5	21.9	...	46.7	20.7	30.3	9.2	2.2
	2013	...	...	...	...	...	24.7	31.7	12.5	2.8
Chile Chili	2005	17.5	78.1	4.4	9.6	37.4	39.0	14.0	16.2	3.2
	2009	18.1	78.9	3.0	12.8	36.4	35.2	15.6	17.0	4.2
	2010	...	...	...	13.4	31.7	32.5	22.3	17.8	4.2
	2015	...	...	...	13.2	25.6	29.4	25.7	18.9	4.9
China, Hong Kong SAR Chine, Hong Kong RAS	2005	...	...	...	2.3	23.1	33.8	28.4	22.5	4.1
	2010	...	...	12.7	3.8	20.9	35.5	27.8	20.2	3.5
	2012	...	...	18.2	3.9	18.7	33.6	32.8	18.6	3.5
	2015	...	...	...	4.7	20.9	33.9	29.5	18.6	3.3
China, Macao SAR Chine, Macao RAS	2000	...	...	...	* 7.6	* 24.8	* 25.0	28.4	...	3.7
	2003	...	...	...	...	* 24.8	...	41.1	11.7	2.8
	2005	...	...	...	...	...	...	45.6	10.5	2.3
	2010	19.5	39.0	41.5	...	...	...	48.4	15.4	2.6
	2013	23.5	49.8	26.7	...	...	55.1	44.9	16.4	2.0
	2014	30.8	57.0	12.2	...	...	...	42.7	13.4	2.0
Colombia Colombie	2004	23.3	71.0	5.7	* 2.7	* 48.3	* 35.7	13.3	15.4	4.1
	2005	...	...	...	2.6	47.4	36.1	13.8	15.5	4.0
	2010	6.8	71.0	22.3	5.8	35.9	34.8	22.1	16.4	4.8
	2015	5.8	69.0	25.2	5.9	36.7	35.4	21.4	15.0	4.5
Comoros Comores	2002	...	...	...	* 0.4	* 45.2	* 40.1	* 7.7	15.8	3.9
	2008	...	...	...	...	61.7	23.7	14.6	29.2	7.7
	2015	4.8	95.2	...	7.1	54.6	27.7	10.4	15.3	4.3
Congo Congo	2005	...	...	...	* 2.9	* 27.3	* 41.2	* 25.9	7.6	1.8
	2010	...	...	...	4.6	31.0	53.3	10.9	29.0	6.2

Public expenditure on education *(continued)*
By expenditure type, level of education, total government expenditure and GDP

Dépenses publiques afférentes à l'éducation *(suite)*
Par type de dépenses, niveau de scolarité, dépenses publiques totales et PIB

Country or area Pays ou zone	Year Année	Percentage of total expenditure in public institutions / Pourcentage des dépenses publiques totales en faveur de l'éducation: Current expenditure Dépenses courantes	Staff Compensation Rémunération du personnel	Capital expenditure Dépenses en Capital	Percentage of government expenditure on education by level / Pourcentage des dépenses publiques selon le niveau d'enseignement: Pre-primary Préprimaire	Primary Primaire	Secondary Secondaire	Tertiary Tertiaire	As % of Govt. Expenditure En % des dépenses du gouvt.	As % of GDP En % du PIB
Cook Islands	2000	...	...	...	7.1	50.6	36.5	...	6.7	...
Îles Cook	2013	...	...	...	11.4	40.4	40.6	7.6	8.8	3.0
	2014	15.7	84.3	...	...	...	...	9.2	11.6	3.9
	2015	16.3	82.4	1.3	...	...	...	8.9	...	3.9
Costa Rica	2004	...	...	...	7.9	45.5	27.8	18.8	20.4	4.9
Costa Rica	2010	...	...	...	5.4	41.9	31.5	18.4	22.9	6.6
	2015	...	...	...	6.0	36.8	33.7	22.3	23.4	7.2
Côte d'Ivoire	2000	...	...	...	* ~0.0	* 41.6	* 32.7	22.0	20.8	3.7
Côte d'Ivoire	2001	...	...	...	...	* 42.2	...	19.4	23.2	3.7
	2005	...	...	...	...	...	...	20.0	21.8	4.1
	2010	21.8	71.2	7.0	2.0	42.7	33.1	22.2	22.8	4.6
	*2015	21.4	72.7	5.9	3.0	41.4	34.2	21.4	21.2	5.0
Croatia	2004	30.0	65.6	4.4	9.2	...	...	18.1	8.1	3.8
Croatie	2010	23.0	70.6	6.4	13.8	...	...	18.3	9.0	4.3
	2011	21.3	74.4	4.3	14.1	...	...	22.2	8.5	4.2
	2013	27.3	69.4	3.2	...	...	...	21.9	9.6	4.6
Cuba	2005	34.3	52.6	13.2	8.3	30.3	37.7	22.1	...	10.6
Cuba	2007	46.7	50.2	3.1	8.1	30.1	36.0	25.1	...	11.9
	2010	40.5	58.6	0.9	6.8	29.0	29.1	...	...	12.8
Curaçao Curaçao	2013	13.9	86.1	...	9.2	27.5	33.9	5.3	...	4.9
Cyprus	2005	9.8	76.9	13.4	4.9	27.3	44.9	22.9	15.8	6.2
Chypre	2010	11.5	77.5	11.0	5.5	31.0	43.0	20.5	15.7	6.6
	2014	12.2	85.0	2.8	5.8	32.8	43.8	17.6	15.5	6.1
Czechia	2005	34.4	56.0	9.7	9.8	14.5	51.3	21.0	9.3	3.9
Tchéquie	2010	38.4	51.5	10.1	11.4	16.2	45.7	22.5	9.5	4.1
	2013	38.9	51.4	9.7	13.2	17.8	43.9	21.5	9.6	4.1
Dem. Rep. of the Congo	2010	2.6	87.8	9.6	0.6	33.3	33.7	24.0	9.0	1.6
Rép. dém. du Congo	2013	1.7	81.4	16.9	1.0	61.6	14.4	22.0	16.9	2.2
Denmark	2005	20.7	74.1	5.3	8.6	23.3	36.3	28.7	15.8	8.1
Danemark	2010	18.0	74.9	7.1	11.5	23.7	34.5	27.3	15.1	8.6
	2013	20.1	73.5	6.3	13.9	24.9	32.4	26.9	15.2	8.6
Djibouti	2005	...	42.2	2.7	...	...	...	...	22.7	8.4
Djibouti	2007	...	38.8	4.6	...	19.0	...	...	22.3	8.4
	2010	...	...	...	...	34.1	37.3	16.5	12.3	4.5
Dominica Dominique	2012	...	100.0	...	...	...	...	...	...	...
Dominican Republic	2002	16.6	76.7	6.7	2.1	62.8	...	...	12.1	2.0
République dominicaine	*2003	...	...	...	...	...	...	...	9.7	1.9
	2004	24.1	72.6	3.4	...	...	...	...	...	...
	2007	15.5	66.9	17.6	4.2	58.7	18.0	14.5	12.6	2.0
Ecuador	2000	16.7	78.1	5.2	...	38.3	34.6	5.2	5.0	1.2
Équateur	2010	...	...	...	21.4	32.4	10.4	35.8	13.0	4.5
	2015	...	...	...	21.1	23.3	12.1	43.5	12.8	5.0
Egypt	2005	...	...	...	...	...	...	...	14.4	4.8
Égypte	2008	...	...	...	...	...	...	...	10.5	3.8
El Salvador	2005	27.3	66.9	5.8	* 8.5	* 51.0	* 29.1	* 11.1	* 14.7	* 2.7
El Salvador	2008	37.8	51.7	10.5	9.1	38.0	22.0	...	19.4	3.7
	2010	...	...	...	7.9	42.7	30.1	12.2	16.2	3.5
	2015	19.0	67.1	6.2	7.2	40.6	31.8	7.9	16.6	3.5
Eritrea	2002	8.6	31.0	60.4	...	26.0	35.4	14.9	5.6	3.5
Érythrée	2004	...	...	41.7	...	23.1	21.1	31.9	5.7	3.1
	2006	22.7	57.7	19.6	...	...	...	...	5.2	2.1

Public expenditure on education *(continued)*

By expenditure type, level of education, total government expenditure and GDP

Dépenses publiques afférentes à l'éducation *(suite)*

Par type de dépenses, niveau de scolarité, dépenses publiques totales et PIB

		Percentage of total expenditure in public institutions / Pourcentage des dépenses publiques totales en faveur de l'éducation			Percentage of government expenditure on education by level / Pourcentage des dépenses publiques selon le niveau d'enseignement					
Country or area / Pays ou zone	**Year / Année**	**Current expenditure / Dépenses courantes**	**Staff Compensation / Rémunération du personnel**	**Capital expenditure / Dépenses en Capital**	**Pre-primary / Préprimaire**	**Primary / Primaire**	**Secondary / Secondaire**	**Tertiary / Tertiaire**	**As % of Govt. Expenditure / En % des dépenses du gouvt.**	**As % of GDP / En % du PIB**
Estonia / Estonie	2002	28.8	56.3	15.0	5.2	28.0	40.9	19.7	15.3	5.5
	2004	...	...	9.5	6.4	25.8	46.3	17.4	14.5	4.9
	2005	...	...	...	7.4	25.3	43.7	18.9	14.5	4.8
	2010	...	...	...	7.8	24.6	40.1	21.7	13.7	5.5
	2013	28.9	57.7	13.4	7.3	30.7	29.4	28.2	12.6	4.8
	2014	26.7	64.0	9.3	...	24.6	26.1	26.2	14.3	5.5
Ethiopia / Éthiopie	*2002	...	...	...	...	...	...	...	16.2	3.6
	2010	21.0	44.8	34.1	~0.0	28.4	25.0	43.9	26.3	4.5
	2013	19.7	44.2	36.1	0.4	24.0	29.3	42.7	27.0	4.5
Fiji / Fidji	2004	...	...	...	0.2	39.1	32.6	15.9	22.0	6.2
	2005	...	...	...	...	...	...	...	18.8	5.1
	2009	...	...	...	...	...	...	...	15.4	4.5
	2011	...	...	...	0.4	44.4	15.9	13.0	14.9	4.2
	2013	1.2	98.7	0.1	...	38.6	...	22.6	14.0	3.9
Finland / Finlande	2005	32.1	60.9	7.0	5.5	20.8	41.9	31.8	12.2	6.1
	2010	33.6	60.3	6.1	5.8	19.9	42.4	31.8	11.9	6.5
	2011	33.4	59.5	7.2	6.0	20.0	42.0	32.0	11.9	6.5
	2014	34.0	59.7	6.3	10.7	19.1	...	27.9	12.3	7.2
France / France	2005	15.6	74.5	9.9	11.4	20.2	47.1	21.1	10.4	5.5
	2010	17.4	73.2	9.4	11.6	20.4	45.0	22.6	10.1	5.7
	2013	17.9	73.4	8.7	12.7	20.7	43.7	22.6	9.7	5.5
Gabon / Gabon	*2000	...	...	...	...	...	...	...	17.7	3.8
	2010	...	...	...	3.6	29.6	28.3	37.8	13.3	3.1
	2014	...	45.5	...	3.8	29.2	28.9	37.8	11.4	2.7
Gambia / Gambie	2005	...	...	...	...	61.4	23.1	14.3	5.3	1.1
	2010	10.8	46.4	42.8	...	65.3	23.4	9.9	17.6	4.2
	2012	7.4	50.4	42.2	...	60.0	31.4	7.4	13.8	4.1
	2013	...	...	...	...	51.8	35.5	10.7	10.3	2.8
Georgia / Géorgie	2005	...	...	...	...	...	...	...	11.2	2.5
	2008	...	...	...	10.7	36.0	37.0	11.6	8.9	2.9
	*2009	...	...	...	12.3	...	...	...	9.0	3.2
	2012	...	...	...	14.4	34.3	32.1	19.2	6.7	2.0
Germany / Allemagne	2010	19.8	70.6	9.6	9.1	13.5	45.5	27.2	10.4	4.9
	2014	20.0	72.9	7.1	8.9	12.8	42.0	26.6	11.1	5.0
Ghana / Ghana	2005	22.3	63.0	14.7	5.9	39.5	32.5	22.1	23.4	7.4
	2010	14.3	68.8	16.9	6.1	30.9	37.1	25.9	20.9	5.5
	2014	18.2	73.3	8.6	7.3	21.7	37.0	18.3	21.0	6.2
Greece / Grèce	2005	11.0	67.3	21.7	...	...	33.9	36.1	8.7	4.0
Grenada / Grenade	2003	8.3	82.2	9.5	5.7	36.4	35.8	9.8	10.8	3.9
Guatemala / Guatemala	2008	9.9	65.2	11.5	10.0	59.8	12.8	10.8	23.3	3.2
	2010	...	...	0.1	11.2	55.6	14.8	11.3	19.3	2.8
	2015	20.9	75.3	3.8	17.3	49.9	12.9	13.8	24.1	3.0
Guinea / Guinée	2005	...	...	...	...	...	...	30.6	10.9	1.8
	2010	...	...	7.7	...	38.9	24.9	36.2	12.4	3.7
	2014	12.6	75.0	12.4	0.1	38.9	21.9	39.1	12.0	3.2
Guinea-Bissau / Guinée-Bissau	2010	12.5	61.5	26.0	0.7	46.7	46.7	5.0	10.0	1.9
	2013	0.9	48.3	50.8	0.8	64.4	30.4	3.9	16.2	2.2
Guyana / Guyana	2004	37.6	51.8	10.6	11.6	32.1	26.5	6.2	11.1	5.5
	2005	23.1	62.3	14.6	...	...	...	...	13.8	8.1
	2010	22.8	68.4	8.7	11.5	29.1	33.4	5.3	12.0	3.7
	2012	22.5	62.9	14.6	11.6	30.6	33.3	5.1	10.3	3.2
Honduras / Honduras	2013	15.6	79.7	4.7	7.3	48.9	25.3	18.5	19.2	5.9

Public expenditure on education *(continued)*

By expenditure type, level of education, total government expenditure and GDP

Dépenses publiques afférentes à l'éducation *(suite)*

Par type de dépenses, niveau de scolarité, dépenses publiques totales et PIB

Country or area Pays ou zone	Year Année	Percentage of total expenditure in public institutions / Pourcentage des dépenses publiques totales en faveur de l'éducation: Current expenditure Dépenses courantes	Staff Compensation Rémunération du personnel	Capital expenditure Dépenses en Capital	Percentage of government expenditure on education by level / Pourcentage des dépenses publiques selon le niveau d'enseignement: Pre-primary Préprimaire	Primary Primaire	Secondary Secondaire	Tertiary Tertiaire	As % of Govt. Expenditure En % des dépenses du gouvt.	As % of GDP En % du PIB
Hungary Hongrie	2005	21.0	71.6	7.4	14.2	20.1	40.4	18.9	10.8	5.3
	2010	27.1	62.5	10.4	14.4	17.8	40.3	20.1	9.7	4.8
	2013	31.6	63.7	4.7	15.5	20.5	34.5	21.3	8.5	4.2
	2014	25.1	66.3	8.7	...	12.5	42.8	16.4	9.4	4.7
Iceland Islande	2005	23.6	67.9	8.5	6.7	35.0	33.6	19.1	17.8	7.4
	2010	20.8	72.6	6.6	9.6	32.4	31.2	21.5	14.6	7.2
	2013	32.1	62.7	5.3	11.5	28.6	27.7	19.4	17.7	7.8
India Inde	2005	9.0	86.2	4.8	1.3	35.6	42.9	19.6	11.5	3.1
	2010	...	...	...	1.1	25.2	37.0	36.1	11.7	3.4
	2013	...	...	...	1.6	28.4	41.4	28.5	14.1	3.8
Indonesia Indonésie	*2005	...	...	...	...	...	...	...	15.1	2.9
	2010	33.6	54.5	11.9	0.7	44.4	24.3	16.1	16.7	2.8
	2014	25.0	63.3	11.7	1.8	43.7	26.8	15.1	17.7	3.3
	2015	24.1	64.1	11.9	...	42.6	27.0	15.8	20.5	3.6
Iran (Islamic Republic of) Iran (Rép. islamique d')	2002	...	...	8.2	0.9	25.9	36.3	18.5	26.3	4.5
	2005	...	...	...	1.0	22.4	34.6	15.4	22.3	4.2
	2010	...	...	...	1.0	24.7	49.2	21.4	18.8	3.9
	2015	25.6	68.2	6.2	0.2	26.7	37.9	29.4	18.6	2.9
Ireland Irlande	2005	17.3	74.2	8.4	0.1	33.6	34.8	23.3	13.6	4.5
	2010	19.7	71.6	8.7	1.6	35.3	33.8	22.2	9.3	6.1
	2013	20.6	73.6	5.8	2.0	36.2	33.5	21.5	13.5	5.3
Israel Israël	2005	25.1	68.8	6.1	10.7	37.5	28.9	16.6	12.7	5.7
	2010	18.7	72.9	8.4	11.0	41.2	25.7	16.9	13.5	5.5
	2014	15.8	75.1	9.1	12.3	38.1	29.1	15.3	14.3	5.8
Italy Italie	2005	20.9	71.9	7.2	10.3	24.6	46.5	17.2	9.0	4.2
	2010	20.5	74.7	4.8	10.0	25.0	42.9	18.8	8.7	4.4
	2014	22.8	72.4	4.8	11.2	24.5	42.4	19.6	8.0	4.1
Jamaica Jamaïque	2004	7.5	88.1	4.5	5.6	32.6	41.9	18.8	11.7	3.9
	2005	...	...	...	4.9	*34.2	*38.0	22.1	14.3	4.6
	2008	4.9	85.6	9.4	5.5	30.2	42.6	15.7	19.1	6.2
	2009	7.0	93.0	...	8.2	33.2	37.1	20.3	17.6	6.2
	2010	...	...	...	4.0	36.3	36.6	21.8	16.1	6.3
	2015	18.7	78.9	2.3	3.6	36.7	39.4	17.4	20.1	5.5
Japan Japon	2005	20.2	70.8	9.1	2.7	35.7	38.4	17.3	10.3	3.4
	2010	20.3	66.4	13.3	2.7	34.9	36.8	20.1	9.5	3.6
	2014	21.3	64.8	13.9	2.8	33.1	37.8	20.8	9.3	3.6
Kazakhstan Kazakhstan	2005	40.6	53.2	6.2	3.8	...	...	12.3	10.2	2.3
	2009	34.2	56.8	9.0	6.8	...	...	13.1	13.0	3.1
	2010	32.8	57.8	9.4	...	...	...	...	...	...
	2015	36.6	59.9	3.5	10.9	...	65.8	15.3	11.9	2.8
Kenya Kenya	2004	...	...	...	1.6	62.1	23.4	12.9	26.7	6.8
	2005	...	...	...	...	...	...	...	27.5	7.4
	2006	...	...	...	0.1	54.1	21.7	15.4	25.1	7.0
	2010	...	...	...	...	...	...	...	20.6	5.5
	2015	31.6	60.9	7.5	1.8	36.3	41.8	13.1	16.5	5.3
Kiribati Kiribati	2001	...	...	...	...	34.3	...	...	11.5	12.0
Kuwait Koweït	2005	17.4	74.9	7.7	9.8	19.8	36.2	32.6	13.9	4.7
	*2006	...	...	...	9.6	20.4	36.2	32.6	13.4	3.8
Kyrgyzstan Kirghizistan	2005	28.4	66.2	5.4	6.2	...	...	19.2	16.5	4.9
	2010	29.1	64.5	6.5	8.1	...	...	15.5	15.7	5.8
	2014	17.6	69.1	13.3	10.7	...	...	4.6	16.1	5.5
Lao People's Dem. Rep. Rép. dém. populaire lao	2002	...	...	...	1.9	45.0	19.0	12.6	16.2	2.8
	2005	...	...	...	1.6	62.5	...	...	13.7	2.4
	2010	16.7	65.0	18.3	6.8	46.5	29.9	16.2	7.3	1.7
	2014	12.4	72.6	15.0	6.6	40.6	38.6	13.8	12.2	3.3

Public expenditure on education *(continued)*
By expenditure type, level of education, total government expenditure and GDP

Dépenses publiques afférentes à l'éducation *(suite)*
Par type de dépenses, niveau de scolarité, dépenses publiques totales et PIB

Country or area Pays ou zone	Year Année	Percentage of total expenditure in public institutions / Pourcentage des dépenses publiques totales en faveur de l'éducation: Current expenditure Dépenses courantes	Staff Compensation Rémunération du personnel	Capital expenditure Dépenses en Capital	Percentage of government expenditure on education by level / Pourcentage des dépenses publiques selon le niveau d'enseignement: Pre-primary Préprimaire	Primary Primaire	Secondary Secondaire	Tertiary Tertiaire	As % of Govt. Expenditure En % des dépenses du gouvt.	As % of GDP En % du PIB
Latvia	2004	21.9	69.7	8.4	13.0	16.3	56.4	13.4	14.5	4.9
Lettonie	2010	21.6	65.7	12.7	16.8	28.5	38.4	15.9	11.8	5.1
	2014	24.1	58.0	17.9	16.2	30.0	31.2	21.3	14.0	5.3
Lebanon	2005	1.6	94.7	3.7	...	...	...	28.8	8.4	2.7
Liban	2010	0.1	88.0	11.9	...	...	...	27.2	5.5	1.6
	2011	0.1	86.8	13.1	...	...	...	26.5	5.7	1.6
	2013	2.4	97.6	...	...	...	17.1	28.7	8.6	2.6
Lesotho	2001	...	...	8.7	...	53.2	23.8	18.6	23.8	9.4
Lesotho	2005	...	...	...	...	* 43.0	* 18.3	* 36.4	32.4	12.1
	2008	...	...	* 1.7	0.1	36.0	20.5	36.4	24.7	11.4
Liberia	2008	47.4	41.4	11.2	...	...	...	...	7.3	3.2
Libéria	2012	...	...	...	...	30.7	34.5	* 31.6	8.1	2.8
Liechtenstein	2004	...	...	...	6.5	29.0	42.6	13.9	...	2.4
Liechtenstein	2007	19.3	80.7	...	6.9	30.6	47.2	9.1	...	1.9
	2008	30.2	69.8	...	7.3	31.1	52.4	...	...	2.0
	2010	18.9	68.4	12.6	...	...	...	...	...	...
	2011	20.7	73.9	5.4	7.1	38.6	47.4	...	...	2.6
Lithuania	2005	20.1	73.0	6.8	12.1	14.9	50.6	21.0	14.6	4.9
Lituanie	2010	19.5	72.9	7.6	12.9	16.7	44.9	23.6	12.9	5.3
	2012	20.1	67.4	12.5	13.1	15.3	39.7	29.0	13.5	4.8
	2013	...	...	...	...	15.2	38.5	28.8	13.3	4.6
Luxembourg	2001	11.2	71.3	17.5	...	...	...	...	9.3	3.6
Luxembourg	2014	13.9	74.3	11.8	14.3	30.8	42.2	12.6	9.6	4.1
Madagascar	2005	* 24.4	* 43.8	31.8	...	57.3	18.9	10.1	18.0	3.8
Madagascar	2008	31.3	58.7	10.0	0.4	53.6	22.1	15.4	16.3	2.9
	2009	...	...	...	0.3	52.3	18.2	15.4	22.6	3.2
	2012	...	...	* 4.6	0.2	47.4	19.3	15.2	20.3	2.7
	2013	29.5	67.4	3.1	...	...	...	...	14.0	2.1
Malawi	2001	...	...	...	...	45.2	22.5	15.3	...	4.5
Malawi	2003	...	...	...	...	54.9	21.1	...	16.6	3.2
	2010	...	...	4.9	~0.0	34.8	24.1	29.8	12.5	3.5
	2013	14.5	71.7	13.8	~0.0	36.7	24.4	28.4	20.4	5.4
	2015	...	...	1.2	...	44.0	27.8	24.2	21.6	5.6
Malaysia	2004	30.2	56.8	13.1	1.1	29.6	35.1	33.4	21.0	5.9
Malaisie	2009	15.7	68.8	15.5	1.2	27.7	32.8	35.9	18.5	6.0
	2010	...	...	...	1.2	28.6	33.7	34.5	18.4	5.0
	2015	28.7	65.7	5.6	3.1	33.2	36.4	27.3	19.7	5.0
Maldives	2005	...	...	...	...	54.1	...	...	13.0	5.2
Maldives	2010	20.5	78.3	1.2	12.7	42.5	25.0	7.3	12.5	4.6
	2015	43.5	55.6	1.0	11.8	39.7	24.3	12.7	12.9	5.2
Mali	2005	...	...	...	...	...	...	...	16.3	3.5
Mali	2010	40.9	54.1	5.0	0.2	25.3	53.8	20.7	16.5	3.3
	2012	34.9	62.7	2.4	0.3	38.3	39.9	20.3	22.4	3.5
	2014	...	...	2.9	0.2	43.2	34.1	21.6	18.2	3.7
Malta	2004	14.5	79.9	5.6	5.2	21.1	39.8	11.0	10.6	4.5
Malte	2010	17.5	72.4	10.1	7.4	21.6	45.7	22.8	15.7	6.5
	2013	12.0	73.2	14.7	5.6	20.2	35.8	19.2	18.8	7.8
Marshall Islands	2002	* 22.6	* 75.0	* 2.4	...	45.5	38.9	14.7	14.8	8.7
Îles Marshall	2003	...	...	...	...	...	...	...	22.5	12.2
	2006	42.8	35.8	21.4	...	...	...	...	...	...
Mauritania	*2004	...	...	...	...	...	...	...	8.2	2.5
Mauritanie	2010	...	...	...	0.5	47.5	23.2	18.8	16.0	3.6
	2013	...	...	...	...	43.2	23.3	11.6	11.4	2.9
Mauritius	2005	...	...	...	1.5	27.2	44.2	11.3	15.8	4.2
Maurice	2010	...	...	13.5	1.4	27.0	52.6	9.4	14.6	3.6
	2015	...	...	...	1.2	20.6	64.1	6.8	19.0	4.9

Public expenditure on education *(continued)*
By expenditure type, level of education, total government expenditure and GDP

Dépenses publiques afférentes à l'éducation *(suite)*
Par type de dépenses, niveau de scolarité, dépenses publiques totales et PIB

		Percentage of total expenditure in public institutions Pourcentage des dépenses publiques totales en faveur de l'éducation			Percentage of government expenditure on education by level Pourcentage des dépenses publiques selon le niveau d'enseignement					
Country or area Pays ou zone	Year Année	Current expenditure Dépenses courantes	Staff Compensation Rémunération du personnel	Capital expenditure Dépenses en Capital	Pre-primary Préprimaire	Primary Primaire	Secondary Secondaire	Tertiary Tertiaire	As % of Govt. Expenditure En % des dépenses du gouvt.	As % of GDP En % du PIB
Mexico	2005	11.2	85.7	3.1	10.4	39.1	30.3	17.5	22.2	4.9
Mexique	2010	10.3	85.7	3.9	10.2	36.0	30.3	19.7	19.4	5.2
	2011	10.6	85.5	3.9	10.4	35.5	30.7	18.1	19.0	5.1
	2014	12.9	82.8	4.3	...	32.8	32.0	21.3	19.1	5.3
Micronesia (Fed. States of)	*2000	...	...	...	...	...	...	...	10.0	6.7
Micronésie (États féd.)	2015	...	...	...	...	...	...	...	20.7	12.5
Monaco	2004	2.1	90.9	7.0	4.3	15.4	45.8	4.4	5.9	1.2
Monaco	2010	8.4	90.7	0.9	3.2	15.3	37.7	...	6.4	1.3
	2014	4.3	87.3	8.4	3.6	16.0	41.1	...	5.0	1.0
	2015	8.5	83.7	7.8	...	...	...	...	...	...
Mongolia	2000	55.8	43.4	0.8	...	...	...	...	16.1	5.6
Mongolie	2002	...	...	4.9	14.1	...	...	15.5	20.3	7.2
	2004	...	...	...	18.5	25.1	32.8	18.4	13.6	4.3
	2010	...	...	...	22.0	26.9	33.7	6.7	14.7	4.6
	2011	...	...	...	23.8	32.7	30.4	3.8	12.2	4.6
Montserrat	2001	* 27.5	* 41.4	* 31.2	13.6	20.6	29.5	5.5	...	...
Montserrat	2004	...	...	...	...	20.5	...	...	...	...
	2009	...	...	...	...	...	...	...	...	5.1
Morocco	2008	...	...	...	~0.0	35.5	43.1	...	17.5	5.3
Maroc	2009	...	...	...	...	37.7	41.9	20.2	17.3	5.3
Mozambique	2005	...	...	22.6	...	...	...	...	22.7	4.4
Mozambique	2006	...	...	26.8	...	57.7	29.3	12.1	18.6	4.3
	2013	22.2	58.5	19.3	...	49.2	30.6	13.7	19.0	6.5
Namibia	2000	19.3	73.6	7.2	0.2	58.8	27.2	12.0	21.9	7.0
Namibie	2003	...	...	...	0.5	63.1	25.8	9.1	20.3	6.1
	2008	...	* 79.9	...	0.4	47.6	18.7	9.9	25.1	6.5
	2010	22.1	77.0	0.8	...	40.0	23.5	23.1	26.2	8.3
Nauru	2002	...	...	...	...	67.5	...	...	...	...
Nauru	*2007	20.8	56.9	...	...	...	...	...	...	...
Nepal	2003	...	...	...	...	* 56.5	22.1	10.3	21.3	3.1
Népal	2005	...	...	...	...	...	...	...	22.3	3.4
	2010	18.0	69.2	12.8	1.0	55.7	30.5	12.7	16.0	3.6
	2015	24.9	64.1	11.0	2.1	53.8	33.3	10.8	17.1	3.7
Netherlands	2005	17.5	69.8	12.7	7.7	25.9	39.4	26.8	12.2	5.2
Pays-Bas	2010	18.5	69.6	11.9	6.9	24.3	40.7	28.0	11.5	5.6
	2014	20.3	67.7	12.1	6.7	22.5	40.3	30.6	12.0	5.5
New Zealand	2005	...	...	...	3.3	25.7	42.6	23.1	18.0	6.3
Nouvelle-Zélande	2010	...	...	...	6.7	24.4	38.7	26.8	16.9	7.0
	2015	...	...	...	7.6	23.2	37.0	25.6	18.0	6.4
Nicaragua	2002	10.7	80.1	9.2	...	...	...	...	15.7	2.4
Nicaragua	*2003	...	...	...	...	...	...	...	14.9	2.4
	2004	...	...	11.7	...	...	...	...	...	...
	2010	10.7	46.2	11.4	3.6	39.8	13.2	26.0	22.8	4.5
Niger	2003	...	...	...	...	72.6	...	...	13.8	2.4
Niger	2010	14.2	77.9	7.9	2.4	61.0	21.3	12.6	18.1	3.7
	2014	15.0	59.1	25.9	4.5	52.2	29.1	13.9	21.7	6.7
Niue										
Nioué	2002	...	...	...	...	28.8	50.7	...	...	...
Norway	2005	22.4	66.9	10.7	4.1	25.0	35.7	32.4	16.8	6.9
Norvège	2010	21.3	67.4	11.3	4.9	26.7	35.3	29.6	15.3	6.8
	2011	20.9	69.0	10.1	5.5	26.0	35.2	29.9	15.0	6.5
	2013	19.1	69.9	11.0	9.9	22.7	...	25.9	17.0	7.4
Oman	2002	...	...	14.4	...	46.8	43.2	10.0	11.1	4.3
Oman	2005	...	...	...	...	50.5	41.8	7.6	10.1	3.5
	2009	...	...	...	...	33.0	40.2	26.9	10.9	4.2
	2013	20.7	67.6	11.7	...	...	32.1	...	11.1	5.0

Public expenditure on education *(continued)*

By expenditure type, level of education, total government expenditure and GDP

Dépenses publiques afférentes à l'éducation *(suite)*

Par type de dépenses, niveau de scolarité, dépenses publiques totales et PIB

Country or area Pays ou zone	Year Année	Percentage of total expenditure in public institutions / Pourcentage des dépenses publiques totales en faveur de l'éducation: Current expenditure Dépenses courantes	Staff Compensation Rémunération du personnel	Capital expenditure Dépenses en Capital	Percentage of government expenditure on education by level / Pourcentage des dépenses publiques selon le niveau d'enseignement: Pre-primary Préprimaire	Primary Primaire	Secondary Secondaire	Tertiary Tertiaire	As % of Govt. Expenditure En % des dépenses du gouvt.	As % of GDP En % du PIB
Pakistan	2005	12.3	49.2	38.5	...	...	...	...	13.8	2.3
Pakistan	2007	14.8	59.1	26.1	...	...	...	...	15.4	2.6
	2010	...	...	...	...	...	...	...	11.9	2.3
	2013	...	...	24.6	...	32.7	25.1	32.2	11.5	2.5
	2015	...	...	...	...	31.1	37.4	22.8	13.2	2.6
Palau	2001	...	...	...	* 14.6	* 44.9	9.6	20.7	15.1	7.6
Palaos	*2002	...	...	...	...	...	...	...	15.3	7.5
Panama	2002	11.1	67.9	21.0	2.2	32.1	29.2	28.1	17.0	4.2
Panama	*2004	...	...	...	4.0	34.5	25.9	28.4	14.6	3.6
	2008	...	...	14.1	...	...	...	...	14.9	3.6
	2011	...	...	...	3.0	23.5	22.4	22.2	13.0	3.2
Paraguay	2004	6.2	89.4	4.4	7.6	46.6	29.8	15.9	18.2	3.4
Paraguay	2010	9.5	65.5	6.5	6.7	38.5	36.1	18.5	18.8	3.8
	2012	11.7	79.9	8.4	6.1	38.3	33.0	22.4	19.6	5.0
Peru	2005	9.3	81.3	9.4	8.1	35.6	31.4	10.7	14.3	2.8
Pérou	2010	14.5	64.6	20.9	12.0	39.9	34.2	13.8	13.6	2.9
	2015	28.3	49.5	22.2	16.6	36.5	30.8	16.1	17.6	4.0
Philippines	2005	11.1	85.5	3.4	0.1	52.0	26.8	13.3	12.4	2.4
Philippines	2009	18.4	73.4	8.2	1.7	55.0	29.7	12.0	13.2	2.7
Poland	2005	32.6	60.5	6.9	9.9	31.0	36.6	21.8	12.3	5.4
Pologne	2010	29.3	61.4	9.3	10.0	31.0	35.5	22.8	11.1	5.1
	2014	24.7	68.0	7.3	12.4	31.4	31.4	24.1	11.6	4.9
Portugal	2005	10.2	86.2	3.6	7.4	30.6	40.8	18.1	10.9	5.1
Portugal	2010	12.1	84.1	3.8	7.2	27.0	44.0	20.2	10.4	5.4
	2014	12.8	84.3	2.8	8.3	29.9	42.3	17.8	9.9	5.1
Puerto Rico Porto Rico	2013	37.9	57.5	4.6	7.2	21.6	23.6	38.6	21.6	6.4
Qatar	2005	...	...	...	...	...	...	...	13.7	4.0
Qatar	2009	...	...	...	4.4	17.6	14.7	...	14.8	3.4
	2010	...	...	...	...	...	...	...	13.8	4.5
	2014	45.5	22.7	31.9	...	...	...	...	12.7	3.6
Republic of Korea	2005	24.0	58.7	17.4	1.6	35.4	41.5	14.0	...	3.9
République de Corée	2009	27.2	55.8	17.0	2.2	32.6	38.2	17.1	...	4.7
	2015	25.2	62.7	12.1	8.3	31.5	39.4	20.8	...	5.1
Republic of Moldova	2005	...	...	...	...	...	...	...	19.3	7.2
République de Moldova	2010	29.1	62.6	8.2	19.5	18.0	37.3	18.0	22.3	9.1
	2014	28.6	60.8	10.6	21.0	22.7	35.7	17.2	18.8	7.5
	2015	...	52.2	7.5	...	...	...	...	...	...
Romania	2005	34.4	59.1	6.5	9.1	* 13.8	* 44.3	23.2	10.8	3.5
Roumanie	2010	27.1	62.2	10.8	10.0	16.4	35.8	28.5	9.1	3.5
	2014	27.7	67.3	5.0	10.8	13.7	40.9	21.6	9.2	3.1
Russian Federation	2005	...	...	...	13.9	...	...	21.1	12.0	3.8
Fédération de Russie	2008	...	...	...	15.0	...	...	23.1	12.0	4.1
	2012	24.5	66.4	9.1	...	...	...	21.2	11.1	3.9
	2013	23.0	68.8	8.2	...	...	...	...	...	...
Rwanda	2000	...	47.3	20.3	* 0.5	* 48.2	* 16.7	* 34.7	21.1	4.1
Rwanda	2001	24.4	33.8	41.8	...	...	...	...	26.7	5.7
	2010	25.1	58.7	16.1	0.2	36.7	30.7	22.7	17.4	4.9
	*2015	41.4	47.9	10.8	1.3	32.7	42.6	20.9	12.5	3.8
	*2016	44.8	42.2	13.0	7.7	34.6	52.8	...	...	3.6
Saint Kitts and Nevis	2005	...	...	...	...	...	...	...	11.1	3.9
Saint-Kitts-et-Nevis	2007	...	...	...	...	...	...	...	13.1	4.3
	2015	...	...	...	15.6	21.4	40.2	15.4	8.8	2.8

Public expenditure on education *(continued)*

By expenditure type, level of education, total government expenditure and GDP

Dépenses publiques afférentes à l'éducation *(suite)*

Par type de dépenses, niveau de scolarité, dépenses publiques totales et PIB

		Percentage of total expenditure in public institutions Pourcentage des dépenses publiques totales en faveur de l'éducation			Percentage of government expenditure on education by level Pourcentage des dépenses publiques selon le niveau d'enseignement					
Country or area Pays ou zone	Year Année	Current expenditure Dépenses courantes	Staff Compensation Rémunération du personnel	Capital expenditure Dépenses en Capital	Pre-primary Préprimaire	Primary Primaire	Secondary Secondaire	Tertiary Tertiaire	As % of Govt. Expenditure En % des dépenses du gouvt.	As % of GDP En % du PIB
Saint Lucia	2004	26.1	73.2	0.7	0.4	47.2	33.4	...	15.0	4.1
Sainte-Lucie	2005	...	...	...	...	...	...	...	16.3	5.1
	2006	28.4	45.3	26.3	...	...	...	...	19.0	5.5
	*2010	...	...	...	1.8	42.3	45.6	4.6	14.2	4.1
	2011	...	...	...	1.5	42.3	45.1	* 5.0	13.8	4.3
	2015	...	...	11.7	1.4	34.2	43.8	...	16.5	4.9
Saint Vincent & Grenadines	2005	14.6	51.9	33.6	0.3	41.0	31.7	3.7	22.6	6.4
St-Vincent-Grenadines	2010	5.6	94.4	...	2.0	41.4	36.3	7.0	15.5	5.1
Samoa	2001	...	...	...	* 0.7	* 36.2	* 29.8	33.2	12.8	3.8
Samoa	*2002	...	...	...	...	45.8	...	...	12.8	3.8
	2008	...	...	...	...	...	...	...	16.1	5.1
San Marino	2010	4.2	95.8	...	19.0	31.7	39.5	9.8	10.8	2.3
Saint-Marin	2011	5.0	95.0	...	20.2	33.3	35.8	10.8	10.6	2.4
Sao Tome and Principe	2005	...	...	...	...	...	...	...	12.1	5.3
Sao Tomé-et-Principe	2010	...	...	...	...	...	...	...	19.3	9.7
	2014	...	...	...	12.0	55.8	22.6	9.6	12.3	3.8
Saudi Arabia	2005	...	...	...	...	...	...	...	19.3	5.4
Arabie saoudite	2008	...	...	...	...	...	...	...	19.3	5.1
Senegal	2005	...	...	...	0.9	41.8	22.4	22.0	21.8	5.1
Sénégal	2010	18.3	72.6	9.1	1.1	43.2	27.9	26.8	24.0	6.5
	2014	10.6	77.0	12.4	2.9	34.9	33.3	28.8	24.8	7.4
Serbia	2010	22.4	75.1	2.5	0.5	45.9	23.3	29.1	10.5	4.6
Serbie	2011	22.4	75.0	2.6	1.1	45.3	23.1	29.2	10.6	4.5
	2012	22.4	75.1	2.5	...	...	...	29.1	9.6	4.4
	2014	19.4	78.7	1.9	...	...	...	...	9.1	4.2
Seychelles	2002	23.9	66.4	9.7	* 10.5	* 32.0	* 26.1	17.4	9.2	5.2
Seychelles	2003	31.8	59.3	8.9	* 8.6	* 32.8	* 28.9	...	12.0	5.4
	2006	29.8	56.7	13.5	4.1	...	...	17.9	11.0	4.8
	2011	18.7	71.3	10.0	...	24.0	16.2	32.5	10.4	3.6
Sierra Leone	*2005	...	...	...	...	...	...	...	15.5	2.8
Sierra Leone	2010	28.3	69.1	2.5	...	50.7	26.4	19.6	12.8	2.6
	2011	24.5	74.3	1.2	...	52.6	26.3	17.9	12.4	2.7
	2014	...	...	0.5	...	43.1	23.4	30.7	15.1	2.7
Singapore	2005	...	...	...	...	...	...	...	19.8	3.2
Singapour	2010	...	...	9.2	...	20.8	25.0	35.1	17.2	3.1
	2013	...	...	8.2	...	22.0	23.0	35.3	20.0	2.9
Slovakia	2005	34.1	60.2	5.6	10.1	17.1	48.9	21.0	9.5	3.8
Slovaquie	2010	30.8	57.0	12.2	9.4	20.7	46.9	19.6	9.8	4.1
	2014	34.4	58.4	7.2	11.4	19.1	41.8	23.0	10.2	4.2
Slovenia	2003	21.0	69.4	9.6	9.2	* 21.8	* 46.6	22.3	13.7	5.7
Slovénie	2005	20.6	69.4	10.0	10.4	...	...	22.0	13.3	5.6
	2010	21.3	70.0	8.7	10.3	28.5	37.1	24.0	12.1	5.6
	2013	21.0	67.0	12.0	11.1	27.9	33.8	20.5	10.0	5.5
Solomon Islands Îles Salomon	2010	...	...	...	...	...	...	...	17.5	10.0
South Africa	2005	20.9	66.3	2.9	0.6	42.9	32.6	15.1	19.9	5.1
Afrique du Sud	2006	...	69.8	* 3.5	0.5	45.1	31.1	12.8	19.7	5.1
	2009	...	...	* 3.8	0.9	41.1	30.9	12.5	18.3	5.2
	2010	...	...	...	1.1	42.5	31.4	11.9	18.0	5.7
	2014	29.5	67.2	3.3	1.5	38.8	30.7	12.2	19.1	6.0
South Sudan	2014	34.6	48.8	16.5	0.6	57.5	16.6	24.7	4.3	1.7
Soudan du sud	2015	75.5	24.5	...	0.6	53.8	18.0	27.6	2.6	1.5
	2016	6.5	93.5	...	0.3	36.4	12.2	50.4	...	1.8
Spain	2005	16.7	73.5	9.8	12.4	25.8	39.5	22.4	10.8	4.1
Espagne	2010	17.7	71.6	10.8	14.1	25.5	37.0	23.4	10.6	4.8
	2013	19.5	74.6	5.8	11.2	26.1	36.9	22.4	9.5	4.3
	2014	18.4	76.3	5.3	11.3	26.3	...	22.5	9.6	4.3

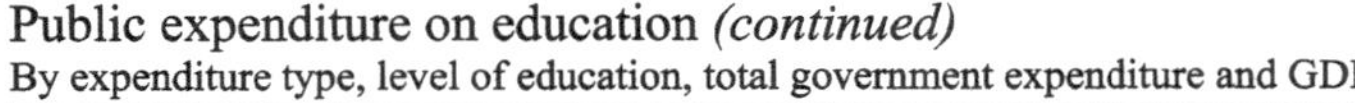

9 Public expenditure on education *(continued)*

By expenditure type, level of education, total government expenditure and GDP

Dépenses publiques afférentes à l'éducation *(suite)*

Par type de dépenses, niveau de scolarité, dépenses publiques totales et PIB

Country or area Pays ou zone	Year Année	Percentage of total expenditure in public institutions / Pourcentage des dépenses publiques totales en faveur de l'éducation: Current expenditure Dépenses courantes	Staff Compensation Rémunération du personnel	Capital expenditure Dépenses en Capital	Percentage of government expenditure on education by level / Pourcentage des dépenses publiques selon le niveau d'enseignement: Pre-primary Préprimaire	Primary Primaire	Secondary Secondaire	Tertiary Tertiaire	As % of Govt. Expenditure En % des dépenses du gouvt.	As % of GDP En % du PIB
Sri Lanka	2010	9.9	75.5	14.6	...	25.0	53.2	16.4	8.6	1.7
Sri Lanka	2015	18.3	62.4	19.3	...	28.3	47.1	19.4	11.0	2.2
	2016	42.8	39.1	18.1	...	32.8	49.3	14.2	...	...
State of Palestine	2010	...	...	...	...	...	...	...	...	1.8
État de Palestine	2015	11.3	85.2	3.5	...	...	...	...	...	1.3
Sudan	2005	...	...	...	...	...	...	...	6.0	1.6
Soudan	2009	...	...	...	...	...	...	...	10.8	2.2
Swaziland	2005	...	...	...	~0.0	39.9	34.9	23.9	20.9	6.5
Swaziland	2010	...	...	...	0.2	47.2	35.5	16.6	18.3	6.1
	2014	36.2	59.3	4.5	1.1	50.8	34.1	13.3	24.9	7.1
Sweden	2005	28.4	65.0	6.6	7.8	26.2	38.2	27.5	12.7	6.6
Suède	2010	31.3	63.1	5.6	10.2	24.3	35.6	29.0	13.0	6.6
	2014	29.7	65.2	5.1	16.9	22.8	27.5	25.3	14.9	7.7
Switzerland	2005	15.5	75.3	9.1	3.6	29.7	37.7	26.0	15.9	5.2
Suisse	2010	16.2	75.2	8.6	3.7	28.0	41.3	25.3	15.4	4.9
	2014	15.6	74.4	10.0	4.7	29.6	37.6	26.4	15.5	5.1
Syrian Arab Republic	2002	...	...	...	...	44.4	33.4	21.0	16.8	5.1
République arabe	2004	...	...	...	...	...	...	24.8	17.1	5.4
syrienne	2009	...	...	...	...	38.9	36.9	24.2	19.2	5.1
Tajikistan	2005	...	...	...	3.8	...	...	7.4	15.3	3.5
Tadjikistan	2010	...	...	...	5.0	...	...	10.1	15.3	4.0
	2015	...	...	14.0	5.3	...	...	9.9	16.3	5.2
Thailand	2004	...	...	...	10.4	31.0	24.0	20.6	21.5	4.0
Thaïlande	2005	...	...	...	13.6	...	...	21.7	20.5	3.9
	2010	45.8	50.9	3.3	5.7	40.1	28.6	16.5	16.2	3.5
	2013	45.8	49.2	5.0	5.4	41.1	29.8	15.6	18.9	4.1
	2014	31.8	62.5	5.7	...	...	...	...	...	...
TFYR of Macedonia ex-R.Y. de Macédoine	2002	10.8	87.1	2.1	...	...	...	15.0	8.6	3.3
Timor-Leste	2010	52.5	37.8	9.7	...	...	...	10.4	12.9	10.4
Timor-Leste	2014	46.4	49.5	4.0	1.2	64.9	29.8	4.1	8.0	7.8
Togo	2000	20.9	69.1	10.0	...	48.6	29.3	17.4	24.4	4.5
Togo	2005	...	...	...	...	41.8	...	...	17.7	3.4
	2010	14.7	74.7	10.6	2.6	51.7	25.6	16.7	19.6	4.4
	2015	7.0	90.5	2.5	1.6	64.5	16.3	17.3	18.0	5.2
Tonga Tonga	2004	...	...	...	...	44.4	30.1	21.7	18.1	3.9
Trinidad and Tobago Trinité-et-Tobago	2003	...	...	...	0.6	39.2	36.8	...	13.3	3.1
Tunisia	2000	8.2	77.3	14.5	...	* 33.3	* 45.0	* 21.7	* 25.0	* 6.2
Tunisie	2002	...	...	11.6	...	* 32.9	* 44.4	22.8	23.1	5.8
	2005	...	...	...	...	* 34.3	* 41.6	24.1	26.7	6.5
	2008	...	...	10.0	...	27.7	47.3	25.0	25.3	6.3
	2010	...	...	10.4	...	...	...	28.2	24.4	6.3
	2012	...	...	...	...	...	...	28.1	20.6	6.3
Turkey	2004	12.6	66.3	21.1	0.6	...	...	27.9	8.8	3.1
Turquie	2006	14.9	74.6	10.6	...	...	...	31.9	8.5	2.9
	2013	23.0	66.2	10.8	3.4	20.5	42.9	33.2	12.4	4.8
Turkmenistan Turkménistan	2012	...	...	33.7	28.1	...	...	9.2	20.8	3.1
Turks and Caicos Islands	2002	9.8	61.1	29.2	* 5.0	* 21.1	31.7	22.9	...	...
Îles Turques-et-Caïques	2003	...	...	...	...	* 21.6	28.0	37.2	...	...
	2005	13.7	69.5	16.8	...	* 30.0	47.7	...	...	...
	2015	...	...	17.6	...	36.1	41.5	22.4	...	3.3
Uganda	2004	12.1	62.7	25.2	...	61.2	17.3	11.9	20.3	5.0
Ouganda	2010	51.1	35.5	13.4	...	47.3	39.4	13.3	10.1	2.4
	2014	48.3	39.1	12.6	...	59.2	24.6	16.3	11.7	2.2

Public expenditure on education *(continued)*

By expenditure type, level of education, total government expenditure and GDP

Dépenses publiques afférentes à l'éducation *(suite)*

Par type de dépenses, niveau de scolarité, dépenses publiques totales et PIB

Country or area Pays ou zone	Year Année	Percentage of total expenditure in public institutions / Pourcentage des dépenses publiques totales en faveur de l'éducation: Current expenditure Dépenses courantes	Staff Compensation Rémunération du personnel	Capital expenditure Dépenses en Capital	Percentage of government expenditure on education by level / Pourcentage des dépenses publiques selon le niveau d'enseignement: Pre-primary Préprimaire	Primary Primaire	Secondary Secondaire	Tertiary Tertiaire	As % of Govt. Expenditure En % des dépenses du gouvt.	As % of GDP En % du PIB
Ukraine	2000	...	...	8.3	11.1	...	...	32.3	11.4	4.2
Ukraine	2005	...	...	...	11.0	...	...	29.5	13.7	6.1
	2009	...	...	...	12.5	...	...	32.4	15.1	7.3
	2014	...	...	2.2	16.3	18.0	27.8	31.5	13.1	5.9
United Kingdom	2005	18.5	73.5	8.0	5.9	26.5	45.4	22.3	13.2	5.0
Royaume-Uni	2010	29.8	58.8	11.4	5.2	30.1	48.3	16.4	13.0	5.8
	2015	23.5	73.9	2.6	3.5	32.2	41.0	22.8	13.9	5.7
United Rep. of Tanzania	2005	...	...	...	5.8	56.0	12.9	21.7	18.1	4.6
Rép.-Unie de Tanzanie	2009	...	...	...	4.4	41.9	16.7	33.8	17.4	4.0
	2010	...	...	...	...	...	11.3	28.3	19.6	4.6
	2014	...	...	...	6.0	49.2	18.3	21.4	17.3	3.5
United States of America	2005	21.0	67.6	11.3	5.8	32.3	36.0	25.8	15.1	5.1
États-Unis d'Amérique	2010	20.5	69.4	10.1	6.5	32.4	35.4	25.7	13.1	5.4
	2014	21.6	69.7	8.7	6.1	28.7	32.0	32.5	14.5	5.4
Uruguay	2005	14.5	80.8	4.7	8.9	33.8	35.5	21.8	9.5	2.7
Uruguay	2006	14.1	80.2	5.7	8.7	33.3	36.0	22.0	9.9	2.9
	2011	14.9	80.5	4.6	10.2	27.9	33.2	26.8	14.9	4.4
	2015	13.4	82.6	4.0	...	...	...	...	...	...
Vanuatu	2001	1.1	51.7	47.2	0.1	27.9	57.4	10.5	40.1	9.0
Vanuatu	2003	...	...	...	...	...	...	...	44.8	8.4
	2008	11.4	87.4	1.2	0.5	49.7	32.9	5.9	21.4	5.8
	2009	8.8	89.5	1.7	0.1	54.3	29.7	...	18.7	5.0
	2015	...	...	...	0.1	41.3	28.7	...	22.3	5.5
Venezuela (Boliv. Rep. of) Venezuela (Rép. boliv.)	2009	20.2	76.9	2.9	11.6	31.5	19.0	22.6	20.7	6.9
Viet Nam	2010	32.3	42.4	25.3	13.3	30.0	42.2	14.5	17.1	5.1
Viet Nam	2013	31.3	46.9	21.9	15.7	29.7	39.6	15.0	18.5	5.7
Yemen	*2001	...	...	...	...	...	...	...	30.3	9.3
Yémen	2008	...	...	25.7	...	...	...	...	12.5	5.1
Zambia	2004	25.2	73.0	1.8	...	63.9	13.3	18.0	10.6	2.5
Zambie	2005	...	...	...	...	59.8	14.5	25.8	7.7	1.7
	2008	...	...	...	...	...	...	...	5.7	1.1
Zimbabwe	2010	...	...	...	...	51.6	25.6	22.8	8.7	2.0
Zimbabwe	2014	...	...	...	2.0	47.8	26.9	16.8	30.0	8.4

Source:

United Nations Educational, Scientific and Cultural Organization (UNESCO) Institute for Statistics, Montreal, the UNESCO Institute for Statistics (UIS) statistics database, last accessed June 2017.

Source:

L'Institut de statistique de l'Organisation des Nations Unies pour l'éducation, la science et la culture (UNESCO), Montréal, la base de données de l'institut de statistique de l'UNESCO (ISU), dernier accès juin 2017.

10 Health Personnel

Number of health workers and workforce density (per 1 000 population)

Le personnel de santé

Personnel de santé et densité (pour 1 000 habitants)

Country or area Pays ou zone	Year Année	Physicians / Médecins Number Nombre	Per 1 000 Pour 1 000	Dentists / Dentistes Number Nombre	Per 1 000 Pour 1 000	Pharmacists / Pharmaciens Number Nombre	Per 1 000 Pour 1 000	Nurses and midwives / Infirmières et Sages-femmes Number Nombre	Per 1 000 Pour 1 000
Afghanistan	2001	4 104	0.2	…	…	525	~0.0	4 752	0.2
Afghanistan	2005	…	…	…	…	900	~0.0	14 930	0.6
	2008	4 834	0.2	382	~0.0	829	~0.0	13 780	0.5
	2009	6 037	0.2	…	…	847	~0.0	17 257	0.6
	2010	6 901	0.2	…	…	814	~0.0	…	…
	2014	9 618	0.3	356	~0.0	1 068	~0.0	11 399	0.4
Albania	2006	…	…	1 035	0.3	…	…	…	…
Albanie	2010	3 640	1.3	…	…	1 324	0.5	…	…
	2013	3 709	1.3	…	…	2 441	0.8	…	…
Algeria	2002	35 368	1.1	9 553	0.3	6 333	0.2	69 749	2.2
Algérie	2005	33 952	1.0	9 022	0.3	6 104	0.2	…	…
	2007	40 857	1.2	11 010	0.3	8 232	0.2	65 919	1.9
Andorra	2003	244	3.3	44	0.6	68	0.9	…	…
Andorre	2009	266	3.1	51	0.6	78	0.9	311	3.6
	2015	260	3.7	64	0.9	82	1.2	313	4.4
Angola	2004	1 165	0.1	222	~0.0	919	0.1	18 485	1.1
Angola	2009	2 956	0.1	…	…	…	…	29 592	1.4
Argentina	2004	122 623	3.2	35 592	0.9	19 510	0.5	18 685	0.5
Argentine	2013	160 041	3.8	…	…	…	…	…	…
Armenia	2010	8 177	2.8	1 257	0.4	123	~0.0	…	…
Arménie	2014	8 425	2.8	1 138	0.4	150	0.1	15 014	5.0
Australia	2001	47 875	2.5	21 296	1.1	13 956	0.7	187 837	9.7
Australie	2009	62 800	2.9	14 500	0.7	21 800	1.0	201 300	9.2
	2010	…	…	…	…	19 237	0.9	…	…
	2013	78 514	3.4	13 088	0.6	19 253	0.8	287 244	12.3
Austria	2010	40 105	4.8	4 685	0.6	5 579	0.7	…	…
Autriche	2014	43 126	5.1	4 893	0.6	5 647	0.7	69 772	8.2
	2015	44 002	5.2	4 906	0.6	…	…	…	…
Azerbaijan	2010	33 085	3.6	2 467	0.3	1 831	0.2	…	…
Azerbaïdjan	2014	32 756	3.4	2 601	0.3	1 897	0.2	61 157	6.4
Bahamas Bahamas	2008	947	2.7	115	0.3	160	0.5	1 391	4.0
Bahrain	2005	928	1.1	243	0.3	164	0.2	2 389	2.8
Bahreïn	2010	1 178	0.9	294	0.2	196	0.2	3 052	2.4
	2014	1 279	0.9	339	0.2	219	0.2	3 330	2.4
Bangladesh	2002	…	…	1 886	~0.0	7 622	0.1	…	…
Bangladesh	2005	42 881	0.3	2 344	~0.0	…	…	39 471	0.3
	2010	53 643	0.4	6 252	~0.0	58 388	0.4	28 228	0.2
	2012	60 413	0.4	6 985	~0.0	64 704	0.4	33 016	0.2
Barbados Barbade	2005	489	1.8	94	0.3	251	0.9	1 311	4.8
Belarus	2010	33 325	3.5	5 087	0.5	2 731	0.3	…	…
Bélarus	2014	38 671	4.1	5 414	0.6	3 240	0.3	103 582	10.9
Belgium	2005	21 599	2.0	7 731	0.7	…	…	…	…
Belgique	2010	31 815	2.9	7 675	0.7	12 629	1.2	110 150	10.1
	2014	33 353	3.0	8 108	0.7	13 508	1.2	…	…
Belize	2000	251	1.0	32	0.1	…	…	303	1.2
Belize	2009	241	0.8	12	~0.0	112	0.4	570	1.8
Benin	2004	311	~0.0	12	~0.0	11	~0.0	5 789	0.7
Bénin	2008	542	0.1	37	~0.0	20	~0.0	7 129	0.8
	2013	1 507	0.1	…	…	…	…	6 236	0.6
Bhutan	2004	118	0.2	58	0.1	79	0.1	515	0.8
Bhoutan	2007	144	0.2	65	0.1	87	0.1	545	0.8
	2008	171	0.2	…	…	89	0.1	666	1.0
	2012	194	0.3	…	…	11	~0.0	736	1.0
	2014	197	0.3	26	~0.0	…	…	827	1.1
Bolivia (Plurin. State of)	2001	10 329	1.2	5 997	0.7	4 670	0.6	18 091	2.1
Bolivie (État plurin. de)	2010	4 406	0.4	976	0.1	567	0.1	8 366	0.8
	2011	4 771	0.5	1 130	0.1	660	0.1	10 139	1.0

10 Health Personnel *(continued)*

Number of health workers and workforce density (per 1 000 population)

Le personnel de santé *(suite)*

Personnel de santé et densité (pour 1 000 habitants)

Country or area Pays ou zone	Year Année	Physicians / Médecins Number Nombre	Physicians / Médecins Per 1 000 Pour 1 000	Dentists / Dentistes Number Nombre	Dentists / Dentistes Per 1 000 Pour 1 000	Pharmacists / Pharmaciens Number Nombre	Pharmacists / Pharmaciens Per 1 000 Pour 1 000	Nurses and midwives / Infirmières et Sages-femmes Number Nombre	Nurses and midwives / Infirmières et Sages-femmes Per 1 000 Pour 1 000
Bosnia and Herzegovina	2010	6 665	1.7	797	0.2	371	0.1	...	...
Bosnie-Herzégovine	2013	7 211	1.9	809	0.2	429	0.1	...	...
	2014	...	...	825	0.2	441	0.1	21 352	5.6
Botswana	2004	715	0.4	38	~0.0	333	0.2	4 753	2.6
Botswana	2005	466	0.3	...	...	...	...	4 468	2.4
	2009	693	0.3	145	0.1	365	0.2	5 816	2.9
	2012	819	0.4	...	...	...	...	5 816	2.7
Brazil	2005	310 138	1.6	207 904	1.1	99 696	0.5	703 813	3.7
Brésil	2010	355 006	1.8	242 266	1.2	142 841	0.7	1 446 403	7.3
	2013	378 354	1.9	...	...	...	...	1 520 533	7.4
Brunei Darussalam	2005	390	1.1	73	0.2	41	0.1	2 006	5.5
Brunéi Darussalam	2010	563	1.4	86	0.2	43	0.1	2 907	7.4
	2012	596	1.5	174	0.4	167	0.4	3 323	8.2
Bulgaria	2001	...	...	...	...	1 020	0.1	...	...
Bulgarie	2010	27 963	3.8	6 389	0.9	...	...	...	...
	2014	28 801	4.0	7 054	1.0	...	...	35 035	4.9
Burkina Faso	2004	708	0.1	58	~0.0	343	~0.0	6 557	0.5
Burkina Faso	2010	713	~0.0	32	~0.0	339	~0.0	8 645	0.6
	2012	787	~0.0	38	~0.0	351	~0.0	10 459	0.6
Burundi	2004	200	~0.0	14	~0.0	76	~0.0	1 348	0.2
Burundi	2011	...	...	...	...	172	~0.0	...	...
Cabo Verde	2004	231	0.5	11	~0.0	43	0.1	410	0.9
Cabo Verde	2010	167	0.3	4	~0.0	4	~0.0	257	0.5
	2011	153	0.3	3	~0.0	5	~0.0	279	0.6
Cambodia	2000	2 047	0.2	209	~0.0	564	~0.0	11 125	0.9
Cambodge	2010	3 294	0.2	242	~0.0	548	~0.0	12 251	0.9
	2013	2 540	0.2	297	~0.0	603	~0.0	14 419	1.0
Cameroon	2005	1 049	0.1	26	~0.0	27	~0.0	6 705	0.4
Cameroun	2010	1 712	0.1	58	~0.0	42	~0.0	10 714	0.5
Canada	2004	60 612	1.9	35 834	1.1	28 537	0.9	316 512	9.9
Canada	2005	...	...	...	...	...	...	321 159	10.0
	2008	65 440	2.0	41 798	1.3	29 010	0.9	343 699	10.3
	2009	...	...	...	...	30 553	0.9	350 547	10.4
	2010	69 648	2.0	...	...	...	...	318 565	9.3
	2012	86 365	2.5	...	...	31 637	0.9	326 227	9.4
	2013	...	...	...	...	32 573	0.9	334 711	9.5
Central African Republic	2004	331	0.1	13	~0.0	17	~0.0	1 613	0.4
République centrafricaine	2009	205	~0.0	12	~0.0	12	~0.0	1 097	0.3
Chad	2004	345	~0.0	15	~0.0	37	~0.0	2 499	0.3
Tchad	2006	368	~0.0	...	...	...	...	1 891	0.2
	2013	573	~0.0	...	...	72	~0.0	4 057	0.3
Chile	2005	15 865	1.0	12	~0.0	36	~0.0	2 103	0.1
Chili	2009	17 382	1.0	15	~0.0	39	~0.0	2 443	0.1
China	2002	1 463 573	1.1	...	...	357 659	0.3	1 246 545	1.0
Chine	2005	...	...	51 012	~0.0	349 533	0.3	1 349 589	1.0
	2010	1 972 840	1.5	...	...	353 916	0.3	2 048 071	1.5
	2011	2 020 154	1.5	...	...	363 993	0.3	2 244 020	1.7
Colombia	2005	62 807	1.5	37 371	0.9	...	...	25 845	0.6
Colombie	2010	71 980	1.6	44 858	1.0	...	...	30 119	0.7
Comoros									
Comores	2004	115	0.2	29	~0.0	41	0.1	588	1.0
Congo	2004	756	0.2	12	~0.0	99	~0.0	3 672	1.1
Congo	2007	401	0.1	...	...	63	~0.0	3 492	0.9
Cook Islands	2004	20	1.0	10	0.5	2	0.1	80	4.2
Îles Cook	2009	24	1.2	19	0.9	8	0.4	116	5.8
Costa Rica	2000	5 204	1.3	1 905	0.5	2 101	0.5	3 653	0.9
Costa Rica	2013	5 411	1.2	599	0.1	891	0.2	3 745	0.8
Côte d'Ivoire	2005	1 698	0.1	204	~0.0	128	~0.0	8 988	0.5
Côte d'Ivoire	2008	2 746	0.1	274	~0.0	413	~0.0	9 231	0.5
Croatia	2010	12 304	2.9	3 158	0.7	2 851	0.7	...	...
Croatie	2014	13 302	3.1	3 327	0.8	3 024	0.7	26 136	6.1

Health Personnel *(continued)*

Number of health workers and workforce density (per 1 000 population)

Le personnel de santé *(suite)*

Personnel de santé et densité (pour 1 000 habitants)

Country or area Pays ou zone	Year Année	Physicians / Médecins Number Nombre	Physicians / Médecins Per 1 000 Pour 1 000	Dentists / Dentistes Number Nombre	Dentists / Dentistes Per 1 000 Pour 1 000	Pharmacists / Pharmaciens Number Nombre	Pharmacists / Pharmaciens Per 1 000 Pour 1 000	Nurses and midwives / Infirmières et Sages-femmes Number Nombre	Nurses and midwives / Infirmières et Sages-femmes Per 1 000 Pour 1 000
Cuba	2002	67 079	6.0	9 955	0.9	...	...	83 880	7.5
Cuba	2005	70 594	6.3	10 554	0.9	...	...	...	...
	2010	76 506	6.8	12 144	1.1	4 656	0.4	103 014	9.1
	2014	85 563	7.5	21 032	1.8	3 058	0.3	90 765	8.0
Cyprus	2002	...	...	...	...	144	0.1	2 994	3.1
Chypre	2009	2 313	2.1	757	0.7	...	...	3 806	3.5
	2010	2 399	2.2	772	0.7	181	0.2	...	...
	2014	2 880	2.5	839	0.7	188	0.2	4 509	3.9
Czechia	2010	37 661	3.6	7 263	0.7	6 061	0.6	...	...
Tchéquie	2013	38 776	3.7	7 426	0.7	6 383	0.6	...	...
	2014	...	...	7 906	0.8	6 724	0.6	87 782	8.3
Dem. People's Rep. Korea	2003	74 597	3.2	8 315	0.4	13 497	0.6	93 414	4.0
Rép. pop. dém. de Corée	2011	68 393	2.8	4 314	0.2	8 622	0.4	100 768	4.1
Dem. Rep. of the Congo Rép. dém. du Congo	2009	5 832	0.1	79	~0.0	495	~0.0	61 368	1.0
Denmark	2005	17 350	3.2	4 634	0.9	...	...	81 219	15.0
Danemark	2009	18 797	3.4	4 438	0.8	...	...	88 335	16.0
	2010	19 881	3.6	4 485	0.8	2 623	0.5	...	...
	2013	20 519	3.6	4 295	0.8	2 841	0.5	94 545	16.8
Djibouti	2004	129	0.2	10	~0.0	18	~0.0	296	0.4
Djibouti	2005	140	0.2	...	...	41	0.1	450	0.6
	2006	185	0.2	...	...	16	~0.0	...	...
	2008	...	...	...	...	266	0.3	...	...
	2014	201	0.2	19	~0.0	210	0.2	488	0.6
Dominica Dominique	2001	124	1.8	21	0.3	18	0.3	438	6.3
Dominican Republic	2000	15 670	1.8	7 000	0.8	3 330	0.4	15 352	1.8
République dominicaine	2008	10 385	1.1	1 205	0.1	...	...	...	...
	2009	...	...	1 785	0.2	...	...	12 686	1.3
	2011	14 983	1.5	1 910	0.2	...	...	13 374	1.3
Ecuador	2003	20 020	1.5	2 213	0.2	497	~0.0	20 372	1.5
Équateur	2009	23 614	1.6	3 363	0.2	664	~0.0	27 764	1.9
	2011	25 277	1.7	4 183	0.3	810	0.1	31 635	2.1
Egypt	2004	...	...	9 917	0.1	...	...	146 761	2.0
Égypte	2005	179 900	2.4	...	...	...	...	...	...
	2009	225 565	2.8	...	...	...	...	...	...
	2014	72 901	0.8	14 753	0.2	29 507	0.3	128 445	1.4
El Salvador	2005	10 355	1.7	4 255	0.7	2 280	0.4	2 084	0.4
El Salvador	2008	11 542	1.9	4 669	0.8	2 316	0.4	2 929	0.5
Equatorial Guinea Guinée équatoriale	2004	153	0.3	15	~0.0	121	0.2	271	0.4
Eritrea Érythrée	2004	215	0.1	16	~0.0	107	~0.0	2 505	0.6
Estonia	2000	6 118	4.4	1 747	1.2	580	0.4	12 087	8.6
Estonie	2010	4 319	3.2	1 198	0.9	842	0.6	...	...
	2014	4 364	3.3	1 215	0.9	889	0.7	7 859	6.0
Ethiopia	2003	1 936	~0.0	93	~0.0	1 343	~0.0	15 544	0.2
Éthiopie	2005	2 453	~0.0	...	...	1 619	~0.0	18 809	0.2
	2009	2 152	~0.0	...	...	2 661	~0.0	21 488	0.3
Fiji	2003	380	0.5	60	0.1	90	0.1	1 660	2.0
Fidji	2009	372	0.4	171	0.2	76	0.1	1 957	2.3
Finland	2002	16 446	3.2	6 674	1.3	5 829	1.1	78 402	15.1
Finlande	2010	16 030	3.0	4 234	0.8	5 944	1.1	...	...
	2012	16 280	3.0	4 234	0.8	6 857	1.3	78 728	14.5
	2013	16 410	3.0	...	...	...	...	...	...
France	2003	...	...	40 648	0.7	63 909	1.1	439 115	7.3
France	2005	...	...	...	...	...	...	469 036	7.7
	2007	227 683	3.7	41 444	0.7	70 498	1.1	500 863	8.1
	2008	...	...	41 422	0.7	72 160	1.2	494 895	7.9
	2015	207 789	3.2	42 602	0.7	70 247	1.1	682 896	10.6
Gabon Gabon	2004	395	0.3	66	~0.0	63	~0.0	6 778	5.0

10 Health Personnel *(continued)*

Number of health workers and workforce density (per 1 000 population)

Le personnel de santé *(suite)*

Personnel de santé et densité (pour 1 000 habitants)

Country or area Pays ou zone	Year Année	Physicians / Médecins Number Nombre	Per 1 000 Pour 1 000	Dentists / Dentistes Number Nombre	Per 1 000 Pour 1 000	Pharmacists / Pharmaciens Number Nombre	Per 1 000 Pour 1 000	Nurses and midwives / Infirmières et Sages-femmes Number Nombre	Per 1 000 Pour 1 000
Gambia	2005	166	0.1	10	~0.0	11	~0.0	732	0.5
Gambie	2008	175	0.1	47	~0.0	75	~0.0	1 411	0.9
Georgia	2009	20 609	4.8	...	...	...	...	13 925	3.2
Géorgie	2010	18 227	4.3	1 257	0.3	353	0.1	...	...
	2014	19 270	4.8	2 152	0.5	308	0.1	15 416	3.8
Germany	2010	303 645	3.8	66 427	0.8	50 604	0.6	...	...
Allemagne	2014	332 695	4.1	69 089	0.9	52 004	0.6	1 087 000	13.5
Ghana	2004	3 240	0.2	393	~0.0	1 388	0.1	19 707	0.9
Ghana	2008	2 587	0.1	148	~0.0	1 673	0.1	22 834	1.0
	2010	2 325	0.1	...	...	...	...	22 507	0.9
Greece	2010	69 265	6.2	14 661	1.3	11 160	1.0	...	...
Grèce	2014	68 807	6.3	13 746	1.3	11 579	1.1	37 842	3.4
Grenada	2003	58	0.6	13	0.1	22	0.2	366	3.6
Grenade	2006	69	0.7	19	0.2	21	0.2	398	3.9
	2011	...	...	...	...	89	0.8	...	...
Guatemala	2007	...	...	2 376	0.2	...	...	...	...
Guatemala	2009	12 940	0.9	...	...	...	...	12 452	0.9
Guinea	2004	987	0.1	60	~0.0	...	...	4 408	0.5
Guinée	2005	940	0.1	33	~0.0	199	~0.0	...	...
Guinea-Bissau	2004	188	0.1	22	~0.0	40	~0.0	1 072	0.7
Guinée-Bissau	2009	124	0.1	13	~0.0	21	~0.0	1 042	0.7
Guyana	2000	366	0.5	30	~0.0	...	...	1 738	2.3
Guyana	2009	161	0.2	46	0.1	87	0.1	989	1.3
	2010	161	0.2	...	...	...	...	399	0.5
Honduras	2000	3 676	0.6	1 371	0.2	926	0.1	8 528	1.4
Honduras	2005	2 680	0.4	...	...	...	...	7 796	1.1
Hungary	2005	32 563	3.2	...	...	...	...	...	...
Hongrie	2010	28 686	2.9	5 257	0.5	5 821	0.6	...	...
	2014	32 791	3.3	6 203	0.6	7 594	0.8	64 956	6.6
Iceland	2005	1 070	3.6	314	1.1	388	1.3	4 378	14.8
Islande	2009	1 167	3.7	308	1.0	583	1.9	5 121	16.3
	2010	1 142	3.6	299	0.9	365	1.1	...	...
	2015	1 249	3.8	278	0.8	370	1.1	5 387	16.4
India	2003	625 400	0.6	47 318	~0.0	559 408	0.5	1 382 901	1.2
Inde	2005	660 801	0.6	55 344	~0.0	...	...	1 481 270	1.3
	2009	757 377	0.6	104 603	0.1	655 801	0.5	1 702 555	1.4
	2010	816 629	0.7	...	...	656 101	0.5	1 894 968	1.5
	2013	...	...	...	...	664 176	0.5	2 621 981	2.0
	2014	938 861	0.7	154 436	0.1	...	...	...	...
Indonesia	2003	29 499	0.1	7 093	~0.0	7 580	~0.0	179 959	0.8
Indonésie	2010	33 736	0.1	18 454	0.1	18 022	0.1	256 625	1.1
	2012	49 853	0.2	24 147	0.1	25 502	0.1	338 501	1.4
Iran (Islamic Republic of)	2005	61 870	0.9	13 210	0.2	13 900	0.2	98 020	1.4
Iran (Rép. islamique d')	2014	116 536	1.5	27 783	0.4	17 750	0.2	121 166	1.6
Iraq	2010	19 738	0.6	4 799	0.2	5 675	0.2	...	...
Iraq	2014	30 131	0.9	7 891	0.2	8 609	0.2	63 850	1.8
Ireland	2010	...	...	2 721	0.6	4 567	1.0	...	...
Irlande	2011	12 215	2.6	2 667	0.6	4 791	1.0	57 685	12.4
	2015	13 075	2.8	2 828	0.6	5 191	1.1	...	...
Israel	2010	25 333	3.4	6 367	0.9	5 733	0.8	...	...
Israël	2014	28 733	3.6	6 300	0.8	5 800	0.7	41 791	5.3
Italy	2010	...	...	34 023	0.6	51 832	0.9	...	...
Italie	2014	235 889	3.9	39 075	0.7	64 759	1.1	387 144	6.5
Jamaica	2003	2 253	0.9	212	0.1	...	...	4 374	1.7
Jamaïque	2008	1 103	0.4	244	0.1	172	0.1	2 930	1.1
Japan	2004	270 371	2.1	95 197	0.8	241 369	1.9	1 210 633	9.6
Japon	2010	283 548	2.2	98 739	0.8	197 616	1.6	1 320 623	10.4
	2012	292 039	2.3	99 686	0.8	205 716	1.6	1 372 738	10.8
Jordan	2005	12 909	2.4	4 194	0.8	7 100	1.3	17 428	3.3
Jordanie	2010	16 212	2.5	5 691	0.9	9 151	1.4	25 661	3.9
	2014	19 651	2.7	6 884	0.9	12 232	1.6	21 189	2.9

Health Personnel *(continued)*

Number of health workers and workforce density (per 1 000 population)

Le personnel de santé *(suite)*

Personnel de santé et densité (pour 1 000 habitants)

Country or area Pays ou zone	Year Année	Physicians / Médecins Number Nombre	Per 1 000 Pour 1 000	Dentists / Dentistes Number Nombre	Per 1 000 Pour 1 000	Pharmacists / Pharmaciens Number Nombre	Per 1 000 Pour 1 000	Nurses and midwives / Infirmières et Sages-femmes Number Nombre	Per 1 000 Pour 1 000
Kazakhstan	2010	57 179	3.5	6 657	0.4	11 265	0.7	...	...
Kazakhstan	2013	59 872	3.5	6 406	0.4	13 828	0.8	136 640	8.0
	2014	56 873	3.3	6 430	0.4	14 163	0.8	...	...
Kenya	2002	4 506	0.1	1 340	~0.0	...	...	...	...
Kenya	2004	...	...	...	...	3 094	0.1	16 146	0.5
	2010	7 129	0.2	898	~0.0	3 097	0.1	29 678	0.7
	2013	8 682	0.2	1 045	~0.0	2 202	0.1	37 907	0.9
Kiribati	2004	...	...	3	~0.0	2	~0.0	260	2.9
Kiribati	2008	25	0.3	18	0.2	22	0.2	361	3.7
	2013	22	0.2	27	0.2	15	0.1	501	4.6
Kuwait	2001	...	...	673	0.3	722	0.4	9 197	4.6
Koweït	2009	5 340	1.9	1 054	0.4	888	0.3	13 554	4.7
	2014	7 316	1.9	2 237	0.6	1 814	0.5	17 747	4.7
Kyrgyzstan	2009	13 135	2.4	...	...	...	...	29 311	5.4
Kirghizistan	2010	10 277	1.9	1 022	0.2	169	~0.0	...	...
	2013	10 838	1.9	981	0.2	317	0.1	34 237	6.0
	2014	10 833	1.9	965	0.2	242	~0.0	...	...
Lao People's Dem. Rep.	2005	1 614	0.3	...	...	...	...	5 724	1.0
Rép. dém. populaire lao	2009	1 211	0.2	324	0.1	...	...	5 322	0.9
	2012	1 160	0.2	225	~0.0	735	0.1	5 581	0.9
Latvia	2005	8 207	3.7	1 450	0.7	...	...	10 350	4.6
Lettonie	2009	7 964	3.8	1 458	0.7	...	...	9 330	4.4
	2010	6 517	3.1	1 488	0.7	1 433	0.7	...	...
	2014	6 412	3.2	1 400	0.7	1 548	0.8	10 010	5.0
	2015	...	...	...	...	1 574	0.8	...	...
Lebanon	2001	11 505	3.4	4 283	1.3	3 359	1.0	4 157	1.2
Liban	2005	...	...	...	...	4 105	1.0	4 720	1.2
	2010	11 583	2.7	5 395	1.2	5 508	1.3	8 791	2.0
	2014	13 358	2.4	5 627	1.0	7 609	1.4	14 377	2.6
Lesotho Lesotho	2003	89	~0.0	16	~0.0	62	~0.0	1 123	0.6
Liberia	2004	103	~0.0	13	~0.0	35	~0.0	1 035	0.3
Libéria	2008	51	~0.0	4	~0.0	269	0.1	978	0.3
Libya	2004	7 070	1.2	850	0.1	1 130	0.2	27 160	4.8
Libye	2009	12 009	1.9	3 792	0.6	2 275	0.4	42 982	6.9
	2014	13 095	2.1	4 583	0.7	3 928	0.6	43 216	6.9
Lithuania	2003	...	...	...	...	2 270	0.7	...	...
Lituanie	2010	12 226	3.9	2 456	0.8	...	...	...	...
	2014	12 631	4.3	2 669	0.9	...	...	23 192	8.0
Luxembourg	2010	1 404	2.8	422	0.8	374	0.7	...	...
Luxembourg	2015	1 656	2.9	506	0.9	396	0.7	6 990	12.3
Madagascar	2005	3 303	0.2	197	~0.0	8	0.0	6 418	0.4
Madagascar	2010	4 130	0.2	195	~0.0	7	0.0	4 724	0.2
	2012	3 188	0.1	181	~0.0	6	0.0	4 858	0.2
Malawi	2004	266	~0.0	...	...	...	...	7 264	0.6
Malawi	2009	265	~0.0	180	~0.0	221	~0.0	4 812	0.3
Malaysia	2002	17 020	0.7	2 160	0.1	2 880	0.1	43 380	1.8
Malaisie	2010	32 979	1.2	9 995	0.4	11 077	0.4	90 199	3.2
	2011	36 607	1.3	4 253	0.1	12 402	0.4	97 054	3.4
Maldives	2004	302	1.0	14	~0.0	241	0.8	886	3.0
Maldives	2010	525	1.6	32	0.1	247	0.7	1 868	5.6
Mali	2004	1 053	0.1	84	~0.0	351	~0.0	8 338	0.7
Mali	2010	1 291	0.1	103	~0.0	135	~0.0	6 715	0.4
Malta	2010	1 279	3.1	184	0.4	301	0.7	...	...
Malte	2015	1 636	3.9	206	0.5	558	1.3	3 629	8.7
Marshall Islands	2007	31	0.6	13	0.2	6	0.1	188	3.6
Îles Marshall	2012	24	0.5	26	0.5	7	0.1	187	3.6
Mauritania	2004	313	0.1	64	~0.0	81	~0.0	1 893	0.6
Mauritanie	2009	445	0.1	93	~0.0	123	~0.0	2 303	0.7
Mauritius Maurice	2004	1 303	1.1	233	0.2	1 428	1.2	4 604	3.8

Health Personnel *(continued)*

Number of health workers and workforce density (per 1 000 population)

Le personnel de santé *(suite)*

Personnel de santé et densité (pour 1 000 habitants)

Country or area Pays ou zone	Year Année	Physicians / Médecins Number Nombre	Per 1 000 Pour 1 000	Dentists / Dentistes Number Nombre	Per 1 000 Pour 1 000	Pharmacists / Pharmaciens Number Nombre	Per 1 000 Pour 1 000	Nurses and midwives / Infirmières et Sages-femmes Number Nombre	Per 1 000 Pour 1 000
Mexico Mexique	2000	195 897	1.9	78 281	0.8	...	...	88 678	0.9
	2010	228 028	1.9	13 225	0.1	...	...	275 171	2.3
	2013	256 281	2.1	14 494	0.1	...	...	310 441	2.5
Micronesia (Fed. States of) Micronésie (États féd. de)	2005	62	0.6	13	0.1	16	0.2	249	2.3
	2008	64	0.6	40	0.4	16	0.2	280	2.7
	2009	20	0.2	...	...	...	...	375	3.6
Monaco Monaco	2014	250	6.6	38	1.0	98	2.6	752	20.0
Mongolia Mongolie	2002	6 732	2.8	337	0.1	1 093	0.4	8 826	3.6
	2010	7 497	2.8	533	0.2	1 176	0.4	9 876	3.6
	2011	7 943	2.9	652	0.2	1 284	0.5	10 143	3.7
Montenegro Monténégro	2010	1 268	2.0	26	~0.0	91	0.1	...	...
	2015	1 466	2.3	25	~0.0	109	0.2	3 346	5.3
Morocco Maroc	2004	15 991	0.5	3 091	0.1	7 366	0.2	24 328	0.8
	2009	20 682	0.7	2 668	0.1	9 006	0.3	29 689	0.9
	2014	20 947	0.6	4 655	0.1	...	...	29 592	0.9
Mozambique Mozambique	2004	514	~0.0	159	~0.0	618	~0.0	6 183	0.3
	2010	1 145	~0.0	448	~0.0	1 221	0.1	9 507	0.4
	2013	1 452	0.1	418	~0.0	1 491	0.1	10 620	0.4
Myanmar Myanmar	2004	17 791	0.4	1 396	~0.0	127	~0.0	...	...
	2005	18 584	0.4	1 756	~0.0	...	...	36 521	0.7
	2010	26 435	0.5	2 849	0.1	...	...	45 200	0.9
	2012	29 832	0.6	3 355	0.1	...	...	48 871	0.9
Namibia Namibie	2004	598	0.3	113	0.1	288	0.1	6 145	3.1
	2007	774	0.4	90	~0.0	376	0.2	5 750	2.8
Nauru Nauru	2004	10	1.0	1	0.1	10	1.0	63	6.2
	2008	10	1.0	1	0.1	...	...	69	6.9
	2009	10	1.0	3	0.3	7	0.7	...	...
	2010	10	1.0	...	...	...	...	...	...
Nepal Népal	2004	5 384	0.2	359	~0.0	358	~0.0	11 825	0.5
	2012	...	...	...	...	4 200	0.2	...	...
Netherlands Pays-Bas	2008	...	...	...	...	...	...	140 703	8.5
	2010	49 242	3.0	8 345	0.5	3 308	0.2	...	...
	2013	55 681	3.3	8 803	0.5	3 566	0.2	...	...
	2014	56 535	3.4	8 750	0.5	...	...	...	...
New Zealand Nouvelle-Zélande	2001	9 027	2.3	2 586	0.7	3 495	0.9	33 249	8.5
	2002	8 190	2.1	1 620	0.4	...	...	...	...
	2007	9 757	2.3	1 877	0.4	2 889	0.7	44 491	10.5
	2010	11 412	2.6	...	...	...	...	46 218	10.6
	2011	11 634	2.6	...	...	4 440	1.0	46 912	10.7
	2014	12 820	2.9	...	...	...	...	48 184	10.7
Nicaragua Nicaragua	2005	2 717	0.5	246	~0.0	...	...	6 294	1.2
	2010	4 239	0.7	258	~0.0	...	...	7 366	1.3
	2014	5 495	0.9	260	~0.0	...	...	8 323	1.4
Niger Niger	2004	296	~0.0	15	~0.0	20	~0.0	2 818	0.2
	2008	288	~0.0	16	~0.0	21	~0.0	2 115	0.1
Nigeria Nigéria	2005	39 210	0.3	2 113	~0.0	12 072	0.1	213 425	1.5
	2008	56 526	0.4	3 781	~0.0	18 682	0.1	224 943	1.5
	2009	58 363	0.4	2 464	~0.0	...	...	...	...
	2011	...	...	...	...	17 022	0.1	...	...
Niue Nioué	2004	4	2.3	2	1.2	1	0.6	22	12.8
	2008	3	1.8	4	2.4	1	0.6	16	9.8
Norway Norvège	2009	19 579	4.1	4 192	0.9	...	...	150 334	31.1
	2010	20 114	4.1	4 293	0.9	3 120	0.6	...	...
	2014	22 754	4.4	4 450	0.9	3 710	0.7	89 607	17.4
Oman Oman	2004	3 871	1.6	544	0.2	1 551	0.6	10 289	4.2
	2005	4 182	1.7	448	0.2	...	...	9 277	3.7
	2010	5 862	2.0	654	0.2	2 784	0.9	12 865	4.4
	2014	6 528	1.5	782	0.2	1 474	0.3	14 169	3.3

Health Personnel *(continued)*

Number of health workers and workforce density (per 1 000 population)

Le personnel de santé *(suite)*

Personnel de santé et densité (pour 1 000 habitants)

Country or area Pays ou zone	Year Année	Physicians / Médecins Number Nombre	Per 1 000 Pour 1 000	Dentists / Dentistes Number Nombre	Per 1 000 Pour 1 000	Pharmacists / Pharmaciens Number Nombre	Per 1 000 Pour 1 000	Nurses and midwives / Infirmières et Sages-femmes Number Nombre	Per 1 000 Pour 1 000
Pakistan	2004	116 298	0.8	7 862	0.1	8 102	0.1	71 764	0.5
Pakistan	2005	126 350	0.8	...	...	...	...	...	...
	2010	144 901	0.9	10 508	0.1	...	...	100 397	0.6
	2014	149 142	0.8	18 642	0.1	26 100	0.1	111 857	0.6
Palau	2004	...	...	...	...	...	...	120	6.1
Palaos	2007	...	...	5	0.2	1	0.1	...	...
	2010	29	1.4	...	...	...	...	120	5.9
Panama	2005	4 488	1.4	938	0.3	...	...	6 675	2.0
Panama	2010	5 121	1.4	1 091	0.3	...	...	9 021	2.5
	2011	5 551	1.5	1 114	0.3	...	...	8 579	2.3
	2013	6 068	1.6	1 037	0.3	...	...	...	...
Papua New Guinea	2000	275	0.1	90	~0.0	...	...	2 841	0.5
Papouasie-Nvl-Guinée	2009	...	...	121	~0.0	...	...	...	...
	2010	376	0.1	...	...	...	...	3 643	0.5
	2012	...	...	...	...	354	~0.0	...	...
Paraguay	2002	6 355	1.2	3 182	0.6	1 868	0.3	10 261	1.9
Paraguay	2012	8 203	1.3	1 054	0.2	...	...	6 689	1.0
Peru	2009	27 272	0.9	3 570	0.1	1 822	0.1	37 672	1.3
Pérou	2012	33 669	1.1	4 471	0.1	1 528	0.1	45 024	1.5
Philippines	2004	93 862	1.1	45 903	0.5	49 667	0.6	488 434	5.8
Philippines	2011	...	...	...	...	84 000	0.9	...	...
Poland	2010	83 201	2.2	12 549	0.3	25 203	0.7	...	...
Pologne	2014	87 687	2.3	13 088	0.3	27 747	0.7	221 569	5.7
Portugal	2005	36 138	3.4	5 056	0.5	9 494	0.9	48 155	4.6
Portugal	2009	40 095	3.8	6 605	0.6	11 347	1.1	59 601	5.6
	2010	40 672	3.8	8 105	0.8	7 674	0.7	...	...
	2014	46 036	4.4	9 125	0.9	8 653	0.8	66 340	6.4
Qatar	2005	2 150	2.6	690	0.8	1 100	1.3	4 880	5.8
Qatar	2006	2 313	2.3	486	0.5	1 056	1.1	6 185	6.3
	2010	6 919	3.9	...	...	...	...	10 615	6.0
	2014	4 267	2.0	1 242	0.6	2 023	0.9	12 381	5.7
Republic of Korea	2005	85 369	1.8	21 581	0.5	54 829	1.2	222 301	4.7
République de Corée	2010	98 293	2.0	20 936	0.4	32 152	0.7	229 819	4.7
	2014	111 694	2.2	22 952	0.5	32 645	0.7	283 897	5.7
Republic of Moldova	2010	9 962	2.4	1 641	0.4	1 779	0.4	...	...
République de Moldova	2013	10 432	2.6	1 751	0.4	1 901	0.5	...	...
	2014	10 333	2.5	1 751	0.4	...	...	21 634	5.3
Romania	2002	43 093	2.0	13 205	0.6	15 121	0.7	...	...
Roumanie	2010	50 778	2.5	12 959	0.6	13 534	0.7	...	...
	2013	52 828	2.7	14 248	0.7	16 231	0.8	123 520	6.2
Russian Federation	2010	343 345	2.4	41 481	0.3	8 344	0.1	...	...
Fédération de Russie	2014	474 242	3.3	41 113	0.3	7 115	0.1	655 814	4.6
Rwanda	2004	432	~0.0	21	~0.0	278	~0.0	3 647	0.4
Rwanda	2010	568	0.1	122	~0.0	56	~0.0	6 975	0.7
Saint Kitts and Nevis Saint-Kitts-et-Nevis	2001	49	1.1	15	0.3	...	...	294	6.4
Saint Lucia	2001	130	0.8	27	0.2	23	0.1	371	2.3
Sainte-Lucie	2004	68	0.4	7	~0.0	...	...	375	2.3
	2005	83	0.5	...	...	...	...	326	2.0
	2009	18	0.1	5	~0.0	...	...	...	...
	2010	...	...	28	0.2	...	...	...	...
Saint Vincent & Grenadines Saint-Vincent-Grenadines	2001	62	0.6	21	0.2	23	0.2	476	4.4
Samoa	2003	50	0.3	10	0.1	20	0.1	310	1.7
Samoa	2005	50	0.3	...	...	3	~0.0	...	...
	2008	85	0.5	63	0.3	59	0.3	348	1.9
San Marino Saint-Marin	2014	201	6.4	22	0.7	22	0.7	270	8.5
Sao Tome and Principe Sao Tomé-et-Principe	2004	81	0.5	11	0.1	24	0.2	308	2.1

Health Personnel *(continued)*

Number of health workers and workforce density (per 1 000 population)

Le personnel de santé *(suite)*

Personnel de santé et densité (pour 1 000 habitants)

Country or area Pays ou zone	Year Année	Physicians / Médecins: Number Nombre	Physicians / Médecins: Per 1 000 Pour 1 000	Dentists / Dentistes: Number Nombre	Dentists / Dentistes: Per 1 000 Pour 1 000	Pharmacists / Pharmaciens: Number Nombre	Pharmacists / Pharmaciens: Per 1 000 Pour 1 000	Nurses and midwives / Infirmières et Sages-femmes: Number Nombre	Nurses and midwives / Infirmières et Sages-femmes: Per 1 000 Pour 1 000
Saudi Arabia	2000	14 950	0.7	...	...	863	~0.0	36 495	1.7
Arabie saoudite	2001	14 464	0.7	1 581	0.1	...	...	...	...
	2010	66 014	2.4	...	...	14 928	0.5	129 792	4.6
	2014	79 313	2.6	12 301	0.4	21 639	0.7	160 811	5.2
Senegal	2004	594	0.1	97	~0.0	85	~0.0	3 287	0.3
Sénégal	2008	741	0.1	105	~0.0	127	~0.0	5 254	0.4
Serbia	2010	22 316	2.5	2 530	0.3	2 247	0.2	...	...
Serbie	2014	21 900	2.5	2 310	0.3	2 344	0.3	44 845	5.0
Seychelles	2005	104	1.2	10	0.1	7	0.1	390	4.4
Seychelles	2010	100	1.1	19	0.2	4	~0.0	412	4.4
	2012	93	1.0	14	0.1	4	~0.0	419	4.4
Sierra Leone	2004	168	~0.0	5	~0.0	340	0.1	2 510	0.5
Sierra Leone	2010	136	~0.0	6	~0.0	114	~0.0	1 842	0.3
Singapore	2005	6 748	1.5	1 277	0.3	1 330	0.3	20 167	4.5
Singapour	2010	8 819	1.7	1 506	0.3	1 814	0.4	29 340	5.8
	2013	10 339	1.9	2 149	0.4	2 186	0.4	30 533	5.6
Slovakia	2009	17 798	3.3	2 633	0.5	2 917	0.5	34 477	6.4
Slovaquie	2013	18 355	3.4	3 777	0.7	5 398	1.0	32 903	6.1
	2014	...	...	...	...	...	...	32 961	6.1
Slovenia	2010	4 979	2.4	1 259	0.6	1 102	0.5	...	...
Slovénie	2014	5 712	2.8	1 365	0.7	1 244	0.6	17 790	8.6
Solomon Islands	2005	89	0.2	52	0.1	53	0.1	694	1.5
Îles Salomon	2009	118	0.2	...	...	...	...	1 080	2.1
	2011	109	0.2	...	...	...	...	...	...
Somalia	2006	300	~0.0	...	...	50	~0.0	965	0.1
Somalie	2014	309	~0.0	...	...	...	...	825	0.1
South Africa	2004	34 829	0.7	5 995	0.1	12 521	0.3	184 459	3.9
Afrique du Sud	2005	...	...	...	...	...	...	191 269	4.0
	2010	37 599	0.7	8 812	0.2	...	...	231 086	4.5
	2015	41 775	0.8	10 770	0.2	34 261	0.6	278 617	5.1
Spain	2005	199 123	4.5	22 150	0.5	59 498	1.4	231 001	5.3
Espagne	2009	219 031	4.7	26 725	0.6	63 377	1.4	255 445	5.5
	2010	175 033	3.8	27 826	0.6	43 000	0.9	...	...
	2014	176 665	3.8	33 286	0.7	54 567	1.2	247 864	5.4
Sri Lanka	2004	10 479	0.5	1 245	0.1	990	0.1	33 233	1.7
Sri Lanka	2005	10 198	0.5	954	~0.0	...	...	27 514	1.4
	2007	11 023	0.6	1 743	0.1	886	~0.0	40 678	2.1
	2010	14 668	0.7	1 046	0.1	...	...	35 367	1.8
	2012	...	...	1 224	0.1	753	~0.0	...	...
Sudan	2004	7 552	0.2	1 082	~0.0	3 558	0.1	31 496	1.0
Soudan	2008	10 813	0.3	772	~0.0	386	~0.0	32 439	0.9
	2014	120 326	3.1	7 670	0.2	19 175	0.5	45 541	1.2
Suriname									
Suriname	2004	400	0.8	42	0.1	...	...	2 580	5.3
Swaziland	2004	171	0.2	32	~0.0	70	0.1	6 828	6.2
Swaziland	2009	173	0.1	59	0.1	51	~0.0	1 626	1.4
Sweden	2007	29 693	3.2	7 541	0.8	...	...	100 480	11.0
Suède	2010	36 501	3.9	7 546	0.8	7 135	0.8	...	...
	2013	39 524	4.1	7 747	0.8	7 266	0.8	114 448	11.9
Switzerland	2010	29 803	3.8	4 109	0.5	4 230	0.5	...	...
Suisse	2014	33 785	4.1	4 217	0.5	4 469	0.5	146 272	17.8
Syrian Arab Republic	2005	28 247	1.6	15 725	0.9	13 218	0.7	34 604	1.9
République arabe syrienne	2010	31 194	1.5	15 984	0.8	16 554	0.8	40 053	1.9
	2014	29 025	1.5	16 585	0.9	27 715	1.5	43 210	2.3
Tajikistan	2003	12 688	1.9	...	...	680	0.1	...	...
Tadjikistan	2005	13 272	2.0	...	...	...	...	...	...
	2010	12 778	1.7	1 234	0.2	...	...	...	...
	2014	14 219	1.7	1 289	0.2	...	...	39 229	4.7
Thailand	2004	18 918	0.3	4 129	0.1	7 413	0.1	96 704	1.5
Thaïlande	2010	26 244	0.4	17 222	0.3	8 700	0.1	138 710	2.1
TFYR of Macedonia	2010	5 541	2.7	1 599	0.8	692	0.3	...	...
ex-R.Y. de Macédoine	2013	5 804	2.8	1 705	0.8	930	0.4	8 728	4.2

Health Personnel *(continued)*

Number of health workers and workforce density (per 1 000 population)

Le personnel de santé *(suite)*

Personnel de santé et densité (pour 1 000 habitants)

Country or area Pays ou zone	Year Année	Physicians / Médecins Number Nombre	Per 1 000 Pour 1 000	Dentists / Dentistes Number Nombre	Per 1 000 Pour 1 000	Pharmacists / Pharmaciens Number Nombre	Per 1 000 Pour 1 000	Nurses and midwives / Infirmières et Sages-femmes Number Nombre	Per 1 000 Pour 1 000
Timor-Leste	2004	79	0.1	45	~0.0	14	~0.0	1 795	1.9
Timor-Leste	2010	84	0.1	44	~0.0	130	0.1	1 255	1.2
	2011	84	0.1	46	~0.0	131	0.1	1 283	1.2
Togo	2004	225	~0.0	19	~0.0	134	~0.0	1 937	0.4
Togo	2008	349	0.1	19	~0.0	11	~0.0	1 816	0.3
Tonga	2001	35	0.4	33	0.3	17	0.2	341	3.5
Tonga	2002	30	0.3	...	...	...	...	350	3.5
	2003	...	...	23	0.2	...	...	...	...
	2009	62	0.6	37	0.4	15	0.1	378	3.7
	2010	58	0.6	...	...	...	...	400	3.8
	2012	...	...	...	...	9	0.1	...	...
Trinidad and Tobago	2003	1 038	0.8	249	0.2	525	0.4	3 980	3.1
Trinité-et-Tobago	2007	1 543	1.2	294	0.2	641	0.5	4 677	3.6
Tunisia	2004	13 330	1.3	2 452	0.2	2 909	0.3	28 537	2.8
Tunisie	2005	9 422	0.9	1 850	0.2	2 114	0.2	...	...
	2009	12 535	1.2	2 528	0.2	2 106	0.2	34 551	3.3
	2010	12 996	1.2	3 130	0.3	3 236	0.3	...	...
	2014	18 346	1.6	4 259	0.4	2 457	0.2	35 492	3.2
Turkey	2005	100 853	1.5	18 149	0.3	22 756	0.3	121 723	1.8
Turquie	2009	118 641	1.7	20 589	0.3	25 201	0.4	154 533	2.2
	2010	123 447	1.7	21 432	0.3	26 506	0.4	...	...
	2014	135 616	1.7	22 996	0.3	27 199	0.4	195 270	2.5
Turkmenistan	2002	20 032	4.4	876	0.2	1 626	0.4	43 359	9.4
Turkménistan	2010	11 570	2.3	586	0.1	928	0.2	...	...
	2014	12 161	2.3	631	0.1	926	0.2	24 201	4.6
Tuvalu	2003	10	1.0	2	0.2	2	0.2	50	5.2
Tuvalu	2008	10	1.0	4	0.4	2	0.2	64	6.5
	2009	12	1.2	...	...	...	...	...	...
Uganda	2005	3 361	0.1	440	~0.0	762	~0.0	37 625	1.3
Ouganda	2012	...	...	...	...	1 200	~0.0	...	...
Ukraine	2001	...	...	...	...	23 576	0.5	...	...
Ukraine	2010	159 495	3.5	30 147	0.7	1 818	~0.0	...	...
	2014	134 986	3.0	26 954	0.6	1 521	~0.0	300 489	6.7
United Arab Emirates	2004	...	...	1 368	0.3	2 006	0.5	14 362	3.6
Émirats arabes unis	2005	6 946	1.6	...	...	...	...	14 844	3.3
	2007	9 215	1.5	2 053	0.3	2 817	0.5	17 336	2.9
	2010	12 752	1.5	...	...	...	...	24 362	2.9
	2014	14 154	1.6	2 814	0.3	3 344	0.4	27 812	3.1
United Kingdom	2010	169 179	2.7	32 423	0.5	40 641	0.6	...	...
Royaume-Uni	2015	181 572	2.8	34 622	0.5	54 380	0.8	545 954	8.4
United Rep. of Tanzania	2002	822	~0.0	267	~0.0	365	~0.0	13 292	0.4
Rép.-Unie de Tanzanie	2006	300	~0.0	230	~0.0	...	...	9 440	0.2
	2012	1 481	~0.0	509	~0.0	656	~0.0	20 800	0.4
United States of America	2000	730 801	2.6	463 663	1.6	249 642	0.9	2 669 603	9.4
États-Unis d'Amérique	2004	793 648	2.7	...	...	...	...	...	...
	2005	...	...	...	...	...	...	2 927 000	9.9
	2010	752 572	2.4	...	...	275 000	0.9	...	...
	2013	809 845	2.6	...	...	...	...	...	...
Uruguay	2002	12 384	3.7	3 936	1.2	...	...	2 880	0.9
Uruguay	2008	13 197	3.9	2 476	0.7	1 877	0.6	19 595	5.8
Uzbekistan	2010	72 522	2.6	4 693	0.2	1 074	~0.0	...	...
Ouzbékistan	2014	72 237	2.5	4 520	0.2	1 243	~0.0	343 223	11.6
Vanuatu	2004	30	0.1	...	...	...	...	360	1.8
Vanuatu	2008	26	0.1	3	~0.0	2	~0.0	380	1.7
	2012	46	0.2	17	0.1	29	0.1	549	2.2
Venezuela (Boliv. Rep. of) Venezuela (Rép. boliv. du)	2001	48 000	1.9	13 680	0.5	...	...	28 000	1.1
Viet Nam	2005	101 117	1.2	...	...	23 218	0.3	69 665	0.8
Viet Nam	2008	107 131	1.2	...	...	28 370	0.3	88 025	1.0
	2010	99 621	1.1	...	...	...	...	94 049	1.1
	2011	102 925	1.2	...	...	27 734	0.3	100 972	1.1
	2013	107 867	1.2	...	...	...	...	112 029	1.2

10 Health Personnel *(continued)*

Number of health workers and workforce density (per 1 000 population)

Le personnel de santé *(suite)*

Personnel de santé et densité (pour 1 000 habitants)

		Physicians Médecins		**Dentists Dentistes**		**Pharmacists Pharmaciens**		**Nurses and midwives Infirmières et Sages-femmes**	
Country or area Pays ou zone	**Year Année**	**Number Nombre**	**Per 1 000 Pour 1 000**	**Number Nombre**	**Per 1 000 Pour 1 000**	**Number Nombre**	**Per 1 000 Pour 1 000**	**Number Nombre**	**Per 1 000 Pour 1 000**
Yemen	2004	6 739	0.3	850	~0.0	2 638	0.1	13 746	0.7
Yémen	2009	7 127	0.3	...	...	...	...	...	...
	2010	...	...	897	~0.0	2 295	0.1	16 590	0.7
	2014	8 148	0.3	543	~0.0	2 716	0.1	19 828	0.8
Zambia	2004	1 499	0.1	491	~0.0	804	0.1	22 010	1.9
Zambie	2005	646	0.1	...	...	...	...	8 369	0.7
	2010	836	0.1	246	~0.0	317	~0.0	9 932	0.7
	2012	2 399	0.2	401	~0.0	1 223	0.1	...	...
Zimbabwe	2004	2 086	0.2	...	...	883	0.1	...	...
Zimbabwe	2010	916	0.1	239	~0.0	472	~0.0	17 029	1.2
	2011	1 054	0.1	255	~0.0	467	~0.0	17 022	1.2

Source:

World Health Organisation (WHO), Geneva, WHO Global Health Workforce statistics database, last accessed June 2017.

Source:

Organisation mondiale de la santé (OMS), Genève, base de données OMS sur les statistiques relatives aux personnels de santé, dernier accès juin 2017.

11 Expenditure on health
Percentage of GDP and of government expenditure

Dépenses de santé
Pourcentage du PIB et des dépenses du gouvernement

Region, country or area	1995	2000	2005	2010	2012	2013	2014	Région, pays ou zone
Afghanistan [1,2]								**Afghanistan [1,2]**
Total expenditure (% GDP)	...	...	* 8.1	* 9.2	* 8.5	* 8.1	* 8.2	Dépenses totales (% du PIB)
General govt.(% expend. total)	...	...	* 5.5	* 14.4	* 11.7	* 10.6	* 12.0	Dépenses publiques (en % du totale)
Albania								**Albanie**
Total expenditure (% GDP)	6.6	6.3	6.1	5.3	5.6	5.7	5.9	Dépenses totales (% du PIB)
General govt.(% expend. total)	5.5	7.1	9.7	8.5	9.7	9.8	9.4	Dépenses publiques (en % du totale)
Algeria								**Algérie**
Total expenditure (% GDP)	3.7	3.5	3.2	5.1	6.1	7.1	7.2	Dépenses totales (% du PIB)
General govt.(% expend. total)	8.5	8.8	8.2	9.6	10.0	9.9	9.9	Dépenses publiques (en % du totale)
Andorra								**Andorre**
Total expenditure (% GDP)	5.8	5.8	5.2	8.0	7.5	11.5	8.1	Dépenses totales (% du PIB)
General govt.(% expend. total)	23.6	19.1	19.5	24.0	18.9	22.3	27.9	Dépenses publiques (en % du totale)
Angola								**Angola**
Total expenditure (% GDP)	6.5	2.8	4.1	3.4	3.3	4.3	3.3	Dépenses totales (% du PIB)
General govt.(% expend. total)	5.2	2.9	6.1	5.4	5.6	7.4	5.0	Dépenses publiques (en % du totale)
Antigua and Barbuda								**Antigua-et-Barbuda**
Total expenditure (% GDP)	* 4.1	* 4.1	* 4.4	* 5.6	* 5.4	* 5.3	* 5.5	Dépenses totales (% du PIB)
General govt.(% expend. total)	* 12.9	* 11.4	* 12.1	* 16.4	* 17.2	* 16.3	* 18.1	Dépenses publiques (en % du totale)
Argentina								**Argentine**
Total expenditure (% GDP)	* 8.3	* 9.2	* 6.8	* 6.6	* 5.0	* 5.0	* 4.8	Dépenses totales (% du PIB)
General govt.(% expend. total)	* 19.4	* 17.6	* 16.7	* 14.1	* 8.7	* 7.7	* 6.9	Dépenses publiques (en % du totale)
Armenia								**Arménie**
Total expenditure (% GDP)	6.4	6.3	5.3	4.6	4.5	4.6	4.5	Dépenses totales (% du PIB)
General govt.(% expend. total)	8.3	5.3	10.2	7.0	7.4	7.3	7.0	Dépenses publiques (en % du totale)
Australia								**Australie**
Total expenditure (% GDP)	7.3	8.1	8.5	9.0	9.4	9.4	9.4	Dépenses totales (% du PIB)
General govt.(% expend. total)	14.9	16.0	16.9	17.1	17.3	17.3	17.3	Dépenses publiques (en % du totale)
Austria								**Autriche**
Total expenditure (% GDP)	9.5	10.1	10.5	11.2	11.2	11.1	11.2	Dépenses totales (% du PIB)
General govt.(% expend. total)	12.7	14.5	15.7	15.9	16.3	16.3	16.3	Dépenses publiques (en % du totale)
Azerbaijan [3]								**Azerbaïdjan [3]**
Total expenditure (% GDP)	5.8	4.7	7.9	5.3	5.4	5.5	6.0	Dépenses totales (% du PIB)
General govt.(% expend. total)	6.9	5.4	5.2	4.2	3.8	3.5	3.9	Dépenses publiques (en % du totale)
Bahamas								**Bahamas**
Total expenditure (% GDP)	6.9	5.2	6.0	7.4	7.4	7.0	7.7	Dépenses totales (% du PIB)
General govt.(% expend. total)	14.2	14.8	14.7	17.6	15.1	13.4	14.8	Dépenses publiques (en % du totale)
Bahrain								**Bahreïn**
Total expenditure (% GDP)	* 4.1	* 3.5	* 3.2	* 3.6	* 4.4	* 4.7	* 5.0	Dépenses totales (% du PIB)
General govt.(% expend. total)	* 10.8	* 10.2	* 8.6	* 9.1	* 9.3	* 10.6	* 10.5	Dépenses publiques (en % du totale)
Bangladesh								**Bangladesh**
Total expenditure (% GDP)	* 3.2	* 2.3	* 2.7	* 3.1	* 3.1	* 2.9	* 2.8	Dépenses totales (% du PIB)
General govt.(% expend. total)	* 8.4	* 8.1	* 7.9	* 8.3	* 6.9	* 5.5	* 5.7	Dépenses publiques (en % du totale)
Barbados								**Barbade**
Total expenditure (% GDP)	5.2	5.2	5.4	6.2	7.4	7.6	7.5	Dépenses totales (% du PIB)
General govt.(% expend. total)	11.4	9.9	9.2	9.7	10.7	10.7	10.9	Dépenses publiques (en % du totale)
Belarus								**Bélarus**
Total expenditure (% GDP)	6.7	6.1	6.9	5.6	5.0	6.1	5.7	Dépenses totales (% du PIB)
General govt.(% expend. total)	11.5	10.1	10.5	13.4	13.2	13.9	13.8	Dépenses publiques (en % du totale)
Belgium								**Belgique**
Total expenditure (% GDP)	7.6	8.1	9.2	10.2	10.5	10.6	10.6	Dépenses totales (% du PIB)
General govt.(% expend. total)	11.2	12.3	13.7	15.0	14.9	15.1	15.1	Dépenses publiques (en % du totale)
Belize								**Belize**
Total expenditure (% GDP)	* 4.2	* 4.0	* 4.5	* 5.8	* 5.5	* 5.8	* 5.8	Dépenses totales (% du PIB)
General govt.(% expend. total)	* 10.5	* 6.5	* 9.3	* 13.1	* 12.5	* 13.4	* 13.8	Dépenses publiques (en % du totale)
Benin								**Bénin**
Total expenditure (% GDP)	4.7	4.3	4.7	4.9	4.9	4.6	4.6	Dépenses totales (% du PIB)
General govt.(% expend. total)	10.4	10.0	11.1	12.4	10.2	9.6	9.6	Dépenses publiques (en % du totale)
Bhutan								**Bhoutan**
Total expenditure (% GDP)	* 4.0	* 6.9	* 5.3	* 5.2	* 3.7	* 3.8	* 3.6	Dépenses totales (% du PIB)
General govt.(% expend. total)	* 6.9	* 12.2	* 11.7	* 11.0	* 7.8	* 8.4	* 8.0	Dépenses publiques (en % du totale)
Bolivia (Plurin. State of) [4]								**Bolivie (État plurin. de) [4]**
Total expenditure (% GDP)	* 3.7	* 5.7	* 5.7	* 5.4	* 5.6	* 6.0	* 6.3	Dépenses totales (% du PIB)
General govt.(% expend. total)	* 7.9	* 8.7	* 11.8	* 11.9	* 11.3	* 12.0	* 11.8	Dépenses publiques (en % du totale)

Expenditure on health *(continued)*
Percentage of GDP and of government expenditure

Dépenses de santé *(suite)*
Pourcentage du PIB et des dépenses du gouvernement

Region, country or area	1995	2000	2005	2010	2012	2013	2014	Région, pays ou zone
Bosnia and Herzegovina								**Bosnie-Herzégovine**
Total expenditure (% GDP)	9.0	7.1	8.5	9.6	9.9	9.5	9.6	Dépenses totales (% du PIB)
General govt.(% expend. total)	9.1	11.3	10.5	13.7	14.7	14.1	14.1	Dépenses publiques (en % du totale)
Botswana								**Botswana**
Total expenditure (% GDP)	4.1	4.6	5.6	5.6	6.3	5.8	5.4	Dépenses totales (% du PIB)
General govt.(% expend. total)	5.5	7.5	11.8	8.6	10.8	10.4	8.8	Dépenses publiques (en % du totale)
Brazil								**Brésil**
Total expenditure (% GDP)	6.5	7.0	8.3	8.3	8.3	8.5	8.3	Dépenses totales (% du PIB)
General govt.(% expend. total)	8.4	4.1	5.0	9.9	6.9	7.1	6.8	Dépenses publiques (en % du totale)
Brunei Darussalam								**Brunéi Darussalam**
Total expenditure (% GDP)	3.0	3.1	2.6	2.7	2.3	2.6	2.6	Dépenses totales (% du PIB)
General govt.(% expend. total)	3.5	6.3	6.9	6.3	6.1	6.4	6.5	Dépenses publiques (en % du totale)
Bulgaria								**Bulgarie**
Total expenditure (% GDP)	4.8	6.1	7.1	7.2	7.1	7.9	8.4	Dépenses totales (% du PIB)
General govt.(% expend. total)	8.5	9.0	11.7	11.0	11.5	11.0	11.0	Dépenses publiques (en % du totale)
Burkina Faso								**Burkina Faso**
Total expenditure (% GDP)	4.9	5.1	6.9	7.2	5.3	5.9	5.0	Dépenses totales (% du PIB)
General govt.(% expend. total)	9.1	8.8	18.7	15.7	11.7	12.7	11.2	Dépenses publiques (en % du totale)
Burundi [5]								**Burundi** [5]
Total expenditure (% GDP)	* 4.4	* 5.0	* 9.8	* 8.8	* 8.2	* 8.0	* 7.5	Dépenses totales (% du PIB)
General govt.(% expend. total)	* 6.8	* 7.1	* 11.2	* 13.5	* 14.1	* 14.0	* 13.2	Dépenses publiques (en % du totale)
Cabo Verde								**Cabo Verde**
Total expenditure (% GDP)	5.3	4.8	4.9	4.8	4.6	4.3	4.8	Dépenses totales (% du PIB)
General govt.(% expend. total)	8.2	9.9	10.4	8.7	9.6	9.2	11.7	Dépenses publiques (en % du totale)
Cambodia [6]								**Cambodge** [6]
Total expenditure (% GDP)	5.4	5.9	5.8	6.0	6.2	5.9	5.7	Dépenses totales (% du PIB)
General govt.(% expend. total)	7.0	8.9	13.1	7.2	7.3	6.8	6.1	Dépenses publiques (en % du totale)
Cameroon								**Cameroun**
Total expenditure (% GDP)	* 3.9	* 4.5	* 4.8	* 5.3	* 4.3	* 4.3	* 4.1	Dépenses totales (% du PIB)
General govt.(% expend. total)	* 6.1	* 6.1	* 7.7	* 8.5	* 5.5	* 4.6	* 4.3	Dépenses publiques (en % du totale)
Canada								**Canada**
Total expenditure (% GDP)	8.9	8.7	9.6	11.2	10.8	10.7	10.4	Dépenses totales (% du PIB)
General govt.(% expend. total)	13.2	15.1	17.5	18.2	18.6	18.6	18.8	Dépenses publiques (en % du totale)
Central African Republic [5]								**République centrafricaine** [5]
Total expenditure (% GDP)	3.6	4.2	4.3	3.9	3.6	3.8	4.2	Dépenses totales (% du PIB)
General govt.(% expend. total)	8.0	12.6	12.5	9.7	10.5	15.5	14.2	Dépenses publiques (en % du totale)
Chad [5]								**Tchad** [5]
Total expenditure (% GDP)	5.8	6.3	3.9	2.9	3.0	3.4	3.6	Dépenses totales (% du PIB)
General govt.(% expend. total)	11.1	12.9	13.5	4.9	5.9	7.8	9.0	Dépenses publiques (en % du totale)
Chile								**Chili**
Total expenditure (% GDP)	5.2	6.4	6.7	7.0	7.2	7.5	7.8	Dépenses totales (% du PIB)
General govt.(% expend. total)	12.7	14.5	12.5	13.8	14.7	15.3	15.9	Dépenses publiques (en % du totale)
China [7]								**Chine** [7]
Total expenditure (% GDP)	3.5	4.6	4.7	4.9	5.3	5.4	5.5	Dépenses totales (% du PIB)
General govt.(% expend. total)	15.9	10.8	9.8	10.2	10.5	10.3	10.4	Dépenses publiques (en % du totale)
Colombia								**Colombie**
Total expenditure (% GDP)	* 6.8	* 5.9	* 5.8	* 6.8	* 6.9	* 6.8	* 7.2	Dépenses totales (% du PIB)
General govt.(% expend. total)	* 17.2	* 19.3	* 15.7	* 18.1	* 18.9	* 18.1	* 18.1	Dépenses publiques (en % du totale)
Comoros								**Comores**
Total expenditure (% GDP)	4.6	3.6	4.3	5.8	7.1	6.5	6.7	Dépenses totales (% du PIB)
General govt.(% expend. total)	8.2	9.3	11.2	6.2	9.9	7.4	8.7	Dépenses publiques (en % du totale)
Congo								**Congo**
Total expenditure (% GDP)	3.2	2.1	2.4	2.3	4.0	5.1	5.2	Dépenses totales (% du PIB)
General govt.(% expend. total)	5.7	4.8	6.2	6.5	8.7	8.7	8.7	Dépenses publiques (en % du totale)
Cook Islands								**Îles Cook**
Total expenditure (% GDP)	5.2	3.5	4.7	3.6	3.4	3.6	3.4	Dépenses totales (% du PIB)
General govt.(% expend. total)	9.9	10.1	13.2	10.3	8.4	7.9	6.1	Dépenses publiques (en % du totale)
Costa Rica								**Costa Rica**
Total expenditure (% GDP)	* 6.5	* 7.1	* 7.7	* 9.7	* 9.6	* 9.5	* 9.3	Dépenses totales (% du PIB)
General govt.(% expend. total)	* 20.9	* 24.3	* 21.3	* 29.0	* 25.7	* 24.1	* 23.3	Dépenses publiques (en % du totale)
Côte d'Ivoire								**Côte d'Ivoire**
Total expenditure (% GDP)	6.4	6.0	5.4	6.3	6.1	5.8	5.7	Dépenses totales (% du PIB)
General govt.(% expend. total)	6.8	10.0	7.0	8.2	8.5	8.2	7.3	Dépenses publiques (en % du totale)
Croatia								**Croatie**
Total expenditure (% GDP)	6.7	7.7	6.9	8.2	7.8	7.8	7.8	Dépenses totales (% du PIB)
General govt.(% expend. total)	12.8	13.0	13.7	15.3	14.0	14.0	14.0	Dépenses publiques (en % du totale)

Expenditure on health *(continued)*
Percentage of GDP and of government expenditure

Dépenses de santé *(suite)*
Pourcentage du PIB et des dépenses du gouvernement

Region, country or area	1995	2000	2005	2010	2012	2013	2014	Région, pays ou zone
Cuba								**Cuba**
Total expenditure (% GDP)	5.2	6.1	9.4	10.2	8.6	9.5	11.1	Dépenses totales (% du PIB)
General govt.(% expend. total)	8.0	10.8	13.7	13.9	11.5	14.1	18.0	Dépenses publiques (en % du totale)
Cyprus [8]								**Chypre** [8]
Total expenditure (% GDP)	4.7	5.8	6.4	# 7.2	# 7.4	# 7.5	# 7.4	Dépenses totales (% du PIB)
General govt.(% expend. total)	5.1	6.5	6.2	# 7.4	# 7.5	# 7.6	# 7.6	Dépenses publiques (en % du totale)
Czechia								**Tchéquie**
Total expenditure (% GDP)	6.7	6.3	6.9	7.4	7.5	7.5	7.4	Dépenses totales (% du PIB)
General govt.(% expend. total)	11.5	13.7	14.1	14.2	14.2	14.9	14.9	Dépenses publiques (en % du totale)
Dem. Rep. of the Congo								**Rép. dém. du Congo**
Total expenditure (% GDP)	* 3.3	* 1.4	* 3.1	* 4.0	* 3.8	* 3.9	* 4.3	Dépenses totales (% du PIB)
General govt.(% expend. total)	* 2.2	* 1.8	* 6.2	* 7.8	* 11.6	* 9.3	* 11.1	Dépenses publiques (en % du totale)
Denmark								**Danemark**
Total expenditure (% GDP)	8.1	8.7	9.8	11.1	11.0	11.2	10.8	Dépenses totales (% du PIB)
General govt.(% expend. total)	11.3	13.6	15.6	16.3	15.9	16.8	16.8	Dépenses publiques (en % du totale)
Djibouti								**Djibouti**
Total expenditure (% GDP)	4.0	5.8	7.2	8.8	8.9	9.1	10.6	Dépenses totales (% du PIB)
General govt.(% expend. total)	6.2	12.0	13.4	14.1	14.1	14.1	14.1	Dépenses publiques (en % du totale)
Dominica								**Dominique**
Total expenditure (% GDP)	5.9	4.7	4.6	5.7	5.4	5.6	5.5	Dépenses totales (% du PIB)
General govt.(% expend. total)	11.9	6.6	7.9	10.6	9.6	10.6	10.5	Dépenses publiques (en % du totale)
Dominican Republic								**République dominicaine**
Total expenditure (% GDP)	* 5.2	* 5.9	* 4.3	* 4.1	* 4.3	* 4.1	* 4.4	Dépenses totales (% du PIB)
General govt.(% expend. total)	* 10.7	* 15.9	* 7.9	* 12.2	* 14.4	* 15.5	* 17.4	Dépenses publiques (en % du totale)
Ecuador								**Équateur**
Total expenditure (% GDP)	* 3.4	* 3.4	* 5.9	* 5.9	* 6.5	* 7.3	* 9.2	Dépenses totales (% du PIB)
General govt.(% expend. total)	* 9.6	* 5.1	* 5.6	* 7.1	* 7.3	* 8.8	* 10.2	Dépenses publiques (en % du totale)
Egypt								**Égypte**
Total expenditure (% GDP)	3.5	5.6	5.1	4.8	5.3	5.5	5.6	Dépenses totales (% du PIB)
General govt.(% expend. total)	5.3	7.3	6.1	5.6	5.8	5.5	5.6	Dépenses publiques (en % du totale)
El Salvador								**El Salvador**
Total expenditure (% GDP)	* 6.4	* 8.2	* 7.2	* 6.9	* 6.7	* 6.9	* 6.8	Dépenses totales (% du PIB)
General govt.(% expend. total)	* 13.5	* 15.1	* 15.5	* 13.5	* 15.5	* 16.8	* 16.7	Dépenses publiques (en % du totale)
Equatorial Guinea [5]								**Guinée équatoriale** [5]
Total expenditure (% GDP)	5.4	2.7	1.6	3.8	4.0	3.7	3.8	Dépenses totales (% du PIB)
General govt.(% expend. total)	15.3	8.7	6.5	7.0	7.0	7.0	7.0	Dépenses publiques (en % du totale)
Eritrea [5]								**Érythrée** [5]
Total expenditure (% GDP)	4.5	4.4	3.0	3.2	3.0	3.0	3.3	Dépenses totales (% du PIB)
General govt.(% expend. total)	3.0	2.6	1.8	3.6	3.6	3.6	3.6	Dépenses publiques (en % du totale)
Estonia								**Estonie**
Total expenditure (% GDP)	6.3	5.3	5.0	6.2	6.4	6.5	6.4	Dépenses totales (% du PIB)
General govt.(% expend. total)	13.7	11.3	11.5	12.3	13.0	13.5	13.5	Dépenses publiques (en % du totale)
Ethiopia								**Éthiopie**
Total expenditure (% GDP)	3.0	4.4	4.2	6.9	5.8	5.2	4.9	Dépenses totales (% du PIB)
General govt.(% expend. total)	7.0	9.4	11.2	19.8	18.5	15.9	15.7	Dépenses publiques (en % du totale)
Fiji								**Fidji**
Total expenditure (% GDP)	* 3.1	* 3.9	* 3.6	* 4.2	* 4.2	* 4.3	* 4.5	Dépenses totales (% du PIB)
General govt.(% expend. total)	* 9.4	* 11.3	* 10.8	* 10.7	* 9.5	* 9.7	* 9.2	Dépenses publiques (en % du totale)
Finland								**Finlande**
Total expenditure (% GDP)	7.8	7.2	8.4	9.0	9.3	9.5	9.7	Dépenses totales (% du PIB)
General govt.(% expend. total)	9.1	10.6	12.4	12.1	12.4	12.3	12.4	Dépenses publiques (en % du totale)
France [9]								**France** [9]
Total expenditure (% GDP)	10.1	9.8	10.6	11.2	11.4	11.6	11.5	Dépenses totales (% du PIB)
General govt.(% expend. total)	14.9	15.2	15.6	15.4	15.5	15.6	15.7	Dépenses publiques (en % du totale)
Gabon								**Gabon**
Total expenditure (% GDP)	3.5	2.9	2.8	3.4	3.1	4.0	3.4	Dépenses totales (% du PIB)
General govt.(% expend. total)	5.2	5.3	5.2	10.7	8.2	10.1	7.4	Dépenses publiques (en % du totale)
Gambia								**Gambie**
Total expenditure (% GDP)	3.3	3.6	5.0	5.8	6.1	6.5	7.3	Dépenses totales (% du PIB)
General govt.(% expend. total)	6.9	10.4	13.0	14.5	12.4	15.3	15.3	Dépenses publiques (en % du totale)
Georgia [10]								**Géorgie** [10]
Total expenditure (% GDP)	5.1	6.9	8.6	10.1	8.6	7.2	7.4	Dépenses totales (% du PIB)
General govt.(% expend. total)	2.5	6.9	6.2	6.6	3.8	4.2	5.0	Dépenses publiques (en % du totale)
Germany								**Allemagne**
Total expenditure (% GDP)	9.4	10.1	10.5	11.3	11.0	11.2	11.3	Dépenses totales (% du PIB)
General govt.(% expend. total)	14.0	17.9	17.3	18.1	18.8	19.3	19.6	Dépenses publiques (en % du totale)

11 Expenditure on health *(continued)*

Percentage of GDP and of government expenditure

Dépenses de santé *(suite)*

Pourcentage du PIB et des dépenses du gouvernement

Region, country or area	1995	2000	2005	2010	2012	2013	2014	Région, pays ou zone
Ghana [11]								**Ghana** [11]
Total expenditure (% GDP)	3.1	3.0	4.5	5.3	4.8	4.6	3.6	Dépenses totales (% du PIB)
General govt.(% expend. total)	10.8	7.8	15.1	14.9	9.3	10.6	6.8	Dépenses publiques (en % du totale)
Greece								**Grèce**
Total expenditure (% GDP)	8.3	7.6	9.4	9.2	9.2	9.3	8.1	Dépenses totales (% du PIB)
General govt.(% expend. total)	9.4	9.8	12.4	11.8	11.4	10.0	10.0	Dépenses publiques (en % du totale)
Grenada								**Grenade**
Total expenditure (% GDP)	6.9	6.6	5.5	6.4	6.4	6.2	6.1	Dépenses totales (% du PIB)
General govt.(% expend. total)	10.4	13.2	10.8	11.0	11.4	9.8	9.2	Dépenses publiques (en % du totale)
Guatemala								**Guatemala**
Total expenditure (% GDP)	* 3.9	* 5.3	* 6.8	* 6.6	* 6.3	* 6.3	* 6.2	Dépenses totales (% du PIB)
General govt.(% expend. total)	* 15.0	* 14.4	* 14.9	* 15.7	* 14.7	* 16.9	* 17.8	Dépenses publiques (en % du totale)
Guinea								**Guinée**
Total expenditure (% GDP)	3.5	3.5	2.8	4.5	5.4	5.5	5.6	Dépenses totales (% du PIB)
General govt.(% expend. total)	7.0	6.4	3.3	6.8	8.0	9.5	9.0	Dépenses publiques (en % du totale)
Guinea-Bissau [5,12]								**Guinée-Bissau** [5,12]
Total expenditure (% GDP)	* 6.4	* 4.9	* 5.7	* 6.7	* 6.0	* 6.1	* 5.6	Dépenses totales (% du PIB)
General govt.(% expend. total)	* 9.2	* 2.3	* 5.0	* 9.1	* 10.4	* 13.3	* 7.8	Dépenses publiques (en % du totale)
Guyana								**Guyana**
Total expenditure (% GDP)	5.1	5.8	5.8	6.6	6.6	5.1	5.2	Dépenses totales (% du PIB)
General govt.(% expend. total)	10.3	10.8	8.1	14.7	13.1	8.8	9.4	Dépenses publiques (en % du totale)
Haiti								**Haïti**
Total expenditure (% GDP)	* 6.6	* 6.1	* 4.4	* 8.1	* 9.9	* 8.1	* 7.6	Dépenses totales (% du PIB)
General govt.(% expend. total)	* 23.6	* 16.0	* 8.2	* 5.5	* 3.4	* 6.1	* 6.1	Dépenses publiques (en % du totale)
Honduras								**Honduras**
Total expenditure (% GDP)	5.3	6.6	7.8	8.5	9.8	9.2	8.7	Dépenses totales (% du PIB)
General govt.(% expend. total)	11.4	15.3	15.5	15.6	16.7	14.6	15.4	Dépenses publiques (en % du totale)
Hungary								**Hongrie**
Total expenditure (% GDP)	7.2	7.1	8.3	7.9	7.7	7.5	7.4	Dépenses totales (% du PIB)
General govt.(% expend. total)	11.0	10.6	11.8	10.5	10.3	10.1	10.1	Dépenses publiques (en % du totale)
Iceland								**Islande**
Total expenditure (% GDP)	8.2	9.3	9.2	8.9	8.7	8.8	8.9	Dépenses totales (% du PIB)
General govt.(% expend. total)	16.1	18.3	18.1	14.4	15.4	16.0	15.7	Dépenses publiques (en % du totale)
India [13]								**Inde** [13]
Total expenditure (% GDP)	* 4.0	* 4.3	* 4.3	* 4.3	* 4.4	# * 4.5	# * 4.7	Dépenses totales (% du PIB)
General govt.(% expend. total)	* 4.5	* 4.4	* 4.5	* 4.3	* 4.5	# * 4.7	# * 5.0	Dépenses publiques (en % du totale)
Indonesia								**Indonésie**
Total expenditure (% GDP)	2.0	2.0	2.8	2.7	2.9	2.9	2.8	Dépenses totales (% du PIB)
General govt.(% expend. total)	4.9	4.4	4.2	6.1	6.1	6.0	5.7	Dépenses publiques (en % du totale)
Iran (Islamic Republic of) [14]								**Iran (Rép. islamique d')** [14]
Total expenditure (% GDP)	3.6	5.1	5.7	7.2	6.9	6.4	7.5	Dépenses totales (% du PIB)
General govt.(% expend. total)	6.2	12.2	9.9	12.7	16.4	16.4	23.6	Dépenses publiques (en % du totale)
Iraq [5,15]								**Iraq** [5,15]
Total expenditure (% GDP)	...	...	# 4.1	# 3.8	# 5.3	# 5.9	# 5.5	Dépenses totales (% du PIB)
General govt.(% expend. total)	...	...	# 3.2	# 4.8	# 6.5	# 6.5	# 6.5	Dépenses publiques (en % du totale)
Ireland [16]								**Irlande** [16]
Total expenditure (% GDP)	6.4	6.0	7.3	8.8	8.3	8.0	7.8	Dépenses totales (% du PIB)
General govt.(% expend. total)	11.4	14.5	16.5	9.3	13.4	13.4	13.4	Dépenses publiques (en % du totale)
Israel								**Israël**
Total expenditure (% GDP)	7.3	7.1	7.4	7.4	7.7	7.9	7.8	Dépenses totales (% du PIB)
General govt.(% expend. total)	9.8	9.3	9.6	11.2	11.8	11.8	11.6	Dépenses publiques (en % du totale)
Italy								**Italie**
Total expenditure (% GDP)	7.1	7.9	8.7	9.4	9.3	9.2	9.2	Dépenses totales (% du PIB)
General govt.(% expend. total)	9.7	12.5	14.1	14.6	13.8	13.7	13.7	Dépenses publiques (en % du totale)
Jamaica								**Jamaïque**
Total expenditure (% GDP)	* 4.2	* 5.8	* 4.1	* 5.3	* 5.7	* 5.9	* 5.4	Dépenses totales (% du PIB)
General govt.(% expend. total)	* 5.6	* 7.4	* 3.5	* 8.5	* 7.1	* 9.7	* 8.1	Dépenses publiques (en % du totale)
Japan								**Japon**
Total expenditure (% GDP)	6.6	7.5	8.2	9.6	10.2	10.2	10.2	Dépenses totales (% du PIB)
General govt.(% expend. total)	15.0	15.4	18.3	19.4	20.0	20.1	20.3	Dépenses publiques (en % du totale)
Jordan [17]								**Jordanie** [17]
Total expenditure (% GDP)	* 8.5	* 9.7	* 8.9	* 8.4	* 8.0	* 7.2	* 7.5	Dépenses totales (% du PIB)
General govt.(% expend. total)	* 14.8	* 13.7	* 12.3	* 19.5	* 17.5	* 13.7	* 13.7	Dépenses publiques (en % du totale)
Kazakhstan								**Kazakhstan**
Total expenditure (% GDP)	4.6	4.2	4.1	4.4	4.3	4.3	4.4	Dépenses totales (% du PIB)
General govt.(% expend. total)	11.5	9.2	9.3	11.4	10.9	10.9	10.9	Dépenses publiques (en % du totale)

Region, country or area	1995	2000	2005	2010	2012	2013	2014	Région, pays ou zone
Kenya [18]								**Kenya** [18]
Total expenditure (% GDP)	4.3	4.7	4.4	4.0	5.5	5.6	5.7	Dépenses totales (% du PIB)
General govt.(% expend. total)	6.4	10.6	7.6	5.9	13.4	13.1	12.8	Dépenses publiques (en % du totale)
Kiribati								**Kiribati**
Total expenditure (% GDP)	9.4	8.1	10.1	10.5	10.4	10.2	10.2	Dépenses totales (% du PIB)
General govt.(% expend. total)	10.9	10.4	9.2	10.2	8.4	8.0	5.8	Dépenses publiques (en % du totale)
Kuwait								**Koweït**
Total expenditure (% GDP)	3.7	2.5	2.4	2.8	2.6	2.6	3.0	Dépenses totales (% du PIB)
General govt.(% expend. total)	5.6	5.2	6.8	5.2	5.8	5.8	5.8	Dépenses publiques (en % du totale)
Kyrgyzstan								**Kirghizistan**
Total expenditure (% GDP)	6.0	4.7	5.8	6.7	7.0	6.7	6.5	Dépenses totales (% du PIB)
General govt.(% expend. total)	10.7	12.0	11.9	11.9	12.2	13.2	11.9	Dépenses publiques (en % du totale)
Lao People's Dem. Rep.								**Rép. dém. populaire lao**
Total expenditure (% GDP)	3.8	3.4	4.3	2.7	# 2.1	# 2.0	# 1.9	Dépenses totales (% du PIB)
General govt.(% expend. total)	7.6	5.2	4.1	5.2	# 3.4	# 3.4	# 3.4	Dépenses publiques (en % du totale)
Latvia								**Lettonie**
Total expenditure (% GDP)	5.8	6.0	6.4	6.6	5.9	5.7	5.9	Dépenses totales (% du PIB)
General govt.(% expend. total)	9.9	8.7	10.2	9.1	9.8	9.8	9.8	Dépenses publiques (en % du totale)
Lebanon								**Liban**
Total expenditure (% GDP)	12.6	10.9	8.4	7.2	7.0	6.6	6.4	Dépenses totales (% du PIB)
General govt.(% expend. total)	13.8	7.6	11.8	9.2	10.7	10.7	10.7	Dépenses publiques (en % du totale)
Lesotho								**Lesotho**
Total expenditure (% GDP)	7.5	6.9	6.3	10.9	11.1	11.1	10.6	Dépenses totales (% du PIB)
General govt.(% expend. total)	6.4	6.3	6.7	13.2	13.1	12.8	13.1	Dépenses publiques (en % du totale)
Liberia								**Libéria**
Total expenditure (% GDP)	...	5.9	8.0	11.9	10.2	9.3	10.0	Dépenses totales (% du PIB)
General govt.(% expend. total)	...	6.7	13.3	12.8	11.6	9.9	11.9	Dépenses publiques (en % du totale)
Libya [5]								**Libye** [5]
Total expenditure (% GDP)	3.3	3.4	2.7	3.1	4.3	4.3	5.0	Dépenses totales (% du PIB)
General govt.(% expend. total)	5.5	6.0	5.8	4.3	7.9	4.9	4.9	Dépenses publiques (en % du totale)
Lithuania [19]								**Lituanie** [19]
Total expenditure (% GDP)	5.4	6.5	5.8	7.1	6.7	6.6	6.6	Dépenses totales (% du PIB)
General govt.(% expend. total)	11.6	11.3	11.6	11.9	12.1	12.5	13.4	Dépenses publiques (en % du totale)
Luxembourg								**Luxembourg**
Total expenditure (% GDP)	5.6	7.5	7.9	7.7	7.2	7.1	6.9	Dépenses totales (% du PIB)
General govt.(% expend. total)	13.0	16.9	16.2	15.2	13.6	13.6	13.6	Dépenses publiques (en % du totale)
Madagascar								**Madagascar**
Total expenditure (% GDP)	* 4.1	* 5.1	* 5.0	* 4.9	* 3.5	* 4.1	* 3.0	Dépenses totales (% du PIB)
General govt.(% expend. total)	* 8.1	* 14.0	* 12.3	* 18.6	* 13.5	* 17.2	* 10.2	Dépenses publiques (en % du totale)
Malawi								**Malawi**
Total expenditure (% GDP)	5.0	6.1	8.2	10.0	12.1	11.0	11.4	Dépenses totales (% du PIB)
General govt.(% expend. total)	5.1	9.0	20.0	20.1	22.1	16.8	16.8	Dépenses publiques (en % du totale)
Malaysia								**Malaisie**
Total expenditure (% GDP)	3.0	3.0	3.3	4.0	4.0	4.0	4.2	Dépenses totales (% du PIB)
General govt.(% expend. total)	5.2	5.3	5.3	6.7	5.7	5.9	6.4	Dépenses publiques (en % du totale)
Maldives								**Maldives**
Total expenditure (% GDP)	6.0	8.0	9.5	7.9	9.2	11.2	13.7	Dépenses totales (% du PIB)
General govt.(% expend. total)	10.0	13.8	17.8	14.4	19.3	22.9	26.6	Dépenses publiques (en % du totale)
Mali								**Mali**
Total expenditure (% GDP)	5.0	6.3	6.3	5.3	5.3	6.9	7.0	Dépenses totales (% du PIB)
General govt.(% expend. total)	12.1	8.9	12.1	7.5	9.2	7.5	7.0	Dépenses publiques (en % du totale)
Malta								**Malte**
Total expenditure (% GDP)	5.7	6.8	8.8	8.3	10.0	9.9	9.7	Dépenses totales (% du PIB)
General govt.(% expend. total)	9.8	11.8	14.2	12.7	15.6	15.6	15.6	Dépenses publiques (en % du totale)
Marshall Islands								**Îles Marshall**
Total expenditure (% GDP)	* 30.8	* 21.9	* 17.4	* 17.3	* 16.7	* 17.2	* 17.1	Dépenses totales (% du PIB)
General govt.(% expend. total)	* 19.4	* 21.1	* 18.9	* 22.7	* 24.4	* 24.0	* 23.8	Dépenses publiques (en % du totale)
Mauritania								**Mauritanie**
Total expenditure (% GDP)	4.6	5.3	4.2	3.3	3.4	3.6	3.8	Dépenses totales (% du PIB)
General govt.(% expend. total)	9.2	10.8	7.1	6.8	4.6	6.0	6.0	Dépenses publiques (en % du totale)
Mauritius								**Maurice**
Total expenditure (% GDP)	3.6	3.8	4.5	5.3	4.8	4.8	4.8	Dépenses totales (% du PIB)
General govt.(% expend. total)	9.0	8.7	9.4	10.3	9.8	9.5	10.0	Dépenses publiques (en % du totale)
Mexico								**Mexique**
Total expenditure (% GDP)	5.1	5.0	6.0	6.4	6.2	6.3	6.3	Dépenses totales (% du PIB)
General govt.(% expend. total)	8.9	10.5	12.0	11.5	11.5	11.6	11.6	Dépenses publiques (en % du totale)

Region, country or area	1995	2000	2005	2010	2012	2013	2014	Région, pays ou zone
Micronesia (Fed. States of)								**Micronésie (Etats féd. de)**
Total expenditure (% GDP)	9.2	7.9	12.1	13.8	12.8	13.4	13.7	Dépenses totales (% du PIB)
General govt.(% expend. total)	11.3	10.9	19.1	18.6	17.8	20.4	21.2	Dépenses publiques (en % du totale)
Monaco [5]								**Monaco [5]**
Total expenditure (% GDP)	3.1	3.3	4.0	4.4	4.3	4.0	4.3	Dépenses totales (% du PIB)
General govt.(% expend. total)	14.3	14.2	16.3	18.8	18.8	18.8	18.8	Dépenses publiques (en % du totale)
Mongolia								**Mongolie**
Total expenditure (% GDP)	3.2	4.9	5.1	4.7	4.2	4.2	4.7	Dépenses totales (% du PIB)
General govt.(% expend. total)	9.8	11.1	9.9	8.4	5.8	5.5	6.7	Dépenses publiques (en % du totale)
Montenegro								**Monténégro**
Total expenditure (% GDP)	7.4	7.3	8.5	6.9	7.2	6.4	6.4	Dépenses totales (% du PIB)
General govt.(% expend. total)	16.9	16.9	14.3	9.5	9.8	9.8	9.8	Dépenses publiques (en % du totale)
Morocco								**Maroc**
Total expenditure (% GDP)	3.6	4.2	5.1	5.9	6.1	5.9	5.9	Dépenses totales (% du PIB)
General govt.(% expend. total)	4.9	4.8	4.4	6.5	6.0	5.8	6.0	Dépenses publiques (en % du totale)
Mozambique								**Mozambique**
Total expenditure (% GDP)	* 5.3	* 6.2	* 6.9	* 5.4	* 5.6	* 5.9	* 7.0	Dépenses totales (% du PIB)
General govt.(% expend. total)	* 14.0	* 17.0	* 18.2	* 10.4	* 8.8	* 8.8	* 8.8	Dépenses publiques (en % du totale)
Myanmar [20]								**Myanmar [20]**
Total expenditure (% GDP)	2.1	1.8	1.8	1.9	2.2	2.2	2.3	Dépenses totales (% du PIB)
General govt.(% expend. total)	1.6	1.3	1.1	1.8	3.3	3.3	3.6	Dépenses publiques (en % du totale)
Namibia								**Namibie**
General govt.(% expend. total)	13.2	13.9	12.8	11.8	10.2	9.3	9.3	Dépenses publiques (en % du totale)
Nauru								**Nauru**
Total expenditure (% GDP)	* 13.2	* 13.5	* 12.6	* 9.1	* 7.0	* 4.7	* 3.3	Dépenses totales (% du PIB)
General govt.(% expend. total)	* 5.9	* 11.2	* 18.5	* 10.3	* 11.5	* 11.5	* 5.2	Dépenses publiques (en % du totale)
Nepal								**Népal**
Total expenditure (% GDP)	5.3	5.4	5.7	6.4	5.9	5.7	5.8	Dépenses totales (% du PIB)
General govt.(% expend. total)	7.9	7.7	10.3	14.3	11.8	11.6	11.2	Dépenses publiques (en % du totale)
Netherlands [21]								**Pays-Bas [21]**
Total expenditure (% GDP)	7.4	7.4	9.6	10.5	11.0	11.0	10.9	Dépenses totales (% du PIB)
General govt.(% expend. total)	10.5	11.4	15.8	19.0	20.3	20.9	20.9	Dépenses publiques (en % du totale)
New Zealand								**Nouvelle-Zélande**
Total expenditure (% GDP)	6.9	7.5	8.2	11.2	11.5	11.2	11.0	Dépenses totales (% du PIB)
General govt.(% expend. total)	13.2	15.7	17.7	19.8	23.1	23.4	23.4	Dépenses publiques (en % du totale)
Nicaragua								**Nicaragua**
Total expenditure (% GDP)	6.5	5.4	6.1	6.6	8.0	8.4	9.0	Dépenses totales (% du PIB)
General govt.(% expend. total)	21.5	13.1	18.6	19.8	18.7	19.8	24.0	Dépenses publiques (en % du totale)
Niger								**Niger**
Total expenditure (% GDP)	6.7	6.0	7.1	6.4	6.1	6.2	6.0	Dépenses totales (% du PIB)
General govt.(% expend. total)	9.0	8.4	14.8	10.7	7.6	7.6	5.6	Dépenses publiques (en % du totale)
Nigeria [22]								**Nigéria [22]**
Total expenditure (% GDP)	2.8	2.8	4.1	3.5	3.3	3.7	3.7	Dépenses totales (% du PIB)
General govt.(% expend. total)	6.1	5.9	7.3	5.7	7.4	6.5	8.2	Dépenses publiques (en % du totale)
Niue								**Nioué**
Total expenditure (% GDP)	8.0	7.9	8.2	8.3	7.0	7.2	7.4	Dépenses totales (% du PIB)
General govt.(% expend. total)	8.1	6.6	7.2	6.5	4.8	5.6	5.9	Dépenses publiques (en % du totale)
Norway								**Norvège**
Total expenditure (% GDP)	7.7	8.3	8.9	9.3	9.2	9.4	9.7	Dépenses totales (% du PIB)
General govt.(% expend. total)	12.9	16.2	17.7	17.4	18.1	18.2	18.2	Dépenses publiques (en % du totale)
Oman								**Oman**
Total expenditure (% GDP)	3.6	3.1	2.6	2.7	2.5	2.8	3.6	Dépenses totales (% du PIB)
General govt.(% expend. total)	6.9	7.0	6.1	6.7	4.8	5.4	6.8	Dépenses publiques (en % du totale)
Pakistan [23]								**Pakistan [23]**
Total expenditure (% GDP)	* 2.5	* 2.8	* 2.9	* 3.0	* 2.8	* 2.7	* 2.6	Dépenses totales (% du PIB)
General govt.(% expend. total)	* 3.8	* 3.5	* 4.3	* 4.7	* 4.7	* 4.7	* 4.7	Dépenses publiques (en % du totale)
Palau								**Palaos**
Total expenditure (% GDP)	* 11.7	* 9.5	* 8.2	* 10.6	* 9.4	* 9.3	* 9.0	Dépenses totales (% du PIB)
General govt.(% expend. total)	* 13.9	* 12.0	* 16.0	* 16.9	* 16.5	* 17.8	* 18.1	Dépenses publiques (en % du totale)
Panama								**Panama**
Total expenditure (% GDP)	7.7	7.8	7.5	8.0	7.2	8.1	8.0	Dépenses totales (% du PIB)
General govt.(% expend. total)	16.1	21.3	12.7	15.1	12.7	14.5	14.6	Dépenses publiques (en % du totale)
Papua New Guinea								**Papouasie-Nvl-Guinée**
Total expenditure (% GDP)	2.9	4.0	6.4	4.2	4.6	4.8	4.3	Dépenses totales (% du PIB)
General govt.(% expend. total)	8.6	9.9	15.5	10.4	11.7	11.2	9.5	Dépenses publiques (en % du totale)

11 Expenditure on health *(continued)*
Percentage of GDP and of government expenditure

Dépenses de santé *(suite)*
Pourcentage du PIB et des dépenses du gouvernement

Region, country or area	1995	2000	2005	2010	2012	2013	2014	Région, pays ou zone
Paraguay								**Paraguay**
Total expenditure (% GDP)	5.9	8.1	6.1	9.1	10.3	10.5	9.8	Dépenses totales (% du PIB)
General govt.(% expend. total)	11.8	17.7	13.2	11.2	11.5	12.8	11.9	Dépenses publiques (en % du totale)
Peru								**Pérou**
Total expenditure (% GDP)	* 4.5	* 4.8	* 4.7	* 5.0	* 5.2	* 5.2	* 5.5	Dépenses totales (% du PIB)
General govt.(% expend. total)	* 13.1	* 14.1	* 14.9	* 13.3	* 13.9	* 14.4	* 15.0	Dépenses publiques (en % du totale)
Philippines [24]								**Philippines [24]**
Total expenditure (% GDP)	3.4	3.2	3.9	4.4	4.5	4.6	4.7	Dépenses totales (% du PIB)
General govt.(% expend. total)	7.4	8.4	8.9	9.3	8.2	8.9	10.0	Dépenses publiques (en % du totale)
Poland								**Pologne**
Total expenditure (% GDP)	5.4	5.5	6.2	6.9	6.6	6.4	6.4	Dépenses totales (% du PIB)
General govt.(% expend. total)	8.2	9.2	9.7	10.7	10.8	10.7	10.7	Dépenses publiques (en % du totale)
Portugal [25]								**Portugal [25]**
Total expenditure (% GDP)	7.4	9.1	10.0	10.4	9.7	9.6	9.5	Dépenses totales (% du PIB)
General govt.(% expend. total)	10.9	14.5	15.0	13.8	12.9	12.5	11.9	Dépenses publiques (en % du totale)
Qatar								**Qatar**
Total expenditure (% GDP)	* 3.7	* 2.2	* 3.0	* 2.1	* 2.2	* 2.1	* 2.2	Dépenses totales (% du PIB)
General govt.(% expend. total)	* 5.2	* 5.0	* 8.1	* 5.1	* 5.8	* 5.8	* 5.8	Dépenses publiques (en % du totale)
Republic of Korea								**République de Corée**
Total expenditure (% GDP)	3.7	4.2	5.3	6.8	7.0	7.2	7.4	Dépenses totales (% du PIB)
General govt.(% expend. total)	6.3	8.4	9.6	12.4	11.8	12.3	12.3	Dépenses publiques (en % du totale)
Republic of Moldova [26]								**République de Moldova [26]**
Total expenditure (% GDP)	9.1	6.7	9.2	12.1	11.9	10.1	10.3	Dépenses totales (% du PIB)
General govt.(% expend. total)	15.9	8.9	11.3	13.8	13.8	13.1	13.3	Dépenses publiques (en % du totale)
Romania								**Roumanie**
Total expenditure (% GDP)	3.2	4.3	5.5	5.8	5.5	5.6	5.6	Dépenses totales (% du PIB)
General govt.(% expend. total)	7.0	9.1	13.2	11.8	12.1	12.8	12.8	Dépenses publiques (en % du totale)
Russian Federation								**Fédération de Russie**
Total expenditure (% GDP)	5.4	5.4	5.2	6.8	6.9	7.1	7.1	Dépenses totales (% du PIB)
General govt.(% expend. total)	9.1	12.7	11.7	9.7	10.2	9.8	9.5	Dépenses publiques (en % du totale)
Rwanda								**Rwanda**
Total expenditure (% GDP)	4.3	4.2	6.8	7.9	7.7	7.7	7.5	Dépenses totales (% du PIB)
General govt.(% expend. total)	8.0	8.5	13.7	11.3	10.4	10.1	9.9	Dépenses publiques (en % du totale)
Saint Kitts and Nevis								**Saint-Kitts-et-Nevis**
Total expenditure (% GDP)	* 5.9	* 5.3	* 4.8	* 5.5	* 5.8	* 6.1	* 5.1	Dépenses totales (% du PIB)
General govt.(% expend. total)	* 10.0	* 9.6	* 4.5	* 6.8	* 7.1	* 7.2	* 6.9	Dépenses publiques (en % du totale)
Saint Lucia								**Sainte-Lucie**
Total expenditure (% GDP)	6.1	5.5	6.2	8.1	8.3	7.9	6.7	Dépenses totales (% du PIB)
General govt.(% expend. total)	11.3	11.7	9.5	13.1	10.2	11.3	11.5	Dépenses publiques (en % du totale)
Saint Vincent & Grenadines								**Saint-Vincent-Grenadines**
Total expenditure (% GDP)	6.7	3.7	3.7	4.7	8.5	5.2	8.6	Dépenses totales (% du PIB)
General govt.(% expend. total)	13.1	10.8	8.4	11.7	15.0	14.6	14.8	Dépenses publiques (en % du totale)
Samoa								**Samoa**
Total expenditure (% GDP)	4.6	5.3	4.5	5.7	5.0	6.9	7.2	Dépenses totales (% du PIB)
General govt.(% expend. total)	7.5	13.7	11.2	12.6	11.6	16.5	15.1	Dépenses publiques (en % du totale)
San Marino								**Saint-Marin**
Total expenditure (% GDP)	5.3	4.8	4.1	5.0	6.3	6.0	6.1	Dépenses totales (% du PIB)
General govt.(% expend. total)	17.7	20.4	12.4	14.6	13.2	13.2	13.2	Dépenses publiques (en % du totale)
Sao Tome and Principe								**Sao Tomé-et-Principe**
Total expenditure (% GDP)	8.1	9.4	9.9	5.3	6.4	8.1	...	Dépenses totales (% du PIB)
General govt.(% expend. total)	7.9	9.0	13.2	5.6	5.9	12.4	12.4	Dépenses publiques (en % du totale)
Saudi Arabia								**Arabie saoudite**
Total expenditure (% GDP)	* 2.9	* 4.2	* 3.4	* 3.5	* 3.9	* 4.2	* 4.7	Dépenses totales (% du PIB)
General govt.(% expend. total)	* 4.4	* 8.6	* 8.1	* 6.2	* 7.7	* 8.2	* 8.2	Dépenses publiques (en % du totale)
Senegal								**Sénégal**
Total expenditure (% GDP)	3.9	4.6	5.4	4.6	4.3	4.5	4.7	Dépenses totales (% du PIB)
General govt.(% expend. total)	7.1	10.1	12.4	8.8	7.5	7.9	8.0	Dépenses publiques (en % du totale)
Serbia [27]								**Serbie [27]**
Total expenditure (% GDP)	6.5	6.5	8.7	10.1	9.9	10.1	10.4	Dépenses totales (% du PIB)
General govt.(% expend. total)	13.6	13.6	14.3	14.3	13.1	13.9	13.9	Dépenses publiques (en % du totale)
Seychelles								**Seychelles**
Total expenditure (% GDP)	5.0	4.6	3.9	3.6	4.1	3.6	3.4	Dépenses totales (% du PIB)
General govt.(% expend. total)	8.0	7.9	10.1	8.9	10.4	9.7	9.7	Dépenses publiques (en % du totale)
Sierra Leone								**Sierra Leone**
Total expenditure (% GDP)	* 11.4	* 13.6	* 12.2	* 10.3	* 11.2	* 11.6	* 11.1	Dépenses totales (% du PIB)
General govt.(% expend. total)	* 14.6	* 14.6	* 14.6	* 11.9	* 9.7	* 10.8	* 10.8	Dépenses publiques (en % du totale)

11 Expenditure on health *(continued)*
Percentage of GDP and of government expenditure

Dépenses de santé *(suite)*
Pourcentage du PIB et des dépenses du gouvernement

Region, country or area	1995	2000	2005	2010	2012	2013	2014	Région, pays ou zone
Singapore								**Singapour**
Total expenditure (% GDP)	2.9	2.7	3.7	4.0	4.2	4.5	4.9	Dépenses totales (% du PIB)
General govt.(% expend. total)	9.3	7.1	7.9	9.8	11.1	12.7	14.1	Dépenses publiques (en % du totale)
Slovakia								**Slovaquie**
Total expenditure (% GDP)	6.1	5.5	7.0	8.5	8.1	8.0	8.1	Dépenses totales (% du PIB)
General govt.(% expend. total)	11.0	9.4	13.8	14.6	14.9	15.0	15.0	Dépenses publiques (en % du totale)
Slovenia								**Slovénie**
Total expenditure (% GDP)	7.5	8.3	8.5	9.1	9.4	9.3	9.2	Dépenses totales (% du PIB)
General govt.(% expend. total)	11.1	13.1	13.8	13.6	14.1	11.2	12.8	Dépenses publiques (en % du totale)
Solomon Islands								**Îles Salomon**
Total expenditure (% GDP)	3.2	4.6	7.8	7.5	5.5	5.4	5.1	Dépenses totales (% du PIB)
General govt.(% expend. total)	14.8	20.7	28.5	20.3	13.3	13.1	12.5	Dépenses publiques (en % du totale)
South Africa								**Afrique du Sud**
Total expenditure (% GDP)	8.3	8.1	7.8	8.5	8.8	8.8	8.8	Dépenses totales (% du PIB)
General govt.(% expend. total)	13.0	13.6	13.0	14.1	14.4	14.2	14.2	Dépenses publiques (en % du totale)
South Sudan [5]								**Soudan du sud** [5]
Total expenditure (% GDP)	...	...	...	...	2.8	2.6	2.7	Dépenses totales (% du PIB)
General govt.(% expend. total)	...	...	...	...	4.0	4.0	4.0	Dépenses publiques (en % du totale)
Spain								**Espagne**
Total expenditure (% GDP)	7.4	7.2	8.1	9.6	9.4	9.1	9.0	Dépenses totales (% du PIB)
General govt.(% expend. total)	12.1	13.2	15.3	15.5	14.1	14.5	14.5	Dépenses publiques (en % du totale)
Sri Lanka								**Sri Lanka**
Total expenditure (% GDP)	3.4	3.8	4.1	3.4	3.2	# 3.7	# 3.5	Dépenses totales (% du PIB)
General govt.(% expend. total)	5.3	6.9	7.8	6.8	6.2	# 11.5	# 11.2	Dépenses publiques (en % du totale)
Sudan [5]								**Soudan** [5]
Total expenditure (% GDP)	* 4.0	* 3.2	* 3.2	* 8.0	* 8.2	* 8.4	* 8.4	Dépenses totales (% du PIB)
General govt.(% expend. total)	* 11.7	* 8.5	* 5.5	* 11.6	* 11.6	* 11.6	* 11.6	Dépenses publiques (en % du totale)
Suriname								**Suriname**
Total expenditure (% GDP)	7.0	9.7	6.8	5.8	6.1	6.0	5.7	Dépenses totales (% du PIB)
General govt.(% expend. total)	18.3	14.0	11.6	11.9	12.1	11.8	11.8	Dépenses publiques (en % du totale)
Swaziland								**Swaziland**
Total expenditure (% GDP)	5.0	5.3	6.8	8.5	8.8	9.7	9.3	Dépenses totales (% du PIB)
General govt.(% expend. total)	12.4	10.5	13.0	15.4	18.1	19.7	16.6	Dépenses publiques (en % du totale)
Sweden [8]								**Suède** [8]
Total expenditure (% GDP)	8.0	8.2	9.1	9.5	# 11.8	# 12.0	# 11.9	Dépenses totales (% du PIB)
General govt.(% expend. total)	10.6	12.6	13.7	14.7	# 19.2	# 19.0	# 19.0	Dépenses publiques (en % du totale)
Switzerland								**Suisse**
Total expenditure (% GDP)	9.3	9.9	10.9	11.1	11.6	11.7	11.7	Dépenses totales (% du PIB)
General govt.(% expend. total)	14.4	15.4	18.3	21.0	22.0	22.6	22.7	Dépenses publiques (en % du totale)
Syrian Arab Republic [28]								**République arabe syrienne** [28]
Total expenditure (% GDP)	5.5	4.9	4.1	3.3	3.3	3.3	3.3	Dépenses totales (% du PIB)
General govt.(% expend. total)	7.4	6.9	7.4	5.3	4.8	4.8	4.8	Dépenses publiques (en % du totale)
Tajikistan								**Tadjikistan**
Total expenditure (% GDP)	3.1	4.6	5.9	6.0	6.4	6.8	6.9	Dépenses totales (% du PIB)
General govt.(% expend. total)	7.4	6.5	5.9	5.9	7.5	7.3	6.8	Dépenses publiques (en % du totale)
Thailand								**Thaïlande**
Total expenditure (% GDP)	* 3.5	* 3.4	* 3.5	* 3.8	* 4.2	* 4.0	* 4.1	Dépenses totales (% du PIB)
General govt.(% expend. total)	* 9.9	* 10.0	* 11.1	* 12.5	* 13.7	* 12.8	* 13.3	Dépenses publiques (en % du totale)
TFYR of Macedonia								**ex-R.Y. de Macédoine**
Total expenditure (% GDP)	8.4	8.5	8.0	6.8	6.8	6.1	6.5	Dépenses totales (% du PIB)
General govt.(% expend. total)	13.3	15.0	14.7	13.2	13.3	13.2	12.9	Dépenses publiques (en % du totale)
Timor-Leste [29]								**Timor-Leste** [29]
Total expenditure (% GDP)	...	3.3	1.0	0.9	1.0	1.3	1.5	Dépenses totales (% du PIB)
General govt.(% expend. total)	...	11.6	10.5	4.5	2.1	2.9	2.4	Dépenses publiques (en % du totale)
Togo								**Togo**
Total expenditure (% GDP)	4.0	4.3	5.2	5.4	5.1	5.1	5.2	Dépenses totales (% du PIB)
General govt.(% expend. total)	7.7	7.7	9.8	8.6	7.4	8.4	7.8	Dépenses publiques (en % du totale)
Tonga								**Tonga**
Total expenditure (% GDP)	4.1	4.8	6.5	4.6	4.5	5.0	5.2	Dépenses totales (% du PIB)
General govt.(% expend. total)	9.9	15.4	26.6	13.0	14.1	13.7	13.5	Dépenses publiques (en % du totale)
Trinidad and Tobago								**Trinité-et-Tobago**
Total expenditure (% GDP)	* 5.1	* 4.2	* 5.3	* 5.3	* 5.8	* 6.0	* 5.9	Dépenses totales (% du PIB)
General govt.(% expend. total)	* 9.4	* 6.8	* 9.6	* 8.3	* 7.8	* 8.1	* 8.2	Dépenses publiques (en % du totale)
Tunisia								**Tunisie**
Total expenditure (% GDP)	* 5.9	* 5.4	* 5.6	* 6.5	* 7.2	* 7.3	* 7.0	Dépenses totales (% du PIB)
General govt.(% expend. total)	* 10.7	* 12.0	* 11.9	* 15.7	* 14.2	* 14.2	* 14.2	Dépenses publiques (en % du totale)

11 Expenditure on health *(continued)*
Percentage of GDP and of government expenditure

Dépenses de santé *(suite)*
Pourcentage du PIB et des dépenses du gouvernement

Region, country or area	1995	2000	2005	2010	2012	2013	2014	Région, pays ou zone
Turkey								**Turquie**
Total expenditure (% GDP)	2.5	4.9	5.4	5.6	5.2	5.4	5.4	Dépenses totales (% du PIB)
General govt.(% expend. total)	10.7	9.8	11.3	11.0	10.8	10.5	10.5	Dépenses publiques (en % du totale)
Turkmenistan [5]								**Turkménistan** [5]
Total expenditure (% GDP)	3.1	3.9	3.5	2.0	2.0	2.1	2.1	Dépenses totales (% du PIB)
General govt.(% expend. total)	9.2	13.7	10.3	8.7	8.7	8.7	8.7	Dépenses publiques (en % du totale)
Tuvalu								**Tuvalu**
Total expenditure (% GDP)	8.2	15.7	18.4	16.8	13.8	16.6	16.5	Dépenses totales (% du PIB)
General govt.(% expend. total)	6.3	8.5	22.9	16.1	17.3	20.2	16.9	Dépenses publiques (en % du totale)
Uganda [30]								**Ouganda** [30]
Total expenditure (% GDP)	5.7	6.8	9.4	11.0	7.6	7.5	7.2	Dépenses totales (% du PIB)
General govt.(% expend. total)	9.9	8.8	14.1	19.5	14.3	13.1	11.0	Dépenses publiques (en % du totale)
Ukraine								**Ukraine**
Total expenditure (% GDP)	7.0	5.6	6.4	7.8	7.5	7.7	7.1[31]	Dépenses totales (% du PIB)
General govt.(% expend. total)	11.4	10.2	11.9	12.7	11.8	12.0	10.8[31]	Dépenses publiques (en % du totale)
United Arab Emirates								**Émirats arabes unis**
Total expenditure (% GDP)	2.6	2.4	2.3	3.9	3.4	3.5	3.6	Dépenses totales (% du PIB)
General govt.(% expend. total)	8.3	7.8	8.7	8.7	8.7	8.7	8.7	Dépenses publiques (en % du totale)
United Kingdom								**Royaume-Uni**
Total expenditure (% GDP)	6.7	6.9	8.2	9.5	9.4	9.3	9.1	Dépenses totales (% du PIB)
General govt.(% expend. total)	13.0	15.2	15.3	15.9	16.2	16.5	16.5	Dépenses publiques (en % du totale)
United Rep. of Tanzania								**Rép.-Unie de Tanzanie**
Total expenditure (% GDP)	3.0	2.6	4.7	5.3	5.7	5.6	5.6	Dépenses totales (% du PIB)
General govt.(% expend. total)	9.2	9.2	19.0	10.9	15.9	13.4	12.3	Dépenses publiques (en % du totale)
United States of America								**États-Unis d'Amérique**
Total expenditure (% GDP)	13.1	13.1	15.2	17.0	17.0	16.9	17.1	Dépenses totales (% du PIB)
General govt.(% expend. total)	15.9	16.8	18.5	19.0	20.1	20.8	21.3	Dépenses publiques (en % du totale)
Uruguay								**Uruguay**
Total expenditure (% GDP)	* 12.6	* 7.8	* 11.1	* 8.6	* 8.7	* 8.7	* 8.6	Dépenses totales (% du PIB)
General govt.(% expend. total)	* 12.6	* 9.0	* 29.2	* 19.5	* 21.3	* 20.9	* 20.8	Dépenses publiques (en % du totale)
Uzbekistan								**Ouzbékistan**
Total expenditure (% GDP)	6.7	5.3	5.1	5.3	6.5	6.3	5.8	Dépenses totales (% du PIB)
General govt.(% expend. total)	9.5	8.7	7.3	8.7	9.6	9.7	10.7	Dépenses publiques (en % du totale)
Vanuatu								**Vanuatu**
Total expenditure (% GDP)	2.7	3.3	3.9	4.7	3.7	3.9	5.0	Dépenses totales (% du PIB)
General govt.(% expend. total)	7.8	10.5	17.9	15.9	13.5	14.1	17.9	Dépenses publiques (en % du totale)
Venezuela (Boliv. Rep. of)								**Venezuela (Rép. boliv. du)**
Total expenditure (% GDP)	5.4	4.9	4.7	5.0	4.8	4.9	5.3	Dépenses totales (% du PIB)
General govt.(% expend. total)	7.8	7.3	8.3	9.1	5.9	6.4	5.8	Dépenses publiques (en % du totale)
Viet Nam								**Viet Nam**
Total expenditure (% GDP)	* 5.2	* 4.9	* 5.4	* 6.4	* 7.0	* 7.2	* 7.1	Dépenses totales (% du PIB)
General govt.(% expend. total)	* 7.9	* 7.2	* 5.4	* 9.9	* 12.7	* 13.2	* 14.2	Dépenses publiques (en % du totale)
Yemen								**Yémen**
Total expenditure (% GDP)	* 4.2	* 4.1	* 4.6	* 5.2	* 5.7	* 5.8	* 5.6	Dépenses totales (% du PIB)
General govt.(% expend. total)	* 6.4	* 8.0	* 4.8	* 4.3	* 3.9	* 3.9	* 3.9	Dépenses publiques (en % du totale)
Zambia								**Zambie**
Total expenditure (% GDP)	5.0	7.2	7.6	4.4	4.9	5.0	5.0	Dépenses totales (% du PIB)
General govt.(% expend. total)	9.5	13.3	17.6	12.6	11.4	11.0	11.3	Dépenses publiques (en % du totale)
Zimbabwe [5]								**Zimbabwe** [5]
Total expenditure (% GDP)	...	5.9	5.8	5.3	6.7	6.7	6.0	Dépenses totales (% du PIB)
General govt.(% expend. total)	...	...	8.1	7.5	9.7	9.6	8.5	Dépenses publiques (en % du totale)

Source:

World Health Organization (WHO), Geneva, WHO Global Health Expenditure database, last accessed June 2017.

Source:

Organisation mondiale de la Santé (OMS), Genève, base de données de l'Observatoire sur les dépenses de santé mondiales, dernier accès juin 2017.

1 Non-profit institutions (such as NGOs) serving households are accounted for in "external assistance" and recorded under government expenditure. GDP includes both licit and illicit GDPs (for example, opium).

2 Government expenditures include external assistance (external budget).

1 Les institutions sans but lucratif (telles que les ONG) desservant les ménages sont prises en compte à la rubrique « aide extérieure » et enregistrées comme dépenses publiques. Le PIB comprend à la fois le PIB licite et illicite (opium, par ex.).

2 Les dépenses publiques comprennent l'aide extérieure (budget externe).

3 Adjustments for currency change (from old to new manat) were made for the entire Azerbaijan series starting from World Health Statistics 2008.

4 Funds previously included in social security were reclassified.

5 Estimates should be viewed with caution as these are derived from scarce data.

6 2012 data are based on a health accounts study based on SHA2011. Numbers were converted to SHA 1.0 format for comparability.

7 General government expenditure series was revised using the one provided by the IMF. As a result, some ratios may have changed from last year.

8 Data is converted from SHA 2011.

9 Estimates are based on different national accounting bases (2000, 2005 and 2010) with major breaks in the data for 2003 and 2011.

10 As a result of recent health-care reforms in Georgia, public compulsory insurance has since 2008 been implemented by private insurance companies. The voucher cost of this insurance is treated as general government health expenditure.

11 In 2010, Ghana revalued its economy from 1993 base to 2006, increasing its overall GDP by more than 60 per cent. Estimates have been updated taking into account 2010 GDP rebasing data series.

12 Government expenditures show fluctuations due to variations in capital investment.

13 General government expenditure series was fully revised.

14 Exchange rate changed in 2002 from multiple to a managed floating exchange rate. Inter-bank market rate used prior to 2002.

15 The estimates do not include expenditures for Northern Iraq.

16 Ireland has reviewed and improved its data collection as part of the transition to SHA 2011 leading to more complete SHA 2011 data than available under SHA 1.0

17 The public expenditure on health includes contributions from the United Nations Relief and Works Agency for Palestine Refugees in the Near East (UNRWA) made to Palestinian refugees residing in Jordanian territories.

18 In 2014, Kenya revalued its base year from 2002 to 2009, which increased its GDP by 25 per cent in 2013.

19 For years 2010 to 2012, total health expenditure (THE) is greater than the sum of government (HF.1) and private expenditure (HF.2) due to rest-of-the-world (external) payments for health goods and services consumed by residents (HF.3).

20 Newly found data for government expenditures for years 2012-2014 (UNICEP) has made some ratios have kinks for these years. The market exchange rate is used to estimate the per capita figures. Revision of PPPs has increased per capita (PPP) values for all years.

21 Total health expenditure does not include capital.

22 In 2014, a revised GDP series was published following a statistical rebasing exercise (the base year changed from 1990 to 2010). Nigeria has emerged as Africa's largest economy, with a GDP increase of 89% for year 2013.

23 Total level of government expenditure on health increased due to the inclusion of local government expenditure, as well as a more-comprehensive estimation of regional expenditure on health.

24 The Philippine Statistics Authority implemented a revision in the estimation methodology for local government units (LGU) health expenditures between 2010 and 2011 resulting to a significant decrease in estimated LGU expenditures between the two years.

25 Portugal is currently reviewing its health expenditure series and new figures will be puiblished consistent with the System of Health Accounts (SHA 2011) methodology

3 Des ajustements ont été apportés à l'ensemble de la série concernant l'Azerbaïdjan à partir des Statistiques sanitaires mondiales de 2008, compte tenu du changement de monnaie (passage du vieux manat au nouveau manat).

4 Les montants précédemment inclus dans la sécurité sociale ont été reclassés.

5 Les montants estimatifs sont à prendre avec prudence, car calculés à partir de données peu nombreuses.

6 Les données de 2012 sont basées sur une étude sur les comptes de santé basée sur SHA2011. Les nombres ont été convertis au format SHA 1.0 pour la comparabilité.

7 Les séries des dépenses des administrations publiques ont été révisées à l'aide de celles fournies par le FMI. En conséquence, certains ratios peuvent avoir changé par rapport à l'année dernière.

8 Les données ont été converties du SCS de 2011.

9 Les montants estimatifs reposent sur des bases de comptabilité nationale différentes (2000, 2005 et 2010) avec des ruptures majeures dans les données pour 2003 et 2011.

10 Du fait de réformes récentes des soins de santé en Géorgie, l'assurance publique obligatoire est réalisée depuis 2008 par des sociétés d'assurance privées. Le coût des coupons correspondant à cette assurance est traité comme dépense publique de santé.

11 En 2010, le Ghana a changé la base de calcul de son économie, passant de la base 1993 à la base 2006, ce qui accru son PIB global de plus de 60 pour cent. Les montants estimatifs ont été actualisés compte tenu du passage des séries de données à la base 2010.

12 Les dépenses publiques manifestent des fluctuations du fait de variations des investissements.

13 Les séries des dépenses des administrations publiques ont été entièrement révisées.

14 Les taux de change, qui étaient précédemment des taux multiples, sont depuis 2002 des taux flottants dirigés. Pour les données antérieures à 2002, les taux utilisés étaient les taux du marché interbancaire.

15 Les montants estimatifs ne comprennent pas les dépenses pour le nord de l'Irak.

16 L'Irlande a examiné et amélioré sa collecte de données dans le cadre de la transition vers SHA 2011 conduisant à des données SHA 2011 plus complètes que celles disponibles dans SHA 1.0

17 Les dépenses publiques de santé comprennent les contributions de l'Office de secours et de travaux pour les réfugiés de Palestine dans le Proche-Orient (UNRWA) versées aux réfugiés de Palestine résidant en Jordanie.

18 En 2014, le Kenya a changé son année de base, qui est passée de 2002 à 2009, de sorte que le PIB a augmenté de 25 pour cent pour 2013.

19 Pour les années 2010 à 2012, les dépenses totales de santé (THE) sont supérieures à la somme des dépenses gouvernementales (HF.1) et privées (HF.2) en raison des paiements externes (externes) pour les biens et services de santé Consommé par les habitants (HF.3).

20 Les données récemment trouvées pour les dépenses du gouvernement pour les années 2012-2014 (UNICEP) ont fait que certains ratios ont des plis pour ces années. Le taux de change du marché est utilisé pour estimer les chiffres par habitant. La révision des PPP a augmenté les valeurs par habitant (PPP) pour toutes les années.

21 Les dépenses totales de santé ne prennent pas en compt pas le capital.

22 En 2014, une série révisée a été publiée pour le PIB à la suite d'une modification de l'année de base utilisée pour les statistiques (de 1990 à 2010). Le Nigéria est de ce fait devenu l'économie la plus importante d'Afrique, avec une augmentation de 89 pour cent du PIB pour 2013.

23 Le montant total des dépenses publiques de santé a augmenté du fait qu'on y a ajouté les dépenses des administrations publiques locales et rendu plus complètes les estimations des dépenses régionales de santé.

24 L'Autorité des statistiques des Philippines a mis en œuvre une révision de la méthode d'estimation pour les dépenses de santé des unités d'administrations locales entre 2010 et 2011, ce qui entraîne une diminution significative des dépenses estimatives des unités d'administrations locales entre les deux années.

25 Le Portugal examine actuellement sa série de dépenses de santé et de nouveaux chiffres seront publiés conformément à la méthodologie du Système de comptabilité de la santé (SHA 2011)

26 The health expenditure data as well as the population data after 2000 do not include Transdniestria. Data on GDP and private final consumption expenditure exclude Transdniestria from 1995.

27 Excluding Kosovo and Metohija.

28 The exchange rate used for the Syrian Arab Republic is the rate for non-commercial transactions from the Central Bank of Syria.

29 From this year oil GDP (includes the income from petroleum) is being used for denominators. Hence the changes in ratios since last year's reporting. The country became independent in 2002. Expenditure data have been allocated exceptionally to the previous calendar year (i.e. 2000 data covers the fiscal year 1999-2000). Drop in health expenditures from previous year is mainly due to revision of Out of pocket expenditure estimates.

30 Unlike other countries, in Uganda fiscal year 2010/2011 corresponds to calendar year 2010.

31 Excludes the temporarily occupied territory of the Autonomous Republic of Crimea and Sevastopol.

26 Les données sur les dépenses de santé ainsi que les données démographiques après 2000 n'incluent pas la Transnniestria. Les données sur le PIB et les dépenses de consommation finale privées excluent la Transnistrie à partir de 1995.

27 Non compris Kosovo et Metohija.

28 Le taux de change utilisé pour la République arabe syrienne est le taux de la Banque centrale syrienne servant pour les transactions non commerciales.

29 À partir de cette année, le PIB pétrolier (comprend le revenu du pétrole) est utilisé pour les dénominateurs. D'où les changements de ratios depuis les rapports de l'an dernier. Le pays est devenu indépendant en 2002. Les données sur les dépenses ont été attribuées exceptionnellement à l'année civile précédente (c.-à-d., 2000 données couvrent l'année financière 1999-2000). La baisse des dépenses de santé par rapport à l'année précédente s'explique principalement par la révision des estimations des dépenses de dépenses.

30 À la différence d'autres pays, en Ouganda l'exercice budgétaire 2010/2011 correspond à l'année civile 2010.

31 Excluent le territoire temporairement occupé de la République autonome de Crimée et de Sébastopol.

12 Intentional homicides and other crimes

By type of crime per 100 000 population and homicide victims by sex

Homicides intentionnels et autres crimes

Par type de crime pour 100 000 habitants et victimes d'homicides par sexe

Country or area Pays ou zone	Year Année	Intentional homicides / Homicides volontaires: Per 100 000 Pour 100 000	Victims (%) / Victimes (%): Male Hommes	Victims (%) / Victimes (%): Female Femmes	Other crimes (per 100 000 pop.) / Autres infractions (pour 100 000 hab.): Assault Agression	Kidnapping Enlèvement	Theft Vol simple	Robbery Vol qualifié	Sexual Violence Violences Sexuelles
Total, all countries or areas [1] **Total, tous pays ou zones [1]**	**2015**	**5.3**	**...**	**...**	**...**	**...**	**...**	**...**	**...**
Sub-Saharan Africa [1] Afrique subsaharienne [1]	2015	9.6	...	...	...	...	...	...	...
Latin America & the Caribb.[1] Amérique latine et Caraïb. [1]	2015	22.3	...	...	...	...	...	...	...
Australia and New Zealand [1] Australie et Nouvelle-Zél. [1]	2015	1.0	...	...	...	...	...	...	...
Afghanistan	2010	3.5	...	...	...	...	...	...	...
Afghanistan	2012	6.6	...	...	...	...	...	...	...
Albania	2005	5.0	86.0	14.0	5.4	...	96.9	6.5	2.9
Albanie	2010	4.4	85.0	15.0	6.1	0.3	137.1	8.1	2.7
	2015	2.3	79.0	21.0	5.8	0.3	248.1	8.1	5.1
Algeria	2005	0.6	...	...	# 99.0	0.3	...	# 75.6	...
Algérie	2010	0.7	...	...	# 114.8	0.5	# 141.7	# 51.3	# 10.5
	2015	1.4	87.0	13.0	# 123.8	1.3	# 125.0	# 65.6	# 8.5
Andorra	2004	1.3	...	...	...	...	...	...	...
Andorre	2010	1.2	100.0	0.0	116.1	...	1 323.2	9.5	11.9
	2011	1.2	100.0	0.0	174.9	...	1 291.2	6.1	20.7
	2012	...	0.0	0.0	205.5	...	1 269.6	7.6	22.7
	2014	...	...	...	169.0	1.4	1 286.0	9.6	22.0
	2015	...	...	...	188.7	...	1 484.3	11.4	15.6
Angola	2005	11.5	...	...	...	...	...	...	...
Angola	2010	10.5	...	...	...	...	...	...	...
	2015	9.7	...	...	...	...	...	...	...
Anguilla	2004	16.2	...	...	...	...	...	...	...
Anguilla	2009	7.4	...	...	...	...	...	...	...
	2014	27.7	...	...	...	...	...	...	...
Antigua and Barbuda	2005	3.6	...	...	...	...	...	...	...
Antigua-et-Barbuda	2010	6.9	...	...	...	...	...	...	...
	2012	11.2	...	...	...	...	...	...	...
Argentina	2005	...	...	...	363.0	...	775.7	907.7	...
Argentine	2008	...	...	...	359.7	...	703.8	957.9	26.3
	2015	6.5	86.0	14.0	417.6	...	626.3	1 020.4	37.1
Armenia	2005	1.9	81.0	19.0	6.0	0.7	81.7	8.9	1.7
Arménie	2010	1.9	82.0	18.0	5.2	1.3	123.6	12.0	2.8
	2012	2.2	71.0	29.0	5.3	1.3	134.9	10.4	3.5
	2015	2.5	72.0	28.0	5.4	1.9	177.8	...	4.0
Aruba	2005	12.0	...	...	...	...	...	...	...
Aruba	2010	3.9	...	...	...	...	...	...	...
Australia	2005	1.3	63.0	38.0	...	...	# 2 556.6	...	...
Australie	2010	1.0	60.0	40.0	309.8	# 2.8	# 2 153.4	# 66.0	# 85.1
	2015	1.0	64.0	36.0	279.9	# 2.2	# 2 122.5	# 37.4	# 89.2
Austria	2005	0.7	56.0	44.0	43.9	0.1	2 149.7	57.9	20.3
Autriche	2010	0.7	48.0	52.0	43.0	0.1	1 857.2	51.4	39.3
	2015	0.5	61.0	39.0	40.5	~0.0	1 630.9	40.0	39.0
Azerbaijan	2005	2.2	...	...	1.9	0.3	25.1	2.3	...
Azerbaïdjan	2010	2.1	70.0	30.0	1.9	~0.0	42.5	3.2	2.2
	2014	2.5	63.0	37.0	1.7	~0.0	60.9	2.5	2.2
Bahamas	2005	15.8	85.0	15.0	...	7.3	440.4	...	133.3
Bahamas	2010	26.1	85.0	15.0	848.9	5.0	545.7	93.1	85.6
	2012	29.8	91.0	9.0	841.1	7.5	533.1	98.6	80.3
Bahrain	2005	0.5	...	...	406.9	1.4	1 114.1	48.4	...
Bahreïn	2006	0.7	...	...	367.2	2.2	888.6	24.8	...
	2008	0.5	...	...	327.5	...	681.0	27.4	15.7
	2010	0.9	...	...	...	...	...	...	...
	2011	0.5	...	...	...	...	...	...	...

Intentional homicides and other crimes *(continued)*

By type of crime per 100 000 population and homicide victims by sex

Homicides intentionnels et autres crimes *(suite)*

Par type de crime pour 100 000 habitants et victimes d'homicides par sexe

Country or area Pays ou zone	Year Année	Intentional homicides Homicides volontaires Per 100 000 Pour 100 000	Victims (%) Victimes (%) Male Hommes	Female Femmes	Other crimes (per 100 000 pop.) Autres infractions (pour 100 000 hab.) Assault Agression	Kidnapping Enlèvement	Theft Vol simple	Robbery Vol qualifié	Sexual Violence Violences Sexuelles
Bangladesh	2005	2.5	...	...	0.4	0.9	8.8	0.6	...
Bangladesh	2006	2.9	...	...	0.4	0.8	9.0	0.6	...
	2010	2.6	...	...	...	...	...	...	...
	2015	2.5	...	...	...	...	...	...	...
Barbados	2005	10.6	...	...	631.7	8.4	412.4	120.4	70.1
Barbade	2010	11.1	74.0	26.0	540.5	4.3	739.4	174.2	60.5
	2015	10.9	90.0	10.0	518.6	4.9	596.0	105.6	68.3
Belarus	2005	8.6	...	...	19.9	0.4	# 1 070.4	119.9	8.5
Bélarus	2010	5.1	66.0	34.0	12.2	0.2	# 775.3	49.9	3.9
	2014	3.6	66.0	34.0	8.7	0.3	# 426.6	25.9	4.8
Belgium	2005	2.1[2]	...	...	638.3	8.7	2 058.2	# 1 814.0	57.3
Belgique	2010	1.7[2]	...	...	711.4	10.3	2 089.3	# 218.3	64.9
	2015	2.0[2]	...	...	600.0	10.1	1 651.3	# 195.6	55.1
Belize	2005	28.6	...	...	...	3.2	592.4	235.5	...
Belize	2009	61.8	91.0	9.0	165.3	0.6	375.6	173.6	64.4
	2010	40.1	88.0	13.0	...	...	259.9	148.3	40.4
	2011	37.7	90.0	10.0	...	0.9	283.1	135.8	36.8
	2014	34.4	...	...	296.3	1.1	234.9	86.4	42.4
Benin	2005	7.0	...	...	...	...	...	...	...
Bénin	2010	6.4	...	...	...	...	...	...	...
	2015	6.0	...	...	...	...	...	...	...
Bermuda	2004	1.5	...	...	668.6	# 3.1	1 541.7	118.4	...
Bermudes	2005	3.1	...	...	...	...	...	...	...
	2010	11.0	100.0	0.0	964.8	# 1.6	950.7	154.8	143.9
	2015	6.5	100.0	0.0	922.5	# 1.6	1 029.0	74.2	137.1
Bhutan	2010	1.9	...	...	9.3	0.1	67.9	6.5	9.9
Bhoutan	2013	2.5	...	...	1.7	0.1	76.5	5.4	8.5
	2014	2.8	...	...	...	0.8	69.5	...	10.6
Bolivia (Plurin. State of)	2005	7.2	...	...	66.0	1.1	41.6	93.9	18.9
Bolivie (État plurin. de)	2010	10.6	...	...	85.2	0.9	50.9	125.7	39.8
	2012	12.4	...	...	72.5	1.0	50.8	140.8	47.1
Bosnia and Herzegovina	2002	...	72.0	28.0	...	...	...	...	...
Bosnie-Herzégovine	2005	...	...	...	# 35.7	0.2	# 480.4	19.7	...
	2008	...	...	...	# 38.4	0.2	# 168.1	19.4	4.4
	2010	1.5	82.0	18.0	# 13.2	~0.0	# 296.3	...	3.8
	2014	1.3	78.0	22.0	# 15.5	0.1	# 155.4	26.9	3.5
	2015	1.5	68.0	32.0	# 26.0	...	# 127.9	...	4.3
Botswana	2005	15.6	...	...	...	...	...	...	...
Botswana	2010	14.8	...	...	852.5	0.2	1 451.1	117.3	...
	2011	10.5	...	...	770.4	0.2	1 210.3	117.8	...
	2014	...	...	...	758.9	0.1	1 335.9	76.5	123.9
Brazil	2010	21.8	...	...	360.4	0.2	696.2	544.3	23.4
Brésil	2013	26.5	91.0	9.0	323.9	0.2	873.8	495.7	27.5
	2015	26.7	...	...	...	...	...	...	...
British Virgin Islands	2004	17.8	...	...	...	...	...	...	...
Îles Vierges britanniques	2006	8.4	...	...	...	...	...	...	...
Brunei Darussalam	2004	0.6	...	...	151.0	0.3	295.8	3.1	...
Brunéi Darussalam	2005	0.6	...	...	146.5	...	332.2	2.5	...
	2006	0.8	...	...	122.5	...	308.6	0.5	...
	2010	0.3	...	...	...	...	...	...	...
	2013	0.5	...	...	...	...	...	...	...
Bulgaria	2005	2.6	74.0	26.0	47.6	2.5	561.3	48.9	13.5
Bulgarie	2010	2.0	82.0	18.0	41.0	1.6	681.5	50.5	9.4
	2015	1.8	78.0	22.0	35.3	1.0	535.9	27.2	8.4
Burkina Faso	2005	0.6	...	...	...	...	...	...	...
Burkina Faso	2010	0.6	...	...	...	...	...	...	...
	2012	0.7	...	...	...	...	...	...	...
Burundi	2010	3.7	...	...	3.2	0.3	...	32.1	7.4
Burundi	2014	4.0	...	...	5.1	0.7	7.5	41.6	11.7

12 Intentional homicides and other crimes *(continued)*
By type of crime per 100 000 population and homicide victims by sex

Homicides intentionnels et autres crimes *(suite)*
Par type de crime pour 100 000 habitants et victimes d'homicides par sexe

Country or area Pays ou zone	Year Année	Intentional homicides / Homicides volontaires: Per 100 000 Pour 100 000	Victims (%) / Victimes (%): Male Hommes	Female Femmes	Other crimes (per 100 000 pop.) / Autres infractions (pour 100 000 hab.): Assault Agression	Kidnapping Enlèvement	Theft Vol simple	Robbery Vol qualifié	Sexual Violence Violences Sexuelles
Cabo Verde	2010	8.0	...	...	834.1	1.2	764.9	626.9	41.4
Cabo Verde	2013	10.7	90.0	10.0	791.1	5.5	748.3	763.7	46.9
	2015	8.8	...	...	807.9	1.0	799.4	1 051.3	42.3
Cambodia	2005	3.4	...	...	...	...	...	...	...
Cambodge	2010	2.3	...	...	...	...	...	...	...
	2011	1.8	...	...	...	...	...	...	...
Cameroon	#2005	...	...	...	17.3	...	66.3	...	...
Cameroun	2010	4.9	...	...	# 23.9	2.2	# 79.7	# 79.7	# 10.0
	2014	2.6	...	...	# 31.5	3.3	# 111.0	# 111.0	# 3.1
	2015	5.9	...	...	# 20.6	4.2	# 69.8	# 69.8	...
Canada	2005	2.1	73.0	27.0	165.7	12.1	2 033.4	100.6	81.7
Canada	2010	1.6	72.0	28.0	162.4	12.6	1 594.8	89.3	78.8
	2015	1.7	71.0	29.0	140.3	9.9	1 402.7	61.4	76.0
Cayman Islands	2004	12.3	...	...	...	...	...	...	...
Îles Caïmanes	2009	14.7	...	...	...	...	...	...	...
Central African Republic	2005	14.9	...	...	...	...	...	...	...
République centrafricaine	2010	13.6	...	...	...	...	...	...	...
	2015	13.1	...	...	...	...	...	...	...
Chad	2005	10.7	...	...	...	...	...	...	...
Tchad	2010	9.7	...	...	...	...	...	...	...
	2015	9.0	...	...	...	...	...	...	...
Chile	2005	3.6	86.0	14.0	...	# 0.9	964.6	403.0	...
Chili	2010	3.2	82.0	18.0	130.8	# 1.5	1 098.9	480.0	76.5
	2014	3.6	81.0	19.0	98.3	# 1.5	1 082.1	598.7	70.9
	2015	...	...	...	89.0	# 1.5	1 025.6	593.2	65.6
China	2005	1.6	...	...	...	...	...	...	...
Chine	2010	1.0	...	...	...	...	...	...	...
	2014	0.7	...	...	...	...	...	...	...
China, Hong Kong SAR	2004	0.7	56.0	44.0	114.2	~0.0	548.1	32.7	20.4
Chine, Hong Kong RAS	2005	0.5	62.0	38.0	118.3	...	514.6	24.5	21.3
	2010	0.5	46.0	54.0	108.7	~0.0	491.1	11.1	26.3
	2013	0.9	40.0	60.0	92.5	~0.0	441.1	7.0	24.9
	2015	0.3	...	...	...	...	...	...	...
China, Macao SAR	2005	1.5	...	...	...	...	...	...	...
Chine, Macao RAS	2010	0.4	100.0	0.0	# 343.4	# 0.4	# 526.0	# 33.3	# 8.4
	2012	0.7	75.0	25.0	# 314.5	...	# 532.5	# 32.1	# 8.8
	2013	0.2	...	...	# 299.3	# 0.2	# 529.2	# 26.4	# 9.3
	2015	0.2	...	...	# 275.7	...	# 450.5	# 19.2	# 9.7
Colombia	2005	39.5	92.0	8.0	70.3	1.9	158.8	93.9	# 10.6
Colombie	2010	32.7	92.0	8.0	115.7	0.6	200.0	133.8	# 14.8
	2015	26.5	92.0	8.0	180.2	0.4	300.5	210.1	# 45.1
Comoros	2005	9.4	...	...	...	...	...	...	...
Comores	2010	8.4	...	...	...	...	...	...	...
	2015	7.6	...	...	...	...	...	...	...
Congo	2005	11.3	...	...	...	...	...	...	...
Congo	2010	10.7	...	...	...	...	...	...	...
	2015	10.1	...	...	...	...	...	...	...
Cook Islands Îles Cook	2012	3.1	...	...	...	...	...	...	...
Costa Rica	2005	7.9	...	...	...	0.3	196.8	# 501.1	...
Costa Rica	2010	11.6	88.0	12.0	175.0	0.2	445.5	# 950.1	143.3
	2013	8.7	91.0	9.0	174.7	0.1	696.6	# 1 018.9	154.7
	2014	10.0	91.0	9.0	...	0.1	...	# 1 095.6	...
	2015	11.8	...	...	...	...	...	...	...
Côte d'Ivoire	2005	14.9	...	...	...	...	...	...	...
Côte d'Ivoire	2008	...	...	...	52.6	...	...	3.1	3.7
	2010	12.8	...	...	...	...	...	...	...
	2015	11.8	...	...	...	...	...	...	...

12 Intentional homicides and other crimes *(continued)*
By type of crime per 100 000 population and homicide victims by sex

Homicides intentionnels et autres crimes *(suite)*
Par type de crime pour 100 000 habitants et victimes d'homicides par sexe

Country or area Pays ou zone	Year Année	Intentional homicides / Homicides volontaires: Per 100 000 Pour 100 000	Victims (%) / Victimes (%): Male Hommes	Female Femmes	Other crimes (per 100 000 pop.) / Autres infractions (pour 100 000 hab.): Assault Agression	Kidnapping Enlèvement	Theft Vol simple	Robbery Vol qualifié	Sexual Violence Violences Sexuelles
Croatia Croatie	2005	1.5	60.0	40.0	26.3	0.5	# 694.3	35.6	14.2
	2010	1.4	48.0	52.0	22.8	0.3	# 314.5	28.8	9.2
	2014	0.9	53.0	47.0	18.0	~0.0	# 283.0	29.8	14.2
	2015	0.9	59.0	41.0	19.0	...	# 319.5	30.9	14.3
Cuba Cuba	2005	6.1	...	...	...	...	...	...	...
	2010	4.5	...	...	...	...	...	...	...
	2011	4.7	...	...	...	...	...	...	...
Cyprus Chypre	2005	1.9	90.0	10.0	12.8	1.6	116.3	8.1	10.9
	2010	0.7	88.0	13.0	15.7	2.5	151.3	14.1	7.2
	2015	1.3	87.0	13.0	12.1	2.1	78.8	8.0	8.6
Czechia Tchéquie	2005	1.1	58.0	42.0	212.0	0.1	1 506.5	54.3	18.1
	2010	1.0	49.0	51.0	172.0	0.1	1 202.2	38.3	12.7
	2015	0.8	59.0	41.0	148.6	~0.0	1 319.3	19.2	13.5
Dem. People's Rep. Korea Rép. pop. dém. de Corée	2005	5.1	...	...	...	...	...	...	...
	2010	4.8	...	...	...	...	...	...	...
	2015	4.4	...	...	...	...	...	...	...
Dem. Rep. of the Congo Rép. dém. du Congo	2005	14.3	...	...	...	...	...	...	...
	2010	14.0	...	...	...	...	...	...	...
	2015	13.4	...	...	...	...	...	...	...
Denmark Danemark	2005	1.0	...	...	205.2	...	3 103.2	53.9	...
	2010	0.8	48.0	52.0	31.6	...	4 354.3	60.8	36.2
	2015	1.0	59.0	41.0	25.8	...	3 430.5	35.9	38.4
Djibouti Djibouti	2005	8.2	...	...	...	...	...	...	...
	2010	7.6	...	...	...	...	...	...	...
	2015	6.8	...	...	...	...	...	...	...
Dominica Dominique	2005	11.3	...	...	...	...	...	...	...
	2010	21.1	...	...	...	...	...	...	...
	2011	8.4	...	...	...	...	...	...	...
Dominican Republic République dominicaine	2005	25.9	...	...	...	0.2	...	...	...
	2006	22.9	...	...	...	0.2	...	...	...
	2010	25.0	91.0	9.0	...	...	...	...	...
	2014	17.4	90.0	10.0	48.3	0.2	235.3	144.2	2.8
Ecuador Équateur	2005	15.4	...	...	56.5	0.3	# 43.4	346.7	...
	2010	17.7	...	...	30.2	0.2	# 33.6	362.3	24.5
	2014	8.2	86.0	14.0	46.7	0.2	# 152.8	570.6	19.0
Egypt Égypte	2005	0.7	88.0	12.0	...	~0.0	46.7	0.6	...
	2010	2.2	89.0	11.0	0.2	0.1	94.1	0.9	0.2
	2011	3.2	88.0	12.0	0.4	0.3	104.0	3.2	0.1
El Salvador El Salvador	2005	63.5	...	...	# 77.8	0.1	# 180.3	# 81.7	...
	2010	66.0	86.0	14.0	# 64.4	0.5	# 160.2	# 89.7	# 37.0
	2015	108.6	91.0	9.0	# 96.1	0.3	# 139.4	# 84.2	# 72.5
Equatorial Guinea Guinée équatoriale	2005	3.5	...	...	...	...	...	...	...
	2010	3.4	...	...	...	...	...	...	...
	2015	3.2	...	...	...	...	...	...	...
Eritrea Érythrée	2005	9.1	...	...	...	...	...	...	...
	2010	8.3	...	...	...	...	...	...	...
	2015	7.5	...	...	...	...	...	...	...
Estonia Estonie	2005	8.3	75.0	25.0	9.7	# 0.2	2 246.3	97.8	29.7
	2008	6.3	78.0	22.0	10.5	# 0.2	1 677.0	67.8	27.5
	2010	5.3	77.0	23.0	7.7	...	1 895.7	45.0	20.6
	2013	3.9	65.0	35.0	7.5	# 0.1	1 247.3	36.1	28.9
	2015	3.2	76.0	24.0	7.5	...	865.0	25.7	42.9
Ethiopia Éthiopie	2005	9.4	...	...	...	...	...	...	...
	2010	8.5	...	...	...	...	...	...	...
	2015	7.6	...	...	...	...	...	...	...
Fiji Fidji	2010	2.8	...	...	...	...	...	...	...
	2012	3.0	...	...	...	...	...	...	...

12 Intentional homicides and other crimes *(continued)*

By type of crime per 100 000 population and homicide victims by sex

Homicides intentionnels et autres crimes *(suite)*

Par type de crime pour 100 000 habitants et victimes d'homicides par sexe

Country or area Pays ou zone	Year Année	Intentional homicides / Homicides volontaires: Per 100 000 Pour 100 000	Victims (%) / Victimes (%): Male Hommes	Female Femmes	Other crimes (per 100 000 pop.) / Autres infractions (pour 100 000 hab.): Assault Agression	Kidnapping Enlèvement	Theft Vol simple	Robbery Vol qualifié	Sexual Violence Violences Sexuelles
Finland Finlande	2005	2.3	70.0	30.0	# 580.7	~0.0	2 384.1	34.6	# 36.6
	2010	2.2	76.0	24.0	# 37.2	~0.0	1 852.5	28.1	# 45.0
	2015	1.6	81.0	19.0	# 28.4	~0.0	1 771.0	28.2	# 54.0
France France	2005	1.6	...	...	# 242.7	3.3	# 1 363.5	# 203.5	# 39.0
	2010	1.3	...	...	# 368.3	3.3	# 1 862.3	# 192.2	# 36.5
	2015	1.6	...	...	# 379.1	6.2	# 1 906.9	# 162.9	# 52.1
French Guiana Guyane française	2005	22.1	...	...	...	...	...	...	...
	2009	13.2	...	...	...	...	...	...	...
French Polynesia Polynésie française	2009	0.4	...	...	...	...	...	...	...
Gabon Gabon	2005	11.2	...	...	...	...	...	...	...
	2010	9.3	...	...	...	...	...	...	...
	2015	9.0	...	...	...	...	...	...	...
Gambia Gambie	2005	9.8	...	...	...	...	...	...	...
	2010	9.8	...	...	...	...	...	...	...
	2015	9.1	...	...	...	...	...	...	...
Georgia Géorgie	2005	9.0	82.0	18.0	8.2	2.0	363.2	46.6	3.7
	2010	4.4	85.0	15.0	3.0	0.1	267.5	15.0	3.9
	2011	...	76.0	24.0	...	...	...	...	...
	2014	2.7	...	...	5.7	...	236.9	11.7	3.3
Germany Allemagne	2005	1.1	55.0	45.0	# 608.4	# 2.1	# 2 750.2	67.5	67.9
	2010	1.0	50.0	50.0	# 177.7	# 6.1	# 1 516.7	59.9	45.5
	2015	0.9	52.0	48.0	# 157.9	# 5.9	# 1 657.2	55.4	42.5
Ghana Ghana	2005	1.8	...	...	...	...	...	...	...
	2010	1.7	...	...	...	...	...	...	...
	2011	1.7	...	...	...	...	...	...	...
Greece Grèce	2005	1.2	96.0	4.0	# 70.3	0.2	557.0	18.8	5.7
	2010	1.6	81.0	19.0	# 9.9	1.6	1 060.3	54.4	4.6
	2015	0.9	68.0	32.0	# 14.8	0.8	915.6	39.4	5.1
Greenland Groenland	2005	17.6	...	...	...	...	...	...	...
	2010	31.8	...	...	...	...	...	...	...
	2015	12.5	...	...	...	...	...	...	...
Grenada Grenade	2005	10.7	73.0	27.0	1 839.7	...	1 761.0	43.7	146.7
	2010	9.6	80.0	20.0	1 100.5	...	918.1	24.8	106.0
	2014	7.5	63.0	38.0	1 342.8	...	1 267.5	22.6	76.2
	2015	...	...	...	462.4	...	1 948.1	71.1	196.6
Guadeloupe Guadeloupe	2005	5.1	...	...	...	...	...	...	...
	2009	7.9	...	...	...	...	...	...	...
Guam Guam	2005	4.4	...	...	...	...	...	...	...
	2010	1.9	...	...	...	...	...	...	...
	2011	2.5	...	...	...	...	...	...	...
Guatemala Guatemala	2004	35.0	89.0	11.0	50.0	0.4	40.2	# 93.8	2.8
	2005	...	90.0	10.0	46.2	0.4	32.6	# 83.3	2.4
	2010	40.5	88.0	12.0	50.6	0.9	44.2	# 22.0	3.4
	2012	33.5	89.0	11.0	39.6	0.5	59.3	# 24.9	4.3
	2014	31.2	87.0	13.0	37.3	0.3	...	# 19.4	...
Guinea Guinée	2005	10.1	...	...	3.0	0.2	...	...	...
	2007	...	...	...	2.9	0.2	13.3	1.5	0.3
	2008	...	...	...	...	0.2	...	...	...
	2010	9.3	...	...	...	...	...	...	...
	2015	8.5	...	...	...	...	...	...	...
Guinea-Bissau Guinée-Bissau	2005	11.0	...	...	...	...	...	...	...
	2010	10.0	...	...	...	...	...	...	...
	2015	9.2	...	...	...	...	...	...	...
Guyana Guyana	2005	19.1	80.0	20.0	...	...	...	...	32.2
	2010	18.6	78.0	22.0	# 1 484.3	0.3	518.5	145.4	19.5
	2011	17.2	74.0	26.0	...	0.1	252.6	157.6	39.3
	2015	19.4	81.0	19.0	# 1 208.3	...	674.1	190.7	49.5

12 Intentional homicides and other crimes *(continued)*

By type of crime per 100 000 population and homicide victims by sex

Homicides intentionnels et autres crimes *(suite)*

Par type de crime pour 100 000 habitants et victimes d'homicides par sexe

Country or area Pays ou zone	Year Année	Intentional homicides Homicides volontaires			Other crimes (per 100 000 pop.) Autres infractions (pour 100 000 hab.)				
			Victims (%) Victimes (%)						
		Per 100 000 Pour 100 000	Male Hommes	Female Femmes	Assault Agression	Kidnapping Enlèvement	Theft Vol simple	Robbery Vol qualifié	Sexual Violence Violences Sexuelles
Haiti Haïti	2010	6.8	...	...	...	...	...	...	...
	2012	10.0	...	...	...	...	...	...	...
Honduras Honduras	2005	46.7	...	...	...	...	...	...	...
	2009	71.5	93.0	7.0	...	...	66.4	...	...
	2010	83.1	...	...	...	...	59.7	...	...
	2015	63.8	91.0	9.0	16.4	0.5	36.1	127.2	18.4
Hungary Hongrie	2005	1.6	53.0	47.0	122.2	0.1	1 250.5	29.5	# 8.5
	2010	1.4	56.0	44.0	145.5	0.2	1 340.0	33.9	# 12.9
	2014	1.5	54.0	46.0	136.3	~0.0	1 081.3	19.8	# 7.8
Iceland Islande	2005	1.0	67.0	33.0	...	...	1 072.0	16.5	97.1
	2010	0.6	100.0	0.0	17.9	...	1 547.0	13.2	68.2
	2015	0.9	100.0	0.0	25.8	...	1 224.0	16.1	108.7
India Inde	2005	3.6	64.0	36.0	23.7	2.0	23.9	1.5	5.5
	2010	3.4	74.0	26.0	23.5	3.1	26.8	1.9	5.9
	2013	3.3	73.0	27.0	26.2	5.1	29.1	2.9	9.2
	2014	3.2	...	...	...	...	...	...	...
Indonesia Indonésie	2004	0.6	...	...	...	...	...	...	...
	2010	0.4	...	...	# 13.2	0.2	10.1	4.1	...
	2014	0.5	...	...	# 14.5	0.1	9.6	4.6	2.2
	2015	...	...	...	# 5.7	0.2	10.2	4.6	2.0
Iran (Islamic Republic of) Iran (Rép. islamique d')	2004	...	...	...	...	...	158.5	...	...
	2005	5.4	...	...	...	...	...	...	...
	2010	5.2	...	...	...	...	...	...	...
	2015	4.1	...	...	...	...	...	...	...
Iraq Iraq	2010	9.7[3]	82.0	18.0	98.3[3]	5.3[3]	31.1[3]	...	...
	2014	10.1[3]	82.0	18.0	83.2[3]	3.7[3]	34.8[3]	...	...
Ireland Irlande	2005	1.2	...	...	296.9	1.8	1 400.7	57.7	42.8
	2010	1.2	...	...	325.7	2.9	1 416.8	69.2	51.2
	2015	0.6	...	...	317.4	3.3	1 481.6	54.9	50.2
Israel Israël	2005	2.5	...	...	774.0	6.3	1 897.3	65.6	69.6
	2010	2.0	...	...	620.0	3.6	974.9	39.2	66.8
	2011	2.0	...	...	569.4	3.5	936.2	36.3	60.5
	2015	1.4	...	...	...	...	...	...	...
Italy Italie	2005	1.0	78.0	22.0	96.5	0.6	# 1 870.8	112.1	6.9
	2010	0.9	71.0	29.0	108.9	0.6	# 1 584.3	80.6	8.1
	2015	0.8	70.0	30.0	107.1	0.5	# 1 748.2	58.6	6.7
Jamaica Jamaïque	2005	62.5	89.0	11.0	...	1.2	...	...	40.8
	2008	59.6	90.0	10.0	...	1.6	...	97.9	54.2
	2010	52.8	90.0	10.0	# 51.3	...	...	104.2	54.2
	2013	43.3	89.0	11.0	# 178.0	0.8	75.4	96.4	95.8
	2015	43.2	90.0	10.0	...	0.5	...	68.3	79.2
Japan Japon	2005	0.5	50.0	50.0	47.5	0.2	727.1	4.7	8.5
	2010	0.4	49.0	51.0	20.9	0.2	485.5	3.2	6.6
	2014	0.3	48.0	52.0	21.0	0.2	356.2	2.4	6.8
Jordan Jordanie	2005	1.3	...	...	275.2	0.5	132.5	11.6	...
	2006	1.8	...	...	283.8	0.6	161.8	14.5	...
	2010	1.8	67.0	33.0	...	...	187.2	...	...
	2012	2.3	84.0	16.0	...	...	193.1	...	...
	2013	2.0	...	...	...	...	...	...	...
Kazakhstan Kazakhstan	2005	# 11.7	...	...	...	0.6	408.6	84.6	...
	2010	# 8.6	77.0	23.0	9.8	0.8	367.8	65.8	2.2
	2013	# 6.6	77.0	23.0	8.0	0.7	1 229.3	110.1	3.0
	2015	# 4.8	...	...	5.1	0.5	1 185.3	69.2	2.7
Kenya Kenya	2005	3.6	...	...	36.0	0.4	34.5	19.6	7.3
	2010	5.6	...	...	34.9	0.2	29.7	7.1	11.9
	2015	5.8	73.0	27.0	32.4	0.2	20.7	6.2	13.4
Kiribati Kiribati	2010	3.9	...	...	...	...	...	...	...
	2012	7.5	...	...	...	...	...	...	...

12 Intentional homicides and other crimes *(continued)*

By type of crime per 100 000 population and homicide victims by sex

Homicides intentionnels et autres crimes *(suite)*

Par type de crime pour 100 000 habitants et victimes d'homicides par sexe

		Intentional homicides Homicides volontaires	Victims (%) Victimes (%)		Other crimes (per 100 000 pop.) Autres infractions (pour 100 000 hab.)				
Country or area Pays ou zone	Year Année	Per 100 000 Pour 100 000	Male Hommes	Female Femmes	Assault Agression	Kidnapping Enlèvement	Theft Vol simple	Robbery Vol qualifié	Sexual Violence Violences Sexuelles
Kosovo	2010	5.8	...	...	205.9	2.4	834.3	31.0	8.2
Kosovo	2014	2.2	...	...	48.7	1.2	834.2	22.9	2.9
	2015	1.6	...	...	...	...	...	...	...
Kuwait	2005	...	...	...	26.3	12.4	432.5	19.0	16.4
Koweït	2009	1.7	...	...	23.8	12.4	282.1	22.8	17.7
	2010	2.0	78.0	22.0	...	...	...	...	...
	2012	1.8	84.0	16.0	...	...	...	...	...
Kyrgyzstan	2005	8.2	...	...	5.2	# 0.5	# 241.1	53.1	# 0.3
Kirghizistan	2009	7.8	...	...	6.7	# 0.1	# 203.3	43.6	# 0.6
	2010	19.6	...	...	9.8	# 1.5	# 180.9	51.2	...
	2013	3.6	...	...	5.3	# 0.7	# 173.6	28.1	# 1.3
	2015	5.1	...	...	6.0	# 0.9	# 166.6	...	# 1.3
Lao People's Dem. Rep.	2005	9.6	...	...	...	...	...	...	...
Rép. dém. populaire lao	2010	8.0	...	...	...	...	...	...	...
	2015	6.9	...	...	...	...	...	...	...
Latvia	2002	...	67.0	33.0	...	...	...	...	...
Lettonie	2005	5.7	...	...	# 49.4	0.3	# 1 090.3	97.1	# 32.4
	2010	3.4	...	...	# 58.7	0.4	# 1 227.4	51.3	# 11.1
	2015	4.1	56.0	44.0	# 27.1	0.9	# 983.9	39.5	# 23.7
Lebanon	2010	3.8	...	...	219.0	12.9	662.1	# 0.5	4.8
Liban	2015	4.0	...	...	132.8	16.9	427.8	# 39.8	3.5
Lesotho	2009	36.3	...	...	368.4	3.1	225.9	63.8	...
Lesotho	2010	38.0	...	...	...	...	...	...	...
Liberia	2010	3.3	...	...	...	...	...	...	...
Libéria	2012	3.2	...	...	...	...	...	...	...
Libya	2005	3.7	...	...	...	...	...	...	...
Libye	2010	3.1	...	...	...	...	...	...	...
	2015	2.5	...	...	...	...	...	...	...
Liechtenstein	2004	2.9	...	...	202.5	...	413.7	5.8	20.3
Liechtenstein	2005	...	...	...	203.7	...	502.1	2.9	51.7
	2010	2.8	100.0	0.0	212.3	...	479.7	5.5	16.5
	2014	2.7	100.0	0.0	321.8	...	573.9	2.7	21.5
	2015	...	...	...	327.7	...	514.2	8.0	24.0
Lithuania	2005	11.1	73.0	27.0	12.2	2.1	826.1	155.7	16.7
Lituanie	2010	7.0	66.0	34.0	7.9	2.2	849.6	87.3	16.5
	2015	6.0	72.0	28.0	7.4	1.7	699.0	55.2	13.0
Luxembourg	2005	...	50.0	50.0	...	...	...	...	...
Luxembourg	2010	2.0	50.0	50.0	487.3	5.3	1 421.2	74.2	# 41.5
	2014	0.7	50.0	50.0	572.6	9.3	1 843.2	110.5	# 51.4
Madagascar	2005	1.8	...	...	...	...	...	...	...
Madagascar	2010	0.6	...	...	16.4	...	0.3	14.9	3.3
	2015	...	...	...	9.0	0.1	0.9	7.2	4.6
Malawi	2005	1.6	...	...	...	...	...	...	...
Malawi	2010	3.5	...	...	...	...	...	...	...
	2012	1.8	...	...	...	...	...	...	...
Malaysia	2005	2.3	...	...	16.5	...	133.0	59.7	...
Malaisie	2006	2.2	...	...	21.8	...	141.4	81.6	...
	2010	1.9	...	...	...	...	...	...	...
Maldives	2004	...	...	...	...	0.3	...	155.7	...
Maldives	2010	1.8	...	...	444.4	7.8	1 203.0	164.5	157.3
	2013	0.9	...	...	367.1	2.3	1 903.4	207.6	163.2
Mali	2005	12.6	...	...	...	...	...	...	...
Mali	2010	12.1	...	...	...	...	...	...	...
	2015	10.8	...	...	...	...	...	...	...
Malta	2005	1.0	50.0	50.0	...	...	2 420.6	# 64.5	...
Malte	2010	1.0	75.0	25.0	# 43.7	...	1 885.4	# 47.6	# 22.1
	2015	1.0	50.0	50.0	# 43.7	...	2 066.8	# 57.8	# 24.8
Marshall Islands Îles Marshall	2012	4.7	...	...	...	...	...	...	...

12 Intentional homicides and other crimes *(continued)*

By type of crime per 100 000 population and homicide victims by sex

Homicides intentionnels et autres crimes *(suite)*

Par type de crime pour 100 000 habitants et victimes d'homicides par sexe

		Intentional homicides Homicides volontaires			Other crimes (per 100 000 pop.) Autres infractions (pour 100 000 hab.)				
			Victims (%) Victimes (%)						
Country or area Pays ou zone	Year Année	Per 100 000 Pour 100 000	Male Hommes	Female Femmes	Assault Agression	Kidnapping Enlèvement	Theft Vol simple	Robbery Vol qualifié	Sexual Violence Violences Sexuelles
Martinique	2005	4.8	...	...	...	...	...	...	...
Martinique	2009	2.8	...	...	...	...	...	...	...
Mauritania	2005	12.3	...	...	...	...	...	...	...
Mauritanie	2010	10.9	...	...	...	...	...	...	...
	2015	10.2	...	...	...	...	...	...	...
Mauritius	2005	...	...	...	10.0	...	# 1 172.3	110.5	25.7
Maurice	2010	2.6	76.0	24.0	19.1	2.8	# 864.0	86.9	34.6
	2011	2.7	76.0	24.0	18.4	4.0	# 729.9	65.0	37.2
Mayotte									
Mayotte	2009	5.9	...	...	...	...	...	...	...
Mexico	2005	9.0	...	...	# 217.9	# 0.3	# 77.3	# 470.1	# 26.1
Mexique	2010	21.7	...	...	# 194.5	# 1.1	# 111.3	# 622.3	# 28.8
	2015	16.4	...	...	# 35.8	# 0.9	# 114.2	# 129.2	# 31.8
Micronesia (Fed. States of)	2005	4.6	...	...	...	...	...	...	...
Micronésie (États féd. de)	2010	4.5	...	...	...	...	...	...	...
	2015	4.7	...	...	...	...	...	...	...
Monaco	2005	3.0	...	...	458.5	...	958.4	20.7	...
Monaco	2006	2.9	...	...	407.2	5.8	1 006.3	11.6	...
Mongolia	2005	15.8	...	...	118.4	~0.0	264.5	23.1	13.4
Mongolie	2009	8.2	73.0	27.0	216.1	~0.0	238.8	28.2	13.0
	2010	8.8	72.0	28.0	214.6	...	213.0	19.2	13.3
	2013	7.3	72.0	28.0	264.6	0.1	275.7	21.7	14.2
	2014	7.5	75.0	25.0	279.5	...	289.5	23.6	12.1
	2015	7.2	...	...	272.5	...	309.9	18.2	12.1
Montenegro	2005	...	...	...	# 25.2	...	249.8	# 14.0	5.7
Monténégro	2010	2.4	53.0	47.0	# 31.0	0.3	85.2	# 0.5	5.8
	2013	1.6	90.0	10.0	# 27.7	0.2	118.3	# 25.8	4.0
	2015	2.7	82.0	18.0	# 22.4	...	132.2	# 24.9	4.2
Montserrat	2005	20.9	...	...	...	...	...	...	...
Montserrat	2008	20.4	...	...	...	...	...	...	...
Morocco	2005	1.5	...	...	107.4	1.0	204.4	49.4	3.1
Maroc	2009	1.4	88.0	12.0	98.1	1.0	247.2	81.8	10.3
	2010	1.4	...	...	...	...	...	...	...
	2013	1.3	85.0	15.0	202.6	2.9	322.3	44.4	12.9
	2014	1.1	...	...	...	...	...	...	...
Mozambique	2005	5.2	...	...	6.0	...	26.3	32.3	3.7
Mozambique	2009	3.5	...	...	2.2	...	20.1	22.3	2.6
	2010	3.6	...	...	...	...	...	...	...
	2011	3.4	...	...	...	...	...	...	...
Myanmar	2005	1.5	...	...	...	...	...	...	...
Myanmar	2010	1.6	81.0	19.0	5.2	...	3.3	~0.0	0.5
	2013	2.4	83.0	17.0	4.7	~0.0	4.8	~0.0	0.7
	2014	2.5	83.0	17.0	10.3	0.0	5.6	0.2	...
	2015	2.4	81.0	19.0	9.0	...	5.4	0.3	...
Namibia	2004	17.6	...	...	...	...	...	...	...
Namibie	2010	14.3	...	...	...	...	...	...	...
	2012	16.9	...	...	...	...	...	...	...
Nauru									
Nauru	2012	1.3	...	...	...	...	...	...	...
Nepal	2005	3.6	...	...	4.1	0.5	2.0	0.9	...
Népal	2006	2.5	...	...	4.1	1.0	2.1	0.6	...
	2010	3.0	...	...	...	...	...	...	...
	2014	2.3	...	...	...	...	...	...	...
Netherlands	2005	1.1	...	...	# 410.6	# 5.6	# 4 641.6	# 100.7	# 44.6
Pays-Bas	2010	0.9	63.0	38.0	# 362.4	# 3.9	# 3 981.0	# 97.0	# 57.8
	2015	0.6	60.0	40.0	# 281.8	# 2.5	# 3 214.8	# 56.8	# 43.5
New Caledonia									
Nouvelle-Calédonie	2009	3.3	...	...	...	...	...	...	...

12 Intentional homicides and other crimes *(continued)*
By type of crime per 100 000 population and homicide victims by sex

Homicides intentionnels et autres crimes *(suite)*
Par type de crime pour 100 000 habitants et victimes d'homicides par sexe

Country or area Pays ou zone	Year Année	Intentional homicides Homicides volontaires Per 100 000 Pour 100 000	Victims (%) Victimes (%) Male Hommes	Female Femmes	Other crimes (per 100 000 pop.) Autres infractions (pour 100 000 hab.) Assault Agression	Kidnapping Enlèvement	Theft Vol simple	Robbery Vol qualifié	Sexual Violence Violences Sexuelles
New Zealand Nouvelle-Zélande	2005	1.5[4]	…	…	234.2	# 7.0	3 088.4	56.2	59.6
	2010	1.0[4]	48.0	52.0	257.7	# 5.2	2 676.6	57.0	66.7
	2013	1.0[4]	74.0	26.0	200.5	# 4.4	2 280.1	45.5	83.7
	2014	0.9[4]	…	…	220.2	# 5.2	…	44.9	83.2
Nicaragua Nicaragua	2005	13.6	…	…	359.4	0.2	269.8	# 397.4	…
	2010	13.7	90.0	10.0	319.7	0.1	182.2	# 495.5	# 63.2
	2012	11.5	…	…	…	…	…	…	…
Niger Niger	2012	4.5	…	…	…	…	…	…	…
Nigeria Nigéria	2005	11.8	…	…	…	…	…	…	…
	2010	10.7	…	…	11.4	0.5	12.9	1.4	1.1
	2013	…	…	…	9.5	0.3	13.9	1.1	1.0
	2015	9.8	…	…	…	…	…	…	…
Niue Nioué	2012	3.1	…	…	…	…	…	…	…
Norway Norvège	2001	…	47.0	53.0	…	…	…	…	…
	2005	0.7	…	…	# 64.0	…	2 996.7	# 31.3	42.4
	2010	0.6	48.0	52.0	# 59.8	…	2 590.0	# 34.5	50.1
	2014	0.6	55.0	45.0	# 46.2	…	2 193.7	# 20.7	51.6
Oman Oman	2008	0.7	…	…	78.5	0.3	207.9	9.6	6.9
	2011	1.1	…	…	…	…	…	…	…
Other non-specified areas Autres zones non-spécifiées	2010	0.8	…	…	…	…	…	…	…
	2015	0.8	…	…	…	…	…	…	…
Pakistan Pakistan	2005	6.3	…	…	…	…	…	…	…
	2010	7.8	…	…	…	…	…	…	…
	2012	7.8	…	…	…	…	…	…	…
Palau Palaos	2012	3.1	…	…	…	…	…	…	…
Panama Panama	2005	11.0	90.0	10.0	…	# 0.5	# 421.1	# 158.1	# 23.6
	2010	21.0	93.0	7.0	167.4	# 1.1	# 504.4	# 262.6	# 27.8
	2015	11.4	89.0	11.0	72.4	# 0.4	# 480.4	# 207.9	# 80.2
Papua New Guinea Papouasie-Nvl-Guinée	2005	9.9	…	…	…	…	…	…	…
	2010	10.4	…	…	…	…	…	…	…
Paraguay Paraguay	2005	18.6	…	…	38.6	~0.0	…	…	…
	2010	11.9	90.0	10.0	31.4	0.1	502.1	220.3	54.7
	2015	9.3	91.0	9.0	10.3	~0.0	572.7	317.2	74.8
Peru Pérou	2005	11.1	…	…	53.2	# 1.8	189.9	165.1	…
	2010	9.2	…	…	64.9	# 1.6	190.1	193.4	18.0
	2015	7.2	82.0	18.0	79.0	# 0.7	301.1	264.4	18.2
Philippines Philippines	2005	# 7.5	…	…	…	0.1	# 13.0	# 9.0	…
	2010	# 9.6	86.0	14.0	…	~0.0	# 78.4	# 38.8	2.3
	2012	# 8.8	87.0	13.0	…	~0.0	# 45.4	# 28.1	1.9
	#2014	9.8	…	…	…	…	113.8	44.1	…
Poland Pologne	2005	1.4	…	…	…	0.1	725.0	109.6	…
	2010	1.1	…	…	28.5	0.1	528.6	50.2	8.0
	2015	0.7	…	…	14.3	0.6	357.8	21.1	7.8
Portugal Portugal	2005	1.3	…	…	374.2	4.2	876.1	192.9	15.5
	2010	1.2	…	…	8.2	4.7	898.1	193.1	20.2
	2015	1.0	…	…	4.5	3.6	835.0	149.5	23.6
Puerto Rico Porto Rico	2005	20.5	…	…	…	…	…	…	…
	2010	26.3	…	…	73.2	…	721.7	175.7	…
	2015	15.9	…	…	76.3	…	665.0	110.5	…
Qatar Qatar	2004	…	…	…	40.7	0.8	100.3	2.9	…
	2005	4.9	…	…	…	…	107.2	…	…
	2006	…	…	…	…	…	105.5	…	…
	2010	6.9	…	…	…	…	…	…	…
	2015	8.1	…	…	…	…	…	…	…

Intentional homicides and other crimes *(continued)*
By type of crime per 100 000 population and homicide victims by sex

Homicides intentionnels et autres crimes *(suite)*
Par type de crime pour 100 000 habitants et victimes d'homicides par sexe

		Intentional homicides Homicides volontaires			Other crimes (per 100 000 pop.) Autres infractions (pour 100 000 hab.)				
			Victims (%) Victimes (%)						
Country or area Pays ou zone	Year Année	Per 100 000 Pour 100 000	Male Hommes	Female Femmes	Assault Agression	Kidnapping Enlèvement	Theft Vol simple	Robbery Vol qualifié	Sexual Violence Violences Sexuelles
Republic of Korea République de Corée	2005	...	...	...	...	...	396.6	10.9	...
	2010	...	...	...	# 595.5	0.5	548.8	9.0	37.1
	2014	0.7	49.0	51.0	# 100.4	0.4	531.7	3.2	42.1
Republic of Moldova République de Moldova	2005	7.1	66.0	34.0	# 9.5	0.4	276.7	4.5	9.5
	2010	6.5	80.0	20.0	# 10.2	0.9	334.1	4.5	13.6
	2014	3.2	63.0	37.0	# 7.9	2.2	410.8	3.1	15.9
Réunion Réunion	2005	3.2	...	...	...	...	...	...	...
	2009	1.8	...	...	...	...	...	...	...
Romania Roumanie	2005	2.1[2]	...	...	# 41.6	# 1.3	# 201.8	# 15.5	...
	2010	2.0[2]	...	...	# 60.6	# 1.6	# 240.6	# 12.2	# 7.3
	2015	1.5[2]	...	...	# 1.5	# 1.5	# 555.8	# 17.2	# 8.9
Russian Federation Fédération de Russie	2005	...	...	...	40.3	0.8	1 095.2	239.8	12.9
	2010	16.0	...	...	21.2	0.4	774.2	114.9	10.6
	2015	11.3	...	...	16.6	0.2	709.9	50.7	11.3
Rwanda Rwanda	2010	4.9	...	...	19.5	0.1	...	20.1	...
	2013	4.5	...	...	29.8	0.2	...	25.0	15.7
Saint Kitts and Nevis Saint-Kitts-et-Nevis	2005	16.3	...	...	...	...	...	...	...
	2010	40.1	90.0	10.0	296.1	3.8	1 018.1	166.2	118.4
	2011	64.2	97.0	3.0	258.5	5.7	926.5	124.5	120.8
	2012	33.6	...	...	...	...	...	...	...
Saint Lucia Sainte-Lucie	2005	24.8	...	...	...	...	...	...	...
	2010	24.8	...	...	...	...	...	...	...
	2012	21.6	...	...	...	...	...	...	...
Saint Pierre and Miquelon Saint-Pierre-et-Miquelon	2009	15.9	...	...	...	...	...	...	...
Saint Vincent & Grenadines Saint-Vincent-Grenadines	2005	21.2	73.0	27.0	1 151.3	1.8	1 777.5	67.1	104.8
	2010	22.9	88.0	12.0	1 197.5	1.8	1 739.0	107.0	153.7
	2012	25.6	...	...	1 017.1	3.7	1 923.5	146.3	160.1
	2013	...	...	...	...	...	...	136.3	209.5
Samoa Samoa	2010	8.6	...	...	...	...	...	...	...
	2013	3.2	...	...	...	...	...	...	...
Sao Tome and Principe Sao Tomé-et-Principe	2004	...	...	...	0.7	...	...	...	...
	2009	3.0	...	...	3.0	...	3.0	...	...
	2010	3.5	...	...	...	...	9.4	0.6	...
	2011	3.4	...	...	2.3	...	11.5	0.6	...
Saudi Arabia Arabie saoudite	2015	1.5	...	...	1.4	...	...	0.3	0.1
Senegal Sénégal	2005	9.3	...	...	2.5	...	...	24.4	...
	2010	8.5	...	...	2.4	...	19.3	19.3	...
	2015	7.3	...	...	...	~0.0	16.5	16.5	1.7
Serbia Serbie	2005	1.6	69.0	31.0	17.6	0.3	# 182.5	32.5	5.8
	2010	1.4	68.0	32.0	15.4	0.2	# 175.7	40.0	5.4
	2015	1.1	70.0	30.0	12.9	0.2	# 255.4	34.2	3.8
Seychelles Seychelles	2005	3.4	...	...	...	...	...	...	...
	2010	2.2	...	...	...	...	...	...	...
Sierra Leone Sierra Leone	2005	2.0	...	...	...	...	...	...	...
	2008	3.3	...	...	359.9	...	190.2	3.3	11.3
	2010	2.8	...	...	...	...	...	...	...
	2015	1.9	...	...	...	...	...	...	...
Singapore Singapour	2003	0.6	...	...	13.9	0.1	354.6	22.9	...
	2005	0.5	...	...	13.5	...	470.9	24.3	...
	2006	0.4	71.0	29.0	13.8	~0.0	413.3	20.5	30.3
	2010	0.4	84.0	16.0	8.5	...	359.8	10.2	31.1
	2014	0.3	50.0	50.0	9.3	...	288.2	4.2	27.9
	2015	0.3	...	...	8.4	...	266.0	2.2	26.0
Slovakia Slovaquie	2005	2.0	66.0	34.0	72.4	0.3	350.9	35.6	...
	2010	1.7	62.0	38.0	44.9	0.1	452.5	22.0	10.4
	2015	0.9	68.0	32.0	35.0	~0.0	444.0	9.9	3.0

12 Intentional homicides and other crimes *(continued)*

By type of crime per 100 000 population and homicide victims by sex

Homicides intentionnels et autres crimes *(suite)*

Par type de crime pour 100 000 habitants et victimes d'homicides par sexe

Country or area Pays ou zone	Year Année	Intentional homicides / Homicides volontaires: Per 100 000 Pour 100 000	Victims (%) / Victimes (%): Male Hommes	Female Femmes	Other crimes (per 100 000 pop.) / Autres infractions (pour 100 000 hab.): Assault Agression	Kidnapping Enlèvement	Theft Vol simple	Robbery Vol qualifié	Sexual Violence Violences Sexuelles
Slovenia Slovénie	2005	1.0	50.0	50.0	115.4	0.2	1 477.0	21.5	15.6
	2010	0.7	47.0	53.0	106.3	0.2	1 408.6	22.6	18.3
	2015	1.2	45.0	55.0	74.5	0.2	1 102.7	11.2	7.4
Solomon Islands Îles Salomon	2005	5.5	...	...	258.5	...	219.3	5.1	43.5
	2008	3.8	...	...	217.9	...	174.4	10.3	24.2
Somalia Somalie	2005	6.1	...	...	...	...	...	...	...
	2010	6.6	...	...	...	...	...	...	...
	2015	5.6	...	...	...	...	...	...	...
South Africa Afrique du Sud	2005	38.9	...	...	...	...	...	...	...
	2010	30.9	...	...	...	...	...	...	...
	2015	34.3	...	...	...	...	...	...	...
South Sudan Soudan du sud	2012	13.7	...	...	...	...	...	...	...
Spain Espagne	2005	1.2	...	...	# 394.1	0.5	...	...	...
	2010	0.9	61.0	39.0	# 53.8	0.3	# 310.3	181.1	21.4
	2015	0.7	60.0	40.0	# 63.0	0.2	# 446.1	140.0	21.4
Sri Lanka Sri Lanka	2004	# 7.1	...	...	109.3	4.5	135.8	41.0	...
	#2005	6.3	...	...	...	...	...	...	...
	2010	# 3.8	78.0	22.0	319.9	1.0	62.8	31.9	4.4
	2013	# 2.9	78.0	22.0	316.4	1.0	55.8	23.1	4.8
State of Palestine État de Palestine	2005	4.1	...	...	# 183.6	# 5.6	# 122.3	# 5.7	...
	2010	0.7	70.0	30.0	# 7.0	# 0.5	# 67.4	# 69.9	4.4
	2012	0.6	85.0	15.0	# 8.1	# 0.3	# 45.3	# 46.4	2.8
	2013	...	...	...	...	...	...	# 84.5	3.0
Sudan Soudan	2005	7.5	...	...	...	...	...	...	...
	2008	...	...	...	...	1.8	220.6	8.9	...
	2010	6.8	...	...	...	...	...	...	...
	2015	6.5	...	...	...	...	...	...	...
Suriname Suriname	2004	...	...	...	...	...	2 778.8	...	...
	2005	3.1	...	...	...	...	...	...	...
	2010	9.5	...	...	...	...	...	...	...
	2015	10.7	...	...	...	...	...	...	...
Swaziland Swaziland	2004	13.3	...	...	1 332.4	8.8	1 904.6	309.8	...
	2005	13.8	...	...	...	...	...	...	...
	2010	17.4	...	...	...	...	...	...	...
	2013	8.2	...	...	...	...	...	...	...
Sweden Suède	2005	0.9	...	...	804.5	...	4 926.0	104.1	129.7
	2010	1.0	68.0	32.0	59.6	...	3 921.9	98.3	150.6
	2015	1.2	74.0	26.0	47.4	...	3 815.5	86.5	155.8
Switzerland Suisse	2005	1.0	...	...	# 109.3	# 3.3	# 1 922.4	# 53.7	...
	2009	0.7	47.0	53.0	# 6.8	# 4.6	# 1 616.4	# 65.0	# 85.9
	2010	0.7	50.0	50.0	# 6.2	...	# 2 059.6	# 56.3	# 31.8
	2015	0.7	47.0	53.0	# 7.4	# 0.1	# 1 759.6	# 39.5	# 32.7
Syrian Arab Republic République arabe syrienne	2004	2.4	...	...	36.0	0.8	65.3	3.1	...
	2005	2.4	...	...	34.0	0.2	...	4.2	...
	2008	2.6	...	...	2.8	0.1	32.4	4.3	0.4
	2010	2.2	...	...	...	...	...	...	...
Tajikistan Tadjikistan	2005	...	...	...	...	...	52.3	...	...
	2010	2.0	87.0	13.0	72.4	1.9	46.9	3.2	2.6
	2011	1.9	87.0	13.0	48.2	2.2	47.3	3.7	2.6
	2013	1.4	...	...	...	...	...	...	...
Thailand Thaïlande	2005	7.3	...	...	# 42.9	~0.0	92.4	...	...
	2010	5.5	...	...	# 13.7	~0.0	81.5	# 2.8	2.9
	2015	3.5	...	...	# 20.1	0.5	57.9	# 2.2	6.0
TFYR of Macedonia ex-R.Y. de Macédoine	2005	2.2	...	...	...	1.2	...	34.7	...
	2010	2.1	65.0	35.0	12.0	0.8	237.4	29.3	6.0
	2014	1.6	70.0	30.0	10.4	0.4	240.1	14.7	6.5
Timor-Leste Timor-Leste	2005	4.7	...	...	...	...	...	...	...
	2010	3.7	...	...	...	...	...	...	...

12 Intentional homicides and other crimes *(continued)*

By type of crime per 100 000 population and homicide victims by sex

Homicides intentionnels et autres crimes *(suite)*

Par type de crime pour 100 000 habitants et victimes d'homicides par sexe

		Intentional homicides Homicides volontaires			Other crimes (per 100 000 pop.) Autres infractions (pour 100 000 hab.)				
			Victims (%) Victimes (%)						
Country or area Pays ou zone	Year Année	Per 100 000 Pour 100 000	Male Hommes	Female Femmes	Assault Agression	Kidnapping Enlèvement	Theft Vol simple	Robbery Vol qualifié	Sexual Violence Violences Sexuelles
Togo	2005	10.9	...	...	...	...	...	...	...
Togo	2010	9.8	...	...	...	...	...	...	...
	2015	9.1	...	...	...	...	...	...	...
Tonga	2005	4.0	...	...	...	...	...	...	...
Tonga	2010	1.0	...	...	...	...	...	...	...
	2012	1.0	...	...	...	...	...	...	...
Trinidad and Tobago	2005	29.8	90.0	10.0	61.8	4.5	212.2	375.4	61.9
Trinité-et-Tobago	2010	35.6	89.0	11.0	46.4	0.5	307.9	385.7	57.8
	2015	30.9	93.0	7.0	44.1	0.3	137.5	181.5	51.1
Tunisia	2005	2.6	...	...	...	...	...	...	...
Tunisie	2010	2.7	...	...	...	...	...	...	...
	2012	3.1	...	...	...	...	...	...	...
Turkey	2005	4.9	82.0	18.0	155.8	12.9	152.9	21.2	4.5
Turquie	2010	4.2	79.0	21.0	305.5	18.8	248.4	11.9	5.8
	2012	4.3	81.0	19.0	350.5	17.9	279.1	13.8	7.4
Turkmenistan	2004	...	...	...	...	2.7	...	3.8	...
Turkménistan	2005	4.9	...	...	1.9	...	35.0	3.4	...
	2006	...	...	...	1.7	...	29.8	2.9	...
	2010	4.5	...	...	...	...	...	...	...
	2015	4.2	...	...	...	...	...	...	...
Turks and Caicos Islands									
Îles Turques-et-Caïques	2009	6.6	...	...	...	...	...	...	...
Tuvalu	2010	10.2	...	...	...	...	...	...	...
Tuvalu	2012	20.3	...	...	...	...	...	...	...
Uganda	2005	8.9	...	...	125.1	...	196.3	26.1	50.3
Ouganda	2010	9.5	81.0	19.0	69.3	# 0.5	70.7	18.2	26.1
	2014	11.8	81.0	19.0	38.4	# 0.6	45.2	9.6	36.2
Ukraine	2005	6.5	...	...	14.3	0.4	398.9	100.5	4.1
Ukraine	2010	4.4	...	...	8.8	0.6	558.1	51.0	3.0
United Arab Emirates	2004	...	...	...	...	12.7	# 277.6	11.0	...
Émirats arabes unis	2005	...	...	...	16.0	19.2	...	9.6	...
	2006	...	...	...	14.7	18.8	...	10.8	...
	2010	0.8	73.0	27.0	...	...	...	...	...
	2015	0.7	84.0	16.0	3.5	0.9	# 67.8	9.0	4.1
United Kingdom	2005	1.5	72.0	28.0	1 010.6[5]	5.2[5]	3 368.8[5]	183.3[5]	88.0[5]
Royaume-Uni	2010	1.2	70.0	30.0	658.8[5]	3.1[5]	2 654.9[5]	136.8[5]	81.5[5]
	2014	0.9	65.0	35.0	649.3[5]	3.8[5]	2 208.6[5]	87.5[5]	137.0[5]
United Rep. of Tanzania	2010	8.5	86.0	14.0	...	...	...	26.1	~0.0
Rép.-Unie de Tanzanie	2015	7.0	82.0	18.0	4.4	...	0.3	17.6	0.1
United States of America	2005	5.7	79.0	21.0	291.2	...	2 290.6	141.0	...
États-Unis d'Amérique	2010	4.8	78.0	22.0	252.3	...	2 002.3	119.1	...
	2015	4.9	79.0	21.0	237.6	...	1 773.4	101.7	...
United States Virgin Islands	2005	32.5	...	...	...	...	...	...	...
Îles Vierges américaines	2010	52.6	...	...	...	...	...	...	...
Uruguay	2003	5.9	...	...	...	0.1	2 904.9	291.7	...
Uruguay	2004	5.8	...	...	...	...	3 179.5	277.5	...
	2005	5.7	...	...	...	...	...	291.7	...
	2010	6.1	80.0	20.0	15.4	...	2 823.3	409.8	...
	2015	8.4	83.0	17.0	13.6	0.3	3 043.6	566.0	46.1
Uzbekistan	2005	3.6	...	...	...	...	...	...	...
Ouzbékistan	2010	3.2	...	...	...	...	...	...	...
	2015	3.0	...	...	...	...	...	...	...
Vanuatu	2005	2.5	...	...	...	...	...	...	...
Vanuatu	2010	2.3	...	...	...	...	...	...	...
	2015	2.1	...	...	...	...	...	...	...
Venezuela (Boliv. Rep. of)	2005	37.2	...	...	...	...	...	...	...
Venezuela (Rép. boliv. du)	2010	45.1	...	...	...	...	...	...	...
	2015	57.2	...	...	...	...	...	...	...

12 Intentional homicides and other crimes *(continued)*

By type of crime per 100 000 population and homicide victims by sex

Homicides intentionnels et autres crimes *(suite)*

Par type de crime pour 100 000 habitants et victimes d'homicides par sexe

		Intentional homicides Homicides volontaires			Other crimes (per 100 000 pop.) Autres infractions (pour 100 000 hab.)				
			Victims (%) Victimes (%)						
Country or area Pays ou zone	Year Année	Per 100 000 Pour 100 000	Male Hommes	Female Femmes	Assault Agression	Kidnapping Enlèvement	Theft Vol simple	Robbery Vol qualifié	Sexual Violence Violences Sexuelles
Viet Nam	2005	1.3	...	...	...	...	...	...	...
Viet Nam	2010	1.5	...	...	...	...	...	...	...
	2011	1.5	...	...	...	...	...	...	...
Yemen	2005	4.6	...	...	...	0.5	...	...	...
Yémen	2009	4.3	...	...	0.1	0.2	...	1.9	0.3
	2010	4.7	...	...	...	...	...	...	...
	2013	6.7	...	...	...	...	...	...	...
Zambia Zambie	2010	5.9	...	...	...	...	...	...	...
Zimbabwe	2005	10.4	...	...	712.5	0.3	851.1	85.8	...
Zimbabwe	2008	...	...	...	379.7	1.6	677.7	65.2	...
	2010	5.1	...	...	...	...	...	...	...
	2012	6.7	...	...	...	...	...	...	...

Source:

United Nations Office on Drugs and Crime, Vienna, UNODC Statistics database, last accessed June 2017.

1 Data is for 2015, or latest available data from 2010 onwards.

2 Data refer to offences, not victims, of intentional homicide.

3 Data refer to Central Iraq.

4 Data for 2000-2006 refer to offences, data for 2007 onwards refer to victims of intentional homicide.

5 England and Wales only.

Source:

Office des Nations Unies contre la drogue et le crime, Vienna, la base de données de l'UNODC, dernier accès juin 2017.

1 Données pour 2015, ou dernières données disponibles à partir de 2010.

2 Les données concernent les infractions, et non les victimes, d'homicides volontaires.

3 Les données se réfèrent l'Iraq central

4 Les données pour 2000-2006 concernent les infractions, les données à partir de 2007 concernent les victimes d' homicides volontaires.

5 Se rapporte seulement a l'Angleterre et au pays de Galles.

Part Two

Economic activity

Chapter VII	National accounts (tables 13 and 14)
Chapter VIII	Finance (table 15 and 16)
Chapter IX	Labour market (tables 17 and 18)
Chapter X	Price and production indices (tables 19)
Chapter XI	International merchandise trade (table 20 and 21)

Deuxième partie

Activité économique

Chapitre VII	Compatibilités nationales (tableaux 13 et 14)
Chapitre VIII	Finances (tableau 15 et 16)
Chapitre IX	Marché du travail (tableaux 17 et 18)
Chapitre X	Indices des prix et de la production (tableaux 19)
Chapitre XI	Commerce international des marchandises (tableau 20 et 21)

13 Gross domestic product and gross domestic product per capita

In millions of US dollars at current and constant 2005 prices; per capita US dollars; real rates of growth

Produit intérieur brut et produit intérieur brut par habitant

En millions de dollars É.-U. aux prix courants et constants de 2005; par habitant en dollars É.U.; taux de croissance réels

Region, country or area	1985	1995	2005	2010	2013	2014	2015	Région, pays ou zone
Total, all countries or areas								**Total, tous pays ou zones**
GDP at current prices	**13 507 658**	**31 032 911**	**47 539 451**	**65 911 732**	**76 830 809**	**78 612 132**	**74 176 854**	**PIB aux prix courants**
GDP per capita	**2 785**	**5 412**	**7 293**	**9 514**	**10 700**	**10 822**	**10 095**	**PIB par habitant**
GDP at constant prices	**26 128 620**	**34 767 584**	**47 539 451**	**53 112 570**	**57 109 121**	**58 560 379**	**60 092 455**	**PIB aux prix constants**
Growth rates	**3.7**	**3.0**	**3.6**	**4.1**	**2.3**	**2.5**	**2.6**	**Taux de croissance**
Africa								**Afrique**
GDP at current prices	510 018	575 740	1 116 958	1 942 476	2 410 732	2 502 053	2 267 610	PIB aux prix courants
GDP per capita	929	800	1 216	1 863	2 141	2 166	1 914	PIB par habitant
GDP at constant prices	592 057	719 063	1 116 958	1 428 275	1 562 669	1 621 603	1 672 435	PIB aux prix constants
Growth rates	3.5	2.9	5.9	5.2	2.4	3.8	3.1	Taux de croissance
Northern Africa								**Afrique septentrionale**
GDP at current prices	142 523	207 392	373 106	647 993	772 172	786 018	736 257	PIB aux prix courants
GDP per capita	1 111	1 275	1 917	3 189	3 591	3 586	3 297	PIB par habitant
GDP at constant prices	192 112	239 901	373 106	460 365	457 443	462 986	478 135	PIB aux prix constants
Growth rates	5.8	1.3	5.7	4.4	-3.0	1.2	3.3	Taux de croissance
Eastern Africa								**Afrique orientale**
GDP at current prices	61 784	67 198	110 318	212 886	291 174	317 620	307 528	PIB aux prix courants
GDP per capita	375	307	382	623	783	830	782	PIB par habitant
GDP at constant prices	54 907	72 993	110 318	164 465	192 200	204 807	216 055	PIB aux prix constants
Growth rates	2.4	4.3	6.3	7.7	6.8	6.6	5.5	Taux de croissance
Middle Africa								**Afrique centrale**
GDP at current prices	33 928	35 261	97 928	182 587	265 718	281 581	231 955	PIB aux prix courants
GDP per capita	555	420	875	1 398	1 857	1 909	1 527	PIB par habitant
GDP at constant prices	65 550	59 410	97 928	130 617	152 044	161 594	167 108	PIB aux prix constants
Growth rates	1.6	6.5	8.5	4.4	4.3	6.3	3.4	Taux de croissance
Southern Africa								**Afrique australe**
GDP at current prices	62 809	168 936	279 299	406 135	401 939	386 706	346 595	PIB aux prix courants
GDP per capita	1 675	3 566	5 053	6 876	6 560	6 240	5 534	PIB par habitant
GDP at constant prices	172 127	200 717	279 299	326 917	355 811	362 424	367 259	PIB aux prix constants
Growth rates	-1.0	3.3	5.2	3.3	2.8	1.9	1.3	Taux de croissance
Western Africa								**Afrique occidentale**
GDP at current prices	208 974	96 952	256 307	492 876	679 730	730 127	645 275	PIB aux prix courants
GDP per capita	1 326	470	955	1 600	2 032	2 124	1 827	PIB par habitant
GDP at constant prices	107 360	146 043	256 307	345 911	405 171	429 792	443 878	PIB aux prix constants
Growth rates	8.9	3.0	6.1	7.3	5.8	6.1	3.3	Taux de croissance
Americas								**Amériques**
GDP at current prices	5 489 745	10 194 789	17 115 581	21 917 163	24 856 629	25 454 584	25 000 541	PIB aux prix courants
GDP per capita	8 173	13 037	19 205	23 249	25 572	25 933	25 229	PIB par habitant
GDP at constant prices	9 329 192	12 336 952	17 115 581	18 233 607	19 440 418	19 818 244	20 217 924	PIB aux prix constants
Growth rates	4.1	2.5	3.5	3.1	1.9	1.9	2.0	Taux de croissance
Northern America								**Amérique septentrionale**
GDP at current prices	4 713 295	8 271 819	14 269 637	16 585 978	18 542 203	19 194 079	19 597 386	PIB aux prix courants
GDP per capita	17 676	27 974	43 436	48 198	52 604	54 044	54 767	PIB par habitant
GDP at constant prices	7 665 580	10 210 248	14 269 637	14 843 618	15 698 411	16 072 931	16 467 482	PIB aux prix constants
Growth rates	4.3	2.8	3.3	2.6	1.7	2.4	2.5	Taux de croissance
Latin America & the Caribbean								**Amérique latine et Caraïbes**
GDP at current prices	776 450	1 922 970	2 845 944	5 331 185	6 314 427	6 260 505	5 403 154	PIB aux prix courants
GDP per capita	1 917	3 954	5 058	8 906	10 192	9 995	8 534	PIB par habitant
GDP at constant prices	1 663 611	2 126 704	2 845 944	3 389 989	3 742 007	3 745 313	3 750 441	PIB aux prix constants
Growth rates	3.2	0.8	4.3	5.7	2.7	0.1	0.1	Taux de croissance
Caribbean								**Caraïbes**
GDP at current prices	68 412	118 569	219 320	286 653	320 420	327 758	337 854	PIB aux prix courants
GDP per capita	2 199	3 341	5 613	7 053	7 703	7 822	8 005	PIB par habitant
GDP at constant prices	125 949	151 934	219 320	242 651	254 135	257 818	264 787	PIB aux prix constants
Growth rates	0.7	4.0	3.7	1.7	1.9	1.4	2.7	Taux de croissance
Central America								**Amérique centrale**
GDP at current prices	250 081	371 585	961 724	1 204 845	1 462 482	1 510 299	1 370 237	PIB aux prix courants
GDP per capita	2 418	2 925	6 455	7 478	8 696	8 860	7 932	PIB par habitant
GDP at constant prices	562 883	671 356	961 724	1 070 132	1 178 701	1 207 170	1 239 263	PIB aux prix constants
Growth rates	2.6	-5.2	3.2	5.0	1.6	2.4	2.7	Taux de croissance
South America								**Amérique du Sud**
GDP at current prices	457 957	1 432 816	1 664 900	3 839 687	4 531 525	4 422 448	3 695 063	PIB aux prix courants
GDP per capita	1 693	4 425	4 444	9 675	11 058	10 682	8 836	PIB par habitant
GDP at constant prices	974 780	1 303 415	1 664 900	2 077 206	2 309 170	2 280 325	2 246 391	PIB aux prix constants
Growth rates	3.9	3.7	5.0	6.5	3.3	-1.2	-1.5	Taux de croissance

13 Gross domestic product and gross domestic product per capita *(continued)*

In millions of US dollars at current and constant 2005 prices; per capita US dollars; real rates of growth

Produit intérieur brut et produit intérieur brut par habitant *(suite)*

En millions de dollars É.-U. aux prix courants et constants de 2005; par habitant en dollars É.U.; taux de croissance réels

Region, country or area	1985	1995	2005	2010	2013	2014	2015	Région, pays ou zone
Asia								**Asie**
GDP at current prices	2 879 411	9 186 371	12 321 485	20 769 947	25 978 074	26 821 657	26 514 784	PIB aux prix courants
GDP per capita	1 016	2 644	3 124	4 981	6 035	6 167	6 036	PIB par habitant
GDP at constant prices	5 268 753	8 517 418	12 321 485	15 474 995	17 677 573	18 389 584	19 127 470	PIB aux prix constants
Growth rates	5.3	4.9	5.3	7.2	4.6	4.0	4.0	Taux de croissance
Central Asia								**Asie centrale**
GDP at current prices	...	38 930	90 474	220 593	348 831	344 636	302 780	PIB aux prix courants
GDP per capita	...	732	1 559	3 550	5 348	5 199	4 498	PIB par habitant
GDP at constant prices	...	51 812	90 474	128 397	159 566	169 416	175 223	PIB aux prix constants
Growth rates	...	-6.9	9.4	7.6	7.3	6.2	3.4	Taux de croissance
Eastern Asia								**Asie orientale**
GDP at current prices	1 927 587	7 179 560	8 547 753	13 584 987	16 964 302	17 701 007	17 826 442	PIB aux prix courants
GDP per capita	1 534	4 955	5 563	8 624	10 615	11 026	11 056	PIB par habitant
GDP at constant prices	3 857 625	6 131 098	8 547 753	10 542 813	11 957 541	12 407 445	12 875 993	PIB aux prix constants
Growth rates	6.9	4.7	4.7	7.1	4.5	3.8	3.8	Taux de croissance
South-eastern Asia								**Asie du Sud-est**
GDP at current prices	243 706	703 063	958 699	1 980 390	2 510 939	2 526 429	2 440 849	PIB aux prix courants
GDP per capita	607	1 444	1 702	3 319	4 058	4 035	3 853	PIB par habitant
GDP at constant prices	325 756	654 942	958 699	1 241 294	1 444 212	1 506 629	1 572 544	PIB aux prix constants
Growth rates	0.5	7.9	5.7	8.0	4.9	4.3	4.4	Taux de croissance
Southern Asia								**Asie méridionale**
GDP at current prices	367 120	611 435	1 251 993	2 500 434	2 927 828	3 018 537	3 104 480	PIB aux prix courants
GDP per capita	346	463	792	1 468	1 649	1 678	1 703	PIB par habitant
GDP at constant prices	463 643	720 987	1 251 993	1 767 998	2 041 796	2 175 053	2 311 959	PIB aux prix constants
Growth rates	4.5	6.3	7.9	8.6	5.2	6.5	6.3	Taux de croissance
Western Asia								**Asie occidentale**
GDP at current prices	340 998	653 382	1 472 566	2 483 544	3 226 174	3 231 049	2 840 232	PIB aux prix courants
GDP per capita	2 945	3 925	7 165	10 685	13 032	12 806	11 053	PIB par habitant
GDP at constant prices	621 729	958 580	1 472 566	1 794 493	2 074 458	2 131 040	2 191 752	PIB aux prix constants
Growth rates	-0.6	4.4	6.7	6.1	3.9	2.7	2.8	Taux de croissance
Europe								**Europe**
GDP at current prices	4 414 541	10 601 737	16 084 260	19 805 957	21 820 425	22 136 240	18 945 444	PIB aux prix courants
GDP per capita	5 733	14 539	22 012	26 867	29 510	29 918	25 590	PIB par habitant
GDP at constant prices	10 466 104	12 559 659	16 084 260	16 951 871	17 316 875	17 592 303	17 906 876	PIB aux prix constants
Growth rates	2.6	2.2	2.3	2.3	0.4	1.6	1.8	Taux de croissance
Eastern Europe								**Europe orientale**
GDP at current prices	1 124 205	785 499	1 619 644	2 851 190	3 716 159	3 497 633	2 575 830	PIB aux prix courants
GDP per capita	3 019	2 537	5 445	9 678	12 655	11 924	8 793	PIB par habitant
GDP at constant prices	1 460 593	1 128 229	1 619 644	1 912 270	2 052 581	2 082 609	2 070 434	PIB aux prix constants
Growth rates	1.6	-0.5	5.4	3.6	1.3	1.5	-0.6	Taux de croissance
Northern Europe								**Europe septentrionale**
GDP at current prices	810 059	2 148 531	3 960 212	4 231 377	4 791 093	5 075 324	4 664 906	PIB aux prix courants
GDP per capita	9 791	23 129	41 271	42 574	47 421	49 986	45 708	PIB par habitant
GDP at constant prices	2 245 384	2 881 674	3 960 212	4 071 048	4 241 352	4 365 123	4 519 027	PIB aux prix constants
Growth rates	4.0	3.1	3.1	2.2	1.6	2.9	3.5	Taux de croissance
Southern Europe								**Europe méridionale**
GDP at current prices	783 494	2 120 828	3 606 117	4 304 152	4 177 804	4 213 271	3 599 558	PIB aux prix courants
GDP per capita	5 528	14 716	24 088	28 071	27 316	27 611	23 632	PIB par habitant
GDP at constant prices	2 285 942	2 824 914	3 606 117	3 657 059	3 458 487	3 479 880	3 536 544	PIB aux prix constants
Growth rates	2.5	3.0	1.9	0.6	-1.7	0.6	1.6	Taux de croissance
Western Europe								**Europe occidentale**
GDP at current prices	1 696 783	5 546 879	6 898 287	8 419 238	9 135 370	9 350 013	8 105 149	PIB aux prix courants
GDP per capita	9 796	30 374	36 777	44 338	47 633	48 588	41 989	PIB par habitant
GDP at constant prices	4 474 185	5 724 842	6 898 287	7 311 493	7 564 455	7 664 691	7 780 871	PIB aux prix constants
Growth rates	2.2	2.0	1.4	2.9	0.5	1.3	1.5	Taux de croissance
Oceania								**Océanie**
GDP at current prices	213 944	474 275	901 167	1 476 189	1 764 948	1 697 598	1 448 476	PIB aux prix courants
GDP per capita	8 673	16 479	27 250	40 863	46 576	44 133	37 107	PIB par habitant
GDP at constant prices	472 514	634 492	901 167	1 023 822	1 111 586	1 138 645	1 167 751	PIB aux prix constants
Growth rates	3.7	3.9	3.0	2.3	2.4	2.4	2.6	Taux de croissance
Australia and New Zealand								**Australie et Nouvelle-Zélande**
GDP at current prices	205 806	455 255	876 503	1 439 785	1 719 288	1 650 009	1 404 276	PIB aux prix courants
GDP per capita	10 798	20 884	35 909	54 266	61 988	58 682	49 277	PIB par habitant
GDP at constant prices	459 239	614 284	876 503	995 413	1 081 124	1 106 763	1 134 534	PIB aux prix constants
Growth rates	3.7	4.0	3.0	2.2	2.4	2.4	2.5	Taux de croissance

Gross domestic product and gross domestic product per capita *(continued)*
In millions of US dollars at current and constant 2005 prices; per capita US dollars; real rates of growth

Produit intérieur brut et produit intérieur brut par habitant *(suite)*
En millions de dollars É.-U. aux prix courants et constants de 2005; par habitant en dollars É.U.; taux de croissance réels

Region, country or area	1985	1995	2005	2010	2013	2014	2015	Région, pays ou zone
Melanesia								**Mélanésie**
GDP at current prices	5 972	13 532	17 354	28 121	37 051	38 828	36 455	PIB aux prix courants
GDP per capita	1 208	2 180	2 220	3 226	4 001	4 113	3 788	PIB par habitant
GDP at constant prices	8 809	14 439	17 354	21 306	23 258	24 502	25 671	PIB aux prix constants
Growth rates	2.2	1.2	3.5	8.2	3.1	5.4	4.8	Taux de croissance
Micronesia								**Micronésie**
GDP at current prices	260	550	707	863	1 065	1 107	1 107	PIB aux prix courants
GDP per capita	1 238	2 088	2 519	2 983	3 597	3 705	3 673	PIB par habitant
GDP at constant prices	551	686	707	702	763	766	804	PIB aux prix constants
Growth rates	2.9	4.6	2.9	1.6	2.7	0.4	5.1	Taux de croissance
Polynesia								**Polynésie**
GDP at current prices	1 906	4 937	6 603	7 421	7 543	7 654	6 639	PIB aux prix courants
GDP per capita	4 184	9 704	11 692	12 617	12 513	12 592	10 831	PIB par habitant
GDP at constant prices	3 915	5 083	6 603	6 401	6 442	6 614	6 741	PIB aux prix constants
Growth rates	5.4	0.8	1.6	-1.8	3.6	2.7	1.9	Taux de croissance
Afghanistan								**Afghanistan**
GDP at current prices	3 322	3 236	6 622	16 078	21 610	21 123	20 270	PIB aux prix courants
GDP per capita	286	193	271	575	704	668	623	PIB par habitant
GDP at constant prices	7 501	4 532	6 622	10 393	13 341	13 628	13 300	PIB aux prix constants
Growth rates	0.3	49.9	9.9	3.2	6.5	2.2	-2.4	Taux de croissance
Albania								**Albanie**
GDP at current prices	2 324	2 393	8 052	11 927	12 781	13 278	11 541	PIB aux prix courants
GDP per capita	783	770	2 612	4 110	4 433	4 595	3 984	PIB par habitant
GDP at constant prices	5 161	4 736	8 052	10 414	10 950	11 172	11 467	PIB aux prix constants
Growth rates	1.8	13.3	5.5	3.7	1.1	2.0	2.6	Taux de croissance
Algeria								**Algérie**
GDP at current prices	57 866	41 971	103 198	161 207	209 783	213 983	164 779	PIB aux prix courants
GDP per capita	2 564	1 452	3 102	4 473	5 494	5 496	4 154	PIB par habitant
GDP at constant prices	64 280	67 626	103 198	116 968	127 937	132 799	137 845	PIB aux prix constants
Growth rates	3.7	3.8	5.9	3.6	2.8	3.8	3.8	Taux de croissance
Andorra								**Andorre**
GDP at current prices	439	1 491	3 256	3 355	3 282	3 351	2 812	PIB aux prix courants
GDP per capita	9 838	23 358	40 084	39 748	43 237	46 034	39 896	PIB par habitant
GDP at constant prices	1 354	1 818	3 256	2 837	2 671	2 731	2 754	PIB aux prix constants
Growth rates	2.3	2.8	7.4	-5.4	0.4	2.3	0.8	Taux de croissance
Angola								**Angola**
GDP at current prices	9 109	6 642	36 971	83 799	136 710	145 712	117 955	PIB aux prix courants
GDP per capita	935	509	2 064	3 949	5 830	6 014	4 714	PIB par habitant
GDP at constant prices	18 070	17 732	36 971	55 017	64 852	67 506	69 536	PIB aux prix constants
Growth rates	3.5	15.0	15.0	4.7	5.0	4.1	3.0	Taux de croissance
Anguilla								**Anguilla**
GDP at current prices	27	104	229	268	282	311	320	PIB aux prix courants
GDP per capita	4 040	10 578	18 130	19 460	19 720	21 531	21 880	PIB par habitant
GDP at constant prices	55	130	229	240	233	245	252	PIB aux prix constants
Growth rates	12.9	-2.3	13.1	-4.5	-0.6	5.1	2.9	Taux de croissance
Antigua and Barbuda								**Antigua-et-Barbuda**
GDP at current prices	245	577	1 015	1 148	1 196	1 274	1 356	PIB aux prix courants
GDP per capita	3 723	8 446	12 293	13 159	13 290	14 019	14 764	PIB par habitant
GDP at constant prices	449	685	1 015	1 024	1 042	1 090	1 135	PIB aux prix constants
Growth rates	7.7	-4.4	6.3	-7.0	-0.2	4.6	4.1	Taux de croissance
Argentina								**Argentine**
GDP at current prices	95 530	279 701	201 388	428 792	615 685	570 723	632 343	PIB aux prix courants
GDP per capita	3 144	7 993	5 145	10 402	14 474	13 279	14 565	PIB par habitant
GDP at constant prices	122 446	161 125	201 388	256 328	275 420	268 374	274 740	PIB aux prix constants
Growth rates	-7.0	-2.8	8.9	10.4	2.3	-2.6	2.4	Taux de croissance
Armenia								**Arménie**
GDP at current prices	...	1 372	5 226	9 875	11 121	11 610	10 529	PIB aux prix courants
GDP per capita	...	426	1 733	3 332	3 717	3 862	3 489	PIB par habitant
GDP at constant prices	...	2 251	5 226	6 315	7 313	7 579	7 808	PIB aux prix constants
Growth rates	...	6.9	13.9	2.2	3.3	3.6	3.0	Taux de croissance
Aruba								**Aruba**
GDP at current prices	385	1 321	2 331	2 391	2 582	2 650	2 702	PIB aux prix courants
GDP per capita	6 107	16 441	23 303	23 529	25 083	25 616	26 005	PIB par habitant
GDP at constant prices	760	1 811	2 331	2 062	2 195	2 213	2 215	PIB aux prix constants
Growth rates	9.1	2.5	1.2	-3.4	4.2	0.8	0.1	Taux de croissance

13

Gross domestic product and gross domestic product per capita *(continued)*
In millions of US dollars at current and constant 2005 prices; per capita US dollars; real rates of growth

Produit intérieur brut et produit intérieur brut par habitant *(suite)*
En millions de dollars É.-U. aux prix courants et constants de 2005; par habitant en dollars É.U.; taux de croissance réels

Region, country or area	1985	1995	2005	2010	2013	2014	2015	Région, pays ou zone
Australia								**Australie**
GDP at current prices	181 698	392 103	761 783	1 293 201	1 529 747	1 451 276	1 230 859	PIB aux prix courants
GDP per capita	11 506	21 634	37 574	58 350	65 738	61 437	51 352	PIB par habitant
GDP at constant prices	390 453	532 668	761 783	871 727	948 574	969 991	993 574	PIB aux prix constants
Growth rates	4.1	3.9	3.0	2.4	2.5	2.3	2.4	Taux de croissance
Austria								**Autriche**
GDP at current prices	69 221	240 474	314 641	390 212	428 248	438 376	376 967	PIB aux prix courants
GDP per capita	9 107	30 162	38 208	46 498	50 460	51 471	44 118	PIB par habitant
GDP at constant prices	192 112	248 960	314 641	335 524	347 949	350 193	353 566	PIB aux prix constants
Growth rates	2.5	2.7	2.1	1.9	0.1	0.6	1.0	Taux de croissance
Azerbaijan								**Azerbaïdjan**
GDP at current prices	...	3 081	13 245	52 906	74 161	75 240	53 049	PIB aux prix courants
GDP per capita	...	396	1 547	5 814	7 808	7 813	5 439	PIB par habitant
GDP at constant prices	...	5 085	13 245	28 277	30 071	30 870	31 075	PIB aux prix constants
Growth rates	...	-11.8	28.0	4.6	5.9	2.7	0.7	Taux de croissance
Bahamas								**Bahamas**
GDP at current prices	2 256	4 009	7 706	7 910	8 522	8 618	8 854	PIB aux prix courants
GDP per capita	9 614	14 309	23 406	21 921	22 554	22 497	22 817	PIB par habitant
GDP at constant prices	4 942	5 540	7 706	7 617	7 901	7 859	7 729	PIB aux prix constants
Growth rates	4.8	4.4	3.4	1.5	~0.0	-0.5	-1.7	Taux de croissance
Bahrain								**Bahreïn**
GDP at current prices	4 475	6 787	15 969	25 713	32 540	33 388	31 126	PIB aux prix courants
GDP per capita	10 669	12 039	18 418	20 386	24 114	24 515	22 600	PIB par habitant
GDP at constant prices	6 462	9 882	15 969	20 928	23 338	24 353	25 050	PIB aux prix constants
Growth rates	-16.1	1.9	6.8	4.3	5.4	4.4	2.9	Taux de croissance
Bangladesh								**Bangladesh**
GDP at current prices	19 169	37 866	57 628	114 508	153 505	173 062	194 466	PIB aux prix courants
GDP per capita	206	320	403	755	977	1 088	1 208	PIB par habitant
GDP at constant prices	22 804	34 316	57 628	77 343	92 987	98 623	105 085	PIB aux prix constants
Growth rates	3.0	4.9	6.0	5.6	6.0	6.1	6.6	Taux de croissance
Barbados								**Barbade**
GDP at current prices	1 425	2 275	3 897	4 447	4 371	4 353	4 385	PIB aux prix courants
GDP per capita	5 569	8 585	14 223	15 906	15 473	15 360	15 429	PIB par habitant
GDP at constant prices	2 975	3 185	3 897	4 054	4 095	4 103	4 139	PIB aux prix constants
Growth rates	1.1	2.0	4.0	0.3	-0.1	0.2	0.9	Taux de croissance
Belarus								**Bélarus**
GDP at current prices	...	13 856	30 210	55 221	73 098	76 104	54 609	PIB aux prix courants
GDP per capita	...	1 364	3 134	5 818	7 697	8 011	5 751	PIB par habitant
GDP at constant prices	...	15 516	30 210	42 921	46 556	47 369	45 503	PIB aux prix constants
Growth rates	...	-10.4	9.4	7.7	1.0	1.7	-3.9	Taux de croissance
Belgium								**Belgique**
GDP at current prices	86 728	289 571	387 356	483 549	520 092	531 762	455 107	PIB aux prix courants
GDP per capita	8 766	28 496	36 676	44 241	46 632	47 367	40 278	PIB par habitant
GDP at constant prices	243 698	307 035	387 356	415 035	420 026	429 776	436 223	PIB aux prix constants
Growth rates	1.7	2.4	2.1	2.7	-0.7	2.3	1.5	Taux de croissance
Belize								**Belize**
GDP at current prices	209	587	1 114	1 397	1 624	1 718	1 721	PIB aux prix courants
GDP per capita	1 269	2 834	3 933	4 344	4 719	4 884	4 789	PIB par habitant
GDP at constant prices	323	639	1 114	1 261	1 357	1 409	1 426	PIB aux prix constants
Growth rates	1.0	4.2	3.0	3.3	1.5	3.9	1.2	Taux de croissance
Benin								**Bénin**
GDP at current prices	1 130	2 345	4 804	6 970	9 111	9 575	8 476	PIB aux prix courants
GDP per capita	263	392	587	733	883	903	779	PIB par habitant
GDP at constant prices	2 167	3 101	4 804	5 800	6 679	7 116	7 489	PIB aux prix constants
Growth rates	7.5	10.1	1.7	2.1	6.9	6.5	5.2	Taux de croissance
Bermuda								**Bermudes**
GDP at current prices	1 428	2 557	4 868	5 855	5 640	5 651	5 853	PIB aux prix courants
GDP per capita	24 239	40 782	74 753	91 555	89 843	90 600	94 400	PIB par habitant
GDP at constant prices	3 106	3 562	4 868	4 881	4 374	4 355	4 370	PIB aux prix constants
Growth rates	4.2	5.4	1.7	-2.5	-2.4	-0.4	0.4	Taux de croissance
Bhutan								**Bhoutan**
GDP at current prices	172	289	819	1 585	1 798	1 959	2 074	PIB aux prix courants
GDP per capita	367	568	1 258	2 201	2 383	2 561	2 677	PIB par habitant
GDP at constant prices	174	399	819	1 288	1 491	1 573	1 655	PIB aux prix constants
Growth rates	5.7	6.8	7.1	11.7	2.1	5.5	5.2	Taux de croissance

13 Gross domestic product and gross domestic product per capita *(continued)*

In millions of US dollars at current and constant 2005 prices; per capita US dollars; real rates of growth

Produit intérieur brut et produit intérieur brut par habitant *(suite)*

En millions de dollars É.-U. aux prix courants et constants de 2005; par habitant en dollars É.U.; taux de croissance réels

Region, country or area	1985	1995	2005	2010	2013	2014	2015	Région, pays ou zone
Bolivia (Plurin. State of)								**Bolivie (État plurin. de)**
GDP at current prices	4 122	6 715	9 549	19 650	30 659	32 996	32 998	PIB aux prix courants
GDP per capita	664	887	1 046	1 981	2 948	3 124	3 077	PIB par habitant
GDP at constant prices	5 064	6 925	9 549	11 954	14 119	14 890	15 611	PIB aux prix constants
Growth rates	-1.0	4.7	4.4	4.1	6.8	5.5	4.8	Taux de croissance
Bosnia and Herzegovina								**Bosnie-Herzégovine**
GDP at current prices	...	2 034	11 225	17 164	18 155	18 522	16 251	PIB aux prix courants
GDP per capita	...	524	2 928	4 475	4 748	4 852	4 265	PIB par habitant
GDP at constant prices	...	3 196	11 225	12 912	13 216	13 359	13 770	PIB aux prix constants
Growth rates	...	20.8	3.9	0.8	2.4	1.1	3.1	Taux de croissance
Botswana								**Botswana**
GDP at current prices	838	4 731	9 931	12 790	14 801	15 872	14 391	PIB aux prix courants
GDP per capita	708	3 001	5 328	6 246	6 800	7 150	6 361	PIB par habitant
GDP at constant prices	2 773	6 454	9 931	12 412	15 105	15 589	15 549	PIB aux prix constants
Growth rates	9.2	7.0	4.6	8.6	9.9	3.2	-0.3	Taux de croissance
Brazil								**Brésil**
GDP at current prices	187 426	778 053	891 634	2 208 838	2 465 786	2 417 095	1 772 591	PIB aux prix courants
GDP per capita	1 370	4 781	4 731	11 121	12 072	11 729	8 528	PIB par habitant
GDP at constant prices	554 072	703 848	891 634	1 109 705	1 210 618	1 176 157	1 130 906	PIB aux prix constants
Growth rates	7.8	4.2	3.2	7.5	3.0	-2.8	-3.8	Taux de croissance
British Virgin Islands								**Îles Vierges britanniques**
GDP at current prices	90	397	870	894	916	902	908	PIB aux prix courants
GDP per capita	6 754	21 547	37 550	32 840	31 509	30 501	30 144	PIB par habitant
GDP at constant prices	185	530	870	929	869	867	857	PIB aux prix constants
Growth rates	1.4	24.2	14.3	1.3	-0.3	-0.3	-1.1	Taux de croissance
Brunei Darussalam								**Brunéi Darussalam**
GDP at current prices	4 425	5 245	10 561	13 707	18 094	17 122	12 930	PIB aux prix courants
GDP per capita	19 841	17 780	29 184	34 851	43 971	41 022	30 553	PIB par habitant
GDP at constant prices	8 356	8 922	10 561	10 914	11 183	10 921	10 860	PIB aux prix constants
Growth rates	-1.5	4.5	0.4	2.6	-2.1	-2.3	-0.6	Taux de croissance
Bulgaria								**Bulgarie**
GDP at current prices	16 486	14 434	29 821	49 939	55 628	56 718	48 953	PIB aux prix courants
GDP per capita	1 840	1 727	3 882	6 742	7 670	7 876	6 847	PIB par habitant
GDP at constant prices	26 007	24 556	29 821	34 705	35 791	36 345	37 424	PIB aux prix constants
Growth rates	2.7	2.9	7.2	0.1	1.3	1.5	3.0	Taux de croissance
Burkina Faso								**Burkina Faso**
GDP at current prices	1 569	2 404	5 463	8 980	11 948	12 596	11 065	PIB aux prix courants
GDP per capita	203	238	407	574	699	716	611	PIB par habitant
GDP at constant prices	2 088	2 926	5 463	7 139	8 573	8 950	9 315	PIB aux prix constants
Growth rates	8.5	5.7	8.7	8.4	5.8	4.4	4.1	Taux de croissance
Burundi								**Burundi**
GDP at current prices	1 168	1 000	1 117	2 032	2 452	2 798	2 735	PIB aux prix courants
GDP per capita	245	160	141	215	234	259	245	PIB par habitant
GDP at constant prices	1 000	1 070	1 117	1 393	1 588	1 663	1 594	PIB aux prix constants
Growth rates	11.7	-7.0	0.9	5.1	4.9	4.7	-4.1	Taux de croissance
Cabo Verde								**Cabo Verde**
GDP at current prices	157	558	1 105	1 664	1 851	1 881	1 603	PIB aux prix courants
GDP per capita	499	1 434	2 331	3 394	3 649	3 661	3 080	PIB par habitant
GDP at constant prices	365	569	1 105	1 413	1 497	1 525	1 547	PIB aux prix constants
Growth rates	8.6	7.5	6.5	1.5	0.8	1.9	1.5	Taux de croissance
Cambodia								**Cambodge**
GDP at current prices	1 059	3 309	6 293	11 242	15 269	16 703	18 050	PIB aux prix courants
GDP per capita	137	309	472	783	1 013	1 090	1 159	PIB par habitant
GDP at constant prices	1 410	2 851	6 293	8 693	10 730	11 489	12 298	PIB aux prix constants
Growth rates	4.7	5.9	13.2	6.0	7.4	7.1	7.0	Taux de croissance
Cameroon								**Cameroun**
GDP at current prices	8 436	8 913	16 588	23 622	29 568	32 051	28 416	PIB aux prix courants
GDP per capita	813	640	915	1 147	1 331	1 407	1 217	PIB par habitant
GDP at constant prices	14 129	10 993	16 588	19 147	22 015	23 320	24 666	PIB aux prix constants
Growth rates	2.4	4.1	2.3	3.3	5.6	5.9	5.8	Taux de croissance
Canada								**Canada**
GDP at current prices	364 761	604 014	1 169 393	1 613 463	1 842 627	1 792 883	1 552 808	PIB aux prix courants
GDP per capita	14 112	20 615	36 253	47 279	52 302	50 379	43 206	PIB par habitant
GDP at constant prices	683 438	845 915	1 169 393	1 237 610	1 330 911	1 365 053	1 377 908	PIB aux prix constants
Growth rates	4.7	2.7	3.2	3.1	2.5	2.6	0.9	Taux de croissance

13 Gross domestic product and gross domestic product per capita *(continued)*

In millions of US dollars at current and constant 2005 prices; per capita US dollars; real rates of growth

Produit intérieur brut et produit intérieur brut par habitant *(suite)*

En millions de dollars É.-U. aux prix courants et constants de 2005; par habitant en dollars É.U.; taux de croissance réels

Region, country or area	1985	1995	2005	2010	2013	2014	2015	Région, pays ou zone
Cayman Islands								**Îles Caïmanes**
GDP at current prices	416	1 296	3 042	3 267	3 478	3 650	3 726	PIB aux prix courants
GDP per capita	21 542	40 930	62 558	58 857	59 586	61 681	62 132	PIB par habitant
GDP at constant prices	899	1 801	3 042	2 953	3 062	3 147	3 171	PIB aux prix constants
Growth rates	3.5	4.8	6.5	-2.7	1.3	2.8	0.7	Taux de croissance
Central African Republic								**République centrafricaine**
GDP at current prices	905	1 167	1 413	2 034	1 565	1 756	1 633	PIB aux prix courants
GDP per capita	344	350	348	458	332	365	333	PIB par habitant
GDP at constant prices	1 169	1 304	1 413	1 667	1 108	1 120	1 173	PIB aux prix constants
Growth rates	3.3	5.2	2.4	3.6	-36.7	1.0	4.8	Taux de croissance
Chad								**Tchad**
GDP at current prices	987	1 643	6 681	9 791	11 895	12 793	10 009	PIB aux prix courants
GDP per capita	194	235	664	823	905	942	713	PIB par habitant
GDP at constant prices	2 110	2 932	6 681	9 700	11 195	13 781	14 691	PIB aux prix constants
Growth rates	7.9	1.4	7.9	13.4	7.4	23.1	6.6	Taux de croissance
Chile								**Chili**
GDP at current prices	18 747	74 160	123 056	217 538	277 079	258 733	240 796	PIB aux prix courants
GDP per capita	1 548	5 225	7 645	12 785	15 765	14 566	13 416	PIB par habitant
GDP at constant prices	38 321	80 487	123 056	147 859	171 596	174 816	178 847	PIB aux prix constants
Growth rates	2.0	10.6	6.2	5.8	4.0	1.9	2.3	Taux de croissance
China [1]								**Chine** [1]
GDP at current prices	312 617	736 869	2 308 800	6 066 351	9 635 026	10 534 527	11 158 457	PIB aux prix courants
GDP per capita	297	600	1 768	4 524	7 072	7 693	8 109	PIB par habitant
GDP at constant prices	366 862	958 040	2 308 800	3 944 168	5 023 539	5 390 257	5 762 185	PIB aux prix constants
Growth rates	13.4	11.0	11.4	10.6	7.8	7.3	6.9	Taux de croissance
China, Hong Kong SAR								**Chine, Hong Kong RAS**
GDP at current prices	35 700	144 652	181 569	228 639	275 659	291 229	309 236	PIB aux prix courants
GDP per capita	6 593	23 542	26 536	32 693	38 479	40 298	42 431	PIB par habitant
GDP at constant prices	69 050	129 722	181 569	220 057	241 817	248 303	254 353	PIB aux prix constants
Growth rates	0.8	2.4	7.4	6.8	3.1	2.7	2.4	Taux de croissance
China, Macao SAR								**Chine, Macao RAS**
GDP at current prices	1 349	6 996	12 092	28 124	51 549	55 523	46 178	PIB aux prix courants
GDP per capita	4 553	17 558	25 830	52 604	90 747	96 075	78 586	PIB par habitant
GDP at constant prices	3 491	7 191	12 092	20 579	30 413	30 154	24 018	PIB aux prix constants
Growth rates	2.0	3.0	8.1	25.3	11.2	-0.9	-20.3	Taux de croissance
Colombia								**Colombie**
GDP at current prices	49 322	110 292	146 566	287 018	380 192	378 416	292 080	PIB aux prix courants
GDP per capita	1 590	2 946	3 386	6 251	8 031	7 918	6 056	PIB par habitant
GDP at constant prices	75 485	117 224	146 566	182 951	212 782	222 114	228 962	PIB aux prix constants
Growth rates	3.1	5.2	4.7	4.0	4.9	4.4	3.1	Taux de croissance
Comoros								**Comores**
GDP at current prices	238	480	782	995	1 186	1 227	1 079	PIB aux prix courants
GDP per capita	666	1 001	1 264	1 425	1 578	1 593	1 369	PIB par habitant
GDP at constant prices	546	644	782	935	1 110	1 151	1 206	PIB aux prix constants
Growth rates	2.0	3.6	2.8	-0.7	9.5	3.7	4.8	Taux de croissance
Congo								**Congo**
GDP at current prices	2 161	2 116	6 087	12 281	14 022	14 077	8 493	PIB aux prix courants
GDP per capita	1 037	778	1 738	3 020	3 191	3 125	1 838	PIB par habitant
GDP at constant prices	4 437	4 428	6 087	7 878	8 734	9 332	9 444	PIB aux prix constants
Growth rates	-1.2	4.0	7.6	8.7	3.3	6.8	1.2	Taux de croissance
Cook Islands								**Îles Cook**
GDP at current prices	28	106	183	255	302	318	294	PIB aux prix courants
GDP per capita	1 592	5 786	9 411	12 579	14 623	15 323	14 119	PIB par habitant
GDP at constant prices	99	143	183	181	189	200	211	PIB aux prix constants
Growth rates	8.8	-4.4	-1.1	-3.0	-1.4	6.2	5.5	Taux de croissance
Costa Rica								**Costa Rica**
GDP at current prices	4 673	10 983	19 952	37 269	49 640	49 657	52 958	PIB aux prix courants
GDP per capita	1 711	3 128	4 697	8 199	10 547	10 437	11 015	PIB par habitant
GDP at constant prices	7 953	12 987	19 952	25 173	28 080	28 911	29 970	PIB aux prix constants
Growth rates	0.7	3.9	3.9	5.0	2.0	3.0	3.7	Taux de croissance
Côte d'Ivoire								**Côte d'Ivoire**
GDP at current prices	6 978	11 105	17 085	24 884	31 264	34 163	32 076	PIB aux prix courants
GDP per capita	687	771	942	1 236	1 446	1 542	1 413	PIB par habitant
GDP at constant prices	11 659	14 519	17 085	19 064	22 040	23 921	26 187	PIB aux prix constants
Growth rates	4.5	7.1	1.7	2.0	9.2	8.5	9.5	Taux de croissance

13 Gross domestic product and gross domestic product per capita *(continued)*

In millions of US dollars at current and constant 2005 prices; per capita US dollars; real rates of growth

Produit intérieur brut et produit intérieur brut par habitant *(suite)*

En millions de dollars É.-U. aux prix courants et constants de 2005; par habitant en dollars É.U.; taux de croissance réels

Region, country or area	1985	1995	2005	2010	2013	2014	2015	Région, pays ou zone
Croatia								**Croatie**
GDP at current prices	...	22 388	45 416	59 665	57 770	57 081	48 676	PIB aux prix courants
GDP per capita	...	4 849	10 374	13 823	13 525	13 412	11 479	PIB par habitant
GDP at constant prices	...	30 834	45 416	46 492	44 865	44 644	45 377	PIB aux prix constants
Growth rates	...	6.8	4.2	-1.7	-1.1	-0.5	1.6	Taux de croissance
Cuba								**Cuba**
GDP at current prices	22 921	30 428	42 644	64 328	77 148	80 656	87 206	PIB aux prix courants
GDP per capita	2 273	2 790	3 787	5 689	6 790	7 088	7 657	PIB par habitant
GDP at constant prices	38 933	26 733	42 644	55 439	60 324	60 956	63 661	PIB aux prix constants
Growth rates	1.6	2.5	11.2	2.4	2.7	1.0	4.4	Taux de croissance
Curaçao								**Curaçao**
GDP at current prices	...	...	2 345	2 951	3 148	3 158	3 152	PIB aux prix courants
GDP per capita	...	...	18 120	19 995	20 399	20 277	20 050	PIB par habitant
GDP at constant prices	...	...	2 345	2 484	2 476	2 448	2 455	PIB aux prix constants
Growth rates	...	...	...	0.1	-0.8	-1.1	0.3	Taux de croissance
Cyprus [2]								**Chypre** [2]
GDP at current prices	2 711	9 933	18 694	25 561	24 056	23 307	19 561	PIB aux prix courants
GDP per capita	5 011	15 265	25 311	30 817	27 543	26 408	21 942	PIB par habitant
GDP at constant prices	7 189	12 952	18 694	21 168	19 341	19 045	19 365	PIB aux prix constants
Growth rates	4.7	9.9	3.7	1.3	-6.0	-1.5	1.7	Taux de croissance
Czechia								**Tchéquie**
GDP at current prices	...	59 536	135 990	207 016	209 402	207 818	185 156	PIB aux prix courants
GDP per capita	...	5 760	13 292	19 703	19 857	19 712	17 562	PIB par habitant
GDP at constant prices	...	102 694	135 990	153 349	154 421	158 614	165 808	PIB aux prix constants
Growth rates	...	6.2	6.4	2.3	-0.5	2.7	4.5	Taux de croissance
Dem. People's Rep. Korea								**Rép. pop. dém. de Corée**
GDP at current prices	12 075	4 849	13 031	13 945	16 565	17 396	16 283	PIB aux prix courants
GDP per capita	722	222	548	570	666	696	648	PIB par habitant
GDP at constant prices	15 015	12 063	13 031	12 958	13 375	13 514	13 360	PIB aux prix constants
Growth rates	3.7	-4.4	3.8	-0.5	1.1	1.0	-1.1	Taux de croissance
Dem. Rep. of the Congo								**Rép. dém. du Congo**
GDP at current prices	7 524	8 947	11 965	21 672	32 672	35 909	37 569	PIB aux prix courants
GDP per capita	251	212	213	329	450	480	486	PIB par habitant
GDP at constant prices	17 720	12 119	11 965	15 669	19 455	21 297	22 784	PIB aux prix constants
Growth rates	0.5	0.7	6.1	7.1	8.5	9.5	7.0	Taux de croissance
Denmark								**Danemark**
GDP at current prices	62 659	185 008	264 467	321 995	343 584	352 297	301 308	PIB aux prix courants
GDP per capita	12 254	35 357	48 815	58 007	61 089	62 388	53 149	PIB par habitant
GDP at constant prices	177 084	213 383	264 467	267 266	273 986	278 578	283 052	PIB aux prix constants
Growth rates	4.0	3.0	2.3	1.9	0.9	1.7	1.6	Taux de croissance
Djibouti								**Djibouti**
GDP at current prices	369	510	709	1 067	1 393	1 589	1 737	PIB aux prix courants
GDP per capita	872	771	910	1 284	1 611	1 814	1 956	PIB par habitant
GDP at constant prices	519	602	709	961	1 105	1 171	1 247	PIB aux prix constants
Growth rates	-0.2	5.6	3.2	3.5	5.0	6.0	6.5	Taux de croissance
Dominica								**Dominique**
GDP at current prices	117	260	370	494	509	523	512	PIB aux prix courants
GDP per capita	1 587	3 639	5 251	6 939	7 073	7 234	7 051	PIB par habitant
GDP at constant prices	218	309	370	443	455	474	466	PIB aux prix constants
Growth rates	1.3	2.0	-0.3	1.2	3.9	4.2	-1.8	Taux de croissance
Dominican Republic								**République dominicaine**
GDP at current prices	5 618	15 747	35 510	53 043	61 198	63 969	67 103	PIB aux prix courants
GDP per capita	866	1 995	3 844	5 359	5 952	6 147	6 374	PIB par habitant
GDP at constant prices	14 371	21 389	35 510	48 067	53 145	57 047	61 013	PIB aux prix constants
Growth rates	-2.1	5.5	9.3	8.3	4.8	7.3	7.0	Taux de croissance
Ecuador								**Équateur**
GDP at current prices	17 141	24 421	41 507	69 555	95 130	102 292	100 177	PIB aux prix courants
GDP per capita	1 895	2 135	3 022	4 657	6 074	6 432	6 205	PIB par habitant
GDP at constant prices	23 423	31 032	41 507	49 036	58 642	60 984	61 080	PIB aux prix constants
Growth rates	3.9	2.3	5.3	3.5	4.9	4.0	0.2	Taux de croissance
Egypt								**Égypte**
GDP at current prices	23 801	65 758	94 456	214 630	268 367	296 979	315 917	PIB aux prix courants
GDP per capita	482	1 053	1 260	2 616	3 063	3 315	3 452	PIB par habitant
GDP at constant prices	37 503	61 117	94 456	127 460	135 392	138 410	144 229	PIB aux prix constants
Growth rates	6.8	4.6	4.5	5.1	2.1	2.2	4.2	Taux de croissance

13 Gross domestic product and gross domestic product per capita *(continued)*

In millions of US dollars at current and constant 2005 prices; per capita US dollars; real rates of growth

Produit intérieur brut et produit intérieur brut par habitant *(suite)*

En millions de dollars É.-U. aux prix courants et constants de 2005; par habitant en dollars É.U.; taux de croissance réels

Region, country or area	1985	1995	2005	2010	2013	2014	2015	Région, pays ou zone
El Salvador								**El Salvador**
GDP at current prices	1 886	9 501	17 094	21 418	24 351	25 054	25 850	PIB aux prix courants
GDP per capita	383	1 700	2 874	3 547	3 999	4 102	4 219	PIB par habitant
GDP at constant prices	8 842	13 093	17 094	18 341	19 453	19 731	20 215	PIB aux prix constants
Growth rates	2.0	6.4	3.6	1.4	1.8	1.4	2.5	Taux de croissance
Equatorial Guinea								**Guinée équatoriale**
GDP at current prices	88	215	8 520	16 299	21 943	21 504	13 812	PIB aux prix courants
GDP per capita	281	480	13 613	22 366	27 529	26 196	16 344	PIB par habitant
GDP at constant prices	396	639	8 520	11 245	12 438	12 376	11 456	PIB aux prix constants
Growth rates	12.9	11.7	8.9	-8.9	-4.1	-0.5	-7.4	Taux de croissance
Eritrea								**Érythrée**
GDP at current prices	...	640	1 098	2 117	3 502	4 052	4 783	PIB aux prix courants
GDP per capita	...	202	262	451	701	793	915	PIB par habitant
GDP at constant prices	...	920	1 098	1 057	1 266	1 330	1 393	PIB aux prix constants
Growth rates	...	20.9	1.5	2.2	3.1	5.0	4.8	Taux de croissance
Estonia								**Estonie**
GDP at current prices	...	4 423	14 003	19 503	25 081	26 214	22 460	PIB aux prix courants
GDP per capita	...	3 086	10 330	14 641	19 000	19 916	17 112	PIB par habitant
GDP at constant prices	...	7 398	14 003	13 748	15 648	16 090	16 322	PIB aux prix constants
Growth rates	...	4.3	9.4	2.4	1.4	2.8	1.4	Taux de croissance
Ethiopia								**Éthiopie**
GDP at current prices	...	7 587	12 164	26 311	46 749	54 326	59 917	PIB aux prix courants
GDP per capita	...	133	159	300	494	560	603	PIB par habitant
GDP at constant prices	...	7 125	12 164	20 386	27 714	30 563	33 499	PIB aux prix constants
Growth rates	...	6.1	11.8	12.6	10.6	10.3	9.6	Taux de croissance
Fiji								**Fidji**
GDP at current prices	1 143	1 993	2 981	3 141	4 190	4 470	4 391	PIB aux prix courants
GDP per capita	1 606	2 571	3 627	3 652	4 759	5 042	4 922	PIB par habitant
GDP at constant prices	1 722	2 381	2 981	3 090	3 372	3 560	3 688	PIB aux prix constants
Growth rates	-3.9	2.5	0.7	3.1	4.7	5.6	3.6	Taux de croissance
Finland								**Finlande**
GDP at current prices	55 914	134 196	204 431	247 800	269 980	272 463	231 960	PIB aux prix courants
GDP per capita	11 406	26 271	38 966	46 165	49 510	49 723	42 148	PIB par habitant
GDP at constant prices	121 263	140 425	204 431	212 913	213 640	212 127	212 573	PIB aux prix constants
Growth rates	3.5	4.2	2.8	3.0	-0.8	-0.7	0.2	Taux de croissance
France [3]								**France** [3]
GDP at current prices	555 202	1 609 794	2 203 624	2 646 837	2 808 511	2 839 162	2 418 946	PIB aux prix courants
GDP per capita	9 775	26 859	34 833	40 667	42 531	42 801	36 304	PIB par habitant
GDP at constant prices	1 397 266	1 758 875	2 203 624	2 289 830	2 355 206	2 370 199	2 400 400	PIB aux prix constants
Growth rates	1.6	2.1	1.6	2.0	0.6	0.6	1.3	Taux de croissance
French Polynesia								**Polynésie française**
GDP at current prices	1 716	4 421	5 703	6 081	5 959	6 039	5 135	PIB aux prix courants
GDP per capita	9 795	20 542	22 374	22 684	21 532	21 586	18 161	PIB par habitant
GDP at constant prices	3 372	4 435	5 703	5 466	5 488	5 634	5 725	PIB aux prix constants
Growth rates	5.4	0.5	1.4	-2.5	4.4	2.7	1.6	Taux de croissance
Gabon								**Gabon**
GDP at current prices	4 639	5 519	9 579	12 882	17 027	17 412	13 735	PIB aux prix courants
GDP per capita	5 589	5 080	6 952	8 354	10 317	10 317	7 961	PIB par habitant
GDP at constant prices	7 428	9 170	9 579	10 123	12 056	12 659	13 147	PIB aux prix constants
Growth rates	-2.3	5.0	1.1	6.8	5.6	5.0	3.9	Taux de croissance
Gambia								**Gambie**
GDP at current prices	654	786	624	952	904	849	942	PIB aux prix courants
GDP per capita	894	738	433	563	484	440	473	PIB par habitant
GDP at constant prices	328	431	624	784	832	840	879	PIB aux prix constants
Growth rates	3.4	0.9	-0.9	6.5	4.8	0.9	4.7	Taux de croissance
Georgia								**Géorgie**
GDP at current prices	...	2 703	6 411	11 638	16 141	16 510	13 965	PIB aux prix courants
GDP per capita	...	534	1 433	2 738	3 953	4 092	3 491	PIB par habitant
GDP at constant prices	...	3 390	6 411	8 280	9 762	10 213	10 496	PIB aux prix constants
Growth rates	...	2.6	9.6	6.2	3.4	4.6	2.8	Taux de croissance
Germany								**Allemagne**
GDP at current prices	729 751	2 591 447	2 861 339	3 417 095	3 752 514	3 879 277	3 363 600	PIB aux prix courants
GDP per capita	9 408	31 753	35 218	42 483	46 577	48 102	41 686	PIB par habitant
GDP at constant prices	1 944 168	2 529 418	2 861 339	3 042 359	3 184 742	3 235 549	3 291 225	PIB aux prix constants
Growth rates	2.3	1.7	0.7	4.1	0.5	1.6	1.7	Taux de croissance

Gross domestic product and gross domestic product per capita *(continued)*

In millions of US dollars at current and constant 2005 prices; per capita US dollars; real rates of growth

Produit intérieur brut et produit intérieur brut par habitant *(suite)*

En millions de dollars É.-U. aux prix courants et constants de 2005; par habitant en dollars É.U.; taux de croissance réels

Region, country or area	1985	1995	2005	2010	2013	2014	2015	Région, pays ou zone
Ghana								**Ghana**
GDP at current prices	6 605	10 361	17 199	32 174	47 806	37 418	37 156	PIB aux prix courants
GDP per capita	519	618	804	1 323	1 827	1 397	1 356	PIB par habitant
GDP at constant prices	6 895	10 740	17 199	23 169	30 990	32 226	33 477	PIB aux prix constants
Growth rates	5.1	4.0	6.2	7.9	7.3	4.0	3.9	Taux de croissance
Greece								**Grèce**
GDP at current prices	47 816	136 886	247 777	299 362	239 862	236 080	194 860	PIB aux prix courants
GDP per capita	4 826	12 864	22 383	26 782	21 697	21 460	17 788	PIB par habitant
GDP at constant prices	151 310	171 209	247 777	243 731	198 649	199 350	198 913	PIB aux prix constants
Growth rates	2.5	2.1	0.6	-5.5	-3.2	0.4	-0.2	Taux de croissance
Greenland								**Groenland**
GDP at current prices	406	1 189	1 650	2 287	2 419	2 441	2 078	PIB aux prix courants
GDP per capita	7 632	21 298	28 969	40 450	42 994	43 430	36 977	PIB par habitant
GDP at constant prices	1 140	1 267	1 650	1 868	1 874	1 844	1 849	PIB aux prix constants
Growth rates	3.7	3.7	3.7	2.5	-1.3	-1.6	0.3	Taux de croissance
Grenada								**Grenade**
GDP at current prices	137	280	701	777	848	884	954	PIB aux prix courants
GDP per capita	1 368	2 793	6 804	7 418	8 011	8 313	8 934	PIB par habitant
GDP at constant prices	282	408	701	669	680	697	740	PIB aux prix constants
Growth rates	8.1	2.1	13.3	-0.5	2.2	2.4	6.2	Taux de croissance
Guatemala								**Guatemala**
GDP at current prices	9 967	13 066	27 211	41 338	53 851	58 722	63 794	PIB aux prix courants
GDP per capita	1 228	1 261	2 064	2 806	3 432	3 667	3 903	PIB par habitant
GDP at constant prices	13 566	19 313	27 211	32 557	36 210	37 722	39 287	PIB aux prix constants
Growth rates	-0.6	5.0	3.3	2.9	3.7	4.2	4.1	Taux de croissance
Guinea								**Guinée**
GDP at current prices	2 848	5 260	4 063	6 853	8 123	8 876	8 875	PIB aux prix courants
GDP per capita	561	669	420	622	680	723	704	PIB par habitant
GDP at constant prices	1 958	2 882	4 063	4 669	5 484	5 544	5 552	PIB aux prix constants
Growth rates	5.0	4.7	3.0	4.2	4.4	1.1	0.1	Taux de croissance
Guinea-Bissau								**Guinée-Bissau**
GDP at current prices	415	800	587	849	1 046	1 027	978	PIB aux prix courants
GDP per capita	440	677	401	520	595	570	530	PIB par habitant
GDP at constant prices	374	525	587	692	759	760	797	PIB aux prix constants
Growth rates	4.3	4.0	4.3	4.6	3.3	0.2	4.8	Taux de croissance
Guyana								**Guyana**
GDP at current prices	737	991	1 315	2 259	2 990	3 077	3 282	PIB aux prix courants
GDP per capita	963	1 364	1 772	2 999	3 929	4 028	4 279	PIB par habitant
GDP at constant prices	888	1 110	1 315	1 628	1 891	1 963	2 024	PIB aux prix constants
Growth rates	2.4	5.0	-2.0	4.4	5.2	3.8	3.1	Taux de croissance
Haiti								**Haïti**
GDP at current prices	2 665	2 696	4 154	6 708	8 387	8 661	8 501	PIB aux prix courants
GDP per capita	417	345	448	671	804	819	794	PIB par habitant
GDP at constant prices	4 275	3 771	4 154	4 313	4 881	5 017	5 100	PIB aux prix constants
Growth rates	0.6	9.9	1.8	-5.5	4.2	2.8	1.7	Taux de croissance
Honduras								**Honduras**
GDP at current prices	4 342	4 724	9 757	15 839	18 511	19 497	20 365	PIB aux prix courants
GDP per capita	1 025	845	1 418	2 111	2 358	2 449	2 522	PIB par habitant
GDP at constant prices	4 822	6 695	9 757	11 648	12 945	13 345	13 830	PIB aux prix constants
Growth rates	4.2	4.1	6.1	3.7	2.8	3.1	3.6	Taux de croissance
Hungary								**Hongrie**
GDP at current prices	23 597	46 301	112 589	130 256	134 680	139 295	121 715	PIB aux prix courants
GDP per capita	2 232	4 473	11 152	13 007	13 570	14 085	12 351	PIB par habitant
GDP at constant prices	86 319	78 786	112 589	111 471	113 955	118 567	122 300	PIB aux prix constants
Growth rates	-0.3	1.5	4.4	0.7	2.1	4.0	3.1	Taux de croissance
Iceland								**Islande**
GDP at current prices	3 008	7 182	16 691	13 255	15 479	17 180	16 780	PIB aux prix courants
GDP per capita	12 462	26 852	56 248	41 676	47 571	52 486	50 936	PIB par habitant
GDP at constant prices	8 977	10 633	16 691	17 460	18 819	19 181	19 981	PIB aux prix constants
Growth rates	3.3	0.1	6.7	-3.6	4.4	1.9	4.2	Taux de croissance
India								**Inde**
GDP at current prices	219 581	358 024	812 059	1 650 635	1 923 751	2 046 257	2 116 239	PIB aux prix courants
GDP per capita	281	373	710	1 341	1 504	1 580	1 614	PIB par habitant
GDP at constant prices	250 308	437 551	812 059	1 210 644	1 454 071	1 559 396	1 677 339	PIB aux prix constants
Growth rates	5.5	7.6	9.3	10.3	6.6	7.2	7.6	Taux de croissance

13 Gross domestic product and gross domestic product per capita *(continued)*

In millions of US dollars at current and constant 2005 prices; per capita US dollars; real rates of growth

Produit intérieur brut et produit intérieur brut par habitant *(suite)*

En millions de dollars É.-U. aux prix courants et constants de 2005; par habitant en dollars É.U.; taux de croissance réels

Region, country or area	1985	1995	2005	2010	2013	2014	2015	Région, pays ou zone
Indonesia								**Indonésie**
GDP at current prices	102 171	236 456	304 372	755 094	912 524	890 487	861 934	PIB aux prix courants
GDP per capita	617	1 195	1 345	3 125	3 632	3 500	3 346	PIB par habitant
GDP at constant prices	114 371	232 971	304 372	402 359	478 114	502 134	526 206	PIB aux prix constants
Growth rates	2.5	8.2	5.7	6.2	5.6	5.0	4.8	Taux de croissance
Iran (Islamic Republic of)								**Iran (Rép. islamique d')**
GDP at current prices	76 257	114 364	219 846	467 790	511 621	425 326	398 563	PIB aux prix courants
GDP per capita	1 613	1 896	3 135	6 300	6 631	5 443	5 038	PIB par habitant
GDP at constant prices	120 226	141 577	219 846	279 059	265 221	276 740	277 792	PIB aux prix constants
Growth rates	1.9	2.4	4.2	6.6	-1.9	4.3	0.4	Taux de croissance
Iraq								**Iraq**
GDP at current prices	12 074	3 477	36 268	117 138	207 124	192 772	164 234	PIB aux prix courants
GDP per capita	775	172	1 342	3 795	6 073	5 465	4 509	PIB par habitant
GDP at constant prices	20 184	12 059	36 268	48 218	75 414	74 932	73 104	PIB aux prix constants
Growth rates	-~0.0	-18.3	4.4	5.5	26.0	-0.6	-2.4	Taux de croissance
Ireland								**Irlande**
GDP at current prices	21 291	69 210	211 680	221 343	239 271	256 271	283 716	PIB aux prix courants
GDP per capita	5 980	18 986	50 356	47 938	51 222	54 815	60 514	PIB par habitant
GDP at constant prices	64 237	101 394	211 680	216 595	216 472	234 790	296 484	PIB aux prix constants
Growth rates	3.1	9.6	5.8	2.0	1.1	8.5	26.3	Taux de croissance
Israel								**Israël**
GDP at current prices	27 672	100 279	142 462	233 756	293 318	308 767	299 413	PIB aux prix courants
GDP per capita	6 778	18 808	21 573	31 502	37 519	38 890	37 129	PIB par habitant
GDP at constant prices	57 901	99 530	142 462	176 500	198 160	204 428	209 555	PIB aux prix constants
Growth rates	4.0	6.8	4.2	5.7	4.4	3.2	2.5	Taux de croissance
Italy								**Italie**
GDP at current prices	450 706	1 170 824	1 852 616	2 125 058	2 130 491	2 149 814	1 821 580	PIB aux prix courants
GDP per capita	7 920	20 498	31 584	35 663	35 644	35 957	30 462	PIB par habitant
GDP at constant prices	1 287 287	1 601 566	1 852 616	1 823 726	1 751 729	1 753 339	1 766 169	PIB aux prix constants
Growth rates	2.8	2.9	0.9	1.7	-1.7	0.1	0.7	Taux de croissance
Jamaica								**Jamaïque**
GDP at current prices	2 380	6 544	11 244	13 220	14 277	13 898	14 262	PIB aux prix courants
GDP per capita	1 029	2 629	4 199	4 823	5 148	4 993	5 106	PIB par habitant
GDP at constant prices	7 101	10 430	11 244	10 974	11 150	11 227	11 339	PIB aux prix constants
Growth rates	-4.6	1.0	0.9	-1.5	0.5	0.7	1.0	Taux de croissance
Japan								**Japon**
GDP at current prices	1 400 715	5 449 118	4 755 410	5 700 098	5 155 717	4 848 733	4 383 076	PIB aux prix courants
GDP per capita	11 674	43 774	37 450	44 770	40 601	38 241	34 629	PIB par habitant
GDP at constant prices	3 076 677	4 245 270	4 755 410	4 778 705	4 941 463	4 958 050	5 018 510	PIB aux prix constants
Growth rates	6.3	2.7	1.7	4.2	2.0	0.3	1.2	Taux de croissance
Jordan								**Jordanie**
GDP at current prices	5 119	6 732	12 589	26 425	33 594	35 827	37 517	PIB aux prix courants
GDP per capita	1 840	1 558	2 361	4 054	4 656	4 831	4 940	PIB par habitant
GDP at constant prices	5 982	7 894	12 589	17 034	18 445	19 016	19 469	PIB aux prix constants
Growth rates	-2.7	6.2	8.1	2.3	2.8	3.1	2.4	Taux de croissance
Kazakhstan								**Kazakhstan**
GDP at current prices	...	20 555	57 124	148 047	236 635	221 416	181 754	PIB aux prix courants
GDP per capita	...	1 291	3 697	9 077	13 839	12 746	10 312	PIB par habitant
GDP at constant prices	...	30 850	57 124	77 245	92 160	96 031	97 183	PIB aux prix constants
Growth rates	...	-8.2	9.7	7.3	6.0	4.2	1.2	Taux de croissance
Kenya								**Kenya**
GDP at current prices	9 110	13 428	21 506	40 000	55 101	61 395	63 399	PIB aux prix courants
GDP per capita	463	491	608	992	1 261	1 368	1 377	PIB par habitant
GDP at constant prices	11 339	16 134	21 506	27 424	32 158	33 873	35 786	PIB aux prix constants
Growth rates	4.3	4.4	5.9	8.4	5.7	5.3	5.6	Taux de croissance
Kiribati								**Kiribati**
GDP at current prices	30	56	112	153	187	186	162	PIB aux prix courants
GDP per capita	468	720	1 215	1 493	1 724	1 684	1 443	PIB par habitant
GDP at constant prices	76	89	112	109	122	125	130	PIB aux prix constants
Growth rates	-4.6	-0.6	5.0	-1.6	5.8	2.4	3.7	Taux de croissance
Kosovo								**Kosovo**
GDP at current prices	...	5 304	3 680	5 830	7 072	7 387	6 440	PIB aux prix courants
GDP per capita	...	2 351	2 108	3 298	3 985	4 183	3 665	PIB par habitant
GDP at constant prices	...	3 417	3 680	4 729	5 249	5 314	5 531	PIB aux prix constants
Growth rates	...	8.1	3.9	3.3	3.4	1.2	4.1	Taux de croissance

Gross domestic product and gross domestic product per capita *(continued)*

In millions of US dollars at current and constant 2005 prices; per capita US dollars; real rates of growth

Produit intérieur brut et produit intérieur brut par habitant *(suite)*

En millions de dollars É.-U. aux prix courants et constants de 2005; par habitant en dollars É.U.; taux de croissance réels

Region, country or area	1985	1995	2005	2010	2013	2014	2015	Région, pays ou zone
Kuwait								**Koweït**
GDP at current prices	21 446	26 554	80 798	115 416	174 168	162 656	114 054	PIB aux prix courants
GDP per capita	12 359	16 221	35 694	37 724	48 465	43 339	29 304	PIB par habitant
GDP at constant prices	31 211	48 626	80 798	85 603	101 214	101 721	103 599	PIB aux prix constants
Growth rates	-4.3	1.4	10.6	-2.4	1.1	0.5	1.8	Taux de croissance
Kyrgyzstan								**Kirghizistan**
GDP at current prices	...	1 492	2 460	4 794	7 335	7 468	6 572	PIB aux prix courants
GDP per capita	...	325	481	877	1 277	1 278	1 106	PIB par habitant
GDP at constant prices	...	1 555	2 460	3 056	3 576	3 720	3 849	PIB aux prix constants
Growth rates	...	-5.4	-0.2	-0.5	10.5	4.0	3.5	Taux de croissance
Lao People's Dem. Rep.								**Rép. dém. populaire lao**
GDP at current prices	601	1 708	2 717	6 744	10 760	11 853	12 585	PIB aux prix courants
GDP per capita	163	352	473	1 077	1 635	1 772	1 850	PIB par habitant
GDP at constant prices	889	1 482	2 717	3 988	5 020	5 399	5 808	PIB aux prix constants
Growth rates	5.1	7.0	6.8	8.1	8.0	7.6	7.6	Taux de croissance
Latvia								**Lettonie**
GDP at current prices	...	5 407	16 922	23 765	30 234	31 321	27 004	PIB aux prix courants
GDP per capita	...	2 173	7 597	11 368	15 028	15 744	13 704	PIB par habitant
GDP at constant prices	...	8 880	16 922	16 539	18 798	19 193	19 719	PIB aux prix constants
Growth rates	...	-0.8	10.7	-3.8	2.9	2.1	2.7	Taux de croissance
Lebanon								**Liban**
GDP at current prices	2 275	11 506	21 490	38 420	47 221	48 688	50 149	PIB aux prix courants
GDP per capita	850	3 793	5 390	8 858	8 931	8 676	8 571	PIB par habitant
GDP at constant prices	16 152	16 338	21 490	31 042	33 162	33 762	34 272	PIB aux prix constants
Growth rates	24.3	6.5	2.7	8.0	3.0	1.8	1.5	Taux de croissance
Lesotho								**Lesotho**
GDP at current prices	248	859	1 368	2 187	2 218	2 181	2 008	PIB aux prix courants
GDP per capita	169	490	711	1 088	1 065	1 034	941	PIB par habitant
GDP at constant prices	621	979	1 368	1 763	2 012	2 085	2 143	PIB aux prix constants
Growth rates	3.4	2.0	2.7	7.9	4.5	3.6	2.8	Taux de croissance
Liberia								**Libéria**
GDP at current prices	881	171	608	1 074	1 947	2 013	2 053	PIB aux prix courants
GDP per capita	401	82	186	271	453	458	456	PIB par habitant
GDP at constant prices	802	117	608	1 099	1 359	1 368	1 372	PIB aux prix constants
Growth rates	-2.0	-4.3	9.5	10.8	8.1	0.7	0.3	Taux de croissance
Libya								**Libye**
GDP at current prices	29 887	28 292	45 451	80 942	76 618	48 094	34 457	PIB aux prix courants
GDP per capita	7 782	5 800	7 834	12 918	12 228	7 684	5 488	PIB par habitant
GDP at constant prices	33 739	32 935	45 451	60 501	25 208	19 158	17 204	PIB aux prix constants
Growth rates	8.3	-2.2	10.3	4.3	-52.1	-24.0	-10.2	Taux de croissance
Liechtenstein								**Liechtenstein**
GDP at current prices	591	2 713	4 087	5 678	6 392	6 664	6 361	PIB aux prix courants
GDP per capita	21 685	88 001	117 279	156 533	172 562	178 723	169 492	PIB par habitant
GDP at constant prices	1 747	2 789	4 087	4 552	4 585	4 726	4 793	PIB aux prix constants
Growth rates	7.0	5.9	4.8	7.4	3.9	3.1	1.4	Taux de croissance
Lithuania								**Lituanie**
GDP at current prices	...	6 702	26 141	37 130	46 465	48 586	41 402	PIB aux prix courants
GDP per capita	...	1 847	7 819	11 890	15 677	16 657	14 384	PIB par habitant
GDP at constant prices	...	14 422	26 141	27 715	31 589	32 693	33 275	PIB aux prix constants
Growth rates	...	3.3	7.7	1.6	3.5	3.5	1.8	Taux de croissance
Luxembourg								**Luxembourg**
GDP at current prices	4 725	21 528	36 976	52 906	61 544	65 372	56 802	PIB aux prix courants
GDP per capita	12 879	52 745	80 762	104 169	112 949	117 454	100 161	PIB par habitant
GDP at constant prices	13 142	22 875	36 976	41 811	44 444	46 535	48 179	PIB aux prix constants
Growth rates	2.8	1.4	3.2	5.8	4.2	4.7	3.5	Taux de croissance
Madagascar								**Madagascar**
GDP at current prices	2 858	3 160	5 039	8 730	10 602	10 674	9 739	PIB aux prix courants
GDP per capita	286	235	275	414	462	453	402	PIB par habitant
GDP at constant prices	3 312	3 730	5 039	5 796	6 195	6 400	6 596	PIB aux prix constants
Growth rates	1.2	1.7	4.6	0.4	2.3	3.3	3.1	Taux de croissance
Malawi								**Malawi**
GDP at current prices	2 028	2 474	3 656	6 960	5 146	5 965	6 420	PIB aux prix courants
GDP per capita	281	252	287	471	318	357	373	PIB par habitant
GDP at constant prices	2 276	2 744	3 656	5 228	5 876	6 211	6 394	PIB aux prix constants
Growth rates	4.7	9.0	3.3	6.9	5.2	5.7	3.0	Taux de croissance

13 Gross domestic product and gross domestic product per capita *(continued)*

In millions of US dollars at current and constant 2005 prices; per capita US dollars; real rates of growth

Produit intérieur brut et produit intérieur brut par habitant *(suite)*

En millions de dollars É.-U. aux prix courants et constants de 2005; par habitant en dollars É.U.; taux de croissance réels

Region, country or area	1985	1995	2005	2010	2013	2014	2015	Région, pays ou zone
Malaysia								**Malaisie**
GDP at current prices	31 200	88 833	143 534	255 018	323 276	338 073	296 284	PIB aux prix courants
GDP per capita	1 979	4 286	5 564	9 069	10 971	11 306	9 768	PIB par habitant
GDP at constant prices	41 539	90 111	143 534	178 674	207 743	220 234	231 175	PIB aux prix constants
Growth rates	-1.1	9.8	5.3	7.4	4.7	6.0	5.0	Taux de croissance
Maldives								**Maldives**
GDP at current prices	165	562	1 120	2 323	2 795	3 094	3 435	PIB aux prix courants
GDP per capita	869	2 211	3 672	6 986	7 961	8 657	9 446	PIB par habitant
GDP at constant prices	253	577	1 120	1 691	1 973	2 091	2 150	PIB aux prix constants
Growth rates	13.0	7.1	-8.1	7.2	4.7	6.0	2.8	Taux de croissance
Mali								**Mali**
GDP at current prices	1 377	3 168	6 245	10 679	13 246	14 388	13 100	PIB aux prix courants
GDP per capita	176	329	485	704	798	842	744	PIB par habitant
GDP at constant prices	2 273	3 364	6 245	10 328	13 245	14 276	15 363	PIB aux prix constants
Growth rates	8.5	0.9	10.4	10.9	7.0	7.8	7.6	Taux de croissance
Malta								**Malte**
GDP at current prices	1 156	3 697	6 393	8 741	10 185	10 737	9 747	PIB aux prix courants
GDP per capita	3 417	9 929	16 100	21 212	24 440	25 704	23 281	PIB par habitant
GDP at constant prices	2 554	4 496	6 393	7 066	7 730	7 998	8 490	PIB aux prix constants
Growth rates	2.6	6.3	3.8	3.5	4.5	3.5	6.2	Taux de croissance
Marshall Islands								**Îles Marshall**
GDP at current prices	44	121	138	164	190	187	183	PIB aux prix courants
GDP per capita	1 155	2 378	2 647	3 124	3 603	3 530	3 453	PIB par habitant
GDP at constant prices	75	145	138	149	160	158	159	PIB aux prix constants
Growth rates	-6.3	8.2	2.6	6.2	1.9	-1.1	0.6	Taux de croissance
Mauritania								**Mauritanie**
GDP at current prices	1 085	1 681	2 184	4 338	5 923	5 694	5 023	PIB aux prix courants
GDP per capita	614	720	693	1 208	1 529	1 434	1 235	PIB par habitant
GDP at constant prices	1 145	1 504	2 184	2 798	3 271	3 488	3 531	PIB aux prix constants
Growth rates	3.4	-2.4	9.0	4.8	5.7	6.6	1.2	Taux de croissance
Mauritius								**Maurice**
GDP at current prices	1 103	4 092	6 489	9 718	11 932	12 613	11 511	PIB aux prix courants
GDP per capita	1 086	3 625	5 310	7 787	9 443	9 943	9 041	PIB par habitant
GDP at constant prices	2 293	4 193	6 489	8 155	9 024	9 352	9 679	PIB aux prix constants
Growth rates	6.9	4.4	1.8	4.1	3.2	3.6	3.5	Taux de croissance
Mexico								**Mexique**
GDP at current prices	219 661	319 551	864 810	1 049 925	1 258 775	1 294 695	1 140 724	PIB aux prix courants
GDP per capita	2 841	3 384	7 880	8 851	10 173	10 326	8 981	PIB par habitant
GDP at constant prices	515 589	604 407	864 810	952 038	1 043 670	1 066 952	1 093 252	PIB aux prix constants
Growth rates	2.8	-6.2	3.1	5.2	1.4	2.2	2.5	Taux de croissance
Micronesia (Fed. States of)								**Micronésie (États féd. de)**
GDP at current prices	108	222	251	297	316	318	315	PIB aux prix courants
GDP per capita	1 262	2 063	2 360	2 867	3 049	3 057	3 015	PIB par habitant
GDP at constant prices	160	245	251	251	242	236	244	PIB aux prix constants
Growth rates	16.6	4.6	2.1	3.3	-3.0	-2.4	3.7	Taux de croissance
Monaco								**Monaco**
GDP at current prices	1 059	3 070	4 203	5 362	6 554	7 060	6 258	PIB aux prix courants
GDP per capita	36 723	100 012	124 319	145 538	174 636	187 650	165 871	PIB par habitant
GDP at constant prices	2 665	3 355	4 203	4 609	5 461	5 854	6 170	PIB aux prix constants
Growth rates	1.6	2.1	1.6	2.2	9.6	7.2	5.4	Taux de croissance
Mongolia								**Mongolie**
GDP at current prices	1 218	1 678	2 926	7 189	12 582	12 227	11 758	PIB aux prix courants
GDP per capita	634	730	1 158	2 650	4 401	4 202	3 973	PIB par habitant
GDP at constant prices	1 774	1 859	2 926	4 005	5 891	6 355	6 501	PIB aux prix constants
Growth rates	5.7	6.3	7.3	6.4	11.6	7.9	2.3	Taux de croissance
Montenegro								**Monténégro**
GDP at current prices	...	1 215	2 272	4 139	4 465	4 588	4 020	PIB aux prix courants
GDP per capita	...	1 958	3 686	6 655	7 147	7 337	6 424	PIB par habitant
GDP at constant prices	...	1 324	2 272	2 821	2 933	2 986	3 119	PIB aux prix constants
Growth rates	...	14.3	4.2	2.5	3.5	1.8	4.5	Taux de croissance
Montserrat								**Montserrat**
GDP at current prices	44	69	49	56	59	59	59	PIB aux prix courants
GDP per capita	3 850	6 729	10 231	11 208	11 749	11 579	11 553	PIB par habitant
GDP at constant prices	92	103	49	51	58	59	60	PIB aux prix constants
Growth rates	5.9	-8.8	3.1	-2.8	5.1	2.0	0.4	Taux de croissance

13 Gross domestic product and gross domestic product per capita *(continued)*

In millions of US dollars at current and constant 2005 prices; per capita US dollars; real rates of growth

Produit intérieur brut et produit intérieur brut par habitant *(suite)*

En millions de dollars É.-U. aux prix courants et constants de 2005; par habitant en dollars É.U.; taux de croissance réels

Region, country or area	1985	1995	2005	2010	2013	2014	2015	Région, pays ou zone
Morocco [4]								**Maroc** [4]
GDP at current prices	15 111	38 728	62 545	93 217	107 235	110 009	100 359	PIB aux prix courants
GDP per capita	669	1 426	2 058	2 903	3 206	3 243	2 919	PIB par habitant
GDP at constant prices	31 288	40 658	62 545	79 350	90 091	92 269	96 329	PIB aux prix constants
Growth rates	6.3	-6.6	3.0	3.8	4.7	2.4	4.4	Taux de croissance
Mozambique								**Mozambique**
GDP at current prices	5 752	2 572	7 724	10 154	16 019	16 961	14 806	PIB aux prix courants
GDP per capita	439	162	366	418	605	623	529	PIB par habitant
GDP at constant prices	2 083	2 926	7 724	11 053	13 599	14 611	15 577	PIB aux prix constants
Growth rates	-8.8	2.2	8.7	6.7	7.1	7.4	6.6	Taux de croissance
Myanmar								**Myanmar**
GDP at current prices	6 606	7 764	11 931	41 445	62 140	66 300	62 601	PIB aux prix courants
GDP per capita	172	174	239	801	1 173	1 241	1 161	PIB par habitant
GDP at constant prices	3 669	4 374	11 931	20 286	24 928	26 920	28 884	PIB aux prix constants
Growth rates	2.9	6.9	13.6	10.2	8.4	8.0	7.3	Taux de croissance
Namibia								**Namibie**
GDP at current prices	1 537	4 011	7 121	11 282	12 713	12 854	11 491	PIB aux prix courants
GDP per capita	1 338	2 425	3 513	5 143	5 418	5 349	4 674	PIB par habitant
GDP at constant prices	3 386	4 866	7 121	8 772	10 233	10 893	11 470	PIB aux prix constants
Growth rates	0.2	4.1	2.5	6.0	5.7	6.5	5.3	Taux de croissance
Nauru								**Nauru**
GDP at current prices	33	35	26	62	153	182	189	PIB aux prix courants
GDP per capita	4 043	3 496	2 599	6 234	15 100	17 857	18 469	PIB par habitant
GDP at constant prices	138	60	26	41	71	80	94	PIB aux prix constants
Growth rates	-2.8	-7.9	-12.1	20.1	26.4	12.6	18.7	Taux de croissance
Nepal								**Népal**
GDP at current prices	2 741	4 534	8 259	16 281	18 227	19 738	20 658	PIB aux prix courants
GDP per capita	164	212	324	606	655	701	725	PIB par habitant
GDP at constant prices	3 416	5 499	8 259	10 299	11 621	12 317	12 653	PIB aux prix constants
Growth rates	6.1	3.5	3.1	4.8	4.1	6.0	2.7	Taux de croissance
Netherlands								**Pays-Bas**
GDP at current prices	142 011	446 514	678 517	836 390	866 680	879 635	750 318	PIB aux prix courants
GDP per capita	9 813	28 899	41 546	50 289	51 560	52 148	44 332	PIB par habitant
GDP at constant prices	388 883	513 546	678 517	722 835	725 709	736 012	750 376	PIB aux prix constants
Growth rates	2.6	3.1	2.2	1.4	-0.2	1.4	2.0	Taux de croissance
Netherlands Antilles [former]								**Antilles néerlandaises [anc.]**
GDP at current prices	1 190	2 571	3 053	3 848	...	...	...	PIB aux prix courants
GDP per capita	6 558	13 560	17 312	...	...	...	...	PIB par habitant
GDP at constant prices	2 410	3 012	3 053	3 291	...	...	...	PIB aux prix constants
Growth rates	-2.1	1.6	1.1	-0.3	...	...	...	Taux de croissance
New Caledonia								**Nouvelle-Calédonie**
GDP at current prices	855	3 628	6 236	9 355	9 858	10 236	8 937	PIB aux prix courants
GDP per capita	5 553	19 178	27 270	37 976	38 437	39 398	33 966	PIB par habitant
GDP at constant prices	2 670	4 982	6 236	7 564	8 036	8 283	8 550	PIB aux prix constants
Growth rates	4.5	5.9	3.6	6.9	1.9	3.1	3.2	Taux de croissance
New Zealand								**Nouvelle-Zélande**
GDP at current prices	24 108	63 151	114 721	146 584	189 541	198 734	173 417	PIB aux prix courants
GDP per capita	7 376	17 185	27 746	33 551	42 448	44 207	38 294	PIB par habitant
GDP at constant prices	68 786	81 617	114 721	123 686	132 550	136 772	140 960	PIB aux prix constants
Growth rates	1.6	4.6	3.3	1.0	1.6	3.2	3.1	Taux de croissance
Nicaragua								**Nicaragua**
GDP at current prices	3 618	4 132	6 321	8 741	10 875	11 790	12 693	PIB aux prix courants
GDP per capita	975	896	1 175	1 523	1 829	1 960	2 087	PIB par habitant
GDP at constant prices	4 589	4 236	6 321	7 154	8 389	8 772	9 204	PIB aux prix constants
Growth rates	-4.1	5.9	4.3	3.2	4.5	4.6	4.9	Taux de croissance
Niger								**Niger**
GDP at current prices	1 531	1 786	3 369	5 719	7 668	8 245	7 143	PIB aux prix courants
GDP per capita	224	191	250	351	418	431	359	PIB par habitant
GDP at constant prices	2 118	2 307	3 369	4 334	5 219	5 587	5 789	PIB aux prix constants
Growth rates	7.7	3.3	7.4	8.4	5.3	7.0	3.6	Taux de croissance
Nigeria								**Nigéria**
GDP at current prices	178 821	49 030	180 502	369 062	514 966	568 499	494 583	PIB aux prix courants
GDP per capita	2 131	452	1 293	2 315	2 980	3 203	2 714	PIB par habitant
GDP at constant prices	67 600	94 219	180 502	249 671	287 811	305 971	314 087	PIB aux prix constants
Growth rates	11.3	2.1	6.5	7.8	5.4	6.3	2.7	Taux de croissance

13 Gross domestic product and gross domestic product per capita *(continued)*

In millions of US dollars at current and constant 2005 prices; per capita US dollars; real rates of growth

Produit intérieur brut et produit intérieur brut par habitant *(suite)*

En millions de dollars É.-U. aux prix courants et constants de 2005; par habitant en dollars É.U.; taux de croissance réels

Region, country or area	1985	1995	2005	2010	2013	2014	2015	Région, pays ou zone
Norway								**Norvège**
GDP at current prices	65 417	152 028	308 722	428 527	522 746	498 340	386 578	PIB aux prix courants
GDP per capita	15 769	34 871	66 760	87 611	102 833	96 803	74 186	PIB par habitant
GDP at constant prices	177 363	231 758	308 722	323 263	338 716	345 215	350 776	PIB aux prix constants
Growth rates	5.6	4.2	2.6	0.6	1.0	1.9	1.6	Taux de croissance
Oman								**Oman**
GDP at current prices	10 281	13 650	31 082	58 641	78 939	81 034	69 832	PIB aux prix courants
GDP per capita	6 861	6 228	12 399	19 921	20 205	19 130	15 551	PIB par habitant
GDP at constant prices	16 487	25 248	31 082	41 164	46 454	47 635	50 327	PIB aux prix constants
Growth rates	14.5	4.8	2.5	4.8	4.4	2.5	5.7	Taux de croissance
Pakistan								**Pakistan**
GDP at current prices	38 840	77 266	117 708	174 508	220 203	247 953	266 458	PIB aux prix courants
GDP per capita	421	630	768	1 026	1 215	1 340	1 410	PIB par habitant
GDP at constant prices	47 300	78 593	117 708	139 224	154 534	161 856	170 820	PIB aux prix constants
Growth rates	7.6	5.0	7.7	1.6	4.4	4.7	5.5	Taux de croissance
Palau								**Palaos**
GDP at current prices	44	116	180	186	219	234	258	PIB aux prix courants
GDP per capita	3 241	6 729	9 037	9 084	10 451	11 092	12 122	PIB par habitant
GDP at constant prices	102	147	180	152	168	167	176	PIB aux prix constants
Growth rates	5.4	10.9	5.5	-6.4	2.0	-0.8	5.7	Taux de croissance
Panama								**Panama**
GDP at current prices	5 725	9 042	15 465	28 917	44 856	49 166	52 132	PIB aux prix courants
GDP per capita	2 580	3 302	4 659	7 987	11 787	12 712	13 268	PIB par habitant
GDP at constant prices	7 198	9 986	15 465	21 961	28 597	30 328	32 080	PIB aux prix constants
Growth rates	5.1	1.8	7.2	5.8	6.6	6.1	5.8	Taux de croissance
Papua New Guinea								**Papouasie-Nvl-Guinée**
GDP at current prices	3 682	7 273	7 312	14 205	21 144	22 207	21 315	PIB aux prix courants
GDP per capita	1 001	1 542	1 201	2 074	2 893	2 975	2 798	PIB par habitant
GDP at constant prices	3 925	6 331	7 312	9 550	10 648	11 431	12 187	PIB aux prix constants
Growth rates	3.6	-3.3	3.9	11.2	3.6	7.4	6.6	Taux de croissance
Paraguay								**Paraguay**
GDP at current prices	4 017[5]	8 066[5]	8 735	20 048	28 966	30 881	27 714	PIB aux prix courants
GDP per capita	1 094	1 694	1 507	3 228	4 480	4 713	4 174	PIB par habitant
GDP at constant prices	4 740[5]	6 776[5]	8 735	11 148	13 101	13 719	14 142	PIB aux prix constants
Growth rates	4.0[5]	5.5[5]	2.1	13.1	14.0	4.7	3.1	Taux de croissance
Peru								**Pérou**
GDP at current prices	14 529	53 371	76 080	147 528	201 023	202 491	190 428	PIB aux prix courants
GDP per capita	743[5]	2 220[5]	2 755	5 022	6 577	6 538	6 069	PIB par habitant
GDP at constant prices	46 436	54 299	76 080	106 102	126 848	129 869	134 093	PIB aux prix constants
Growth rates	2.1	7.4	6.3	8.3	5.9	2.4	3.3	Taux de croissance
Philippines								**Philippines**
GDP at current prices	34 052	82 121	103 072	199 591	271 836	284 834	292 449	PIB aux prix courants
GDP per capita	627	1 176	1 197	2 145	2 786	2 873	2 904	PIB par habitant
GDP at constant prices	49 280	69 129	103 072	131 138	155 268	164 923	174 660	PIB aux prix constants
Growth rates	-7.3	4.7	4.8	7.6	7.1	6.2	5.9	Taux de croissance
Poland								**Pologne**
GDP at current prices	73 333	142 138	306 127	479 321	524 215	545 152	477 066	PIB aux prix courants
GDP per capita	1 956	3 683	7 959	12 426	13 574	14 116	12 355	PIB par habitant
GDP at constant prices	186 629	203 463	306 127	386 375	418 011	431 733	448 747	PIB aux prix constants
Growth rates	3.6	7.0	3.5	3.6	1.4	3.3	3.9	Taux de croissance
Portugal								**Portugal**
GDP at current prices	27 118	118 132	197 300	238 303	226 073	229 630	199 122	PIB aux prix courants
GDP per capita	2 731	11 721	18 826	22 514	21 614	22 075	19 239	PIB par habitant
GDP at constant prices	107 932	154 749	197 300	203 429	189 501	191 194	194 244	PIB aux prix constants
Growth rates	2.8	4.3	0.8	1.9	-1.1	0.9	1.6	Taux de croissance
Puerto Rico								**Porto Rico**
GDP at current prices	20 574	43 246	83 915	98 381	102 450	102 089	102 906	PIB aux prix courants
GDP per capita	6 106	11 721	22 311	26 520	27 760	27 692	27 939	PIB par habitant
GDP at constant prices	39 130	62 809	83 915	78 370	77 872	76 783	76 748	PIB aux prix constants
Growth rates	2.1	4.5	-2.0	-0.4	-0.3	-1.4	-~0.0	Taux de croissance
Qatar								**Qatar**
GDP at current prices	6 153	8 041	43 998	123 627	198 728	206 225	164 641	PIB aux prix courants
GDP per capita	16 583	16 049	52 571	70 023	94 574	94 944	73 653	PIB par habitant
GDP at constant prices	12 711	17 483	43 998	100 718	124 424	129 374	133 968	PIB aux prix constants
Growth rates	-2.1	2.4	7.5	16.7	4.4	4.0	3.6	Taux de croissance
Republic of Korea								**République de Corée**

13 Gross domestic product and gross domestic product per capita *(continued)*

In millions of US dollars at current and constant 2005 prices; per capita US dollars; real rates of growth

Produit intérieur brut et produit intérieur brut par habitant *(suite)*

En millions de dollars É.-U. aux prix courants et constants de 2005; par habitant en dollars É.U.; taux de croissance réels

Region, country or area	1985	1995	2005	2010	2013	2014	2015	Région, pays ou zone
GDP at current prices	100 273	556 129	898 137	1 094 499	1 305 605	1 411 334	1 377 873	PIB aux prix courants
GDP per capita	2 476	12 454	18 866	22 296	26 192	28 185	27 397	PIB par habitant
GDP at constant prices	221 415	545 690	898 137	1 098 694	1 199 006	1 239 070	1 271 434	PIB aux prix constants
Growth rates	7.7	9.6	3.9	6.5	2.9	3.3	2.6	Taux de croissance
Republic of Moldova								**République de Moldova**
GDP at current prices	...	1 767	2 988	5 812	7 985	7 983	6 475	PIB aux prix courants
GDP per capita	...	407	719	1 423	1 960	1 960	1 591	PIB par habitant
GDP at constant prices	...	2 405	2 988	3 502	4 062	4 257	4 225	PIB aux prix constants
Growth rates	...	-1.4	7.5	7.1	9.4	4.8	-0.7	Taux de croissance
Romania								**Roumanie**
GDP at current prices	50 742	37 657	99 699	167 998	191 548	199 326	177 956	PIB aux prix courants
GDP per capita	2 196	1 640	4 657	8 276	9 677	10 143	9 121	PIB par habitant
GDP at constant prices	93 084	76 334	99 699	115 113	121 209	124 938	129 514	PIB aux prix constants
Growth rates	-0.1	7.1	4.2	-0.8	3.5	3.1	3.7	Taux de croissance
Russian Federation								**Fédération de Russie**
GDP at current prices	...	399 472	764 016	1 524 917	2 230 625	2 030 973	1 326 016	PIB aux prix courants
GDP per capita	...	2 694	5 320	10 652	15 559	14 160	9 243	PIB par habitant
GDP at constant prices	...	524 113	764 016	909 266	993 946	1 000 969	963 665	PIB aux prix constants
Growth rates	...	-4.1	6.4	4.5	1.3	0.7	-3.7	Taux de croissance
Rwanda								**Rwanda**
GDP at current prices	1 813	1 230	2 581	5 699	7 522	7 903	8 096	PIB aux prix courants
GDP per capita	296	208	287	554	679	697	697	PIB par habitant
GDP at constant prices	1 612	1 057	2 581	3 847	4 725	5 054	5 405	PIB aux prix constants
Growth rates	4.4	33.5	9.4	7.3	4.7	7.0	6.9	Taux de croissance
Saint Kitts and Nevis								**Saint-Kitts-et-Nevis**
GDP at current prices	106	300	543	705	788	848	876	PIB aux prix courants
GDP per capita	2 524	6 988	11 054	13 467	14 515	15 430	15 772	PIB par habitant
GDP at constant prices	207	359	543	556	601	637	661	PIB aux prix constants
Growth rates	8.6	5.8	8.8	-2.2	6.2	6.0	3.8	Taux de croissance
Saint Lucia								**Sainte-Lucie**
GDP at current prices	249	617	935	1 244	1 336	1 405	1 450	PIB aux prix courants
GDP per capita	1 970	4 199	5 656	7 014	7 327	7 649	7 839	PIB par habitant
GDP at constant prices	447	754	935	1 039	1 030	1 034	1 054	PIB aux prix constants
Growth rates	7.5	1.1	-1.7	-1.0	-0.4	0.4	1.9	Taux de croissance
Saint Vincent & Grenadines								**Saint-Vincent-Grenadines**
GDP at current prices	133	312	551	681	721	728	738	PIB aux prix courants
GDP per capita	1 277	2 887	5 064	6 232	6 597	6 656	6 739	PIB par habitant
GDP at constant prices	255	389	551	589	606	613	622	PIB aux prix constants
Growth rates	6.2	7.8	2.5	-3.4	1.8	1.2	1.6	Taux de croissance
Samoa								**Samoa**
GDP at current prices	85	196	434	679	805	824	774	PIB aux prix courants
GDP per capita	532	1 151	2 414	3 651	4 226	4 296	4 006	PIB par habitant
GDP at constant prices	251	273	434	458	466	475	488	PIB aux prix constants
Growth rates	3.9	6.0	5.1	4.3	0.5	1.9	2.8	Taux de croissance
San Marino								**Saint-Marin**
GDP at current prices	318	1 020	2 027	2 139	1 865	1 845	1 565	PIB aux prix courants
GDP per capita	14 017	39 410	69 333	69 708	59 412	58 390	49 240	PIB par habitant
GDP at constant prices	859	1 305	2 027	1 842	1 496	1 481	1 496	PIB aux prix constants
Growth rates	2.8	9.3	2.3	-4.6	-3.0	-1.0	1.0	Taux de croissance
Sao Tome and Principe								**Sao Tomé-et-Principe**
GDP at current prices	79	99	126	206	318	367	334	PIB aux prix courants
GDP per capita	760	785	824	1 206	1 741	1 968	1 753	PIB par habitant
GDP at constant prices	92	93	126	168	191	204	212	PIB aux prix constants
Growth rates	9.3	2.0	7.1	6.6	5.1	6.8	4.0	Taux de croissance
Saudi Arabia								**Arabie saoudite**
GDP at current prices	103 894	143 152	328 461	526 811	744 336	753 832	653 219	PIB aux prix courants
GDP per capita	7 776	7 593	13 274	18 754	24 646	24 406	20 711	PIB par habitant
GDP at constant prices	147 670	248 623	328 461	374 862	445 987	462 215	477 713	PIB aux prix constants
Growth rates	-9.8	0.2	5.6	4.8	2.7	3.6	3.4	Taux de croissance
Senegal								**Sénégal**
GDP at current prices	2 808	4 873	8 708	12 926	14 828	15 309	13 633	PIB aux prix courants
GDP per capita	436	559	773	998	1 043	1 043	901	PIB par habitant
GDP at constant prices	4 381	5 498	8 708	10 358	11 389	11 880	12 655	PIB aux prix constants
Growth rates	3.8	4.7	5.6	4.2	3.5	4.3	6.5	Taux de croissance

Gross domestic product and gross domestic product per capita *(continued)*

In millions of US dollars at current and constant 2005 prices; per capita US dollars; real rates of growth

Produit intérieur brut et produit intérieur brut par habitant *(suite)*

En millions de dollars É.-U. aux prix courants et constants de 2005; par habitant en dollars É.U.; taux de croissance réels

Region, country or area	1985	1995	2005	2010	2013	2014	2015	Région, pays ou zone
Serbia								**Serbie**
GDP at current prices	...	21 823[6]	26 252[7]	39 460[7]	45 520[7]	44 211[7]	37 160[7]	PIB aux prix courants
GDP per capita	...	2 208[6]	3 528[7]	5 412[7]	6 355[7]	6 203[7]	5 239[7]	PIB par habitant
GDP at constant prices	...	18 246[6]	26 252[7]	29 943[7]	30 827[7]	30 263[7]	30 492[7]	PIB aux prix constants
Growth rates	...	5.7[6]	5.5[7]	0.6[7]	2.6[7]	-1.8[7]	0.8[7]	Taux de croissance
Seychelles								**Seychelles**
GDP at current prices	204	614	919	970	1 316	1 349	1 363	PIB aux prix courants
GDP per capita	2 922	8 005	10 357	10 421	13 817	14 074	14 133	PIB par habitant
GDP at constant prices	460	699	919	1 138	1 306	1 388	1 482	PIB aux prix constants
Growth rates	10.3	-0.6	9.0	5.9	5.0	6.2	6.8	Taux de croissance
Sierra Leone								**Sierra Leone**
GDP at current prices	1 376	1 179	1 650	2 578	4 920	5 015	4 483	PIB aux prix courants
GDP per capita	397	307	325	446	796	794	695	PIB par habitant
GDP at constant prices	1 724	1 548	1 650	2 130	3 148	3 292	2 624	PIB aux prix constants
Growth rates	2.3	-10.0	4.5	5.3	20.7	4.6	-20.3	Taux de croissance
Singapore								**Singapour**
GDP at current prices	18 555	87 892	127 418	236 420	300 289	306 357	292 734	PIB aux prix courants
GDP per capita	6 850	25 237	28 343	46 549	55 557	55 635	52 239	PIB par habitant
GDP at constant prices	33 360	76 309	127 418	176 458	203 373	210 004	214 221	PIB aux prix constants
Growth rates	-0.7	7.0	7.5	15.2	4.7	3.3	2.0	Taux de croissance
Sint Maarten (Dutch part)								**St-Martin (partie néerland.)**
GDP at current prices	...	...	708	896	1 023	1 059	1 094	PIB aux prix courants
GDP per capita	...	...	21 764	27 064	28 070	28 085	28 242	PIB par habitant
GDP at constant prices	...	...	708	788	812	825	830	PIB aux prix constants
Growth rates	...	...	...	1.1	1.3	1.7	0.5	Taux de croissance
Slovakia								**Slovaquie**
GDP at current prices	...	19 959	48 965	89 501	98 478	100 761	87 268	PIB aux prix courants
GDP per capita	...	3 722	9 093	16 553	18 172	18 581	16 082	PIB par habitant
GDP at constant prices	...	32 178	48 965	61 745	65 499	67 183	69 757	PIB aux prix constants
Growth rates	...	5.8	6.8	5.0	1.5	2.6	3.8	Taux de croissance
Slovenia								**Slovénie**
GDP at current prices	...	21 274	36 345	48 014	47 689	49 530	42 777	PIB aux prix courants
GDP per capita	...	10 683	18 204	23 393	23 096	23 973	20 690	PIB par habitant
GDP at constant prices	...	24 719	36 345	39 598	38 362	39 562	40 478	PIB aux prix constants
Growth rates	...	4.1	4.0	1.2	-1.1	3.1	2.3	Taux de croissance
Solomon Islands								**Îles Salomon**
GDP at current prices	160	365	429	720	1 057	1 101	1 075	PIB aux prix courants
GDP per capita	591	1 015	915	1 368	1 885	1 924	1 842	PIB par habitant
GDP at constant prices	252	425	429	599	674	687	709	PIB aux prix constants
Growth rates	2.8	10.0	12.8	10.6	3.0	2.0	3.3	Taux de croissance
Somalia								**Somalie**
GDP at current prices	810	1 122	2 316	1 071	1 399	1 565	1 559	PIB aux prix courants
GDP per capita	133	177	273	112	136	149	145	PIB par habitant
GDP at constant prices	2 480	1 796	2 316	2 628	2 838	2 943	3 022	PIB aux prix constants
Growth rates	9.5	0.0	3.0	2.6	2.6	3.7	2.7	Taux de croissance
South Africa								**Afrique du Sud**
GDP at current prices	59 648	157 434	257 772	375 348	367 595	351 306	314 571	PIB aux prix courants
GDP per capita	1 808	3 800	5 331	7 271	6 882	6 509	5 773	PIB par habitant
GDP at constant prices	164 194	186 154	257 772	300 266	324 379	329 662	333 831	PIB aux prix constants
Growth rates	-1.2	3.1	5.3	3.0	2.3	1.6	1.3	Taux de croissance
South Sudan								**Soudan du sud**
GDP at current prices	...	...	...	15 720	13 694	16 061	13 167	PIB aux prix courants
GDP per capita	...	...	...	1 563	1 196	1 348	1 067	PIB par habitant
GDP at constant prices	...	...	...	10 920	7 115	8 262	8 429	PIB aux prix constants
Growth rates	...	...	...	5.5	26.7	16.1	2.0	Taux de croissance
Spain								**Espagne**
GDP at current prices	180 305	612 943	1 157 248	1 431 588	1 361 776	1 375 856	1 192 955	PIB aux prix courants
GDP per capita	4 655	15 414	26 388	30 720	29 314	29 742	25 865	PIB par habitant
GDP at constant prices	597 137	801 810	1 157 248	1 219 911	1 152 328	1 168 219	1 205 656	PIB aux prix constants
Growth rates	2.3	2.8	3.7	~0.0	-1.7	1.4	3.2	Taux de croissance
Sri Lanka								**Sri Lanka**
GDP at current prices	6 873	15 293	27 932	56 726	74 318	80 025	82 316	PIB aux prix courants
GDP per capita	425	838	1 430	2 808	3 621	3 881	3 974	PIB par habitant
GDP at constant prices	11 660	17 943	27 932	38 058	46 558	48 829	51 166	PIB aux prix constants
Growth rates	5.0	5.5	6.2	8.0	3.4	4.9	4.8	Taux de croissance

13

Gross domestic product and gross domestic product per capita *(continued)*

In millions of US dollars at current and constant 2005 prices; per capita US dollars; real rates of growth

Produit intérieur brut et produit intérieur brut par habitant *(suite)*

En millions de dollars É.-U. aux prix courants et constants de 2005; par habitant en dollars É.U.; taux de croissance réels

Region, country or area	1985	1995	2005	2010	2013	2014	2015	Région, pays ou zone
State of Palestine								**État de Palestine**
GDP at current prices	1 005	3 283	4 832	8 913	12 476	12 716	12 677	PIB aux prix courants
GDP per capita	571	1 254	1 350	2 191	2 824	2 800	2 716	PIB par habitant
GDP at constant prices	1 463	3 324	4 832	6 167	7 532	7 518	7 778	PIB aux prix constants
Growth rates	-0.6	7.1	10.8	8.1	2.2	-0.2	3.5	Taux de croissance
Sudan								**Soudan**
GDP at current prices	...	...	...	53 944	63 912	69 350	79 546	PIB aux prix courants
GDP per capita	...	...	...	1 494	1 659	1 762	1 977	PIB par habitant
GDP at constant prices	...	...	...	35 904	36 865	37 455	39 290	PIB aux prix constants
Growth rates	...	...	...	6.9	5.3	1.6	4.9	Taux de croissance
Sudan [former]								**Soudan [anc.]**
GDP at current prices	6 624	12 847	35 183	69 665	...	...	...	PIB aux prix courants
GDP per capita	294	426	878	...	...	...	...	PIB par habitant
GDP at constant prices	11 109	17 707	35 183	46 910	...	...	...	PIB aux prix constants
Growth rates	5.4	6.0	9.0	6.6	...	...	...	Taux de croissance
Suriname								**Suriname**
GDP at current prices	1 196	844	2 193	4 368	5 146	5 241	4 879	PIB aux prix courants
GDP per capita	3 221	1 894	4 457	8 431	9 646	9 737	8 985	PIB par habitant
GDP at constant prices	1 578	1 561	2 193	2 751	3 077	3 089	3 005	PIB aux prix constants
Growth rates	14.0	~0.0	3.9	5.2	2.9	0.4	-2.7	Taux de croissance
Swaziland								**Swaziland**
GDP at current prices	539	1 902	3 107	4 526	4 611	4 493	4 133	PIB aux prix courants
GDP per capita	764	1 974	2 813	3 794	3 687	3 540	3 212	PIB par habitant
GDP at constant prices	1 154	2 263	3 107	3 704	4 083	4 195	4 264	PIB aux prix constants
Growth rates	1.9	4.8	5.2	1.8	4.6	2.7	1.7	Taux de croissance
Sweden								**Suède**
GDP at current prices	112 514	264 053	389 043	488 378	578 742	573 818	495 694	PIB aux prix courants
GDP per capita	13 473	29 915	43 083	52 053	60 134	59 137	50 687	PIB par habitant
GDP at constant prices	245 761	286 677	389 043	420 871	436 196	447 556	465 838	PIB aux prix constants
Growth rates	2.2	4.0	2.8	6.0	1.2	2.6	4.1	Taux de croissance
Switzerland								**Suisse**
GDP at current prices	107 495	341 768	407 543	581 209	684 835	702 706	670 790	PIB aux prix courants
GDP per capita	16 651	48 705	55 009	74 223	84 353	85 577	80 831	PIB par habitant
GDP at constant prices	290 505	337 990	407 543	454 938	476 335	485 847	489 939	PIB aux prix constants
Growth rates	3.7	0.5	3.0	3.0	1.8	2.0	0.8	Taux de croissance
Syrian Arab Republic								**République arabe syrienne**
GDP at current prices	10 050	13 547	28 397	60 465	31 685	34 096	28 393	PIB aux prix courants
GDP per capita	942	945	1 566	2 918	1 640	1 816	1 535	PIB par habitant
GDP at constant prices	13 198	18 570	28 397	36 081	19 729	19 807	18 758	PIB aux prix constants
Growth rates	6.1	7.0	6.2	3.4	-24.8	0.4	-5.3	Taux de croissance
Tajikistan								**Tadjikistan**
GDP at current prices	...	1 218	2 312	5 642	8 506	9 237	7 853	PIB aux prix courants
GDP per capita	...	211	340	744	1 049	1 113	926	PIB par habitant
GDP at constant prices	...	1 455	2 312	3 162	3 742	3 992	4 160	PIB aux prix constants
Growth rates	...	-12.4	6.7	6.5	7.4	6.7	4.2	Taux de croissance
Thailand								**Thaïlande**
GDP at current prices	40 240	168 998	189 318	340 923	419 889	404 320	395 168	PIB aux prix courants
GDP per capita	773	2 852	2 874	5 112	6 225	5 970	5 815	PIB par habitant
GDP at constant prices	56 940	139 809	189 318	227 448	252 573	254 638	261 840	PIB aux prix constants
Growth rates	4.6	8.1	4.2	7.5	2.7	0.8	2.8	Taux de croissance
TFYR of Macedonia								**ex-R.Y. de Macédoine**
GDP at current prices	...	4 707	6 259	9 407	10 818	11 362	10 052	PIB aux prix courants
GDP per capita	...	2 409	3 064	4 561	5 220	5 474	4 836	PIB par habitant
GDP at constant prices	...	4 905	6 259	7 610	7 980	8 269	8 587	PIB aux prix constants
Growth rates	...	-1.1	4.7	3.4	2.9	3.6	3.8	Taux de croissance
Timor-Leste								**Timor-Leste**
GDP at current prices	...	451	1 850	4 274	5 641	4 175	2 873	PIB aux prix courants
GDP per capita	...	527	1 869	4 043	4 995	3 607	2 425	PIB par habitant
GDP at constant prices	...	624	1 850	3 053	3 001	2 168	2 260	PIB aux prix constants
Growth rates	...	9.5	52.7	-1.3	-12.8	-27.8	4.3	Taux de croissance
Togo								**Togo**
GDP at current prices	740	1 446	2 110	3 173	4 180	4 576	4 086	PIB aux prix courants
GDP per capita	228	338	378	496	603	643	559	PIB par habitant
GDP at constant prices	1 484	1 790	2 110	2 462	2 873	3 048	3 215	PIB aux prix constants
Growth rates	3.7	6.8	1.2	4.0	5.1	6.1	5.5	Taux de croissance

13 Gross domestic product and gross domestic product per capita *(continued)*
In millions of US dollars at current and constant 2005 prices; per capita US dollars; real rates of growth

Produit intérieur brut et produit intérieur brut par habitant *(suite)*
En millions de dollars É.-U. aux prix courants et constants de 2005; par habitant en dollars É.U.; taux de croissance réels

Region, country or area	1985	1995	2005	2010	2013	2014	2015	Région, pays ou zone
Tonga								**Tonga**
GDP at current prices	73	203	262	374	439	435	402	PIB aux prix courants
GDP per capita	779	2 120	2 593	3 597	4 178	4 122	3 784	PIB par habitant
GDP at constant prices	185	216	262	272	273	278	289	PIB aux prix constants
Growth rates	6.6	4.0	1.6	3.6	-3.1	2.0	3.8	Taux de croissance
Trinidad and Tobago								**Trinité-et-Tobago**
GDP at current prices	7 376	5 329	15 982	22 158	26 444	27 267	25 927	PIB aux prix courants
GDP per capita	6 299	4 246	12 323	16 684	19 614	20 131	19 063	PIB par habitant
GDP at constant prices	7 868	7 527	15 982	19 358	19 993	19 790	19 825	PIB aux prix constants
Growth rates	-4.1	4.0	6.2	0.2	2.3	-1.0	0.2	Taux de croissance
Tunisia								**Tunisie**
GDP at current prices	9 234	19 795	32 272	44 051	46 257	47 604	41 199	PIB aux prix courants
GDP per capita	1 261	2 172	3 194	4 140	4 203	4 277	3 661	PIB par habitant
GDP at constant prices	14 194	19 858	32 272	40 182	41 949	42 896	43 239	PIB aux prix constants
Growth rates	5.7	2.3	4.0	3.0	2.4	2.3	0.8	Taux de croissance
Turkey								**Turquie**
GDP at current prices	90 379	227 607	482 986	731 144	823 256	798 414	717 888	PIB aux prix courants
GDP per capita	1 838	3 889	7 117	10 111	10 801	10 299	9 126	PIB par habitant
GDP at constant prices	205 784	315 856	482 986	565 099	654 069	673 129	699 952	PIB aux prix constants
Growth rates	4.2	7.2	8.4	9.2	4.2	2.9	4.0	Taux de croissance
Turkmenistan								**Turkménistan**
GDP at current prices	...	2 190	14 182	22 583	39 198	43 486	37 597	PIB aux prix courants
GDP per capita	...	523	2 987	4 479	7 480	8 194	6 997	PIB par habitant
GDP at constant prices	...	8 890	14 182	23 226	32 617	35 976	38 315	PIB aux prix constants
Growth rates	...	-7.2	13.0	9.2	10.2	10.3	6.5	Taux de croissance
Turks and Caicos Islands								**Îles Turques-et-Caïques**
GDP at current prices	58	191	579	687	736	797	863	PIB aux prix courants
GDP per capita	6 144	12 424	21 877	22 159	22 245	23 615	25 122	PIB par habitant
GDP at constant prices	94	258	579	634	655	685	713	PIB aux prix constants
Growth rates	10.7	7.3	14.4	1.0	1.3	4.6	4.1	Taux de croissance
Tuvalu								**Tuvalu**
GDP at current prices	4	12	22	32	38	38	33	PIB aux prix courants
GDP per capita	407	1 275	2 259	3 238	3 880	3 796	3 362	PIB par habitant
GDP at constant prices	8	17	22	24	26	27	28	PIB aux prix constants
Growth rates	-1.8	-5.0	-3.9	-2.7	1.3	2.2	3.5	Taux de croissance
Uganda								**Ouganda**
GDP at current prices	4 742	7 146	11 154	19 803	26 138	28 321	25 282	PIB aux prix courants
GDP per capita	324	350	398	597	715	750	648	PIB par habitant
GDP at constant prices	2 995	5 671	11 154	16 480	18 858	19 773	20 836	PIB aux prix constants
Growth rates	-0.3	9.4	10.0	8.2	4.7	4.9	5.4	Taux de croissance
Ukraine								**Ukraine**
GDP at current prices	...	50 379	89 239	141 209	190 499	133 504[8]	90 615[8]	PIB aux prix courants
GDP per capita	...	991	1 907	3 093	4 218	2 967[8]	2 022[8]	PIB par habitant
GDP at constant prices	...	68 183	89 239	93 824	99 129	92 634[8]	83 491[8]	PIB aux prix constants
Growth rates	...	-12.2	3.1	4.1	~0.0	-6.6[8]	-9.9[8]	Taux de croissance
United Arab Emirates								**Émirats arabes unis**
GDP at current prices	40 604	65 744	180 617	286 185	388 598	401 958	370 296	PIB aux prix courants
GDP per capita	30 067	27 974	40 299	34 358	42 987	44 239	40 439	PIB par habitant
GDP at constant prices	72 917	101 625	180 617	203 435	239 376	246 749	256 021	PIB aux prix constants
Growth rates	-2.4	8.2	4.9	1.6	4.7	3.1	3.8	Taux de croissance
United Kingdom								**Royaume-Uni**
GDP at current prices	489 256	1 320 322	2 508 111	2 429 680	2 719 509	2 998 834	2 858 003	PIB aux prix courants
GDP per capita	8 672	22 802	41 656	38 741	42 522	46 615	44 162	PIB par habitant
GDP at constant prices	1 450 700	1 866 706	2 508 111	2 554 677	2 677 488	2 759 700	2 821 007	PIB aux prix constants
Growth rates	4.2	2.5	3.0	1.9	1.9	3.1	2.2	Taux de croissance
United Rep. of Tanzania [9]								**Rép.-Unie de Tanzanie** [9]
GDP at current prices	11 654	7 575	18 072	31 105	44 333	48 197	45 628	PIB aux prix courants
GDP per capita	534	260	476	701	908	955	877	PIB par habitant
GDP at constant prices	7 120	10 467	18 072	24 275	29 540	31 598	33 797	PIB aux prix constants
Growth rates	4.6	3.6	7.4	6.4	7.3	7.0	7.0	Taux de croissance
Zanzibar								**Zanzibar**
GDP at current prices	...	186	438	746	1 156	1 291	1 159	PIB aux prix courants
GDP per capita	...	235	408	588	835	936	794	PIB par habitant
GDP at constant prices	...	225	438	570	701	749	799	PIB aux prix constants
Growth rates	...	3.5	4.9	4.3	7.2	7.0	6.6	Taux de croissance

13 Gross domestic product and gross domestic product per capita *(continued)*

In millions of US dollars at current and constant 2005 prices; per capita US dollars; real rates of growth

Produit intérieur brut et produit intérieur brut par habitant *(suite)*

En millions de dollars É.-U. aux prix courants et constants de 2005; par habitant en dollars É.U.; taux de croissance réels

Region, country or area	1985	1995	2005	2010	2013	2014	2015	Région, pays ou zone
United States of America								**États-Unis d'Amérique**
GDP at current prices	4 346 700	7 664 060	13 093 726	14 964 372	16 691 517	17 393 103	18 036 648	PIB aux prix courants
GDP per capita	18 059	28 782	44 215	48 291	52 632	54 447	56 054	PIB par habitant
GDP at constant prices	6 977 897	9 359 504	13 093 726	13 599 258	14 361 252	14 701 679	15 083 356	PIB aux prix constants
Growth rates	4.2	2.8	3.3	2.5	1.7	2.4	2.6	Taux de croissance
Uruguay								**Uruguay**
GDP at current prices	5 226	21 312	17 363	40 287	57 531	57 236	53 442	PIB aux prix courants
GDP per capita	1 735	6 609	5 221	11 939	16 881	16 738	15 574	PIB par habitant
GDP at constant prices	10 537	15 453	17 363	23 193	26 425	27 281	27 549	PIB aux prix constants
Growth rates	1.5	-1.5	7.5	7.8	4.6	3.2	1.0	Taux de croissance
Uzbekistan								**Ouzbékistan**
GDP at current prices	...	13 474	14 396	39 526	57 157	63 030	69 004	PIB aux prix courants
GDP per capita	...	594	555	1 425	1 969	2 139	2 308	PIB par habitant
GDP at constant prices	...	9 061	14 396	21 707	27 472	29 697	31 716	PIB aux prix constants
Growth rates	...	-0.9	7.0	8.5	8.0	8.1	6.8	Taux de croissance
Vanuatu								**Vanuatu**
GDP at current prices	133	273	395	701	802	815	737	PIB aux prix courants
GDP per capita	1 020	1 621	1 886	2 966	3 167	3 148	2 783	PIB par habitant
GDP at constant prices	240	321	395	504	529	541	536	PIB aux prix constants
Growth rates	1.1	4.7	5.3	1.6	2.0	2.3	-1.0	Taux de croissance
Venezuela (Boliv. Rep. of)								**Venezuela (Rép. boliv. du)**
GDP at current prices	59 963	74 889	145 514	393 806	371 338	363 266	344 331	PIB aux prix courants
GDP per capita	3 425	3 375	5 436	13 581	12 265	11 835	11 069	PIB par habitant
GDP at constant prices	91 790	123 574	145 514	174 551	194 651	187 071	175 432	PIB aux prix constants
Growth rates	0.2	4.0	10.3	-1.5	1.3	-3.9	-6.2	Taux de croissance
Viet Nam								**Viet Nam**
GDP at current prices	4 797	20 736	57 633	115 932	171 222	186 205	193 241	PIB aux prix courants
GDP per capita	79	276	684	1 312	1 874	2 015	2 068	PIB par habitant
GDP at constant prices	15 942	28 984	57 633	78 282	92 277	97 799	104 331	PIB aux prix constants
Growth rates	5.6	9.5	7.5	6.4	5.4	6.0	6.7	Taux de croissance
Yemen								**Yémen**
GDP at current prices	...	5 936	19 041	30 907	34 714	34 011	29 688	PIB aux prix courants
GDP per capita	...	389	929	1 310	1 360	1 299	1 106	PIB par habitant
GDP at constant prices	...	9 843	19 041	23 604	20 669	18 692	13 440	PIB aux prix constants
Growth rates	...	16.7	5.1	5.7	-1.6	-9.6	-28.1	Taux de croissance
Zambia								**Zambie**
GDP at current prices	2 772	3 807	8 332	20 265	28 046	27 135	21 255	PIB aux prix courants
GDP per capita	395	411	692	1 456	1 840	1 726	1 311	PIB par habitant
GDP at constant prices	4 880	5 164	8 332	12 647	15 107	15 866	16 321	PIB aux prix constants
Growth rates	-~0.0	2.9	7.2	10.3	5.1	5.0	2.9	Taux de croissance
Zimbabwe								**Zimbabwe**
GDP at current prices	7 548	9 576	6 223	9 422	13 490	14 197	13 893	PIB aux prix courants
GDP per capita	852	820	479	674	905	931	890	PIB par habitant
GDP at constant prices	5 897	7 826	6 223	9 573	12 376	12 853	12 991	PIB aux prix constants
Growth rates	6.9	0.2	-4.1	11.4	4.5	3.8	1.1	Taux de croissance

Source:

United Nations Statistics Division, New York, National Accounts Analysis of Main Aggregates (AMA) database, last accessed February 2017.

Source:

Organisation des Nations Unies, Division de statistique, New York, base de données des estimations des principaux agrégats de comptes nationaux, denier accès février 2017.

1 For statistical purposes, the data for China do not include those for the Hong Kong Special Administrative Region (Hong Kong SAR), Macao Special Administrative Region (Macao SAR) and Taiwan Province of China.
2 Excluding northern Cyprus.
3 Including Guadeloupe, Martinique, Réunion and French Guiana.
4 Including Western Sahara.
5 Does not incorporate value added generated by binational hydroelectric plants.
6 Including Kosovo and Metohija.
7 Excluding Kosovo and Metohija.

1 Pour la présentation des statistiques, les données pour la Chine ne comprennent pas la Région Administrative Spéciale de Hong Kong (Hong Kong RAS), la Région Administrative Spéciale de Macao (Macao RAS) et la province de Taiwan.
2 Chypre du nord non compris.
3 Y compris Guadeloupe, Martinique, Réunion et Guyane française.
4 Y compris les données de Sahara occidental.
5 Ne comprend pas la valeur ajoutée produite par les centrales hydroélectriques binationales.
6 Y compris Kosovo et Metohija.
7 Non compris Kosovo et Metohija.

8 Data for GDP and its components excludes the temporarily occupied territory of the Autonomous Republic of Crimea and Sevastopol.
9 Tanzania mainland only.

8 Les données concernant le PIB et ses composantes excluent le territoire temporairement occupé de la République autonome de Crimée et de Sébastopol.
9 Tanzanie continentale seulement.

14 Gross value added by kind of economic activity

Percentage distribution, current prices

Valeur ajoutée brute par type d'activité économique

Répartition en pourcentage, aux prix courants

Country or area &	1985	1995	2005	2010	2013	2014	2015	Pays ou zone &
Afghanistan								**Afghanistan**
Agriculture	51.2	65.7	36.6	29.6	26.2	25.7	23.3	Agriculture
Industry	24.9	10.5	26.9	21.9	20.8	22.1	23.3	Industrie
Services	23.9	23.8	36.5	48.5	52.9	52.2	53.3	Services
Albania [1]								**Albanie** [1]
Agriculture	38.7	54.3	21.5	20.7	22.5	22.9	22.4	Agriculture
Industry	43.1	26.5	28.7	28.7	26.4	25.1	26.0	Industrie
Services	18.3	19.2	49.8	50.7	51.1	52.0	51.7	Services
Algeria								**Algérie**
Agriculture	8.4	10.4	8.0	8.6	10.2	10.7	12.2	Agriculture
Industry	49.8	47.9	59.7	51.4	45.9	43.8	37.3	Industrie
Services	41.9	41.7	32.3	40.0	43.8	45.5	50.5	Services
Andorra [1]								**Andorre** [1]
Agriculture	0.5	0.5	0.4	0.5	0.6	0.6	0.5	Agriculture
Industry	18.3	18.8	17.3	14.6	11.4	11.0	10.8	Industrie
Services	81.2	80.7	82.3	84.8	88.0	88.4	88.6	Services
Angola								**Angola**
Agriculture	13.6	7.4	5.0	6.2	6.3	8.1	6.8	Agriculture
Industry	43.4	67.4	59.8	52.1	52.0	46.2	51.2	Industrie
Services	43.0	25.2	35.2	41.7	41.7	45.8	42.0	Services
Anguilla								**Anguilla**
Agriculture	5.6	3.3	2.7	2.0	2.3	2.2	2.3	Agriculture
Industry	16.6	14.5	19.3	15.8	13.6	15.0	15.7	Industrie
Services	77.8	82.2	78.0	82.2	84.1	82.7	82.0	Services
Antigua and Barbuda								**Antigua-et-Barbuda**
Agriculture	2.2	1.9	2.0	1.8	2.2	1.8	1.9	Agriculture
Industry	11.4	14.4	16.5	18.3	17.4	17.9	18.3	Industrie
Services	86.4	83.7	81.5	79.9	80.3	80.3	79.8	Services
Argentina								**Argentine**
Agriculture	7.4	5.3	9.3	8.4	7.2	8.0	6.0	Agriculture
Industry	37.7	26.0	33.5	29.9	28.5	28.7	27.8	Industrie
Services	54.9	68.7	57.2	61.7	64.3	63.4	66.2	Services
Armenia								**Arménie**
Agriculture [1]	...	40.6	20.0	18.0	20.3	19.9	19.0	Agriculture [1]
Industry	0.0	28.6[1]	44.0[1]	35.1[1]	29.4[1]	27.8[1]	28.3[1]	Industrie
Services [1]	...	30.8	36.0	46.9	50.3	52.2	52.8	Services [1]
Aruba								**Aruba**
Agriculture [2]	0.5	0.5	0.4	0.5	0.5	0.5	0.5	Agriculture [2]
Industry [3]	15.9	15.6	19.6	15.4	15.4	15.4	15.4	Industrie [3]
Services	83.5	83.9	80.0	84.2	84.2	84.2	84.1	Services
Australia [1]								**Australie** [1]
Agriculture	4.5	3.7	3.0	2.5	2.4	2.5	2.5	Agriculture
Industry	35.5	28.5	27.9	28.5	27.1	25.5	26.5	Industrie
Services	60.0	67.8	69.1	69.0	70.5	72.0	71.1	Services
Austria [1]								**Autriche** [1]
Agriculture	3.6	2.4	1.4	1.4	1.4	1.4	1.3	Agriculture
Industry	34.6	32.2	30.4	28.7	28.6	28.3	28.3	Industrie
Services	61.8	65.4	68.2	69.9	70.0	70.4	70.4	Services
Azerbaijan [1]								**Azerbaïdjan** [1]
Agriculture	...	26.9	9.8	5.9	5.7	5.7	6.7	Agriculture
Industry	...	32.9	63.2	64.0	60.8	57.6	49.9	Industrie
Services	...	40.3	27.0	30.1	33.5	36.7	43.4	Services
Bahamas [1,4]								**Bahamas** [1,4]
Agriculture	2.2	3.6	2.1	2.2	1.7	1.8	1.6	Agriculture
Industry	13.9	12.7	14.6	15.2	17.8	18.5	12.7	Industrie
Services	84.0	83.7	83.4	82.6	80.5	79.8	85.7	Services
Bahrain [4]								**Bahreïn** [4]
Agriculture	0.8	0.7	0.3	0.3	0.3	0.3	0.3	Agriculture
Industry	38.9	36.1	42.8	45.5	48.4	46.9	40.7	Industrie
Services	60.2	63.2	56.9	54.2	51.3	52.8	59.0	Services
Bangladesh								**Bangladesh**
Agriculture	35.7	26.4	20.1	17.8	16.3	16.1	15.5	Agriculture
Industry	21.5	24.6	27.2	26.1	27.6	27.6	28.1	Industrie
Services	42.8	49.1	52.6	56.0	56.1	56.3	56.3	Services

14 Gross value added by kind of economic activity *(continued)*
Percentage distribution, current prices

Valeur ajoutée brute par type d'activité économique *(suite)*
Répartition en pourcentage, aux prix courants

Country or area &	1985	1995	2005	2010	2013	2014	2015	Pays ou zone &
Barbados								**Barbade**
Agriculture	4.5	3.5	1.8	1.5	1.8	1.7	1.7	Agriculture
Industry	23.0	16.6	16.9	14.4	11.9	11.2	12.1	Industrie
Services	72.5	79.9	81.3	84.0	86.2	87.1	86.2	Services
Belarus								**Bélarus**
Agriculture	...	16.8	9.8	10.2	7.9	8.4	7.5	Agriculture
Industry	...	37.7	43.4	40.8	41.0	40.2	38.9	Industrie
Services	...	45.5	46.8	49.0	51.1	51.4	53.6	Services
Belgium [1]								**Belgique** [1]
Agriculture	2.5	1.4	0.9	0.9	0.8	0.7	0.7	Agriculture
Industry	30.4	29.0	25.1	23.2	22.2	22.1	22.2	Industrie
Services	67.1	69.6	74.0	76.0	77.0	77.2	77.1	Services
Belize								**Belize**
Agriculture	19.8	19.8	14.7	12.6	14.7	14.9	14.6	Agriculture
Industry	24.3	23.5	16.5	20.7	18.3	17.8	18.5	Industrie
Services	55.9	56.8	68.8	66.7	67.0	67.3	66.9	Services
Benin								**Bénin**
Agriculture	32.4	23.7	27.1	25.4	23.6	23.0	23.2	Agriculture
Industry	15.5	32.5	30.3	24.7	22.5	22.7	24.9	Industrie
Services	52.0	43.8	42.5	49.9	53.9	54.3	51.9	Services
Bermuda								**Bermudes**
Agriculture	0.8	0.8	0.8	0.7	0.7	0.6	0.7	Agriculture
Industry	10.4	10.4	9.7	7.1	5.3	5.3	5.3	Industrie
Services	88.9	88.8	89.5	92.2	94.0	94.1	94.0	Services
Bhutan								**Bhoutan**
Agriculture	42.3	33.2	23.2	17.5	17.0	17.7	17.2	Agriculture
Industry	21.4	33.5	37.3	44.6	44.7	42.9	43.9	Industrie
Services	36.4	33.3	39.5	37.9	38.3	39.4	38.8	Services
Bolivia (Plurinational State of)								**Bolivie (État plurinational de)**
Agriculture	28.7	16.4	13.9	12.4	12.7	12.4	12.6	Agriculture
Industry	28.5	32.1	30.9	35.8	36.2	35.0	31.0	Industrie
Services	42.8	51.5	55.2	51.8	51.1	52.6	56.5	Services
Bosnia and Herzegovina								**Bosnie-Herzégovine**
Agriculture	...	22.0	9.8[1]	8.0[1]	8.0[1]	7.0[1]	7.3[1]	Agriculture
Industry	...	31.8	25.3[1]	26.4[1]	26.1[1]	26.0[1]	26.5[1]	Industrie
Services	...	46.2	64.9[1]	65.6[1]	65.9[1]	66.9[1]	66.2[1]	Services
Botswana								**Botswana**
Agriculture	7.4	4.9	2.0	2.8	2.6	2.3	2.4	Agriculture
Industry	54.3	46.5	47.6	35.6	36.6	38.6	33.4	Industrie
Services	38.3	48.6	50.3	61.6	60.8	59.1	64.2	Services
Brazil								**Brésil**
Agriculture	11.1	5.5[1]	5.5[1]	4.8[1]	5.3[1]	5.2[1]	5.2[1]	Agriculture
Industry	42.3	26.0[1]	28.5[1]	27.4[1]	24.9[1]	24.0[1]	22.7[1]	Industrie
Services	46.6	68.5[1]	66.0[1]	67.8[1]	69.8[1]	70.8[1]	72.0[1]	Services
British Virgin Islands								**Îles Vierges britanniques**
Agriculture	4.3	1.8	1.1	1.0	1.0	1.0	1.0	Agriculture
Industry	13.1	13.3	11.9	10.0	11.2	11.1	11.1	Industrie
Services	82.6	84.9	87.1	89.0	87.7	87.9	87.8	Services
Brunei Darussalam [1]								**Brunéi Darussalam** [1]
Agriculture	0.4	1.1	0.9	0.7	0.7	0.8	1.1	Agriculture
Industry	78.5	53.4	72.0	67.4	68.7	66.7	60.2	Industrie
Services	21.1	45.5	27.1	31.9	30.6	32.4	38.7	Services
Bulgaria [1]								**Bulgarie** [1]
Agriculture	13.0	13.4	8.5	4.9	5.3	5.3	5.1	Agriculture
Industry	53.9	25.6	28.2	27.5	27.6	27.2	27.6	Industrie
Services	33.1	61.0	63.3	67.6	67.1	67.6	67.2	Services
Burkina Faso								**Burkina Faso**
Agriculture	34.9	34.3	38.5	35.1	34.7	35.8	34.5	Agriculture
Industry	19.8	24.8	17.7	20.2	21.8	21.0	21.8	Industrie
Services	45.4	40.9	43.8	44.7	43.5	43.2	43.7	Services
Burundi								**Burundi**
Agriculture	56.1	48.2	43.0	40.7	41.4	35.9	36.3	Agriculture
Industry	17.0	19.2	17.8	16.3	16.8	16.2	13.9	Industrie
Services	26.9	32.6	39.1	43.0	41.8	47.9	49.8	Services

14 Gross value added by kind of economic activity *(continued)*
Percentage distribution, current prices

Valeur ajoutée brute par type d'activité économique *(suite)*
Répartition en pourcentage, aux prix courants

Country or area &	1985	1995	2005	2010	2013	2014	2015	Pays ou zone &
Cabo Verde								**Cabo Verde**
Agriculture	17.3	15.6	11.7	9.2	9.4	9.4	9.5	Agriculture
Industry	25.4	30.0	22.8	20.8	20.0	20.0	19.8	Industrie
Services	57.3	54.4	65.5	70.1	70.6	70.6	70.7	Services
Cambodia								**Cambodge**
Agriculture	47.0	51.4	32.4	36.0	33.5	30.7	28.2	Agriculture
Industry	13.6	12.9	26.4	23.3	25.6	27.2	29.4	Industrie
Services	39.4	35.7	41.2	40.7	40.8	42.2	42.3	Services
Cameroon								**Cameroun**
Agriculture	19.8	23.7	20.4	23.3	22.7	22.0	22.7	Agriculture
Industry	32.4	29.8	31.8	29.7	29.7	29.9	28.3	Industrie
Services	47.8	46.5	47.8	47.0	47.6	48.1	49.1	Services
Canada								**Canada**
Agriculture	3.5	2.9	1.8	1.4[1]	1.8[1]	1.8[1]	1.8[1]	Agriculture
Industry	35.1	30.7	32.4	28.6[1]	28.2[1]	28.8[1]	28.6[1]	Industrie
Services	61.4	66.4	65.8	70.0[1]	70.0[1]	69.4[1]	69.6[1]	Services
Cayman Islands [1]								**Îles Caïmanes [1]**
Agriculture	0.3	0.2	0.2	0.3	0.3	0.3	0.3	Agriculture
Industry	9.8	9.2	9.1	7.7	7.5	7.4	7.5	Industrie
Services	89.9	90.5	90.6	92.0	92.2	92.3	92.2	Services
Central African Rep.								**Rép. centrafricaine**
Agriculture	35.7	36.1	45.0	41.2	34.1	34.8	34.9	Agriculture
Industry	22.2	26.9	18.6	24.0	28.6	26.4	24.8	Industrie
Services	42.1	37.0	36.5	34.8	37.3	38.8	40.4	Services
Chad								**Tchad**
Agriculture	32.0	27.9	26.1	35.9	23.9	24.3	25.4	Agriculture
Industry	14.3	14.4	34.9	36.7	42.6	39.7	39.0	Industrie
Services	53.7	57.6	39.0	27.4	33.5	36.0	35.6	Services
Chile [4]								**Chili [4]**
Agriculture	5.4	5.4	4.1	3.5	3.3	3.7	3.9	Agriculture
Industry	37.0	41.4	40.3	39.6	35.0	34.6	32.8	Industrie
Services	57.6	53.2	55.6	57.0	61.7	61.7	63.3	Services
China [4,5]								**Chine [4,5]**
Agriculture	28.2	19.8	12.0	9.8	9.6	9.3	9.2	Agriculture
Industry	42.8	46.9	47.2	46.6	44.2	43.3	41.1	Industrie
Services	29.0	33.3	40.9	43.6	46.2	47.4	49.7	Services
China, Hong Kong SAR								**Chine, Hong Kong RAS**
Agriculture [6]	0.5	0.1	0.1	0.1	0.1	0.1	0.1	Agriculture [6]
Industry	26.9	14.1	8.7	7.0	7.1	7.2	7.2	Industrie
Services [7]	72.6	85.7	91.3	93.0	92.9	92.7	92.7	Services [7]
China, Macao SAR								**Chine, Macao RAS**
Industry	24.7	14.5	14.9	7.4	5.8	7.7	6.6	Industrie
Services	75.3	85.5	85.1	92.6	94.2	92.3	93.4	Services
Colombia								**Colombie**
Agriculture	12.3	9.3	8.4	7.1	6.1	6.3	6.8	Agriculture
Industry	31.2	30.0	32.8	35.0	37.1	35.6	34.0	Industrie
Services	56.5	60.7	58.8	57.9	56.8	58.0	59.2	Services
Comoros								**Comores**
Agriculture	33.0	40.9	34.4	32.5	31.0	31.3	30.7	Agriculture
Industry	18.0	11.9	4.0	4.2	4.2	4.1	4.0	Industrie
Services	49.0	47.2	61.7	63.3	64.8	64.7	65.3	Services
Congo								**Congo**
Agriculture	7.6	10.9	4.6	3.7	4.5	5.1	4.7	Agriculture
Industry	54.9	46.9	73.4	78.1	73.4	70.9	70.0	Industrie
Services	37.5	42.2	22.0	18.2	22.1	24.0	25.3	Services
Cook Islands [4]								**Îles Cook [4]**
Agriculture	6.8	7.4	6.9	4.9	7.2	9.0	8.1	Agriculture
Industry	8.8	7.8	9.6	8.5	9.5	7.5	9.0	Industrie
Services	84.5	84.8	83.5	86.6	83.3	83.5	82.9	Services
Costa Rica [1]								**Costa Rica [1]**
Agriculture	16.3	14.8	9.6	7.2	5.5	5.6	5.1	Agriculture
Industry	30.2	26.3	26.9	25.4	22.6	22.1	21.5	Industrie
Services	53.5	58.9	63.6	67.4	71.9	72.4	73.4	Services

14 Gross value added by kind of economic activity *(continued)*
Percentage distribution, current prices

Valeur ajoutée brute par type d'activité économique *(suite)*
Répartition en pourcentage, aux prix courants

Country or area &	1985	1995	2005	2010	2013	2014	2015	Pays ou zone &
Côte d'Ivoire								**Côte d'Ivoire**
Agriculture	28.1	26.7	25.2	27.0	23.4	23.7	23.7	Agriculture
Industry	21.8	22.4	25.5	24.7	28.9	27.7	28.3	Industrie
Services	50.1	50.9	49.3	48.3	47.7	48.5	48.1	Services
Croatia [1]								**Croatie** [1]
Agriculture	...	7.2	5.0	4.9	4.4	4.1	4.1	Agriculture
Industry	...	32.3	29.0	27.1	26.6	26.6	26.6	Industrie
Services	...	60.5	66.0	68.1	69.0	69.2	69.3	Services
Cuba								**Cuba**
Agriculture	12.5	8.8	5.6	5.0	5.0	5.0	5.0	Agriculture
Industry	19.2	22.9	19.4	20.5	20.5	20.5	20.5	Industrie
Services	68.2	68.4	75.0	74.5	74.5	74.5	74.5	Services
Curaçao								**Curaçao**
Agriculture [2]	...	...	0.6	0.5	0.4	0.4	0.5	Agriculture [2]
Industry	...	...	16.4	16.0	19.9	19.9	19.8	Industrie
Services	...	...	83.0	83.5	79.6	79.7	79.8	Services
Cyprus [1,8]								**Chypre** [1,8]
Agriculture	7.6	5.2	3.1	2.4	2.3	2.1	2.3	Agriculture
Industry	27.0	22.0	20.5	16.7	11.3	10.7	10.6	Industrie
Services	65.4	72.8	76.4	80.9	86.5	87.2	87.2	Services
Czechia [1]								**Tchéquie** [1]
Agriculture	...	4.4	2.4	1.7	2.7	2.7	2.5	Agriculture
Industry	...	39.0	37.7	36.8	36.7	37.9	37.8	Industrie
Services	...	56.7	59.8	61.5	60.6	59.4	59.7	Services
Dem. P. R. Korea								**R. p. dém. de Corée**
Agriculture	28.3	27.6	25.0	20.8	22.4	21.8	21.6	Agriculture
Industry	48.5	42.0	42.8	48.2	47.6	46.9	46.2	Industrie
Services	23.2	30.3	32.2	31.0	30.0	31.3	32.2	Services
Dem. Rep. of the Congo								**Rép. dém. du Congo**
Agriculture	31.8	57.0	22.3	22.4	20.8	19.9	19.9	Agriculture
Industry	31.0	17.0	32.9	40.5	44.4	46.1	44.2	Industrie
Services	37.1	26.0	44.9	37.0	34.8	34.0	35.9	Services
Denmark [1]								**Danemark** [1]
Agriculture	4.8	3.3	1.3	1.4	1.5	1.6	1.2	Agriculture
Industry	27.0	25.5	26.2	22.8	23.2	22.5	22.9	Industrie
Services	68.3	71.2	72.5	75.8	75.3	75.9	75.8	Services
Djibouti								**Djibouti**
Agriculture	3.1[9]	3.2[9]	3.6	3.6	3.6	3.2	3.3	Agriculture
Industry	21.2[10]	15.4[10]	16.2	19.0	19.2	22.7	21.4	Industrie
Services	75.7	81.3	80.2	77.4	77.3	74.0	75.3	Services
Dominica								**Dominique**
Agriculture	22.7	13.7	13.2	13.8	14.7	14.9	15.4	Agriculture
Industry	13.7	16.0	15.0	14.4	13.9	14.7	13.2	Industrie
Services	63.6	70.3	71.9	71.8	71.4	70.4	71.5	Services
Dominican Republic [1]								**Rép. dominicaine** [1]
Agriculture	13.4	10.7	7.7	6.5	6.3	6.2	6.6	Agriculture
Industry	41.9	35.1	32.5	30.1	28.8	28.7	28.0	Industrie
Services	44.7	54.3	59.8	63.4	64.9	65.1	65.4	Services
Ecuador [1]								**Équateur** [1]
Agriculture	19.6	22.6	10.0	10.2	9.2	9.5	10.1	Agriculture
Industry	30.7	28.0	33.4	36.3	39.0	38.6	34.1	Industrie
Services	49.7	49.4	56.6	53.5	51.8	51.9	55.8	Services
Egypt [11]								**Égypte** [11]
Agriculture	18.3	16.8	14.4	14.0	11.0	11.1	11.2	Agriculture
Industry	31.7	32.7	36.9	37.5	38.9	39.0	36.3	Industrie
Services	50.0	50.9	48.8	48.5	50.1	49.9	52.5	Services
El Salvador [4]								**El Salvador** [4]
Agriculture	18.2	14.0	10.2	12.1	10.6	10.8	10.8	Agriculture
Industry	21.9	28.7	28.7	25.9	26.3	25.7	25.8	Industrie
Services	59.9	57.3	61.1	62.1	63.1	63.4	63.3	Services
Equatorial Guinea								**Guinée équatoriale**
Agriculture	14.5	12.5	1.5	1.1	1.2	1.3	1.2	Agriculture
Industry	20.6	35.8	81.3	74.3	71.9	71.1	73.1	Industrie
Services	64.9	51.6	17.2	24.6	26.9	27.6	25.7	Services

Gross value added by kind of economic activity *(continued)*
Percentage distribution, current prices

Valeur ajoutée brute par type d'activité économique *(suite)*
Répartition en pourcentage, aux prix courants

Country or area &	1985	1995	2005	2010	2013	2014	2015	Pays ou zone &
Eritrea								**Érythrée**
Agriculture	...	20.9	24.2	19.1	17.6	17.2	17.2	Agriculture
Industry	...	16.8	21.9	23.1	23.5	23.6	23.5	Industrie
Services	...	62.3	53.9	57.8	58.9	59.2	59.3	Services
Estonia [1]								**Estonie** [1]
Agriculture	...	5.7	3.5	3.2	3.5	3.6	3.4	Agriculture
Industry	...	31.9	29.8	28.0	28.8	28.6	27.4	Industrie
Services	...	62.4	66.7	68.8	67.7	67.8	69.2	Services
Ethiopia								**Éthiopie**
Agriculture	...	57.3	45.2	45.3	44.5	41.5	40.5	Agriculture
Industry	...	10.2	13.1	10.4	11.8	14.5	16.0	Industrie
Services	...	32.4	41.7	44.3	43.7	44.0	43.5	Services
Fiji [1]								**Fidji** [1]
Agriculture	16.7	16.4	12.8	10.2	12.1	11.4	11.3	Agriculture
Industry	16.3	17.8	17.9	19.9	19.6	18.2	18.1	Industrie
Services	67.0	65.8	69.2	69.9	68.3	70.4	70.7	Services
Finland [1]								**Finlande** [1]
Agriculture	7.8	4.3	2.6	2.7	3.0	2.8	2.5	Agriculture
Industry	35.1	33.7	33.5	30.0	27.0	26.7	26.8	Industrie
Services	57.1	62.0	63.8	67.3	70.0	70.5	70.6	Services
France [1,12]								**France** [1,12]
Agriculture	3.8	2.7	1.9	1.8	1.6	1.7	1.7	Agriculture
Industry	28.4	24.5	21.5	19.6	19.8	19.6	19.5	Industrie
Services	67.9	72.7	76.6	78.6	78.5	78.7	78.8	Services
French Polynesia								**Polynésie française**
Agriculture	4.7	5.2	3.4	2.5	2.7	2.8	2.8	Agriculture
Industry	21.0	12.5	12.7	12.3	12.0	11.9	11.9	Industrie
Services	74.3	82.3	83.9	85.2	85.3	85.3	85.2	Services
Gabon								**Gabon**
Agriculture	5.0	7.3	5.2	4.6	3.6	3.9	3.8	Agriculture
Industry	58.5	54.5	62.6	55.6	55.2	50.9	54.5	Industrie
Services	36.5	38.2	32.2	39.8	41.2	45.2	41.7	Services
Gambia								**Gambie**
Agriculture	23.3	20.6	28.6	30.7	22.6	20.3	21.1	Agriculture
Industry	10.7	14.3	14.9	13.1	15.0	14.5	14.9	Industrie
Services	66.0	65.1	56.5	56.3	62.4	65.2	64.0	Services
Georgia								**Géorgie**
Agriculture	...	44.4	16.5	8.3	9.3	9.1	9.0	Agriculture
Industry	...	14.3	26.5	22.0	23.7	23.6	24.1	Industrie
Services	...	41.3	57.0	69.8	67.0	67.3	66.9	Services
Germany [1]								**Allemagne** [1]
Agriculture	1.6	1.0	0.8	0.7	0.9	0.8	0.6	Agriculture
Industry	39.4	32.9	29.4	30.2	30.2	30.5	30.5	Industrie
Services	59.0	66.0	69.8	69.1	68.9	68.7	68.9	Services
Ghana								**Ghana**
Agriculture	37.8	34.0	31.8	29.8[1]	22.4[1]	21.5[1]	19.0[1]	Agriculture
Industry	15.8	20.9	20.3	19.1[1]	27.8[1]	26.6[1]	26.9[1]	Industrie
Services	46.4	45.1	47.9	51.1[1]	49.8[1]	51.9[1]	54.1[1]	Services
Greece [1]								**Grèce** [1]
Agriculture	10.2	8.1	4.8	3.3	3.6	3.7	4.1	Agriculture
Industry	27.0	21.6	19.8	15.7	16.5	15.9	15.7	Industrie
Services	62.7	70.3	75.4	81.1	79.9	80.3	80.2	Services
Greenland								**Groenland**
Agriculture	10.2	10.2	10.2	7.5	9.8	10.6	10.0	Agriculture
Industry	14.8	14.8	15.3	17.6	15.9	13.9	15.9	Industrie
Services	75.0	75.0	74.5	74.9	74.3	75.4	74.1	Services
Grenada								**Grenade**
Agriculture	16.1	9.5	3.4	5.2	5.5	6.5	8.3	Agriculture
Industry	16.3	18.6	26.1	16.8	15.0	14.0	13.9	Industrie
Services	67.7	71.9	70.5	78.1	79.5	79.5	77.8	Services
Guatemala								**Guatemala**
Agriculture	16.8	15.8	13.1	11.4	10.9	11.0	10.8	Agriculture
Industry	29.7	29.0	28.6	28.0	28.1	28.1	27.2	Industrie
Services	53.5	55.3	58.3	60.6	60.9	60.9	62.0	Services

14 Gross value added by kind of economic activity *(continued)*

Percentage distribution, current prices

Valeur ajoutée brute par type d'activité économique *(suite)*

Répartition en pourcentage, aux prix courants

Country or area &	1985	1995	2005	2010	2013	2014	2015	Pays ou zone &
Guinea								**Guinée**
Agriculture	18.3	25.7	14.9	18.6	19.8	19.6	19.8	Agriculture
Industry	31.9	27.2	34.9	34.3	32.0	32.0	32.8	Industrie
Services	49.9	47.1	50.3	47.1	48.2	48.4	47.4	Services
Guinea-Bissau								**Guinée-Bissau**
Agriculture	46.5	55.1	45.4	46.2	44.7	42.7	45.0	Agriculture
Industry	15.6	12.2	14.7	13.5	14.6	15.1	14.5	Industrie
Services	37.9	32.7	39.9	40.3	40.7	42.1	40.5	Services
Guyana								**Guyana**
Agriculture	20.0	37.1	25.7	17.6	18.2	17.9	17.6	Agriculture
Industry	31.6	33.3	28.7	34.5	34.4	32.9	31.7	Industrie
Services	48.4	29.6	45.6	47.9	47.4	49.2	50.6	Services
Haiti								**Haïti**
Agriculture	33.3	24.3	22.4	21.0	18.5	17.6	16.7	Agriculture
Industry	24.7	31.4	32.9	33.7	36.8	37.7	38.2	Industrie
Services	42.0	44.3	44.8	45.4	44.7	44.7	45.1	Services
Honduras								**Honduras**
Agriculture	20.4	20.4	13.1	11.9	12.4	13.0	13.0	Agriculture
Industry	23.8	29.9	27.6	26.2	25.8	24.8	25.1	Industrie
Services	55.8	49.7	59.3	62.0	61.9	62.2	61.9	Services
Hungary [1]								**Hongrie** [1]
Agriculture	16.0	8.4	4.3	3.6	4.6	4.5	4.1	Agriculture
Industry	42.9	30.6	31.4	30.2	30.1	31.2	31.9	Industrie
Services	41.1	61.0	64.3	66.3	65.3	64.4	64.0	Services
Iceland [1]								**Islande** [1]
Agriculture	11.2	10.9	5.7	7.4	6.9	6.2	6.4	Agriculture
Industry	35.0	29.2	24.9	24.8	23.7	23.2	24.0	Industrie
Services	53.8	59.9	69.3	67.8	69.4	70.6	69.7	Services
India [1]								**Inde** [1]
Agriculture	32.7	27.5	19.5	18.9	18.3	17.4	17.0	Agriculture
Industry	31.0	32.8	33.6	32.5	30.8	30.0	29.7	Industrie
Services	36.3	39.6	46.9	48.7	50.9	52.6	53.2	Services
Indonesia [1]								**Indonésie** [1]
Agriculture	19.8	14.2	12.1	14.3	13.7	13.7	14.0	Agriculture
Industry	33.1	38.3	43.1	43.9	43.7	43.0	41.3	Industrie
Services	47.1	47.6	44.8	41.8	42.6	43.3	44.7	Services
Iran (Islamic Rep. of)								**Iran (Rép. islamique d')**
Agriculture	13.1	12.4	6.4	6.7	8.9	9.2	8.6	Agriculture
Industry	31.4	38.7	45.7	40.3	39.4	37.7	39.1	Industrie
Services	55.4	48.9	47.9	53.1	51.7	53.1	52.3	Services
Iraq								**Iraq**
Agriculture	13.9 [13]	12.3	6.9	5.1	4.7	4.9	4.6	Agriculture
Industry	42.2 [13,14]	66.0	63.3	55.4	57.4	56.3	58.0	Industrie
Services	43.9 [14]	21.7	29.9	39.4	37.8	38.8	37.4	Services
Ireland [1]								**Irlande** [1]
Agriculture	9.4	6.4	1.2	1.1	1.3	1.5	1.0	Agriculture
Industry	30.6	32.1	34.3	26.1	27.3	26.7	41.7	Industrie
Services	59.9	61.5	64.5	72.9	71.4	71.9	57.3	Services
Israel [1]								**Israël** [1]
Agriculture	4.2	2.0	1.8	1.7	1.3	1.3	1.3	Agriculture
Industry	26.9	26.2	23.0	22.8	22.0	21.9	21.2	Industrie
Services	68.8	71.9	75.2	75.5	76.7	76.8	77.5	Services
Italy [1]								**Italie** [1]
Agriculture	4.6	3.3	2.2	2.0	2.3	2.2	2.2	Agriculture
Industry	33.0	29.1	25.8	24.4	23.7	23.4	23.5	Industrie
Services	62.4	67.6	71.9	73.7	74.0	74.5	74.2	Services
Jamaica								**Jamaïque**
Agriculture	6.0	8.9	5.7	5.9	6.8	6.8	7.1	Agriculture
Industry	30.3	29.3	23.9	20.0	20.4	20.8	22.3	Industrie
Services	63.7	61.7	70.4	74.1	72.8	72.4	70.5	Services
Japan [1]								**Japon** [1]
Agriculture	3.0	1.8	1.2	1.2	1.2	1.2	1.2	Agriculture
Industry	37.7	33.1	28.1	27.5	26.4	26.9	26.4	Industrie
Services	59.4	65.2	70.6	71.3	72.4	72.0	72.4	Services

14 Gross value added by kind of economic activity *(continued)*
Percentage distribution, current prices

Valeur ajoutée brute par type d'activité économique *(suite)*
Répartition en pourcentage, aux prix courants

Country or area &	1985	1995	2005	2010	2013	2014	2015	Pays ou zone &
Jordan								**Jordanie**
Agriculture	5.0	4.3	3.0	3.2	3.2	3.6	4.0	Agriculture
Industry	26.5	27.5	26.9	28.7	27.6	27.8	27.7	Industrie
Services	68.5	68.3	70.1	68.1	69.1	68.6	68.4	Services
Kazakhstan [1]								**Kazakhstan** [1]
Agriculture	...	12.9	6.6	4.6	4.9	4.7	5.0	Agriculture
Industry	...	30.2	39.2	41.8	36.9	35.9	32.5	Industrie
Services	...	56.9	54.2	53.6	58.2	59.4	62.5	Services
Kenya [1]								**Kenya** [1]
Agriculture	28.7	27.6	23.2	27.1	28.6	29.4	32.0	Agriculture
Industry	25.2	20.9	22.3	20.3	19.4	18.8	19.0	Industrie
Services	46.1	51.5	54.5	52.6	52.0	51.8	49.0	Services
Kiribati [11]								**Kiribati** [11]
Agriculture	44.0	26.9	21.8	24.6	23.7	23.5	24.1	Agriculture
Industry	9.4	9.1	9.3	10.3	14.5	14.6	13.6	Industrie
Services	46.6	64.0	68.9	65.0	61.8	62.0	62.2	Services
Kosovo [1]								**Kosovo** [1]
Agriculture	...	7.2	17.2	16.2	14.4	14.3	12.6	Agriculture
Industry	...	32.6	26.6	28.4	28.2	26.7	29.1	Industrie
Services	...	60.2	56.2	55.4	57.4	59.0	58.2	Services
Kuwait								**Koweït**
Agriculture	0.6	0.4	0.3	0.4	0.3	0.4	0.6	Agriculture
Industry	56.4	52.8	60.2	58.2	65.5	62.3	48.7	Industrie
Services	43.0	46.7	39.5	41.4	34.2	37.3	50.7	Services
Kyrgyzstan [1]								**Kirghizistan** [1]
Agriculture	...	43.1	31.3	18.8	16.4	16.5	15.4	Agriculture
Industry	...	21.8	22.1	28.2	27.9	26.8	25.9	Industrie
Services	...	35.1	46.6	53.0	55.7	56.7	58.7	Services
Lao People's Dem. Rep.								**Rép. dém. pop. lao**
Agriculture	37.5	41.8	36.3	29.7	24.1	23.9	23.6	Agriculture
Industry	15.6	15.3	23.2	28.9	34.1	33.5	32.8	Industrie
Services	46.9	42.9	40.5	41.4	41.7	42.5	43.6	Services
Latvia [1]								**Lettonie** [1]
Agriculture	...	8.9	4.3	4.4	3.4	3.3	3.2	Agriculture
Industry	...	30.3	22.9	23.9	23.8	23.5	23.3	Industrie
Services	...	60.8	72.8	71.7	72.8	73.3	73.5	Services
Lebanon [1]								**Liban** [1]
Agriculture	3.7	5.7	4.0	4.3	4.2	4.3	3.2	Agriculture
Industry	22.4	31.7	16.7	15.7	18.8	20.3	19.6	Industrie
Services	73.8	62.6	79.3	80.1	77.0	75.5	77.2	Services
Lesotho								**Lesotho**
Agriculture	22.4	13.2	8.9	8.3	7.9	7.8	7.7	Agriculture
Industry	12.3	26.5	32.8	31.2	31.3	31.4	31.3	Industrie
Services	65.3	60.3	58.2	60.5	60.8	60.8	61.0	Services
Liberia								**Libéria**
Agriculture	35.9	80.5	68.8	70.0	70.1	70.7 [15]	70.8 [15]	Agriculture
Industry	24.7	5.2	9.8	11.3	11.3	11.4 [15]	11.4 [15]	Industrie
Services	39.4	14.3	21.5	18.7	18.6	17.9 [15]	17.9 [15]	Services
Libya								**Libye**
Agriculture	3.5	6.7	2.2	2.5	0.9	0.9	0.9	Agriculture
Industry	58.8	40.3	75.7	74.0	67.1	67.1	67.1	Industrie
Services	37.7	53.0	22.2	23.5	32.0	32.0	32.0	Services
Liechtenstein [1]								**Liechtenstein** [1]
Agriculture	2.5	1.5	0.9	0.8	0.7	0.7	0.7	Agriculture
Industry	32.2	29.7	38.6	39.0	40.7	41.0	40.1	Industrie
Services	65.4	68.8	60.5	60.2	58.7	58.4	59.2	Services
Lithuania [1]								**Lituanie** [1]
Agriculture	...	11.1	4.8	3.3	3.9	3.8	3.6	Agriculture
Industry	...	31.5	32.7	29.1	30.1	30.4	29.8	Industrie
Services	...	57.4	62.5	67.6	66.0	65.8	66.5	Services
Luxembourg [1]								**Luxembourg** [1]
Agriculture	2.0	1.0	0.4	0.3	0.3	0.3	0.2	Agriculture
Industry	27.8	21.0	16.6	12.7	12.2	12.9	12.1	Industrie
Services	70.2	78.0	83.0	87.0	87.5	86.8	87.7	Services

Country or area &	1985	1995	2005	2010	2013	2014	2015	Pays ou zone &
Madagascar								**Madagascar**
Agriculture	34.5	32.3	28.1	27.6	25.7	25.7	24.9	Agriculture
Industry	13.1	14.8	18.6	19.5	18.8	18.6	18.4	Industrie
Services	52.4	52.8	53.3	52.9	55.5	55.6	56.7	Services
Malawi [1]								**Malawi** [1]
Agriculture	50.0	31.9	37.1	31.9	27.5	27.5	26.1	Agriculture
Industry	28.1	21.9	16.8	16.4	16.4	16.2	16.6	Industrie
Services	21.8	46.1	46.1	51.7	56.2	56.3	57.3	Services
Malaysia								**Malaisie**
Agriculture	20.3	12.7[1,4]	8.4[1,4]	10.2[1,4]	9.2[1,4]	9.0[1,4]	8.6[1,4]	Agriculture
Industry	39.2	40.5[1,4]	46.9[1,4]	40.9[1,4]	40.3[1,4]	40.4[1,4]	39.6[1,4]	Industrie
Services	40.5	46.8[1,4]	44.7[1,4]	48.9[1,4]	50.5[1,4]	50.6[1,4]	51.8[1,4]	Services
Maldives								**Maldives**
Agriculture [2]	10.4	7.3	7.5[4]	4.1[4]	3.7[4]	3.4[4]	3.1	Agriculture [2]
Industry	8.4	10.0	14.8[4]	14.9[4]	16.6[4]	18.5[4]	22.0	Industrie
Services	81.1	82.7	77.7[4]	81.0[4]	79.8[4]	78.1[4]	74.9	Services
Mali								**Mali**
Agriculture	32.2	40.3	34.4	34.9	38.8	39.3	39.9	Agriculture
Industry	15.5	18.6	25.9	25.3	20.5	20.8	19.6	Industrie
Services	52.4	41.1	39.6	39.7	40.7	39.9	40.5	Services
Malta [1]								**Malte** [1]
Agriculture	4.3	2.8	2.2	1.7	1.4	1.3	1.4	Agriculture
Industry	34.2	28.7	23.3	19.1	16.2	15.4	15.0	Industrie
Services	61.5	68.5	74.5	79.3	82.4	83.2	83.6	Services
Marshall Islands								**Îles Marshall**
Agriculture	9.6	10.3	9.1	15.4	21.6	18.3	16.4	Agriculture
Industry	12.5	14.1	9.2	11.6	10.1	10.3	10.2	Industrie
Services	77.8	75.5	81.6	72.9	68.2	71.5	73.3	Services
Mauritania								**Mauritanie**
Agriculture	36.1	43.6	29.8	21.3	19.6	23.8	20.9	Agriculture
Industry	27.0	24.7	32.4	40.9	44.9	37.0	41.7	Industrie
Services	36.9	31.6	37.9	37.8	35.5	39.2	37.4	Services
Mauritius								**Maurice**
Agriculture	14.8	9.8	5.7	3.6[1]	3.2[1]	3.2[1]	2.9[1]	Agriculture
Industry	32.2	31.3	26.6	26.6[1]	24.6[1]	23.5[1]	22.7[1]	Industrie
Services	53.1	58.9	67.8	69.8[1]	72.2[1]	73.3[1]	74.4[1]	Services
Mexico [1]								**Mexique** [1]
Agriculture	8.3	4.7	3.2	3.3	3.5	3.5	3.6	Agriculture
Industry	41.9	37.2	38.8	38.3	37.7	37.6	36.0	Industrie
Services	49.9	58.1	58.1	58.3	58.7	58.9	60.4	Services
Micronesia (Fed. States of)								**Micronésie (États féd. de)**
Agriculture	24.5	24.9	24.2	26.7	28.1	26.1	27.8	Agriculture
Industry	7.4	7.2	5.7	7.8	7.9	6.4	6.5	Industrie
Services	68.1	68.0	70.2	65.5	64.0	67.6	65.8	Services
Monaco [1,4]								**Monaco** [1,4]
Industry	12.8	12.8	12.2	12.9	14.0	12.6	13.4	Industrie
Services	87.2	87.2	87.8	87.1	86.0	87.4	86.6	Services
Mongolia [1]								**Mongolie** [1]
Agriculture	10.1[4]	28.9[4]	17.8	13.1	15.1	14.7	14.8	Agriculture
Industry	33.1[4]	34.3[4]	37.4	37.0	34.4	34.7	34.1	Industrie
Services	56.7[4]	36.7[4]	44.8	50.0	50.4	50.5	51.1	Services
Montenegro [1]								**Monténégro** [1]
Agriculture	...	12.2	10.4	9.2	9.8	10.0	9.8	Agriculture
Industry	...	24.8	21.6	20.5	18.8	17.7	17.5	Industrie
Services	...	63.1	68.0	70.3	71.4	72.3	72.6	Services
Montserrat								**Montserrat**
Agriculture	4.0	4.9	0.9	1.1	1.4	1.6	1.4	Agriculture
Industry	17.7	12.3	16.7	13.3	15.0	16.0	12.7	Industrie
Services	78.3	82.8	82.5	85.7	83.7	82.5	85.9	Services
Morocco [16]								**Maroc** [16]
Agriculture	17.4	15.1	13.1	14.4	14.7	13.0	13.7	Agriculture
Industry	32.8	29.6	28.9	28.6	28.7	29.3	28.9	Industrie
Services	49.8	55.3	58.0	56.9	56.6	57.7	57.4	Services

Country or area &	1985	1995	2005	2010	2013	2014	2015	Pays ou zone &
Mozambique								**Mozambique**
Agriculture	47.5	33.5[1]	25.4[1]	28.9[1]	25.9[1]	24.5[1]	24.6[1]	Agriculture
Industry	13.2	14.4[1]	20.7[1]	18.6[1]	18.2[1]	20.2[1]	21.0[1]	Industrie
Services	39.3	52.1[1]	53.8[1]	52.5[1]	55.9[1]	55.3[1]	54.4[1]	Services
Myanmar [4]								**Myanmar** [4]
Agriculture	48.2	60.0	46.7	36.9	29.5	27.8	26.7	Agriculture
Industry	13.1	9.9	17.5	26.5	32.4	34.5	34.5	Industrie
Services [17]	38.7	30.1	35.8	36.7	38.1	37.7	38.7	Services [17]
Namibia								**Namibie**
Agriculture	10.0	12.7	11.4	9.2	6.8	7.0	6.6	Agriculture
Industry	43.7	27.4	27.3	29.8	32.0	31.4	30.6	Industrie
Services	46.3	59.9	61.3	61.1	61.2	61.6	62.8	Services
Nauru [4]								**Nauru** [4]
Agriculture	6.0	6.4	7.8	4.2	3.4	3.1	3.0	Agriculture
Industry	32.9	27.7	-6.5	47.4	55.5	58.2	59.9	Industrie
Services	61.1	65.8	98.7	48.4	41.1	38.6	37.1	Services
Nepal								**Népal**
Agriculture	49.0	38.9	35.2	35.4	33.8	32.6	31.8	Agriculture
Industry	11.5	17.7	17.1	15.1	15.2	14.9	14.9	Industrie
Services	39.5	43.4	47.7	49.5	51.0	52.5	53.3	Services
Netherlands [1]								**Pays-Bas** [1]
Agriculture	4.2	3.4	2.0	1.9	1.9	1.8	1.8	Agriculture
Industry	33.4	27.0	24.0	22.1	21.4	20.5	20.0	Industrie
Services	62.4	69.6	74.0	76.0	76.7	77.7	78.2	Services
Netherlands Antilles [former]								**Antilles néerlandaises [anc.]**
Agriculture [2]	1.1	0.9	0.8	0.6	...	...	...	Agriculture [2]
Industry	20.5	18.4	15.6	15.7	...	...	...	Industrie
Services	78.4	80.7	83.7	83.7	...	...	...	Services
New Caledonia								**Nouvelle-Calédonie**
Agriculture	1.8	1.8	1.7	1.4	1.4	1.4	1.4	Agriculture
Industry	25.9	22.0	26.6	25.5	26.2	26.4	26.0	Industrie
Services	72.2	76.2	71.7	73.1	72.4	72.2	72.6	Services
New Zealand [1]								**Nouvelle-Zélande** [1]
Agriculture	7.4	7.0	4.9	7.1	6.7	6.6	6.5	Agriculture
Industry	34.1	27.8	25.8	23.0	23.0	23.0	23.0	Industrie
Services	58.5	65.3	69.3	69.9	70.3	70.5	70.6	Services
Nicaragua								**Nicaragua**
Agriculture	14.8	22.3	17.7	18.8	18.0	19.1	18.8	Agriculture
Industry	33.9	22.2	23.0	24.3	27.1	26.6	26.8	Industrie
Services	51.3	55.5	59.3	56.9	54.9	54.3	54.4	Services
Niger [1]								**Niger** [1]
Agriculture	37.0	35.9	45.5	43.8	38.2	39.0	39.6	Agriculture
Industry	20.2	14.3	11.8	16.7	23.0	21.2	19.1	Industrie
Services	42.8	49.7	42.7	39.4	38.8	39.8	41.3	Services
Nigeria [1]								**Nigéria** [1]
Agriculture	23.2	27.0	25.6	23.9	21.0	20.2	20.9	Agriculture
Industry	18.2	25.1	23.7	25.3	26.0	24.9	20.4	Industrie
Services	58.6	47.9	50.7	50.8	53.0	54.8	58.8	Services
Norway [1]								**Norvège** [1]
Agriculture	3.3	3.0	1.6	1.8	1.5	1.6	1.8	Agriculture
Industry	38.3	33.1	42.5	39.0	39.8	38.1	34.6	Industrie
Services	58.3	63.9	55.9	59.2	58.8	60.3	63.5	Services
Oman								**Oman**
Agriculture	2.3	2.9	1.6	1.4	1.2	1.2	1.5	Agriculture
Industry	63.3	49.7	62.1	62.8	63.4	60.2	51.1	Industrie
Services	34.4	47.4	36.3	35.9	35.4	38.6	47.3	Services
Pakistan [1]								**Pakistan** [1]
Agriculture	30.5	28.2	24.5	24.3	24.9	25.1	25.5	Agriculture
Industry	16.8	17.9	21.3	20.6	21.1	20.9	19.0	Industrie
Services	52.7	53.9	54.2	55.1	54.1	54.0	55.5	Services
Palau [1]								**Palaos** [1]
Agriculture	14.1	6.9	4.2	4.6	4.6	4.2	3.8	Agriculture
Industry	19.0	11.3	17.5	9.9	8.4	8.7	8.0	Industrie
Services	66.9	81.8	78.2	85.5	87.0	87.1	88.2	Services

14 Gross value added by kind of economic activity *(continued)*
Percentage distribution, current prices

Valeur ajoutée brute par type d'activité économique *(suite)*
Répartition en pourcentage, aux prix courants

Country or area &	1985	1995	2005	2010	2013	2014	2015	Pays ou zone &
Panama								**Panama**
Agriculture	7.3	7.4	6.8	3.9	3.1	3.1	2.8	Agriculture
Industry	22.1	19.8	16.3	20.3	25.3	26.6	27.1	Industrie
Services	70.6	72.8	76.9	75.8	71.7	70.3	70.0	Services
Papua New Guinea								**Papouasie-Nvl-Guinée**
Agriculture	18.6	22.0	22.7	20.3	20.2	20.0	20.1	Agriculture
Industry	14.4	23.0	34.0	33.6	27.0	29.0	28.2	Industrie
Services	67.0	55.0	43.3	46.0	52.8	51.0	51.8	Services
Paraguay								**Paraguay**
Agriculture	26.5	22.8	19.6	22.5	21.5	20.5	19.0	Agriculture
Industry	24.2[18]	25.7[18]	34.8	30.1	28.3	28.8	29.5	Industrie
Services	49.3	51.5	45.7	47.4	50.1	50.6	51.6	Services
Peru [1]								**Pérou** [1]
Agriculture	10.7	8.9	7.5	7.5	7.2	7.2	7.6	Agriculture
Industry	33.3	32.3	37.7	39.1	37.5	35.3	33.3	Industrie
Services	56.0	58.8	54.7	53.5	55.3	57.5	59.2	Services
Philippines [1,15]								**Philippines** [1,15]
Agriculture	21.3	18.9	12.7	12.3	11.3	10.8	10.5	Agriculture
Industry	38.1	35.0	33.8	32.6	31.1	34.4	31.3	Industrie
Services	40.5	46.1	53.5	55.1	57.6	54.8	58.2	Services
Poland [1]								**Pologne** [1]
Agriculture	14.6	5.6	3.3	2.9	3.2	2.9	2.6	Agriculture
Industry	51.4	37.4	32.2	33.2	32.2	33.2	34.1	Industrie
Services	34.0	57.0	64.5	63.9	64.5	63.8	63.3	Services
Portugal [1]								**Portugal** [1]
Agriculture	13.3	5.4	2.6	2.2	2.4	2.3	2.3	Agriculture
Industry	26.8	28.2	24.6	22.6	21.5	21.6	22.3	Industrie
Services	59.9	66.4	72.7	75.2	76.2	76.0	75.4	Services
Puerto Rico [4]								**Porto Rico** [4]
Agriculture	2.5	1.0	0.6	0.8	0.8	0.9	0.8	Agriculture
Industry	45.3	47.6	47.3	50.7	49.5	50.0	50.0	Industrie
Services	52.2	51.4	52.1	48.4	49.7	49.1	49.1	Services
Qatar [1]								**Qatar** [1]
Agriculture	1.0	1.0	0.1	0.1	0.1	0.1	0.2	Agriculture
Industry	57.8	53.0	74.6	67.5	70.2	67.9	56.4	Industrie
Services	41.3	46.0	25.3	32.4	29.7	32.0	43.5	Services
Republic of Korea [1]								**République de Corée** [1]
Agriculture	13.0	5.9	3.1	2.5	2.3	2.3	2.3	Agriculture
Industry	37.2	39.5	37.5	38.3	38.4	38.1	38.0	Industrie
Services	49.7	54.6	59.4	59.3	59.3	59.6	59.7	Services
Republic of Moldova								**République de Moldova**
Agriculture	...	32.2	19.1	14.1	14.5	15.1	13.4	Agriculture
Industry	...	31.4	22.2	19.5	20.7	21.0	20.8	Industrie
Services	...	36.4	58.7	66.4	64.8	63.8	65.8	Services
Romania [1]								**Roumanie** [1]
Agriculture	15.5	19.2	9.5	6.3	6.1	5.3	4.8	Agriculture
Industry	54.0	38.4	36.0	41.3	36.6	36.2	34.9	Industrie
Services	30.4	42.5	54.5	52.4	57.3	58.4	60.3	Services
Russian Federation								**Fédération de Russie**
Agriculture	...	7.2	5.0	3.9	3.8	4.2	4.7	Agriculture
Industry	...	39.3	38.1	34.7	32.9	31.9	31.8	Industrie
Services	...	53.5	57.0	61.4	63.3	63.9	63.5	Services
Rwanda [1]								**Rwanda** [1]
Agriculture	53.8	44.5	41.3	34.7	35.1	35.0	34.6	Agriculture
Industry	15.7	12.4	12.5	13.8	15.7	15.2	15.1	Industrie
Services	30.5	43.1	46.2	51.5	49.2	49.8	50.3	Services
Saint Kitts and Nevis								**Saint-Kitts-et-Nevis**
Agriculture	5.7	3.3	1.9	1.6	1.5	1.3	1.2	Agriculture
Industry	19.1	24.0	25.4	28.1	25.3	27.2	28.1	Industrie
Services	75.2	72.6	72.7	70.3	73.2	71.4	70.7	Services
Saint Lucia								**Sainte-Lucie**
Agriculture	12.0	7.5	3.5	2.9	3.0	2.6	2.7	Agriculture
Industry	16.0	16.2	18.7	15.5	14.1	12.6	12.9	Industrie
Services	72.1	76.3	77.8	81.6	82.9	84.7	84.4	Services

14 Gross value added by kind of economic activity *(continued)*

Percentage distribution, current prices

Valeur ajoutée brute par type d'activité économique *(suite)*

Répartition en pourcentage, aux prix courants

Country or area &	1985	1995	2005	2010	2013	2014	2015	Pays ou zone &
Saint Vincent-Grenadines								**Saint-Vincent-Grenadines**
Agriculture	15.1	11.2	6.2	7.1	7.5	7.7	7.5	Agriculture
Industry	19.6	20.9	18.6	19.2	17.7	17.2	17.2	Industrie
Services	65.3	67.9	75.1	73.7	74.8	75.1	75.3	Services
Samoa [4]								**Samoa** [4]
Agriculture	22.4	20.1	12.3	9.1	9.6	9.2	9.3	Agriculture
Industry	27.3	27.1	30.6	25.8	25.8	25.0	24.2	Industrie
Services	50.3	52.7	57.2	65.1	64.6	65.8	66.6	Services
San Marino [1]								**Saint-Marin** [1]
Agriculture	0.1	0.1	0.1	0.1	0.1	0.1	0.1	Agriculture
Industry	40.9	40.8	38.2	35.6	34.6	32.9	33.3	Industrie
Services	59.0	59.1	61.7	64.4	65.4	67.0	66.6	Services
Sao Tome and Principe								**Sao Tomé-et-Principe**
Agriculture	27.6	26.4	18.3	11.8	12.1	11.6	12.3	Agriculture
Industry	17.9	19.6	14.9	18.2	16.1	17.3	14.7	Industrie
Services	54.5	53.9	66.8	70.1	71.8	71.1	73.0	Services
Saudi Arabia								**Arabie saoudite**
Agriculture	3.7	5.9	3.2	2.4	1.9	1.9	2.3	Agriculture
Industry	41.5	48.8	62.1	58.7	60.3	57.6	46.0	Industrie
Services	54.8	45.2	34.7	38.9	37.9	40.5	51.8	Services
Senegal								**Sénégal**
Agriculture	18.1	19.4	16.8	17.5	15.6	15.4	15.5	Agriculture
Industry	22.2	24.7	23.6	23.4	23.7	24.2	24.1	Industrie
Services	59.6	55.9	59.6	59.2	60.7	60.4	60.4	Services
Serbia [1]								**Serbie** [1]
Agriculture	...	20.9	12.0[19]	10.2[19]	9.4[19]	9.3[19]	8.2[19]	Agriculture
Industry	...	35.5	29.3[19]	28.4[19]	31.7[19]	30.2[19]	31.4[19]	Industrie
Services	...	43.6	58.7[19]	61.4[19]	59.0[19]	60.5[19]	60.5[19]	Services
Seychelles								**Seychelles**
Agriculture	6.7	5.9	3.8[1]	2.7[1]	3.2[1]	2.8[1]	2.7[1]	Agriculture
Industry	9.2	13.5	19.4[1]	16.5[1]	15.0[1]	14.4[1]	13.6[1]	Industrie
Services	84.1	80.6	76.8[1]	80.8[1]	81.9[1]	82.8[1]	83.8[1]	Services
Sierra Leone								**Sierra Leone**
Agriculture	41.0	48.1	51.0	55.2	49.1	53.3	51.4	Agriculture
Industry	20.4	9.1	11.6	8.1	21.7	16.1	17.6	Industrie
Services	38.7	42.8	37.4	36.7	29.2	30.7	31.1	Services
Singapore [1]								**Singapour** [1]
Agriculture [2]	1.0	0.2	0.1	~0.0	~0.0	~0.0	~0.0	Agriculture [2]
Industry [3]	33.4	33.8	32.4	27.6	25.0	25.5	26.4	Industrie [3]
Services	65.6	66.1	67.6	72.3	75.0	74.5	73.6	Services
Sint Maarten (Dutch part)								**Saint-Martin (partie néerlandaise)**
Agriculture	...	...	0.3	0.1	0.1	0.1	0.1	Agriculture
Industry	...	...	16.4	13.4	12.2	12.0	12.3	Industrie
Services	...	...	83.3	86.5	87.7	87.9	87.6	Services
Slovakia [1]								**Slovaquie** [1]
Agriculture	...	5.6	3.6	2.8	4.0	4.4	3.7	Agriculture
Industry	...	36.8	36.1	35.2	33.1	34.5	34.8	Industrie
Services	...	57.5	60.3	62.0	63.0	61.1	61.5	Services
Slovenia [1]								**Slovénie** [1]
Agriculture	...	4.3	2.6	2.0	2.1	2.4	2.4	Agriculture
Industry	...	34.7	34.1	30.6	32.3	33.0	32.7	Industrie
Services	...	61.0	63.3	67.4	65.6	64.5	64.9	Services
Solomon Islands								**Îles Salomon**
Agriculture	50.4	44.7	30.4	28.7	28.4	28.2	28.2	Agriculture
Industry	8.3	14.4	7.5	13.3	15.2	15.8	15.6	Industrie
Services	41.3	41.0	62.1	57.9	56.4	55.9	56.3	Services
Somalia								**Somalie**
Agriculture	66.1	60.1	60.1	60.2	60.2	60.2	60.2	Agriculture
Industry	7.6	7.3	7.4	7.4	7.4	7.4	7.4	Industrie
Services	26.3	32.6	32.6	32.5	32.5	32.5	32.5	Services
South Africa								**Afrique du Sud**
Agriculture	5.1	3.8	2.7	2.6	2.3	2.4	2.4	Agriculture
Industry	42.8	33.9	30.3	30.2	29.8	29.7	28.9	Industrie
Services	52.1	62.4	67.1	67.2	67.8	67.8	68.7	Services

14 Gross value added by kind of economic activity *(continued)*
Percentage distribution, current prices

Valeur ajoutée brute par type d'activité économique *(suite)*
Répartition en pourcentage, aux prix courants

Country or area &	1985	1995	2005	2010	2013	2014	2015	Pays ou zone &
South Sudan								**Soudan du sud**
Agriculture	...	...	...	5.1	4.7	4.9	4.6	Agriculture
Industry	...	...	...	55.4	57.4	56.3	58.0	Industrie
Services	...	...	...	39.4	37.8	38.8	37.4	Services
Spain [1]								**Espagne** [1]
Agriculture	5.7	4.2	3.0	2.6	2.8	2.5	2.6	Agriculture
Industry	34.9	30.7	30.4	26.0	23.3	23.2	23.6	Industrie
Services	59.4	65.3	66.4	71.4	74.1	74.2	73.7	Services
Sri Lanka [1]								**Sri Lanka** [1]
Agriculture	23.1	17.0	9.1	9.5	8.2	8.6	8.7	Agriculture
Industry	25.9	26.5	28.5	29.7	31.3	30.6	30.7	Industrie
Services	51.0	56.5	62.4	60.9	60.5	60.8	60.6	Services
State of Palestine [1]								**État de Palestine** [1]
Agriculture	13.2	12.6	5.8	6.4	4.7	4.4	4.8	Agriculture
Industry	30.7	31.6	25.8	23.3	23.0	22.7	23.4	Industrie
Services	56.1	55.8	68.3	70.2	72.2	72.9	71.9	Services
Sudan								**Soudan**
Agriculture	...	...	...	42.9	30.6	32.1	32.4	Agriculture
Industry	...	...	...	13.7	20.9	21.3	20.1	Industrie
Services	...	...	...	43.4	48.5	46.6	47.6	Services
Sudan [former]								**Soudan [anc.]**
Agriculture	36.7	37.1	34.5	34.6	...	...	...	Agriculture
Industry	13.2	9.9	21.7	22.9	...	...	...	Industrie
Services	50.1	53.0	43.7	42.5	...	...	...	Services
Suriname								**Suriname**
Agriculture	8.6[11]	29.9	11.3	10.2	9.3	10.0	11.4	Agriculture
Industry	28.5[11]	27.5	37.4	37.9	35.2	32.7	27.4	Industrie
Services	62.9[11]	42.6	51.3	51.9	55.5	57.3	61.1	Services
Swaziland [1]								**Swaziland** [1]
Agriculture	14.5	7.9	8.0	7.5	6.6	6.0	6.6	Agriculture
Industry	24.8	41.2	40.6	41.0	41.6	42.0	42.1	Industrie
Services	60.7	51.0	51.4	51.5	51.8	52.0	51.3	Services
Sweden [1]								**Suède** [1]
Agriculture	4.5	2.8	1.1	1.6	1.4	1.3	1.3	Agriculture
Industry	33.7	31.3	29.7	28.9	26.1	25.7	26.3	Industrie
Services	61.9	65.9	69.2	69.4	72.5	72.9	72.4	Services
Switzerland [1]								**Suisse** [1]
Agriculture	2.5	1.5	0.9	0.7	0.7	0.8	0.7	Agriculture
Industry	32.2	29.7	26.8	26.3	26.1	25.7	25.5	Industrie
Services	65.4	68.8	72.3	73.0	73.2	73.6	73.8	Services
Syrian Arab Republic [15]								**Rép. arabe syrienne** [15]
Agriculture	21.0	28.2	20.3	19.7	20.4	20.6	20.7	Agriculture
Industry	21.9	18.1	31.2	30.7	30.3	30.2	30.0	Industrie
Services	57.1	53.7	48.5	49.6	49.3	49.2	49.3	Services
Tajikistan								**Tadjikistan**
Agriculture	...	31.6	23.8	21.8	23.1	26.8	25.0	Agriculture
Industry	...	48.4	30.7	27.9	25.9	25.5	28.0	Industrie
Services	...	20.0	45.6	50.3	51.0	47.6	47.1	Services
Thailand [4]								**Thaïlande** [4]
Agriculture	15.8	9.1	9.2	10.5	11.4	10.2	9.1	Agriculture
Industry	31.8	37.6	38.6	40.0	37.0	36.8	35.7	Industrie
Services	52.3	53.3	52.2	49.4	51.6	53.0	55.1	Services
TFYR of Macedonia [1]								**ex-R.Y. de Macédoine** [1]
Agriculture	...	12.5	11.3	11.7	11.5	11.7	12.0	Agriculture
Industry	...	24.7	23.7	24.4	25.4	26.3	27.9	Industrie
Services	...	62.8	64.9	63.9	63.0	62.0	65.1	Services
Timor-Leste								**Timor-Leste**
Agriculture	...	20.0	7.3[1]	4.5[1]	4.9[1]	6.7[1]	5.2[1]	Agriculture
Industry	...	49.3	76.8[1]	82.3[1]	81.2[1]	73.4[1]	79.9[1]	Industrie
Services	...	30.7	15.8[1]	13.2[1]	13.9[1]	19.9[1]	14.9[1]	Services
Togo								**Togo**
Agriculture	37.9	41.9	43.2	46.1	44.8	47.4	45.7	Agriculture
Industry	24.4	24.6	18.9	18.2	20.6	19.6	19.7	Industrie
Services	37.8	33.4	37.5	35.7	35.1	34.4	34.6	Services

14 Gross value added by kind of economic activity *(continued)*
Percentage distribution, current prices

Valeur ajoutée brute par type d'activité économique *(suite)*
Répartition en pourcentage, aux prix courants

Country or area &	1985	1995	2005	2010	2013	2014	2015	Pays ou zone &
Tonga								**Tonga**
Agriculture	37.8	22.1	20.2	18.3	19.9	19.4	22.4	Agriculture
Industry	14.9	22.0	19.1	20.0	18.2	18.2	21.5	Industrie
Services	47.3	55.9	60.6	61.7	61.9	62.4	56.1	Services
Trinidad and Tobago								**Trinité-et-Tobago**
Agriculture	2.9	1.9	0.5	0.5	0.5	0.4	0.5	Agriculture
Industry	42.5	41.7	56.7	51.3	47.8	46.8	42.5	Industrie
Services	54.6	56.3	42.8	48.2	51.8	52.8	57.0	Services
Tunisia [11]								**Tunisie** [11]
Agriculture	14.4	10.5	10.0	8.1	9.3	9.5	10.3	Agriculture
Industry	34.7	29.6	28.8	31.1	29.8	28.8	27.8	Industrie
Services	50.8	59.9	61.3	60.8	60.9	61.6	62.0	Services
Turkey [1]								**Turquie** [1]
Agriculture	15.3	11.9	10.7	9.7	8.3	8.0	8.6	Agriculture
Industry	33.7	38.2	28.3	27.0	26.6	27.0	26.4	Industrie
Services	51.0	50.0	61.0	63.4	65.0	64.9	65.0	Services
Turkmenistan								**Turkménistan**
Agriculture	...	16.9	18.8	14.5	13.6	13.3	13.4	Agriculture
Industry	...	65.3	37.6	48.4	50.6	51.3	51.0	Industrie
Services	...	17.9	43.6	37.0	35.8	35.4	35.6	Services
Turks and Caicos Islands								**Îles Turques-et-Caïques**
Agriculture	1.3	1.3	1.2	0.6	0.6	0.6	0.6	Agriculture
Industry	16.3	16.4	19.7	12.4	11.0	11.0	10.4	Industrie
Services	82.4	82.3	79.1	86.9	88.5	88.4	89.0	Services
Tuvalu								**Tuvalu**
Agriculture	10.8	24.0	21.6	27.6	25.5	25.9	26.0	Agriculture
Industry	13.5	14.0	8.5	5.7	9.2	8.3	7.6	Industrie
Services	75.6	62.0	69.9	66.7	65.3	65.8	66.4	Services
Uganda [1]								**Ouganda** [1]
Agriculture	50.2	40.2	28.6	26.1	26.6	26.7	25.6	Agriculture
Industry	9.5	17.0	22.2	20.4	21.9	21.3	21.5	Industrie
Services	40.3	42.8	49.1	53.5	51.5	52.0	52.9	Services
Ukraine [1]								**Ukraine** [1]
Agriculture	...	14.5	10.0	8.4	10.0	11.7[20]	14.0[20]	Agriculture
Industry	...	41.8	34.1	29.0	25.9	26.2[20]	26.3[20]	Industrie
Services	...	43.7	55.8	62.7	64.1	62.2[20]	59.7[20]	Services
United Arab Emirates [4]								**Émirats arabes unis** [4]
Agriculture	0.9	1.7	1.4	0.8	0.6	0.6	0.7	Agriculture
Industry	60.4	47.3	53.8	52.4	54.3	52.4	44.9	Industrie
Services	38.7	51.0	44.8	46.8	45.0	47.0	54.4	Services
United Kingdom [1]								**Royaume-Uni** [1]
Agriculture	1.5	1.4	0.6	0.7	0.7	0.7	0.7	Agriculture
Industry	37.7	27.8	22.0	20.1	20.5	20.1	19.4	Industrie
Services	60.9	70.8	77.3	79.2	78.8	79.2	79.9	Services
United Rep. of Tanzania [21]								**Rép.-Unie de Tanzanie** [21]
Agriculture	27.6	34.2[1]	30.1[1]	31.7[1]	32.9[1]	31.0[1]	31.1[1]	Agriculture
Industry	13.0	16.7[1]	20.8[1]	21.5[1]	23.9[1]	25.0[1]	26.1[1]	Industrie
Services	59.4	49.2[1]	49.1[1]	46.8[1]	43.2[1]	44.0[1]	42.9[1]	Services
United States [1,15]								**États-Unis** [1,15]
Agriculture	1.6	1.2	1.0	1.1	1.3	1.2	1.0	Agriculture
Industry	28.4	24.3	21.5	20.2	20.5	20.6	19.7	Industrie
Services	70.0	74.5	77.5	78.8	78.2	78.2	79.3	Services
Uruguay								**Uruguay**
Agriculture	12.5	8.1	9.8	8.0	8.4	7.4	6.8	Agriculture
Industry	30.8	25.9	26.6	27.3	26.2	27.3	28.0	Industrie
Services	56.7	66.0	63.6	64.7	65.4	65.3	65.2	Services
Uzbekistan								**Ouzbékistan**
Agriculture	...	31.4	29.5	19.8	19.1	19.3	19.2	Agriculture
Industry	...	30.9	29.1	33.4	32.8	32.9	32.9	Industrie
Services	...	37.7	41.4	46.8	48.0	47.8	47.9	Services
Vanuatu [1]								**Vanuatu** [1]
Agriculture	32.6	30.5	24.1	21.9	26.7	26.8	26.7	Agriculture
Industry	5.9	9.1	8.5	13.0	8.4	8.7	8.4	Industrie
Services	61.5	60.4	67.4	65.0	64.9	64.5	64.9	Services

14 Gross value added by kind of economic activity *(continued)*

Percentage distribution, current prices

Valeur ajoutée brute par type d'activité économique *(suite)*

Répartition en pourcentage, aux prix courants

Country or area &	1985	1995	2005	2010	2013	2014	2015	Pays ou zone &
Venezuela (Boliv. Rep. of)								**Venezuela (Rép. boliv. du)**
Agriculture	6.4	5.9	4.0	5.7	5.2	5.4	5.3	Agriculture
Industry	51.9	47.1	56.9	51.0	47.0	39.6	44.7	Industrie
Services	41.7	47.0	39.2	43.4	47.9	55.0	50.0	Services
Viet Nam [1]								**Viet Nam [1]**
Agriculture	41.7	26.7	21.3	21.0	20.0	19.7	18.9	Agriculture
Industry	18.6	24.4	36.1	36.7	36.9	36.9	37.0	Industrie
Services	39.7	48.9	42.6	42.2	43.1	43.4	44.2	Services
Yemen								**Yémen**
Agriculture	...	17.5	9.6	12.0	15.4	14.0	14.7	Agriculture
Industry	...	27.7	43.8	38.3	37.0	38.2	36.9	Industrie
Services	...	56.1	46.5	49.5	47.7	47.8	48.4	Services
Zambia								**Zambie**
Agriculture	13.3	15.1	15.5	10.0[1]	8.8[1]	9.2[1]	8.2[1]	Agriculture
Industry	50.8	36.8	28.6	34.1[1]	34.7[1]	32.0[1]	32.3[1]	Industrie
Services	35.9	48.1	55.9	55.9[1]	56.6[1]	58.8[1]	59.5[1]	Services
Zanzibar [1]								**Zanzibar [1]**
Agriculture	...	21.3	23.0	32.5	33.8	30.7	28.2	Agriculture
Industry	...	22.5	17.5	19.2	19.7	18.6	19.8	Industrie
Services	...	56.2	59.5	48.3	46.5	50.7	52.0	Services
Zimbabwe								**Zimbabwe**
Agriculture	20.8	14.0	12.3	14.4	11.9	13.9	13.0	Agriculture
Industry	27.8	28.8	41.9	30.7	30.9	29.2	30.5	Industrie
Services	51.4	57.2	45.9	54.9	57.2	56.9	56.5	Services

Source:

United Nations Statistics Division, New York, National Accounts Analysis of Main Aggregates (AMA) database, last accessed February 2017.

& Table is in ISIC Rev. 3 unless otherwise indicated.

1 Data classified according to ISIC Rev. 4.
2 Includes mining and quarrying.
3 Excludes mining and quarrying.
4 At producers' prices.
5 For statistical purposes, the data for China do not include those for the Hong Kong Special Administrative Region (Hong Kong SAR), Macao Special Administrative Region (Macao SAR) and Taiwan Province of China.
6 Excludes hunting and forestry.
7 Excludes waste management.
8 Excluding northern Cyprus.
9 Excludes hunting.
10 Excludes gas.
11 At factor cost.
12 Including Guadeloupe, Martinique, Réunion and French Guiana.
13 Agricultural services and related activities such as cotton ginning and pressing are included in Industry.
14 Gas distribution is included in wholesale and retail trade.
15 Includes Taxes less subsidies on production and imports.
16 Including Western Sahara.
17 Includes gas and water.
18 Does not incorporate value added generated by binational hydroelectric plants.
19 Excluding Kosovo and Metohija.
20 Data for GDP and its components excludes the temporarily occupied territory of the Autonomous Republic of Crimea and Sevastopol.
21 Tanzania mainland only.

Source:

Organisation des Nations Unies, Division de statistique, New York, base de données des estimations des principaux agrégats de comptes nationaux, denier accès février 2017.

& Sauf indication contraire la classification utilisée dans ce tableau est la CITI Rev. 3.

1 Données classifiées selon la CITI, Rév. 4.
2 Y compris les industries extractives.
3 Non compris les industries extractives.
4 Aux prix à la production.
5 Pour la présentation des statistiques, les données pour la Chine ne comprennent pas la Région Administrative Spéciale de Hong Kong (Hong Kong RAS), la Région Administrative Spéciale de Macao (Macao RAS) et la province de Taiwan.
6 Non compris la chasse et la sylviculture.
7 Gestion des déchets non-compris.
8 Chypre du nord non compris.
9 Non compris la chasse.
10 Non compris le gaz.
11 Au coût des facteurs.
12 Y compris Guadeloupe, Martinique, Réunion et Guyane française.
13 Les services agricoles et les activités connexes (par exemple l'égrenage du coton, tressage) figurent sous « Industrie».
14 La distribution de gaz est comprise dans le commerce de gros et de détail.
15 Inclut les impôts moins subventions sur la production et les importations.
16 Y compris les données de Sahara occidental.
17 Y compris le gaz et l'eau.
18 Ne comprend pas la valeur ajoutée produite par les centrales hydroélectriques binationales.
19 Non compris Kosovo et Metohija.
20 Les données concernant le PIB et ses composantes excluent le territoire temporairement occupé de la République autonome de Crimée et de Sébastopol.
21 Tanzanie continentale seulement.

15 Balance of payments summary
Millions of US dollars

Résumé de la balance des paiements
Millions de dollars É.-U.

Country or area	1985	1995	2005	2010	2013	2014	2015	Pays ou zone
Afghanistan								**Afghanistan**
Current account	-243	...	...	-1 673	-5 049	-3 921	-5 121	Compte des transac. courantes
Capital account, n.i.e.	...	...	...	2 882	2 821	2 252	1 321	Compte de capital, n.i.a.
Financial account, n.i.e.	-101	...	...	236	76	22	87	Compte financier, n.i.a.
Reserves and related items	26	...	...	1 780	639	771	-139	Réserves et postes apparentés
Albania								**Albanie**
Current account	-36	-12	-571	-1 354	# -1 395	-1 703	-1 222	Compte des transac. courantes
Capital account, n.i.e.	...	389	123	112	# 64	115	139	Compte de capital, n.i.a.
Financial account, n.i.e.	-13	411	-393	-724	# -1 224	-1 306	-1 362	Compte financier, n.i.a.
Reserves and related items	-18	21	148	-75	# 150	68	576	Réserves et postes apparentés
Algeria								**Algérie**
Current account	1 015	...	21 180	# 12 220	1 188	-9 507	-27 229	Compte des transac. courantes
Capital account, n.i.e.	...	...	-3	# 4	~0	-3	~0	Compte de capital, n.i.a.
Financial account, n.i.e.	121	...	4 084	# -4 286	282	-3 735	-226	Compte financier, n.i.a.
Reserves and related items	1 020	...	16 904	# 15 207	107	-5 941	-27 446	Réserves et postes apparentés
Angola								**Angola**
Current account	195	-295	5 138	7 506	8 348	-3 748	-10 273	Compte des transac. courantes
Capital account, n.i.e.	...	...	...	1	...	2	6	Compte de capital, n.i.a.
Financial account, n.i.e.	-454	925	3 126	1 661	7 948	-13	-7 260	Compte financier, n.i.a.
Reserves and related items	-6	-1 239	1 438	5 200	593	-3 430	-2 694	Réserves et postes apparentés
Anguilla								**Anguilla**
Current account	...	-10	-52	-51	-48	...	...	Compte des transac. courantes
Capital account, n.i.e.	...	1	2	4	6	...	...	Compte de capital, n.i.a.
Financial account, n.i.e.	...	1	-47	-37	-36	...	...	Compte financier, n.i.a.
Reserves and related items	...	4	5	2	1	...	...	Réserves et postes apparentés
Antigua and Barbuda								**Antigua-et-Barbuda**
Current account	-23	-1	-171	-167	-204	...	...	Compte des transac. courantes
Capital account, n.i.e.	...	4	211	17	12	...	...	Compte de capital, n.i.a.
Financial account, n.i.e.	-20	11	25	-138	-201	...	...	Compte financier, n.i.a.
Reserves and related items	-3	14	7	-20	12	...	...	Réserves et postes apparentés
Argentina								**Argentine**
Current account	-952	-5 118	5 274	-1 516	-12 143	-8 031	-15 944	Compte des transac. courantes
Capital account, n.i.e.	...	14	89	89	33	59	51	Compte de capital, n.i.a.
Financial account, n.i.e.	-638	-5 466	-1 955	-13 383	-1 554	-7 179	-9 498	Compte financier, n.i.a.
Reserves and related items	-846	-2 311	7 654	10 281	-13 736	-850	-7 550	Réserves et postes apparentés
Armenia								**Arménie**
Current account	...	-221	-124	-1 261	-813	-883	-279	Compte des transac. courantes
Capital account, n.i.e.	...	8	84	99	84	70	65	Compte de capital, n.i.a.
Financial account, n.i.e.	...	-227	-442	-1 027	-1 690	-301	-901	Compte financier, n.i.a.
Reserves and related items	...	30	239	-291	662	-545	341	Réserves et postes apparentés
Aruba								**Aruba**
Current account	...	-~0	105	-460	-331	-137	96	Compte des transac. courantes
Capital account, n.i.e.	...	...	16	4	...	...	...	Compte de capital, n.i.a.
Financial account, n.i.e.	...	-42	170	-435	-340	-181	-35	Compte financier, n.i.a.
Reserves and related items	...	43	-22	-11	-43	9	146	Réserves et postes apparentés
Australia								**Australie**
Current account	...	# -18 671	-43 342	-44 714	-50 397	-43 202	-57 746	Compte des transac. courantes
Capital account, n.i.e.	...	# -300	-121	-287	-461	-360	-402	Compte de capital, n.i.a.
Financial account, n.i.e.	...	# -19 262	-49 428	-44 535	-60 138	-44 965	-51 481	Compte financier, n.i.a.
Reserves and related items	...	# 396	7 254	430	5 507	3 644	-2 346	Réserves et postes apparentés
Austria								**Autriche**
Current account	-158	-7 014	6 245	11 480	8 375	10 151	7 020	Compte des transac. courantes
Capital account, n.i.e.	...	-359	-84	270	-649	-463	-1 863	Compte de capital, n.i.a.
Financial account, n.i.e.	-332	-8 339	917	3 313	13 902	489	6 220	Compte financier, n.i.a.
Reserves and related items	15	1 391	-750	1 445	526	2 890	-364	Réserves et postes apparentés
Azerbaijan								**Azerbaïdjan**
Current account	...	-401	167	15 040	# 12 232	10 209	-222	Compte des transac. courantes
Capital account, n.i.e.	...	-2	-~0	...	# -13	-7	-44	Compte de capital, n.i.a.
Financial account, n.i.e.	...	-400	-78	12 695	# 8 106	7 182	6 077	Compte financier, n.i.a.
Reserves and related items	...	58	161	1 370	# 2 233	214	-8 429	Réserves et postes apparentés
Bahamas								**Bahamas**
Current account	-3	-146	-701	-814	-1 494	-1 928	-1 409	Compte des transac. courantes
Financial account, n.i.e.	12	-105	-822	-1 145	-981	-1 509	-370	Compte financier, n.i.a.
Reserves and related items	19	-3	-88	48	-69	52	28	Réserves et postes apparentés

15 Balance of payments summary *(continued)*
Millions of US dollars

Résumé de la balance des paiements *(suite)*
Millions de dollars É.-U.

Country or area	1985	1995	2005	2010	2013	2014	2015	Pays ou zone
Bahrain								**Bahreïn**
Current account	39	237	1 474	770	2 560	1 124	...	Compte des transac. courantes
Capital account, n.i.e.	...	157	50	50	100	100	...	Compte de capital, n.i.a.
Financial account, n.i.e.	476	1 727	1 380	-352	2 363	-3 707	...	Compte financier, n.i.a.
Reserves and related items	357	169	294	1 280	173	556	...	Réserves et postes apparentés
Bangladesh								**Bangladesh**
Current account	-458	-824	# 508	2 109	2 058	756	2 687	Compte des transac. courantes
Capital account, n.i.e.	...	...	# 263	603	725	497	418	Compte de capital, n.i.a.
Financial account, n.i.e.	-442	-179	# 206	-2 765	-4 325	-4 413	-3 231	Compte financier, n.i.a.
Reserves and related items	-84	-512	# -104	1 020	5 277	4 571	5 417	Réserves et postes apparentés
Barbados								**Barbade**
Current account	51	9	-467	-236	-248	...	...	Compte des transac. courantes
Capital account, n.i.e.	...	...	...	...	-7	...	...	Compte de capital, n.i.a.
Financial account, n.i.e.	~0	26	-418	-257	-46	...	...	Compte financier, n.i.a.
Reserves and related items	14	42	22	-45	-156	...	...	Réserves et postes apparentés
Belarus								**Bélarus**
Current account	...	-458	459	-8 280	-7 567	-5 228	-2 037	Compte des transac. courantes
Capital account, n.i.e.	...	7	...	...	10	8	5	Compte de capital, n.i.a.
Financial account, n.i.e.	...	-204	37	-6 101	-8 402	-3 524	-778	Compte financier, n.i.a.
Reserves and related items	...	-78	548	-1 477	-94	-2 146	-544	Réserves et postes apparentés
Belgium								**Belgique**
Current account	...	...	7 703	7 973	-1 577	-3 605	1 936	Compte des transac. courantes
Capital account, n.i.e.	...	...	-922	-1 142	-537	-1 379	124	Compte de capital, n.i.a.
Financial account, n.i.e.	...	...	11 397	5 747	329	-3 099	4 091	Compte financier, n.i.a.
Reserves and related items	...	...	-2 176	820	-472	-1 356	-1 075	Réserves et postes apparentés
Belize								**Belize**
Current account	9	-17	-151	-46	-73	-136	-175	Compte des transac. courantes
Capital account, n.i.e.	...	...	3	5	38	34	9	Compte de capital, n.i.a.
Financial account, n.i.e.	-9	1	-144	-27	-136	-164	-45	Compte financier, n.i.a.
Reserves and related items	2	4	-11	5	117	85	-104	Réserves et postes apparentés
Benin								**Bénin**
Current account	-39	-213	-270	-618	-673	-885	...	Compte des transac. courantes
Capital account, n.i.e.	...	84	79	115	186	253	...	Compte de capital, n.i.a.
Financial account, n.i.e.	7	125	-111	-176	-415	-732	...	Compte financier, n.i.a.
Reserves and related items	-29	-254	-52	-294	-53	106	...	Réserves et postes apparentés
Bermuda								**Bermudes**
Current account	...	...	...	696	841	818	817	Compte des transac. courantes
Financial account, n.i.e.	...	...	...	711	927	973	811	Compte financier, n.i.a.
Reserves and related items	...	...	...	3	8	-15	7	Réserves et postes apparentés
Bhutan								**Bhoutan**
Current account	...	...	...	-323	-472	-484	-579	Compte des transac. courantes
Capital account, n.i.e.	...	...	...	150	263	276	226	Compte de capital, n.i.a.
Financial account, n.i.e.	...	...	...	-195	-357	-228	-387	Compte financier, n.i.a.
Reserves and related items	...	...	...	90	168	71	-5	Réserves et postes apparentés
Bolivia (Plurinational State of)								**Bolivie (État plurinational de)**
Current account	-286	-303	622	874	1 054	# 478	-1 854	Compte des transac. courantes
Capital account, n.i.e.	...	...	...	...	...	# 5	5	Compte de capital, n.i.a.
Financial account, n.i.e.	295	-505	-181	-860	-2 022	# -449	-1 030	Compte financier, n.i.a.
Reserves and related items	-387	92	437	924	1 124	# 932	-1 610	Réserves et postes apparentés
Bosnia and Herzegovina								**Bosnie-Herzégovine**
Current account	...	...	-1 844	-1 031	-962	-1 369	-923	Compte des transac. courantes
Capital account, n.i.e.	...	...	276	264	229	299	207	Compte de capital, n.i.a.
Financial account, n.i.e.	...	...	-1 828	-586	-1 105	-1 345	-1 136	Compte financier, n.i.a.
Reserves and related items	...	...	491	-60	524	377	550	Réserves et postes apparentés
Botswana								**Botswana**
Current account	82	300	1 598	-352	1 388	2 481	1 120	Compte des transac. courantes
Capital account, n.i.e.	...	12	...	...	...	...	...	Compte de capital, n.i.a.
Financial account, n.i.e.	-123	34	774	363	965	-296	848	Compte financier, n.i.a.
Reserves and related items	254	207	2 021	-1 033	986	1 260	549	Réserves et postes apparentés
Brazil								**Brésil**
Current account	-280	-18 136	13 984	# -75 760	-74 788	-104 181	-58 882	Compte des transac. courantes
Capital account, n.i.e.	...	...	52	# 242	322	231	440	Compte de capital, n.i.a.
Financial account, n.i.e.	8 676	-29 306	-13 144	# -125 000	-66 496	-111 431	-56 303	Compte financier, n.i.a.
Reserves and related items	-9 479	12 969	27 566	# 49 080	-5 924	10 833	1 569	Réserves et postes apparentés

15 Balance of payments summary *(continued)*
Millions of US dollars

Résumé de la balance des paiements *(suite)*
Millions de dollars É.-U.

Country or area	1985	1995	2005	2010	2013	2014	2015	Pays ou zone
Brunei Darussalam								**Brunéi Darussalam**
Current account	…	…	4 033	# 5 016	3 778	5 251	2 071	Compte des transac. courantes
Capital account, n.i.e.	…	…	-8	…	…	…	…	Compte de capital, n.i.a.
Financial account, n.i.e.	…	…	82	# 4 842	2 698	4 063	4 779	Compte financier, n.i.a.
Reserves and related items	…	…	-63	# 76	178	246	-34	Réserves et postes apparentés
Bulgaria								**Bulgarie**
Current account	-136	-26	-3 347	# -965	679	100	196	Compte des transac. courantes
Capital account, n.i.e.	…	…	290	# 398	624	1 251	1 556	Compte de capital, n.i.a.
Financial account, n.i.e.	165	-327	-4 985	# 1 275	1 912	-2 708	-596	Compte financier, n.i.a.
Reserves and related items	298	445	709	# -414	-755	2 338	4 045	Réserves et postes apparentés
Burkina Faso								**Burkina Faso**
Current account	…	…	-819	-549	-1 345	-998	…	Compte des transac. courantes
Capital account, n.i.e.	…	…	209	200	483	405	…	Compte de capital, n.i.a.
Financial account, n.i.e.	…	…	-149	382	-444	-325	…	Compte financier, n.i.a.
Reserves and related items	…	…	-466	-733	-424	-283	…	Réserves et postes apparentés
Burundi								**Burundi**
Current account	-41	10	# -222	-301	-258	-393	-375	Compte des transac. courantes
Capital account, n.i.e.	…	…	# 24	78	104	82	56	Compte de capital, n.i.a.
Financial account, n.i.e.	-66	-21	# 11	-217	-163	-378	-145	Compte financier, n.i.a.
Reserves and related items	16	37	# -293	-9	-19	7	-110	Réserves et postes apparentés
Cabo Verde								**Cabo Verde**
Current account	-9	-62	-41	-223	-107	-168	-73	Compte des transac. courantes
Capital account, n.i.e.	…	21	21	38	6	8	19	Compte de capital, n.i.a.
Financial account, n.i.e.	-18	-45	-83	-298	-173	-222	-114	Compte financier, n.i.a.
Reserves and related items	14	-32	65	28	70	91	37	Réserves et postes apparentés
Cambodia								**Cambodge**
Current account	…	-186	# -321	-410	-1 607	-1 657	…	Compte des transac. courantes
Capital account, n.i.e.	…	78	# 83	331	342	278	…	Compte de capital, n.i.a.
Financial account, n.i.e.	…	-122	# -311	-256	-1 666	-2 165	…	Compte financier, n.i.a.
Reserves and related items	…	26	# 74	150	352	754	…	Réserves et postes apparentés
Cameroon								**Cameroun**
Current account	-562	90	-495	-856	-1 128	-1 400	-1 173	Compte des transac. courantes
Capital account, n.i.e.	…	20	204	147	97	95	22	Compte de capital, n.i.a.
Financial account, n.i.e.	-512	-168	78	-527	-1 103	-1 517	-1 863	Compte financier, n.i.a.
Reserves and related items	59	152	-397	7	-71	130	738	Réserves et postes apparentés
Canada								**Canada**
Current account	-5 839	-5 061	21 931	-58 160	-59 445	-43 575	-53 083	Compte des transac. courantes
Capital account, n.i.e.	-1	-433	-191	-121	-103	361	-85	Compte de capital, n.i.a.
Financial account, n.i.e.	-9 924	-4 332	19 070	-62 114	-61 629	-48 808	-62 285	Compte financier, n.i.a.
Reserves and related items	-63	2 711	1 335	3 815	4 751	5 245	8 456	Réserves et postes apparentés
Chile								**Chili**
Current account	-1 413	-1 350	1 449	3 581	-10 311	-3 316	-4 761	Compte des transac. courantes
Capital account, n.i.e.	…	…	41	6 240	11	10	585	Compte de capital, n.i.a.
Financial account, n.i.e.	1 394	-2 357	-1 550	5 943	-12 232	-4 901	-4 952	Compte financier, n.i.a.
Reserves and related items	-2 877	1 139	1 711	3 023	312	1 057	226	Réserves et postes apparentés
China								**Chine**
Current account	-11 417	1 618	# 132 378	237 810	148 204	277 434	330 602	Compte des transac. courantes
Capital account, n.i.e.	…	…	# 4 102	4 630	3 052	-33	316	Compte de capital, n.i.a.
Financial account, n.i.e.	-8 971	-38 674	# -91 247	-282 234	-343 048	51 361	485 614	Compte financier, n.i.a.
Reserves and related items	-2 440	22 469	# 250 975	471 659	431 382	117 784	-342 941	Réserves et postes apparentés
China, Hong Kong SAR								**Chine, Hong Kong RAS**
Current account	…	…	21 575	16 012	4 153	3 788	10 101	Compte des transac. courantes
Capital account, n.i.e.	…	…	-74	-571	-208	-96	-28	Compte de capital, n.i.a.
Financial account, n.i.e.	…	…	21 143	3 251	3 460	-8 516	-19 813	Compte financier, n.i.a.
Reserves and related items	…	…	-1 773	7 616	7 464	17 939	36 381	Réserves et postes apparentés
China, Macao SAR								**Chine, Macao RAS**
Current account	…	…	2 902	11 089	20 746	18 931	11 557	Compte des transac. courantes
Capital account, n.i.e.	…	…	515	20	-1	-2	-3	Compte de capital, n.i.a.
Financial account, n.i.e.	…	…	320	1 629	18 239	12 569	2 449	Compte financier, n.i.a.
Reserves and related items	…	…	1 126	5 158	-572	77	2 325	Réserves et postes apparentés
Colombia								**Colombie**
Current account	-1 809	-4 516	-1 892	-8 663	-12 449	-19 563	-18 922	Compte des transac. courantes
Financial account, n.i.e.	-2 236	-4 560	-3 231	-12 539	-18 829	-23 838	-18 770	Compte financier, n.i.a.
Reserves and related items	154	-4	1 724	3 117	6 941	4 436	417	Réserves et postes apparentés

15 Balance of payments summary *(continued)*
Millions of US dollars

Résumé de la balance des paiements *(suite)*
Millions de dollars É.-U.

Country or area	1985	1995	2005	2010	2013	2014	2015	Pays ou zone
Comoros								**Comores**
Current account	-14	-19	-29	-91	...	...	...	Compte des transac. courantes
Capital account, n.i.e.	...	...	15	30	...	...	...	Compte de capital, n.i.a.
Financial account, n.i.e.	-19	-11	-1	32	...	...	...	Compte financier, n.i.a.
Reserves and related items	6	-10	-6	-90	...	...	...	Réserves et postes apparentés
Congo								**Congo**
Current account	-161	-625	696	...	...	...	...	Compte des transac. courantes
Capital account, n.i.e.	...	19	11	...	...	...	...	Compte de capital, n.i.a.
Financial account, n.i.e.	-39	-81	227	...	...	...	...	Compte financier, n.i.a.
Reserves and related items	-81	-581	510	...	...	...	...	Réserves et postes apparentés
Costa Rica								**Costa Rica**
Current account	-291	-358	-860	-1 214	-2 431	-2 364	-2 493	Compte des transac. courantes
Capital account, n.i.e.	...	...	15	54	8	-25	31	Compte de capital, n.i.a.
Financial account, n.i.e.	287	-517	-1 552	-2 203	-3 544	-2 856	-3 189	Compte financier, n.i.a.
Reserves and related items	-435	216	393	561	461	-113	644	Réserves et postes apparentés
Côte d'Ivoire								**Côte d'Ivoire**
Current account	...	...	40	465	-633	...	...	Compte des transac. courantes
Capital account, n.i.e.	...	...	185	1 178	192	...	...	Compte de capital, n.i.a.
Financial account, n.i.e.	...	...	483	162	-125	...	...	Compte financier, n.i.a.
Reserves and related items	...	...	-315	1 427	-17	...	...	Réserves et postes apparentés
Croatia								**Croatie**
Current account	...	-1 442	-2 479	-894	567	448	2 492	Compte des transac. courantes
Capital account, n.i.e.	...	...	64	77	78	102	345	Compte de capital, n.i.a.
Financial account, n.i.e.	...	-1 143	-4 768	-1 885	-2 994	586	1 277	Compte financier, n.i.a.
Reserves and related items	...	40	1 019	18	2 473	-765	845	Réserves et postes apparentés
Curaçao								**Curaçao**
Current account	...	...	...	...	-662	-376	-517	Compte des transac. courantes
Capital account, n.i.e.	...	...	...	...	23	8	~0	Compte de capital, n.i.a.
Financial account, n.i.e.	...	...	...	...	-596	-517	-492	Compte financier, n.i.a.
Reserves and related items	...	...	...	...	-35	187	11	Réserves et postes apparentés
Cyprus								**Chypre**
Current account	-180	-205	-971	-2 906	-1 193	-1 008	-576	Compte des transac. courantes
Capital account, n.i.e.	...	...	35	78	339	195	55	Compte de capital, n.i.a.
Financial account, n.i.e.	-112	213	-1 421	-1 969	-54	-1 498	850	Compte financier, n.i.a.
Reserves and related items	-30	-363	703	-296	-386	-225	-458	Réserves et postes apparentés
Czechia								**Tchéquie**
Current account	...	-1 374	-2 810	-7 351	-1 106	438	1 683	Compte des transac. courantes
Capital account, n.i.e.	...	6	1 028	1 953	4 216	1 572	4 302	Compte de capital, n.i.a.
Financial account, n.i.e.	...	-8 225	-5 992	-8 521	-6 075	-421	-6 457	Compte financier, n.i.a.
Reserves and related items	...	7 453	3 879	2 076	9 614	3 540	14 288	Réserves et postes apparentés
Dem. Rep. of the Congo								**Rép. dém. du Congo**
Current account	...	...	-389	-2 174	-3 109	-1 723	-1 546	Compte des transac. courantes
Capital account, n.i.e.	...	...	-93	-161	193	321	252	Compte de capital, n.i.a.
Financial account, n.i.e.	...	...	-334	9 464	-2 996	-1 531	-1 291	Compte financier, n.i.a.
Reserves and related items	...	...	-43	-10 650	59	76	-195	Réserves et postes apparentés
Denmark								**Danemark**
Current account	-2 767	1 855	11 104	18 183	# 24 248	31 194	27 582	Compte des transac. courantes
Capital account, n.i.e.	...	...	518	83	# 10	-733	-1 069	Compte de capital, n.i.a.
Financial account, n.i.e.	-4 603	432	10 579	-5 327	# 30 149	35 161	23 617	Compte financier, n.i.a.
Reserves and related items	1 532	2 498	-1 506	4 280	# -647	-8 158	-3 084	Réserves et postes apparentés
Djibouti								**Djibouti**
Current account	...	78	20	50	-309	-395	-548	Compte des transac. courantes
Capital account, n.i.e.	...	5	27	55	50	65	94	Compte de capital, n.i.a.
Financial account, n.i.e.	...	2	8	-31	-273	-325	-295	Compte financier, n.i.a.
Reserves and related items	...	-7	-7	13	176	-30	-26	Réserves et postes apparentés
Dominica								**Dominique**
Current account	-6	-40	-76	-80	-72	...	...	Compte des transac. courantes
Capital account, n.i.e.	...	22	15	30	5	...	...	Compte de capital, n.i.a.
Financial account, n.i.e.	-7	-42	-57	-55	-43	...	...	Compte financier, n.i.a.
Reserves and related items	-1	8	11	1	-5	...	...	Réserves et postes apparentés
Dominican Republic								**Rép. dominicaine**
Current account	-108	-183	-473	# -4 024	-2 537	-2 170	-1 335	Compte des transac. courantes
Capital account, n.i.e.	...	...	...	...	41	...	2 087	Compte de capital, n.i.a.
Financial account, n.i.e.	-44	-254	-1 641	# -5 059	-4 148	-3 762	-1 518	Compte financier, n.i.a.
Reserves and related items	92	146	748	# 73	1 340	651	774	Réserves et postes apparentés

15 Balance of payments summary *(continued)*
Millions of US dollars

Résumé de la balance des paiements *(suite)*
Millions de dollars É.-U.

Country or area	1985	1995	2005	2010	2013	2014	2015	Pays ou zone
Ecuador								**Équateur**
Current account	76	-1 000	474	-1 586	-932	-574	-2 201	Compte des transac. courantes
Capital account, n.i.e.	...	17	16	15	12	13	-124	Compte de capital, n.i.a.
Financial account, n.i.e.	1 122	43	246	-393	-2 858	-307	-746	Compte financier, n.i.a.
Reserves and related items	-878	-1 459	865	-1 282	1 792	-474	-1 541	Réserves et postes apparentés
Egypt								**Égypte**
Current account	-2 166	-254	2 103	-4 504	-3 534	-5 972	-16 787	Compte des transac. courantes
Capital account, n.i.e.	...	...	-40	-39	-83	-141	-148	Compte de capital, n.i.a.
Financial account, n.i.e.	-1 381	1 845	-5 591	-6 470	-5 837	-1 186	-21 258	Compte financier, n.i.a.
Reserves and related items	-200	-1 827	5 226	-218	903	-3 259	-424	Réserves et postes apparentés
El Salvador								**El Salvador**
Current account	-189	-262	-622	-533	-1 586	-1 312	-920	Compte des transac. courantes
Capital account, n.i.e.	...	...	94	232	101	64	66	Compte de capital, n.i.a.
Financial account, n.i.e.	-3	-438	-787	33	-1 020	-702	-1 097	Compte financier, n.i.a.
Reserves and related items	-163	148	-190	-297	-327	-33	113	Réserves et postes apparentés
Estonia								**Estonie**
Current account	...	-158	-1 386	344	-86	225	493	Compte des transac. courantes
Capital account, n.i.e.	...	-1	103	681	651	284	467	Compte de capital, n.i.a.
Financial account, n.i.e.	...	-233	-1 520	2 210	483	153	1 087	Compte financier, n.i.a.
Reserves and related items	...	84	386	-1 112	12	164	26	Réserves et postes apparentés
Ethiopia								**Éthiopie**
Current account	106	39	-1 568	-425	...	...	...	Compte des transac. courantes
Capital account, n.i.e.	...	3	...	...	...	...	...	Compte de capital, n.i.a.
Financial account, n.i.e.	-225	25	-759	-2 369	...	...	...	Compte financier, n.i.a.
Reserves and related items	162	-105	-323	-987	...	...	...	Réserves et postes apparentés
Euro Area								**Zone euro**
Current account	...	...	19 191	31 043	288 275	315 068	358 322	Compte des transac. courantes
Capital account, n.i.e.	...	...	14 237	16 312	25 844	17 099	-13 685	Compte de capital, n.i.a.
Financial account, n.i.e.	...	...	71 432	-66 425	575 725	414 982	287 647	Compte financier, n.i.a.
Reserves and related items	...	...	-22 911	37	-9 869	19 183	42 144	Réserves et postes apparentés
Faroe Islands								**Îles Féroé**
Current account	...	...	31	144	...	...	...	Compte des transac. courantes
Fiji								**Fidji**
Current account	19	-113	# -206	-149	-407	-339	-72	Compte des transac. courantes
Capital account, n.i.e.	...	116	# 3	3	5	4	3	Compte de capital, n.i.a.
Financial account, n.i.e.	2	-88	# -204	-294	-407	-539	-317	Compte financier, n.i.a.
Reserves and related items	-4	93	# -134	137	74	22	67	Réserves et postes apparentés
Finland								**Finlande**
Current account	-806	5 231	# 7 788	3 168	-4 312	-3 205	-979	Compte des transac. courantes
Capital account, n.i.e.	...	66	# 324	234	308	247	178	Compte de capital, n.i.a.
Financial account, n.i.e.	-1 433	4 284	# 3 966	6 482	-10 428	-11 063	-2 005	Compte financier, n.i.a.
Reserves and related items	583	-372	# -180	-2 118	1 052	-284	-242	Réserves et postes apparentés
France								**France**
Current account	-35	10 840	-137	-22 034	-24 381	-31 475	-4 861	Compte des transac. courantes
Capital account, n.i.e.	...	442	1 161	1 637	2 556	2 861	2 305	Compte de capital, n.i.a.
Financial account, n.i.e.	-2 441	7 517	-2 114	-7 003	-16 889	-12 860	-16 303	Compte financier, n.i.a.
Reserves and related items	2 696	712	-9 028	7 784	-2 018	1 111	7 991	Réserves et postes apparentés
French Polynesia								**Polynésie française**
Current account	...	...	9	-18	159	208	...	Compte des transac. courantes
Capital account, n.i.e.	...	...	-1	-1	4	-1	...	Compte de capital, n.i.a.
Financial account, n.i.e.	...	...	32	-119	175	271	...	Compte financier, n.i.a.
Reserves and related items	...	...	...	...	-~0	...	...	Réserves et postes apparentés
Gabon								**Gabon**
Current account	-162	515	1 983	...	...	...	...	Compte des transac. courantes
Capital account, n.i.e.	...	5	...	...	...	...	...	Compte de capital, n.i.a.
Financial account, n.i.e.	-164	516	1 342	...	...	...	...	Compte financier, n.i.a.
Reserves and related items	-61	-228	226	...	...	...	...	Réserves et postes apparentés
Gambia								**Gambie**
Current account	8	-8	-50	21	...	...	...	Compte des transac. courantes
Financial account, n.i.e.	4	-25	-43	25	...	...	...	Compte financier, n.i.a.
Reserves and related items	-8	2	-42	-93	...	...	...	Réserves et postes apparentés
Georgia								**Géorgie**
Current account	...	...	-757	-1 330	-1 014	-1 831	-1 775	Compte des transac. courantes
Capital account, n.i.e.	...	...	54	155	123	108	62	Compte de capital, n.i.a.
Financial account, n.i.e.	...	...	-725	-996	-763	-1 705	-1 436	Compte financier, n.i.a.
Reserves and related items	...	...	49	-212	-170	-98	-365	Réserves et postes apparentés

15 Balance of payments summary *(continued)*
Millions of US dollars

Résumé de la balance des paiements *(suite)*
Millions de dollars É.-U.

Country or area	1985	1995	2005	2010	2013	2014	2015	Pays ou zone
Germany								**Allemagne**
Current account	17 994	-32 185	131 661	193 034	253 483	281 301	279 969	Compte des transac. courantes
Capital account, n.i.e.	-741	-3 119	-2 998	1 617	-861	1 772	-144	Compte de capital, n.i.a.
Financial account, n.i.e.	18 494	-44 430	123 102	121 606	290 412	327 231	252 106	Compte financier, n.i.a.
Reserves and related items	2 220	7 224	-2 600	2 132	1 158	-3 295	-2 423	Réserves et postes apparentés
Ghana								**Ghana**
Current account	-134	-144	-1 105	-2 747	-5 704	-3 695	-2 809	Compte des transac. courantes
Capital account, n.i.e.	...	...	331	338	349	...	474	Compte de capital, n.i.a.
Financial account, n.i.e.	-85	-459	-834	-4 146	-5 427	-3 753	-2 640	Compte financier, n.i.a.
Reserves and related items	14	183	125	561	-1 190	-85	-172	Réserves et postes apparentés
Greece								**Grèce**
Current account	-3 276	-2 864	-18 233	-30 275	-4 947	-3 736	218	Compte des transac. courantes
Capital account, n.i.e.	...	...	2 563	2 776	4 032	3 355	2 192	Compte de capital, n.i.a.
Financial account, n.i.e.	-2 924	-3 162	-15 633	-14 180	9 794	-3 295	-6 912	Compte financier, n.i.a.
Reserves and related items	-396	-23	-104	-13 936	-6 456	5 472	10 584	Réserves et postes apparentés
Grenada								**Grenade**
Current account	2	-42	-193	-204	-213	...	...	Compte des transac. courantes
Capital account, n.i.e.	...	9	24	36	36	...	...	Compte de capital, n.i.a.
Financial account, n.i.e.	-6	-7	-144	-125	-155	...	...	Compte financier, n.i.a.
Reserves and related items	6	6	-27	-16	32	...	...	Réserves et postes apparentés
Guatemala								**Guatemala**
Current account	-246	-572	-1 301	-563	-1 351	-1 230	-96	Compte des transac. courantes
Capital account, n.i.e.	...	62	...	3	...	...	...	Compte de capital, n.i.a.
Financial account, n.i.e.	124	-495	-612	-1 584	-2 220	-1 797	-1 042	Compte financier, n.i.a.
Reserves and related items	-327	-152	109	677	302	73	475	Réserves et postes apparentés
Guinea								**Guinée**
Current account	...	-216	-160	-329	-1 240	...	...	Compte des transac. courantes
Capital account, n.i.e.	...	...	21	5	29	...	...	Compte de capital, n.i.a.
Financial account, n.i.e.	...	-109	-91	-313	-666	...	...	Compte financier, n.i.a.
Reserves and related items	...	-72	71	40	-184	...	...	Réserves et postes apparentés
Guinea-Bissau								**Guinée-Bissau**
Current account	-76	-51	-46	-99	-53	...	...	Compte des transac. courantes
Capital account, n.i.e.	31	49	36	64	32	...	...	Compte de capital, n.i.a.
Financial account, n.i.e.	-63	28	9	908	-27	...	...	Compte financier, n.i.a.
Reserves and related items	8	-41	-23	-946	14	...	...	Réserves et postes apparentés
Guyana								**Guyana**
Current account	-97	-135	-96	-246	-456	-385	-144	Compte des transac. courantes
Capital account, n.i.e.	...	11	52	27	7	4	18	Compte de capital, n.i.a.
Financial account, n.i.e.	38	-71	-127	-160	-290	-382	39	Compte financier, n.i.a.
Reserves and related items	-139	-43	14	-195	49	22	25	Réserves et postes apparentés
Haiti								**Haïti**
Current account	-95	-87	-356	-1 942	-1 287	-1 365	-723	Compte des transac. courantes
Capital account, n.i.e.	...	...	...	658	20	26	25	Compte de capital, n.i.a.
Financial account, n.i.e.	-46	-99	-15	752	-1 495	-226	-151	Compte financier, n.i.a.
Reserves and related items	-2	137	-331	-1 670	-739	-1 046	-656	Réserves et postes apparentés
Honduras								**Honduras**
Current account	-309	-201	-304	-682	-1 763	-1 444	-1 291	Compte des transac. courantes
Capital account, n.i.e.	...	...	581	48	28	32	21	Compte de capital, n.i.a.
Financial account, n.i.e.	-175	-115	-689	-1 341	-2 501	-1 658	-1 384	Compte financier, n.i.a.
Reserves and related items	-172	-41	788	567	483	456	281	Réserves et postes apparentés
Hungary								**Hongrie**
Current account	-455	# -1 577	-7 883	346	5 094	2 765	3 946	Compte des transac. courantes
Capital account, n.i.e.	...	# 60	740	2 365	4 846	5 126	5 504	Compte de capital, n.i.a.
Financial account, n.i.e.	-1 066	# -4 979	-14 977	-2 783	-8	4 724	13 572	Compte financier, n.i.a.
Reserves and related items	536	# 5 381	4 904	4 162	8 342	1 199	-5 389	Réserves et postes apparentés
Iceland								**Islande**
Current account	-115	# -47	-2 339	-308	936	673	854	Compte des transac. courantes
Capital account, n.i.e.	...	# -4	-6	-11	-11	-14	-11	Compte de capital, n.i.a.
Financial account, n.i.e.	-233	# -71	-6 286	11 967	962	-3 004	-70 152	Compte financier, n.i.a.
Reserves and related items	64	# ~0	71	-10 023	132	3 588	71 177	Réserves et postes apparentés
India								**Inde**
Current account	-4 177	-5 563	-10 284	-54 516	-49 123	-27 314	-22 457	Compte des transac. courantes
Capital account, n.i.e.	...	...	...	50	962	-74	37	Compte de capital, n.i.a.
Financial account, n.i.e.	-3 281	-3 861	-25 284	-69 597	-59 115	-68 354	-67 659	Compte financier, n.i.a.
Reserves and related items	-397	-733	14 554	14 127	10 928	37 583	44 065	Réserves et postes apparentés

15 Balance of payments summary *(continued)*
Millions of US dollars

Résumé de la balance des paiements *(suite)*
Millions de dollars É.-U.

Country or area	1985	1995	2005	2010	2013	2014	2015	Pays ou zone
Indonesia								**Indonésie**
Current account	-1 923	-6 431	278	# 5 144	-29 109	-27 510	-17 697	Compte des transac. courantes
Capital account, n.i.e.	...	...	334	# 50	45	27	17	Compte de capital, n.i.a.
Financial account, n.i.e.	-1 782	-10 259	2 587	# -26 476	-21 926	-44 916	-17 082	Compte financier, n.i.a.
Reserves and related items	510	1 573	-2 111	# 30 342	-7 325	15 248	-1 098	Réserves et postes apparentés
Iraq								**Iraq**
Current account	...	...	-7 513	6 488	# 22 590	24 428	4 121	Compte des transac. courantes
Capital account, n.i.e.	...	...	3 889	25	# 20	-10	-2	Compte de capital, n.i.a.
Financial account, n.i.e.	...	...	1 350	-7 703	# -13 365	-3 585	-4 971	Compte financier, n.i.a.
Reserves and related items	...	...	-4 523	5 066	# 8 032	-11 130	-14 191	Réserves et postes apparentés
Ireland								**Irlande**
Current account	...	...	-7 150	2 319	14 438	# 8 914	28 967	Compte des transac. courantes
Capital account, n.i.e.	...	...	418	-827	100	# 180	-1 397	Compte de capital, n.i.a.
Financial account, n.i.e.	...	...	2 501	-8 378	17 726	# -2 526	13 475	Compte financier, n.i.a.
Reserves and related items	...	...	-1 776	-42	-4 421	# 11 309	11 769	Réserves et postes apparentés
Israel								**Israël**
Current account	988	-4 790	4 043	7 855	9 746	11 817	# 13 642	Compte des transac. courantes
Capital account, n.i.e.	151	285	253	143	307	355	# 332	Compte de capital, n.i.a.
Financial account, n.i.e.	-377	-4 179	8 282	17	5 162	8 573	# 6 684	Compte financier, n.i.a.
Reserves and related items	399	458	1 623	12 076	4 672	7 159	# 7 336	Réserves et postes apparentés
Italy								**Italie**
Current account	-4 088	25 096	-29 744	-73 118	20 766	39 533	29 348	Compte des transac. courantes
Capital account, n.i.e.	222	1 721	1 628	69	329	4 226	2 873	Compte de capital, n.i.a.
Financial account, n.i.e.	-98	3 040	-25 286	-111 705	14 554	57 911	27 280	Compte financier, n.i.a.
Reserves and related items	-7 637	2 585	-1 030	1 335	1 997	-1 213	593	Réserves et postes apparentés
Jamaica								**Jamaïque**
Current account	-273	-99	-1 071	-934	-1 357	-1 114	-400	Compte des transac. courantes
Capital account, n.i.e.	...	21	~0	4	19	9	1 467	Compte de capital, n.i.a.
Financial account, n.i.e.	-217	-108	-1 310	-437	-918	-2 151	-434	Compte financier, n.i.a.
Reserves and related items	-71	27	230	-348	-179	800	428	Réserves et postes apparentés
Japan								**Japon**
Current account	...	...	170 123	220 888	46 379	36 025	135 608	Compte des transac. courantes
Capital account, n.i.e.	...	...	-4 878	-4 964	-7 681	-1 993	-2 252	Compte de capital, n.i.a.
Financial account, n.i.e.	...	...	126 662	203 004	-43 013	49 915	169 723	Compte financier, n.i.a.
Reserves and related items	...	...	22 325	43 854	38 776	8 477	5 127	Réserves et postes apparentés
Jordan								**Jordanie**
Current account	-260	-259	-2 271	# -1 882	-3 504	-2 608	-3 332	Compte des transac. courantes
Capital account, n.i.e.	...	...	8	# ~0	2	4	7	Compte de capital, n.i.a.
Financial account, n.i.e.	-248	-230	-1 849	# -2 577	-7 135	-3 250	-2 455	Compte financier, n.i.a.
Reserves and related items	-42	-171	261	# 1 460	4 584	1 986	228	Réserves et postes apparentés
Kazakhstan								**Kazakhstan**
Current account	...	-213	-1 036	1 386	1 187	5 957	-5 464	Compte des transac. courantes
Capital account, n.i.e.	...	...	5	7 898	-6	29	132	Compte de capital, n.i.a.
Financial account, n.i.e.	...	-1 163	2 294	10 632	-303	-7 270	-9 972	Compte financier, n.i.a.
Reserves and related items	...	299	-1 944	4 706	-2 380	4 255	-764	Réserves et postes apparentés
Kenya								**Kenya**
Current account	-118	-1 578	-252	-2 369	-4 872	-6 339	...	Compte des transac. courantes
Capital account, n.i.e.	...	124	103	240	98	24	...	Compte de capital, n.i.a.
Financial account, n.i.e.	-32	266	-511	-2 128	-4 924	-6 833	...	Compte financier, n.i.a.
Reserves and related items	-52	-14	117	142	394	1 378	...	Réserves et postes apparentés
Kiribati								**Kiribati**
Current account	-3	...	...	-3	15	45	...	Compte des transac. courantes
Capital account, n.i.e.	7	...	...	13	23	32	...	Compte de capital, n.i.a.
Financial account, n.i.e.	-~0	...	...	-7	15	97	...	Compte financier, n.i.a.
Reserves and related items	-~0	...	...	10	12	2	...	Réserves et postes apparentés
Kosovo								**Kosovo**
Current account	...	...	-308	-678	# -241	-502	-547	Compte des transac. courantes
Capital account, n.i.e.	...	...	20	28	# 46	27	28	Compte de capital, n.i.a.
Financial account, n.i.e.	...	...	-27	-451	# -123	-131	-384	Compte financier, n.i.a.
Reserves and related items	...	...	-40	32	# -50	-58	82	Réserves et postes apparentés
Kuwait								**Koweït**
Current account	4 798	5 017	30 071	36 989	69 493	53 966	8 584	Compte des transac. courantes
Capital account, n.i.e.	...	-194	710	2 096	4 461	3 991	-288	Compte de capital, n.i.a.
Financial account, n.i.e.	2 334	-157	32 762	45 577	68 676	57 003	14 371	Compte financier, n.i.a.
Reserves and related items	545	-139	619	611	3 356	1 253	-2 829	Réserves et postes apparentés

15 Balance of payments summary *(continued)*
Millions of US dollars

Résumé de la balance des paiements *(suite)*
Millions de dollars É.-U.

Country or area	1985	1995	2005	2010	2013	2014	2015	Pays ou zone
Kyrgyzstan								**Kirghizistan**
Current account	...	-235	-62	# -448	-1 009	-1 301	-721	Compte des transac. courantes
Capital account, n.i.e.	...	2	43	# -11	91	66	79	Compte de capital, n.i.a.
Financial account, n.i.e.	...	-260	-85	# -462	-700	-540	-689	Compte financier, n.i.a.
Reserves and related items	...	-81	68	# 103	79	-251	-67	Réserves et postes apparentés
Lao People's Dem. Rep.								**Rép. dém. pop. lao**
Current account	-164	-346	-174	29	-376	-1 178	-2 264	Compte des transac. courantes
Financial account, n.i.e.	11	-90	-162	-477	-777	-1 725	-2 819	Compte financier, n.i.a.
Reserves and related items	-136	-151	-6	103	-76	160	175	Réserves et postes apparentés
Latvia								**Lettonie**
Current account	...	-16	-1 988	492	-826	-624	-210	Compte des transac. courantes
Capital account, n.i.e.	...	...	212	470	763	1 006	758	Compte de capital, n.i.a.
Financial account, n.i.e.	...	-636	-2 598	849	-213	1 036	-563	Compte financier, n.i.a.
Reserves and related items	...	-33	525	579	520	-155	348	Réserves et postes apparentés
Lebanon								**Liban**
Current account	...	...	-2 748	-7 552	-11 471	-11 667	-8 146	Compte des transac. courantes
Capital account, n.i.e.	...	...	27	39	1 539	1 392	1 801	Compte de capital, n.i.a.
Financial account, n.i.e.	...	...	-3 786	-3 516	-9 220	-13 932	-8 783	Compte financier, n.i.a.
Reserves and related items	...	...	458	3 059	2 055	3 308	-915	Réserves et postes apparentés
Lesotho								**Lesotho**
Current account	-12	-323	# 166	-158	-168	-184	-168	Compte des transac. courantes
Capital account, n.i.e.	...	44	# 26	108	156	33	37	Compte de capital, n.i.a.
Financial account, n.i.e.	-16	-349	# 134	201	-113	-272	-240	Compte financier, n.i.a.
Reserves and related items	6	98	# 44	-209	212	125	113	Réserves et postes apparentés
Liberia								**Libéria**
Current account	1	...	-208	-737	-536	# -1 617	-860	Compte des transac. courantes
Capital account, n.i.e.	...	...	...	1 594	33	# 118	105	Compte de capital, n.i.a.
Financial account, n.i.e.	3	...	-61	-447	-794	# -913	-1 036	Compte financier, n.i.a.
Reserves and related items	2	...	-186	2 003	19	# -53	-9	Réserves et postes apparentés
Libya								**Libye**
Current account	1 906	1 672	14 945	16 801	-108	...	...	Compte des transac. courantes
Financial account, n.i.e.	-784	207	-392	10 339	4 109	...	...	Compte financier, n.i.a.
Reserves and related items	2 362	1 701	13 840	4 170	-6 912	...	...	Réserves et postes apparentés
Lithuania								**Lituanie**
Current account	...	-614	-1 891	-119	726	1 701	-977	Compte des transac. courantes
Capital account, n.i.e.	...	-39	261	1 422	1 455	1 287	1 242	Compte de capital, n.i.a.
Financial account, n.i.e.	...	-534	-1 951	448	2 217	-1 037	2 192	Compte financier, n.i.a.
Reserves and related items	...	168	712	491	-575	1 615	-1 481	Réserves et postes apparentés
Luxembourg								**Luxembourg**
Current account	...	...	4 107	3 585	3 417	3 329	2 962	Compte des transac. courantes
Capital account, n.i.e.	...	...	1 278	-263	-1 065	-1 411	-662	Compte de capital, n.i.a.
Financial account, n.i.e.	...	...	5 453	3 264	2 209	2 026	2 251	Compte financier, n.i.a.
Reserves and related items	...	...	-69	34	74	-130	-55	Réserves et postes apparentés
Madagascar								**Madagascar**
Current account	-184	-276	-767	-896	-622	...	...	Compte des transac. courantes
Capital account, n.i.e.	...	40	286	75	134	...	...	Compte de capital, n.i.a.
Financial account, n.i.e.	-6	198	-15	-943	-274	...	...	Compte financier, n.i.a.
Reserves and related items	-167	-330	-378	-41	-397	...	...	Réserves et postes apparentés
Malawi								**Malawi**
Current account	-127	-78	-507	-969	-1 236	-1 129	-710	Compte des transac. courantes
Capital account, n.i.e.	...	...	363	710	611	457	533	Compte de capital, n.i.a.
Financial account, n.i.e.	4	-88	-150	-121	-931	-924	-916	Compte financier, n.i.a.
Reserves and related items	-26	-75	41	114	177	181	101	Réserves et postes apparentés
Malaysia								**Malaisie**
Current account	-600	-8 644	19 980	# 25 644	11 205	14 846	8 960	Compte des transac. courantes
Capital account, n.i.e.	...	...	...	# -34	-5	103	-311	Compte de capital, n.i.a.
Financial account, n.i.e.	-1 929	-7 643	9 806	# 5 961	6 175	24 169	13 321	Compte financier, n.i.a.
Reserves and related items	1 148	-1 763	3 620	# -37	4 399	-11 080	346	Réserves et postes apparentés
Maldives								**Maldives**
Current account	-6	-18	-273	-196	-127	-118	-326	Compte des transac. courantes
Capital account, n.i.e.	...	...	...	9	8	7	10	Compte de capital, n.i.a.
Financial account, n.i.e.	4	-68	-223	-153	-67	-544	-461	Compte financier, n.i.a.
Reserves and related items	2	17	-23	82	69	253	51	Réserves et postes apparentés

Country or area	1985	1995	2005	2010	2013	2014	2015	Pays ou zone
Mali								**Mali**
Current account	-210	-284	# -438	-1 190	-375	-676	...	Compte des transac. courantes
Capital account, n.i.e.	81	126	# 149	230	210	201	...	Compte de capital, n.i.a.
Financial account, n.i.e.	-121	-119	# -333	-752	14	-164	...	Compte financier, n.i.a.
Reserves and related items	-27	-52	# 16	-177	-213	-485	...	Réserves et postes apparentés
Malta								**Malte**
Current account	-26	-380	-418	-420	289	755	539	Compte des transac. courantes
Capital account, n.i.e.	...	13	197	171	178	190	186	Compte de capital, n.i.a.
Financial account, n.i.e.	25	-39	-356	-91	6	128	-651	Compte financier, n.i.a.
Reserves and related items	-67	-307	219	27	-47	30	-98	Réserves et postes apparentés
Marshall Islands								**Îles Marshall**
Current account	...	...	# -3	-14	-29	-5	...	Compte des transac. courantes
Capital account, n.i.e.	...	...	# 6	19	13	9	...	Compte de capital, n.i.a.
Financial account, n.i.e.	...	...	# -4	19	-34	-14	...	Compte financier, n.i.a.
Reserves and related items	...	...	...	0	~0	0	...	Réserves et postes apparentés
Mauritania								**Mauritanie**
Current account	-116	22	...	...	-1 349	-1 537	-1 066	Compte des transac. courantes
Capital account, n.i.e.	...	...	...	...	5	16	31	Compte de capital, n.i.a.
Financial account, n.i.e.	-91	10	...	...	-1 588	-1 194	-1 246	Compte financier, n.i.a.
Reserves and related items	-31	-6	...	...	-63	-386	78	Réserves et postes apparentés
Mauritius								**Maurice**
Current account	-30	-22	-324	-1 006	# -750	-714	-566	Compte des transac. courantes
Financial account, n.i.e.	24	-25	-142	-1 065	# -1 061	-1 367	-1 081	Compte financier, n.i.a.
Reserves and related items	-3	109	-165	209	# 541	756	567	Réserves et postes apparentés
Mexico								**Mexique**
Current account	800	-1 576	-9 069	-5 270	-30 952	-26 131	-33 216	Compte des transac. courantes
Financial account, n.i.e.	612	10 487	-15 276	-49 476	-69 358	-60 958	-34 924	Compte financier, n.i.a.
Reserves and related items	-2 729	-16 312	9 996	20 698	17 778	16 722	-15 417	Réserves et postes apparentés
Micronesia (Fed. States of)								**Micronésie (États féd. de)**
Current account	...	...	...	-25	-2	22	...	Compte des transac. courantes
Capital account, n.i.e.	...	...	...	64	42	21	...	Compte de capital, n.i.a.
Financial account, n.i.e.	...	...	...	24	15	28	...	Compte financier, n.i.a.
Reserves and related items	...	...	...	5	1	11	...	Réserves et postes apparentés
Mongolia								**Mongolie**
Current account	-814	39	88	-885	-4 732	-1 934	-948	Compte des transac. courantes
Capital account, n.i.e.	...	...	...	152	141	136	116	Compte de capital, n.i.a.
Financial account, n.i.e.	-755	17	-161	-1 669	-2 808	-1 504	-788	Compte financier, n.i.a.
Reserves and related items	25	33	54	875	-1 867	-471	-268	Réserves et postes apparentés
Montenegro								**Monténégro**
Current account	...	...	...	-952	# -649	-699	-533	Compte des transac. courantes
Capital account, n.i.e.	...	...	...	-1	# 3	-~0	-~0	Compte de capital, n.i.a.
Financial account, n.i.e.	...	...	...	-710	# -420	-320	-323	Compte financier, n.i.a.
Reserves and related items	...	...	...	13	# 105	161	147	Réserves et postes apparentés
Montserrat								**Montserrat**
Current account	...	-2	-16	-19	-27	...	...	Compte des transac. courantes
Capital account, n.i.e.	...	7	7	13	30	...	...	Compte de capital, n.i.a.
Financial account, n.i.e.	...	-2	-10	-9	-8	...	...	Compte financier, n.i.a.
Reserves and related items	...	1	-~0	3	8	...	...	Réserves et postes apparentés
Morocco								**Maroc**
Current account	-891	-1 296	949	-4 209	-8 692	# -6 267	-2 161	Compte des transac. courantes
Capital account, n.i.e.	...	...	...	...	...	# 2	1	Compte de capital, n.i.a.
Financial account, n.i.e.	-815	984	88	-1 364	-3 056	# -8 833	-5 791	Compte financier, n.i.a.
Reserves and related items	-32	-1 895	449	-3 012	-5 258	# 3 726	4 307	Réserves et postes apparentés
Mozambique								**Mozambique**
Current account	...	...	-761	-1 679	-6 253	-5 797	-5 833	Compte des transac. courantes
Capital account, n.i.e.	...	...	188	355	423	375	288	Compte de capital, n.i.a.
Financial account, n.i.e.	...	...	-427	-1 471	-6 204	-5 339	-4 848	Compte financier, n.i.a.
Reserves and related items	...	...	-121	201	396	-107	-679	Réserves et postes apparentés
Myanmar								**Myanmar**
Current account	-205	-258	582	1 574	# -389	-2 725	-3 921	Compte des transac. courantes
Capital account, n.i.e.	...	...	...	...	# 6 467	-2	-6	Compte de capital, n.i.a.
Financial account, n.i.e.	-149	-243	-165	-1 117	# 948	-1 309	-4 709	Compte financier, n.i.a.
Reserves and related items	-15	-32	142	559	# 2 617	673	106	Réserves et postes apparentés

Country or area	1985	1995	2005	2010	2013	2014	2015	Pays ou zone
Namibia								**Namibie**
Current account	...	176	267	-717	-660	-1 146	-1 700	Compte des transac. courantes
Capital account, n.i.e.	...	40	80	113	129	138	138	Compte de capital, n.i.a.
Financial account, n.i.e.	...	205	875	64	1 782	-73	-819	Compte financier, n.i.a.
Reserves and related items	...	24	-401	-1 023	-2 559	-1 255	-974	Réserves et postes apparentés
Nepal								**Népal**
Current account	-122	-356	153	-128	1 160	496	2 447	Compte des transac. courantes
Capital account, n.i.e.	...	...	40	185	167	141	162	Compte de capital, n.i.a.
Financial account, n.i.e.	-26	-369	162	-285	-67	-35	183	Compte financier, n.i.a.
Reserves and related items	-93	15	171	162	1 457	846	2 329	Réserves et postes apparentés
Netherlands								**Pays-Bas**
Current account	4 248	25 773	41 599	61 820	85 496	78 607	65 129	Compte des transac. courantes
Capital account, n.i.e.	-39	-497	84	-4 121	999	-733	-37 551	Compte de capital, n.i.a.
Financial account, n.i.e.	2 373	18 839	34 149	50 863	83 999	83 129	47 261	Compte financier, n.i.a.
Reserves and related items	771	-1 911	-1 790	492	-129	-1 596	-463	Réserves et postes apparentés
Netherlands Antilles [former]								**Antilles néerlandaises [anc.]**
Current account	403	128	-106	...	...	...	...	Compte des transac. courantes
Capital account, n.i.e.	...	63	96	...	...	...	...	Compte de capital, n.i.a.
Financial account, n.i.e.	324	142	-27	...	...	...	...	Compte financier, n.i.a.
Reserves and related items	72	60	48	...	...	...	...	Réserves et postes apparentés
New Caledonia								**Nouvelle-Calédonie**
Current account	...	...	-112	-1 360	-1 861	-1 469	...	Compte des transac. courantes
Capital account, n.i.e.	...	...	9	2	8	11	...	Compte de capital, n.i.a.
Financial account, n.i.e.	...	...	-19	-1 279	-2 060	-1 519	...	Compte financier, n.i.a.
New Zealand								**Nouvelle-Zélande**
Current account	...	...	-8 025	-3 430	-5 850	-6 370	-5 501	Compte des transac. courantes
Capital account, n.i.e.	...	...	-1	4 354	2	33	226	Compte de capital, n.i.a.
Financial account, n.i.e.	...	...	-11 368	-99	1 415	-3 261	2 100	Compte financier, n.i.a.
Reserves and related items	...	...	2 417	847	-842	-140	-521	Réserves et postes apparentés
Nicaragua								**Nicaragua**
Current account	-771	-722	# -784	-791	-1 180	-913	-1 045	Compte des transac. courantes
Capital account, n.i.e.	...	227	# 479	264	229	298	363	Compte de capital, n.i.a.
Financial account, n.i.e.	-110	612	# -403	-550	-1 393	-1 317	-1 406	Compte financier, n.i.a.
Reserves and related items	9	-964	# 34	202	112	313	231	Réserves et postes apparentés
Niger								**Niger**
Current account	-69	-152	-312	-1 136	-1 150	...	...	Compte des transac. courantes
Capital account, n.i.e.	...	65	49	196	571	...	...	Compte de capital, n.i.a.
Financial account, n.i.e.	8	46	-174	-1 031	-689	...	...	Compte financier, n.i.a.
Reserves and related items	-50	-18	33	106	98	...	...	Réserves et postes apparentés
Nigeria								**Nigéria**
Current account	2 604	-2 578	36 529	13 111	19 049	899	-15 763	Compte des transac. courantes
Capital account, n.i.e.	...	-46	7 336	...	...	...	...	Compte de capital, n.i.a.
Financial account, n.i.e.	3 678	46	15 184	7 890	-6 706	-3 803	7 026	Compte financier, n.i.a.
Reserves and related items	-1 209	-2 774	11 336	-9 693	-980	-8 384	-5 977	Réserves et postes apparentés
Norway								**Norvège**
Current account	3 030	5 233	49 967	50 258	53 450	54 965	33 746	Compte des transac. courantes
Capital account, n.i.e.	...	-170	-279	-164	-243	-201	-118	Compte de capital, n.i.a.
Financial account, n.i.e.	-1 506	542	45 214	39 186	47 889	56 514	25 272	Compte financier, n.i.a.
Reserves and related items	3 460	575	4 382	3 762	3 197	7 179	-4 974	Réserves et postes apparentés
Oman								**Oman**
Current account	-10	-801	5 178	4 884	5 215	4 188	-10 807	Compte des transac. courantes
Capital account, n.i.e.	...	...	-16	-65	-113	-131	543	Compte de capital, n.i.a.
Financial account, n.i.e.	-458	19	1 501	4 216	-6 452	1 693	-11 786	Compte financier, n.i.a.
Reserves and related items	122	-432	2 809	1 510	12 298	1 117	605	Réserves et postes apparentés
Pakistan								**Pakistan**
Current account	-1 083	-3 349	# -3 606	-1 354	-4 416	-3 616	-1 603	Compte des transac. courantes
Capital account, n.i.e.	...	...	# 202	109	329	1 961	307	Compte de capital, n.i.a.
Financial account, n.i.e.	-634	-2 449	# -3 811	-3 127	-2 049	-8 777	-5 692	Compte financier, n.i.a.
Reserves and related items	-419	-1 204	# 260	694	-2 556	7 099	3 851	Réserves et postes apparentés
Palau								**Palaos**
Current account	...	...	# -40	-19	-29	-48	-24	Compte des transac. courantes
Capital account, n.i.e.	...	...	# 51	30	24	21	21	Compte de capital, n.i.a.
Financial account, n.i.e.	...	...	# 7	6	-2	-15	29	Compte financier, n.i.a.
Reserves and related items	...	...	...	0	~0	0	...	Réserves et postes apparentés

Country or area	1985	1995	2005	2010	2013	2014	2015	Pays ou zone
Panama								**Panama**
Current account	75	-471	-1 064	-3 113	-4 401	-4 795	# -3 377	Compte des transac. courantes
Capital account, n.i.e.	…	9	16	43	28	24	# 27	Compte de capital, n.i.a.
Financial account, n.i.e.	83	-116	-1 785	-1 528	-4 368	-5 699	# -3 959	Compte financier, n.i.a.
Reserves and related items	-128	-331	497	-1 276	-110	397	# -78	Réserves et postes apparentés
Papua New Guinea								**Papouasie-Nvl-Guinée**
Current account	-122	492	539	-914	-3 973	1 932	5 326	Compte des transac. courantes
Capital account, n.i.e.	…	…	33	37	24	10	8	Compte de capital, n.i.a.
Financial account, n.i.e.	-124	445	606	-1 037	-2 742	2 762	4 632	Compte financier, n.i.a.
Reserves and related items	-1	-39	-30	85	180	-105	-90	Réserves et postes apparentés
Paraguay								**Paraguay**
Current account	-252	-217	-68	-57	477	-127	-462	Compte des transac. courantes
Capital account, n.i.e.	…	11	20	40	61	141	154	Compte de capital, n.i.a.
Financial account, n.i.e.	-39	-1 012	-565	-155	-29	-1 482	477	Compte financier, n.i.a.
Reserves and related items	-140	48	163	319	1 036	1 138	-560	Réserves et postes apparentés
Peru								**Pérou**
Current account	102	-4 625	1 148	-3 782	-8 582	-8 196	-9 210	Compte des transac. courantes
Capital account, n.i.e.	32	65	6	7	12	12	6	Compte de capital, n.i.a.
Financial account, n.i.e.	200	-3 718	-24	-13 391	-10 168	-5 648	-10 078	Compte financier, n.i.a.
Reserves and related items	-1 594	-590	1 411	10 970	1 650	-3 307	-769	Réserves et postes apparentés
Philippines								**Philippines**
Current account	-36	-1 980	# 1 990	7 179	11 384	10 756	7 694	Compte des transac. courantes
Capital account, n.i.e.	…	…	# 79	88	134	108	110	Compte de capital, n.i.a.
Financial account, n.i.e.	-328	-5 309	# 2 583	-13 775	2 230	9 631	3 220	Compte financier, n.i.a.
Reserves and related items	838	1 235	# 1 662	17 528	5 085	-2 858	2 616	Réserves et postes apparentés
Poland								**Pologne**
Current account	-982	854	-7 981	-25 875	-6 749	-11 444	-2 932	Compte des transac. courantes
Capital account, n.i.e.	…	285	996	8 612	11 962	13 305	11 331	Compte de capital, n.i.a.
Financial account, n.i.e.	1 476	-9 260	-15 171	-46 129	-6 963	-6 709	388	Compte financier, n.i.a.
Reserves and related items	-2 340	9 835	8 143	15 109	946	371	1 098	Réserves et postes apparentés
Portugal								**Portugal**
Current account	380	-132	-19 537	-24 199	3 515	93	842	Compte des transac. courantes
Capital account, n.i.e.	…	…	2 782	3 317	3 716	3 390	2 474	Compte de capital, n.i.a.
Financial account, n.i.e.	-580	-3 025	-15 564	-21 653	11 727	4 069	-7 777	Compte financier, n.i.a.
Reserves and related items	707	-300	-1 743	1 270	-3 986	-186	10 786	Réserves et postes apparentés
Qatar								**Qatar**
Current account	…	…	…	…	60 461	49 410	13 751	Compte des transac. courantes
Capital account, n.i.e.	…	…	…	…	-1 961	-2 722	-737	Compte de capital, n.i.a.
Financial account, n.i.e.	…	…	…	…	47 366	43 647	18 936	Compte financier, n.i.a.
Reserves and related items	…	…	…	…	9 064	1 294	-5 503	Réserves et postes apparentés
Republic of Korea								**République de Corée**
Current account	-2 079	-9 752	12 655	28 850	81 148	84 373	105 871	Compte des transac. courantes
Capital account, n.i.e.	…	…	-1	-63	-27	-9	-65	Compte de capital, n.i.a.
Financial account, n.i.e.	-3 861	-18 562	-1 035	-3 781	63 809	71 448	97 677	Compte financier, n.i.a.
Reserves and related items	201	7 039	19 864	26 971	16 296	17 412	11 733	Réserves et postes apparentés
Republic of Moldova								**République de Moldova**
Current account	…	-88	-248	-534	-516	-569	-415	Compte des transac. courantes
Capital account, n.i.e.	…	…	…	5	58	97	23	Compte de capital, n.i.a.
Financial account, n.i.e.	…	69	-200	-522	-667	-54	-178	Compte financier, n.i.a.
Reserves and related items	…	-175	114	67	304	-509	-266	Réserves et postes apparentés
Romania								**Roumanie**
Current account	1 381	-1 780	# -8 541	-8 479	-2 077	-1 382	-2 096	Compte des transac. courantes
Capital account, n.i.e.	…	32	# 714	258	4 048	5 206	4 337	Compte de capital, n.i.a.
Financial account, n.i.e.	1 580	-812	# -14 162	-6 392	-6 754	3	1 609	Compte financier, n.i.a.
Reserves and related items	-317	-480	# 6 804	-1 156	8 825	3 960	895	Réserves et postes apparentés
Russian Federation								**Fédération de Russie**
Current account	…	6 963	84 389	67 452	33 428	57 513	69 000	Compte des transac. courantes
Capital account, n.i.e.	…	786	-12 387	-41	-395	-42 005	-309	Compte de capital, n.i.a.
Financial account, n.i.e.	…	6 290	2 048	21 529	46 213	131 049	70 852	Compte financier, n.i.a.
Reserves and related items	…	-8 325	64 968	36 749	-22 078	-107 546	1 702	Réserves et postes apparentés
Rwanda								**Rwanda**
Current account	-64	57	-98	-412	# -815	-1 047	-1 099	Compte des transac. courantes
Capital account, n.i.e.	…	…	93	286	# 235	337	300	Compte de capital, n.i.a.
Financial account, n.i.e.	-69	11	-82	-214	# -751	-591	-795	Compte financier, n.i.a.
Reserves and related items	2	53	88	72	# 228	-90	-29	Réserves et postes apparentés

Country or area	1985	1995	2005	2010	2013	2014	2015	Pays ou zone
Saint Kitts and Nevis								**Saint-Kitts-et-Nevis**
Current account	-7	-45	-65	-139	-63	...	...	Compte des transac. courantes
Capital account, n.i.e.	...	6	12	56	128	...	...	Compte de capital, n.i.a.
Financial account, n.i.e.	-9	-25	-29	-142	62	...	...	Compte financier, n.i.a.
Reserves and related items	2	2	-7	33	34	...	...	Réserves et postes apparentés
Saint Lucia								**Sainte-Lucie**
Current account	-13	-36	-129	-203	-100	...	...	Compte des transac. courantes
Capital account, n.i.e.	...	12	4	42	27	...	...	Compte de capital, n.i.a.
Financial account, n.i.e.	-12	-31	-123	-157	-57	...	...	Compte financier, n.i.a.
Reserves and related items	1	6	-17	21	-40	...	...	Réserves et postes apparentés
Saint Vincent-Grenadines								**Saint-Vincent-Grenadines**
Current account	4	-40	-102	-208	-210	...	...	Compte des transac. courantes
Capital account, n.i.e.	...	5	12	52	11	...	...	Compte de capital, n.i.a.
Financial account, n.i.e.	-1	-33	-108	-179	-210	...	...	Compte financier, n.i.a.
Reserves and related items	6	-1	-3	31	24	...	...	Réserves et postes apparentés
Samoa								**Samoa**
Current account	2	9	# -48	-44	-45	-48	-44	Compte des transac. courantes
Capital account, n.i.e.	...	...	# 35	31	43	45	44	Compte de capital, n.i.a.
Financial account, n.i.e.	~0	6	# -8	-46	-19	-24	-23	Compte financier, n.i.a.
Reserves and related items	5	2	# -1	24	-19	-25	40	Réserves et postes apparentés
Sao Tome and Principe								**Sao Tomé-et-Principe**
Current account	-18	...	-36	-88	-81	-104	-69	Compte des transac. courantes
Capital account, n.i.e.	...	...	66	42	28	29	27	Compte de capital, n.i.a.
Financial account, n.i.e.	-1	...	4	-75	-16	17	-30	Compte financier, n.i.a.
Reserves and related items	-11	...	31	13	6	-2	4	Réserves et postes apparentés
Saudi Arabia								**Arabie saoudite**
Current account	-12 932	-5 318	# 90 060	66 751	135 442	73 758	-56 724	Compte des transac. courantes
Capital account, n.i.e.	...	...	...	...	-335	-329	-1 062	Compte de capital, n.i.a.
Financial account, n.i.e.	-12 222	-6 533	# -8 361	-2 657	57 382	57 357	42 853	Compte financier, n.i.a.
Reserves and related items	-709	1 215	# 63 969	35 255	69 127	7 477	-115 369	Réserves et postes apparentés
Senegal								**Sénégal**
Current account	-361	-244	# -676	-589	-1 550	-1 348	...	Compte des transac. courantes
Capital account, n.i.e.	88	187	# 200	302	367	437	...	Compte de capital, n.i.a.
Financial account, n.i.e.	-179	-44	# -118	224	-1 252	-987	...	Compte financier, n.i.a.
Reserves and related items	-91	-33	# -362	-529	88	65	...	Réserves et postes apparentés
Serbia								**Serbie**
Current account	...	...	...	-2 692	-2 795	-2 635	-1 751	Compte des transac. courantes
Capital account, n.i.e.	...	...	...	-1	20	9	-19	Compte de capital, n.i.a.
Financial account, n.i.e.	...	...	...	-402	-4 007	-669	-1 685	Compte financier, n.i.a.
Reserves and related items	...	...	...	-1 676	1 838	-1 597	346	Réserves et postes apparentés
Seychelles								**Seychelles**
Current account	-19	-3	-188	-214	-159	-310	-256	Compte des transac. courantes
Capital account, n.i.e.	...	1	30	275	71	39	37	Compte de capital, n.i.a.
Financial account, n.i.e.	-16	1	-129	-164	-134	-236	-289	Compte financier, n.i.a.
Reserves and related items	-~0	-32	-29	302	95	41	71	Réserves et postes apparentés
Sierra Leone								**Sierra Leone**
Current account	3	-118	-171	-746	-775	-1 317	...	Compte des transac. courantes
Capital account, n.i.e.	...	...	37	79	93	163	...	Compte de capital, n.i.a.
Financial account, n.i.e.	-4	-98	-63	-325	-753	-624	...	Compte financier, n.i.a.
Reserves and related items	-74	1	-130	-319	-69	-505	...	Réserves et postes apparentés
Singapore								**Singapour**
Current account	-4	# 14 445	28 133	56 292	53 771	53 516	57 922	Compte des transac. courantes
Financial account, n.i.e.	-698	# 5 580	16 837	17 605	37 326	46 231	56 045	Compte financier, n.i.a.
Reserves and related items	1 337	# 8 594	12 283	42 353	18 097	6 819	1 052	Réserves et postes apparentés
Sint Maarten (Dutch part)								**Saint-Martin (partie néerland)**
Current account	...	...	...	...	4	-110	23	Compte des transac. courantes
Capital account, n.i.e.	...	...	...	...	7	4	-~0	Compte de capital, n.i.a.
Financial account, n.i.e.	...	...	...	...	87	-141	37	Compte financier, n.i.a.
Reserves and related items	...	...	...	...	-21	64	3	Réserves et postes apparentés
Slovakia								**Slovaquie**
Current account	...	390	-5 125	-4 211	1 768	1 244	193	Compte des transac. courantes
Capital account, n.i.e.	...	46	-13	1 392	1 422	937	3 078	Compte de capital, n.i.a.
Financial account, n.i.e.	...	-1 211	-6 035	-3 177	-849	-927	684	Compte financier, n.i.a.
Reserves and related items	...	1 791	1 294	37	96	552	336	Réserves et postes apparentés

15 Balance of payments summary *(continued)*
Millions of US dollars

Résumé de la balance des paiements *(suite)*
Millions de dollars É.-U.

Country or area	1985	1995	2005	2010	2013	2014	2015	Pays ou zone
Slovenia								**Slovénie**
Current account	...	-75	-681	-55	2 295	3 086	2 216	Compte des transac. courantes
Capital account, n.i.e.	...	-6	-137	72	252	219	410	Compte de capital, n.i.a.
Financial account, n.i.e.	...	-516	-844	-1 879	1 376	3 040	2 096	Compte financier, n.i.a.
Reserves and related items	...	240	206	-31	5	124	-123	Réserves et postes apparentés
Solomon Islands								**Îles Salomon**
Current account	-28	8	-90	-144	-39	-50	-36	Compte des transac. courantes
Capital account, n.i.e.	...	1	28	50	87	71	55	Compte de capital, n.i.a.
Financial account, n.i.e.	-14	8	9	-209	-9	9	-33	Compte financier, n.i.a.
Reserves and related items	-15	-1	-18	94	59	1	53	Réserves et postes apparentés
South Africa								**Afrique du Sud**
Current account	2 261	-2 493	-8 015	-5 492	-21 638	-18 633	-13 644	Compte des transac. courantes
Capital account, n.i.e.	...	...	30	31	25	22	19	Compte de capital, n.i.a.
Financial account, n.i.e.	2 092	-4 295	-12 612	-11 304	-13 970	-15 412	-10 805	Compte financier, n.i.a.
Reserves and related items	-742	911	5 766	3 796	499	1 398	-757	Réserves et postes apparentés
South Sudan								**Soudan du sud**
Current account	...	...	...	...	...	# -935	...	Compte des transac. courantes
Capital account, n.i.e.	...	...	...	...	...	# 223	...	Compte de capital, n.i.a.
Financial account, n.i.e.	...	...	...	...	...	# -136	...	Compte financier, n.i.a.
Reserves and related items	...	...	...	...	...	# -521	...	Réserves et postes apparentés
Spain								**Espagne**
Current account	2 785	-1 967	-87 006	-56 363	20 756	14 148	16 208	Compte des transac. courantes
Capital account, n.i.e.	...	5 861	9 048	6 501	8 806	6 599	7 733	Compte de capital, n.i.a.
Financial account, n.i.e.	3 217	6 675	-73 517	-58 118	43 769	9 511	22 110	Compte financier, n.i.a.
Reserves and related items	-2 275	-6 414	-1 921	1 052	689	4 855	5 704	Réserves et postes apparentés
Sri Lanka								**Sri Lanka**
Current account	-418	-770	-743	-1 127	-2 541	-1 988	-2 009	Compte des transac. courantes
Capital account, n.i.e.	...	116	242	150	71	58	46	Compte de capital, n.i.a.
Financial account, n.i.e.	-373	-730	-67	952	-4 628	-3 804	-3 127	Compte financier, n.i.a.
Reserves and related items	-88	239	-498	-2 782	1 566	2 268	857	Réserves et postes apparentés
State of Palestine								**Etat de Palestine**
Current account	...	-984	-1 365	-1 307	-2 384	-2 149	-1 713	Compte des transac. courantes
Capital account, n.i.e.	...	262	386	828	546	683	407	Compte de capital, n.i.a.
Financial account, n.i.e.	...	-557	-892	-238	-1 614	-1 062	-1 042	Compte financier, n.i.a.
Reserves and related items	...	...	7	36	16	-20	-100	Réserves et postes apparentés
Sudan								**Soudan**
Current account	149	-500	-2 473	# -1 725	-5 822	-3 545	-5 933	Compte des transac. courantes
Capital account, n.i.e.	...	...	165	# 378	314	213	250	Compte de capital, n.i.a.
Financial account, n.i.e.	444	-474	-1 991	# 69	-1 965	-1 543	-4 589	Compte financier, n.i.a.
Reserves and related items	-444	-3	542	# -1 702	-2 157	-352	-1 101	Réserves et postes apparentés
Suriname								**Suriname**
Current account	...	...	-144	651	-196	-415	-808	Compte des transac. courantes
Capital account, n.i.e.	...	...	15	54	~0	-~0	1	Compte de capital, n.i.a.
Financial account, n.i.e.	...	...	21	502	-429	-688	-702	Compte financier, n.i.a.
Reserves and related items	...	...	20	35	-148	-150	-302	Réserves et postes apparentés
Swaziland								**Swaziland**
Current account	-38	-30	-103	-389	150	58	281	Compte des transac. courantes
Capital account, n.i.e.	...	-~0	-3	14	26	78	29	Compte de capital, n.i.a.
Financial account, n.i.e.	-22	25	-148	-88	189	339	1 076	Compte financier, n.i.a.
Reserves and related items	-5	24	1	-231	90	-128	-170	Réserves et postes apparentés
Sweden								**Suède**
Current account	-1 010	4 940	23 583	29 196	30 466	26 539	23 250	Compte des transac. courantes
Capital account, n.i.e.	...	...	290	-681	-1 439	-808	-981	Compte de capital, n.i.a.
Financial account, n.i.e.	2 893	5 052	27 739	35 800	4 674	16 627	9 112	Compte financier, n.i.a.
Reserves and related items	-4 651	-1 664	250	-1 190	14 910	486	1 311	Réserves et postes apparentés
Switzerland								**Suisse**
Current account	6 039	20 703	55 428	86 609	78 750	61 445	77 378	Compte des transac. courantes
Capital account, n.i.e.	...	-462	-2 297	-4 460	792	-11 756	-14 361	Compte de capital, n.i.a.
Financial account, n.i.e.	7 272	11 231	97 549	-16 296	100 273	11 225	-1 694	Compte financier, n.i.a.
Reserves and related items	1 228	29	-17 673	125 382	13 994	35 900	98 770	Réserves et postes apparentés
Syrian Arab Republic								**Rép. arabe syrienne**
Current account	-958	263	295	-367	...	...	...	Compte des transac. courantes
Capital account, n.i.e.	...	20	18	50	...	...	...	Compte de capital, n.i.a.
Financial account, n.i.e.	-789	-521	162	-1 252	...	...	...	Compte financier, n.i.a.
Reserves and related items	-186	839	14	2 076	...	...	...	Réserves et postes apparentés

15 Balance of payments summary *(continued)*
Millions of US dollars

Résumé de la balance des paiements *(suite)*
Millions de dollars É.-U.

Country or area	1985	1995	2005	2010	2013	2014	2015	Pays ou zone
Tajikistan								**Tadjikistan**
Current account	...	...	-19	# -540	-659	-261	-472	Compte des transac. courantes
Capital account, n.i.e.	...	...	...	# 59	134	124	144	Compte de capital, n.i.a.
Financial account, n.i.e.	...	...	-101	# -287	-148	-298	-504	Compte financier, n.i.a.
Reserves and related items	...	...	6	# -123	-44	-85	30	Réserves et postes apparentés
Thailand								**Thaïlande**
Current account	-1 537	-13 582	# -7 642	11 486	-4 845	15 100	32 149	Compte des transac. courantes
Capital account, n.i.e.	...	...	...	245	281	100	~0	Compte de capital, n.i.a.
Financial account, n.i.e.	-1 538	-21 937	# -7 857	-23 573	2 488	16 204	17 102	Compte financier, n.i.a.
Reserves and related items	105	7 159	# 5 422	31 324	-5 049	-1 210	5 859	Réserves et postes apparentés
TFYR of Macedonia								**ex-R.Y. de Macédoine**
Current account	...	...	-159	-198	-177	-72	-204	Compte des transac. courantes
Capital account, n.i.e.	...	...	~0	4	20	4	8	Compte de capital, n.i.a.
Financial account, n.i.e.	...	...	-576	-272	-90	-710	-154	Compte financier, n.i.a.
Reserves and related items	...	...	411	78	-48	660	-46	Réserves et postes apparentés
Timor-Leste								**Timor-Leste**
Current account	...	...	...	1 671	2 390	1 106	# 238	Compte des transac. courantes
Capital account, n.i.e.	...	...	...	31	20	-3	# 29	Compte de capital, n.i.a.
Financial account, n.i.e.	...	...	...	1 547	2 569	1 402	# -29	Compte financier, n.i.a.
Reserves and related items	...	...	...	156	-202	-390	# 220	Réserves et postes apparentés
Togo								**Togo**
Current account	-33	-122	-204	-200	-568	-458	-461	Compte des transac. courantes
Capital account, n.i.e.	...	...	51	1 388	315	319	269	Compte de capital, n.i.a.
Financial account, n.i.e.	-31	53	-31	1 177	-295	-218	-314	Compte financier, n.i.a.
Reserves and related items	-3	-194	-110	14	49	73	132	Réserves et postes apparentés
Tonga								**Tonga**
Current account	2	...	-21	-80	-33	...	...	Compte des transac. courantes
Capital account, n.i.e.	...	...	13	34	33	...	...	Compte de capital, n.i.a.
Financial account, n.i.e.	1	...	-3	-43	-11	...	...	Compte financier, n.i.a.
Reserves and related items	1	...	-17	-14	8	...	...	Réserves et postes apparentés
Trinidad and Tobago								**Trinité-et-Tobago**
Current account	-48	294	3 881	4 172	...	...	...	Compte des transac. courantes
Financial account, n.i.e.	-20	215	1 510	3 763	...	...	...	Compte financier, n.i.a.
Reserves and related items	-301	84	1 387	436	...	...	...	Réserves et postes apparentés
Tunisia								**Tunisie**
Current account	-581	-774	-299	-2 104	-3 879	-4 341	-3 850	Compte des transac. courantes
Capital account, n.i.e.	...	47	127	82	115	300	225	Compte de capital, n.i.a.
Financial account, n.i.e.	-381	-958	-1 136	-1 757	-2 815	-3 894	-3 711	Compte financier, n.i.a.
Reserves and related items	-226	97	936	-170	-848	-132	83	Réserves et postes apparentés
Turkey								**Turquie**
Current account	-1 013	-2 338	# -20 980	-44 616	-63 608	-43 552	-32 278	Compte des transac. courantes
Capital account, n.i.e.	...	...	...	-51	-96	-70	-21	Compte de capital, n.i.a.
Financial account, n.i.e.	-1 065	-4 643	# -42 685	-60 099	-73 059	-41 594	-11 146	Compte financier, n.i.a.
Reserves and related items	-784	4 660	# 23 176	14 971	10 774	-484	-11 831	Réserves et postes apparentés
Tuvalu								**Tuvalu**
Current account	...	...	-4	-14	7	...	...	Compte des transac. courantes
Capital account, n.i.e.	...	...	2	9	4	...	...	Compte de capital, n.i.a.
Financial account, n.i.e.	...	...	2	3	-2	...	...	Compte financier, n.i.a.
Reserves and related items	...	...	-1	-4	10	...	...	Réserves et postes apparentés
Uganda								**Ouganda**
Current account	5	-339	-13	-1 659	-1 845	-2 431	-2 353	Compte des transac. courantes
Capital account, n.i.e.	...	48	...	...	80	95	108	Compte de capital, n.i.a.
Financial account, n.i.e.	-81	-211	-565	-1 070	-1 367	-1 850	-1 418	Compte financier, n.i.a.
Reserves and related items	33	-51	102	-91	181	24	-450	Réserves et postes apparentés
Ukraine								**Ukraine**
Current account	...	-1 152	# 2 534	-3 016	-16 518	-4 596	-189	Compte des transac. courantes
Capital account, n.i.e.	...	6	# -43	188	-60	400	456	Compte de capital, n.i.a.
Financial account, n.i.e.	...	526	# -8 126	-6 508	-19 241	9 644	-726	Compte financier, n.i.a.
Reserves and related items	...	-1 624	# 10 725	5 045	2 005	-13 308	793	Réserves et postes apparentés
United Kingdom								**Royaume-Uni**
Current account	3 314	-13 436	-30 220	-66 842	-119 919	-139 686	-122 571	Compte des transac. courantes
Capital account, n.i.e.	...	486	-1 439	-3	-777	-658	-1 694	Compte de capital, n.i.a.
Financial account, n.i.e.	1 788	-3 669	-22 270	-57 252	-130 805	-139 941	-134 432	Compte financier, n.i.a.
Reserves and related items	2 570	-853	1 732	10 010	6 956	10 140	31 316	Réserves et postes apparentés

15 Balance of payments summary *(continued)*
Millions of US dollars

Résumé de la balance des paiements *(suite)*
Millions de dollars É.-U.

Country or area	1985	1995	2005	2010	2013	2014	2015	Pays ou zone
United Rep. of Tanzania								**Rép.-Unie de Tanzanie**
Current account	-375	-646	-1 570	# -2 211	-4 988	-5 017	-3 312	Compte des transac. courantes
Capital account, n.i.e.	...	191	393	# 538	713	535	421	Compte de capital, n.i.a.
Financial account, n.i.e.	72	-67	-1 422	# -3 061	-5 021	-3 898	-3 596	Compte financier, n.i.a.
Reserves and related items	-487	-359	-595	# 349	523	-257	-231	Réserves et postes apparentés
United States								**États-Unis**
Current account	-124 455	-113 561	-745 445	-441 963	-366 424	-392 066	-462 961	Compte des transac. courantes
Capital account, n.i.e.	...	-222	13 115	-158	-413	-46	-43	Compte de capital, n.i.a.
Financial account, n.i.e.	-108 512	-92 562	-686 624	-438 809	-387 885	-283 796	-188 933	Compte financier, n.i.a.
Reserves and related items	3 835	9 747	-14 096	1 825	-3 087	-3 583	-6 305	Réserves et postes apparentés
Uruguay								**Uruguay**
Current account	-98	-213	24	-756	-2 883	-2 599	-1 141	Compte des transac. courantes
Capital account, n.i.e.	...	...	4	...	201	12	159	Compte de capital, n.i.a.
Financial account, n.i.e.	75	-422	-924	-1 057	-4 520	-4 023	228	Compte financier, n.i.a.
Reserves and related items	66	228	778	-387	2 901	1 337	-1 810	Réserves et postes apparentés
Vanuatu								**Vanuatu**
Current account	-10	-18	-53	# -42	-5	19	-82	Compte des transac. courantes
Capital account, n.i.e.	10	31	20	# 21	21	32	84	Compte de capital, n.i.a.
Financial account, n.i.e.	-5	-25	-38	# -155	-131	-~0	-24	Compte financier, n.i.a.
Reserves and related items	-~0	5	-11	# 6	10	12	76	Réserves et postes apparentés
Venezuela (Boliv. Rep. of)								**Venezuela (Rép. boliv. du)**
Current account	3 327	2 014	# 25 447	5 585	4 604	3 598	-20 360	Compte des transac. courantes
Capital account, n.i.e.	...	...	...	-211	...	...	-3 980	Compte de capital, n.i.a.
Financial account, n.i.e.	629	2 964	# 16 430	9 583	5 596	641	-22 523	Compte financier, n.i.a.
Reserves and related items	1 699	-1 444	# 5 425	-7 939	-4 410	-609	-4 470	Réserves et postes apparentés
Viet Nam								**Viet Nam**
Current account	...	...	-560	-4 276	# 7 745	9 359	906	Compte des transac. courantes
Financial account, n.i.e.	...	...	-3 087	-6 201	# 280	-5 571	-1 575	Compte financier, n.i.a.
Reserves and related items	...	...	2 130	-1 765	# 557	8 375	-6 032	Réserves et postes apparentés
Yemen								**Yémen**
Current account	...	...	624	-1 398	-1 530	-1 488	-3 026	Compte des transac. courantes
Capital account, n.i.e.	...	...	202	88	...	...	...	Compte de capital, n.i.a.
Financial account, n.i.e.	...	...	606	317	227	193	274	Compte financier, n.i.a.
Reserves and related items	...	...	434	-1 561	-1 040	-1 296	-2 638	Réserves et postes apparentés
Zambia								**Zambie**
Current account	-395	...	# -363	1 377	-218	-401	-768	Compte des transac. courantes
Capital account, n.i.e.	...	...	# 287	150	278	51	81	Compte de capital, n.i.a.
Financial account, n.i.e.	-363	...	# 1 888	1 564	277	-699	-278	Compte financier, n.i.a.
Reserves and related items	-181	...	# -2 086	-66	-263	301	-446	Réserves et postes apparentés
Zimbabwe								**Zimbabwe**
Current account	-64	...	...	-1 444	-2 526	-2 254	-1 521	Compte des transac. courantes
Capital account, n.i.e.	...	...	...	231	251	369	398	Compte de capital, n.i.a.
Financial account, n.i.e.	-121	...	...	-186	-1 157	-1 666	-907	Compte financier, n.i.a.
Reserves and related items	82	...	...	-225	27	-304	-187	Réserves et postes apparentés

Source:

International Monetary Fund (IMF), Washington, D.C., the database on International Financial Statistics, last accessed February 2017.

Source:

Fonds monétaire international (FMI), Washington, D.C., la base de données de Statistiques Financières Internationales, dernier accès février 2017.

16 Exchange rates

National currency per US dollar

Cours des changes

Valeur du dollar E.-U. en monnaie nationale

Country or area	National currency Monnaie nationale	1985	1995	2005	2010	2013	2014	2015	2016	Pays ou zone
Afghanistan										**Afghanistan**
End of period	Afghani (AFN)	50.6	47.5	50.4	45.3	56.6	57.8	68.1	66.8	Fin de période
Period average		43.5	36.6	49.5	46.5	55.4	57.2	61.1	67.9	Moy. sur période
Åland Islands										**Îles d'Åland**
End of period	Euro (EUR)	...	...	0.8	0.7	0.7	0.8	0.9	0.9	Fin de période
Period average		...	...	0.8	0.8	0.8	0.8	0.9	0.9	Moy. sur période
Albania										**Albanie**
End of period	Lek (ALL)	...	94.2	103.6	104.0	101.9	115.2	125.8	128.2	Fin de période
Period average		...	92.7	99.9	103.9	105.7	105.5	126.0	124.1	Moy. sur période
Algeria										**Algérie**
End of period	Algerian Dinar (DZD)	4.8	52.2	73.4	74.9	78.2	87.9	107.1	110.5	Fin de période
Period average	dinar algérien (DZD)	5.0	47.7	73.3	74.4	79.4	80.6	100.7	109.4	Moy. sur période
Andorra										**Andorre**
End of period	Euro (EUR)	...	...	0.8	0.7	0.7	0.8	0.9	0.9	Fin de période
Period average		...	...	0.8	0.8	0.8	0.8	0.9	0.9	Moy. sur période
Angola										**Angola**
End of period	Kwanza (AOA)	0.0	~0.0	80.8	92.6	97.6	102.9	135.3	165.9	Fin de période
Period average		0.0	~0.0	87.2	91.9	96.5	98.3	120.1	163.7	Moy. sur période
Anguilla										**Anguilla**
End of period	E. Caribbean Dollar (XCD),	2.7	2.7	2.7	2.7	2.7	2.7	2.7	2.7	Fin de période
Period average	dollar des Caraïb. (XCD) [1]	2.7	2.7	2.7	2.7	2.7	2.7	2.7	2.7	Moy. sur période
Antigua and Barbuda										**Antigua-et-Barbuda**
End of period	E. Caribbean Dollar (XCD),	2.7	2.7	2.7	2.7	2.7	2.7	2.7	2.7	Fin de période
Period average	dollar des Caraïb. (XCD) [1]	2.7	2.7	2.7	2.7	2.7	2.7	2.7	2.7	Moy. sur période
Argentina										**Argentine**
End of period	Argentine Peso (ARS),	~0.0	1.0	3.0	4.0	6.5	8.5	13.1	15.9	Fin de période
Period average	peso argentin (ARS)	~0.0	1.0	2.9	3.9	5.5	8.1	9.2	14.8	Moy. sur période
Armenia										**Arménie**
End of period	Armenian Dram (AMD),	...	402.0	450.2	363.4	405.6	475.0	483.8	483.9	Fin de période
Period average	dram arménien (AMD)	...	405.9	457.7	373.7	409.6	415.9	477.9	480.5	Moy. sur période
Aruba										**Aruba**
End of period	Aruban Florin (AWG), florin	...	1.8	1.8	1.8	1.8	1.8	1.8	1.8	Fin de période
Period average	de Aruba (AWG)	...	1.8	1.8	1.8	1.8	1.8	1.8	1.8	Moy. sur période
Australia										**Australie**
End of period	Australian Dollar (AUD),	1.5	1.3	1.4	1.0	1.1	1.2	1.4	1.4	Fin de période
Period average	dollar australien (AUD)	1.4	1.3	1.3	1.1	1.0	1.1	1.3	1.3	Moy. sur période
Austria										**Autriche**
End of period	Euro (EUR)	...	...	0.8	0.7	0.7	0.8	0.9	0.9	Fin de période
Period average		...	...	0.8	0.8	0.8	0.8	0.9	0.9	Moy. sur période
Azerbaijan										**Azerbaïdjan**
End of period	Azerbaijan manat (AZN),	...	0.9	0.9	0.8	0.8	0.8	1.6	1.8	Fin de période
Period average	manat azerbaïd. (AZN)	...	0.9	0.9	0.8	0.8	0.8	1.0	1.6	Moy. sur période
Bahamas										**Bahamas**
End of period	Bahamian Dollar (BSD),	1.0	1.0	1.0	1.0	1.0	1.0	1.0	1.0	Fin de période
Period average	dollar des Bahamas (BSD)	1.0	1.0	1.0	1.0	1.0	1.0	1.0	1.0	Moy. sur période
Bahrain										**Bahreïn**
End of period	Bahraini Dinar (BHD)	0.4	0.4	0.4	0.4	0.4	0.4	0.4	0.4	Fin de période
Period average	dinar de Bahreïn (BHD)	0.4	0.4	0.4	0.4	0.4	0.4	0.4	0.4	Moy. sur période
Bangladesh										**Bangladesh**
End of period	Taka (BDT)	31.0	40.8	66.2	70.7	77.8	77.9	78.5	78.7	Fin de période
Period average		28.0	40.3	64.3	69.6	78.1	77.6	77.9	78.5	Moy. sur période
Barbados										**Barbade**
End of period	Barbados Dollar (BBD),	2.0	2.0	2.0	2.0	2.0	2.0	2.0	2.0	Fin de période
Period average	dollar de la Barbade (BBD)	2.0	2.0	2.0	2.0	2.0	2.0	2.0	2.0	Moy. sur période
Belarus										**Bélarus**
End of period	Belarusian Ruble (BYR),	...	0.0	0.2	0.3	1.0	1.2	1.9	2.0	Fin de période
Period average	rouble bélarussien (BYR)	...	~0.0	0.2	0.3	0.9	1.0	1.6	2.0	Moy. sur période
Belgium										**Belgique**
End of period	Euro (EUR)	...	...	0.8	0.7	0.7	0.8	0.9	0.9	Fin de période
Period average		...	...	0.8	0.8	0.8	0.8	0.9	0.9	Moy. sur période
Belize										**Belize**
End of period	Belize Dollar (BZD)	2.0	2.0	2.0	2.0	2.0	2.0	2.0	2.0	Fin de période
Period average	dollar du Belize (BZD)	2.0	2.0	2.0	2.0	2.0	2.0	2.0	2.0	Moy. sur période

Country or area	National currency Monnaie nationale	1985	1995	2005	2010	2013	2014	2015	2016	Pays ou zone
Benin										**Bénin**
End of period	CFA Franc (XOF), franc	378.1	490.0	556.0	490.9	475.6	540.3	602.5	622.3	Fin de période
Period average	CFA (XOF)	449.3	499.1	527.5	495.3	494.0	494.4	591.4	593.0	Moy. sur période
Bermuda										**Bermudes**
End of period	Bermudian Dollar (BMD),	1.0	1.0	1.0	1.0	1.0	1.0	1.0	1.0	Fin de période
Period average	dollar des Bermudes (BMD)	1.0	1.0	1.0	1.0	1.0	1.0	1.0	1.0	Moy. sur période
Bhutan										**Bhoutan**
End of period	Ngultrum (BTN)	12.2	35.2	45.1	44.8	61.9	63.3	66.3	68.0	Fin de période
Period average		12.4	32.4	44.1	45.7	58.6	61.0	64.2	67.2	Moy. sur période
Bolivia (Plurin. State of)										**Bolivie (État plurin. de)**
End of period	Boliviano (BOB)	1.7	4.9	8.0	7.0	6.9	6.9	6.9	6.9	Fin de période
Period average		0.4	4.8	8.1	7.0	6.9	6.9	6.9	6.9	Moy. sur période
Bosnia and Herzegovina										**Bosnie-Herzégovine**
End of period	Convertible Mark (BAM),	...	...	1.7	1.5	1.4	1.6	1.8	1.9	Fin de période
Period average	marka convertible (BAM)	...	...	1.6	1.5	1.5	1.5	1.8	1.8	Moy. sur période
Botswana										**Botswana**
End of period	Pula (BWP)	2.1	2.8	5.5	6.4	8.7	9.5	11.2	10.6	Fin de période
Period average		1.9	2.8	5.1	6.8	8.4	9.0	10.1	10.9	Moy. sur période
Bouvet Island										**Île Bouvet**
End of period	Norwegian Krone (NOK),	7.6	6.3	6.8	5.9	6.1	7.4	8.8	8.6	Fin de période
Period average	couronne norv. (NOK)	8.6	6.3	6.4	6.0	5.9	6.3	8.1	8.4	Moy. sur période
Brazil										**Brésil**
End of period	Brazilian Real (BRL)	0.0	1.0	2.3	1.7	2.4	2.7	3.9	3.3	Fin de période
Period average	real brésilien (BRL)	0.0	0.9	2.4	1.8	2.2	2.4	3.3	3.5	Moy. sur période
British Indian Ocean Terr.										**Terr. brit. de l'océan Indien**
End of period	Pound Sterling (GBP)	0.7	0.6	0.6	0.6	0.6	0.6	0.7	0.8	Fin de période
Period average	livre sterling (GBP)	0.8	0.6	0.6	0.6	0.6	0.6	0.7	0.7	Moy. sur période
Brunei Darussalam										**Brunéi Darussalam**
End of period	Brunei Dollar (BND)	2.1	1.4	1.7	1.3	1.3	1.3	1.4	1.4	Fin de période
Period average	dollar du Brunéi (BND)	2.2	1.4	1.7	1.4	1.3	1.3	1.4	1.4	Moy. sur période
Bulgaria										**Bulgarie**
End of period	Bulgarian Lev (BGN)	~0.0	0.1	1.7	1.5	1.4	1.6	1.8	1.9	Fin de période
Period average	lev bulgare (BGN)	~0.0	0.1	1.6	1.5	1.5	1.5	1.8	1.8	Moy. sur période
Burkina Faso										**Burkina Faso**
End of period	CFA Franc (XOF)	378.0	490.0	556.0	490.9	475.6	540.3	602.5	622.3	Fin de période
Period average	franc CFA (XOF)	449.3	499.1	527.5	495.3	494.0	494.4	591.4	593.0	Moy. sur période
Burundi										**Burundi**
End of period	Burundi Franc (BIF)	112.0	277.9	997.8	1 232.5	1 542.0	1 553.1	1 617.1	1 688.6	Fin de période
Period average	franc burundais (BIF)	120.7	249.8	1 081.6	1 230.7	1 555.1	1 546.7	1 571.9	1 654.6	Moy. sur période
Cabo Verde										**Cabo Verde**
End of period	Cabo Verde Escudo (CVE),	85.4	77.5	93.5	82.5	80.0	90.8	101.3	104.6	Fin de période
Period average	esc. du Cabo Verde (CVE)	91.6	76.9	88.7	83.3	83.1	83.1	99.4	99.7	Moy. sur période
Cambodia										**Cambodge**
End of period	Riel (KHR)	...	2 526.0	4 112.0	4 051.0	3 995.0	4 075.0	4 051.5	4 044.5	Fin de période
Period average		...	2 450.8	4 092.5	4 184.9	4 027.3	4 037.5	4 067.8	4 058.7	Moy. sur période
Cameroon										**Cameroun**
End of period	CFA Franc (XAF)	378.1	490.0	556.0	490.9	475.6	540.3	602.5	622.3	Fin de période
Period average	franc CFA (XAF)	449.3	499.1	527.5	495.3	494.0	494.4	591.4	593.0	Moy. sur période
Canada										**Canada**
End of period	Canadian Dollar (CAD),	1.4	1.4	1.2	1.0	1.1	1.2	1.4	1.3	Fin de période
Period average	dollar canadien (CAD)	1.4	1.4	1.2	1.0	1.0	1.1	1.3	1.3	Moy. sur période
Cayman Islands [2]										**Îles Caïmanes** [2]
End of period	Cayman Isl. Dollar (KYD), dollar des Îles Caïm. (KYD)	...	...	...	...	...	...	0.8	0.8	Fin de période
Central African Republic										**République centrafricaine**
End of period	CFA Franc (XAF)	378.0	490.0	556.0	490.9	475.6	540.3	602.5	622.3	Fin de période
Period average	franc CFA (XAF)	449.3	499.1	527.5	495.3	494.0	494.4	591.4	593.0	Moy. sur période
Chad										**Tchad**
End of period	CFA Franc (XAF)	378.1	490.0	556.0	490.9	475.6	540.3	602.5	622.3	Fin de période
Period average	franc CFA (XAF)	449.3	499.1	527.5	495.3	494.0	494.4	591.4	593.0	Moy. sur période
Channel Islands										**Îles Anglo-Normandes**
End of period	Pound Sterling (GBP)	0.7	0.6	0.6	0.6	0.6	0.6	0.7	0.8	Fin de période
Period average	livre sterling (GBP)	0.8	0.6	0.6	0.6	0.6	0.6	0.7	0.7	Moy. sur période

Country or area	National currency Monnaie nationale	1985	1995	2005	2010	2013	2014	2015	2016	Pays ou zone
Chile										**Chili**
End of period	Chilean Peso (CLP)	183.7	407.1	514.2	468.4	523.8	607.4	707.3	667.3	Fin de période
Period average	peso chilien (CLP)	160.9	396.8	559.8	510.2	495.3	570.3	654.1	677.0	Moy. sur période
China										**Chine**
End of period	Yuan Renminbi (CNY),	3.2	8.3	8.1	6.6	6.1	6.1	6.5	6.9	Fin de période
Period average	yuan (CNY)	2.9	8.4	8.2	6.8	6.2	6.1	6.2	6.6	Moy. sur période
China, Hong Kong SAR										**Chine, Hong Kong RAS**
End of period	Hong Kong Dollar (HKD),	7.8	7.7	7.8	7.8	7.8	7.8	7.8	7.8	Fin de période
Period average	dollar de Hong Kong (HKD)	7.8	7.7	7.8	7.8	7.8	7.8	7.8	7.8	Moy. sur période
China, Macao SAR										**Chine, Macao RAS**
End of period	Pataca (MOP)	8.0	8.0	8.0	8.0	8.0	8.0	8.0	8.0	Fin de période
Period average		8.0	8.0	8.0	8.0	8.0	8.0	8.0	8.0	Moy. sur période
Christmas Island										**Île Christmas**
End of period	Australian dollar (AUD),	1.5	1.3	1.4	1.0	1.1	1.2	1.4	1.4	Fin de période
Period average	dollar australien (AUD)	1.4	1.3	1.3	1.1	1.0	1.1	1.3	1.3	Moy. sur période
Cocos (Keeling) Islands										**Îles des Cocos (Keeling)**
End of period	Australian dollar (AUD),	1.5	1.3	1.4	1.0	1.1	1.2	1.4	1.4	Fin de période
Period average	dollar australien (AUD)	1.4	1.3	1.3	1.1	1.0	1.1	1.3	1.3	Moy. sur période
Colombia										**Colombie**
End of period	Colombian Peso (COP),	172.2	987.7	2 284.2	1 989.9	1 922.6	2 392.5	3 149.5	3 000.7	Fin de période
Period average	peso colombien (COP)	142.3	912.8	2 320.8	1 898.6	1 868.8	2 001.8	2 741.9	3 054.1	Moy. sur période
Comoros										**Comores**
End of period	Comorian Franc (KMF),	378.0	367.5	417.0	368.2	356.7	405.2	451.9	466.7	Fin de période
Period average	franc comorien (KMF)	449.3	374.4	395.6	371.5	370.5	370.8	443.6	444.8	Moy. sur période
Congo										**Congo**
End of period	CFA Franc (XAF)	378.0	490.0	556.0	490.9	475.6	540.3	602.5	622.3	Fin de période
Period average	franc CFA (XAF)	449.3	499.1	527.5	495.3	494.0	494.4	591.4	593.0	Moy. sur période
Cook Islands										**Îles Cook**
End of period	New Zealand Dollar (NZD),	2.0	1.5	1.5	1.3	1.2	1.3	1.5	1.4	Fin de période
Period average	dollar néo-zélandais (NZD)	2.0	1.5	1.4	1.4	1.2	1.2	1.4	1.4	Moy. sur période
Costa Rica										**Costa Rica**
End of period	Costa Rican Colon (CRC),	53.7	194.9	496.7	513.0	501.4	539.4	538.4	554.6	Fin de période
Period average	colon costaricien (CRC)	50.5	179.7	477.8	525.8	499.8	538.3	534.6	544.7	Moy. sur période
Côte d'Ivoire										**Côte d'Ivoire**
End of period	CFA Franc (XOF)	378.0	490.0	556.0	490.9	475.6	540.3	602.5	622.3	Fin de période
Period average	franc CFA (XOF)	449.3	499.1	527.5	495.3	494.0	494.4	591.4	593.0	Moy. sur période
Croatia										**Croatie**
End of period	Kuna (HRK)	...	5.3	6.2	5.6	5.5	6.3	7.0	7.2	Fin de période
Period average		...	5.2	5.9	5.5	5.7	5.7	6.9	6.8	Moy. sur période
Cuba [2]										**Cuba** [2]
End of period	Cuban Peso (CUP), peso cubain (CUP) [3]	...	...	...	...	...	...	1.0	1.0	Fin de période
Curaçao										**Curaçao**
End of period	Neth. Ant. Guilder (ANG),	...	...	...	1.8	1.8	1.8	1.8	1.8	Fin de période
Period average	flor. des Ant. néer. (ANG) [4]	...	...	...	1.8	1.8	1.8	1.8	1.8	Moy. sur période
Cyprus										**Chypre**
End of period	Euro (EUR)	...	...	...	0.7	0.7	0.8	0.9	0.9	Fin de période
Period average		...	...	...	0.8	0.8	0.8	0.9	0.9	Moy. sur période
Czechia										**Tchéquie**
End of period	Czech Koruna (CZK),	...	26.6	24.6	18.8	19.9	22.8	24.8	25.6	Fin de période
Period average	couronne tchèque (CZK)	...	26.5	24.0	19.1	19.6	20.8	24.6	24.4	Moy. sur période
Dem. People's Rep. Korea [2]										**Rép. pop. dém. de Corée** [2]
End of period	North Korean Won (KPW), won nord-coréen (KPW)	...	...	...	...	97.8	103.0	109.0	110.9	Fin de période
Dem. Rep. of the Congo										**Rép. dém. du Congo**
End of period	Congolese Franc (CDF),	0.0	0.1	431.3	915.1	925.5	924.5	926.8	1 215.6	Fin de période
Period average	franc congolais (CDF)	0.0	0.1	473.9	905.9	919.6	925.2	926.0	1 010.3	Moy. sur période
Denmark										**Danemark**
End of period	Danish Krone (DKK),	9.0	5.5	6.3	5.6	5.4	6.1	6.8	7.1	Fin de période
Period average	couronne danoise (DKK)	10.6	5.6	6.0	5.6	5.6	5.6	6.7	6.7	Moy. sur période
Djibouti										**Djibouti**
End of period	Djibouti Franc (DJF)	177.7	177.7	177.7	177.7	177.7	177.7	177.7	177.7	Fin de période
Period average	franc Djibouti (DJF)	177.7	177.7	177.7	177.7	177.7	177.7	177.7	177.7	Moy. sur période

Country or area	National currency Monnaie nationale	1985	1995	2005	2010	2013	2014	2015	2016	Pays ou zone
Dominica										**Dominique**
End of period	E. Caribbean Dollar (XCD),	2.7	2.7	2.7	2.7	2.7	2.7	2.7	2.7	Fin de période
Period average	dollar des Caraïb. (XCD) [1]	2.7	2.7	2.7	2.7	2.7	2.7	2.7	2.7	Moy. sur période
Dominican Republic										**République dominicaine**
End of period	Dominican Peso (DOP),	2.9	13.5	34.9	37.9	42.8	44.4	45.7	46.7	Fin de période
Period average	peso dominicain (DOP)	3.1	13.6	30.5	37.3	41.8	43.6	45.1	46.1	Moy. sur période
Egypt										**Égypte**
End of period	Egyptian Pound (EGP),	0.7	3.4	5.7	5.8	6.9	7.1	7.8	18.1	Fin de période
Period average	livre égyptienne (EGP)	0.7	3.4	5.8	5.6	6.9	7.1	7.7	10.0	Moy. sur période
El Salvador										**El Salvador**
End of period	El Salvador Colon (SVC),	2.5	8.8	8.8	8.8	8.8	8.8	8.8	8.8	Fin de période
Period average	colon salvadorien (SVC) [5]	2.5	8.8	8.8	8.8	8.8	8.8	8.8	8.8	Moy. sur période
Equatorial Guinea										**Guinée équatoriale**
End of period	CFA Franc (XAF)	378.0	490.0	556.0	490.9	475.6	540.3	602.5	622.3	Fin de période
Period average	franc CFA (XAF)	449.3	499.1	527.5	495.3	494.0	494.4	591.4	593.0	Moy. sur période
Eritrea										**Érythrée**
End of period	Nakfa (ERN)	2.1	6.3	15.4	15.4	15.4	15.4	...	...	Fin de période
Period average		2.1	6.2	15.4	15.4	15.4	15.4	...	...	Moy. sur période
Estonia										**Estonie**
End of period	Euro (EUR)	...	...	...	...	0.7	0.8	0.9	0.9	Fin de période
Period average		...	...	...	...	0.8	0.8	0.9	0.9	Moy. sur période
Ethiopia										**Éthiopie**
End of period	Ethiopian Birr (ETB)	2.1	6.3	8.7	16.6	19.0[2]	20.1[2]	21.2[2]	22.6[2]	Fin de période
Period average	birr éthiopien (ETB)	2.1	6.2	8.7	14.4	...	...	...	...	Moy. sur période
Falkland Islands (Malvinas)										**Îles Falkland (Malvinas)**
End of period	Falkland Isl. Pound (FKP),	0.7	0.6	0.6	0.6	0.6	0.6	0.7	0.8	Fin de période
Period average	livre de Îles Falkland (FKP)	0.8	0.6	0.6	0.6	0.6	0.6	0.7	0.7	Moy. sur période
Faroe Islands										**Îles Féroé**
End of period	Danish Krone (DKK),	9.0	5.5	6.3	5.6	5.4	6.1	6.8	7.1	Fin de période
Period average	couronne danoise (DKK)	10.6	5.6	6.0	5.6	5.6	5.6	6.7	6.7	Moy. sur période
Fiji										**Fidji**
End of period	Fiji Dollar (FJD)	1.1	1.4	1.7	1.8	1.9	2.0	2.1	2.1	Fin de période
Period average	dollar des Fidji (FJD)	1.2	1.4	1.7	1.9	1.8	1.9	2.1	2.1	Moy. sur période
Finland										**Finlande**
End of period	Euro (EUR)	...	...	0.8	0.7	0.7	0.8	0.9	0.9	Fin de période
Period average		...	...	0.8	0.8	0.8	0.8	0.9	0.9	Moy. sur période
France										**France**
End of period	Euro (EUR)	...	...	0.8	0.7	0.7	0.8	0.9	0.9	Fin de période
Period average		...	...	0.8	0.8	0.8	0.8	0.9	0.9	Moy. sur période
French Guiana										**Guyane française**
End of period	Euro (EUR)	...	...	0.8	0.7	0.7	0.8	0.9	0.9	Fin de période
Period average		...	...	0.8	0.8	0.8	0.8	0.9	0.9	Moy. sur période
French Polynesia										**Polynésie française**
End of period	CFP Franc (XPF)	137.5	89.1	101.2	89.3	86.5	98.3	109.6	113.2	Fin de période
Period average	franc CFP (XPF)	163.4	90.8	96.0	90.1	89.9	89.9	107.6	107.9	Moy. sur période
French Southern Territories										**Terres australes françaises**
End of period	Euro (EUR)	...	...	0.8	0.7	0.7	0.8	0.9	0.9	Fin de période
Period average		...	...	0.8	0.8	0.8	0.8	0.9	0.9	Moy. sur période
Gabon										**Gabon**
End of period	CFA Franc (XAF)	378.0	490.0	556.0	490.9	475.6	540.3	602.5	622.3	Fin de période
Period average	franc CFA (XAF)	449.3	499.1	527.5	495.3	494.0	494.4	591.4	593.0	Moy. sur période
Gambia										**Gambie**
End of period	Dalasi (GMD)	3.5	9.6	28.1	28.4	37.9	45.3	...	...	Fin de période
Period average		3.9	9.5	28.6	28.0	36.0	41.7	...	...	Moy. sur période
Georgia										**Géorgie**
End of period	Lari (GEL)	...	1.2	1.8	1.8	1.7	1.9	2.4	2.6	Fin de période
Period average		...	...	1.8	1.8	1.7	1.8	2.3	2.4	Moy. sur période
Germany										**Allemagne**
End of period	Euro (EUR)	...	...	0.8	0.7	0.7	0.8	0.9	0.9	Fin de période
Period average		...	...	0.8	0.8	0.8	0.8	0.9	0.9	Moy. sur période
Ghana										**Ghana**
End of period	Ghana Cedi (GHS)	~0.0	0.1	0.9	1.5	2.2	3.2	3.8	4.2	Fin de période
Period average	cedi ghanéen (GHS)	~0.0	0.1	0.9	1.4	2.0	...	...	...	Moy. sur période

Country or area	National currency Monnaie nationale	1985	1995	2005	2010	2013	2014	2015	2016	Pays ou zone
Gibraltar										**Gibraltar**
End of period	Gibraltar Pound (GIP)	0.7	0.6	0.6	0.6	0.6	0.6	0.7	0.8	Fin de période
Period average	livre de Gibraltar (GIP)	0.8	0.6	0.6	0.6	0.6	0.6	0.7	0.7	Moy. sur période
Greece										**Grèce**
End of period	Euro (EUR)	...	...	0.8	0.7	0.7	0.8	0.9	0.9	Fin de période
Period average		...	...	0.8	0.8	0.8	0.8	0.9	0.9	Moy. sur période
Greenland										**Groenland**
End of period	Danish Krone (DKK),	9.0	5.5	6.3	5.6	5.4	6.1	6.8	7.1	Fin de période
Period average	couronne danoise (DKK)	10.6	5.6	6.0	5.6	5.6	5.6	6.7	6.7	Moy. sur période
Grenada										**Grenade**
End of period	E. Caribbean Dollar (XCD),	2.7	2.7	2.7	2.7	2.7	2.7	2.7	2.7	Fin de période
Period average	dollar des Caraïb. (XCD) [1]	2.7	2.7	2.7	2.7	2.7	2.7	2.7	2.7	Moy. sur période
Guadeloupe										**Guadeloupe**
End of period	Euro (EUR)	...	...	0.8	0.7	0.7	0.8	0.9	0.9	Fin de période
Period average		...	...	0.8	0.8	0.8	0.8	0.9	0.9	Moy. sur période
Guatemala										**Guatemala**
End of period	Quetzal (GTQ)	1.0	6.0	7.6	8.0	7.9	7.6	7.7	7.5	Fin de période
Period average		1.0	5.8	7.6	8.1	7.9	7.7	7.7	7.6	Moy. sur période
Guernsey										**Guernesey**
End of period	Pound Sterling (GBP)	0.7	0.6	0.6	0.6	0.6	0.6	0.7	0.8	Fin de période
Period average	livre sterling (GBP)	0.8	0.6	0.6	0.6	0.6	0.6	0.7	0.7	Moy. sur période
Guinea										**Guinée**
End of period	Guinean Franc (GNF),	22.5	998.0	4 500.0	6 083.9	7 005.8	7 227.7	8 003.7	9 225.3	Fin de période
Period average	franc guinéen (GNF)	24.3	991.4	3 644.3	5 726.1	6 907.9	7 014.1	7 485.5	...	Moy. sur période
Guinea-Bissau										**Guinée-Bissau**
End of period	CFA Franc (XOF)	...	...	556.0	490.9	475.6	540.3	602.5	622.3	Fin de période
Period average	franc CFA (XOF)	...	...	527.5	495.3	494.0	494.4	591.4	593.0	Moy. sur période
Guyana										**Guyana**
End of period	Guyana Dollar (GYD),	4.2	140.5	200.3	203.5	206.3	206.5	206.5	206.5	Fin de période
Period average	dollar du Guyana (GYD)	4.3	142.0	199.9	203.6	205.4	206.4	206.5	206.5	Moy. sur période
Haiti										**Haïti**
End of period	Gourde (HTG)	5.0	16.2	43.0	39.9	43.9	46.7	56.7	67.4	Fin de période
Period average		5.0	15.1	40.4	39.8	43.5	45.2	50.7	63.3	Moy. sur période
Heard Is. and McDonald Is.										**Île Heard-et-Îles MacDonald**
End of period	Australian Dollar (AUD),	1.5	1.3	1.4	1.0	1.1	1.2	1.4	1.4	Fin de période
Period average	dollar australien (AUD)	1.4	1.3	1.3	1.1	1.0	1.1	1.3	1.3	Moy. sur période
Holy See										**Saint-Siège**
End of period	Euro (EUR)	...	...	0.8	0.7	0.7	0.8	0.9	0.9	Fin de période
Period average		...	...	0.8	0.8	0.8	0.8	0.9	0.9	Moy. sur période
Honduras										**Honduras**
End of period	Lempira (HNL)	2.0	10.3	18.9	18.9	20.6	21.5	22.4	23.5	Fin de période
Period average		2.0	9.5	18.8	18.9	20.4	21.0	21.9	22.8	Moy. sur période
Hungary										**Hongrie**
End of period	Forint (HUF)	47.3	139.5	213.6	208.7	215.7	259.1	286.6	293.7	Fin de période
Period average		50.1	125.7	199.6	207.9	223.7	232.6	279.3	281.5	Moy. sur période
Iceland										**Islande**
End of period	Iceland Krona (ISK),	42.1	65.2	63.0	115.1	115.6	126.9	129.6	112.8	Fin de période
Period average	couronne islandaise (ISK)	41.5	64.7	63.0	122.2	122.2	116.8	131.9	120.8	Moy. sur période
India										**Inde**
End of period	Indian Rupee (INR)	12.2	35.2	45.1	44.8	61.9	63.3	66.3	68.0	Fin de période
Period average	roupie indienne (INR)	12.4	32.4	44.1	45.7	58.6	61.0	64.2	67.2	Moy. sur période
Indonesia										**Indonésie**
End of period	Rupiah (IDR)	1 125.0	2 308.0	9 830.0	8 991.0	12 189.0	12 440.0	13 795.0	13 436.0	Fin de période
Period average	rupiah indonésienne (IDR)	1 110.6	2 248.6	9 704.7	9 090.4	10 461.2	11 865.2	13 389.4	13 308.3	Moy. sur période
Iran (Islamic Republic of)										**Iran (Rép. islamique d')**
End of period	Iranian Rial (IRR)	84.2	1 747.5	9 091.0	10 353.0	24 774.0	27 138.0	30 130.0	32 376.0	Fin de période
Period average	rial iranien (IRR)	91.1	1 748.4	8 964.0	10 254.2	18 414.4	25 941.7	29 011.5	30 914.9	Moy. sur période
Iraq										**Iraq**
End of period	Iraqi Dinar (IQD)	0.3	0.3	1 487.0	1 170.0	1 166.0	1 166.0	1 182.0	1 182.0	Fin de période
Period average	dinar iraquien (IQD)	0.3	0.3	1 472.0	1 170.0	1 166.0	1 166.0	1 167.3	1 182.0	Moy. sur période
Ireland										**Irlande**
End of period	Euro (EUR)	...	...	0.8	0.7	0.7	0.8	0.9	0.9	Fin de période
Period average		...	...	0.8	0.8	0.8	0.8	0.9	0.9	Moy. sur période

Exchange rates *(continued)*
National currency per US dollar

Cours des changes *(suite)*
Valeur du dollar E.-U. en monnaie nationale

Country or area	National currency Monnaie nationale	1985	1995	2005	2010	2013	2014	2015	2016	Pays ou zone
Isle of Man										**Île de Man**
End of period	Pound Sterling (GBP)	0.7	0.6	0.6	0.6	0.6	0.6	0.7	0.8	Fin de période
Period average	livre sterling (GBP)	0.8	0.6	0.6	0.6	0.6	0.6	0.7	0.7	Moy. sur période
Israel										**Israël**
End of period	New Israeli Sheqel (ILS),	1.5	3.1	4.6	3.5	3.5	3.9	3.9	3.8	Fin de période
Period average	nouv. shekel israélien (ILS)	1.2	3.0	4.5	3.7	3.6	3.6	3.9	3.8	Moy. sur période
Italy										**Italie**
End of period	Euro (EUR)	...	...	0.8	0.7	0.7	0.8	0.9	0.9	Fin de période
Period average		...	...	0.8	0.8	0.8	0.8	0.9	0.9	Moy. sur période
Jamaica										**Jamaïque**
End of period	Jamaican Dollar (JMD),	5.5	39.6	64.4	85.6	106.0	114.4	120.0	128.0	Fin de période
Period average	dollar jamaïcain (JMD)	5.6	35.1	62.3	87.2	100.2	110.9	116.9	125.1	Moy. sur période
Japan										**Japon**
End of period	Yen (JPY)	200.5	102.8	118.0	81.5	105.3	120.6	120.5	116.8	Fin de période
Period average		238.5	94.1	110.2	87.8	97.6	105.9	121.0	108.8	Moy. sur période
Jersey										**Jersey**
End of period	Pound Sterling (GBP)	0.7	0.6	0.6	0.6	0.6	0.6	0.7	0.8	Fin de période
Period average	livre sterling (GBP)	0.8	0.6	0.6	0.6	0.6	0.6	0.7	0.7	Moy. sur période
Jordan										**Jordanie**
End of period	Jordanian Dinar (JOD),	0.4	0.7	0.7	0.7	0.7	0.7	0.7	0.7	Fin de période
Period average	dinar jordanien (JOD)	0.4	0.7	0.7	0.7	0.7	0.7	0.7	0.7	Moy. sur période
Kazakhstan										**Kazakhstan**
End of period	Tenge (KZT)	...	64.0	134.0	147.5	154.1	182.4	340.0	333.3	Fin de période
Period average		...	61.0	132.9	147.4	152.1	179.2	221.7	342.2	Moy. sur période
Kenya										**Kenya**
End of period	Kenyan Shilling (KES),	16.3	55.9	72.4	80.8	86.3	90.5	102.3	...	Fin de période
Period average	shilling kényan (KES)	16.4	51.4	75.6	79.2	86.1	87.9	98.2	...	Moy. sur période
Kiribati										**Kiribati**
End of period	Australian Dollar (AUD),	1.5	1.3	1.4	1.0	1.1	1.2	1.4	1.4	Fin de période
Period average	dollar australien (AUD)	1.4	1.3	1.3	1.1	1.0	1.1	1.3	1.3	Moy. sur période
Kuwait										**Koweït**
End of period	Kuwaiti Dinar (KWD)	0.3	0.3	0.3	0.3	0.3	0.3	0.3	0.3	Fin de période
Period average	dinar koweïtien (KWD)	0.3	0.3	0.3	0.3	0.3	0.3	0.3	0.3	Moy. sur période
Kyrgyzstan										**Kirghizistan**
End of period	Som (KGS)	...	11.2	41.3	47.1	49.2	58.9	75.9	69.2	Fin de période
Period average		...	10.8	41.0	46.0	48.4	53.7	64.5	69.9	Moy. sur période
Lao People's Dem. Rep.										**Rép. dém. populaire lao**
End of period	Lao Kip (LAK)	95.0	923.0	10 743.0	8 058.8	8 027.8	8 097.8	8 172.6	8 204.0	Fin de période
Period average		55.0	804.7	10 655.2	8 258.8	7 860.1	8 049.0	8 147.9	8 129.1	Moy. sur période
Latvia										**Lettonie**
End of period	Euro (EUR)	...	...	...	...	...	0.8	0.9	0.9	Fin de période
Period average		...	...	...	...	...	0.8	0.9	0.9	Moy. sur période
Lebanon										**Liban**
End of period	Lebanese Pound (LBP),	18.1	1 596.0	1 507.5	1 507.5	1 507.5	1 507.5	1 507.5	1 507.5	Fin de période
Period average	livre libanaise (LBP)	16.4	1 621.4	1 507.5	1 507.5	1 507.5	1 507.5	1 507.5	1 507.5	Moy. sur période
Lesotho										**Lesotho**
End of period	Loti (LSL)	2.6	3.6	6.3	6.6	10.5	11.6	15.5	13.7	Fin de période
Period average		2.2	3.6	6.4	7.3	9.7	10.9	12.8	14.7	Moy. sur période
Liberia										**Libéria**
End of period	Liberian Dollar (LRD),	43.3	43.8	56.5	71.5	82.5	82.5	88.5	102.5	Fin de période
Period average	dollar libérien (LRD)	46.4	49.8	57.1	71.4	77.5	83.9	86.2	...	Moy. sur période
Libya										**Libye**
End of period	Libyan Dinar (LYD)	0.3	0.4	1.4	1.3	1.3	1.3	1.4	1.4	Fin de période
Period average	dinar libyen (LYD)	0.3	0.4	1.3	1.3	1.3	1.3	1.4	1.4	Moy. sur période
Liechtenstein										**Liechtenstein**
End of period	Swiss Franc (CHF)	2.1	1.2	1.3	0.9	0.9	1.0	1.0	1.0	Fin de période
Period average	franc suisse (CHF)	2.5	1.2	1.2	1.0	0.9	0.9	1.0	1.0	Moy. sur période
Lithuania										**Lituanie**
End of period	Euro (EUR)	...	...	...	...	...	...	0.9	0.9	Fin de période
Period average		...	...	...	...	...	...	0.9	0.9	Moy. sur période
Luxembourg										**Luxembourg**
End of period	Euro (EUR)	...	...	0.8	0.7	0.7	0.8	0.9	0.9	Fin de période
Period average		...	...	0.8	0.8	0.8	0.8	0.9	0.9	Moy. sur période

Exchange rates *(continued)*
National currency per US dollar

Cours des changes *(suite)*
Valeur du dollar E.-U. en monnaie nationale

Country or area	National currency Monnaie nationale	1985	1995	2005	2010	2013	2014	2015	2016	Pays ou zone
Madagascar										**Madagascar**
End of period	Malagasy Ariary (MGA),	127.2	684.6	2 159.8	2 146.1	2 236.1	2 596.7	3 199.2	3 347.9	Fin de période
Period average	ariary malgache (MGA)	132.5	853.1	2 003.0	2 090.0	2 206.9	2 414.8	2 933.5	3 176.5	Moy. sur période
Malawi										**Malawi**
End of period	Malawi Kwacha (MWK),	1.7	15.3	123.8	150.8	435.0	470.8	664.4	725.0	Fin de période
Period average	kwacha malawien (MWK)	1.7	15.3	118.4	150.5	364.4	424.9	496.4	713.8	Moy. sur période
Malaysia										**Malaisie**
End of period	Malaysian Ringgit (MYR),	2.4	2.5	3.8	3.1	3.3	3.5	4.3	4.5	Fin de période
Period average	ringgit malaisien (MYR)	2.5	2.5	3.8	3.2	3.2	3.3	3.9	4.1	Moy. sur période
Maldives										**Maldives**
End of period	Rufiyaa (MVR)	7.1	11.8	12.8	12.8	15.4	15.4	15.4	15.4	Fin de période
Period average		7.1	11.8	12.8	12.8	15.4	15.4	15.4	15.4	Moy. sur période
Mali										**Mali**
End of period	CFA Franc (XOF)	378.0	490.0	556.0	490.9	475.6	540.3	602.5	622.3	Fin de période
Period average	franc CFA (XOF)	449.3	499.1	527.5	495.3	494.0	494.4	591.4	593.0	Moy. sur période
Malta										**Malte**
End of period	Euro (EUR)	...	...	...	0.7	0.7	0.8	0.9	0.9	Fin de période
Period average		...	...	...	0.8	0.8	0.8	0.9	0.9	Moy. sur période
Martinique										**Martinique**
End of period	Euro (EUR)	...	...	0.8	0.7	0.7	0.8	0.9	0.9	Fin de période
Period average		...	...	0.8	0.8	0.8	0.8	0.9	0.9	Moy. sur période
Mauritania										**Mauritanie**
End of period	Ouguiya (MRO)	77.1	137.1	270.6	282.0	299.0	312.6	339.0	...	Fin de période
Period average		77.1	129.8	265.5	275.9	300.7	302.7	324.7	...	Moy. sur période
Mauritius										**Maurice**
End of period	Mauritius Rupee (MUR),	14.3	17.7	30.7	30.4	30.1	31.7	35.9	36.0	Fin de période
Period average	roupie mauricienne (MUR)	15.4	17.4	29.5	30.8	30.7	30.6	35.1	35.5	Moy. sur période
Mayotte										**Mayotte**
End of period	Euro (EUR)	...	...	0.8	0.7	0.7	0.8	0.9	0.9	Fin de période
Period average		...	...	0.8	0.8	0.8	0.8	0.9	0.9	Moy. sur période
Mexico										**Mexique**
End of period	Mexican Peso (MXN)	0.4	7.6	10.8	12.4	13.1	14.7	17.2	20.7	Fin de période
Period average	peso mexicain (MXN)	0.3	6.4	10.9	12.6	12.8	13.3	15.8	18.7	Moy. sur période
Monaco										**Monaco**
End of period	Euro (EUR)	...	...	0.8	0.7	0.7	0.8	0.9	0.9	Fin de période
Period average		...	...	0.8	0.8	0.8	0.8	0.9	0.9	Moy. sur période
Mongolia										**Mongolie**
End of period	Tugrik (MNT)	...	473.6	1 221.0	1 256.5	1 654.1	1 885.6	1 996.0	2 489.5	Fin de période
Period average		...	448.6	1 205.2	1 357.1	1 523.9	1 817.9	1 970.3	2 140.3	Moy. sur période
Montenegro										**Monténégro**
End of period	Euro (EUR)	...	...	0.8	0.7	0.7	0.8	0.9	0.9	Fin de période
Period average		...	...	0.8	0.8	0.8	0.8	0.9	0.9	Moy. sur période
Montserrat										**Montserrat**
End of period	E. Caribbean Dollar (XCD),	2.7	2.7	2.7	2.7	2.7	2.7	2.7	2.7	Fin de période
Period average	dollar des Caraïb. (XCD) [1]	2.7	2.7	2.7	2.7	2.7	2.7	2.7	2.7	Moy. sur période
Morocco										**Maroc**
End of period	Moroccan Dirham (MAD),	9.6	8.5	9.2	8.4	8.2	9.0	9.9	10.1	Fin de période
Period average	dirham marocain (MAD)	10.1	8.5	8.9	8.4	8.4	8.4	9.8	9.8	Moy. sur période
Mozambique										**Mozambique**
End of period	Mozam. Metical (MZN),	~0.0	10.9	24.2	32.6	30.1	33.6	45.9	71.4	Fin de période
Period average	metical de Mozam. (MZN)	~0.0	9.0	23.1	34.0	30.1	31.4	40.0	63.1	Moy. sur période
Myanmar										**Myanmar**
End of period	Kyat (MMK)	7.8	5.8	6.0	5.6	988.0	1 031.5	1 304.0	1 357.5	Fin de période
Period average		8.5	5.7	5.8	5.6	933.6	984.3	1 162.6	1 234.9	Moy. sur période
Namibia										**Namibie**
End of period	Namibia Dollar (NAD),	2.6	3.6	6.3	6.6	10.5	11.6	15.5	13.7	Fin de période
Period average	dollar namibien (NAD)	2.2	3.6	6.4	7.3	9.7	10.9	12.8	14.7	Moy. sur période
Nauru										**Nauru**
End of period	Australian Dollar (AUD),	1.5	1.3	1.4	1.0	1.1	1.2	1.4	1.4	Fin de période
Period average	dollar australien (AUD)	1.4	1.3	1.3	1.1	1.0	1.1	1.3	1.3	Moy. sur période
Nepal										**Népal**
End of period	Nepalese Rupee (NPR),	20.7	56.0	74.1	71.7	99.1	99.4	107.0	109.0	Fin de période
Period average	roupie népalaise (NPR)	18.2	51.9	71.4	73.3	93.0	97.6	102.4	107.5	Moy. sur période

16 Exchange rates *(continued)*
National currency per US dollar

Cours des changes *(suite)*
Valeur du dollar E.-U. en monnaie nationale

Country or area	National currency Monnaie nationale	1985	1995	2005	2010	2013	2014	2015	2016	Pays ou zone
Netherlands										**Pays-Bas**
End of period	Euro (EUR)	...	...	0.8	0.7	0.7	0.8	0.9	0.9	Fin de période
Period average		...	...	0.8	0.8	0.8	0.8	0.9	0.9	Moy. sur période
Netherlands Antilles [former]										**Antilles néerlandaises [anc.]**
End of period	Neth. Ant. Guilder (ANG),	1.8	1.8	1.8	...	...	...	...	...	Fin de période
Period average	flor. des Ant. néer. (ANG) [4]	1.8	1.8	1.8	...	...	...	...	...	Moy. sur période
New Caledonia										**Nouvelle-Calédonie**
End of period	CFP Franc (XPF)	137.5	89.1	101.2	89.3	86.5	98.3	109.6	113.2	Fin de période
Period average	franc CFP (XPF)	163.4	90.8	96.0	90.1	89.9	89.9	107.6	107.9	Moy. sur période
New Zealand										**Nouvelle-Zélande**
End of period	New Zealand Dollar (NZD),	2.0	1.5	1.5	1.3	1.2	1.3	1.5	1.4	Fin de période
Period average	dollar néo-zélandais (NZD)	2.0	1.5	1.4	1.4	1.2	1.2	1.4	1.4	Moy. sur période
Nicaragua										**Nicaragua**
End of period	Cordoba Oro (NIO)	0.0	8.0	17.1	21.9	25.3	26.6	27.9	29.3	Fin de période
Period average		0.0	7.5	16.7	21.4	24.7	26.0	27.3	28.6	Moy. sur période
Niger										**Niger**
End of period	CFA Franc (XOF)	378.0	490.0	556.0	490.9	475.6	540.3	602.5	622.3	Fin de période
Period average	franc CFA (XOF)	449.3	499.1	527.5	495.3	494.0	494.4	591.4	593.0	Moy. sur période
Nigeria										**Nigéria**
End of period	Naira (NGN)	1.0	21.9	129.0	150.7	157.3	169.7	197.0	305.0	Fin de période
Period average		0.9	21.9	131.3	150.3	157.3	158.6	192.4	253.5	Moy. sur période
Niue										**Nioué**
End of period	New Zealand Dollar (NZD),	2.0	1.5	1.5	1.3	1.2	1.3	1.5	1.4	Fin de période
Period average	dollar néo-zélandais (NZD)	2.0	1.5	1.4	1.4	1.2	1.2	1.4	1.4	Moy. sur période
Norfolk Island										**Île Norfolk**
End of period	Australian dollar (AUD),	1.5	1.3	1.4	1.0	1.1	1.2	1.4	1.4	Fin de période
Period average	dollar australien (AUD)	1.4	1.3	1.3	1.1	1.0	1.1	1.3	1.3	Moy. sur période
Norway										**Norvège**
End of period	Norwegian Krone (NOK),	7.6	6.3	6.8	5.9	6.1	7.4	8.8	8.6	Fin de période
Period average	couronne norvég. (NOK)	8.6	6.3	6.4	6.0	5.9	6.3	8.1	8.4	Moy. sur période
Oman										**Oman**
End of period	Rial Omani (OM	0.3	0.4	0.4	0.4	0.4	0.4	0.4	0.4	Fin de période
Period average	rial omanais (OMR)	0.3	0.4	0.4	0.4	0.4	0.4	0.4	0.4	Moy. sur période
Pakistan										**Pakistan**
End of period	Pakistan Rupee (PKR),	16.0	34.3	59.8	85.7	105.7	100.5	104.9	104.8	Fin de période
Period average	roupie pakistanaise (PKR)	15.9	31.6	59.5	85.2	101.6	101.1	102.8	104.8	Moy. sur période
Panama										**Panama**
End of period	Balboa (PAB)	1.0	1.0	1.0	1.0	1.0	1.0	1.0	1.0	Fin de période
Period average		1.0	1.0	1.0	1.0	1.0	1.0	1.0	1.0	Moy. sur période
Papua New Guinea										**Papouasie-Nvl-Guinée**
End of period	Kina (PGK)	1.0	1.3	3.1	2.6	2.4	2.6	3.0	3.2	Fin de période
Period average		1.0	1.3	3.1	2.7	2.2	2.5	2.8	3.1	Moy. sur période
Paraguay										**Paraguay**
End of period	Guarani (PYG)	320.0	1 979.7	6 120.0	4 573.8	4 524.0	4 626.3	5 806.9	5 766.9	Fin de période
Period average	guaraní (PYG)	306.7	1 963.0	6 178.0	4 735.5	4 320.7	4 462.2	5 204.9	5 670.5	Moy. sur période
Peru										**Pérou**
End of period	Sol (PEN)	0.0	2.3	3.4	2.8	2.8	3.0	3.4	3.4	Fin de période
Period average		0.0	2.3	3.3	2.8	2.7	2.8	3.2	3.4	Moy. sur période
Philippines										**Philippines**
End of period	Philippine Peso (PHP),	19.0	26.2	53.1	43.9	44.4	44.6	47.2	49.8	Fin de période
Period average	peso philippin (PHP)	18.6	25.7	55.1	45.1	42.4	44.4	45.5	47.5	Moy. sur période
Pitcairn										**Pitcairn**
End of period	New Zealand dollar (NZD),	2.0	1.5	1.5	1.3	1.2	1.3	1.5	1.4	Fin de période
Period average	dollar néo-zélandais (NZD)	2.0	1.5	1.4	1.4	1.2	1.2	1.4	1.4	Moy. sur période
Poland										**Pologne**
End of period	Zloty (PLN)	~0.0	2.5	3.3	3.0	3.0	3.5	3.9	4.2	Fin de période
Period average		~0.0	2.4	3.2	3.0	3.2	3.2	3.8	3.9	Moy. sur période
Portugal										**Portugal**
End of period	Euro (EUR)	...	...	0.8	0.7	0.7	0.8	0.9	0.9	Fin de période
Period average		...	...	0.8	0.8	0.8	0.8	0.9	0.9	Moy. sur période
Qatar										**Qatar**
End of period	Qatari Rial (QAR)	3.6	3.6	3.6	3.6	3.6	3.6	3.6	3.6	Fin de période
Period average	riyal qatari (QAR)	3.6	3.6	3.6	3.6	3.6	3.6	3.6	3.6	Moy. sur période

Country or area	National currency Monnaie nationale	1985	1995	2005	2010	2013	2014	2015	2016	Pays ou zone
Republic of Korea										**République de Corée**
End of period	South Korean Won (KRW),	890.2	774.7	1 011.6	1 134.8	1 055.4	1 099.3	1 172.5	1 208.5	Fin de période
Period average	won sud-coréen (KRW)	870.0	771.3	1 024.1	1 156.1	1 094.9	1 053.0	1 131.2	1 160.3	Moy. sur période
Republic of Moldova										**République de Moldova**
End of period	Moldovan Leu (MDL)	...	4.5	12.8	12.2	13.1	15.6	19.7	20.0	Fin de période
Period average	leu moldove (MDL)	...	4.5	12.6	12.4	12.6	14.0	18.8	19.9	Moy. sur période
Réunion										**Réunion**
End of period	Euro (EUR)	...	...	0.8	0.7	0.7	0.8	0.9	0.9	Fin de période
Period average		...	...	0.8	0.8	0.8	0.8	0.9	0.9	Moy. sur période
Romania										**Roumanie**
End of period	Romanian Leu (RON)	~0.0	0.3	3.1	3.2	3.3	3.7	4.1	4.3	Fin de période
Period average	leu roumain (RON)	~0.0	0.2	2.9	3.2	3.3	3.3	4.0	4.1	Moy. sur période
Russian Federation										**Fédération de Russie**
End of period	Russian Ruble (RUB)	...	4.6	28.8	30.5	32.7	56.3	72.9	60.7	Fin de période
Period average	ruble russe (RUB)	...	4.6	28.3	30.4	31.8	38.4	60.9	67.1	Moy. sur période
Rwanda										**Rwanda**
End of period	Rwanda Franc (RWF),	93.5	299.8	553.7	594.5	670.1	694.4	747.4	819.8	Fin de période
Period average	franc rwandais (RWF)	101.2	262.2	557.8	583.1	646.6	681.9	721.0	...	Moy. sur période
Saint Barthélemy										**Saint-Barthélemy**
End of period	Euro (EUR)	...	...	0.8	0.7	0.7	0.8	0.9	0.9	Fin de période
Period average		...	...	0.8	0.8	0.8	0.8	0.9	0.9	Moy. sur période
Saint Helena										**Sainte-Hélène**
End of period	Saint Helena Pound (SHP),	0.7	0.6	0.6	0.6	0.6	0.6	0.7	0.8	Fin de période
Period average	livre de St.-Hélène (SHP)	0.8	0.6	0.6	0.6	0.6	0.6	0.7	0.7	Moy. sur période
Saint Kitts and Nevis										**Saint-Kitts-et-Nevis**
End of period	E. Caribbean Dollar (XCD),	2.7	2.7	2.7	2.7	2.7	2.7	2.7	2.7	Fin de période
Period average	dollar des Caraïb. (XCD) [1]	2.7	2.7	2.7	2.7	2.7	2.7	2.7	2.7	Moy. sur période
Saint Lucia										**Sainte-Lucie**
End of period	E. Caribbean Dollar (XCD),	2.7	2.7	2.7	2.7	2.7	2.7	2.7	2.7	Fin de période
Period average	dollar des Caraïb. (XCD) [1]	2.7	2.7	2.7	2.7	2.7	2.7	2.7	2.7	Moy. sur période
Saint Martin (French part)										**St-Martin (partie française)**
End of period	Euro (EUR)	...	...	0.8	0.7	0.7	0.8	0.9	0.9	Fin de période
Period average		...	...	0.8	0.8	0.8	0.8	0.9	0.9	Moy. sur période
Saint Pierre and Miquelon										**Saint-Pierre-et-Miquelon**
End of period	Euro (EUR)	...	...	0.8	0.7	0.7	0.8	0.9	0.9	Fin de période
Period average		...	...	0.8	0.8	0.8	0.8	0.9	0.9	Moy. sur période
Saint Vincent & Grenadines										**Saint-Vincent-Grenadines**
End of period	E. Caribbean Dollar (XCD),	2.7	2.7	2.7	2.7	2.7	2.7	2.7	2.7	Fin de période
Period average	dollar des Caraïb. (XCD) [1]	2.7	2.7	2.7	2.7	2.7	2.7	2.7	2.7	Moy. sur période
Samoa										**Samoa**
End of period	Tala (WST)	2.3	2.5	2.8	2.3	2.3	2.4	2.6	2.6	Fin de période
Period average		2.2	2.5	2.7	2.5	2.3	2.3	2.6	2.6	Moy. sur période
San Marino										**Saint-Marin**
End of period	Euro (EUR)	...	...	0.8	0.7	0.7	0.8	0.9	0.9	Fin de période
Period average		...	...	0.8	0.8	0.8	0.8	0.9	0.9	Moy. sur période
Sao Tome and Principe										**Sao Tomé-et-Principe**
End of period	Dobra (STD)	41.2	1 756.9	11 929.7	18 335.6	17 765.2	20 179.6	22 503.9	23 242.6	Fin de période
Period average		44.6	1 420.3	10 558.0	18 498.6	18 450.0	18 466.4	22 090.6	22 148.9	Moy. sur période
Saudi Arabia										**Arabie saoudite**
End of period	Saudi Riyal (SAR)	3.6	3.8	3.7	3.8	3.8	3.8	3.8	3.8	Fin de période
Period average	rial saoudien (SAR)	3.6	3.8	3.7	3.8	3.8	3.8	3.8	3.8	Moy. sur période
Senegal										**Sénégal**
End of period	CFA Franc (XOF)	378.0	490.0	556.0	490.9	475.6	540.3	602.5	622.3	Fin de période
Period average	franc CFA (XOF)	449.3	499.1	527.5	495.3	494.0	494.4	591.4	593.0	Moy. sur période
Serbia										**Serbie**
End of period	Serbian Dinar (RSD)	...	...	72.2	79.3	83.1	99.5	111.2	117.1	Fin de période
Period average	dinar de Serbie (RSD)	...	...	66.7	77.7	85.2	88.4	108.8	111.3	Moy. sur période
Seychelles										**Seychelles**
End of period	Seychelles Rupee (SCR),	6.6	4.9	5.5	12.1	12.1	14.0	13.2	13.5	Fin de période
Period average	roupie seychelloise (SCR)	7.1	4.8	5.5	12.1	12.1	12.7	13.3	13.3	Moy. sur période
Sierra Leone										**Sierra Leone**
End of period	Leone (SLL)	5.2	943.4	2 932.5	4 198.0	4 356.4	4 953.3	5 639.1	...	Fin de période
Period average		5.1	755.2	2 889.6	3 978.1	4 332.5	4 524.2	5 080.7	...	Moy. sur période

16 Exchange rates (continued)
National currency per US dollar

Cours des changes (suite)
Valeur du dollar E.-U. en monnaie nationale

Country or area	National currency Monnaie nationale	1985	1995	2005	2010	2013	2014	2015	2016	Pays ou zone
Singapore										**Singapour**
End of period	Singapore Dollar (SGD),	2.1	1.4	1.7	1.3	1.3	1.3	1.4	1.4	Fin de période
Period average	dollar singapourien (SGD)	2.2	1.4	1.7	1.4	1.3	1.3	1.4	1.4	Moy. sur période
Sint Maarten (Dutch part)										**St-Martin (partie néerland.)**
End of period	Neth. Ant. Guilder (ANG),	...	...	...	1.8	1.8	1.8	1.8	1.8	Fin de période
Period average	flor. des Ant. néer. (ANG) [4]	...	...	...	1.8	1.8	1.8	1.8	1.8	Moy. sur période
Slovakia										**Slovaquie**
End of period	Euro (EUR)	...	...	...	0.7	0.7	0.8	0.9	0.9	Fin de période
Period average		...	...	...	0.8	0.8	0.8	0.9	0.9	Moy. sur période
Slovenia										**Slovénie**
End of period	Euro (EUR)	...	...	...	0.7	0.7	0.8	0.9	0.9	Fin de période
Period average		...	...	...	0.8	0.8	0.8	0.9	0.9	Moy. sur période
Solomon Islands										**Îles Salomon**
End of period	Solomon Is. Dollar (SBD),	1.6	3.5	7.6	8.1	7.4	7.4	8.1	...	Fin de période
Period average	dollar des Îl. Sal. (SBD) [6]	1.5	3.4	7.5	8.1	7.3	7.4	7.9	...	Moy. sur période
Somalia [2]										**Somalie** [2]
End of period	Somali Shilling (SOS), shilling somalien (SOS)	...	...	...	...	2 300.0	2 300.0	2 300.0	2 300.0	Fin de période
South Africa										**Afrique du Sud**
End of period	Rand (ZAR)	2.6	3.6	6.3	6.6	10.5	11.6	15.5	13.7	Fin de période
Period average		2.2	3.6	6.4	7.3	9.7	10.9	12.8	14.7	Moy. sur période
South Georgia & Sandwich Is.										**Géorgie du S.-Îles Sandwich**
End of period	Pound Sterling (GBP), livre	0.7	0.6	0.6	0.6	0.6	0.6	0.7	0.8	Fin de période
Period average	sterling (GBP)	0.8	0.6	0.6	0.6	0.6	0.6	0.7	0.7	Moy. sur période
South Sudan										**Soudan du sud**
End of period	S. Sudanese Pound (SSP),	...	...	...	...	3.0	3.0	16.6	83.9	Fin de période
Period average	livre s.-soudanaise (SSP) [7]	...	...	...	...	3.0	3.0	4.1	49.4	Moy. sur période
Spain										**Espagne**
End of period	Euro (EUR)	...	...	0.8	0.7	0.7	0.8	0.9	0.9	Fin de période
Period average		...	...	0.8	0.8	0.8	0.8	0.9	0.9	Moy. sur période
Sri Lanka										**Sri Lanka**
End of period	Sri Lanka Rupee (LKR),	27.4	54.0	102.1	111.0	130.8	131.0	144.1	149.8	Fin de période
Period average	roupie sri-lankaise (LKR)	27.2	51.3	100.5	113.1	129.1	130.6	135.9	145.6	Moy. sur période
Sudan										**Soudan**
End of period	Sudanese Pound (SDG),	~0.0	0.5	2.3	2.5	5.7	6.0	6.1	...	Fin de période
Period average	livre soudanaise (SDG)	~0.0	0.6	2.4	2.3	4.8	5.7	6.0	...	Moy. sur période
Suriname										**Suriname**
End of period	Surinam Dollar (SRD),	~0.0	0.4	2.7	2.7	3.3	3.3	4.0	7.4	Fin de période
Period average	dollar surinamais (SRD)	~0.0	0.4	2.7	2.7	3.3	3.3	3.4	6.2	Moy. sur période
Svalbard and Jan Mayen Is.										**Îles Svalbard-et-Jan Mayen**
End of period	Norwegian Krone (NOK),	7.6	6.3	6.8	5.9	6.1	7.4	8.8	8.6	Fin de période
Period average	couronne norvég. (NOK)	8.6	6.3	6.4	6.0	5.9	6.3	8.1	8.4	Moy. sur période
Swaziland										**Swaziland**
End of period	Lilangeni (SZL)	2.6	3.6	6.3	6.6	10.5	11.6	15.5	13.7	Fin de période
Period average		2.2	3.6	6.4	7.3	9.7	10.9	12.8	14.7	Moy. sur période
Sweden										**Suède**
End of period	Swedish Krona (SEK),	7.6	6.7	8.0	6.7	6.4	7.7	8.4	9.1	Fin de période
Period average	couronne suédoise (SEK)	8.6	7.1	7.5	7.2	6.5	6.9	8.4	8.6	Moy. sur période
Switzerland										**Suisse**
End of period	Swiss Franc (CHF)	2.1	1.2	1.3	0.9	0.9	1.0	1.0	1.0	Fin de période
Period average	franc suisse (CHF)	2.5	1.2	1.2	1.0	0.9	0.9	1.0	1.0	Moy. sur période
Syrian Arab Republic [2]										**République arabe syrienne** [2]
End of period	Syrian Pound (SYP), livre syrienne (SYP)	...	...	...	46.6	143.6	196.0	338.0	514.9	Fin de période
Tajikistan										**Tadjikistan**
End of period	Somoni (TJS)	...	0.3	3.2	4.4	4.8	5.3	7.0	7.9	Fin de période
Period average		...	0.1	3.1	4.4	4.8	4.9	6.2	7.8	Moy. sur période
Thailand										**Thaïlande**
End of period	Baht (THB)	26.7	25.2	41.0	30.2	32.8	33.0	36.1	35.8	Fin de période
Period average		27.2	24.9	40.2	31.7	30.7	32.5	34.2	35.3	Moy. sur période
TFYR of Macedonia										**ex-R.Y. de Macédoine**
End of period	Denar (MKD)	...	38.0	51.9	46.3	44.6	50.6	56.4	58.3	Fin de période
Period average		...	37.9	49.3	46.5	46.4	46.4	55.5	55.7	Moy. sur période

Country or area	National currency Monnaie nationale	1985	1995	2005	2010	2013	2014	2015	2016	Pays ou zone
Togo										**Togo**
End of period	CFA Franc (XOF)	378.1	490.0	556.0	490.9	475.6	540.3	602.5	622.3	Fin de période
Period average	franc CFA (XOF)	449.3	499.1	527.5	495.3	494.0	494.4	591.4	593.0	Moy. sur période
Tokelau										**Tokélaou**
End of period	New Zealand Dollar (NZD),	2.0	1.5	1.5	1.3	1.2	1.3	1.5	1.4	Fin de période
Period average	dollar néo-zélandais (NZD)	2.0	1.5	1.4	1.4	1.2	1.2	1.4	1.4	Moy. sur période
Tonga										**Tonga**
End of period	Pa'anga (TOP)	1.5	1.3	2.1	1.8	1.8	2.0	2.2	2.2	Fin de période
Period average		1.4	1.3	1.9	1.9	1.8	1.8	2.1	2.2	Moy. sur période
Trinidad and Tobago										**Trinité-et-Tobago**
End of period	TT Dollar (TTD)	3.6	6.0	6.3	6.4	6.5	6.4	6.4	6.8	Fin de période
Period average	dollar de la T-et-T (TTD) [8]	2.5	5.9	6.3	6.4	6.4	6.4	6.4	6.7	Moy. sur période
Tunisia										**Tunisie**
End of period	Tunisian Dinar (TND)	0.8	1.0	1.4	1.4	1.6	1.9	2.0	2.3	Fin de période
Period average	dinar tunisien (TND)	0.8	0.9	1.3	1.4	1.6	1.7	2.0	2.1	Moy. sur période
Turkey										**Turquie**
End of period	Turkish Lira (TRY)	~0.0	0.1	1.3	1.5	2.1	2.3	2.9	3.5	Fin de période
Period average	livre turque (TRY)	~0.0	~0.0	1.3	1.5	1.9	2.2	2.7	3.0	Moy. sur période
Turkmenistan [2]										**Turkménistan** [2]
End of period	Turkmen. Manat (TMT), manat turkmène (TMT) [9]	...	...	...	3.5	3.5	3.5	3.5	3.5	Fin de période
Tuvalu										**Tuvalu**
End of period	Australian Dollar (AUD),	1.5	1.3	1.4	1.0	1.1	1.2	1.4	1.4	Fin de période
Period average	dollar australien (AUD)	1.4	1.3	1.3	1.1	1.0	1.1	1.3	1.3	Moy. sur période
Uganda										**Ouganda**
End of period	Uganda Shilling (UGX),	14.0	1 009.5	1 816.9	2 308.3	2 528.0	2 773.1	3 377.0	3 610.5	Fin de période
Period average	shilling ougandais (UGX)	6.7	968.9	1 780.7	2 177.6	2 586.9	2 599.8	3 240.6	3 420.1	Moy. sur période
Ukraine										**Ukraine**
End of period	Hryvnia (UAH)	...	1.8	5.1	8.0	8.0	15.8	24.0	27.2	Fin de période
Period average		...	1.5	5.1	7.9	8.0	11.9	21.8	25.6	Moy. sur période
United Arab Emirates										**Émirats arabes unis**
End of period	UAE Dirham (AED)	3.7	3.7	3.7	3.7	3.7	3.7	3.7	3.7	Fin de période
Period average	dirham des É.A.U. (AED) [10]	3.7	3.7	3.7	3.7	3.7	3.7	3.7	3.7	Moy. sur période
United Kingdom										**Royaume-Uni**
End of period	Pound Sterling (GBP)	0.7	0.6	0.6	0.6	0.6	0.6	0.7	0.8	Fin de période
Period average	livre sterling (GBP)	0.8	0.6	0.6	0.6	0.6	0.6	0.7	0.7	Moy. sur période
United Rep. of Tanzania										**Rép.-Unie de Tanzanie**
End of period	Tanzanian Shilling (TZS),	16.5	550.4	1 165.5	1 453.5	1 578.6	1 725.8	2 148.5	2 172.6	Fin de période
Period average	shilling tanzanien (TZS)	17.5	574.8	1 128.9	1 395.6	1 597.6	1 653.2	1 991.4	2 177.1	Moy. sur période
Uruguay										**Uruguay**
End of period	Peso Uruguayo (UYU),	0.1	7.1	24.1	20.1	21.4	24.3	29.9	29.3	Fin de période
Period average	peso uruguayen (UYU)	0.1	6.3	24.5	20.1	20.5	23.2	27.3	30.2	Moy. sur période
Uzbekistan [2]										**Ouzbékistan** [2]
End of period	Uzbekistan Sum (UZS), sum ouzbek (UZS)	...	...	...	1 640.0	2 202.0	2 418.0	2 780.1	3 218.0	Fin de période
Vanuatu										**Vanuatu**
End of period	Vatu (VUV)	100.3	113.7	112.3	93.2	97.3	102.7	110.5	112.3	Fin de période
Period average		106.0	112.1	109.2	96.9	94.5	97.1	109.0	108.5	Moy. sur période
Venezuela (Boliv. Rep. of)										**Venezuela (Rép. boliv. du)**
End of period	Bolívar (VEF)	~0.0	0.3	2.1	2.6	6.3	6.3	6.3	10.0	Fin de période
Period average	bolivar (VEF)	~0.0	0.2	2.1	2.6	6.0	6.3	6.3	9.3	Moy. sur période
Viet Nam										**Viet Nam**
End of period	Dong (VND)	22.5	11 015.0	15 916.0	18 932.0	21 036.0	21 246.0	21 890.0	22 159.0	Fin de période
Period average		...	11 038.3	15 858.9	18 612.9	20 933.4	21 148.0	21 697.6	21 935.0	Moy. sur période
Wallis and Futuna Islands										**Îles Wallis-et-Futuna**
End of period	CFP Franc (XPF)	137.5	89.1	101.2	89.3	86.5	98.3	109.6	113.2	Fin de période
Period average	franc CFP (XPF)	163.4	90.8	96.0	90.1	89.9	89.9	107.6	107.9	Moy. sur période
Western Sahara										**Sahara occidental**
End of period	Moroccan Dirham (MAD),	9.6	8.5	9.2	8.4	8.2	9.0	9.9	10.1	Fin de période
Period average	dirham marocain (MAD)	10.1	8.5	8.9	8.4	8.4	8.4	9.8	9.8	Moy. sur période
Yemen										**Yémen**
End of period	Yemeni Rial (YER)	...	53.8	195.1	213.8	214.9	214.9	214.9	214.9	Fin de période
Period average	rial yéménite (YER)	...	40.8	191.5	219.6	214.9	214.9	214.9	214.9	Moy. sur période

16 Exchange rates *(continued)*

National currency per US dollar

Cours des changes *(suite)*

Valeur du dollar E.-U. en monnaie nationale

Country or area	National currency Monnaie nationale	1985	1995	2005	2010	2013	2014	2015	2016	Pays ou zone
Zambia										**Zambie**
End of period	Zambian Kwacha (ZMW),	~0.0	1.0	3.5	4.8	5.5	6.4	11.0	9.9	Fin de période
Period average	kwacha zambien (ZMW)	~0.0	0.9	4.5	4.8	5.4	6.2	8.6	10.3	Moy. sur période
Zimbabwe										**Zimbabwe**
End of period	Zimbabwe Dollar (ZWL),	~0.0	~0.0	80.8	...	...	...	...	...	Fin de période
Period average	dollar du Zimbabwe (ZWL)	~0.0	~0.0	22.4	...	...	...	...	...	Moy. sur période

Source:

International Monetary Fund (IMF), Washington, D.C., the database on International Financial Statistics supplemented by operational rates of exchange for United Nations programmes, last accessed June 2017.

1 East Caribbean Dollar.
2 UN operational exchange rate.
3 The national currency of Cuba is the Cuban Peso (CUP). The convertible peso (CUC) is used by foreigners and tourists in Cuba.
4 Netherlands Antillean Guilder.
5 The Colon is still legal tender as banks in El Salvador accept Colons in small quantities. However, nearly all transactions are settled in US Dollars since 95 per cent of the Colons are no longer in circulation.
6 Solomon Islands Dollar.
7 South Sudanese Pound.
8 Trinidad and Tobago Dollar.
9 Turkmenistan New Manat.
10 United Arab Emirates Dirham.

Source:

Fonds monétaire international (FMI), Washington, D.C., la base de données de Statistiques Financières Internationales complétée par les taux de change opérationnels pour les programmes des Nations Unies, dernier accès juin 2017.

1 dollar des Caraïbes orientales.
2 Taux de change opérationnel des Nations Unies.
3 La monnaie nationale du Cuba est le Peso Cubain (CUP). Le Peso Cubain Convertible (CUC) est utilisé par les touristes et les étrangers à Cuba.
4 florin des Antilles néerlandaises.
5 Le Colón Salvadorien est encore la monnaie légale étant donné que les banques en El Salvador acceptent les Colón Salvadorien en petites quantités. Toutefois, presque toutes les opérations sont réglées en dollars américains comme 90 pour cent des Colón Salvadorien ne sont plus en circulation.
6 dollar des Îles Salomon.
7 livre sud-soudanaise.
8 dollar de la Trinité-et-Tobago.
9 nouveau manat turkmène.
10 dirham des Émirats arabes unis.

17 Labour force participation rate and unemployment rate

Labour force (LF) participation rate and unemployment rate by sex (percent)

Taux d'activité et taux de chômage

Taux d'activité et taux de chômage par sexe (pourcentage)

Region, country or area & Région, pays ou zone &	Year Année	Male and Female Hommes et femmes: LF particip. rate Taux d'activité	Male and Female Hommes et femmes: Unemp. rate Taux de Chômage	Male Hommes: LF particip. rate Taux d'activité	Male Hommes: Unemp. rate Taux de Chômage	Female Femmes: LF particip. rate Taux d'activité	Female Femmes: Unemp. rate Taux de Chômage
Total, all countries or areas	***2005**	**64.7**	**6.2**	**77.6**	**5.9**	**51.9**	**6.8**
Total, tous pays ou zones	***2010**	**63.2**	**6.1**	**76.5**	**5.8**	**50.0**	**6.6**
	***2016**	**62.8**	**5.7**	**76.1**	**5.5**	**49.5**	**6.2**
	***2017**	**62.8**	**5.8**	**76.1**	**...**	**49.4**	**...**
Africa	*2005	64.5	8.6	75.4	7.5	53.8	10.2
Afrique	*2010	64.8	8.1	75.4	6.9	54.5	9.6
	*2016	65.5	8.0	75.7	6.9	55.4	9.4
	*2017	65.6	8.0	75.8	...	55.6	...
Northern Africa	*2005	47.7	12.7	74.3	10.1	21.4	21.7
Afrique septentrionale	*2010	47.8	10.3	73.8	7.6	22.0	19.3
	*2016	48.3	12.1	74.0	9.7	22.7	20.0
	*2017	48.3	12.0	74.1	...	22.9	...
Sub-Saharan Africa	*2005	69.7	7.8	75.8	6.7	63.7	9.0
Afrique subsaharienne	*2010	69.9	7.6	75.8	6.7	64.1	8.7
	*2016	70.3	7.2	76.2	6.2	64.5	8.3
	*2017	70.4	7.2	76.3	...	64.6	...
Eastern Africa	*2005	80.8	6.9	84.8	5.5	77.0	8.3
Afrique orientale	*2010	80.2	6.8	84.1	5.7	76.5	8.1
	*2016	79.2	6.5	83.5	5.2	75.1	7.9
	*2017	79.3	6.5	83.5	...	75.1	...
Middle Africa	*2005	71.7	5.2	75.7	4.5	67.8	6.0
Afrique centrale	*2010	71.6	5.1	75.5	4.4	67.7	5.9
	*2016	71.5	5.0	75.3	4.3	67.8	5.7
	*2017	71.5	5.0	75.3	...	67.8	...
Southern Africa	*2005	55.1	24.2	62.9	21.9	48.0	26.9
Afrique australe	*2010	52.9	24.3	60.9	22.5	45.5	26.6
	*2016	54.8	25.6	62.0	23.4	47.9	28.2
	*2017	55.1	25.6	62.5	...	48.0	...
Western Africa	*2005	60.7	6.6	69.5	6.0	51.9	7.4
Afrique occidentale	*2010	62.2	6.5	70.8	5.9	53.7	7.3
	*2016	63.4	5.6	71.8	5.1	55.0	6.4
	*2017	63.5	5.8	71.9	...	55.1	...
Americas	*2005	65.4	7.6	77.1	6.7	54.3	8.9
Amériques	*2010	65.0	8.3	75.9	7.9	54.4	8.9
	*2016	64.1	7.0	74.6	6.2	54.1	8.0
	*2017	64.1	7.2	74.5	...	54.0	...
Northern America	*2005	65.2	5.3	72.2	5.3	58.5	5.3
Amérique septentrionale	*2010	64.0	9.4	70.2	10.3	58.0	8.4
	*2016	62.3	5.1	68.5	5.3	56.4	5.0
	*2017	62.2	5.1	68.3	...	56.2	...
Latin America & the Caribbean	*2005	65.6	9.2	80.4	7.6	51.4	11.6
Amérique latine et Caraïbes	*2010	65.6	7.7	79.6	6.5	52.1	9.3
	*2016	65.2	8.1	78.4	6.7	52.7	10.0
	*2017	65.2	8.4	78.3	...	52.7	...
Caribbean	*2005	59.1	10.7	71.2	8.0	47.4	14.6
Caraïbes	*2010	59.6	10.1	70.6	8.3	49.0	12.6
	*2016	60.4	10.3	70.7	7.9	50.4	13.5
	*2017	60.4	10.3	70.7	...	50.5	...
Central America	*2005	61.1	4.0	81.4	3.7	41.7	4.5
Amérique centrale	*2010	62.2	5.5	81.1	5.4	44.0	5.6
	*2016	62.5	4.3	80.0	4.1	45.7	4.8
	*2017	62.6	4.3	80.1	...	45.8	...
South America	*2005	67.9	10.8	80.9	8.9	55.4	13.3
Amérique du Sud	*2010	67.5	8.2	80.0	6.8	55.5	10.1
	*2016	66.8	9.2	78.5	7.7	55.6	11.3
	*2017	66.7	9.8	78.4	...	55.6	...
Central Asia	*2005	63.5	9.1	73.8	8.9	53.9	9.4
Asie centrale	*2010	64.4	8.4	75.3	8.4	54.1	8.5
	*2016	65.4	7.9	77.0	7.9	54.6	8.0
	*2017	65.5	8.1	77.2	...	54.6	...
Eastern Asia	*2005	71.8	4.2	78.9	4.6	64.4	3.6
Asie orientale	*2010	69.5	4.3	77.0	4.7	61.9	3.7
	*2017	69.1	4.5	76.8	5.1	61.3	3.7
South-eastern Asia	*2005	70.4	6.2	82.7	5.9	58.5	6.7
Asie du Sud-Est	*2010	70.5	4.6	82.1	4.4	59.1	4.8
	*2016	70.2	3.7	81.9	3.7	58.8	3.7
	*2017	70.1	3.7	81.8	...	58.7	...

17 Labour force participation rate and unemployment rate *(continued)*

Labour force (LF) participation rate and unemployment rate by sex (percent)

Taux d'activité et taux de chômage *(suite)*

Taux d'activité et taux de chômage par sexe (pourcentage)

Region, country or area & / Région, pays ou zone &	Year / Année	Male and Female / Hommes et femmes: LF particip. rate / Taux d'activité	Male and Female / Hommes et femmes: Unemp. rate / Taux de Chômage	Male / Hommes: LF particip. rate / Taux d'activité	Male / Hommes: Unemp. rate / Taux de Chômage	Female / Femmes: LF particip. rate / Taux d'activité	Female / Femmes: Unemp. rate / Taux de Chômage
Southern Asia / Asie méridionale	*2005	59.9	5.0	82.8	4.6	35.8	6.0
	*2010	55.6	4.3	80.5	3.9	29.5	5.4
	*2016	54.5	4.1	79.4	3.8	28.5	5.0
	*2017	54.6	4.1	79.4	...	28.6	...
Western Asia [1] / Asie occidentale [1]	*2005	49.0	10.9	74.5	9.0	18.7	20.3
	*2010	50.9	9.8	75.6	7.0	20.0	23.1
	*2016	52.0	10.7	76.5	8.3	21.2	21.9
	*2017	51.9	10.6	76.4	...	21.2	...
Caucasus [2] / Caucase [2]	*2005	50.5	10.7	69.9	10.5	32.3	11.2
	*2010	52.6	10.5	70.6	10.3	35.7	10.7
	*2016	54.0	9.6	71.3	9.1	37.8	10.6
	*2017	54.0	10.0	71.3	...	37.7	...
Eastern Europe / Europe orientale	*2005	58.8	8.5	65.8	8.5	52.7	8.4
	*2010	59.6	7.8	67.3	8.3	52.9	7.3
	*2016	60.2	6.2	68.3	6.4	53.2	5.9
	*2017	60.0	6.1	68.1	...	53.0	...
Northern Europe / Europe septentrionale	*2005	62.1	5.5	69.0	5.7	55.6	5.2
	*2010	62.2	8.6	68.3	9.5	56.4	7.5
	*2016	62.4	5.7	67.9	6.0	57.1	5.4
	*2017	62.4	5.8	67.9	...	57.1	...
Southern Europe / Europe méridionale	*2005	53.2	10.1	64.4	8.2	42.7	12.7
	*2010	53.4	14.3	62.9	13.4	44.4	15.5
	*2016	52.7	15.9	60.9	14.8	45.1	17.4
	*2017	52.6	15.3	60.7	...	45.0	...
Western Europe / Europe occidentale	*2005	58.2	9.2	65.8	8.9	51.0	9.4
	*2010	58.8	7.3	65.3	7.4	52.7	7.2
	*2016	58.7	6.6	64.4	6.7	53.4	6.4
	*2017	58.6	6.4	64.1	...	53.3	...
Oceania / Océanie	*2005	65.8	4.9	72.9	4.7	58.9	5.2
	*2010	66.3	5.3	72.7	5.1	60.1	5.6
	*2016	65.5	5.6	71.1	5.4	60.0	5.8
	*2017	65.4	5.5	71.0	...	59.9	...
Afghanistan / Afghanistan	2005	* 51.7	8.5	* 84.3	7.7	* 16.4	13.0
	*2010	51.3	8.2	84.0	7.5	16.5	12.2
	*2017	52.6	8.6	83.6	7.8	19.3	12.6
Albania / Albanie	*2005	58.0	13.8	68.5	13.3	47.6	14.7
	2010	* 53.9	14.2	* 63.6	12.3	* 44.1	17.0
	*2017	50.4	15.8	61.0	16.1	40.2	15.4
Algeria / Algérie	2005	* 42.5	15.3	* 71.8	13.1	* 12.8	27.6
	2010	* 42.3	10.0	* 70.0	8.1	* 14.4	19.3
	*2017	43.9	11.4	70.7	9.2	17.0	20.3
American Samoa [3] / Samoa américaines [3]	2000	52.9	5.1	58.8	4.9	41.2	6.0
	#2005	59.9	...	...	...	...	...
	2010	52.8	# 9.2	...	...	...	...
Angola / Angola	*2005	69.0	7.0	76.9	6.6	61.4	7.4
	*2010	68.2	6.8	77.4	6.4	59.3	7.3
	*2017	68.3	6.6	77.1	6.2	59.8	7.1
Anguilla / Anguilla	2002	72.3	7.8	77.2	6.3	67.2	9.5
Antigua and Barbuda / Antigua-et-Barbuda	2001	71.7	8.4	78.4	8.0	65.9	8.8
Argentina / Argentine	2005	* 62.2	11.5	* 76.6	10.1	* 48.8	13.6
	2010	* 60.5	7.7	* 74.9	6.7	* 47.0	9.2
	*2017	61.1	6.5	74.4	5.7	48.6	7.6
Armenia / Arménie	*2005	57.6	17.2	67.7	15.3	48.5	19.7
	2010	* 61.6	19.0	* 72.3	17.3	* 50.9	21.4
	*2017	63.8	16.6	74.2	14.9	55.3	18.4
Aruba / Aruba	2001	...	6.9	...	6.5	...	7.4
	#2010[4]	63.9[5]	10.6	68.9[5]	10.8	59.5[5]	10.4
	#2011	63.8	...	69.6	...	58.8	...
Australia / Australie	2005	* 64.5	5.0	* 72.2	4.9	* 57.0	5.2
	2010	* 65.5	5.2	* 72.5	5.1	* 58.7	5.4
	*2017	64.5	5.5	70.7	5.4	58.4	5.5
Austria / Autriche	2005	* 59.0	5.6	* 67.3	5.5	* 51.2	5.8
	2010	* 60.5	4.8	* 67.6	5.0	* 53.9	4.6
	*2017	60.1	6.2	65.8	6.5	54.6	5.9
Azerbaijan / Azerbaïdjan	2005	* 63.3	7.3	* 66.3	6.1	* 60.5	8.6
	2010	* 64.5	5.6	* 67.4	4.4	* 61.8	6.8
	*2017	65.3	5.2	68.8	4.4	62.0	6.0
Bahamas / Bahamas	2005	* 72.6	10.2	* 77.8	9.2	* 67.7	11.3
	*2010	74.2	14.3	79.2	14.1	69.5	14.5
	*2017	74.1	14.7	79.1	14.2	69.4	15.3

17 Labour force participation rate and unemployment rate *(continued)*
Labour force (LF) participation rate and unemployment rate by sex (percent)

Taux d'activité et taux de chômage *(suite)*
Taux d'activité et taux de chômage par sexe (pourcentage)

Region, country or area [&] Région, pays ou zone [&]	Year Année	Male and Female Hommes et femmes		Male Hommes		Female Femmes	
		LF particip. rate Taux d'activité	Unemp. rate Taux de Chômage	LF particip. rate Taux d'activité	Unemp. rate Taux de Chômage	LF particip. rate Taux d'activité	Unemp. rate Taux de Chômage
Bahrain Bahreïn	*2005	66.8	1.3	84.5	0.6	36.2	4.5
	2010	* 71.0	1.1	* 87.0	0.4	* 41.3	3.9
	*2017	68.6	1.3	84.9	0.6	38.5	4.4
Bangladesh Bangladesh	2005	* 66.4	4.3	* 84.1	3.0	* 48.1	6.5
	2010	* 62.3	4.5	* 82.3	4.1	* 42.0	5.4
	*2017	62.3	4.0	81.1	3.7	43.2	4.6
Barbados Barbade	2005	* 69.5	9.1	* 75.4	7.6	* 64.2	10.7
	2010	* 68.0	10.7	* 73.1	11.0	* 63.5	10.4
	*2017	65.7	11.3	70.0	11.6	61.8	11.1
Belarus Bélarus	*2005	59.6	0.7	66.6	0.7	53.8	0.7
	2010	* 60.5	0.7	* 67.7	0.7	* 54.5	0.7
	*2017	60.3	0.5	67.8	0.6	54.0	0.5
Belgium Belgique	2005	* 53.4	8.4	* 61.4	7.6	* 45.8	9.5
	2010	* 54.1	8.3	* 60.8	8.1	* 47.8	8.5
	*2017	53.4	8.3	58.9	8.5	48.1	8.1
Belize Belize	2005	* 63.8	11.0	* 81.8	7.5	* 45.7	17.3
	*2010	67.2	13.2	82.6	8.3	51.9	21.0
	*2017	70.1	11.5	83.8	7.5	56.7	17.3
Benin Bénin	*2005	72.1	0.9	77.0	1.0	67.4	0.8
	2010	* 71.5	1.0	* 73.7	0.9	* 69.3	1.2
	*2017	71.7	1.0	73.4	1.1	70.0	0.9
Bermuda Bermudes	2000	73.8	2.7[3]	79.2	3.1[3]	67.4	2.3[3]
	#2009[3]	82.0	4.5	86.0	6.0	79.0	3.0
	2010[3]	84.0	...	87.0	...	81.0	...
	2012[3,6]	76.1	8.4	80.0	8.7	72.6	8.2
	2013[3,6]	...	6.7	...	...	...	...
Bhutan Bhoutan	2005	* 72.0	3.1	* 77.7	2.9	* 65.2	3.3
	2010	* 69.7	3.3	* 74.5	2.7	* 63.8	4.3
	*2017	67.1	2.4	73.5	1.9	59.4	3.1
Bolivia (Plurin. State of) Bolivie (État plurin. de)	2005	* 71.0	5.4	* 81.4	4.6	* 60.7	6.5
	2010	* 72.3	6.0	* 82.3	4.8	* 62.5	7.6
	*2017	73.3	3.8	82.6	3.1	64.1	4.6
Bosnia and Herzegovina Bosnie-Herzégovine	*2005	44.9	21.6	58.3	21.0	31.8	22.5
	2010	* 46.9	27.2	* 59.6	25.5	* 34.6	30.0
	*2017	45.8	25.4	57.5	27.0	34.3	22.9
Botswana Botswana	*2005	76.1	20.5	80.9	17.8	71.4	23.5
	2010	* 76.8	17.9	* 81.0	14.4	* 72.7	21.6
	*2017	77.5	18.6	81.6	15.9	73.6	21.5
Brazil Brésil	*2005	70.5	11.4	82.4	9.5	59.1	13.9
	*2010	68.8	8.5	80.7	7.0	57.6	10.5
	*2017	66.8	12.4	78.2	10.3	56.0	15.0
Brunei Darussalam Brunéi Darussalam	*2005	66.9	2.4	78.1	2.2	55.2	2.6
	*2010	65.9	1.7	76.9	1.6	54.1	1.9
	*2017	63.2	2.1	75.0	2.0	50.6	2.3
Bulgaria Bulgarie	2005	* 50.2	10.1	* 56.3	10.3	* 44.6	9.8
	2010	* 53.3	10.3	* 59.5	10.9	* 47.5	9.6
	*2017	54.1	8.1	60.1	8.5	48.5	7.7
Burkina Faso Burkina Faso	2005	* 83.5	4.0	* 91.0	5.1	* 76.5	2.8
	*2010	83.6	3.3	91.0	4.2	76.6	2.3
	*2017	83.4	2.9	90.5	3.7	76.5	2.1
Burundi Burundi	*2005	82.9	1.7	81.8	1.4	84.0	1.9
	*2010	82.8	1.6	81.6	1.3	84.0	1.9
	*2017	83.7	1.7	82.7	1.3	84.6	1.9
Cabo Verde Cabo Verde	*2005	64.4	11.1	82.2	9.4	48.0	13.6
	2010	* 66.4	10.7	* 82.8	* 9.1	* 50.9	* 13.1
	*2017	68.8	10.5	84.6	9.1	53.7	12.6
Cambodia Cambodge	*2005	80.9	1.8	86.6	2.2	75.9	1.4
	2010	* 84.9	0.4	* 88.6	0.4	* 81.6	0.3
	*2017	81.0	0.3	87.0	0.4	75.6	0.3
Cameroon Cameroun	2005	* 73.2	4.4	* 79.5	3.7	* 67.1	5.2
	2010	* 75.8	4.1	* 81.2	3.5	* 70.5	4.9
	*2017	76.2	4.6	81.2	3.9	71.1	5.4
Canada Canada	2005	* 66.6	6.8	* 72.6	7.1	* 60.9	6.5
	2010	* 66.6	8.1	* 71.5	8.9	* 61.8	7.3
	*2017	65.2	7.1	69.9	7.7	60.7	6.5
Cayman Islands Îles Caïmanes	2005	...	3.5	...	...	...	...
	#2009	84.2[5]	6.0	88.0[5]	7.0	80.6[5]	5.0
	2010	81.8	6.7	...	...	...	...
	2013	83.1	6.3	85.6	6.7	80.6	5.8
Central African Republic République centrafricaine	*2005	77.6	6.8	85.7	6.4	69.9	7.2
	*2010	77.3	6.8	85.2	6.4	69.8	7.2
	*2017	78.1	6.9	84.6	6.6	71.9	7.3

17 Labour force participation rate and unemployment rate *(continued)*

Labour force (LF) participation rate and unemployment rate by sex (percent)

Taux d'activité et taux de chômage *(suite)*

Taux d'activité et taux de chômage par sexe (pourcentage)

Region, country or area & / Région, pays ou zone &	Year / Année	Male and Female / Hommes et femmes: LF particip. rate / Taux d'activité	Male and Female / Hommes et femmes: Unemp. rate / Taux de Chômage	Male / Hommes: LF particip. rate / Taux d'activité	Male / Hommes: Unemp. rate / Taux de Chômage	Female / Femmes: LF particip. rate / Taux d'activité	Female / Femmes: Unemp. rate / Taux de Chômage
Chad / Tchad	*2005	71.8	5.8	79.5	4.8	64.2	7.0
	*2010	71.6	5.8	79.3	4.9	64.1	7.0
	*2017	71.6	5.8	79.3	4.8	64.0	7.0
Channel Islands / Îles Anglo-Normandes	*2005	59.7	8.6	68.8	9.6	51.1	7.4
	*2010	59.5	8.9	67.0	10.1	52.2	7.4
	*2017	57.6	8.7	65.4	9.7	49.9	7.3
Chile / Chili	2005	* 55.3	8.0	* 73.1	7.0	* 38.2	9.8
	2010	* 60.4	8.1	* 74.7	7.1	* 46.8	9.7
	*2017	62.5	6.8	74.7	6.3	50.7	7.5
China [7] / Chine [7]	*2005	73.5	4.1	79.8	4.6	66.9	3.6
	*2010	70.9	4.2	77.8	4.7	63.7	3.6
	*2017	70.5	4.6	77.7	5.3	63.0	3.7
China, Hong Kong SAR / Chine, Hong Kong RAS	2005	* 60.9	5.6	* 71.3	6.5	* 51.7	4.4
	2010	* 59.5	4.3	* 68.5	5.0	* 51.8	3.5
	*2017	59.6	3.5	67.8	3.9	52.6	3.1
China, Macao SAR / Chine, Macao RAS	2005	* 66.2	4.2	* 74.3	4.4	* 59.0	4.0
	2010	* 71.0	2.8	* 77.1	3.5	* 65.5	2.1
	*2017	70.8	3.2	76.4	3.9	65.6	2.5
Colombia / Colombie	2005	* 66.7	11.9	* 81.2	9.1	* 53.0	15.9
	2010	* 67.6	11.8	* 80.3	9.0	* 55.5	15.7
	*2017	68.6	10.5	79.8	7.9	58.0	13.8
Comoros / Comores	*2005	55.5	20.3	78.7	18.8	32.2	23.9
	*2010	56.6	19.9	79.0	18.4	34.1	23.5
	*2017	57.6	20.0	79.5	18.4	35.7	23.7
Congo / Congo	*2005	69.5	15.9	71.5	13.1	67.4	18.7
	*2010	69.9	14.6	72.3	12.1	67.5	17.3
	*2017	69.8	11.5	72.6	9.5	67.1	13.7
Cook Islands / Îles Cook	2001	74.5[8]	13.1	75.5[8]	11.7	63.0[8]	14.8
	#2006[5]	70.2	6.9	76.1	6.7	64.2	7.3
	2011[5]	71.0	8.2	76.6	8.2	65.4	8.1
Costa Rica / Costa Rica	2005	* 61.8	6.6	* 80.2	5.0	* 43.6	9.4
	2010	* 60.5	8.9	* 77.1	7.6	* 44.1	11.2
	*2017	61.6	8.6	76.5	7.1	46.9	11.0
Côte d'Ivoire / Côte d'Ivoire	*2005	67.0	9.2	82.0	8.2	50.5	11.1
	*2010	67.1	9.2	81.4	8.2	51.8	11.0
	*2017	67.0	9.3	80.9	8.3	52.6	11.0
Croatia / Croatie	2005	* 53.3	12.6	* 61.1	11.5	* 46.2	13.9
	2010	* 52.2	11.6	* 59.2	11.1	* 45.8	12.2
	*2017	52.1	11.7	58.4	11.1	46.3	12.5
Cuba / Cuba	2005	* 52.8	1.9	* 67.3	1.7	* 38.2	2.3
	2010	* 55.7	2.5	* 68.9	2.4	* 42.4	2.7
	*2017	55.2	3.0	68.3	2.7	42.1	3.5
Curaçao / Curaçao	2005	59.4	18.2	65.4	17.1	54.8	19.2
	2008	59.0	10.3	66.5	8.0	53.2	12.5
	#2009[6]	…	9.6	…	7.8	…	11.2
	2013[6]	…	13.0	…	10.5	…	15.4
Cyprus / Chypre	2005	* 63.4	5.3	* 73.1	4.5	* 53.6	6.4
	2010	* 64.4	6.3	* 71.3	6.1	* 57.1	6.4
	*2017	64.2	10.3	70.4	10.0	57.8	10.6
Czechia / Tchéquie	2005	* 59.5	7.9	* 68.9	6.4	* 50.8	9.8
	2010	* 58.4	7.3	* 68.0	6.4	* 49.3	8.5
	*2017	59.4	3.9	67.8	3.2	51.3	4.9
Dem. People's Rep. Korea / Rép. pop. dém. de Corée	*2005	81.3	4.5	88.6	5.3	74.5	3.6
	*2010	80.2	4.4	86.9	5.2	73.9	3.5
	*2017	79.6	4.3	85.9	5.0	73.6	3.4
Dem. Rep. of the Congo / Rép. dém. du Congo	2005	* 72.0	3.7	* 73.0	3.0	* 70.9	4.4
	*2010	71.5	3.7	72.2	3.0	70.7	4.4
	*2017	71.1	3.6	71.8	2.9	70.4	4.3
Denmark / Danemark	2005	* 65.9	4.8	* 71.4	4.4	* 60.5	5.3
	2010	* 64.4	7.5	* 69.1	8.4	* 59.8	6.5
	*2017	62.0	6.0	66.0	5.7	58.1	6.4
Djibouti / Djibouti	*2005	49.6	6.8	66.2	6.2	33.0	8.0
	*2010	51.2	6.7	66.8	6.2	35.6	7.7
	*2017	52.5	6.6	68.5	6.1	36.5	7.6
Dominica / Dominique	2001	57.7	11.0	70.2	12.0	45.0	9.5
Dominican Republic / République dominicaine	2005	* 64.6	18.0	* 80.7	11.4	* 48.8	28.7
	2010	* 63.9	12.4	* 78.7	8.4	* 49.3	18.6
	*2017	65.3	14.4	78.6	9.0	52.3	22.3
Ecuador / Équateur	2005	* 69.8	7.7	* 84.6	5.6	* 55.3	10.9
	2010	* 65.1	5.0	* 80.6	4.0	* 49.9	6.6
	*2017	64.3	5.8	79.9	4.7	49.1	7.6

17 Labour force participation rate and unemployment rate *(continued)*

Labour force (LF) participation rate and unemployment rate by sex (percent)

Taux d'activité et taux de chômage *(suite)*

Taux d'activité et taux de chômage par sexe (pourcentage)

Region, country or area & / Région, pays ou zone &	Year / Année	Male and Female / Hommes et femmes: LF particip. rate / Taux d'activité	Male and Female / Hommes et femmes: Unemp. rate / Taux de Chômage	Male / Hommes: LF particip. rate / Taux d'activité	Male / Hommes: Unemp. rate / Taux de Chômage	Female / Femmes: LF particip. rate / Taux d'activité	Female / Femmes: Unemp. rate / Taux de Chômage
Egypt / Égypte	2005	* 47.8	11.2	* 75.3	7.0	* 20.5	26.6
	2010	* 49.1	9.0	* 75.6	4.8	* 22.7	22.8
	*2017	49.7	11.5	76.2	7.9	23.1	23.5
El Salvador / El Salvador	2005	* 60.6	7.2	* 78.5	9.3	* 45.2	4.2
	2010	* 61.3	7.1	* 78.9	8.4	* 46.4	5.1
	*2017	63.1	6.4	79.5	7.9	49.5	4.3
Equatorial Guinea / Guinée équatoriale	*2005	81.4	6.7	92.6	6.5	69.3	7.0
	*2010	81.8	6.6	92.3	6.3	70.4	7.0
	*2017	82.0	7.7	91.8	7.7	71.5	7.8
Eritrea / Érythrée	*2005	82.7	7.5	89.2	7.0	76.5	8.1
	*2010	83.6	7.2	89.8	6.8	77.6	7.7
	*2017	83.9	7.3	90.1	6.8	77.8	7.8
Estonia / Estonie	2005	* 59.0	8.0	* 65.6	9.1	* 53.4	6.9
	2010	* 61.4	16.7	* 67.7	19.3	* 56.0	14.0
	*2017	61.8	7.2	69.4	7.7	55.4	6.7
Ethiopia / Éthiopie	2005	* 84.5	5.4	* 90.8	2.8	* 78.4	8.3
	*2010	83.6	5.2	90.0	3.0	77.5	7.6
	*2017	83.0	5.7	89.1	3.2	77.1	8.6
Falkland Islands (Malvinas) [9] / Îles Falkland (Malvinas) [9]	2013	# 81.9	1.2	# 86.0	1.1	# 77.2	1.4
Faroe Islands / Îles Féroé	2005[3]	...	3.2	...	2.6	...	3.9
	2010[6,10]	81.7	# 6.4	85.3	# 5.1	77.5	# 8.0
	2013[6,10]	82.9	4.0	86.0	3.4	79.4	4.9
Fiji / Fidji	2005	* 56.2	4.6	* 73.8	3.7	* 38.1	6.4
	2010	* 54.9	8.9	* 71.8	7.1	* 37.4	12.5
	*2017	54.2	7.7	71.2	6.2	37.0	10.8
Finland / Finlande	2005	* 61.0	8.4	* 65.4	8.3	* 56.8	8.5
	2010	* 60.3	8.4	* 64.6	9.1	* 56.2	7.6
	*2017	58.0	8.9	61.7	9.2	54.5	8.6
France / France	2005	* 55.8	8.9	* 61.9	8.2	* 50.0	9.8
	2010	* 55.9	9.3	* 61.3	9.1	* 50.9	9.5
	*2017	54.7	9.8	59.4	10.1	50.3	9.6
French Guiana [6] / Guyane française [6]	2005	42.1	24.8	48.2	22.8	36.3	27.0
	2010	48.9	21.0	54.9	17.8	43.2	25.1
	#2013	53.4	21.3	58.8	16.7	48.4	26.3
French Polynesia / Polynésie française	*2005	56.7	16.1	65.8	15.0	47.2	17.7
	*2010	55.7	11.9	64.1	10.9	47.0	13.4
	*2017	54.9	17.0	63.0	16.2	46.4	18.2
Gabon / Gabon	2005	* 59.1	16.9	* 64.1	15.3	* 54.1	18.8
	2010	* 47.8	20.4	* 56.3	14.7	* 39.0	28.8
	*2017	49.6	18.1	58.3	16.4	40.7	20.7
Gambia / Gambie	*2005	77.5	29.7	83.5	21.6	71.7	38.6
	*2010	77.6	29.8	83.2	21.7	72.2	38.6
	*2017	77.3	29.7	82.6	21.7	72.2	38.4
Georgia / Géorgie	2005	* 63.6	13.8	* 73.3	14.8	* 55.4	12.7
	2010	* 65.1	16.3	* 75.4	17.9	* 56.2	14.5
	*2017	67.8	11.4	79.0	12.6	57.9	10.0
Germany / Allemagne	2005	* 58.5	11.2	* 66.9	11.4	* 50.6	10.9
	2010	* 59.4	7.0	* 66.5	7.4	* 52.8	6.5
	*2017	60.2	4.2	66.1	4.4	54.5	3.9
Ghana / Ghana	*2005	69.6	4.9	71.7	4.7	67.6	5.2
	2010	* 73.3	4.2	* 75.2	3.9	* 71.6	4.5
	*2017	77.2	5.9	78.8	5.5	75.7	6.3
Gibraltar / Gibraltar	2001	68.4	...	78.8	...	57.5	...
Greece / Grèce	2005	* 52.9	10.0	* 64.2	6.3	* 42.1	15.4
	2010	* 53.7	12.7	* 63.7	10.1	* 44.2	16.3
	*2017	51.8	23.0	60.1	18.8	44.1	28.4
Greenland / Groenland	2005	...	9.3	...	10.4	...	8.0
	2006[11,1]	...	8.4	...	10.0	...	6.7
	#2013[2]	...	9.7	...	9.6	...	9.8
Grenada / Grenade	2001	...	10.2	...	9.6	...	10.9
Guadeloupe [6] / Guadeloupe [6]	2005	41.8	25.9	46.8	22.4	37.7	29.5
	2010	41.6	23.8	44.2	21.4	39.5	26.0
	#2013	52.7	26.1	56.5	23.8	49.6	28.3
Guam / Guam	2005	* 63.0	7.0	* 69.7	6.4	* 56.1	7.8
	2010	* 62.5	8.2	* 70.1	7.4	* 54.8	9.3
	*2017	62.0	10.7	68.7	10.1	55.2	11.4

17 Labour force participation rate and unemployment rate *(continued)*

Labour force (LF) participation rate and unemployment rate by sex (percent)

Taux d'activité et taux de chômage *(suite)*

Taux d'activité et taux de chômage par sexe (pourcentage)

Region, country or area & / Région, pays ou zone &	Year / Année	Male and Female / Hommes et femmes: LF particip. rate / Taux d'activité	Male and Female / Hommes et femmes: Unemp. rate / Taux de Chômage	Male / Hommes: LF particip. rate / Taux d'activité	Male / Hommes: Unemp. rate / Taux de Chômage	Female / Femmes: LF particip. rate / Taux d'activité	Female / Femmes: Unemp. rate / Taux de Chômage
Guatemala / Guatemala	*2005	65.3	2.5	87.6	2.1	45.1	3.1
	2010	* 62.7	3.7	* 85.7	3.4	* 41.8	4.3
	*2017	61.9	2.4	84.0	2.1	41.7	3.0
Guinea / Guinée	*2005	71.7	6.9	80.9	6.4	62.7	7.5
	*2010	73.5	6.9	80.9	6.4	66.1	7.5
	*2017	82.3	6.8	85.1	6.3	79.4	7.4
Guinea-Bissau / Guinée-Bissau	*2005	72.3	6.7	78.8	6.3	65.9	7.2
	*2010	72.4	6.7	78.4	6.2	66.6	7.1
	*2017	72.9	6.5	78.5	6.1	67.4	7.0
Guyana / Guyana	*2005	60.1	10.2	82.1	8.6	38.7	13.5
	*2010	60.0	10.9	79.7	8.9	40.4	14.8
	*2017	59.5	11.3	77.0	9.0	41.9	15.4
Haiti / Haïti	*2005	63.7	14.2	69.4	12.3	58.4	16.4
	*2010	65.2	14.5	70.5	12.6	60.2	16.6
	*2017	66.7	12.9	71.7	11.2	62.0	14.9
Honduras / Honduras	2005	* 59.4	4.2	* 83.1	3.2	* 36.3	6.4
	2010	* 64.2	4.8	* 84.6	3.9	* 44.2	6.4
	*2017	65.9	5.6	84.5	4.1	47.6	8.3
Hungary / Hongrie	2005	* 50.1	7.2	* 58.3	7.0	* 42.9	7.4
	2010	* 50.5	11.2	* 58.3	11.6	* 43.7	10.7
	*2017	54.0	4.5	62.4	4.4	46.6	4.5
Iceland / Islande	2005	* 75.5	2.5	* 80.2	2.6	* 70.8	2.5
	2010	* 74.5	7.6	* 78.6	8.3	* 70.4	6.7
	*2017	73.7	3.6	77.2	3.5	70.3	3.7
India / Inde	2005	* 60.6	4.4	* 83.1	4.1	* 36.8	5.0
	2010	* 55.3	3.6	* 80.5	3.3	* 28.6	4.4
	*2017	53.8	3.4	79.1	3.3	27.0	3.8
Indonesia / Indonésie	2005	* 67.6	11.2	* 85.3	9.5	* 50.0	14.1
	2010	* 68.1	7.1	* 84.3	6.2	* 51.9	8.7
	*2017	67.3	5.8	83.7	5.3	51.0	6.6
Iran (Islamic Republic of) / Iran (Rép. islamique d')	2005	* 47.4	12.1	* 74.2	10.5	* 19.4	18.4
	2010	* 43.1	13.5	* 69.9	11.9	* 16.0	20.8
	*2017	44.8	11.3	73.2	9.7	16.3	18.5
Iraq / Iraq	2005	* 41.2	18.0	* 68.9	15.8	* 13.7	28.9
	*2010	41.9	15.2	69.3	13.2	14.5	25.0
	*2017	42.7	16.1	69.9	13.8	15.3	26.7
Ireland / Irlande	2005	* 62.6	4.3	* 72.9	4.6	* 52.4	4.0
	2010	* 61.2	13.9	* 69.2	17.0	* 53.3	9.8
	*2017	59.4	7.6	67.1	8.4	51.9	6.5
Isle of Man / Île de Man	2001	63.3	1.6	71.4	1.7	55.7	1.5
	2006	62.8	2.4	69.9	2.8	56.3	2.0
	#2011[3]	63.3	3.3[11]	69.3	3.8[11]	57.5	2.8[11]
	#2013[13]	...	2.6	...	3.4	...	1.7
Israel / Israël	2005	* 62.2	11.3	* 69.3	11.1	* 55.4	11.6
	2010	* 63.2	8.5	* 69.7	8.9	* 57.1	8.0
	*2017	63.7	5.9	69.0	5.7	58.5	6.1
Italy / Italie	2005	* 49.0	7.7	* 61.0	6.2	* 37.8	10.0
	2010	* 48.0	8.4	* 59.0	7.5	* 37.8	9.6
	*2017	48.2	11.4	57.8	10.4	39.2	12.8
Jamaica / Jamaïque	2005	* 66.0	10.9	* 75.1	7.1	* 57.3	15.6
	2010	* 62.9	12.4	* 71.0	9.4	* 55.1	16.1
	*2017	65.3	13.1	72.7	9.0	58.1	18.0
Japan / Japon	2005	* 60.5	4.4	* 73.3	4.5	* 48.4	4.2
	2010	* 60.2	5.1	* 71.6	5.5	* 49.4	4.6
	*2017	58.9	3.0	69.7	3.2	48.9	2.8
Jordan / Jordanie	2005	* 41.1	14.8	* 67.6	12.8	* 12.3	27.1
	2010	* 42.4	12.5	* 67.6	10.3	* 15.4	22.9
	*2017	40.1	13.4	64.5	11.1	14.5	24.0
Kazakhstan / Kazakhstan	2005	* 69.5	8.1	* 75.2	6.9	* 64.4	9.3
	2010	* 70.4	5.8	* 75.8	4.9	* 65.5	6.6
	*2017	71.6	5.6	77.5	4.7	66.3	6.6
Kenya / Kenya	*2005	64.8	10.7	69.8	9.0	59.9	12.7
	*2010	66.2	12.2	71.4	10.1	61.0	14.6
	*2017	67.3	10.8	72.4	9.0	62.4	13.0
Kiribati / Kiribati	2005	# 26.4[14]	14.7[15]	# 32.8[14]	12.3[15]	# 20.4[14]	18.2[15]
	2010	# 59.3[14]	30.6[15]	66.8[14]	27.6[15]	52.3[14]	34.1[15]
Kosovo [13] / Kosovo [13]	2005	48.7	41.4	68.3	32.9	29.7	60.5
	2009	47.7	# 45.4	66.9	# 56.4	28.7	# 40.7
	#2012	37.1	30.9	55.5	28.1	17.9	40.0
	#2013	40.6	...	60.2	...	21.1	...

17 Labour force participation rate and unemployment rate *(continued)*

Labour force (LF) participation rate and unemployment rate by sex (percent)

Taux d'activité et taux de chômage *(suite)*

Taux d'activité et taux de chômage par sexe (pourcentage)

Region, country or area & Région, pays ou zone &	Year Année	Male and Female / Hommes et femmes: LF particip. rate Taux d'activité	Male and Female / Hommes et femmes: Unemp. rate Taux de Chômage	Male / Hommes: LF particip. rate Taux d'activité	Male / Hommes: Unemp. rate Taux de Chômage	Female / Femmes: LF particip. rate Taux d'activité	Female / Femmes: Unemp. rate Taux de Chômage
Kuwait	2005	* 67.7	2.0	* 81.9	1.9	* 45.0	2.0
Koweït	2010	* 68.3	1.8	* 83.8	1.9	* 46.9	1.6
	*2017	68.4	2.2	83.6	2.4	47.7	1.8
Kyrgyzstan	2005	* 64.9	8.1	* 76.1	7.4	* 54.1	9.0
Kirghizistan	2010	* 64.1	8.6	* 76.6	7.7	* 52.2	9.9
	*2017	63.3	7.7	77.5	6.8	49.7	9.2
Lao People's Dem. Rep.	2005	* 78.8	1.4	* 78.8	1.6	* 78.9	1.2
Rép. dém. populaire lao	*2010	77.5	1.4	77.0	1.6	77.9	1.2
	*2017	77.8	1.5	77.8	1.8	77.9	1.3
Latvia	2005	* 57.8	10.0	* 66.3	10.1	* 50.9	9.9
Lettonie	2010	* 59.0	19.5	* 65.4	22.7	* 53.8	16.3
	*2017	60.4	9.6	67.7	10.5	54.5	8.7
Lebanon	*2005	46.1	8.1	70.6	7.5	20.3	10.4
Liban	*2010	46.7	6.2	70.0	4.4	22.0	12.2
	*2017	47.3	7.0	70.6	5.6	23.8	11.0
Lesotho	*2005	68.4	36.0	75.5	28.6	61.8	44.3
Lesotho	*2010	65.6	25.6	73.2	21.9	58.6	30.0
	*2017	67.0	27.5	74.6	23.9	59.7	31.9
Liberia	*2005	60.7	4.9	62.9	5.7	58.5	4.2
Libéria	2010	* 61.2	3.7	* 64.3	3.4	* 58.1	4.1
	*2017	61.0	4.1	64.1	4.2	57.9	3.9
Libya	*2005	53.2	19.2	75.9	15.5	28.6	29.9
Libye	*2010	54.3	18.4	77.7	14.7	29.8	28.4
	*2017	53.0	19.2	78.4	15.8	27.8	28.7
Liechtenstein	2005	63.0	…	73.7	…	52.8	…
Liechtenstein	2010	61.6	2.6[13]	70.9	2.3[13]	52.6	3.1[13]
	2013	61.9	2.6[13]	70.6	2.3[13]	53.5	3.1[13]
Lithuania	2005	* 56.1	8.3	* 62.7	8.1	* 50.5	8.5
Lituanie	2010	* 56.9	17.8	* 62.1	21.2	* 52.6	14.5
	*2017	59.5	9.2	66.1	10.1	54.1	8.3
Luxembourg	2005	* 54.8	4.5	* 64.7	3.5	* 45.4	5.8
Luxembourg	2010	* 57.0	4.4	* 65.4	3.8	* 48.8	5.1
	*2017	58.8	5.6	65.5	4.9	52.0	6.5
Madagascar	2005	* 86.6	2.6	* 89.1	1.8	* 84.1	3.5
Madagascar	2010	* 89.0	3.8	* 91.0	2.8	* 87.2	4.9
	*2017	86.4	2.3	89.0	1.7	83.8	3.0
Malawi	2005	* 82.2	7.8	* 85.8	7.5	* 78.7	8.1
Malawi	*2010	82.1	6.5	80.6	6.1	83.6	6.8
	*2017	81.1	6.8	81.0	6.4	81.3	7.1
Malaysia	2005	* 61.2	3.5	* 77.8	3.3	* 44.2	3.9
Malaisie	2010	* 59.8	3.4	* 75.9	3.2	* 43.8	3.7
	*2017	63.4	3.3	77.8	3.2	49.3	3.6
Maldives	*2005	62.4	7.0	74.5	4.6	50.4	10.6
Maldives	2010	* 65.7	11.7	* 76.3	10.9	* 55.2	12.8
	*2017	68.6	2.9	79.6	2.1	57.8	3.9
Mali	*2005	54.0	9.6	70.1	7.4	38.3	13.6
Mali	2010	* 65.8	7.3	* 81.4	5.6	* 50.3	10.1
	*2017	66.5	8.1	82.3	6.1	50.5	11.3
Malta	2005	* 48.5	6.9	* 68.8	6.3	* 29.1	8.3
Malte	2010	* 49.3	6.8	* 66.0	6.8	* 32.6	7.0
	*2017	52.5	5.4	65.7	5.2	39.4	5.7
Marshall Islands	2006[3]	44.6	…	…	…	…	…
Îles Marshall	2011	41.3	# 4.7	53.3	# 4.9	29.0	# 4.5
Martinique [6]	2005	43.6	18.7	48.5	16.9	39.6	20.4
Martinique [6]	2010	45.9	21.0	49.1	19.7	43.3	22.2
	#2013	53.1	22.8	53.8	22.8	52.6	22.8
Mauritania	*2005	46.8	10.9	65.9	10.1	27.8	12.9
Mauritanie	*2010	47.1	10.8	65.5	10.0	28.8	12.7
	*2017	47.4	12.0	65.5	11.1	29.3	13.9
Mauritius	2005	* 58.7	9.6	* 76.8	5.8	* 41.1	16.5
Maurice	2010	* 58.6	7.7	* 74.4	4.6	* 43.2	12.8
	*2017	60.3	7.6	74.3	5.1	46.9	11.4
Mexico	2005	* 60.6	3.6	* 80.9	3.4	* 41.0	3.9
Mexique	2010	* 62.0	5.3	* 80.7	5.4	* 43.8	5.2
	*2017	62.3	4.1	79.5	3.9	45.5	4.3
Monaco [16]							
Monaco [16]	2000	45.7	3.6	57.3	2.5	35.1	5.2
Mongolia	2005	* 60.3	3.3	* 65.2	3.4	* 55.4	3.2
Mongolie	2010	* 61.3	6.5	* 67.6	7.0	* 55.1	5.9
	*2017	62.9	6.3	69.3	6.8	56.8	5.8

17 Labour force participation rate and unemployment rate *(continued)*

Labour force (LF) participation rate and unemployment rate by sex (percent)

Taux d'activité et taux de chômage *(suite)*

Taux d'activité et taux de chômage par sexe (pourcentage)

Region, country or area & / Région, pays ou zone &	Year / Année	Male and Female / Hommes et femmes: LF particip. rate / Taux d'activité	Male and Female / Hommes et femmes: Unemp. rate / Taux de Chômage	Male / Hommes: LF particip. rate / Taux d'activité	Male / Hommes: Unemp. rate / Taux de Chômage	Female / Femmes: LF particip. rate / Taux d'activité	Female / Femmes: Unemp. rate / Taux de Chômage
Montenegro / Monténégro	*2005	50.6	19.6	59.0	18.8	42.6	20.6
	2010	* 50.7	19.7	* 58.9	18.9	* 42.9	20.7
	*2017	48.7	17.4	55.9	17.4	41.8	17.4
Montserrat / Montserrat	#2001	85.2	9.5	89.2	...	80.6	...
	2011	...	5.6	...	7.7	...	3.3
Morocco / Maroc	2005	* 51.7	11.0	* 77.2	10.8	* 27.6	11.6
	2010	* 49.7	9.1	* 75.2	8.9	* 25.7	9.7
	*2017	49.5	10.4	74.5	10.1	25.6	11.1
Mozambique / Mozambique	*2005	85.0	23.2	82.8	20.5	87.0	25.4
	*2010	81.6	23.5	78.7	21.2	84.3	25.5
	*2017	79.1	24.1	75.6	22.0	82.2	25.9
Myanmar / Myanmar	*2005	78.0	0.9	80.8	0.8	75.4	0.9
	*2010	78.5	0.8	81.5	0.8	75.8	0.9
	*2017	77.7	0.8	80.8	0.8	74.7	0.9
Namibia / Namibie	*2005	61.4	23.1	67.7	20.7	55.5	25.8
	2010	* 61.2	22.1	* 66.3	20.5	* 56.5	23.8
	*2017	60.2	24.9	64.3	22.7	56.4	27.2
Nauru / Nauru	2002[3]	78.0	22.7	86.8	17.1	69.6	29.6
	2011	64.0	# 23.0	78.9	# 21.4	49.3	# 25.5
Nepal / Népal	*2005	84.6	3.2	89.0	3.4	80.4	2.9
	*2010	83.4	2.5	87.5	2.7	79.8	2.3
	*2017	83.0	3.0	86.7	3.3	79.7	2.7
Netherlands / Pays-Bas	2005	* 64.5	4.7	* 72.5	4.4	* 56.7	5.1
	2010	* 64.6	4.5	* 71.2	4.4	* 58.1	4.5
	*2017	63.4	5.6	69.7	5.2	57.3	6.1
Netherlands Antilles [former] [6,14,17] / Antilles néerland. [anc.] [6,14,17]	#2009	56.3	...	61.1	...	52.6	...
	2011	57.9	...	62.2	...	54.5	...
New Caledonia / Nouvelle-Calédonie	*2005	58.8	16.7	69.9	14.2	47.8	20.3
	*2010	56.7	13.9	67.3	11.7	45.8	17.3
	*2017	56.2	15.1	66.9	12.7	45.5	18.6
New Zealand / Nouvelle-Zélande	2005	* 67.3	3.8	* 74.8	3.5	* 60.3	4.1
	2010	* 67.7	6.1	* 74.2	5.9	* 61.5	6.4
	*2017	67.2	5.5	72.8	5.0	62.1	6.0
Nicaragua / Nicaragua	2005	* 61.5	5.6	* 80.4	5.7	* 43.7	5.5
	2010	* 63.1	8.0	* 80.5	7.6	* 46.8	8.7
	*2017	64.6	6.1	80.6	6.1	49.6	6.2
Niger / Niger	2005	* 64.6	3.1	* 90.7	3.4	* 39.2	2.4
	*2010	64.7	2.4	90.1	3.0	39.8	1.2
	*2017	64.7	2.7	89.2	3.2	40.4	1.6
Nigeria / Nigéria	*2005	54.9	7.1	62.1	6.2	47.6	8.2
	*2010	55.6	7.3	63.2	6.4	47.9	8.4
	*2017	56.5	5.4	64.3	4.8	48.5	6.3
Niue / Nioué	2001	75.5	2.2	76.7	2.3	74.8	2.1
	#2002	...	9.7	...	...	...	...
Northern Mariana Islands [3] / Îles Mariannes du Nord [3]	2003	81.8	4.6	82.5	5.0	81.3	4.3
	2005	...	6.5	...	7.3	...	5.8
	#2010	72.3	11.2	77.6	9.7	66.6	13.0
Norway / Norvège	2005	* 65.3	4.4	* 70.5	4.6	* 60.3	4.2
	2010	* 65.7	3.5	* 70.0	4.0	* 61.4	2.9
	*2017	64.7	5.1	68.3	5.5	61.1	4.7
Oman / Oman	*2005	55.6	19.2	77.1	14.7	25.4	38.5
	*2010	60.9	18.3	80.7	14.8	27.6	35.4
	*2017	68.9	17.8	85.4	15.0	30.1	36.9
Pakistan / Pakistan	2005	* 52.6	7.7	* 84.1	6.5	* 19.3	13.3
	2010	* 54.0	5.6	* 82.8	4.4	* 23.9	9.8
	*2017	54.3	5.9	82.5	4.5	24.8	10.7
Palau [3] / Palaos [3]	2005	67.5	4.2	75.4	3.7	58.1	4.9
Panama / Panama	2005	* 64.5	9.8	* 81.1	7.7	* 47.9	13.3
	2010	* 65.4	6.5	* 82.0	5.3	* 49.0	8.6
	*2017	65.4	6.2	80.4	4.9	50.5	8.1
Papua New Guinea / Papouasie-Nvl-Guinée	*2005	72.9	2.6	74.4	2.1	71.3	3.0
	*2010	71.7	2.4	72.9	2.0	70.5	2.8
	*2017	70.5	2.5	71.2	2.1	69.6	3.0
Paraguay / Paraguay	2005	* 70.2	5.8	* 85.7	5.0	* 54.3	7.1
	2010	* 69.8	5.7	* 84.6	4.6	* 54.6	7.4
	*2017	71.7	5.5	84.7	5.0	58.3	6.3
Peru / Pérou	2005	* 68.1	8.3	* 78.9	7.2	* 57.5	9.8
	2010	* 74.9	4.0	* 84.3	3.7	* 65.6	4.4
	*2017	74.4	5.3	82.8	4.8	66.1	6.0

17 Labour force participation rate and unemployment rate *(continued)*

Labour force (LF) participation rate and unemployment rate by sex (percent)

Taux d'activité et taux de chômage *(suite)*

Taux d'activité et taux de chômage par sexe (pourcentage)

Region, country or area [&] Région, pays ou zone [&]	Year Année	Male and Female / Hommes et femmes LF particip. rate Taux d'activité	Male and Female / Hommes et femmes Unemp. rate Taux de Chômage	Male / Hommes LF particip. rate Taux d'activité	Male / Hommes Unemp. rate Taux de Chômage	Female / Femmes LF particip. rate Taux d'activité	Female / Femmes Unemp. rate Taux de Chômage
Philippines Philippines	2005	* 64.9	7.7	* 80.0	7.7	* 49.8	7.8
	2010	* 64.9	7.4	* 79.6	7.6	* 50.2	7.0
	*2017	64.8	5.9	78.9	5.9	50.8	5.8
Poland Pologne	2005	* 54.7	17.7	* 62.5	16.6	* 47.5	19.1
	2010	* 56.0	9.6	* 64.3	9.3	* 48.3	10.0
	*2017	56.6	5.3	64.9	5.1	49.1	5.6
Portugal Portugal	2005	* 62.0	7.6	* 69.3	6.7	* 55.4	8.6
	2010	* 61.0	10.8	* 66.8	9.8	* 55.8	11.9
	*2017	58.2	10.5	63.7	10.2	53.3	10.8
Puerto Rico Porto Rico	2005	* 48.9	11.4	* 61.0	12.2	* 38.1	10.1
	2010	* 43.9	16.1	* 53.7	18.7	* 35.1	12.6
	*2017	42.6	12.8	51.7	14.0	34.4	11.1
Qatar Qatar	*2005	79.6	1.6	94.1	0.9	43.5	4.9
	2010	* 86.6	0.5	* 95.7	0.1	* 51.5	2.6
	*2017	83.7	0.3	93.6	0.1	53.1	1.2
Republic of Korea République de Corée	2005	* 60.9	3.7	* 72.6	4.0	* 49.5	3.2
	2010	* 60.3	3.7	* 71.7	4.0	* 49.3	3.3
	*2017	60.9	3.6	71.9	3.8	50.2	3.3
Republic of Moldova République de Moldova	2005	* 49.0	7.3	* 50.4	8.7	* 47.9	6.0
	2010	* 41.8	7.5	* 45.3	9.1	* 38.6	5.8
	*2017	42.6	5.0	46.5	6.1	39.1	3.8
Réunion [6] Réunion [6]	2005	50.1	30.1	60.3	27.6	41.1	33.3
	2010	52.1	28.9	59.9	28.0	45.3	30.0
	#2013	54.9	28.9	61.3	28.3	49.1	29.7
Romania Roumanie	2005	* 54.5	7.2	* 62.1	7.8	* 47.4	6.4
	2010	* 55.1	7.0	* 63.6	7.6	* 47.3	6.2
	*2017	55.5	7.1	64.5	7.8	47.3	6.3
Russian Federation Fédération de Russie	2005	* 61.9	7.1	* 68.6	7.3	* 56.2	6.9
	2010	* 63.0	7.3	* 70.7	7.9	* 56.5	6.8
	*2017	63.1	5.8	71.3	6.1	56.3	5.5
Rwanda Rwanda	*2005	84.2	2.4	82.5	2.2	85.6	2.6
	*2010	85.3	2.7	84.0	2.3	86.4	3.0
	*2017	84.8	2.4	83.3	2.3	86.1	2.5
Saint Helena Sainte-Hélène	2005	…	5.2	…	…	…	…
	2010	…	2.0	…	…	…	…
Saint Kitts and Nevis Saint-Kitts-et-Nevis	2001	# 68.8	5.1	# 62.8	4.3	# 74.9	5.9
Saint Lucia Sainte-Lucie	2005	* 70.1	18.7	* 77.6	14.9	* 63.1	23.1
	2010	* 68.5	20.6	* 75.5	16.4	* 61.9	25.6
	*2017	69.6	19.0	76.6	15.8	63.1	22.6
Saint Vincent & Grenadines Saint-Vincent-Grenadines	*2005	65.8	19.4	78.0	19.7	53.3	19.0
	*2010	66.7	18.9	77.9	18.3	55.4	19.6
	*2017	66.7	19.1	76.9	19.2	56.4	19.0
Samoa Samoa	*2005	49.4	4.8	69.2	4.4	28.3	5.8
	*2010	42.8	8.8	60.5	8.0	24.1	10.9
	*2017	41.3	6.5	58.2	5.9	23.3	7.9
San Marino Saint-Marin	2003	66.2	…	79.2	…	53.8	…
	2010	…	4.4	…	2.1	…	7.3
	#2014[4]	…	6.6	…	4.3	…	9.5
Sao Tome and Principe Sao Tomé-et-Principe	2005	* 57.9	16.5	* 72.9	13.7	* 43.4	20.9
	*2010	59.7	14.3	75.2	11.9	44.6	18.3
	*2017	60.6	13.6	76.2	11.4	45.4	17.3
Saudi Arabia Arabie saoudite	2005	* 51.3	6.1	* 75.4	4.1	* 17.5	18.0
	2010	* 52.1	5.6	* 75.8	3.5	* 18.3	17.6
	*2017	54.2	5.5	78.5	2.9	20.0	20.1
Senegal Sénégal	*2005	52.6	8.5	71.2	6.7	35.6	11.6
	*2010	55.4	9.2	69.6	7.2	42.4	12.3
	*2017	57.4	9.3	70.5	7.2	45.3	12.3
Serbia Serbie	2005	* 54.1	20.9	* 63.9	17.1	* 44.9	25.9
	2010	* 50.6	19.2	* 59.1	17.3	* 42.6	21.7
	*2017	51.4	15.5	59.9	14.3	43.4	17.0
Seychelles Seychelles	2005	72.1	5.5	…	6.1	…	4.9
	#2011[6,18]	65.0	4.1	68.3	3.8	61.9	4.5
Sierra Leone Sierra Leone	*2005	65.9	3.3	66.7	4.4	65.1	2.2
	*2010	66.5	3.0	67.9	4.0	65.1	2.0
	*2017	66.9	3.1	68.8	4.1	65.1	2.0
Singapore Singapour	2005	* 64.9	5.6	* 76.7	5.2	* 53.5	6.1
	2010	* 67.2	3.1	* 77.5	2.9	* 57.3	3.4
	*2017	66.8	2.0	76.1	1.9	57.8	2.1
Slovakia Slovaquie	2005	* 59.5	16.3	* 68.5	15.5	* 51.2	17.2
	2010	* 59.0	14.4	* 67.8	14.2	* 50.8	14.6
	*2017	59.3	9.9	68.0	8.9	51.4	11.2

17 Labour force participation rate and unemployment rate *(continued)*
Labour force (LF) participation rate and unemployment rate by sex (percent)

Taux d'activité et taux de chômage *(suite)*
Taux d'activité et taux de chômage par sexe (pourcentage)

Region, country or area & Région, pays ou zone &	Year Année	Male and Female Hommes et femmes: LF particip. rate Taux d'activité	Male and Female Hommes et femmes: Unemp. rate Taux de Chômage	Male Hommes: LF particip. rate Taux d'activité	Male Hommes: Unemp. rate Taux de Chômage	Female Femmes: LF particip. rate Taux d'activité	Female Femmes: Unemp. rate Taux de Chômage
Slovenia	2005	* 59.2	6.5	* 66.0	6.0	* 52.8	7.0
Slovénie	2010	* 59.3	7.2	* 65.5	7.4	* 53.2	7.1
	*2017	57.0	8.1	62.2	7.4	51.8	8.8
Solomon Islands	*2005	67.9	31.3	74.3	30.1	61.3	32.8
Îles Salomon	*2010	67.7	31.1	74.2	29.9	61.2	32.6
	*2017	67.3	31.4	73.5	30.3	61.1	32.9
Somalia	*2005	54.2	6.7	76.8	6.4	32.4	7.4
Somalie	*2010	54.0	6.7	76.3	6.4	32.4	7.4
	*2017	54.3	6.6	75.9	6.2	33.3	7.4
South Africa	2005	* 53.7	23.8	* 61.5	21.8	* 46.7	26.3
Afrique du Sud	2010	* 51.3	24.7	* 59.4	22.9	* 43.8	26.9
	*2017	53.6	26.0	61.1	24.0	46.4	28.5
South Sudan [19]							
Soudan du sud [19]	2008	74.2	13.7	76.7	12.9	71.6	14.6
Spain	2005	* 56.9	9.1	* 68.3	7.1	* 45.9	12.0
Espagne	2010	* 59.3	19.9	* 67.5	19.6	* 51.4	20.2
	*2017	58.0	18.3	64.2	16.6	52.1	20.3
Sri Lanka	2005	* 54.8	7.7	* 76.2	5.7	* 34.4	12.0
Sri Lanka	2010	* 54.8	4.9	* 76.6	3.5	* 34.6	7.7
	*2017	51.5	5.2	75.0	3.6	30.4	8.8
State of Palestine	2005	* 40.6	23.5	* 66.8	24.4	* 14.1	19.0
État de Palestine	2010	* 40.7	23.7	* 66.2	23.1	* 14.8	26.6
	*2017	44.3	24.2	69.7	23.8	18.4	25.6
Sudan	*2005	49.1	14.1	73.9	12.0	24.5	20.4
Soudan	*2010	47.9	13.0	72.9	10.8	23.2	19.7
	*2017	48.2	13.4	72.2	11.4	24.4	19.3
Suriname	*2005	52.4	8.7	67.2	6.5	37.6	12.5
Suriname	2010	* 54.1	7.6	* 68.4	5.3	* 39.9	11.3
	*2017	54.4	9.9	68.6	6.8	40.5	15.1
Swaziland	*2005	49.0	25.5	64.3	24.0	35.1	28.1
Swaziland	*2010	49.9	27.8	62.7	26.6	37.8	29.6
	*2017	52.6	25.1	65.1	23.5	40.6	27.6
Sweden	2005	* 63.7	7.5	* 68.1	7.6	* 59.3	7.4
Suède	2010	* 63.5	8.6	* 68.1	8.7	* 59.0	8.5
	*2017	64.4	7.3	68.0	7.5	60.7	7.2
Switzerland	2005	* 67.0	4.4	* 75.0	3.9	* 59.5	5.1
Suisse	2010	* 67.9	4.5	* 75.3	4.2	* 60.8	5.0
	*2017	68.4	4.6	74.5	4.5	62.5	4.7
Syrian Arab Republic	*2005	46.8	9.2	76.1	6.5	16.3	22.6
République arabe syrienne	2010	* 43.2	8.4	* 72.7	5.8	* 13.3	22.6
	*2017	41.7	13.8	70.9	10.7	12.4	31.8
Tajikistan	*2005	66.2	11.7	74.7	12.8	57.7	10.3
Tadjikistan	*2010	67.3	11.6	76.3	12.6	58.3	10.2
	*2017	68.8	10.8	77.9	11.6	59.6	9.9
Thailand	2005	* 73.6	1.4	* 81.4	1.5	* 66.0	1.2
Thaïlande	2010	* 72.5	1.0	* 81.0	1.1	* 64.4	1.0
	*2017	71.0	0.6	79.8	0.6	62.7	0.5
TFYR of Macedonia	2005	* 53.5	37.3	* 64.6	36.5	* 42.6	38.4
ex-R.Y. de Macédoine	2010	* 56.1	32.0	* 69.3	31.9	* 43.1	32.2
	*2017	55.7	27.3	67.8	27.6	43.9	26.7
Timor-Leste	*2005	49.3	7.3	66.2	6.2	32.0	9.6
Timor-Leste	2010	* 40.8	3.1	* 55.3	2.4	* 26.1	4.4
	*2017	41.4	4.3	55.6	3.5	26.9	5.9
Togo	*2005	80.1	7.0	80.4	6.5	79.8	7.4
Togo	*2010	80.7	6.9	80.3	6.4	81.0	7.3
	*2017	80.9	6.8	80.7	6.3	81.0	7.2
Tonga	*2005	63.8	5.2	75.0	3.5	53.1	7.4
Tonga	*2010	63.9	5.0	75.2	3.4	53.1	7.2
	*2017	63.3	4.8	73.9	3.3	52.9	6.9
Trinidad and Tobago	2005	* 64.7	8.0	* 76.2	5.8	* 53.5	11.0
Trinité-et-Tobago	2010	* 63.8	5.9	* 75.4	5.1	* 52.5	7.0
	*2017	62.6	4.2	73.2	3.6	52.4	5.1
Tunisia	2005	* 45.7	12.9	* 68.0	11.9	* 24.0	15.7
Tunisie	2010	* 46.7	13.1	* 69.7	10.9	* 24.5	19.0
	*2017	47.7	14.6	71.3	12.3	25.1	20.8
Turkey	2005	* 46.1	10.6	* 70.3	10.5	* 23.4	11.0
Turquie	2010	* 48.5	10.7	* 70.7	10.4	* 27.6	11.2
	*2017	50.3	10.8	71.4	10.1	30.4	12.4
Turkmenistan	*2005	60.5	9.2	74.8	9.3	47.0	9.1
Turkménistan	*2010	60.6	9.2	75.7	9.3	46.4	9.1
	*2017	62.1	8.6	77.7	8.7	47.3	8.4

Labour force participation rate and unemployment rate *(continued)*

Labour force (LF) participation rate and unemployment rate by sex (percent)

Taux d'activité et taux de chômage *(suite)*

Taux d'activité et taux de chômage par sexe (pourcentage)

Region, country or area & Région, pays ou zone &	Year Année	Male and Female Hommes et femmes LF particip. rate Taux d'activité	Male and Female Hommes et femmes Unemp. rate Taux de Chômage	Male Hommes LF particip. rate Taux d'activité	Male Hommes Unemp. rate Taux de Chômage	Female Femmes LF particip. rate Taux d'activité	Female Femmes Unemp. rate Taux de Chômage
Turks and Caicos Islands	2005	# 62.0	8.0	...	...	...	...
Îles Turques-et-Caïques	#2008	64.0	8.3	...	...	...	...
Tuvalu							
Tuvalu	2005	58.2	6.5	69.6	4.9	47.9	8.6
Uganda	2005	* 78.4	1.9	* 79.7	2.4	* 77.1	1.4
Ouganda	*2010	82.9	3.1	85.4	3.8	80.6	2.3
	*2017	85.0	2.4	87.7	2.8	82.3	1.9
Ukraine	2005	* 58.3	7.2	* 65.6	7.5	* 52.2	6.8
Ukraine	2010	* 58.6	8.1	* 65.9	9.3	* 52.4	6.8
	*2017	59.2	8.8	67.5	9.8	52.3	7.7
United Arab Emirates	2005	* 77.8	3.1	* 91.2	2.6	* 37.1	7.0
Émirats arabes unis	*2010	80.7	4.2	91.3	3.3	42.4	10.9
	*2017	79.0	3.7	90.8	2.8	41.7	9.5
United Kingdom	2005	* 61.9	4.8	* 69.3	5.2	* 54.9	4.3
Royaume-Uni	2010	* 62.1	7.8	* 68.7	8.6	* 55.8	6.9
	*2017	62.7	5.0	68.6	5.3	57.0	4.7
United Rep. of Tanzania	*2005	89.6	3.1	90.6	2.2	88.7	3.9
Rép.-Unie de Tanzanie	*2010	84.8	2.9	86.0	2.1	83.6	3.7
	*2017	78.5	2.7	83.2	2.0	73.9	3.5
United States of America	2005	* 65.1	5.1	* 72.2	5.1	* 58.3	5.1
États-Unis d'Amérique	2010	* 63.7	9.6	* 70.0	10.5	* 57.6	8.6
	*2017	61.8	4.9	68.1	5.0	55.7	4.8
United States Virgin Islands	*2005	64.9	9.3	76.1	8.0	54.9	10.9
Îles Vierges américaines	*2010	64.0	9.0	73.9	7.8	55.2	10.6
	*2017	61.0	9.0	70.7	7.8	52.5	10.4
Uruguay	2005	* 62.8	12.2	* 74.1	9.5	* 52.7	15.6
Uruguay	2010	* 65.4	6.8	* 76.7	5.0	* 55.1	9.1
	*2017	65.4	8.8	76.3	6.2	55.6	12.0
Uzbekistan	*2005	59.2	9.3	72.1	9.4	47.2	9.2
Ouzbékistan	*2010	60.6	9.3	74.4	9.3	47.6	9.1
	*2017	62.1	8.9	76.6	9.0	48.5	8.7
Vanuatu	*2005	73.6	5.6	81.7	5.1	65.3	6.3
Vanuatu	*2010	71.0	5.4	80.7	4.8	61.5	6.2
	*2017	71.0	5.3	80.5	4.7	61.7	6.1
Venezuela (Boliv. Rep. of)	2005	* 66.5	11.4	* 81.5	9.9	* 51.7	13.7
Venezuela (Rép. boliv. du)	2010	* 64.8	8.5	* 79.3	7.8	* 50.6	9.4
	*2017	64.7	6.6	78.3	6.1	51.5	7.2
Viet Nam	*2005	77.0	2.3	81.8	2.4	72.5	2.3
Viet Nam	2010	* 76.9	2.6	* 81.6	2.5	* 72.5	2.8
	*2017	78.4	2.2	83.3	2.2	73.9	2.2
Western Sahara	*2005	55.9	7.2	83.1	5.7	24.1	13.0
Sahara occidental	*2010	57.6	7.0	83.5	5.4	27.7	12.4
	*2017	57.5	6.8	83.3	5.2	28.6	12.0
Yemen	2005	* 47.5	16.1	* 71.3	14.2	* 23.6	21.9
Yémen	2010	* 48.2	17.8	* 71.4	9.7	* 24.8	41.3
	*2017	50.0	16.1	73.7	12.5	26.2	26.4
Zambia	2005	* 79.5	15.9	* 85.6	15.2	* 73.5	16.7
Zambie	*2010	75.0	10.8	79.8	11.1	70.4	10.6
	*2017	75.3	7.4	80.9	7.3	69.9	7.5
Zimbabwe	*2005	86.3	4.8	90.2	5.3	82.5	4.4
Zimbabwe	*2010	83.2	6.3	88.7	7.7	78.0	4.7
	*2017	82.6	5.0	87.5	5.5	78.0	4.5
European Union (EU)	*2005	56.7	9.0	65.3	8.3	48.7	9.7
Union européenne (UE)	*2010	57.2	9.6	64.8	9.6	50.1	9.5
	*2016	57.3	8.6	64.0	8.4	51.0	8.8
	*2017	57.2	8.3	63.9	...	50.9	...

Source:

International Labour Organization (ILO), Geneva, Key Indicators of the Labour Market (KILM 9th edition), the ILOSTAT database, last accessed March 2017.

& Population aged 15 years and over, unless otherwise footnoted.

1 Data excludes Armenia, Azerbaijan, Cyprus, Georgia, Israel and Turkey.

2 Caucasus refers to Armenia, Azerbaijan, Cyprus, Georgia, Israel and Turkey.

Source:

Bureau international du travail (BIT), Genève, Indicateurs clés du marché du travail (ICMT 9e édition), ILOSTAT base de données du BIT, dernier accès mars 2017.

& Sauf indication contraire, population âgée de 15 ans et plus.

1 Les données excluent l'Arménie, l'Azerbaïdjan, Chypre, la Géorgie, l'Israël et la Turquie.

2 Le Caucase se rapportent à l'Arménie, l'Azerbaïdjan, Chypre, la Géorgie, l'Israël et la Turquie.

17

Labour force participation rate and unemployment rate *(continued)*
Labour force (LF) participation rate and unemployment rate by sex (percent)

Taux d'activité et taux de chômage *(suite)*
Taux d'activité et taux de chômage par sexe (pourcentage)

3 Population aged 16 years and over.
4 Population aged 14 years and over.
5 Resident population (de jure).
6 Excluding the institutional population.
7 For statistical purposes, the data for China do not include those for the Hong Kong Special Administrative Region (Hong Kong SAR), Macao Special Administrative Region (Macao SAR) and Taiwan Province of China.
8 Population aged 15 to 69 years.
9 Population aged 16 to 65 years.
10 Population aged 15 to 74 years.
11 Nationals, residents.
12 Population aged 18 to 64 years.
13 Population aged 15 to 64 years.
14 Persons present (de facto).
15 De facto population.
16 Population aged 17 years and over.
17 Main city or metropolitan area.
18 Excluding some areas.
19 Population aged 10 years and over.

3 Population âgée de 16 ans et plus.
4 Population âgée de 14 ans et plus.
5 Population résidente (de droit).
6 Non compris la population dans les institutions.
7 Pour la présentation des statistiques, les données pour la Chine ne comprennent pas la région administrative spéciale de Hong Kong (Hong Kong RAS), la région administrative spéciale de Macao (Macao RAS) et la province chinoise de Taïwan.
8 Population âgée de 15 à 69 ans.
9 Population âgée de 16 à 65 ans.
10 Population âgée de 15 à 74 ans.
11 Ressortissants, résidents.
12 Population âgée de 18 à 64 ans.
13 Population âgée de 15 à 64 ans.
14 Personnes présentes (de facto)
15 Population de fait.
16 Population âgée de 17 ans et plus.
17 Ville principale ou zone métropolitaine.
18 Certaines régions sont exclues.
19 Population âgée de 10 ans et plus.

18 Employment by economic activity

Percentage of persons employed by sex and ISIC 4 categories; agriculture (agr.), industry (ind.) and services (ser.)

Emploi par activité économique

Personnes employées par sexe et branches de la CITI rév. 4; agriculture (agr.), industrie (ind.) et services (ser.), pourcentage

Region, country or area & / Région, pays ou zone &	Year / Année	Male and Female / Hommes et femmes			Male / Hommes			Female / Femmes		
		Agr.	Ind.	Ser.	Agr.	Ind.	Ser.	Agr.	Ind.	Ser.
Total, all countries or areas	***2005**	**36.0**	**20.5**	**43.5**	**34.2**	**24.5**	**41.3**	**38.6**	**14.6**	**46.7**
Total, tous pays ou zones	***2010**	**32.4**	**21.3**	**46.3**	**31.2**	**25.9**	**42.9**	**34.2**	**14.3**	**51.6**
	***2017**	**28.8**	**21.5**	**49.7**	**27.6**	**26.6**	**45.7**	**30.5**	**13.6**	**55.9**
Africa	*2005	53.3	11.9	34.8	49.5	15.2	35.3	58.6	7.4	34.0
Afrique	*2010	52.3	12.8	34.9	48.9	16.3	34.8	57.1	7.9	35.0
	*2017	50.9	12.9	36.2	47.7	16.6	35.7	55.2	7.9	36.9
Northern Africa	*2005	30.2	22.1	47.7	29.1	23.2	47.7	34.3	18.0	47.8
Afrique septentrionale	*2010	27.0	25.7	47.4	25.8	27.7	46.5	31.5	17.9	50.6
	*2017	24.5	25.5	50.0	23.4	27.6	49.0	28.3	18.1	53.7
Sub-Saharan Africa	*2005	57.9	9.9	32.2	55.5	12.8	31.7	60.8	6.5	32.7
Afrique subsaharienne	*2010	57.4	10.2	32.4	55.6	13.0	31.4	59.4	7.0	33.6
	*2017	55.6	10.7	33.7	54.0	13.7	32.2	57.4	7.0	35.5
Eastern Africa	*2005	66.3	7.7	26.0	62.5	10.5	26.9	70.3	4.6	25.0
Afrique orientale	*2010	70.6	7.1	22.3	68.1	9.5	22.5	73.4	4.4	22.1
	*2017	69.4	7.5	23.1	66.8	10.2	23.0	72.2	4.4	23.3
Middle Africa	*2005	58.1	11.5	30.4	50.0	16.4	33.6	66.9	6.2	26.9
Afrique centrale	*2010	57.5	11.5	31.0	49.4	16.7	34.0	66.4	5.8	27.8
	*2017	55.4	11.4	33.1	47.4	16.7	35.9	64.3	5.5	30.1
Southern Africa	*2005	10.9	23.2	66.0	12.7	32.0	55.4	8.6	11.9	79.5
Afrique australe	*2010	8.7	22.1	69.2	10.0	30.6	59.4	7.0	11.0	82.0
	*2017	9.7	24.7	65.7	11.5	34.5	53.9	7.2	11.7	81.1
Western Africa	*2005	54.8	9.8	35.4	56.6	10.7	32.7	52.3	8.5	39.2
Afrique occidentale	*2010	47.1	12.0	40.9	50.2	12.9	36.9	42.9	10.9	46.2
	*2017	43.7	12.6	43.7	47.1	13.8	39.1	39.0	11.0	50.0
Americas	*2005	10.8	21.4	67.8	14.2	28.3	57.5	6.0	11.8	82.2
Amériques	*2010	10.9	20.4	68.8	14.4	27.5	58.0	6.0	10.7	83.3
	*2017	10.3	20.0	69.8	13.8	27.5	58.7	5.5	9.8	84.7
Northern America	*2005	1.7	20.4	77.9	2.4	29.7	68.0	0.9	9.4	89.7
Amérique septentrionale	*2010	1.7	18.0	80.3	2.4	27.0	70.6	0.8	7.8	91.4
	*2017	1.5	17.5	81.0	2.1	26.2	71.6	0.8	7.2	92.0
Latin America & the Caribbean	*2005	17.0	22.1	60.9	21.4	27.5	51.1	10.1	13.7	76.2
Amérique latine et Caraïbes	*2010	16.5	21.8	61.7	21.0	27.8	51.2	9.7	12.8	77.5
	*2017	15.6	21.5	63.0	20.2	28.2	51.7	8.8	11.6	79.7
Caribbean	*2005	22.6	18.5	58.8	28.5	23.9	47.6	13.4	10.2	76.4
Caraïbes	*2010	22.8	16.4	60.8	29.0	21.6	49.3	13.6	8.8	77.5
	*2017	20.6	14.8	64.7	26.1	19.8	54.2	12.6	7.6	79.8
Central America	*2005	18.4	24.5	57.1	25.1	27.5	47.4	5.8	18.8	75.4
Amérique centrale	*2010	17.1	23.8	59.1	23.8	27.5	48.7	5.4	17.1	77.5
	*2017	16.3	23.6	60.1	23.3	28.0	48.8	4.6	16.2	79.2
South America	*2005	16.0	21.6	62.4	19.3	27.8	52.8	11.2	12.5	76.4
Amérique du Sud	*2010	15.7	21.6	62.7	19.2	28.5	52.3	10.8	11.7	77.5
	*2017	14.8	21.2	64.0	18.3	29.0	52.7	9.9	10.3	79.8
Central Asia	*2005	37.6	20.3	42.1	36.7	23.6	39.7	38.8	16.1	45.2
Asie centrale	*2010	32.3	22.2	45.5	32.2	26.0	41.8	32.6	17.2	50.2
	*2017	28.3	22.4	49.3	27.8	27.2	45.0	29.0	15.9	55.1
Eastern Asia	*2005	38.5	22.5	39.0	35.1	26.5	38.4	42.7	17.6	39.7
Asie orientale	*2010	31.1	24.2	44.7	27.6	29.5	42.9	35.6	17.4	47.0
	*2017	24.8	24.1	51.0	21.9	30.3	47.9	28.6	16.3	55.0
South-eastern Asia	*2005	43.8	17.7	38.5	43.2	19.7	37.0	44.6	14.9	40.5
Asie du Sud-Est	*2010	39.3	18.5	42.2	39.4	21.1	39.5	39.3	15.0	45.7
	*2017	31.9	20.8	47.2	32.5	24.7	42.8	31.1	15.6	53.3
Southern Asia	*2005	53.2	18.9	27.9	46.6	20.6	32.7	69.5	14.5	16.0
Asie méridionale	*2010	49.5	21.6	28.9	44.0	23.3	32.7	65.4	16.4	18.2
	*2017	43.4	23.3	33.3	37.7	25.5	36.8	60.4	16.8	22.8
Western Asia [1]	*2005	14.6	22.8	62.7	12.5	26.0	61.5	25.7	5.5	68.8
Asie occidentale [1]	*2010	11.0	24.3	64.8	10.2	27.4	62.4	15.5	6.3	78.2
	*2017	12.6	25.1	62.3	11.4	28.8	59.8	19.0	5.8	75.2
Caucasus [2]	*2005	29.8	21.6	48.6	23.9	26.4	49.7	41.8	12.0	46.2
Caucase [2]	*2010	25.2	22.7	52.1	19.4	28.5	52.1	35.8	12.0	52.2
	*2017	21.5	23.7	54.8	17.4	29.9	52.7	28.9	12.5	58.6

18 Employment by economic activity *(continued)*

Percentage of persons employed by sex and ISIC 4 categories; agriculture (agr.), industry (ind.) and services (ser.)

Emploi par activité économique *(suite)*

Personnes employées par sexe et branches de la CITI rév. 4; agriculture (agr.), industrie (ind.) et services (ser.), pourcentage

Region, country or area & / Région, pays ou zone &	Year / Année	Male and Female / Hommes et femmes			Male / Hommes			Female / Femmes		
		Agr.	Ind.	Ser.	Agr.	Ind.	Ser.	Agr.	Ind.	Ser.
Eastern Europe / Europe orientale	*2005	15.1	29.6	55.4	16.1	36.5	47.4	14.0	22.0	64.0
	*2010	11.7	28.7	59.5	13.4	37.1	49.5	10.0	19.6	70.4
	*2017	9.8	28.0	62.3	11.4	36.8	51.9	8.0	18.3	73.7
Northern Europe / Europe septentrionale	*2005	2.8	23.1	74.1	3.8	34.0	62.2	1.6	10.5	87.9
	*2010	2.1	20.0	77.8	3.0	30.4	66.6	1.1	8.3	90.5
	*2017	2.0	19.0	78.9	2.9	28.8	68.3	1.1	8.0	90.9
Southern Europe / Europe méridionale	*2005	8.6	29.2	62.1	8.9	38.4	52.7	8.3	15.5	76.2
	*2010	7.7	25.8	66.5	8.3	35.5	56.3	6.8	12.6	80.6
	*2017	6.8	23.3	69.9	8.0	32.1	59.9	5.3	11.9	82.9
Western Europe / Europe occidentale	*2005	3.0	26.3	70.7	3.8	36.9	59.4	2.2	13.4	84.5
	*2010	2.4	24.6	73.0	3.0	35.7	61.2	1.7	11.7	86.6
	*2017	2.1	23.4	74.5	2.7	34.2	63.1	1.4	11.1	87.4
Oceania / Océanie	*2005	17.0	18.0	65.0	16.4	25.8	57.8	17.8	8.4	73.8
	*2010	16.9	17.6	65.5	16.0	25.9	58.2	18.0	7.6	74.3
	*2017	16.3	17.8	65.9	15.4	26.9	57.7	17.3	7.1	75.6
Afghanistan / Afghanistan	*2005	65.3	11.2	23.5	62.0	11.9	26.1	84.5	6.8	8.7
	*2010	64.2	9.4	26.4	60.7	10.1	29.1	84.1	5.2	10.7
	*2017	61.6	10.0	28.5	57.4	10.9	31.7	81.9	5.3	12.8
Albania / Albanie	*2005	49.3	17.8	32.9	42.1	21.5	36.5	59.8	12.4	27.9
	*2010	42.6	19.9	37.5	34.9	26.0	39.1	54.3	10.7	35.0
	*2017	41.4	18.3	40.3	36.6	23.7	39.7	48.2	10.6	41.2
Algeria / Algérie	*2005	17.2	27.1	55.7	18.5	26.7	54.7	8.0	29.5	62.5
	*2010	12.5	33.9	53.6	13.8	33.9	52.3	5.1	33.9	61.0
	*2017	10.8	34.5	54.7	12.2	34.6	53.3	4.4	34.2	61.4
American Samoa [3,4] / Samoa américaines [3,4]	2000	3.1	41.7	51.9	...	...	...	...	...	...
	#2010	3.0	23.2	73.8	...	...	...	...	...	...
Angola / Angola	*2005	7.1	38.0	54.9	1.6	52.6	45.8	13.7	20.4	65.9
	*2010	4.9	37.9	57.2	0.8	52.8	46.4	10.1	19.1	70.8
	*2017	4.2	37.6	58.2	0.7	52.4	46.9	8.7	19.0	72.3
Anguilla [4] / Anguilla [4]	#2001	2.9	18.9	76.7	4.8	32.1	61.7	0.7	3.7	93.9
Antigua and Barbuda [4] / Antigua-et-Barbuda [4]	2005	2.8	15.6	81.6	4.4	26.1	69.5	1.2	5.0	93.8
	2008	2.8	15.6	81.6	4.4	26.1	69.5	1.2	5.0	93.8
Argentina / Argentine	*2005	1.1	23.5	75.4	1.4	32.0	66.5	0.6	10.6	88.8
	*2010	1.3	23.3	75.4	1.9	32.6	65.5	0.4	9.3	90.3
	*2017	2.0	24.8	73.1	3.2	36.2	60.6	0.3	8.3	91.4
Armenia / Arménie	*2005	38.7	18.3	43.0	33.0	25.5	41.5	46.3	8.7	45.0
	*2010	38.6	17.3	44.0	32.9	25.3	41.8	47.2	5.4	47.4
	*2017	35.0	15.7	49.3	30.9	23.2	45.9	39.6	7.3	53.1
Aruba [4] / Aruba [4]	#2000	0.5	16.4	82.3	0.8	26.7	71.6	0.2	4.5	94.7
	#2010[5]	0.6	14.5	84.4	1.0	24.4	74.1	0.3	4.5	94.8
	#2011	0.6	14.0	85.1	0.8	24.4	74.4	0.4	3.3	96.1
Australia / Australie	*2005	3.5	21.4	75.1	4.4	30.8	64.9	2.4	9.8	87.8
	*2010	3.3	20.9	75.7	4.1	30.8	65.1	2.3	8.9	88.8
	*2017	2.7	21.2	76.1	3.6	32.0	64.4	1.7	8.2	90.2
Austria / Autriche	*2005	5.3	27.6	67.2	5.3	39.6	55.1	5.3	12.9	81.9
	*2010	5.2	24.8	70.0	5.4	36.3	58.3	5.0	11.4	83.6
	*2017	4.7	25.6	69.7	4.9	37.0	58.0	4.4	12.5	83.1
Azerbaijan / Azerbaïdjan	*2005	39.3	12.0	48.6	41.0	15.3	43.7	37.6	8.6	53.8
	*2010	38.2	13.7	48.1	32.3	20.9	46.8	44.4	6.1	49.5
	*2017	36.7	14.2	49.1	31.3	21.9	46.9	42.5	6.0	51.5
Bahamas / Bahamas	*2005	3.5	17.8	78.7	5.9	29.0	65.1	0.9	5.7	93.5
	*2010	3.3	14.4	82.3	5.7	24.3	70.0	0.8	3.8	95.4
	*2017	3.9	14.2	81.9	6.6	23.8	69.6	0.9	3.8	95.3
Bahrain / Bahreïn	*2005	1.4	30.2	68.4	1.8	35.3	63.0	0.1	8.9	91.0
	*2010	1.1	35.7	63.2	1.3	42.3	56.3	~0.0	8.8	91.1
	*2017	1.0	33.4	65.6	1.3	39.5	59.3	~0.0	7.8	92.2
Bangladesh / Bangladesh	*2005	48.1	14.5	37.5	38.2	15.1	46.6	66.6	13.2	20.2
	*2010	47.3	17.6	35.1	38.8	19.6	41.6	64.3	13.6	22.2
	*2017	40.6	19.1	40.3	31.2	21.3	47.5	58.7	14.8	26.6
Barbados / Barbade	*2005	3.1	16.5	80.3	4.0	25.5	70.6	2.2	6.7	91.0
	*2010	3.0	19.3	77.7	3.9	29.3	66.7	2.1	9.0	88.9
	*2017	2.8	19.3	77.9	4.2	29.1	66.7	1.5	9.4	89.1

18 Employment by economic activity *(continued)*

Percentage of persons employed by sex and ISIC 4 categories; agriculture (agr.), industry (ind.) and services (ser.)

Emploi par activité économique *(suite)*

Personnes employées par sexe et branches de la CITI rév. 4; agriculture (agr.), industrie (ind.) et services (ser.), pourcentage

Region, country or area & / Région, pays ou zone &	Year / Année	Male and Female / Hommes et femmes			Male / Hommes			Female / Femmes		
		Agr.	Ind.	Ser.	Agr.	Ind.	Ser.	Agr.	Ind.	Ser.
Belarus / Bélarus	*2005	12.1	35.1	52.8	16.7	34.4	48.9	7.4	35.8	56.8
	*2010	11.1	33.8	55.1	15.4	34.9	49.7	6.7	32.5	60.8
	*2017	9.6	32.0	58.4	13.3	33.1	53.6	5.8	30.8	63.4
Belgium / Belgique	*2005	2.0	24.7	73.3	2.5	35.0	62.5	1.5	11.4	87.2
	*2010	1.4	23.4	75.2	1.8	34.4	63.8	0.9	10.2	88.9
	*2017	1.2	21.2	77.6	1.5	32.4	66.1	0.8	8.1	91.1
Belize / Belize	*2005	19.5	17.8	62.7	27.6	21.6	50.8	3.2	10.2	86.6
	*2010	17.3	17.6	65.1	24.7	21.9	53.4	3.8	9.7	86.5
	*2017	16.1	15.9	67.9	23.1	20.9	56.0	5.0	7.8	87.2
Benin / Bénin	*2005	46.1	9.9	44.0	57.2	11.0	31.9	34.0	8.8	57.2
	*2010	45.3	10.5	44.2	53.8	13.8	32.4	36.5	7.0	56.5
	*2017	43.2	10.2	46.6	52.2	14.1	33.7	33.9	6.3	59.8
Bermuda / Bermudes	2004[6]	1.7	12.1	86.2	3.0	20.5	76.6	0.3	3.1	96.6
	#2010[3,4]	1.4	12.9	85.7	2.4	22.6	75.0	0.4	3.2	96.4
	#2012[4,7]	1.7	9.6	88.7	3.0	16.5	80.5	0.3	2.6	97.1
	#2013[3,4,8]	1.6	10.3	87.6	...	...	...	...	...	...
Bhutan / Bhoutan	*2005	49.7	19.5	30.8	35.6	28.3	36.1	70.1	6.9	23.0
	*2010	59.4	6.8	33.8	55.0	6.7	38.3	65.7	6.9	27.4
	*2017	56.6	9.7	33.7	51.3	10.1	38.6	64.5	9.2	26.3
Bolivia (Plurin. State of) / Bolivie (État plurin. de)	*2005	34.9	20.2	44.9	36.0	27.6	36.4	33.3	10.3	56.4
	*2010	31.1	21.9	47.1	34.2	29.9	35.9	26.9	11.1	62.0
	*2017	29.5	21.1	49.4	32.6	29.6	37.8	25.5	10.2	64.3
Bosnia and Herzegovina / Bosnie-Herzégovine	*2005	26.9	27.0	46.1	24.7	33.7	41.6	31.0	14.7	54.3
	*2010	20.2	28.7	51.2	18.5	36.6	44.9	23.2	14.4	62.3
	*2017	18.0	30.4	51.7	18.6	38.0	43.4	17.0	18.5	64.5
Botswana / Botswana	*2005	26.4	17.4	56.2	33.1	21.5	45.4	18.3	12.6	69.1
	*2010	28.8	15.3	55.9	34.6	19.1	46.4	21.9	10.8	67.3
	*2017	25.7	14.9	59.4	30.2	19.3	50.4	20.4	9.7	69.9
Brazil / Brésil	*2005	20.4	21.4	58.1	23.7	27.3	49.0	15.9	13.3	70.8
	*2010	16.1	22.4	61.6	19.4	29.2	51.4	11.4	13.0	75.6
	*2017	15.2	21.5	63.2	18.4	29.2	52.5	10.9	10.9	78.2
British Virgin Islands [4] / Îles Vierges britanniques [4]	2010	0.5	11.1	87.4	...	...	...	...	...	...
Brunei Darussalam / Brunéi Darussalam	*2005	1.0	21.0	78.0	1.4	28.1	70.5	0.4	10.5	89.1
	*2010	0.8	20.2	79.1	0.9	26.2	72.9	0.5	10.9	88.6
	*2017	0.6	19.4	80.1	0.7	24.4	74.9	0.5	11.3	88.2
Bulgaria / Bulgarie	*2005	8.9	34.2	56.8	10.7	38.9	50.4	6.8	28.8	64.4
	*2010	6.8	33.4	59.8	8.2	40.8	51.0	5.2	24.8	70.0
	*2017	6.5	29.4	64.1	8.6	35.6	55.8	4.2	22.3	73.5
Burkina Faso / Burkina Faso	*2005	84.7	3.1	12.2	82.3	3.9	13.9	87.4	2.3	10.4
	*2010	80.8	5.1	14.1	78.9	6.7	14.4	83.0	3.3	13.8
	*2017	80.0	4.9	15.1	77.5	6.6	15.9	82.8	3.0	14.2
Burundi / Burundi	*2005	91.1	2.8	6.1	86.2	4.6	9.2	95.7	1.1	3.2
	*2010	90.8	2.6	6.5	85.8	4.5	9.7	95.6	0.9	3.5
	*2017	91.1	2.6	6.3	86.2	4.4	9.4	95.8	0.9	3.3
Cabo Verde / Cabo Verde	*2005	35.3	9.9	54.9	25.8	15.1	59.1	51.0	1.2	47.9
	*2010	30.2	11.3	58.5	21.3	17.6	61.1	44.6	1.2	54.2
	*2017	27.2	11.5	61.3	19.4	18.0	62.6	39.5	1.3	59.2
Cambodia / Cambodge	*2005	59.8	14.6	25.7	59.0	14.1	26.8	60.5	15.0	24.5
	*2010	54.2	16.2	29.6	52.9	17.0	30.1	55.4	15.5	29.1
	*2017	42.4	19.6	38.0	44.4	20.8	34.8	40.4	18.3	41.3
Cameroon / Cameroun	*2005	64.1	8.8	27.2	59.4	10.0	30.5	69.5	7.3	23.2
	*2010	63.7	8.8	27.4	59.0	10.4	30.6	69.2	7.0	23.8
	*2017	61.8	8.7	29.5	57.1	10.6	32.3	67.2	6.5	26.2
Canada / Canada	*2005	2.7	22.1	75.2	3.7	32.1	64.2	1.6	10.6	87.8
	*2010	2.2	20.2	77.6	3.0	30.4	66.6	1.2	9.0	89.8
	*2017	2.1	19.5	78.4	2.9	29.4	67.7	1.2	8.6	90.2
Cayman Islands / Îles Caïmanes	2005[4]	1.7	22.2	75.5	2.6	39.3	57.3	0.6	3.3	95.7
	#2010	0.6	14.9	84.2	1.1	26.2	72.5	0.1	3.2	96.4
	#2013	0.8	15.5	83.6	1.5	29.0	69.5	0.2	2.0	97.7
Central African Republic / République centrafricaine	*2005	69.9	4.5	25.6	60.1	7.5	32.4	81.5	0.9	17.6
	*2010	69.6	4.6	25.8	60.0	7.8	32.3	80.9	0.9	18.2
	*2017	72.2	4.3	23.4	63.3	7.3	29.4	82.4	1.0	16.7

18 Employment by economic activity *(continued)*

Percentage of persons employed by sex and ISIC 4 categories; agriculture (agr.), industry (ind.) and services (ser.)

Emploi par activité économique *(suite)*

Personnes employées par sexe et branches de la CITI rév. 4; agriculture (agr.), industrie (ind.) et services (ser.), pourcentage

Region, country or area & / Région, pays ou zone &	Year / Année	Male and Female / Hommes et femmes			Male / Hommes			Female / Femmes		
		Agr.	Ind.	Ser.	Agr.	Ind.	Ser.	Agr.	Ind.	Ser.
Chad	*2005	76.7	1.8	21.5	72.2	2.7	25.1	82.3	0.6	17.1
Tchad	*2010	78.0	1.9	20.0	73.4	3.0	23.7	83.9	0.7	15.4
	*2017	76.6	2.0	21.4	72.3	3.0	24.7	82.1	0.7	17.3
Channel Islands	*2005	5.3	25.1	69.6	8.8	30.9	60.3	0.9	17.9	81.2
Îles Anglo-Normandes	*2010	5.2	24.8	70.0	8.7	30.8	60.5	0.9	17.5	81.5
	*2017	5.0	24.5	70.5	8.3	30.5	61.2	0.9	17.0	82.1
Chile	*2005	13.1	22.8	64.1	17.1	29.0	53.9	5.6	11.0	83.4
Chili	*2010	10.9	23.5	65.6	14.5	31.7	53.8	5.3	10.6	84.1
	*2017	9.6	22.9	67.5	12.8	31.0	56.2	4.9	11.3	83.8
China [9]	*2005	42.6	21.8	35.6	38.9	25.4	35.7	47.1	17.4	35.5
Chine [9]	*2010	34.1	24.0	41.9	30.1	29.1	40.8	39.2	17.6	43.3
	*2017	27.0	23.9	49.1	23.5	29.9	46.6	31.3	16.3	52.4
China, Hong Kong SAR	*2005	0.3	20.1	79.5	0.4	28.5	71.2	0.3	10.0	89.7
Chine, Hong Kong RAS	*2010	0.2	16.5	83.3	0.3	25.0	74.8	0.2	6.9	92.9
	*2017	0.2	14.9	84.9	0.2	23.0	76.7	0.1	5.9	93.9
China, Macao SAR	*2005	0.1	26.8	73.1	0.1	27.0	72.9	0.1	26.6	73.3
Chine, Macao RAS	*2010	0.2	15.6	84.2	0.2	20.2	79.6	0.2	10.9	88.9
	*2017	0.3	17.7	82.1	0.3	26.3	73.4	0.3	8.6	91.1
Colombia	*2005	18.5	16.4	65.2	26.5	18.8	54.7	5.9	12.5	81.6
Colombie	*2010	16.0	17.1	66.9	23.4	20.4	56.2	4.9	12.4	82.7
	*2017	13.5	16.6	69.9	20.2	20.9	58.9	4.2	10.6	85.2
Comoros	*2005	61.8	5.5	32.7	55.5	7.4	37.1	78.2	0.5	21.3
Comores	*2010	62.2	5.3	32.5	56.0	7.2	36.8	77.7	0.5	21.8
	*2017	62.0	5.2	32.8	56.2	7.1	36.7	76.1	0.6	23.3
Congo	*2005	43.2	25.9	31.0	37.1	24.7	38.3	50.0	27.2	22.8
Congo	*2010	41.7	25.2	33.0	35.1	24.5	40.4	49.1	26.1	24.7
	*2017	40.7	25.8	33.5	34.6	25.3	40.1	47.5	26.4	26.1
Cook Islands [10] / Îles Cook [10]	2011	4.3	11.7	84.0	6.4	17.7	75.9	1.8	5.0	93.3
Costa Rica	*2005	15.2	21.7	63.1	20.7	26.5	52.8	4.7	12.4	82.8
Costa Rica	*2010	15.1	19.6	65.3	20.9	24.2	54.9	4.7	11.4	83.9
	*2017	11.6	19.1	69.3	16.4	24.8	58.8	3.5	9.4	87.1
Côte d'Ivoire	*2005	60.9	5.1	34.0	51.3	7.4	41.3	78.4	0.8	20.8
Côte d'Ivoire	*2010	60.3	5.1	34.6	50.4	7.5	42.1	77.6	0.9	21.6
	*2017	56.0	5.7	38.4	44.7	8.6	46.7	74.5	0.9	24.6
Croatia	*2005	17.3	28.6	54.1	16.0	37.2	46.8	18.9	18.1	63.0
Croatie	*2010	14.3	27.6	58.1	13.3	38.3	48.4	15.5	14.9	69.7
	*2017	9.2	26.8	64.0	10.5	37.0	52.4	7.7	14.8	77.5
Cuba	*2005	20.1	19.1	60.9	26.0	22.3	51.7	9.5	13.4	77.2
Cuba	*2010	18.6	17.1	64.3	24.8	20.5	54.7	8.5	11.5	80.0
	*2017	12.9	11.7	75.3	17.8	14.7	67.6	5.0	6.9	88.1
Curaçao [4]	2000	1.1	18.0	80.9	2.0	28.6	69.4	0.2	5.6	94.2
Curaçao [4]	2005	0.9	15.3	83.8	...	...	...	...	...	...
	2008	1.1	17.6	81.3	...	...	...	...	...	...
Cyprus	*2005	4.7	24.0	71.2	5.7	33.8	60.6	3.4	10.3	86.2
Chypre	*2010	3.8	20.4	75.8	4.9	29.2	65.9	2.4	9.0	88.6
	*2017	4.1	16.7	79.2	5.8	24.7	69.5	1.9	6.6	91.6
Czechia	*2005	4.0	39.5	56.5	4.9	49.4	45.7	2.8	26.5	70.7
Tchéquie	*2010	3.1	38.0	58.9	4.0	49.0	47.0	1.9	23.3	74.8
	*2017	2.5	37.0	60.5	3.3	48.3	48.4	1.5	22.5	76.0
Dem. People's Rep. Korea	*2005	59.7	18.5	21.9	61.5	16.5	22.1	57.7	20.6	21.7
Rép. pop. dém. de Corée	*2010	58.9	19.6	21.4	61.4	16.9	21.7	56.3	22.5	21.2
	*2017	58.9	19.3	21.8	61.3	16.8	21.9	56.3	22.0	21.7
Dem. Rep. of the Congo	*2005	68.7	6.1	25.2	59.0	10.0	31.0	78.5	2.2	19.3
Rép. dém. du Congo	*2010	68.1	6.0	25.9	58.3	9.9	31.8	78.0	2.0	20.0
	*2017	65.3	5.9	28.9	55.1	9.9	35.0	75.6	1.7	22.7
Denmark	*2005	3.2	23.9	72.9	4.6	33.9	61.6	1.6	12.4	86.0
Danemark	*2010	2.4	19.6	78.0	3.8	29.1	67.1	0.9	9.2	89.9
	*2017	2.4	19.2	78.4	3.8	28.2	67.9	0.9	9.1	90.1
Djibouti	*2005	27.0	21.2	51.8	30.5	16.5	53.0	19.8	30.9	49.3
Djibouti	*2010	25.5	22.9	51.5	28.7	18.9	52.4	19.4	30.7	49.9
	*2017	22.8	23.9	53.2	25.8	20.9	53.3	17.2	29.7	53.2
Dominica [6] / Dominique [6]	#2001	21.0	20.0	58.8	29.4	26.8	43.9	8.3	9.7	81.5

18 Employment by economic activity *(continued)*

Percentage of persons employed by sex and ISIC 4 categories; agriculture (agr.), industry (ind.) and services (ser.)

Emploi par activité économique *(suite)*

Personnes employées par sexe et branches de la CITI rév. 4; agriculture (agr.), industrie (ind.) et services (ser.), pourcentage

Region, country or area & Région, pays ou zone &	Year Année	Male and Female Hommes et femmes			Male Hommes			Female Femmes		
		Agr.	Ind.	Ser.	Agr.	Ind.	Ser.	Agr.	Ind.	Ser.
Dominican Republic République dominicaine	*2005	14.5	22.3	63.3	20.5	26.6	52.9	2.4	13.5	84.1
	*2010	14.6	18.1	67.3	21.3	22.9	55.8	2.7	9.7	87.5
	*2017	13.1	16.9	70.0	19.2	21.7	59.0	2.5	8.7	88.8
Ecuador Équateur	*2005	8.3	21.2	70.5	10.9	27.1	62.0	4.2	11.9	83.9
	*2010	27.3	18.1	54.6	31.1	22.4	46.5	21.0	11.1	67.9
	*2017	25.7	19.2	55.1	28.8	24.4	46.7	20.5	10.5	69.0
Egypt Égypte	*2005	30.9	21.4	47.6	27.6	25.0	47.5	46.6	4.9	48.6
	*2010	28.8	25.9	45.3	25.0	30.8	44.2	44.5	5.8	49.7
	*2017	25.4	25.3	49.3	21.5	30.3	48.2	41.1	5.2	53.8
El Salvador El Salvador	*2005	20.0	22.3	57.7	30.8	23.8	45.4	4.8	20.2	75.0
	*2010	20.8	21.5	57.7	31.9	23.6	44.5	5.4	18.6	76.0
	*2017	18.6	20.2	61.2	29.8	22.6	47.6	4.2	17.1	78.7
Equatorial Guinea Guinée équatoriale	*2005	16.8	17.3	65.9	3.5	25.6	71.0	36.2	5.2	58.6
	*2010	16.9	20.4	62.7	3.8	30.9	65.3	35.6	5.5	58.9
	*2017	18.8	18.0	63.2	5.0	27.6	67.4	37.8	4.7	57.5
Eritrea Érythrée	*2005	61.1	6.5	32.4	49.1	11.3	39.6	74.8	0.9	24.3
	*2010	61.2	6.6	32.2	50.2	11.5	38.3	73.8	1.0	25.3
	*2017	57.0	7.6	35.4	45.7	13.3	40.9	69.8	1.0	29.1
Estonia Estonie	*2005	5.2	34.1	60.7	7.2	44.0	48.8	3.2	24.1	72.7
	*2010	4.2	30.6	65.2	5.7	43.6	50.6	2.7	18.1	79.2
	*2017	3.8	29.0	67.3	5.2	40.3	54.5	2.2	17.0	80.8
Ethiopia Éthiopie	*2005	46.7	13.6	39.8	51.1	15.4	33.5	41.4	11.4	47.3
	*2010	66.8	9.1	24.1	73.9	9.0	17.1	58.3	9.2	32.5
	*2017	70.5	8.4	21.1	77.9	8.0	14.1	61.7	8.8	29.5
Faroe Islands [3,6] Îles Féroé [3,6]	2005	11.1	22.2	66.7	20.0	33.3	53.3	8.3	8.3	83.3
Fiji Fidji	*2005	23.3	3.0	73.7	23.3	3.5	73.1	23.3	1.8	74.8
	*2010	23.0	3.0	74.0	22.0	3.6	74.4	25.2	1.8	73.0
	*2017	21.3	2.9	75.8	20.7	3.5	75.8	22.4	1.6	76.0
Finland Finlande	*2005	4.8	25.8	69.4	6.6	38.3	55.1	2.9	12.3	84.8
	*2010	4.4	23.3	72.3	6.0	35.7	58.3	2.8	10.0	87.3
	*2017	4.2	22.0	73.8	6.0	34.4	59.6	2.3	8.7	89.0
France France	*2005	3.6	23.8	72.6	4.8	33.8	61.4	2.3	12.0	85.7
	*2010	2.9	22.2	74.9	3.9	33.0	63.1	1.8	10.1	88.1
	*2017	2.7	20.5	76.8	3.7	30.4	65.9	1.6	9.7	88.7
French Guiana [8,11] Guyane française [8,11]	2010	...	14.1	51.5	...	...	...	...	...	...
	2012	...	14.9	58.3	...	...	...	...	...	...
French Polynesia Polynésie française	*2005	9.1	17.5	73.4	11.7	24.3	64.0	5.0	7.4	87.7
	*2010	9.6	17.5	72.9	12.0	24.5	63.5	6.0	7.2	86.8
	*2017	8.9	16.9	74.2	11.3	24.2	64.6	5.5	6.4	88.1
Gabon Gabon	*2005	26.7	14.1	59.2	15.8	22.3	62.0	40.2	4.1	55.8
	*2010	17.9	17.5	64.6	10.9	24.7	64.4	30.1	4.8	65.1
	*2017	16.2	19.1	64.8	9.2	27.9	62.9	27.0	5.4	67.7
Gambia Gambie	*2005	40.3	9.5	50.2	30.2	14.8	55.0	54.7	1.8	43.5
	*2010	34.4	11.7	53.8	23.8	18.6	57.6	49.3	2.2	48.5
	*2017	30.4	14.4	55.3	21.7	22.6	55.7	42.4	3.0	54.6
Georgia Géorgie	*2005	54.4	9.2	36.4	51.7	13.6	34.6	57.3	4.3	38.4
	*2010	49.1	10.4	40.5	47.7	16.4	35.9	50.7	3.6	45.7
	*2017	44.7	11.2	44.1	43.9	17.8	38.2	45.5	3.6	50.9
Germany Allemagne	*2005	2.4	29.8	67.8	2.9	41.0	56.1	1.7	16.0	82.3
	*2010	1.6	28.4	70.0	2.0	40.2	57.8	1.2	14.3	84.5
	*2017	1.4	27.5	71.2	1.7	39.5	58.8	1.0	13.6	85.5
Ghana Ghana	*2005	59.3	13.2	27.5	61.6	14.0	24.4	56.9	12.4	30.7
	*2010	53.4	13.1	33.5	57.3	14.5	28.2	49.5	11.8	38.7
	*2017	41.9	14.2	43.8	45.5	17.9	36.5	38.3	10.5	51.2
Greece Grèce	*2005	12.2	22.4	65.5	11.3	30.1	58.6	13.5	9.9	76.6
	*2010	12.5	19.6	67.9	12.4	27.6	60.0	12.7	7.9	79.4
	*2017	12.9	15.0	72.1	13.3	20.2	66.5	12.2	7.5	80.4
Greenland [11,12] Groenland [11,12]	2011	4.6	12.6	82.5	8.1	20.3	71.3	0.3	3.3	96.2
Guadeloupe [8,11] Guadeloupe [8,11]	2010	...	13.8	64.4	...	...	...	...	...	...
	2012	3.3	13.5	65.5	...	...	...	...	...	...

18 Employment by economic activity *(continued)*

Percentage of persons employed by sex and ISIC 4 categories; agriculture (agr.), industry (ind.) and services (ser.)

Emploi par activité économique *(suite)*

Personnes employées par sexe et branches de la CITI rév. 4; agriculture (agr.), industrie (ind.) et services (ser.), pourcentage

Region, country or area [&] / Région, pays ou zone [&]	Year / Année	Male and Female / Hommes et femmes			Male / Hommes			Female / Femmes		
		Agr.	Ind.	Ser.	Agr.	Ind.	Ser.	Agr.	Ind.	Ser.
Guam / Guam	*2005	0.4	12.6	87.1	0.3	17.1	82.6	0.4	6.6	92.9
	*2010	0.3	13.8	85.9	0.2	19.0	80.7	0.3	6.9	92.7
	*2017	0.2	14.0	85.7	0.2	19.5	80.2	0.3	6.9	92.8
Guatemala / Guatemala	*2005	36.7	21.2	42.2	49.8	20.7	29.5	13.3	22.1	64.6
	*2010	38.8	19.5	41.7	51.5	19.2	29.3	14.9	20.1	65.0
	*2017	32.0	18.5	49.4	44.3	19.7	36.0	9.2	16.4	74.4
Guernsey / Guernesey	2013	1.5	13.6	84.8	1.0	12.2	40.9	0.5	1.4	44.3
Guinea / Guinée	*2005	74.5	5.6	19.9	69.5	9.2	21.3	80.9	1.0	18.2
	*2010	74.3	5.8	19.9	68.2	9.7	22.1	81.8	0.9	17.3
	*2017	69.7	7.4	22.9	62.3	13.0	24.6	77.6	1.3	21.0
Guinea-Bissau / Guinée-Bissau	*2005	63.6	5.3	31.1	52.8	8.9	38.3	76.3	1.0	22.7
	*2010	62.4	5.3	32.3	51.2	9.1	39.8	75.5	1.0	23.6
	*2017	60.1	5.8	34.1	49.4	9.9	40.7	72.3	1.1	26.6
Guyana / Guyana	*2005	22.5	23.3	54.1	29.8	29.0	41.2	6.6	11.2	82.2
	*2010	20.7	25.9	53.3	26.4	32.5	41.1	8.9	12.2	78.9
	*2017	18.4	25.4	56.2	23.9	33.0	43.1	7.5	10.2	82.3
Haiti / Haïti	*2005	50.5	10.6	39.0	62.7	13.7	23.7	36.1	6.9	57.0
	*2010	49.8	10.6	39.6	60.8	14.1	25.1	37.1	6.4	56.5
	*2017	46.9	12.6	40.6	57.2	16.6	26.2	35.1	7.9	57.0
Honduras / Honduras	*2005	36.7	19.5	43.8	47.9	19.0	33.1	10.8	20.7	68.5
	*2010	35.0	18.9	46.1	47.5	18.2	34.3	10.8	20.5	68.7
	*2017	29.4	21.6	49.0	41.6	22.0	36.4	7.2	20.8	72.0
Hungary / Hongrie	*2005	4.9	32.5	62.7	6.7	41.9	51.4	2.6	21.2	76.2
	*2010	4.5	30.7	64.8	6.4	40.2	53.4	2.3	19.6	78.1
	*2017	4.3	29.8	65.9	5.8	39.6	54.5	2.5	18.2	79.3
Iceland / Islande	*2005	6.5	21.7	71.7	9.6	31.5	58.9	3.0	10.7	86.3
	*2010	5.5	18.4	76.0	8.5	28.2	63.3	2.2	7.7	90.1
	*2017	4.0	17.7	78.2	6.0	27.2	66.8	1.9	7.3	90.8
India / Inde	*2005	55.8	19.0	25.2	49.5	20.9	29.6	71.1	14.4	14.6
	*2010	51.0	22.5	26.5	46.2	24.0	29.8	65.4	17.8	16.8
	*2017	44.3	24.5	31.2	39.3	26.4	34.3	59.9	18.3	21.8
Indonesia / Indonésie	*2005	43.3	17.9	38.9	42.3	19.7	38.0	45.0	14.6	40.4
	*2010	38.7	18.4	42.9	38.9	21.0	40.0	38.4	14.0	47.6
	*2017	31.4	22.4	46.2	32.2	26.5	41.3	30.1	15.7	54.2
Iran (Islamic Republic of) / Iran (Rép. islamique d')	*2005	24.7	30.4	44.9	22.7	30.9	46.4	33.4	28.4	38.2
	*2010	19.2	32.2	48.6	17.5	33.8	48.8	28.0	24.4	47.6
	*2017	16.6	32.5	50.9	15.9	34.1	50.1	20.5	24.5	55.0
Iraq / Iraq	*2005	22.6	18.3	59.1	18.0	20.6	61.4	49.6	5.0	45.5
	*2010	22.4	18.8	58.9	17.8	21.6	60.7	47.8	3.3	48.9
	*2017	20.4	21.0	58.6	16.1	24.2	59.7	43.7	3.9	52.3
Ireland / Irlande	*2005	5.9	27.6	66.5	9.3	39.2	51.5	1.3	11.9	86.8
	*2010	4.5	19.5	76.0	7.5	28.7	63.8	1.0	8.7	90.3
	*2017	4.8	17.7	77.4	7.7	26.4	65.9	1.3	7.0	91.7
Isle of Man [4] / Île de Man [4]	2001	1.4	16.1	82.5	2.2	25.0	72.9	0.5	5.5	94.0
	2006	1.9	14.8	83.3	2.9	24.0	73.0	0.7	3.9	95.4
Israel / Israël	*2005	2.0	21.6	76.4	3.1	31.0	65.9	0.8	10.4	88.8
	*2010	1.6	20.2	78.1	2.4	29.6	68.0	0.8	9.5	89.8
	*2017	1.0	17.9	81.0	1.5	26.8	71.8	0.6	7.8	91.6
Italy / Italie	*2005	4.2	30.7	65.1	4.8	39.2	56.0	3.3	17.4	79.4
	*2010	3.8	28.7	67.5	4.5	38.5	57.0	2.8	14.1	83.1
	*2017	3.5	27.1	69.4	4.4	36.7	58.9	2.3	13.5	84.2
Jamaica / Jamaïque	*2005	18.4	18.0	63.6	25.3	27.1	47.7	9.0	5.5	85.5
	*2010	20.2	15.9	63.8	28.4	22.6	49.0	9.3	6.9	83.8
	*2017	17.9	15.3	66.8	25.3	22.4	52.3	7.8	5.8	86.4
Japan / Japon	*2005	4.5	28.3	67.2	4.5	35.6	59.9	4.6	17.9	77.5
	*2010	4.1	26.1	69.8	4.3	34.3	61.5	3.9	15.1	81.0
	*2017	3.7	26.5	69.8	3.9	35.0	61.1	3.3	15.4	81.3
Jersey / Jersey	2013	4.1	11.7	70.2	...	...	...	...	...	...
Jordan / Jordanie	*2005	3.4	20.7	75.9	3.6	22.0	74.4	2.0	11.0	87.0
	*2010	2.0	18.7	79.3	2.2	20.5	77.3	1.0	9.2	89.8
	*2017	2.0	17.8	80.2	2.2	19.5	78.3	0.9	8.5	90.6

18 Employment by economic activity *(continued)*

Percentage of persons employed by sex and ISIC 4 categories; agriculture (agr.), industry (ind.) and services (ser.)

Emploi par activité économique *(suite)*

Personnes employées par sexe et branches de la CITI rév. 4; agriculture (agr.), industrie (ind.) et services (ser.), pourcentage

Region, country or area & Région, pays ou zone &	Year Année	Male and Female Hommes et femmes Agr.	Ind.	Ser.	Male Hommes Agr.	Ind.	Ser.	Female Femmes Agr.	Ind.	Ser.
Kazakhstan Kazakhstan	*2005	32.4	17.9	49.7	33.5	24.5	42.0	31.3	10.9	57.8
	*2010	28.3	18.7	53.0	29.1	25.6	45.3	27.4	11.4	61.2
	*2017	18.1	20.4	61.6	19.0	29.0	52.0	17.1	11.2	71.7
Kenya Kenya	*2005	66.3	7.4	26.3	56.7	11.2	32.0	77.7	2.7	19.5
	*2010	64.8	8.0	27.2	54.9	12.2	32.9	77.0	2.8	20.2
	*2017	61.9	8.6	29.5	50.9	13.6	35.5	75.0	2.6	22.4
Kiribati Kiribati	2005[6]	7.1	8.4	81.1	8.7	10.9	77.3	4.7	4.5	87.8
	2010	22.1	16.1	61.8	32.1	9.1	58.8	9.0	25.3	65.7
Kosovo [11,13] Kosovo [11,13]	2012	4.6	28.4	67.1	4.3	33.3	62.3	5.4	10.1	84.7
Kuwait Koweït	*2005	2.7	21.2	76.1	3.6	27.3	69.1	0.1	3.4	96.5
	*2010	2.5	25.9	71.6	3.5	34.2	62.3	0.1	5.5	94.4
	*2017	2.6	27.3	70.1	3.7	36.2	60.1	0.1	6.2	93.7
Kyrgyzstan Kirghizistan	*2005	38.5	17.6	43.9	39.3	23.0	37.6	37.3	10.2	52.4
	*2010	29.1	23.5	47.3	31.0	29.4	39.7	26.6	15.3	58.2
	*2017	29.2	21.0	49.8	27.6	27.7	44.7	31.6	10.8	57.6
Lao People's Dem. Rep. Rép. dém. populaire lao	*2005	83.4	3.5	13.1	79.4	4.5	16.1	87.2	2.5	10.3
	*2010	81.9	3.5	14.6	77.3	4.9	17.8	86.2	2.3	11.5
	*2017	78.3	4.0	17.7	73.3	5.7	21.1	83.2	2.3	14.5
Latvia Lettonie	*2005	12.1	26.5	61.5	15.9	35.2	48.9	8.0	17.2	74.8
	*2010	8.8	24.0	67.1	12.0	34.8	53.1	5.9	14.2	79.9
	*2017	7.3	23.0	69.7	10.3	34.1	55.6	4.2	12.0	83.8
Lebanon Liban	*2005	8.5	16.6	74.9	10.7	20.2	69.2	0.2	3.3	96.6
	*2010	8.0	17.3	74.7	10.1	21.0	68.8	0.2	3.5	96.3
	*2017	8.2	22.4	69.4	10.7	27.4	61.9	0.2	6.5	93.2
Lesotho Lesotho	*2005	53.2	14.1	32.7	63.0	13.6	23.3	39.3	14.7	46.1
	*2010	42.0	20.2	37.9	51.8	20.2	28.0	29.1	20.1	50.8
	*2017	39.7	20.0	40.3	48.8	21.9	29.4	27.5	17.4	55.1
Liberia Libéria	*2005	52.5	6.8	40.7	54.3	9.7	36.0	50.6	3.8	45.7
	*2010	47.3	10.6	42.0	47.3	15.5	37.2	47.4	5.3	47.3
	*2017	45.3	11.7	43.0	44.4	17.4	38.2	46.4	5.4	48.2
Libya Libye	*2005	14.9	25.6	59.5	11.9	26.4	61.8	25.3	23.1	51.6
	*2010	14.2	28.5	57.3	10.8	29.8	59.4	25.2	24.3	50.5
	*2017	19.1	25.1	55.8	16.5	25.1	58.4	27.5	25.2	47.3
Lithuania Lituanie	*2005	14.3	29.1	56.7	16.9	37.0	46.1	11.5	20.8	67.7
	*2010	9.0	24.6	66.4	11.5	33.5	55.0	6.8	16.5	76.7
	*2017	8.7	24.5	66.8	11.1	33.5	55.4	6.4	15.5	78.1
Luxembourg Luxembourg	*2005	1.7	17.3	81.0	2.2	25.5	72.3	1.1	5.8	93.1
	*2010	1.1	13.3	85.6	1.3	19.8	78.9	0.7	4.8	94.5
	*2017	1.3	10.2	88.5	1.8	15.2	83.0	0.8	3.7	95.5
Madagascar Madagascar	*2005	81.5	3.4	15.1	81.4	5.1	13.6	81.6	1.6	16.8
	*2010	79.6	5.2	15.2	79.0	7.7	13.3	80.2	2.6	17.1
	*2017	74.2	9.4	16.5	72.1	13.9	14.0	76.4	4.5	19.1
Malawi Malawi	*2005	72.4	4.3	23.2	62.7	7.4	29.9	82.9	1.0	16.1
	*2010	70.5	4.8	24.7	60.0	8.6	31.4	80.5	1.1	18.4
	*2017	69.9	4.8	25.4	59.0	8.5	32.4	80.6	1.1	18.4
Malaysia Malaisie	*2005	14.6	29.8	55.6	17.1	32.8	50.1	10.1	24.4	65.5
	*2010	14.2	27.7	58.1	17.2	31.8	51.0	9.0	20.6	70.4
	*2017	11.8	27.3	60.9	14.6	32.8	52.7	7.5	18.8	73.6
Maldives Maldives	*2005	13.3	27.4	59.3	16.4	21.1	62.5	8.5	37.2	54.3
	*2010	15.0	16.1	68.8	20.7	15.7	63.6	7.2	16.7	76.1
	*2017	7.7	22.8	69.5	10.6	24.4	64.9	3.7	20.4	75.8
Mali Mali	*2005	51.2	14.8	34.0	56.9	15.1	27.9	40.0	14.3	45.7
	*2010	58.9	13.8	27.3	61.5	15.0	23.5	54.6	11.7	33.7
	*2017	56.7	14.7	28.6	59.9	15.5	24.6	51.2	13.2	35.6
Malta Malte	*2005	2.1	29.8	68.1	2.7	35.5	61.8	0.6	16.8	82.6
	*2010	1.3	25.2	73.5	1.8	31.3	66.9	0.4	12.8	86.8
	*2017	1.2	20.9	77.9	1.7	27.9	70.4	0.4	9.3	90.4
Marshall Islands [4] Îles Marshall [4]	#2010	11.0	9.4	79.6	...	...	...	...	...	...
Martinique [8,11] Martinique [8,11]	2010	4.1	11.9	65.3	...	...	...	...	...	...
	2012	3.9	11.8	69.0	...	...	...	...	...	...

Employment by economic activity *(continued)*

Percentage of persons employed by sex and ISIC 4 categories; agriculture (agr.), industry (ind.) and services (ser.)

Emploi par activité économique *(suite)*

Personnes employées par sexe et branches de la CITI rév. 4; agriculture (agr.), industrie (ind.) et services (ser.), pourcentage

Region, country or area & / Région, pays ou zone &	Year / Année	Male and Female / Hommes et femmes			Male / Hommes			Female / Femmes		
		Agr.	Ind.	Ser.	Agr.	Ind.	Ser.	Agr.	Ind.	Ser.
Mauritania / Mauritanie	*2005	48.4	9.0	42.5	40.3	12.1	47.6	68.2	1.4	30.3
	*2010	44.1	9.2	46.7	35.1	12.4	52.5	65.1	1.7	33.2
	*2017	40.3	9.5	50.2	31.1	12.9	56.0	61.6	1.5	36.9
Mauritius / Maurice	*2005	10.0	32.5	57.5	10.6	34.2	55.2	8.9	28.9	62.3
	*2010	8.5	28.8	62.7	9.1	32.8	58.1	7.4	21.6	71.0
	*2017	7.3	25.2	67.5	8.3	30.5	61.3	5.7	16.5	77.7
Mexico / Mexique	*2005	15.0	25.8	59.2	20.3	29.5	50.2	4.7	18.8	76.5
	*2010	13.1	25.5	61.5	18.3	30.0	51.7	3.8	17.3	78.9
	*2017	13.4	25.2	61.3	19.2	30.3	50.6	3.7	16.6	79.7
Mongolia / Mongolie	*2005	47.9	11.3	40.8	50.1	12.9	37.0	45.4	9.4	45.2
	*2010	33.5	16.2	50.2	34.8	20.2	45.1	32.1	11.6	56.3
	*2017	28.4	20.7	51.0	29.2	26.9	43.9	27.4	13.5	59.1
Montenegro / Monténégro	*2005	8.6	19.2	72.1	8.5	26.5	65.0	8.8	9.6	81.6
	*2010	6.8	18.6	74.7	8.7	26.0	65.3	4.1	8.6	87.3
	*2017	7.5	17.3	75.2	7.1	25.3	67.6	8.0	6.9	85.0
Morocco / Maroc	*2005	40.3	18.4	41.3	41.5	18.8	39.7	37.2	17.2	45.6
	*2010	36.3	20.0	43.7	36.9	21.4	41.8	34.5	16.3	49.1
	*2017	32.6	20.7	46.8	32.7	22.5	44.8	32.4	15.4	52.2
Mozambique / Mozambique	*2005	76.4	3.7	20.0	65.6	7.5	26.9	86.0	0.3	13.7
	*2010	75.5	3.8	20.7	63.6	7.8	28.6	86.1	0.2	13.6
	*2017	75.0	4.1	21.0	63.3	8.4	28.3	85.3	0.2	14.4
Myanmar / Myanmar	*2005	44.0	11.7	44.3	37.6	10.9	51.5	50.5	12.5	37.0
	*2010	38.3	13.8	48.0	31.5	12.7	55.8	45.0	14.8	40.1
	*2017	23.6	14.6	61.7	16.5	17.0	66.5	30.9	12.2	56.9
Namibia / Namibie	*2005	35.6	13.4	51.0	38.3	17.9	43.9	32.3	8.1	59.6
	*2010	31.7	12.7	55.5	32.9	19.2	47.9	30.4	5.6	64.0
	*2017	29.1	14.6	56.3	30.5	23.3	46.2	27.5	5.0	67.5
Nepal / Népal	*2005	71.6	11.9	16.6	62.3	14.6	23.1	81.1	9.0	9.8
	*2010	74.3	10.5	15.2	63.8	14.6	21.6	84.7	6.4	8.9
	*2017	72.6	10.9	16.5	61.7	15.5	22.9	83.1	6.5	10.4
Netherlands / Pays-Bas	*2005	3.3	20.5	76.1	4.3	30.2	65.5	2.2	8.5	89.3
	*2010	3.1	17.6	79.3	4.2	26.8	69.0	1.8	6.6	91.6
	*2017	2.2	15.9	81.9	2.9	24.4	72.8	1.4	5.7	92.9
Netherlands Antilles [former] / Antilles néerlandaises [anc.]	2009	0.8	16.0	83.2	1.6	28.2	70.1	0.2	4.4	95.4
	2011	0.7	15.3	84.0	1.4	27.7	71.0	0.2	4.1	95.7
	2013	0.2	15.9	83.2	...	...	...	...	...	...
New Caledonia / Nouvelle-Calédonie	*2005	3.8	26.1	70.1	4.7	35.0	60.4	2.5	12.2	85.3
	*2010	3.4	27.4	69.2	4.1	36.2	59.7	2.3	13.4	84.4
	*2017	3.0	26.9	70.1	3.6	36.1	60.3	2.0	12.4	85.6
New Zealand / Nouvelle-Zélande	*2005	7.1	22.2	70.7	9.0	32.1	59.0	5.0	10.6	84.4
	*2010	6.9	21.0	72.2	9.0	30.7	60.2	4.4	9.8	85.8
	*2017	5.9	21.4	72.6	7.9	32.1	60.0	3.7	9.7	86.6
Nicaragua / Nicaragua	*2005	29.0	19.6	51.4	41.1	20.0	39.0	8.1	19.0	72.8
	*2010	27.4	14.0	58.7	38.0	15.8	46.2	10.1	11.0	78.9
	*2017	24.1	14.5	61.4	34.8	17.1	48.2	7.9	10.4	81.7
Niger / Niger	*2005	64.2	13.0	22.8	66.7	8.9	24.4	58.7	22.1	19.3
	*2010	64.0	13.8	22.3	67.6	9.1	23.3	55.9	23.9	20.2
	*2017	62.3	14.4	23.3	66.3	9.5	24.2	53.6	24.9	21.5
Nigeria / Nigéria	*2005	47.0	10.2	42.8	52.6	10.4	37.0	39.3	9.9	50.8
	*2010	30.6	14.1	55.3	39.2	13.6	47.1	18.6	14.8	66.5
	*2017	27.9	14.7	57.4	37.6	14.1	48.3	14.5	15.5	70.0
Niue [4] / Nioué [4]	2001	9.0	20.4	70.1	11.4	28.7	59.4	5.8	8.7	85.1
	#2002	4.8	9.3	85.9	...	...	...	...	...	...
Northern Mariana Islands [3,6] / Îles Marianne du Nord [3,6]	#2000	1.5	47.2	45.8	...	...	...	...	...	...
Norway / Norvège	*2005	3.3	20.9	75.8	4.8	32.4	62.8	1.6	8.0	90.4
	*2010	2.5	19.7	77.8	3.9	31.1	65.0	1.0	7.0	92.0
	*2017	2.2	20.2	77.6	3.3	31.7	65.0	1.0	7.3	91.7
Oman / Oman	*2005	9.5	24.6	66.0	10.9	26.7	62.4	1.4	11.7	86.9
	*2010	5.1	36.8	58.1	5.8	41.7	52.5	0.4	5.4	94.2
	*2017	5.0	39.6	55.4	5.5	43.4	51.0	0.4	4.9	94.7
Pakistan / Pakistan	*2005	43.4	20.5	36.1	38.7	21.6	39.6	66.7	15.0	18.2
	*2010	45.0	19.1	35.9	38.0	21.4	40.6	72.2	10.2	17.6
	*2017	42.1	19.8	38.1	34.9	22.4	42.7	68.9	10.2	20.9

18

Employment by economic activity *(continued)*

Percentage of persons employed by sex and ISIC 4 categories; agriculture (agr.), industry (ind.) and services (ser.)

Emploi par activité économique *(suite)*

Personnes employées par sexe et branches de la CITI rév. 4; agriculture (agr.), industrie (ind.) et services (ser.), pourcentage

Region, country or area & Région, pays ou zone &	Year Année	Male and Female Hommes et femmes			Male Hommes			Female Femmes		
		Agr.	Ind.	Ser.	Agr.	Ind.	Ser.	Agr.	Ind.	Ser.
Palau [3]	2000[6]	7.1	13.8	79.1	9.6	20.7	69.7	3.1	2.6	94.4
Palaos [3]	2008[4]	2.4	11.8	85.9	...	...	...	...	...	...
Panama	*2005	15.7	17.3	67.0	22.0	21.7	56.2	4.2	9.3	86.5
Panama	*2010	17.4	18.7	63.9	23.1	23.9	53.0	7.5	9.7	82.8
	*2017	14.5	19.6	65.9	18.9	26.0	55.1	7.4	9.2	83.5
Papua New Guinea	*2005	73.5	3.8	22.7	67.4	5.6	27.0	80.1	1.9	18.1
Papouasie-Nvl-Guinée	*2010	72.8	4.5	22.7	65.1	7.1	27.8	81.1	1.7	17.2
	*2017	68.3	5.7	26.0	61.0	9.3	29.6	75.9	1.9	22.2
Paraguay	*2005	31.9	15.6	52.5	38.0	19.7	42.3	21.9	8.8	69.3
Paraguay	*2010	26.8	18.8	54.3	31.6	25.1	43.3	19.1	8.5	72.4
	*2017	19.6	19.5	61.0	23.8	26.1	50.1	13.1	9.5	77.4
Peru	*2005	1.6	24.4	74.0	2.0	31.8	66.2	1.2	14.1	84.8
Pérou	*2010	25.7	17.7	56.6	28.0	23.3	48.8	22.8	10.6	66.6
	*2017	24.4	17.3	58.3	28.2	23.7	48.1	19.6	9.4	71.0
Philippines	*2005	35.9	15.6	48.5	43.6	17.8	38.6	23.7	12.0	64.3
Philippines	*2010	33.2	15.0	51.8	40.5	18.2	41.3	21.7	9.9	68.4
	*2017	27.7	16.3	56.1	34.1	20.5	45.3	17.6	9.7	72.7
Poland	*2005	17.4	29.2	53.4	18.0	39.0	43.0	16.6	17.1	66.3
Pologne	*2010	12.8	30.1	57.1	13.1	41.6	45.4	12.4	16.0	71.6
	*2017	10.9	29.6	59.5	11.9	41.2	46.9	9.7	15.5	74.8
Portugal	*2005	12.1	30.4	57.6	11.2	40.6	48.2	13.1	18.4	68.5
Portugal	*2010	10.9	27.7	61.4	11.0	38.0	51.0	10.7	16.3	72.9
	*2017	8.0	23.8	68.2	10.1	32.5	57.4	5.8	14.6	79.6
Puerto Rico	*2005	2.2	20.1	77.7	3.6	29.5	66.9	0.2	7.0	92.8
Porto Rico	*2010	1.8	16.9	81.3	3.1	25.6	71.3	0.1	5.9	94.0
	*2017	2.0	17.5	80.5	3.4	26.2	70.4	0.1	6.3	93.6
Qatar	*2005	2.8	41.4	55.8	3.2	48.1	48.7	0.1	4.0	95.9
Qatar	*2010	1.5	56.8	41.8	1.7	63.8	34.6	~0.0	5.8	94.2
	*2017	1.2	54.1	44.7	1.4	62.7	35.8	0.2	6.4	93.4
Republic of Korea	*2005	7.9	26.8	65.3	7.2	33.9	58.9	8.9	16.6	74.5
République de Corée	*2010	6.6	24.9	68.5	6.4	32.5	61.2	6.9	14.4	78.7
	*2017	5.0	24.7	70.3	4.9	32.8	62.3	5.1	13.3	81.6
Republic of Moldova	*2005	32.9	32.5	34.6	34.4	27.6	37.9	31.5	37.0	31.5
République de Moldova	*2010	27.5	32.2	40.3	32.4	28.0	39.6	22.5	36.4	41.1
	*2017	28.8	30.9	40.3	32.4	27.6	40.0	24.9	34.4	40.7
Réunion [8]	2010[11]	4.2	14.1	67.1	...	...	...	...	...	...
Réunion [8]	#2012	4.3	12.7	81.7	6.3	20.0	72.0	2.1	4.1	93.0
Romania	*2005	32.3	30.5	37.3	31.7	35.2	33.2	33.1	24.8	42.2
Roumanie	*2010	30.1	28.6	41.3	29.0	35.5	35.5	31.4	20.1	48.5
	*2017	25.5	27.7	46.8	25.7	34.6	39.6	25.2	19.2	55.5
Russian Federation	*2005	10.1	29.8	60.1	12.2	38.2	49.6	7.9	21.3	70.7
Fédération de Russie	*2010	7.9	27.7	64.4	10.0	37.3	52.7	5.7	17.8	76.5
	*2017	6.8	27.1	66.1	8.3	37.5	54.2	5.2	16.3	78.6
Rwanda	*2005	77.9	3.8	18.3	67.3	6.9	25.8	86.8	1.1	12.1
Rwanda	*2010	77.9	5.5	16.5	66.6	10.5	22.9	87.5	1.4	11.2
	*2017	75.0	7.2	17.8	61.2	14.0	24.9	86.7	1.5	11.8
Saint Helena [4,14]										
Sainte-Hélène [4,14]	2008	7.3	20.0	72.7	11.8	33.9	54.3	1.7	2.9	95.4
Saint Kitts and Nevis [6]										
Saint-Kitts-et-Nevis [6]	#2001	0.2	48.8	42.1	0.4	51.6	34.7	0.1	45.5	50.6
Saint Lucia	*2005	13.8	20.3	65.9	17.9	27.8	54.4	8.6	10.8	80.5
Sainte-Lucie	*2010	14.7	18.7	66.6	18.8	26.8	54.5	9.5	8.2	82.3
	*2017	14.8	17.6	67.6	18.9	25.7	55.4	9.7	7.5	82.8
Saint Vincent & Grenadines	*2005	19.3	18.1	62.7	25.0	26.9	48.1	10.7	5.0	84.2
Saint-Vincent-Grenadines	*2010	23.7	17.1	59.2	29.7	26.0	44.2	15.0	4.0	81.0
	*2017	22.1	16.1	61.8	28.4	25.1	46.5	13.5	3.7	82.8
Samoa	*2005	29.4	35.5	35.0	38.8	26.4	34.8	4.6	59.7	35.7
Samoa	*2010	38.6	13.5	47.9	44.6	14.1	41.3	22.2	11.9	65.9
	*2017	5.3	14.8	79.8	6.1	17.7	76.2	3.2	7.2	89.6
San Marino	2005[4]	0.5	39.3	60.2	0.6	50.4	49.1	0.3	23.4	76.3
Saint-Marin	#2010	0.3	34.3	65.4	0.4	45.6	54.0	0.2	18.7	81.1
Sao Tome and Principe	*2005	27.9	17.2	54.9	34.7	24.7	40.6	15.9	3.9	80.3
Sao Tomé-et-Principe	*2010	25.8	15.8	58.5	30.3	21.3	48.5	17.9	6.1	76.1
	*2017	22.2	13.5	64.3	26.0	18.6	55.4	15.4	4.8	79.8

18 Employment by economic activity *(continued)*

Percentage of persons employed by sex and ISIC 4 categories; agriculture (agr.), industry (ind.) and services (ser.)

Emploi par activité économique *(suite)*

Personnes employées par sexe et branches de la CITI rév. 4; agriculture (agr.), industrie (ind.) et services (ser.), pourcentage

Region, country or area & Région, pays ou zone &	Year Année	Male and Female Hommes et femmes Agr.	Ind.	Ser.	Male Hommes Agr.	Ind.	Ser.	Female Femmes Agr.	Ind.	Ser.
Saudi Arabia Arabie saoudite	*2005	4.1	20.3	75.6	4.6	23.0	72.3	0.4	1.0	98.6
	*2010	4.3	21.7	74.0	4.8	24.7	70.5	0.2	1.5	98.3
	*2017	5.9	22.7	71.4	6.7	25.9	67.5	0.5	1.5	98.0
Senegal Sénégal	*2005	41.0	16.8	42.1	41.3	22.3	36.4	40.5	6.1	53.4
	*2010	55.5	21.0	23.5	51.1	28.0	20.9	62.5	10.0	27.6
	*2017	51.4	20.7	27.9	48.0	28.0	24.0	56.7	9.5	33.9
Serbia Serbie	*2005	23.3	27.6	49.1	23.3	34.3	42.4	23.3	17.6	59.1
	*2010	22.2	26.0	51.8	23.2	33.3	43.5	20.8	16.0	63.2
	*2017	19.4	24.5	56.1	21.8	30.2	48.0	16.2	16.9	66.8
Seychelles [8,15] Seychelles [8,15]	2011	3.6	17.9	78.2	6.4	25.3	68.1	0.7	10.4	88.5
Sierra Leone Sierra Leone	*2005	68.4	6.4	25.2	65.6	10.6	23.9	71.1	2.5	26.5
	*2010	68.7	6.4	25.0	66.5	10.2	23.3	70.8	2.5	26.6
	*2017	68.0	6.5	25.5	65.0	10.6	24.4	71.0	2.3	26.7
Singapore Singapour	*2005	0.4	22.1	77.6	0.5	25.3	74.3	0.2	17.6	82.2
	*2010	0.3	21.4	78.3	0.5	25.5	74.0	0.2	16.0	83.8
	*2017	0.3	17.0	82.6	0.5	21.0	78.5	0.2	12.0	87.8
Slovakia Slovaquie	*2005	4.8	38.8	56.4	6.4	49.6	43.9	2.6	25.2	72.1
	*2010	3.2	37.0	59.8	4.3	49.9	45.7	1.8	21.1	77.1
	*2017	3.3	34.5	62.2	4.6	47.2	48.3	1.6	18.7	79.7
Slovenia Slovénie	*2005	9.1	37.1	53.8	9.1	46.9	44.0	9.1	25.4	65.5
	*2010	8.8	32.5	58.7	9.1	42.6	48.3	8.5	20.4	71.0
	*2017	8.9	29.6	61.5	9.2	40.7	50.1	8.5	16.4	75.1
Solomon Islands Îles Salomon	*2005	52.9	2.1	45.0	49.5	2.4	48.1	57.3	1.7	41.0
	*2010	51.8	2.5	45.7	48.9	2.7	48.4	55.4	2.3	42.3
	*2017	48.1	2.4	49.5	46.0	2.7	51.3	50.8	2.0	47.2
Somalia Somalie	*2005	72.6	4.7	22.7	67.3	6.3	26.4	85.0	0.9	14.1
	*2010	72.4	4.7	22.8	67.1	6.4	26.5	84.7	0.9	14.4
	*2017	72.0	4.8	23.2	66.6	6.5	26.9	84.2	1.0	14.8
South Africa Afrique du Sud	*2005	7.1	24.4	68.5	8.5	34.0	57.5	5.4	12.1	82.5
	*2010	4.6	23.1	72.3	5.7	32.3	62.0	3.2	11.0	85.8
	*2017	6.1	26.2	67.7	8.0	36.7	55.3	3.6	12.1	84.2
Spain Espagne	*2005	5.3	29.6	65.1	6.5	41.0	52.6	3.5	12.4	84.1
	*2010	4.3	22.9	72.7	5.7	33.6	60.7	2.5	9.4	88.2
	*2017	3.9	19.2	76.8	5.5	28.3	66.2	2.0	8.1	89.9
Sri Lanka Sri Lanka	*2005	38.5	22.1	39.4	38.3	19.6	42.0	38.9	27.7	33.4
	*2010	36.6	20.2	43.2	35.6	18.0	46.4	38.9	24.8	36.3
	*2017	27.4	25.9	46.7	26.0	26.2	47.8	30.7	25.3	44.0
State of Palestine État de Palestine	*2005	14.6	26.3	59.1	10.7	30.2	59.2	32.3	8.8	58.9
	*2010	11.7	26.4	61.9	9.7	29.6	60.6	21.0	11.1	67.8
	*2017	8.7	29.8	61.5	7.6	34.1	58.3	13.3	12.5	74.2
Sudan Soudan	*2005	38.3	19.9	41.9	39.4	16.6	44.0	34.5	30.6	34.9
	*2010	34.3	20.2	45.4	36.1	17.7	46.2	28.1	29.1	42.9
	*2017	32.9	20.4	46.7	35.8	17.4	46.8	23.2	30.4	46.4
Suriname Suriname	*2005	7.3	24.4	68.3	9.0	32.7	58.3	3.9	8.6	87.5
	*2010	4.3	24.5	71.2	5.5	34.2	60.3	2.2	6.8	91.1
	*2017	3.4	22.3	74.3	4.4	31.9	63.7	1.7	4.7	93.7
Swaziland Swaziland	*2005	23.3	17.5	59.3	10.5	25.8	63.8	45.9	2.8	51.3
	*2010	22.2	17.9	59.9	8.4	26.7	64.9	44.5	3.7	51.8
	*2017	22.0	17.0	61.0	8.9	25.7	65.5	43.6	2.7	53.8
Sweden Suède	*2005	2.3	22.0	75.6	3.5	33.5	63.0	1.0	9.3	89.7
	*2010	2.1	19.9	78.0	3.1	30.8	66.1	1.0	7.5	91.5
	*2017	1.8	18.2	79.9	2.7	28.6	68.7	0.9	6.8	92.3
Switzerland Suisse	*2005	3.7	22.8	73.5	4.5	32.2	63.3	2.8	11.5	85.7
	*2010	3.5	22.2	74.4	4.2	31.7	64.0	2.6	10.8	86.7
	*2017	3.5	20.4	76.1	4.3	28.9	66.8	2.6	10.4	87.0
Syrian Arab Republic République arabe syrienne	*2005	21.6	27.4	51.0	19.5	30.8	49.6	34.0	6.9	59.1
	*2010	14.3	32.8	52.9	13.5	36.3	50.1	19.4	9.1	71.6
	*2017	18.5	39.2	42.3	16.8	42.8	40.4	30.8	12.9	56.4
Tajikistan Tadjikistan	*2005	57.0	16.3	26.7	42.9	25.6	31.5	74.6	4.7	20.7
	*2010	53.8	15.3	31.0	41.2	23.3	35.4	69.6	5.1	25.3
	*2017	57.2	13.4	29.4	45.0	21.1	33.9	72.9	3.5	23.5

18 Employment by economic activity *(continued)*

Percentage of persons employed by sex and ISIC 4 categories; agriculture (agr.), industry (ind.) and services (ser.)

Emploi par activité économique *(suite)*

Personnes employées par sexe et branches de la CITI rév. 4; agriculture (agr.), industrie (ind.) et services (ser.), pourcentage

Region, country or area & Région, pays ou zone &	Year Année	Male and Female Hommes et femmes Agr.	Ind.	Ser.	Male Hommes Agr.	Ind.	Ser.	Female Femmes Agr.	Ind.	Ser.
Thailand	*2005	42.6	20.2	37.2	44.2	21.6	34.2	40.6	18.6	40.7
Thaïlande	*2010	38.2	20.7	41.0	40.0	22.8	37.1	36.1	18.2	45.7
	*2017	34.0	22.7	43.3	35.9	25.5	38.6	31.7	19.3	49.1
TFYR of Macedonia	*2005	18.1	29.4	52.4	19.8	31.1	49.1	15.5	26.9	57.6
ex-R.Y. de Macédoine	*2010	18.0	29.4	52.7	19.4	31.4	49.2	15.6	26.2	58.2
	*2017	16.2	29.2	54.5	18.5	31.7	49.8	12.9	25.5	61.6
Timor-Leste	*2005	55.4	1.6	42.9	51.1	1.9	47.0	65.0	1.1	33.9
Timor-Leste	*2010	50.7	1.5	47.8	46.0	1.7	52.3	61.3	0.9	37.8
	*2017	50.8	2.0	47.2	45.7	2.3	52.0	61.9	1.4	36.7
Togo	*2005	64.7	8.2	27.1	57.2	10.6	32.2	71.8	6.0	22.2
Togo	*2010	63.1	8.6	28.2	57.9	10.8	31.4	68.2	6.5	25.3
	*2017	62.5	8.7	28.7	54.2	12.2	33.6	70.5	5.4	24.0
Tonga	*2005	32.0	30.0	38.0	51.3	13.1	35.6	4.6	54.0	41.5
Tonga	*2010	33.2	29.7	37.1	52.8	13.1	34.1	5.5	53.2	41.4
	*2017	33.3	28.2	38.5	53.1	12.4	34.5	5.1	50.7	44.2
Trinidad and Tobago	*2005	4.5	32.8	62.7	6.9	47.7	45.5	1.1	11.0	87.8
Trinité-et-Tobago	*2010	4.2	33.7	62.2	6.2	49.7	44.1	1.3	10.9	87.8
	*2017	4.1	31.6	64.3	6.2	47.6	46.2	1.3	9.8	88.9
Tunisia	*2005	16.4	28.6	55.1	20.2	26.3	53.6	5.5	35.1	59.3
Tunisie	*2010	15.1	29.4	55.6	18.4	27.6	53.9	4.9	34.7	60.5
	*2017	11.7	29.4	58.9	14.8	28.6	56.7	2.5	32.0	65.5
Turkey	*2005	29.4	24.8	45.8	21.7	28.1	50.1	51.0	15.3	33.7
Turquie	*2010	23.7	26.1	50.2	17.4	30.3	52.3	39.1	16.0	44.8
	*2017	19.6	27.5	52.9	15.4	32.3	52.3	29.1	16.8	54.1
Turkmenistan	*2005	22.2	35.7	42.1	23.4	33.6	43.0	20.5	38.8	40.7
Turkménistan	*2010	19.4	41.0	39.6	21.5	37.7	40.8	16.0	46.0	37.9
	*2017	17.9	37.4	44.7	18.7	36.8	44.5	16.8	38.2	45.0
Turks and Caicos Islands [4]	2005	1.4	16.8	70.9	...	...	...	...	...	...
Îles Turques-et-Caïques [4]	#2008	1.2	23.1	74.0	...	...	...	...	...	...
Uganda	*2005	73.7	5.6	20.7	67.8	8.4	23.7	79.5	2.7	17.7
Ouganda	*2010	73.7	6.9	19.4	69.9	9.4	20.7	77.6	4.4	18.0
	*2017	72.1	7.4	20.5	68.3	10.2	21.5	76.0	4.5	19.5
Ukraine	*2005	27.9	22.7	49.4	24.9	25.2	49.9	30.9	20.1	49.0
Ukraine	*2010	20.3	25.7	54.0	21.8	28.7	49.5	18.8	22.6	58.5
	*2017	15.7	24.6	59.7	18.1	27.5	54.4	13.2	21.6	65.2
United Arab Emirates	*2005	4.9	40.1	54.9	5.6	44.5	50.0	0.1	5.9	94.0
Émirats arabes unis	*2010	3.8	23.1	73.1	4.2	25.3	70.5	0.1	4.7	95.2
	*2017	3.5	21.1	75.4	4.0	23.3	72.7	0.1	4.8	95.2
United Kingdom	*2005	1.4	22.2	76.4	1.9	33.1	64.9	0.7	9.4	89.9
Royaume-Uni	*2010	1.2	19.3	79.5	1.7	29.6	68.6	0.6	7.5	91.9
	*2017	1.2	18.4	80.4	1.6	27.9	70.5	0.7	7.5	91.9
United Rep. of Tanzania	*2005	75.5	4.2	20.3	72.5	6.2	21.3	78.7	2.0	19.3
Rép.-Unie de Tanzanie	*2010	72.2	5.5	22.3	68.8	7.9	23.3	75.7	3.0	21.4
	*2017	66.9	6.4	26.7	64.3	9.4	26.3	69.8	3.0	27.2
United States of America	*2005	1.6	20.2	78.2	2.2	29.4	68.4	0.8	9.3	89.9
États-Unis d'Amérique	*2010	1.6	17.8	80.6	2.3	26.6	71.1	0.8	7.6	91.6
	*2017	1.5	17.2	81.3	2.1	25.8	72.1	0.8	7.0	92.2
United States Virgin Islands	*2005	10.1	23.9	66.1	15.1	37.8	47.1	3.7	6.2	90.1
Îles Vierges américaines	*2010	9.7	23.9	66.4	14.6	38.3	47.1	3.7	6.4	89.9
	*2017	10.9	24.0	65.2	16.3	37.8	45.9	4.3	7.1	88.6
Uruguay	*2005	11.1	23.1	65.8	15.7	30.4	54.0	4.9	13.3	81.8
Uruguay	*2010	11.6	21.4	67.0	16.5	28.8	54.7	5.1	11.8	83.2
	*2017	8.7	20.5	70.8	12.3	28.7	59.0	4.0	9.6	86.4
Uzbekistan	*2005	39.3	20.9	39.7	39.4	20.7	39.9	39.3	21.3	39.5
Ouzbékistan	*2010	32.6	23.0	44.4	34.1	24.1	41.8	30.6	21.4	48.1
	*2017	29.0	23.9	47.1	30.2	26.0	43.8	27.2	20.8	52.0
Vanuatu	*2005	63.3	6.2	30.5	61.3	8.9	29.8	65.9	2.6	31.4
Vanuatu	*2010	60.9	7.3	31.8	58.8	10.6	30.6	63.6	2.9	33.4
	*2017	61.4	6.8	31.8	59.7	9.8	30.5	63.7	2.8	33.4
Venezuela (Boliv. Rep. of)	*2005	10.6	26.9	62.5	14.8	37.9	47.2	3.9	8.9	87.2
Venezuela (Rép. boliv. du)	*2010	10.3	25.8	63.9	14.2	37.5	48.3	4.3	7.5	88.2
	*2017	11.9	26.8	61.3	16.8	38.6	44.7	4.5	9.3	86.1

18 Employment by economic activity *(continued)*

Percentage of persons employed by sex and ISIC 4 categories; agriculture (agr.), industry (ind.) and services (ser.)

Emploi par activité économique *(suite)*

Personnes employées par sexe et branches de la CITI rév. 4; agriculture (agr.), industrie (ind.) et services (ser.), pourcentage

Region, country or area & Région, pays ou zone &	Year Année	Male and Female Hommes et femmes			Male Hommes			Female Femmes		
		Agr.	Ind.	Ser.	Agr.	Ind.	Ser.	Agr.	Ind.	Ser.
Viet Nam	*2005	55.5	18.8	25.7	53.3	22.6	24.2	57.8	14.8	27.4
Viet Nam	*2010	49.9	21.3	28.9	47.8	25.3	26.9	52.1	17.0	31.0
	*2017	41.8	22.9	35.2	41.2	27.0	31.8	42.5	18.6	38.9
Western Sahara	*2005	38.6	26.6	34.8	42.6	21.6	35.8	20.8	48.5	30.7
Sahara occidental	*2010	38.0	27.5	34.5	42.8	22.1	35.2	20.0	47.9	32.1
	*2017	37.4	27.9	34.7	43.0	22.1	34.9	17.7	48.6	33.7
Yemen	*2005	33.1	15.9	51.0	25.9	18.1	56.0	57.2	8.3	34.5
Yémen	*2010	24.1	19.0	56.9	22.7	20.1	57.1	30.3	14.1	55.6
	*2017	32.9	17.9	49.2	29.1	20.9	50.0	45.7	7.7	46.6
Zambia	*2005	72.1	7.1	20.8	65.3	10.6	24.1	80.0	3.1	16.9
Zambie	*2010	65.0	8.7	26.3	55.7	13.8	30.5	75.2	3.1	21.7
	*2017	54.8	9.9	35.3	44.3	15.7	40.0	66.7	3.4	29.9
Zimbabwe	*2005	70.1	10.6	19.4	62.1	15.9	22.0	78.4	5.0	16.6
Zimbabwe	*2010	68.4	9.4	22.2	63.8	14.7	21.4	73.3	3.8	22.9
	*2017	67.5	7.3	25.2	63.8	12.1	24.1	71.4	2.2	26.4
European Union (EU)	*2005	6.2	27.6	66.2	6.9	37.6	55.5	5.3	14.8	79.9
Union européenne (UE)	*2010	5.2	25.3	69.6	5.8	35.8	58.3	4.3	12.5	83.2
	*2017	4.4	23.7	71.9	5.3	33.9	60.8	3.4	11.7	84.9

Source:

International Labour Organization (ILO), Geneva, Key Indicators of the Labour Market (KILM 9th edition), the ILOSTAT database, last accessed March 2017.

& Ages 15 years and over unless indicated otherwise. Table is in ISIC Rev. 4 unless otherwise indicated.

1 Data excludes Armenia, Azerbaijan, Cyprus, Georgia, Israel and Turkey.
2 Refers to Armenia, Azerbaijan, Cyprus, Georgia, Israel and Turkey.
3 Persons aged 16 years and over.
4 Data classified according to ISIC Rev. 3.
5 Persons aged 14 years and over.
6 Data classified according to ISIC Rev. 2.
7 Persons aged 13 years and over.
8 Excluding the institutional population.
9 For statistical purposes, the data for China do not include those for the Hong Kong Special Administrative Region (Hong Kong SAR), Macao Special Administrative Region (Macao SAR) and Taiwan Province of China.
10 Resident population (de jure).
11 Persons aged 15 to 64 years.
12 Nationals, residents.
13 Civilians only.
14 Persons aged 15 to 69 years.
15 Excluding some areas.

Source:

Bureau international du travail (BIT), Genève, Indicateurs clés du marché du travail (ICMT 9e édition), ILOSTAT base de données du BIT, dernier accès mars 2017.

& Sauf indication contraire, Age 15 ans et plus. Sauf indication contraire, la classification utilisée dans ce tableau est la CITI Rév. 4.

1 Les données excluent l'Arménie, l'Azerbaïdjan, Chypre, la Géorgie, l'Israël et la Turquie.
2 Les données se rapportent à l'Arménie, l'Azerbaïdjan, Chypre, la Géorgie, l'Israël et la Turquie.
3 Personnes âgées de 16 ans et plus.
4 Données classifiées selon la CITI, Rév. 3.
5 Population âgée de plus de 14 ans.
6 Données classifiées selon la CITI, Rév. 2.
7 Personnes âgées de 13 ans et plus.
8 Non compris la population dans les institutions.
9 Pour la présentation des statistiques, les données pour la Chine ne comprennent pas la Région Administrative Spéciale de Hong Kong (Hong Kong RAS), la Région Administrative Spéciale de Macao (Macao RAS) et la province de Taiwan.
10 Population résidente (de droit).
11 Personnes âgées de 15 à 64 ans.
12 Ressortissants, résidents.
13 Civils uniquement.
14 Personnes âgées de 15 à 69 ans.
15 Certaines régions sont exclues.

19 Agricultural production indices
Index base: 2004 - 2006 = 100

Indices de la production agricole
Indices base: 2004 - 2006 = 100

Région, pays ou zone	1975	1985	1995	2005	2010	2012	2013	2014	Région, pays ou zone
Total, all countries or areas									**Total, tous pays ou zones**
Agriculture (gross)	**51**	**66**	**78**	**100**	**113**	**118**	**122**	**124**	**Agriculture (brut)**
Food (gross)	**51**	**65**	**78**	**100**	**113**	**118**	**123**	**124**	**Produits ailmentaires (brut)**
Africa									**Afrique**
Agriculture (gross)	43	51	69	100	118	123	127	129	Agriculture (brut)
Food (gross)	42	50	68	100	118	124	127	129	Produits ailmentaires (brut)
Eastern Africa									**Afrique orientale**
Agriculture (gross)	52	61	71	100	126	135	141	140	Agriculture (brut)
Food (gross)	52	60	70	100	127	136	142	141	Produits ailmentaires (brut)
Middle Africa									**Afrique centrale**
Agriculture (gross)	58	66	78	102	133	138	146	137	Agriculture (brut)
Food (gross)	54	64	77	102	135	139	148	139	Produits ailmentaires (brut)
Northern Africa									**Afrique septentrionale**
Agriculture (gross)	37	47	64	99	111	117	121	123	Agriculture (brut)
Food (gross)	35	45	64	99	112	118	122	124	Produits ailmentaires (brut)
Southern Africa									**Afrique australe**
Agriculture (gross)	66	76	76	102	116	119	121	123	Agriculture (brut)
Food (gross)	64	74	75	102	117	120	122	124	Produits ailmentaires (brut)
Western Africa									**Afrique occidentale**
Agriculture (gross)	34	40	68	100	113	118	118	125	Agriculture (brut)
Food (gross)	34	39	68	100	115	120	119	126	Produits ailmentaires (brut)
Americas									**Amériques**
Agriculture (gross)	52	67	78	100	111	112	118	120	Agriculture (brut)
Food (gross)	51	66	78	100	112	112	119	120	Produits ailmentaires (brut)
Northern America									**Amérique septentrionale**
Agriculture (gross)	63	77	84	100	105	104	109	111	Agriculture (brut)
Food (gross)	63	77	83	100	106	104	111	112	Produits ailmentaires (brut)
Caribbean									**Caraïbes**
Agriculture (gross)	87	106	84	98	107	111	117	118	Agriculture (brut)
Food (gross)	86	105	84	98	107	112	117	119	Produits ailmentaires (brut)
Central America									**Amérique centrale**
Agriculture (gross)	46	62	77	98	111	117	119	123	Agriculture (brut)
Food (gross)	43	61	76	98	110	116	119	123	Produits ailmentaires (brut)
South America									**Amérique du Sud**
Agriculture (gross)	38	53	70	100	118	121	129	129	Agriculture (brut)
Food (gross)	37	51	71	100	119	121	130	130	Produits ailmentaires (brut)
Asia									**Asie**
Agriculture (gross)	34	49	73	100	118	127	130	132	Agriculture (brut)
Food (gross)	34	48	73	100	119	127	131	132	Produits ailmentaires (brut)
Central Asia									**Asie centrale**
Agriculture (gross)	...	...	79	100	115	124	135	136	Agriculture (brut)
Food (gross)	...	...	76	100	119	129	141	143	Produits ailmentaires (brut)
South-eastern Asia									**Asie du Sud-est**
Agriculture (gross)	33	50	71	99	120	131	132	133	Agriculture (brut)
Food (gross)	33	50	71	99	121	131	132	133	Produits ailmentaires (brut)
Southern Asia									**Asie méridionale**
Agriculture (gross)	42	57	79	100	121	129	135	138	Agriculture (brut)
Food (gross)	42	57	79	101	121	129	135	138	Produits ailmentaires (brut)
Western Asia									**Asie occidentale**
Agriculture (gross)	43	60	80	101	106	115	117	111	Agriculture (brut)
Food (gross)	43	60	80	101	107	116	119	113	Produits ailmentaires (brut)
Europe									**Europe**
Agriculture (gross)	102	116	97	99	99	100	106	108	Agriculture (brut)
Food (gross)	100	114	97	99	99	101	106	108	Produits ailmentaires (brut)
Eastern Europe									**Europe orientale**
Agriculture (gross)	140	156	102	99	97	105	114	118	Agriculture (brut)
Food (gross)	135	151	102	99	97	105	114	118	Produits ailmentaires (brut)
Northern Europe									**Europe septentrionale**
Agriculture (gross)	77	92	102	101	101	100	102	107	Agriculture (brut)
Food (gross)	77	92	102	101	101	100	102	107	Produits ailmentaires (brut)
Southern Europe									**Europe méridionale**
Agriculture (gross)	77	88	87	98	98	92	100	95	Agriculture (brut)
Food (gross)	78	88	87	98	99	93	100	95	Produits ailmentaires (brut)

Région, pays ou zone	1975	1985	1995	2005	2010	2012	2013	2014	Région, pays ou zone
Western Europe									**Europe occidentale**
Agriculture (gross)	86	101	98	100	101	102	102	108	Agriculture (brut)
Food (gross)	86	101	98	100	101	102	102	108	Produits ailmentaires (brut)
Oceania									**Océanie**
Agriculture (gross)	60	71	85	105	102	114	114	111	Agriculture (brut)
Food (gross)	57	67	83	105	103	113	113	111	Produits ailmentaires (brut)
Australia and New Zealand									**Australie et Nouvelle-Zélande**
Agriculture (gross)	60	71	85	105	101	114	114	113	Agriculture (brut)
Food (gross)	57	67	83	105	103	113	113	113	Produits ailmentaires (brut)
Melanesia									**Mélanésie**
Agriculture (gross)	53	69	81	99	110	114	116	86	Agriculture (brut)
Food (gross)	53	68	81	99	110	115	116	86	Produits ailmentaires (brut)
Micronesia									**Micronésie**
Agriculture (gross)	79	105	82	97	77	75	76	79	Agriculture (brut)
Food (gross)	79	105	82	97	77	75	76	79	Produits ailmentaires (brut)
Polynesia									**Polynésie**
Agriculture (gross)	115	108	89	101	111	112	111	111	Agriculture (brut)
Food (gross)	114	107	89	101	111	112	111	111	Produits ailmentaires (brut)
Afghanistan									**Afghanistan**
Agriculture (gross)	82	70	85	107	117	123	121	125	Agriculture (brut)
Food (gross)	79	69	84	107	117	123	121	125	Produits ailmentaires (brut)
Albania									**Albanie**
Agriculture (gross)	51	65	86	98	119	132	133	134	Agriculture (brut)
Food (gross)	48	61	85	98	119	132	133	134	Produits ailmentaires (brut)
Algeria									**Algérie**
Agriculture (gross)	40	50	65	99	125	148	164	160	Agriculture (brut)
Food (gross)	40	50	65	99	125	149	165	161	Produits ailmentaires (brut)
American Samoa									**Samoa américaines**
Agriculture (gross)	66	51	63	100	110	105	113	112	Agriculture (brut)
Food (gross)	66	51	63	100	110	105	113	112	Produits ailmentaires (brut)
Angola									**Angola**
Agriculture (gross)	48	37	46	102	167	152	206	175	Agriculture (brut)
Food (gross)	36	35	45	102	168	153	207	176	Produits ailmentaires (brut)
Antigua and Barbuda									**Antigua-et-Barbuda**
Agriculture (gross)	60	97	98	95	87	86	86	88	Agriculture (brut)
Food (gross)	59	97	98	95	87	86	86	88	Produits ailmentaires (brut)
Argentina									**Argentine**
Agriculture (gross)	52	63	75	105	112	107	118	119	Agriculture (brut)
Food (gross)	50	62	74	105	112	107	118	119	Produits ailmentaires (brut)
Armenia									**Arménie**
Agriculture (gross)	...	...	73	103	102	127	133	135	Agriculture (brut)
Food (gross)	...	...	73	103	102	127	133	135	Produits ailmentaires (brut)
Australia									**Australie**
Agriculture (gross)	61	69	87	108	100	116	115	111	Agriculture (brut)
Food (gross)	59	66	85	108	102	114	114	111	Produits ailmentaires (brut)
Austria									**Autriche**
Agriculture (gross)	86	94	93	100	105	101	102	108	Agriculture (brut)
Food (gross)	86	94	93	100	105	101	102	108	Produits ailmentaires (brut)
Azerbaijan									**Azerbaïdjan**
Agriculture (gross)	...	...	60	104	118	132	137	131	Agriculture (brut)
Food (gross)	...	...	56	103	122	137	142	136	Produits ailmentaires (brut)
Bahamas									**Bahamas**
Agriculture (gross)	71	67	80	99	124	129	130	132	Agriculture (brut)
Food (gross)	71	67	80	99	124	129	130	132	Produits ailmentaires (brut)
Bahrain									**Bahreïn**
Agriculture (gross)	97	116	120	91	113	157	192	167	Agriculture (brut)
Food (gross)	97	116	120	91	113	157	192	167	Produits ailmentaires (brut)
Bangladesh									**Bangladesh**
Agriculture (gross)	49	58	67	103	129	134	137	141	Agriculture (brut)
Food (gross)	48	56	67	103	130	133	136	140	Produits ailmentaires (brut)
Barbados									**Barbade**
Agriculture (gross)	99	106	97	106	91	95	89	88	Agriculture (brut)
Food (gross)	99	106	97	106	91	95	89	88	Produits ailmentaires (brut)
Belarus									**Bélarus**
Agriculture (gross)	...	...	91	98	117	122	116	122	Agriculture (brut)
Food (gross)	...	...	91	98	117	122	116	123	Produits ailmentaires (brut)

19 Agricultural production indices *(continued)*
Index base: 2004 - 2006 = 100

Indices de la production agricole *(suite)*
Indices base: 2004 - 2006 = 100

Région, pays ou zone	1975	1985	1995	2005	2010	2012	2013	2014	Région, pays ou zone
Belgium									**Belgique**
Agriculture (gross)	...	...	...	100	100	97	101	108	Agriculture (brut)
Food (gross)	...	...	...	100	99	97	101	107	Produits ailmentaires (brut)
Belize									**Belize**
Agriculture (gross)	28	39	65	97	93	102	96	97	Agriculture (brut)
Food (gross)	28	39	65	97	93	102	96	97	Produits ailmentaires (brut)
Benin									**Bénin**
Agriculture (gross)	25	40	67	102	116	134	143	152	Agriculture (brut)
Food (gross)	27	41	63	102	123	140	148	158	Produits ailmentaires (brut)
Bermuda									**Bermudes**
Agriculture (gross)	85	92	97	100	111	117	115	115	Agriculture (brut)
Food (gross)	85	92	97	100	111	117	115	115	Produits ailmentaires (brut)
Bhutan									**Bhoutan**
Agriculture (gross)	46	62	73	106	94	102	95	98	Agriculture (brut)
Food (gross)	46	62	73	106	94	102	95	98	Produits ailmentaires (brut)
Bolivia (Plurinational State of)									**Bolivie (État plurinational de)**
Agriculture (gross)	41	49	71	100	119	133	138	142	Agriculture (brut)
Food (gross)	39	49	70	100	120	134	139	143	Produits ailmentaires (brut)
Bosnia and Herzegovina									**Bosnie-Herzégovine**
Agriculture (gross)	...	...	63	98	107	98	112	96	Agriculture (brut)
Food (gross)	...	...	63	98	108	98	113	97	Produits ailmentaires (brut)
Botswana									**Botswana**
Agriculture (gross)	83	93	110	102	125	128	127	110	Agriculture (brut)
Food (gross)	83	93	111	102	125	129	128	110	Produits ailmentaires (brut)
Brazil									**Brésil**
Agriculture (gross)	31	49	67	99	122	126	135	135	Agriculture (brut)
Food (gross)	30	48	68	99	123	127	136	136	Produits ailmentaires (brut)
British Virgin Islands									**Îles Vierges britanniques**
Agriculture (gross)	76	95	94	100	102	104	104	103	Agriculture (brut)
Food (gross)	76	95	94	100	102	104	104	103	Produits ailmentaires (brut)
Brunei Darussalam									**Brunéi Darussalam**
Agriculture (gross)	33	54	46	75	139	154	167	157	Agriculture (brut)
Food (gross)	31	53	46	75	140	155	168	157	Produits ailmentaires (brut)
Bulgaria									**Bulgarie**
Agriculture (gross)	167	171	131	91	106	99	120	117	Agriculture (brut)
Food (gross)	162	167	134	91	107	101	121	119	Produits ailmentaires (brut)
Burkina Faso									**Burkina Faso**
Agriculture (gross)	27	40	60	104	118	125	125	131	Agriculture (brut)
Food (gross)	31	44	66	104	125	132	127	134	Produits ailmentaires (brut)
Burundi									**Burundi**
Agriculture (gross)	71	81	83	92	108	90	128	109	Agriculture (brut)
Food (gross)	82	91	95	100	114	99	145	122	Produits ailmentaires (brut)
Cabo Verde									**Cabo Verde**
Agriculture (gross)	22	36	70	99	103	95	99	98	Agriculture (brut)
Food (gross)	22	36	70	99	103	95	99	98	Produits ailmentaires (brut)
Cambodia									**Cambodge**
Agriculture (gross)	26	37	63	105	149	174	175	175	Agriculture (brut)
Food (gross)	25	36	61	105	148	175	176	177	Produits ailmentaires (brut)
Cameroon									**Cameroun**
Agriculture (gross)	46	53	69	103	140	152	156	155	Agriculture (brut)
Food (gross)	45	51	67	102	144	157	161	160	Produits ailmentaires (brut)
Canada									**Canada**
Agriculture (gross)	54	68	81	102	102	105	116	109	Agriculture (brut)
Food (gross)	53	68	81	102	103	106	117	109	Produits ailmentaires (brut)
Cayman Islands									**Îles Caïmanes**
Agriculture (gross)	229	230	105	100	100	105	105	104	Agriculture (brut)
Food (gross)	229	230	105	100	100	105	105	104	Produits ailmentaires (brut)
Central African Rep.									**Rép. centrafricaine**
Agriculture (gross)	51	57	78	101	116	122	124	114	Agriculture (brut)
Food (gross)	46	53	74	101	115	121	123	113	Produits ailmentaires (brut)
Chad									**Tchad**
Agriculture (gross)	48	53	73	107	154	163	146	146	Agriculture (brut)
Food (gross)	44	52	72	107	163	171	153	151	Produits ailmentaires (brut)
Chile									**Chili**
Agriculture (gross)	36	44	77	100	108	111	112	111	Agriculture (brut)
Food (gross)	35	43	76	100	108	112	112	111	Produits ailmentaires (brut)

Région, pays ou zone	1975	1985	1995	2005	2010	2012	2013	2014	Région, pays ou zone
China [1]									**Chine** [1]
Agriculture (gross)	26	40	67	100	120	129	131	132	Agriculture (brut)
Food (gross)	25	39	67	100	120	129	132	133	Produits ailmentaires (brut)
China, Hong Kong SAR									**Chine, Hong Kong RAS**
Agriculture (gross)	163	222	84	99	55	58	59	34	Agriculture (brut)
Food (gross)	163	222	84	99	55	58	59	34	Produits ailmentaires (brut)
China, Macao SAR									**Chine, Macao RAS**
Agriculture (gross)	59	66	70	100	95	86	88	86	Agriculture (brut)
Food (gross)	59	66	70	100	95	86	88	86	Produits ailmentaires (brut)
Colombia									**Colombie**
Agriculture (gross)	49	58	82	99	101	109	114	114	Agriculture (brut)
Food (gross)	45	55	79	99	102	112	116	115	Produits ailmentaires (brut)
Comoros									**Comores**
Agriculture (gross)	58	64	89	96	107	102	107	107	Agriculture (brut)
Food (gross)	58	64	89	96	107	102	107	107	Produits ailmentaires (brut)
Congo									**Congo**
Agriculture (gross)	49	62	72	100	124	131	133	106	Agriculture (brut)
Food (gross)	48	61	73	100	125	131	133	106	Produits ailmentaires (brut)
Cook Islands									**Îles Cook**
Agriculture (gross)	320	285	153	100	93	89	92	91	Agriculture (brut)
Food (gross)	320	285	152	100	93	89	92	91	Produits ailmentaires (brut)
Costa Rica									**Costa Rica**
Agriculture (gross)	39	47	78	98	114	120	122	127	Agriculture (brut)
Food (gross)	37	43	75	98	115	121	125	129	Produits ailmentaires (brut)
Côte d'Ivoire									**Côte d'Ivoire**
Agriculture (gross)	41	56	78	100	107	120	123	122	Agriculture (brut)
Food (gross)	39	54	79	98	109	121	124	123	Produits ailmentaires (brut)
Croatia									**Croatie**
Agriculture (gross)	...	...	97	98	100	89	98	91	Agriculture (brut)
Food (gross)	...	...	98	98	100	88	98	91	Produits ailmentaires (brut)
Cuba									**Cuba**
Agriculture (gross)	95	130	80	97	88	96	100	100	Agriculture (brut)
Food (gross)	94	130	80	97	88	97	101	101	Produits ailmentaires (brut)
Cyprus									**Chypre**
Agriculture (gross)	65	90	111	98	83	81	77	80	Agriculture (brut)
Food (gross)	65	90	111	98	84	82	77	80	Produits ailmentaires (brut)
Czechia									**Tchéquie**
Agriculture (gross)	...	...	108	100	91	89	92	102	Agriculture (brut)
Food (gross)	...	...	108	100	91	89	92	102	Produits ailmentaires (brut)
Dem. P. R. Korea									**R. p. dém. de Corée**
Agriculture (gross)	67	88	76	101	98	102	104	104	Agriculture (brut)
Food (gross)	66	87	75	101	97	102	103	103	Produits ailmentaires (brut)
Dem. Rep. of the Congo									**Rép. dém. du Congo**
Agriculture (gross)	82	103	108	100	106	112	110	104	Agriculture (brut)
Food (gross)	79	100	107	100	106	112	111	104	Produits ailmentaires (brut)
Denmark									**Danemark**
Agriculture (gross)	68	85	94	101	101	103	100	105	Agriculture (brut)
Food (gross)	68	85	94	101	101	103	100	105	Produits ailmentaires (brut)
Djibouti									**Djibouti**
Agriculture (gross)	24	68	76	95	116	134	134	133	Agriculture (brut)
Food (gross)	24	68	76	95	116	134	134	133	Produits ailmentaires (brut)
Dominica									**Dominique**
Agriculture (gross)	98	114	110	99	108	110	111	110	Agriculture (brut)
Food (gross)	99	115	111	99	108	111	111	111	Produits ailmentaires (brut)
Dominican Republic									**Rép. dominicaine**
Agriculture (gross)	64	77	77	99	127	124	133	136	Agriculture (brut)
Food (gross)	61	73	76	99	129	126	135	138	Produits ailmentaires (brut)
Eastern Asia									**Asie orientale**
Agriculture (gross)	30	45	70	100	118	127	129	129	Agriculture (brut)
Food (gross)	30	44	70	100	119	127	129	130	Produits ailmentaires (brut)
Ecuador									**Équateur**
Agriculture (gross)	45	55	80	99	122	116	112	118	Agriculture (brut)
Food (gross)	44	53	78	98	123	118	113	119	Produits ailmentaires (brut)
Egypt									**Égypte**
Agriculture (gross)	31	41	67	99	109	119	116	120	Agriculture (brut)
Food (gross)	29	39	67	99	110	121	118	122	Produits ailmentaires (brut)

19 Agricultural production indices *(continued)*
Index base: 2004 - 2006 = 100

Indices de la production agricole *(suite)*
Indices base: 2004 - 2006 = 100

Région, pays ou zone	1975	1985	1995	2005	2010	2012	2013	2014	Région, pays ou zone
El Salvador									**El Salvador**
Agriculture (gross)	82	78	88	99	107	116	109	111	Agriculture (brut)
Food (gross)	60	65	80	99	105	117	116	117	Produits ailmentaires (brut)
Equatorial Guinea									**Guinée équatoriale**
Agriculture (gross)	66	69	85	101	110	114	115	117	Agriculture (brut)
Food (gross)	58	57	82	101	111	114	116	118	Produits ailmentaires (brut)
Eritrea									**Érythrée**
Agriculture (gross)	...	...	77	108	105	109	112	109	Agriculture (brut)
Food (gross)	...	...	77	108	105	109	112	109	Produits ailmentaires (brut)
Estonia									**Estonie**
Agriculture (gross)	...	...	110	103	110	123	127	136	Agriculture (brut)
Food (gross)	...	...	110	103	110	123	127	136	Produits ailmentaires (brut)
Ethiopia									**Éthiopie**
Agriculture (gross)	...	...	59	102	137	146	153	158	Agriculture (brut)
Food (gross)	...	...	58	103	137	147	152	157	Produits ailmentaires (brut)
Falkland Is. (Malvinas)									**Îles Falkland (Malvinas)**
Agriculture (gross)	99	104	112	103	96	97	96	96	Agriculture (brut)
Food (gross)	118	122	133	100	105	106	105	105	Produits ailmentaires (brut)
Faroe Islands									**Îles Féroé**
Agriculture (gross)	94	94	101	100	100	101	102	102	Agriculture (brut)
Food (gross)	94	94	101	100	100	101	102	102	Produits ailmentaires (brut)
Fiji									**Fidji**
Agriculture (gross)	63	88	107	99	82	86	86	88	Agriculture (brut)
Food (gross)	63	88	107	99	82	86	86	88	Produits ailmentaires (brut)
Finland									**Finlande**
Agriculture (gross)	99	106	95	102	94	94	99	101	Agriculture (brut)
Food (gross)	99	106	95	102	94	94	99	101	Produits ailmentaires (brut)
France									**France**
Agriculture (gross)	84	99	99	100	97	97	98	103	Agriculture (brut)
Food (gross)	83	99	99	100	97	98	98	103	Produits ailmentaires (brut)
French Guiana									**Guyane française**
Agriculture (gross)	21	52	105	97	95	113	119	120	Agriculture (brut)
Food (gross)	21	52	105	97	95	113	119	120	Produits ailmentaires (brut)
French Polynesia									**Polynésie française**
Agriculture (gross)	106	91	91	104	100	106	100	98	Agriculture (brut)
Food (gross)	105	91	91	104	100	106	100	98	Produits ailmentaires (brut)
Gabon									**Gabon**
Agriculture (gross)	51	70	85	100	113	117	121	97	Agriculture (brut)
Food (gross)	54	74	88	100	111	114	117	92	Produits ailmentaires (brut)
Gambia									**Gambie**
Agriculture (gross)	79	64	64	94	137	107	98	82	Agriculture (brut)
Food (gross)	79	64	64	94	137	107	98	82	Produits ailmentaires (brut)
Georgia									**Géorgie**
Agriculture (gross)	...	...	119	121	67	71	86	85	Agriculture (brut)
Food (gross)	...	...	117	121	68	72	88	86	Produits ailmentaires (brut)
Germany									**Allemagne**
Agriculture (gross)	95	110	92	100	103	105	105	111	Agriculture (brut)
Food (gross)	95	110	92	100	103	105	105	111	Produits ailmentaires (brut)
Ghana									**Ghana**
Agriculture (gross)	38	36	64	100	124	139	143	144	Agriculture (brut)
Food (gross)	37	36	63	100	124	139	143	144	Produits ailmentaires (brut)
Greece									**Grèce**
Agriculture (gross)	79	93	104	103	83	95	86	86	Agriculture (brut)
Food (gross)	81	96	103	103	86	99	88	87	Produits ailmentaires (brut)
Greenland									**Groenland**
Agriculture (gross)	61	103	100	100	99	99	99	99	Agriculture (brut)
Food (gross)	59	103	101	99	99	99	99	99	Produits ailmentaires (brut)
Grenada									**Grenade**
Agriculture (gross)	141	140	138	79	97	100	101	103	Agriculture (brut)
Food (gross)	141	140	138	79	98	100	101	103	Produits ailmentaires (brut)
Guadeloupe									**Guadeloupe**
Agriculture (gross)	136	116	80	103	89	90	85	100	Agriculture (brut)
Food (gross)	136	116	80	103	89	89	85	100	Produits ailmentaires (brut)
Guam									**Guam**
Agriculture (gross)	67	72	87	99	96	88	87	88	Agriculture (brut)
Food (gross)	67	72	87	99	96	88	87	88	Produits ailmentaires (brut)

19 Agricultural production indices *(continued)*
Index base: 2004 - 2006 = 100

Indices de la production agricole *(suite)*
Indices base: 2004 - 2006 = 100

Région, pays ou zone	1975	1985	1995	2005	2010	2012	2013	2014	Région, pays ou zone
Guatemala									**Guatemala**
Agriculture (gross)	40	47	70	99	133	145	153	158	Agriculture (brut)
Food (gross)	35	43	71	97	132	142	152	158	Produits ailmentaires (brut)
Guinea									**Guinée**
Agriculture (gross)	42	50	72	100	120	128	133	130	Agriculture (brut)
Food (gross)	42	50	71	101	120	129	133	131	Produits ailmentaires (brut)
Guinea-Bissau									**Guinée-Bissau**
Agriculture (gross)	39	53	69	101	129	134	140	137	Agriculture (brut)
Food (gross)	39	53	69	100	129	134	140	138	Produits ailmentaires (brut)
Guyana									**Guyana**
Agriculture (gross)	78	68	99	94	108	113	129	142	Agriculture (brut)
Food (gross)	78	68	99	94	108	113	129	143	Produits ailmentaires (brut)
Haiti									**Haïti**
Agriculture (gross)	91	104	84	102	135	145	159	163	Agriculture (brut)
Food (gross)	89	103	83	101	136	146	159	166	Produits ailmentaires (brut)
Honduras									**Honduras**
Agriculture (gross)	40	55	72	103	111	122	121	122	Agriculture (brut)
Food (gross)	41	57	72	104	109	115	118	119	Produits ailmentaires (brut)
Hungary									**Hongrie**
Agriculture (gross)	108	126	91	97	80	80	88	99	Agriculture (brut)
Food (gross)	107	126	91	97	80	80	88	99	Produits ailmentaires (brut)
Iceland									**Islande**
Agriculture (gross)	105	107	86	99	110	115	114	117	Agriculture (brut)
Food (gross)	104	105	85	99	110	115	114	117	Produits ailmentaires (brut)
India									**Inde**
Agriculture (gross)	44	59	81	100	124	135	140	143	Agriculture (brut)
Food (gross)	44	60	81	100	123	134	139	142	Produits ailmentaires (brut)
Indonesia									**Indonésie**
Agriculture (gross)	31	50	77	98	123	135	137	139	Agriculture (brut)
Food (gross)	31	50	77	98	124	136	137	140	Produits ailmentaires (brut)
Iran (Islamic Rep. of)									**Iran (Rép. islamique d')**
Agriculture (gross)	26	42	70	102	106	103	104	106	Agriculture (brut)
Food (gross)	25	42	69	102	106	103	105	107	Produits ailmentaires (brut)
Iraq									**Iraq**
Agriculture (gross)	61	103	97	104	104	113	129	123	Agriculture (brut)
Food (gross)	60	102	98	104	104	113	129	123	Produits ailmentaires (brut)
Ireland									**Irlande**
Agriculture (gross)	76	92	97	99	100	95	100	102	Agriculture (brut)
Food (gross)	76	92	97	99	100	95	99	102	Produits ailmentaires (brut)
Israel									**Israël**
Agriculture (gross)	54	69	80	100	104	112	112	112	Agriculture (brut)
Food (gross)	52	65	78	100	105	113	112	112	Produits ailmentaires (brut)
Italy									**Italie**
Agriculture (gross)	88	95	95	100	97	91	90	89	Agriculture (brut)
Food (gross)	88	95	95	100	97	92	91	89	Produits ailmentaires (brut)
Jamaica									**Jamaïque**
Agriculture (gross)	73	75	102	97	98	102	101	102	Agriculture (brut)
Food (gross)	74	76	103	97	98	103	102	102	Produits ailmentaires (brut)
Japan									**Japon**
Agriculture (gross)	103	117	110	101	97	97	97	96	Agriculture (brut)
Food (gross)	100	115	110	101	97	98	97	97	Produits ailmentaires (brut)
Jordan									**Jordanie**
Agriculture (gross)	20	45	80	97	129	132	136	134	Agriculture (brut)
Food (gross)	19	44	79	97	129	132	136	135	Produits ailmentaires (brut)
Kazakhstan									**Kazakhstan**
Agriculture (gross)	...	...	88	100	107	111	126	126	Agriculture (brut)
Food (gross)	...	...	88	100	108	111	126	127	Produits ailmentaires (brut)
Kenya									**Kenya**
Agriculture (gross)	36	53	71	103	123	121	125	126	Agriculture (brut)
Food (gross)	36	52	69	103	124	123	126	126	Produits ailmentaires (brut)
Kiribati									**Kiribati**
Agriculture (gross)	41	72	65	95	60	61	61	61	Agriculture (brut)
Food (gross)	41	72	65	95	60	61	61	61	Produits ailmentaires (brut)
Kuwait									**Koweït**
Agriculture (gross)	18	55	54	95	136	153	176	199	Agriculture (brut)
Food (gross)	17	54	54	95	136	153	177	199	Produits ailmentaires (brut)

Agricultural production indices *(continued)*
Index base: 2004 - 2006 = 100

Indices de la production agricole *(suite)*
Indices base: 2004 - 2006 = 100

Région, pays ou zone	1975	1985	1995	2005	2010	2012	2013	2014	Région, pays ou zone
Kyrgyzstan									**Kirghizistan**
Agriculture (gross)	...	...	66	98	105	106	111	108	Agriculture (brut)
Food (gross)	...	...	65	98	106	108	113	110	Produits ailmentaires (brut)
Lao People's Dem. Rep.									**Rép. dém. pop. lao**
Agriculture (gross)	28	42	53	100	132	159	165	193	Agriculture (brut)
Food (gross)	26	43	52	100	130	151	160	186	Produits ailmentaires (brut)
Latvia									**Lettonie**
Agriculture (gross)	...	...	113	105	110	127	124	130	Agriculture (brut)
Food (gross)	...	...	113	105	110	127	124	130	Produits ailmentaires (brut)
Lebanon									**Liban**
Agriculture (gross)	41	60	111	97	94	88	94	95	Agriculture (brut)
Food (gross)	41	60	112	97	94	88	93	95	Produits ailmentaires (brut)
Lesotho									**Lesotho**
Agriculture (gross)	83	91	89	103	112	99	111	101	Agriculture (brut)
Food (gross)	84	91	86	102	113	98	111	100	Produits ailmentaires (brut)
Liberia									**Libéria**
Agriculture (gross)	76	95	49	103	104	114	110	104	Agriculture (brut)
Food (gross)	75	94	67	102	127	134	131	121	Produits ailmentaires (brut)
Libya									**Libye**
Agriculture (gross)	49	66	90	101	110	116	115	113	Agriculture (brut)
Food (gross)	49	66	90	101	110	116	115	114	Produits ailmentaires (brut)
Liechtenstein									**Liechtenstein**
Agriculture (gross)	47	93	94	100	100	103	99	102	Agriculture (brut)
Food (gross)	47	93	94	100	100	103	99	102	Produits ailmentaires (brut)
Lithuania									**Lituanie**
Agriculture (gross)	...	...	97	106	99	121	117	125	Agriculture (brut)
Food (gross)	...	...	97	106	99	121	117	125	Produits ailmentaires (brut)
Luxembourg									**Luxembourg**
Agriculture (gross)	...	...	...	99	94	91	94	98	Agriculture (brut)
Food (gross)	...	...	...	99	94	91	94	98	Produits ailmentaires (brut)
Madagascar									**Madagascar**
Agriculture (gross)	71	78	87	103	122	128	117	119	Agriculture (brut)
Food (gross)	68	76	86	103	123	129	118	120	Produits ailmentaires (brut)
Malawi									**Malawi**
Agriculture (gross)	38	48	60	86	156	173	186	149	Agriculture (brut)
Food (gross)	38	45	52	85	157	182	193	150	Produits ailmentaires (brut)
Malaysia									**Malaisie**
Agriculture (gross)	32	47	70	100	111	120	122	122	Agriculture (brut)
Food (gross)	20	38	67	100	115	125	129	130	Produits ailmentaires (brut)
Maldives									**Maldives**
Agriculture (gross)	87	110	98	89	75	65	63	65	Agriculture (brut)
Food (gross)	87	110	98	89	75	65	63	65	Produits ailmentaires (brut)
Mali									**Mali**
Agriculture (gross)	36	45	68	102	141	144	140	154	Agriculture (brut)
Food (gross)	38	46	65	102	152	151	148	157	Produits ailmentaires (brut)
Malta									**Malte**
Agriculture (gross)	64	75	92	97	98	91	92	96	Agriculture (brut)
Food (gross)	64	75	92	97	98	91	92	96	Produits ailmentaires (brut)
Marshall Islands									**Îles Marshall**
Agriculture (gross)	...	...	173	97	112	109	115	115	Agriculture (brut)
Food (gross)	...	...	173	97	112	109	115	115	Produits ailmentaires (brut)
Martinique									**Martinique**
Agriculture (gross)	100	99	94	99	82	76	79	78	Agriculture (brut)
Food (gross)	100	99	94	99	82	76	79	78	Produits ailmentaires (brut)
Mauritania									**Mauritanie**
Agriculture (gross)	50	66	79	100	111	119	121	125	Agriculture (brut)
Food (gross)	50	66	79	100	111	119	121	125	Produits ailmentaires (brut)
Mauritius									**Maurice**
Agriculture (gross)	67	89	94	98	99	96	94	96	Agriculture (brut)
Food (gross)	66	85	92	98	99	96	94	96	Produits ailmentaires (brut)
Mexico									**Mexique**
Agriculture (gross)	45	65	78	98	108	113	116	120	Agriculture (brut)
Food (gross)	43	64	77	98	108	113	116	120	Produits ailmentaires (brut)
Micronesia (Fed. States of)									**Micronésie (États féd. de)**
Agriculture (gross)	...	...	93	99	85	83	88	99	Agriculture (brut)
Food (gross)	...	...	93	99	85	83	88	99	Produits ailmentaires (brut)

Région, pays ou zone	1975	1985	1995	2005	2010	2012	2013	2014	Région, pays ou zone
Mongolia									**Mongolie**
Agriculture (gross)	132	136	115	97	114	133	144	147	Agriculture (brut)
Food (gross)	132	136	113	97	115	134	146	149	Produits ailmentaires (brut)
Montenegro									**Monténégro**
Agriculture (gross)	...	...	...	...	91	88	67	66	Agriculture (brut)
Food (gross)	...	...	...	...	91	88	67	66	Produits ailmentaires (brut)
Montserrat									**Montserrat**
Agriculture (gross)	66	82	100	99	102	104	104	103	Agriculture (brut)
Food (gross)	66	82	100	99	103	104	104	103	Produits ailmentaires (brut)
Morocco									**Maroc**
Agriculture (gross)	38	50	57	93	126	124	131	130	Agriculture (brut)
Food (gross)	38	50	56	93	126	124	132	130	Produits ailmentaires (brut)
Mozambique									**Mozambique**
Agriculture (gross)	63	52	68	96	151	129	130	137	Agriculture (brut)
Food (gross)	65	57	73	95	157	130	129	137	Produits ailmentaires (brut)
Myanmar									**Myanmar**
Agriculture (gross)	28	45	53	99	135	124	128	130	Agriculture (brut)
Food (gross)	27	44	53	99	135	122	126	128	Produits ailmentaires (brut)
Namibia									**Namibie**
Agriculture (gross)	73	70	89	104	90	91	90	88	Agriculture (brut)
Food (gross)	72	70	89	104	90	92	90	89	Produits ailmentaires (brut)
Nauru									**Nauru**
Agriculture (gross)	62	68	88	100	106	108	111	112	Agriculture (brut)
Food (gross)	62	68	88	100	106	108	111	112	Produits ailmentaires (brut)
Nepal									**Népal**
Agriculture (gross)	39	51	76	100	114	141	132	139	Agriculture (brut)
Food (gross)	38	51	76	100	114	141	132	139	Produits ailmentaires (brut)
Netherlands									**Pays-Bas**
Agriculture (gross)	72	97	106	100	112	111	113	115	Agriculture (brut)
Food (gross)	72	97	106	100	112	111	113	115	Produits ailmentaires (brut)
Netherlands Antilles [former]									**Antilles néerlandaises [anc.]**
Agriculture (gross)	126	102	88	99	118	...	...	...	Agriculture (brut)
Food (gross)	126	102	88	99	118	...	...	...	Produits ailmentaires (brut)
New Caledonia									**Nouvelle-Calédonie**
Agriculture (gross)	83	95	93	100	100	102	104	102	Agriculture (brut)
Food (gross)	76	93	93	100	100	102	104	103	Produits ailmentaires (brut)
New Zealand									**Nouvelle-Zélande**
Agriculture (gross)	57	74	80	99	104	109	110	116	Agriculture (brut)
Food (gross)	54	70	78	99	105	111	111	118	Produits ailmentaires (brut)
Nicaragua									**Nicaragua**
Agriculture (gross)	74	56	60	104	118	131	138	130	Agriculture (brut)
Food (gross)	60	49	58	102	119	131	140	130	Produits ailmentaires (brut)
Niger									**Niger**
Agriculture (gross)	28	35	53	102	146	140	144	148	Agriculture (brut)
Food (gross)	28	35	53	102	146	140	144	148	Produits ailmentaires (brut)
Nigeria									**Nigéria**
Agriculture (gross)	30	34	68	100	105	109	106	116	Agriculture (brut)
Food (gross)	30	34	68	100	105	109	107	117	Produits ailmentaires (brut)
Niue									**Nioué**
Agriculture (gross)	102	109	92	100	98	98	100	101	Agriculture (brut)
Food (gross)	102	109	92	100	98	98	100	101	Produits ailmentaires (brut)
Norway									**Norvège**
Agriculture (gross)	89	104	103	99	102	101	102	103	Agriculture (brut)
Food (gross)	89	104	103	99	102	101	102	104	Produits ailmentaires (brut)
Oman									**Oman**
Agriculture (gross)	20	45	70	112	120	124	130	134	Agriculture (brut)
Food (gross)	20	45	69	113	120	124	130	134	Produits ailmentaires (brut)
Pakistan									**Pakistan**
Agriculture (gross)	33	49	78	100	110	116	133	135	Agriculture (brut)
Food (gross)	34	48	78	101	113	118	137	138	Produits ailmentaires (brut)
Panama									**Panama**
Agriculture (gross)	77	88	92	99	107	115	113	117	Agriculture (brut)
Food (gross)	78	89	92	99	108	115	114	118	Produits ailmentaires (brut)
Papua New Guinea									**Papouasie-Nvl-Guinée**
Agriculture (gross)	51	65	78	99	112	116	118	84	Agriculture (brut)
Food (gross)	51	64	77	99	113	117	119	83	Produits ailmentaires (brut)

19 Agricultural production indices *(continued)*
Index base: 2004 - 2006 = 100

Indices de la production agricole *(suite)*
Indices base: 2004 - 2006 = 100

Région, pays ou zone	1975	1985	1995	2005	2010	2012	2013	2014	Région, pays ou zone
Paraguay									**Paraguay**
Agriculture (gross)	30	56	72	97	137	112	158	160	Agriculture (brut)
Food (gross)	28	50	68	98	141	116	163	166	Produits ailmentaires (brut)
Peru									**Pérou**
Agriculture (gross)	43	47	62	99	128	140	144	145	Agriculture (brut)
Food (gross)	42	46	62	100	130	141	147	148	Produits ailmentaires (brut)
Philippines									**Philippines**
Agriculture (gross)	46	57	76	100	113	119	121	122	Agriculture (brut)
Food (gross)	45	56	76	100	113	120	119	120	Produits ailmentaires (brut)
Poland									**Pologne**
Agriculture (gross)	121	118	103	98	101	107	107	113	Agriculture (brut)
Food (gross)	121	118	103	98	101	107	107	113	Produits ailmentaires (brut)
Portugal									**Portugal**
Agriculture (gross)	81	82	99	97	105	100	104	104	Agriculture (brut)
Food (gross)	81	82	99	97	105	100	105	104	Produits ailmentaires (brut)
Puerto Rico									**Porto Rico**
Agriculture (gross)	140	125	117	96	106	109	109	110	Agriculture (brut)
Food (gross)	139	123	117	97	107	110	110	111	Produits ailmentaires (brut)
Qatar									**Qatar**
Agriculture (gross)	11	43	105	97	127	141	157	154	Agriculture (brut)
Food (gross)	11	43	105	97	127	141	157	154	Produits ailmentaires (brut)
Republic of Korea									**République de Corée**
Agriculture (gross)	49	71	93	100	101	99	103	104	Agriculture (brut)
Food (gross)	47	70	92	100	101	99	104	104	Produits ailmentaires (brut)
Republic of Moldova									**République de Moldova**
Agriculture (gross)	...	...	132	100	93	77	101	109	Agriculture (brut)
Food (gross)	...	...	130	100	93	77	101	109	Produits ailmentaires (brut)
Réunion									**Réunion**
Agriculture (gross)	56	66	87	99	105	106	104	104	Agriculture (brut)
Food (gross)	55	66	87	99	105	106	104	104	Produits ailmentaires (brut)
Romania									**Roumanie**
Agriculture (gross)	89	116	96	95	91	79	96	100	Agriculture (brut)
Food (gross)	88	115	96	95	91	79	96	100	Produits ailmentaires (brut)
Russian Federation									**Fédération de Russie**
Agriculture (gross)	...	...	100	100	94	108	117	120	Agriculture (brut)
Food (gross)	...	...	100	100	94	108	117	120	Produits ailmentaires (brut)
Rwanda									**Rwanda**
Agriculture (gross)	45	68	55	101	140	162	166	139	Agriculture (brut)
Food (gross)	44	67	54	101	141	163	168	139	Produits ailmentaires (brut)
Saint Kitts and Nevis									**Saint-Kitts-et-Nevis**
Agriculture (gross)	156	184	138	91	35	40	40	39	Agriculture (brut)
Food (gross)	155	184	138	91	35	40	40	39	Produits ailmentaires (brut)
Saint Lucia									**Sainte-Lucie**
Agriculture (gross)	186	252	298	91	89	80	67	69	Agriculture (brut)
Food (gross)	186	252	298	91	89	80	67	69	Produits ailmentaires (brut)
Saint Pierre and Miquelon									**Saint-Pierre-et-Miquelon**
Agriculture (gross)	2	33	68	94	110	111	111	112	Agriculture (brut)
Food (gross)	2	33	68	94	110	111	111	112	Produits ailmentaires (brut)
Saint Vincent-Grenadines									**Saint-Vincent-Grenadines**
Agriculture (gross)	63	123	102	104	119	109	109	115	Agriculture (brut)
Food (gross)	64	124	102	104	119	110	109	115	Produits ailmentaires (brut)
Samoa									**Samoa**
Agriculture (gross)	97	113	83	101	107	106	106	107	Agriculture (brut)
Food (gross)	97	113	83	101	107	106	105	107	Produits ailmentaires (brut)
Sao Tome and Principe									**Sao Tomé-et-Principe**
Agriculture (gross)	62	52	64	101	107	103	112	119	Agriculture (brut)
Food (gross)	62	52	64	101	107	103	112	119	Produits ailmentaires (brut)
Saudi Arabia									**Arabie saoudite**
Agriculture (gross)	21	52	75	100	103	103	105	96	Agriculture (brut)
Food (gross)	21	52	75	100	103	103	105	96	Produits ailmentaires (brut)
Senegal									**Sénégal**
Agriculture (gross)	94	74	89	110	151	125	121	126	Agriculture (brut)
Food (gross)	95	75	90	110	153	126	122	127	Produits ailmentaires (brut)
Serbia									**Serbie**
Agriculture (gross)	...	...	...	...	103	84	102	102	Agriculture (brut)
Food (gross)	...	...	...	...	103	84	102	102	Produits ailmentaires (brut)

19 Agricultural production indices *(continued)*

Index base: 2004 - 2006 = 100

Indices de la production agricole *(suite)*

Indices base: 2004 - 2006 = 100

Région, pays ou zone	1975	1985	1995	2005	2010	2012	2013	2014	Région, pays ou zone
Serbia and Montenegro [former]									**Serbie-et-Monténégro [anc.]**
Agriculture (gross)	...	...	98	96	...	...	...	...	Agriculture (brut)
Food (gross)	...	...	98	96	...	...	...	...	Produits ailmentaires (brut)
Seychelles									**Seychelles**
Agriculture (gross)	126	138	154	99	92	103	105	105	Agriculture (brut)
Food (gross)	131	141	157	98	96	107	109	109	Produits ailmentaires (brut)
Sierra Leone									**Sierra Leone**
Agriculture (gross)	49	53	55	93	146	161	169	168	Agriculture (brut)
Food (gross)	49	51	52	93	147	161	169	168	Produits ailmentaires (brut)
Singapore									**Singapour**
Agriculture (gross)	974	857	163	90	92	105	112	112	Agriculture (brut)
Food (gross)	968	857	163	90	92	105	112	112	Produits ailmentaires (brut)
Slovakia									**Slovaquie**
Agriculture (gross)	...	...	115	102	82	77	84	97	Agriculture (brut)
Food (gross)	...	...	114	102	82	77	84	97	Produits ailmentaires (brut)
Slovenia									**Slovénie**
Agriculture (gross)	...	...	96	99	92	85	81	89	Agriculture (brut)
Food (gross)	...	...	96	99	92	85	81	89	Produits ailmentaires (brut)
Solomon Islands									**Îles Salomon**
Agriculture (gross)	42	73	78	103	111	112	115	118	Agriculture (brut)
Food (gross)	42	73	78	103	111	112	115	118	Produits ailmentaires (brut)
Somalia									**Somalie**
Agriculture (gross)	70	91	89	102	105	111	117	112	Agriculture (brut)
Food (gross)	70	91	89	102	105	111	117	112	Produits ailmentaires (brut)
South Africa									**Afrique du Sud**
Agriculture (gross)	65	75	74	102	118	121	123	125	Agriculture (brut)
Food (gross)	63	73	74	102	118	121	123	126	Produits ailmentaires (brut)
Spain									**Espagne**
Agriculture (gross)	61	74	70	95	103	93	113	102	Agriculture (brut)
Food (gross)	61	74	70	94	104	93	114	102	Produits ailmentaires (brut)
Sri Lanka									**Sri Lanka**
Agriculture (gross)	69	90	96	102	123	123	135	120	Agriculture (brut)
Food (gross)	64	90	97	102	125	125	139	122	Produits ailmentaires (brut)
State of Palestine									**État de Palestine**
Agriculture (gross)	...	...	49	107	77	93	90	90	Agriculture (brut)
Food (gross)	...	...	49	107	77	93	90	90	Produits ailmentaires (brut)
Sudan [former]									**Soudan [anc.]**
Agriculture (gross)	38	47	61	101	98	...	...	...	Agriculture (brut)
Food (gross)	35	45	61	101	100	...	...	...	Produits ailmentaires (brut)
Suriname									**Suriname**
Agriculture (gross)	91	139	126	99	137	136	145	152	Agriculture (brut)
Food (gross)	90	139	126	99	137	136	145	152	Produits ailmentaires (brut)
Swaziland									**Swaziland**
Agriculture (gross)	63	89	83	103	107	112	115	114	Agriculture (brut)
Food (gross)	60	87	83	103	107	113	115	115	Produits ailmentaires (brut)
Sweden									**Suède**
Agriculture (gross)	99	113	101	100	94	97	96	100	Agriculture (brut)
Food (gross)	99	113	101	100	94	97	96	100	Produits ailmentaires (brut)
Switzerland									**Suisse**
Agriculture (gross)	97	108	103	99	103	104	101	106	Agriculture (brut)
Food (gross)	97	108	103	99	103	104	101	106	Produits ailmentaires (brut)
Syrian Arab Republic									**Rép. arabe syrienne**
Agriculture (gross)	31	49	65	100	89	92	82	65	Agriculture (brut)
Food (gross)	30	48	64	99	92	94	84	68	Produits ailmentaires (brut)
Tajikistan									**Tadjikistan**
Agriculture (gross)	...	...	70	99	123	145	159	155	Agriculture (brut)
Food (gross)	...	...	66	99	137	158	176	172	Produits ailmentaires (brut)
Thailand									**Thaïlande**
Agriculture (gross)	41	62	79	98	113	132	130	129	Agriculture (brut)
Food (gross)	45	66	81	98	115	131	129	126	Produits ailmentaires (brut)
TFYR of Macedonia									**ex-R.Y. de Macédoine**
Agriculture (gross)	...	...	88	99	115	109	114	111	Agriculture (brut)
Food (gross)	...	...	89	99	115	109	114	112	Produits ailmentaires (brut)
Timor-Leste									**Timor-Leste**
Agriculture (gross)	89	82	95	98	121	112	111	111	Agriculture (brut)
Food (gross)	97	85	98	97	126	119	117	117	Produits ailmentaires (brut)

19 Agricultural production indices *(continued)*
Index base: 2004 - 2006 = 100

Indices de la production agricole *(suite)*
Indices base: 2004 - 2006 = 100

Région, pays ou zone	1975	1985	1995	2005	2010	2012	2013	2014	Région, pays ou zone
Togo									**Togo**
Agriculture (gross)	46	56	77	97	124	135	125	140	Agriculture (brut)
Food (gross)	48	54	73	100	130	139	128	143	Produits ailmentaires (brut)
Tokelau									**Tokélaou**
Agriculture (gross)	82	66	90	100	107	111	111	112	Agriculture (brut)
Food (gross)	82	66	90	100	107	111	111	112	Produits ailmentaires (brut)
Tonga									**Tonga**
Agriculture (gross)	155	111	97	98	135	134	134	134	Agriculture (brut)
Food (gross)	155	111	97	98	135	134	134	134	Produits ailmentaires (brut)
Trinidad and Tobago									**Trinité-et-Tobago**
Agriculture (gross)	109	84	92	99	96	96	96	95	Agriculture (brut)
Food (gross)	107	82	92	99	96	96	97	95	Produits ailmentaires (brut)
Tunisia									**Tunisie**
Agriculture (gross)	53	60	59	101	106	118	117	108	Agriculture (brut)
Food (gross)	53	60	59	101	106	118	118	108	Produits ailmentaires (brut)
Turkey									**Turquie**
Agriculture (gross)	53	69	83	101	110	122	126	120	Agriculture (brut)
Food (gross)	53	69	82	101	111	124	128	122	Produits ailmentaires (brut)
Turkmenistan									**Turkménistan**
Agriculture (gross)	...	...	65	104	98	101	105	103	Agriculture (brut)
Food (gross)	...	...	53	102	102	107	112	109	Produits ailmentaires (brut)
Tuvalu									**Tuvalu**
Agriculture (gross)	48	82	82	100	105	107	110	110	Agriculture (brut)
Food (gross)	48	82	82	100	105	107	110	110	Produits ailmentaires (brut)
Uganda									**Ouganda**
Agriculture (gross)	68	55	76	100	102	92	94	93	Agriculture (brut)
Food (gross)	67	55	75	100	101	91	92	90	Produits ailmentaires (brut)
Ukraine									**Ukraine**
Agriculture (gross)	...	...	105	100	106	121	138	137	Agriculture (brut)
Food (gross)	...	...	104	100	106	121	138	137	Produits ailmentaires (brut)
United Arab Emirates									**Émirats arabes unis**
Agriculture (gross)	7	22	68	105	112	66	68	70	Agriculture (brut)
Food (gross)	7	22	68	105	112	66	68	70	Produits ailmentaires (brut)
United Kingdom									**Royaume-Uni**
Agriculture (gross)	86	105	107	100	102	98	101	108	Agriculture (brut)
Food (gross)	86	105	107	100	102	98	101	108	Produits ailmentaires (brut)
United Rep. of Tanzania									**Rép.-Unie de Tanzanie**
Agriculture (gross)	43	58	69	98	129	147	167	176	Agriculture (brut)
Food (gross)	41	58	68	97	130	149	169	180	Produits ailmentaires (brut)
United States									**États-Unis**
Agriculture (gross)	64	78	84	100	106	103	108	111	Agriculture (brut)
Food (gross)	65	79	84	100	107	104	110	113	Produits ailmentaires (brut)
United States Virgin Is.									**Îles Vierges américaines**
Agriculture (gross)	114	126	91	99	108	109	106	109	Agriculture (brut)
Food (gross)	114	126	91	99	108	109	106	109	Produits ailmentaires (brut)
Uruguay									**Uruguay**
Agriculture (gross)	57	59	74	101	119	123	127	129	Agriculture (brut)
Food (gross)	55	56	72	101	120	124	128	130	Produits ailmentaires (brut)
Uzbekistan									**Ouzbékistan**
Agriculture (gross)	...	...	81	100	127	143	152	158	Agriculture (brut)
Food (gross)	...	...	75	99	135	155	167	174	Produits ailmentaires (brut)
Vanuatu									**Vanuatu**
Agriculture (gross)	80	100	101	100	128	127	134	123	Agriculture (brut)
Food (gross)	80	100	101	100	128	127	134	122	Produits ailmentaires (brut)
Venezuela (Boliv. Rep. of)									**Venezuela (Rép. boliv. du)**
Agriculture (gross)	47	65	79	101	109	117	120	118	Agriculture (brut)
Food (gross)	46	64	78	101	109	117	121	119	Produits ailmentaires (brut)
Viet Nam									**Viet Nam**
Agriculture (gross)	22	37	58	100	120	133	134	136	Agriculture (brut)
Food (gross)	23	39	60	100	118	131	131	134	Produits ailmentaires (brut)
Wallis and Futuna Islands									**Îles Wallis-et-Futuna**
Agriculture (gross)	77	83	88	102	104	107	109	115	Agriculture (brut)
Food (gross)	77	83	88	102	104	107	109	115	Produits ailmentaires (brut)
Western Sahara									**Sahara occidental**
Agriculture (gross)	66	84	97	100	101	107	104	100	Agriculture (brut)
Food (gross)	66	84	97	100	101	107	104	100	Produits ailmentaires (brut)

19 Agricultural production indices *(continued)*
Index base: 2004 - 2006 = 100

Indices de la production agricole *(suite)*
Indices base: 2004 - 2006 = 100

Région, pays ou zone	1975	1985	1995	2005	2010	2012	2013	2014	Région, pays ou zone
Yemen									**Yémen**
Agriculture (gross)	41	45	65	98	136	141	138	136	Agriculture (brut)
Food (gross)	41	46	66	98	137	142	139	137	Produits ailmentaires (brut)
Zambia									**Zambie**
Agriculture (gross)	52	55	63	101	169	188	186	179	Agriculture (brut)
Food (gross)	59	60	70	98	172	185	188	180	Produits ailmentaires (brut)
Zimbabwe									**Zimbabwe**
Agriculture (gross)	80	104	85	93	102	103	99	99	Agriculture (brut)
Food (gross)	78	97	71	91	97	99	97	98	Produits ailmentaires (brut)
European Union (EU)									**Union européenne (UE)**
Agriculture (gross)	83	95	96	99	99	97	101	103	Agriculture (brut)
Food (gross)	83	95	95	99	99	97	101	104	Produits ailmentaires (brut)

Source:

Food and Agriculture Organization of the United Nations (FAO), Rome, FAOSTAT database, last accessed February 2017.

1 For statistical purposes, the data for China do not include those for the Hong Kong Special Administrative Region (Hong Kong SAR) and Macao Special Administrative Region (Macao SAR).

Source:

Organisation des Nations Unies pour l'alimentation et l'agriculture (FAO), Rome, la base de données FAOSTAT, dernier accès février 2017.

1 Pour la présentation des statistiques, les données pour la Chine ne comprennent pas la Région Administrative Spéciale de Hong Kong (Hong Kong RAS) et la Région Administrative Spéciale de Macao (Macao RAS).

20 Total imports, exports and balance of trade

Imports CIF, exports FOB and balance: millions of US dollars

Total des importations, des exportations et balance commerciale

Importations CAF, exportations FAB et balance: en millions de dollars É.-U.

Region, country or area	Sys.[&]	1995	2005	2010	2013	2014	2015	2016	Région, pays ou zone
Total, all countries or areas									**Total, tous pays ou zones**
Imports		**5 099 057**	**10 576 337**	**15 258 942**	**18 746 318**	**18 727 075**	**16 498 603**	**15 931 970**	**Importations**
Exports		**5 050 238**	**10 372 753**	**15 097 799**	**18 819 756**	**18 812 157**	**16 470 749**	**15 840 182**	**Exportations**
Balance		**-48 819**	**-203 584**	**-161 143**	**73 438**	**85 081**	**-27 854**	**-91 788**	**Balance**
Africa									**Afrique**
Imports		114 352	246 228	467 978	609 877	616 725	540 120	475 287	Importations
Exports		103 460	306 656	496 304	587 771	556 584	441 304	401 945	Exportations
Balance		-10 892	60 428	28 325	-22 106	-60 141	-98 816	-73 342	Balance
Northern Africa									**Afrique septentrionale**
Imports		45 062	87 571	181 147	227 951	229 144	205 345	182 830	Importations
Exports		33 043	114 104	165 544	182 579	153 120	108 178	95 253	Exportations
Balance		-12 019	26 533	-15 603	-45 372	-76 024	-97 167	-87 577	Balance
Sub-Saharan Africa									**Afrique subsaharienne**
Imports		69 290	158 657	286 832	381 926	387 582	334 775	292 458	Importations
Exports		70 417	192 552	330 760	405 192	403 464	333 126	306 692	Exportations
Balance		1 127	33 895	43 928	23 266	15 882	-1 649	14 234	Balance
Eastern Africa									**Afrique orientale**
Imports		17 980	31 243	62 505	95 776	103 500	102 541	81 096	Importations
Exports		9 499	16 297	31 282	44 253	49 721	42 943	37 487	Exportations
Balance		-8 481	-14 945	-31 223	-51 523	-53 779	-59 598	-43 609	Balance
Middle Africa									**Afrique centrale**
Imports		5 412	18 680	43 639	62 235	59 725	48 576	39 432	Importations
Exports		10 954	48 958	90 869	117 033	101 741	64 916	43 292	Exportations
Balance		5 542	30 278	47 231	54 797	42 016	16 340	3 860	Balance
Southern Africa									**Afrique australe**
Imports		26 745	63 786	97 572	122 258	119 656	97 800	90 027	Importations
Exports		28 214	56 076	95 227	111 851	107 328	83 236	88 777	Exportations
Balance		1 470	-7 711	-2 345	-10 407	-12 328	-14 564	-1 251	Balance
Western Africa									**Afrique occidentale**
Imports		19 153	44 948	83 116	101 656	104 701	85 858	81 902	Importations
Exports		21 750	71 221	113 381	132 056	144 675	142 031	137 136	Exportations
Balance		2 597	26 273	30 265	30 400	39 974	56 173	55 234	Balance
Americas									**Amériques**
Imports		1 178 848	2 557 148	3 228 875	3 910 786	3 990 150	3 735 613	3 558 310	Importations
Exports		997 709	1 835 325	2 550 359	3 133 086	3 169 679	2 828 555	2 711 385	Exportations
Balance		-181 139	-721 823	-678 516	-777 700	-820 471	-907 058	-846 925	Balance
Northern America									**Amérique septentrionale**
Imports		936 343	2 048 668	2 362 939	2 791 702	2 877 573	2 736 892	2 656 839	Importations
Exports		774 525	1 265 374	1 665 222	2 035 018	2 095 899	1 911 586	1 843 292	Exportations
Balance		-161 818	-783 295	-697 718	-756 685	-781 675	-825 306	-813 547	Balance
Latin America & the Caribbean									**Amérique latine et Caraïbes**
Imports		242 505	508 480	865 935	1 119 084	1 112 577	998 721	901 471	Importations
Exports		223 184	569 951	885 137	1 098 068	1 073 780	916 969	868 093	Exportations
Balance		-19 321	61 471	19 202	-21 016	-38 797	-81 752	-33 378	Balance
Caribbean									**Caraïbes**
Imports		20 945	36 923	51 256	58 055	56 331	50 911	50 576	Importations
Exports		8 346	21 331	24 192	38 285	40 217	37 341	29 845	Exportations
Balance		-12 598	-15 592	-27 064	-19 770	-16 114	-13 570	-20 731	Balance
Central America									**Amérique centrale**
Imports		87 084	259 847	366 171	455 606	474 335	466 161	456 251	Importations
Exports		87 067	233 506	336 529	416 478	434 971	416 220	406 463	Exportations
Balance		-17	-26 340	-29 642	-39 128	-39 364	-49 941	-49 789	Balance
South America									**Amérique du Sud**
Imports		134 476	211 710	448 508	605 424	581 911	481 649	394 644	Importations
Exports		127 771	315 113	524 416	643 305	598 592	463 407	431 786	Exportations
Balance		-6 706	103 404	75 908	37 882	16 681	-18 241	37 142	Balance
Asia									**Asie**
Imports		1 500 432	3 171 536	5 445 416	7 204 143	7 118 779	6 222 250	5 889 037	Importations
Exports		1 557 385	3 569 166	5 893 524	7 628 798	7 689 308	6 862 536	6 430 832	Exportations
Balance		56 953	397 630	448 108	424 655	570 529	640 286	541 795	Balance
Central Asia									**Asie centrale**
Imports		9 375	25 644	40 684	75 251	70 828	61 498	60 317	Importations
Exports		10 782	36 890	74 850	106 253	104 462	74 712	70 785	Exportations
Balance		1 407	11 246	34 166	31 001	33 634	13 214	10 468	Balance

Total imports, exports and balance of trade *(continued)*

Imports CIF, exports FOB and balance: millions of US dollars

Total des importations, des exportations et balance commerciale *(suite)*

Importations CAF, exportations FAB et balance: en millions de dollars É.-U.

Region, country or area	Sys.[&]	1995	2005	2010	2013	2014	2015	2016	Région, pays ou zone
Eastern Asia									**Asie orientale**
Imports		804 190	1 744 378	2 967 502	3 938 970	3 915 363	3 320 014	3 163 966	Importations
Exports		894 718	1 937 757	3 219 262	4 025 261	4 137 680	3 951 011	3 783 102	Exportations
Balance		90 528	193 379	251 759	86 291	222 316	630 997	619 136	Balance
South-eastern Asia									**Asie du Sud-Est**
Imports		353 943	583 336	951 476	1 241 324	1 230 114	1 088 741	1 081 570	Importations
Exports		320 454	654 380	1 051 658	1 270 038	1 290 883	1 157 475	1 142 558	Exportations
Balance		-33 489	71 044	100 182	28 714	60 768	68 734	60 988	Balance
Southern Asia									**Asie méridionale**
Imports		74 082	229 179	497 340	630 597	604 858	561 650	523 794	Importations
Exports		65 912	193 182	354 892	480 250	456 830	393 491	375 981	Exportations
Balance		-8 171	-35 997	-142 448	-150 347	-148 028	-168 160	-147 813	Balance
Western Asia									**Asie occidentale**
Imports		155 335	407 407	737 099	1 048 745	1 023 770	961 838	828 459	Importations
Exports		154 177	557 564	919 156	1 443 270	1 385 890	1 005 827	777 927	Exportations
Balance		-1 159	150 158	182 058	394 525	362 121	43 989	-50 532	Balance
Europe									**Europe**
Imports		2 228 669	4 439 990	5 869 522	6 729 082	6 709 753	5 743 644	5 761 863	Importations
Exports		2 320 042	4 527 059	5 904 713	7 167 778	7 100 187	6 102 187	6 059 004	Exportations
Balance		91 373	87 068	35 191	438 695	390 434	358 542	297 141	Balance
Eastern Europe									**Europe orientale**
Imports		161 835	490 657	867 387	1 076 946	1 054 924	847 830	852 440	Importations
Exports		176 871	594 285	993 297	1 284 181	1 276 700	1 024 049	975 327	Exportations
Balance		15 036	103 628	125 910	207 235	221 776	176 219	122 888	Balance
Northern Europe									**Europe septentrionale**
Imports		470 870	937 990	1 118 189	1 226 315	1 272 043	1 133 040	1 135 048	Importations
Exports		494 552	913 599	1 043 670	1 241 412	1 193 436	1 046 613	981 599	Exportations
Balance		23 682	-24 391	-74 519	15 097	-78 607	-86 426	-153 449	Balance
Southern Europe									**Europe méridionale**
Imports		400 631	861 881	1 039 442	1 054 222	1 075 792	925 499	921 887	Importations
Exports		372 435	660 817	830 354	1 002 492	1 026 036	887 598	899 660	Exportations
Balance		-28 196	-201 064	-209 088	-51 730	-49 756	-37 901	-22 227	Balance
Western Europe									**Europe occidentale**
Imports		1 195 333	2 149 462	2 844 504	3 371 600	3 306 994	2 837 275	2 852 488	Importations
Exports		1 276 184	2 358 357	3 037 392	3 639 693	3 604 015	3 143 926	3 202 418	Exportations
Balance		80 851	208 895	192 888	268 093	297 021	306 651	349 929	Balance
Oceania									**Océanie**
Imports		76 756	161 435	247 151	292 430	291 668	256 977	247 473	Importations
Exports		71 642	134 548	252 899	302 324	296 399	236 167	237 017	Exportations
Balance		-5 114	-26 888	5 748	9 893	4 731	-20 809	-10 457	Balance
Australia and New Zealand									**Australie et Nouvelle-Zélande**
Imports		71 338	151 453	231 861	272 100	270 042	236 642	225 829	Importations
Exports		66 374	127 740	243 041	291 599	282 080	222 150	223 463	Exportations
Balance		-4 965	-23 714	11 179	19 498	12 038	-14 493	-2 365	Balance
Melanesia									**Mélanésie**
Imports		3 432	5 397	9 665	13 629	14 717	13 442	14 483	Importations
Exports		4 039	5 199	8 112	8 824	12 366	12 059	11 517	Exportations
Balance		607	-197	-1 553	-4 805	-2 351	-1 382	-2 966	Balance
Micronesia									**Micronésie**
Imports		897	2 379	3 292	4 149	4 362	4 618	4 948	Importations
Exports		1 028	1 295	1 508	1 658	1 694	1 736	1 778	Exportations
Balance		131	-1 084	-1 783	-2 491	-2 667	-2 882	-3 170	Balance
Polynesia									**Polynésie**
Imports		1 089	2 206	2 333	2 552	2 548	2 275	2 214	Importations
Exports		201	314	238	243	259	223	258	Exportations
Balance		-887	-1 893	-2 095	-2 309	-2 289	-2 052	-1 956	Balance
Afghanistan									**Afghanistan**
Imports	G	...	...	5 154	8 554	7 697	7 723	3 568	Importations
Exports	G	...	...	388	515	571	571	1 458	Exportations
Balance	G	...	...	-4 766	-8 039	-7 127	-7 151	-2 110	Balance
Albania									**Albanie**
Imports	G	713	2 614	4 603	4 881	5 230	4 320	4 669	Importations
Exports	G	202	658	1 550	2 332	2 431	1 930	1 962	Exportations
Balance	G	-511	-1 956	-3 053	-2 549	-2 799	-2 391	-2 707	Balance

Total imports, exports and balance of trade *(continued)*
Imports CIF, exports FOB and balance: millions of US dollars

Total des importations, des exportations et balance commerciale *(suite)*
Importations CAF, exportations FAB et balance: en millions de dollars É.-U.

Region, country or area	Sys.[&]	1995	2005	2010	2013	2014	2015	2016	Région, pays ou zone
Algeria									**Algérie**
Imports	S	10 782	20 357	41 000	54 910	58 618	51 803	47 091	Importations
Exports	S	9 357	46 002	57 051	65 998	60 388	34 796	29 992	Exportations
Balance	S	-1 426	25 645	16 051	11 088	1 770	-17 007	-17 099	Balance
Andorra									**Andorre**
Imports	S	1 025	1 796	1 541	1 487	1 556	1 295	1 355	Importations
Exports	S	48	143	92	99	95	89	100	Exportations
Balance	S	-978	-1 653	-1 448	-1 388	-1 461	-1 206	-1 255	Balance
Angola [1]									**Angola** [1]
Imports	S	1 466	8 321	18 143	26 756	28 753	16 758	8 790	Importations
Exports	S	3 592	23 835	52 612	67 713	58 672	33 048	21 011	Exportations
Balance	S	2 126	15 514	34 469	40 956	29 919	16 290	12 221	Balance
Anguilla									**Anguilla**
Imports	S	53	133	157	145	152	158	154	Importations
Exports	S	1	7	12	4	4	2	2	Exportations
Balance	S	-52	-126	-145	-141	-148	-156	-153	Balance
Antigua and Barbuda									**Antigua-et-Barbuda**
Imports	G	344	525	501	508	552	465	491	Importations
Exports	G	53	121	35	33	23	26	61	Exportations
Balance	G	-291	-405	-466	-475	-529	-439	-429	Balance
Argentina									**Argentine**
Imports	S	20 122	28 689	56 792	74 442	65 230	59 757	55 610	Importations
Exports	S	20 963	40 106	68 174	75 963	68 407	56 788	57 733	Exportations
Balance	S	841	11 418	11 382	1 521	3 178	-2 969	2 124	Balance
Armenia									**Arménie**
Imports	S	674	1 692	3 782	4 256	4 160	3 257	3 230	Importations
Exports	S	271	937	1 011	1 468	1 490	1 483	1 776	Exportations
Balance	S	-403	-755	-2 770	-2 788	-2 669	-1 774	-1 455	Balance
Aruba									**Aruba**
Imports	S	566	1 030	1 071	1 303	1 284	1 165	1 117	Importations
Exports	S	15	106	125	168	116	80	95	Exportations
Balance	S	-551	-924	-947	-1 136	-1 168	-1 085	-1 022	Balance
Australia [1]									**Australie** [1]
Imports	G	57 381	125 221	201 703	232 481	227 544	200 114	189 406	Importations
Exports	G	52 628	106 011	212 109	252 155	240 445	187 792	189 630	Exportations
Balance	G	-4 752	-19 210	10 405	19 674	12 900	-12 322	224	Balance
Austria									**Autriche**
Imports	S	66 331	119 950	150 593	173 358	172 447	147 935	149 299	Importations
Exports	S	53 460	117 722	144 882	166 271	169 715	145 277	145 503	Exportations
Balance	S	-12 871	-2 228	-5 711	-7 086	-2 732	-2 658	-3 795	Balance
Azerbaijan									**Azerbaïdjan**
Imports	G	666	4 211	6 597	10 763	9 179	9 211	8 532	Importations
Exports	G	637	4 347	21 278	23 904	21 752	11 327	9 143	Exportations
Balance	G	-30	136	14 682	13 141	12 573	2 116	611	Balance
Bahamas [2]									**Bahamas** [2]
Imports	G	1 243	2 567	2 862	3 365	3 790	3 161	2 904	Importations
Exports	G	176	271	620	811	689	443	365	Exportations
Balance	G	-1 067	-2 296	-2 242	-2 554	-3 101	-2 719	-2 539	Balance
Bahrain									**Bahreïn**
Imports	G	3 679	9 339	16 002	18 618	20 074	16 378	14 749	Importations
Exports	G	3 475	10 239	16 059	20 036	23 746	16 684	12 892	Exportations
Balance	G	-204	899	58	1 419	3 672	307	-1 856	Balance
Bangladesh									**Bangladesh**
Imports	G	5 438	12 631	30 504	35 493	7 047	48 059	52 624	Importations
Exports	G	3 407	9 332	19 231	24 537	12 302	31 734	36 031	Exportations
Balance	G	-2 031	-3 299	-11 273	-10 956	5 255	-16 325	-16 593	Balance
Barbados									**Barbade**
Imports	G	766	1 672	1 196	1 769	1 740	1 618	1 621	Importations
Exports	G	238	361	314	467	481	483	517	Exportations
Balance	G	-528	-1 311	-883	-1 301	-1 260	-1 135	-1 104	Balance
Belarus									**Bélarus**
Imports	G	5 382	16 699	34 884	43 023	40 502	30 291	27 464	Importations
Exports	G	4 623	15 977	25 283	37 203	36 081	26 660	23 414	Exportations
Balance	G	-759	-722	-9 601	-5 820	-4 422	-3 631	-4 050	Balance

20 Total imports, exports and balance of trade *(continued)*
Imports CIF, exports FOB and balance: millions of US dollars

Total des importations, des exportations et balance commerciale *(suite)*
Importations CAF, exportations FAB et balance: en millions de dollars É.-U.

Region, country or area	Sys.&	1995	2005	2010	2013	2014	2015	2016	Région, pays ou zone
Belgium									**Belgique**
Imports	S	153 388[3]	319 085[3]	391 256	488 527	452 773	371 025	372 713	Importations
Exports	S	168 154[3]	335 692[3]	407 596	511 505	472 201	397 739	398 033	Exportations
Balance	S	14 765[3]	16 606[3]	16 340	22 978	19 429	26 714	25 321	Balance
Belize									**Belize**
Imports	G	259	439	700	906	962	996	952	Importations
Exports	G	162	208	282	413	358	314	246	Exportations
Balance	G	-97	-231	-418	-493	-604	-682	-706	Balance
Benin									**Bénin**
Imports	S	745	899	2 134	2 941	3 704	2 475	2 630	Importations
Exports	S	415	288	534	602	968	626	410	Exportations
Balance	S	-329	-611	-1 600	-2 339	-2 735	-1 849	-2 220	Balance
Bermuda									**Bermudes**
Imports	G	633	988	970	995	961	929	971	Importations
Exports	G	63	49	15	22	12	9	8	Exportations
Balance	G	-570	-939	-955	-973	-949	-920	-963	Balance
Bhutan									**Bhoutan**
Imports	G	113	387	854	911	810	1 170	1 688	Importations
Exports	G	103	258	413	544	555	585	616	Exportations
Balance	G	-9	-129	-440	-367	-255	-585	-1 072	Balance
Bolivia (Plurin. State of)									**Bolivie (État plurin. de)**
Imports	G	1 396	2 343	5 604	9 353	10 492	9 766	8 374	Importations
Exports	G	1 181	2 797	6 965	12 207	12 856	8 726	6 969	Exportations
Balance	G	-215	454	1 361	2 854	2 364	-1 041	-1 405	Balance
Bosnia and Herzegovina									**Bosnie-Herzégovine**
Imports	S	1 068	7 054	9 223	10 295	10 990	8 994	9 130	Importations
Exports	S	152	2 388	4 803	5 687	5 891	5 099	5 327	Exportations
Balance	S	-917	-4 665	-4 420	-4 608	-5 100	-3 895	-3 803	Balance
Botswana									**Botswana**
Imports	G	...	3 162	5 657	7 433	7 830	7 626	6 103	Importations
Exports	G	...	4 431	4 693	7 573	7 915	6 319	7 321	Exportations
Balance	G	...	1 268	-964	140	85	-1 307	1 218	Balance
Brazil									**Brésil**
Imports	G	53 734	73 600	181 768	239 748	229 060	171 446	137 552	Importations
Exports	G	46 505	118 529	201 915	242 033	225 098	191 127	185 235	Exportations
Balance	G	-7 229	44 928	20 147	2 285	-3 962	19 681	47 683	Balance
British Virgin Islands									**Îles Vierges britanniques**
Imports		122	227	313	379	403	430	444	Importations
Exports		11	~0	~0	~0	~0	~0	~0	Exportations
Balance		-110	-226	-313	-379	-403	-430	-444	Balance
Brunei Darussalam									**Brunéi Darussalam**
Imports	S	2 078	1 447	3 364	3 612	3 599	3 229	2 679	Importations
Exports	S	2 379	6 242	9 172	11 447	10 509	6 353	4 875	Exportations
Balance	S	301	4 794	5 809	7 835	6 910	3 124	2 197	Balance
Bulgaria									**Bulgarie**
Imports	S	5 469	18 162	25 360	34 317	34 740	29 265	28 875	Importations
Exports	S	5 220	11 739	20 608	29 511	29 387	25 779	26 088	Exportations
Balance	S	-249	-6 423	-4 752	-4 806	-5 354	-3 486	-2 787	Balance
Burkina Faso									**Burkina Faso**
Imports	G	484	1 161	2 048	4 365	3 575	2 980	3 699	Importations
Exports	G	171	332	1 288	2 651	2 846	2 177	2 019	Exportations
Balance	G	-313	-828	-760	-1 715	-729	-802	-1 680	Balance
Burundi									**Burundi**
Imports	S	270	258	404	722	673	561	625	Importations
Exports	S	179	114	118	206	142	114	123	Exportations
Balance	S	-92	-144	-286	-516	-531	-447	-502	Balance
Cabo Verde									**Cabo Verde**
Imports	G	252	438	731	726	769	606	485	Importations
Exports	G	9	89	220	333	357	215	29	Exportations
Balance	G	-243	-349	-511	-394	-412	-391	-455	Balance
Cambodia									**Cambodge**
Imports	S	217	2 552	4 903	8 232	9 702	10 669	15 313	Importations
Exports	S	76	3 019	5 590	6 666	6 846	8 542	13 204	Exportations
Balance	S	-142	467	688	-1 566	-2 856	-2 126	-2 109	Balance

20 Total imports, exports and balance of trade *(continued)*
Imports CIF, exports FOB and balance: millions of US dollars

Total des importations, des exportations et balance commerciale *(suite)*
Importations CAF, exportations FAB et balance: en millions de dollars É.-U.

Region, country or area	Sys.[&]	1995	2005	2010	2013	2014	2015	2016	Région, pays ou zone
Cameroon									**Cameroun**
Imports	S	1 079	2 800	5 133	6 657	7 561	6 037	4 899	Importations
Exports	S	1 539	2 849	3 878	4 521	5 160	4 053	2 130	Exportations
Balance	S	460	49	-1 255	-2 136	-2 402	-1 984	-2 768	Balance
Canada [1]									**Canada [1]**
Imports	G	164 371	314 444	392 109	461 785	463 089	419 693	402 954	Importations
Exports	G	191 118	360 552	386 580	456 598	475 177	408 804	388 911	Exportations
Balance	G	26 747	46 108	-5 529	-5 187	12 088	-10 889	-14 043	Balance
Cayman Islands									**Îles Caïmanes**
Imports	G	390	1 191	828	929	976	915	991	Importations
Exports	G	4	52	13	30	26	20	18	Exportations
Balance	G	-386	-1 138	-815	-899	-950	-895	-972	Balance
Central African Republic									**République centrafricaine**
Imports	S	265	185	210	130	308	457	147	Importations
Exports	S	120	111	90	49	21	97	213	Exportations
Balance	S	-146	-75	-120	-81	-287	-360	66	Balance
Chad									**Tchad**
Imports	S	214	953	2 507	2 997	3 494	2 198	1 371	Importations
Exports	S	243	3 095	3 410	4 496	4 194	2 900	1 990	Exportations
Balance	S	28	2 142	904	1 499	700	702	619	Balance
Chile									**Chili**
Imports	S	14 903	32 926	59 207	79 173	72 344	63 038	58 804	Importations
Exports	S	15 901	41 973	71 106	76 684	76 639	63 360	59 884	Exportations
Balance	S	998	9 047	11 899	-2 489	4 295	322	1 080	Balance
China [4]									**Chine [4]**
Imports	S	131 353	659 953	1 396 002	1 949 992	1 958 021	1 681 671	1 588 696	Importations
Exports	S	148 616	761 953	1 577 764	2 209 007	2 342 343	2 281 856	2 118 981	Exportations
Balance	S	17 263	102 001	181 762	259 015	384 322	600 185	530 285	Balance
China, Hong Kong SAR									**Chine, Hong Kong RAS**
Imports	G	196 072	300 160	441 369	621 417	600 613	559 284	547 124	Importations
Exports	G	173 871	292 119	400 692	535 187	524 065	510 533	516 588	Exportations
Balance	G	-22 201	-8 042	-40 677	-86 230	-76 548	-48 751	-30 536	Balance
China, Macao SAR									**Chine, Macao RAS**
Imports	G	2 025	4 514	5 629	10 141	11 396	10 603	8 924	Importations
Exports	G	2 025	2 474	870	1 138	1 240	1 339	1 257	Exportations
Balance	G	-1	-2 040	-4 760	-9 002	-10 156	-9 264	-7 668	Balance
Colombia									**Colombie**
Imports	G	13 883	21 204	40 683	59 381	64 028	54 036	44 831	Importations
Exports	G	10 201	21 190	39 820	58 822	54 795	35 691	31 045	Exportations
Balance	G	-3 682	-14	-863	-559	-9 233	-18 345	-13 786	Balance
Comoros									**Comores**
Imports	S	62	85	181	115	106	92	193	Importations
Exports	S	11	4	14	10	10	9	20	Exportations
Balance	S	-51	-81	-167	-105	-96	-83	-173	Balance
Congo									**Congo**
Imports	S	556	1 342	4 369	8 372	3 348	7 747	9 793	Importations
Exports	S	1 090	4 744	6 918	10 453	6 550	4 650	2 540	Exportations
Balance	S	534	3 402	2 548	2 081	3 202	-3 097	-7 253	Balance
Cook Islands									**Îles Cook**
Imports	G	49	81	91	116	121	109	98	Importations
Exports	G	5	5	5	11	18	14	14	Exportations
Balance	G	-44	-76	-85	-105	-103	-95	-84	Balance
Costa Rica									**Costa Rica**
Imports	S	3 205	9 173	13 920	18 124	17 185	15 504	15 322	Importations
Exports	S	2 702	7 151	9 045	11 472	11 243	9 578	9 908	Exportations
Balance	S	-504	-2 023	-4 875	-6 652	-5 942	-5 926	-5 414	Balance
Côte d'Ivoire									**Côte d'Ivoire**
Imports	S	2 472	5 865	7 849	12 483	11 178	9 532	8 380	Importations
Exports	S	3 736	7 248	10 284	12 084	12 985	11 845	10 661	Exportations
Balance	S	1 264	1 383	2 434	-399	1 807	2 313	2 281	Balance
Croatia									**Croatie**
Imports	G	7 509	18 560	20 067	21 932	22 907	20 580	21 830	Importations
Exports	G	4 633	8 773	11 811	12 742	13 844	12 844	13 648	Exportations
Balance	G	-2 877	-9 788	-8 256	-9 190	-9 063	-7 737	-8 182	Balance

Total imports, exports and balance of trade *(continued)*
Imports CIF, exports FOB and balance: millions of US dollars

Total des importations, des exportations et balance commerciale *(suite)*
Importations CAF, exportations FAB et balance: en millions de dollars É.-U.

Region, country or area	Sys.[&]	1995	2005	2010	2013	2014	2015	2016	Région, pays ou zone
Cuba									**Cuba**
Imports	S	2 874	8 084	10 913	7 326	6 413	5 613	4 911	Importations
Exports	S	1 491	2 319	4 945	9 436	11 703	14 515	18 000	Exportations
Balance	S	-1 384	-5 766	-5 968	2 109	5 289	8 902	13 089	Balance
Cyprus									**Chypre**
Imports	G	3 694	6 382	8 645	6 418	6 829	5 699	6 604	Importations
Exports	G	1 231	1 546	1 506	2 134	1 924	1 935	1 920	Exportations
Balance	G	-2 463	-4 836	-7 138	-4 284	-4 905	-3 764	-4 684	Balance
Czechia									**Tchéquie**
Imports	S	25 303	76 527	125 691	142 526	153 225	140 716	140 316	Importations
Exports	S	21 686	78 209	132 141	161 524	174 279	157 194	161 248	Exportations
Balance	S	-3 618	1 681	6 450	18 998	21 054	16 478	20 932	Balance
Dem. People's Rep. Korea									**Rép. pop. dém. de Corée**
Imports		3 122	1 466	1 957	2 323	2 460	2 604	2 757	Importations
Exports		1 739	787	882	944	965	987	1 010	Exportations
Balance		-1 382	-679	-1 075	-1 379	-1 495	-1 617	-1 748	Balance
Dem. Rep. of the Congo									**Rép. dém. du Congo**
Imports	S	869	2 268	4 500	6 296	6 494	6 196	5 906	Importations
Exports	S	1 562	2 190	5 300	6 300	6 599	5 789	5 103	Exportations
Balance	S	693	-78	800	4	105	-407	-803	Balance
Denmark									**Danemark**
Imports	S	43 142	72 716	82 724	97 252	99 568	85 327	85 133	Importations
Exports	S	48 789	82 278	96 217	110 470	110 749	94 619	94 355	Exportations
Balance	S	5 648	9 562	13 492	13 218	11 181	9 291	9 222	Balance
Djibouti									**Djibouti**
Imports	G	176	277	420	560	803	890	987	Importations
Exports	G	13	39	100	120	129	132	134	Exportations
Balance	G	-163	-238	-320	-440	-674	-758	-852	Balance
Dominica									**Dominique**
Imports	S	117	165	225	203	230	218	214	Importations
Exports	S	45	42	34	35	36	30	23	Exportations
Balance	S	-72	-124	-190	-168	-194	-188	-191	Balance
Dominican Republic [1,5]									**République dominicaine** [1,5]
Imports	G	3 155	6 804	15 138	17 845	17 752	17 348	22 725	Importations
Exports	G	872	6 183	4 767	7 961	9 928	8 384	3 747	Exportations
Balance	G	-2 283	-621	-10 371	-9 884	-7 824	-8 964	-18 978	Balance
Ecuador									**Équateur**
Imports	G	4 195	9 609	20 591	27 064	27 518	21 387	16 189	Importations
Exports	G	4 361	9 869	17 490	24 958	25 724	18 331	16 798	Exportations
Balance	G	166	261	-3 101	-2 107	-1 794	-3 057	609	Balance
Egypt [6,7]									**Égypte** [6,7]
Imports	G	11 739	19 812	53 003	66 666	71 338	74 361	58 053	Importations
Exports	G	3 444	10 646	26 332	28 779	26 812	21 967	22 507	Exportations
Balance	G	-8 295	-9 166	-26 672	-37 887	-44 526	-52 394	-35 545	Balance
El Salvador									**El Salvador**
Imports	S	2 628	6 809	8 416	10 772	10 513	10 415	9 855	Importations
Exports	S	985	3 436	4 499	5 491	5 273	5 485	5 335	Exportations
Balance	S	-1 642	-3 373	-3 917	-5 281	-5 240	-4 930	-4 519	Balance
Equatorial Guinea									**Guinée équatoriale**
Imports	G	50	1 309	5 679	6 990	6 492	6 010	5 456	Importations
Exports	G	86	7 062	9 964	13 981	11 587	9 301	7 443	Exportations
Balance	G	36	5 753	4 285	6 991	5 094	3 291	1 987	Balance
Eritrea									**Érythrée**
Imports		432	503	1 187	1 987	2 359	2 800	3 325	Importations
Exports		73	11	13	14	15	15	16	Exportations
Balance		-359	-493	-1 175	-1 973	-2 344	-2 785	-3 310	Balance
Estonia									**Estonie**
Imports	S	2 546	11 018	13 197	20 186	20 185	15 747	15 759	Importations
Exports	S	1 840	8 247	12 811	18 284	17 466	13 897	13 952	Exportations
Balance	S	-706	-2 770	-385	-1 902	-2 719	-1 850	-1 807	Balance
Ethiopia									**Éthiopie**
Imports	G	1 141	4 095	8 602	14 899	21 914	25 815	19 121	Importations
Exports	G	422	926	2 330	4 077	5 667	5 028	1 724	Exportations
Balance	G	-719	-3 169	-6 272	-10 822	-16 247	-20 788	-17 397	Balance

Total imports, exports and balance of trade *(continued)*

Imports CIF, exports FOB and balance: millions of US dollars

Total des importations, des exportations et balance commerciale *(suite)*

Importations CAF, exportations FAB et balance: en millions de dollars É.-U.

Region, country or area	Sys.&	1995	2005	2010	2013	2014	2015	2016	Région, pays ou zone
Falkland Islands (Malvinas)									**Iles Falkland (Malvinas)**
Imports		27	8	50	30	26	21	17	Importations
Exports		4	11	9	6	5	4	4	Exportations
Balance		-23	2	-41	-24	-21	-17	-13	Balance
Faroe Islands									**Îles Féroé**
Imports	G	314	747	780	1 110	1 040	909	976	Importations
Exports	G	362	602	839	1 080	1 110	1 024	1 192	Exportations
Balance	G	48	-145	59	-29	71	114	216	Balance
Fiji									**Fidji**
Imports	G	891	1 607	1 808	2 826	3 250	2 081	2 316	Importations
Exports	G	619	702	841	1 108	1 373	895	926	Exportations
Balance	G	-273	-906	-967	-1 718	-1 877	-1 186	-1 391	Balance
Finland									**Finlande**
Imports	G	29 520	58 473	68 767	77 587	76 773	60 174	60 502	Importations
Exports	G	40 409	65 238	70 117	74 445	74 339	59 682	57 326	Exportations
Balance	G	10 889	6 766	1 349	-3 142	-2 434	-492	-3 176	Balance
France [8]									**France** [8]
Imports	S	273 387	475 857	599 172	671 254	659 872	563 398	560 555	Importations
Exports	S	277 079	434 354	511 651	567 988	566 656	493 941	488 885	Exportations
Balance	S	3 692	-41 503	-87 520	-103 266	-93 216	-69 457	-71 670	Balance
French Guiana [8]									**Guyane française** [8]
Imports	S	783	...	...	...	...	...	...	Importations
Exports	S	158	...	...	...	...	...	...	Exportations
Balance	S	-625	...	...	...	...	...	...	Balance
French Polynesia									**Polynésie française**
Imports	S	848	1 702	1 726	1 815	1 762	1 527	1 491	Importations
Exports	S	173	210	153	151	170	130	173	Exportations
Balance	S	-675	-1 491	-1 573	-1 663	-1 592	-1 397	-1 319	Balance
Gabon									**Gabon**
Imports	S	884	1 451	2 984	3 886	3 104	3 032	2 930	Importations
Exports	S	2 718	5 068	8 691	9 514	8 949	5 069	2 851	Exportations
Balance	S	1 834	3 617	5 706	5 628	5 844	2 037	-79	Balance
Gambia									**Gambie**
Imports	G	215	260	284	350	387	426	471	Importations
Exports	G	19	7	68	106	104	23	32	Exportations
Balance	G	-196	-252	-215	-244	-283	-403	-439	Balance
Georgia									**Géorgie**
Imports	G	396	2 490	5 236	8 022	8 602	7 730	7 236	Importations
Exports	G	152	865	1 677	2 911	2 861	2 205	2 114	Exportations
Balance	G	-245	-1 624	-3 558	-5 112	-5 741	-5 525	-5 122	Balance
Germany									**Allemagne**
Imports	S	464 145	779 819	1 066 817	1 187 315	1 214 956	1 057 616	1 060 672	Importations
Exports	S	518 224	977 132	1 271 096	1 450 951	1 498 158	1 328 549	1 340 752	Exportations
Balance	S	54 079	197 313	204 280	263 636	283 202	270 933	280 080	Balance
Ghana									**Ghana**
Imports	G	1 897	4 878	8 057	12 787	14 682	13 290	11 939	Importations
Exports	G	1 755	3 060	5 233	12 644	12 548	9 550	7 221	Exportations
Balance	G	-142	-1 819	-2 824	-143	-2 134	-3 740	-4 718	Balance
Gibraltar									**Gibraltar**
Imports		408	501	627	742	701	657	533	Importations
Exports		114	195	259	279	267	254	234	Exportations
Balance		-294	-306	-368	-463	-434	-403	-299	Balance
Greece									**Grèce**
Imports	S	25 805	54 894	66 453	61 148	62 181	47 264	47 595	Importations
Exports	S	10 896	17 434	27 586	36 262	35 755	28 289	27 811	Exportations
Balance	S	-14 909	-37 459	-38 867	-24 886	-26 425	-18 975	-19 784	Balance
Greenland									**Groenland**
Imports	G	421	700	854	822	768	586	623	Importations
Exports	G	364	402	391	490	540	395	553	Exportations
Balance	G	-57	-297	-463	-332	-228	-191	-71	Balance
Grenada									**Grenade**
Imports	S	129	334	317	368	336	344	350	Importations
Exports	S	22	28	24	33	40	33	30	Exportations
Balance	S	-107	-306	-293	-336	-296	-311	-320	Balance

Total imports, exports and balance of trade *(continued)*
Imports CIF, exports FOB and balance: millions of US dollars

Total des importations, des exportations et balance commerciale *(suite)*
Importations CAF, exportations FAB et balance: en millions de dollars É.-U.

Region, country or area	Sys.&	1995	2005	2010	2013	2014	2015	2016	Région, pays ou zone
Guadeloupe [8]									**Guadeloupe** [8]
Imports	S	1 901	...	...	...	...	...	...	Importations
Exports	S	162	...	...	...	...	...	...	Exportations
Balance	S	-1 739	...	...	...	...	...	...	Balance
Guatemala									**Guatemala**
Imports	S	3 292	10 500	13 830	17 504	18 263	17 637	16 987	Importations
Exports	S	1 936	5 381	8 460	10 065	10 891	10 677	10 572	Exportations
Balance	S	-1 357	-5 119	-5 370	-7 439	-7 373	-6 960	-6 415	Balance
Guinea									**Guinée**
Imports	S	819	1 648	1 405	2 401	2 509	2 139	2 082	Importations
Exports	S	702	796	1 471	1 780	1 947	1 574	1 753	Exportations
Balance	S	-117	-852	66	-621	-563	-565	-329	Balance
Guinea-Bissau									**Guinée-Bissau**
Imports	G	134	112	197	240	230	221	212	Importations
Exports	G	45	23	120	210	339	548	885	Exportations
Balance	G	-89	-88	-77	-30	109	327	673	Balance
Guyana									**Guyana**
Imports	S	472	778	1 452	1 866	1 783	2 186	1 625	Importations
Exports	S	455	539	901	1 376	1 174	1 286	1 453	Exportations
Balance	S	-17	-239	-551	-490	-609	-900	-172	Balance
Haiti									**Haïti**
Imports	G	650	1 449	3 147	3 400	3 734	3 523	3 316	Importations
Exports	G	35	470	579	885	950	1 018	984	Exportations
Balance	G	-615	-979	-2 568	-2 515	-2 785	-2 505	-2 332	Balance
Honduras									**Honduras**
Imports	S	1 728	4 419	6 895	8 566	7 984	8 381	8 448	Importations
Exports	S	656	1 294	3 104	3 649	4 533	4 201	3 657	Exportations
Balance	S	-1 072	-3 125	-3 791	-4 917	-3 450	-4 179	-4 791	Balance
Hungary									**Hongrie**
Imports	S	15 186	65 920	87 432	99 296	104 178	90 761	92 044	Importations
Exports	S	12 452	62 272	94 749	108 015	112 536	100 297	103 071	Exportations
Balance	S	-2 734	-3 648	7 317	8 719	8 358	9 536	11 027	Balance
Iceland									**Islande**
Imports	G	1 751	4 979	3 914	5 019	5 372	5 285	5 703	Importations
Exports	G	1 803	3 091	4 603	4 998	5 051	4 722	4 450	Exportations
Balance	G	51	-1 888	689	-22	-321	-563	-1 254	Balance
India [9]									**Inde** [9]
Imports	G	36 592	140 862	350 029	466 046	459 369	390 745	356 705	Importations
Exports	G	31 699	100 353	220 408	336 611	317 545	264 381	260 327	Exportations
Balance	G	-4 893	-40 509	-129 621	-129 434	-141 825	-126 364	-96 378	Balance
Indonesia									**Indonésie**
Imports	S	40 629	57 701	135 663	186 629	178 179	142 695	135 653	Importations
Exports	S	45 418	85 660	157 779	182 552	176 036	150 366	144 490	Exportations
Balance	S	4 789	27 959	22 116	-4 077	-2 143	7 671	8 837	Balance
Iran (Islamic Republic of) [10,11]									**Iran (Rép. islamique d')** [10,11]
Imports	S	13 882	38 869	54 697	49 701	53 563	42 488	35 333	Importations
Exports	S	18 360	60 012	83 785	81 887	88 795	62 886	45 627	Exportations
Balance	S	4 478	21 143	29 088	32 186	35 232	20 398	10 294	Balance
Iraq									**Iraq**
Imports		445	12 861	31 764	61 000	37 064	52 000	45 831	Importations
Exports		555	19 773	52 483	89 742	84 506	49 403	27 341	Exportations
Balance		110	6 912	20 718	28 742	47 442	-2 597	-18 490	Balance
Ireland									**Irlande**
Imports	G	32 321	70 284	60 550	65 951	71 049	77 760	76 997	Importations
Exports	G	43 789	110 003	118 338	115 323	118 287	124 671	129 315	Exportations
Balance	G	11 468	39 719	57 788	49 373	47 238	46 911	52 318	Balance
Israel [12]									**Israël** [12]
Imports	S	28 328	45 032	59 194	71 995	72 332	62 068	65 803	Importations
Exports	S	19 046	42 771	58 413	66 781	68 965	64 062	60 571	Exportations
Balance	S	-9 282	-2 262	-781	-5 214	-3 367	1 994	-5 232	Balance
Italy									**Italie**
Imports	S	200 320	384 836	486 984	479 336	474 083	410 933	404 578	Importations
Exports	S	230 441	372 957	446 840	518 095	529 529	456 989	461 529	Exportations
Balance	S	30 122	-11 878	-40 145	38 759	55 446	46 055	56 951	Balance

Total imports, exports and balance of trade *(continued)*
Imports CIF, exports FOB and balance: millions of US dollars

Total des importations, des exportations et balance commerciale *(suite)*
Importations CAF, exportations FAB et balance: en millions de dollars É.-U.

Region, country or area	Sys.[&]	1995	2005	2010	2013	2014	2015	2016	Région, pays ou zone
Jamaica									**Jamaïque**
Imports	G	2 773	4 885	5 225	6 216	5 836	4 993	4 767	Importations
Exports	G	1 424	1 514	1 328	1 569	1 452	1 263	1 202	Exportations
Balance	G	-1 349	-3 370	-3 898	-4 647	-4 384	-3 730	-3 565	Balance
Japan									**Japon**
Imports	G	336 094	515 866	694 059	833 166	812 185	625 568	606 924	Importations
Exports	G	442 937	594 941	769 774	715 097	690 217	624 874	644 932	Exportations
Balance	G	106 843	79 074	75 715	-118 069	-121 967	-695	38 008	Balance
Jordan									**Jordanie**
Imports	G	3 696	10 455	15 262	21 549	22 740	20 475	19 207	Importations
Exports	G	1 769	4 284	7 023	7 920	8 385	7 833	7 509	Exportations
Balance	G	-1 928	-6 170	-8 239	-13 629	-14 355	-12 642	-11 698	Balance
Kazakhstan									**Kazakhstan**
Imports	G	3 805	17 333	24 024	48 805	41 295	30 567	25 175	Importations
Exports	G	5 227	27 846	57 244	84 699	79 459	45 954	36 775	Exportations
Balance	G	1 422	10 513	33 220	35 894	38 163	15 387	11 601	Balance
Kenya									**Kenya**
Imports	G	2 818	5 846	12 093	16 394	18 397	16 097	14 109	Importations
Exports	G	1 826	3 420	5 169	5 537	6 046	5 908	5 688	Exportations
Balance	G	-992	-2 426	-6 924	-10 858	-12 351	-10 189	-8 420	Balance
Kiribati									**Kiribati**
Imports	G	34	74	73	97	95	100	116	Importations
Exports	G	7	4	4	7	5	9	3	Exportations
Balance	G	-27	-70	-69	-90	-90	-91	-113	Balance
Kuwait									**Koweït**
Imports	S	7 790	15 801	22 691	29 646	31 489	31 907	30 825	Importations
Exports	S	12 944	44 869	62 698	114 404	101 132	55 162	46 238	Exportations
Balance	S	5 155	29 068	40 007	84 758	69 643	23 254	15 413	Balance
Kyrgyzstan									**Kirghizistan**
Imports	S	522	1 108	3 223	5 983	5 732	4 068	3 844	Importations
Exports	S	412	672	1 488	1 773	1 897	1 441	1 423	Exportations
Balance	S	-110	-436	-1 734	-4 210	-3 836	-2 627	-2 421	Balance
Lao People's Dem. Rep.									**Rép. dém. populaire lao**
Imports	S	588	874	2 059	3 020	3 300	3 859	4 513	Importations
Exports	S	311	552	1 746	2 264	2 650	2 340	2 066	Exportations
Balance	S	-277	-322	-312	-756	-650	-1 519	-2 447	Balance
Latvia									**Lettonie**
Imports	S	1 818	8 770	11 143	16 779	16 798	13 850	13 596	Importations
Exports	S	1 305	5 303	8 851	13 325	13 603	11 491	11 433	Exportations
Balance	S	-513	-3 468	-2 292	-3 454	-3 196	-2 359	-2 163	Balance
Lebanon									**Liban**
Imports	G	7 295	9 327	17 970	21 234	20 487	18 439	20 409	Importations
Exports	G	826	1 879	4 254	3 937	3 312	3 982	3 402	Exportations
Balance	G	-6 469	-7 448	-13 716	-17 297	-17 175	-14 458	-17 007	Balance
Lesotho									**Lesotho**
Imports	G	...	1 410	1 277	2 284	2 207	1 949	1 727	Importations
Exports	G	...	650	503	934	924	773	648	Exportations
Balance	G	...	-760	-773	-1 350	-1 283	-1 177	-1 079	Balance
Liberia									**Libéria**
Imports	S	358	309	710	1 210	1 045	898	727	Importations
Exports	S	452	130	222	540	583	627	641	Exportations
Balance	S	94	-179	-488	-670	-462	-270	-86	Balance
Libya									**Libye**
Imports	G	4 912	6 058	17 674	27 004	18 991	12 999	8 876	Importations
Exports	G	9 363	31 272	36 440	43 986	20 994	9 717	4 615	Exportations
Balance	G	4 451	25 215	18 766	16 982	2 003	-3 282	-4 261	Balance
Lithuania									**Lituanie**
Imports	G	3 649	15 704	23 378	34 813	35 217	28 176	27 501	Importations
Exports	G	2 706	12 070	20 814	32 600	32 394	25 411	25 025	Exportations
Balance	G	-943	-3 634	-2 564	-2 213	-2 823	-2 765	-2 476	Balance
Luxembourg									**Luxembourg**
Imports	S	...	17 586[13]	20 400	23 934	23 850	19 296	19 124	Importations
Exports	S	...	12 715[13]	13 911	13 826	14 791	12 626	12 838	Exportations
Balance	S	...	-4 871[13]	-6 489	-10 108	-9 059	-6 671	-6 285	Balance

Total imports, exports and balance of trade *(continued)*
Imports CIF, exports FOB and balance: millions of US dollars

Total des importations, des exportations et balance commerciale *(suite)*
Importations CAF, exportations FAB et balance: en millions de dollars É.-U.

Region, country or area	Sys.&	1995	2005	2010	2013	2014	2015	2016	Région, pays ou zone
Madagascar									**Madagascar**
Imports	S	550	1 686	2 546	2 699	3 355	2 961	2 965	Importations
Exports	S	360	836	1 082	1 627	2 243	2 164	2 256	Exportations
Balance	S	-190	-850	-1 464	-1 073	-1 112	-796	-709	Balance
Malawi									**Malawi**
Imports	G	500	1 165	2 173	2 845	2 774	2 312	1 649	Importations
Exports	G	433	495	1 066	1 208	1 342	1 080	875	Exportations
Balance	G	-67	-670	-1 107	-1 637	-1 432	-1 232	-774	Balance
Malaysia									**Malaisie**
Imports	G	77 046	114 290	164 586	205 814	208 823	176 175	168 375	Importations
Exports	G	73 778	141 624	198 791	228 316	234 135	200 211	189 414	Exportations
Balance	G	-3 267	27 334	34 204	22 503	25 312	24 036	21 039	Balance
Maldives									**Maldives**
Imports	G	268	745	1 095	1 733	1 993	1 897	2 128	Importations
Exports	G	50	154	74	167	145	144	140	Exportations
Balance	G	-218	-591	-1 021	-1 567	-1 848	-1 753	-1 988	Balance
Mali									**Mali**
Imports	S	774	1 544	4 704	3 699	3 951	3 159	2 510	Importations
Exports	S	443	1 075	1 996	2 601	2 097	2 532	3 030	Exportations
Balance	S	-331	-468	-2 707	-1 098	-1 854	-626	520	Balance
Malta									**Malte**
Imports	G	2 942	3 865	5 732	7 525	8 445	6 788	7 182	Importations
Exports	G	1 913	2 431	3 717	5 206	4 971	3 915	4 039	Exportations
Balance	G	-1 029	-1 435	-2 015	-2 319	-3 474	-2 873	-3 143	Balance
Marshall Islands									**Îles Marshall**
Imports	G	75	68	76	81	83	84	86	Importations
Exports	G	23	11	17	22	23	25	27	Exportations
Balance	G	-52	-57	-60	-60	-59	-59	-58	Balance
Martinique [8]									**Martinique** [8]
Imports	S	1 970	...	...	...	...	...	...	Importations
Exports	S	242	...	...	...	...	...	...	Exportations
Balance	S	-1 728	...	...	...	...	...	...	Balance
Mauritania									**Mauritanie**
Imports	S	326	1 342	1 708	3 978	3 642	3 657	2 174	Importations
Exports	S	550	556	1 819	2 463	2 140	1 630	1 623	Exportations
Balance	S	225	-786	111	-1 516	-1 502	-2 027	-551	Balance
Mauritius									**Maurice**
Imports	G	2 000	3 160	4 402	5 395	5 607	4 458	4 655	Importations
Exports	G	1 538	2 144	1 850	2 341	2 663	2 481	2 194	Exportations
Balance	G	-462	-1 016	-2 553	-3 054	-2 944	-1 977	-2 461	Balance
Mayotte									**Mayotte**
Imports		...	309	...	...	...	...	...	Importations
Exports		...	6	...	...	...	...	...	Exportations
Balance		...	-303	...	...	...	...	...	Balance
Mexico [1,14]									**Mexique** [1,14]
Imports	G	72 453	221 819	301 482	381 210	399 977	395 232	387 064	Importations
Exports	G	79 541	214 207	298 305	379 949	396 882	380 601	373 883	Exportations
Balance	G	7 088	-7 612	-3 177	-1 261	-3 095	-14 631	-13 181	Balance
Micronesia (Fed. States of) [1]									**Micronésie (États féd. de)** [1]
Imports	S	100	128	168	188	117	68	40	Importations
Exports	S	43	13	23	28	19	11	6	Exportations
Balance	S	-56	-115	-145	-160	-98	-58	-34	Balance
Mongolia									**Mongolie**
Imports	G	415	1 183	3 278	6 358	5 131	3 797	3 358	Importations
Exports	G	473	1 064	2 899	4 269	5 774	4 669	4 917	Exportations
Balance	G	58	-118	-378	-2 089	643	873	1 559	Balance
Montenegro									**Monténégro**
Imports	S	...	...	2 182	2 349	2 367	2 050	2 263	Importations
Exports	S	...	...	437	494	441	353	354	Exportations
Balance	S	...	...	-1 745	-1 854	-1 926	-1 697	-1 908	Balance
Montserrat									**Montserrat**
Imports	S	51	30	29	42	42	39	36	Importations
Exports	S	2	1	1	6	3	3	4	Exportations
Balance	S	-49	-28	-28	-36	-39	-36	-32	Balance

20 Total imports, exports and balance of trade *(continued)*
Imports CIF, exports FOB and balance: millions of US dollars

Total des importations, des exportations et balance commerciale *(suite)*
Importations CAF, exportations FAB et balance: en millions de dollars É.-U.

Region, country or area	Sys.[&]	1995	2005	2010	2013	2014	2015	2016	Région, pays ou zone
Morocco									**Maroc**
Imports	S	8 540	20 803	35 379	45 186	46 192	37 546	41 696	Importations
Exports	S	4 719	11 185	17 765	21 965	23 816	22 037	22 858	Exportations
Balance	S	-3 822	-9 618	-17 614	-23 221	-22 376	-15 509	-18 838	Balance
Mozambique									**Mozambique**
Imports	S	727	2 408	3 564	10 099	8 743	7 908	5 295	Importations
Exports	S	174	1 745	2 243	4 024	4 725	3 196	3 352	Exportations
Balance	S	-553	-663	-1 321	-6 075	-4 018	-4 712	-1 943	Balance
Myanmar									**Myanmar**
Imports	G	1 346	1 907	4 164	12 042	16 227	16 844	15 696	Importations
Exports	G	860	3 776	7 625	11 232	11 299	11 432	11 673	Exportations
Balance	G	-487	1 869	3 461	-810	-4 928	-5 412	-4 023	Balance
Namibia									**Namibie**
Imports	G	...	2 525	5 980	7 575	8 531	7 697	6 721	Importations
Exports	G	...	2 726	5 848	6 337	5 984	4 628	4 816	Exportations
Balance	G	...	201	-131	-1 237	-2 547	-3 069	-1 905	Balance
Nepal									**Népal**
Imports	G	1 330	2 282	5 116	6 452	7 590	6 612	5 249	Importations
Exports	G	345	863	874	863	901	660	703	Exportations
Balance	G	-985	-1 419	-4 242	-5 588	-6 689	-5 952	-4 547	Balance
Netherlands									**Pays-Bas**
Imports	S	157 929	310 591	439 987	506 162	508 042	424 851	420 969	Importations
Exports	S	177 626	349 813	492 646	571 247	571 348	473 834	511 714	Exportations
Balance	S	19 697	39 222	52 659	65 085	63 305	48 983	90 745	Balance
Netherlands Antilles [former] [15]									**Antilles néerlandaises [anc.]** [15]
Imports	S	1 830	894	1 254	...	...	...	...	Importations
Exports	S	1 354	91	109	...	...	...	...	Exportations
Balance	S	-476	-803	-1 145	...	...	...	...	Balance
New Caledonia									**Nouvelle-Calédonie**
Imports	S	840	1 774	3 303	3 237	3 315	2 529	2 422	Importations
Exports	S	570	1 114	1 268	1 237	1 619	1 239	1 344	Exportations
Balance	S	-270	-660	-2 036	-2 000	-1 696	-1 291	-1 079	Balance
New Zealand									**Nouvelle-Zélande**
Imports	G	13 958	26 232	30 158	39 619	42 498	36 528	36 423	Importations
Exports	G	13 745	21 729	30 932	39 444	41 636	34 357	33 833	Exportations
Balance	G	-212	-4 504	774	-176	-862	-2 171	-2 589	Balance
Nicaragua									**Nicaragua**
Imports	G	1 009	2 536	4 191	5 499	5 746	5 866	5 927	Importations
Exports	G	509	866	1 848	4 594	4 974	4 667	2 225	Exportations
Balance	G	-500	-1 670	-2 343	-905	-773	-1 199	-3 701	Balance
Niger									**Niger**
Imports	S	345	736	2 273	1 714	2 151	2 458	1 861	Importations
Exports	S	273	486	479	1 337	1 050	790	927	Exportations
Balance	S	-71	-250	-1 794	-377	-1 101	-1 669	-933	Balance
Nigeria									**Nigéria**
Imports	G	8 221	21 314	44 235	44 598	46 532	34 891	36 533	Importations
Exports	G	12 342	55 145	86 568	90 554	102 878	106 479	104 084	Exportations
Balance	G	4 121	33 831	42 333	45 956	56 346	71 587	67 551	Balance
Northern Mariana Islands									**Îles Mariannes du Nord**
Imports	G	628	1 952	2 867	3 614	3 902	4 215	4 553	Importations
Exports	G	941	1 254	1 453	1 588	1 635	1 684	1 735	Exportations
Balance	G	313	-699	-1 414	-2 026	-2 266	-2 531	-2 818	Balance
Norway									**Norvège**
Imports	G	32 706	55 488	77 330	89 807	89 439	77 193	72 473	Importations
Exports	G	41 740	103 759	130 657	155 351	144 611	104 800	89 120	Exportations
Balance	G	9 034	48 271	53 327	65 543	55 172	27 607	16 647	Balance
Oman									**Oman**
Imports	G	4 249	8 970	19 775	34 331	29 303	29 007	23 260	Importations
Exports	G	5 917	18 692	36 600	55 497	50 718	31 927	24 455	Exportations
Balance	G	1 669	9 722	16 825	21 166	21 415	2 919	1 195	Balance
Other non-specified areas [16]									**Autres zones non-spécifiées** [16]
Imports		103 506	181 592	251 315	269 256	273 845	228 508	230 930	Importations
Exports		111 343	189 393	273 706	303 726	313 563	280 019	280 479	Exportations
Balance		7 838	7 801	22 391	34 470	39 718	51 511	49 549	Balance

Total imports, exports and balance of trade *(continued)*

Imports CIF, exports FOB and balance: millions of US dollars

Total des importations, des exportations et balance commerciale *(suite)*

Importations CAF, exportations FAB et balance: en millions de dollars É.-U.

Region, country or area	Sys.&	1995	2005	2010	2013	2014	2015	2016	Région, pays ou zone
Pakistan									**Pakistan**
Imports	G	11 704	25 097	37 537	43 775	47 545	43 990	46 998	Importations
Exports	G	8 158	16 050	21 413	25 121	24 722	22 089	20 534	Exportations
Balance	G	-3 546	-9 046	-16 124	-18 654	-22 823	-21 901	-26 464	Balance
Palau									**Palaos**
Imports	S	60	156	107	169	165	150	154	Importations
Exports	S	14	14	12	14	11	6	7	Exportations
Balance	S	-47	-143	-96	-154	-154	-144	-147	Balance
Panama									**Panama**
Imports	S	2 511	4 152	16 737	13 024	13 705	12 129	11 697	Importations
Exports	S	577	963	10 987	844	818	696	636	Exportations
Balance	S	-1 933	-3 189	-5 751	-12 180	-12 887	-11 433	-11 061	Balance
Papua New Guinea									**Papouasie-Nvl-Guinée**
Imports	G	1 451	1 728	3 950	6 673	7 343	8 011	8 874	Importations
Exports	G	2 653	3 276	5 742	5 951	8 852	9 486	8 760	Exportations
Balance	G	1 202	1 548	1 792	-722	1 509	1 475	-114	Balance
Paraguay									**Paraguay**
Imports	S	3 136	3 274	10 033	12 142	12 169	10 291	9 753	Importations
Exports	S	919	3 153	6 517	9 456	9 636	8 328	8 494	Exportations
Balance	S	-2 217	-121	-3 517	-2 686	-2 533	-1 964	-1 259	Balance
Peru [1]									**Pérou** [1]
Imports	S	7 584	12 502	29 966	43 322	42 194	38 105	36 185	Importations
Exports	S	5 440	17 114	35 807	42 569	38 459	33 245	36 040	Exportations
Balance	S	-2 144	4 612	5 842	-753	-3 734	-4 860	-145	Balance
Philippines									**Philippines**
Imports	G	28 487	49 487	58 468	65 705	67 719	70 153	85 909	Importations
Exports	G	17 447	41 255	51 498	56 698	61 810	58 648	56 313	Exportations
Balance	G	-11 040	-8 233	-6 970	-9 008	-5 909	-11 505	-29 596	Balance
Poland									**Pologne**
Imports	S	29 019	101 539	174 128	205 614	216 687	189 696	188 518	Importations
Exports	S	22 862	89 378	157 065	203 848	214 477	194 461	196 455	Exportations
Balance	S	-6 157	-12 161	-17 063	-1 766	-2 210	4 765	7 937	Balance
Portugal									**Portugal**
Imports	S	33 565	63 904	77 682	75 714	78 396	66 871	67 580	Importations
Exports	S	23 370	38 672	49 414	62 794	63 834	55 259	55 658	Exportations
Balance	S	-10 195	-25 232	-28 268	-12 920	-14 562	-11 612	-11 922	Balance
Qatar									**Qatar**
Imports	S	3 398	10 061	23 240	27 034	30 448	32 610	32 058	Importations
Exports	S	3 557	25 762	74 964	136 855	131 592	77 971	57 254	Exportations
Balance	S	159	15 702	51 725	109 821	101 144	45 361	25 196	Balance
Republic of Korea									**République de Corée**
Imports	G	135 109	261 236	425 208	515 573	525 557	436 487	406 182	Importations
Exports	G	125 056	284 418	466 381	559 619	573 075	526 753	495 418	Exportations
Balance	G	-10 052	23 183	41 173	44 046	47 518	90 266	89 236	Balance
Republic of Moldova									**République de Moldova**
Imports	G	841	2 292	3 855	5 492	5 317	3 987	4 020	Importations
Exports	G	746	1 091	1 541	2 428	2 340	1 967	2 045	Exportations
Balance	G	-95	-1 201	-2 314	-3 064	-2 977	-2 020	-1 975	Balance
Réunion [8]									**Réunion** [8]
Imports	S	2 711	...	...	...	...	...	...	Importations
Exports	S	209	...	...	...	...	...	...	Exportations
Balance	S	-2 502	...	...	...	...	...	...	Balance
Romania									**Roumanie**
Imports	S	10 278	40 463	62 007	73 452	77 889	69 858	74 605	Importations
Exports	S	7 910	27 730	49 413	65 881	69 878	60 605	63 581	Exportations
Balance	S	-2 368	-12 733	-12 593	-7 571	-8 011	-9 253	-11 024	Balance
Russian Federation									**Fédération de Russie**
Imports	G	46 710	98 707	228 912	314 945	286 649	182 782	182 257	Importations
Exports	G	79 869	241 452	397 068	527 266	497 834	343 908	285 491	Exportations
Balance	G	33 159	142 744	168 156	212 321	211 185	161 126	103 234	Balance
Rwanda									**Rwanda**
Imports	G	241	374	1 405	1 989	1 954	1 858	1 778	Importations
Exports	G	8	150	242	608	653	579	622	Exportations
Balance	G	-233	-224	-1 163	-1 381	-1 301	-1 279	-1 157	Balance

20 Total imports, exports and balance of trade *(continued)*

Imports CIF, exports FOB and balance: millions of US dollars

Total des importations, des exportations et balance commerciale *(suite)*

Importations CAF, exportations FAB et balance: en millions de dollars É.-U.

Region, country or area	Sys.&	1995	2005	2010	2013	2014	2015	2016	Région, pays ou zone
Saint Helena [17]									**Sainte-Hélène** [17]
Imports	G	13	12	20	26	33	41	48	Importations
Exports	G	1	1	~0	~0	~0	~0	~0	Exportations
Balance	G	-12	-12	-20	-25	-33	-40	-48	Balance
Saint Kitts and Nevis									**Saint-Kitts-et-Nevis**
Imports	S	132	210	270	249	268	297	332	Importations
Exports	S	19	34	32	40	39	56	51	Exportations
Balance	S	-113	-176	-238	-208	-229	-241	-280	Balance
Saint Lucia									**Sainte-Lucie**
Imports	S	306	486	647	888	642	583	654	Importations
Exports	S	109	64	215	155	146	181	120	Exportations
Balance	S	-197	-422	-432	-733	-496	-403	-535	Balance
Saint Pierre and Miquelon									**Saint-Pierre-et-Miquelon**
Imports		96	216	747	1 510	1 900	2 259	2 629	Importations
Exports		16	31	137	320	426	533	653	Exportations
Balance		-80	-185	-610	-1 190	-1 473	-1 726	-1 976	Balance
Saint Vincent & Grenadines									**Saint-Vincent-Grenadines**
Imports	S	134	240	379	378	362	334	335	Importations
Exports	S	59	40	42	48	48	46	47	Exportations
Balance	S	-75	-201	-338	-330	-314	-288	-288	Balance
Samoa									**Samoa**
Imports	S	95	239	310	367	388	371	350	Importations
Exports	S	9	87	70	62	51	59	56	Exportations
Balance	S	-86	-151	-240	-304	-337	-312	-294	Balance
Sao Tome and Principe									**Sao Tomé-et-Principe**
Imports	S	29	50	112	152	170	142	139	Importations
Exports	S	5	3	6	7	10	9	10	Exportations
Balance	S	-24	-46	-106	-145	-159	-133	-129	Balance
Saudi Arabia									**Arabie saoudite**
Imports	S	28 085	57 233	103 622	163 013	168 240	163 821	135 904	Importations
Exports	S	49 030	180 278	250 577	375 361	341 947	201 492	182 329	Exportations
Balance	S	20 944	123 045	146 955	212 347	173 708	37 671	46 426	Balance
Senegal									**Sénégal**
Imports	G	1 413	3 498	4 782	6 552	6 503	5 595	5 478	Importations
Exports	G	412	1 471	2 088	2 661	2 750	2 612	2 640	Exportations
Balance	G	-1 001	-2 027	-2 694	-3 891	-3 753	-2 984	-2 838	Balance
Serbia									**Serbie**
Imports	S	...	...	16 735	20 551	20 609	18 210	19 231	Importations
Exports	S	...	...	9 795	14 611	14 843	13 379	14 852	Exportations
Balance	S	...	...	-6 940	-5 940	-5 765	-4 831	-4 379	Balance
Serbia and Monten. [former]									**Serbie-et-Monténégro [anc.]**
Imports		2 666	11 393	...	...	...	...	...	Importations
Exports		1 531	4 430	...	...	...	...	...	Exportations
Balance		-1 135	-6 963	...	...	...	...	...	Balance
Seychelles									**Seychelles**
Imports	G	255	675	1 180	925	1 075	975	833	Importations
Exports	G	53	340	418	574	551	474	335	Exportations
Balance	G	-202	-335	-763	-351	-524	-501	-498	Balance
Sierra Leone									**Sierra Leone**
Imports	S	131	341	776	1 617	2 057	1 759	958	Importations
Exports	S	42	154	342	344	279	93	466	Exportations
Balance	S	-89	-187	-434	-1 274	-1 778	-1 666	-492	Balance
Singapore									**Singapour**
Imports	G	124 503	200 050	310 791	373 016	366 247	296 745	283 009	Importations
Exports	G	118 263	229 652	351 867	410 250	409 769	346 638	329 871	Exportations
Balance	G	-6 240	29 602	41 076	37 234	43 521	49 893	46 862	Balance
Slovakia									**Slovaquie**
Imports	S	8 162	34 226	64 382	81 295	81 354	72 958	75 156	Importations
Exports	S	8 374	32 210	63 999	85 184	85 976	75 051	77 565	Exportations
Balance	S	212	-2 016	-383	3 889	4 622	2 094	2 409	Balance
Slovenia									**Slovénie**
Imports	S	9 492	19 626	26 592	29 375	30 049	25 870	26 646	Importations
Exports	S	8 316	17 896	24 435	28 629	30 522	26 587	27 585	Exportations
Balance	S	-1 176	-1 730	-2 157	-747	473	717	939	Balance

20

Total imports, exports and balance of trade *(continued)*
Imports CIF, exports FOB and balance: millions of US dollars

Total des importations, des exportations et balance commerciale *(suite)*
Importations CAF, exportations FAB et balance: en millions de dollars É.-U.

Region, country or area	Sys.[&]	1995	2005	2010	2013	2014	2015	2016	Région, pays ou zone
Solomon Islands									**Iles Salomon**
Imports	S	154	139	328	580	500	466	454	Importations
Exports	S	168	70	215	489	459	400	437	Exportations
Balance	S	14	-68	-112	-91	-41	-65	-17	Balance
Somalia									**Somalie**
Imports	G	38	469	496	513	519	525	530	Importations
Exports	G	38	379	568	725	786	853	925	Exportations
Balance	G	-~0	-90	72	212	267	328	394	Balance
South Africa [1,18]									**Afrique du Sud** [1,18]
Imports	G	...	55 033	82 949	103 441	99 893	79 591	74 744	Importations
Exports	G	...	46 991	82 626	95 112	90 612	69 631	74 111	Exportations
Balance	G	...	-8 042	-323	-8 330	-9 281	-9 960	-633	Balance
South Sudan									**Soudan du sud**
Imports		...	...	...	424	537	635	750	Importations
Exports		...	...	...	2 260	4 030	3 103	2 389	Exportations
Balance		...	...	...	1 836	3 493	2 469	1 640	Balance
Spain									**Espagne**
Imports	S	113 399	289 611	315 547	332 267	350 978	305 266	302 539	Importations
Exports	S	89 616	192 798	246 265	310 964	318 649	278 122	281 777	Exportations
Balance	S	-23 783	-96 812	-69 282	-21 303	-32 328	-27 144	-20 762	Balance
Sri Lanka									**Sri Lanka**
Imports	G	4 756	8 307	12 354	17 931	19 244	18 967	19 501	Importations
Exports	G	3 790	6 160	8 304	10 005	11 295	10 440	10 546	Exportations
Balance	G	-966	-2 147	-4 050	-7 926	-7 949	-8 528	-8 955	Balance
State of Palestine									**État de Palestine**
Imports	S	...	2 668	3 959	5 164	5 683	5 225	5 058	Importations
Exports	S	...	335	576	901	944	958	929	Exportations
Balance	S	...	-2 332	-3 383	-4 263	-4 739	-4 268	-4 128	Balance
Sudan									**Soudan**
Imports		...	...	...	9 918	9 211	8 413	7 658	Importations
Exports		...	...	...	4 790	4 350	5 588	1 797	Exportations
Balance		...	...	...	-5 128	-4 861	-2 826	-5 861	Balance
Sudan [former]									**Soudan [anc.]**
Imports	G	1 185	7 367	11 875	...	...	...	...	Importations
Exports	G	685	4 506	11 529	...	...	...	...	Exportations
Balance	G	-500	-2 861	-346	...	...	...	...	Balance
Suriname									**Suriname**
Imports	G	583	1 050	1 397	2 308	1 827	1 981	1 244	Importations
Exports	G	483	997	2 026	2 204	1 918	1 617	1 437	Exportations
Balance	G	-100	-53	628	-104	91	-364	193	Balance
Swaziland									**Swaziland**
Imports	G	...	1 656	1 710	1 525	1 195	936	733	Importations
Exports	G	...	1 278	1 557	1 894	1 892	1 884	1 881	Exportations
Balance	G	...	-378	-153	370	697	948	1 149	Balance
Sweden									**Suède**
Imports	G	61 647	111 351	148 788	160 589	162 257	138 365	140 838	Importations
Exports	G	77 436	130 264	158 411	167 495	164 680	140 001	139 574	Exportations
Balance	G	15 790	18 912	9 622	6 906	2 423	1 635	-1 263	Balance
Switzerland									**Suisse**
Imports	S	80 152	126 574	176 281	321 050	275 054	253 152	269 157	Importations
Exports	S	81 641	130 930	195 609	357 905	311 146	291 959	304 691	Exportations
Balance	S	1 489	4 356	19 329	36 855	36 092	38 807	35 534	Balance
Syrian Arab Republic									**République arabe syrienne**
Imports	S	4 645	7 898	17 562	5 800	4 311	3 206	2 383	Importations
Exports	S	3 561	6 450	11 353	2 998	2 250	1 683	1 265	Exportations
Balance	S	-1 084	-1 448	-6 209	-2 802	-2 061	-1 522	-1 118	Balance
Tajikistan									**Tadjikistan**
Imports	G	809	1 329	2 657	4 151	4 296	3 435	3 030	Importations
Exports	G	748	905	1 195	1 162	977	891	899	Exportations
Balance	G	-61	-424	-1 462	-2 989	-3 319	-2 544	-2 132	Balance
Thailand									**Thaïlande**
Imports	S	70 781	118 164	182 393	250 708	227 932	202 019	195 666	Importations
Exports	S	56 439	110 110	195 312	228 527	227 573	210 883	213 927	Exportations
Balance	S	-14 341	-8 054	12 918	-22 181	-359	8 864	18 260	Balance

20 Total imports, exports and balance of trade *(continued)*

Imports CIF, exports FOB and balance: millions of US dollars

Total des importations, des exportations et balance commerciale *(suite)*

Importations CAF, exportations FAB et balance: en millions de dollars É.-U.

Region, country or area	Sys.&	1995	2005	2010	2013	2014	2015	2016	Région, pays ou zone
TFYR of Macedonia									**ex-R.Y. de Macédoine**
Imports	S	1 719	3 228	5 474	6 620	7 301	6 400	6 757	Importations
Exports	S	1 204	2 041	3 351	4 299	4 964	4 490	4 785	Exportations
Balance	S	-515	-1 187	-2 123	-2 321	-2 337	-1 910	-1 972	Balance
Timor-Leste									**Timor-Leste**
Imports	S	112	102	246	514	547	578	647	Importations
Exports	S	34	43	42	53	39	45	94	Exportations
Balance	S	-78	-58	-205	-461	-508	-533	-553	Balance
Togo									**Togo**
Imports	S	556	593	1 205	1 967	1 753	1 731	1 716	Importations
Exports	S	383	360	648	1 146	804	710	715	Exportations
Balance	S	-174	-233	-557	-821	-949	-1 021	-1 001	Balance
Tokelau									**Tokélaou**
Imports		1	1	1	1	1	1	1	Importations
Exports		~0	~0	~0	~0	~0	~0	~0	Exportations
Balance		-~0	-1	-1	-1	-1	-1	-1	Balance
Tonga									**Tonga**
Imports	G	77	120	159	198	218	206	209	Importations
Exports	G	15	10	8	17	19	18	14	Exportations
Balance	G	-63	-110	-151	-181	-199	-188	-196	Balance
Trinidad and Tobago									**Trinité-et-Tobago**
Imports	S	1 386	5 694	6 480	12 396	11 412	9 298	4 826	Importations
Exports	S	2 007	9 611	10 982	16 597	14 526	10 756	4 576	Exportations
Balance	S	622	3 918	4 502	4 202	3 114	1 458	-249	Balance
Tunisia									**Tunisie**
Imports	G	7 903	13 174	22 215	24 266	24 793	20 223	19 456	Importations
Exports	G	5 475	10 494	16 427	17 060	16 760	14 073	13 483	Exportations
Balance	G	-2 428	-2 681	-5 789	-7 206	-8 034	-6 149	-5 973	Balance
Turkey									**Turquie**
Imports	S	35 707	116 774	185 544	251 661	242 177	207 207	198 602	Importations
Exports	S	21 599	73 476	113 883	151 803	157 610	143 850	142 606	Exportations
Balance	S	-14 109	-43 298	-71 661	-99 859	-84 567	-63 356	-55 996	Balance
Turkmenistan									**Turkménistan**
Imports	G	1 364	2 217	2 400	2 515	2 533	2 554	2 616	Importations
Exports	G	677	3 009	3 335	3 532	3 600	3 670	3 741	Exportations
Balance	G	-687	792	935	1 018	1 068	1 116	1 125	Balance
Turks and Caicos Islands									**Îles Turques-et-Caïques**
Imports	G	51	304	302	345	406	410	389	Importations
Exports	G	5	15	16	6	6	5	4	Exportations
Balance	G	-46	-289	-286	-339	-400	-405	-385	Balance
Tuvalu									**Tuvalu**
Imports	G	6	13	12	12	12	12	12	Importations
Exports	G	~0	~0	~0	~0	~0	~0	~0	Exportations
Balance	G	-6	-13	-12	-12	-12	-12	-12	Balance
Uganda									**Ouganda**
Imports	G	1 038	2 054	4 664	5 818	6 074	5 528	3 750	Importations
Exports	G	575	813	1 619	2 408	2 262	2 267	2 755	Exportations
Balance	G	-462	-1 241	-3 046	-3 410	-3 812	-3 261	-996	Balance
Ukraine									**Ukraine**
Imports	G	15 484	36 122	60 737	76 986	54 381	37 516	39 184	Importations
Exports	G	13 128	34 228	51 430	63 320	53 913	38 127	36 369	Exportations
Balance	G	-2 356	-1 894	-9 307	-13 666	-468	611	-2 815	Balance
United Arab Emirates									**Émirats arabes unis**
Imports	G	20 776	80 814	187 001	294 967	298 611	287 025	201 908	Importations
Exports	G	27 691	115 453	198 362	379 489	380 340	333 362	195 613	Exportations
Balance	G	6 915	34 639	11 361	84 522	81 728	46 338	-6 296	Balance
United Kingdom									**Royaume-Uni**
Imports	G	261 456	528 461	627 618	657 223	694 344	630 251	635 570	Importations
Exports	G	234 372	392 744	422 014	548 042	511 145	466 296	415 856	Exportations
Balance	G	-27 084	-135 717	-205 603	-109 181	-183 199	-163 955	-219 713	Balance
United Rep. of Tanzania									**Rép.-Unie de Tanzanie**
Imports	G	1 653	3 247	8 013	12 525	12 691	14 706	7 876	Importations
Exports	G	685	1 672	4 051	4 413	5 705	5 854	4 742	Exportations
Balance	G	-968	-1 575	-3 962	-8 113	-6 986	-8 852	-3 134	Balance

20 Total imports, exports and balance of trade *(continued)*

Imports CIF, exports FOB and balance: millions of US dollars

Total des importations, des exportations et balance commerciale *(suite)*

Importations CAF, exportations FAB et balance: en millions de dollars É.-U.

Region, country or area	Sys.&	1995	2005	2010	2013	2014	2015	2016	Région, pays ou zone
United States of America [19]									**États-Unis d'Amérique [19]**
Imports	G	770 821	1 732 321	1 968 260	2 326 590	2 410 855	2 313 425	2 249 661	Importations
Exports	G	582 965	904 339	1 278 099	1 577 587	1 619 743	1 501 846	1 453 167	Exportations
Balance	G	-187 857	-827 981	-690 161	-749 003	-791 113	-811 579	-796 494	Balance
Uruguay									**Uruguay**
Imports	G	2 866	3 879	8 622	11 642	10 762	9 489	8 137	Importations
Exports	G	2 106	3 422	6 724	9 066	9 166	7 670	6 964	Exportations
Balance	G	-760	-457	-1 898	-2 577	-1 597	-1 820	-1 173	Balance
Uzbekistan									**Ouzbékistan**
Imports	G	2 874	3 657	8 381	13 798	16 972	20 874	25 652	Importations
Exports	G	3 718	4 458	11 587	15 087	18 529	22 756	27 947	Exportations
Balance	G	844	801	3 206	1 289	1 557	1 881	2 295	Balance
Vanuatu									**Vanuatu**
Imports	G	95	149	276	313	308	355	416	Importations
Exports	G	28	38	46	39	63	39	50	Exportations
Balance	G	-67	-111	-230	-275	-246	-316	-366	Balance
Venezuela (Boliv. Rep. of)									**Venezuela (Rép. boliv. du)**
Imports	G	10 791	21 848	32 343	44 952	44 478	40 146	16 324	Importations
Exports	G	19 093	55 413	66 963	87 961	74 714	37 236	19 731	Exportations
Balance	G	8 302	33 565	34 620	43 009	30 236	-2 910	3 407	Balance
Viet Nam									**Viet Nam**
Imports	G	8 155	36 761	84 839	132 033	147 839	165 776	174 111	Importations
Exports	G	5 449	32 447	72 237	132 033	150 217	162 017	176 632	Exportations
Balance	G	-2 706	-4 314	-12 602	~0	2 378	-3 759	2 520	Balance
Wallis and Futuna Islands									**Îles Wallis-et-Futuna**
Imports	S	13	51	35	43	46	49	53	Importations
Exports	S	~0	1	1	1	1	1	1	Exportations
Balance	S	-13	-50	-34	-42	-45	-48	-51	Balance
Yemen									**Yémen**
Imports	S	1 812	5 400	9 255	13 273	12 042	6 573	6 861	Importations
Exports	S	1 917	5 608	6 437	7 130	2 417	510	570	Exportations
Balance	S	105	208	-2 818	-6 143	-9 625	-6 063	-6 291	Balance
Zambia									**Zambie**
Imports	S	708	2 558	5 321	10 162	9 539	8 420	7 442	Importations
Exports	S	1 055	1 810	7 200	10 594	9 688	6 983	6 505	Exportations
Balance	S	347	-748	1 879	432	149	-1 437	-937	Balance
Zimbabwe									**Zimbabwe**
Imports	G	2 659	2 072	5 852	7 704	6 380	6 002	5 212	Importations
Exports	G	1 846	1 394	3 199	3 507	3 064	2 704	2 832	Exportations
Balance	G	-813	-679	-2 653	-4 197	-3 316	-3 298	-2 379	Balance

Source:

United Nations Statistics Division, New York, UN Comtrade database, last accessed June 2017.

& Systems of trade: Two systems of recording trade, the General trade system (G) and the Special trade system (S), are in common use. They differ mainly in the way warehoused and re-exported goods are recorded. See the Technical notes for an explanation of the trade systems.

1 Imports FOB.
2 Trade statistics exclude certain oil and chemical products.
3 Prior to 1997, the data refer to the Economic Union of Belgium and Luxembourg and intertrade between the two countries is excluded. Beginning January 1997, data refer to Belgium only and include trade between Belgium and Luxembourg.

Source:

Organisation des Nations Unies, Division de statistique, New York, Comtrade base de données de l'ONU, dernier accès juin 2017.

& Systèmes de commerce : Deux systèmes d'enregistrement du commerce sont couramment utilisés, le Commerce général (G) et le Commerce spécial (S). Ils ne diffèrent que par la façon dont sont enregistrées les marchandises entreposées et les marchandises réexportées. Voir les Notes techniques pour une explication des Systèmes de commerce.

1 Importations FAB.
2 Les statistiques commerciales font exclusion de certains produits pétroliers et chimiques.
3 Avant 1997, les données se rapportent à l'Union économique belgo-luxembourgeoise et ne comprennent pas le commerce entre ces pays. A partir de janvier 1997, les données se rapportent à Belgique seulement et recouvrent les échanges entre la Belgique et le Luxembourg.

4 For statistical purposes, the data for China do not include those for the Hong Kong Special Administrative Region (Hong Kong SAR), Macao Special Administrative Region (Macao SAR) and Taiwan Province of China.
5 Export and import values exclude trade in the processing zone.
6 Imports exclude petroleum imported without stated value. Exports cover domestic exports.
7 Prior to 2008, special trade.
8 Beginning 1997, trade data for France include the import and export values of French Guiana, Guadeloupe, Martinique, and Réunion.
9 Excluding military goods, fissionable materials, bunkers, ships and aircraft.
10 Data include oil and gas. The value of oil exports and total exports are rough estimates based on information published in various petroleum industry journals.
11 Year ending 20 March of the year stated.
12 Imports and exports net of returned goods. The figures also exclude Judea and Samaria and the Gaza area.
13 Prior to 1997, included under Belgium. See also footnote for Belgium.
14 Trade data include maquiladoras and exclude goods from customs-bonded warehouses. Total exports include revaluation and exports of silver.
15 The Netherlands Antilles was dissolved on October 10, 2010. Beginning 2011, data are reported separately for Curaçao, Sint Maarten (Dutch part), Bonaire, Saint Eustatius and Saba.
16 Asia not elsewhere specified.
17 Year ending 31 March of the following year.
18 Exports include gold.
19 Including the trade with the U.S. Virgin Islands and Puerto Rico but excluding with Guam and American Samoa. Including non-monetary gold imports and exports.

4 Pour la présentation des statistiques, les données pour la Chine ne comprennent pas la région administrative spéciale de Hong Kong (Hong Kong RAS), la région administrative spéciale de Macao (Macao RAS) et la province chinoise de Taïwan.
5 Les valeurs à l'exportation et à l'importation excluent le commerce de la zone de transformation.
6 Non compris le pétrole brute dont la valeur des importations ne sont pas stipulée. Les exportations sont les exportations d'intérieur.
7 Avant 2008, commerce special.
8 A partir de 1997, les valeurs de commerce pour la France comprennent les valeurs des importations et des exportations de la Guyane française, la Guadeloupe, la Martinique, et la Réunion.
9 A l'exclusion des marchandises militaires, des matières fissibles, des soutes, des bateaux et de l'avion.
10 Les données comprennent le pétrole et le gaz. La valeur des exportations de pétrole et des exportations totales sont des évaluations grossières basées sur l'information publiée à divers journaux d'industrie de pétrole.
11 Année finissant le 20 mars de l'année indiquée.
12 Importations et exportations nets, ne comprenant pas les marchandises retournées. Sont également exclues les données de la Judée et de Samara et ainsi que la zone de Gaza.
13 Avant 1997, inclus sous la Belgique. Voir également l'apostille pour la Belgique.
14 Les statistiques du commerce extérieur comprennent maquiladoras et ne comprennent pas les marchandises provenant des entrepôts en douane. Les exportations comprennent la réévaluation et les données sur les exportations d'argent.
15 Les Antilles néerlandaises a été dissous le 10 Octobre 2010. Début 2011, les données sont présentées séparément pour Curaçao, Sint Maarten (partie néerlandaise), Bonaire, Saint-Eustache et Saba.
16 Asie non spécifiées ailleurs.
17 Année finissant le 31 Mars de l'année suivante.
18 Les exportations comprennent l'or.
19 Y compris le commerce des Iles Vierges américaines et de Porto Rico mais non compris les échanges de marchandises, entre les Etats-Unis et leurs autres possessions (Guam et Samoa américaines). Les données comprennent les importations et exportations d'or non-monétaire.

21 Major trading partner

Three largest trade partners as a percentage of total international merchandise trade in US dollars, as at 2016

Partenaire commercial principal

Trois principaux partenaires commerciaux en pourcentage du total de commerce international de marchandises en dollars américains, en 2016

Country or area	Major trading partner	Percentage of exports 2005	2010	2016	Major trading partner	Percentage of imports 2005	2010	2016	Pays ou zone
Afghanistan									**Afghanistan**
Partner 1	Pakistan	...	39.0	39.7	Iran (Islamic Rep.), Iran (Rép. islamique)	...	7.5	23.4	Partenaire 1
Partner 2	India, Inde	...	16.8	33.1	Pakistan	...	11.6	17.4	Partenaire 2
Partner 3	Iran (Islamic Rep.), Iran (Rép. islamique)	...	8.2	5.1	China, Chine	...	13.7	13.5	Partenaire 3
Albania									**Albanie**
Partner 1	Italy, Italie	72.4	50.8	54.6	Italy, Italie	29.3	28.2	29.3	Partenaire 1
Partner 2	Serbia, Serbie	...	8.3	8.7	Germany, Allemagne	5.4	5.6	9.5	Partenaire 2
Partner 3	Greece, Grèce	10.5	5.4	4.6	China, Chine	6.6	6.3	8.8	Partenaire 3
Algeria									**Algérie**
Partner 1	Italy, Italie	16.4	15.4	17.4	China, Chine	6.5	11.2	17.9	Partenaire 1
Partner 2	Spain, Espagne	11.0	10.4	12.9	France	22.0	14.9	10.1	Partenaire 2
Partner 3	United States, États-Unis	23.0	24.2	12.9	Italy, Italie	7.5	10.0	9.9	Partenaire 3
Andorra									**Andorre**
Partner 1	Spain, Espagne	59.2	67.4	59.0	Spain, Espagne	51.5	59.9	61.7	Partenaire 1
Partner 2	France	17.0	16.8	17.9	France	22.3	17.6	15.5	Partenaire 2
Partner 3	Norway, Norvège	~0.0	4.3	5.5	China, Chine	2.2	4.1	4.1	Partenaire 3
Angola									**Angola**
Partner 1	China, Chine	29.8	39.8	43.2	China, Chine	4.8	10.1	16.9	Partenaire 1
Partner 2	India, Inde	~0.0	9.7	8.1	Portugal	12.9	14.4	14.6	Partenaire 2
Partner 3	Spain, Espagne	3.1	1.9	6.8	Republic of Korea, République de Corée	19.6	1.1	8.6	Partenaire 3
Anguilla									**Anguilla**
Partner 1	United States, États-Unis	26.5	17.0	51.9	United States, États-Unis	61.7	59.4	65.6	Partenaire 1
Partner 2	Saint Lucia, Sainte-Lucie	8.5	...	8.1	Japan, Japon	2.8	1.5	4.6	Partenaire 2
Partner 3	Israel, Israël	...	0.9	5.4	United Kingdom, Royaume-Uni	5.6	0.7	3.8	Partenaire 3
Antigua and Barbuda									**Antigua-et-Barbuda**
Partner 1	United Kingdom, Royaume-Uni	16.7	19.7	52.5	United States, États-Unis	48.9	34.5	53.5	Partenaire 1
Partner 2	United States, États-Unis	7.7	29.7	16.2	China, Chine	0.9	8.4	6.3	Partenaire 2
Partner 3	Spain, Espagne	~0.0	0.7	12.8	Japan, Japon	2.8	2.7	4.7	Partenaire 3
Argentina									**Argentine**
Partner 1	Brazil, Brésil	15.8	21.2	15.6	Brazil, Brésil	37.0	32.5	24.5	Partenaire 1
Partner 2	United States, États-Unis	12.1	5.4	8.4	China, Chine	5.3	13.5	18.8	Partenaire 2
Partner 3	China, Chine	7.9	8.5	7.7	United States, États-Unis	16.3	11.8	13.1	Partenaire 3
Armenia									**Arménie**
Partner 1	Russian Federation, Fédération de Russie	12.4	17.5	20.9	Russian Federation, Fédération de Russie	14.8	22.0	30.8	Partenaire 1
Partner 2	Bulgaria, Bulgarie	0.1	15.5	8.6	China, Chine	1.5	10.6	11.0	Partenaire 2
Partner 3	Georgia, Géorgie	3.6	4.8	8.0	Iran (Islamic Rep.), Iran (Rép. islamique)	6.0	5.8	5.1	Partenaire 3
Aruba									**Aruba**
Partner 1	Colombia, Colombie	11.9	27.2	24.3	United States, États-Unis	55.7	50.0	55.1	Partenaire 1
Partner 2	United States, États-Unis	11.3	6.1	19.4	Netherlands, Pays-Bas	12.7	11.3	12.8	Partenaire 2
Partner 3	Netherlands, Pays-Bas	33.5	5.1	16.6	Areas nes, Zones nsa [1]	0.1	2.0	12.0	Partenaire 3
Australia									**Australie**
Partner 1	China, Chine	11.6	25.3	31.6	China, Chine	13.8	18.8	23.4	Partenaire 1
Partner 2	Japan, Japon	20.5	18.9	13.9	United States, États-Unis	13.9	11.2	11.5	Partenaire 2
Partner 3	Republic of Korea, République de Corée	7.9	8.9	6.7	Japan, Japon	11.0	8.7	7.7	Partenaire 3
Austria									**Autriche**
Partner 1	Germany, Allemagne	31.8	31.6	29.5	Germany, Allemagne	42.2	39.5	36.4	Partenaire 1
Partner 2	United States, États-Unis	5.6	4.5	6.7	Italy, Italie	6.6	6.8	6.0	Partenaire 2
Partner 3	Italy, Italie	8.6	7.8	6.2	China, Chine	3.1	4.8	5.9	Partenaire 3
Azerbaijan									**Azerbaïdjan**
Partner 1	Italy, Italie	30.3	33.1	21.3	Russian Federation, Fédération de Russie	17.0	17.4	15.6	Partenaire 1
Partner 2	Germany, Allemagne	0.8	~0.0	10.8	Turkey, Turquie	7.4	11.7	12.7	Partenaire 2
Partner 3	Spain, Espagne	1.7	0.8	9.6	United States, États-Unis	3.4	3.1	9.2	Partenaire 3
Bahamas									**Bahamas**
Partner 1	United States, États-Unis	60.9	76.0	83.1	United States, États-Unis	85.9	90.9	81.9	Partenaire 1
Partner 2	France	13.1	3.5	4.4	Areas nes, Zones nsa [1]	0.1	0.8	3.0	Partenaire 2
Partner 3	Finland, Finlande	...	...	3.2	Dominica, Dominique	...	...	1.5	Partenaire 3
Bahrain									**Bahreïn**
Partner 1	Saudi Arabia, Arabie saoudite	6.3	7.2	18.1	Areas nes, Zones nsa [1]	44.6	36.6	21.4	Partenaire 1
Partner 2	United Arab Emirates, Émirats arabes unis	1.6	2.7	17.3	China, Chine	4.1	7.4	9.7	Partenaire 2
Partner 3	United States, États-Unis	2.7	1.5	11.5	United States, États-Unis	3.7	4.5	8.6	Partenaire 3

21 Major trading partner *(continued)*

Three largest trade partners as a percentage of total international merchandise trade in US dollars, as at 2016

Partenaire commercial principal *(suite)*

Trois principaux partenaires commerciaux en pourcentage du total de commerce international de marchandises en dollars américains, en 2016

Country or area	Major trading partner	Percentage of exports 2005	2010	2016	Major trading partner	Percentage of imports 2005	2010	2016	Pays ou zone
Bangladesh									**Bangladesh**
Partner 1	United States, États-Unis	28.5	24.3	19.3	China, Chine	15.9	17.5	21.5	Partenaire 1
Partner 2	Germany, Allemagne	15.7	13.8	14.7	India, Inde	10.9	11.5	12.2	Partenaire 2
Partner 3	United Kingdom, Royaume-Uni	10.1	8.9	11.0	Singapore, Singapour	3.5	5.4	9.2	Partenaire 3
Barbados									**Barbade**
Partner 1	United States, États-Unis	13.4	24.9	34.4	United States, États-Unis	35.9	43.9	39.1	Partenaire 1
Partner 2	Jamaica, Jamaïque	5.8	5.6	9.4	Trinidad and Tobago, Trinité-et-Tobago	21.2	7.2	13.4	Partenaire 2
Partner 3	Trinidad and Tobago, Trinité-et-Tobago	10.6	8.4	7.8	China, Chine	2.9	4.8	7.3	Partenaire 3
Belarus									**Bélarus**
Partner 1	Russian Federation, Fédération de Russie	35.8	39.4	45.8	Russian Federation, Fédération de Russie	60.4	55.8	56.3	Partenaire 1
Partner 2	Ukraine	5.7	10.1	12.0	China, Chine	1.7	4.6	7.6	Partenaire 2
Partner 3	United Kingdom, Royaume-Uni	7.0	3.7	4.7	Germany, Allemagne	6.7	6.8	4.9	Partenaire 3
Belgium									**Belgique**
Partner 1	Germany, Allemagne	19.2	18.6	16.7	Netherlands, Pays-Bas	17.6	18.6	16.1	Partenaire 1
Partner 2	France	17.2	16.6	15.4	Germany, Allemagne	17.1	16.1	13.6	Partenaire 2
Partner 3	Netherlands, Pays-Bas	11.7	11.9	11.2	France	11.3	11.0	9.5	Partenaire 3
Belize									**Belize**
Partner 1	United States, États-Unis	53.9	49.1	33.2	United States, États-Unis	40.3	47.9	37.4	Partenaire 1
Partner 2	United Kingdom, Royaume-Uni	19.9	26.1	28.4	China, Chine	2.2	9.7	11.7	Partenaire 2
Partner 3	Jamaica, Jamaïque	4.6	2.6	5.6	Mexico, Mexique	11.6	10.0	10.8	Partenaire 3
Benin									**Bénin**
Partner 1	India, Inde	6.9	4.6	15.4	India, Inde	1.6	0.9	14.9	Partenaire 1
Partner 2	Malaysia, Malaisie	2.8	1.5	13.2	Thailand, Thaïlande	6.7	8.6	12.4	Partenaire 2
Partner 3	Bangladesh	0.4	0.6	10.2	France	18.4	14.7	10.1	Partenaire 3
Bermuda									**Bermudes**
Partner 1	United States, États-Unis	7.0	10.7	90.0	United States, États-Unis	77.0	71.7	70.0	Partenaire 1
Partner 2	United Kingdom, Royaume-Uni	1.1	0.5	5.2	Canada	4.0	8.0	11.3	Partenaire 2
Partner 3	Canada	20.2	1.3	2.7	United Kingdom, Royaume-Uni	3.3	3.7	3.2	Partenaire 3
Bhutan									**Bhoutan**
Partner 1	India, Inde	87.6	82.4	68.3	India, Inde	75.1	75.1	82.9	Partenaire 1
Partner 2	Bangladesh	4.9	4.8	23.5	Singapore, Singapour	2.6	2.3	3.1	Partenaire 2
Partner 3	United States, États-Unis	~0.0	~0.0	2.3	Thailand, Thaïlande	1.6	2.5	2.6	Partenaire 3
Bolivia (Plurin. State of)									**Bolivie (État plurin. de)**
Partner 1	Brazil, Brésil	36.3	34.6	28.0	China, Chine	5.8	11.7	17.9	Partenaire 1
Partner 2	Argentina, Argentine	9.5	8.0	16.9	Brazil, Brésil	21.9	18.0	16.5	Partenaire 2
Partner 3	United States, États-Unis	14.6	9.9	12.1	Argentina, Argentine	16.7	12.7	11.8	Partenaire 3
Bosnia and Herzegovina									**Bosnie-Herzégovine**
Partner 1	Germany, Allemagne	11.3	15.8	16.4	Germany, Allemagne	14.4	10.5	12.3	Partenaire 1
Partner 2	Italy, Italie	13.1	12.2	12.2	Italy, Italie	8.9	8.9	11.7	Partenaire 2
Partner 3	Serbia, Serbie	...	14.2	10.7	Serbia, Serbie	...	10.5	11.3	Partenaire 3
Botswana									**Botswana**
Partner 1	Belgium, Belgique	0.2	3.3	18.9	South Africa, Afrique du Sud	84.1	72.8	64.6	Partenaire 1
Partner 2	India, Inde	0.1	0.9	15.1	Namibia, Namibie	0.5	1.2	10.5	Partenaire 2
Partner 3	South Africa, Afrique du Sud	8.8	12.9	13.6	Canada	0.5	0.1	5.6	Partenaire 3
Brazil									**Brésil**
Partner 1	China, Chine	5.8	15.2	19.0	United States, États-Unis	17.5	15.0	17.5	Partenaire 1
Partner 2	United States, États-Unis	19.9	10.0	13.3	China, Chine	7.3	14.1	17.0	Partenaire 2
Partner 3	Argentina, Argentine	8.4	9.2	7.2	Germany, Allemagne	8.3	6.9	6.6	Partenaire 3
British Virgin Islands									**Îles Vierges britanniques**
Partner 1	United States, États-Unis	24.3	14.0	26.0	United States, États-Unis	8.9	9.9	41.1	Partenaire 1
Partner 2	Mexico, Mexique	1.3	0.1	12.3	Switzerland, Suisse	2.0	3.9	11.2	Partenaire 2
Partner 3	United Kingdom, Royaume-Uni	12.7	9.4	6.3	Italy, Italie	6.8	1.7	6.7	Partenaire 3
Brunei Darussalam									**Brunéi Darussalam**
Partner 1	Japan, Japon	37.7	45.8	34.7	Malaysia, Malaisie	20.1	15.5	21.1	Partenaire 1
Partner 2	Republic of Korea, République de Corée	12.9	17.0	14.3	Singapore, Singapour	18.3	32.5	19.2	Partenaire 2
Partner 3	India, Inde	5.7	2.3	9.4	China, Chine	6.2	12.6	13.0	Partenaire 3
Bulgaria									**Bulgarie**
Partner 1	Germany, Allemagne	9.8	10.6	15.4	Germany, Allemagne	13.6	11.7	13.1	Partenaire 1
Partner 2	Romania, Roumanie	3.8	9.2	9.9	Russian Federation, Fédération de Russie	15.6	16.1	8.9	Partenaire 2
Partner 3	Italy, Italie	12.0	9.7	9.2	Italy, Italie	9.0	7.4	7.9	Partenaire 3

21 Major trading partner *(continued)*

Three largest trade partners as a percentage of total international merchandise trade in US dollars, as at 2016

Partenaire commercial principal *(suite)*

Trois principaux partenaires commerciaux en pourcentage du total de commerce international de marchandises en dollars américains, en 2016

Country or area	Major trading partner	Percentage of exports 2005	2010	2016	Major trading partner	Percentage of imports 2005	2010	2016	Pays ou zone
Burkina Faso									**Burkina Faso**
Partner 1	Switzerland, Suisse	9.4	63.5	50.6	China, Chine	2.7	9.7	11.1	Partenaire 1
Partner 2	India, Inde	~0.0	0.1	10.3	France	18.7	10.3	9.0	Partenaire 2
Partner 3	Singapore, Singapour	2.2	4.9	10.0	Côte d'Ivoire	17.9	16.0	8.4	Partenaire 3
Burundi									**Burundi**
Partner 1	Dem. Rep. of Congo, Rép. Dém. du Congo	0.9	6.2	22.3	China, Chine	4.2	12.0	16.6	Partenaire 1
Partner 2	Switzerland, Suisse	36.2	26.9	17.9	India, Inde	4.1	6.0	14.1	Partenaire 2
Partner 3	United Arab Emirates, Émirats arabes unis	25.3	8.8	13.1	United Rep. Tanzania, Rép.-Unie Tanzanie	4.9	6.0	8.2	Partenaire 3
Cabo Verde									**Cabo Verde**
Partner 1	Areas nes, Zones nsa [1]	0.1	19.1	27.5	Portugal	40.4	45.5	43.5	Partenaire 1
Partner 2	Portugal	22.9	24.4	25.4	Netherlands, Pays-Bas	8.7	13.8	12.3	Partenaire 2
Partner 3	Spain, Espagne	8.1	32.2	24.7	Spain, Espagne	7.0	6.8	7.3	Partenaire 3
Cambodia									**Cambodge**
Partner 1	United States, États-Unis	52.9	34.1	25.0	China, Chine	16.6	24.2	36.8	Partenaire 1
Partner 2	United Kingdom, Royaume-Uni	4.1	4.2	10.2	Thailand, Thaïlande	11.4	14.1	14.6	Partenaire 2
Partner 3	Germany, Allemagne	7.5	2.0	8.8	Viet Nam	7.1	9.9	8.7	Partenaire 3
Cameroon									**Cameroun**
Partner 1	Netherlands, Pays-Bas	7.5	13.1	21.4	China, Chine	4.4	10.6	21.4	Partenaire 1
Partner 2	Belgium, Belgique	4.0	1.9	9.3	France	18.0	14.6	12.0	Partenaire 2
Partner 3	Italy, Italie	16.3	9.7	7.8	Nigeria, Nigéria	26.8	18.2	4.6	Partenaire 3
Canada									**Canada**
Partner 1	United States, États-Unis	83.8	74.9	76.2	United States, États-Unis	56.5	50.4	52.2	Partenaire 1
Partner 2	China, Chine	1.7	3.3	4.1	China, Chine	7.8	11.0	12.1	Partenaire 2
Partner 3	United Kingdom, Royaume-Uni	1.9	4.1	3.3	Mexico, Mexique	3.8	5.5	6.2	Partenaire 3
Cayman Islands									**Îles Caïmanes**
Partner 1	United States, États-Unis	67.0	26.7	62.2	United States, États-Unis	50.8	42.8	78.4	Partenaire 1
Partner 2	Guatemala	~0.0	...	16.4	Bahamas	0.0	~0.0	4.9	Partenaire 2
Partner 3	France	~0.0	2.1	4.5	Brazil, Brésil	2.1	33.9	2.4	Partenaire 3
Central African Republic									**République centrafricaine**
Partner 1	France	19.6	16.0	63.6	France	14.0	24.1	21.1	Partenaire 1
Partner 2	Chad, Tchad	~0.0	1.3	11.5	United States, États-Unis	0.5	4.6	12.2	Partenaire 2
Partner 3	Cameroon, Cameroun	12.5	1.1	8.8	Zambia, Zambie	...	...	9.6	Partenaire 3
Chad									**Tchad**
Partner 1	United States, États-Unis	72.7	68.0	61.1	France	23.5	12.2	16.8	Partenaire 1
Partner 2	India, Inde	~0.0	~0.0	9.0	China, Chine	3.7	22.5	13.3	Partenaire 2
Partner 3	China, Chine	8.8	16.0	6.7	Cameroon, Cameroun	6.5	24.7	12.7	Partenaire 3
Chile									**Chili**
Partner 1	China, Chine	11.7	24.4	28.5	China, Chine	9.8	16.8	24.1	Partenaire 1
Partner 2	United States, États-Unis	16.0	9.9	14.1	United States, États-Unis	15.6	17.7	17.4	Partenaire 2
Partner 3	Japan, Japon	11.9	10.9	8.6	Brazil, Brésil	11.6	8.3	8.0	Partenaire 3
China									**Chine**
Partner 1	United States, États-Unis	21.4	18.0	18.3	Republic of Korea, République de Corée	11.6	9.9	10.0	Partenaire 1
Partner 2	China, Hong Kong SAR, Chine, Hong Kong RAS	16.3	13.8	13.8	Japan, Japon	15.2	12.7	9.2	Partenaire 2
Partner 3	Japan, Japon	11.0	7.7	6.1	Asia nes, Asie nsa [2]	11.3	8.3	8.8	Partenaire 3
China, Hong Kong SAR									**Chine, Hong Kong RAS**
Partner 1	China, Chine	44.6	52.5	55.3	China, Chine	45.0	44.7	44.7	Partenaire 1
Partner 2	United States, États-Unis	15.9	10.7	8.1	Asia nes, Asie nsa	7.2	6.6	8.9	Partenaire 2
Partner 3	India, Inde	1.0	2.5	3.0	Japan, Japon	11.0	9.3	6.3	Partenaire 3
China, Macao SAR									**Chine, Macao RAS**
Partner 1	Areas nes, Zones nsa [1]	4.1	29.8	58.7	China, Chine	37.4	30.5	35.1	Partenaire 1
Partner 2	China, Hong Kong SAR, Chine, Hong Kong RAS	9.8	30.4	31.6	China, Hong Kong SAR, Chine, Hong Kong RAS	8.6	10.3	8.9	Partenaire 2
Partner 3	China, Chine	14.9	11.4	6.8	France	2.9	9.0	8.0	Partenaire 3
Colombia									**Colombie**
Partner 1	United States, États-Unis	41.8	43.1	32.9	United States, États-Unis	28.5	25.9	26.7	Partenaire 1
Partner 2	Panama	1.2	2.4	6.2	China, Chine	7.6	13.5	19.3	Partenaire 2
Partner 3	Netherlands, Pays-Bas	2.1	4.1	3.9	Mexico, Mexique	8.3	9.5	7.6	Partenaire 3
Comoros									**Comores**
Partner 1	India, Inde	6.1	5.2	30.0	United Rep. Tanzania, Rép.-Unie Tanzanie	1.7	1.6	41.7	Partenaire 1
Partner 2	France	74.9	22.0	12.2	China, Chine	1.6	7.7	12.2	Partenaire 2
Partner 3	United Arab Emirates, Émirats arabes unis	1.7	3.6	11.3	France	17.9	20.6	10.9	Partenaire 3

21 Major trading partner *(continued)*

Three largest trade partners as a percentage of total international merchandise trade in US dollars, as at 2016

Partenaire commercial principal *(suite)*

Trois principaux partenaires commerciaux en pourcentage du total de commerce international de marchandises en dollars américains, en 2016

Country or area	Major trading partner	Percentage of exports 2005	2010	2016	Major trading partner	Percentage of imports 2005	2010	2016	Pays ou zone
Congo									**Congo**
Partner 1	China, Chine	36.1	20.9	34.9	France	20.9	12.2	17.2	Partenaire 1
Partner 2	Australia, Australie	0.1	~0.0	9.0	China, Chine	9.2	3.5	15.4	Partenaire 2
Partner 3	Gabon	0.2	4.7	8.3	Belgium, Belgique	4.4	3.7	13.5	Partenaire 3
Cook Islands									**Îles Cook**
Partner 1	Japan, Japon	30.8	49.7	39.0	New Zealand, Nouvelle-Zélande	73.9	76.4	46.7	Partenaire 1
Partner 2	Germany, Allemagne	4.5	...	11.7	Italy, Italie	~0.0	~0.0	16.0	Partenaire 2
Partner 3	France	...	...	7.0	Fiji, Fidji	1.2	9.4	8.2	Partenaire 3
Costa Rica									**Costa Rica**
Partner 1	United States, États-Unis	42.8	37.4	41.0	United States, États-Unis	41.1	46.8	37.3	Partenaire 1
Partner 2	Netherlands, Pays-Bas	6.3	7.0	5.8	China, Chine	3.8	7.1	13.6	Partenaire 2
Partner 3	Panama	2.6	4.8	5.7	Mexico, Mexique	4.7	6.4	7.0	Partenaire 3
Côte d'Ivoire									**Côte d'Ivoire**
Partner 1	Netherlands, Pays-Bas	11.0	14.2	12.1	Nigeria, Nigéria	24.5	26.3	15.2	Partenaire 1
Partner 2	United States, États-Unis	14.1	10.3	8.1	France	27.7	11.9	13.8	Partenaire 2
Partner 3	Belgium, Belgique	2.2	0.1	6.5	China, Chine	3.1	7.0	11.7	Partenaire 3
Croatia									**Croatie**
Partner 1	Italy, Italie	21.2	18.7	13.7	Germany, Allemagne	14.8	12.5	16.1	Partenaire 1
Partner 2	Slovenia, Slovénie	8.1	7.8	12.5	Italy, Italie	16.0	15.2	12.6	Partenaire 2
Partner 3	Germany, Allemagne	10.7	10.3	11.8	Slovenia, Slovénie	6.8	5.8	10.9	Partenaire 3
Cuba									**Cuba**
Partner 1	Canada	20.3	22.7	17.2	China, Chine	11.5	18.6	27.2	Partenaire 1
Partner 2	China, Chine	4.9	27.4	16.0	Spain, Espagne	8.7	13.6	15.3	Partenaire 2
Partner 3	Netherlands, Pays-Bas	27.8	5.0	9.4	Italy, Italie	3.8	4.3	5.3	Partenaire 3
Cyprus									**Chypre**
Partner 1	Greece, Grèce	11.4	21.5	12.3	Greece, Grèce	17.1	18.7	21.3	Partenaire 1
Partner 2	United Kingdom, Royaume-Uni	16.8	7.6	7.6	Germany, Allemagne	8.3	9.1	16.3	Partenaire 2
Partner 3	Libya, Libye	0.5	0.7	7.5	Italy, Italie	10.1	9.3	6.6	Partenaire 3
Czechia									**Tchéquie**
Partner 1	Germany, Allemagne	33.5	31.9	32.5	Germany, Allemagne	30.0	25.5	26.7	Partenaire 1
Partner 2	Slovakia, Slovaquie	8.6	8.8	8.4	China, Chine	5.1	12.2	12.7	Partenaire 2
Partner 3	Poland, Pologne	5.5	6.2	5.7	Poland, Pologne	5.0	6.4	8.3	Partenaire 3
Dem. People's Rep. Korea									**Rép. pop. dém. de Corée**
Partner 1	China, Chine	35.0	56.1	84.0	China, Chine	45.0	62.8	88.4	Partenaire 1
Partner 2	India, Inde	0.6	6.9	2.8	Thailand, Thaïlande	8.6	0.8	2.3	Partenaire 2
Partner 3	Philippines	...	...	1.7	Russian Federation, Fédération de Russie	9.3	1.3	2.1	Partenaire 3
Dem. Rep. of the Congo									**Rép. dém. du Congo**
Partner 1	China, Chine	11.6	43.3	37.4	China, Chine	3.1	10.8	20.3	Partenaire 1
Partner 2	Zambia, Zambie	1.4	21.9	15.0	South Africa, Afrique du Sud	17.0	19.3	15.9	Partenaire 2
Partner 3	Saudi Arabia, Arabie saoudite	~0.0	3.4	9.0	Zambia, Zambie	6.0	7.6	9.9	Partenaire 3
Denmark									**Danemark**
Partner 1	Germany, Allemagne	17.2	19.8	20.3	Germany, Allemagne	21.0	20.7	21.6	Partenaire 1
Partner 2	Sweden, Suède	14.8	14.2	14.1	Sweden, Suède	14.1	13.3	12.1	Partenaire 2
Partner 3	Norway, Norvège	5.2	6.1	6.2	Netherlands, Pays-Bas	6.7	7.1	8.0	Partenaire 3
Djibouti									**Djibouti**
Partner 1	United States, États-Unis	1.0	0.4	23.3	China, Chine	11.0	3.2	49.2	Partenaire 1
Partner 2	Saudi Arabia, Arabie saoudite	0.1	0.8	21.3	India, Inde	19.2	3.2	6.1	Partenaire 2
Partner 3	United Arab Emirates, Émirats arabes unis	5.3	1.0	15.1	Indonesia, Indonésie	4.2	0.2	4.7	Partenaire 3
Dominica									**Dominique**
Partner 1	Bahamas	0.4	0.4	43.0	United States, États-Unis	36.6	41.8	24.4	Partenaire 1
Partner 2	Poland, Pologne	...	...	20.5	China, Chine	2.2	4.0	16.8	Partenaire 2
Partner 3	Saudi Arabia, Arabie saoudite	...	...	6.9	United Kingdom, Royaume-Uni	6.8	4.0	5.7	Partenaire 3
Dominican Republic									**République dominicaine**
Partner 1	United States, États-Unis	70.3	57.7	53.6	United States, États-Unis	54.8	39.0	41.3	Partenaire 1
Partner 2	Haiti, Haïti	2.7	16.8	12.1	China, Chine	5.4	10.7	13.4	Partenaire 2
Partner 3	Canada	0.6	0.5	8.4	Mexico, Mexique	2.8	6.0	4.6	Partenaire 3
Ecuador									**Équateur**
Partner 1	United States, États-Unis	50.1	34.7	32.4	United States, États-Unis	19.2	27.9	23.2	Partenaire 1
Partner 2	Chile, Chili	3.1	4.8	6.8	China, Chine	6.5	7.8	19.1	Partenaire 2
Partner 3	Viet Nam	~0.0	~0.0	6.6	Colombia, Colombie	14.4	9.8	8.1	Partenaire 3

21 Major trading partner *(continued)*

Three largest trade partners as a percentage of total international merchandise trade in US dollars, as at 2016

Partenaire commercial principal *(suite)*

Trois principaux partenaires commerciaux en pourcentage du total de commerce international de marchandises en dollars américains, en 2016

Country or area	Major trading partner	Percentage of exports 2005	2010	2016	Major trading partner	Percentage of imports 2005	2010	2016	Pays ou zone
Egypt									**Égypte**
Partner 1	United Arab Emirates, Émirats arabes unis	2.9	2.3	12.6	China, Chine	5.0	9.2	13.0	Partenaire 1
Partner 2	Saudi Arabia, Arabie saoudite	3.6	5.9	7.8	Germany, Allemagne	10.4	7.6	8.7	Partenaire 2
Partner 3	Italy, Italie	10.1	8.4	6.5	United States, États-Unis	10.9	9.4	5.3	Partenaire 3
El Salvador									**El Salvador**
Partner 1	United States, États-Unis	52.9	48.4	48.2	United States, États-Unis	36.5	37.0	37.3	Partenaire 1
Partner 2	Honduras	14.1	12.9	14.1	Guatemala	8.7	9.6	10.0	Partenaire 2
Partner 3	Guatemala	12.4	14.0	13.5	China, Chine	3.2	5.7	8.7	Partenaire 3
Equatorial Guinea									**Guinée équatoriale**
Partner 1	India, Inde	~0.0	1.3	19.7	Netherlands, Pays-Bas	2.4	0.9	21.4	Partenaire 1
Partner 2	China, Chine	21.7	6.2	13.7	United States, États-Unis	24.8	5.3	18.0	Partenaire 2
Partner 3	Republic of Korea, République de Corée	...	7.9	13.4	Spain, Espagne	11.2	5.8	16.9	Partenaire 3
Eritrea									**Érythrée**
Partner 1	China, Chine	0.7	5.8	55.3	China, Chine	2.7	7.6	21.8	Partenaire 1
Partner 2	India, Inde	7.2	3.0	20.4	Egypt, Égypte	2.3	10.9	21.6	Partenaire 2
Partner 3	United Arab Emirates, Émirats arabes unis	0.3	13.3	4.7	United Arab Emirates, Émirats arabes unis	12.2	14.2	9.8	Partenaire 3
Estonia									**Estonie**
Partner 1	Sweden, Suède	12.2	14.0	16.8	Germany, Allemagne	12.8	10.6	10.7	Partenaire 1
Partner 2	Finland, Finlande	24.6	15.3	15.0	Finland, Finlande	11.7	11.5	9.6	Partenaire 2
Partner 3	Russian Federation, Fédération de Russie	9.8	14.8	9.3	China, Chine	5.7	7.0	8.0	Partenaire 3
Ethiopia									**Éthiopie**
Partner 1	United States, États-Unis	4.7	4.4	9.8	China, Chine	12.6	24.0	31.9	Partenaire 1
Partner 2	Saudi Arabia, Arabie saoudite	6.3	6.3	9.7	United States, États-Unis	9.2	5.6	8.8	Partenaire 2
Partner 3	Germany, Allemagne	13.1	11.4	8.6	India, Inde	6.0	7.2	7.5	Partenaire 3
Falkland Islands (Malvinas)									**Îles Falkland (Malvinas)**
Partner 1	Spain, Espagne	78.1	79.5	71.7	United Kingdom, Royaume-Uni	73.1	77.7	73.1	Partenaire 1
Partner 2	Namibia, Namibie	...	...	9.5	Greece, Grèce	...	6.7	9.0	Partenaire 2
Partner 3	United States, États-Unis	5.6	3.1	7.7	Spain, Espagne	0.8	1.2	5.9	Partenaire 3
Faroe Islands									**Îles Féroé**
Partner 1	United Kingdom, Royaume-Uni	28.4	17.3	20.9	Denmark, Danemark	26.7	30.4	51.2	Partenaire 1
Partner 2	Russian Federation, Fédération de Russie	3.6	4.0	19.1	Germany, Allemagne	6.6	6.1	11.0	Partenaire 2
Partner 3	Denmark, Danemark	14.6	11.0	13.7	Norway, Norvège	17.4	18.1	8.8	Partenaire 3
Fiji									**Fidji**
Partner 1	United States, États-Unis	15.4	11.4	15.7	Singapore, Singapour	29.9	33.1	19.0	Partenaire 1
Partner 2	Australia, Australie	20.4	21.1	15.1	Australia, Australie	24.6	20.3	15.4	Partenaire 2
Partner 3	Areas nes, Zones nsa [1]	1.4	10.5	6.5	China, Chine	3.3	6.1	14.6	Partenaire 3
Finland									**Finlande**
Partner 1	Germany, Allemagne	10.6	9.5	12.8	Germany, Allemagne	14.9	13.2	14.6	Partenaire 1
Partner 2	Sweden, Suède	10.7	11.4	10.6	Sweden, Suède	10.6	10.0	11.2	Partenaire 2
Partner 3	United States, États-Unis	5.8	6.7	7.2	Russian Federation, Fédération de Russie	13.9	17.7	11.1	Partenaire 3
France									**France**
Partner 1	Germany, Allemagne	14.5	16.2	16.1	Germany, Allemagne	17.2	17.3	16.9	Partenaire 1
Partner 2	Spain, Espagne	10.2	7.4	7.5	China, Chine	5.5	8.2	9.1	Partenaire 2
Partner 3	United States, États-Unis	7.2	5.7	7.4	Italy, Italie	8.6	7.5	7.5	Partenaire 3
French Polynesia									**Polynésie française**
Partner 1	Japan, Japon	28.3	20.1	26.1	France	35.5	28.1	25.6	Partenaire 1
Partner 2	China, Hong Kong SAR, Chine, Hong Kong RAS	28.0	30.0	24.5	China, Chine	6.4	9.4	13.2	Partenaire 2
Partner 3	United States, États-Unis	13.8	11.6	18.0	United States, États-Unis	10.0	10.1	10.4	Partenaire 3
Gabon									**Gabon**
Partner 1	China, Chine	4.0	8.0	29.3	France	39.3	32.9	22.7	Partenaire 1
Partner 2	Trinidad and Tobago, Trinité-et-Tobago	...	...	12.6	China, Chine	1.7	4.9	16.7	Partenaire 2
Partner 3	Australia, Australie	1.3	~0.0	9.2	Congo	0.7	0.8	9.2	Partenaire 3
Gambia									**Gambie**
Partner 1	Mali	0.1	3.4	37.9	Côte d'Ivoire	12.6	19.4	20.6	Partenaire 1
Partner 2	Guinea, Guinée	33.4	18.9	24.7	Brazil, Brésil	4.3	10.0	11.0	Partenaire 2
Partner 3	Senegal, Sénégal	7.1	26.3	16.0	China, Chine	9.3	8.7	8.3	Partenaire 3
Georgia									**Géorgie**
Partner 1	Russian Federation, Fédération de Russie	17.8	2.7	9.8	Turkey, Turquie	11.5	16.9	18.7	Partenaire 1
Partner 2	Turkey, Turquie	14.1	12.5	8.2	Russian Federation, Fédération de Russie	15.4	4.6	9.3	Partenaire 2
Partner 3	China, Chine	0.6	1.6	8.0	China, Chine	1.9	6.4	7.6	Partenaire 3

21 Major trading partner *(continued)*

Three largest trade partners as a percentage of total international merchandise trade in US dollars, as at 2016

Partenaire commercial principal *(suite)*

Trois principaux partenaires commerciaux en pourcentage du total de commerce international de marchandises en dollars américains, en 2016

Country or area	Major trading partner	Percentage of exports 2005	2010	2016	Major trading partner	Percentage of imports 2005	2010	2016	Pays ou zone
Germany									**Allemagne**
Partner 1	United States, États-Unis	8.8	6.8	8.8	China, Chine	6.5	9.5	9.9	Partenaire 1
Partner 2	France	10.1	9.5	8.3	Netherlands, Pays-Bas	8.3	8.5	8.7	Partenaire 2
Partner 3	United Kingdom, Royaume-Uni	7.7	6.2	7.0	France	8.6	7.7	6.9	Partenaire 3
Ghana									**Ghana**
Partner 1	Switzerland, Suisse	4.5	4.1	23.0	China, Chine	8.1	13.2	30.9	Partenaire 1
Partner 2	India, Inde	1.4	0.9	13.9	Nigeria, Nigéria	11.7	0.4	6.3	Partenaire 2
Partner 3	China, Chine	1.4	1.0	12.5	Netherlands, Pays-Bas	3.7	3.5	6.2	Partenaire 3
Gibraltar									**Gibraltar**
Partner 1	Spain, Espagne	15.5	14.1	28.6	United States, États-Unis	3.9	22.7	22.6	Partenaire 1
Partner 2	Poland, Pologne	1.2	1.3	24.9	Russian Federation, Fédération de Russie	14.9	0.3	14.5	Partenaire 2
Partner 3	Belgium, Belgique	0.2	2.8	12.5	United Kingdom, Royaume-Uni	16.7	14.8	12.4	Partenaire 3
Greece									**Grèce**
Partner 1	Italy, Italie	10.5	9.2	11.2	Germany, Allemagne	13.3	10.7	10.9	Partenaire 1
Partner 2	Germany, Allemagne	12.5	9.3	7.7	Italy, Italie	12.3	9.7	8.3	Partenaire 2
Partner 3	Cyprus, Chypre	5.2	6.4	6.1	China, Chine	3.9	5.7	6.7	Partenaire 3
Greenland									**Groenland**
Partner 1	Denmark, Danemark	86.7	88.9	81.3	Denmark, Danemark	71.5	57.6	72.2	Partenaire 1
Partner 2	Portugal	...	4.1	8.3	Sweden, Suède	16.1	21.6	9.8	Partenaire 2
Partner 3	Areas nes, Zones nsa [1]	~0.0	2.3	6.0	China, Chine	~0.0	1.8	2.6	Partenaire 3
Grenada									**Grenade**
Partner 1	United States, États-Unis	21.4	16.3	32.5	United States, États-Unis	37.5	31.9	39.1	Partenaire 1
Partner 2	Saint Lucia, Sainte-Lucie	9.3	11.2	12.3	Trinidad and Tobago, Trinité-et-Tobago	20.9	25.2	10.4	Partenaire 2
Partner 3	Germany, Allemagne	1.6	6.0	6.1	United Kingdom, Royaume-Uni	5.8	4.2	5.0	Partenaire 3
Guatemala									**Guatemala**
Partner 1	United States, États-Unis	50.1	38.8	35.0	United States, États-Unis	33.9	37.1	37.1	Partenaire 1
Partner 2	El Salvador	12.1	11.7	11.6	Mexico, Mexique	8.7	11.2	11.6	Partenaire 2
Partner 3	Honduras	7.3	8.3	8.5	China, Chine	7.2	7.1	10.6	Partenaire 3
Guinea									**Guinée**
Partner 1	Ghana	~0.0	~0.0	22.0	China, Chine	3.9	6.7	14.9	Partenaire 1
Partner 2	India, Inde	0.2	0.3	16.4	Netherlands, Pays-Bas	1.2	20.6	13.4	Partenaire 2
Partner 3	United Arab Emirates, Émirats arabes unis	~0.0	0.2	9.9	India, Inde	2.3	2.6	10.9	Partenaire 3
Guinea-Bissau									**Guinée-Bissau**
Partner 1	India, Inde	86.6	76.2	70.3	Portugal	37.2	24.2	28.1	Partenaire 1
Partner 2	Viet Nam	...	4.2	11.0	Senegal, Sénégal	40.9	21.4	17.2	Partenaire 2
Partner 3	Belarus, Bélarus	...	~0.0	10.9	India, Inde	~0.0	1.6	7.1	Partenaire 3
Guyana									**Guyana**
Partner 1	Canada	16.0	39.6	30.6	Trinidad and Tobago, Trinité-et-Tobago	33.3	22.0	29.1	Partenaire 1
Partner 2	United States, États-Unis	15.5	10.2	20.6	United States, États-Unis	31.1	27.7	27.6	Partenaire 2
Partner 3	Trinidad and Tobago, Trinité-et-Tobago	5.5	3.5	11.4	China, Chine	4.1	5.8	7.3	Partenaire 3
Haiti									**Haïti**
Partner 1	United States, États-Unis	83.7	81.2	80.6	United States, États-Unis	49.3	35.2	36.8	Partenaire 1
Partner 2	Dominican Republic, République dominicaine	4.2	2.3	5.9	China, Chine	2.2	7.4	15.2	Partenaire 2
Partner 3	Mexico, Mexique	1.2	2.0	2.6	Dominican Republic, République dominicaine	12.0	23.4	15.1	Partenaire 3
Honduras									**Honduras**
Partner 1	United States, États-Unis	41.6	38.9	44.2	United States, États-Unis	36.8	38.5	35.0	Partenaire 1
Partner 2	Germany, Allemagne	8.3	7.5	8.0	China, Chine	2.3	7.7	15.4	Partenaire 2
Partner 3	El Salvador	9.8	10.2	6.5	Guatemala	7.8	8.9	8.0	Partenaire 3
Hungary									**Hongrie**
Partner 1	Germany, Allemagne	30.1	25.1	27.5	Germany, Allemagne	27.6	24.0	26.4	Partenaire 1
Partner 2	Romania, Roumanie	3.7	5.4	5.0	Austria, Autriche	6.6	6.2	6.4	Partenaire 2
Partner 3	Slovakia, Slovaquie	2.8	5.4	4.9	Poland, Pologne	3.8	5.2	5.6	Partenaire 3
Iceland									**Islande**
Partner 1	Netherlands, Pays-Bas	12.5	34.0	25.5	Germany, Allemagne	13.8	7.5	10.0	Partenaire 1
Partner 2	United Kingdom, Royaume-Uni	17.8	10.1	11.3	United States, États-Unis	9.3	7.9	10.0	Partenaire 2
Partner 3	Spain, Espagne	7.4	4.7	10.4	Norway, Norvège	7.0	9.1	9.0	Partenaire 3
India									**Inde**
Partner 1	United States, États-Unis	16.5	11.2	16.1	China, Chine	7.2	11.8	16.7	Partenaire 1
Partner 2	United Arab Emirates, Émirats arabes unis	8.4	12.3	11.5	United States, États-Unis	6.0	5.5	6.4	Partenaire 2
Partner 3	China, Hong Kong SAR, Chine, Hong Kong RAS	4.4	4.3	5.1	United Arab Emirates, Émirats arabes unis	3.6	8.8	5.4	Partenaire 3

21 Major trading partner *(continued)*

Three largest trade partners as a percentage of total international merchandise trade in US dollars, as at 2016

Partenaire commercial principal *(suite)*

Trois principaux partenaires commerciaux en pourcentage du total de commerce international de marchandises en dollars américains, en 2016

Country or area	Major trading partner	Percentage of exports 2005	2010	2016	Major trading partner	Percentage of imports 2005	2010	2016	Pays ou zone
Indonesia									**Indonésie**
Partner 1	China, Chine	7.8	9.9	11.6	China, Chine	10.1	15.1	22.7	Partenaire 1
Partner 2	United States, États-Unis	11.5	9.1	11.2	Singapore, Singapour	16.4	14.9	10.7	Partenaire 2
Partner 3	Japan, Japon	21.1	16.3	11.1	Japan, Japon	12.0	12.5	9.6	Partenaire 3
Iran (Islamic Republic of)									**Iran (Rép. islamique d')**
Partner 1	China, Chine	0.8	5.3	31.3	China, Chine	6.4	10.4	31.3	Partenaire 1
Partner 2	India, Inde	1.1	2.0	17.3	United Arab Emirates, Émirats arabes unis	18.7	28.6	12.0	Partenaire 2
Partner 3	Turkey, Turquie	3.6	4.8	9.7	Turkey, Turquie	2.2	4.2	9.4	Partenaire 3
Iraq									**Iraq**
Partner 1	China, Chine	...	12.9	22.9	Areas nes, Zones nsa [1]	69.0	94.8	70.4	Partenaire 1
Partner 2	India, Inde	0.0	14.9	21.3	China, Chine	1.0	0.2	9.0	Partenaire 2
Partner 3	United States, États-Unis	56.0	25.9	13.5	United Arab Emirates, Émirats arabes unis	5.5	0.4	4.7	Partenaire 3
Ireland									**Irlande**
Partner 1	United States, États-Unis	18.7	23.3	25.8	United Kingdom, Royaume-Uni	31.2	32.2	23.8	Partenaire 1
Partner 2	United Kingdom, Royaume-Uni	17.1	15.5	12.8	United States, États-Unis	14.1	14.1	16.5	Partenaire 2
Partner 3	Belgium, Belgique	15.1	15.1	12.6	France	3.4	4.0	12.5	Partenaire 3
Israel									**Israël**
Partner 1	United States, États-Unis	37.8	33.2	33.2	United States, États-Unis	13.6	11.2	12.3	Partenaire 1
Partner 2	China, Hong Kong SAR, Chine, Hong Kong RAS	5.6	6.7	7.3	China, Chine	4.2	8.0	9.0	Partenaire 2
Partner 3	United Kingdom, Royaume-Uni	3.9	3.9	6.6	Switzerland, Suisse	5.4	5.4	6.5	Partenaire 3
Italy									**Italie**
Partner 1	Germany, Allemagne	13.1	14.3	12.6	Germany, Allemagne	18.1	16.0	16.3	Partenaire 1
Partner 2	France	12.2	11.5	10.5	France	10.2	8.7	8.9	Partenaire 2
Partner 3	United States, États-Unis	8.0	6.1	8.9	China, Chine	4.6	7.8	7.5	Partenaire 3
Jamaica									**Jamaïque**
Partner 1	United States, États-Unis	25.6	49.6	41.5	United States, États-Unis	42.8	37.4	39.5	Partenaire 1
Partner 2	Canada	19.4	12.3	12.1	Trinidad and Tobago, Trinité-et-Tobago	15.0	13.8	7.3	Partenaire 2
Partner 3	Netherlands, Pays-Bas	2.3	5.1	10.4	China, Chine	2.9	4.6	6.5	Partenaire 3
Japan									**Japon**
Partner 1	United States, États-Unis	22.9	15.6	20.2	China, Chine	21.0	22.1	25.8	Partenaire 1
Partner 2	China, Chine	13.5	19.4	17.6	United States, États-Unis	12.7	10.0	11.4	Partenaire 2
Partner 3	Republic of Korea, République de Corée	7.8	8.1	7.2	Australia, Australie	4.8	6.5	5.0	Partenaire 3
Jordan									**Jordanie**
Partner 1	United States, États-Unis	26.1	13.2	20.9	China, Chine	9.2	10.8	14.0	Partenaire 1
Partner 2	Saudi Arabia, Arabie saoudite	5.9	9.6	13.2	Saudi Arabia, Arabie saoudite	23.7	19.8	12.1	Partenaire 2
Partner 3	India, Inde	8.1	11.2	7.6	United States, États-Unis	5.6	5.6	7.0	Partenaire 3
Kazakhstan									**Kazakhstan**
Partner 1	Italy, Italie	15.0	16.7	20.3	Russian Federation, Fédération de Russie	38.0	22.8	36.3	Partenaire 1
Partner 2	China, Chine	8.7	17.7	11.5	China, Chine	7.2	16.5	14.6	Partenaire 2
Partner 3	Russian Federation, Fédération de Russie	10.5	5.3	9.5	Germany, Allemagne	7.5	7.6	5.7	Partenaire 3
Kenya									**Kenya**
Partner 1	United States, États-Unis	6.7	5.5	10.8	China, Chine	5.2	12.6	34.7	Partenaire 1
Partner 2	Netherlands, Pays-Bas	7.1	6.6	8.2	India, Inde	5.6	10.8	15.0	Partenaire 2
Partner 3	Pakistan	5.4	4.4	7.7	Japan, Japon	5.2	6.1	4.5	Partenaire 3
Kiribati									**Kiribati**
Partner 1	Thailand, Thaïlande	...	...	63.7	Fiji, Fidji	20.9	26.8	27.0	Partenaire 1
Partner 2	Viet Nam	...	3.6	9.2	China, Chine	2.3	5.4	18.8	Partenaire 2
Partner 3	China, Chine	0.5	...	7.4	Japan, Japon	17.1	7.4	13.5	Partenaire 3
Kuwait									**Koweït**
Partner 1	Republic of Korea, République de Corée	15.1	15.2	15.2	China, Chine	6.8	12.5	16.0	Partenaire 1
Partner 2	China, Chine	2.1	8.4	12.4	United States, États-Unis	10.8	11.4	9.4	Partenaire 2
Partner 3	Japan, Japon	19.3	14.8	9.0	United Arab Emirates, Émirats arabes unis	4.5	4.5	9.3	Partenaire 3
Kyrgyzstan									**Kirghizistan**
Partner 1	Switzerland, Suisse	9.7	26.1	45.5	China, Chine	9.3	20.7	38.1	Partenaire 1
Partner 2	Kazakhstan	17.3	12.2	10.6	Russian Federation, Fédération de Russie	34.2	33.6	20.8	Partenaire 2
Partner 3	Russian Federation, Fédération de Russie	20.0	17.3	10.2	Kazakhstan	16.3	12.0	16.5	Partenaire 3
Lao People's Dem. Rep.									**Rép. dém. populaire lao**
Partner 1	Thailand, Thaïlande	37.0	36.2	33.4	Thailand, Thaïlande	68.4	65.5	66.1	Partenaire 1
Partner 2	China, Chine	4.2	29.0	31.7	China, Chine	9.2	14.8	15.7	Partenaire 2
Partner 3	Viet Nam	15.9	14.1	14.5	Viet Nam	6.2	6.1	8.9	Partenaire 3

21 Major trading partner *(continued)*

Three largest trade partners as a percentage of total international merchandise trade in US dollars, as at 2016

Partenaire commercial principal *(suite)*

Trois principaux partenaires commerciaux en pourcentage du total de commerce international de marchandises en dollars américains, en 2016

Country or area	Major trading partner	Percentage of exports 2005	2010	2016	Major trading partner	Percentage of imports 2005	2010	2016	Pays ou zone
Latvia									**Lettonie**
Partner 1	Lithuania, Lituanie	10.5	16.2	18.3	Lithuania, Lituanie	13.5	17.1	17.5	Partenaire 1
Partner 2	Estonia, Estonie	10.4	13.5	12.1	Germany, Allemagne	13.6	11.5	11.9	Partenaire 2
Partner 3	Russian Federation, Fédération de Russie	8.3	10.6	7.6	Poland, Pologne	6.3	7.9	10.8	Partenaire 3
Lebanon									**Liban**
Partner 1	Saudi Arabia, Arabie saoudite	7.4	5.8	11.4	China, Chine	7.9	9.1	12.1	Partenaire 1
Partner 2	United Arab Emirates, Émirats arabes unis	8.5	9.8	9.7	Italy, Italie	10.4	7.8	8.0	Partenaire 2
Partner 3	South Africa, Afrique du Sud	0.2	8.1	9.0	France	8.5	6.7	6.2	Partenaire 3
Lesotho									**Lesotho**
Partner 1	United States, États-Unis	44.5	21.4	35.1	South Africa, Afrique du Sud	77.1	78.9	84.6	Partenaire 1
Partner 2	South Africa, Afrique du Sud	42.3	74.9	32.0	China, Chine	3.8	2.6	4.1	Partenaire 2
Partner 3	Belgium, Belgique	0.8	...	24.8	Asia nes, Asie nsa [2]	5.6	5.3	4.0	Partenaire 3
Liberia									**Libéria**
Partner 1	Areas nes, Zones nsa [1]	20.1	...	21.1	China, Chine	10.0	29.6	32.2	Partenaire 1
Partner 2	Switzerland, Suisse	0.2	0.5	13.2	Singapore, Singapour	11.8	11.8	12.3	Partenaire 2
Partner 3	United Arab Emirates, Émirats arabes unis	0.1	6.0	9.5	Republic of Korea, République de Corée	6.2	7.2	8.2	Partenaire 3
Libya									**Libye**
Partner 1	Italy, Italie	36.7	42.3	26.0	China, Chine	3.3	9.8	11.7	Partenaire 1
Partner 2	United Arab Emirates, Émirats arabes unis	0.2	0.4	12.4	Italy, Italie	18.3	9.4	11.5	Partenaire 2
Partner 3	Spain, Espagne	9.8	9.2	12.2	Turkey, Turquie	1.8	10.6	8.7	Partenaire 3
Lithuania									**Lituanie**
Partner 1	Russian Federation, Fédération de Russie	11.4	15.6	13.5	Russian Federation, Fédération de Russie	27.5	32.7	14.4	Partenaire 1
Partner 2	Latvia, Lettonie	10.0	9.5	9.9	Germany, Allemagne	14.8	10.9	12.1	Partenaire 2
Partner 3	Poland, Pologne	5.3	7.7	9.1	Poland, Pologne	8.2	8.8	10.8	Partenaire 3
Luxembourg									**Luxembourg**
Partner 1	Germany, Allemagne	25.4	28.4	26.9	Germany, Allemagne	26.1	25.6	24.4	Partenaire 1
Partner 2	France	17.2	16.2	14.8	Belgium, Belgique	33.9	24.9	22.9	Partenaire 2
Partner 3	Belgium, Belgique	11.4	12.6	11.7	France	11.8	14.9	11.5	Partenaire 3
Madagascar									**Madagascar**
Partner 1	France	34.4	33.1	23.8	China, Chine	13.9	12.2	21.3	Partenaire 1
Partner 2	United States, États-Unis	22.0	4.2	13.0	France	15.6	14.4	6.9	Partenaire 2
Partner 3	Germany, Allemagne	6.4	7.3	8.4	India, Inde	5.9	2.4	6.5	Partenaire 3
Malawi									**Malawi**
Partner 1	Belgium, Belgique	1.4	12.4	10.6	South Africa, Afrique du Sud	32.7	30.1	18.1	Partenaire 1
Partner 2	Zimbabwe	2.2	5.4	9.3	China, Chine	2.9	9.1	13.1	Partenaire 2
Partner 3	Mozambique	3.5	3.4	9.2	United Arab Emirates, Émirats arabes unis	2.3	5.0	11.0	Partenaire 3
Malaysia									**Malaisie**
Partner 1	Singapore, Singapour	15.6	13.4	14.6	China, Chine	11.5	12.6	20.4	Partenaire 1
Partner 2	China, Chine	6.6	12.6	12.5	Singapore, Singapour	11.7	11.4	10.4	Partenaire 2
Partner 3	United States, États-Unis	19.6	9.5	10.2	Japan, Japon	14.5	12.6	8.2	Partenaire 3
Maldives									**Maldives**
Partner 1	Thailand, Thaïlande	15.3	29.9	34.4	United Arab Emirates, Émirats arabes unis	15.7	18.8	15.7	Partenaire 1
Partner 2	Sri Lanka	12.2	19.6	10.2	Singapore, Singapour	24.1	17.9	14.3	Partenaire 2
Partner 3	United States, États-Unis	2.9	0.7	8.9	China, Chine	2.1	2.9	13.4	Partenaire 3
Mali									**Mali**
Partner 1	United Arab Emirates, Émirats arabes unis	~0.0	1.0	59.6	Senegal, Sénégal	11.5	13.6	13.8	Partenaire 1
Partner 2	Switzerland, Suisse	30.3	12.1	18.8	Côte d'Ivoire	10.2	7.9	13.1	Partenaire 2
Partner 3	India, Inde	0.2	~0.0	6.0	France	12.6	13.4	12.2	Partenaire 3
Malta									**Malte**
Partner 1	United States, États-Unis	13.5	7.0	20.5	Italy, Italie	30.7	24.6	19.2	Partenaire 1
Partner 2	Germany, Allemagne	12.3	10.5	11.1	Cayman Islands, Îles Caïmanes	~0.0	1.0	10.2	Partenaire 2
Partner 3	Bunkers, Com. de soute [3]	0.1	0.1	9.4	Canada	0.2	2.2	9.0	Partenaire 3
Marshall Islands									**Îles Marshall**
Partner 1	United States, États-Unis	25.9	12.9	23.4	Singapore, Singapour	29.2	29.7	29.0	Partenaire 1
Partner 2	Spain, Espagne	~0.0	~0.0	11.5	China, Chine	11.4	24.3	23.5	Partenaire 2
Partner 3	Thailand, Thaïlande	35.4	33.6	10.9	Republic of Korea, République de Corée	15.1	16.7	16.1	Partenaire 3
Mauritania									**Mauritanie**
Partner 1	China, Chine	1.5	39.4	36.9	United States, États-Unis	9.8	3.7	13.4	Partenaire 1
Partner 2	Switzerland, Suisse	...	13.1	13.5	United Arab Emirates, Émirats arabes unis	0.9	12.1	11.9	Partenaire 2
Partner 3	Spain, Espagne	10.7	7.2	8.9	Belgium, Belgique	3.6	9.9	9.2	Partenaire 3

21

Major trading partner *(continued)*

Three largest trade partners as a percentage of total international merchandise trade in US dollars, as at 2016

Partenaire commercial principal *(suite)*

Trois principaux partenaires commerciaux en pourcentage du total de commerce international de marchandises en dollars américains, en 2016

		Percentage of exports				Percentage of imports			
Country or area	Major trading partner	2005	2010	2016	Major trading partner	2005	2010	2016	Pays ou zone
Mauritius									**Maurice**
Partner 1	France	15.7	16.2	14.8	China, Chine	9.8	13.3	17.7	Partenaire 1
Partner 2	United Kingdom, Royaume-Uni	30.0	23.7	12.0	India, Inde	6.9	22.3	16.5	Partenaire 2
Partner 3	United States, États-Unis	9.2	10.9	11.4	France	7.6	8.8	7.8	Partenaire 3
Mexico									**Mexique**
Partner 1	United States, États-Unis	85.8	80.1	81.0	United States, États-Unis	53.6	48.2	46.5	Partenaire 1
Partner 2	Canada	2.0	3.6	2.8	China, Chine	8.0	15.1	18.0	Partenaire 2
Partner 3	China, Chine	0.5	1.4	1.4	Japan, Japon	5.9	5.0	4.6	Partenaire 3
Micronesia (Fed. States of)									**Micronésie (États féd. de)**
Partner 1	Thailand, Thaïlande	82.0	30.6	30.1	Republic of Korea, République de Corée	4.0	2.4	29.6	Partenaire 1
Partner 2	Indonesia, Indonésie	...	...	25.3	United States, États-Unis	42.9	48.7	24.0	Partenaire 2
Partner 3	China, Chine	...	3.8	17.9	Asia nes, Asie nsa [2]	1.7	0.8	13.6	Partenaire 3
Mongolia									**Mongolie**
Partner 1	China, Chine	48.1	81.8	83.5	China, Chine	24.9	41.5	35.8	Partenaire 1
Partner 2	United Kingdom, Royaume-Uni	8.2	2.1	7.2	Russian Federation, Fédération de Russie	35.3	26.8	26.9	Partenaire 2
Partner 3	Switzerland, Suisse	0.4	~0.0	2.3	Japan, Japon	6.4	4.6	7.2	Partenaire 3
Montenegro									**Monténégro**
Partner 1	Serbia, Serbie	...	28.2	25.7	Serbia, Serbie	...	26.2	22.3	Partenaire 1
Partner 2	Hungary, Hongrie	...	8.8	10.9	Germany, Allemagne	...	7.1	10.5	Partenaire 2
Partner 3	Areas nes, Zones nsa [1]	...	0.1	8.7	China, Chine	...	5.4	9.0	Partenaire 3
Montserrat									**Montserrat**
Partner 1	United States, États-Unis	23.6	28.5	29.0	United States, États-Unis	56.6	68.5	72.8	Partenaire 1
Partner 2	France	1.2	25.9	23.0	Trinidad and Tobago, Trinité-et-Tobago	14.6	6.1	6.0	Partenaire 2
Partner 3	Saint Kitts and Nevis, Saint-Kitts-et-Nevis	3.0	3.9	22.2	United Kingdom, Royaume-Uni	7.8	5.6	4.1	Partenaire 3
Morocco									**Maroc**
Partner 1	Spain, Espagne	20.0	17.0	23.8	Spain, Espagne	11.6	10.6	15.7	Partenaire 1
Partner 2	France	30.1	22.5	21.1	France	18.2	15.6	13.2	Partenaire 2
Partner 3	Italy, Italie	5.0	4.5	4.6	China, Chine	5.1	8.4	9.1	Partenaire 3
Mozambique									**Mozambique**
Partner 1	South Africa, Afrique du Sud	16.5	20.8	21.0	South Africa, Afrique du Sud	40.6	34.4	30.0	Partenaire 1
Partner 2	Netherlands, Pays-Bas	59.7	52.7	20.9	Singapore, Singapour	1.0	0.2	8.1	Partenaire 2
Partner 3	India, Inde	1.8	1.4	20.2	China, Chine	2.9	3.6	7.9	Partenaire 3
Myanmar									**Myanmar**
Partner 1	China, Chine	7.2	6.2	40.8	China, Chine	29.0	27.1	34.4	Partenaire 1
Partner 2	Thailand, Thaïlande	47.1	41.7	19.2	Singapore, Singapour	18.5	27.0	14.5	Partenaire 2
Partner 3	India, Inde	12.9	12.6	8.9	Thailand, Thaïlande	21.9	11.4	12.7	Partenaire 3
Namibia									**Namibie**
Partner 1	Switzerland, Suisse	0.3	0.9	18.8	South Africa, Afrique du Sud	83.2	72.4	57.2	Partenaire 1
Partner 2	South Africa, Afrique du Sud	28.2	29.0	16.0	Botswana	0.2	0.3	6.8	Partenaire 2
Partner 3	Botswana	0.4	0.7	14.1	Zambia, Zambie	0.1	1.3	4.1	Partenaire 3
Nepal									**Népal**
Partner 1	India, Inde	52.4	65.3	63.5	India, Inde	53.0	63.6	60.6	Partenaire 1
Partner 2	United States, États-Unis	29.1	6.3	10.7	China, Chine	8.4	11.0	13.9	Partenaire 2
Partner 3	Germany, Allemagne	3.4	4.1	4.1	United Arab Emirates, Émirats arabes unis	0.7	3.8	4.0	Partenaire 3
Netherlands									**Pays-Bas**
Partner 1	Germany, Allemagne	23.8	24.3	23.9	Germany, Allemagne	19.0	17.8	18.0	Partenaire 1
Partner 2	Belgium, Belgique	11.7	11.1	10.4	Belgium, Belgique	10.8	9.6	10.1	Partenaire 2
Partner 3	United Kingdom, Royaume-Uni	9.2	8.0	8.9	China, Chine	7.6	9.3	9.0	Partenaire 3
New Caledonia									**Nouvelle-Calédonie**
Partner 1	China, Chine	5.6	3.5	35.7	France	32.3	22.3	25.7	Partenaire 1
Partner 2	Japan, Japon	18.3	18.8	15.9	China, Chine	4.7	17.6	10.2	Partenaire 2
Partner 3	Republic of Korea, République de Corée	13.1	11.6	15.1	Singapore, Singapour	15.0	12.9	8.2	Partenaire 3
New Zealand									**Nouvelle-Zélande**
Partner 1	China, Chine	5.1	11.1	19.4	China, Chine	10.8	16.0	19.9	Partenaire 1
Partner 2	Australia, Australie	21.0	23.0	17.0	Australia, Australie	20.6	18.2	12.5	Partenaire 2
Partner 3	United States, États-Unis	15.0	8.6	10.9	United States, États-Unis	11.0	10.4	11.4	Partenaire 3
Nicaragua									**Nicaragua**
Partner 1	United States, États-Unis	35.4	32.8	53.7	United States, États-Unis	20.7	20.7	18.0	Partenaire 1
Partner 2	Mexico, Mexique	5.1	2.8	11.1	China, Chine	5.9	8.7	14.4	Partenaire 2
Partner 3	Venezuela (Bol. Rep.), Venezuela (Rép. bol.)	0.4	13.5	6.2	Mexico, Mexique	8.5	7.7	10.4	Partenaire 3

21 Major trading partner *(continued)*

Three largest trade partners as a percentage of total international merchandise trade in US dollars, as at 2016

Partenaire commercial principal *(suite)*

Trois principaux partenaires commerciaux en pourcentage du total de commerce international de marchandises en dollars américains, en 2016

Country or area	Major trading partner	Percentage of exports 2005	2010	2016	Major trading partner	Percentage of imports 2005	2010	2016	Pays ou zone
Niger									**Niger**
Partner 1	France	22.2	9.0	31.3	France	15.8	11.0	28.3	Partenaire 1
Partner 2	Thailand, Thaïlande	~0.0	1.2	11.6	China, Chine	5.5	43.8	16.2	Partenaire 2
Partner 3	Malaysia, Malaisie	...	0.7	11.1	United States, États-Unis	5.4	6.1	7.8	Partenaire 3
Nigeria									**Nigéria**
Partner 1	India, Inde	9.3	10.5	14.6	China, Chine	13.8	16.6	21.9	Partenaire 1
Partner 2	Netherlands, Pays-Bas	2.6	4.5	10.2	United States, États-Unis	15.7	17.9	10.4	Partenaire 2
Partner 3	Spain, Espagne	8.0	3.3	9.3	Belgium, Belgique	5.1	3.9	7.2	Partenaire 3
Northern Mariana Islands									**Îles Mariannes du Nord**
Partner 1	Areas nes, Zones nsa [1]	91.1	91.1	91.1	Areas nes, Zones nsa [1]	56.5	66.2	66.1	Partenaire 1
Partner 2	Singapore, Singapour	0.1	0.7	3.2	China, Hong Kong SAR, Chine, Hong Kong RAS	12.3	11.4	8.5	Partenaire 2
Partner 3	Republic of Korea, République de Corée	0.5	0.6	1.8	Viet Nam	~0.0	...	8.3	Partenaire 3
Norway									**Norvège**
Partner 1	United Kingdom, Royaume-Uni	25.0	27.5	20.7	Germany, Allemagne	13.4	12.3	12.0	Partenaire 1
Partner 2	Germany, Allemagne	12.6	11.1	14.3	Sweden, Suède	14.4	14.0	12.0	Partenaire 2
Partner 3	Netherlands, Pays-Bas	9.9	11.9	10.6	China, Chine	5.6	8.5	11.1	Partenaire 3
Oman									**Oman**
Partner 1	China, Chine	27.5	25.6	43.6	United Arab Emirates, Émirats arabes unis	26.1	28.4	45.1	Partenaire 1
Partner 2	Areas nes, Zones nsa [1]	9.7	16.8	10.3	Areas nes, Zones nsa [1]	1.6	...	11.2	Partenaire 2
Partner 3	United Arab Emirates, Émirats arabes unis	7.3	11.6	7.5	China, Chine	2.4	4.8	4.8	Partenaire 3
Other non-specified areas									**Autres zones non-spécifiées**
Partner 1	China, Chine	21.6	28.0	26.3	China, Chine	11.0	14.3	19.1	Partenaire 1
Partner 2	China, Hong Kong SAR, Chine, Hong Kong RAS	16.2	13.8	13.7	Japan, Japon	25.3	20.7	17.6	Partenaire 2
Partner 3	United States, États-Unis	15.1	11.5	12.0	United States, États-Unis	11.6	10.2	12.5	Partenaire 3
Pakistan									**Pakistan**
Partner 1	United States, États-Unis	24.8	17.2	16.7	China, Chine	9.4	14.0	29.1	Partenaire 1
Partner 2	China, Chine	2.7	6.7	7.7	United Arab Emirates, Émirats arabes unis	9.9	14.0	13.2	Partenaire 2
Partner 3	United Kingdom, Royaume-Uni	5.7	5.2	7.6	Indonesia, Indonésie	2.7	1.8	4.4	Partenaire 3
Palau									**Palaos**
Partner 1	Areas nes, Zones nsa [1]	...	2.9	73.9	United States, États-Unis	31.5	34.9	42.0	Partenaire 1
Partner 2	United States, États-Unis	2.4	0.8	8.4	Japan, Japon	14.2	12.3	13.0	Partenaire 2
Partner 3	Japan, Japon	90.8	87.3	5.7	Singapore, Singapour	...	17.9	11.4	Partenaire 3
Panama									**Panama**
Partner 1	United States, États-Unis	44.8	19.8	19.9	United States, États-Unis	26.8	20.5	28.7	Partenaire 1
Partner 2	Germany, Allemagne	0.2	0.1	13.2	China, Chine	6.4	24.9	15.9	Partenaire 2
Partner 3	Costa Rica	4.0	5.1	7.9	Mexico, Mexique	4.2	4.3	5.3	Partenaire 3
Papua New Guinea									**Papouasie-Nvl-Guinée**
Partner 1	Australia, Australie	56.7	42.8	30.4	Australia, Australie	58.7	39.5	30.7	Partenaire 1
Partner 2	Japan, Japon	3.9	7.0	23.0	China, Chine	3.2	7.3	15.8	Partenaire 2
Partner 3	China, Chine	4.0	6.4	18.6	Singapore, Singapour	7.2	11.1	9.2	Partenaire 3
Paraguay									**Paraguay**
Partner 1	Brazil, Brésil	48.9	33.7	35.4	China, Chine	19.6	34.2	27.1	Partenaire 1
Partner 2	Argentina, Argentine	11.9	8.5	10.7	Brazil, Brésil	27.2	24.1	24.2	Partenaire 2
Partner 3	Russian Federation, Fédération de Russie	3.2	6.6	7.6	Argentina, Argentine	19.9	15.7	14.7	Partenaire 3
Peru									**Pérou**
Partner 1	China, Chine	10.9	15.2	23.5	China, Chine	8.5	17.2	22.8	Partenaire 1
Partner 2	United States, États-Unis	30.7	17.1	17.3	United States, États-Unis	17.8	19.4	19.6	Partenaire 2
Partner 3	Switzerland, Suisse	4.6	10.7	7.1	Brazil, Brésil	8.2	7.3	5.9	Partenaire 3
Philippines									**Philippines**
Partner 1	Japan, Japon	17.5	15.2	20.7	China, Chine	6.3	8.5	18.5	Partenaire 1
Partner 2	United States, États-Unis	18.0	14.7	15.4	Japan, Japon	17.1	12.5	11.9	Partenaire 2
Partner 3	China, Hong Kong SAR, Chine, Hong Kong RAS	8.1	8.4	11.7	United States, États-Unis	18.9	10.8	8.9	Partenaire 3
Poland									**Pologne**
Partner 1	Germany, Allemagne	28.2	26.1	27.0	Germany, Allemagne	24.7	21.7	22.9	Partenaire 1
Partner 2	United Kingdom, Royaume-Uni	5.6	6.3	6.6	China, Chine	5.4	9.5	12.4	Partenaire 2
Partner 3	Czechia, Tchéquie	4.6	5.9	6.5	Russian Federation, Fédération de Russie	8.8	10.5	6.1	Partenaire 3
Portugal									**Portugal**
Partner 1	Spain, Espagne	27.5	27.0	26.2	Spain, Espagne	30.7	32.0	32.8	Partenaire 1
Partner 2	France	13.4	12.0	12.6	Germany, Allemagne	14.3	13.9	13.5	Partenaire 2
Partner 3	Germany, Allemagne	12.3	13.0	11.7	France	8.7	7.2	7.8	Partenaire 3

21 Major trading partner *(continued)*

Three largest trade partners as a percentage of total international merchandise trade in US dollars, as at 2016

Partenaire commercial principal *(suite)*

Trois principaux partenaires commerciaux en pourcentage du total de commerce international de marchandises en dollars américains, en 2016

Country or area	Major trading partner	Percentage of exports 2005	2010	2016	Major trading partner	Percentage of imports 2005	2010	2016	Pays ou zone
Qatar									**Qatar**
Partner 1	Japan, Japon	40.0	28.7	20.8	China, Chine	5.2	9.1	11.5	Partenaire 1
Partner 2	Republic of Korea, République de Corée	15.8	16.0	17.3	United States, États-Unis	11.6	11.8	11.0	Partenaire 2
Partner 3	India, Inde	3.5	8.6	11.9	United Arab Emirates, Émirats arabes unis	6.4	6.9	8.8	Partenaire 3
Republic of Korea									**République de Corée**
Partner 1	China, Chine	21.8	25.1	25.1	China, Chine	14.8	16.8	21.4	Partenaire 1
Partner 2	United States, États-Unis	14.6	10.7	13.5	Japan, Japon	18.5	15.1	11.7	Partenaire 2
Partner 3	China, Hong Kong SAR, Chine, Hong Kong RAS	5.5	5.4	6.6	United States, États-Unis	11.8	9.5	10.7	Partenaire 3
Republic of Moldova									**République de Moldova**
Partner 1	Romania, Roumanie	10.2	16.0	25.1	Romania, Roumanie	11.2	10.0	13.7	Partenaire 1
Partner 2	Russian Federation, Fédération de Russie	31.8	26.2	11.4	Russian Federation, Fédération de Russie	11.7	15.2	13.3	Partenaire 2
Partner 3	Italy, Italie	12.2	9.6	9.7	China, Chine	3.2	8.3	9.8	Partenaire 3
Romania									**Roumanie**
Partner 1	Germany, Allemagne	14.0	18.1	21.5	Germany, Allemagne	14.0	16.7	20.5	Partenaire 1
Partner 2	Italy, Italie	19.4	13.8	11.6	Italy, Italie	15.5	11.6	10.3	Partenaire 2
Partner 3	France	7.4	8.3	7.2	Hungary, Hongrie	3.3	8.7	7.5	Partenaire 3
Russian Federation									**Fédération de Russie**
Partner 1	Netherlands, Pays-Bas	10.2	13.4	10.2	China, Chine	7.4	17.0	20.9	Partenaire 1
Partner 2	China, Chine	5.4	5.0	9.8	Germany, Allemagne	13.4	11.6	10.7	Partenaire 2
Partner 3	Germany, Allemagne	8.2	4.0	7.4	United States, États-Unis	4.6	4.3	6.1	Partenaire 3
Rwanda									**Rwanda**
Partner 1	Dem. Rep. of Congo, Rép. Dém. du Congo	2.6	7.5	31.8	China, Chine	3.7	15.0	21.2	Partenaire 1
Partner 2	Kenya	22.0	16.3	16.0	Uganda, Ouganda	13.2	12.7	11.2	Partenaire 2
Partner 3	United Arab Emirates, Émirats arabes unis	~0.0	0.2	14.0	Kenya	13.5	10.1	7.8	Partenaire 3
Saint Helena									**Sainte-Hélène**
Partner 1	United States, États-Unis	22.3	34.2	57.1	United Kingdom, Royaume-Uni	49.4	45.9	45.3	Partenaire 1
Partner 2	Japan, Japon	19.8	21.5	15.8	South Africa, Afrique du Sud	13.9	14.1	32.1	Partenaire 2
Partner 3	Australia, Australie	...	~0.0	7.0	Austria, Autriche	~0.0	0.1	6.4	Partenaire 3
Saint Kitts and Nevis									**Saint-Kitts-et-Nevis**
Partner 1	United States, États-Unis	91.9	74.2	75.6	United States, États-Unis	57.9	68.0	63.8	Partenaire 1
Partner 2	Trinidad and Tobago, Trinité-et-Tobago	2.0	1.9	3.9	Trinidad and Tobago, Trinité-et-Tobago	14.1	6.5	3.5	Partenaire 2
Partner 3	Saint Lucia, Sainte-Lucie	0.3	3.5	3.4	Japan, Japon	3.8	2.6	3.0	Partenaire 3
Saint Lucia									**Sainte-Lucie**
Partner 1	United States, États-Unis	14.0	57.8	47.5	United States, États-Unis	44.0	42.0	44.4	Partenaire 1
Partner 2	United Kingdom, Royaume-Uni	26.0	6.7	15.8	Trinidad and Tobago, Trinité-et-Tobago	14.2	21.0	19.7	Partenaire 2
Partner 3	Areas nes, Zones nsa [1]	2.1	...	8.5	United Kingdom, Royaume-Uni	6.5	4.9	4.5	Partenaire 3
Saint Pierre and Miquelon									**Saint-Pierre-et-Miquelon**
Partner 1	Canada	0.2	21.4	33.8	France	49.3	62.5	52.6	Partenaire 1
Partner 2	Portugal	0.2	12.0	19.9	Canada	31.7	33.1	42.1	Partenaire 2
Partner 3	Slovakia, Slovaquie	0.3	2.2	19.6	Belgium, Belgique	3.9	1.9	2.0	Partenaire 3
Saint Vincent & Grenadines									**Saint-Vincent-Grenadines**
Partner 1	Barbados, Barbade	12.7	11.3	17.8	United States, États-Unis	33.3	33.0	38.2	Partenaire 1
Partner 2	Saint Lucia, Sainte-Lucie	10.9	20.6	17.2	Trinidad and Tobago, Trinité-et-Tobago	23.6	27.1	17.6	Partenaire 2
Partner 3	Antigua and Barbuda, Antigua-et-Barbuda	6.2	7.4	14.5	United Kingdom, Royaume-Uni	9.4	5.7	7.2	Partenaire 3
Samoa									**Samoa**
Partner 1	Australia, Australie	74.8	65.3	35.9	New Zealand, Nouvelle-Zélande	33.4	30.7	23.9	Partenaire 1
Partner 2	American Samoa, Samoa américaines	13.4	4.5	25.8	Singapore, Singapour	4.4	5.9	14.6	Partenaire 2
Partner 3	New Zealand, Nouvelle-Zélande	2.0	9.3	12.0	China, Chine	3.1	6.1	14.1	Partenaire 3
Sao Tome and Principe									**Sao Tomé-et-Principe**
Partner 1	Poland, Pologne	...	0.6	31.9	Portugal	57.0	62.4	59.1	Partenaire 1
Partner 2	Belgium, Belgique	10.8	21.2	20.1	Angola	20.4	15.6	15.2	Partenaire 2
Partner 3	Spain, Espagne	...	~0.0	16.0	China, Chine	0.2	2.2	5.4	Partenaire 3
Saudi Arabia									**Arabie saoudite**
Partner 1	Asia nes, Asie nsa [2]	49.5	56.1	48.1	China, Chine	7.5	11.9	14.6	Partenaire 1
Partner 2	N & C Ame nes, Amér c-et-n nsa [4]	15.8	13.6	10.5	United States, États-Unis	15.1	13.4	13.4	Partenaire 2
Partner 3	Other Europe nes, Autres d'Europe nsa [5]	13.7	7.9	9.5	Germany, Allemagne	8.3	7.9	7.2	Partenaire 3
Senegal									**Sénégal**
Partner 1	Mali	19.2	26.1	17.5	France	20.9	19.7	15.9	Partenaire 1
Partner 2	Switzerland, Suisse	0.2	7.9	10.2	China, Chine	3.6	8.3	10.3	Partenaire 2
Partner 3	India, Inde	12.9	10.0	7.9	Nigeria, Nigéria	10.4	10.2	7.8	Partenaire 3

21 Major trading partner *(continued)*

Three largest trade partners as a percentage of total international merchandise trade in US dollars, as at 2016

Partenaire commercial principal *(suite)*

Trois principaux partenaires commerciaux en pourcentage du total de commerce international de marchandises en dollars américains, en 2016

Country or area	Major trading partner	Percentage of exports 2005	2010	2016	Major trading partner	Percentage of imports 2005	2010	2016	Pays ou zone
Serbia									**Serbie**
Partner 1	Italy, Italie	...	11.4	14.6	Germany, Allemagne	...	10.6	12.9	Partenaire 1
Partner 2	Germany, Allemagne	...	10.3	13.1	Italy, Italie	...	8.6	10.3	Partenaire 2
Partner 3	Bosnia-Herzegovina, Bosnie-Herzégovine	...	11.1	8.3	China, Chine	...	7.2	8.3	Partenaire 3
Seychelles									**Seychelles**
Partner 1	United Arab Emirates, Émirats arabes unis	0.1	37.9	30.3	United Arab Emirates, Émirats arabes unis	3.8	48.0	26.1	Partenaire 1
Partner 2	France	14.7	19.2	19.7	Spain, Espagne	7.8	6.6	8.2	Partenaire 2
Partner 3	United Kingdom, Royaume-Uni	28.5	18.6	17.8	France	6.6	5.0	7.9	Partenaire 3
Sierra Leone									**Sierra Leone**
Partner 1	Côte d'Ivoire	~0.0	0.2	34.7	China, Chine	5.5	12.2	12.6	Partenaire 1
Partner 2	United States, États-Unis	3.6	8.1	31.0	United States, États-Unis	3.5	7.5	9.8	Partenaire 2
Partner 3	Belgium, Belgique	87.5	26.6	19.3	India, Inde	2.8	5.4	7.8	Partenaire 3
Singapore									**Singapour**
Partner 1	China, Chine	8.6	10.3	13.0	China, Chine	10.3	10.8	14.3	Partenaire 1
Partner 2	China, Hong Kong SAR, Chine, Hong Kong RAS	9.4	11.7	12.6	Malaysia, Malaisie	13.7	11.7	11.4	Partenaire 2
Partner 3	Malaysia, Malaisie	13.2	11.9	10.6	United States, États-Unis	11.7	11.5	10.9	Partenaire 3
Slovakia									**Slovaquie**
Partner 1	Germany, Allemagne	25.6	19.2	21.9	Germany, Allemagne	20.6	16.1	17.0	Partenaire 1
Partner 2	Czechia, Tchéquie	14.3	13.7	11.8	Czechia, Tchéquie	12.8	10.3	10.7	Partenaire 2
Partner 3	Poland, Pologne	6.2	7.3	7.6	Other Europe nes, Autres d'Europe nsa [5]	8.4	12.1	9.1	Partenaire 3
Slovenia									**Slovénie**
Partner 1	Germany, Allemagne	19.9	19.6	20.9	Germany, Allemagne	17.2	16.2	17.4	Partenaire 1
Partner 2	Italy, Italie	12.7	12.1	11.2	Italy, Italie	17.4	15.6	14.7	Partenaire 2
Partner 3	Austria, Autriche	8.1	8.1	8.3	Austria, Autriche	7.9	7.9	8.6	Partenaire 3
Solomon Islands									**Îles Salomon**
Partner 1	China, Chine	45.8	49.1	62.5	Australia, Australie	42.0	32.4	20.4	Partenaire 1
Partner 2	Italy, Italie	...	3.1	7.0	Singapore, Singapour	6.3	24.1	15.5	Partenaire 2
Partner 3	United Kingdom, Royaume-Uni	~0.0	7.4	4.4	China, Chine	3.8	12.9	14.8	Partenaire 3
Somalia									**Somalie**
Partner 1	Saudi Arabia, Arabie saoudite	3.4	35.8	41.1	India, Inde	6.5	5.8	23.9	Partenaire 1
Partner 2	Oman	3.4	19.0	23.5	China, Chine	3.0	5.9	19.0	Partenaire 2
Partner 3	United Arab Emirates, Émirats arabes unis	38.0	21.4	13.4	United Arab Emirates, Émirats arabes unis	39.1	23.6	15.3	Partenaire 3
South Africa									**Afrique du Sud**
Partner 1	China, Chine	2.9	9.9	9.9	China, Chine	9.0	13.8	18.1	Partenaire 1
Partner 2	United States, États-Unis	10.4	8.7	7.5	Germany, Allemagne	14.0	10.9	11.8	Partenaire 2
Partner 3	Germany, Allemagne	7.1	6.7	7.1	United States, États-Unis	7.9	7.2	6.7	Partenaire 3
South Sudan									**Soudan du sud**
Partner 1	China, Chine	...	...	98.8	Uganda, Ouganda	...	...	60.6	Partenaire 1
Partner 2	Pakistan	...	...	0.5	China, Chine	...	...	8.6	Partenaire 2
Partner 3	Algeria, Algérie	...	...	0.5	Pakistan	...	...	7.2	Partenaire 3
Spain									**Espagne**
Partner 1	France	19.2	18.2	15.1	Germany, Allemagne	14.7	11.7	13.5	Partenaire 1
Partner 2	Germany, Allemagne	11.4	11.5	12.6	France	14.1	10.7	11.1	Partenaire 2
Partner 3	Italy, Italie	8.4	8.9	8.1	China, Chine	5.0	7.9	8.7	Partenaire 3
Sri Lanka									**Sri Lanka**
Partner 1	United States, États-Unis	32.8	21.3	26.6	China, Chine	7.6	10.0	21.9	Partenaire 1
Partner 2	United Kingdom, Royaume-Uni	12.6	12.3	9.9	India, Inde	17.3	20.6	19.6	Partenaire 2
Partner 3	India, Inde	9.1	5.6	7.6	United Arab Emirates, Émirats arabes unis	2.7	2.7	5.5	Partenaire 3
State of Palestine									**État de Palestine**
Partner 1	Areas nes, Zones nsa [1]	0.3	...	86.1	Areas nes, Zones nsa [1]	~0.0	0.1	93.5	Partenaire 1
Partner 2	Israel, Israël	86.6	84.9	11.7	Israel, Israël	70.2	72.6	3.8	Partenaire 2
Partner 3	Jordan, Jordanie	5.2	5.4	0.9	Turkey, Turquie	4.5	4.5	0.5	Partenaire 3
Sudan									**Soudan**
Partner 1	China, Chine	...	...	56.4	China, Chine	...	...	22.8	Partenaire 1
Partner 2	United Arab Emirates, Émirats arabes unis	...	...	14.4	Jordan, Jordanie	...	...	8.6	Partenaire 2
Partner 3	Saudi Arabia, Arabie saoudite	...	...	14.4	India, Inde	...	...	8.5	Partenaire 3
Suriname									**Suriname**
Partner 1	United States, États-Unis	0.9	7.6	24.3	United States, États-Unis	18.9	24.6	27.5	Partenaire 1
Partner 2	United Arab Emirates, Émirats arabes unis	5.4	13.7	22.0	Netherlands, Pays-Bas	17.7	17.5	14.4	Partenaire 2
Partner 3	Switzerland, Suisse	0.3	8.8	13.6	Trinidad and Tobago, Trinité-et-Tobago	19.1	23.7	10.6	Partenaire 3

21 Major trading partner *(continued)*

Three largest trade partners as a percentage of total international merchandise trade in US dollars, as at 2016

Partenaire commercial principal *(suite)*

Trois principaux partenaires commerciaux en pourcentage du total de commerce international de marchandises en dollars américains, en 2016

Country or area	Major trading partner	Percentage of exports 2005	2010	2016	Major trading partner	Percentage of imports 2005	2010	2016	Pays ou zone
Swaziland									**Swaziland**
Partner 1	South Africa, Afrique du Sud	37.5	51.1	59.7	South Africa, Afrique du Sud	80.9	81.2	72.3	Partenaire 1
Partner 2	Nigeria, Nigéria	...	2.4	6.7	Nigeria, Nigéria	~0.0	0.1	10.3	Partenaire 2
Partner 3	Mozambique	7.6	0.9	2.7	China, Chine	4.0	1.4	2.7	Partenaire 3
Sweden									**Suède**
Partner 1	Germany, Allemagne	10.4	11.4	12.0	Germany, Allemagne	18.1	18.0	18.8	Partenaire 1
Partner 2	Norway, Norvège	8.7	10.0	10.2	Netherlands, Pays-Bas	6.7	6.2	8.3	Partenaire 2
Partner 3	United States, États-Unis	10.6	7.3	7.4	Norway, Norvège	8.2	8.7	8.2	Partenaire 3
Switzerland									**Suisse**
Partner 1	Germany, Allemagne	19.4	19.3	14.3	Germany, Allemagne	31.6	31.9	19.3	Partenaire 1
Partner 2	United States, États-Unis	10.9	10.1	12.1	United States, États-Unis	5.6	5.4	8.9	Partenaire 2
Partner 3	United Kingdom, Royaume-Uni	5.4	5.9	10.7	Italy, Italie	10.5	10.2	7.3	Partenaire 3
Syrian Arab Republic									**République arabe syrienne**
Partner 1	Lebanon, Liban	2.9	3.8	15.9	Turkey, Turquie	4.3	9.5	28.3	Partenaire 1
Partner 2	Egypt, Égypte	2.3	3.4	15.5	China, Chine	8.1	8.8	20.1	Partenaire 2
Partner 3	Jordan, Jordanie	2.4	3.6	11.4	Lebanon, Liban	2.3	1.0	5.3	Partenaire 3
Tajikistan									**Tadjikistan**
Partner 1	Kazakhstan	2.1	1.4	27.3	China, Chine	13.7	43.4	52.0	Partenaire 1
Partner 2	Turkey, Turquie	6.0	23.1	20.3	Russian Federation, Fédération de Russie	22.8	21.2	20.1	Partenaire 2
Partner 3	Italy, Italie	5.0	2.6	10.0	Kazakhstan	14.3	8.2	11.3	Partenaire 3
Thailand									**Thaïlande**
Partner 1	United States, États-Unis	15.5	10.4	11.2	China, Chine	9.4	13.3	20.3	Partenaire 1
Partner 2	China, Chine	8.3	11.0	11.1	Japan, Japon	22.0	20.8	15.4	Partenaire 2
Partner 3	Japan, Japon	13.6	10.5	9.4	United States, États-Unis	7.4	5.9	6.9	Partenaire 3
TFYR of Macedonia									**ex-R.Y. de Macédoine**
Partner 1	Germany, Allemagne	17.8	21.3	47.0	Germany, Allemagne	10.4	11.2	12.3	Partenaire 1
Partner 2	Serbia, Serbie	...	21.2	8.9	United Kingdom, Royaume-Uni	1.4	5.2	10.8	Partenaire 2
Partner 3	Bulgaria, Bulgarie	3.7	8.8	5.2	Serbia, Serbie	...	8.1	8.0	Partenaire 3
Timor-Leste									**Timor-Leste**
Partner 1	Thailand, Thaïlande	0.2	~0.0	40.2	Indonesia, Indonésie	47.0	28.9	41.0	Partenaire 1
Partner 2	United States, États-Unis	23.9	20.1	12.0	China, Chine	1.7	17.7	30.3	Partenaire 2
Partner 3	Singapore, Singapour	0.4	5.2	10.6	Singapore, Singapour	14.6	8.3	7.7	Partenaire 3
Togo									**Togo**
Partner 1	Benin, Bénin	11.6	5.3	17.6	China, Chine	13.2	15.1	28.7	Partenaire 1
Partner 2	Burkina Faso	18.8	10.5	16.0	France	17.6	13.6	8.9	Partenaire 2
Partner 3	India, Inde	5.9	9.2	7.7	Netherlands, Pays-Bas	3.9	3.6	4.3	Partenaire 3
Tokelau									**Tokélaou**
Partner 1	Bangladesh	32.4	25.3	21.4	United States, États-Unis	51.5	9.7	30.6	Partenaire 1
Partner 2	Myanmar	...	7.3	16.5	Samoa	0.8	0.1	21.0	Partenaire 2
Partner 3	France	5.4	5.8	13.1	Netherlands, Pays-Bas	0.3	3.7	14.8	Partenaire 3
Tonga									**Tonga**
Partner 1	New Zealand, Nouvelle-Zélande	13.4	16.5	23.2	New Zealand, Nouvelle-Zélande	38.3	31.9	28.6	Partenaire 1
Partner 2	China, Hong Kong SAR, Chine, Hong Kong RAS	0.8	44.1	17.7	Singapore, Singapour	2.4	20.4	21.1	Partenaire 2
Partner 3	Areas nes, Zones nsa [1]	...	0.2	15.5	United States, États-Unis	9.0	13.0	10.9	Partenaire 3
Trinidad and Tobago									**Trinité-et-Tobago**
Partner 1	United States, États-Unis	58.6	48.1	41.7	United States, États-Unis	29.2	28.0	32.0	Partenaire 1
Partner 2	Argentina, Argentine	0.2	0.8	6.8	Gabon	2.1	12.9	12.5	Partenaire 2
Partner 3	Colombia, Colombie	1.6	2.6	4.1	China, Chine	3.0	5.8	7.1	Partenaire 3
Tunisia									**Tunisie**
Partner 1	France	32.9	28.7	29.3	France	23.5	18.9	17.8	Partenaire 1
Partner 2	Italy, Italie	24.1	19.9	18.5	Italy, Italie	20.9	17.6	14.9	Partenaire 2
Partner 3	Germany, Allemagne	8.5	8.5	10.5	China, Chine	2.9	6.1	8.4	Partenaire 3
Turkey									**Turquie**
Partner 1	Germany, Allemagne	12.9	10.1	9.8	China, Chine	5.9	9.3	12.8	Partenaire 1
Partner 2	United Kingdom, Royaume-Uni	8.1	6.4	8.2	Germany, Allemagne	11.7	9.5	10.8	Partenaire 2
Partner 3	Iraq	3.7	5.3	5.4	Russian Federation, Fédération de Russie	11.1	11.6	7.6	Partenaire 3
Turkmenistan									**Turkménistan**
Partner 1	China, Chine	0.4	39.0	70.9	Turkey, Turquie	8.6	23.5	24.9	Partenaire 1
Partner 2	Turkey, Turquie	3.3	14.4	5.4	Russian Federation, Fédération de Russie	10.6	14.8	11.4	Partenaire 2
Partner 3	Italy, Italie	4.7	7.2	5.4	Japan, Japon	0.7	0.5	7.9	Partenaire 3

21 Major trading partner *(continued)*

Three largest trade partners as a percentage of total international merchandise trade in US dollars, as at 2016

Partenaire commercial principal *(suite)*

Trois principaux partenaires commerciaux en pourcentage du total de commerce international de marchandises en dollars américains, en 2016

Country or area	Major trading partner	Percentage of exports 2005	2010	2016	Major trading partner	Percentage of imports 2005	2010	2016	Pays ou zone
Turks and Caicos Islands									**Îles Turques-et-Caïques**
Partner 1	Bahamas	...	~0.0	30.7	United States, États-Unis	98.3	98.3	89.3	Partenaire 1
Partner 2	United States, États-Unis	99.7	99.1	29.6	Japan, Japon	~0.0	~0.0	2.0	Partenaire 2
Partner 3	Zimbabwe	...	...	22.4	United Kingdom, Royaume-Uni	...	...	1.1	Partenaire 3
Tuvalu									**Tuvalu**
Partner 1	Thailand, Thaïlande	...	75.2	86.2	Singapore, Singapour	17.5	0.4	30.1	Partenaire 1
Partner 2	Japan, Japon	...	7.8	5.5	Japan, Japon	3.7	16.3	26.7	Partenaire 2
Partner 3	China, Hong Kong SAR, Chine, Hong Kong RAS	...	...	1.8	Fiji, Fidji	19.7	23.9	16.6	Partenaire 3
Uganda									**Ouganda**
Partner 1	Kenya	8.9	11.8	18.8	India, Inde	6.4	14.7	20.9	Partenaire 1
Partner 2	South Sudan, Soudan du Sud	...	...	11.7	China, Chine	5.3	8.9	15.8	Partenaire 2
Partner 3	Rwanda	4.4	9.2	10.5	Kenya	25.3	11.0	10.0	Partenaire 3
Ukraine									**Ukraine**
Partner 1	Russian Federation, Fédération de Russie	21.9	26.1	12.7	Russian Federation, Fédération de Russie	35.6	36.5	20.0	Partenaire 1
Partner 2	Turkey, Turquie	5.9	5.9	7.3	Germany, Allemagne	9.4	7.6	10.6	Partenaire 2
Partner 3	China, Chine	2.1	2.6	6.3	China, Chine	5.0	7.7	10.1	Partenaire 3
United Arab Emirates									**Émirats arabes unis**
Partner 1	Areas nes, Zones nsa [1]	29.2	26.4	53.3	Areas nes, Zones nsa [1]	0.7	30.2	35.8	Partenaire 1
Partner 2	Asia nes, Asie nsa [2]	10.6	34.3	14.0	China, Chine	8.5	7.3	8.0	Partenaire 2
Partner 3	Iran (Islamic Rep.), Iran (Rép. islamique)	5.0	4.7	3.2	United States, États-Unis	7.0	6.0	6.7	Partenaire 3
United Kingdom									**Royaume-Uni**
Partner 1	United States, États-Unis	14.4	13.9	15.0	Germany, Allemagne	13.0	12.2	14.0	Partenaire 1
Partner 2	Germany, Allemagne	10.6	10.6	10.6	United States, États-Unis	8.4	9.0	9.7	Partenaire 2
Partner 3	France	9.3	7.5	6.4	China, Chine	6.8	9.8	9.3	Partenaire 3
United Rep. of Tanzania									**Rép.-Unie de Tanzanie**
Partner 1	Switzerland, Suisse	8.7	17.5	16.2	China, Chine	6.9	10.9	20.8	Partenaire 1
Partner 2	India, Inde	4.7	5.6	14.8	India, Inde	5.9	11.2	18.1	Partenaire 2
Partner 3	South Africa, Afrique du Sud	17.6	10.7	13.3	United Arab Emirates, Émirats arabes unis	6.3	8.4	7.5	Partenaire 3
United States of America									**États-Unis d'Amérique**
Partner 1	Canada	23.4	19.5	18.3	China, Chine	15.0	19.5	21.4	Partenaire 1
Partner 2	Mexico, Mexique	13.3	12.8	15.9	Mexico, Mexique	10.0	11.8	13.2	Partenaire 2
Partner 3	China, Chine	4.6	7.2	8.0	Canada	16.8	14.2	12.6	Partenaire 3
Uruguay									**Uruguay**
Partner 1	China, Chine	4.5	10.4	17.8	China, Chine	6.2	13.0	18.8	Partenaire 1
Partner 2	Brazil, Brésil	13.4	23.4	17.5	Brazil, Brésil	21.3	18.3	18.0	Partenaire 2
Partner 3	Free zones, Zones franches	0.9	4.1	9.6	Argentina, Argentine	20.3	17.0	13.3	Partenaire 3
Uzbekistan									**Ouzbékistan**
Partner 1	Switzerland, Suisse	0.1	0.5	38.1	China, Chine	7.0	14.2	21.0	Partenaire 1
Partner 2	China, Chine	11.5	19.3	21.4	Russian Federation, Fédération de Russie	26.0	20.0	20.3	Partenaire 2
Partner 3	Russian Federation, Fédération de Russie	22.0	22.5	10.1	Republic of Korea, République de Corée	15.0	17.3	9.6	Partenaire 3
Vanuatu									**Vanuatu**
Partner 1	Mauritania, Mauritanie	...	...	37.9	China, Chine	5.2	9.9	18.4	Partenaire 1
Partner 2	Japan, Japon	4.1	4.5	25.1	Australia, Australie	41.3	30.9	16.8	Partenaire 2
Partner 3	Republic of Korea, République de Corée	~0.0	0.3	5.7	Japan, Japon	2.2	3.7	9.9	Partenaire 3
Venezuela (Boliv. Rep. of)									**Venezuela (Rép. boliv. du)**
Partner 1	United States, États-Unis	45.2	7.6	38.3	United States, États-Unis	31.6	30.5	33.8	Partenaire 1
Partner 2	China, Chine	0.4	5.8	18.4	China, Chine	3.7	11.1	16.3	Partenaire 2
Partner 3	India, Inde	~0.0	~0.0	17.0	Brazil, Brésil	9.1	9.8	8.2	Partenaire 3
Viet Nam									**Viet Nam**
Partner 1	United States, États-Unis	18.3	19.7	20.7	China, Chine	16.0	23.8	30.0	Partenaire 1
Partner 2	China, Chine	10.0	10.7	10.6	Republic of Korea, République de Corée	9.8	11.5	16.6	Partenaire 2
Partner 3	Japan, Japon	13.4	10.7	8.7	Japan, Japon	11.1	10.6	8.6	Partenaire 3
Wallis and Futuna Islands									**Îles Wallis-et-Futuna**
Partner 1	United States, États-Unis	2.3	0.8	53.8	France	32.0	23.1	26.2	Partenaire 1
Partner 2	Cambodia, Cambodge	...	...	12.1	Fiji, Fidji	5.8	13.4	20.5	Partenaire 2
Partner 3	France	6.8	1.6	7.6	New Caledonia, Nouvelle-Calédonie	5.6	17.1	20.4	Partenaire 3
Yemen									**Yémen**
Partner 1	Saudi Arabia, Arabie saoudite	1.8	3.2	32.2	United Arab Emirates, Émirats arabes unis	8.2	11.7	11.5	Partenaire 1
Partner 2	Oman	0.1	0.2	17.0	China, Chine	6.4	7.9	10.8	Partenaire 2
Partner 3	Areas nes, Zones nsa [1]	0.5	0.9	10.5	Saudi Arabia, Arabie saoudite	6.4	6.1	8.6	Partenaire 3

21 Major trading partner *(continued)*

Three largest trade partners as a percentage of total international merchandise trade in US dollars, as at 2016

Partenaire commercial principal *(suite)*

Trois principaux partenaires commerciaux en pourcentage du total de commerce international de marchandises en dollars américains, en 2016

Country or area	Major trading partner	Percentage of exports 2005	2010	2016	Major trading partner	Percentage of imports 2005	2010	2016	Pays ou zone
Zambia									**Zambie**
Partner 1	Switzerland, Suisse	28.7	51.0	44.3	South Africa, Afrique du Sud	47.6	34.4	30.9	Partenaire 1
Partner 2	China, Chine	2.1	20.2	14.5	Dem. Rep. of Congo, Rép. Dém. du Congo	0.9	23.8	11.2	Partenaire 2
Partner 3	Singapore, Singapour	0.1	~0.0	7.8	China, Chine	3.3	5.4	8.2	Partenaire 3
Zimbabwe									**Zimbabwe**
Partner 1	South Africa, Afrique du Sud	41.5	54.2	79.4	South Africa, Afrique du Sud	15.0	48.0	41.3	Partenaire 1
Partner 2	Mozambique	2.8	2.9	9.5	Singapore, Singapour	0.2	0.3	21.5	Partenaire 2
Partner 3	United Arab Emirates, Émirats arabes unis	0.7	10.3	4.1	China, Chine	2.4	5.5	7.0	Partenaire 3

Source:

United Nations Statistics Division, New York, UN Comtrade database, last accessed June 2017.

1 Areas not elsewhere specified.
2 Asia not elsewhere specified.
3 Bunkers, ship stores.
4 North and Central America not elsewhere specified.
5 Other Europe, not elsewhere specified.

Source:

Organisation des Nations Unies, Division de statistique, New York, Comtrade base de données de l'ONU, dernier accès juin 2017.

1 Zones non spécifiées ailleurs.
2 Asie non spécifiées ailleurs.
3 Combustible de soute et provisions de bord.
4 Amérique centrale et du nord non spécifiées ailleurs.
5 Autres zones d'Europe, non spécifiées ailleurs

Part Three

Energy, environment and infrastructure

Chapter XII	Energy (table 22)
Chapter XIII	Environment (tables 23 - 26)
Chapter XIV	Science and technology (table 27 - 29)
Chapter XV	International tourism and transport (table 30 and 31)
Chapter XVI	Development assistance (tables 32 and 33)

Troisième partie

Energie, environnement et infrastructures

Chapitre XII	Énergie (tableau 22)
Chapitre XIII	Environnement (tableaux 23 - 26)
Chapitre XIV	Science et technologie (tableau 27 - 29)
Chapitre XV	Tourisme international et transport (tableau 30 et 31)
Chapitre XVI	Aide au développement (tableaux 32 et 33)

22 Production, trade and supply of energy
Petajoules and gigajoules per capita

Production, commerce et fourniture d'énergie
pétajoules et gigajoules par habitant

Region, country or area	1990	1995	2000	2005	2010	2012	2013	2014	Région, pays ou zone
Total, all countries or areas									**Total, tous pays ou zones**
Primary Energy production	**357 498**	**377 087**	**408 413**	**476 824**	**530 011**	**554 058**	**560 493**	**567 417**	**Prod. d'énergie primaire**
Net imports	**-7 192**	**-8 877**	**-10 731**	**-14 076**	**-13 179**	**-14 856**	**-18 269**	**-16 753**	**Importations nettes**
Changes in stocks	**3 992**	**164**	**-2 731**	**-302**	**-2**	**795**	**454**	**3 131**	**Variations des stocks**
Total supply	**346 313**	**368 047**	**400 413**	**463 050**	**516 833**	**538 409**	**541 770**	**547 533**	**Approv. total**
Supply per capita	**62**	**64**	**65**	**71**	**75**	**76**	**75**	**75**	**Approv. par habitant**
Africa									**Afrique**
Primary Energy production	27 741	32 055	37 223	44 944	47 607	47 122	45 731	45 612	Prod. d'énergie primaire
Net imports	-12 195	-13 008	-16 305	-20 492	-19 452	-17 242	-15 279	-14 193	Importations nettes
Changes in stocks	-10	289	31	10	-62	-19	-49	208	Variations des stocks
Total supply	15 556	18 758	20 886	24 442	28 218	29 898	30 501	31 211	Approv. total
Supply per capita	24	26	26	27	27	27	27	27	Approv. par habitant
North America									**Amérique du Nord**
Primary Energy production	89 522	93 198	96 299	98 288	100 331	105 022	108 320	114 496	Prod. d'énergie primaire
Net imports	7 813	9 160	15 607	19 994	13 037	6 630	3 554	1 635	Importations nettes
Changes in stocks	1 782	-922	-2 220	-144	-602	-175	-1 542	887	Variations des stocks
Total supply	95 554	103 281	114 127	118 427	113 970	111 827	113 417	115 244	Approv. total
Supply per capita	223	226	234	230	208	200	201	203	Approv. par habitant
South America									**Amérique du Sud**
Primary Energy production	16 239	20 310	24 108	26 630	29 391	30 633	30 904	31 217	Prod. d'énergie primaire
Net imports	-3 752	-5 789	-7 316	-8 057	-7 260	-7 362	-7 151	-6 665	Importations nettes
Changes in stocks	86	-6	-13	-323	-60	-143	15	149	Variations des stocks
Total supply	12 401	14 527	16 804	18 897	22 192	23 415	23 739	24 404	Approv. total
Supply per capita	42	45	48	51	56	58	58	59	Approv. par habitant
Asia									**Asie**
Primary Energy production	103 898	129 676	145 570	192 217	235 722	254 438	257 360	259 583	Prod. d'énergie primaire
Net imports	-11 657	-8 984	-9 629	-9 786	98	3 445	3 621	7 530	Importations nettes
Changes in stocks	1 551	598	-539	-391	1 615	1 127	1 817	1 391	Variations des stocks
Total supply	90 689	120 093	136 481	182 822	234 205	256 756	259 164	265 722	Approv. total
Supply per capita	29	35	37	46	56	60	60	61	Approv. par habitant
Europe									**Europe**
Primary Energy production	112 784	93 236	94 616	102 532	102 460	102 440	102 878	100 312	Prod. d'énergie primaire
Net imports	15 352	13 532	12 273	10 783	8 103	7 417	5 649	4 628	Importations nettes
Changes in stocks	381	102	243	583	-1 175	-115	57	452	Variations des stocks
Total supply	127 755	106 665	106 646	112 731	111 737	109 972	108 471	104 490	Approv. total
Supply per capita	118	147	147	154	152	149	147	142	Approv. par habitant
Oceania									**Océanie**
Primary Energy production	7 314	8 611	10 598	12 213	14 500	14 403	15 299	16 196	Prod. d'énergie primaire
Net imports	-2 752	-3 785	-5 363	-6 518	-7 706	-7 742	-8 665	-9 690	Importations nettes
Changes in stocks	203	103	-233	-37	282	120	155	43	Variations des stocks
Total supply	4 358	4 723	5 468	5 732	6 512	6 540	6 479	6 462	Approv. total
Supply per capita	160	163	176	171	179	174	170	167	Approv. par habitant
Afghanistan									**Afghanistan**
Primary Energy production	19	16	18	23	41	56	59	63	Prod. d'énergie primaire
Net imports	* 28	* 13	* 8	* 14	96	113	* 100	* 91	Importations nettes
Changes in stocks	* 0	* 0	* 0	...	...	...	...	...	Variations des stocks
Total supply	* 46	* 29	25	36	137	169	158	* 154	Approv. total
Supply per capita	* 4	* 1	1	1	5	6	5	* 5	Approv. par habitant
Albania									**Albanie**
Primary Energy production	99	43	34	48	69	70	85	84	Prod. d'énergie primaire
Net imports	* 15	4	31	43	* 22	* 18	* 27	33	Importations nettes
Changes in stocks	* 23	0	...	0	0	0	10	13	Variations des stocks
Total supply	92	47	65	91	91	88	102	103	Approv. total
Supply per capita	28	15	21	29	31	30	35	36	Approv. par habitant
Algeria									**Algérie**
Primary Energy production	4 380	4 748	6 556	7 534	6 200	5 928	5 676	5 900	Prod. d'énergie primaire
Net imports	* -3 263	* -3 485	* -5 414	-5 952	-4 551	-4 043	-3 714	-3 732	Importations nettes
Changes in stocks	* 41	-8	-27	0	9	-5	3	44	Variations des stocks
Total supply	1 075	1 270	1 170	1 583	1 641	1 890	1 959	2 123	Approv. total
Supply per capita	43	45	38	48	46	50	51	55	Approv. par habitant
Andorra									**Andorre**
Primary Energy production	* 0	* 0	* 0	0	1	0	1	1	Prod. d'énergie primaire
Net imports	* 6	* 7	* 9	* 10	* 9	* 9	8	8	Importations nettes
Total supply	* 7	7	9	10	10	9	9	9	Approv. total
Supply per capita	* 130	111	138	130	114	115	118	119	Approv. par habitant

Region, country or area	1990	1995	2000	2005	2010	2012	2013	2014	Région, pays ou zone
Angola									**Angola**
Primary Energy production	1 198	1 585	1 803	2 934	4 057	3 967	4 001	3 902	Prod. d'énergie primaire
Net imports	* -960	-1 224	-1 475	-2 565	-3 547	-3 385	-3 421	-3 280	Importations nettes
Changes in stocks	...	17	21	5	1	3	0	8	Variations des stocks
Total supply	238	343	308	363	509	580	581	613	Approv. total
Supply per capita	23	28	22	22	24	26	25	25	Approv. par habitant
Anguilla									**Anguilla**
Primary Energy production	* 0	* 0	* 0	* 0	* 0	* 0	* 0	* 0	Prod. d'énergie primaire
Net imports	* 1	* 1	* 1	* 2	* 2	* 2	* 2	* 2	Importations nettes
Total supply	* 1	* 1	* 1	* 2	* 2	* 2	* 2	* 2	Approv. total
Supply per capita	* 87	* 94	* 117	* 132	* 155	* 140	* 136	* 136	Approv. par habitant
Antigua and Barbuda									**Antigua-et-Barbuda**
Net imports	* 5	* 4	* 5	* 7	* 8	* 8	* 8	* 8	Importations nettes
Total supply	* 4	* 4	* 5	* 6	* 8	* 8	* 8	* 8	Approv. total
Supply per capita	* 68	* 60	* 65	* 75	* 86	* 85	* 84	* 84	Approv. par habitant
Argentina									**Argentine**
Primary Energy production	2 064	2 722	3 404	3 609	3 343	3 160	2 981	3 167	Prod. d'énergie primaire
Net imports	-144	-535	-866	-683	-21	205	403	465	Importations nettes
Changes in stocks	-8	-6	-17	8	16	-17	4	-6	Variations des stocks
Total supply	1 928	2 194	2 556	2 919	3 307	3 382	3 379	3 638	Approv. total
Supply per capita	59	63	69	75	80	80	79	85	Approv. par habitant
Armenia									**Arménie**
Primary Energy production	...	10	27	36	52	52	47	48	Prod. d'énergie primaire
Net imports	...	59	57	69	* 70	* 92	* 90	* 91	Importations nettes
Changes in stocks	...	...	...	...	* 3	0	0	...	Variations des stocks
Total supply	...	68	84	105	* 119	145	138	139	Approv. total
Supply per capita	...	21	27	34	* 40	49	46	46	Approv. par habitant
Aruba									**Aruba**
Primary Energy production	0	0	* 5	* 5	* 5	* 4	* 1	* 1	Prod. d'énergie primaire
Net imports	* 22	* 24	* 21	* 26	* 23	* 13	* 12	* 12	Importations nettes
Changes in stocks	0	...	...	...	...	...	...	...	Variations des stocks
Total supply	* 23	* 23	* 26	30	* 28	* 17	* 12	* 12	Approv. total
Supply per capita	* 363	* 285	* 284	299	* 273	* 168	* 119	* 120	Approv. par habitant
Australia [1]									**Australie** [1]
Primary Energy production	6 547	7 784	9 731	11 451	13 620	13 538	14 429	15 282	Prod. d'énergie primaire
Net imports	-2 694	-3 752	-5 412	-6 717	-7 924	-7 971	-8 952	-9 981	Importations nettes
Changes in stocks	203	104	-221	-28	264	143	145	49	Variations des stocks
Total supply	3 650	3 928	4 540	4 762	5 431	5 423	5 333	5 252	Approv. total
Supply per capita	213	217	237	233	245	237	229	222	Approv. par habitant
Austria									**Autriche**
Primary Energy production	340	367	410	418	503	530	507	505	Prod. d'énergie primaire
Net imports	712	737	777	1 003	886	876	855	880	Importations nettes
Changes in stocks	14	-14	-10	0	-37	24	-28	38	Variations des stocks
Total supply	1 038	1 119	1 197	1 421	1 426	1 382	1 391	1 346	Approv. total
Supply per capita	135	141	150	173	170	163	164	158	Approv. par habitant
Azerbaijan									**Azerbaïdjan**
Primary Energy production	...	628	803	1 155	2 759	2 458	2 486	2 459	Prod. d'énergie primaire
Net imports	...	-91	-319	-547	-2 239	-1 887	-1 907	-1 885	Importations nettes
Changes in stocks	...	0	-2	35	34	13	11	-9	Variations des stocks
Total supply	...	536	485	573	486	558	567	584	Approv. total
Supply per capita	...	69	60	67	53	60	60	61	Approv. par habitant
Bahamas									**Bahamas**
Primary Energy production	0	...	...	0	0	0	0	0	Prod. d'énergie primaire
Net imports	* 35	* 21	* 23	* 26	* 24	* 29	* 44	* 31	Importations nettes
Changes in stocks	* 8	* -1	* 0	...	...	...	* 4	* -4	Variations des stocks
Total supply	* 27	* 23	* 23	* 25	24	29	40	35	Approv. total
Supply per capita	* 106	* 83	* 78	* 79	67	77	107	90	Approv. par habitant
Bahrain									**Bahreïn**
Primary Energy production	294	341	706	672	849	828	911	961	Prod. d'énergie primaire
Net imports	* -87	* -94	-388	-377	-334	-332	-355	-403	Importations nettes
Changes in stocks	* -6	-10	-6	-28	-3	3	0	-5	Variations des stocks
Total supply	213	257	324	323	517	494	556	563	Approv. total
Supply per capita	433	459	508	446	410	370	412	413	Approv. par habitant

Production, trade and supply of energy *(continued)*
Petajoules and gigajoules per capita

Production, commerce et fourniture d'énergie *(suite)*
pétajoules et gigajoules par habitant

Region, country or area	1990	1995	2000	2005	2010	2012	2013	2014	Région, pays ou zone
Bangladesh									**Bangladesh**
Primary Energy production	682	792	857	1 027	1 300	1 347	1 410	1 438	Prod. d'énergie primaire
Net imports	* 97	* 125	139	165	163	212	212	236	Importations nettes
Changes in stocks	-6	-4	-6	3	-21	-34	0	-13	Variations des stocks
Total supply	785	921	1 001	1 189	1 485	1 594	1 623	1 687	Approv. total
Supply per capita	7	8	8	8	10	10	10	11	Approv. par habitant
Barbados									**Barbade**
Primary Energy production	5	5	6	5	4	3	3	2	Prod. d'énergie primaire
Net imports	9	8	10	* 12	* 16	* 17	* 17	* 15	Importations nettes
Changes in stocks	-1	0	-1	0	0	0	0	0	Variations des stocks
Total supply	16	13	16	18	20	20	19	17	Approv. total
Supply per capita	62	49	61	66	73	70	69	59	Approv. par habitant
Belarus									**Bélarus**
Primary Energy production	...	138	147	159	166	173	167	155	Prod. d'énergie primaire
Net imports	...	912	881	962	980	1 116	982	1 012	Importations nettes
Changes in stocks	...	6	-1	-4	-8	9	7	5	Variations des stocks
Total supply	...	1 043	1 029	1 125	1 155	1 280	1 142	1 162	Approv. total
Supply per capita	...	102	102	115	122	135	120	122	Approv. par habitant
Belgium									**Belgique**
Primary Energy production	544	495	570	577	644	587	621	520	Prod. d'énergie primaire
Net imports	1 457	1 771	1 835	1 877	1 887	1 637	1 732	1 705	Importations nettes
Changes in stocks	-4	29	-21	19	7	-24	21	23	Variations des stocks
Total supply	2 005	2 237	2 426	2 436	2 524	2 249	2 332	2 203	Approv. total
Supply per capita	202	222	238	234	231	203	209	196	Approv. par habitant
Belize									**Belize**
Primary Energy production	4	4	5	4	14	12	10	9	Prod. d'énergie primaire
Net imports	4	6	6	* 7	-2	1	3	3	Importations nettes
Changes in stocks	...	...	...	...	0	0	0	0	Variations des stocks
Total supply	8	10	11	11	13	13	13	13	Approv. total
Supply per capita	44	44	44	39	40	37	38	36	Approv. par habitant
Benin									**Bénin**
Primary Energy production	74	79	62	70	86	91	94	96	Prod. d'énergie primaire
Net imports	* 1	* 10	20	37	66	71	76	83	Importations nettes
Changes in stocks	0	0	0	2	0	0	0	0	Variations des stocks
Total supply	74	89	83	105	153	163	170	179	Approv. total
Supply per capita	16	16	13	14	16	16	16	17	Approv. par habitant
Bermuda									**Bermudes**
Primary Energy production	...	...	...	...	* 1	* 1	* 1	* 1	Prod. d'énergie primaire
Net imports	* 7	* 7	* 7	* 7	* 9	* 7	* 6	* 8	Importations nettes
Total supply	* 7	* 8	* 7	* 8	* 9	7	7	9	Approv. total
Supply per capita	* 118	* 123	* 115	* 124	* 138	115	108	136	Approv. par habitant
Bhutan									**Bhoutan**
Primary Energy production	41	43	46	53	73	72	75	75	Prod. d'énergie primaire
Net imports	-3	* -4	* -2	-5	-14	-11	* -12	* -11	Importations nettes
Total supply	37	39	44	48	59	61	63	63	Approv. total
Supply per capita	67	76	77	73	81	82	83	82	Approv. par habitant
Bolivia (Plurinational State of)									**Bolivie (État plurinational de)**
Primary Energy production	202	235	282	586	659	804	910	962	Prod. d'énergie primaire
Net imports	-97	-85	-78	-366	-397	-485	-592	-621	Importations nettes
Changes in stocks	0	1	-2	0	-1	1	-1	0	Variations des stocks
Total supply	105	149	206	220	263	319	319	341	Approv. total
Supply per capita	16	20	25	24	27	31	31	32	Approv. par habitant
Bonaire, Sint Eustatius and Saba									**Bonaire, Saint-Eustache et Saba**
Primary Energy production	...	...	...	...	...	...	...	0	Prod. d'énergie primaire
Net imports	...	...	...	...	...	* 6	* 5	* 5	Importations nettes
Total supply	...	...	...	...	...	* 5	* 5	* 5	Approv. total
Supply per capita	...	...	...	...	...	* 215	* 213	* 208	Approv. par habitant
Bosnia and Herzegovina									**Bosnie-Herzégovine**
Primary Energy production	...	28	126	152	182	188	192	252	Prod. d'énergie primaire
Net imports	...	29	52	54	84	93	79	72	Importations nettes
Changes in stocks	...	...	-1	-1	-3	3	5	-1	Variations des stocks
Total supply	...	56	179	206	269	278	266	325	Approv. total
Supply per capita	...	17	48	54	70	73	70	85	Approv. par habitant

Region, country or area	1990	1995	2000	2005	2010	2012	2013	2014	Région, pays ou zone
Botswana									**Botswana**
Primary Energy production	24	27	28	29	30	41	42	47	Prod. d'énergie primaire
Net imports	15	17	29	36	46	48	50	45	Importations nettes
Changes in stocks	0	...	...	0	0	18	10	-7	Variations des stocks
Total supply	39	44	57	65	76	73	83	98	Approv. total
Supply per capita	28	28	32	35	37	34	38	44	Approv. par habitant
Brazil									**Brésil**
Primary Energy production	4 490	5 038	6 308	8 344	10 050	10 305	10 360	10 948	Prod. d'énergie primaire
Net imports	1 555	1 918	1 713	900	859	1 235	1 760	1 642	Importations nettes
Changes in stocks	86	-106	1	-8	-8	-91	-30	41	Variations des stocks
Total supply	5 960	7 062	8 020	9 252	10 916	11 631	12 149	12 549	Approv. total
Supply per capita	40	44	46	50	55	57	59	61	Approv. par habitant
British Virgin Islands									**Îles Vierges britanniques**
Primary Energy production	0	0	0	0	0	0	0	0	Prod. d'énergie primaire
Net imports	* 1	* 1	* 1	* 2	* 2	* 2	* 2	* 3	Importations nettes
Total supply	* 1	* 1	* 1	* 2	* 2	* 2	* 2	* 3	Approv. total
Supply per capita	* 56	* 66	* 72	* 85	* 89	* 87	* 85	* 85	Approv. par habitant
Brunei Darussalam									**Brunéi Darussalam**
Primary Energy production	668	752	813	848	775	773	710	679	Prod. d'énergie primaire
Net imports	* -594	-683	-744	-772	-648	-612	-582	-528	Importations nettes
Changes in stocks	* -33	-1	-4	-1	-7	1	0	3	Variations des stocks
Total supply	107	71	73	76	136	160	127	149	Approv. total
Supply per capita	424	246	224	210	345	396	310	357	Approv. par habitant
Bulgaria									**Bulgarie**
Primary Energy production	407	428	410	444	442	491	444	474	Prod. d'énergie primaire
Net imports	730	546	358	384	291	275	265	258	Importations nettes
Changes in stocks	-44	7	-5	2	-9	-1	6	-14	Variations des stocks
Total supply	1 181	966	773	826	741	767	703	745	Approv. total
Supply per capita	134	116	97	107	100	105	97	103	Approv. par habitant
Burkina Faso									**Burkina Faso**
Primary Energy production	85	96	69	98	118	121	123	123	Prod. d'énergie primaire
Net imports	* 9	10	12	16	* 25	* 34	* 42	* 39	Importations nettes
Changes in stocks	* 0	1	-1	0	...	...	...	...	Variations des stocks
Total supply	93	104	83	114	143	156	164	162	Approv. total
Supply per capita	10	10	7	8	9	9	10	9	Approv. par habitant
Burundi									**Burundi**
Primary Energy production	54	62	51	79	86	54	56	56	Prod. d'énergie primaire
Net imports	* 4	* 4	* 5	3	4	4	4	6	Importations nettes
Changes in stocks	0	0	0	0	0	0	0	0	Variations des stocks
Total supply	58	66	55	81	89	58	60	62	Approv. total
Supply per capita	10	11	9	11	9	6	6	6	Approv. par habitant
Cabo Verde									**Cabo Verde**
Primary Energy production	1	1	1	2	1	2	2	2	Prod. d'énergie primaire
Net imports	* 1	* 2	* 4	* 6	7	7	7	7	Importations nettes
Changes in stocks	0	...	...	...	...	...	...	...	Variations des stocks
Total supply	* 2	* 3	* 4	8	9	9	9	9	Approv. total
Supply per capita	* 7	* 7	* 10	16	19	17	17	17	Approv. par habitant
Cambodia									**Cambodge**
Primary Energy production	103	98	114	105	152	165	171	178	Prod. d'énergie primaire
Net imports	* 18	22	28	39	70	78	79	89	Importations nettes
Total supply	121	119	142	144	222	242	250	267	Approv. total
Supply per capita	13	11	11	11	15	16	17	17	Approv. par habitant
Cameroon									**Cameroun**
Primary Energy production	501	457	532	442	351	352	376	408	Prod. d'énergie primaire
Net imports	* -308	* -204	-268	-152	-73	-61	-69	-89	Importations nettes
Changes in stocks	* 0	* 0	0	-5	-13	0	0	...	Variations des stocks
Total supply	193	253	264	295	291	291	307	318	Approv. total
Supply per capita	16	18	17	17	14	13	14	14	Approv. par habitant
Canada									**Canada**
Primary Energy production	11 460	14 587	15 531	16 756	16 450	17 507	18 309	19 276	Prod. d'énergie primaire
Net imports	-2 538	-5 047	-5 377	-5 654	-5 856	-6 515	-7 285	-7 574	Importations nettes
Changes in stocks	170	-145	-351	-127	-303	-75	-145	171	Variations des stocks
Total supply	8 752	9 684	10 504	11 229	10 896	11 066	11 168	11 530	Approv. total
Supply per capita	316	331	343	348	319	317	317	324	Approv. par habitant

Production, trade and supply of energy *(continued)*
Petajoules and gigajoules per capita

Production, commerce et fourniture d'énergie *(suite)*
pétajoules et gigajoules par habitant

Region, country or area	1990	1995	2000	2005	2010	2012	2013	2014	Région, pays ou zone
Cayman Islands									**Îles Caïmanes**
Net imports	4	* 6	* 7	* 7	* 8	* 7	8	8	Importations nettes
Total supply	4	* 5	* 7	7	8	8	8	8	Approv. total
Supply per capita	138	* 159	* 166	130	144	134	131	130	Approv. par habitant
Central African Rep.									**Rép. centrafricaine**
Primary Energy production	28	28	19	19	19	19	19	19	Prod. d'énergie primaire
Net imports	* 3	* 3	* 4	* 3	* 4	* 5	* 5	* 5	Importations nettes
Changes in stocks	0	* 0	* 0	...	...	...	...	...	Variations des stocks
Total supply	31	31	22	22	23	23	23	23	Approv. total
Supply per capita	11	9	6	5	5	5	5	5	Approv. par habitant
Chad									**Tchad**
Primary Energy production	43	48	55	433	324	288	275	288	Prod. d'énergie primaire
Net imports	* 2	* 2	* 2	* -367	* -252	* -213	* -198	* -209	Importations nettes
Changes in stocks	0	0	...	...	...	...	...	...	Variations des stocks
Total supply	45	50	57	66	73	75	77	79	Approv. total
Supply per capita	7	7	7	7	6	6	6	6	Approv. par habitant
Chile									**Chili**
Primary Energy production	326	344	358	390	384	544	626	540	Prod. d'énergie primaire
Net imports	284	437	722	791	888	1 002	1 013	975	Importations nettes
Changes in stocks	24	10	7	3	-6	-5	26	10	Variations des stocks
Total supply	587	772	1 073	1 178	1 278	1 551	1 613	1 505	Approv. total
Supply per capita	45	54	70	72	75	89	92	85	Approv. par habitant
China [2]									**Chine** [2]
Primary Energy production	32 727	39 692	40 783	63 831	88 553	99 224	101 306	101 394	Prod. d'énergie primaire
Net imports	* -1 378	* -397	* 1 426	4 251	14 219	17 730	18 884	19 627	Importations nettes
Changes in stocks	959	132	-251	-752	1 247	1 324	1 894	1 443	Variations des stocks
Total supply	30 390	39 163	42 461	68 833	101 525	115 631	118 296	119 578	Approv. total
Supply per capita	27	32	33	53	76	85	87	87	Approv. par habitant
China, Hong Kong SAR									**Chine, Hong Kong RAS**
Net imports	321	382	571	578	680	582	592	590	Importations nettes
Changes in stocks	5	* -16	1	-2	130	9	6	-10	Variations des stocks
Total supply	316	398	570	579	550	573	585	599	Approv. total
Supply per capita	54	65	84	85	79	81	82	83	Approv. par habitant
China, Macao SAR									**Chine, Macao RAS**
Primary Energy production	...	...	...	* 2	* 2	* 2	* 2	* 2	Prod. d'énergie primaire
Net imports	15	18	23	26	31	32	32	33	Importations nettes
Changes in stocks	0	0	0	0	0	0	0	0	Variations des stocks
Total supply	15	18	24	28	33	34	33	36	Approv. total
Supply per capita	40	45	55	58	62	61	58	62	Approv. par habitant
Colombia									**Colombie**
Primary Energy production	1 882	2 419	3 046	3 335	4 486	5 283	5 697	5 380	Prod. d'énergie primaire
Net imports	* -891	-1 267	-1 987	-2 139	* -3 089	* -3 822	-4 160	-3 751	Importations nettes
Changes in stocks	7	48	-43	16	6	0	26	124	Variations des stocks
Total supply	983	1 104	1 103	1 180	1 390	1 461	1 511	1 505	Approv. total
Supply per capita	30	30	28	27	30	31	32	31	Approv. par habitant
Comoros									**Comores**
Primary Energy production	1	2	2	2	2	3	3	3	Prod. d'énergie primaire
Net imports	* 1	* 1	* 1	* 2	* 2	* 2	* 3	* 2	Importations nettes
Total supply	2	3	3	* 4	* 5	5	* 5	5	Approv. total
Supply per capita	5	6	6	* 6	* 7	6	* 7	6	Approv. par habitant
Congo									**Congo**
Primary Energy production	361	419	609	563	724	676	612	648	Prod. d'énergie primaire
Net imports	* -325	* -375	-569	-519	-649	-570	-516	-525	Importations nettes
Changes in stocks	0	0	...	0	6	0	-12	14	Variations des stocks
Total supply	36	44	40	45	70	106	109	109	Approv. total
Supply per capita	15	16	13	13	17	25	25	24	Approv. par habitant
Cook Islands									**Îles Cook**
Net imports	* 1	* 1	* 1	* 1	* 1	* 1	* 1	* 1	Importations nettes
Total supply	* 0	* 1	* 1	1	* 1	* 1	* 1	* 1	Approv. total
Supply per capita	* 28	* 30	* 36	45	* 49	* 49	* 48	* 48	Approv. par habitant
Costa Rica									**Costa Rica**
Primary Energy production	30	46	67	93	104	106	110	110	Prod. d'énergie primaire
Net imports	40	65	70	85	99	99	98	102	Importations nettes
Changes in stocks	1	0	-1	0	0	-2	0	1	Variations des stocks
Total supply	68	110	137	177	203	207	208	212	Approv. total
Supply per capita	22	32	35	41	45	44	44	44	Approv. par habitant

22 Production, trade and supply of energy *(continued)*
Petajoules and gigajoules per capita

Production, commerce et fourniture d'énergie *(suite)*
pétajoules et gigajoules par habitant

Region, country or area	1990	1995	2000	2005	2010	2012	2013	2014	Région, pays ou zone
Côte d'Ivoire									**Côte d'Ivoire**
Primary Energy production	179	178	242	451	467	523	540	540	Prod. d'énergie primaire
Net imports	* 26	* 68	* 28	-27	-39	3	24	38	Importations nettes
Changes in stocks	* 1	* 0	* -8	* 5	3	-2	-2	-3	Variations des stocks
Total supply	204	245	278	418	425	528	566	580	Approv. total
Supply per capita	16	17	17	23	21	25	26	26	Approv. par habitant
Croatia									**Croatie**
Primary Energy production	...	209	178	199	215	176	186	182	Prod. d'énergie primaire
Net imports	...	115	166	212	180	177	164	146	Importations nettes
Changes in stocks	...	-2	-4	4	5	-6	-2	-8	Variations des stocks
Total supply	...	325	349	407	390	359	352	335	Approv. total
Supply per capita	...	70	77	92	90	84	82	79	Approv. par habitant
Cuba									**Cuba**
Primary Energy production	* 213	170	241	205	200	206	202	212	Prod. d'énergie primaire
Net imports	* 410	286	232	* 207	* 366	* 336	* 323	* 320	Importations nettes
Changes in stocks	-5	4	10	...	...	...	...	...	Variations des stocks
Total supply	628	452	462	412	566	542	524	531	Approv. total
Supply per capita	59	41	42	37	50	48	46	47	Approv. par habitant
Curaçao									**Curaçao**
Primary Energy production	...	...	...	...	...	0	0	0	Prod. d'énergie primaire
Net imports	...	...	...	...	...	86	77	85	Importations nettes
Total supply	...	...	...	...	...	87	77	85	Approv. total
Supply per capita	...	...	...	...	...	570	499	545	Approv. par habitant
Cyprus									**Chypre**
Primary Energy production	0	0	0	0	4	4	5	5	Prod. d'énergie primaire
Net imports	57	78	88	94	104	91	78	76	Importations nettes
Changes in stocks	2	10	1	3	5	1	1	-2	Variations des stocks
Total supply	54	69	87	92	103	94	82	83	Approv. total
Supply per capita	70	80	93	89	94	83	71	72	Approv. par habitant
Czechia									**Tchéquie**
Primary Energy production	...	1 356	1 281	1 374	1 321	1 363	1 258	1 221	Prod. d'énergie primaire
Net imports	...	367	411	527	469	443	478	517	Importations nettes
Changes in stocks	...	-30	-49	16	-71	28	-16	13	Variations des stocks
Total supply	...	1 753	1 741	1 885	1 860	1 779	1 751	1 725	Approv. total
Supply per capita	...	170	170	184	177	169	166	164	Approv. par habitant
Dem. P. R. Korea									**R. p. dém. de Corée**
Primary Energy production	1 211	838	787	923	872	849	853	871	Prod. d'énergie primaire
Net imports	181	83	41	-28	-77	-246	-395	-367	Importations nettes
Changes in stocks	...	...	2	...	...	...	...	...	Variations des stocks
Total supply	1 391	921	826	896	795	603	459	505	Approv. total
Supply per capita	69	42	36	38	32	24	18	20	Approv. par habitant
Dem. Rep. of the Congo									**Rép. dém. du Congo**
Primary Energy production	490	616	677	866	855	1 112	1 149	1 179	Prod. d'énergie primaire
Net imports	* -13	-33	-43	-41	-24	-17	2	23	Importations nettes
Changes in stocks	0	0	-1	0	0	...	...	...	Variations des stocks
Total supply	477	584	635	825	831	1 095	1 151	1 202	Approv. total
Supply per capita	13	13	13	14	13	16	16	16	Approv. par habitant
Denmark [3]									**Danemark [3]**
Primary Energy production	420	649	1 149	1 298	968	779	692	666	Prod. d'énergie primaire
Net imports	298	217	-383	-498	-204	-78	44	25	Importations nettes
Changes in stocks	-7	57	-19	14	-47	-17	6	18	Variations des stocks
Total supply	725	811	785	786	812	718	729	673	Approv. total
Supply per capita	141	155	147	145	146	128	130	119	Approv. par habitant
Djibouti									**Djibouti**
Primary Energy production	2	2	3	3	3	3	3	3	Prod. d'énergie primaire
Net imports	* 5	* 5	* 5	* 6	* 7	* 7	* 7	* 7	Importations nettes
Changes in stocks	0	...	...	...	* 0	0	0	0	Variations des stocks
Total supply	* 6	* 7	8	* 9	11	* 11	* 11	* 11	Approv. total
Supply per capita	* 12	* 11	10	* 11	13	* 13	* 13	* 13	Approv. par habitant
Dominica									**Dominique**
Primary Energy production	0	0	0	0	0	0	0	0	Prod. d'énergie primaire
Net imports	* 1	* 1	* 1	* 2	* 2	* 2	* 2	* 2	Importations nettes
Changes in stocks	...	* 0	...	...	...	...	...	...	Variations des stocks
Total supply	* 1	1	2	2	* 2	* 2	* 2	* 2	Approv. total
Supply per capita	* 14	19	24	26	* 29	* 29	* 28	* 29	Approv. par habitant

22 Production, trade and supply of energy *(continued)*
Petajoules and gigajoules per capita

Production, commerce et fourniture d'énergie *(suite)*
pétajoules et gigajoules par habitant

Region, country or area	1990	1995	2000	2005	2010	2012	2013	2014	Région, pays ou zone
Dominican Republic									**Rép. dominicaine**
Primary Energy production	22	24	24	28	27	29	29	28	Prod. d'énergie primaire
Net imports	122	212	259	* 239	271	287	278	270	Importations nettes
Changes in stocks	1	0	0	2	0	0	0	3	Variations des stocks
Total supply	143	236	283	266	298	316	307	295	Approv. total
Supply per capita	20	30	33	29	30	31	30	28	Approv. par habitant
Ecuador									**Équateur**
Primary Energy production	683	915	959	1 251	1 077	1 141	1 188	1 247	Prod. d'énergie primaire
Net imports	-428	* -577	-612	-772	-513	-555	-565	-582	Importations nettes
Changes in stocks	0	...	20	4	2	-2	0	2	Variations des stocks
Total supply	255	339	328	475	562	588	623	663	Approv. total
Supply per capita	25	30	27	35	38	38	40	42	Approv. par habitant
Egypt									**Égypte**
Primary Energy production	2 376	2 684	2 773	3 383	3 692	3 669	3 448	3 509	Prod. d'énergie primaire
Net imports	* -1 084	* -709	-449	-645	-511	-224	-20	-298	Importations nettes
Changes in stocks	* 21	369	36	-4	-60	-5	0	-48	Variations des stocks
Total supply	1 271	1 605	2 288	2 742	3 242	3 450	3 428	3 259	Approv. total
Supply per capita	22	26	34	37	40	40	39	36	Approv. par habitant
El Salvador									**El Salvador**
Primary Energy production	60	70	89	104	95	91	86	86	Prod. d'énergie primaire
Net imports	32	67	77	85	81	83	81	82	Importations nettes
Changes in stocks	-1	2	0	0	-2	-3	0	-1	Variations des stocks
Total supply	92	135	166	189	178	177	167	170	Approv. total
Supply per capita	17	24	28	31	29	29	27	28	Approv. par habitant
Equatorial Guinea									**Guinée équatoriale**
Primary Energy production	4	34	285	823	813	819	801	841	Prod. d'énergie primaire
Net imports	* 1	* -28	-276	* -770	* -745	* -743	* -733	* -770	Importations nettes
Changes in stocks	...	* 1	...	...	...	...	...	...	Variations des stocks
Total supply	5	5	9	52	69	76	69	72	Approv. total
Supply per capita	13	11	18	86	94	98	86	87	Approv. par habitant
Eritrea									**Érythrée**
Primary Energy production	...	31	21	21	24	25	26	27	Prod. d'énergie primaire
Net imports	...	13	9	10	7	7	7	8	Importations nettes
Changes in stocks	...	...	0	-2	0	0	0	0	Variations des stocks
Total supply	...	43	30	32	31	33	33	34	Approv. total
Supply per capita	...	14	8	7	7	7	7	7	Approv. par habitant
Estonia									**Estonie**
Primary Energy production	...	139	129	163	205	213	237	242	Prod. d'énergie primaire
Net imports	...	74	66	57	30	32	21	16	Importations nettes
Changes in stocks	...	-3	-1	0	-2	12	1	5	Variations des stocks
Total supply	...	217	196	220	236	233	258	254	Approv. total
Supply per capita	...	151	143	164	177	176	195	193	Approv. par habitant
Ethiopia									**Éthiopie**
Primary Energy production	...	885	977	1 070	1 212	1 259	1 285	1 308	Prod. d'énergie primaire
Net imports	...	31	43	60	82	94	111	121	Importations nettes
Changes in stocks	...	* -2	-2	-3	1	0	1	1	Variations des stocks
Total supply	...	918	1 022	1 132	1 293	1 352	1 394	1 428	Approv. total
Supply per capita	...	16	16	15	15	15	15	15	Approv. par habitant
Falkland Is. (Malvinas)									**Îles Falkland (Malvinas)**
Primary Energy production	0	* 0	* 0	* 0	* 0	* 0	* 0	* 0	Prod. d'énergie primaire
Net imports	0	* 0	* 0	* 1	* 1	* 1	* 1	* 1	Importations nettes
Total supply	1	* 1	* 1	* 1	* 1	* 1	* 1	* 1	Approv. total
Supply per capita	271	* 239	* 178	* 235	* 261	* 259	* 258	* 257	Approv. par habitant
Faroe Islands									**Îles Féroé**
Primary Energy production	0	0	0	0	0	0	0	1	Prod. d'énergie primaire
Net imports	* 11	* 9	* 10	* 11	* 9	* 8	* 9	* 8	Importations nettes
Total supply	10	* 8	* 10	* 10	* 9	* 9	* 10	* 9	Approv. total
Supply per capita	220	* 191	* 216	* 216	* 184	* 177	* 202	* 182	Approv. par habitant
Fiji									**Fidji**
Primary Energy production	10	13	11	9	6	6	8	8	Prod. d'énergie primaire
Net imports	9	* 11	* 11	* 16	* 16	* 13	* 15	* 15	Importations nettes
Changes in stocks	-1	...	...	* 0	...	...	...	...	Variations des stocks
Total supply	21	* 23	22	24	22	20	* 23	* 23	Approv. total
Supply per capita	28	* 30	27	29	26	23	* 26	* 26	Approv. par habitant

Region, country or area	1990	1995	2000	2005	2010	2012	2013	2014	Région, pays ou zone
Finland									**Finlande**
Primary Energy production	459	507	622	695	727	720	759	757	Prod. d'énergie primaire
Net imports	713	636	727	767	722	642	658	676	Importations nettes
Changes in stocks	36	-26	1	26	-78	-55	30	25	Variations des stocks
Total supply	1 135	1 170	1 348	1 436	1 527	1 416	1 386	1 408	Approv. total
Supply per capita	228	229	261	274	284	261	254	257	Approv. par habitant
France [4]									**France** [4]
Primary Energy production	4 652	5 314	5 427	5 692	5 623	5 565	5 638	5 694	Prod. d'énergie primaire
Net imports	4 801	4 619	5 258	5 689	5 197	4 901	4 914	4 509	Importations nettes
Changes in stocks	71	10	148	49	-109	-71	-32	54	Variations des stocks
Total supply	9 381	9 924	10 537	11 332	10 929	10 538	10 584	10 149	Approv. total
Supply per capita	165	171	178	186	173	166	166	158	Approv. par habitant
French Guiana									**Guyane française**
Primary Energy production	0	1	2	* 2	3	3	3	3	Prod. d'énergie primaire
Net imports	* 9	* 8	* 6	* 8	* 8	* 7	* 8	* 10	Importations nettes
Total supply	9	9	8	10	* 11	* 11	* 11	* 13	Approv. total
Supply per capita	79	62	47	49	* 48	* 45	* 45	* 50	Approv. par habitant
French Polynesia									**Polynésie française**
Primary Energy production	0	0	1	1	1	* 1	* 1	* 1	Prod. d'énergie primaire
Net imports	* 6	* 6	* 8	* 11	* 12	* 11	* 11	* 10	Importations nettes
Total supply	* 7	7	9	12	13	12	12	12	Approv. total
Supply per capita	* 34	32	37	48	49	44	44	43	Approv. par habitant
Gabon									**Gabon**
Primary Energy production	609	822	630	622	590	604	558	559	Prod. d'énergie primaire
Net imports	-509	-765	-572	-545	-527	-502	-451	-451	Importations nettes
Changes in stocks	50	2	-4	5	-29	-1	0	...	Variations des stocks
Total supply	50	56	62	72	93	102	107	109	Approv. total
Supply per capita	54	52	50	53	60	63	65	64	Approv. par habitant
Gambia									**Gambie**
Primary Energy production	4	5	6	6	6	7	7	7	Prod. d'énergie primaire
Net imports	* 3	* 3	* 4	* 5	* 6	* 6	* 6	* 7	Importations nettes
Changes in stocks	0	...	...	...	...	...	...	...	Variations des stocks
Total supply	7	7	9	10	12	13	13	14	Approv. total
Supply per capita	7	6	7	7	7	7	7	7	Approv. par habitant
Georgia									**Géorgie**
Primary Energy production	...	22	28	53	58	48	63	61	Prod. d'énergie primaire
Net imports	...	37	65	82	82	115	104	127	Importations nettes
Changes in stocks	...	0	0	0	0	0	0	0	Variations des stocks
Total supply	...	59	93	135	140	164	167	188	Approv. total
Supply per capita	...	12	20	30	33	40	41	47	Approv. par habitant
Germany									**Allemagne**
Primary Energy production	...	6 050	5 645	5 704	5 377	5 126	5 032	5 004	Prod. d'énergie primaire
Net imports	...	7 849	8 207	8 354	8 088	7 872	8 202	7 765	Importations nettes
Changes in stocks	...	-137	-183	48	-192	-8	-27	-8	Variations des stocks
Total supply	...	14 037	14 034	14 009	13 656	13 005	13 261	12 776	Approv. total
Supply per capita	...	171	170	170	170	162	165	158	Approv. par habitant
Ghana									**Ghana**
Primary Energy production	138	211	192	164	148	347	401	410	Prod. d'énergie primaire
Net imports	* 49	* 66	79	87	120	-24	-30	-33	Importations nettes
Changes in stocks	* 1	...	...	...	0	0	5	4	Variations des stocks
Total supply	187	277	271	251	267	323	367	372	Approv. total
Supply per capita	13	16	14	12	11	13	14	14	Approv. par habitant
Gibraltar									**Gibraltar**
Net imports	3	5	6	7	8	8	8	9	Importations nettes
Changes in stocks	0	...	...	...	...	...	...	...	Variations des stocks
Total supply	2	4	5	6	7	7	8	8	Approv. total
Supply per capita	90	162	197	219	238	231	245	259	Approv. par habitant
Greece									**Grèce**
Primary Energy production	385	391	419	432	396	437	389	368	Prod. d'énergie primaire
Net imports	506	581	741	831	762	706	573	613	Importations nettes
Changes in stocks	-10	10	12	-18	-11	18	-28	-2	Variations des stocks
Total supply	902	963	1 148	1 280	1 169	1 124	989	983	Approv. total
Supply per capita	89	90	104	115	105	101	89	89	Approv. par habitant

22 Production, trade and supply of energy *(continued)*
Petajoules and gigajoules per capita

Production, commerce et fourniture d'énergie *(suite)*
pétajoules et gigajoules par habitant

Region, country or area	1990	1995	2000	2005	2010	2012	2013	2014	Région, pays ou zone
Greenland									**Groenland**
Primary Energy production	...	...	1	1	1	1	1	2	Prod. d'énergie primaire
Net imports	8	* 7	* 8	9	10	8	8	7	Importations nettes
Changes in stocks	...	...	...	* 1	1	0	0	0	Variations des stocks
Total supply	8	* 7	* 8	9	11	9	9	9	Approv. total
Supply per capita	140	* 128	* 146	165	186	166	165	154	Approv. par habitant
Grenada									**Grenade**
Primary Energy production	0	0	0	0	0	0	0	0	Prod. d'énergie primaire
Net imports	* 2	* 2	* 3	3	4	4	5	4	Importations nettes
Changes in stocks	0	0	0	0	0	0	0	0	Variations des stocks
Total supply	2	2	3	3	4	4	5	4	Approv. total
Supply per capita	17	23	29	33	38	39	43	35	Approv. par habitant
Guadeloupe									**Guadeloupe**
Primary Energy production	1	* 2	* 2	* 3	* 4	4	5	5	Prod. d'énergie primaire
Net imports	* 16	* 19	* 24	* 28	* 29	* 32	* 32	* 32	Importations nettes
Total supply	18	21	26	32	* 33	* 36	* 37	* 37	Approv. total
Supply per capita	47	52	61	71	* 72	* 78	* 80	* 80	Approv. par habitant
Guatemala									**Guatemala**
Primary Energy production	143	178	229	255	279	309	310	327	Prod. d'énergie primaire
Net imports	52	75	75	117	111	122	122	174	Importations nettes
Changes in stocks	0	* 1	-4	7	0	4	-20	-15	Variations des stocks
Total supply	195	252	307	365	391	427	452	517	Approv. total
Supply per capita	22	25	27	29	27	28	29	32	Approv. par habitant
Guernsey									**Guernesey**
Net imports	...	...	...	1	1	1	0	1	Importations nettes
Total supply	...	...	...	1	1	1	0	1	Approv. total
Supply per capita	...	...	...	17	14	18	6	9	Approv. par habitant
Guinea									**Guinée**
Primary Energy production	91	110	107	109	111	112	113	113	Prod. d'énergie primaire
Net imports	* 14	* 16	* 21	* 26	* 36	* 35	* 31	* 32	Importations nettes
Changes in stocks	0	...	...	...	...	...	...	...	Variations des stocks
Total supply	105	126	128	135	147	148	144	145	Approv. total
Supply per capita	18	17	15	15	13	13	12	12	Approv. par habitant
Guinea-Bissau									**Guinée-Bissau**
Primary Energy production	17	18	20	22	24	24	25	25	Prod. d'énergie primaire
Net imports	* 3	* 4	* 3	* 4	* 5	* 5	* 5	* 4	Importations nettes
Total supply	20	21	23	26	28	29	29	30	Approv. total
Supply per capita	20	19	19	19	17	17	17	17	Approv. par habitant
Guyana									**Guyana**
Primary Energy production	9	8	9	9	8	8	7	7	Prod. d'énergie primaire
Net imports	* 16	* 21	22	20	24	27	27	28	Importations nettes
Changes in stocks	...	0	0	0	0	0	0	0	Variations des stocks
Total supply	24	29	32	29	32	36	34	35	Approv. total
Supply per capita	34	39	43	39	43	47	45	46	Approv. par habitant
Haiti									**Haïti**
Primary Energy production	51	58	65	115	131	140	140	136	Prod. d'énergie primaire
Net imports	* 11	* 13	20	28	28	31	31	38	Importations nettes
Changes in stocks	-1	...	...	...	...	...	-1	0	Variations des stocks
Total supply	64	71	84	142	159	170	171	174	Approv. total
Supply per capita	9	9	10	15	16	17	16	16	Approv. par habitant
Honduras									**Honduras**
Primary Energy production	91	92	96	77	93	104	106	105	Prod. d'énergie primaire
Net imports	32	51	65	89	98	111	112	110	Importations nettes
Changes in stocks	0	1	5	-4	0	0	0	-9	Variations des stocks
Total supply	122	142	157	170	191	214	217	224	Approv. total
Supply per capita	25	25	25	25	25	28	28	28	Approv. par habitant
Hungary									**Hongrie**
Primary Energy production	615	583	486	434	461	442	426	423	Prod. d'énergie primaire
Net imports	594	521	573	729	627	517	499	591	Importations nettes
Changes in stocks	-2	11	10	8	9	-30	-22	55	Variations des stocks
Total supply	1 211	1 093	1 049	1 155	1 079	989	947	959	Approv. total
Supply per capita	117	106	103	115	108	99	95	97	Approv. par habitant

Production, trade and supply of energy *(continued)*
Petajoules and gigajoules per capita

Production, commerce et fourniture d'énergie *(suite)*
pétajoules et gigajoules par habitant

Region, country or area	1990	1995	2000	2005	2010	2012	2013	2014	Région, pays ou zone
Iceland									**Islande**
Primary Energy production	59	63	109	127	252	281	283	284	Prod. d'énergie primaire
Net imports	28	27	31	31	26	26	26	27	Importations nettes
Changes in stocks	0	0	2	1	-1	0	1	0	Variations des stocks
Total supply	87	90	139	158	278	306	309	312	Approv. total
Supply per capita	341	338	494	534	875	945	951	952	Approv. par habitant
India									**Inde**
Primary Energy production	9 218	10 985	12 090	18 315	22 598	23 320	22 401	23 103	Prod. d'énergie primaire
Net imports	1 196	* 2 010	3 890	4 689	6 558	9 283	10 690	* 12 056	Importations nettes
Changes in stocks	45	* -41	-155	194	252	-28	-103	-169	Variations des stocks
Total supply	10 370	13 035	16 135	22 809	28 903	32 630	33 195	35 327	Approv. total
Supply per capita	12	14	15	20	23	26	26	27	Approv. par habitant
Indonesia [5]									**Indonésie** [5]
Primary Energy production	6 735	8 320	8 129	11 351	16 854	18 812	19 776	19 481	Prod. d'énergie primaire
Net imports	* -2 753	* -3 634	* -3 577	-4 243	-8 522	-8 214	-10 747	-10 397	Importations nettes
Changes in stocks	223	100	-417	21	2	-72	62	282	Variations des stocks
Total supply	3 759	4 587	4 970	7 087	8 330	10 669	8 966	8 801	Approv. total
Supply per capita	20	23	23	31	34	43	36	35	Approv. par habitant
Iran (Islamic Rep. of)									**Iran (Rép. islamique d')**
Primary Energy production	7 454	9 302	11 121	13 006	14 283	12 506	12 544	13 291	Prod. d'énergie primaire
Net imports	-4 634	-5 415	-5 787	* -5 682	-5 634	-3 557	-3 369	-3 376	Importations nettes
Changes in stocks	0	0	-52	103	69	-107	-30	-43	Variations des stocks
Total supply	2 819	3 887	5 386	7 221	8 579	9 055	9 205	9 958	Approv. total
Supply per capita	51	65	82	104	116	119	119	127	Approv. par habitant
Iraq									**Iraq**
Primary Energy production	4 411	1 265	5 482	4 147	5 274	6 423	6 507	6 744	Prod. d'énergie primaire
Net imports	* -3 697	-193	-4 487	-2 656	-3 835	-4 540	-4 443	-4 629	Importations nettes
Changes in stocks	* 169	0	0	3	1	11	13	61	Variations des stocks
Total supply	546	1 072	995	1 488	1 437	1 871	2 049	2 054	Approv. total
Supply per capita	31	53	42	54	47	57	60	58	Approv. par habitant
Ireland									**Irlande**
Primary Energy production	145	172	90	69	77	53	94	84	Prod. d'énergie primaire
Net imports	281	303	482	544	522	466	486	454	Importations nettes
Changes in stocks	10	28	-2	2	-8	-31	34	2	Variations des stocks
Total supply	416	446	573	610	608	549	546	535	Approv. total
Supply per capita	118	124	151	147	132	118	117	114	Approv. par habitant
Isle of Man									**Île de Man**
Primary Energy production	...	...	...	* 0	* 0	* 0	* 0	* 0	Prod. d'énergie primaire
Net imports	...	...	...	0	0	1	* 0	* 0	Importations nettes
Total supply	...	...	...	* 0	0	1	* 0	* 0	Approv. total
Supply per capita	...	...	...	* 6	2	11	* 4	* 3	Approv. par habitant
Israel									**Israël**
Primary Energy production	18	23	27	87	162	136	273	313	Prod. d'énergie primaire
Net imports	450	625	719	685	804	886	712	634	Importations nettes
Changes in stocks	-12	-1	-17	5	0	11	21	3	Variations des stocks
Total supply	480	649	763	767	966	1 012	963	945	Approv. total
Supply per capita	107	122	127	116	130	132	123	119	Approv. par habitant
Italy [6]									**Italie** [6]
Primary Energy production	1 072	1 235	1 183	1 269	1 384	1 466	1 542	1 539	Prod. d'énergie primaire
Net imports	5 375	5 481	6 239	6 509	6 009	5 344	4 965	4 628	Importations nettes
Changes in stocks	80	3	190	-70	69	6	-23	-1	Variations des stocks
Total supply	6 366	6 714	7 230	7 847	7 324	6 804	6 530	6 168	Approv. total
Supply per capita	112	118	127	134	123	114	109	103	Approv. par habitant
Jamaica									**Jamaïque**
Primary Energy production	13	9	11	15	6	7	7	8	Prod. d'énergie primaire
Net imports	* 97	* 118	144	139	95	99	104	96	Importations nettes
Changes in stocks	-2	-3	7	1	-2	1	-1	1	Variations des stocks
Total supply	113	130	148	151	103	105	113	104	Approv. total
Supply per capita	48	53	57	56	38	38	41	37	Approv. par habitant
Japan									**Japon**
Primary Energy production	3 121	4 086	4 387	4 172	4 116	1 168	1 159	1 114	Prod. d'énergie primaire
Net imports	15 344	16 665	17 456	17 704	16 743	17 766	17 803	17 244	Importations nettes
Changes in stocks	146	56	165	101	-6	51	-20	-118	Variations des stocks
Total supply	18 318	20 696	21 678	21 774	20 863	18 882	18 982	18 477	Approv. total
Supply per capita	150	166	172	172	164	149	149	146	Approv. par habitant

Region, country or area	1990	1995	2000	2005	2010	2012	2013	2014	Région, pays ou zone
Jersey									**Jersey**
Primary Energy production	...	...	...	* 0	* 1	* 1	* 1	* 1	Prod. d'énergie primaire
Net imports	...	1	1	2	2	2	2	2	Importations nettes
Total supply	...	1	1	3	3	3	3	3	Approv. total
Supply per capita	...	9	17	28	30	32	30	28	Approv. par habitant
Jordan									**Jordanie**
Primary Energy production	2	10	10	10	9	8	7	7	Prod. d'énergie primaire
Net imports	136	160	190	285	300	330	* 310	348	Importations nettes
Changes in stocks	4	-2	-5	7	5	7	-10	5	Variations des stocks
Total supply	133	172	205	289	303	332	328	350	Approv. total
Supply per capita	39	39	42	54	46	47	45	47	Approv. par habitant
Kazakhstan									**Kazakhstan**
Primary Energy production	...	2 663	3 367	5 131	6 770	7 030	7 198	7 091	Prod. d'énergie primaire
Net imports	...	-477	-1 819	-2 771	* -3 318	* -3 674	-3 568	-3 722	Importations nettes
Changes in stocks	...	...	-12	8	88	107	80	16	Variations des stocks
Total supply	...	2 185	1 560	2 352	3 363	3 249	3 550	3 352	Approv. total
Supply per capita	...	137	104	155	206	193	208	193	Approv. par habitant
Kenya									**Kenya**
Primary Energy production	217	239	248	338	* 650	* 690	* 719	750	Prod. d'énergie primaire
Net imports	* 71	98	141	109	137	150	149	159	Importations nettes
Changes in stocks	0	...	...	4	-5	0	-1	0	Variations des stocks
Total supply	289	337	388	443	* 793	* 841	* 868	909	Approv. total
Supply per capita	12	12	12	12	* 20	* 20	* 20	20	Approv. par habitant
Kiribati									**Kiribati**
Primary Energy production	0	0	0	0	0	0	0	0	Prod. d'énergie primaire
Net imports	* 0	* 0	* 0	* 1	* 1	* 1	* 1	* 1	Importations nettes
Total supply	* 0	* 0	0	* 1	* 1	* 1	* 1	1	Approv. total
Supply per capita	* 5	* 5	5	* 10	* 9	* 8	* 8	8	Approv. par habitant
Kuwait [7]									**Koweït** [7]
Primary Energy production	2 799	4 802	4 748	6 080	5 557	7 136	7 113	6 941	Prod. d'énergie primaire
Net imports	* -2 088	-3 968	-3 941	-4 915	-4 229	-5 573	-5 659	-5 536	Importations nettes
Changes in stocks	* -36	-1	-17	31	-22	-21	-21	-22	Variations des stocks
Total supply	746	835	824	1 133	1 350	1 584	1 475	1 427	Approv. total
Supply per capita	358	513	424	500	441	463	410	380	Approv. par habitant
Kyrgyzstan									**Kirghizistan**
Primary Energy production	...	53	60	61	53	73	74	80	Prod. d'énergie primaire
Net imports	...	51	38	53	63	104	96	91	Importations nettes
Changes in stocks	...	3	-2	0	1	4	2	11	Variations des stocks
Total supply	...	101	101	114	115	174	167	159	Approv. total
Supply per capita	...	22	20	23	21	31	29	27	Approv. par habitant
Lao People's Dem. Rep.									**Rép. dém. pop. lao**
Primary Energy production	54	57	76	80	79	78	77	72	Prod. d'énergie primaire
Net imports	* 1	* 3	* -7	* -5	* -4	* -5	* 2	* 7	Importations nettes
Total supply	55	59	68	74	75	73	79	78	Approv. total
Supply per capita	13	12	13	13	12	11	12	12	Approv. par habitant
Latvia									**Lettonie**
Primary Energy production	...	60	59	78	95	109	98	108	Prod. d'énergie primaire
Net imports	...	138	94	116	78	102	100	70	Importations nettes
Changes in stocks	...	1	-4	5	-29	11	2	-17	Variations des stocks
Total supply	...	197	157	190	203	200	196	196	Approv. total
Supply per capita	...	79	66	82	97	98	98	99	Approv. par habitant
Lebanon									**Liban**
Primary Energy production	5	8	7	10	9	9	10	7	Prod. d'énergie primaire
Net imports	* 108	166	198	197	253	283	279	300	Importations nettes
Changes in stocks	...	...	-1	...	...	...	...	...	Variations des stocks
Total supply	* 113	173	207	206	262	292	289	306	Approv. total
Supply per capita	* 38	50	55	51	60	59	55	55	Approv. par habitant
Lesotho									**Lesotho**
Primary Energy production	19	22	28	25	27	30	31	31	Prod. d'énergie primaire
Net imports	* 17	* 19	* 20	* 22	* 25	* 27	* 27	* 28	Importations nettes
Total supply	36	41	48	47	52	58	58	59	Approv. total
Supply per capita	22	23	24	23	26	28	28	28	Approv. par habitant

22 Production, trade and supply of energy *(continued)*
Petajoules and gigajoules per capita

Production, commerce et fourniture d'énergie *(suite)*
pétajoules et gigajoules par habitant

Region, country or area	1990	1995	2000	2005	2010	2012	2013	2014	Région, pays ou zone
Liberia									**Libéria**
Primary Energy production	32	25	43	53	64	69	71	73	Prod. d'énergie primaire
Net imports	* 7	* 5	* 5	* 9	* 11	* 14	* 12	* 11	Importations nettes
Total supply	38	30	49	63	75	82	83	85	Approv. total
Supply per capita	18	14	17	20	19	20	19	19	Approv. par habitant
Libya									**Libye**
Primary Energy production	3 020	3 190	3 117	4 062	4 294	3 590	2 635	1 505	Prod. d'énergie primaire
Net imports	-2 676	-2 538	-2 433	-3 335	-3 365	-2 891	-2 016	-688	Importations nettes
Changes in stocks	-124	...	...	...	69	-17	-185	74	Variations des stocks
Total supply	468	653	685	727	860	716	805	743	Approv. total
Supply per capita	108	137	131	126	137	114	129	119	Approv. par habitant
Liechtenstein									**Liechtenstein**
Primary Energy production	...	...	...	...	1	1	1	1	Prod. d'énergie primaire
Net imports	...	...	...	...	2	2	2	2	Importations nettes
Total supply	...	...	...	...	3	3	3	3	Approv. total
Supply per capita	...	...	...	...	81	78	79	74	Approv. par habitant
Lithuania									**Lituanie**
Primary Energy production	...	157	139	170	64	65	69	74	Prod. d'énergie primaire
Net imports	...	234	175	196	225	230	210	214	Importations nettes
Changes in stocks	...	14	8	4	3	-4	-2	1	Variations des stocks
Total supply	...	376	306	362	286	299	282	287	Approv. total
Supply per capita	...	104	87	106	92	99	95	98	Approv. par habitant
Luxembourg									**Luxembourg**
Primary Energy production	1	2	3	4	5	5	6	6	Prod. d'énergie primaire
Net imports	143	130	140	179	173	168	163	156	Importations nettes
Changes in stocks	0	-1	2	-1	-1	1	0	1	Variations des stocks
Total supply	143	133	142	185	178	173	168	161	Approv. total
Supply per capita	376	327	325	405	351	325	308	290	Approv. par habitant
Madagascar									**Madagascar**
Primary Energy production	72	89	92	104	124	124	127	129	Prod. d'énergie primaire
Net imports	* 13	* 18	* 26	* 24	* 25	* 35	* 39	* 39	Importations nettes
Changes in stocks	* 0	0	...	0	-1	1	0	* 0	Variations des stocks
Total supply	85	107	118	127	150	158	166	167	Approv. total
Supply per capita	8	8	8	7	7	7	7	7	Approv. par habitant
Malawi									**Malawi**
Primary Energy production	56	55	76	80	86	88	88	89	Prod. d'énergie primaire
Net imports	* 8	* 11	* 8	* 10	* 13	* 12	* 13	* 13	Importations nettes
Total supply	64	65	85	90	98	100	101	102	Approv. total
Supply per capita	7	7	8	7	7	6	6	6	Approv. par habitant
Malaysia									**Malaisie**
Primary Energy production	1 794	2 791	3 082	3 770	3 450	3 369	3 529	3 738	Prod. d'énergie primaire
Net imports	-1 019	* -1 018	-1 116	-1 120	* -505	-298	-57	-240	Importations nettes
Changes in stocks	3	* 5	8	18	* -9	-76	54	-37	Variations des stocks
Total supply	773	1 768	1 958	2 632	2 955	3 146	3 417	3 535	Approv. total
Supply per capita	42	85	84	101	105	108	116	118	Approv. par habitant
Maldives									**Maldives**
Primary Energy production	0	0	0	0	0	0	0	0	Prod. d'énergie primaire
Net imports	* 3	* 4	* 6	* 9	* 13	* 16	* 15	* 19	Importations nettes
Total supply	* 2	4	6	9	13	16	16	19	Approv. total
Supply per capita	* 11	14	24	30	40	46	45	54	Approv. par habitant
Mali									**Mali**
Primary Energy production	37	42	45	49	52	53	53	55	Prod. d'énergie primaire
Net imports	* 5	* 6	* 11	* 12	* 12	* 13	* 13	* 19	Importations nettes
Total supply	43	48	57	60	64	66	66	73	Approv. total
Supply per capita	5	5	5	5	4	4	4	4	Approv. par habitant
Malta									**Malte**
Primary Energy production	...	...	...	0	0	0	0	1	Prod. d'énergie primaire
Net imports	* 28	* 30	28	37	35	39	37	31	Importations nettes
Changes in stocks	0	1	1	0	-1	1	4	-2	Variations des stocks
Total supply	28	29	28	37	35	37	32	33	Approv. total
Supply per capita	76	74	70	91	86	90	78	78	Approv. par habitant
Marshall Islands									**Îles Marshall**
Primary Energy production	...	...	...	...	...	* 0	0	* 0	Prod. d'énergie primaire
Net imports	...	* 1	* 1	* 1	* 1	1	* 1	* 1	Importations nettes
Total supply	...	* 1	* 1	* 1	* 1	1	* 1	* 1	Approv. total
Supply per capita	...	* 19	* 20	* 23	* 28	27	* 28	* 27	Approv. par habitant

Region, country or area	1990	1995	2000	2005	2010	2012	2013	2014	Région, pays ou zone
Martinique									**Martinique**
Primary Energy production	0	0	* 0	* 0	* 1	* 1	* 1	* 1	Prod. d'énergie primaire
Net imports	* 21	* 21	* 22	* 28	* 26	* 29	* 29	* 30	Importations nettes
Changes in stocks	0	...	...	...	...	...	...	...	Variations des stocks
Total supply	21	* 21	* 22	29	27	30	* 30	* 31	Approv. total
Supply per capita	57	* 57	* 58	73	69	77	* 76	* 79	Approv. par habitant
Mauritania									**Mauritanie**
Primary Energy production	11	12	13	15	34	31	31	31	Prod. d'énergie primaire
Net imports	* 13	* 14	16	21	7	18	* 20	* 20	Importations nettes
Changes in stocks	0	...	...	0	* -3	* -1	0	...	Variations des stocks
Total supply	* 23	* 26	29	36	45	51	* 51	* 51	Approv. total
Supply per capita	* 11	* 11	11	12	12	13	* 13	* 13	Approv. par habitant
Mauritius									**Maurice**
Primary Energy production	13	15	13	12	11	10	11	10	Prod. d'énergie primaire
Net imports	21	28	34	44	49	52	55	53	Importations nettes
Changes in stocks	1	2	-3	-1	-2	1	2	* -2	Variations des stocks
Total supply	33	41	49	57	63	62	63	65	Approv. total
Supply per capita	31	36	41	45	50	49	50	51	Approv. par habitant
Mayotte									**Mayotte**
Primary Energy production	* 0	0	0	0	0	0	0	* 0	Prod. d'énergie primaire
Net imports	* 1	* 1	* 2	* 3	4	* 4	* 4	* 4	Importations nettes
Changes in stocks	...	...	...	...	0	...	...	...	Variations des stocks
Total supply	* 1	* 2	* 2	* 3	4	* 4	* 4	* 4	Approv. total
Supply per capita	* 12	* 13	* 14	* 17	20	* 19	* 19	* 19	Approv. par habitant
Mexico									**Mexique**
Primary Energy production	8 170	8 488	9 613	10 716	9 040	8 886	8 843	8 514	Prod. d'énergie primaire
Net imports	-2 985	-2 997	-3 167	-3 301	-1 623	-928	-858	-656	Importations nettes
Changes in stocks	7	-7	91	-19	5	14	9	45	Variations des stocks
Total supply	5 179	5 498	6 356	7 434	7 413	7 944	7 976	7 812	Approv. total
Supply per capita	61	60	64	70	62	65	64	62	Approv. par habitant
Micronesia (Fed. States of)									**Micronésie (États féd. de)**
Primary Energy production	...	* 0	0	0	0	0	0	0	Prod. d'énergie primaire
Net imports	...	* 2	* 2	* 2	* 2	* 2	* 2	* 2	Importations nettes
Total supply	...	* 2	* 2	2	2	* 2	* 2	* 2	Approv. total
Supply per capita	...	* 15	* 17	16	17	* 20	* 21	* 22	Approv. par habitant
Mongolia									**Mongolie**
Primary Energy production	82	72	66	138	655	780	799	677	Prod. d'énergie primaire
Net imports	33	* 17	21	-35	-446	-404	-327	-384	Importations nettes
Changes in stocks	...	...	...	-1	41	74	29	47	Variations des stocks
Total supply	116	89	87	104	168	302	444	245	Approv. total
Supply per capita	53	39	36	41	62	108	155	84	Approv. par habitant
Montenegro									**Monténégro**
Primary Energy production	...	...	...	25	35	29	32	29	Prod. d'énergie primaire
Net imports	...	...	...	17	14	13	10	11	Importations nettes
Changes in stocks	...	...	...	...	...	...	...	0	Variations des stocks
Total supply	...	...	...	42	48	43	42	40	Approv. total
Supply per capita	...	...	...	67	77	69	67	64	Approv. par habitant
Montserrat									**Montserrat**
Net imports	* 0	* 1	* 0	* 1	* 1	* 1	* 1	* 1	Importations nettes
Changes in stocks	...	...	...	...	0	* 0	* 0	0	Variations des stocks
Total supply	* 0	* 0	* 0	* 1	1	1	1	1	Approv. total
Supply per capita	* 41	* 48	* 75	* 93	175	118	146	133	Approv. par habitant
Morocco									**Maroc**
Primary Energy production	83	85	73	72	81	73	81	78	Prod. d'énergie primaire
Net imports	267	* 354	401	530	* 686	* 759	752	785	Importations nettes
Changes in stocks	-2	10	-2	0	10	10	42	63	Variations des stocks
Total supply	352	428	477	603	758	824	791	800	Approv. total
Supply per capita	14	16	17	20	23	25	23	23	Approv. par habitant
Mozambique									**Mozambique**
Primary Energy production	236	248	302	430	516	671	734	779	Prod. d'énergie primaire
Net imports	* 12	16	-11	-66	-95	-182	-195	-195	Importations nettes
Changes in stocks	0	0	0	-1	0	42	70	35	Variations des stocks
Total supply	248	264	292	364	421	447	469	549	Approv. total
Supply per capita	18	17	16	18	17	17	18	20	Approv. par habitant

Production, trade and supply of energy *(continued)*
Petajoules and gigajoules per capita

Production, commerce et fourniture d'énergie *(suite)*
pétajoules et gigajoules par habitant

Region, country or area	1990	1995	2000	2005	2010	2012	2013	2014	Région, pays ou zone
Myanmar									**Myanmar**
Primary Energy production	446	464	648	927	962	954	973	1 078	Prod. d'énergie primaire
Net imports	6	27	-113	-307	-305	-305	-290	-305	Importations nettes
Changes in stocks	2	-7	-3	1	2	2	1	-31	Variations des stocks
Total supply	449	498	538	619	656	646	683	805	Approv. total
Supply per capita	11	12	12	13	13	12	13	15	Approv. par habitant
Namibia									**Namibie**
Primary Energy production	...	13	16	17	17	18	19	19	Prod. d'énergie primaire
Net imports	...	24	26	37	48	* 48	* 40	54	Importations nettes
Changes in stocks	...	...	...	...	0	0	* 0	...	Variations des stocks
Total supply	...	38	42	53	65	66	59	74	Approv. total
Supply per capita	...	23	22	26	30	29	25	31	Approv. par habitant
Nauru									**Nauru**
Primary Energy production	...	...	...	...	* 0	* 0	* 0	0	Prod. d'énergie primaire
Net imports	* 2	* 2	* 2	* 1	* 1	* 1	* 1	* 1	Importations nettes
Changes in stocks	...	...	...	...	* 0	* 0	0	0	Variations des stocks
Total supply	* 2	* 1	* 1	* 1	1	* 1	* 1	* 1	Approv. total
Supply per capita	* 188	* 148	* 119	* 84	58	* 55	* 61	* 63	Approv. par habitant
Nepal									**Népal**
Primary Energy production	146	271	310	349	384	365	409	451	Prod. d'énergie primaire
Net imports	8	25	39	39	62	* 65	* 74	* 91	Importations nettes
Changes in stocks	-1	-1	...	...	...	...	...	* 0	Variations des stocks
Total supply	154	297	349	388	446	430	483	542	Approv. total
Supply per capita	8	14	14	14	17	16	17	19	Approv. par habitant
Netherlands									**Pays-Bas**
Primary Energy production	2 534	2 796	2 416	2 610	2 917	2 701	2 894	2 447	Prod. d'énergie primaire
Net imports	198	183	769	783	565	503	327	552	Importations nettes
Changes in stocks	8	-74	82	41	35	-4	40	-4	Variations des stocks
Total supply	2 723	3 053	3 103	3 352	3 447	3 208	3 180	3 004	Approv. total
Supply per capita	183	198	196	206	207	192	189	178	Approv. par habitant
Netherlands Antilles [former]									**Antilles néerlandaises [anc.]**
Primary Energy production	0	0	0	0	0	...	...	...	Prod. d'énergie primaire
Net imports	* 71	* 94	83	84	68	...	...	...	Importations nettes
Changes in stocks	* -11	...	...	...	...	...	...	...	Variations des stocks
Total supply	82	* 95	83	84	69	...	...	...	Approv. total
Supply per capita	432	* 500	464	452	334	...	...	...	Approv. par habitant
New Caledonia									**Nouvelle-Calédonie**
Primary Energy production	2	1	2	1	1	2	2	1	Prod. d'énergie primaire
Net imports	* 20	* 26	* 28	* 36	* 49	* 45	* 56	* 55	Importations nettes
Changes in stocks	...	...	...	...	3	-1	2	* 0	Variations des stocks
Total supply	21	27	30	37	46	48	56	56	Approv. total
Supply per capita	125	140	141	161	186	188	219	215	Approv. par habitant
New Zealand									**Nouvelle-Zélande**
Primary Energy production	500	544	628	572	770	739	739	783	Prod. d'énergie primaire
Net imports	58	82	106	167	77	107	143	144	Importations nettes
Changes in stocks	1	-3	-12	-8	12	-22	11	-3	Variations des stocks
Total supply	555	629	747	747	834	868	871	931	Approv. total
Supply per capita	163	171	194	181	191	196	195	207	Approv. par habitant
Nicaragua									**Nicaragua**
Primary Energy production	59	66	56	62	66	78	89	91	Prod. d'énergie primaire
Net imports	28	37	49	57	56	60	59	62	Importations nettes
Changes in stocks	0	0	-1	0	-3	0	-1	-1	Variations des stocks
Total supply	86	102	107	119	125	138	148	154	Approv. total
Supply per capita	21	22	21	22	22	24	25	26	Approv. par habitant
Niger									**Niger**
Primary Energy production	54	65	74	* 70	56	88	101	* 101	Prod. d'énergie primaire
Net imports	* 7	* 9	* 7	* 7	13	-4	-13	* -9	Importations nettes
Changes in stocks	0	0	0	0	0	0	1	* 1	Variations des stocks
Total supply	62	73	81	* 77	70	84	87	* 91	Approv. total
Supply per capita	8	8	7	* 6	4	5	5	* 5	Approv. par habitant
Nigeria									**Nigéria**
Primary Energy production	6 091	6 856	8 247	9 734	10 595	11 097	10 656	10 851	Prod. d'énergie primaire
Net imports	-3 312	-3 804	-4 595	-5 342	-5 615	-5 575	-5 046	-5 240	Importations nettes
Changes in stocks	-2	-30	53	-9	-35	-65	3	-26	Variations des stocks
Total supply	2 780	3 082	3 599	4 402	5 015	5 588	5 606	5 637	Approv. total
Supply per capita	29	28	29	31	31	33	32	32	Approv. par habitant

Production, trade and supply of energy *(continued)*
Petajoules and gigajoules per capita

Production, commerce et fourniture d'énergie *(suite)*
pétajoules et gigajoules par habitant

Region, country or area	1990	1995	2000	2005	2010	2012	2013	2014	Région, pays ou zone
Niue									**Nioué**
Primary Energy production	0	0	0	0	0	0	0	0	Prod. d'énergie primaire
Net imports	* 0	* 0	* 0	* 0	0	0	0	0	Importations nettes
Total supply	* 0	* 0	* 0	0	0	0	0	0	Approv. total
Supply per capita	* 34	* 34	* 42	42	53	58	61	62	Approv. par habitant
Norway [8]									**Norvège** [8]
Primary Energy production	4 977	7 543	9 340	9 372	8 759	8 560	8 134	8 204	Prod. d'énergie primaire
Net imports	-4 024	-6 559	-8 250	-8 240	-7 334	-7 302	-6 770	-7 026	Importations nettes
Changes in stocks	77	20	15	15	-1	10	-2	-20	Variations des stocks
Total supply	876	964	1 075	1 117	1 425	1 248	1 365	1 199	Approv. total
Supply per capita	207	221	239	242	291	249	269	233	Approv. par habitant
Oman									**Oman**
Primary Energy production	1 531	1 931	2 359	2 351	2 793	3 014	3 150	3 101	Prod. d'énergie primaire
Net imports	* -1 392	* -1 710	-2 079	-1 906	-2 022	-2 027	-2 136	-2 090	Importations nettes
Changes in stocks	-14	-15	-41	0	-7	2	-4	-2	Variations des stocks
Total supply	153	236	322	445	778	985	1 018	1 014	Approv. total
Supply per capita	82	106	142	183	264	278	261	239	Approv. par habitant
Other non-specified areas									**Autres zones non-spécifiées**
Primary Energy production	462	468	505	532	538	551	562	566	Prod. d'énergie primaire
Net imports	1 601	2 260	3 150	3 747	4 112	3 901	3 947	4 095	Importations nettes
Changes in stocks	114	104	243	37	-1	6	-8	60	Variations des stocks
Total supply	1 947	2 623	3 413	4 242	4 651	4 446	4 517	4 601	Approv. total
Supply per capita	95	123	153	186	200	191	194	197	Approv. par habitant
Pakistan									**Pakistan**
Primary Energy production	906	1 192	1 403	2 020	2 105	* 2 216	* 2 193	* 2 202	Prod. d'énergie primaire
Net imports	385	529	680	633	843	815	858	894	Importations nettes
Changes in stocks	...	...	0	10	2	* -7	* -5	* -6	Variations des stocks
Total supply	1 290	1 722	2 082	2 642	2 946	3 039	3 056	3 101	Approv. total
Supply per capita	12	14	14	17	17	17	17	17	Approv. par habitant
Palau									**Palaos**
Net imports	...	* 3	* 3	* 3	* 3	* 3	* 3	* 3	Importations nettes
Total supply	...	* 3	* 4	* 4	* 4	* 3	* 4	* 4	Approv. total
Supply per capita	...	* 190	* 183	* 184	* 172	* 169	* 170	* 172	Approv. par habitant
Panama									**Panama**
Primary Energy production	24	22	28	32	26	31	31	31	Prod. d'énergie primaire
Net imports	42	41	75	88	97	* 112	129	121	Importations nettes
Changes in stocks	4	1	-1	0	-20	-10	-1	16	Variations des stocks
Total supply	62	62	104	120	143	152	161	136	Approv. total
Supply per capita	26	23	35	37	40	41	42	35	Approv. par habitant
Papua New Guinea									**Papouasie-Nvl-Guinée**
Primary Energy production	251	263	220	174	95	112	114	* 114	Prod. d'énergie primaire
Net imports	* -163	* -171	* -121	* -48	* 47	* 34	* 44	* 44	Importations nettes
Changes in stocks	0	* 3	* 0	0	2	0	-2	* -3	Variations des stocks
Total supply	88	89	99	126	141	145	160	* 161	Approv. total
Supply per capita	21	19	18	21	21	20	22	* 22	Approv. par habitant
Paraguay									**Paraguay**
Primary Energy production	* 145	194	276	288	327	344	340	325	Prod. d'énergie primaire
Net imports	* -59	-80	-122	-109	-98	-105	-108	-77	Importations nettes
Changes in stocks	* 1	-4	2	-1	-4	2	-5	1	Variations des stocks
Total supply	* 84	118	153	180	234	237	237	247	Approv. total
Supply per capita	* 20	25	29	31	38	37	37	38	Approv. par habitant
Peru									**Pérou**
Primary Energy production	420	408	419	455	783	899	954	1 020	Prod. d'énergie primaire
Net imports	-28	60	130	108	-22	-119	-162	-93	Importations nettes
Changes in stocks	-3	23	7	-3	-12	-55	-38	12	Variations des stocks
Total supply	396	444	542	565	773	835	830	914	Approv. total
Supply per capita	18	19	21	20	26	28	27	30	Approv. par habitant
Philippines									**Philippines**
Primary Energy production	540	533	695	762	865	969	936	991	Prod. d'énergie primaire
Net imports	512	759	860	* 697	718	771	817	871	Importations nettes
Changes in stocks	13	28	4	-10	11	14	-27	-38	Variations des stocks
Total supply	1 039	1 264	1 551	1 469	1 572	1 726	1 780	1 899	Approv. total
Supply per capita	17	18	20	17	17	18	18	19	Approv. par habitant

Region, country or area	1990	1995	2000	2005	2010	2012	2013	2014	Région, pays ou zone
Poland									**Pologne**
Primary Energy production	4 350	4 161	3 318	3 280	2 808	2 986	2 969	2 819	Prod. d'énergie primaire
Net imports	99	58	438	686	1 351	1 295	1 091	1 144	Importations nettes
Changes in stocks	43	-36	-24	82	-93	171	-61	21	Variations des stocks
Total supply	4 406	4 256	3 780	3 886	4 251	4 110	4 122	3 941	Approv. total
Supply per capita	116	111	99	102	110	106	107	102	Approv. par habitant
Portugal [9]									**Portugal** [9]
Primary Energy production	142	139	161	151	242	197	241	250	Prod. d'énergie primaire
Net imports	596	714	864	969	717	694	631	608	Importations nettes
Changes in stocks	19	12	0	16	-15	0	-16	-16	Variations des stocks
Total supply	720	840	1 026	1 104	975	890	888	874	Approv. total
Supply per capita	73	83	99	105	92	85	85	84	Approv. par habitant
Puerto Rico									**Porto Rico**
Primary Energy production	* 1	0	1	0	0	0	1	1	Prod. d'énergie primaire
Net imports	...	...	12	24	27	48	55	58	Importations nettes
Total supply	* 1	0	13	24	27	48	56	60	Approv. total
Supply per capita	* 0	0	3	6	7	13	15	16	Approv. par habitant
Qatar									**Qatar**
Primary Energy production	1 009	1 364	2 449	3 718	7 428	9 184	9 271	9 166	Prod. d'énergie primaire
Net imports	-832	-811	-1 921	-2 991	-6 261	-7 618	-7 861	-7 300	Importations nettes
Changes in stocks	-22	0	-56	-1	3	-13	15	29	Variations des stocks
Total supply	199	553	584	728	1 165	1 579	1 395	1 837	Approv. total
Supply per capita	420	1 102	988	886	660	783	664	846	Approv. par habitant
Republic of Korea									**République de Corée**
Primary Energy production	941	878	1 420	1 776	1 855	1 908	1 799	2 023	Prod. d'énergie primaire
Net imports	2 840	5 319	6 505	6 810	8 703	9 034	9 257	9 192	Importations nettes
Changes in stocks	-69	115	71	-179	117	-49	49	50	Variations des stocks
Total supply	3 851	6 083	7 854	8 764	10 441	10 992	11 007	11 164	Approv. total
Supply per capita	90	136	171	186	213	222	221	223	Approv. par habitant
Republic of Moldova									**République de Moldova**
Primary Energy production	...	1	3	4	8	10	12	15	Prod. d'énergie primaire
Net imports	...	* 184	* 64	* 85	80	80	82	80	Importations nettes
Changes in stocks	...	2	0	0	-2	0	1	0	Variations des stocks
Total supply	...	183	66	89	91	91	93	95	Approv. total
Supply per capita	...	42	16	24	22	22	23	23	Approv. par habitant
Réunion									**Réunion**
Primary Energy production	8	9	7	7	8	8	9	8	Prod. d'énergie primaire
Net imports	* 16	* 23	* 36	* 44	* 50	* 50	* 48	* 49	Importations nettes
Changes in stocks	0	0	1	1	0	-2	0	-1	Variations des stocks
Total supply	24	31	42	49	58	59	57	58	Approv. total
Supply per capita	39	47	57	61	70	70	67	68	Approv. par habitant
Romania									**Roumanie**
Primary Energy production	1 695	1 335	1 194	1 173	1 155	1 142	1 090	1 109	Prod. d'énergie primaire
Net imports	936	591	331	446	311	328	240	214	Importations nettes
Changes in stocks	11	2	-8	-7	-7	2	-11	-9	Variations des stocks
Total supply	2 620	1 925	1 532	1 626	1 474	1 469	1 342	1 331	Approv. total
Supply per capita	113	85	69	75	73	74	68	68	Approv. par habitant
Russian Federation									**Fédération de Russie**
Primary Energy production	...	40 589	41 030	50 506	53 679	55 216	56 263	54 829	Prod. d'énergie primaire
Net imports	...	-13 397	-14 842	-22 870	-24 601	-24 070	-25 405	-24 793	Importations nettes
Changes in stocks	...	472	195	298	147	69	225	150	Variations des stocks
Total supply	...	26 720	25 994	27 338	28 932	31 078	30 634	29 886	Approv. total
Supply per capita	...	180	177	190	202	217	214	208	Approv. par habitant
Rwanda									**Rwanda**
Primary Energy production	28	48	46	63	76	* 81	* 83	* 84	Prod. d'énergie primaire
Net imports	* 8	* 7	* 8	* 7	* 8	* 10	* 11	* 12	Importations nettes
Changes in stocks	...	...	...	0	...	...	...	...	Variations des stocks
Total supply	35	54	54	71	84	* 91	* 95	* 96	Approv. total
Supply per capita	5	10	7	8	8	* 8	* 9	* 8	Approv. par habitant
Saint Helena									**Sainte-Hélène**
Primary Energy production	* 0	0	0	0	0	0	0	* 0	Prod. d'énergie primaire
Net imports	0	* 0	0	0	0	0	0	* 0	Importations nettes
Total supply	0	* 0	0	0	0	0	0	* 0	Approv. total
Supply per capita	17	* 27	36	33	38	41	40	* 41	Approv. par habitant

Production, trade and supply of energy *(continued)*
Petajoules and gigajoules per capita

Production, commerce et fourniture d'énergie *(suite)*
pétajoules et gigajoules par habitant

Region, country or area	1990	1995	2000	2005	2010	2012	2013	2014	Région, pays ou zone
Saint Kitts and Nevis									**Saint-Kitts-et-Nevis**
Primary Energy production	1	1	1	1	0	0	* 0	* 0	Prod. d'énergie primaire
Net imports	* 2	* 2	* 3	* 3	3	3	* 3	* 3	Importations nettes
Changes in stocks	...	...	...	...	...	0	...	...	Variations des stocks
Total supply	* 2	* 2	* 3	* 3	3	3	* 3	* 3	Approv. total
Supply per capita	* 53	* 56	* 63	* 67	61	60	* 59	* 59	Approv. par habitant
Saint Lucia									**Sainte-Lucie**
Primary Energy production	0	0	0	0	0	0	0	0	Prod. d'énergie primaire
Net imports	2	4	* 5	* 6	* 6	* 6	* 6	* 6	Importations nettes
Changes in stocks	0	...	...	...	...	...	...	...	Variations des stocks
Total supply	2	5	5	* 5	6	6	6	6	Approv. total
Supply per capita	18	31	31	* 33	33	33	33	33	Approv. par habitant
Saint Pierre and Miquelon									**Saint-Pierre-et-Miquelon**
Primary Energy production	...	...	* 0	* 0	0	0	* 0	* 0	Prod. d'énergie primaire
Net imports	2	1	* 1	* 1	* 1	* 1	* 1	* 1	Importations nettes
Total supply	1	1	* 1	* 1	* 1	* 1	* 1	* 1	Approv. total
Supply per capita	206	164	* 125	* 148	* 159	* 158	* 162	* 174	Approv. par habitant
Saint Vincent-Grenadines									**Saint-Vincent-Grenadines**
Primary Energy production	0	0	0	0	* 0	* 0	* 0	* 0	Prod. d'énergie primaire
Net imports	* 1	* 2	2	* 3	* 3	* 4	* 3	* 3	Importations nettes
Total supply	* 1	* 2	2	* 3	3	4	3	* 3	Approv. total
Supply per capita	* 12	* 19	21	* 31	31	35	29	* 29	Approv. par habitant
Samoa									**Samoa**
Primary Energy production	1	1	1	2	* 2	* 2	* 2	* 2	Prod. d'énergie primaire
Net imports	* 2	* 2	* 2	* 3	* 3	* 3	3	* 3	Importations nettes
Changes in stocks	...	...	...	...	0	...	0	...	Variations des stocks
Total supply	* 3	* 3	* 3	* 4	* 5	* 4	5	* 5	Approv. total
Supply per capita	* 16	* 17	* 19	* 21	* 24	* 23	24	* 24	Approv. par habitant
Sao Tome and Principe									**Sao Tomé-et-Principe**
Primary Energy production	1	1	1	1	1	1	1	1	Prod. d'énergie primaire
Net imports	* 1	* 1	* 1	* 1	2	* 2	* 2	* 2	Importations nettes
Total supply	* 1	1	* 2	* 2	2	* 3	* 3	* 3	Approv. total
Supply per capita	* 12	12	* 12	* 13	14	* 15	* 14	* 14	Approv. par habitant
Saudi Arabia [7]									**Arabie saoudite** [7]
Primary Energy production	16 769	19 932	20 284	24 162	22 115	26 010	25 573	25 904	Prod. d'énergie primaire
Net imports	* -13 721	-16 427	-15 797	-18 116	-14 727	-17 929	-17 702	-17 114	Importations nettes
Changes in stocks	* 172	-12	0	0	-319	-243	-114	-87	Variations des stocks
Total supply	2 875	3 516	4 487	6 047	7 707	8 324	7 985	8 876	Approv. total
Supply per capita	178	190	224	252	274	282	264	287	Approv. par habitant
Senegal									**Sénégal**
Primary Energy production	40	44	50	52	86	92	75	77	Prod. d'énergie primaire
Net imports	* 41	* 43	46	65	74	74	79	87	Importations nettes
Changes in stocks	0	0	1	3	-4	-2	-2	-1	Variations des stocks
Total supply	* 81	* 87	96	114	165	168	155	165	Approv. total
Supply per capita	* 11	* 10	10	11	13	12	11	11	Approv. par habitant
Serbia [10]									**Serbie** [10]
Primary Energy production	...	...	...	431	440	450	474	393	Prod. d'énergie primaire
Net imports	...	...	...	243	212	166	145	148	Importations nettes
Changes in stocks	...	...	...	2	4	11	0	-7	Variations des stocks
Total supply	...	...	...	672	648	605	618	550	Approv. total
Supply per capita	...	...	...	68	72	67	69	62	Approv. par habitant
Serbia and Montenegro [former]									**Serbie-et-Monténégro [anc.]**
Primary Energy production	...	497	479	...	...	...	...	...	Prod. d'énergie primaire
Net imports	...	* 25	77	...	...	...	...	...	Importations nettes
Total supply	...	522	556	...	...	...	...	...	Approv. total
Supply per capita	...	48	52	...	...	...	...	...	Approv. par habitant
Seychelles									**Seychelles**
Primary Energy production	0	0	0	0	0	0	0	0	Prod. d'énergie primaire
Net imports	1	* 4	* 9	* 10	6	6	6	* 7	Importations nettes
Changes in stocks	* 0	0	* 0	...	...	...	...	...	Variations des stocks
Total supply	2	* 3	8	10	6	6	6	7	Approv. total
Supply per capita	31	* 39	102	115	66	64	59	72	Approv. par habitant

Region, country or area	1990	1995	2000	2005	2010	2012	2013	2014	Région, pays ou zone
Sierra Leone									**Sierra Leone**
Primary Energy production	43	42	49	50	52	52	53	53	Prod. d'énergie primaire
Net imports	* 7	* 5	* 6	* 7	* 9	* 13	* 15	* 17	Importations nettes
Changes in stocks	0	...	...	...	...	...	...	...	Variations des stocks
Total supply	50	47	55	56	60	65	67	69	Approv. total
Supply per capita	13	12	13	11	10	11	11	11	Approv. par habitant
Singapore									**Singapour**
Primary Energy production	...	...	...	...	25	26	27	27	Prod. d'énergie primaire
Net imports	493	641	783	* 774	* 1 024	* 812	* 1 087	* 1 129	Importations nettes
Changes in stocks	-163	2	27	-31	-25	15	-11	4	Variations des stocks
Total supply	656	640	756	805	1 075	823	1 125	1 151	Approv. total
Supply per capita	218	184	193	189	212	155	208	209	Approv. par habitant
Sint Maarten (Dutch part)									**Saint-Martin (partie néerlandaise)**
Net imports	...	...	...	...	...	* 11	* 11	* 11	Importations nettes
Total supply	...	...	...	...	...	* 11	* 11	* 11	Approv. total
Supply per capita	...	...	...	...	...	* 311	* 306	* 303	Approv. par habitant
Slovakia									**Slovaquie**
Primary Energy production	...	210	263	265	250	261	269	264	Prod. d'énergie primaire
Net imports	...	514	485	516	475	422	424	408	Importations nettes
Changes in stocks	...	-22	4	4	-12	-4	-7	15	Variations des stocks
Total supply	...	746	744	778	737	688	700	658	Approv. total
Supply per capita	...	139	138	144	136	127	129	121	Approv. par habitant
Slovenia									**Slovénie**
Primary Energy production	...	124	129	146	157	150	151	154	Prod. d'énergie primaire
Net imports	...	129	141	160	149	150	133	124	Importations nettes
Changes in stocks	...	-1	2	0	0	4	-3	-2	Variations des stocks
Total supply	...	254	269	306	306	296	287	280	Approv. total
Supply per capita	...	129	136	153	149	143	139	135	Approv. par habitant
Solomon Islands									**Îles Salomon**
Primary Energy production	* 3	* 3	* 3	* 3	* 3	* 3	* 3	* 3	Prod. d'énergie primaire
Net imports	* 2	* 2	* 2	* 3	* 3	* 3	* 3	* 3	Importations nettes
Total supply	* 5	* 5	* 5	* 6	* 6	* 6	* 6	* 6	Approv. total
Supply per capita	* 17	* 15	* 13	* 12	* 11	* 11	* 11	* 11	Approv. par habitant
Somalia									**Somalie**
Primary Energy production	58	69	85	103	124	128	128	129	Prod. d'énergie primaire
Net imports	* 10	* 8	* 5	* 4	* 1	* 0	* 0	* 0	Importations nettes
Changes in stocks	* 0	* 0	...	...	...	...	...	...	Variations des stocks
Total supply	68	77	90	107	126	128	128	129	Approv. total
Supply per capita	10	12	12	13	13	13	12	12	Approv. par habitant
South Africa									**Afrique du Sud**
Primary Energy production	4 767	5 691	6 175	6 648	6 909	6 995	6 999	7 102	Prod. d'énergie primaire
Net imports	* -587	-1 009	-1 171	-1 183	-584	-719	-694	-545	Importations nettes
Changes in stocks	0	-68	-41	0	1	6	18	-12	Variations des stocks
Total supply	4 179	4 750	5 044	5 465	6 323	6 269	6 287	6 568	Approv. total
Supply per capita	114	115	113	114	122	119	118	122	Approv. par habitant
South Sudan									**Soudan du sud**
Primary Energy production	...	...	...	...	...	74	217	337	Prod. d'énergie primaire
Net imports	...	...	...	...	...	-47	-190	-308	Importations nettes
Total supply	...	...	...	...	...	27	28	29	Approv. total
Supply per capita	...	...	...	...	...	2	2	2	Approv. par habitant
Spain [11]									**Espagne** [11]
Primary Energy production	1 442	1 313	1 314	1 256	1 419	1 374	1 420	1 432	Prod. d'énergie primaire
Net imports	2 308	2 949	3 812	4 738	3 991	3 690	3 295	3 352	Importations nettes
Changes in stocks	6	69	52	78	73	-142	-125	52	Variations des stocks
Total supply	3 744	4 191	5 074	5 915	5 337	5 207	4 841	4 732	Approv. total
Supply per capita	96	106	126	136	115	112	104	102	Approv. par habitant
Sri Lanka									**Sri Lanka**
Primary Energy production	135	146	156	163	184	173	184	179	Prod. d'énergie primaire
Net imports	54	80	144	161	170	217	188	211	Importations nettes
Changes in stocks	2	-1	4	1	-7	8	-16	-24	Variations des stocks
Total supply	187	225	296	324	360	381	388	414	Approv. total
Supply per capita	11	12	16	16	18	19	19	20	Approv. par habitant

Region, country or area	1990	1995	2000	2005	2010	2012	2013	2014	Région, pays ou zone
State of Palestine									**État de Palestine**
Primary Energy production	* 4	* 5	* 5	8	9	8	8	9	Prod. d'énergie primaire
Net imports	* 16	* 18	33	49	45	50	53	57	Importations nettes
Changes in stocks	...	...	...	0	0	0	0	-2	Variations des stocks
Total supply	* 20	* 22	38	58	54	58	61	69	Approv. total
Supply per capita	...	* 8	12	16	13	13	14	15	Approv. par habitant
Sudan									**Soudan**
Primary Energy production	...	...	...	...	...	619	679	682	Prod. d'énergie primaire
Net imports	...	...	...	...	...	-30	* -63	-56	Importations nettes
Changes in stocks	...	...	...	...	...	* 0	* -1	...	Variations des stocks
Total supply	...	...	...	...	...	590	617	626	Approv. total
Supply per capita	...	...	...	...	...	16	16	16	Approv. par habitant
Sudan [former]									**Soudan [anc.]**
Primary Energy production	379	448	851	1 145	1 473	...	...	...	Prod. d'énergie primaire
Net imports	* 73	* 59	-287	-480	-762	...	...	...	Importations nettes
Changes in stocks	* 1	1	8	12	...	...	...	...	Variations des stocks
Total supply	451	506	556	654	711	...	...	...	Approv. total
Supply per capita	17	17	16	17	16	...	...	...	Approv. par habitant
Suriname									**Suriname**
Primary Energy production	15	17	33	32	43	45	42	44	Prod. d'énergie primaire
Net imports	* 15	* 16	* 1	* -4	* -4	* -7	* -11	* -11	Importations nettes
Changes in stocks	0	0	...	...	0	0	0	0	Variations des stocks
Total supply	30	34	36	26	40	38	31	34	Approv. total
Supply per capita	73	78	76	53	77	72	59	62	Approv. par habitant
Swaziland									**Swaziland**
Primary Energy production	20	19	34	36	33	37	38	39	Prod. d'énergie primaire
Net imports	...	* 2	* 7	* 3	* 11	* 10	* 10	* 11	Importations nettes
Changes in stocks	...	...	...	* 0	* 0	0	0	0	Variations des stocks
Total supply	20	21	41	40	44	46	48	50	Approv. total
Supply per capita	23	22	39	36	37	38	38	40	Approv. par habitant
Sweden									**Suède**
Primary Energy production	1 235	1 312	1 257	1 430	1 364	1 494	1 450	1 428	Prod. d'énergie primaire
Net imports	726	747	724	739	714	542	594	581	Importations nettes
Changes in stocks	-5	-29	9	32	-33	-42	-6	11	Variations des stocks
Total supply	1 967	2 089	1 971	2 137	2 112	2 079	2 050	1 998	Approv. total
Supply per capita	230	237	222	237	225	218	213	206	Approv. par habitant
Switzerland [12]									**Suisse** [12]
Primary Energy production	428	468	500	458	526	530	540	552	Prod. d'énergie primaire
Net imports	584	521	524	628	564	545	569	491	Importations nettes
Changes in stocks	-5	-14	-18	6	-2	7	-5	0	Variations des stocks
Total supply	1 017	1 003	1 041	1 080	1 091	1 068	1 113	1 043	Approv. total
Supply per capita	152	142	145	145	139	133	136	126	Approv. par habitant
Syrian Arab Republic									**Rép. arabe syrienne**
Primary Energy production	1 036	1 403	1 417	1 171	1 165	590	304	237	Prod. d'énergie primaire
Net imports	* -554	-813	-690	-431	-233	59	226	218	Importations nettes
Changes in stocks	6	* 5	...	1	20	0	0	0	Variations des stocks
Total supply	476	585	729	740	911	650	530	454	Approv. total
Supply per capita	39	41	46	40	44	33	27	24	Approv. par habitant
Tajikistan									**Tadjikistan**
Primary Energy production	...	56	53	66	65	71	73	76	Prod. d'énergie primaire
Net imports	...	40	38	33	29	29	32	43	Importations nettes
Total supply	...	95	91	99	94	99	106	119	Approv. total
Supply per capita	...	17	15	15	12	12	13	14	Approv. par habitant
Thailand									**Thaïlande**
Primary Energy production	1 089	1 322	1 700	2 144	2 952	3 041	3 060	3 338	Prod. d'énergie primaire
Net imports	* 699	* 1 289	* 1 308	* 1 869	* 2 027	* 2 100	2 137	2 248	Importations nettes
Changes in stocks	4	-25	-67	-54	33	* -26	-163	-57	Variations des stocks
Total supply	1 784	2 635	3 075	4 067	4 945	5 167	5 359	5 643	Approv. total
Supply per capita	31	44	49	61	74	77	79	83	Approv. par habitant
TFYR of Macedonia									**ex-R.Y. de Macédoine**
Primary Energy production	...	112	118	108	68	64	57	53	Prod. d'énergie primaire
Net imports	...	43	48	52	53	61	55	57	Importations nettes
Changes in stocks	...	5	-4	-4	-1	-2	-2	0	Variations des stocks
Total supply	...	151	169	163	121	126	113	110	Approv. total
Supply per capita	...	77	84	80	59	61	54	53	Approv. par habitant

Region, country or area	1990	1995	2000	2005	2010	2012	2013	2014	Région, pays ou zone
Timor-Leste									**Timor-Leste**
Primary Energy production	...	...	...	201	186	169	168	143	Prod. d'énergie primaire
Net imports	...	...	...	* -196	* -182	* -164	* -161	* -135	Importations nettes
Total supply	...	...	...	* 4	* 4	* 5	* 7	* 8	Approv. total
Supply per capita	...	...	...	* 4	* 4	* 5	* 6	* 7	Approv. par habitant
Togo									**Togo**
Primary Energy production	44	57	74	84	99	105	108	111	Prod. d'énergie primaire
Net imports	* 11	* 15	* 16	15	29	24	26	27	Importations nettes
Changes in stocks	0	0	0	-1	-1	-2	-2	-2	Variations des stocks
Total supply	55	71	89	99	131	131	135	139	Approv. total
Supply per capita	15	17	19	18	20	19	20	20	Approv. par habitant
Tonga									**Tonga**
Primary Energy production	0	0	0	0	0	0	0	0	Prod. d'énergie primaire
Net imports	1	1	1	* 2	* 2	* 2	* 2	* 2	Importations nettes
Total supply	1	1	1	* 2	2	2	2	2	Approv. total
Supply per capita	12	14	15	* 16	16	15	15	15	Approv. par habitant
Trinidad and Tobago									**Trinité-et-Tobago**
Primary Energy production	529	511	799	1 464	1 786	1 670	1 673	1 663	Prod. d'énergie primaire
Net imports	-271	-264	-378	-777	-954	-861	-863	-847	Importations nettes
Changes in stocks	6	-12	7	10	-13	0	-13	-6	Variations des stocks
Total supply	251	258	414	678	845	809	824	822	Approv. total
Supply per capita	206	205	321	516	636	603	611	607	Approv. par habitant
Tunisia									**Tunisie**
Primary Energy production	222	205	253	274	341	309	298	274	Prod. d'énergie primaire
Net imports	* -27	* 6	47	71	79	115	135	162	Importations nettes
Changes in stocks	2	-9	7	-4	-7	1	2	2	Variations des stocks
Total supply	192	220	293	349	427	422	430	435	Approv. total
Supply per capita	23	25	31	35	40	39	39	39	Approv. par habitant
Turkey									**Turquie**
Primary Energy production	1 087	1 112	1 085	1 004	1 352	1 282	1 310	1 303	Prod. d'énergie primaire
Net imports	1 139	1 532	2 114	2 517	3 039	3 694	3 587	3 745	Importations nettes
Changes in stocks	35	45	-3	-28	-28	57	23	-4	Variations des stocks
Total supply	2 191	2 598	3 202	3 549	4 419	4 918	4 874	5 052	Approv. total
Supply per capita	40	44	50	52	61	66	64	65	Approv. par habitant
Turkmenistan									**Turkménistan**
Primary Energy production	...	1 376	1 928	2 584	1 982	2 852	3 208	3 270	Prod. d'énergie primaire
Net imports	...	-802	-1 303	-1 779	-1 030	-1 780	-2 109	-2 148	Importations nettes
Total supply	...	574	625	805	951	1 072	1 100	1 123	Approv. total
Supply per capita	...	137	139	170	189	207	210	212	Approv. par habitant
Turks and Caicos Islands									**Îles Turques-et-Caïques**
Primary Energy production	0	0	0	0	0	0	0	0	Prod. d'énergie primaire
Net imports	* 0	* 1	* 1	* 2	* 3	* 3	* 3	* 3	Importations nettes
Total supply	* 0	* 1	* 1	* 2	* 3	* 3	* 3	* 3	Approv. total
Supply per capita	* 34	* 43	* 52	* 57	* 86	* 86	* 85	* 86	Approv. par habitant
Tuvalu									**Tuvalu**
Net imports	* 0	* 0	* 0	* 0	0	* 0	* 0	* 0	Importations nettes
Total supply	* 0	* 0	* 0	* 0	0	* 0	* 0	* 0	Approv. total
Supply per capita	* 8	* 9	* 10	* 13	13	* 13	* 13	* 13	Approv. par habitant
Uganda									**Ouganda**
Primary Energy production	271	300	321	350	379	398	401	409	Prod. d'énergie primaire
Net imports	* 9	* 12	* 17	* 26	* 46	* 46	* 53	57	Importations nettes
Changes in stocks	0	...	...	...	...	...	...	...	Variations des stocks
Total supply	281	312	338	376	425	443	454	466	Approv. total
Supply per capita	16	15	14	13	13	13	12	12	Approv. par habitant
Ukraine									**Ukraine**
Primary Energy production	...	3 661	3 231	3 328	3 238	3 552	3 578	3 203	Prod. d'énergie primaire
Net imports	...	3 411	2 343	2 458	1 762	1 605	* 1 320	* 1 159	Importations nettes
Changes in stocks	...	0	0	-86	-490	21	54	-68	Variations des stocks
Total supply	...	7 073	5 574	5 872	5 491	5 135	4 844	4 431	Approv. total
Supply per capita	...	138	114	125	120	113	107	98	Approv. par habitant
United Arab Emirates									**Émirats arabes unis**
Primary Energy production	5 177	5 661	6 571	7 293	7 541	8 470	8 681	8 642	Prod. d'énergie primaire
Net imports	* -4 375	* -4 533	-4 853	-5 450	* -4 955	* -5 593	* -5 877	-5 317	Importations nettes
Changes in stocks	12	21	...	...	...	...	...	...	Variations des stocks
Total supply	791	1 108	1 719	1 842	2 587	2 877	2 805	3 326	Approv. total
Supply per capita	437	472	567	453	311	321	310	366	Approv. par habitant

Production, trade and supply of energy *(continued)*
Petajoules and gigajoules per capita

Production, commerce et fourniture d'énergie *(suite)*
pétajoules et gigajoules par habitant

Region, country or area	1990	1995	2000	2005	2010	2012	2013	2014	Région, pays ou zone
United Kingdom [13]									**Royaume-Uni** [13]
Primary Energy production	8 595	10 588	11 247	8 483	6 217	4 880	4 576	4 482	Prod. d'énergie primaire
Net imports	-151	-1 928	-2 169	736	1 959	3 065	3 402	3 095	Importations nettes
Changes in stocks	-84	-265	-138	0	-265	-78	26	130	Variations des stocks
Total supply	8 527	8 925	9 216	9 219	8 442	8 024	7 951	7 448	Approv. total
Supply per capita	149	154	157	153	135	126	124	116	Approv. par habitant
United Rep. of Tanzania									**Rép.-Unie de Tanzanie**
Primary Energy production	178	434	543	665	789	843	889	935	Prod. d'énergie primaire
Net imports	* 29	* 44	30	57	64	89	113	111	Importations nettes
Changes in stocks	0	...	...	...	...	...	...	...	Variations des stocks
Total supply	206	477	572	722	854	932	1 002	1 046	Approv. total
Supply per capita	8	16	17	19	19	19	20	20	Approv. par habitant
United States [14]									**États-Unis** [14]
Primary Energy production	68 646	68 864	69 431	68 344	71 997	75 832	78 361	83 887	Prod. d'énergie primaire
Net imports	12 528	16 273	23 218	28 307	19 895	13 268	10 884	8 999	Importations nettes
Changes in stocks	1 606	-764	-1 980	-16	-263	-104	-1 374	688	Variations des stocks
Total supply	79 568	85 901	94 630	96 666	92 155	89 204	90 619	92 198	Approv. total
Supply per capita	314	323	335	326	297	283	286	289	Approv. par habitant
Uruguay									**Uruguay**
Primary Energy production	51	45	46	45	89	83	95	113	Prod. d'énergie primaire
Net imports	44	66	70	75	85	126	94	85	Importations nettes
Changes in stocks	-2	4	-2	-5	1	8	-7	-1	Variations des stocks
Total supply	96	107	119	126	173	202	197	199	Approv. total
Supply per capita	31	33	36	38	51	60	58	58	Approv. par habitant
Uzbekistan									**Ouzbékistan**
Primary Energy production	...	2 045	2 307	2 446	2 309	2 382	2 268	2 339	Prod. d'énergie primaire
Net imports	...	-170	-177	-395	-499	-354	-469	-510	Importations nettes
Changes in stocks	...	88	...	...	...	...	...	...	Variations des stocks
Total supply	...	1 788	2 130	2 050	1 809	2 027	1 799	1 829	Approv. total
Supply per capita	...	78	86	79	65	71	62	62	Approv. par habitant
Vanuatu									**Vanuatu**
Primary Energy production	0	0	1	1	1	1	1	1	Prod. d'énergie primaire
Net imports	* 1	* 1	* 1	* 1	* 2	* 2	* 2	* 3	Importations nettes
Changes in stocks	...	...	...	...	* 0	* 0	* 0	* 0	Variations des stocks
Total supply	1	1	* 2	2	3	3	3	3	Approv. total
Supply per capita	8	7	* 11	8	11	11	10	12	Approv. par habitant
Venezuela (Boliv. Rep. of)									**Venezuela (Rép. boliv. du)**
Primary Energy production	5 953	7 962	8 965	8 283	8 139	8 013	7 699	7 460	Prod. d'énergie primaire
Net imports	-4 027	-5 772	-6 320	-5 883	* -4 983	-4 873	-4 858	-4 733	Importations nettes
Changes in stocks	-18	24	15	-336	-54	17	39	-33	Variations des stocks
Total supply	1 944	2 167	2 629	2 737	3 211	3 123	2 803	2 760	Approv. total
Supply per capita	99	98	108	103	111	105	93	90	Approv. par habitant
Viet Nam									**Viet Nam**
Primary Energy production	787	1 136	1 733	2 612	2 747	2 856	2 878	2 977	Prod. d'énergie primaire
Net imports	-3	-207	-421	-795	-424	-324	-281	-162	Importations nettes
Changes in stocks	-6	20	50	70	5	* 82	* 86	* 56	Variations des stocks
Total supply	791	908	1 262	1 747	2 318	2 450	2 510	2 759	Approv. total
Supply per capita	12	12	16	21	26	27	27	30	Approv. par habitant
Wallis and Futuna Islands									**Îles Wallis-et-Futuna**
Net imports	...	...	...	0	0	0	0	0	Importations nettes
Total supply	...	...	...	0	0	0	0	0	Approv. total
Supply per capita	...	...	...	26	27	26	26	26	Approv. par habitant
Yemen									**Yémen**
Primary Energy production	...	713	908	844	804	619	759	668	Prod. d'énergie primaire
Net imports	...	-571	-712	-529	-477	-369	-416	-359	Importations nettes
Changes in stocks	...	0	0	40	...	...	...	...	Variations des stocks
Total supply	...	142	197	274	326	250	344	309	Approv. total
Supply per capita	...	9	11	13	14	10	13	12	Approv. par habitant
Zambia									**Zambie**
Primary Energy production	207	224	248	280	319	346	362	374	Prod. d'énergie primaire
Net imports	* 14	* 19	13	25	29	37	35	34	Importations nettes
Changes in stocks	...	-1	1	0	0	-1	-1	-6	Variations des stocks
Total supply	222	244	260	305	348	383	398	415	Approv. total
Supply per capita	28	27	25	27	25	26	26	26	Approv. par habitant

22 Production, trade and supply of energy *(continued)*
Petajoules and gigajoules per capita

Production, commerce et fourniture d'énergie *(suite)*
pétajoules et gigajoules par habitant

Region, country or area	1990	1995	2000	2005	2010	2012	2013	2014	Région, pays ou zone
Zimbabwe									**Zimbabwe**
Primary Energy production	372	362	379	379	368	353	400	482	Prod. d'énergie primaire
Net imports	* 30	64	53	36	24	49	54	49	Importations nettes
Changes in stocks	0	5	-5	1	...	...	...	67	Variations des stocks
Total supply	402	422	438	414	392	402	454	464	Approv. total
Supply per capita	38	36	35	33	28	28	30	30	Approv. par habitant

Source:

United Nations Statistics Division, New York, Energy Statistics Yearbook 2014, last accessed January 2017.

1 Excluding overseas territories.
2 For statistical purposes, the data for China do not include those for the Hong Kong Special Administrative Region (Hong Kong SAR), Macao Special Administrative Region (Macao SAR) and Taiwan Province of China.
3 Excluding the Faeroe Islands and Greenland.
4 Including Monaco.
5 Data include Timor-Leste.
6 Data include San Marino and the Holy See.
7 The data for crude oil production include 50 per cent of the output of the Neutral Zone.
8 Including Svalbard and Jan Mayen Islands.
9 Data includes the Azores and Madeira.
10 Excluding Kosovo.
11 Data include the Canary Islands.
12 Including Liechtenstein.
13 Shipments of coal and oil to Jersey, Guernsey and the isle of Man from the United Kingdom are not classed as exports. Supplies of coal and oil to these islands are, therefore, included as part of UK supply. Exports of natural gas to the Isle of Man included with the exports to Ireland.

14 Includes the 50 states and the District of Columbia. Oil statistics as well as coal trade statistics also include Puerto Rico, Guam, the U.S. Virgin Islands, American Samoa, Johnston Atoll, Midway Islands, Wake Island and the Northern Mariana Islands.

Source:

Organisation des Nations Unies, Division de statistique, New York, Annuaire des statistiques de l'Energie 2014, dernier accès janvièr 2017.

1 Non compris les départements d'outre-mer.
2 Pour la présentation des statistiques, les données pour la Chine ne comprennent pas la Région Administrative Spéciale de Hong Kong (Hong Kong RAS), la Région Administrative Spéciale de Macao (Macao RAS) et la province de Taiwan.
3 Non compris les îles Féroé et Groenland.
4 Y compris Monaco.
5 Les données comprennent Timor-Leste.
6 Les données comprennent Saint-Marin et le Saint-Siège.
7 Les données relatives à la production de pétrole brut comprennent 50 pour cent de la production de la Zone Neutre.
8 Y compris îles Svalbard et Jan Mayen.
9 Les données comprennent Azores et Madère.
10 Non compris Kosovo.
11 Les données comprennent les Iles Canaries.
12 Y compris Liechtenstein.
13 Les livraisons de charbon et de pétrole du Royaume-Uni à Jersey, Guernesey et à l'île de Man ne sont pas considérées comme des exportations ; l'approvisionnement de charbon et pétrole à ces îles fait donc partie de l'approvisionnement du Royaume-Uni. Les exportations de gaz naturel vers l'île de Man sont inclues dans les exportations vers l'Irlande.
14 Comprend les 50 États et le District de Columbia. Les statistiques pétrolières et les statistiques du commerce de charbon incluent également Puerto Rico, Guam, les îles Vierges américaines, les Samoa américaines, Johnston Atoll, les îles Midway, l'île de Wake et les îles Mariannes septentrionale.

23 Land

Thousand hectares and percent of total land

Terres

Milliers d'hectares et pourcentage de la superficie totale

Region, country or area Région, pays ou zone	Year Année	Area – Superficie ('000 hectares) Total land Superficie totale	 Arable land Terres arables	 Permanent crops Cultures permanentes	 Forest cover Superficie forestière	Area – Superficie (Percent of total)[&] Arable land Terres arables	 Permanent crops Cultures Permanentes[&]	 Forest cover Superficie forestière	Sites protected for terre-strial biodiversity Sites pour la bio. terre. dans aires protég. (%)[&&]
Total, all countries or areas	**2005**	**13 011 699**	**1 405 845**	**148 372**	**4 032 743**	**10.8**	**1.1**	**31.0**	**40.67**
Total, tous pays ou zones	**2010**	**13 009 625**	**1 388 256**	**159 210**	**4 015 673**	**10.7**	**1.2**	**30.9**	**44.79**
	2014	**13 009 010**	**1 417 153**	**164 650**	**4 002 442**	**10.9**	**1.3**	**30.8**	**46.52**
	2017	**...**	**...**	**...**	**...**	**...**	**...**	**...**	**46.62**
Africa	2005	2 964 823	216 296	30 844	654 679	7.3	1.0	22.1	...
Afrique	2010	2 964 894	226 593	33 026	638 282	7.6	1.1	21.5	...
	2014	2 964 921	234 056	34 012	626 939	7.9	1.1	21.1	...
Northern Africa	2005	838 039	41 430	5 310	36 954	4.9	0.6	4.4	22.11[1]
Afrique septentrionale	2010	838 039	42 525	5 806	36 813	5.1	0.7	4.4	25.25[1]
	2014	838 039	42 717	6 336	29 000	5.1	0.8	3.5	38.63[1]
	2017[1]	...	...	...	...	...	...	...	38.63
Sub-Saharan Africa	2005	2 126 784[2]	174 866[2]	25 534[2]	617 725[2]	8.2[2]	1.2[2]	29.0[2]	41.53
Afrique subsaharienne	2010	2 126 855[2]	184 068[2]	27 221[2]	601 469[2]	8.7[2]	1.3[2]	28.3[2]	45.72
	2014	2 126 882[2]	191 339[2]	27 676[2]	597 939[2]	9.0[2]	1.3[2]	28.1[2]	47.16
	2017	...	...	...	...	...	...	...	47.38
Eastern Africa	2005	605 629	55 768	6 913	203 745	9.2	1.1	33.6	...
Afrique orientale	2010	605 700	62 720	7 604	196 249	10.4	1.3	32.4	...
	2014	605 727	66 395	7 908	198 527	11.0	1.3	32.8	...
Middle Africa	2005	649 682	23 346	2 762	310 491	3.6	0.4	47.8	...
Afrique centrale	2010	649 682	24 364	3 015	306 378	3.8	0.5	47.2	...
	2014	649 682	25 904	3 201	303 876	4.0	0.5	46.8	...
Southern Africa	2005	265 067	14 730	406	29 429	5.6	0.2	11.1	...
Afrique australe	2010	265 067	14 089	460	28 489	5.3	0.2	10.7	...
	2014	265 067	14 146	444	27 806	5.3	0.2	10.5	...
Western Africa	2005	606 406	81 022	15 453	74 060	13.4	2.5	12.2	...
Afrique occidentale	2010	606 406	82 895	16 142	70 353	13.7	2.7	11.6	...
	2014	606 406	84 894	16 123	67 729	14.0	2.7	11.2	...
Americas	2005	3 880 552	367 910	29 413	1 616 564	9.5	0.8	41.7	...
Amériques	2010	3 879 102	364 013	27 990	1 602 412	9.4	0.7	41.3	...
	2014	3 878 860	376 185	27 584	1 594 613	9.7	0.7	41.1	...
Northern America	2005	1 866 616	210 385	9 573	652 337	11.3	0.5	34.9	...
Amérique septentrionale	2010	1 865 166	199 327	7 621	656 026	10.7	0.4	35.2	...
	2014	1 865 166	200 623	7 241	656 940	10.8	0.4	35.2	...
Latin America & the Caribbean	2005	2 013 936[2]	157 525[2]	19 840[2]	964 227[2]	7.8[2]	1.0[2]	47.9[2]	32.75
Amérique latine et Caraïbes	2010	2 013 936[2]	164 686[2]	20 369[2]	946 386[2]	8.2[2]	1.0[2]	47.0[2]	36.26
	2014	2 013 694[2]	175 563[2]	20 343[2]	937 673[2]	8.7[2]	1.0[2]	46.6[2]	37.79
	2017	...	...	...	...	...	...	...	37.96
Caribbean	2005	22 598	5 699	1 324	6 340	25.2	5.9	28.1	...
Caraïbes	2010	22 598	5 579	1 317	6 744	24.7	5.8	29.8	...
	2014	22 356	5 257	1 278	7 104	23.5	5.7	31.8	...
Central America	2005	245 227	29 276	4 837	89 276	11.9	2.0	36.4	...
Amérique centrale	2010	245 227	28 796	5 127	87 508	11.7	2.1	35.7	...
	2014	245 227	28 074	5 225	86 534	11.4	2.1	35.3	...
South America	2005	1 746 111	122 551	13 679	868 611	7.0	0.8	49.7	...
Amérique du Sud	2010	1 746 111	130 311	13 925	852 133	7.5	0.8	48.8	...
	2014	1 746 111	142 232	13 840	844 035	8.1	0.8	48.3	...
Asia	2005	3 103 540	492 151	70 530	580 868	15.9	2.3	18.7	...
Asie	2010	3 103 331	480 787	81 156	589 405	15.5	2.6	19.0	...
	2014	3 103 224	481 539	86 213	592 570	15.5	2.8	19.1	...
Central Asia	2005	392 679	37 043	705	12 038	9.4	0.2	3.1	...
Asie centrale	2010	392 679	37 001	701	11 799	9.4	0.2	3.0	...
	2014	392 562	37 746	777	11 724	9.6	0.2	3.0	...
Eastern Asia	2005	1 156 002	121 906	13 296	241 841	10.5	1.2	20.9	44.87[3]
Asie orientale	2010	1 156 045	116 625	15 468	250 504	10.1	1.3	21.7	45.89[3]
	2014	1 156 071	114 914	16 972	255 738	9.9	1.5	22.1	46.65[3]
	2017[3]	...	...	...	...	...	...	...	46.66
South-eastern Asia	2005	434 076	65 548	36 521	217 123	15.1	8.4	50.0	31.37
Asie du Sud-Est	2010	434 067	68 194	42 500	214 594	15.7	9.8	49.4	33.65
	2014	434 050	69 538	44 727	211 526	16.0	10.3	48.7	35.17
	2017	...	...	...	...	...	...	...	35.20

Land *(continued)*
Thousand hectares and percent of total land

Terres *(suite)*
Milliers d'hectares et pourcentage de la superficie totale

Region, country or area Région, pays ou zone	Year Année	Area – Superficie ('000 hectares) Total land Superficie totale	Arable land Terres arables	Permanent crops Cultures permanentes	Forest cover Superficie forestière	Area – Superficie (Percent of total)[&] Arable land Terres arables	Permanent crops Cultures Permanentes[&]	Forest cover Superficie forestière	Sites protected for terre-strial biodiversity Sites pour la bio. terre. dans aires protég. (%)[&&]
Southern Asia Asie méridionale	2005	640 034	225 413	14 631	91 519	35.2	2.3	14.3	29.48
	2010	640 034	220 858	16 865	93 406	34.5	2.6	14.6	30.57
	2014	640 034	220 445	17 798	93 951	34.4	2.8	14.7	33.14
	2017	...	...	...	...	...	...	...	33.14
Western Asia Asie occidentale	2005	480 749	42 240	5 377	18 347	8.8	1.1	3.8	6.25[4]
	2010	480 506	38 110	5 623	19 103	7.9	1.2	4.0	8.04[4]
	2014	480 507	38 897	5 939	19 632	8.1	1.2	4.1	9.32[4]
	2017[4]	...	...	...	...	...	...	...	9.33
Europe Europe	2005	2 214 130	279 163	16 166	1 004 147	12.6	0.7	45.4	...
	2010	2 213 644	273 243	15 435	1 013 572	12.3	0.7	45.8	...
	2014	2 213 351	277 271	15 294	1 015 100	12.5	0.7	45.9	...
Eastern Europe Europe orientale	2005	1 805 641	195 108	4 505	852 968	10.8	0.2	47.2	...
	2010	1 805 269	190 941	4 275	859 827	10.6	0.2	47.6	...
	2014	1 805 260	195 273	4 107	860 305	10.8	0.2	47.7	...
Northern Europe Europe septentrionale	2005	170 310	18 781	139	74 437	11.0	0.1	43.7	...
	2010	170 245	19 208	115	74 570	11.3	0.1	43.8	...
	2014	169 915	19 707	113	74 702	11.6	0.1	44.0	...
Southern Europe Europe méridionale	2005	129 659	31 187	10 069	43 296	24.1	7.8	33.4	...
	2010	129 633	29 256	9 685	45 100	22.6	7.5	34.8	...
	2014	129 655	28 408	9 725	45 531	21.9	7.5	35.1	...
Western Europe Europe occidentale	2005	108 521	34 086	1 453	33 446	31.4	1.3	30.8	...
	2010	108 497	33 837	1 359	34 076	31.2	1.3	31.4	...
	2014	108 522	33 883	1 349	34 562	31.2	1.2	31.8	...
Oceania Océanie	2005	848 655	50 326	1 419	176 485	5.9	0.2	20.8	10.67
	2010	848 655	43 620	1 602	172 002	5.1	0.2	20.3	20.61
	2014	848 655	48 102	1 548	173 219	5.7	0.2	20.4	21.03
	2017	...	...	...	...	...	...	...	21.48
Australia and New Zealand Australie et Nouvelle-Zélande	2005	794 565	49 827	403	137 824	6.3	0.1	17.3	46.58
	2010	794 565	43 067	471	133 362	5.4	0.1	16.8	51.29
	2014	794 565	47 547	417	134 595	6.0	0.1	16.9	53.14
	2017	...	...	...	...	...	...	...	53.14
Melanesia Mélanésie	2005	52 959	453	873	38 103	0.9	1.6	71.9	...
	2010	52 959	511	994	38 058	1.0	1.9	71.9	...
	2014	52 959	511	994	38 044	1.0	1.9	71.8	...
Micronesia Micronésie	2005	317	11	70	185	3.3	22.2	58.4	...
	2010	317	9	69	185	2.8	21.9	58.2	...
	2014	317	9	68	184	2.8	21.4	58.0	...
Polynesia Polynésie	2005	814	36	73	372	4.4	9.0	45.8	...
	2010	814	33	68	397	4.1	8.3	48.8	...
	2014	814	35	69	396	4.2	8.5	48.7	...
Afghanistan Afghanistan	2005	* 65 286	7 805	105	* 1 350	* 12.0	* 0.2	* 2.1	0.04
	2010	* 65 286	7 793	118	* 1 350	* 11.9	* 0.2	* 2.1	6.14
	2014	* 65 286	7 771	139	* 1 350	* 11.9	* 0.2	* 2.1	6.14
	2017	...	...	...	...	...	...	...	6.14
Albania Albanie	2005	2 740	538	121	* 782	19.6	4.4	* 28.6	43.98
	2010	2 740	626	70	* 776	22.8	2.6	* 28.3	58.81
	2014	2 740	616	80	* 772	22.5	2.9	* 28.2	68.50
	2017	...	...	...	...	...	...	...	68.50
Algeria Algérie	2005	238 174	7 511	852	1 536	3.2	0.4	0.6	38.43
	2010	238 174	7 502	909	1 918	3.1	0.4	0.8	38.43
	2014	238 174	7 469	970	* 1 948	3.1	0.4	* 0.8	38.81
	2017	...	...	...	...	...	...	...	38.81
American Samoa Samoa américaines	2005	20	* 3	* 2	* 18	* 16.5	* 8.5	* 89.4	61.50
	2010	20	* 3	* 2	* 18	* 15.0	* 9.5	* 88.6	61.50
	2014	20	* 3	* 2	* 18	* 15.0	* 9.5	* 87.9	61.50
	2017	...	...	...	...	...	...	...	61.50
Andorra Andorre	2005	47	3	...	* 16	5.3	...	* 34.0	5.73
	2010	47	3	...	* 16	5.3	...	* 34.0	5.73
	2014	47	3	...	* 16	6.0	...	* 34.0	19.40
	2017	...	...	...	...	...	...	...	19.40

23 Land *(continued)*
Thousand hectares and percent of total land

Terres *(suite)*
Milliers d'hectares et pourcentage de la superficie totale

Region, country or area Région, pays ou zone	Year Année	Area – Superficie ('000 hectares) Total land Superficie totale	Arable land Terres arables	Permanent crops Cultures permanentes	Forest cover Superficie forestière	Area – Superficie (Percent of total)[&] Arable land Terres arables	Permanent crops Cultures Permanentes[&]	Forest cover Superficie forestière	Sites protected for terre-strial biodiversity Sites pour la bio. terre. dans aires protég. (%)[&&]
Angola Angola	2005	124 670	* 3 300	* 290	59 104	* 2.6	* 0.2	47.4	28.37
	2010	124 670	* 4 100	* 290	58 480	* 3.3	* 0.2	46.9	28.37
	2014	124 670	* 4 900	* 290	* 57 981	* 3.9	* 0.2	* 46.5	28.37
	2017	...	...	...	...	...	...	...	28.37
Anguilla Anguilla	2005	9	...	...	* 6	...	...	* 61.1	6.30
	2010	9	...	...	* 6	...	...	* 61.1	6.30
	2014	9	...	...	* 6	...	...	* 61.1	6.30
	2017	...	...	...	...	...	...	...	6.30
Antigua and Barbuda Antigua-et-Barbuda	2005	44	* 4	* 1	* 10	* 9.1	* 2.3	* 22.3	18.96
	2010	44	* 4	* 1	* 10	* 9.1	* 2.3	* 22.3	18.96
	2014	44	* 4	* 1	* 10	* 9.1	* 2.3	* 22.3	18.96
	2017	...	...	...	...	...	...	...	18.96
Argentina Argentine	2005	* 273 669	* 32 898	* 1 000	30 186	* 12.0	* 0.4	* 11.0	29.69
	2010	* 273 669	* 37 981	* 1 000	28 596	* 13.9	* 0.4	* 10.4	32.00
	2014	* 273 669	* 39 200	* 1 000	* 27 409	* 14.3	* 0.4	* 10.0	32.49
	2017	...	...	...	...	...	...	...	33.21
Armenia Arménie	2005	2 847	* 455	50	332	* 16.0	1.8	11.7	24.84
	2010	2 847	449	55	331	15.8	1.9	11.6	30.54
	2014	* 2 847	448	58	* 332	* 15.7	* 2.0	* 11.7	30.54
	2017	...	...	...	...	...	...	...	30.54
Aruba Aruba	2005	18	* 2	...	* ~0	* 11.1	...	* 2.3	0.00
	2010	18	* 2	...	* ~0	* 11.1	...	* 2.3	0.00
	2014	18	* 2	...	* ~0	* 11.1	...	* 2.3	0.00
	2017	...	...	...	...	...	...	...	0.00
Australia Australie	2005	768 230	* 49 402	* 340	127 641	* 6.4	* ~0.0	16.6	46.25
	2010	768 230	* 42 568	* 400	123 211	* 5.5	* 0.1	16.0	51.30
	2014	768 230	* 46 957	* 350	* 124 443	* 6.1	* ~0.0	* 16.2	53.23
	2017	...	...	...	...	...	...	...	53.23
Austria Autriche	2005	* 8 258	1 381	66	3 851	* 16.7	* 0.8	* 46.6	62.61
	2010	8 257	1 364	65	3 860	16.5	0.8	46.7	64.90
	2014	8 252	1 352	65	* 3 867	16.4	0.8	* 46.9	65.02
	2017	...	...	...	...	...	...	...	65.03
Azerbaijan Azerbaïdjan	2005	8 266	1 843	222	* 877	22.3	2.7	* 10.6	33.27
	2010	8 266	1 884	227	* 1 008	22.8	2.8	* 12.2	39.42
	2014	8 266	1 927	234	* 1 113	23.3	2.8	* 13.5	39.42
	2017	...	...	...	...	...	...	...	39.42
Bahamas Bahamas	2005	* 1 001	* 7	* 4	* 515	* 0.7	* 0.4	* 51.4	9.75
	2010	* 1 001	* 9	* 4	* 515	* 0.9	* 0.4	* 51.4	9.81
	2014	* 1 001	* 8	* 4	* 515	* 0.8	* 0.4	* 51.4	9.81
	2017	...	...	...	...	...	...	...	9.81
Bahrain Bahreïn	2005	74	* 2	* 3	* ~0	* 2.0	* 4.3	* 0.6	19.61
	2010	76	* 2	* 3	* 1	* 2.1	* 3.9	* 0.7	27.46
	2014	77	* 2	* 3	* 1	* 2.1	* 3.9	* 0.8	27.46
	2017	...	...	...	...	...	...	...	27.46
Bangladesh Bangladesh	2005	13 017	* 7 911	* 800	1 455	* 60.8	* 6.1	11.2	37.92
	2010	* 13 017	* 7 791	* 850	1 442	* 59.9	* 6.5	* 11.1	48.00
	2014	* 13 017	* 7 669	* 830	* 1 432	* 58.9	* 6.4	* 11.0	48.02
	2017	...	...	...	...	...	...	...	48.02
Barbados Barbade	2005	43	* 13	* 1	6	* 30.2	* 2.3	14.7	2.07
	2010	43	* 12	* 1	6	* 27.9	* 2.3	14.7	2.07
	2014	43	* 11	* 1	* 6	* 25.6	* 2.3	* 14.7	2.07
	2017	...	...	...	...	...	...	...	2.07
Belarus Bélarus	2005	20 283	5 542	118	8 436	27.3	0.6	41.6	36.95
	2010	20 290	5 535	122	8 534	27.3	0.6	42.1	37.26
	2014	* 20 291	* 5 670	118	* 8 614	* 27.9	* 0.6	* 42.5	45.41
	2017	...	...	...	...	...	...	...	47.06
Belgium Belgique	2005	3 028	843	21	674	27.8	0.7	22.3	79.39
	2010	3 028	834	22	681	27.5	0.7	22.5	79.44
	2014	* 3 028	817	22	* 683	* 27.0	* 0.7	* 22.6	79.44
	2017	...	...	...	...	...	...	...	79.44

23 Land (continued)

Thousand hectares and percent of total land

Terres (suite)

Milliers d'hectares et pourcentage de la superficie totale

Region, country or area Région, pays ou zone	Year Année	Area – Superficie ('000 hectares) Total land Superficie totale	Arable land Terres arables	Permanent crops Cultures permanentes	Forest cover Superficie forestière	Area – Superficie (Percent of total)& Arable land Terres arables	Permanent crops Cultures Permanentes&	Forest cover Superficie forestière	Sites protected for terre-strial biodiversity Sites pour la bio. terre. dans aires protég. (%)&&
Belize	2005	2 281	* 70	* 32	* 1 417	* 3.1	* 1.4	* 62.1	45.75
Belize	2010	* 2 281	* 75	* 32	* 1 391	* 3.3	* 1.4	* 61.0	45.77
	2014	* 2 281	* 78	* 32	* 1 371	* 3.4	* 1.4	* 60.1	45.96
	2017	...	...	...	...	...	...	...	45.96
Benin	2005	* 11 276	* 2 700	* 270	4 811	* 23.9	* 2.4	* 42.7	77.38
Bénin	2010	* 11 276	* 2 540	* 350	4 561	* 22.5	* 3.1	* 40.4	77.38
	2014	* 11 276	* 2 700	* 500	* 4 361	* 23.9	* 4.4	* 38.7	77.38
	2017	...	...	...	...	...	...	...	77.38
Bermuda	2005	5	~0	...	* 1	8.0	...	* 20.0	57.66
Bermudes	2010	5	~0	...	* 1	6.0	...	* 20.0	57.66
	2014	* 5	* ~0	...	* 1	* 6.0	...	* 20.0	57.66
	2017	...	...	...	...	...	...	...	57.66
Bhutan	2005	3 812	* 167	* 19	2 656	* 4.4	* 0.5	69.7	38.56
Bhoutan	2010	3 812	101	12	2 705	2.6	0.3	71.0	41.23
	2014	3 812	100	12	* 2 745	2.6	0.3	* 72.0	42.92
	2017	...	...	...	...	...	...	...	42.92
Bolivia (Plurin. State of)	2005	108 330	3 806	199	58 734	3.5	0.2	54.2	53.50
Bolivie (État plurin. de)	2010	* 108 330	* 4 297	* 219	56 209	* 4.0	* 0.2	* 51.9	55.41
	2014	* 108 330	* 4 473	* 232	* 55 053	* 4.1	* 0.2	* 50.8	57.04
	2017	...	...	...	...	...	...	...	57.04
Bonaire, St. Eustatius & Saba	2005	...	...	...	...	...	...	...	41.87
Bonaire, St-Eustache et	2010	...	...	...	...	...	...	...	41.87
Saba	2017	...	...	...	...	...	...	...	41.87
Bosnia and Herzegovina	2005	5 120	1 025	95	* 2 185	20.0	1.9	* 42.7	~0.00
Bosnie-Herzégovine	2010	5 120	1 004	105	* 2 185	19.6	2.1	* 42.7	12.46
	2014	5 120	1 011	106	* 2 185	19.7	2.1	* 42.7	12.46
	2017	...	...	...	...	...	...	...	12.46
Botswana	2005	* 56 673	* 240	2	11 943	* 0.4	* ~0.0	* 21.1	47.10
Botswana	2010	* 56 673	259	* 2	11 351	* 0.5	* ~0.0	* 20.0	47.10
	2014	* 56 673	* 399	* 2	* 10 942	* 0.7	* ~0.0	* 19.3	47.10
	2017	...	...	...	...	...	...	...	47.10
Brazil	2005	* 835 814	* 69 157	* 7 276	506 734	* 8.3	* 0.9	* 60.6	42.07
Brésil	2010	* 835 814	* 70 363	* 7 100	498 458	* 8.4	* 0.8	* 59.6	47.25
	2014	* 835 814	* 80 017	* 6 572	* 494 522	* 9.6	* 0.8	* 59.2	47.36
	2017	...	...	...	...	...	...	...	47.36
British Indian Ocean Terr.	2005	...	...	...	...	...	...	...	99.91
Terr. brit. de l'océan Indien	2010	...	...	...	...	...	...	...	99.91
	2017	...	...	...	...	...	...	...	99.91
British Virgin Islands	2005	15	* 1	* 1	* 4	* 6.7	* 6.7	* 24.4	6.98
Îles Vierges britanniques	2010	15	* 1	* 1	* 4	* 6.7	* 6.7	* 24.3	6.98
	2014	15	* 1	* 1	* 4	* 6.7	* 6.7	* 24.1	6.98
	2017	...	...	...	...	...	...	...	6.98
Brunei Darussalam	2005	527	* 2	* 5	* 389	* 0.4	* 0.9	* 73.8	62.88
Brunéi Darussalam	2010	* 527	* 4	* 6	* 380	* 0.8	* 1.1	* 72.1	62.88
	2014	* 527	* 5	* 6	* 380	* 0.9	* 1.1	* 72.1	62.88
	2017	...	...	...	...	...	...	...	62.88
Bulgaria	2005	10 864	3 173	188	3 651	29.2	1.7	33.6	40.88
Bulgarie	2010	* 10 856	3 186	164	3 737	* 29.3	* 1.5	* 34.4	95.56
	2014	* 10 856	3 486	127	* 3 806	* 32.1	* 1.2	* 35.1	95.57
	2017	...	...	...	...	...	...	...	95.57
Burkina Faso	2005	* 27 360	* 4 900	* 70	5 949	* 17.9	* 0.3	* 21.7	66.71
Burkina Faso	2010	* 27 360	* 6 000	* 80	5 649	* 21.9	* 0.3	* 20.6	71.83
	2014	* 27 360	* 6 000	* 100	* 5 410	* 21.9	* 0.4	* 19.8	71.83
	2017	...	...	...	...	...	...	...	71.83
Burundi	2005	* 2 568	* 956	* 380	181	* 37.2	* 14.8	* 7.0	45.51
Burundi	2010	* 2 568	* 950	* 400	253	* 37.0	* 15.6	* 9.9	45.51
	2014	* 2 568	* 1 200	* 350	* 271	* 46.7	* 13.6	* 10.6	51.19
	2017	...	...	...	...	...	...	...	51.19
Cabo Verde	2005	403	* 48	* 2	84	* 11.9	* 0.5	20.7	0.00
Cabo Verde	2010	403	* 50	* 3	85	* 12.4	* 0.7	21.1	0.00
	2014	403	* 55	* 4	* 89	* 13.6	* 1.0	* 22.1	7.08
	2017	...	...	...	...	...	...	...	7.08

Land *(continued)*
Thousand hectares and percent of total land

Terres *(suite)*
Milliers d'hectares et pourcentage de la superficie totale

Region, country or area Région, pays ou zone	Year Année	Area – Superficie ('000 hectares) Total land Superficie totale	Arable land Terres arables	Permanent crops Cultures permanentes	Forest cover Superficie forestière	Area – Superficie (Percent of total)& Arable land Terres arables	Permanent crops Cultures Permanentes&	Forest cover Superficie forestière	Sites protected for terre-strial biodiversity Sites pour la bio. terre. dans aires protég. (%)&&
Cambodia Cambodge	2005	17 652	* 3 700	156	10 731	* 21.0	0.9	60.8	38.12
	2010	* 17 652	* 3 800	* 155	10 094	* 21.5	* 0.9	* 57.2	39.54
	2014	* 17 652	* 3 800	* 155	* 9 584	* 21.5	* 0.9	* 54.3	39.54
	2017	...	...	...	...	...	...	...	39.54
Cameroon Cameroun	2005	47 271	5 963	* 1 250	21 016	12.6	* 2.6	44.5	30.49
	2010	* 47 271	* 6 200	* 1 500	19 916	* 13.1	* 3.2	* 42.1	33.05
	2014	* 47 271	* 6 200	* 1 550	* 19 036	* 13.1	* 3.3	* 40.3	36.31
	2017	...	...	...	...	...	...	...	36.31
Canada Canada	2005	909 351	* 45 266	* 6 873	347 576	* 5.0	* 0.8	38.2	21.16
	2010	909 351	* 43 397	* 5 021	347 302	* 4.8	* 0.6	38.2	25.39
	2014	909 351	* 46 015	* 4 641	* 347 116	* 5.1	* 0.5	* 38.2	25.54
	2017	...	...	...	...	...	...	...	25.66
Cayman Islands Îles Caïmanes	2005	24	* ~0	* 1	* 13	* 0.8	* 2.1	* 52.9	31.64
	2010	24	* ~0	* 1	* 13	* 0.8	* 2.1	* 52.9	31.67
	2014	24	* ~0	* 1	* 13	* 0.8	* 2.1	* 52.9	32.51
	2017	...	...	...	...	...	...	...	32.51
Central African Republic République centrafricaine	2005	62 298	* 1 930	* 85	22 326	* 3.1	* 0.1	35.8	74.23
	2010	62 298	* 1 800	* 80	22 248	* 2.9	* 0.1	35.7	74.37
	2014	62 298	* 1 800	* 80	* 22 186	* 2.9	* 0.1	* 35.6	74.37
	2017	...	...	...	...	...	...	...	74.37
Chad Tchad	2005	125 920	* 4 500	* 30	6 141	* 3.6	* ~0.0	4.9	70.63
	2010	125 920	* 4 500	* 35	5 508	* 3.6	* ~0.0	4.4	70.63
	2014	* 125 920	* 4 900	* 35	* 5 002	* 3.9	* ~0.0	* 4.0	70.63
	2017	...	...	...	...	...	...	...	70.63
Channel Islands Îles Anglo-Normandes	2005	19	* 4	...	* 1	* 20.0	...	* 4.2	...
	2010	19	* 4	...	* 1	* 22.6	...	* 4.2	...
	2014	19	* 4	...	* 1	* 21.9	...	* 4.2	...
Chile Chili	2005	74 353	* 1 450	* 435	16 042	* 2.0	* 0.6	21.6	33.42
	2010	74 353	* 1 271	* 457	16 231	* 1.7	* 0.6	21.8	35.19
	2014	* 74 353	* 1 289	* 457	* 17 434	* 1.7	* 0.6	* 23.4	35.19
	2017	...	...	...	...	...	...	...	35.66
China [5] Chine [5]	2005	* 938 821	* 112 250	* 12 350	193 044	* 12.0	* 1.3	* 20.6	51.20
	2010	* 938 821	* 107 220	* 14 500	200 610	* 11.4	* 1.5	* 21.4	51.40
	2014	* 938 821	* 105 700	* 16 020	* 206 779	* 11.3	* 1.7	* 22.0	52.04
	2017	...	...	...	...	...	...	...	52.05
China, Hong Kong SAR Chine, Hong Kong RAS	2005	105	* 5	* 1	...	* 4.8	* 1.0	...	56.66
	2010	* 105	* 4	* 1	...	* 3.3	* 1.0	...	56.66
	2014	* 105	* 3	* 1	...	* 3.0	* 1.0	...	56.66
	2017	...	...	...	...	...	...	...	56.66
China, Macao SAR Chine, Macao RAS	2005	3	...	...	...	...	...	...	0.00
	2010	3	...	...	...	...	...	...	0.00
	2014	3	...	...	...	...	...	...	0.00
	2017	...	...	...	...	...	...	...	0.00
Christmas Island Île Christmas	2005	...	...	...	...	...	...	...	79.63
	2010	...	...	...	...	...	...	...	79.63
	2017	...	...	...	...	...	...	...	79.63
Colombia Colombie	2005	110 950	* 2 026	* 1 587	60 201	* 1.8	* 1.4	54.3	25.56
	2010	110 950	* 1 763	* 1 590	58 635	* 1.6	* 1.4	52.8	30.92
	2014	110 950	* 1 675	* 1 873	* 58 528	* 1.5	* 1.7	* 52.8	38.61
	2017	...	...	...	...	...	...	...	38.61
Comoros Comores	2005	186	* 65	* 53	* 42	* 34.9	* 28.5	* 22.6	0.00
	2010	186	* 65	* 53	* 39	* 34.9	* 28.5	* 21.0	14.84
	2014	186	* 65	* 53	* 37	* 34.9	* 28.5	* 20.1	14.84
	2017	...	...	...	...	...	...	...	14.84
Congo Congo	2005	* 34 150	* 490	* 57	22 471	* 1.4	* 0.2	* 65.8	51.53
	2010	* 34 150	* 510	* 66	22 411	* 1.5	* 0.2	* 65.6	61.21
	2014	* 34 150	* 550	* 77	* 22 349	* 1.6	* 0.2	* 65.4	72.12
	2017	...	...	...	...	...	...	...	72.12
Cook Islands Îles Cook	2005	24	* 1	* 1	15	* 5.2	* 6.2	62.9	16.75
	2010	24	* 1	* 1	15	* 2.9	* 2.7	62.9	16.75
	2014	24	* 1	* 1	* 15	* 4.2	* 2.1	* 62.9	16.75
	2017	...	...	...	...	...	...	...	16.75

Region, country or area Région, pays ou zone	Year Année	Area – Superficie ('000 hectares) Total land Superficie totale	Arable land Terres arables	Permanent crops Cultures permanentes	Forest cover Superficie forestière	Area – Superficie (Percent of total)[&] Arable land Terres arables	Permanent crops Cultures Permanentes[&]	Forest cover Superficie forestière	Sites protected for terre-strial biodiversity Sites pour la bio. terre. dans aires protég. (%)[&&]
Costa Rica Costa Rica	2005	* 5 106	* 210	* 280	2 491	* 4.1	* 5.5	* 48.8	44.76
	2010	* 5 106	* 225	* 315	2 605	* 4.4	* 6.2	* 51.0	45.33
	2014	* 5 106	232	314	* 2 726	* 4.5	* 6.1	* 53.4	45.33
	2017	...	...	...	...	...	...	...	45.33
Côte d'Ivoire Côte d'Ivoire	2005	* 31 800	* 2 800	* 4 200	* 10 405	* 8.8	* 13.2	* 32.7	77.66
	2010	* 31 800	* 2 900	* 4 500	* 10 403	* 9.1	* 14.2	* 32.7	77.66
	2014	* 31 800	* 2 900	* 4 500	* 10 401	* 9.1	* 14.2	* 32.7	77.66
	2017	...	...	...	...	...	...	...	77.66
Croatia Croatie	2005	5 596	873	73	1 903	15.6	1.3	34.0	20.53
	2010	5 596	904	84	1 920	16.2	1.5	34.3	22.25
	2014	5 596	813	78	* 1 922	14.5	1.4	* 34.3	65.22
	2017	...	...	...	...	...	...	...	65.23
Cuba Cuba	2005	10 644	* 3 672	425	2 697	* 34.5	4.0	25.3	44.10
	2010	* 10 644	* 3 384	* 420	2 932	* 31.8	* 3.9	* 27.5	69.42
	2014	10 402	* 3 088	427	* 3 146	* 29.7	4.1	* 30.2	74.32
	2017	...	...	...	...	...	...	...	74.32
Curaçao Curaçao	2005	...	...	...	...	...	...	...	6.07
	2010	...	...	...	...	...	...	...	6.07
	2017	...	...	...	...	...	...	...	40.41
Cyprus Chypre	2005	924	123	43	173	13.3	4.7	18.7	36.08
	2010	924	83	30	173	8.9	3.2	18.7	54.55
	2014	924	80	27	* 173	8.6	2.9	* 18.7	57.81
	2017	...	...	...	...	...	...	...	57.81
Czechia Tchéquie	2005	7 726	3 209	77	2 647	41.5	1.0	34.3	89.21
	2010	7 724	3 171	77	2 657	41.1	1.0	34.4	93.79
	2014	7 721	3 143	76	* 2 665	40.7	1.0	* 34.5	93.79
	2017	...	...	...	...	...	...	...	93.79
Dem. People's Rep. Korea Rép. pop. dém. de Corée	2005	* 12 041	* 2 350	* 200	* 6 299	* 19.5	* 1.7	* 52.3	10.16
	2010	* 12 041	* 2 400	* 230	* 5 666	* 19.9	* 1.9	* 47.1	10.16
	2014	* 12 041	* 2 350	* 230	* 5 158	* 19.5	* 1.9	* 42.8	10.16
	2017	...	...	...	...	...	...	...	10.16
Dem. Rep. of the Congo Rép. dém. du Congo	2005	* 226 705	* 6 700	* 750	155 692	* 3.0	* 0.3	* 68.7	34.72
	2010	* 226 705	* 6 800	* 765	154 135	* 3.0	* 0.3	* 68.0	36.69
	2014	* 226 705	* 7 100	* 900	* 152 889	* 3.1	* 0.4	* 67.4	36.69
	2017	...	...	...	...	...	...	...	36.69
Denmark Danemark	2005	4 243	2 332	7	558	55.0	0.2	13.1	89.80
	2010	4 243	2 421	5	587	57.1	0.1	13.8	90.26
	2014	* 4 226	2 432	4	* 607	* 57.5	* 0.1	* 14.4	90.29
	2017	...	...	...	...	...	...	...	90.29
Djibouti Djibouti	2005	* 2 318	* 1	...	* 6	* ~0.0	...	* 0.2	0.00
	2010	* 2 318	2	...	* 6	* 0.1	...	* 0.2	0.00
	2014	* 2 318	* 2	...	* 6	* 0.1	...	* 0.2	0.95
	2017	...	...	...	...	...	...	...	0.95
Dominica Dominique	2005	75	* 5	* 15	* 46	* 6.7	* 20.0	* 61.3	44.26
	2010	75	* 6	* 17	* 45	* 8.0	* 22.7	* 59.5	44.26
	2014	75	* 6	* 17	* 44	* 8.0	* 22.7	* 58.1	44.26
	2017	...	...	...	...	...	...	...	44.26
Dominican Republic République dominicaine	2005	4 831	* 820	* 400	1 652	* 17.0	* 8.3	34.2	71.41
	2010	4 831	* 800	* 400	1 817	* 16.6	* 8.3	37.6	71.41
	2014	4 831	* 800	* 355	* 1 950	* 16.6	* 7.3	* 40.4	74.59
	2017	...	...	...	...	...	...	...	74.59
Ecuador Équateur	2005	24 836	1 296	1 214	13 335	5.2	4.9	53.7	25.74
	2010	24 836	1 186	1 391	12 942	4.8	5.6	52.1	28.02
	2014	24 836	1 018	1 461	* 12 627	4.1	5.9	* 50.8	29.14
	2017	...	...	...	...	...	...	...	29.14
Egypt Égypte	2005	99 545	* 2 563	960	67	* 2.6	1.0	0.1	37.86
	2010	* 99 545	2 873	798	70	* 2.9	* 0.8	* 0.1	39.64
	2014	* 99 545	2 670	1 075	* 72	* 2.7	* 1.1	* 0.1	39.64
	2017	...	...	...	...	...	...	...	39.64

23 Land *(continued)*
Thousand hectares and percent of total land

Terres *(suite)*
Milliers d'hectares et pourcentage de la superficie totale

		Area – Superficie ('000 hectares)				Area – Superficie (Percent of total)&			
Region, country or area Région, pays ou zone	Year Année	Total land Superficie totale	Arable land Terres arables	Permanent crops Cultures permanentes	Forest cover Superficie forestière	Arable land Terres arables	Permanent crops Cultures Permanentes&	Forest cover Superficie forestière	Sites protected for terre-strial biodiversity Sites pour la bio. terre. dans aires protég. (%)&&
El Salvador El Salvador	2005	* 2 072	* 702	227	309	* 33.9	* 11.0	* 14.9	9.88
	2010	* 2 072	* 673	* 225	287	* 32.5	* 10.9	* 13.9	22.39
	2014	* 2 072	* 750	* 215	* 269	* 36.2	* 10.4	* 13.0	26.58
	2017	...	...	...	...	...	...	...	26.58
Equatorial Guinea Guinée équatoriale	2005	2 805	* 130	* 90	1 685	* 4.6	* 3.2	60.1	100.00
	2010	2 805	* 120	* 70	1 626	* 4.3	* 2.5	58.0	100.00
	2014	2 805	* 120	* 60	* 1 580	* 4.3	* 2.1	* 56.3	100.00
	2017	...	...	...	...	...	...	...	100.00
Eritrea Érythrée	2005	* 10 100	* 620	* 2	* 1 554	* 6.1	* ~0.0	* 15.4	13.34
	2010	* 10 100	* 690	* 2	* 1 532	* 6.8	* ~0.0	* 15.2	13.34
	2014	* 10 100	* 690	* 2	* 1 514	* 6.8	* ~0.0	* 15.0	13.34
	2017	...	...	...	...	...	...	...	13.34
Estonia Estonie	2005	4 239	592	11	2 252	14.0	0.3	53.1	94.67
	2010	4 239	645	7	2 234	15.2	0.2	52.7	94.75
	2014	4 239	648	6	* 2 232	15.3	0.1	* 52.7	94.91
	2017	...	...	...	...	...	...	...	94.91
Ethiopia Éthiopie	2005	* 100 000	12 823	768	13 000	* 12.8	* 0.8	* 13.0	18.59
	2010	* 100 000	14 565	1 118	12 296	* 14.6	* 1.1	* 12.3	19.77
	2014	* 100 000	* 15 119	* 1 140	* 12 458	* 15.1	* 1.1	* 12.5	19.77
	2017	...	...	...	...	...	...	...	19.77
Falkland Islands (Malvinas) Îles Falkland (Malvinas)	2005	1 217	...	...	* 0	...	...	* 0.0	10.90
	2010	1 217	...	...	* 0	...	...	* 0.0	10.90
	2014	1 217	...	...	* 0	...	...	* 0.0	10.90
	2017	...	...	...	...	...	...	...	10.90
Faroe Islands Îles Féroé	2005	140	* 3	...	* ~0	* 2.1	...	* 0.1	0.00
	2010	140	* 3	...	* ~0	* 2.1	...	* 0.1	0.00
	2014	140	* 3	...	* ~0	* 2.1	...	* 0.1	6.67
	2017	...	...	...	...	...	...	...	6.67
Fiji Fidji	2005	* 1 827	* 170	* 83	997	* 9.3	* 4.5	* 54.6	3.84
	2010	* 1 827	* 165	* 85	993	* 9.0	* 4.7	* 54.3	7.19
	2014	* 1 827	* 165	* 85	* 1 012	* 9.0	* 4.7	* 55.4	7.19
	2017	...	...	...	...	...	...	...	7.19
Finland Finlande	2005	30 459	2 237	4	22 143	7.3	~0.0	72.7	73.14
	2010	30 390	2 255	4	22 218	7.4	~0.0	73.1	73.35
	2014	30 389	2 231	3	* 22 218	7.3	~0.0	* 73.1	73.75
	2017	...	...	...	...	...	...	...	73.75
France France	2005	* 54 756	18 378	1 111	15 861	* 33.6	* 2.0	* 29.0	69.34
	2010	* 54 756	18 301	1 011	16 424	* 33.4	* 1.8	* 30.0	80.60
	2014	* 54 756	18 333	995	* 16 876	* 33.5	* 1.8	* 30.8	81.61
	2017	...	...	...	...	...	...	...	81.61
French Guiana Guyane française	2005	* 8 220	12	4	8 168	* 0.1	* ~0.0	* 99.4	58.40
	2010	* 8 220	12	4	8 138	* 0.1	* ~0.0	* 99.0	70.82
	2014	* 8 220	13	5	* 8 132	* 0.2	* 0.1	* 98.9	70.82
	2017	...	...	...	...	...	...	...	70.82
French Polynesia Polynésie française	2005	* 366	* 3	* 22	* 130	* 0.8	* 6.0	* 35.5	5.21
	2010	* 366	* 3	* 22	* 155	* 0.7	* 6.0	* 42.3	6.33
	2014	* 366	* 3	* 23	* 155	* 0.7	* 6.3	* 42.3	6.33
	2017	...	...	...	...	...	...	...	6.33
French Southern Territories Terres australes françaises	2005	...	...	...	...	...	...	...	0.00
	2010	...	...	...	...	...	...	...	75.76
	2017	...	...	...	...	...	...	...	81.32
Gabon Gabon	2005	25 767	* 325	* 170	22 000	* 1.3	* 0.7	85.4	61.17
	2010	25 767	* 325	* 170	22 000	* 1.3	* 0.7	85.4	61.17
	2014	25 767	* 325	* 170	* 22 800	* 1.3	* 0.7	* 88.5	61.17
	2017	...	...	...	...	...	...	...	61.17
Gambia Gambie	2005	1 012	* 325	* 5	471	* 32.1	* 0.5	46.5	34.59
	2010	1 012	450	* 5	480	44.5	* 0.5	47.4	34.59
	2014	* 1 012	* 440	* 5	* 486	* 43.5	* 0.5	* 48.1	34.59
	2017	...	...	...	...	...	...	...	34.59

Land *(continued)*
Thousand hectares and percent of total land

Terres *(suite)*
Milliers d'hectares et pourcentage de la superficie totale

		Area – Superficie ('000 hectares)				Area – Superficie (Percent of total)[&]			Sites protected for terre-strial biodiversity Sites pour la bio. terre. dans aires protég. (%)[&&]
Region, country or area Région, pays ou zone	Year Année	Total land Superficie totale	Arable land Terres arables	Permanent crops Cultures permanentes	Forest cover Superficie forestière	Arable land Terres arables	Permanent crops Cultures Permanentes[&]	Forest cover Superficie forestière	
Georgia Géorgie	2005	6 949	* 470	* 110	2 773	* 6.8	* 1.6	39.9	19.78
	2010	* 6 949	* 415	* 125	2 822	* 6.0	* 1.8	* 40.6	21.96
	2014	* 6 949	* 457	* 160	* 2 822	* 6.6	* 2.3	* 40.6	29.30
	2017	...	...	...	...	...	...	...	29.30
Germany Allemagne	2005	34 876	11 904	198	11 384	34.1	0.6	32.6	71.20
	2010	34 857	11 846	199	11 409	34.0	0.6	32.7	78.30
	2014	34 890	11 871	203	* 11 417	34.0	0.6	* 32.7	78.67
	2017	...	...	...	...	...	...	...	78.67
Ghana Ghana	2005	* 22 754	* 4 000	* 2 800	9 053	* 17.6	* 12.3	* 39.8	84.96
	2010	22 754	* 4 620	* 2 700	9 195	* 20.3	* 11.9	40.4	84.96
	2014	22 754	* 4 700	* 2 700	* 9 309	* 20.7	* 11.9	* 40.9	84.96
	2017	...	...	...	...	...	...	...	84.96
Gibraltar Gibraltar	2005	1	...	...	* 0	...	...	* 0.0	34.98
	2010	1	...	...	* 0	...	...	* 0.0	34.98
	2014	1	...	...	* 0	...	...	* 0.0	34.98
	2017	...	...	...	...	...	...	...	34.98
Greece Grèce	2005	* 12 890	2 639	1 136	* 3 752	* 20.5	* 8.8	* 29.1	65.71
	2010	* 12 890	2 567	1 137	* 3 903	* 19.9	* 8.8	* 30.3	72.55
	2014	* 12 890	* 2 600	* 1 125	* 4 024	* 20.2	* 8.7	* 31.2	72.55
	2017	...	...	...	...	...	...	...	72.55
Greenland Groenland	2005	41 045	1	...	* ~0	~0.0	...	* ~0.0	26.11
	2010	41 045	1	...	* ~0	~0.0	...	* ~0.0	26.37
	2014	41 045	1	...	* ~0	~0.0	...	* ~0.0	30.26
	2017	...	...	...	...	...	...	...	30.26
Grenada Grenade	2005	34	* 2	* 4	* 17	* 5.9	* 11.8	* 50.0	30.16
	2010	34	* 3	* 4	* 17	* 8.8	* 11.8	* 50.0	30.16
	2014	34	* 3	* 4	* 17	* 8.8	* 11.8	* 50.0	42.66
	2017	...	...	...	...	...	...	...	42.66
Guadeloupe Guadeloupe	2005	169	19	4	* 74	11.2	2.4	* 43.8	54.17
	2010	* 169	21	3	* 73	* 12.4	* 2.0	* 43.1	80.62
	2014	* 169	22	3	* 73	* 13.2	* 1.8	* 43.0	80.73
	2017	...	...	...	...	...	...	...	80.73
Guam Guam	2005	54	* 2	* 10	* 25	* 3.7	* 18.5	* 46.3	60.25
	2010	54	* 1	* 9	* 25	* 1.9	* 16.7	* 46.3	60.25
	2014	54	* 1	* 9	* 25	* 1.9	* 16.7	* 46.3	60.25
	2017	...	...	...	...	...	...	...	60.25
Guatemala Guatemala	2005	10 716	1 400	841	3 938	13.1	7.8	36.7	27.65
	2010	* 10 716	* 1 196	* 970	3 722	* 11.2	* 9.1	* 34.7	30.75
	2014	* 10 716	934	1 061	* 3 576	* 8.7	* 9.9	* 33.4	30.75
	2017	...	...	...	...	...	...	...	30.75
Guinea Guinée	2005	* 24 572	* 2 741	* 680	6 724	* 11.2	* 2.8	* 27.4	67.22
	2010	* 24 572	* 2 900	* 700	6 544	* 11.8	* 2.8	* 26.6	67.22
	2014	* 24 572	* 3 100	* 700	* 6 400	* 12.6	* 2.8	* 26.0	67.22
	2017	...	...	...	...	...	...	...	67.22
Guinea-Bissau Guinée-Bissau	2005	* 2 812	* 280	* 250	* 2 072	* 10.0	* 8.9	* 73.7	52.18
	2010	* 2 812	* 300	* 250	* 2 022	* 10.7	* 8.9	* 71.9	52.18
	2014	* 2 812	* 300	* 250	* 1 982	* 10.7	* 8.9	* 70.5	52.22
	2017	...	...	...	...	...	...	...	52.60
Guyana Guyana	2005	* 19 685	* 420	* 28	16 602	* 2.1	* 0.1	* 84.3	...
	2010	* 19 685	* 420	* 28	16 576	* 2.1	* 0.1	* 84.2	...
	*2014	19 685	420	30	16 536	2.1	0.2	84.0	...
Haiti Haïti	2005	* 2 756	* 900	* 280	105	* 32.7	* 10.2	* 3.8	5.42
	2010	* 2 756	* 1 100	* 280	101	* 39.9	* 10.2	* 3.7	5.42
	2014	* 2 756	* 1 070	* 280	* 98	* 38.8	* 10.2	* 3.5	5.42
	2017	...	...	...	...	...	...	...	5.42
Heard Is. and McDonald Is. Île Heard-et-Îles MacDonald	2005	...	...	...	...	...	...	...	100.00
	2010	...	...	...	...	...	...	...	100.00
	2017	...	...	...	...	...	...	...	100.00
Honduras Honduras	2005	* 11 189	* 1 050	* 400	5 792	* 9.4	* 3.6	* 51.8	57.46
	2010	* 11 189	* 1 020	* 450	5 192	* 9.1	* 4.0	* 46.4	57.57
	2014	* 11 189	* 1 020	* 455	* 4 712	* 9.1	* 4.1	* 42.1	65.02
	2017	...	...	...	...	...	...	...	65.02

23 Land *(continued)*

Thousand hectares and percent of total land

Terres *(suite)*

Milliers d'hectares et pourcentage de la superficie totale

Region, country or area Région, pays ou zone	Year Année	Area – Superficie ('000 hectares) Total land Superficie totale	Arable land Terres arables	Permanent crops Cultures permanentes	Forest cover Superficie forestière	Area – Superficie (Percent of total)[&] Arable land Terres arables	Permanent crops Cultures Permanentes[&]	Forest cover Superficie forestière	Sites protected for terre-strial biodiversity Sites pour la bio. terre. dans aires protég. (%)[&&]
Hungary Hongrie	2005	8 961	4 601	205	1 983	51.3	2.3	22.1	79.89
	2010	9 053	4 392	188	2 046	48.5	2.1	22.6	81.74
	2014	9 053	4 404	181	* 2 064	48.6	2.0	* 22.8	81.78
	2017	...	...	...	...	...	...	...	81.78
Iceland Islande	2005	10 025	129	...	37	1.3	...	0.4	15.00
	2010	10 025	123	...	43	1.2	...	0.4	15.65
	2014	10 025	121	...	* 48	1.2	...	* 0.5	18.02
	2017	...	...	...	...	...	...	...	18.02
India Inde	2005	297 319	* 159 444	* 10 230	67 709	* 53.6	* 3.4	22.8	22.86
	2010	* 297 319	* 157 009	* 12 225	69 790	* 52.8	* 4.1	* 23.5	22.86
	2014	* 297 319	* 156 360	* 13 000	* 70 504	* 52.6	* 4.4	* 23.7	26.46
	2017	...	...	...	...	...	...	...	26.46
Indonesia Indonésie	2005	181 157	* 22 946	* 17 900	97 857	* 12.7	* 9.9	54.0	21.25
	2010	* 181 157	* 23 600	* 21 000	94 432	* 13.0	* 11.6	* 52.1	22.81
	2014	* 181 157	* 23 500	* 22 500	* 91 694	* 13.0	* 12.4	* 50.6	23.48
	2017	...	...	...	...	...	...	...	23.48
Iran (Islamic Republic of) Iran (Rép. islamique d')	2005	162 876	16 533	1 574	10 692	10.2	1.0	6.6	47.90
	2010	162 876	15 390	1 672	10 692	9.4	1.0	6.6	48.62
	2014	162 876	14 687	1 789	* 10 692	9.0	1.1	* 6.6	48.62
	2017	...	...	...	...	...	...	...	48.62
Iraq Iraq	2005	* 43 737	* 5 200	* 190	* 825	* 11.9	* 0.4	* 1.9	0.00
	2010	* 43 432	* 4 000	* 220	* 825	* 9.2	* 0.5	* 1.9	1.34
	2014	* 43 432	* 5 034	* 235	* 825	* 11.6	* 0.5	* 1.9	4.93
	2017	...	...	...	...	...	...	...	5.10
Ireland Irlande	2005	6 889	1 184	3	695	17.2	~0.0	10.1	86.74
	2010	6 889	1 011	2	726	14.7	~0.0	10.5	89.33
	2014	6 889	1 058	1	* 748	15.4	~0.0	* 10.9	89.96
	2017	...	...	...	...	...	...	...	89.96
Isle of Man Île de Man	2005	57	18	...	* 3	31.2	...	* 6.1	...
	2010	57	25	...	* 3	44.5	...	* 6.1	...
	2014	57	22	...	* 3	38.8	...	* 6.1	...
Israel Israël	2005	2 164	* 311	70	155	* 14.4	3.2	7.2	13.82
	2010	2 164	* 294	77	154	* 13.6	3.6	7.1	15.58
	2014	2 164	* 301	97	* 163	* 13.9	4.5	* 7.5	15.66
	2017	...	...	...	...	...	...	...	15.66
Italy Italie	2005	29 414	7 780	2 554	8 759	26.5	8.7	29.8	75.38
	2010	* 29 414	7 042	2 588	9 028	* 23.9	* 8.8	* 30.7	78.20
	2014	* 29 414	6 728	2 393	* 9 243	* 22.9	* 8.1	* 31.4	78.20
	2017	...	...	...	...	...	...	...	78.20
Jamaica Jamaïque	2005	* 1 083	* 128	* 110	339	* 11.8	* 10.2	* 31.3	22.01
	2010	* 1 083	* 120	* 95	337	* 11.1	* 8.8	* 31.1	22.01
	2014	* 1 083	* 120	* 95	* 336	* 11.1	* 8.8	* 31.0	22.01
	2017	...	...	...	...	...	...	...	22.03
Japan Japon	2005	* 36 450	4 360	332	24 935	* 12.0	* 0.9	* 68.4	64.47
	2010	* 36 455	4 282	311	24 966	* 11.7	* 0.9	* 68.5	64.65
	2014	* 36 456	4 223	296	* 24 960	* 11.6	* 0.8	* 68.5	68.47
	2017	...	...	...	...	...	...	...	68.47
Jordan Jordanie	2005	8 824	185	86	* 98	2.1	1.0	* 1.1	6.19
	2010	8 878	178	83	* 98	2.0	0.9	* 1.1	6.19
	2014	8 878	238	85	* 98	2.7	1.0	* 1.1	7.66
	2017	...	...	...	...	...	...	...	7.66
Kazakhstan Kazakhstan	2005	* 269 970	* 28 562	116	* 3 337	* 10.6	* ~0.0	* 1.2	10.27
	2010	* 269 970	28 684	116	* 3 309	* 10.6	* ~0.0	* 1.2	14.75
	2014	* 269 970	* 29 395	* 132	* 3 309	* 10.9	* ~0.0	* 1.2	15.99
	2017	...	...	...	...	...	...	...	16.29
Kenya Kenya	2005	* 56 914	* 5 264	438	4 047	* 9.2	* 0.8	* 7.1	35.50
	2010	* 56 914	* 5 500	* 520	4 230	* 9.7	* 0.9	* 7.4	36.80
	2014	56 914	* 5 800	* 530	* 4 376	* 10.2	* 0.9	* 7.7	37.50
	2017	...	...	...	...	...	...	...	37.50

23 Land *(continued)*
Thousand hectares and percent of total land

Terres *(suite)*
Milliers d'hectares et pourcentage de la superficie totale

Region, country or area Région, pays ou zone	Year Année	Area – Superficie ('000 hectares) Total land Superficie totale	Arable land Terres arables	Permanent crops Cultures permanentes	Forest cover Superficie forestière	Area – Superficie (Percent of total)[&] Arable land Terres arables	Permanent crops Cultures Permanentes[&]	Forest cover Superficie forestière	Sites protected for terre-strial biodiversity Sites pour la bio. terre. dans aires protég. (%)[&&]
Kiribati	2005	81	* 2	* 32	* 12	* 2.5	* 39.5	* 15.0	27.66
Kiribati	2010	* 81	* 2	* 32	* 12	* 2.5	* 39.5	* 15.0	65.68
	2014	* 81	* 2	* 32	* 12	* 2.5	* 39.5	* 15.0	65.68
	2017	...	...	...	...	...	...	...	65.68
Kuwait	2005	1 782	* 11	3	* 6	* 0.6	0.2	* 0.3	35.38
Koweït	2010	1 782	* 10	* 6	* 6	* 0.6	* 0.3	* 0.4	35.38
	2014	1 782	* 10	* 7	* 6	* 0.5	* 0.4	* 0.4	59.03
	2017	...	...	...	...	...	...	...	59.03
Kyrgyzstan	2005	* 19 180	1 284	72	869	* 6.7	* 0.4	* 4.5	22.36
Kirghizistan	2010	* 19 180	1 276	74	677	* 6.7	* 0.4	* 3.5	22.36
	2014	* 19 180	1 281	75	* 645	* 6.7	* 0.4	* 3.4	22.62
	2017	...	...	...	...	...	...	...	22.62
Lao People's Dem. Rep.	2005	23 080	* 1 150	* 85	16 870	* 5.0	* 0.4	73.1	44.04
Rép. dém. populaire lao	2010	* 23 080	* 1 400	* 130	17 816	* 6.1	* 0.6	* 77.2	45.48
	2014	* 23 080	* 1 525	* 169	* 18 572	* 6.6	* 0.7	* 80.5	45.48
	2017	...	...	...	...	...	...	...	45.48
Latvia	2005	6 220	1 092	13	3 297	17.6	0.2	53.0	97.22
Lettonie	2010	6 224	1 173	7	3 354	18.8	0.1	53.9	97.26
	2014	6 218	1 209	6	* 3 356	19.4	0.1	* 54.0	97.26
	2017	...	...	...	...	...	...	...	97.26
Lebanon	2005	* 1 023	* 142	141	137	* 13.9	* 13.8	* 13.3	11.57
Liban	2010	* 1 023	114	126	137	* 11.1	* 12.3	* 13.4	11.57
	2014	* 1 023	* 132	* 126	* 137	* 12.9	* 12.3	* 13.4	13.08
	2017	...	...	...	...	...	...	...	13.08
Lesotho	2005	3 036	323	* 4	43	10.6	* 0.1	1.4	15.27
Lesotho	2010	3 036	322	* 4	44	10.6	* 0.1	1.4	15.27
	2014	3 036	272	* 5	* 48	9.0	* 0.2	* 1.6	15.27
	2017	...	...	...	...	...	...	...	15.27
Liberia	2005	9 632	* 400	* 215	4 479	* 4.2	* 2.2	46.5	14.82
Libéria	2010	9 632	* 480	* 180	4 329	* 5.0	* 1.9	44.9	14.82
	2014	9 632	* 500	* 200	* 4 209	* 5.2	* 2.1	* 43.7	14.82
	2017	...	...	...	...	...	...	...	14.82
Libya	2005	175 954	* 1 750	* 335	* 217	* 1.0	* 0.2	* 0.1	4.60
Libye	2010	175 954	* 1 716	* 335	* 217	* 1.0	* 0.2	* 0.1	4.60
	2014	175 954	* 1 720	* 330	* 217	* 1.0	* 0.2	* 0.1	4.60
	2017	...	...	...	...	...	...	...	4.60
Liechtenstein	2005	16	* 4	...	* 7	* 24.4	...	* 43.1	80.82
Liechtenstein	2010	16	* 3	...	* 7	* 20.6	...	* 43.1	80.82
	2014	16	* 2	...	* 7	* 14.5	...	* 43.1	80.82
	2017	...	...	...	...	...	...	...	80.82
Lithuania	2005	6 268	1 907	40	2 121	30.4	0.6	33.8	89.61
Lituanie	2010	6 268	2 127	31	2 170	33.9	0.5	34.6	91.59
	2014	6 265	2 350	34	* 2 178	37.5	0.5	* 34.8	91.59
	2017	...	...	...	...	...	...	...	91.59
Luxembourg	2005	259	60	2	* 87	23.2	0.8	* 33.5	56.91
Luxembourg	2010	259	62	2	* 87	23.9	0.6	* 33.5	56.91
	2014	259	63	2	* 87	24.2	0.6	* 33.5	56.94
	2017	...	...	...	...	...	...	...	71.78
Madagascar	2005	* 58 154	* 3 000	* 600	12 838	* 5.2	* 1.0	* 22.1	39.32
Madagascar	2010	* 58 154	* 3 500	* 600	12 553	* 6.0	* 1.0	* 21.6	40.13
	2014	* 58 180	* 3 500	* 620	* 12 489	* 6.0	* 1.1	* 21.5	40.80
	2017	...	...	...	...	...	...	...	40.82
Malawi	2005	9 428	* 3 200	* 130	3 402	* 33.9	* 1.4	36.1	81.64
Malawi	2010	9 428	* 3 700	* 135	3 237	* 39.2	* 1.4	34.3	81.64
	2014	9 428	* 3 800	* 140	* 3 165	* 40.3	* 1.5	* 33.6	81.64
	2017	...	...	...	...	...	...	...	81.64
Malaysia	2005	* 32 855	* 958	* 5 900	20 890	* 2.9	* 18.0	* 63.6	38.84
Malaisie	2010	* 32 855	* 931	* 6 250	22 124	* 2.8	* 19.0	* 67.3	39.27
	2014	* 32 855	* 954	* 6 600	* 22 181	* 2.9	* 20.1	* 67.5	39.27
	2017	...	...	...	...	...	...	...	39.27

Land *(continued)*
Thousand hectares and percent of total land

Terres *(suite)*
Milliers d'hectares et pourcentage de la superficie totale

Region, country or area Région, pays ou zone	Year Année	Area – Superficie ('000 hectares) Total land Superficie totale	Arable land Terres arables	Permanent crops Cultures permanentes	Forest cover Superficie forestière	Area – Superficie (Percent of total)& Arable land Terres arables	Permanent crops Cultures Permanentes&	Forest cover Superficie forestière	Sites protected for terre-strial biodiversity Sites pour la bio. terre. dans aires protég. (%)&&
Maldives Maldives	2005	30	* 3	* 5	* 1	* 10.0	* 16.7	* 3.3	0.00
	2010	30	* 4	* 3	* 1	* 13.0	* 10.0	* 3.3	0.00
	2014	30	4	* 3	* 1	13.0	* 10.0	* 3.3	0.00
	2017	...	...	...	...	...	...	...	0.00
Mali Mali	2005	122 019	* 5 603	* 150	5 505	* 4.6	* 0.1	4.5	33.77
	2010	* 122 019	* 6 261	* 150	5 110	* 5.1	* 0.1	* 4.2	33.77
	2014	* 122 019	* 6 411	* 150	* 4 794	* 5.3	* 0.1	* 3.9	33.77
	2017	...	...	...	...	...	...	...	33.77
Malta Malte	2005	32	8	1	* ~0	25.6	3.4	* 1.1	83.09
	2010	32	9	1	* ~0	28.4	3.9	* 1.1	84.29
	2014	32	9	1	* ~0	28.0	3.9	* 1.1	85.90
	2017	...	...	...	...	...	...	...	90.42
Marshall Islands Îles Marshall	2005	18	2	8	* 13	11.1	44.4	* 70.2	32.08
	2010	18	* 2	* 8	* 13	* 11.1	* 44.4	* 70.2	32.08
	2014	18	* 2	* 7	* 13	* 11.1	* 36.1	* 70.2	32.08
	2017	...	...	...	...	...	...	...	32.08
Martinique Martinique	2005	* 106	10	8	49	* 9.4	* 7.5	* 45.8	75.06
	2010	* 106	10	7	49	* 9.6	* 7.0	* 45.8	99.12
	2014	* 106	10	7	* 49	* 9.5	* 6.3	* 45.8	99.12
	2017	...	...	...	...	...	...	...	99.12
Mauritania Mauritanie	2005	103 070	* 400	* 11	267	* 0.4	* ~0.0	0.3	14.62
	2010	103 070	* 450	* 11	242	* 0.4	* ~0.0	0.2	14.62
	2014	103 070	* 450	* 11	* 228	* 0.4	* ~0.0	* 0.2	14.62
	2017	...	...	...	...	...	...	...	14.62
Mauritius Maurice	2005	203	* 85	* 4	38	* 41.9	* 2.0	18.8	24.46
	2010	203	* 80	* 4	38	* 39.4	* 2.0	18.9	24.57
	2014	203	* 75	* 4	* 39	* 36.9	* 2.0	* 19.0	25.73
	2017	...	...	...	...	...	...	...	25.73
Mayotte Mayotte	2005	37	* 8	* 10	* 8	* 20.6	* 26.7	* 20.7	2.72
	2010	37	* 9	3	* 7	* 23.3	9.1	* 18.2	14.53
	2014	37	* 9	* 3	* 6	* 23.8	* 8.7	* 16.1	14.53
	2017	...	...	...	...	...	...	...	14.53
Mexico Mexique	2005	194 395	* 23 296	2 607	67 083	* 12.0	1.3	34.5	24.15
	2010	194 395	* 23 507	2 651	66 498	* 12.1	1.4	34.2	29.05
	2014	194 395	* 22 993	2 677	* 66 132	* 11.8	1.4	* 34.0	31.03
	2017	...	...	...	...	...	...	...	31.03
Micronesia (Fed. States of) Micronésie (États féd. de)	2005	70	* 3	* 17	* 64	* 3.6	* 24.3	* 91.4	0.00
	2010	70	* 2	* 17	* 64	* 2.9	* 24.3	* 91.6	0.00
	2014	70	* 2	* 17	* 64	* 2.9	* 24.3	* 91.8	0.00
	2017	...	...	...	...	...	...	...	0.00
Mongolia Mongolie	2005	* 155 356	* 695	* 2	11 308	* 0.4	* ~0.0	* 7.3	36.45
	2010	* 155 356	* 614	* 3	13 039	* 0.4	* ~0.0	* 8.4	39.09
	2014	* 155 356	* 567	* 5	* 12 650	* 0.4	* ~0.0	* 8.1	41.98
	2017	...	...	...	...	...	...	...	41.98
Montenegro Monténégro	2005	...	...	...	...	...	...	...	2.07
	2010	* 1 345	172	16	827	* 12.8	* 1.2	* 61.5	2.07
	2014	* 1 345	9	5	* 827	* 0.6	* 0.4	* 61.5	2.07
	2017	...	...	...	...	...	...	...	2.07
Montserrat Montserrat	2005	10	* 2	...	* 3	* 20.0	...	* 25.0	0.00
	2010	10	* 2	...	* 3	* 20.0	...	* 25.0	0.00
	2014	10	* 2	...	* 3	* 20.0	...	* 25.0	30.63
	2017	...	...	...	...	...	...	...	30.63
Morocco Maroc	2005	* 44 630	8 122	867	5 401	* 18.2	* 1.9	* 12.1	13.85
	2010	* 44 630	7 729	1 259	5 672	* 17.3	* 2.8	* 12.7	15.24
	2014	* 44 630	* 8 130	1 462	* 5 640	* 18.2	* 3.3	* 12.6	43.53
	2017	...	...	...	...	...	...	...	43.53
Mozambique Mozambique	2005	78 638	* 5 000	* 250	40 079	* 6.4	* 0.3	51.0	22.18
	2010	78 638	* 5 650	* 300	38 972	* 7.2	* 0.4	49.6	22.18
	2014	78 638	* 5 650	* 300	* 38 146	* 7.2	* 0.4	* 48.5	36.52
	2017	...	...	...	...	...	...	...	36.52

Region, country or area Région, pays ou zone	Year Année	Area – Superficie ('000 hectares) Total land Superficie totale	Arable land Terres arables	Permanent crops Cultures permanentes	Forest cover Superficie forestière	Area – Superficie (Percent of total)& Arable land Terres arables	Permanent crops Cultures Permanentes&	Forest cover Superficie forestière	Sites protected for terre-strial biodiversity Sites pour la bio. terre. dans aires protég. (%)&&
Myanmar	2005	65 336	10 059	896	33 321	15.4	1.4	51.0	22.56
Myanmar	2010	65 326	10 811	1 406	31 773	16.5	2.2	48.6	22.56
	2014	* 65 308	* 10 789	* 1 550	* 29 587	* 16.5	* 2.4	* 45.3	22.56
	2017	...	...	...	...	...	...	...	22.56
Namibia	2005	* 82 329	* 814	* 6	7 661	* 1.0	* ~0.0	* 9.3	44.58
Namibie	2010	* 82 329	* 800	* 9	7 290	* 1.0	* ~0.0	* 8.9	82.37
	2014	* 82 329	* 800	* 9	* 6 993	* 1.0	* ~0.0	* 8.5	85.38
	2017	...	...	...	...	...	...	...	85.38
Nauru	2005	2	...	* ~0	* 0	...	* 20.0	* 0.0	...
Nauru	2010	2	...	* ~0	* 0	...	* 20.0	* 0.0	...
	2014	2	...	* ~0	* 0	...	* 20.0	* 0.0	...
Nepal	2005	14 335	* 2 280	* 133	3 636	* 15.9	* 0.9	25.4	50.32
Népal	2010	14 335	* 2 180	* 152	3 636	* 15.2	* 1.1	25.4	54.63
	2014	14 335	* 2 114	* 212	* 3 636	* 14.7	* 1.5	* 25.4	54.63
	2017	...	...	...	...	...	...	...	54.64
Netherlands	2005	3 376	1 111	32	365	32.9	0.9	10.8	90.70
Pays-Bas	2010	3 373	1 023	36	373	30.3	1.1	11.1	90.75
	2014	3 369	1 045	36	* 375	31.0	1.1	* 11.1	90.75
	2017	...	...	...	...	...	...	...	90.75
Netherlands Antilles [former]	2005	80	* 8	...	* 1	* 10.0	...	* 1.5	...
Antilles néerlandaises [anc.]	2010	80	* 8	...	* 1	* 10.0	...	* 1.5	...
	2014	80	* 8	...	* 1	* 10.0	...	* 1.5	...
New Caledonia	2005	* 1 828	* 7	* 4	* 839	* 0.4	* 0.2	* 45.9	15.50
Nouvelle-Calédonie	2010	1 828	* 7	* 4	* 839	* 0.4	* 0.2	* 45.9	67.78
	2014	1 828	* 6	* 4	* 839	* 0.3	* 0.2	* 45.9	68.04
	2017	...	...	...	...	...	...	...	68.04
New Zealand	2005	26 331	425	63	10 183	1.6	0.2	38.7	45.78
Nouvelle-Zélande	2010	26 331	499	71	10 151	1.9	0.3	38.6	47.05
	2014	26 331	590	67	* 10 152	2.2	0.3	* 38.6	47.15
	2017	...	...	...	...	...	...	...	47.15
Nicaragua	2005	12 034	* 2 000	* 290	3 464	* 16.6	* 2.4	28.8	73.74
Nicaragua	2010	12 034	* 1 531	* 295	3 114	* 12.7	* 2.5	25.9	73.74
	2014	12 034	* 1 504	* 286	* 3 114	* 12.5	* 2.4	* 25.9	73.74
	2017	...	...	...	...	...	...	...	73.74
Niger	2005	* 126 670	* 14 123	* 60	1 266	* 11.1	* ~0.0	* 1.0	40.66
Niger	2010	* 126 670	* 15 100	* 100	1 204	* 11.9	* 0.1	* 1.0	40.66
	2014	* 126 670	* 15 900	* 100	* 1 154	* 12.6	* 0.1	* 0.9	42.75
	2017	...	...	...	...	...	...	...	42.75
Nigeria	2005	* 91 077	* 36 000	* 6 400	11 089	* 39.5	* 7.0	* 12.2	76.00
Nigéria	2010	* 91 077	* 33 000	* 6 700	9 041	* 36.2	* 7.4	* 9.9	79.62
	2014	* 91 077	* 34 000	* 6 500	* 7 403	* 37.3	* 7.1	* 8.1	79.62
	2017	...	...	...	...	...	...	...	79.62
Niue	2005	26	* 1	* 3	* 19	* 3.8	* 10.8	* 73.5	...
Nioué	2010	26	* 1	* 3	* 19	* 3.8	* 11.5	* 71.5	...
	2014	26	* 1	* 3	* 18	* 3.8	* 11.5	* 70.0	...
Norfolk Island	2005	4	...	...	* ~0	...	...	* 11.5	44.38
Île Norfolk	2010	4	...	...	* ~0	...	...	* 11.5	44.38
	2014	4	...	...	* ~0	...	...	* 11.5	55.87
	2017	...	...	...	...	...	...	...	55.87
Northern Mariana Islands	2005	46	* 1	* 1	* 31	* 2.2	* 2.2	* 67.7	15.51
Îles Mariannes du Nord	2010	46	* 1	* 1	* 30	* 2.2	* 2.2	* 65.9	40.59
	2014	46	* 1	* 1	* 30	* 2.2	* 2.2	* 64.5	40.59
	2017	...	...	...	...	...	...	...	40.59
Norway	2005	36 525	862	5	12 092	2.4	~0.0	33.1	52.23
Norvège	2010	36 525	826	5	12 102	2.3	~0.0	33.1	54.27
	2014	36 525	807	5	* 12 110	2.2	~0.0	* 33.2	54.71
	2017	...	...	...	...	...	...	...	54.71
Oman	2005	30 950	28	37	2	0.1	0.1	~0.0	7.82
Oman	2010	30 950	34	38	2	0.1	0.1	~0.0	7.82
	2014	30 950	38	31	* 2	0.1	0.1	* ~0.0	11.46
	2017	...	...	...	...	...	...	...	11.46

Region, country or area Région, pays ou zone	Year Année	Area – Superficie ('000 hectares) Total land Superficie totale	 Arable land Terres arables	 Permanent crops Cultures permanentes	 Forest cover Superficie forestière	Area – Superficie (Percent of total)[&] Arable land Terres arables	 Permanent crops Cultures Permanentes[&]	 Forest cover Superficie forestière	Sites protected for terre-strial biodiversity Sites pour la bio. terre. dans aires protég. (%)[&&]
Other non-specified areas	*2005	3 541	603	230	...	17.0	6.5	...	...
Autres zones non-spécifiées	*2010	3 541	598	215	...	16.9	6.1	...	...
	*2014	3 541	595	205	...	16.8	5.8	...	...
Pakistan	2005	77 088	30 170	795	* 1 902	39.1	1.0	* 2.5	40.27
Pakistan	2010	* 77 088	29 390	852	* 1 687	* 38.1	* 1.1	* 2.2	40.27
	2014	* 77 088	30 440	812	* 1 515	* 39.5	* 1.1	* 2.0	40.27
	2017	...	...	...	...	...	...	...	40.27
Palau	2005	* 46	* 1	* 2	40	* 2.2	* 4.3	* 87.6	17.28
Palaos	2010	* 46	* 1	* 2	40	* 2.2	* 4.3	* 87.6	17.28
	2014	* 46	* 1	* 2	* 40	* 2.2	* 4.3	* 87.6	32.82
	2017	...	...	...	...	...	...	...	50.73
Panama	2005	7 434	* 548	* 160	4 782	* 7.4	* 2.2	64.3	37.84
Panama	2010	* 7 434	569	189	4 699	* 7.7	* 2.5	* 63.2	38.84
	2014	* 7 434	* 563	* 185	* 4 633	* 7.6	* 2.5	* 62.3	38.84
	2017	...	...	...	...	...	...	...	38.84
Papua New Guinea	2005	* 45 286	* 240	* 600	33 586	* 0.5	* 1.3	* 74.2	7.32
Papouasie-Nvl-Guinée	2010	* 45 286	* 300	* 700	33 573	* 0.7	* 1.5	* 74.1	7.32
	2014	* 45 286	* 300	* 700	* 33 562	* 0.7	* 1.5	* 74.1	7.32
	2017	...	...	...	...	...	...	...	7.32
Paraguay	2005	* 39 730	* 3 460	* 100	18 475	* 8.7	* 0.3	* 46.5	23.31
Paraguay	2010	* 39 730	* 4 145	* 85	16 950	* 10.4	* 0.2	* 42.7	23.31
	2014	* 39 730	* 4 800	* 85	* 15 648	* 12.1	* 0.2	* 39.4	23.31
	2017	...	...	...	...	...	...	...	23.31
Peru	2005	* 128 000	* 3 930	* 1 090	75 528	* 3.1	* 0.9	* 59.0	23.11
Pérou	2010	* 128 000	* 4 085	* 1 307	74 811	* 3.2	* 1.0	* 58.4	28.86
	2014	* 128 000	* 4 152	* 1 379	* 74 141	* 3.2	* 1.1	* 57.9	30.07
	2017	...	...	...	...	...	...	...	30.67
Philippines	2005	29 817	* 5 005	* 4 850	7 074	* 16.8	* 16.3	23.7	38.72
Philippines	2010	29 817	* 5 300	* 5 300	6 840	* 17.8	* 17.8	22.9	41.40
	2014	29 817	* 5 590	* 5 350	* 7 800	* 18.7	* 17.9	* 26.2	41.68
	2017	...	...	...	...	...	...	...	41.68
Pitcairn	2005	5	...	...	* 4	...	...	* 74.5	21.77
Pitcairn	2010	5	...	...	* 4	...	...	* 74.5	21.77
	2014	5	...	...	* 4	...	...	* 74.5	21.77
	2017	...	...	...	...	...	...	...	51.65
Poland	2005	30 633	12 141	378	9 200	39.6	1.2	30.0	73.41
Pologne	2010	30 628	10 829	390	9 329	35.4	1.3	30.5	87.88
	2014	30 619	10 928	376	* 9 414	35.7	1.2	* 30.7	88.11
	2017	...	...	...	...	...	...	...	88.11
Portugal	2005	* 9 147	1 278	774	3 296	* 14.0	* 8.5	* 36.0	60.46
Portugal	2010	* 9 159	1 148	714	3 239	* 12.5	* 7.8	* 35.4	70.97
	2014	* 9 161	1 137	748	* 3 193	* 12.4	* 8.2	* 34.9	73.84
	2017	...	...	...	...	...	...	...	73.84
Puerto Rico	2005	887	* 66	* 37	463	* 7.5	* 4.2	52.2	33.98
Porto Rico	2010	* 887	* 57	* 50	479	* 6.4	* 5.6	* 54.0	33.98
	2014	* 887	* 61	* 50	* 493	* 6.9	* 5.6	* 55.5	33.98
	2017	...	...	...	...	...	...	...	33.98
Qatar	2005	1 161	* 12	3	* 0	* 1.0	0.2	* 0.0	12.44
Qatar	2010	1 161	* 13	3	* 0	* 1.1	0.2	* 0.0	12.44
	2014	1 161	* 13	3	* 0	* 1.1	0.2	* 0.0	12.44
	2017	...	...	...	...	...	...	...	12.44
Republic of Korea	2005	9 685	1 643	181	6 255	17.0	1.9	64.6	27.31
République de Corée	2010	* 9 723	* 1 507	208	6 222	* 15.5	* 2.1	* 64.0	36.40
	2014	* 9 748	* 1 476	215	* 6 192	* 15.1	* 2.2	* 63.5	36.54
	2017	...	...	...	...	...	...	...	36.55
Republic of Moldova	2005	3 289	1 833	302	* 363	55.7	9.2	* 11.0	23.61
République de Moldova	2010	3 285	1 813	299	* 386	55.2	9.1	* 11.8	23.61
	2014	3 287	1 817	292	* 404	55.3	8.9	* 12.3	23.61
	2017	...	...	...	...	...	...	...	23.61

Region, country or area Région, pays ou zone	Year Année	Area – Superficie ('000 hectares) Total land Superficie totale	 Arable land Terres arables	 Permanent crops Cultures permanentes	 Forest cover Superficie forestière	Area – Superficie (Percent of total)& Arable land Terres arables	 Permanent crops Cultures Permanentes&	 Forest cover Superficie forestière	Sites protected for terre-strial biodiversity Sites pour la bio. terre. dans aires protég. (%)&&
Réunion Réunion	2005	* 250	35	3	85	* 14.0	* 1.2	* 34.0	3.16
	2010	* 250	35	3	88	* 14.1	* 1.2	* 35.2	90.59
	2014	* 251	36	3	* 88	* 14.2	* 1.2	* 35.1	90.59
	2017	...	...	...	...	...	...	...	90.59
Romania Roumanie	2005	22 998	8 985	510	6 391	39.1	2.2	27.8	14.78
	2010	23 005	9 146	463	6 515	39.8	2.0	28.3	65.40
	2014	23 008	8 778	425	* 6 792	38.2	1.8	* 29.5	77.76
	2017	...	...	...	...	...	...	...	77.76
Russian Federation Fédération de Russie	2005	1 638 139 *	121 781	1 800	808 790	7.4	0.1	49.4	27.13
	2010	1 637 687 *	* 119 000	* 1 650	815 136	* 7.3	* 0.1	* 49.8	27.16
	2014	1 637 687	* 123 122	* 1 600	* 814 972	* 7.5	* 0.1	* 49.8	27.16
	2017	...	...	...	...	...	...	...	27.16
Rwanda Rwanda	2005	* 2 467	* 1 083	* 250	385	* 43.9	* 10.1	* 15.6	45.67
	2010	* 2 467	* 1 124	* 250	446	* 45.6	* 10.1	* 18.1	45.67
	2014	* 2 467	* 1 150	* 250	* 473	* 46.6	* 10.1	* 19.2	45.67
	2017	...	...	...	...	...	...	...	45.67
Saint Barthélemy Saint-Barthélemy	2005	...	...	...	...	...	...	...	23.26
	2010	...	...	...	...	...	...	...	62.29
	2017	...	...	...	...	...	...	...	62.29
Saint Helena Sainte-Hélène	2005	39[6]	* 4[6]	...	* 2[6]	* 10.3[6]	...	* 5.1[6]	16.67
	2010	* 39[6]	* 4[6]	...	* 2[6]	* 10.3[6]	...	* 5.1[6]	16.67
	2014	* 39[6]	* 4[6]	...	* 2[6]	* 10.3[6]	...	* 5.1[6]	51.11
	2017	...	...	...	...	...	...	...	54.85
Saint Kitts and Nevis Saint-Kitts-et-Nevis	2005	26	4	~0	11	15.3	0.1	42.3	29.20
	2010	26	5	~0	11	17.3	0.4	42.3	29.20
	2014	26	5	~0	* 11	19.2	0.4	* 42.3	29.20
	2017	...	...	...	...	...	...	...	29.20
Saint Lucia Sainte-Lucie	2005	* 61	* 2	* 8	21	* 3.6	* 12.6	* 34.3	40.32
	2010	* 61	* 3	* 7	21	* 4.9	* 11.5	* 33.8	46.05
	2014	* 61	* 3	* 7	* 20	* 4.9	* 11.5	* 33.4	46.05
	2017	...	...	...	...	...	...	...	46.05
Saint Martin (French part) St-Martin (partie française)	2005	...	...	...	...	...	...	...	29.21
	2010	...	...	...	...	...	...	...	59.34
	2017	...	...	...	...	...	...	...	59.39
Saint Pierre and Miquelon Saint-Pierre-et-Miquelon	2005	* 23	* 3	...	3	* 13.0	...	* 13.0	...
	2010	* 23	* 3	...	3	* 13.0	...	* 12.6	...
	*2014	23	2	...	3	8.7	...	12.3	...
Saint Vincent & Grenadines Saint-Vincent-Grenadines	2005	39	* 5	* 3	* 26	* 12.8	* 7.7	* 66.7	42.66
	2010	39	* 5	* 3	* 27	* 12.8	* 7.7	* 69.2	42.66
	2014	39	* 5	* 3	* 27	* 12.8	* 7.7	* 69.2	42.66
	2017	...	...	...	...	...	...	...	42.66
Samoa Samoa	2005	* 283	* 11	* 27	* 171	* 3.9	* 9.5	* 60.4	17.52
	2010	* 283	* 8	* 22	* 171	* 2.8	* 7.8	* 60.4	17.52
	2014	* 283	* 8	* 22	* 171	* 2.8	* 7.8	* 60.4	17.52
	2017	...	...	...	...	...	...	...	17.52
San Marino Saint-Marin	2005	6	* 1	...	* 0	* 16.7	...	* 0.0	...
	2010	6	* 1	...	* 0	* 16.7	...	* 0.0	...
	2014	6	* 1	...	* 0	* 16.7	...	* 0.0	...
Sao Tome and Principe Sao Tomé-et-Principe	2005	* 96	* 8	* 40	56	* 8.3	* 41.7	* 58.3	0.00
	2010	* 96	* 9	* 39	54	* 8.9	* 40.6	* 55.8	54.36
	2014	* 96	* 9	* 39	* 54	* 9.1	* 40.6	* 55.8	54.36
	2017	...	...	...	...	...	...	...	54.36
Saudi Arabia Arabie saoudite	2005	214 969	* 3 500	217	* 977	* 1.6	0.1	* 0.5	15.13
	2010	214 969	* 3 180	226	* 977	* 1.5	0.1	* 0.5	15.13
	2014	214 969	* 3 502	145	* 977	* 1.6	0.1	* 0.5	15.13
	2017	...	...	...	...	...	...	...	15.13
Senegal Sénégal	2005	* 19 253	* 3 126	* 50	8 673	* 16.2	* 0.3	* 45.0	41.12
	2010	* 19 253	* 3 800	* 58	8 473	* 19.7	* 0.3	* 44.0	41.12
	2014	* 19 253	* 3 200	* 68	* 8 313	* 16.6	* 0.4	* 43.2	41.16
	2017	...	...	...	...	...	...	...	41.16

Region, country or area Région, pays ou zone	Year Année	Area – Superficie ('000 hectares) Total land Superficie totale	Arable land Terres arables	Permanent crops Cultures permanentes	Forest cover Superficie forestière	Area – Superficie (Percent of total)& Arable land Terres arables	Permanent crops Cultures Permanentes&	Forest cover Superficie forestière	Sites protected for terre-strial biodiversity Sites pour la bio. terre. dans aires protég. (%)&&
Serbia Serbie	2005	...	...	...	...	...	...	...	23.27
	2010	* 8 746	2 654	190	2 713	* 30.3	* 2.2	* 31.0	25.53
	2014	* 8 746	2 606	188	* 2 719	* 29.8	* 2.1	* 31.1	26.15
	2017	...	...	...	...	...	...	...	26.15
Serbia and Monten. [former] Serbie-et-Monténégro [anc.]	2005	* 10 200	* 3 505	* 317	3 102	* 34.4	* 3.1	* 30.4	...
Seychelles Seychelles	2005	46	* 1	* 3	41	* 2.2	* 6.5	88.4	21.85
	2010	* 46	* 1	* 2	41	* 2.0	* 3.5	* 88.4	21.85
	2014	* 46	* ~0	* 1	* 41	* 0.2	* 3.0	* 88.4	21.85
	2017	...	...	...	...	...	...	...	21.85
Sierra Leone Sierra Leone	2005	* 7 218	* 1 472	* 140	2 824	* 20.4	* 1.9	* 39.1	54.61
	2010	* 7 218	* 1 580	* 150	2 726	* 21.9	* 2.1	* 37.8	68.98
	2014	* 7 218	* 1 584	* 165	* 2 980	* 21.9	* 2.3	* 41.3	80.32
	2017	...	...	...	...	...	...	...	80.32
Singapore Singapour	2005	* 69	* 1	* ~0	16	* 1.0	* 0.1	* 23.7	21.14
	2010	* 70	* 1	* ~0	16	* 0.9	* 0.1	* 23.3	21.14
	2014	* 71	* 1	* ~0	* 16	* 0.8	* 0.1	* 23.1	21.14
	2017	...	...	...	...	...	...	...	21.14
Sint Maarten (Dutch part) St-Martin (partie néerland.)	2005	...	...	...	...	...	...	...	0.00
	2010	...	...	...	...	...	...	...	0.00
	2017	...	...	...	...	...	...	...	0.00
Slovakia Slovaquie	2005	4 810	1 391	26	1 932	28.9	0.5	40.2	73.02
	2010	4 809	1 392	25	1 939	28.9	0.5	40.3	76.24
	2014	4 809	1 394	19	* 1 940	29.0	0.4	* 40.3	83.56
	2017	...	...	...	...	...	...	...	83.56
Slovenia Slovénie	2005	2 014	176	28	1 243	8.7	1.4	61.7	82.97
	2010	2 014	185	52	1 247	9.2	2.6	61.9	82.98
	2014	2 014	184	53	* 1 248	9.1	2.6	* 62.0	85.55
	2017	...	...	...	...	...	...	...	85.55
Solomon Islands Îles Salomon	2005	* 2 799	* 16	* 65	* 2 241	* 0.6	* 2.3	* 80.1	7.11
	2010	* 2 799	* 19	* 80	* 2 213	* 0.7	* 2.9	* 79.1	9.53
	2014	* 2 799	* 20	* 80	* 2 191	* 0.7	* 2.9	* 78.3	9.53
	2017	...	...	...	...	...	...	...	9.53
Somalia Somalie	2005	* 62 734	* 1 350	* 27	7 131	* 2.2	* ~0.0	* 11.4	0.00
	2010	* 62 734	* 1 100	* 28	6 747	* 1.8	* ~0.0	* 10.8	0.00
	2014	* 62 734	* 1 100	* 25	* 6 440	* 1.8	* ~0.0	* 10.3	0.00
	2017	...	...	...	...	...	...	...	0.00
South Africa Afrique du Sud	2005	121 309	* 13 175	* 380	9 241	* 10.9	* 0.3	7.6	47.73
	2010	121 309	12 533	430	9 241	10.3	0.4	7.6	50.34
	2014	* 121 309	* 12 500	* 413	* 9 241	* 10.3	* 0.3	* 7.6	52.21
	2017	...	...	...	...	...	...	...	54.48
South Georgia & Sandwich Is. Géorgie du S.-Îles Sandwich	2005	...	...	...	...	...	...	...	0.00
	2010	...	...	...	...	...	...	...	0.00
	2017	...	...	...	...	...	...	...	100.00
South Sudan Soudan du sud	2005	...	...	...	...	...	...	...	30.26
	2010	...	...	...	...	...	...	...	33.64
	2014	...	...	...	* 7 157	...	...	...	33.64
	2017	...	...	...	...	...	...	...	33.64
Spain Espagne	2005	49 909	12 913	4 931	17 282	25.9	9.9	34.6	57.84
	2010	50 001	12 528	4 693	18 247	25.1	9.4	36.5	59.45
	2014	* 50 021	12 278	4 910	* 18 384	* 24.5	* 9.8	* 36.8	61.02
	2017	...	...	...	...	...	...	...	61.03
Sri Lanka Sri Lanka	2005	6 271	* 1 100	* 970	2 118	* 17.5	* 15.5	33.8	41.76
	2010	6 271	* 1 200	* 980	2 103	* 19.1	* 15.6	33.5	47.49
	2014	6 271	* 1 300	* 1 000	* 2 077	* 20.7	* 15.9	* 33.1	49.85
	2017	...	...	...	...	...	...	...	49.85
State of Palestine État de Palestine	2005	602	* 99	115	* 9	* 16.4	19.1	* 1.5	0.00
	2010	602	44	54	* 9	7.3	9.0	* 1.5	0.00
	2014	602	* 64	84	* 9	* 10.6	14.0	* 1.5	0.00
	2017	...	...	...	...	...	...	...	0.00

Land *(continued)*
Thousand hectares and percent of total land

Terres *(suite)*
Milliers d'hectares et pourcentage de la superficie totale

Region, country or area Région, pays ou zone	Year Année	Area – Superficie ('000 hectares) Total land Superficie totale	Arable land Terres arables	Permanent crops Cultures permanentes	Forest cover Superficie forestière	Area – Superficie (Percent of total)[&] Arable land Terres arables	Permanent crops Cultures Permanentes[&]	Forest cover Superficie forestière	Sites protected for terre-strial biodiversity Sites pour la bio. terre. dans aires protég. (%)[&&]
Sudan	2005	...	...	...	...	...	...	...	9.09
Soudan	2010	...	...	...	...	...	...	...	18.62
	2014	...	19 823	168	* 19 384	...	...	...	18.62
	2017	...	...	...	...	...	...	...	25.00
Sudan [former]	2005	237 600	18 750	* 130	28 111	7.9	* 0.1	11.8	...
Soudan [anc.]	2010	237 600	19 878	142	27 239	8.4	0.1	11.5	...
Suriname	2005	* 15 600	49	* 6	15 371	* 0.3	* ~0.0	* 98.5	51.19
Suriname	2010	* 15 600	55	6	15 351	* 0.4	* ~0.0	* 98.4	51.19
	2014	15 600	65	6	* 15 336	0.4	~0.0	* 98.3	51.19
	2017	...	...	...	...	...	...	...	51.19
Svalbard and Jan Mayen Is.	2005	...	...	...	...	...	...	...	63.12
Îles Svalbard-et-Jan Mayen	2010	...	...	...	...	...	...	...	67.67
	2017	...	...	...	...	...	...	...	67.69
Swaziland	2005	* 1 720	* 178	* 14	541	* 10.3	* 0.8	* 31.5	57.40
Swaziland	2010	* 1 720	* 175	* 15	563	* 10.2	* 0.9	* 32.7	57.40
	2014	* 1 720	* 175	* 15	* 581	* 10.2	* 0.9	* 33.8	57.40
	2017	...	...	...	...	...	...	...	57.40
Sweden	2005	41 034	* 2 694	* 9	28 218	* 6.6	* ~0.0	68.8	56.73
Suède	2010	41 034	* 2 625	* 9	28 073	* 6.4	* ~0.0	68.4	57.86
	2014	40 731	* 2 588	* 9	* 28 073	* 6.4	* ~0.0	* 68.9	58.21
	2017	...	...	...	...	...	...	...	58.25
Switzerland	2005	3 952	406	23	1 217	10.3	0.6	30.8	27.62
Suisse	2010	3 952	405	24	1 235	10.2	0.6	31.3	35.13
	2014	3 952	400	26	* 1 250	10.1	0.6	* 31.6	35.15
	2017	...	...	...	...	...	...	...	35.15
Syrian Arab Republic	2005	18 357	4 675	887	* 461	25.5	4.8	* 2.5	1.12
République arabe syrienne	2010	18 363	4 687	1 009	* 491	25.5	5.5	* 2.7	1.12
	2014	* 18 363	* 4 662	* 1 071	* 491	* 25.4	* 5.8	* 2.7	1.12
	2017	...	...	...	...	...	...	...	1.12
Tajikistan	2005	13 996	* 757	117	410	* 5.4	0.8	2.9	20.46
Tadjikistan	2010	* 13 996	* 751	* 130	410	* 5.4	* 0.9	* 2.9	20.46
	2014	* 13 879	* 730	* 140	* 412	* 5.3	* 1.0	* 3.0	20.99
	2017	...	...	...	...	...	...	...	20.99
Thailand	2005	* 51 089	* 15 200	* 3 610	16 100	* 29.8	* 7.1	* 31.5	67.95
Thaïlande	2010	* 51 089	* 15 760	* 4 500	16 249	* 30.8	* 8.8	* 31.8	71.01
	2014	* 51 089	* 16 810	* 4 500	* 16 369	* 32.9	* 8.8	* 32.0	71.74
	2017	...	...	...	...	...	...	...	71.74
TFYR of Macedonia	2005	2 543	448	39	* 975	17.6	1.5	* 38.3	20.78
ex-R.Y. de Macédoine	2010	2 522	414	35	* 998	16.4	1.4	* 39.6	21.06
	2014	2 522	414	38	* 998	16.4	1.5	* 39.6	21.06
	2017	...	...	...	...	...	...	...	21.06
Timor-Leste	2005	1 487	* 170	* 65	* 798	* 11.4	* 4.4	* 53.7	14.91
Timor-Leste	2010	* 1 487	* 150	* 72	* 742	* 10.1	* 4.8	* 49.9	38.73
	2014	* 1 487	* 155	* 75	* 697	* 10.4	* 5.0	* 46.9	38.73
	2017	...	...	...	...	...	...	...	38.73
Togo	2005	* 5 439	* 2 100	* 150	386	* 38.6	* 2.8	* 7.1	75.00
Togo	2010	* 5 439	* 2 460	* 205	287	* 45.2	* 3.8	* 5.3	96.98
	2014	* 5 439	* 2 650	* 170	* 208	* 48.7	* 3.1	* 3.8	96.98
	2017	...	...	...	...	...	...	...	96.98
Tokelau	2005	1	...	* 1	* 0	...	* 60.0	* 0.0	0.00
Tokélaou	2010	1	...	* 1	* 0	...	* 60.0	* 0.0	0.00
	2014	1	...	* 1	* 0	...	* 60.0	* 0.0	0.00
	2017	...	...	...	...	...	...	...	0.00
Tonga	2005	* 72	* 15	* 11	9	* 20.8	* 15.3	* 12.5	11.27
Tonga	2010	72	* 17	* 11	9	* 23.6	* 15.3	12.5	11.27
	2014	72	* 18	* 11	* 9	* 25.0	* 15.3	* 12.5	11.27
	2017	...	...	...	...	...	...	...	11.27
Trinidad and Tobago	2005	513	* 25	* 22	230	* 4.9	* 4.3	44.8	40.67
Trinité-et-Tobago	2010	513	* 25	* 22	226	* 4.9	* 4.3	44.1	40.67
	2014	513	* 25	* 22	* 233	* 4.9	* 4.3	* 45.4	40.67
	2017	...	...	...	...	...	...	...	40.67

Land *(continued)*
Thousand hectares and percent of total land

Terres *(suite)*
Milliers d'hectares et pourcentage de la superficie totale

Region, country or area Région, pays ou zone	Year Année	Area – Superficie ('000 hectares) Total land Superficie totale	 Arable land Terres arables	 Permanent crops Cultures permanentes	 Forest cover Superficie forestière	Area – Superficie (Percent of total)[&] Arable land Terres arables	 Permanent crops Cultures Permanentes[&]	 Forest cover Superficie forestière	Sites protected for terre-strial biodiversity Sites pour la bio. terre. dans aires protég. (%)[&&]
Tunisia Tunisie	2005	15 536	2 730	2 166	915	17.6	13.9	5.9	17.33
	2010	15 536	2 823	2 363	990	18.2	15.2	6.4	27.21
	2014	* 15 536	* 2 900	2 332	* 1 031	* 18.7	* 15.0	* 6.6	40.85
	2017	...	...	...	...	...	...	...	40.85
Turkey Turquie	2005	76 963	23 830	2 776	10 662	31.0	3.6	13.9	2.11
	2010	76 963	21 384	3 011	11 203	27.8	3.9	14.6	2.24
	2014	76 963	20 706	3 238	* 11 613	26.9	4.2	* 15.1	2.29
	2017	...	...	...	...	...	...	...	2.29
Turkmenistan Turkménistan	2005	* 46 993	* 2 040	* 60	* 4 127	* 4.3	* 0.1	* 8.8	14.41
	2010	* 46 993	* 1 940	* 60	* 4 127	* 4.1	* 0.1	* 8.8	14.60
	2014	* 46 993	* 1 940	* 60	* 4 127	* 4.1	* 0.1	* 8.8	14.60
	2017	...	...	...	...	...	...	...	14.60
Turks and Caicos Islands Îles Turques-et-Caïques	2005	95	* 1	...	* 34	* 1.1	...	* 36.2	27.96
	2010	95	* 1	...	* 34	* 1.1	...	* 36.2	27.96
	2014	95	* 1	...	* 34	* 1.1	...	* 36.2	27.96
	2017	...	...	...	...	...	...	...	27.96
Tuvalu Tuvalu	2005	3	...	* 2	* 1	...	* 56.7	* 33.3	...
	2010	3	...	* 2	* 1	...	* 60.0	* 33.3	...
	2014	3	...	* 2	* 1	...	* 60.0	* 33.3	...
Uganda Ouganda	2005	19 981	* 5 950	* 2 200	3 429	* 29.8	* 11.0	17.2	62.37
	2010	20 052	* 6 750	* 2 200	2 753	* 33.7	* 11.0	13.7	73.65
	2014	20 052	* 6 900	* 2 200	* 2 212	* 34.4	* 11.0	* 11.0	73.65
	2017	...	...	...	...	...	...	...	73.65
Ukraine Ukraine	2005	57 938	32 452	901	9 575	56.0	1.6	16.5	23.26
	2010	57 932	32 477	897	9 548	56.1	1.5	16.5	23.32
	2014	57 929	32 531	893	* 9 635	56.2	1.5	* 16.6	23.32
	2017	...	...	...	...	...	...	...	23.32
United Arab Emirates Émirats arabes unis	2005	8 360	* 68	189	* 312	* 0.8	2.3	* 3.7	0.00
	2010	* 8 360	51	42	* 317	* 0.6	* 0.5	* 3.8	14.78
	2014	* 8 360	* 38	* 40	* 322	* 0.4	* 0.5	* 3.8	29.94
	2017	...	...	...	...	...	...	...	29.94
United Kingdom Royaume-Uni	2005	24 193	5 729	47	3 021	23.7	0.2	12.5	77.59
	2010	24 193	5 970	46	3 059	24.7	0.2	12.6	79.97
	2014	24 193	6 234	45	* 3 127	25.8	0.2	* 12.9	80.20
	2017	...	...	...	...	...	...	...	80.20
United Rep. of Tanzania Rép.-Unie de Tanzanie	2005	88 580	* 9 700	* 1 660	49 920	* 11.0	* 1.9	56.4	50.94
	2010	* 88 580	* 11 600	* 1 850	47 920	* 13.1	* 2.1	* 54.1	53.61
	2014	* 88 580	* 13 500	* 2 150	* 46 432	* 15.2	* 2.4	* 52.4	53.61
	2017	...	...	...	...	...	...	...	53.61
U.S. Minor Outlying islands Îles min. éloignées des É-U	2005	...	...	...	...	...	...	...	75.00
	2010	...	...	...	...	...	...	...	100.00
	2017	...	...	...	...	...	...	...	100.00
United States of America États-Unis d'Amérique	2005	916 192	* 165 115	* 2 700	304 757	* 18.0	* 0.3	33.3	26.68
	2010	914 742	* 155 926	* 2 600	308 720	* 17.0	* 0.3	33.7	30.14
	2014	* 914 742	* 154 605	* 2 600	* 309 820	* 16.9	* 0.3	* 33.9	31.25
	2017	...	...	...	...	...	...	...	31.25
United States Virgin Islands Îles Vierges américaines	2005	35	* 2	* 1	19	* 5.7	* 2.9	53.5	32.80
	2010	35	* 1	* 1	18	* 2.9	* 2.9	51.9	32.80
	2014	35	* 1	* 1	* 18	* 2.9	* 2.9	* 50.6	39.38
	2017	...	...	...	...	...	...	...	39.38
Uruguay Uruguay	2005	17 502	* 1 392	* 40	1 522	* 8.0	* 0.2	8.7	10.38
	2010	17 502	* 2 033	38	1 731	* 11.6	0.2	9.9	20.72
	2014	17 502	* 2 411	* 39	* 1 822	* 13.8	* 0.2	* 10.4	20.75
	2017	...	...	...	...	...	...	...	20.80
Uzbekistan Ouzbékistan	2005	42 540	* 4 400	* 340	3 295	* 10.3	* 0.8	7.7	11.90
	2010	* 42 540	* 4 350	* 320	3 276	* 10.2	* 0.8	* 7.7	16.15
	2014	* 42 540	* 4 400	* 370	* 3 231	* 10.3	* 0.9	* 7.6	16.15
	2017	...	...	...	...	...	...	...	16.15
Vanuatu Vanuatu	2005	* 1 219	* 20	* 121	* 440	* 1.6	* 9.9	* 36.1	6.39
	2010	* 1 219	* 20	* 125	* 440	* 1.6	* 10.3	* 36.1	6.39
	2014	* 1 219	* 20	* 125	* 440	* 1.6	* 10.3	* 36.1	6.39
	2017	...	...	...	...	...	...	...	6.39

23 Land *(continued)*

Thousand hectares and percent of total land

Terres *(suite)*

Milliers d'hectares et pourcentage de la superficie totale

Region, country or area Région, pays ou zone	Year Année	Area – Superficie ('000 hectares) Total land Superficie totale	Arable land Terres arables	Permanent crops Cultures permanentes	Forest cover Superficie forestière	Area – Superficie (Percent of total)& Arable land Terres arables	Permanent crops Cultures Permanentes&	Forest cover Superficie forestière	Sites protected for terre-strial biodiversity Sites pour la bio. terre. dans aires protég. (%)&&
Venezuela (Boliv. Rep. of)	2005	* 88 205	* 2 655	* 700	47 713	* 3.0	* 0.8	* 54.1	66.98
Venezuela (Rép. boliv. du)	2010	* 88 205	* 2 700	* 700	47 505	* 3.1	* 0.8	* 53.9	66.98
	2014	* 88 205	* 2 700	* 700	* 46 847	* 3.1	* 0.8	* 53.1	66.98
	2017	...	...	...	...	...	...	...	66.98
Viet Nam	2005	* 31 007	6 358	3 054	13 077	* 20.5	* 9.8	* 42.2	27.16
Viet Nam	2010	* 31 007	6 437	3 681	14 128	* 20.8	* 11.9	* 45.6	29.97
	2014	* 31 007	6 410	3 822	* 14 644	* 20.7	* 12.3	* 47.2	40.65
	2017	...	...	...	...	...	...	...	40.88
Wallis and Futuna Islands	2005	14	* 1	* 5	6	* 7.1	* 35.7	41.5	0.00
Îles Wallis-et-Futuna	2010	14	* 1	* 5	6	* 7.1	* 35.7	41.6	0.00
	2014	14	* 1	* 5	* 6	* 7.1	* 35.7	* 41.6	0.00
	2017	...	...	...	...	...	...	...	0.00
Western Sahara	2005	26 600	* 4	...	* 707	* ~0.0	...	* 2.7	...
Sahara occidental	2010	26 600	* 4	...	* 707	* ~0.0	...	* 2.7	...
	2014	26 600	* 4	...	* 707	* ~0.0	...	* 2.7	...
Yemen	2005	52 797	* 1 287	236	* 549	* 2.4	0.4	* 1.0	20.04
Yémen	2010	* 52 797	* 1 291	288	* 549	* 2.4	* 0.5	* 1.0	31.08
	2014	* 52 797	* 1 248	* 298	* 549	* 2.4	* 0.6	* 1.0	31.08
	2017	...	...	...	...	...	...	...	31.08
Zambia	2005	* 74 339	* 2 727	* 35	50 301	* 3.7	* ~0.0	* 67.7	46.29
Zambie	2010	* 74 339	* 3 400	* 36	49 468	* 4.6	* ~0.0	* 66.5	48.33
	2014	* 74 339	* 3 800	* 36	* 48 802	* 5.1	* ~0.0	* 65.6	48.33
	2017	...	...	...	...	...	...	...	48.33
Zimbabwe	2005	* 38 685	* 3 900	* 100	17 259	* 10.1	* 0.3	* 44.6	80.73
Zimbabwe	2010	* 38 685	* 4 000	* 100	15 624	* 10.3	* 0.3	* 40.4	80.73
	2014	* 38 685	* 4 000	* 100	* 14 374	* 10.3	* 0.3	* 37.2	85.88
	2017	...	...	...	...	...	...	...	85.88
European Union (EU)	2005	424 015	110 732	12 488	156 739	26.1	2.9	37.0	...
Union européenne (UE)	2010	424 114	108 237	12 052	159 235	25.5	2.8	37.5	...
	2014	423 821	108 193	11 970	160 712	25.5	2.8	37.9	...

Source:

Food and Agriculture Organization of the United Nations (FAO), Rome, FAOSTAT data last accessed December 2016.
United Nations Environment Programme (UNEP) World Conservation Monitoring Centre (WCWC) and World Conservation Union (IUCN) and BirdLife International, Cambridge, Sustainable Development Goals database, June 2017.

Source:

Organisation des Nations Unies pour l'alimentation et l'agriculture (FAO), Rome, données FAOSTAT, dernier accès décembre 2016.
Le Programme des Nations Unies pour l'environnement (PNUE) Le Centre mondial de surveillance de la conservation (CMSC) et l'Union mondiale pour la nature (IUCN) et BirdLife International, Cambridge, base de données sur les Objectifs de développement durable (ODD), Juin 2017.

& Figures calculated by the United Nations Statistics Division. && Based on spatial overlap between polygons for Key Biodiversity Areas from the World Database of key Biodiveristy Areas and polygons for protected areas from the World Database on Protected Areas.

& Chiffres calculés par la Division de statistique des Nations Unies. && basées sur un chevauchement spatial entre les zones clés pour la biodiversité de la base de données mondiale pour les zones clés pour la biodiversité et les polygones pour les zones protégées de la base de données mondiale sur les zones protégées.

1 Excluding Sudan.
2 Calculated by the United Nations Statistics Division.
3 Excludes Japan.
4 Data excludes Armenia, Azerbaijan, Cyprus, Georgia, Israel and Turkey.
5 For statistical purposes, the data for China do not include those for the Hong Kong Special Administrative Region (Hong Kong SAR), Macao Special Administrative Region (Macao SAR) and Taiwan Province of China.
6 Including Ascension and Tristan da Cunha.

1 Exclut le Soudan.
2 Calculés par la Division de statistique des Nations Unies.
3 Exclut le Japon.
4 Les données excluent l'Arménie, l'Azerbaïdjan, Chypre, la Géorgie, l'Israël et la Turquie.
5 Pour la présentation des statistiques, les données pour la Chine ne comprennent pas la région administrative spéciale de Hong Kong (Hong Kong RAS), la région administrative spéciale de Macao (Macao RAS) et la province chinoise de Taïwan.
6 Y compris Ascension et Tristan da Cunha.

24 Threatened species

Number of species by taxonomic group

Espèces menacées

Nombre d'espèces menacées par groupe taxonomique

Country or area &	2004	2010	2013	2014	2015	2016	2017	Pays ou zone &
Afghanistan								**Afghanistan**
Vertebrates	31	31	32	32	31	35	35	Vertébrés
Invertebrates	1	1	1	2	2	2	2	Invertébrés
Plants	1	2	3	3	5	5	5	Plantes
Total	33	34	36	37	38	42	42	Total
Albania								**Albanie**
Vertebrates	33	53	54	53	54	63	62	Vertébrés
Invertebrates	4	47	55	56	58	62	68	Invertébrés
Plants	0	0	0	0	0	0	0	Plantes
Total	37	100	109	109	112	125	130	Total
Algeria								**Algérie**
Vertebrates	36	69	72	71	71	78	79	Vertébrés
Invertebrates	12	21	22	25	26	29	38	Invertébrés
Plants	2	15	17	17	17	18	18	Plantes
Total	50	105	111	113	114	125	135	Total
American Samoa								**Samoa américaines**
Vertebrates	18	21	24	25	25	27	27	Vertébrés
Invertebrates	5	57	64	64	64	64	64	Invertébrés
Plants	1	1	1	1	1	1	1	Plantes
Total	24	79	89	90	90	92	92	Total
Andorra								**Andorre**
Vertebrates	1	4	4	4	4	5	5	Vertébrés
Invertebrates	4	4	8	7	7	7	8	Invertébrés
Plants	0	0	0	0	0	0	0	Plantes
Total	5	8	12	11	11	12	13	Total
Angola								**Angola**
Vertebrates	44	77	85	87	87	99	103	Vertébrés
Invertebrates	6	7	7	9	9	9	9	Invertébrés
Plants	26	33	34	34	34	34	34	Plantes
Total	76	117	126	130	130	142	146	Total
Anguilla								**Anguilla**
Vertebrates	15	20	28	29	37	38	38	Vertébrés
Invertebrates	0	10	10	10	10	10	10	Invertébrés
Plants	3	3	3	3	4	4	4	Plantes
Total	18	33	41	42	51	52	52	Total
Antarctica								**Antarctique**
Vertebrates	8	6	6	6	6	6	6	Vertébrés
Invertebrates	0	0	0	0	0	0	0	Invertébrés
Plants	0	0	0	0	0	0	0	Plantes
Total	8	6	6	6	6	6	6	Total
Antigua and Barbuda								**Antigua-et-Barbuda**
Vertebrates	18	23	29	30	38	38	40	Vertébrés
Invertebrates	0	11	11	11	11	11	11	Invertébrés
Plants	4	4	4	4	4	4	4	Plantes
Total	22	38	44	45	53	53	55	Total
Argentina								**Argentine**
Vertebrates	134	157	160	160	160	172	172	Vertébrés
Invertebrates	10	12	13	13	13	14	14	Invertébrés
Plants	42	44	69	70	70	70	70	Plantes
Total	186	213	242	243	243	256	256	Total
Armenia								**Arménie**
Vertebrates	27	29	32	31	31	34	34	Vertébrés
Invertebrates	7	6	7	9	9	9	9	Invertébrés
Plants	1	1	1	71	71	71	71	Plantes
Total	35	36	40	111	111	114	114	Total
Aruba								**Aruba**
Vertebrates	17	20	20	19	25	28	28	Vertébrés
Invertebrates	1	1	2	2	2	2	2	Invertébrés
Plants	0	1	2	2	2	2	2	Plantes
Total	18	22	24	23	29	32	32	Total
Australia [1]								**Australie** [1]
Vertebrates	282	297	301	304	304	319	323	Vertébrés
Invertebrates	283	489	505	511	514	514	531	Invertébrés
Plants	56	67	90	91	91	# 93	94	Plantes
Total	621	853	896	906	909	926	948	Total

24 Threatened species *(continued)*
Number of species by taxonomic group

Espèces menacées *(suite)*
Nombre d'espèces menacées par groupe taxonomique

Country or area &	2004	2010	2013	2014	2015	2016	2017	Pays ou zone &
Austria								**Autriche**
Vertebrates	20	23	24	24	24	27	26	Vertébrés
Invertebrates	44	55	70	70	69	69	71	Invertébrés
Plants	3	4	13	13	13	# 21	21	Plantes
Total	67	82	107	107	106	117	118	Total
Azerbaijan								**Azerbaïdjan**
Vertebrates	32	41	42	43	43	47	48	Vertébrés
Invertebrates	6	4	6	7	7	7	7	Invertébrés
Plants	0	0	0	42	42	42	42	Plantes
Total	38	45	48	92	92	96	97	Total
Bahamas								**Bahamas**
Vertebrates	36	44	51	52	61	65	66	Vertébrés
Invertebrates	1	11	12	12	12	12	12	Invertébrés
Plants	5	7	8	8	8	8	8	Plantes
Total	42	62	71	72	81	85	86	Total
Bahrain								**Bahreïn**
Vertebrates	18	19	19	20	19	23	23	Vertébrés
Invertebrates	0	13	14	13	13	13	13	Invertébrés
Plants	0	0	0	0	0	0	0	Plantes
Total	18	32	33	33	32	36	36	Total
Bangladesh								**Bangladesh**
Vertebrates	73	104	106	108	109	120	123	Vertébrés
Invertebrates	0	2	7	7	7	7	7	Invertébrés
Plants	12	16	17	17	21	21	21	Plantes
Total	85	122	130	132	137	148	151	Total
Barbados								**Barbade**
Vertebrates	18	24	30	31	37	39	42	Vertébrés
Invertebrates	0	10	11	11	11	11	11	Invertébrés
Plants	2	2	3	3	3	3	3	Plantes
Total	20	36	44	45	51	53	56	Total
Belarus								**Bélarus**
Vertebrates	10	10	12	12	11	14	15	Vertébrés
Invertebrates	8	6	9	9	9	9	9	Invertébrés
Plants	0	0	1	1	1	1	1	Plantes
Total	18	16	22	22	21	24	25	Total
Belgium								**Belgique**
Vertebrates	25	15	17	17	16	23	22	Vertébrés
Invertebrates	11	11	14	14	14	14	14	Invertébrés
Plants	0	1	0	0	0	# 1	1	Plantes
Total	36	27	31	31	30	38	37	Total
Belize								**Belize**
Vertebrates	36	48	58	60	70	70	69	Vertébrés
Invertebrates	1	12	12	12	12	12	12	Invertébrés
Plants	30	32	33	33	35	36	36	Plantes
Total	67	92	103	105	117	118	117	Total
Benin								**Bénin**
Vertebrates	17	47	53	55	55	66	68	Vertébrés
Invertebrates	0	1	1	3	3	3	3	Invertébrés
Plants	14	14	15	16	16	17	17	Plantes
Total	31	62	69	74	74	86	88	Total
Bermuda								**Bermudes**
Vertebrates	18	18	24	25	28	35	36	Vertébrés
Invertebrates	25	28	28	28	28	28	28	Invertébrés
Plants	4	4	4	7	8	8	8	Plantes
Total	47	50	56	60	64	71	72	Total
Bhutan								**Bhoutan**
Vertebrates	40	50	52	52	52	54	52	Vertébrés
Invertebrates	1	1	1	1	1	1	1	Invertébrés
Plants	7	8	9	12	18	18	18	Plantes
Total	48	59	62	65	71	73	71	Total
Bolivia (Plurin. State of)								**Bolivie (État plurin. de)**
Vertebrates	79	90	111	114	114	124	124	Vertébrés
Invertebrates	1	1	3	3	3	3	3	Invertébrés
Plants	70	72	98	99	99	104	104	Plantes
Total	150	163	212	216	216	231	231	Total

Threatened species *(continued)*
Number of species by taxonomic group

Espèces menacées *(suite)*
Nombre d'espèces menacées par groupe taxonomique

Country or area &	2004	2010	2013	2014	2015	2016	2017	Pays ou zone &
Bonaire, St. Eustatius & Saba								**Bonaire, St-Eustache et Saba**
Vertebrates	...	...	2	32	41	42	42	Vertébrés
Invertebrates	...	...	0	11	11	11	11	Invertébrés
Plants	...	...	0	3	3	3	3	Plantes
Total	...	...	2	46	55	56	56	Total
Bosnia and Herzegovina								**Bosnie-Herzégovine**
Vertebrates	29	44	45	46	48	51	51	Vertébrés
Invertebrates	10	22	34	36	36	36	39	Invertébrés
Plants	1	1	1	1	1	1	1	Plantes
Total	40	67	80	83	85	88	91	Total
Botswana								**Botswana**
Vertebrates	15	18	20	22	22	24	26	Vertébrés
Invertebrates	0	0	0	0	0	0	0	Invertébrés
Plants	0	0	2	2	2	2	2	Plantes
Total	15	18	22	24	24	26	28	Total
Bouvet Island								**Île Bouvet**
Vertebrates	1	2	3	3	3	3	3	Vertébrés
Invertebrates	0	0	0	0	0	0	0	Invertébrés
Plants	0	0	0	0	0	0	0	Plantes
Total	1	2	3	3	3	3	3	Total
Brazil								**Brésil**
Vertebrates	282[2]	341[2]	379	395	396	397	403	Vertébrés
Invertebrates	34	45	54	54	54	55	55	Invertébrés
Plants	381	387	504	516	516	521	532	Plantes
Total	697	773	937	965	966	973	990	Total
British Indian Ocean Terr.								**Terr. brit. de l'océan Indien**
Vertebrates	6	10	11	11	11	14	15	Vertébrés
Invertebrates	0	65	69	69	69	69	69	Invertébrés
Plants	1	1	1	1	1	1	1	Plantes
Total	7	76	81	81	81	84	85	Total
British Virgin Islands								**Îles Vierges britanniques**
Vertebrates	20	23	32	33	41	41	47	Vertébrés
Invertebrates	0	10	10	10	10	10	10	Invertébrés
Plants	10	10	10	10	10	10	10	Plantes
Total	30	43	52	53	61	61	67	Total
Brunei Darussalam								**Brunéi Darussalam**
Vertebrates	49	70	75	75	77	80	81	Vertébrés
Invertebrates	0	1	8	8	8	8	8	Invertébrés
Plants	99	99	104	104	104	104	104	Plantes
Total	148	170	187	187	189	192	193	Total
Bulgaria								**Bulgarie**
Vertebrates	35	39	42	43	42	49	50	Vertébrés
Invertebrates	9	27	36	37	37	38	48	Invertébrés
Plants	0	0	6	6	6	6	6	Plantes
Total	44	66	84	86	85	93	104	Total
Burkina Faso								**Burkina Faso**
Vertebrates	9	20	24	25	25	27	27	Vertébrés
Invertebrates	0	1	1	1	1	1	1	Invertébrés
Plants	2	3	3	3	3	3	3	Plantes
Total	11	24	28	29	29	31	31	Total
Burundi								**Burundi**
Vertebrates	22	43	46	46	45	44	46	Vertébrés
Invertebrates	4	7	7	7	7	7	7	Invertébrés
Plants	2	2	6	7	8	8	8	Plantes
Total	28	52	59	60	60	59	61	Total
Cabo Verde								**Cabo Verde**
Vertebrates	21	28	36	35	35	49	49	Vertébrés
Invertebrates	0	0	12	13	13	13	13	Invertébrés
Plants	2	3	3	3	3	3	3	Plantes
Total	23	31	51	51	51	65	65	Total
Cambodia								**Cambodge**
Vertebrates	72	107	125	128	130	137	141	Vertébrés
Invertebrates	0	67	77	77	77	79	79	Invertébrés
Plants	31	30	32	32	36	36	35	Plantes
Total	103	204	234	237	243	252	255	Total

24 Threatened species *(continued)*
Number of species by taxonomic group

Espèces menacées *(suite)*
Nombre d'espèces menacées par groupe taxonomique

Country or area &	2004	2010	2013	2014	2015	2016	2017	Pays ou zone &
Cameroon								**Cameroun**
Vertebrates	146	222	235	236	237	255	258	Vertébrés
Invertebrates	4	24	25	27	27	27	27	Invertébrés
Plants	334	378	379	425	433	490	490	Plantes
Total	484	624	639	688	697	772	775	Total
Canada								**Canada**
Vertebrates	62	63	69	69	68	79	81	Vertébrés
Invertebrates	11	12	15	18	22	25	27	Invertébrés
Plants	1	2	2	6	7	# 14	14	Plantes
Total	74	77	86	93	97	118	122	Total
Cayman Islands								**Îles Caïmanes**
Vertebrates	16	21	27	28	38	38	41	Vertébrés
Invertebrates	1	11	11	11	11	11	11	Invertébrés
Plants	2	2	2	22	22	22	22	Plantes
Total	19	34	40	61	71	71	74	Total
Central African Republic								**République centrafricaine**
Vertebrates	15	19	26	31	32	33	36	Vertébrés
Invertebrates	0	0	0	0	0	0	0	Invertébrés
Plants	15	17	18	22	22	24	24	Plantes
Total	30	36	44	53	54	57	60	Total
Chad								**Tchad**
Vertebrates	18	24	27	29	29	31	33	Vertébrés
Invertebrates	1	4	4	4	4	4	4	Invertébrés
Plants	2	2	4	5	5	6	6	Plantes
Total	21	30	35	38	38	41	43	Total
Chile								**Chili**
Vertebrates	83	95	96	98	98	111	112	Vertébrés
Invertebrates	0	9	12	12	12	13	13	Invertébrés
Plants	40	41	71	72	72	72	72	Plantes
Total	123	145	179	182	182	196	197	Total
China [3]								**Chine [3]**
Vertebrates	326	374	407	416	420	428	430	Vertébrés
Invertebrates	4	32	76	76	76	76	76	Invertébrés
Plants	443	453	475	503	544	# 575	574	Plantes
Total	773	859	958	995	1 040	1 079	1 080	Total
China, Hong Kong SAR								**Chine, Hong Kong RAS**
Vertebrates	32	37	44	45	45	46	47	Vertébrés
Invertebrates	1	6	8	8	8	8	8	Invertébrés
Plants	6	6	6	6	7	9	9	Plantes
Total	39	49	58	59	60	63	64	Total
China, Macao SAR								**Chine, Macao RAS**
Vertebrates	5	9	9	10	10	10	10	Vertébrés
Invertebrates	0	0	1	1	1	1	1	Invertébrés
Plants	0	0	0	0	0	0	0	Plantes
Total	5	9	10	11	11	11	11	Total
Christmas Island								**Île Christmas**
Vertebrates	12	16	17	18	18	20	20	Vertébrés
Invertebrates	0	16	18	18	18	18	18	Invertébrés
Plants	1	1	1	1	1	1	1	Plantes
Total	13	33	36	37	37	39	39	Total
Cocos (Keeling) Islands								**Îles des Cocos (Keeling)**
Vertebrates	5	11	12	12	11	12	13	Vertébrés
Invertebrates	0	17	20	20	20	20	20	Invertébrés
Plants	0	0	0	0	0	0	0	Plantes
Total	5	28	32	32	31	32	33	Total
Colombia								**Colombie**
Vertebrates	371	424	459	463	473	518	525	Vertébrés
Invertebrates	0	30	33	33	33	52	52	Invertébrés
Plants	222	227	238	245	245	257	258	Plantes
Total	593	681	730	741	751	827	835	Total
Comoros								**Comores**
Vertebrates	18	21	25	26	26	29	33	Vertébrés
Invertebrates	4	63	72	73	73	73	74	Invertébrés
Plants	5	5	7	7	7	7	7	Plantes
Total	27	89	104	106	106	109	114	Total

24 Threatened species *(continued)*

Number of species by taxonomic group

Espèces menacées *(suite)*

Nombre d'espèces menacées par groupe taxonomique

Country or area &	2004	2010	2013	2014	2015	2016	2017	Pays ou zone &
Congo								**Congo**
Vertebrates	29	61	66	70	71	81	82	Vertébrés
Invertebrates	1	5	5	7	7	7	7	Invertébrés
Plants	35	37	38	41	41	45	45	Plantes
Total	65	103	109	118	119	133	134	Total
Cook Islands								**Îles Cook**
Vertebrates	22	27	30	30	30	31	32	Vertébrés
Invertebrates	0	25	32	32	32	32	32	Invertébrés
Plants	1	1	1	11	11	11	11	Plantes
Total	23	53	63	73	73	74	75	Total
Costa Rica								**Costa Rica**
Vertebrates	112	142	156	156	162	166	169	Vertébrés
Invertebrates	9	27	30	30	30	31	31	Invertébrés
Plants	110	116	129	131	131	140	140	Plantes
Total	231	285	315	317	323	337	340	Total
Côte d'Ivoire								**Côte d'Ivoire**
Vertebrates	61	100	108	113	113	127	130	Vertébrés
Invertebrates	1	4	4	6	6	6	6	Invertébrés
Plants	105	106	105	107	107	112	113	Plantes
Total	167	210	217	226	226	245	249	Total
Croatia								**Croatie**
Vertebrates	46	77	85	84	84	93	94	Vertébrés
Invertebrates	11	21	63	66	67	68	73	Invertébrés
Plants	0	3	8	8	8	# 9	9	Plantes
Total	57	101	156	158	159	170	176	Total
Cuba								**Cuba**
Vertebrates	106	123	132	133	138	138	137	Vertébrés
Invertebrates	3	15	23	23	23	23	23	Invertébrés
Plants	163	166	176	176	176	179	179	Plantes
Total	272	304	331	332	337	340	339	Total
Curaçao								**Curaçao**
Vertebrates	...	...	12	29	36	36	38	Vertébrés
Invertebrates	...	...	0	11	11	11	11	Invertébrés
Plants	...	...	0	2	2	2	2	Plantes
Total	...	...	12	42	49	49	51	Total
Cyprus								**Chypre**
Vertebrates	24	31	34	33	34	41	42	Vertébrés
Invertebrates	0	4	5	7	8	12	12	Invertébrés
Plants	1	8	18	18	18	18	18	Plantes
Total	25	43	57	58	60	71	72	Total
Czechia								**Tchéquie**
Vertebrates	22	10	11	11	11	14	14	Vertébrés
Invertebrates	19	19	24	25	24	24	24	Invertébrés
Plants	4	4	11	10	10	# 15	15	Plantes
Total	45	33	46	46	45	53	53	Total
Dem. People's Rep. Korea								**Rép. pop. dém. de Corée**
Vertebrates	40	44	51	52	53	57	58	Vertébrés
Invertebrates	1	2	3	3	3	3	3	Invertébrés
Plants	3	6	8	8	8	17	17	Plantes
Total	44	52	62	63	64	77	78	Total
Dem. Rep. of the Congo								**Rép. dém. du Congo**
Vertebrates	84	162	168	172	171	183	182	Vertébrés
Invertebrates	22	51	51	53	53	53	53	Invertébrés
Plants	65	83	95	107	109	113	114	Plantes
Total	171	296	314	332	333	349	349	Total
Denmark								**Danemark**
Vertebrates	21	18	20	20	20	27	28	Vertébrés
Invertebrates	11	12	15	15	15	15	15	Invertébrés
Plants	3	3	2	1	1	# 4	4	Plantes
Total	35	33	37	36	36	46	47	Total
Djibouti								**Djibouti**
Vertebrates	19	29	33	34	34	38	38	Vertébrés
Invertebrates	0	50	57	57	57	57	57	Invertébrés
Plants	2	2	3	3	3	3	3	Plantes
Total	21	81	93	94	94	98	98	Total

24 Threatened species *(continued)*
Number of species by taxonomic group

Espèces menacées *(suite)*
Nombre d'espèces menacées par groupe taxonomique

Country or area &	2004	2010	2013	2014	2015	2016	2017	Pays ou zone &
Dominica								**Dominique**
Vertebrates	22	27	32	33	40	42	44	Vertébrés
Invertebrates	0	11	11	11	11	11	11	Invertébrés
Plants	11	10	10	11	11	11	11	Plantes
Total	33	48	53	55	62	64	66	Total
Dominican Republic								**République dominicaine**
Vertebrates	72	80	89	90	95	95	126	Vertébrés
Invertebrates	2	16	16	16	16	16	16	Invertébrés
Plants	30	30	38	41	42	42	42	Plantes
Total	104	126	143	147	153	153	184	Total
Ecuador								**Équateur**
Vertebrates	288	356	393	394	395	417	426	Vertébrés
Invertebrates	48	62	65	65	65	70	70	Invertébrés
Plants	1 815	1 837	1 843	1 840	1 848	# 1 866	1 862	Plantes
Total	2 151	2 255	2 301	2 299	2 308	2 353	2 358	Total
Egypt								**Égypte**
Vertebrates	43	73	80	82	83	96	97	Vertébrés
Invertebrates	1	46	53	54	55	56	56	Invertébrés
Plants	2	2	2	3	3	3	3	Plantes
Total	46	121	135	139	141	155	156	Total
El Salvador								**El Salvador**
Vertebrates	23	39	44	47	47	47	47	Vertébrés
Invertebrates	1	6	7	7	7	10	10	Invertébrés
Plants	25	27	29	29	29	29	29	Plantes
Total	49	72	80	83	83	86	86	Total
Equatorial Guinea								**Guinée équatoriale**
Vertebrates	38	60	64	69	71	85	85	Vertébrés
Invertebrates	2	2	3	5	5	5	5	Invertébrés
Plants	61	68	68	77	79	88	87	Plantes
Total	101	130	135	151	155	178	177	Total
Eritrea								**Érythrée**
Vertebrates	31	44	51	51	51	58	59	Vertébrés
Invertebrates	0	50	58	58	58	58	58	Invertébrés
Plants	3	3	4	4	4	4	5	Plantes
Total	34	97	113	113	113	120	122	Total
Estonia								**Estonie**
Vertebrates	8	8	11	11	11	14	15	Vertébrés
Invertebrates	4	3	6	6	6	6	6	Invertébrés
Plants	0	0	0	0	0	# 2	2	Plantes
Total	12	11	17	17	17	22	23	Total
Ethiopia								**Éthiopie**
Vertebrates	65	79	86	89	89	92	90	Vertébrés
Invertebrates	6	15	15	15	15	15	15	Invertébrés
Plants	22	26	40	40	41	41	43	Plantes
Total	93	120	141	144	145	148	148	Total
Falkland Islands (Malvinas)								**Îles Falkland (Malvinas)**
Vertebrates	21	18	18	18	18	18	18	Vertébrés
Invertebrates	0	0	0	0	0	0	0	Invertébrés
Plants	5	5	5	5	5	5	5	Plantes
Total	26	23	23	23	23	23	23	Total
Faroe Islands								**Îles Féroé**
Vertebrates	11	13	13	13	14	20	20	Vertébrés
Invertebrates	0	0	0	0	0	0	0	Invertébrés
Plants	0	0	0	0	0	# 1	1	Plantes
Total	11	13	13	13	14	21	21	Total
Fiji								**Fidji**
Vertebrates	33	37	48	48	48	52	55	Vertébrés
Invertebrates	2	90	165	165	165	165	165	Invertébrés
Plants	66	65	65	65	65	65	71	Plantes
Total	101	192	278	278	278	282	291	Total
Finland								**Finlande**
Vertebrates	14	10	13	13	13	17	18	Vertébrés
Invertebrates	10	7	10	10	10	10	10	Invertébrés
Plants	1	1	2	2	2	# 8	8	Plantes
Total	25	18	25	25	25	35	36	Total

Threatened species *(continued)*
Number of species by taxonomic group

Espèces menacées *(suite)*
Nombre d'espèces menacées par groupe taxonomique

Country or area &	2004	2010	2013	2014	2015	2016	2017	Pays ou zone &
France								**France**
Vertebrates	53	62	70	70	70	80	82	Vertébrés
Invertebrates	65	91	127	132	133	137	153	Invertébrés
Plants	2	15	32	32	33	# 43	43	Plantes
Total	120	168	229	234	236	260	278	Total
French Guiana								**Guyane française**
Vertebrates	33	40	50	50	51	55	55	Vertébrés
Invertebrates	0	0	0	0	0	0	0	Invertébrés
Plants	16	16	16	16	16	18	18	Plantes
Total	49	56	66	66	67	73	73	Total
French Polynesia								**Polynésie française**
Vertebrates	46	54	61	63	63	63	66	Vertébrés
Invertebrates	29	59	65	65	65	65	62	Invertébrés
Plants	47	47	47	47	47	47	47	Plantes
Total	122	160	173	175	175	175	175	Total
French Southern Territories								**Terres australes françaises**
Vertebrates	17	21	22	22	22	24	25	Vertébrés
Invertebrates	0	0	0	0	0	0	0	Invertébrés
Plants	0	0	0	0	0	0	0	Plantes
Total	17	21	22	22	22	24	25	Total
Gabon								**Gabon**
Vertebrates	31	84	89	92	93	105	105	Vertébrés
Invertebrates	1	0	1	3	3	3	3	Invertébrés
Plants	107	120	120	132	135	162	162	Plantes
Total	139	204	210	227	231	270	270	Total
Gambia								**Gambie**
Vertebrates	17	39	47	48	48	60	60	Vertébrés
Invertebrates	0	0	0	2	2	2	2	Invertébrés
Plants	4	4	5	5	5	5	5	Plantes
Total	21	43	52	55	55	67	67	Total
Georgia								**Géorgie**
Vertebrates	33	37	38	39	38	42	43	Vertébrés
Invertebrates	10	9	13	15	15	15	15	Invertébrés
Plants	0	0	0	61	61	# 62	62	Plantes
Total	43	46	51	115	114	119	120	Total
Germany								**Allemagne**
Vertebrates	35	33	35	35	33	39	40	Vertébrés
Invertebrates	31	34	58	58	57	57	57	Invertébrés
Plants	12	12	17	17	17	# 24	19	Plantes
Total	78	79	110	110	107	120	116	Total
Ghana								**Ghana**
Vertebrates	43	83	95	99	99	112	114	Vertébrés
Invertebrates	0	1	3	5	5	5	5	Invertébrés
Plants	117	118	117	119	119	119	119	Plantes
Total	160	202	215	223	223	236	238	Total
Gibraltar								**Gibraltar**
Vertebrates	16	20	20	20	21	28	26	Vertébrés
Invertebrates	2	2	3	4	5	5	5	Invertébrés
Plants	0	0	0	0	0	0	0	Plantes
Total	18	22	23	24	26	33	31	Total
Greece								**Grèce**
Vertebrates	62	107	111	111	111	120	121	Vertébrés
Invertebrates	11	36	113	117	122	181	192	Invertébrés
Plants	2	13	57	58	58	# 60	61	Plantes
Total	75	156	281	286	291	361	374	Total
Greenland								**Groenland**
Vertebrates	11	13	15	16	16	21	22	Vertébrés
Invertebrates	0	0	0	0	0	0	0	Invertébrés
Plants	1	1	1	1	1	1	1	Plantes
Total	12	14	16	17	17	22	23	Total
Grenada								**Grenade**
Vertebrates	20	24	31	32	38	40	41	Vertébrés
Invertebrates	0	10	10	10	10	10	10	Invertébrés
Plants	3	3	3	3	3	3	3	Plantes
Total	23	37	44	45	51	53	54	Total

Country or area &	2004	2010	2013	2014	2015	2016	2017	Pays ou zone &
Guadeloupe [4]								**Guadeloupe** [4]
Vertebrates	25	30	36	37	45	45	48	Vertébrés
Invertebrates	1	16	16	16	16	16	16	Invertébrés
Plants	7	8	8	9	9	9	9	Plantes
Total	33	54	60	62	70	70	73	Total
Guam								**Guam**
Vertebrates	16	24	29	31	31	34	35	Vertébrés
Invertebrates	5	6	13	60	60	60	60	Invertébrés
Plants	3	4	4	4	4	4	4	Plantes
Total	24	34	46	95	95	98	99	Total
Guatemala								**Guatemala**
Vertebrates	115	140	162	168	176	176	176	Vertébrés
Invertebrates	8	8	9	9	9	13	13	Invertébrés
Plants	85	82	93	94	97	102	101	Plantes
Total	208	230	264	271	282	291	290	Total
Guernsey								**Guernesey**
Vertebrates	...	2	2	2	2	5	5	Vertébrés
Invertebrates	...	0	0	0	0	0	0	Invertébrés
Plants	...	0	0	0	0	0	0	Plantes
Total	...	2	2	2	2	5	5	Total
Guinea								**Guinée**
Vertebrates	42	107	119	122	122	132	134	Vertébrés
Invertebrates	3	5	5	7	7	7	7	Invertébrés
Plants	22	22	28	34	34	44	44	Plantes
Total	67	134	152	163	163	183	185	Total
Guinea-Bissau								**Guinée-Bissau**
Vertebrates	17	48	56	59	59	69	70	Vertébrés
Invertebrates	1	0	0	2	2	2	2	Invertébrés
Plants	4	4	5	5	5	5	5	Plantes
Total	22	52	61	66	66	76	77	Total
Guyana								**Guyana**
Vertebrates	41	46	62	62	63	65	67	Vertébrés
Invertebrates	1	1	1	1	1	1	1	Invertébrés
Plants	23	22	23	23	23	26	26	Plantes
Total	65	69	86	86	87	92	94	Total
Haiti								**Haïti**
Vertebrates	86	94	104	106	113	113	149	Vertébrés
Invertebrates	2	14	14	14	14	14	14	Invertébrés
Plants	28	29	38	39	42	42	42	Plantes
Total	116	137	156	159	169	169	205	Total
Heard Is. and McDonald Is.								**Île Heard-et-Îles MacDonald**
Vertebrates	12	12	12	12	12	12	12	Vertébrés
Invertebrates	0	0	0	0	0	0	0	Invertébrés
Plants	0	0	0	0	0	0	0	Plantes
Total	12	12	12	12	12	12	12	Total
Holy See								**Saint-Siège**
Vertebrates	...	1	1	1	1	1	1	Vertébrés
Invertebrates	...	0	0	0	0	0	0	Invertébrés
Plants	...	0	0	0	0	0	0	Plantes
Total	...	1	1	1	1	1	1	Total
Honduras								**Honduras**
Vertebrates	93	110	139	147	156	156	157	Vertébrés
Invertebrates	2	17	18	18	18	21	21	Invertébrés
Plants	111	113	118	119	120	123	123	Plantes
Total	206	240	275	284	294	300	301	Total
Hungary								**Hongrie**
Vertebrates	25	20	22	22	22	25	26	Vertébrés
Invertebrates	25	26	34	36	35	35	29	Invertébrés
Plants	1	1	10	10	10	# 12	11	Plantes
Total	51	47	66	68	67	72	66	Total
Iceland								**Islande**
Vertebrates	15	17	19	19	21	26	27	Vertébrés
Invertebrates	0	0	0	0	0	0	0	Invertébrés
Plants	0	0	0	0	0	0	0	Plantes
Total	15	17	19	19	21	26	27	Total

24 Threatened species (continued)

Number of species by taxonomic group

Espèces menacées (suite)

Nombre d'espèces menacées par groupe taxonomique

Country or area &	2004	2010	2013	2014	2015	2016	2017	Pays ou zone &
India								**Inde**
Vertebrates	283	390	514	521	520	528	530	Vertébrés
Invertebrates	23	113	134	135	135	135	135	Invertébrés
Plants	246	255	325	332	384	388	387	Plantes
Total	552	758	973	988	1 039	1 051	1 052	Total
Indonesia								**Indonésie**
Vertebrates	419	503	515	529	530	540	564	Vertébrés
Invertebrates	31	246	287	288	290	290	290	Invertébrés
Plants	383	393	404	408	426	427	427	Plantes
Total	833	1 142	1 206	1 225	1 246	1 257	1 281	Total
Iran (Islamic Republic of)								**Iran (Rép. islamique d')**
Vertebrates	65	82	87	94	94	105	106	Vertébrés
Invertebrates	3	19	23	24	24	24	24	Invertébrés
Plants	1	1	2	3	3	3	4	Plantes
Total	69	102	112	121	121	132	134	Total
Iraq								**Iraq**
Vertebrates	33	45	45	51	51	54	53	Vertébrés
Invertebrates	2	15	16	17	17	17	17	Invertébrés
Plants	0	0	1	1	1	1	2	Plantes
Total	35	60	62	69	69	72	72	Total
Ireland								**Irlande**
Vertebrates	18	24	30	31	32	40	41	Vertébrés
Invertebrates	3	2	3	6	6	6	6	Invertébrés
Plants	1	1	1	1	1	# 3	3	Plantes
Total	22	27	34	38	39	49	50	Total
Isle of Man								**Île de Man**
Vertebrates	...	2	3	3	3	3	3	Vertébrés
Invertebrates	...	0	0	0	0	0	0	Invertébrés
Plants	...	0	0	0	0	0	0	Plantes
Total	...	2	3	3	3	3	3	Total
Israel								**Israël**
Vertebrates	47	73	76	78	78	89	90	Vertébrés
Invertebrates	10	58	67	73	74	74	74	Invertébrés
Plants	0	0	0	0	0	9	10	Plantes
Total	57	131	143	151	152	172	174	Total
Italy								**Italie**
Vertebrates	53	70	77	76	76	85	87	Vertébrés
Invertebrates	58	77	130	134	136	141	194	Invertébrés
Plants	3	27	66	66	67	# 79	78	Plantes
Total	114	174	273	276	279	305	359	Total
Jamaica								**Jamaïque**
Vertebrates	54	58	62	63	69	71	82	Vertébrés
Invertebrates	5	15	15	15	15	15	15	Invertébrés
Plants	208	209	212	214	214	214	214	Plantes
Total	267	282	289	292	298	300	311	Total
Japan								**Japon**
Vertebrates	148	158	164	171	171	180	184	Vertébrés
Invertebrates	45	157	170	170	170	171	171	Invertébrés
Plants	12	15	17	21	23	# 46	49	Plantes
Total	205	330	351	362	364	397	404	Total
Jersey								**Jersey**
Vertebrates	...	2	2	2	2	5	5	Vertébrés
Invertebrates	...	0	0	1	1	1	1	Invertébrés
Plants	...	0	0	0	0	0	0	Plantes
Total	...	2	2	3	3	6	6	Total
Jordan								**Jordanie**
Vertebrates	27	41	42	41	40	47	47	Vertébrés
Invertebrates	3	48	56	61	61	61	61	Invertébrés
Plants	0	1	1	1	1	5	5	Plantes
Total	30	90	99	103	102	113	113	Total
Kazakhstan								**Kazakhstan**
Vertebrates	48	53	55	55	55	57	59	Vertébrés
Invertebrates	4	4	6	7	7	7	7	Invertébrés
Plants	1	16	15	15	16	16	16	Plantes
Total	53	73	76	77	78	80	82	Total

24 Threatened species *(continued)*
Number of species by taxonomic group

Espèces menacées *(suite)*
Nombre d'espèces menacées par groupe taxonomique

Country or area &	2004	2010	2013	2014	2015	2016	2017	Pays ou zone &
Kenya								**Kenya**
Vertebrates	99	137	149	157	157	162	162	Vertébrés
Invertebrates	27	72	83	84	84	84	86	Invertébrés
Plants	103	129	187	187	222	222	232	Plantes
Total	229	338	419	428	463	468	480	Total
Kiribati								**Kiribati**
Vertebrates	10	17	20	19	19	21	23	Vertébrés
Invertebrates	1	73	81	81	81	81	81	Invertébrés
Plants	0	0	0	0	0	0	0	Plantes
Total	11	90	101	100	100	102	104	Total
Kuwait								**Koweït**
Vertebrates	20	28	28	29	29	36	36	Vertébrés
Invertebrates	0	13	14	13	13	13	13	Invertébrés
Plants	0	0	0	0	0	0	0	Plantes
Total	20	41	42	42	42	49	49	Total
Kyrgyzstan								**Kirghizistan**
Vertebrates	12	23	23	23	23	26	26	Vertébrés
Invertebrates	3	3	3	4	4	4	4	Invertébrés
Plants	1	14	14	14	14	14	14	Plantes
Total	16	40	40	41	41	44	44	Total
Lao People's Dem. Rep.								**Rép. dém. populaire lao**
Vertebrates	72	107	144	147	148	153	147	Vertébrés
Invertebrates	0	3	21	21	21	21	21	Invertébrés
Plants	19	22	32	32	41	41	41	Plantes
Total	91	132	197	200	210	215	209	Total
Latvia								**Lettonie**
Vertebrates	15	9	13	13	13	16	17	Vertébrés
Invertebrates	8	9	12	12	12	12	12	Invertébrés
Plants	0	0	0	0	0	# 1	1	Plantes
Total	23	18	25	25	25	29	30	Total
Lebanon								**Liban**
Vertebrates	25	44	47	47	48	58	58	Vertébrés
Invertebrates	1	5	10	15	16	16	17	Invertébrés
Plants	0	1	2	2	5	10	12	Plantes
Total	26	50	59	64	69	84	87	Total
Lesotho								**Lesotho**
Vertebrates	11	10	10	10	10	11	11	Vertébrés
Invertebrates	1	2	2	3	3	3	3	Invertébrés
Plants	1	4	4	4	4	4	4	Plantes
Total	13	16	16	17	17	18	18	Total
Liberia								**Libéria**
Vertebrates	45	91	94	98	98	108	109	Vertébrés
Invertebrates	3	9	9	11	11	11	11	Invertébrés
Plants	46	47	48	49	49	52	52	Plantes
Total	94	147	151	158	158	171	172	Total
Libya								**Libye**
Vertebrates	24	42	46	45	49	55	56	Vertébrés
Invertebrates	0	0	0	1	2	4	4	Invertébrés
Plants	1	2	3	3	3	3	3	Plantes
Total	25	44	49	49	54	62	63	Total
Liechtenstein								**Liechtenstein**
Vertebrates	3	0	0	0	0	2	2	Vertébrés
Invertebrates	5	2	4	4	4	4	4	Invertébrés
Plants	0	0	0	0	0	0	0	Plantes
Total	8	2	4	4	4	6	6	Total
Lithuania								**Lituanie**
Vertebrates	12	12	15	15	14	17	17	Vertébrés
Invertebrates	5	5	7	7	7	7	7	Invertébrés
Plants	0	0	1	1	1	# 2	2	Plantes
Total	17	17	23	23	22	26	26	Total
Luxembourg								**Luxembourg**
Vertebrates	6	1	2	2	2	4	4	Vertébrés
Invertebrates	4	4	7	7	7	7	7	Invertébrés
Plants	0	0	0	0	0	0	0	Plantes
Total	10	5	9	9	9	11	11	Total

Country or area &	2004	2010	2013	2014	2015	2016	2017	Pays ou zone &
Madagascar								**Madagascar**
Vertebrates	222	283	392	445	446	527	543	Vertébrés
Invertebrates	32	100	108	110	110	110	172	Invertébrés
Plants	276	280	373	374	409	607	609	Plantes
Total	530	663	873	929	965	1 244	1 324	Total
Malawi								**Malawi**
Vertebrates	25	127	131	132	130	135	136	Vertébrés
Invertebrates	11	17	16	16	16	16	16	Invertébrés
Plants	14	14	23	23	25	24	24	Plantes
Total	50	158	170	171	171	175	176	Total
Malaysia								**Malaisie**
Vertebrates	190	246	262	268	269	282	288	Vertébrés
Invertebrates	19	242	259	262	262	262	264	Invertébrés
Plants	683	692	705	706	721	721	720	Plantes
Total	892	1 180	1 226	1 236	1 252	1 265	1 272	Total
Maldives								**Maldives**
Vertebrates	12	20	23	23	23	29	29	Vertébrés
Invertebrates	0	39	46	46	46	46	46	Invertébrés
Plants	0	0	0	0	0	0	0	Plantes
Total	12	59	69	69	69	75	75	Total
Mali								**Mali**
Vertebrates	19	23	30	31	31	34	34	Vertébrés
Invertebrates	0	0	0	0	0	0	0	Invertébrés
Plants	6	6	7	8	8	8	8	Plantes
Total	25	29	37	39	39	42	42	Total
Malta								**Malte**
Vertebrates	22	20	23	23	23	30	30	Vertébrés
Invertebrates	3	3	3	4	4	5	5	Invertébrés
Plants	0	3	4	4	4	4	4	Plantes
Total	25	26	30	31	31	39	39	Total
Marshall Islands								**Îles Marshall**
Vertebrates	12	17	21	22	22	25	28	Vertébrés
Invertebrates	1	67	73	73	73	73	73	Invertébrés
Plants	0	0	0	0	0	0	0	Plantes
Total	13	84	94	95	95	98	101	Total
Martinique								**Martinique**
Vertebrates	20	22	27	28	34	33	37	Vertébrés
Invertebrates	1	1	2	2	2	2	2	Invertébrés
Plants	8	8	8	9	9	9	9	Plantes
Total	29	31	37	39	45	44	48	Total
Mauritania								**Mauritanie**
Vertebrates	25	57	65	66	66	80	83	Vertébrés
Invertebrates	1	1	1	3	3	3	3	Invertébrés
Plants	0	0	0	0	0	0	0	Plantes
Total	26	58	66	69	69	83	86	Total
Mauritius								**Maurice**
Vertebrates	28	36	39	41	41	45	47	Vertébrés
Invertebrates	32	98	107	118	118	118	120	Invertébrés
Plants	87	88	91	91	90	90	90	Plantes
Total	147	222	237	250	249	253	257	Total
Mayotte								**Mayotte**
Vertebrates	6	9	15	15	15	18	18	Vertébrés
Invertebrates	1	60	69	69	69	69	70	Invertébrés
Plants	0	0	0	0	0	0	0	Plantes
Total	7	69	84	84	84	87	88	Total
Mexico								**Mexique**
Vertebrates	446	609	622	628	639	648	655	Vertébrés
Invertebrates	41	79	90	92	93	102	106	Invertébrés
Plants	261	255	362	371	377	402	401	Plantes
Total	748	943	1 074	1 091	1 109	1 152	1 162	Total
Micronesia (Fed. States of)								**Micronésie (États féd. de)**
Vertebrates	22	35	43	43	44	48	49	Vertébrés
Invertebrates	4	108	115	115	115	115	114	Invertébrés
Plants	4	5	5	5	4	4	4	Plantes
Total	30	148	163	163	163	167	167	Total

24 Threatened species *(continued)*
Number of species by taxonomic group

Espèces menacées *(suite)*
Nombre d'espèces menacées par groupe taxonomique

Country or area &	2004	2010	2013	2014	2015	2016	2017	Pays ou zone &
Monaco								**Monaco**
Vertebrates	9	11	13	13	13	17	18	Vertébrés
Invertebrates	0	0	1	2	3	3	3	Invertébrés
Plants	0	0	0	0	0	0	0	Plantes
Total	9	11	14	15	16	20	21	Total
Mongolia								**Mongolie**
Vertebrates	36	33	33	33	33	37	38	Vertébrés
Invertebrates	3	3	3	3	3	3	3	Invertébrés
Plants	0	0	0	0	0	0	0	Plantes
Total	39	36	36	36	36	40	41	Total
Montenegro								**Monténégro**
Vertebrates	...	44	48	47	49	57	57	Vertébrés
Invertebrates	...	28	34	34	34	35	39	Invertébrés
Plants	...	0	2	2	2	2	2	Plantes
Total	...	72	84	83	85	94	98	Total
Montserrat								**Montserrat**
Vertebrates	18	21	28	29	37	36	38	Vertébrés
Invertebrates	0	11	11	11	11	11	11	Invertébrés
Plants	3	3	5	5	6	6	6	Plantes
Total	21	35	44	45	54	53	55	Total
Morocco								**Maroc**
Vertebrates	40	86	87	89	90	101	103	Vertébrés
Invertebrates	8	40	42	46	52	60	66	Invertébrés
Plants	2	31	34	34	34	# 38	38	Plantes
Total	50	157	163	169	176	199	207	Total
Mozambique								**Mozambique**
Vertebrates	64	98	105	117	117	127	129	Vertébrés
Invertebrates	5	59	67	67	67	67	67	Invertébrés
Plants	46	52	58	77	84	84	113	Plantes
Total	115	209	230	261	268	278	309	Total
Myanmar								**Myanmar**
Vertebrates	107	143	159	161	163	178	183	Vertébrés
Invertebrates	2	64	77	77	77	77	77	Invertébrés
Plants	38	42	46	47	61	61	61	Plantes
Total	147	249	282	285	301	316	321	Total
Namibia								**Namibie**
Vertebrates	44	66	72	74	73	81	84	Vertébrés
Invertebrates	1	0	1	4	4	4	4	Invertébrés
Plants	24	26	27	27	28	28	27	Plantes
Total	69	92	100	105	105	113	115	Total
Nauru								**Nauru**
Vertebrates	5	12	12	12	12	14	14	Vertébrés
Invertebrates	0	62	68	68	68	68	68	Invertébrés
Plants	0	0	0	0	0	0	0	Plantes
Total	5	74	80	80	80	82	82	Total
Nepal								**Népal**
Vertebrates	69	83	83	85	85	87	84	Vertébrés
Invertebrates	1	3	3	3	3	3	3	Invertébrés
Plants	7	7	9	12	17	17	17	Plantes
Total	77	93	95	100	105	107	104	Total
Netherlands								**Pays-Bas**
Vertebrates	27	18	20	20	19	26	27	Vertébrés
Invertebrates	7	6	10	10	10	10	10	Invertébrés
Plants	0	0	0	0	0	# 3	3	Plantes
Total	34	24	30	30	29	39	40	Total
Netherlands Antilles [former]								**Antilles néerlandaises [anc.]**
Vertebrates	26	24	31	...	...	...	...	Vertébrés
Invertebrates	0	11	11	...	...	...	...	Invertébrés
Plants	2	3	3	...	...	...	...	Plantes
Total	28	38	45	...	...	...	...	Total
New Caledonia								**Nouvelle-Calédonie**
Vertebrates	34	61	108	109	109	114	116	Vertébrés
Invertebrates	11	97	124	125	125	125	125	Invertébrés
Plants	217	257	258	259	259	286	285	Plantes
Total	262	415	490	493	493	525	526	Total

24 Threatened species *(continued)*
Number of species by taxonomic group

Espèces menacées *(suite)*
Nombre d'espèces menacées par groupe taxonomique

Country or area &	2004	2010	2013	2014	2015	2016	2017	Pays ou zone &
New Zealand								**Nouvelle-Zélande**
Vertebrates	114	117	118	130	130	128	130	Vertébrés
Invertebrates	14	15	42	46	46	46	46	Invertébrés
Plants	21	21	21	21	21	# 23	23	Plantes
Total	149	153	181	197	197	197	199	Total
Nicaragua								**Nicaragua**
Vertebrates	49	61	73	73	79	78	78	Vertébrés
Invertebrates	2	17	18	18	18	20	20	Invertébrés
Plants	39	43	43	43	44	46	46	Plantes
Total	90	121	134	134	141	144	144	Total
Niger								**Niger**
Vertebrates	12	22	27	27	27	29	30	Vertébrés
Invertebrates	1	2	1	1	1	1	1	Invertébrés
Plants	2	2	3	3	3	3	3	Plantes
Total	15	26	31	31	31	33	34	Total
Nigeria								**Nigéria**
Vertebrates	61	113	126	127	127	145	148	Vertébrés
Invertebrates	1	12	15	17	17	17	17	Invertébrés
Plants	170	172	168	188	189	197	196	Plantes
Total	232	297	309	332	333	359	361	Total
Niue								**Nioué**
Vertebrates	12	20	20	20	20	22	22	Vertébrés
Invertebrates	0	23	30	30	30	30	30	Invertébrés
Plants	0	0	0	0	0	0	0	Plantes
Total	12	43	50	50	50	52	52	Total
Norfolk Island								**Île Norfolk**
Vertebrates	21	19	17	17	17	18	19	Vertébrés
Invertebrates	12	21	23	23	23	23	23	Invertébrés
Plants	1	1	1	1	1	1	2	Plantes
Total	34	41	41	41	41	42	44	Total
Northern Mariana Islands								**Îles Mariannes du Nord**
Vertebrates	22	29	35	37	37	39	40	Vertébrés
Invertebrates	2	51	57	57	57	57	57	Invertébrés
Plants	4	5	5	5	5	5	5	Plantes
Total	28	85	97	99	99	101	102	Total
Norway								**Norvège**
Vertebrates	22	27	30	30	30	38	40	Vertébrés
Invertebrates	9	7	11	10	10	10	10	Invertébrés
Plants	2	2	3	3	4	# 14	14	Plantes
Total	33	36	44	43	44	62	64	Total
Oman								**Oman**
Vertebrates	48	47	53	54	53	62	62	Vertébrés
Invertebrates	1	26	32	31	31	31	31	Invertébrés
Plants	6	6	6	6	6	6	6	Plantes
Total	55	79	91	91	90	99	99	Total
Other non-specified areas								**Autres zones non-spécifiées**
Vertebrates	79	104	110	115	114	123	123	Vertébrés
Invertebrates	0	122	128	128	128	128	128	Invertébrés
Plants	78	78	79	82	83	# 85	86	Plantes
Total	157	304	317	325	325	336	337	Total
Pakistan								**Pakistan**
Vertebrates	70	92	97	100	99	110	110	Vertébrés
Invertebrates	0	15	18	18	18	18	18	Invertébrés
Plants	2	2	4	5	12	12	12	Plantes
Total	72	109	119	123	129	140	140	Total
Palau								**Palaos**
Vertebrates	13	22	26	27	27	31	32	Vertébrés
Invertebrates	5	102	146	146	146	146	146	Invertébrés
Plants	3	4	4	4	4	4	4	Plantes
Total	21	128	176	177	177	181	182	Total
Panama								**Panama**
Vertebrates	113	125	135	138	148	151	153	Vertébrés
Invertebrates	2	20	22	22	22	22	22	Invertébrés
Plants	195	202	202	203	203	208	208	Plantes
Total	310	347	359	363	373	381	383	Total

Threatened species *(continued)*
Number of species by taxonomic group

Espèces menacées *(suite)*
Nombre d'espèces menacées par groupe taxonomique

Country or area &	2004	2010	2013	2014	2015	2016	2017	Pays ou zone &
Papua New Guinea								**Papouasie-Nvl-Guinée**
Vertebrates	141	139	142	145	146	155	160	Vertébrés
Invertebrates	12	171	181	181	181	181	181	Invertébrés
Plants	142	143	145	145	151	152	152	Plantes
Total	295	453	468	471	478	488	493	Total
Paraguay								**Paraguay**
Vertebrates	40	38	39	39	39	40	40	Vertébrés
Invertebrates	0	0	0	0	0	0	0	Invertébrés
Plants	10	10	19	19	19	19	19	Plantes
Total	50	48	58	58	58	59	59	Total
Peru								**Pérou**
Vertebrates	232	274	310	316	317	351	351	Vertébrés
Invertebrates	2	3	8	8	8	8	8	Invertébrés
Plants	274	274	318	318	318	334	326	Plantes
Total	508	551	636	642	643	693	685	Total
Philippines								**Philippines**
Vertebrates	225	262	271	291	291	302	306	Vertébrés
Invertebrates	19	213	237	237	237	237	238	Invertébrés
Plants	212	222	229	233	239	239	239	Plantes
Total	456	697	737	761	767	778	783	Total
Pitcairn								**Pitcairn**
Vertebrates	15	20	20	20	20	21	21	Vertébrés
Invertebrates	5	15	16	16	16	16	16	Invertébrés
Plants	7	7	7	7	7	7	7	Plantes
Total	27	42	43	43	43	44	44	Total
Poland								**Pologne**
Vertebrates	27	17	20	20	19	23	23	Vertébrés
Invertebrates	15	16	23	23	22	22	22	Invertébrés
Plants	4	4	11	10	10	# 13	13	Plantes
Total	46	37	54	53	51	58	58	Total
Portugal								**Portugal**
Vertebrates	51	71	79	79	81	92	94	Vertébrés
Invertebrates	82	79	89	94	94	97	103	Invertébrés
Plants	15	21	81	81	81	# 83	84	Plantes
Total	148	171	249	254	256	272	281	Total
Puerto Rico								**Porto Rico**
Vertebrates	44	49	61	62	70	69	69	Vertébrés
Invertebrates	1	1	0	0	0	0	0	Invertébrés
Plants	52	53	54	57	57	57	57	Plantes
Total	97	103	115	119	127	126	126	Total
Qatar								**Qatar**
Vertebrates	12	19	21	22	22	26	26	Vertébrés
Invertebrates	0	13	14	13	13	13	13	Invertébrés
Plants	0	0	0	0	0	0	0	Plantes
Total	12	32	35	35	35	39	39	Total
Republic of Korea								**République de Corée**
Vertebrates	54	58	59	64	65	72	74	Vertébrés
Invertebrates	1	3	4	4	4	5	5	Invertébrés
Plants	0	3	6	7	7	# 32	32	Plantes
Total	55	64	69	75	76	109	111	Total
Republic of Moldova								**République de Moldova**
Vertebrates	22	24	22	22	22	26	27	Vertébrés
Invertebrates	5	3	6	5	5	5	6	Invertébrés
Plants	0	0	2	2	2	2	2	Plantes
Total	27	27	30	29	29	33	35	Total
Réunion								**Réunion**
Vertebrates	18	16	21	22	22	24	24	Vertébrés
Invertebrates	16	73	85	87	87	87	89	Invertébrés
Plants	14	15	17	17	17	17	17	Plantes
Total	48	104	123	126	126	128	130	Total
Romania								**Roumanie**
Vertebrates	40	39	42	43	42	49	50	Vertébrés
Invertebrates	22	24	38	39	38	38	49	Invertébrés
Plants	1	1	6	5	5	5	5	Plantes
Total	63	64	86	87	85	92	104	Total

24 Threatened species *(continued)*
Number of species by taxonomic group

Espèces menacées *(suite)*
Nombre d'espèces menacées par groupe taxonomique

Country or area &	2004	2010	2013	2014	2015	2016	2017	Pays ou zone &
Russian Federation								**Fédération de Russie**
Vertebrates	114	93	76	126	126	134	136	Vertébrés
Invertebrates	30	25	36	37	36	36	39	Invertébrés
Plants	7	8	12	54	55	# 60	60	Plantes
Total	151	126	124	217	217	230	235	Total
Rwanda								**Rwanda**
Vertebrates	30	49	50	53	51	51	50	Vertébrés
Invertebrates	4	2	2	2	2	2	4	Invertébrés
Plants	3	4	6	6	8	8	8	Plantes
Total	37	55	58	61	61	61	62	Total
Saint Barthélemy								**Saint-Barthélemy**
Vertebrates	...	4	6	7	16	18	18	Vertébrés
Invertebrates	...	11	11	11	11	11	11	Invertébrés
Plants	...	2	2	2	2	2	2	Plantes
Total	...	17	19	20	29	31	31	Total
Saint Helena 5								**Sainte-Hélène** 5
Vertebrates	32	31	34	37	37	39	41	Vertébrés
Invertebrates	2	2	2	13	13	15	15	Invertébrés
Plants	26	27	30	30	30	44	44	Plantes
Total	60	60	66	80	80	98	100	Total
Saint Kitts and Nevis								**Saint-Kitts-et-Nevis**
Vertebrates	17	24	30	32	39	39	40	Vertébrés
Invertebrates	0	10	10	10	10	10	10	Invertébrés
Plants	2	2	2	2	2	2	2	Plantes
Total	19	36	42	44	51	51	52	Total
Saint Lucia								**Sainte-Lucie**
Vertebrates	23	29	34	35	41	43	45	Vertébrés
Invertebrates	0	11	11	11	11	11	11	Invertébrés
Plants	6	6	6	6	6	6	6	Plantes
Total	29	46	51	52	58	60	62	Total
Saint Martin (French part)								**St-Martin (partie française)**
Vertebrates	...	4	10	30	38	37	39	Vertébrés
Invertebrates	...	11	11	10	10	10	10	Invertébrés
Plants	...	2	2	3	3	3	3	Plantes
Total	...	17	23	43	51	50	52	Total
Saint Pierre and Miquelon								**Saint-Pierre-et-Miquelon**
Vertebrates	2	4	6	7	7	11	12	Vertébrés
Invertebrates	0	0	0	0	0	0	0	Invertébrés
Plants	0	0	0	0	0	0	0	Plantes
Total	2	4	6	7	7	11	12	Total
Saint Vincent & Grenadines								**Saint-Vincent-Grenadines**
Vertebrates	20	24	32	33	39	41	43	Vertébrés
Invertebrates	0	10	10	10	10	10	10	Invertébrés
Plants	4	4	4	5	5	5	5	Plantes
Total	24	38	46	48	54	56	58	Total
Samoa								**Samoa**
Vertebrates	15	23	26	26	26	29	29	Vertébrés
Invertebrates	1	53	62	62	62	62	62	Invertébrés
Plants	2	2	2	2	2	2	2	Plantes
Total	18	78	90	90	90	93	93	Total
San Marino								**Saint-Marin**
Vertebrates	...	0	...	0	0	0	0	Vertébrés
Invertebrates	...	0	...	1	1	1	1	Invertébrés
Plants	...	0	...	0	0	0	0	Plantes
Total	...	0	...	1	1	1	1	Total
Sao Tome and Principe								**Sao Tomé-et-Principe**
Vertebrates	24	33	39	38	38	51	52	Vertébrés
Invertebrates	2	2	3	5	5	5	5	Invertébrés
Plants	35	35	36	38	38	38	37	Plantes
Total	61	70	78	81	81	94	94	Total
Saudi Arabia								**Arabie saoudite**
Vertebrates	37	47	52	54	57	66	68	Vertébrés
Invertebrates	1	53	60	59	59	59	59	Invertébrés
Plants	3	3	3	3	3	3	4	Plantes
Total	41	103	115	116	119	128	131	Total

24 Threatened species *(continued)*
Number of species by taxonomic group

Espèces menacées *(suite)*
Nombre d'espèces menacées par groupe taxonomique

Country or area &	2004	2010	2013	2014	2015	2016	2017	Pays ou zone &
Senegal								**Sénégal**
Vertebrates	40	72	82	83	82	95	98	Vertébrés
Invertebrates	0	1	11	13	13	13	13	Invertébrés
Plants	7	9	10	11	11	12	12	Plantes
Total	47	82	103	107	106	120	123	Total
Serbia								**Serbie**
Vertebrates	...	29	29	29	29	35	35	Vertébrés
Invertebrates	...	16	23	23	22	24	30	Invertébrés
Plants	...	1	5	5	5	# 6	6	Plantes
Total	...	46	57	57	56	65	71	Total
Serbia and Monten. [former]								**Serbie-et-Monténégro [anc.]**
Vertebrates	42	...	...	...	...	...	...	Vertébrés
Invertebrates	19	...	...	...	...	...	...	Invertébrés
Plants	1	...	...	...	...	...	...	Plantes
Total	62	...	...	...	...	...	...	Total
Seychelles								**Seychelles**
Vertebrates	35	45	52	54	54	55	57	Vertébrés
Invertebrates	4	100	158	319	319	319	320	Invertébrés
Plants	45	45	62	62	62	62	62	Plantes
Total	84	190	272	435	435	436	439	Total
Sierra Leone								**Sierra Leone**
Vertebrates	35	77	86	90	92	103	103	Vertébrés
Invertebrates	4	6	6	8	8	8	8	Invertébrés
Plants	47	48	54	58	58	65	66	Plantes
Total	86	131	146	156	158	176	177	Total
Singapore								**Singapour**
Vertebrates	30	58	56	56	56	63	63	Vertébrés
Invertebrates	1	162	173	173	173	173	173	Invertébrés
Plants	54	57	58	58	58	58	57	Plantes
Total	85	277	287	287	287	294	293	Total
Sint Maarten (Dutch part)								**St-Martin (partie néerland.)**
Vertebrates	...	...	3	29	37	37	39	Vertébrés
Invertebrates	...	...	0	10	10	10	10	Invertébrés
Plants	...	...	0	2	2	2	2	Plantes
Total	...	...	3	41	49	49	51	Total
Slovakia								**Slovaquie**
Vertebrates	27	15	16	16	16	19	20	Vertébrés
Invertebrates	19	17	22	23	22	22	24	Invertébrés
Plants	2	2	8	7	7	# 10	10	Plantes
Total	48	34	46	46	45	51	54	Total
Slovenia								**Slovénie**
Vertebrates	32	36	42	41	42	50	51	Vertébrés
Invertebrates	42	59	74	75	76	77	81	Invertébrés
Plants	0	0	7	7	7	# 11	11	Plantes
Total	74	95	123	123	125	138	143	Total
Solomon Islands								**Îles Salomon**
Vertebrates	52	63	66	70	70	75	77	Vertébrés
Invertebrates	6	141	151	151	151	151	151	Invertébrés
Plants	16	16	17	17	17	17	17	Plantes
Total	74	220	234	238	238	243	245	Total
Somalia								**Somalie**
Vertebrates	46	56	60	62	60	66	67	Vertébrés
Invertebrates	1	51	62	62	62	62	62	Invertébrés
Plants	17	21	42	42	43	43	46	Plantes
Total	64	128	164	166	165	171	175	Total
South Africa								**Afrique du Sud**
Vertebrates	155	185	194	210	209	219	233	Vertébrés
Invertebrates	127	159	166	202	202	202	202	Invertébrés
Plants	75	97	101	116	116	116	146	Plantes
Total	357	441	461	528	527	537	581	Total
South Georgia & Sandwich Is.								**Géorgie du S.-Îles Sandwich**
Vertebrates	12	10	9	9	9	9	9	Vertébrés
Invertebrates	0	0	0	0	0	0	0	Invertébrés
Plants	0	0	0	0	0	0	0	Plantes
Total	12	10	9	9	9	9	9	Total

24 Threatened species (continued)

Number of species by taxonomic group

Espèces menacées (suite)

Nombre d'espèces menacées par groupe taxonomique

Country or area &	2004	2010	2013	2014	2015	2016	2017	Pays ou zone &
South Sudan								**Soudan du sud**
Vertebrates	...	...	15	27	26	30	34	Vertébrés
Invertebrates	...	...	0	0	0	0	0	Invertébrés
Plants	...	...	2	15	16	15	15	Plantes
Total	...	...	17	42	42	45	49	Total
Spain								**Espagne**
Vertebrates	76	118	124	122	123	135	138	Vertébrés
Invertebrates	63	67	211	216	215	236	258	Invertébrés
Plants	14	55	213	214	213	# 221	221	Plantes
Total	153	240	548	552	551	592	617	Total
Sri Lanka								**Sri Lanka**
Vertebrates	112	149	155	159	159	167	167	Vertébrés
Invertebrates	2	120	130	130	130	130	130	Invertébrés
Plants	280	283	286	287	291	291	290	Plantes
Total	394	552	571	576	580	588	587	Total
State of Palestine								**État de Palestine**
Vertebrates	4	16	18	18	20	23	24	Vertébrés
Invertebrates	0	2	2	4	4	4	4	Invertébrés
Plants	0	0	0	0	0	3	3	Plantes
Total	4	18	20	22	24	30	31	Total
Sudan								**Soudan**
Vertebrates	36	49	58	56	57	63	67	Vertébrés
Invertebrates	2	45	50	50	50	50	50	Invertébrés
Plants	17	18	19	16	16	16	16	Plantes
Total	55	112	127	122	123	129	133	Total
Suriname								**Suriname**
Vertebrates	32	38	48	48	49	55	55	Vertébrés
Invertebrates	0	1	1	1	1	1	1	Invertébrés
Plants	27	26	26	26	26	27	27	Plantes
Total	59	65	75	75	76	83	83	Total
Svalbard and Jan Mayen Is.								**Îles Svalbard-et-Jan Mayen**
Vertebrates	9	3	5	5	5	7	7	Vertébrés
Invertebrates	0	0	0	0	0	0	0	Invertébrés
Plants	0	0	0	0	0	0	0	Plantes
Total	9	3	5	5	5	7	7	Total
Swaziland								**Swaziland**
Vertebrates	12	18	22	23	23	25	23	Vertébrés
Invertebrates	0	0	0	0	0	0	0	Invertébrés
Plants	11	11	11	11	11	11	11	Plantes
Total	23	29	33	34	34	36	34	Total
Sweden								**Suède**
Vertebrates	20	15	17	17	16	24	25	Vertébrés
Invertebrates	13	11	15	15	15	15	15	Invertébrés
Plants	3	3	5	4	5	# 14	14	Plantes
Total	36	29	37	36	36	53	54	Total
Switzerland								**Suisse**
Vertebrates	17	14	15	15	15	18	20	Vertébrés
Invertebrates	30	28	43	43	43	43	44	Invertébrés
Plants	2	3	4	4	4	# 10	10	Plantes
Total	49	45	62	62	62	71	74	Total
Syrian Arab Republic								**République arabe syrienne**
Vertebrates	26	68	72	84	84	94	94	Vertébrés
Invertebrates	3	7	9	19	20	20	20	Invertébrés
Plants	0	3	4	4	4	13	18	Plantes
Total	29	78	85	107	108	127	132	Total
Tajikistan								**Tadjikistan**
Vertebrates	20	24	27	27	26	29	30	Vertébrés
Invertebrates	2	2	2	3	3	3	3	Invertébrés
Plants	2	14	12	12	12	12	12	Plantes
Total	24	40	41	42	41	44	45	Total
Thailand								**Thaïlande**
Vertebrates	136	201	231	233	234	245	248	Vertébrés
Invertebrates	1	185	211	211	211	211	211	Invertébrés
Plants	84	91	131	133	150	150	152	Plantes
Total	221	477	573	577	595	606	611	Total

24 Threatened species *(continued)*
Number of species by taxonomic group

Espèces menacées *(suite)*
Nombre d'espèces menacées par groupe taxonomique

Country or area &	2004	2010	2013	2014	2015	2016	2017	Pays ou zone &
TFYR of Macedonia								**ex-R.Y. de Macédoine**
Vertebrates	24	31	31	31	31	34	35	Vertébrés
Invertebrates	5	59	68	69	69	70	75	Invertébrés
Plants	0	0	0	0	0	0	0	Plantes
Total	29	90	99	100	100	104	110	Total
Timor-Leste								**Timor-Leste**
Vertebrates	11	18	19	19	19	20	22	Vertébrés
Invertebrates	0	0	1	1	1	1	1	Invertébrés
Plants	0	0	1	1	1	1	1	Plantes
Total	11	18	21	21	21	22	24	Total
Togo								**Togo**
Vertebrates	22	43	49	50	51	63	65	Vertébrés
Invertebrates	0	1	1	3	3	3	3	Invertébrés
Plants	10	10	12	12	12	12	12	Plantes
Total	32	54	62	65	66	78	80	Total
Tokelau								**Tokélaou**
Vertebrates	6	10	11	11	11	14	14	Vertébrés
Invertebrates	0	31	35	35	35	35	35	Invertébrés
Plants	0	0	0	0	0	0	0	Plantes
Total	6	41	46	46	46	49	49	Total
Tonga								**Tonga**
Vertebrates	11	19	23	23	23	26	28	Vertébrés
Invertebrates	2	35	47	47	47	47	47	Invertébrés
Plants	3	4	4	4	4	4	4	Plantes
Total	16	58	74	74	74	77	79	Total
Trinidad and Tobago								**Trinité-et-Tobago**
Vertebrates	32	37	44	45	53	56	57	Vertébrés
Invertebrates	0	10	10	10	10	10	10	Invertébrés
Plants	1	1	1	2	2	2	2	Plantes
Total	33	48	55	57	65	68	69	Total
Tunisia								**Tunisie**
Vertebrates	31	57	62	61	61	70	70	Vertébrés
Invertebrates	5	11	11	14	15	17	19	Invertébrés
Plants	0	7	7	7	7	7	7	Plantes
Total	36	75	80	82	83	94	96	Total
Turkey								**Turquie**
Vertebrates	76	130	134	191	191	199	199	Vertébrés
Invertebrates	13	15	38	70	76	78	82	Invertébrés
Plants	3	5	10	103	103	# 105	107	Plantes
Total	92	150	182	364	370	382	388	Total
Turkmenistan								**Turkménistan**
Vertebrates	35	37	38	38	38	42	43	Vertébrés
Invertebrates	5	5	6	7	7	7	7	Invertébrés
Plants	0	3	4	4	4	4	4	Plantes
Total	40	45	48	49	49	53	54	Total
Turks and Caicos Islands								**Îles Turques-et-Caïques**
Vertebrates	18	22	28	29	37	37	41	Vertébrés
Invertebrates	0	10	10	10	10	10	10	Invertébrés
Plants	2	2	7	9	9	9	9	Plantes
Total	20	34	45	48	56	56	60	Total
Tuvalu								**Tuvalu**
Vertebrates	7	14	15	15	15	17	18	Vertébrés
Invertebrates	1	71	78	78	78	78	78	Invertébrés
Plants	0	0	0	0	0	0	0	Plantes
Total	8	85	93	93	93	95	96	Total
Uganda								**Ouganda**
Vertebrates	77	110	116	121	117	116	119	Vertébrés
Invertebrates	19	15	19	19	19	19	24	Invertébrés
Plants	38	41	48	49	52	52	53	Plantes
Total	134	166	183	189	188	187	196	Total
Ukraine								**Ukraine**
Vertebrates	40	45	47	48	47	52	53	Vertébrés
Invertebrates	14	15	24	24	23	23	31	Invertébrés
Plants	1	1	17	16	17	# 19	18	Plantes
Total	55	61	88	88	87	94	102	Total

24 Threatened species *(continued)*

Number of species by taxonomic group

Espèces menacées *(suite)*

Nombre d'espèces menacées par groupe taxonomique

Country or area &	2004	2010	2013	2014	2015	2016	2017	Pays ou zone &
United Arab Emirates								**Émirats arabes unis**
Vertebrates	23	32	34	34	33	41	41	Vertébrés
Invertebrates	0	16	16	15	15	15	15	Invertébrés
Plants	0	0	0	0	0	0	0	Plantes
Total	23	48	50	49	48	56	56	Total
United Kingdom								**Royaume-Uni**
Vertebrates	32	48	53	53	53	61	62	Vertébrés
Invertebrates	10	11	15	17	18	18	18	Invertébrés
Plants	13	14	15	15	16	# 22	22	Plantes
Total	55	73	83	85	87	101	102	Total
United Rep. of Tanzania								**Rép.-Unie de Tanzanie**
Vertebrates	144	313	332	346	346	355	355	Vertébrés
Invertebrates	33	80	107	129	129	129	125	Invertébrés
Plants	239	298	475	504	602	602	602	Plantes
Total	416	691	914	979	1 077	1 086	1 082	Total
U.S. Minor Outlying islands								**Îles min. éloignées des É-U**
Vertebrates	15	23	24	24	24	25	26	Vertébrés
Invertebrates	0	44	47	47	47	47	47	Invertébrés
Plants	0	0	0	0	0	0	0	Plantes
Total	15	67	71	71	71	72	73	Total
United States of America								**États-Unis d'Amérique**
Vertebrates	342	376	441	438	444	454	456	Vertébrés
Invertebrates	561	531	566	570	575	578	580	Invertébrés
Plants	240	245	271	279	280	# 447	477	Plantes
Total	1 143	1 152	1 278	1 287	1 299	1 479	1 513	Total
United States Virgin Islands								**Îles Vierges américaines**
Vertebrates	22	21	31	32	41	42	46	Vertébrés
Invertebrates	0	0	0	0	0	0	0	Invertébrés
Plants	9	12	12	12	12	12	12	Plantes
Total	31	33	43	44	53	54	58	Total
Uruguay								**Uruguay**
Vertebrates	48	78	80	79	79	82	82	Vertébrés
Invertebrates	1	1	2	2	2	2	2	Invertébrés
Plants	1	1	22	22	22	22	22	Plantes
Total	50	80	104	103	103	106	106	Total
Uzbekistan								**Ouzbékistan**
Vertebrates	29	34	35	35	34	39	39	Vertébrés
Invertebrates	1	1	2	3	3	3	3	Invertébrés
Plants	1	15	17	17	17	17	17	Plantes
Total	31	50	54	55	54	59	59	Total
Vanuatu								**Vanuatu**
Vertebrates	19	32	35	35	35	37	36	Vertébrés
Invertebrates	0	79	92	92	92	92	91	Invertébrés
Plants	10	10	10	10	10	10	10	Plantes
Total	29	121	137	137	137	139	137	Total
Venezuela (Boliv. Rep. of)								**Venezuela (Rép. boliv. du)**
Vertebrates	151	179	202	202	209	212	220	Vertébrés
Invertebrates	1	21	26	26	26	26	26	Invertébrés
Plants	67	70	77	77	77	82	82	Plantes
Total	219	270	305	305	312	320	328	Total
Viet Nam								**Viet Nam**
Vertebrates	144	186	229	235	239	260	260	Vertébrés
Invertebrates	0	92	125	126	127	152	152	Invertébrés
Plants	145	146	169	177	199	204	204	Plantes
Total	289	424	523	538	565	616	616	Total
Wallis and Futuna Islands								**Îles Wallis-et-Futuna**
Vertebrates	12	16	22	22	22	24	24	Vertébrés
Invertebrates	0	57	65	65	65	65	64	Invertébrés
Plants	1	1	1	1	1	1	1	Plantes
Total	13	74	88	88	88	90	89	Total
Western Sahara								**Sahara occidental**
Vertebrates	18	38	36	37	36	44	46	Vertébrés
Invertebrates	1	1	1	3	3	3	3	Invertébrés
Plants	0	0	0	0	0	0	0	Plantes
Total	19	39	37	40	39	47	49	Total

24

Threatened species *(continued)*
Number of species by taxonomic group

Espèces menacées *(suite)*
Nombre d'espèces menacées par groupe taxonomique

Country or area &	2004	2010	2013	2014	2015	2016	2017	Pays ou zone &
Yemen								**Yémen**
Vertebrates	34	48	55	55	57	67	68	Vertébrés
Invertebrates	2	62	69	68	68	68	68	Invertébrés
Plants	159	159	162	162	162	162	162	Plantes
Total	195	269	286	285	287	297	298	Total
Zambia								**Zambie**
Vertebrates	24	44	47	51	49	51	53	Vertébrés
Invertebrates	7	14	14	14	14	14	14	Invertébrés
Plants	8	9	14	14	20	20	21	Plantes
Total	39	67	75	79	83	85	88	Total
Zimbabwe								**Zimbabwe**
Vertebrates	24	34	36	38	38	39	41	Vertébrés
Invertebrates	2	5	5	5	5	5	5	Invertébrés
Plants	17	16	17	17	17	17	43	Plantes
Total	43	55	58	60	60	61	89	Total
Areas n.e.s								**Zones n.s.a**
Vertebrates	1	1	1	1	1	3	3	Vertébrés
Invertebrates	0	0	1	1	1	1	1	Invertébrés
Plants	0	0	0	0	0	0	0	Plantes
Total	1	1	2	2	2	4	4	Total

Source:

World Conservation Union (IUCN) / Species Survival Commission (SSC), Gland, Switzerland and Cambridge, United Kingdom, IUCN Red List of Threatened Species publication, last accessed May 2017.

Source:

Union mondiale pour la nature (UICN) / Commission de la sauvegarde des espèces, Gland, Suisse, et Cambridge, Royaume-Uni, La liste rouge des espèces menacées de l'UICN, dernier accès mai 2017.

& Vertebrates consists of mammals, birds, reptiles, amphibians and fish. Invertebrates consists of molluscs and other invertebrates. Plants consists of plants, and since 2016, fungi and protists. Reptiles, fishes, molluscs, other invertebrates, plants, fungi & protists: please note that for these groups, there are still many species that have not yet been assessed for the IUCN Red List and therefore their status is not known (i.e. these groups have not yet been completely assessed). Therefore the figures presented below for these groups should be interpreted as the number of species known to be threatened within those species that have been assessed to date, and not as the overall total number of threatened species for each group.

& Les vertébrés se composent de mammifères, oiseaux, reptiles, amphibiens et poissons; les invertébrés se composent de mollusques et autres invertébrés. A partir de 2016, les plantes incluent aussi les champignons et les protistes. Veuillez noter que beaucoup d'espèces tels que les reptiles, les poissons, les mollusques et autres invertébrés, les plantes, les champignons et les protistes n'ont pas été encore évaluées dans le cadre de la Liste rouge de l'UICN , donc leur statut est inconnu pour le moment (c.-à-d. ces groupes ne sont que partiellement évalués). En conséquent, les données présentées ci-dessous pour chaque groupe doivent être interprétées comme le nombre d'espèces connues et menacées parmi les espèces évaluées à ce jour, et non comme le nombre total d'espèces menacées dans chaque groupe.

1 Excluding overseas territories.
2 The figures for Amphibians displayed here are those that were agreed at the GAA Brazil workshop in April 2003; the "consistent Red List Categories" were not yet accepted by the Brazilian experts.
3 For statistical purposes, the data for China do not include those for the Hong Kong Special Administrative Region (Hong Kong SAR), Macao Special Administrative Region (Macao SAR) and Taiwan Province of China.
4 Excluding the north islands, Saint Barthélémy and Saint Martin (French part).
5 Including Ascension and Tristan da Cunha.

1 Non compris les départements d'outre-mer.
2 Les chiffres concernant les amphibiens sont ceux qui ont été convenus lors de l'atelier de l'Évaluation mondiale des amphibiens du Brésil en avril 2003 ; les "catégories conformes à la Liste rouge" n'ont pas encore été acceptées par les experts brésiliens.
3 Pour la présentation des statistiques, les données pour la Chine ne comprennent pas la région administrative spéciale de Hong Kong (Hong Kong RAS), la région administrative spéciale de Macao (Macao RAS) et la province chinoise de Taïwan.
4 Les îles du Nord, Saint-Barthélémy et Saint-Martin (partie français), sont exclues.
5 Y compris Ascension et Tristan da Cunha.

25 CO2 emission estimates

From fossil fuel combustion, cement production and gas flared (thousand metric tons of carbon dioxide) and per capita

Estimation des émissions de CO2

Dues à la combustion de combustibles fossiles, à la production de ciment et au gaz brûlés à la torchère (milliers de tonnes de dioxyde de carbone) et par habitant

Country or area&	1975	1985	1995	2005	2010	2012	2013	2014	Pays ou zone&
Total, all countries or areas									**Total, tous pays ou zones**
Thousand metric tons	16 853 532	19 864 139	23 120 435	29 490 014	33 472 376	35 470 891	35 837 591	36 138 285	Milliers de tonnes
Metric tons per capita	4.1	4.1	4.0	4.5	4.8	5.0	5.0	5.0	Tonnes par habitant
Afghanistan									**Afghanistan**
Thousand metric tons	2 127	3 509	1 243	1 327	8 463	10 755	10 015	9 809	Milliers de tonnes
Metric tons per capita	0.1	0.3	0.1	~0.0	0.3	0.4	0.3	0.3	Tonnes par habitant
Albania									**Albanie**
Thousand metric tons	4 595	7 880	2 087	4 254	4 598	4 910	5 064	5 717	Milliers de tonnes
Metric tons per capita	1.9	2.7	0.7	1.4	1.6	1.7	1.8	2.0	Tonnes par habitant
Algeria									**Algérie**
Thousand metric tons	32 031	72 786	95 294	107 278	119 178	129 988	134 465	145 400	Milliers de tonnes
Metric tons per capita	2.0	3.3	3.4	3.3	3.3	3.5	3.5	3.7	Tonnes par habitant
Andorra									**Andorre**
Thousand metric tons	...	...	425	576	517	488	477	462	Milliers de tonnes
Metric tons per capita	...	...	6.6	7.4	6.2	6.2	6.3	6.4	Tonnes par habitant
Angola									**Angola**
Thousand metric tons	4 415	4 701	10 975	19 156	29 057	33 399	32 618	34 763	Milliers de tonnes
Metric tons per capita	0.7	0.5	0.9	1.2	1.4	1.5	1.4	1.4	Tonnes par habitant
Anguilla									**Anguilla**
Thousand metric tons	...	...	66	128	150	143	136	143	Milliers de tonnes
Metric tons per capita	...	...	6.9	9.5	10.9	10.0	9.5	9.8	Tonnes par habitant
Antigua and Barbuda									**Antigua-et-Barbuda**
Thousand metric tons	708	249	275	429	524	524	524	532	Milliers de tonnes
Metric tons per capita	10.2	3.8	4.0	5.1	6.0	5.9	5.8	5.8	Tonnes par habitant
Argentina									**Argentine**
Thousand metric tons	94 931	100 597	127 964	162 111	187 919	192 356	189 852	204 025	Milliers de tonnes
Metric tons per capita	3.6	3.3	3.7	4.2	4.5	4.6	4.5	4.7	Tonnes par habitant
Armenia									**Arménie**
Thousand metric tons	...	...	3 410	4 353	4 217	5 695	5 497	5 530	Milliers de tonnes
Metric tons per capita	...	...	1.1	1.4	1.4	1.9	1.8	1.8	Tonnes par habitant
Aruba									**Aruba**
Thousand metric tons	...	...	1 668	2 721	2 508	1 349	862	873	Milliers de tonnes
Metric tons per capita	...	...	20.8	26.9	24.7	13.2	8.4	8.4	Tonnes par habitant
Australia									**Australie**
Thousand metric tons	175 884	241 230	281 860	350 173	390 862	388 126	372 267	361 262	Milliers de tonnes
Metric tons per capita	12.7	15.3	15.5	17.2	17.6	16.9	16.0	15.3	Tonnes par habitant
Austria									**Autriche**
Thousand metric tons	54 393	54 701	59 783	74 216	67 502	62 273	62 486	58 712	Milliers de tonnes
Metric tons per capita	7.2	7.2	7.5	9.0	8.0	7.4	7.4	6.9	Tonnes par habitant
Azerbaijan									**Azerbaïdjan**
Thousand metric tons	...	...	33 333	34 338	30 678	35 555	35 643	37 488	Milliers de tonnes
Metric tons per capita	...	...	4.3	4.0	3.4	3.8	3.7	3.9	Tonnes par habitant
Bahamas									**Bahamas**
Thousand metric tons	8 254	1 511	1 683	1 742	1 654	1 969	2 802	2 417	Milliers de tonnes
Metric tons per capita	43.7	6.5	6.0	5.5	4.6	5.3	7.4	6.3	Tonnes par habitant
Bahrain									**Bahreïn**
Thousand metric tons	5 754	10 194	14 818	19 208	29 266	26 674	31 313	31 338	Milliers de tonnes
Metric tons per capita	21.7	24.5	26.5	26.5	23.2	20.0	23.2	23.0	Tonnes par habitant
Bangladesh									**Bangladesh**
Thousand metric tons	4 870	10 235	22 816	39 479	59 937	67 506	69 710	73 190	Milliers de tonnes
Metric tons per capita	0.1	0.1	0.2	0.3	0.4	0.4	0.4	0.5	Tonnes par habitant
Barbados									**Barbade**
Thousand metric tons	568	847	829	1 353	1 478	1 470	1 448	1 272	Milliers de tonnes
Metric tons per capita	2.3	3.3	3.2	5.0	5.3	5.2	5.1	4.5	Tonnes par habitant
Belarus									**Bélarus**
Thousand metric tons	...	...	60 773	59 167	63 043	63 223	63 769	63 498	Milliers de tonnes
Metric tons per capita	...	...	5.9	6.0	6.6	6.7	6.7	6.7	Tonnes par habitant
Belgium									**Belgique**
Thousand metric tons	122 100	104 473	112 328	108 510	110 824	95 107	96 970	93 351	Milliers de tonnes
Metric tons per capita	12.5	10.6	11.1	10.4	10.2	8.6	8.7	8.3	Tonnes par habitant
Belize									**Belize**
Thousand metric tons	176	191	378	422	539	477	513	495	Milliers de tonnes
Metric tons per capita	1.3	1.1	1.7	1.5	1.7	1.4	1.5	1.4	Tonnes par habitant

25 CO2 emission estimates *(continued)*

From fossil fuel combustion, cement production and gas flared (thousand metric tons of carbon dioxide) and per capita

Estimation des émissions de CO2 *(suite)*

Dues à la combustion de combustibles fossiles, à la production de ciment et au gaz brûlés à la torchère (milliers de tonnes de dioxyde de carbone) et par habitant

Country or area&	1975	1985	1995	2005	2010	2012	2013	2014	Pays ou zone&
Benin									**Bénin**
Thousand metric tons	444	744	1 327	2 395	5 090	5 471	5 812	6 318	Milliers de tonnes
Metric tons per capita	0.1	0.2	0.2	0.3	0.6	0.6	0.6	0.6	Tonnes par habitant
Bermuda									**Bermudes**
Thousand metric tons	458	451	532	583	609	477	458	576	Milliers de tonnes
Metric tons per capita	8.5	7.8	8.7	9.1	9.5	7.5	7.3	9.2	Tonnes par habitant
Bhutan									**Bhoutan**
Thousand metric tons	4	62	249	396	488	818	920	1 001	Milliers de tonnes
Metric tons per capita	0.0	0.1	0.5	0.6	0.7	1.1	1.2	1.3	Tonnes par habitant
Bolivia (Plurin. State of)									**Bolivie (État plurin. de)**
Thousand metric tons	4 059	4 125	9 850	12 185	15 203	18 793	18 918	20 411	Milliers de tonnes
Metric tons per capita	0.8	0.7	1.3	1.3	1.5	1.8	1.8	1.9	Tonnes par habitant
Bonaire, Sint Eustatius and Saba									**Bonaire, Saint-Eustache et Saba**
Thousand metric tons	...	...	...	...	...	312	323	323	Milliers de tonnes
Metric tons per capita	...	...	...	...	...	13.6	13.6	13.3	Tonnes par habitant
Bosnia and Herzegovina									**Bosnie-Herzégovine**
Thousand metric tons	...	...	3 429	16 204	21 276	22 259	21 921	22 233	Milliers de tonnes
Metric tons per capita	...	...	1.0	4.3	5.5	5.8	5.7	5.8	Tonnes par habitant
Botswana									**Botswana**
Thousand metric tons	187	1 159	3 047	4 096	4 686	4 232	5 229	7 033	Milliers de tonnes
Metric tons per capita	0.2	1.0	1.9	2.2	2.3	2.0	2.4	3.2	Tonnes par habitant
Brazil									**Brésil**
Thousand metric tons	151 165	181 249	258 347	347 309	419 754	470 029	503 677	529 808	Milliers de tonnes
Metric tons per capita	1.4	1.3	1.6	1.9	2.1	2.3	2.5	2.6	Tonnes par habitant
British Virgin Islands									**Îles Vierges britanniques**
Thousand metric tons	26	48	84	132	172	176	176	180	Milliers de tonnes
Metric tons per capita	2.3	3.7	4.7	6.0	6.3	6.1	6.0	6.0	Tonnes par habitant
Brunei Darussalam									**Brunéi Darussalam**
Thousand metric tons	7 081	2 596	4 789	5 005	8 203	9 666	7 803	9 109	Milliers de tonnes
Metric tons per capita	45.2	11.8	16.5	13.8	20.9	23.8	19.0	21.8	Tonnes par habitant
Bulgaria									**Bulgarie**
Thousand metric tons	73 061	89 541	58 005	47 917	44 114	44 708	39 600	42 416	Milliers de tonnes
Metric tons per capita	8.4	10.0	6.9	6.2	5.9	6.1	5.5	5.9	Tonnes par habitant
Burkina Faso									**Burkina Faso**
Thousand metric tons	220	477	627	1 126	1 962	2 629	3 058	2 849	Milliers de tonnes
Metric tons per capita	~0.0	0.1	0.1	0.1	0.1	0.1	0.2	0.1	Tonnes par habitant
Burundi									**Burundi**
Thousand metric tons	77	231	238	154	213	282	290	440	Milliers de tonnes
Metric tons per capita	~0.0	~0.0	~0.0	~0.0	~0.0	~0.0	~0.0	~0.0	Tonnes par habitant
Cabo Verde									**Cabo Verde**
Thousand metric tons	77	84	121	440	557	506	499	491	Milliers de tonnes
Metric tons per capita	0.3	0.3	0.3	0.9	1.1	1.0	1.0	1.0	Tonnes par habitant
Cambodia									**Cambodge**
Thousand metric tons	73	418	1 551	2 776	5 013	5 456	5 603	6 685	Milliers de tonnes
Metric tons per capita	0.0	~0.0	0.1	0.2	0.4	0.4	0.4	0.4	Tonnes par habitant
Cameroon									**Cameroun**
Thousand metric tons	1 162	6 476	4 228	3 696	6 780	6 128	6 773	7 004	Milliers de tonnes
Metric tons per capita	0.1	0.6	0.3	0.2	0.3	0.3	0.3	0.3	Tonnes par habitant
Canada									**Canada**
Thousand metric tons	397 143	422 079	467 638	557 417	534 671	517 458	517 161	537 193	Milliers de tonnes
Metric tons per capita	17.2	16.3	16.0	17.3	15.7	14.9	14.7	15.1	Tonnes par habitant
Cayman Islands									**Îles Caïmanes**
Thousand metric tons	55	191	363	473	557	535	535	543	Milliers de tonnes
Metric tons per capita	4.3	9.4	11.0	9.1	10.1	9.3	9.2	9.2	Tonnes par habitant
Central African Rep.									**Rép. centrafricaine**
Thousand metric tons	103	161	235	235	264	293	297	301	Milliers de tonnes
Metric tons per capita	~0.0	0.1	0.1	0.1	0.1	0.1	0.1	0.1	Tonnes par habitant
Chad									**Tchad**
Thousand metric tons	183	180	110	400	517	612	700	730	Milliers de tonnes
Metric tons per capita	~0.0	~0.0	0.0	~0.0	~0.0	~0.0	~0.0	~0.0	Tonnes par habitant
Chile									**Chili**
Thousand metric tons	23 014	21 503	41 745	61 818	72 251	80 975	83 226	82 563	Milliers de tonnes
Metric tons per capita	2.2	1.8	2.9	3.8	4.3	4.7	4.7	4.7	Tonnes par habitant

25 CO2 emission estimates *(continued)*

From fossil fuel combustion, cement production and gas flared (thousand metric tons of carbon dioxide) and per capita

Estimation des émissions de CO2 *(suite)*

Dues à la combustion de combustibles fossiles, à la production de ciment et au gaz brûlés à la torchère (milliers de tonnes de dioxyde de carbone) et par habitant

Country or area&	1975	1985	1995	2005	2010	2012	2013	2014	Pays ou zone&
China [1]									**Chine** [1]
Thousand metric tons	1 145 607	1 966 553	3 320 285	5 896 958	8 776 040	10 028 574	10 258 007	10 291 927	Milliers de tonnes
Metric tons per capita	1.2	1.9	2.8	4.5	6.5	7.4	7.5	7.5	Tonnes par habitant
China, Hong Kong SAR									**Chine, Hong Kong RAS**
Thousand metric tons	11 019	23 014	31 470	43 872	40 678	43 425	45 005	46 223	Milliers de tonnes
Metric tons per capita	2.5	4.3	5.1	6.5	5.8	6.1	6.3	6.4	Tonnes par habitant
China, Macao SAR									**Chine, Macao RAS**
Thousand metric tons	297	733	1 232	1 830	1 408	1 313	1 181	1 283	Milliers de tonnes
Metric tons per capita	1.2	2.5	3.1	3.8	2.6	2.3	2.1	2.2	Tonnes par habitant
Colombia									**Colombie**
Thousand metric tons	35 896	48 379	59 614	60 946	76 175	79 952	89 625	84 092	Milliers de tonnes
Metric tons per capita	1.5	1.6	1.7	1.4	1.7	1.7	1.9	1.8	Tonnes par habitant
Comoros									**Comores**
Thousand metric tons	33	48	73	139	161	143	176	154	Milliers de tonnes
Metric tons per capita	0.1	0.1	0.1	0.2	0.2	0.2	0.2	0.2	Tonnes par habitant
Congo									**Congo**
Thousand metric tons	1 100	1 280	1 566	983	1 980	2 970	3 088	3 095	Milliers de tonnes
Metric tons per capita	0.7	0.6	0.6	0.3	0.5	0.7	0.7	0.7	Tonnes par habitant
Cook Islands									**Îles Cook**
Thousand metric tons	15	22	40	62	70	70	70	70	Milliers de tonnes
Metric tons per capita	0.8	1.2	2.2	3.2	3.5	3.4	3.4	3.4	Tonnes par habitant
Costa Rica									**Costa Rica**
Thousand metric tons	2 039	2 266	4 866	6 868	7 569	7 767	7 598	7 759	Milliers de tonnes
Metric tons per capita	1.0	0.8	1.4	1.6	1.7	1.7	1.6	1.6	Tonnes par habitant
Côte d'Ivoire									**Côte d'Ivoire**
Thousand metric tons	3 990	7 327	6 619	7 825	6 967	9 296	10 686	11 045	Milliers de tonnes
Metric tons per capita	0.6	0.7	0.4	0.4	0.3	0.4	0.5	0.5	Tonnes par habitant
Croatia									**Croatie**
Thousand metric tons	...	...	16 986	22 592	20 172	17 994	17 550	16 843	Milliers de tonnes
Metric tons per capita	...	...	3.6	5.1	4.7	4.2	4.1	4.0	Tonnes par habitant
Cuba									**Cuba**
Thousand metric tons	27 066	32 578	25 709	26 006	38 375	36 157	34 800	34 837	Milliers de tonnes
Metric tons per capita	2.9	3.2	2.3	2.3	3.4	3.2	3.1	3.0	Tonnes par habitant
Curaçao									**Curaçao**
Thousand metric tons	...	...	...	...	...	5 999	5 214	5 882	Milliers de tonnes
Metric tons per capita	...	...	...	...	...	39.3	33.8	37.8	Tonnes par habitant
Cyprus									**Chypre**
Thousand metric tons	1 980	3 102	5 383	7 503	7 708	6 920	5 948	6 062	Milliers de tonnes
Metric tons per capita	3.0	4.4	6.3	7.3	7.0	6.1	5.2	5.2	Tonnes par habitant
Czechia									**Tchéquie**
Thousand metric tons	...	...	123 831	120 109	111 579	101 030	98 675	96 475	Milliers de tonnes
Metric tons per capita	...	...	12.0	11.7	10.6	9.6	9.4	9.2	Tonnes par habitant
Dem. P. R. Korea									**R. p. dém. de Corée**
Thousand metric tons	107 740	144 898	82 911	75 573	66 453	49 057	36 010	40 528	Milliers de tonnes
Metric tons per capita	6.7	7.7	3.8	3.2	2.7	2.0	1.4	1.6	Tonnes par habitant
Dem. Rep. of the Congo									**Rép. dém. du Congo**
Thousand metric tons	3 238	3 641	2 123	1 500	2 021	2 402	3 590	4 672	Milliers de tonnes
Metric tons per capita	0.1	0.1	~0.0	~0.0	~0.0	~0.0	~0.0	0.1	Tonnes par habitant
Denmark									**Danemark**
Thousand metric tons	55 779	60 073	57 172	47 095	46 641	36 428	38 533	33 498	Milliers de tonnes
Metric tons per capita	11.0	11.7	10.9	8.7	8.4	6.5	6.9	5.9	Tonnes par habitant
Djibouti									**Djibouti**
Thousand metric tons	198	359	304	414	517	517	609	722	Milliers de tonnes
Metric tons per capita	0.9	0.9	0.5	0.5	0.6	0.6	0.7	0.8	Tonnes par habitant
Dominica									**Dominique**
Thousand metric tons	29	48	81	117	139	136	132	136	Milliers de tonnes
Metric tons per capita	0.4	0.7	1.1	1.7	1.9	1.9	1.8	1.9	Tonnes par habitant
Dominican Republic									**Rép. dominicaine**
Thousand metric tons	6 340	7 294	15 885	18 639	21 023	22 123	21 441	21 540	Milliers de tonnes
Metric tons per capita	1.2	1.1	2.0	2.0	2.1	2.2	2.1	2.1	Tonnes par habitant
Ecuador									**Équateur**
Thousand metric tons	7 363	19 431	22 842	30 264	36 461	38 140	40 997	43 920	Milliers de tonnes
Metric tons per capita	1.1	2.1	2.0	2.2	2.5	2.5	2.6	2.8	Tonnes par habitant

25 CO2 emission estimates *(continued)*

From fossil fuel combustion, cement production and gas flared (thousand metric tons of carbon dioxide) and per capita

Estimation des émissions de CO2 *(suite)*

Dues à la combustion de combustibles fossiles, à la production de ciment et au gaz brûlés à la torchère (milliers de tonnes de dioxyde de carbone) et par habitant

Country or area&	1975	1985	1995	2005	2010	2012	2013	2014	Pays ou zone&
Egypt									**Égypte**
Thousand metric tons	31 100	63 938	95 723	167 208	202 715	217 068	213 412	201 894	Milliers de tonnes
Metric tons per capita	0.8	1.2	1.5	2.2	2.5	2.5	2.4	2.2	Tonnes par habitant
El Salvador									**El Salvador**
Thousand metric tons	2 109	1 988	5 027	6 454	6 458	6 663	6 230	6 285	Milliers de tonnes
Metric tons per capita	0.5	0.4	0.9	1.1	1.1	1.1	1.0	1.0	Tonnes par habitant
Equatorial Guinea									**Guinée équatoriale**
Thousand metric tons	62	66	128	4 712	4 679	5 115	5 163	5 346	Milliers de tonnes
Metric tons per capita	0.3	0.2	0.3	7.7	6.4	6.6	6.5	6.5	Tonnes par habitant
Eritrea									**Érythrée**
Thousand metric tons	...	...	935	766	513	660	667	697	Milliers de tonnes
Metric tons per capita	...	...	0.3	0.2	0.1	0.1	0.1	0.1	Tonnes par habitant
Estonia									**Estonie**
Thousand metric tons	...	...	17 521	16 755	18 108	17 624	19 893	19 519	Milliers de tonnes
Metric tons per capita	...	...	12.2	12.4	13.6	13.3	15.1	14.8	Tonnes par habitant
Ethiopia									**Éthiopie**
Thousand metric tons	1 210	1 815	2 563	5 119	6 586	8 562	10 634	11 599	Milliers de tonnes
Metric tons per capita	~0.0	~0.0	~0.0	0.1	0.1	0.1	0.1	0.1	Tonnes par habitant
Falkland Is. (Malvinas)									**Îles Falkland (Malvinas)**
Thousand metric tons	15	29	44	51	55	55	55	55	Milliers de tonnes
Metric tons per capita	6.7	15.5	18.1	17.5	19.1	19.1	19.0	18.9	Tonnes par habitant
Faroe Islands									**Îles Féroé**
Thousand metric tons	348	517	572	722	631	590	678	598	Milliers de tonnes
Metric tons per capita	8.7	11.4	13.1	15.0	12.9	12.2	14.0	12.4	Tonnes par habitant
Fiji									**Fidji**
Thousand metric tons	623	579	763	1 096	1 221	1 060	1 151	1 170	Milliers de tonnes
Metric tons per capita	1.1	0.8	1.0	1.3	1.4	1.2	1.3	1.3	Tonnes par habitant
Finland									**Finlande**
Thousand metric tons	46 102	49 666	52 713	54 646	62 082	49 134	47 220	47 301	Milliers de tonnes
Metric tons per capita	9.8	10.1	10.3	10.4	11.6	9.1	8.7	8.6	Tonnes par habitant
France [2]									**France** [2]
Thousand metric tons	446 919	400 880	349 161	385 369	353 033	333 228	334 097	303 276	Milliers de tonnes
Metric tons per capita	8.5	7.3	6.1	6.3	5.6	5.2	5.2	4.7	Tonnes par habitant
French Guiana									**Guyane française**
Thousand metric tons	117	367	583	554	638	590	631	733	Milliers de tonnes
Metric tons per capita	2.1	4.2	4.2	2.8	2.8	2.4	2.5	2.8	Tonnes par habitant
French Polynesia									**Polynésie française**
Thousand metric tons	213	587	429	821	858	814	821	803	Milliers de tonnes
Metric tons per capita	1.7	3.4	2.0	3.2	3.2	3.0	3.0	2.9	Tonnes par habitant
Gabon									**Gabon**
Thousand metric tons	5 368	6 318	4 624	4 888	4 811	5 104	5 280	5 192	Milliers de tonnes
Metric tons per capita	9.0	8.0	4.3	3.6	3.1	3.2	3.2	3.1	Tonnes par habitant
Gambia									**Gambie**
Thousand metric tons	99	172	198	293	433	455	433	513	Milliers de tonnes
Metric tons per capita	0.2	0.2	0.2	0.2	0.3	0.3	0.2	0.3	Tonnes par habitant
Georgia									**Géorgie**
Thousand metric tons	...	...	2 303	5 068	6 315	8 441	7 858	8 988	Milliers de tonnes
Metric tons per capita	...	...	0.4	1.1	1.5	2.1	1.9	2.2	Tonnes par habitant
Germany									**Allemagne**
Thousand metric tons	...	...	864 110	797 180	758 860	739 861	757 313	719 883	Milliers de tonnes
Metric tons per capita	...	...	10.6	9.6	9.4	9.2	9.4	8.9	Tonnes par habitant
Ghana									**Ghana**
Thousand metric tons	2 747	3 326	5 277	6 993	9 956	11 877	14 620	14 466	Milliers de tonnes
Metric tons per capita	0.3	0.3	0.3	0.3	0.4	0.5	0.6	0.6	Tonnes par habitant
Gibraltar									**Gibraltar**
Thousand metric tons	88	44	275	400	466	462	491	528	Milliers de tonnes
Metric tons per capita	3.5	1.6	10.1	13.7	15.2	14.7	15.5	16.5	Tonnes par habitant
Greece									**Grèce**
Thousand metric tons	38 874	60 601	78 782	98 675	83 857	80 043	69 482	67 319	Milliers de tonnes
Metric tons per capita	4.3	6.1	7.4	8.8	7.5	7.2	6.3	6.1	Tonnes par habitant
Greenland									**Groenland**
Thousand metric tons	506	510	502	609	664	568	554	506	Milliers de tonnes
Metric tons per capita	10.2	9.6	9.1	10.6	11.7	10.1	9.8	9.0	Tonnes par habitant

25 CO2 emission estimates *(continued)*

From fossil fuel combustion, cement production and gas flared (thousand metric tons of carbon dioxide) and per capita

Estimation des émissions de CO2 *(suite)*

Dues à la combustion de combustibles fossiles, à la production de ciment et au gaz brûlés à la torchère (milliers de tonnes de dioxyde de carbone) et par habitant

Country or area[&]	1975	1985	1995	2005	2010	2012	2013	2014	Pays ou zone[&]
Grenada									**Grenade**
Thousand metric tons	48	62	150	216	260	271	304	242	Milliers de tonnes
Metric tons per capita	0.5	0.6	1.5	2.1	2.5	2.6	2.9	2.3	Tonnes par habitant
Guadeloupe									**Guadeloupe**
Thousand metric tons	403	891	1 463	2 222	2 299	2 545	2 556	2 567	Milliers de tonnes
Metric tons per capita	1.2	2.5	3.6	5.0	5.0	5.5	5.5	5.5	Tonnes par habitant
Guatemala									**Guatemala**
Thousand metric tons	3 524	3 524	7 165	12 570	11 665	11 973	13 634	18 328	Milliers de tonnes
Metric tons per capita	0.6	0.4	0.7	1.0	0.8	0.8	0.9	1.1	Tonnes par habitant
Guinea									**Guinée**
Thousand metric tons	843	994	1 291	1 826	2 604	2 582	2 299	2 450	Milliers de tonnes
Metric tons per capita	0.2	0.2	0.2	0.2	0.2	0.2	0.2	0.2	Tonnes par habitant
Guinea-Bissau									**Guinée-Bissau**
Thousand metric tons	114	172	183	213	238	253	257	271	Milliers de tonnes
Metric tons per capita	0.1	0.2	0.1	0.1	0.1	0.1	0.1	0.1	Tonnes par habitant
Guyana									**Guyana**
Thousand metric tons	1 826	1 419	1 463	1 437	1 720	1 995	1 936	2 010	Milliers de tonnes
Metric tons per capita	2.5	1.9	2.0	1.9	2.3	2.6	2.5	2.6	Tonnes par habitant
Haiti									**Haïti**
Thousand metric tons	484	942	902	2 076	2 127	2 314	2 406	2 860	Milliers de tonnes
Metric tons per capita	0.1	0.1	0.1	0.2	0.2	0.2	0.2	0.3	Tonnes par habitant
Honduras									**Honduras**
Thousand metric tons	1 668	1 907	3 880	7 554	7 976	8 984	9 065	9 472	Milliers de tonnes
Metric tons per capita	0.6	0.4	0.7	1.1	1.1	1.2	1.1	1.2	Tonnes par habitant
Hungary									**Hongrie**
Thousand metric tons	75 390	86 105	60 370	58 019	50 223	44 583	42 141	42 086	Milliers de tonnes
Metric tons per capita	7.2	8.2	5.8	5.8	5.0	4.5	4.3	4.3	Tonnes par habitant
Iceland									**Islande**
Thousand metric tons	1 617	1 628	1 947	2 230	1 962	1 800	1 900	1 984	Milliers de tonnes
Metric tons per capita	7.4	6.7	7.3	7.5	6.2	5.6	5.8	6.1	Tonnes par habitant
India									**Inde**
Thousand metric tons	252 202	426 674	811 562	1 222 563	1 719 691	2 018 504	2 034 752	2 238 377	Milliers de tonnes
Metric tons per capita	0.4	0.6	0.8	1.1	1.4	1.6	1.6	1.7	Tonnes par habitant
Indonesia									**Indonésie**
Thousand metric tons	53 964	121 246	224 941	341 992	428 760	637 079	490 227	464 176	Milliers de tonnes
Metric tons per capita	0.4	0.7	1.1	1.5	1.8	2.6	1.9	1.8	Tonnes par habitant
Iran (Islamic Rep. of)									**Iran (Rép. islamique d')**
Thousand metric tons	139 350	160 769	272 942	468 808	573 031	611 758	619 778	649 481	Milliers de tonnes
Metric tons per capita	4.3	3.4	4.6	6.7	7.7	8.0	8.0	8.3	Tonnes par habitant
Iraq									**Iraq**
Thousand metric tons	33 157	44 675	74 348	113 523	112 196	152 723	165 506	168 444	Milliers de tonnes
Metric tons per capita	2.8	2.9	3.7	4.1	3.6	4.6	4.8	4.8	Tonnes par habitant
Ireland									**Irlande**
Thousand metric tons	22 053	26 725	32 970	43 538	40 055	35 592	34 855	34 066	Milliers de tonnes
Metric tons per capita	6.9	7.6	9.1	10.5	8.7	7.6	7.4	7.3	Tonnes par habitant
Israel									**Israël**
Thousand metric tons	19 648	24 870	51 100	56 952	68 881	75 529	67 069	64 602	Milliers de tonnes
Metric tons per capita	5.9	6.1	9.6	8.6	9.3	9.8	8.6	8.1	Tonnes par habitant
Italy [3]									**Italie** [3]
Thousand metric tons	342 311	372 134	430 484	473 384	405 361	369 469	345 318	320 411	Milliers de tonnes
Metric tons per capita	6.2	6.6	7.6	8.1	6.8	6.2	5.8	5.4	Tonnes par habitant
Jamaica									**Jamaïque**
Thousand metric tons	8 188	5 046	9 179	10 499	7 297	7 462	8 093	7 422	Milliers de tonnes
Metric tons per capita	4.1	2.2	3.7	3.9	2.7	2.7	2.9	2.7	Tonnes par habitant
Japan									**Japon**
Thousand metric tons	870 073	915 397	1 183 447	1 239 255	1 171 625	1 230 168	1 246 516	1 214 048	Milliers de tonnes
Metric tons per capita	7.8	7.6	9.5	9.8	9.2	9.7	9.8	9.6	Tonnes par habitant
Jordan									**Jordanie**
Thousand metric tons	2 494	8 540	13 557	21 060	21 181	24 444	24 389	26 450	Milliers de tonnes
Metric tons per capita	1.2	3.0	3.1	4.0	3.3	3.5	3.4	3.6	Tonnes par habitant
Kazakhstan									**Kazakhstan**
Thousand metric tons	...	...	169 166	177 329	248 549	242 972	262 847	248 315	Milliers de tonnes
Metric tons per capita	...	...	10.6	11.7	15.3	14.4	15.4	14.3	Tonnes par habitant

25 CO2 emission estimates *(continued)*

From fossil fuel combustion, cement production and gas flared (thousand metric tons of carbon dioxide) and per capita

Estimation des émissions de CO2 *(suite)*

Dues à la combustion de combustibles fossiles, à la production de ciment et au gaz brûlés à la torchère (milliers de tonnes de dioxyde de carbone) et par habitant

Country or area&	1975	1985	1995	2005	2010	2012	2013	2014	Pays ou zone&
Kenya									**Kenya**
Thousand metric tons	4 976	3 770	7 554	8 562	12 174	12 515	13 333	14 287	Milliers de tonnes
Metric tons per capita	0.4	0.2	0.3	0.3	0.3	0.3	0.3	0.3	Tonnes par habitant
Kiribati									**Kiribati**
Thousand metric tons	33	22	29	62	62	62	62	62	Milliers de tonnes
Metric tons per capita	0.7	0.3	0.4	0.7	0.6	0.6	0.6	0.6	Tonnes par habitant
Kuwait									**Koweït**
Thousand metric tons	16 828	29 160	54 822	71 547	89 625	102 335	98 345	95 408	Milliers de tonnes
Metric tons per capita	16.0	16.7	33.7	31.6	29.3	29.9	27.4	25.4	Tonnes par habitant
Kyrgyzstan									**Kirghizistan**
Thousand metric tons	...	...	4 529	5 592	6 384	10 132	9 842	9 608	Milliers de tonnes
Metric tons per capita	...	...	1.0	1.1	1.2	1.8	1.7	1.7	Tonnes par habitant
Lao People's Dem. Rep.									**Rép. dém. pop. lao**
Thousand metric tons	253	202	348	1 404	1 639	1 698	1 577	1 955	Milliers de tonnes
Metric tons per capita	0.1	0.1	0.1	0.3	0.3	0.3	0.3	0.3	Tonnes par habitant
Latvia									**Lettonie**
Thousand metric tons	...	...	9 443	7 506	8 075	7 063	7 081	6 975	Milliers de tonnes
Metric tons per capita	...	...	3.8	3.3	3.9	3.5	3.5	3.5	Tonnes par habitant
Lebanon									**Liban**
Thousand metric tons	6 432	8 056	13 579	16 208	20 047	22 633	22 581	24 070	Milliers de tonnes
Metric tons per capita	2.3	2.8	3.9	4.0	4.6	4.6	4.3	4.3	Tonnes par habitant
Lesotho									**Lesotho**
Thousand metric tons	...	...	1 709	2 013	2 277	2 406	2 435	2 468	Milliers de tonnes
Metric tons per capita	...	...	1.0	1.0	1.1	1.2	1.2	1.2	Tonnes par habitant
Liberia									**Libéria**
Thousand metric tons	1 485	722	326	726	792	1 027	957	935	Milliers de tonnes
Metric tons per capita	0.9	0.3	0.1	0.2	0.2	0.3	0.2	0.2	Tonnes par habitant
Libya									**Libye**
Thousand metric tons	11 580	31 419	46 021	52 108	61 961	52 684	56 266	56 996	Milliers de tonnes
Metric tons per capita	4.7	8.2	9.6	9.0	9.9	8.4	9.0	9.1	Tonnes par habitant
Liechtenstein									**Liechtenstein**
Thousand metric tons	...	...	...	...	55	48	51	44	Milliers de tonnes
Metric tons per capita	...	...	...	...	1.5	1.3	1.4	1.1	Tonnes par habitant
Lithuania									**Lituanie**
Thousand metric tons	...	...	16 204	13 902	13 469	13 832	12 640	12 838	Milliers de tonnes
Metric tons per capita	...	...	4.5	4.1	4.3	4.6	4.3	4.4	Tonnes par habitant
Luxembourg									**Luxembourg**
Thousand metric tons	11 844	9 168	8 317	11 547	10 968	10 664	10 051	9 659	Milliers de tonnes
Metric tons per capita	33.0	25.0	20.4	25.3	21.6	20.0	18.4	17.3	Tonnes par habitant
Madagascar									**Madagascar**
Thousand metric tons	1 694	1 056	1 265	1 742	1 958	2 706	3 117	3 077	Milliers de tonnes
Metric tons per capita	0.2	0.1	0.1	0.1	0.1	0.1	0.1	0.1	Tonnes par habitant
Malawi									**Malawi**
Thousand metric tons	579	557	920	876	1 144	1 096	1 225	1 276	Milliers de tonnes
Metric tons per capita	0.1	0.1	0.1	0.1	0.1	0.1	0.1	0.1	Tonnes par habitant
Malaysia									**Malaisie**
Thousand metric tons	19 446	36 237	121 132	174 487	218 476	218 707	236 510	242 821	Milliers de tonnes
Metric tons per capita	1.6	2.3	5.8	6.7	7.8	7.6	8.0	8.1	Tonnes par habitant
Maldives									**Maldives**
Thousand metric tons	7	66	249	601	935	1 111	1 093	1 335	Milliers de tonnes
Metric tons per capita	~0.0	0.3	1.0	2.1	2.8	3.2	3.1	3.7	Tonnes par habitant
Mali									**Mali**
Thousand metric tons	341	407	469	898	964	994	1 027	1 412	Milliers de tonnes
Metric tons per capita	~0.0	~0.0	~0.0	0.1	0.1	0.1	0.1	0.1	Tonnes par habitant
Malta									**Malte**
Thousand metric tons	667	1 199	2 123	2 699	2 560	2 681	2 340	2 347	Milliers de tonnes
Metric tons per capita	2.2	3.4	5.5	6.6	6.2	6.5	5.6	5.6	Tonnes par habitant
Marshall Islands									**Îles Marshall**
Thousand metric tons	...	...	66	84	103	103	103	103	Milliers de tonnes
Metric tons per capita	...	...	1.3	1.7	2.0	1.9	2.0	1.9	Tonnes par habitant
Martinique									**Martinique**
Thousand metric tons	902	1 210	1 639	2 204	2 010	2 215	2 211	2 299	Milliers de tonnes
Metric tons per capita	2.8	3.6	4.4	5.5	5.1	5.6	5.6	5.8	Tonnes par habitant

25 CO2 emission estimates *(continued)*

From fossil fuel combustion, cement production and gas flared (thousand metric tons of carbon dioxide) and per capita

Estimation des émissions de CO2 *(suite)*

Dues à la combustion de combustibles fossiles, à la production de ciment et au gaz brûlés à la torchère (milliers de tonnes de dioxyde de carbone) et par habitant

Country or area&	1975	1985	1995	2005	2010	2012	2013	2014	Pays ou zone&
Mauritania									**Mauritanie**
Thousand metric tons	510	656	1 074	1 588	2 237	2 655	2 670	2 710	Milliers de tonnes
Metric tons per capita	0.4	0.4	0.5	0.5	0.6	0.7	0.7	0.7	Tonnes par habitant
Mauritius									**Maurice**
Thousand metric tons	590	708	1 830	3 297	3 916	3 968	4 070	4 228	Milliers de tonnes
Metric tons per capita	0.7	0.7	1.6	2.6	3.2	3.2	3.2	3.3	Tonnes par habitant
Mexico									**Mexique**
Thousand metric tons	164 472	288 501	332 817	466 362	464 308	496 325	490 340	480 271	Milliers de tonnes
Metric tons per capita	2.7	3.8	3.6	4.4	3.9	4.1	4.0	3.8	Tonnes par habitant
Micronesia (Fed. States of)									**Micronésie (États féd. de)**
Thousand metric tons	...	...	106	121	114	136	143	150	Milliers de tonnes
Metric tons per capita	...	...	1.0	1.1	1.1	1.3	1.4	1.4	Tonnes par habitant
Mongolia									**Mongolie**
Thousand metric tons	4 067	9 028	7 921	8 562	13 821	26 226	38 753	20 840	Milliers de tonnes
Metric tons per capita	2.8	4.7	3.4	3.4	5.1	9.4	13.6	7.2	Tonnes par habitant
Montenegro									**Monténégro**
Thousand metric tons	...	...	...	...	2 582	2 336	2 248	2 211	Milliers de tonnes
Metric tons per capita	...	...	...	...	4.1	3.7	3.6	3.5	Tonnes par habitant
Montserrat									**Montserrat**
Thousand metric tons	11	26	33	37	66	44	51	48	Milliers de tonnes
Metric tons per capita	1.0	2.2	3.3	6.6	13.0	8.5	10.3	9.6	Tonnes par habitant
Morocco									**Maroc**
Thousand metric tons	11 111	17 866	30 374	45 771	55 958	62 731	59 083	59 864	Milliers de tonnes
Metric tons per capita	0.7	0.8	1.1	1.5	1.7	1.9	1.7	1.7	Tonnes par habitant
Mozambique									**Mozambique**
Thousand metric tons	2 886	1 148	1 115	1 822	2 736	3 121	4 019	8 427	Milliers de tonnes
Metric tons per capita	0.3	0.1	0.1	0.1	0.1	0.1	0.1	0.3	Tonnes par habitant
Myanmar									**Myanmar**
Thousand metric tons	4 587	6 711	6 960	11 599	12 515	11 071	12 860	21 632	Milliers de tonnes
Metric tons per capita	0.1	0.2	0.2	0.3	0.3	0.2	0.3	0.4	Tonnes par habitant
Namibia									**Namibie**
Thousand metric tons	...	...	1 632	2 310	3 102	3 385	2 629	3 755	Milliers de tonnes
Metric tons per capita	...	...	1.0	1.1	1.4	1.5	1.1	1.6	Tonnes par habitant
Nauru									**Nauru**
Thousand metric tons	103	125	106	62	44	40	44	48	Milliers de tonnes
Metric tons per capita	14.8	15.4	10.8	6.1	4.3	4.0	4.3	4.8	Tonnes par habitant
Nepal									**Népal**
Thousand metric tons	352	678	2 035	3 084	5 057	5 856	6 637	8 031	Milliers de tonnes
Metric tons per capita	~0.0	~0.0	0.1	0.1	0.2	0.2	0.3	0.3	Tonnes par habitant
Netherlands									**Pays-Bas**
Thousand metric tons	153 020	147 949	178 634	181 480	183 053	170 310	173 255	167 303	Milliers de tonnes
Metric tons per capita	11.3	10.2	11.6	11.1	11.0	10.2	10.3	9.9	Tonnes par habitant
Netherlands Antilles [former]									**Antilles néerlandaises [anc.]**
Thousand metric tons	...	...	5 225	5 735	4 562	...	...	...	Milliers de tonnes
Metric tons per capita	...	...	27.5	30.8	22.0	...	...	...	Tonnes par habitant
New Caledonia									**Nouvelle-Calédonie**
Thousand metric tons	2 530	1 456	2 076	2 824	3 542	3 630	4 243	4 290	Milliers de tonnes
Metric tons per capita	19.7	9.4	10.9	12.2	14.4	14.3	16.5	16.5	Tonnes par habitant
New Zealand									**Nouvelle-Zélande**
Thousand metric tons	18 262	21 804	27 132	34 140	31 782	34 151	33 458	34 664	Milliers de tonnes
Metric tons per capita	5.9	6.7	7.4	8.3	7.3	7.7	7.5	7.7	Tonnes par habitant
Nicaragua									**Nicaragua**
Thousand metric tons	1 929	1 991	2 780	4 320	4 536	4 620	4 551	4 862	Milliers de tonnes
Metric tons per capita	0.7	0.6	0.6	0.8	0.8	0.8	0.8	0.8	Tonnes par habitant
Niger									**Niger**
Thousand metric tons	334	997	810	715	1 173	1 867	1 940	2 127	Milliers de tonnes
Metric tons per capita	0.1	0.1	0.1	0.1	0.1	0.1	0.1	0.1	Tonnes par habitant
Nigeria									**Nigéria**
Thousand metric tons	47 396	69 893	35 841	106 068	91 517	98 503	98 136	96 281	Milliers de tonnes
Metric tons per capita	0.7	0.8	0.3	0.8	0.6	0.6	0.6	0.6	Tonnes par habitant
Niue									**Nioué**
Thousand metric tons	4	4	7	4	4	7	7	11	Milliers de tonnes
Metric tons per capita	0.8	1.1	2.8	1.8	1.9	3.8	3.8	5.7	Tonnes par habitant

25 CO2 emission estimates *(continued)*

From fossil fuel combustion, cement production and gas flared (thousand metric tons of carbon dioxide) and per capita

Estimation des émissions de CO2 *(suite)*

Dues à la combustion de combustibles fossiles, à la production de ciment et au gaz brûlés à la torchère (milliers de tonnes de dioxyde de carbone) et par habitant

Country or area[&]	1975	1985	1995	2005	2010	2012	2013	2014	Pays ou zone[&]
Norway									**Norvège**
Thousand metric tons	29 673	40 715	33 439	42 438	60 106	49 890	58 162	47 627	Milliers de tonnes
Metric tons per capita	7.4	9.8	7.7	9.2	12.3	9.9	11.4	9.2	Tonnes par habitant
Oman									**Oman**
Thousand metric tons	7 257	8 661	15 896	29 893	47 418	59 160	61 378	61 169	Milliers de tonnes
Metric tons per capita	8.1	5.6	7.1	12.3	16.1	16.7	15.7	14.4	Tonnes par habitant
Pakistan									**Pakistan**
Thousand metric tons	23 219	47 176	84 484	136 636	161 396	163 497	164 326	166 298	Milliers de tonnes
Metric tons per capita	0.3	0.5	0.7	0.8	1.0	0.9	0.9	0.9	Tonnes par habitant
Palau									**Palaos**
Thousand metric tons	194	161	235	260	253	253	257	260	Milliers de tonnes
Metric tons per capita	4.7	2.3	13.5	13.1	12.3	12.1	12.3	12.4	Tonnes par habitant
Panama									**Panama**
Thousand metric tons	3 663	2 629	2 985	6 839	9 164	10 114	10 719	8 801	Milliers de tonnes
Metric tons per capita	2.1	1.2	1.1	2.1	2.5	2.7	2.8	2.3	Tonnes par habitant
Papua New Guinea									**Papouasie-Nvl-Guinée**
Thousand metric tons	1 533	2 127	2 061	4 386	4 763	5 079	6 186	6 318	Milliers de tonnes
Metric tons per capita	0.6	0.6	0.4	0.7	0.7	0.7	0.8	0.8	Tonnes par habitant
Paraguay									**Paraguay**
Thousand metric tons	840	1 551	3 964	3 832	5 097	5 284	5 434	5 702	Milliers de tonnes
Metric tons per capita	0.3	0.4	0.8	0.7	0.8	0.8	0.8	0.9	Tonnes par habitant
Peru									**Pérou**
Thousand metric tons	21 965	19 512	23 883	37 136	57 594	55 071	57 154	61 745	Milliers de tonnes
Metric tons per capita	1.5	1.0	1.0	1.4	1.9	1.8	1.9	2.0	Tonnes par habitant
Philippines									**Philippines**
Thousand metric tons	32 526	28 049	60 711	74 832	84 869	91 206	98 129	105 654	Milliers de tonnes
Metric tons per capita	0.8	0.5	0.9	0.9	0.9	1.0	1.0	1.1	Tonnes par habitant
Poland									**Pologne**
Thousand metric tons	375 559	445 900	344 214	302 539	316 264	299 931	302 278	285 740	Milliers de tonnes
Metric tons per capita	11.0	12.0	8.9	7.9	8.2	7.8	7.8	7.4	Tonnes par habitant
Portugal									**Portugal**
Thousand metric tons	21 357	27 407	51 870	65 280	48 137	46 014	45 427	45 053	Milliers de tonnes
Metric tons per capita	2.3	2.8	5.1	6.2	4.5	4.4	4.3	4.3	Tonnes par habitant
Qatar									**Qatar**
Thousand metric tons	10 957	12 405	31 789	50 957	72 508	94 125	85 023	107 854	Milliers de tonnes
Metric tons per capita	67.3	33.7	63.4	62.1	41.1	46.7	40.4	49.7	Tonnes par habitant
Republic of Korea									**République de Corée**
Thousand metric tons	81 829	178 334	374 771	462 922	566 717	583 966	592 499	587 156	Milliers de tonnes
Metric tons per capita	2.3	4.4	8.4	9.8	11.6	11.8	11.9	11.7	Tonnes par habitant
Republic of Moldova									**République de Moldova**
Thousand metric tons	...	...	11 192	4 895	4 932	4 925	4 998	4 932	Milliers de tonnes
Metric tons per capita	...	...	2.6	1.3	1.2	1.2	1.2	1.2	Tonnes par habitant
Réunion									**Réunion**
Thousand metric tons	484	994	1 764	3 447	4 169	4 250	4 100	4 173	Milliers de tonnes
Metric tons per capita	1.0	1.8	2.6	4.3	5.0	5.0	4.8	4.9	Tonnes par habitant
Romania									**Roumanie**
Thousand metric tons	162 257	194 344	126 049	96 457	79 413	81 723	70 945	70 003	Milliers de tonnes
Metric tons per capita	7.6	8.5	5.6	4.4	3.9	4.1	3.6	3.6	Tonnes par habitant
Russian Federation									**Fédération de Russie**
Thousand metric tons	...	...	1 631 474	1 615 090	1 670 531	1 830 830	1 778 561	1 705 346	Milliers de tonnes
Metric tons per capita	...	...	11.0	11.2	11.7	12.8	12.4	11.9	Tonnes par habitant
Rwanda									**Rwanda**
Thousand metric tons	176	616	462	528	590	737	803	840	Milliers de tonnes
Metric tons per capita	~0.0	0.1	0.1	0.1	0.1	0.1	0.1	0.1	Tonnes par habitant
Saint Helena									**Sainte-Hélène**
Thousand metric tons	...	4	11	11	11	11	11	11	Milliers de tonnes
Metric tons per capita	...	0.6	1.8	2.0	2.9	3.0	3.0	3.1	Tonnes par habitant
Saint Kitts and Nevis									**Saint-Kitts-et-Nevis**
Thousand metric tons	...	51	128	198	220	220	224	231	Milliers de tonnes
Metric tons per capita	...	1.2	3.0	4.0	4.2	4.1	4.1	4.2	Tonnes par habitant
Saint Lucia									**Sainte-Lucie**
Thousand metric tons	77	128	312	367	403	407	407	407	Milliers de tonnes
Metric tons per capita	0.7	1.0	2.1	2.2	2.3	2.2	2.2	2.2	Tonnes par habitant

25 CO2 emission estimates *(continued)*

From fossil fuel combustion, cement production and gas flared (thousand metric tons of carbon dioxide) and per capita

Estimation des émissions de CO2 *(suite)*

Dues à la combustion de combustibles fossiles, à la production de ciment et au gaz brûlés à la torchère (milliers de tonnes de dioxyde de carbone) et par habitant

Country or area[&]	1975	1985	1995	2005	2010	2012	2013	2014	Pays ou zone[&]
Saint Pierre and Miquelon									**Saint-Pierre-et-Miquelon**
Thousand metric tons	33	33	70	66	70	70	73	77	Milliers de tonnes
Metric tons per capita	5.7	5.5	11.2	10.5	11.3	11.3	11.7	12.2	Tonnes par habitant
Saint Vincent-Grenadines									**Saint-Vincent-Grenadines**
Thousand metric tons	33	66	128	220	220	253	209	209	Milliers de tonnes
Metric tons per capita	0.4	0.6	1.2	2.0	2.0	2.3	1.9	1.9	Tonnes par habitant
Samoa									**Samoa**
Thousand metric tons	59	114	117	161	187	198	198	198	Milliers de tonnes
Metric tons per capita	0.4	0.7	0.7	0.9	1.0	1.0	1.0	1.0	Tonnes par habitant
Sao Tome and Principe									**Sao Tomé-et-Principe**
Thousand metric tons	18	55	48	77	99	114	114	114	Milliers de tonnes
Metric tons per capita	0.2	0.6	0.4	0.5	0.6	0.6	0.6	0.6	Tonnes par habitant
Saudi Arabia									**Arabie saoudite**
Thousand metric tons	83 336	172 653	235 161	397 642	518 492	564 843	541 048	601 047	Milliers de tonnes
Metric tons per capita	11.3	13.1	12.7	16.5	18.4	19.1	17.9	19.5	Tonnes par habitant
Senegal									**Sénégal**
Thousand metric tons	2 582	2 677	3 495	5 812	7 745	7 913	8 423	8 856	Milliers de tonnes
Metric tons per capita	0.6	0.4	0.4	0.6	0.6	0.6	0.6	0.6	Tonnes par habitant
Serbia									**Serbie**
Thousand metric tons	...	...	...	...	45 955	44 063	44 884	37 667	Milliers de tonnes
Metric tons per capita	...	...	...	...	5.1	4.9	5.0	4.3	Tonnes par habitant
Serbia and Monten. [former]									**Serbie-et-Monténégro [anc.]**
Thousand metric tons	...	...	40 579	52 302	...	...	...	...	Milliers de tonnes
Metric tons per capita	...	...	3.7	5.0	...	...	...	...	Tonnes par habitant
Seychelles									**Seychelles**
Thousand metric tons	59	150	198	689	444	440	403	495	Milliers de tonnes
Metric tons per capita	1.0	2.2	2.7	8.3	4.8	4.7	4.2	5.2	Tonnes par habitant
Sierra Leone									**Sierra Leone**
Thousand metric tons	524	664	400	546	726	1 030	1 192	1 309	Milliers de tonnes
Metric tons per capita	0.2	0.2	0.1	0.1	0.1	0.2	0.2	0.2	Tonnes par habitant
Singapore									**Singapour**
Thousand metric tons	24 543	33 417	42 174	30 359	55 643	36 373	55 676	56 373	Milliers de tonnes
Metric tons per capita	10.9	12.3	12.1	7.1	11.0	6.9	10.3	10.2	Tonnes par habitant
Sint Maarten (Dutch part)									**Saint-Martin (partie néerlandaise)**
Thousand metric tons	...	...	...	...	...	697	715	733	Milliers de tonnes
Metric tons per capita	...	...	...	...	...	19.8	19.6	19.5	Tonnes par habitant
Slovakia									**Slovaquie**
Thousand metric tons	...	...	42 115	39 358	36 241	32 765	33 091	30 678	Milliers de tonnes
Metric tons per capita	...	...	7.8	7.3	6.7	6.1	6.1	5.6	Tonnes par habitant
Slovenia									**Slovénie**
Thousand metric tons	...	...	14 404	15 867	15 335	14 782	14 151	12 812	Milliers de tonnes
Metric tons per capita	...	...	7.3	7.9	7.5	7.2	6.9	6.2	Tonnes par habitant
Solomon Islands									**Îles Salomon**
Thousand metric tons	59	150	143	161	198	198	202	202	Milliers de tonnes
Metric tons per capita	0.3	0.6	0.4	0.3	0.4	0.4	0.4	0.4	Tonnes par habitant
Somalia									**Somalie**
Thousand metric tons	502	858	590	594	612	609	609	609	Milliers de tonnes
Metric tons per capita	0.1	0.1	0.1	0.1	0.1	0.1	0.1	0.1	Tonnes par habitant
South Africa									**Afrique du Sud**
Thousand metric tons	185 202	324 214	362 259	416 916	474 099	468 771	466 376	489 772	Milliers de tonnes
Metric tons per capita	7.2	9.8	8.8	8.7	9.2	8.9	8.7	9.1	Tonnes par habitant
South Sudan									**Soudan du sud**
Thousand metric tons	...	...	...	...	...	1 331	1 448	1 496	Milliers de tonnes
Metric tons per capita	...	...	...	...	...	0.1	0.1	0.1	Tonnes par habitant
Spain									**Espagne**
Thousand metric tons	181 645	201 234	241 611	353 462	270 911	264 779	237 035	233 977	Milliers de tonnes
Metric tons per capita	5.1	5.2	6.1	8.1	5.8	5.7	5.1	5.1	Tonnes par habitant
Sri Lanka									**Sri Lanka**
Thousand metric tons	2 897	3 957	5 904	12 101	13 264	16 032	15 489	18 394	Milliers de tonnes
Metric tons per capita	0.2	0.3	0.3	0.6	0.7	0.8	0.8	0.9	Tonnes par habitant
State of Palestine									**État de Palestine**
Thousand metric tons	...	...	946	2 743	2 035	2 200	2 439	2 838	Milliers de tonnes
Metric tons per capita	...	...	0.4	0.8	0.5	0.5	0.6	0.6	Tonnes par habitant

25

CO2 emission estimates *(continued)*

From fossil fuel combustion, cement production and gas flared (thousand metric tons of carbon dioxide) and per capita

Estimation des émissions de CO2 *(suite)*

Dues à la combustion de combustibles fossiles, à la production de ciment et au gaz brûlés à la torchère (milliers de tonnes de dioxyde de carbone) et par habitant

Country or area&	1975	1985	1995	2005	2010	2012	2013	2014	Pays ou zone&
Sudan									**Soudan**
Thousand metric tons	...	...	...	...	...	14 642	15 475	15 365	Milliers de tonnes
Metric tons per capita	...	...	...	...	...	0.4	0.4	0.4	Tonnes par habitant
Sudan [former]									**Soudan [anc.]**
Thousand metric tons	4 239	4 074	4 298	10 983	15 940	...	...	...	Milliers de tonnes
Metric tons per capita	0.3	0.2	0.1	0.3	0.4	...	...	...	Tonnes par habitant
Suriname									**Suriname**
Thousand metric tons	2 021	1 599	2 065	1 595	2 402	2 259	1 918	1 991	Milliers de tonnes
Metric tons per capita	5.5	4.3	4.7	3.2	4.6	4.3	3.6	3.7	Tonnes par habitant
Swaziland									**Swaziland**
Thousand metric tons	337	440	455	1 019	1 038	1 206	1 089	1 203	Milliers de tonnes
Metric tons per capita	0.7	0.6	0.5	0.9	0.9	1.0	0.9	1.0	Tonnes par habitant
Sweden									**Suède**
Thousand metric tons	80 824	62 394	55 155	51 562	52 024	47 048	44 847	43 421	Milliers de tonnes
Metric tons per capita	9.9	7.5	6.2	5.7	5.5	4.9	4.7	4.5	Tonnes par habitant
Switzerland									**Suisse**
Thousand metric tons	39 098	39 827	39 226	41 338	38 995	37 774	40 227	35 306	Milliers de tonnes
Metric tons per capita	6.1	6.1	5.5	5.5	5.0	4.7	5.0	4.3	Tonnes par habitant
Syrian Arab Republic									**Rép. arabe syrienne**
Thousand metric tons	11 184	29 651	41 664	50 627	61 606	44 730	36 439	30 704	Milliers de tonnes
Metric tons per capita	1.5	2.8	2.9	2.8	3.0	2.2	1.9	1.7	Tonnes par habitant
Tajikistan									**Tadjikistan**
Thousand metric tons	...	...	2 450	2 442	2 545	2 934	3 480	5 189	Milliers de tonnes
Metric tons per capita	...	...	0.4	0.4	0.3	0.4	0.4	0.6	Tonnes par habitant
Thailand									**Thaïlande**
Thousand metric tons	24 408	48 672	161 154	247 467	281 926	296 598	300 089	316 213	Milliers de tonnes
Metric tons per capita	0.6	0.9	2.7	3.7	4.2	4.4	4.4	4.7	Tonnes par habitant
TFYR of Macedonia									**ex-R.Y. de Macédoine**
Thousand metric tons	...	...	10 840	11 280	8 603	8 966	7 847	7 510	Milliers de tonnes
Metric tons per capita	...	...	5.5	5.5	4.2	4.3	3.8	3.6	Tonnes par habitant
Timor-Leste									**Timor-Leste**
Thousand metric tons	...	...	...	176	235	293	440	469	Milliers de tonnes
Metric tons per capita	...	...	...	0.2	0.2	0.3	0.4	0.4	Tonnes par habitant
Togo									**Togo**
Thousand metric tons	312	550	953	1 338	2 640	2 486	2 659	2 622	Milliers de tonnes
Metric tons per capita	0.1	0.2	0.2	0.3	0.4	0.4	0.4	0.4	Tonnes par habitant
Tonga									**Tonga**
Thousand metric tons	33	48	95	114	117	106	114	121	Milliers de tonnes
Metric tons per capita	0.4	0.5	1.0	1.1	1.1	1.0	1.1	1.1	Tonnes par habitant
Trinidad and Tobago									**Trinité-et-Tobago**
Thousand metric tons	9 622	20 755	17 022	38 151	47 935	45 419	46 542	46 274	Milliers de tonnes
Metric tons per capita	9.5	17.7	13.5	29.0	36.1	33.8	34.5	34.2	Tonnes par habitant
Tunisia									**Tunisie**
Thousand metric tons	5 548	11 940	15 735	22 662	27 660	27 004	27 668	28 830	Milliers de tonnes
Metric tons per capita	1.0	1.6	1.8	2.3	2.6	2.5	2.5	2.6	Tonnes par habitant
Turkey									**Turquie**
Thousand metric tons	65 698	106 717	171 975	237 391	298 002	329 561	324 772	345 981	Milliers de tonnes
Metric tons per capita	1.7	2.2	2.9	3.5	4.1	4.4	4.3	4.5	Tonnes par habitant
Turkmenistan									**Turkménistan**
Thousand metric tons	...	...	34 000	48 338	57 290	64 873	66 736	68 423	Milliers de tonnes
Metric tons per capita	...	...	8.1	10.2	11.4	12.5	12.7	12.9	Tonnes par habitant
Turks and Caicos Islands									**Îles Turques-et-Caïques**
Thousand metric tons	...	...	48	121	191	198	198	205	Milliers de tonnes
Metric tons per capita	...	...	3.0	4.0	6.1	6.2	6.0	6.1	Tonnes par habitant
Tuvalu									**Tuvalu**
Thousand metric tons	...	...	7	11	7	11	11	11	Milliers de tonnes
Uganda									**Ouganda**
Thousand metric tons	1 133	620	939	2 171	3 920	4 070	4 870	5 229	Milliers de tonnes
Metric tons per capita	0.1	~0.0	~0.0	0.1	0.1	0.1	0.1	0.1	Tonnes par habitant
Ukraine									**Ukraine**
Thousand metric tons	...	...	445 944	333 877	304 643	295 791	271 875	227 299	Milliers de tonnes
Metric tons per capita	...	...	8.7	7.1	6.7	6.5	6.0	5.1	Tonnes par habitant

25

CO2 emission estimates *(continued)*

From fossil fuel combustion, cement production and gas flared (thousand metric tons of carbon dioxide) and per capita

Estimation des émissions de CO2 *(suite)*

Dues à la combustion de combustibles fossiles, à la production de ciment et au gaz brûlés à la torchère (milliers de tonnes de dioxyde de carbone) et par habitant

Country or area&	1975	1985	1995	2005	2010	2012	2013	2014	Pays ou zone&
United Arab Emirates									**Émirats arabes unis**
Thousand metric tons	31 070	49 926	70 641	116 149	160 813	176 386	170 706	211 370	Milliers de tonnes
Metric tons per capita	58.2	37.0	30.1	28.5	19.3	19.7	18.9	23.2	Tonnes par habitant
United Kingdom									**Royaume-Uni**
Thousand metric tons	603 643	559 856	538 118	542 580	493 208	468 573	458 250	419 820	Milliers de tonnes
Metric tons per capita	10.7	9.9	9.2	9.0	7.8	7.4	7.2	6.5	Tonnes par habitant
United Rep. of Tanzania									**Rép.-Unie de Tanzanie**
Thousand metric tons	2 285	2 358	3 553	5 504	7 107	9 545	11 177	11 562	Milliers de tonnes
Metric tons per capita	0.1	0.1	0.1	0.1	0.1	0.2	0.2	0.2	Tonnes par habitant
United States 4									**États-Unis** 4
Thousand metric tons	4 406 330	4 492 555	5 132 920	5 789 727	5 395 532	5 119 436	5 159 161	5 254 279	Milliers de tonnes
Metric tons per capita	19.8	18.4	19.0	19.3	17.2	16.1	16.1	16.2	Tonnes par habitant
Uruguay									**Uruguay**
Thousand metric tons	5 970	3 297	4 591	5 776	6 388	8 694	7 587	6 747	Milliers de tonnes
Metric tons per capita	2.1	1.1	1.4	1.7	1.9	2.6	2.2	2.0	Tonnes par habitant
Uzbekistan									**Ouzbékistan**
Thousand metric tons	...	...	103 435	117 249	104 168	115 815	103 354	105 214	Milliers de tonnes
Metric tons per capita	...	...	4.5	4.5	3.7	4.0	3.6	3.6	Tonnes par habitant
Vanuatu									**Vanuatu**
Thousand metric tons	55	121	66	59	121	114	106	154	Milliers de tonnes
Metric tons per capita	0.6	1.0	0.4	0.3	0.5	0.5	0.4	0.6	Tonnes par habitant
Venezuela (Boliv. Rep. of)									**Venezuela (Rép. boliv. du)**
Thousand metric tons	63 817	101 279	133 350	165 096	189 071	198 766	183 922	185 220	Milliers de tonnes
Metric tons per capita	5.0	5.9	6.1	6.2	6.5	6.7	6.1	6.1	Tonnes par habitant
Viet Nam									**Viet Nam**
Thousand metric tons	21 800	21 166	29 090	98 144	142 738	142 221	147 230	166 911	Milliers de tonnes
Metric tons per capita	0.4	0.4	0.4	1.2	1.6	1.6	1.6	1.8	Tonnes par habitant
Wallis and Futuna Islands									**Îles Wallis-et-Futuna**
Thousand metric tons	...	...	...	29	29	26	22	22	Milliers de tonnes
Metric tons per capita	...	...	...	1.9	2.1	1.8	1.6	1.6	Tonnes par habitant
Yemen									**Yémen**
Thousand metric tons	...	...	10 466	20 044	23 432	18 669	25 497	22 699	Milliers de tonnes
Metric tons per capita	...	...	0.7	1.0	1.0	0.7	1.0	0.9	Tonnes par habitant
Zambia									**Zambie**
Thousand metric tons	4 081	2 754	2 171	2 288	2 692	3 667	3 957	4 503	Milliers de tonnes
Metric tons per capita	0.8	0.4	0.3	0.2	0.2	0.3	0.3	0.3	Tonnes par habitant
Zimbabwe									**Zimbabwe**
Thousand metric tons	8 320	10 264	15 130	10 770	7 778	7 792	11 676	12 020	Milliers de tonnes
Metric tons per capita	1.4	1.2	1.3	0.8	0.6	0.6	0.8	0.8	Tonnes par habitant

Source:

Carbon Dioxide Information Analysis Center (CDIAC) of the Oak Ridge National Laboratory, Oak Ridge, Tennessee, U.S.A., database on national CO2 emission estimates, last accessed March 2017.

& These data are transformed from the original CDIAC data in metric tons of Carbon to metric tons of Carbon Dioxide by a factor of 3.667.

1 For statistical purposes, the data for China do not include those for the Hong Kong Special Administrative Region (Hong Kong SAR), Macao Special Administrative Region (Macao SAR) and Taiwan Province of China.
2 Including Monaco.
3 Including San Marino.
4 Including overseas territories.

Source:

"Carbon Dioxide Information Analysis Center (CDIAC) of the Oak Ridge National Laboratory, Oak Ridge, Tennessee, U.S.A.", la base de données des estimations nationales des émissions de CO2, dernier accès mars 2017.

& Les données originales fournies par CDIAC en tonnes métriques de carbone sont converties en tonnes métriques de dioxyde de carbone en multipliant par un facteur de 3,667.

1 Pour la présentation des statistiques, les données pour la Chine ne comprennent pas la Région Administrative Spéciale de Hong Kong (Hong Kong RAS), la Région Administrative Spéciale de Macao (Macao RAS) et la province de Taiwan.
2 Y compris Monaco.
3 Y compris Saint-Marin.
4 Y compris Samoa américaines, Guam, Porto Rico, les Iles Vierges des Etats-Unis et l'Ile de Wake.

26 Water supply and sanitation services

Proportion of population using

Services d'alimentation en eau potable et d'assainissement

Proportion de la population utilisant des services

Country or area& / Pays ou zone&	Year / Année	Proportion of population using: - Proportion de la population utilisant des: Safely managed drinking water services / Services d'alimentation en eau potable gérés en toute sécurité: Urban (%) / Urbaine (%)	Rural (%) / Rurale (%)	Total (%) / Totale (%)	Safely managed sanitation facilities / Services d'assainissement gérés en toute sécurité: Urban (%) / Urbaine (%)	Rural (%) / Rurale (%)	Total (%) / Totale (%)
Total, all countries or areas	**2005**	**85**	**48**	**66**	**35**	**28**	**31**
Total, tous pays ou zones	**2010**	**85**	**56**	**71**	**40**	**31**	**36**
	2015	**85**	**55**	**71**	**43**	**35**	**39**
Northern Africa	2005	...	...	...	31	...	18
Afrique septentrionale	2010	...	...	...	34	...	22
	2015	...	...	...	37	...	25
Sub-Saharan Africa	2005	44	...	20	...	...	...
Afrique subsaharienne	2010	45	...	22	...	...	...
	2015	46	...	24	...	...	...
Eastern Africa	2005	41	4	12	...	...	...
Afrique orientale	2010	44	6	15	...	...	...
	2015	48	7	18	...	...	...
Southern Africa	2005	89	...	...	...	...	...
Afrique australe	2010	89	...	...	...	...	...
	2015	85	...	...	...	...	...
Western Africa	2005	...	...	21	...	...	...
Afrique occidentale	2010	...	...	23	...	...	...
	2015	...	...	25	...	...	...
Northern America	2005	100	...	99	90	...	79
Amérique septentrionale	2010	100	...	99	90	...	79
	2015	100	...	99	89	...	79
Latin America & the Caribbean	2005	77	...	62	16	...	13
Amérique latine et Caraïbes	2010	77	...	64	21	...	18
	2015	77	...	65	27	...	22
Caribbean							
Caraïbes	2001	...	...	...	13	...	...
Central America	2005	...	...	44	18	...	14
Amérique centrale	2010	...	...	47	26	...	21
	2015	...	...	50	34	...	28
South America	2005	81	36	72	16	...	13
Amérique du Sud	2010	81	39	73	21	...	17
	2015	81	41	74	25	...	22
Asia	2005	86	51	65	24	26	25
Asie	2010	86	62	72	31	30	31
	2015	85	61	73	38	35	36
Central Asia	2005	86	34	56	39	...	...
Asie centrale	2010	87	40	59	40	...	...
	2012	88	43	61	40	...	...
	2015	89	...	...	40	...	...
Eastern Asia	2005	94	...	...	43	33	38
Asie orientale	2010	94	...	...	57	37	48
	2015	93	...	...	70	41	59
Southern Asia	2005	63	43	49	...	16	...
Asie méridionale	2010	61	49	53	...	21	...
	2015	59	55	56	...	27	...
Western Asia	2005	...	...	...	51	...	32
Asie occidentale	2010	...	...	...	56	...	38
	2015	...	...	...	58	...	51
Europe	2005	...	...	90	84	46	73
Europe	2010	...	...	91	86	51	76
	2015	...	...	92	86	52	77
Eastern Europe	2005	...	...	81	...	...	...
Europe orientale	2010	...	...	84	...	...	58
	2015	...	...	85	...	...	59
Northern Europe	2005	...	...	95	93	68	87
Europe septentrionale	2010	...	...	96	93	69	89
	2015	...	...	96	94	69	90
Southern Europe	2005	...	...	88	73	41	63
Europe méridionale	2010	...	...	91	83	63	77
	2015	...	...	94	84	64	78

26 Water supply and sanitation services *(continued)*

Proportion of population using

Services d'alimentation en eau potable et d'assainissement *(suite)*

Proportion de la population utilisant des services

Country or area[&] Pays ou zone[&]	Year Année	Proportion of population using: - Proportion de la population utilisant des: Safely managed drinking water services Services d'alimentation en eau potable gérés en toute sécurité			Safely managed sanitation facilities Services d'assainissement gérés en toute sécurité		
		Urban (%) Urbaine (%)	Rural (%) Rurale (%)	Total (%) Totale (%)	Urban (%) Urbaine (%)	Rural (%) Rurale (%)	Total (%) Totale (%)
Western Europe Europe occidentale	2005	...	...	97	96	87	94
	2010	...	...	97	96	87	94
	2015	...	...	97	96	86	94
Oceania Océanie	2005	93	...	...	57	20	46
	2010	95	...	...	61	20	49
	2015	96	...	...	64	20	51
Australia and New Zealand Australie et Nouvelle-Zélande	2005	94	...	...	...	...	61
	2010	96	...	...	...	...	65
	2015	97	...	...	...	...	68
Albania Albanie	2005	...	...	53	65	54	59
	2010	...	...	62	65	60	62
	2015	...	...	69	65	64	65
Algeria Algérie	2005	...	...	...	19	24	21
	2010	...	...	...	18	24	20
	2015	...	...	...	17	24	19
Andorra Andorre	2005	...	...	...	51	51	51
	2010	...	...	...	95	95	95
	2015	...	...	...	100	100	100
Argentina Argentine	2005	98	...	98	26	...	28
	2010	99	...	98	26	...	27
	2015	98	...	99	25	...	26
Armenia Arménie	2005	...	...	44	...	...	...
	2010	...	...	58	...	...	...
	2015	...	...	61	...	...	...
Australia Australie	2005	98	...	...	...	...	66
	2010	99	...	...	...	...	70
	2015	99	...	...	...	...	74
Austria Autriche	2005	...	...	98	99	92	97
	2010	...	...	98	99	92	97
	2015	...	...	99	99	92	97
Azerbaijan Azerbaïdjan	2005	...	...	57	73	...	...
	2010	...	...	68	73	...	...
	2015	...	...	72	73	...	...
Bahrain Bahreïn	2005	...	...	99	...	...	...
	2010	...	...	99	...	...	...
	2015	...	...	99	...	...	...
Bangladesh Bangladesh	2005	45	60	56	...	21	...
	2010	45	61	56	...	26	...
	2015	45	61	56	...	32	...
Belarus Bélarus	2005	...	...	82	86	68	81
	2010	...	...	89	82	70	79
	2015	...	...	94	78	71	76
Belgium Belgique	2005	...	...	99	...	...	74
	2010	...	...	99	...	...	86
	2015	...	...	98	...	...	97
Bhutan Bhoutan	2005	44	24	30	...	...	...
	2010	45	26	32	...	...	...
	2015	45	28	34	...	...	...
Bolivia (Plurin. State of) Bolivie (État plurin. de)	2005	...	...	...	20	...	16
	2010	...	...	...	21	...	18
	2015	...	...	...	22	...	19
Bosnia and Herzegovina Bosnie-Herzégovine	2005	...	...	88	11	...	23
	2010	...	...	88	10	...	23
	2015	...	...	89	9	...	23
Botswana Botswana	2005	84	...	...	...	...	...
	2010	84	...	...	...	...	...
	2015	84	...	...	...	...	...
Brazil Brésil	2005	95	...	...	32	...	30
	2010	97	...	...	36	...	34
	2015	97	...	...	40	...	39

Water supply and sanitation services *(continued)*
Proportion of population using

Services d'alimentation en eau potable et d'assainissement *(suite)*
Proportion de la population utilisant des services

Country or area[&] Pays ou zone[&]	Year Année	Proportion of population using: - Proportion de la population utilisant des: Safely managed drinking water services Services d'alimentation en eau potable gérés en toute sécurité Urban (%) Urbaine (%)	Rural (%) Rurale (%)	Total (%) Totale (%)	Safely managed sanitation facilities Services d'assainissement gérés en toute sécurité Urban (%) Urbaine (%)	Rural (%) Rurale (%)	Total (%) Totale (%)
Bulgaria	2005	...	...	97	80	...	71
Bulgarie	2010	...	...	97	66	...	61
	2015	...	...	97	51	...	49
Cambodia	2005	47	13	19	...	...	...
Cambodge	2010	51	14	22	...	...	...
	2015	55	16	24	...	...	...
Canada	2005	...	...	...	...	...	74
Canada	2010	...	...	...	...	...	76
	2015	...	...	...	...	...	77
Channel Islands	2010	...	...	92	...	...	...
Îles Anglo-Normandes	2015	...	...	92	...	...	...
Chile	2005	99	...	95	53	...	45
Chili	2010	99	...	97	67	...	65
	2015	98	...	98	81	...	85
China [1]	2005	93	...	...	38	33	35
Chine [1]	2010	92	...	...	56	38	47
	2015	91	...	...	73	42	60
China, Hong Kong SAR	2005	99	...	99	17	...	17
Chine, Hong Kong RAS	2010	99	...	99	16	...	16
	2015	100	...	100	16	...	16
China, Macao SAR	2005	100	...	100	...	...	...
Chine, Macao RAS	2010	100	...	100	...	...	...
	2015	100	...	100	...	...	...
Colombia	2005	82	35	69	16	...	18
Colombie	2010	81	37	70	16	...	19
	2015	81	40	71	16	...	20
Congo	2005	...	...	32	...	...	...
Congo	2010	...	...	35	...	...	...
	2015	...	...	37	...	...	...
Costa Rica	2005	...	...	79	...	...	...
Costa Rica	2010	...	...	87	...	...	...
	2015	...	...	90	...	...	...
Côte d'Ivoire	2005	66	17	40	...	...	...
Côte d'Ivoire	2010	65	20	43	...	...	...
	2015	65	23	46	...	...	...
Croatia	2005	...	...	92	64	...	60
Croatie	2010	...	...	93	65	...	60
	2015	...	...	90	65	...	60
Cuba	2005	...	...	...	31	...	32
Cuba	2010	...	...	...	29	...	32
	2015	...	...	...	28	...	31
Cyprus	2005	...	...	96	86	...	76
Chypre	2010	...	...	98	86	...	76
	2015	...	...	100	86	...	76
Czechia	2005	...	...	97	89	78	86
Tchéquie	2010	...	...	97	87	76	84
	2015	...	...	98	85	75	82
Denmark	2005	...	...	94	...	...	93
Danemark	2010	...	...	96	...	...	93
	2015	...	...	97	...	...	93
Ecuador	2005	80	52	69	40	48	42
Équateur	2010	82	54	72	37	52	42
	2015	85	56	74	34	57	42
Egypt	2005	...	...	...	64	...	55
Égypte	2010	...	...	...	67	...	58
	2015	...	...	...	70	...	61
El Salvador	2005	82	...	...	...	...	...
El Salvador	2010	76	...	...	...	...	...
	2015	77	...	...	...	...	...

26 Water supply and sanitation services *(continued)*

Proportion of population using

Services d'alimentation en eau potable et d'assainissement *(suite)*

Proportion de la population utilisant des services

Country or area& Pays ou zone&	Year Année	Proportion of population using: - Proportion de la population utilisant des: Safely managed drinking water services Services d'alimentation en eau potable gérés en toute sécurité Urban (%) Urbaine (%)	Rural (%) Rurale (%)	Total (%) Totale (%)	Safely managed sanitation facilities Services d'assainissement gérés en toute sécurité Urban (%) Urbaine (%)	Rural (%) Rurale (%)	Total (%) Totale (%)
Estonia Estonie	2005	...	...	94	95	76	89
	2010	...	...	89	97	79	91
	2015	...	...	82	99	81	93
Ethiopia Éthiopie	2005	36	~0	6	...	2	...
	2010	37	2	8	...	3	...
	2015	38	4	11	...	4	...
Finland Finlande	2005	...	...	95	97	...	91
	2010	...	...	98	98	...	91
	2015	...	...	97	98	...	92
France France	2005	...	...	93	...	...	89
	2010	...	...	93	...	...	91
	2015	...	...	93	...	...	92
French Guiana Guyane française	2005	...	...	...	...	...	50
	2010	...	...	...	...	...	54
	2015	...	...	...	...	...	58
Gambia Gambie	2005	50	...	...	...	...	...
	2010	60	...	...	...	...	...
	2015	70	...	...	...	...	...
Georgia Géorgie	2005	...	...	76	9	...	...
	2010	...	...	74	14	...	...
	2015	...	...	73	17	...	...
Germany Allemagne	2005	...	...	99	98	92	96
	2010	...	...	99	97	92	96
	2015	...	...	99	97	92	95
Ghana Ghana	2005	37	3	19	...	...	...
	2010	40	5	23	...	...	...
	2015	44	7	27	...	...	...
Gibraltar Gibraltar	2005	...	...	99	...	...	...
	2010	...	...	99	...	...	...
	2015	...	...	99	...	...	...
Greece Grèce	2005	...	...	99	81	...	74
	2010	...	...	99	81	...	74
	2015	...	...	99	81	...	75
Greenland Groenland	2005	...	...	94	...	...	93
	2010	...	...	96	...	...	93
	2015	...	...	97	...	...	93
Guatemala Guatemala	2005	...	...	54	...	...	...
	2010	...	...	57	...	...	...
	2015	...	...	61	...	...	...
Honduras Honduras	2005	...	...	...	15	...	...
	2010	...	...	...	15	...	...
	2015	...	...	...	15	...	...
Hungary Hongrie	2005	...	...	57	60	...	57
	2010	...	...	69	75	...	69
	2015	...	...	82	83	...	76
Iceland Islande	2005	...	...	93	70	...	69
	2010	...	...	96	70	...	69
	2015	...	...	98	70	...	69
India Inde	2005	...	36	...	...	16	...
	2010	...	42	...	...	23	...
	2015	...	49	...	...	31	...
Iran (Islamic Republic of) Iran (Rép. islamique d')	2005	96	83	91	...	...	...
	2010	95	83	91	...	...	...
	2015	94	83	91	...	...	...
Iraq Iraq	2005	...	...	...	27	17	24
	2010	...	...	...	32	23	29
	2015	...	...	...	35	26	32
Ireland Irlande	2005	...	...	94	59	...	47
	2010	...	...	97	75	...	60
	2015	...	...	99	88	...	70

26 Water supply and sanitation services *(continued)*

Proportion of population using

Services d'alimentation en eau potable et d'assainissement *(suite)*

Proportion de la population utilisant des services

		Proportion of population using: - Proportion de la population utilisant des:					
		Safely managed drinking water services Services d'alimentation en eau potable gérés en toute sécurité			Safely managed sanitation facilities Services d'assainissement gérés en toute sécurité		
Country or area[&] Pays ou zone[&]	Year Année	Urban (%) Urbaine (%)	Rural (%) Rurale (%)	Total (%) Totale (%)	Urban (%) Urbaine (%)	Rural (%) Rurale (%)	Total (%) Totale (%)
Isle of Man Île de Man	2015	...	...	96	...	...	...
Israel Israël	2005	99	99	99	84	82	84
	2010	99	99	99	89	87	88
	2015	99	99	99	93	91	93
Italy Italie	2005	...	...	89	...	...	...
	2010	...	...	92	96	94	96
	2015	...	...	94	96	94	95
Japan Japon	2005	...	...	97	...	...	99
	2010	...	...	97	...	...	100
	2015	...	...	97	...	...	100
Jordan Jordanie	2005	...	...	94	83	...	77
	2010	...	...	94	83	...	77
	2015	...	...	93	82	...	77
Kazakhstan Kazakhstan	2005	...	...	...	69	...	...
	2010	...	...	...	68	...	...
	2015	...	...	...	67	...	...
Kenya Kenya	2005	60	...	...	...	...	...
	2010	57	...	...	...	...	...
	2015	54	...	...	...	...	...
Kuwait Koweït	2005	...	...	100	...	...	100
	2010	...	...	100	...	...	100
	2015	...	...	100	...	...	100
Kyrgyzstan Kirghizistan	2005	82	30	49	...	...	...
	2010	88	41	57	...	...	...
	2015	93	52	66	...	...	...
Latvia Lettonie	2005	...	...	81	79	59	73
	2010	...	...	82	82	62	75
	2015	...	...	82	85	66	78
Lebanon Liban	2005	...	...	45	...	...	17
	2010	...	...	46	...	...	19
	2015	...	...	48	...	...	20
Libya Libye	2005	...	...	...	...	...	29
	2010	...	...	...	...	...	27
	2015	...	...	...	...	...	26
Liechtenstein Liechtenstein	2005	...	...	100	...	...	99
	2010	...	...	100	...	...	99
	2015	...	...	100	...	...	99
Lithuania Lituanie	2005	...	...	75	62	46	57
	2010	...	...	84	63	51	59
	2015	...	...	92	64	55	61
Luxembourg Luxembourg	2005	...	...	98	94	87	93
	2010	...	...	98	94	87	94
	2015	...	...	98	94	87	94
Malaysia Malaisie	2005	...	...	93	...	...	80
	2010	...	...	93	...	...	81
	2015	...	...	92	...	...	82
Malta Malte	2005	...	...	100	93	93	93
	2010	...	...	100	93	93	93
	2015	...	...	100	93	93	93
Martinique Martinique	2005	...	...	95	...	...	...
	2010	...	...	99	...	...	...
	2015	...	...	100	...	...	...
Mayotte Mayotte	2010	...	...	85	...	...	...
	2015	...	...	85	...	...	...
Mexico Mexique	2005	...	...	40	28	...	27
	2010	...	...	41	37	...	36
	2015	...	...	43	46	...	45
Monaco Monaco	2005	100	...	100	100	...	100
	2010	100	...	100	100	...	100
	2015	100	...	100	100	...	100

Country or area[&] Pays ou zone[&]	Year Année	Proportion of population using: - Proportion de la population utilisant des: Safely managed drinking water services Services d'alimentation en eau potable gérés en toute sécurité			Safely managed sanitation facilities Services d'assainissement gérés en toute sécurité		
		Urban (%) Urbaine (%)	Rural (%) Rurale (%)	Total (%) Totale (%)	Urban (%) Urbaine (%)	Rural (%) Rurale (%)	Total (%) Totale (%)
Montenegro	2010	95	...	89	36	...	...
Monténégro	2015	94	...	90	36	...	...
Morocco	2005	87	26	59	38	...	34
Maroc	2010	88	32	64	39	...	36
	2015	89	39	69	39	...	38
Mozambique	2005	...	...	...	...	6	...
Mozambique	2010	...	...	...	...	9	...
	2015	...	...	...	...	12	...
Nepal	2005	35	23	25	...	...	...
Népal	2010	34	24	26	...	...	...
	2015	34	25	27	...	...	...
Netherlands	2005	...	...	100	98	97	97
Pays-Bas	2010	...	...	100	98	97	97
	2015	...	...	100	98	97	97
New Caledonia	2005	...	...	89	...	...	...
Nouvelle-Calédonie	2010	...	...	93	...	...	...
	2015	...	...	97	...	...	...
New Zealand	2005	...	...	77	...	...	76
Nouvelle-Zélande	2010	...	...	89	...	...	76
	2015	...	...	100	...	...	76
Nicaragua	2005	78	30	57	...	...	...
Nicaragua	2010	79	30	58	...	...	...
	2015	79	30	59	...	...	...
Niger	2005	...	...	...	19	3	6
Niger	2010	...	...	...	21	4	7
	2015	...	...	...	24	5	9
Nigeria	2005	...	...	18	...	...	...
Nigéria	2010	...	...	19	...	...	...
	2015	...	...	19	...	...	...
Niue	2005	...	...	98	...	...	...
Nioué	2010	...	...	98	...	...	...
	2015	...	...	97	...	...	...
Northern Mariana Islands	2005	...	...	82	...	...	...
Îles Mariannes du Nord	2010	...	...	82	...	...	...
	2015	...	...	82	...	...	...
Norway	2005	...	...	95	...	...	77
Norvège	2010	...	...	95	...	...	77
	2015	...	...	95	...	...	78
Oman	2005	...	...	75	...	...	...
Oman	2010	...	...	82	...	...	...
	2015	...	...	89	...	...	...
Pakistan	2005	49	32	38	...	...	...
Pakistan	2010	45	32	37	...	...	...
	2015	41	32	36	...	...	...
Palau	2005	...	...	...	14	...	19
Palaos	2010	...	...	...	16	...	20
	2015	...	...	...	16	...	20
Panama	2005	...	...	...	26	...	...
Panama	2010	...	...	...	27	...	...
	2015	...	...	...	29	...	...
Peru	2005	57	16	47	23	...	20
Pérou	2010	58	18	49	29	...	25
	2015	58	20	50	35	...	30
Poland	2005	...	...	94	88	...	73
Pologne	2010	...	...	94	90	...	75
	2015	...	...	94	91	...	77
Portugal	2005	...	...	94	65	...	60
Portugal	2010	...	...	95	65	...	61
	2015	...	...	95	65	...	62

Water supply and sanitation services *(continued)*
Proportion of population using

Services d'alimentation en eau potable et d'assainissement *(suite)*
Proportion de la population utilisant des services

Country or area& Pays ou zone&	Year Année	Proportion of population using: - Proportion de la population utilisant des: Safely managed drinking water services Services d'alimentation en eau potable gérés en toute sécurité			Safely managed sanitation facilities Services d'assainissement gérés en toute sécurité		
		Urban (%) Urbaine (%)	Rural (%) Rurale (%)	Total (%) Totale (%)	Urban (%) Urbaine (%)	Rural (%) Rurale (%)	Total (%) Totale (%)
Puerto Rico Porto Rico	2005	...	...	...	...	...	32
	2010	...	...	...	...	...	32
	2015	...	...	...	...	...	32
Qatar Qatar	2005	...	...	...	...	...	88
	2010	...	...	...	...	...	88
	2015	...	...	...	...	...	88
Republic of Korea République de Corée	2005	...	...	97	...	...	90
	2010	...	...	98	...	...	94
	2015	...	...	98	...	...	98
Republic of Moldova République de Moldova	2005	...	...	48	...	...	...
	2010	...	...	60	...	...	...
	2015	...	...	70	...	...	...
Romania Roumanie	2005	...	...	96	...	...	...
	2010	...	...	93	...	...	49
	2015	...	...	88	...	...	57
Russian Federation Fédération de Russie	2005	...	...	75	...	...	...
	2010	...	...	75	...	...	...
	2015	...	...	76	...	...	...
Rwanda Rwanda	2005	29	...	...	...	...	...
	2010	33	...	...	...	...	...
	2015	36	...	...	...	...	...
Saint Pierre and Miquelon Saint-Pierre-et-Miquelon	2010	...	...	83	...	...	...
	2015	...	...	83	...	...	...
San Marino Saint-Marin	2005	...	...	100	...	...	78
	2010	...	...	100	...	...	78
	2015	...	...	100	...	...	78
Saudi Arabia Arabie saoudite	2005	...	...	...	...	...	70
	2010	...	...	...	...	...	81
	2015	...	...	...	...	...	84
Senegal Sénégal	2005	...	...	...	22	18	20
	2010	...	...	...	23	20	22
	2015	...	...	...	24	22	24
Serbia Serbie	2005	...	...	78	17	...	28
	2010	...	...	83	15	...	26
	2015	...	...	88	14	...	24
Singapore Singapour	2005	100	...	100	100	...	100
	2010	100	...	100	100	...	100
	2015	100	...	100	100	...	100
Slovakia Slovaquie	2005	...	...	93	88	75	82
	2010	...	...	93	88	75	82
	2015	...	...	93	88	75	82
Slovenia Slovénie	2005	...	...	82	...	...	74
	2010	...	...	90	...	...	75
	2015	...	...	98	...	...	76
Somalia Somalie	2005	...	...	...	37	8	18
	2010	...	...	...	30	7	16
	2015	...	...	...	24	7	14
South Africa Afrique du Sud	2005	91	...	...	...	...	...
	2010	89	...	...	...	...	...
	2015	85	...	...	...	...	...
Spain Espagne	2005	...	...	98	94	93	94
	2010	...	...	98	96	96	96
	2015	...	...	98	97	98	97
Sri Lanka Sri Lanka	2005	85	...	...	...	...	...
	2010	89	...	...	...	...	...
	2015	93	...	...	...	...	...
State of Palestine État de Palestine	2005	...	...	...	61	...	59
	2010	...	...	...	62	...	59
	2015	...	...	...	63	...	60

Water supply and sanitation services *(continued)*
Proportion of population using

Services d'alimentation en eau potable et d'assainissement *(suite)*
Proportion de la population utilisant des services

Country or area& Pays ou zone&	Year Année	Proportion of population using: - Proportion de la population utilisant des: Safely managed drinking water services Services d'alimentation en eau potable gérés en toute sécurité			Safely managed sanitation facilities Services d'assainissement gérés en toute sécurité		
		Urban (%) Urbaine (%)	Rural (%) Rurale (%)	Total (%) Totale (%)	Urban (%) Urbaine (%)	Rural (%) Rurale (%)	Total (%) Totale (%)
Swaziland Swaziland	2005	75	...	...	...	...	...
	2010	83	...	...	...	...	...
	2015	88	...	...	...	...	...
Sweden Suède	2005	...	...	98	92	87	92
	2010	...	...	98	93	87	92
	2015	...	...	98	93	87	92
Switzerland Suisse	2005	...	...	93	99	98	98
	2010	...	...	94	99	97	99
	2015	...	...	95	100	96	99
Tajikistan Tadjikistan	2005	...	...	41	...	...	...
	2010	...	...	45	...	...	...
	2015	...	...	47	...	...	...
TFYR of Macedonia ex-R.Y. de Macédoine	2005	97	83	91	...	...	...
	2010	93	89	91	...	...	...
	2015	90	75	83	...	...	...
Tunisia Tunisie	2005	...	...	63	79	...	63
	2010	...	...	89	85	...	69
	2015	...	...	93	89	...	73
Turkey Turquie	2005	...	...	...	45	...	27
	2010	...	...	...	47	...	36
	2015	...	...	...	48	...	44
Turkmenistan Turkménistan	2005	87	61	74	...	...	...
	2010	86	74	80	...	...	...
	2015	86	87	86	...	...	...
Tuvalu Tuvalu	2005	0	...	...	7	8	8
	2010	0	...	...	6	12	9
	2015	0	...	...	6	14	9
Uganda Ouganda	2005	23	2	5	...	...	...
	2010	20	3	6	...	...	...
	2015	18	4	6	...	...	...
Ukraine Ukraine	2005	...	...	70	...	...	...
	2010	...	...	84	...	...	...
	2015	...	...	92	...	...	...
United Arab Emirates Émirats arabes unis	2005	...	...	...	95	81	93
	2010	...	...	...	95	81	93
	2015	...	...	...	95	81	93
United Kingdom Royaume-Uni	2005	...	...	96	99	92	97
	2010	...	...	96	99	92	98
	2015	...	...	96	99	92	98
United Rep. of Tanzania Rép.-Unie de Tanzanie	2005	14	...	...	...	...	...
	2010	27	...	...	...	...	...
	2015	34	...	...	...	...	...
United States of America États-Unis d'Amérique	2005	100	...	99	95	...	89
	2010	100	...	99	95	...	89
	2015	100	...	99	95	...	89
Uruguay Uruguay	2005	94	...	...	63	...	62
	2010	94	...	...	64	...	63
	2015	94	...	...	64	...	64
Uzbekistan Ouzbékistan	2005	86	32	52	...	...	...
	2010	87	31	51	...	...	...
	2012	87	31	51	...	...	...
	2015	87	...	...	...	...	...
Venezuela (Boliv. Rep. of) Venezuela (Rép. boliv. du)	2005	...	...	...	17	...	18
	2010	...	...	...	17	...	19
	2015	...	...	...	17	...	19
Yemen Yémen	2005	...	...	...	56	...	...
	2010	...	...	...	62	...	...
	2015	...	...	...	67	...	...
Zambia Zambie	2005	48	...	...	...	...	...
	2010	47	...	...	...	...	...
	2015	47	...	...	...	...	...

Source:

World Health Organization (WHO) and United Nations Children's Fund (UNICEF), Geneva and New York, the WHO/UNICEF Joint Monitoring Programme for the Water and Sanitation database, last accessed July 2017.

& The figures are estimated by the international agency, when corresponding country data on a specific year or set of years are not available, or when multiple sources exist, or there are issues of data quality. Estimates are based on national data, such as surveys or administrative records, or other sources but on the same variable being estimated.

1 For statistical purposes, the data for China do not include those for the Hong Kong Special Administrative Region (Hong Kong SAR), Macao Special Administrative Region (Macao SAR) and Taiwan Province of China.

Source:

Organisation mondial de la santé (OMS) et Fonds des Nations Unies pour l'enfance (UNICEF), Genève et New York, la base de données de la Programme commun OMS/UNICEF de surveillance de l'eau et de l'assainissement, dernier accès juillet 2017.

& Lorsque les données d'un pays sur une ou plusieurs années ne sont pas disponibles, ou lorsque plusieurs sources existent, ou s'il y a un problème de qualité des données, les chiffres sont estimés par l'organisme international. Ces estimations sont basées sur de données nationales comme les enquêtes, les registres administratifs, ou autres sources de la même variable estimée.

1 Pour la présentation des statistiques, les données pour la Chine ne comprennent pas la région administrative spéciale de Hong Kong (Hong Kong RAS), la région administrative spéciale de Macao (Macao RAS) et la province chinoise de Taïwan.

27 Population employed in research and development (R&D)

Full-time equivalent (FTE)

Population employé dans la recherche et le développement (R-D)

Equivalent temps plein (ETP)

Country or area Pays ou zone	Year Année	Total R & D personnel Total du personnel de R - D	Researchers Chercheurs Total M & F Total H & F	 Females Femmes	Technicians and equivalent staff Techniciens et personnel assimilé Total M & F Total H & F	 Females Femmes	Other supporting staff Autre personnel de soutien Total M & F Total H & F	 Females Femmes
Albania [1]								
Albanie [1]	2008	779	467	207	120	…	192	…
Algeria [1]								
Algérie [1]	2005	7 331	5 593	2 043	1 134	…	604	…
American Samoa [1]								
Samoa américaines [1]	2005	6	6	…	…	…	…	…
Angola								
Angola	2011	2 038	1 150	320	858	242	30	6
Argentina	2005	45 361	31 868	15 416	7 788	…	5 705	…
Argentine	2010	65 299	46 199	23 041[2]	10 143	…	8 957	…
	2013	74 866	50 785	25 269[2]	13 561	…	10 521	…
	2014	…	51 665	26 280[2]	…	…	…	…
Armenia [3]	2005[1]	6 892[4]	5 056	2 329	345	…	1 491[4]	…
Arménie [3]	2010[1]	6 558[4]	4 981	2 261	479	…	672	…
	2014[2]	5 627[4]	4 144	2 227	370	230	673	360
Australia	2004	116 194	81 192	…	…	…	…	…
Australie	2008	137 489	92 649	…	24 243	…	20 597	…
	*2010	…	100 414	…	…	…	…	…
Austria	2004	42 891	25 955	4 740	12 067	2 901	4 869	2 471
Autriche	*2005	47 625	28 470	…	…	…	…	…
	2009	56 438	34 664	7 765	16 709	3 903	5 065	2 398
	*2010	59 923	36 581	…	…	…	…	…
	2013	66 186	40 426	9 286	20 310	4 263	5 451	2 343
	*2014	67 135	41 005	…	…	…	…	…
Azerbaijan [3]	2005	18 164[4]	11 603	6 056	1 825	…	3 086	…
Azerbaïdjan [3]	2010	17 924[4]	11 037	6 101	1 819	1 087	3 531	1 866
	2014	23 329[4]	16 337	8 866	1 933	1 099	2 487	1 429
Bahrain								
Bahreïn	2014	562	493	205	23	12	41	16
Belarus [3]	2005	30 222[4]	18 267	7 897	2 112	…	5 763	…
Bélarus [3]	2010	31 712[4]	19 879	8 392	2 248	…	9 585[4]	…
	2013	28 937[4]	18 353	7 535	2 162	…	8 422[4]	…
Belgium	2005	53 517	33 146	9 769	15 047	4 585	5 324	2 702
Belgique	2010	60 075	40 832	12 962	14 401	5 079	4 841	2 517
	2011	62 895	42 686	13 545	15 176	5 232	5 033	2 575
	*2014	68 701	46 880	…	…	…	…	…
Benin [1,3]								
Bénin [1,3]	2007	…	1 000	…	…	…	…	…
Bermuda [3]	2010	80	41	17	10	…	29	13
Bermudes [3]	2014	55	31	11	6	…	18	9
Bolivia (Plurin. State of)	2002	1 090	1 040	…	…	…	50	…
Bolivie (État pl.. de)	2010	2 497	1 646	…	258	…	593	…
Bosnia and Herzegovina	2005[1]	731	253	…	198	…	280	…
Bosnie-Herzégovine	2007[1]	1 554	745	…	270	…	536	…
	2014	1 767	1 018	507	182	90	167	85
Botswana [3]	2005[1]	2 140	1 732	533	408	…	…	…
Botswana [3]	#2012	1 139	690	188	256	110	193	113
Brazil	2005	196 283	109 410	…	86 873	…	…	…
Brésil	2010	266 709	138 653	…	128 056	…	…	…
Brunei Darussalam [1]	2003	140	98	…	…	…	…	…
Brunéi Darussalam [1]	#2004	…	102	…	…	…	…	…
Bulgaria	2005	15 853	10 053	4 673	3 778	2 256	2 022	1 349
Bulgarie	2010	16 574	10 979	5 506	3 704	2 189	1 891	1 172
	2011	16 986	11 902	5 940	3 263	1 970	1 821	1 139
	2013	17 545	12 275	6 196	…	…	…	…
	2014	19 335	13 201	…	…	…	…	…
Burkina Faso [3]	2005	942[1,5]	301[1,5]	37	225[1,5]	…	416[1,5]	…
Burkina Faso [3]	#2010	2 548	1 144	264	608	149	796	256

27 Population employed in research and development (R&D) *(continued)*

Full-time equivalent (FTE)

Population employé dans la recherche et le développement (R-D) *(suite)*

Equivalent temps plein (ETP)

Country or area Pays ou zone	Year Année	Total R & D personnel Total du personnel de R - D	Researchers Chercheurs Total M & F Total H & F	Researchers Chercheurs Females Femmes	Technicians and equivalent staff Techniciens et personnel assimilé Total M & F Total H & F	Technicians and equivalent staff Techniciens et personnel assimilé Females Femmes	Other supporting staff Autre personnel de soutien Total M & F Total H & F	Other supporting staff Autre personnel de soutien Females Femmes
Burundi [3]	2010	744[1]	374[1]	56	117[1]	...	253[1]	...
Burundi [3]	2011	746[1]	379[1]	55	125[1]	...	242[1]	...
Cabo Verde [1]	2002	151	60	...	15	...	76	...
Cabo Verde [1]	2011[6]	# 37	# 25	9	# 4	2	# 8	5
Cambodia [1] Cambodge [1]	*2002	494	223	50	170	...	102	...
Cameroon [3] Cameroun [3]	2008	5 600	4 562	994	338	...	700	...
Canada Canada	2005	218 590	136 700	...	52 825	...	29 072	...
	2010	233 060	158 660	...	51 930	...	22 470	...
	2013	226 620	159 190	...	46 540	...	20 890	...
Central African Republic [3] République centrafricaine [3]	2005[1]	...	11	...	...	...	...	...
	2007[6]	...	41[1]	17	...	...	...	...
	#2009[1]	...	134	...	...	...	...	...
Chile Chili	2010[7]	11 491	5 440	1 671	3 909	1 590	2 142	941
	*2014	15 910	7 602	2 409	5 575	2 406	2 733	1 182
China [8] Chine [8]	2005[9]	1 364 799	1 118 698	...	...	...	...	...
	2010	2 553 829	1 210 841	...	...	...	...	...
	2014	3 710 580	1 524 280	...	...	...	...	...
China, Hong Kong SAR Chine, Hong Kong RAS	2005	22 053	18 024	...	2 346	...	1 683	...
	2010	24 060	20 582	...	2 159	...	1 319	...
	2013	26 045	22 466	...	2 080	...	1 499	...
China, Macao SAR [1] Chine, Macao RAS [1]	#2005	413	298	77	110	...	5	...
	2010	676	350	116	313	158	13	9
	2014	1 067	609	192	440	209	18	13
Colombia Colombie	2005	...	5 462	1 872	...	...	...	...
	2010	...	8 862	3 246	...	...	...	...
	2013	...	7 193	2 817	...	...	...	...
Congo Congo	2000	217[1]	102[1]	13	111[1]	22	4[1]	...
Costa Rica [3] Costa Rica [3]	2005	...	1 444	569	...	...	...	...
	2010	10 383[4]	7 796[4]	1 475[2]	1 326[2]	388	1 261[2]	476
	2013[2]	7 193	4 291	1 846	1 746	597	1 156	425
Côte d'Ivoire [1] Côte d'Ivoire [1]	2005	...	1 269	210	...	...	...	...
Croatia Croatie	2005	9 270	5 727	2 710	2 633	1 196	910	584
	2010	10 859	7 104	3 485	2 601	1 280	1 154	768
	2013	10 448	6 529	3 256	2 820	1 337	1 099	710
	2014	10 027	6 117	...	2 879	...	1 031	...
Cuba [3] Cuba [3]	2005	33 988	5 526	2 703	...	...	28 462[10]	...
	2010	16 641	4 872	2 381	...	...	11 769	...
	2014	14 418	4 355	2 098	...	...	10 063	...
Cyprus Chypre	2005	1 157	682	239	273	98	201	105
	2010	1 302	905	337	216	89	181	101
	2013	1 239	881	338	203	90	155	84
	*2014	1 260	865	...	...	...	...	...
Czechia Tchéquie	#2005	43 370	24 169	6 349	13 773	5 153	5 429	2 633
	2010	52 290	29 228	7 429	15 971	5 141	7 092	3 369
	2013	61 976	34 271	8 401	18 932	5 921	8 772	4 191
	*2014	64 444	36 040	...	19 846	...	8 558	...
Dem. Rep. of the Congo [3,4] Rép. dém. du Congo [3,4]	2005	33 478	10 411	...	1 510	...	21 557	...
	2009	34 820	12 470	...	1 843	...	20 507	...
Denmark Danemark	2005	43 499	28 179	8 113	10 781	5 364	4 538	2 534
	2010	56 623	37 435	* 11 654	12 557	* 4 959	6 631	* 3 433
	2011	57 585	39 181	12 376	11 856	4 694	6 548	3 112
	2013	58 246	40 316	13 159	...	...	...	...
	*2014	58 745	40 647	...	...	...	...	...
Ecuador Équateur	2003	...	645	...	...	...	...	...
	2010	4 769	2 110	854	1 029	300	1 630	783
	2011	4 599	2 736	1 075	1 177	370	686	277

27 Population employed in research and development (R&D) *(continued)*

Full-time equivalent (FTE)

Population employé dans la recherche et le développement (R-D) *(suite)*

Equivalent temps plein (ETP)

Country or area Pays ou zone	Year Année	Total R & D personnel Total du personnel de R - D	Researchers Chercheurs		Technicians and equivalent staff Techniciens et personnel assimilé		Other supporting staff Autre personnel de soutien	
			Total M & F Total H & F	Females Femmes	Total M & F Total H & F	Females Femmes	Total M & F Total H & F	Females Femmes
Egypt	2010	86 455[1]	40 752[1,11]	16 972	20 758[1,5]	...	24 945[1,5]	...
Égypte	2014[11]	111 602	61 059	25 138	31 795	...	18 748	...
El Salvador [3]	2005	...	260	81	...	...	...	...
El Salvador [3]	2010	...	516	190	...	...	...	...
	2015	...	828	315	...	...	...	...
Estonia	2005	4 362	3 331	1 317	567	274	464	305
Estonie	2010	5 277	4 077	1 688	907	404	293	211
	2013	5 858	4 407	1 871	1 058	486	393	256
	2014	5 796	4 323	...	896	...	577	...
Ethiopia	2005	5 112	1 608	111	779	...	2 725	...
Éthiopie	2007	6 051	1 615	125	978	...	3 458	...
	#2010	8 282	3 701	...	1 441	...	3 140	...
	2013	11 501	4 267	556	3 157	757	4 078	1 316
Faroe Islands Îles Féroé	2003	131	86	21	41	...	4	...
Finland	2005	57 471	39 582	...	...	...	...	...
Finlande	2010	55 897	41 425	...	...	...	...	...
	2014	52 130	38 281	...	...	...	...	...
France	2005	349 681	202 507	...	105 171	...	42 003	...
France	2010	# 397 756	# 243 533	46 001[7]	# 118 364	...	# 35 860	...
	2013	418 141	266 222	69 418[7]	117 424	...	34 495	...
	*2014	422 452	269 377	...	116 856	...	36 219	...
Gabon [1,3]	2004[5]	188	80	25	68	...	40	...
Gabon [1,3]	2009	# 839	# 531	# 118	# 142	55	# 166	66
Gambia [3]	2005[1]	84	46	4	28	...	10	...
Gambie [3]	2008	# 855	# 155	31	# 200	...	# 500	...
	2009	926	179	...	198	...	549	...
	2011	# 1 055	# 60[1]	12	# 737	...	# 233	...
Georgia [3]	2005	13 415	8 112	4 275	1 810	...	3 493	...
Géorgie [3]	2014[6]	5 776	2 893	1 481	835	490	2 043	1 168
Germany	2005	475 278	272 148	47 666	94 578	29 657	108 553	44 729
Allemagne	2009	534 975	317 307	65 258	111 660	34 277	106 008	44 018
	2010	548 723	* 327 996	...	* 113 211	...	* 107 515	...
	2013	588 615	354 463	80 353	138 770	38 432	95 382	44 089
	*2014	601 406	353 276	...	...	...	...	...
Ghana Ghana	2010	# 3 005	# 941	163	# 731	186	# 1 333	288
Greece	2005	33 603	19 593	6 213	8 450	3 070	5 559	3 007
Grèce	*2007	35 531	21 014	...	...	...	...	...
	#2011	36 913	24 674	9 602	6 336	2 973	5 903	2 897
	2013	42 188	29 228	11 361	...	...	...	...
	2014	43 316	29 877	...	...	...	...	...
Greenland Groenland	2004	48	40	11	8[12]	...	...	...
Guam Guam	2005	51	48	...	...	...	...	...
Guatemala [1]	2005	851	388	...	139	...	324	...
Guatemala [1]	2010	876	363	145	273	...	240	...
	2012	920	411	172	276	...	233	...
Guinea [1,3]	2000	3 711	2 117	122	768	...	826	...
Guinée [1,3]	2013	# 752	# 214	# 21	# 33	3	# 75	22
Honduras [3] Honduras [3]	2003	2 280	539	143	...	...	1 741	731
Hungary	2005	23 239	15 878	...	4 591	...	2 770	...
Hongrie	2010	31 480	21 342	6 447	5 967	3 230	4 171	2 346
	2013	38 163	25 038	6 748	7 748	3 720	5 377	2 417
	2014	37 329	26 213	...	6 833	...	4 283	...
Iceland	2005	3 226	2 155	784	669	299	402	181
Islande	2009	3 397	2 505	1 000	626	279	266	96
	#2011	3 244	2 258	812	604	192	381	246
	#2013	2 766	1 950	...	481	...	332	...

27 Population employed in research and development (R&D) *(continued)*
Full-time equivalent (FTE)

Population employé dans la recherche et le développement (R-D) *(suite)*
Equivalent temps plein (ETP)

Country or area Pays ou zone	Year Année	Total R & D personnel Total du personnel de R - D	Researchers Chercheurs Total M & F Total H & F	 Females Femmes	Technicians and equivalent staff Techniciens et personnel assimilé Total M & F Total H & F	 Females Femmes	Other supporting staff Autre personnel de soutien Total M & F Total H & F	 Females Femmes
India	2000	318 443	115 936	11 304[7]	90 045[13]	10 363	112 462[13]	19 531
Inde	2005	391 149	154 827	19 707[7]	105 808[13]	...	130 514[13]	...
	2010	441 126	192 819	27 532	124 188[13]	...	124 119[13]	...
Indonesia [3]	2005	# 55 118[1]	# 35 564[1]	10 874	# 9 253[1]	...	# 10 301[1]	...
Indonésie [3]	*							
	#2009[1]	...	41 143	...	...	...	...	...
Iran (Islamic Republic of)	2010[11,14]	...	54 813	14 775	...	...	...	...
Iran (Rép. islamique d')	2012	80 886	52 656	15 484	14 189	3 978	14 041	4 705
Iraq [11]	2010[2]	16 857[4]	12 849[4]	4 380	1 927[4]	...	1 988[4]	...
Iraq [11]	#2014	3 861	2 394	878	875	325	592	215
Ireland	2005	16 690	11 587	3 241	3 043	797	2 060	881
Irlande	*2010	19 722	14 176	4 672	3 052	813	2 494	1 044
	2013	24 129	16 844	4 933	4 490	877	2 795	1 086
	*2014	25 029	17 448	...	4 676	...	2 905	...
Israel [15]	2011	70 401	55 184	11 700	9 818	2 320	5 399	2 006
Israël [15]	*2012	77 143	63 521	...	7 676	...	5 946	...
Italy	2005	175 248	82 489	26 797	...	...	...	...
Italie	2010	225 632	103 424	35 792	...	...	...	...
	2013	246 764	116 163	42 004	...	...	...	...
	*2014	246 423	119 977	...	...	...	...	...
Japan	2005	896 855	680 631	...	71 726	...	144 498	...
Japon	2010	877 928	656 032	...	74 857	...	147 039	...
	2014	895 285	682 935	...	68 822	...	143 528	...
Jordan [3]	2003	42 153	15 891	3 385	19 322	2 073	6 940	2 101
Jordanie [3]	#2007[1]	...	10 887	...	...	...	...	...
Kazakhstan	2010	8 325	6 022	...	454	...	1 179	...
Kazakhstan	#2013	17 586	12 552	...	3 012	...	2 022	...
Kenya Kenya	2010	# 42 566	# 9 305	1 861	# 26 384	12 024	# 6 877	2 735
Kuwait [1,5]	2005	800	384	...	96	...	320	...
Koweït [1,5]	2010	829	407	152	87	23	335	145
	2012	825	439	159	66	17	320	155
Kyrgyzstan [3]	2005	3 419[4]	2 187	977	226	...	498	...
Kirghizistan [3]	2010	3 129[4]	1 974	876	261	...	428	...
	2014	4 242[4]	3 013	1 446	388	160	409	247
Lao People's Dem. Rep. [1] Rép. dém. pop. lao [1]	2002	268	87	...	...	...	...	...
Latvia	2005	5 483	3 282	1 636	1 062	554	1 139	594
Lettonie	2010	5 563	3 896	1 823	915	401	752	439
	2011	5 432	3 947	2 045	819	387	666	440
	2013	5 396	3 625	1 829	...	...	...	...
	*2014	5 739	3 748	...	...	...	...	...
Lesotho	2004	51[1]	20[1]	10[7]	21[1]	...	10[1]	...
Lesotho	2009[1]	105	46	16[7]	47	...	11	...
	2011[1]	14[16]	12[6]	4	2[6]	1[6]	...	...
Libya [3]	2004[1]	772	215	...	164	...	...	...
Libye [3]	2009	1 131[1]	460[1]	101	229[1]	...	268[1]	...
Lithuania	2005	11 002	7 637	3 706	1 436	939	1 929	1 280
Lituanie	2010	12 315	8 599	4 367	1 691	887	2 025	1 281
	2011	11 173	8 390	4 099	1 426	812	1 357	888
	2013	11 080	8 557	4 140	...	...	...	...
	2014	11 283	8 638	...	...	...	...	...
Luxembourg	2005	4 392	2 227	392	1 558	258	607	250
Luxembourg	2009	4 711	2 396	534	1 423	384	891	437
	2010	4 972	2 613	...	1 708	...	651	...
	2013	4 975	2 504	683	1 596	284	875	267
	*2014	5 061	2 548	...	...	...	...	...
Madagascar [3]	2005	2 414[1]	1 607[1]	563	195[1]	...	612[1]	...
Madagascar [3]	2010	# 3 020[1]	# 2 334[1]	821	# 326[1]	...	# 360[1]	...
	2014[1]	# 5 782	# 1 828	# 587	# 575	246	# 2 369	929

Population employed in research and development (R&D) *(continued)*
Full-time equivalent (FTE)

Population employé dans la recherche et le développement (R-D) *(suite)*
Equivalent temps plein (ETP)

Country or area Pays ou zone	Year Année	Total R & D personnel Total du personnel de R - D	Researchers Chercheurs		Technicians and equivalent staff Techniciens et personnel assimilé		Other supporting staff Autre personnel de soutien	
			Total M & F Total H & F	Females Femmes	Total M & F Total H & F	Females Femmes	Total M & F Total H & F	Females Femmes
Malawi Malawi	2010	1 721[2]	732[2]	136	873[2]	155	116[2]	15
Malaysia Malaisie	2004	17 887	12 670	4 701	1 598	…	3 619	…
	2010	50 484	41 253	19 029	3 676	…	5 555	…
	2012	62 807	52 052	24 471	4 734	1 467	6 021	2 843
	2014	75 062	61 351	…	6 337	…	7 374	…
Mali Mali	2010	856	443	62	342	44	71	34
Malta Malte	2005	825	479	121	222	20	124	65
	2010	1 125	595	153	349	36	181	88
	2013	1 441	857	244	344	35	240	122
	*2014	1 586	891	…	411	…	284	…
Mauritius [2] Maurice [2]	2012	627	228	94	68	34	331	57
Mexico Mexique	2005	83 685	43 922	…	25 796	…	13 967	…
	2009	83 642	42 973	…	26 809	…	13 860	…
	2010	…	36 990	…	…	…	…	…
	2011	…	38 823	…	…	…	…	…
Monaco [1] Monaco [1]	2005	18	10	5	5	…	3	…
Mongolia [3] Mongolie [3]	2000	2 113[1]	1 631[1]	…	294[1]	150	188[1]	…
	2005	2 283[1]	1 731[1]	819	81[1]	…	471[1]	…
	2010	2 517[1]	1 739[1]	865[1]	129[1]	48	649[1]	399
	2014[1]	2 724	1 903	931	157	66	664	414
Montenegro Monténégro	2011	642	474	198	70	…	98	…
	2014	600	421	…	127	…	51	…
Morocco Maroc	2010	28 041[1]	23 280[1]	7 744	1 697[1,5]	…	1 747[1,5]	…
	2012	31 099[1]	# 28 265	9 018[2,11]	1 414[1,5]	217[5]	1 420[1,5]	341[5]
Mozambique [3] Mozambique [3]	2002	2 467[7]	468[7]	…	1 999[12]	…	…	…
	2010	# 3 313[2]	# 1 588[2]	512	# 1 390[2]	447	# 335[2]	151
Myanmar [1] Myanmar [1]	2002	7 418	837	…	6 499	…	82	…
Namibia [3] Namibie [3]	2010	949	748	327	118	…	83	41
Nauru [1,3] Nauru [1,3]	2003	77	19	3	18	…	36	…
Nepal [3] Népal [3]	*2002	13 500	3 000	450	6 000	…	4 500	…
	2010	# 41 911[1,17]	# 5 123[1]	399	# 12 053[1]	…	# 21 167[1]	…
Netherlands Pays-Bas	2005	93 599	47 854	…	23 265	…	22 480	…
	2010	100 544	53 703	…	22 128	…	24 714	…
	#2011	117 436	61 335	15 629	34 107	7 340	21 994	8 723
	2013	123 206	76 670	19 576	…	…	…	…
	*2014	123 096	75 536	…	…	…	…	…
New Zealand Nouvelle-Zélande	2005	18 929	12 986	…	3 200	…	2 800	…
	2009	23 200	16 100	…	4 100	…	2 900	…
	2013	24 900	17 900	…	4 520	…	2 580	…
Nicaragua [3] Nicaragua [3]	2002	456	256	96[7]	…	…	200	…
	2004	371	326	…	45	15	…	…
	#2011	…	755	…	…	…	…	…
Niger [1] Niger [1]	2005	595	101	…	137	…	357	…
Nigeria [1,3] Nigéria [1,3]	2005	66 574	28 533	4 839	10 854	…	27 187	…
	#2007	32 802[2]	17 624[2]	4 106	4 647[2]	1 026	10 531[2]	3 759
Norway Norvège	2005	29 966	21 200	…	…	…	…	…
	2010	36 121	26 451	…	…	…	…	…
	2014	40 297	29 237	…	…	…	…	…
Oman [2] Oman [2]	2013	1 071	497	117	198	57	376	67
Pakistan Pakistan	2005	53 159[2,11]	12 689[2,11]	2 053	6 471[2,11]	…	33 999[2,11]	…
	2009	74 695[2,11]	27 602[2,11]	6 534	10 993[2,11]	…	36 100[2,11]	…
	2013[2,11]	75 658	30 244	9 456	13 079	939	32 335	1 602

27 Population employed in research and development (R&D) *(continued)*

Full-time equivalent (FTE)

Population employé dans la recherche et le développement (R-D) *(suite)*

Equivalent temps plein (ETP)

Country or area Pays ou zone	Year Année	Total R & D personnel Total du personnel de R - D	Researchers Chercheurs		Technicians and equivalent staff Techniciens et personnel assimilé		Other supporting staff Autre personnel de soutien	
			Total M & F Total H & F	Females Femmes	Total M & F Total H & F	Females Femmes	Total M & F Total H & F	Females Femmes
Panama	2002	1 331[18]	297	...	...	...	1 034	...
Panama	2005	1 302[18]	344	...	...	...	...	...
	2008	1 449	463	...	377	...	609	...
	2009	531[18]	394	...	...	...	# 137	...
	2011	893	438	134	# 169	76	286	150
	2013	...	150	74	...	...	...	...
Paraguay	2005	# 614	419	...	...	...	# 195	...
Paraguay	2008	667	466	...	...	...	201	...
	2011	# 496	317	...	79	...	100	...
	#2012	...	1 081	...	...	...	...	...
Peru [3]	2004	8 434	4 965	...	1 757	...	1 712	...
Pérou [3]	#2010	...	434	...	...	...	...	...
	#2014	...	5 737	...	...	...	...	...
Philippines	2005	9 407[4]	6 896	3 500	897	...	1 440	...
Philippines	2009	10 366	7 505	3 882	1 116	381	1 743	708
	2013	26 577	18 481	8 872	2 765	1 041	5 140	2 086
Poland	2005	76 761	62 162	24 521	8 947	...	5 652	...
Pologne	2010	81 843	64 511	24 745	10 939	...	6 393	...
	2013	93 751	71 472	25 901	14 678	...	7 600	...
	2014	104 359	78 622	...	16 703	...	9 034	...
Portugal	2005	25 728	21 126	9 530	2 918	1 177	1 683	954
Portugal	2010	47 616	41 523	18 175	4 004	1 481	2 088	894
	2013	46 711	# 37 813	# 16 921	# 7 774	# 2 884	# 1 124	# 591
	*2014	47 236	38 487	...	...	...	...	...
Puerto Rico [3]	2009	5 776	2 986	...	2 790	...	...	...
Porto Rico [3]	2013	4 793	1 976	...	2 516	...	301[13]	...
Qatar Qatar	2012	1 952	1 203	243	394	135	354	147
Republic of Korea	2005[19]	215 345	179 812	...	26 272	...	9 261	...
République de Corée	2010	335 228	264 118	...	47 557	...	23 554	...
	2014	430 868	345 463	...	62 155	...	23 250	...
Republic of Moldova	2005	4 672[7]	2 583[7]	1 120	334[7]	...	1 755[7]	...
République de Moldova	2010	4 316	2 709	1 258	287	202	1 320	773
	2014	4 149	2 655	1 275	244	179	1 250	683
Romania	2005	33 222	22 958	10 617	4 998	2 859	5 266	2 414
Roumanie	2010	26 171	19 780	8 797	3 139	1 695	3 252	1 424
	2013	32 507	18 576	8 405	4 993	2 372	8 938	4 202
	2014	31 391	18 109	...	4 510	...	8 772	...
Russian Federation	2005	919 716	464 577	...	74 253	...	380 886	...
Fédération de Russie	2010	839 992	442 071	...	68 042	...	329 879	...
	2014	829 190	444 865	...	71 843	...	312 481	...
Rwanda [3,6] Rwanda [3,6]	2009	1 001[1]	564[1]	123	8[1]	...	429[1]	...
Saint Helena Sainte-Hélène	2000	33[1]	2[1]	...	8[1]	4	23[1]	...
Saint Vincent & Grenadines [3] Saint-Vincent-Grenadines [3]	2002	131	21	...	110	...	...	...
Saudi Arabia [3]	2002[1,6]	4 182	1 513	263	1 674	...	995	...
Arabie saoudite [3]	2009	2 655[1,5]	1 271[1,5]	18	658[1,5]	...	726[1,5]	...
Senegal Sénégal	2010	5 642	4 679	1 162	441	101	523	161
Serbia	2010[20]	17 274	10 985	5 370	2 428	1 475	3 861	1 954
Serbie	2014	19 446[20]	13 026[20]	6 360	2 495[20]	1 390	3 924[20]	1 880
Seychelles [1] Seychelles [1]	2005	180	13	4	53	...	114	...
Singapore	2005	28 586	23 789	...	2 375	...	2 422	...
Singapour	2010	37 013	32 031	...	2 342	...	2 641	...
	2013	41 582	36 025	...	2 478	...	3 079	...
	2014	...	36 666	...	...	...	...	...

27 Population employed in research and development (R&D) *(continued)*

Full-time equivalent (FTE)

Population employé dans la recherche et le développement (R-D) *(suite)*

Equivalent temps plein (ETP)

Country or area Pays ou zone	Year Année	Total R & D personnel Total du personnel de R - D	Researchers Chercheurs		Technicians and equivalent staff Techniciens et personnel assimilé		Other supporting staff Autre personnel de soutien	
			Total M & F Total H & F	Females Femmes	Total M & F Total H & F	Females Femmes	Total M & F Total H & F	Females Femmes
Slovakia Slovaquie	2005	14 404	10 921	4 484	2 245	1 218	1 238	670
	2010	18 188	15 183	6 376	2 087	1 046	918	589
	2014	17 594	14 742	6 090	1 990	833	862	508
Slovenia Slovénie	2005	8 994	5 253	1 777	2 820	1 067	921	501
	2010	12 940	7 703	2 668	3 928	1 386	1 309	642
	2013	15 229	8 707	3 017	5 205	1 727	1 316	569
	2014	14 866	8 574	…	4 946	…	1 345	…
South Africa Afrique du Sud	2005	28 798	17 303	6 272	5 248	1 749	6 247	2 928
	2010	29 486	18 720	7 649	5 410	2 016	5 357	2 546
	2012	35 050	21 383	9 285	6 582	2 401	7 086	3 397
Spain Espagne	2005	174 773	109 720	41 371	39 904	13 259	25 149	11 390
	2010	222 022	134 653	51 831	60 697	24 052	26 672	12 988
	2013	203 302	123 225	47 760	56 822	22 315	23 256	11 587
	2014	200 233	122 235	…	54 405	…	23 592	…
Sri Lanka Sri Lanka	#2004	5 475	2 679	861	1 474	…	1 322	…
	2010	5 714	2 140	842	1 851	…	1 723	…
	2013	* 4 601	2 276	851	* 1 258	303	1 067	347
State of Palestine État de Palestine	2007[1,14,20]	566	280	94	91	…	195	…
	2010[2]	2 074	1 312	…	291	…	471[21]	…
	2013[2]	5 161	2 492	…	772	…	# 1 483	…
Sudan [former] [3] Soudan [anc.] [3]	*2005	23 726	11 208	4 483	5 569	…	6 949	…
Sweden [7] Suède [7]	#2005	77 557	55 001	15 960[22]	…	…	…	…
	2009	77 363	47 308	14 080	19 686	4 849	10 369	3 817
	*2010	77 418	49 312	…	…	…	…	…
	2011	78 445	48 702	14 721	19 194	4 860	10 551	3 941
	2013	80 957	# 64 194	# 17 989	…	…	…	…
	*2014	83 473	66 643	…	…	…	…	…
Switzerland Suisse	2004	52 250	25 400	…	17 130	…	9 720	…
	2008	62 066	25 142	…	21 763	…	15 161	…
	2012	75 476	35 950	…	22 179	…	17 347	…
Tajikistan [3] Tadjikistan [3]	2004	2 487[4]	1 548	407	247	…	692[4]	…
	2005	3 220[4]	1 993	…	324	…	903[4]	…
	2006	3 110[4]	1 895	735	202	…	1 013[4]	…
	2010[2,11]	2 827[4]	1 802	…	329	…	427	…
	2013	3 389[2,4,11]	2 152[2,11]	728	301[2,11]	108	577[2,11]	275
Thailand Thaïlande	2005	36 967	20 506	10 241	10 520	…	5 941	…
	2009	# 60 344	22 000	11 064	# 15 036	…	# 23 308	…
	2011	# 53 123	36 360	19 306	# 11 313	5 966	# 5 450	3 652
	2014	84 216	65 965	…	13 090	…	4 023	…
TFYR of Macedonia ex-R.Y. de Macédoine	2005	1 434	1 113	576	168	94	153	81
	2010	1 434	1 102	620	170	104	162	106
	2014	1 965	1 740	880	141	85	83	50
Togo Togo	#2005[6]	312	186	…	126	…	…	…
	2010	# 444[2]	# 220[2]	21	# 54[2]	10	# 169[2]	14
	2014[2]	539	272	24	64	20	204	42
Trinidad and Tobago [3] Trinité-et-Tobago [3]	2005	954	548	183	406	180	…	…
	2010	1 351	951	462	400	152	…	…
	2013	1 619	1 244	618	375	137	…	…
	2014	…	1 228	671	…	…	…	…
Tunisia Tunisie	2010	15 589	14 727	7 654	499[5]	197[5]	363[5]	228[5]
	2014	21 177	20 070	11 675	650[5]	290[5]	457[5]	277[5]
Turkey Turquie	2005	49 251[7]	39 139	13 381	4 753[7]	988[7]	5 360[7]	978[7]
	2010	81 792[7]	64 341	21 056	10 352[7]	1 741[7]	7 099[7]	1 551[7]
	2014	115 444[7]	89 657	29 240	16 084[7]	2 977[7]	9 703[7]	2 609[7]
Uganda [3] Ouganda [3]	2005	1 686	776	291	472	…	438	…
	2010	4 270	# 2 823	687	# 922	254	# 525	155
Ukraine Ukraine	2007	132 926[7]	67 493[7]	29 620	15 045[7]	…	25 160[7]	…
	2010[7]	116 321	60 812	…	13 053	…	21 593	…
	2014[7,20]	87 390	46 191	…	8 609	…	16 151	…

27 Population employed in research and development (R&D) *(continued)*

Full-time equivalent (FTE)

Population employé dans la recherche et le développement (R-D) *(suite)*

Equivalent temps plein (ETP)

Country or area Pays ou zone	Year Année	Total R & D personnel Total du personnel de R - D	Researchers Chercheurs: Total M & F Total H & F	Researchers Chercheurs: Females Femmes	Technicians and equivalent staff Techniciens et personnel assimilé: Total M & F Total H & F	Technicians and equivalent staff Techniciens et personnel assimilé: Females Femmes	Other supporting staff Autre personnel de soutien: Total M & F Total H & F	Other supporting staff Autre personnel de soutien: Females Femmes
United Arab Emirates Émirats arabes unis	*2011	11 400	...	...	...	...	...	...
United Kingdom Royaume-Uni	*2005	# 324 917[7]	# 248 599	...	41 494	...	34 824[7]	...
	*2010	350 766[7]	256 585	...	59 290	...	34 891[7]	...
	*2014	387 934[7]	273 560	...	80 313	...	34 060	...
United Rep. of Tanzania Rép.-Unie de Tanzanie	2010	2 929[1,2]	1 600[1,2]	393	472[1,2]	112	857[1,2]	310
	2013[1,2]	1 967	929	228	301	62	737	277
United States of America États-Unis d'Amérique	*2005	...	1 101 062	...	...	...	...	...
	*2010	...	1 198 280	...	...	...	...	...
	*2012	...	1 265 064	...	...	...	...	...
United States Virgin Islands [1,3] Îles Vierges américaines [1,3]	2005	37	6	...	12	...	11	...
	2007	42	6	...	13	...	14	...
Uruguay [3] Uruguay [3]	2002	4 323	3 839	1 813	...	...	484	114
	2006	3 436	3 182	1 349	172	84	# 82	# 69
	2010	...	2 889	1 473	...	...	...	...
	2015	...	2 288	1 117	...	...	...	...
Uzbekistan [3] Ouzbékistan [3]	2010	36 358[4]	30 343	12 487	1 900	...	1 978	...
	2014	35 836[4]	30 785	12 514	1 780	935	1 899	857
Venezuela (Boliv. Rep. of) [1] Venezuela (Rép. boliv. du) [1]	2005	...	3 248	...	...	...	...	...
	2009	...	5 209	2 782	...	...	...	...
	2010	...	5 803	...	...	...	...	...
	2012	...	8 686	...	...	...	...	...
Viet Nam [3] Viet Nam [3]	2002	...	41 117	17 585	...	...	...	...
	#2011	134 781	105 230	43 845	9 781	4 236	14 245	6 943
Zambia [3] Zambie [3]	2005	3 285[1]	792[1]	116[7]	1 240[1]	...	1 253[1]	...
	#2008	2 219	612	188	835	270	772	360
Zimbabwe Zimbabwe	2012	1 741[2]	1 305[2]	332	141[2]	41	295[2]	100

Source:

United Nations Educational, Scientific and Cultural Organization (UNESCO) Institute for Statistics, Montreal, the UNESCO Institute for Statistics database, last accessed February 2017.

Source:

L'Institut de statistique de l'Organisation des Nations Unies pour l'éducation, la science et la culture (UNESCO), Montréal, la base de données de l'Institut de statistique de l'UNESCO, dernier accès février 2017.

1 Partial data.
2 Excluding business enterprise.
3 Head count instead of Full-time equivalent.
4 Overestimated or based on overestimated data.
5 Government only.
6 Higher Education only.
7 Underestimated or based on underestimated data.
8 For statistical purposes, the data for China do not include those for the Hong Kong Special Administrative Region (Hong Kong SAR), Macao Special Administrative Region (Macao SAR) and Taiwan Province of China.
9 Do not correspond exactly to Frascati Manual recommendations.
10 Including technicians and equivalent staff.
11 Excluding private non-profit.
12 Including other supporting staff.
13 Excluding Higher Education.
14 Excluding government.
15 Excluding Defence (all or mostly).
16 Higher Education only.
17 Including other classes.
18 Excluding technicians and equivalent staff.

1 Données partielles.
2 Ne comprend pas les entreprises commerciales.
3 Personnes physiques au lieu d'Equivalents temps plein.
4 Surestimé ou fondé sur des données surestimées.
5 Etat seulement.
6 Enseignement supérieur seulement.
7 Sous-estimé ou basé sur des données sous-estimées.
8 Pour la présentation des statistiques, les données pour la Chine ne comprennent pas la région administrative spéciale de Hong Kong (Hong Kong RAS), la région administrative spéciale de Macao (Macao RAS) et la province chinoise de Taïwan.
9 Ne corresponds pas exactement aux recommendations du Manuel de Frascati.
10 Y compris les techniciens y le personnel assimilé.
11 Non compris les organisations privées à but non lucratif.
12 Y compris autre personnel de soutien.
13 Non compris l'enseignement supérieur.
14 Non compris l'état.
15 A l'exclusion de la défense (en totalité ou en grande partie).
16 Enseignement supérieur seulement.
17 Comprend d'autres catégories.
18 Non compris les techniciens y le personnel assimilé.

27 Population employed in research and development (R&D) *(continued)*

Full-time equivalent (FTE)

Population employé dans la recherche et le développement (R-D) *(suite)*

Equivalent temps plein (ETP)

19 Excluding social sciences and humanities.
20 Excluding data from some regions, provinces or states.
21 Included in others/Not specified.
22 University graduates instead of researchers.

19 Non compris les sciences sociales et les sciences humaines.
20 Non compris les données de certaines régions, provinces ou états.
21 Inclus dans autres/Non spécifié.
22 Diplômes universitaires au lieu de chercheurs.

28 Gross domestic expenditure on research and development (R&D)

As a percentage of GDP and by source of funds

Dépenses intérieures brutes de recherche et développement (R-D)

En pourcentage du PIB et répartition par source de financement

Country or area Pays ou zone	Year Année	Expenditure on R&D as a % of GDP Dépenses en R&D en % du PIB	Source of funds (%) / Source de financement (%)					
			Business enterprises Entreprises	Govern-ment Etat	Higher education Enseigne-ment supérieur	Private non-profit Institut. Institut. privées sans but lucratif	Funds from abroad Fonds de l'étranger	Not specified/ Non précisé
Total, all countries or areas **Total, tous pays ou zones**	**2005**	**1.5**	**...**	**...**	**...**	**...**	**...**	**...**
	2010	**1.6**	**...**	**...**	**...**	**...**	**...**	**...**
	2014	**1.7**	**...**	**...**	**...**	**...**	**...**	**...**
Northern Africa Afrique septentrionale	2005	0.3	...	...	...	...	...	...
	2010	0.4	...	...	...	...	...	...
	2014	0.5	...	...	...	...	...	...
Sub-Saharan Africa Afrique subsaharienne	2005	0.4	...	...	...	...	...	...
	2010	0.4	...	...	...	...	...	...
	2014	0.4	...	...	...	...	...	...
Northern America Amérique septentrionale	2005	2.5	...	...	...	...	...	...
	2010	2.7	...	...	...	...	...	...
	2014	2.6	...	...	...	...	...	...
Latin America & the Caribbean Amérique latine et Caraïbes	2005	0.6	...	...	...	...	...	...
	2010	0.6	...	...	...	...	...	...
	2014	0.7	...	...	...	...	...	...
Central Asia Asie centrale	2005	0.2	...	...	...	...	...	...
	2010	0.2	...	...	...	...	...	...
	2014	0.2	...	...	...	...	...	...
Eastern Asia Asie orientale	2005	2.1	...	...	...	...	...	...
	2010	2.2	...	...	...	...	...	...
	2014	2.5	...	...	...	...	...	...
South-eastern Asia Asie du Sud-Est	2005	0.6	...	...	...	...	...	...
	2010	0.8	...	...	...	...	...	...
	2014	0.8	...	...	...	...	...	...
Southern Asia Asie méridionale	2005	0.7	...	...	...	...	...	...
	2010	0.7	...	...	...	...	...	...
	2014	0.7	...	...	...	...	...	...
Western Asia Asie occidentale	2005	0.5	...	...	...	...	...	...
	2010	0.5	...	...	...	...	...	...
	2014	0.6	...	...	...	...	...	...
Europe Europe	2005	1.6	...	...	...	...	...	...
	2010	1.7	...	...	...	...	...	...
	2014	1.8	...	...	...	...	...	...
Oceania Océanie	2005	1.9	...	...	...	...	...	...
	2010	2.2	...	...	...	...	...	...
	2014	2.0	...	...	...	...	...	...
Australia and New Zealand Australie et Nouvelle-Zélande	2005	1.9	...	...	...	...	...	...
	2010	2.2	...	...	...	...	...	...
	2014	2.1	...	...	...	...	...	...
Albania [1] Albanie [1]	2008	0.2	3.3	80.8	8.6	...	7.4	...
Algeria [1] Algérie [1]	2005	0.1	...	...	...	...	...	...
Argentina Argentine	2005	0.4	31.0	59.6	5.7	3.0	0.7	~0.0
	2008	0.4	26.5	67.6	4.4	1.0	0.6	~0.0
	2010	0.5	...	...	...	...	...	...
	2014	0.6	...	...	...	...	...	...
Armenia Arménie	2005[1]	0.3	...	77.5	...	...	4.7	17.8
	2010[1]	0.2	...	84.5	...	...	11.7	3.8
	2014[2]	0.2	...	71.0	...	...	5.1	23.8
Australia Australie	2004	1.9	54.6	40.3	0.4	1.9	2.9	...
	2008	2.4	61.9	34.6	0.1	1.8	1.6	...
	*2010	2.4	...	...	...	...	...	...
	*2013	2.2	...	...	...	...	...	...

28 Gross domestic expenditure on research and development (R&D) *(continued)*

As a percentage of GDP and by source of funds

Dépenses intérieures brutes de recherche et développement (R-D) *(suite)*

En pourcentage du PIB et répartition par source de financement

Country or area Pays ou zone	Year Année	Expenditure on R&D as a % of GDP Dépenses en R&D en % du PIB	Source of funds (%) / Source de financement (%) Business enterprises Entreprises	Govern-ment Etat	Higher education Enseigne-ment supérieur	Private non-profit Institut. privées sans but lucratif	Funds from abroad Fonds de l'étranger	Not specified/ Non précisé
Austria Autriche	2004	2.2	47.2	32.6	0.4	0.5	19.4	...
	*2005	2.4	45.6	35.9	...	0.4	18.0	...
	2009	2.6	47.1	34.9	0.7	0.6	16.8	...
	*2010	2.7	45.1	38.3[3]	...	0.5	16.1	...
	2013	3.0	48.7	33.6	0.6	0.5	16.6	...
	*2014	3.0	46.6	37.7[3]	...	0.4	15.2	...
	*2015	...	47.2	37.3[3]	...	0.4	15.1	...
Azerbaijan Azerbaïdjan	2005	0.2[4]	18.7	77.5	~0.0	1.3	2.4	...
	2010	0.2	# 9.6	# 88.2	0.3	1.9	~0.0	...
	2014	0.2	30.5	67.6	0.8	0.9	0.2	...
Bahrain Bahreïn	2014	0.1	21.8	41.5	21.2	2.0	12.4	1.1
Belarus Bélarus	2005	0.7	21.2	71.9	0.7	...	6.3	...
	2008	0.7	36.5	57.6	0.3	0.1	5.5	...
	2010	0.7	27.1	58.7	...	0.6	13.6	...
	2011	0.7	45.8	45.5	...	~0.0	8.7	...
	2013	0.7	43.8	48.3	...	...	7.9	...
Belgium Belgique	2005	1.8	59.7	24.7	2.6	0.6	12.4	...
	2010	2.1	57.6	25.4	3.1	0.6	13.3	...
	2013	2.4	57.0	28.5	1.0	0.4	13.1	...
	*2014	2.5	...	...	...	...	...	...
Bermuda [5] Bermudes [5]	2010[6]	0.2	...	...	...	...	...	...
	2014	0.2	...	...	...	...	...	...
Bolivia (Plurin. State of) Bolivie (État plurin. de)	2002	0.3	16.0	20.0	31.0	19.0	14.0	...
	#2009	0.2	5.2	51.2	26.5	2.1	1.9	13.2
Bosnia and Herzegovina Bosnie-Herzégovine	2005[1]	~0.0	...	...	...	...	...	...
	2009[1]	~0.0	...	...	...	...	...	...
	2013	0.3[1]	1.8	25.3	...	~0.0	53.9	18.9
	2014	0.3	24.2	51.4	12.2	0.1	12.1	...
Botswana Botswana	2005	0.5	...	...	...	...	...	...
	#2012	0.3	5.8	73.9	12.6	0.7	6.8	0.2
Brazil Brésil	2005	1.0	50.4	47.7	1.9	...	...	...
	2010	1.2	47.0	51.1	1.8	...	...	~0.0
	2013	1.2	40.3	57.7	1.9	...	...	...
Brunei Darussalam Brunéi Darussalam	2003	~0.0[1]	6.7[1]	86.8	...	...	6.6	...
	#2004	~0.0[1]	1.6	91.0	7.4	...	...	...
Bulgaria Bulgarie	2005	0.4	27.8	63.9	0.4	0.3	7.6	...
	2010	0.6	16.7	43.2	0.5	0.1	39.6	...
	2013	0.6	19.5	31.6	0.1	0.5	48.3	...
	2014	0.8	...	...	...	...	...	...
Burkina Faso Burkina Faso	2005	0.2[1]	...	100.0	...	...	...	...
	2009	0.2	11.9	9.1	12.2	1.3	59.6	5.9
Burundi [1] Burundi [1]	2008	0.2	...	59.9	0.2	...	39.9	...
	2010	0.1	...	...	...	...	...	...
	2011	0.1	...	...	...	...	...	...
Cabo Verde [1,7] Cabo Verde [1,7]	2011	0.1	...	100.0	...	...	...	...
Cambodia [1] Cambodge [1]	2002	~0.0	...	17.9	...	43.0	28.4	10.6
Canada Canada	2005	2.0	49.3	* 31.8	* 7.3	2.8	8.8	...
	2010	1.8	47.0	* 35.2	* 7.8	3.5	6.5	...
	2014	* 1.6	* 45.4	* 34.6	* 10.3	* 3.7	* 6.0	...
Chile Chili	2010	0.3	25.4	40.4	12.7	1.7	19.8	...
	*2014	0.4	32.0	44.1	9.5	0.7	13.8	...
China Chine	2005	1.3	67.0	26.3	...	...	0.9	...
	2010	1.7	71.7	24.0	...	...	1.3	...
	2014	2.0	75.4	20.3	...	...	0.8	...

28 Gross domestic expenditure on research and development (R&D) *(continued)*

As a percentage of GDP and by source of funds

Dépenses intérieures brutes de recherche et développement (R-D) *(suite)*

En pourcentage du PIB et répartition par source de financement

Country or area Pays ou zone	Year Année	Expenditure on R&D as a % of GDP Dépenses en R&D en % du PIB	Source of funds (%) / Source de financement (%) Business enterprises Entreprises	Govern-ment Etat	Higher education Enseigne-ment supérieur	Private non-profit Institut. Institut. privées sans but lucratif	Funds from abroad Fonds de l'étranger	Not specified/ Non précisé
China, Hong Kong SAR Chine, Hong Kong RAS	2005	0.8	53.0[8]	44.1	0.4	...	2.5	...
	2010	0.7	47.6[8]	47.3	0.1	...	4.9	...
	2013	0.7	47.6[8]	45.6	~0.0	...	6.8	...
China, Macao SAR Chine, Macao RAS	2005	0.1[1]	0.2	88.0	10.0	0.4	...	1.4
	2007	# 0.1[1]	0.1	89.3	5.8	2.8	0.6	1.6
	2008	0.1[1]	0.2	91.7	6.4	1.4	...	0.3
	2010[1]	~0.0	...	...	...	...	...	...
	2014	0.1[1]	...	92.5[1]	3.9[1]	3.2[1]	...	0.5
Colombia Colombie	2005	0.2	25.4	36.9	29.4	3.8	4.5	...
	2010	0.2	28.5	37.4	25.1	5.8	3.2	...
	2014	0.2	30.5	39.2	22.5	4.7	3.2	...
Costa Rica Costa Rica	2004	0.4	...	...	...	...	...	...
	2010	0.5	20.7	62.6	...	0.4	11.8	4.6
	2013	0.6	5.0	52.1	...	0.4	7.3	35.2
Croatia Croatie	2005	0.9	34.3	58.1	4.9	~0.0	2.6	...
	2010	0.7	38.8	49.2	2.0	0.2	9.9	...
	2014	0.8	42.9	41.7	2.1	0.5	12.8	...
Cuba Cuba	2005	0.5	35.0	60.0	...	...	5.0	...
	2010	0.6	15.0	75.0	...	...	10.0	...
	2014	0.4	15.0	80.0	...	...	5.0	...
Cyprus Chypre	2005	0.4	16.8	67.0	4.2	1.2	10.9	...
	2010	0.5	12.7	68.3	3.5	0.5	15.0	...
	2013	0.5	12.1	62.1	5.6	0.6	19.6	...
	*2014	0.5	...	...	...	...	...	...
Czechia Tchéquie	2005	1.2	48.2	45.2	1.2	~0.0	5.4	...
	2010	1.3	40.8	44.4	0.9	~0.0	13.9	...
	2013	1.9	37.6	34.7	0.5	0.1	27.2	...
	*2014	2.0	...	32.9	0.6	0.1	...	...
Dem. Rep. of the Congo Rép. dém. du Congo	2005	# 0.1[9,10]	...	100.0	...	...	...	...
	2009	0.1[9,10]	...	100.0	...	...	...	...
Denmark Danemark	2005	2.4	59.5	27.6	...	2.8	10.1	...
	2010	2.9	* 61.1	* 28.2[3]	...	* 3.5	* 7.2	...
	*2014	3.1	57.9	30.4[3]	...	4.3	7.4	...
Ecuador Équateur	2003	0.1	...	...	...	...	...	...
	2010	0.4	1.0[2]	40.2[2]	9.6[2]	0.5[2]	5.3[2]	43.4[11]
	2011	0.3	0.4[2]	28.4[2]	8.1[2]	0.5[2]	4.5[2]	58.1[11]
Egypt Égypte	2005[1,9]	0.2	...	...	...	...	...	...
	2010[2,12]	0.4	...	...	...	...	...	...
	2014	0.7	8.1	91.7[13]	...	0.1	0.1	...
El Salvador El Salvador	2010	0.1	0.6	70.1	20.8	~0.0	8.3	0.1
	2013	0.1	0.7	42.7	37.0	2.8	16.4	0.3
	2014	0.1	0.7	33.0	48.6	0.9	16.9	...
Estonia Estonie	2005	0.9	38.5	43.5	0.8	0.2	17.1	...
	2010	1.6	43.6	44.1	0.6	0.2	11.4	...
	2014	1.4	37.1	49.5	0.9	0.1	12.5	...
Ethiopia Éthiopie	2005	0.2[1]	...	69.2	...	0.1	30.8	...
	2010	# 0.2	10.8	56.0	1.1	~0.0	30.0	2.2
	2013	0.6	0.7	79.1	1.8	0.2	2.1	16.0
Faroe Islands Îles Féroé	2003	...	20.4	...	...	0.3	18.7	60.6[5,13,14]
Finland Finlande	2005	3.3	66.9	25.7	0.2	1.0	# 6.3	...
	2010	3.7	66.1	25.7	0.2	1.1	6.9	...
	2014	3.2	53.5	27.5	0.2	1.4	17.3	...
France France	2005	2.0	51.9	38.6	1.0	0.9	7.5	...
	#2010	2.2	53.5	37.1	1.0	0.8	7.5	...
	2013	2.2	55.0	35.2	1.0	0.8	8.0	...
	*2014	2.3	...	...	...	...	...	...

28 Gross domestic expenditure on research and development (R&D) *(continued)*

As a percentage of GDP and by source of funds

Dépenses intérieures brutes de recherche et développement (R-D) *(suite)*

En pourcentage du PIB et répartition par source de financement

Country or area Pays ou zone	Year Année	Expenditure on R&D as a % of GDP Dépenses en R&D en % du PIB	Source of funds (%) / Source de financement (%) Business enterprises Entreprises	Govern-ment Etat	Higher education Enseigne-ment supérieur	Private non-profit Institut. Institut. privées sans but lucratif	Funds from abroad Fonds de l'étranger	Not specified/ Non précisé
Gabon Gabon	2009	0.6	29.3	58.1	9.5	...	3.1	~0.0
Gambia	2009[1]	~0.0	...	...	...	...	...	...
Gambie	2011[5]	0.1	...	38.5	...	45.6	15.9	...
Georgia	2005	0.2	...	...	...	...	...	...
Géorgie	2014[7]	0.1[15]	...	42.1[16]	41.8[16]	2.1[16]	14.3[16]	0.3[16]
Germany	2005	2.4	67.6	28.4	...	0.3	3.7	...
Allemagne	2010	* 2.7	* 65.5	* 30.4	...	0.2	3.9	...
	2013	2.8	65.4	29.1	...	0.3	5.2	...
	*2014	2.9	...	...	...	...	...	...
Ghana Ghana	#2010	0.4	0.1	68.3	0.3	0.1	31.2	...
Greece	2005	0.6	31.1	46.8	1.7	1.5	19.0	...
Grèce	*2010	0.6	36.5	48.3	2.3	1.0	11.9	...
	2014	0.8	29.8	53.3	2.8	0.9	13.2	...
Guam Guam	2001	...	...	100.0	...	...	...	...
Guatemala [1]	2005	~0.0	...	42.1	57.9	...	...	...
Guatemala [1]	2010	~0.0	...	18.3	30.9	...	50.8	...
	2012	~0.0	...	23.5	27.5	...	49.0	...
Honduras Honduras	2004	~0.0	...	...	...	...	...	...
Hungary	2005	0.9	39.4[16]	49.4[16]	...	0.3[16]	10.7[16]	...
Hongrie	2010	1.1	47.4	39.3	...	0.9	12.4	...
	2014	1.4	48.3	33.5	...	0.7	17.5	...
Iceland	2005	2.7	48.0	40.5	...	0.3	11.2	...
Islande	2009	2.7	47.8	40.2	...	0.6	11.4	...
	#2013	1.9	39.2	35.0	5.7	0.1	20.1	...
	2014	1.9	...	...	...	...	...	...
India	2005	0.8	...	...	...	...	...	...
Inde	2010	0.8	...	...	...	...	...	...
	2011	0.8	...	...	...	...	...	...
Indonesia	2001	~0.0[1]	14.7[1,8]	84.5	0.2	...	...	0.7
Indonésie	#2009[1]	0.1	...	...	...	...	...	...
	2013	0.1	...	...	...	...	...	...
Iran (Islamic Republic of)	2005	0.6	12.2	76.2	11.6	...	...	...
Iran (Rép. islamique d')	2008	0.7	30.9	61.6	7.4	...	...	...
	2010[12,17]	0.3	...	...	...	...	...	...
	2012	0.3	...	...	...	...	...	...
Iraq	2010	~0.0[2,12,15]	...	100.0[13]	...	...	...	...
Iraq	2014[12]	# ~0.0	1.8	# 98.0	...	0.2	~0.0	...
Ireland	2005	1.2	57.4	32.0	1.7	0.2	8.6	...
Irlande	*2010	1.6	52.2	29.4	0.9	0.5	17.0	...
	*2014	1.5	53.6	25.9	0.6	0.6	19.3	...
Israel [18]	2005	4.0	56.2	14.5	2.8	1.8	24.7	...
Israël [18]	2010	3.9	36.2	14.2	1.2	1.1	47.3	...
	2013	4.1	36.5	12.7	0.8	1.1	48.8	...
	2014	4.1	...	...	...	...	...	...
Italy	2005	1.0	39.7	50.7	0.1	1.6	8.0	...
Italie	2010	1.2	44.7	41.6	0.9	3.1	9.8	...
	2013	1.3	45.2	41.4	1.0	2.7	9.7	...
	*2014	1.3	...	...	...	...	...	...
Jamaica Jamaïque	2002	0.1	...	...	...	...	...	...
Japan	2005	3.3	76.1	* 16.8	* 6.1	0.7	0.3	...
Japon	2010	3.3	75.9	* 17.2	* 5.7	0.8	0.4	...
	2014	3.6	77.3	* 16.0	* 5.5	0.7	0.4	...

28 Gross domestic expenditure on research and development (R&D) *(continued)*

As a percentage of GDP and by source of funds

Dépenses intérieures brutes de recherche et développement (R-D) *(suite)*

En pourcentage du PIB et répartition par source de financement

Country or area Pays ou zone	Year Année	Expenditure on R&D as a % of GDP Dépenses en R&D en % du PIB	Source of funds (%) / Source de financement (%) Business enterprises Entreprises	Govern-ment Etat	Higher education Enseigne-ment supérieur	Private non-profit Institut. privées sans but lucratif	Funds from abroad Fonds de l'étranger	Not specified/ Non précisé
Jordan	2002	0.3	...	...	...	...	...	...
Jordanie	2008	0.4	...	...	...	...	...	...
Kazakhstan	2005	0.3	39.1	44.5	13.4	1.3	1.5	...
Kazakhstan	2010	0.2	36.6	36.7	17.2	8.9	0.6	...
	2011	0.2	51.6	24.9	16.3	6.9	0.3	...
	2013	0.2	28.9	63.7	...	...	0.8	6.6
Kenya Kenya	#2010	0.8	4.3	26.0	19.0	3.5	47.1	...
Kuwait	2003[9]	0.1[1]	# 4.4	# 94.7	~0.0	...	0.9	...
Koweït	2004[9]	0.1[1]	6.0	93.2	...	...	0.8	...
	2005[9]	0.1[1]	7.3	92.3	...	0.4	...	...
	2009[9]	0.1[1]	2.3	96.5	...	...	1.2	...
	2010[9]	0.1[1]	5.2	94.8	...	~0.0	...	...
	2013[2,12]	# 0.3	1.4	92.9	0.2	5.5	...	...
Kyrgyzstan	2003	0.2	53.7	45.1	0.1	...	1.1	...
Kirghizistan	2005	0.2	36.4	63.6	...	...	~0.0	...
	2010	0.2	...	...	...	...	...	...
	2014	0.1	7.4	90.4	0.2	...	1.0	1.0
Lao People's Dem. Rep. [1] Rép. dém. populaire lao [1]	2002	~0.0	36.0	8.0	2.0	...	54.0	...
Latvia	2005	0.5	34.3	46.0	1.2	...	18.5	...
Lettonie	2010	0.6	38.8	26.4	1.4	...	33.4	...
	*2014	0.7	27.8	25.6	2.3	...	44.2	...
Lesotho [1]	2004	0.1	...	...	...	...	...	...
Lesotho [1]	2009	~0.0	3.4	15.0	2.8	...	...	78.9
	2011	~0.0[7]	...	...	44.7[14]	...	3.4	51.9
Lithuania	2005	0.7	20.8	62.7	5.7	0.2	10.5	...
Lituanie	2010	0.8	32.4	46.0	1.5	0.2	19.9	...
	*2014	1.0	31.7	33.7	0.2	0.2	34.3	...
Luxembourg	2005	1.6	79.7	16.6	~0.0	0.1	3.6	...
Luxembourg	2010	1.5	43.5	35.1	0.6	0.1	20.6	...
	2013	1.3	16.5	48.4	1.7	1.0	32.3	...
	*2014	1.3	...	...	...	...	...	...
Madagascar	2005	0.2[1]	...	89.8[13]	...	...	10.2	...
Madagascar	2009	0.1[1]	...	89.4[13]	...	...	10.6	...
	2010	0.1[1]	...	# 100.0[13]	...	...	...	...
	2011	0.1[1]	...	100.0[14]	...	...	...	...
	#2014[1,9]	~0.0	...	...	...	...	...	...
Malaysia	2004	0.6	71.2	21.5	6.9	...	0.4	...
Malaisie	2010	1.0	59.6	36.4	3.5	...	0.4	0.1
	2014	1.3	# 6.9[19]	# 12.3[19]	3.8	...	0.2	# 76.8[3]
Mali	2007[1]	0.2[17]	10.1	40.9	...	...	49.0	...
Mali	2010	0.7[2]	...	# 91.2	...	...	8.8	...
Malta	2005	0.6	# 46.8	# 25.9	0.4	0.1	26.9	...
Malte	2010	0.7	53.6	33.3	1.2	0.1	11.7	...
	*2014	0.8	50.0	27.2	1.1	0.2	21.5	...
Mauritius	2005[5,15]	0.4	...	100.0	...	...	...	...
Maurice	2012[2]	# 0.2	0.3	72.4	20.7	0.1	6.4	...
Mexico	2005	0.4	41.5	49.2	7.3	0.9	1.1	...
Mexique	2010	0.5	36.2	60.5	2.3	0.5	0.5	...
	*2014	0.5	23.8	73.6	1.6	0.6	0.5	...
Monaco [1] Monaco [1]	2005	~0.0	...	98.8	...	...	...	1.2
Mongolia	2005	0.2[1]	10.4	77.8	0.8	...	4.4	6.5
Mongolie	2010[1]	0.2	7.2	61.1	1.5	...	4.2	25.9
	2014[1]	0.2	7.5	75.8	3.2	...	2.8	10.7

28 Gross domestic expenditure on research and development (R&D) *(continued)*

As a percentage of GDP and by source of funds

Dépenses intérieures brutes de recherche et développement (R-D) *(suite)*

En pourcentage du PIB et répartition par source de financement

Country or area Pays ou zone	Year Année	Expenditure on R&D as a % of GDP Dépenses en R&D en % du PIB	Source of funds (%) / Source de financement (%) Business enterprises Entreprises	Govern-ment Etat	Higher education Enseigne-ment supérieur	Private non-profit Institut. privées sans but lucratif	Funds from abroad Fonds de l'étranger	Not specified/ Non précisé
Montenegro Monténégro	2005	0.9	...	...	...	...	...	...
	2007	1.1	...	...	...	...	...	...
	2014[20]	0.4	28.5	46.6	4.2	~0.0	20.7	...
Morocco Maroc	2003	0.7	12.3	40.3	47.4	...	...	...
	2010	0.7	29.9	23.1	45.3	...	1.7	...
Mozambique Mozambique	2002[5,10]	0.4	...	34.7	...	...	65.3	...
	2010	# 0.4[2]	...	18.8[13]	...	3.0	78.1	...
Myanmar [1] Myanmar [1]	2002	0.2	...	...	...	...	...	...
Namibia Namibie	2010	0.1[1,17]	19.8	78.6	...	...	1.5	...
Nepal [1,15] Népal [1,15]	2010	0.3	...	...	...	...	...	...
Netherlands Pays-Bas	2005	1.8	46.3	38.8	0.3	2.6	12.0	...
	2009	1.7	45.1	40.9	0.3	2.8	10.8	...
	2010	1.7	...	...	...	...	...	...
	*2014	2.0	51.5	32.7	0.2	3.1	12.5	...
New Zealand Nouvelle-Zélande	2005	1.1	41.1	43.2	8.9	1.7	5.2	...
	2009	1.3	39.0	44.7	8.3	2.8	5.2	...
	2013	1.2	39.8	39.8	10.1	3.1	7.2	...
Nicaragua Nicaragua	2002	~0.0	...	...	...	...	...	...
Nigeria Nigéria	2007	0.2[2]	0.2	96.4	0.1	1.7	1.0	0.6
Norway Norvège	2005	1.5	46.8	43.6	0.7	0.9	8.1	...
	2009	1.7	43.6	46.8	0.4	1.0	8.2	...
	2010	1.7	...	...	...	...	...	...
	2013	1.7	43.1	45.8	0.5	1.0	9.5	...
	2014	1.7	...	...	...	...	...	...
Oman Oman	2013	0.2	24.5	48.6	24.4	0.1	~0.0	2.3
Pakistan Pakistan	2005	0.4[2,12]	...	87.0	11.9	...	0.3	0.8
	2009	0.4[2,12]	...	84.0	12.1	1.7	0.9	1.3
	2013[2,12]	0.3	...	75.3	20.0	1.7	1.3	1.7
Panama Panama	2003	0.3	0.6	25.5	1.8	1.0	71.0	0.1
	2005	0.2	0.4	38.5	1.4	0.7	58.9	...
	2010	0.1	3.4	53.9	6.0	14.0	22.7	~0.0
	2011	0.2	18.9	46.7	5.0	8.7	20.7	~0.0
	2013	0.1	10.8	80.9	8.0	...	0.3	...
Paraguay Paraguay	2005	0.1	# 0.3	# 74.9	# 8.6	# 2.0	# 14.2	...
	2008	0.1	0.3	76.2	9.2	2.1	12.3	...
	2012	0.1	0.8	82.5	3.7	2.9	7.7	2.3
Peru Pérou	2004	0.2	...	...	...	...	...	...
Philippines Philippines	2005	0.1	62.6	25.6	6.0	0.7	4.8	0.3
	2009	0.1	57.5	26.7	7.8	0.4	4.2	3.4
	2013	0.1	36.9	51.6	9.0	0.2	1.8	0.5
Poland Pologne	2005	0.6	33.4	57.7	2.9	0.3	5.7	...
	2010	0.7	24.4	60.9	2.5	0.3	11.8	...
	2014	0.9	39.0	45.2	2.2	0.2	13.4	...
Portugal Portugal	2005	0.8	36.3	55.2	1.0	2.8	4.7	...
	2010	1.5	43.9	45.1	3.2	4.6	3.2	...
	2013	1.3	42.3	46.4	3.9	1.3	6.1	...
	*2014	1.3	...	...	...	...	...	...
Puerto Rico Porto Rico	2009	0.5	...	...	...	...	...	...
	2013	0.4	65.4	24.9	8.9	0.5	...	0.3
Qatar Qatar	2012	0.5	24.2	31.2	36.6	5.6	2.4	0.1

Gross domestic expenditure on research and development (R&D) *(continued)*

As a percentage of GDP and by source of funds

Dépenses intérieures brutes de recherche et développement (R-D) *(suite)*

En pourcentage du PIB et répartition par source de financement

			Source of funds (%) / Source de financement (%)					
Country or area Pays ou zone	Year Année	Expenditure on R&D as a % of GDP Dépenses en R&D en % du PIB	Business enterprises Entreprises	Govern-ment Etat	Higher education Enseigne-ment supérieur	Private non-profit Institut. privées sans but lucratif	Funds from abroad Fonds de l'étranger	Not specified/ Non précisé
Republic of Korea	2005[21]	2.6	75.0	23.0	0.9	0.4	0.7	...
République de Corée	2010	3.5	71.8	26.7	0.9	0.4	0.2	...
	2014	4.3	75.3	23.0	0.7	0.3	0.7	...
Republic of Moldova	2005	0.4	...	...	...	...	3.8	96.2[3]
République de Moldova	2010	0.4	...	...	...	...	7.4	92.6[3]
	2014	0.4	...	...	...	...	12.8	87.2[3]
Romania	2005	0.4	37.2	53.5	4.0	~0.0	5.3	...
Roumanie	2010	0.5	32.3	54.4	2.2	~0.0	11.1	...
	2014	0.4	32.9	48.5	1.4	0.1	17.0	...
Russian Federation	2005	1.1	30.0	61.9	0.4	~0.0	7.6	...
Fédération de Russie	2010	1.1	25.5	70.3	0.5	0.1	3.5	...
	2014	1.2	27.1	69.2	1.1	0.2	2.5	...
Saint Vincent & Grenadines Saint-Vincent-Grenadines	2002	0.1	...	...	...	...	...	...
Saudi Arabia [1]	2005[15]	~0.0	...	...	...	...	...	...
Arabie saoudite [1]	2009	0.1	...	...	...	...	...	...
Senegal Sénégal	2010	0.5	4.1	47.6	~0.0	3.2	40.5	4.5
Serbia	2005[22,23]	0.4	...	...	...	...	...	...
Serbie	2010	0.7[22]	8.6	59.4	28.4	~0.0	3.6	...
	2014	0.8[22]	8.2	53.5	25.9	~0.0	12.5	...
Seychelles Seychelles	2005	0.3	...	...	...	...	...	...
Singapore	2005	2.2	58.8	36.4	0.5	...	4.4	...
Singapour	2010	2.0	53.1	40.2	1.8	...	4.9	...
	2013	2.0	52.7	39.3	2.2	...	5.8	...
	2014	2.2	...	...	...	...	...	...
Slovakia	2005	0.5	36.6	57.0[19]	0.3	~0.0	6.0	...
Slovaquie	2010	0.6	35.1	49.6[19]	0.4	0.3	14.7	...
	2014	0.9	32.2	41.4[19]	2.2	0.5	23.7	...
Slovenia	2005	1.4	54.8	37.2	0.7	~0.0	7.3	...
Slovénie	2010	2.1	58.4	35.3	0.3	0.1	6.0	...
	2014	2.4	68.4	21.8	0.5	~0.0	9.3	...
South Africa	2005	0.9	43.9	38.2	3.0	1.4	13.6	...
Afrique du Sud	2010	0.7	40.1	44.5	0.1	3.2	12.1	...
	2012	0.7	38.3	45.4	0.8	2.5	13.1	...
Spain	2005	1.1	46.3	43.0	4.1	0.9	5.7	...
Espagne	2010	1.3	43.0	46.6	3.9	0.7	5.7	...
	2014	1.2	46.4	41.4	4.1	0.7	7.4	...
Sri Lanka	#2000[1]	0.1	7.7	51.7	18.5	~0.0	4.5	17.5
Sri Lanka	#2004	0.2	0.6[8]	67.5[13]	...	...	22.6	9.3
	2010	0.1	# 40.9	55.9	0.2	~0.0	2.7	0.3
	2013	0.1	40.7	53.9	...	...	5.0	0.4
Sudan [5] Soudan [5]	2005	0.3	...	...	...	...	...	...
Sweden	#2005	3.4	63.9	24.4	0.7	2.9	8.1	...
Suède	2009	3.4	59.5	27.0	0.6	2.6	10.3	...
	*2010	3.2	...	...	...	...	...	...
	2013[19]	3.3	61.0	28.3	1.0	3.1	6.7	...
	*2014	3.2	...	...	...	...	...	...
Switzerland	2004	2.7	69.7	22.7	1.5	0.8	5.2	...
Suisse	2008	2.7	68.2	22.8	2.3	0.7	6.0	...
	2012	3.0	60.8	25.4	1.2	0.6	12.1	...

28 Gross domestic expenditure on research and development (R&D) *(continued)*

As a percentage of GDP and by source of funds

Dépenses intérieures brutes de recherche et développement (R-D) *(suite)*

En pourcentage du PIB et répartition par source de financement

Country or area Pays ou zone	Year Année	Expenditure on R&D as a % of GDP Dépenses en R&D en % du PIB	Source of funds (%) / Source de financement (%) Business enterprises Entreprises	Govern-ment Etat	Higher education Enseigne-ment supérieur	Private non-profit Institut. privées sans but lucratif	Funds from abroad Fonds de l'étranger	Not specified/ Non précisé
Tajikistan Tadjikistan	2001	0.1	0.6	97.3	...	...	0.2	1.9
	2005	0.1	2.2[16]	91.5[16]	0.3[16]	...	...	5.5[16]
	2006	0.1	0.2[16]	76.3[16]	0.2[16]	...	0.6[16]	19.9[16]
	2010	0.1[2,12]	1.9[16]	76.2[16]	0.4[16]	...	...	19.7[16]
	2011	0.1[2,12]	1.6[16]	82.1[16]	0.1[16]	...	...	15.1[16]
	2013	0.1[2,12]	...	92.5	0.2	...	0.2	7.1
Thailand Thaïlande	2005	0.2	48.7	31.5	14.9	0.7	1.8	2.4
	2009	0.2	41.4	37.9	17.8	0.3	1.0	1.6
	2014	0.5	38.8	24.3	17.1	0.4	1.6	17.8
TFYR of Macedonia ex-R.Y. de Macédoine	2002	0.2	7.8	76.3	7.3	~0.0	8.6	...
	2004	0.2	...	...	...	...	...	...
	2010	0.2	...	...	...	...	...	...
	2013	0.4	...	...	...	...	...	...
Togo Togo	2010	0.3[2]	...	88.3	...	...	11.7	...
	2012	0.2[2]	...	84.9	...	3.1	12.1	...
	2014[2]	0.3[12]	...	94.5	...	...	5.5	...
Trinidad and Tobago Trinité-et-Tobago	2005	0.1	...	...	...	...	...	...
	2010	0.1	...	...	...	...	...	...
	2014	0.1	...	...	...	...	...	...
Tunisia Tunisie	2005	0.7	14.4	79.2	...	...	6.4	...
	2010	0.7	17.1	78.1	...	...	4.8	...
	2014	0.6	18.5	77.5	...	...	4.0	...
Turkey Turquie	2005	0.6	43.3[3]	50.1[3]	...	5.8[3]	0.8	...
	2010	0.8	45.1	30.8	19.6	3.7	0.8	...
	2014	1.0	50.9	26.3	18.4	3.4	1.1	...
Uganda Ouganda	2002	0.4	1.3	33.8	1.3	...	63.6	...
	2005	0.2	1.7	41.5	...	...	56.9	...
	2010	0.5	13.7	21.9	1.0	6.0	57.3	...
Ukraine Ukraine	2005	1.2	# 32.3	# 40.1	# 0.1	# 0.4	# 24.4	# 2.8
	2010	0.8	26.2	46.7	0.2	0.1	25.7	1.1
	2014	0.7[22]	35.2	43.8	0.2	~0.0	19.8	1.1
United Arab Emirates Émirats arabes unis	2014	0.7	74.3[24]	25.7[9]	...	...	...	...
United Kingdom Royaume-Uni	2005	1.6	42.1	32.7	1.2	4.7	19.3	...
	2010	* 1.7	* 44.0	32.3	* 1.2	* 4.8	* 17.6	...
	*2014	1.7	46.5	28.8	1.3	4.6	18.9	...
United Rep. of Tanzania Rép.-Unie de Tanzanie	2010	0.4[1,2]	0.1	57.5	0.3	0.1	42.0	...
	2013[2]	0.5	...	...	...	...	...	...
United States of America États-Unis d'Amérique	2005[6]	2.5	63.3	30.8	2.8	3.1	...	...
	2010	2.7[6]	56.9[6]	32.6[6]	3.0[6]	3.8[6]	3.7	...
	*2013	2.7[6]	60.9[6]	27.7[6]	3.3[6]	3.6[6]	4.5	...
United States Virgin Islands [1] Îles Vierges américaines [1]	2002	...	...	70.8	28.0	1.2	...	...
	2005	...	...	100.0	...	...	...	...
	2007	...	...	100.0	...	...	...	...
Uruguay Uruguay	2000	0.2	39.3	20.3	35.7	...	4.8	~0.0
	2002	0.2	46.7	17.1	31.4	0.1	4.7	...
	2010	0.3	47.1	22.9	26.6	0.9	1.7	0.8
	2011	0.3	8.5	30.8	45.2	0.1	6.5	8.9
	2014	0.3	4.6	28.6	59.2	0.3	7.4	...
Uzbekistan Ouzbékistan	2014	0.2	35.9	58.9[13]	...	...	0.8	4.4
Viet Nam Viet Nam	2002	0.2	18.1	74.1	0.7[8]	...	6.3	0.8
	2011	0.2	28.4	64.5	3.1	...	4.0	...
Zambia Zambie	2005[1]	~0.0	...	...	...	...	...	...
	#2008	0.3	3.2	94.8	...	0.3	1.6	...

28 Gross domestic expenditure on research and development (R&D) *(continued)*
As a percentage of GDP and by source of funds

Dépenses intérieures brutes de recherche et développement (R-D) *(suite)*
En pourcentage du PIB et répartition par source de financement

Source:

United Nations Educational, Scientific and Cultural Organization (UNESCO) Institute for Statistics, Montreal, the UNESCO Institute for Statistics database, last accessed February 2017.

1 Partial data.
2 Excluding business enterprise.
3 Including other classes.
4 Data have been converted from the former national currency using the appropriate conversion rate.
5 Overestimated or based on overestimated data.
6 Excluding most or all capital expenditures.
7 Higher Education only.
8 Including private non-profit.
9 Government only.
10 S&T budget instead of R&D expenditure.
11 Including business enterprise.
12 Excluding private non-profit.
13 Including higher education.
14 Including Government.
15 R&D budget instead of R&D expenditure or based on R&D budget.
16 The sum of the breakdown does not add to the total.
17 Excluding government.
18 Excluding Defence (all or mostly).
19 Underestimated or based on underestimated data.
20 Source: EUROSTAT.
21 Excluding social sciences and humanities.
22 Excluding data from some regions, provinces or states.
23 Do not correspond exactly to Frascati Manual recommendations.
24 Business enterprise only.

Source:

L'Institut de statistique de l'Organisation des Nations Unies pour l'éducation, la science et la culture (UNESCO), Montréal, la base de données de l'Institut de statistique de l'UNESCO, dernier accès février 2017.

1 Données partielles.
2 Ne comprend pas les entreprises commerciales.
3 Comprend d'autres catégories.
4 Les données ont été converties à partir de l'ancienne monnaie nationale et du taux de conversion approprié.
5 Surestimé ou fondé sur des données surestimées.
6 A l'exclusion des dépenses d'équipement (en totalité ou en grande partie).
7 Les données se réfèrent au secteur de l'enseignement supérieur seulement.
8 Y compris les fonds privés à but non lucratif.
9 Etat seulement.
10 Budget pour la science et technologie au lieu des dépenses de recherche et développement.
11 Y compris les fonds d'entreprises.
12 Non compris les organisations privées à but non lucratif.
13 Y compris l'enseignement supérieur.
14 Y compris l'état.
15 Basé sur le budget de la recherche-développement au lieu des dépenses.
16 La somme de toutes les valeurs diffère du total.
17 Non compris l'état.
18 A l'exclusion de la défense (en totalité ou en grande partie).
19 Sous-estimé ou basé sur des données sous-estimées.
20 Source: EUROSTAT.
21 Non compris les sciences sociales et les sciences humaines.
22 Non compris les données de certaines régions, provinces ou états.
23 Ne corresponds pas exactement aux recommendations du Manuel de Frascati.
24 Les entreprises commerciales seulement.

29 Patents

Resident filings (per million population), grants and patents in force

Brevets

Demandes émanant de résidents (par million d'habitants), délivrances et brevets en vigueur

Region, country or area	1985	1995	2005	2010	2013	2014	2015	Région, pays ou zone
Total, all countries or areas								**Total, tous pays ou zones**
Grants of patents	**397 580**	**430 500**	**633 900**	**915 700**	**1 175 400**	**1 179 800**	**1 241 100**	**Brevets délivrés**
Africa								**Afrique**
Grants of patents	...	...	4 800	9 600	13 500	14 100	8 800	Brevets délivrés
Northern America								**Amérique septentrionale**
Grants of patents	...	...	159 300	238 700	301 700	324 400	320 600	Brevets délivrés
Latin America and the Caribbean								**Amérique latine et Caraïbes**
Grants of patents	...	...	15 000	18 000	20 100	18 600	18 600	Brevets délivrés
Asia								**Asie**
Grants of patents	...	...	288 700	469 600	656 300	636 700	700 400	Brevets délivrés
Europe								**Europe**
Grants of patents	...	...	150 900	160 800	161 800	161 900	165 200	Brevets délivrés
Oceania								**Océanie**
Grants of patents	...	...	15 200	19 000	22 000	24 100	27 500	Brevets délivrés
Albania								**Albanie**
Resident filings (per mil. pop.)	...	...	...	...	...	4	5	Dem. de rés. (par mil. d'hab.)
Grants of patents	...	...	395	349	9	5	10	Brevets délivrés
Patents in force	...	...	...	349	...	...	...	Brevets en vigueur
Algeria								**Algérie**
Resident filings (per mil. pop.)	...	1	2	2	3	2	2	Dem. de rés. (par mil. d'hab.)
Grants of patents	...	118	443	1 076	5 127	5 372	353	Brevets délivrés
Patents in force	...	...	498	...	4 666	4 340	5 145	Brevets en vigueur
Argentina								**Argentine**
Resident filings (per mil. pop.)	...	19	27	13	15	12	13	Dem. de rés. (par mil. d'hab.)
Grants of patents	...	1 003	1 798	1 366	1 297	1 360	1 559	Brevets délivrés
Armenia								**Arménie**
Resident filings (per mil. pop.)	...	58	68	48	43	40	38	Dem. de rés. (par mil. d'hab.)
Grants of patents	...	52	126	124	99	108	81	Brevets délivrés
Patents in force	...	...	110	278	263	279	248	Brevets en vigueur
Australia								**Australie**
Resident filings (per mil. pop.)	...	99	125	109	132	85	96	Dem. de rés. (par mil. d'hab.)
Grants of patents	6 764	9 406	10 979	14 557	17 112	19 304	23 098	Brevets délivrés
Patents in force	...	...	96 403	96 293	122 811	128 407	117 906	Brevets en vigueur
Austria								**Autriche**
Resident filings (per mil. pop.)	300	217	404	497	490	475	488	Dem. de rés. (par mil. d'hab.)
Grants of patents	2 571	1 777	938	1 130	1 256	962	1 356	Brevets délivrés
Patents in force	...	...	10 126	55 690	42 466	31 923	17 647	Brevets en vigueur
Azerbaijan								**Azerbaïdjan**
Resident filings (per mil. pop.)	...	29	33	30	20	21	23	Dem. de rés. (par mil. d'hab.)
Grants of patents	...	9	195	126	78	97	88	Brevets délivrés
Patents in force	...	...	...	...	248	87	82	Brevets en vigueur
Bahamas								**Bahamas**
Resident filings (per mil. pop.)	13	...	...	...	3	5	...	Dem. de rés. (par mil. d'hab.)
Grants of patents	66	...	...	...	116	120	...	Brevets délivrés
Patents in force	...	...	...	...	...	1 536	...	Brevets en vigueur
Bahrain								**Bahreïn**
Resident filings (per mil. pop.)	...	...	...	...	...	5	7	Dem. de rés. (par mil. d'hab.)
Grants of patents	31	...	...	...	...	...	...	Brevets délivrés
Patents in force	...	...	...	...	123	117	...	Brevets en vigueur
Bangladesh								**Bangladesh**
Resident filings (per mil. pop.)	...	1	...	...	...	...	...	Dem. de rés. (par mil. d'hab.)
Grants of patents	118	80	182	92	134	121	101	Brevets délivrés
Patents in force	...	...	...	...	1 031	1 077	...	Brevets en vigueur
Barbados								**Barbade**
Resident filings (per mil. pop.)	...	...	...	...	11	4	...	Dem. de rés. (par mil. d'hab.)
Grants of patents	...	...	7	...	9	3	10	Brevets délivrés
Patents in force	...	...	49	57	...	...	...	Brevets en vigueur
Belarus								**Bélarus**
Resident filings (per mil. pop.)	...	61	121	197	167	82	75	Dem. de rés. (par mil. d'hab.)
Grants of patents	...	633	955	1 222	1 117	1 938	902	Brevets délivrés
Patents in force	...	...	...	4 444	4 478	5 176	2 676	Brevets en vigueur
Belgium								**Belgique**
Resident filings (per mil. pop.)	78	72	208	244	232	250	265	Dem. de rés. (par mil. d'hab.)
Grants of patents	1 976	1 216	708	532	745	373	567	Brevets délivrés
Patents in force	...	...	708	...	...	...	...	Brevets en vigueur

29 Patents (continued)

Resident filings (per million population), grants and patents in force

Brevets (suite)

Demandes émanant de résidents (par million d'habitants), délivrances et brevets en vigueur

Region, country or area	1985	1995	2005	2010	2013	2014	2015	Région, pays ou zone
Belize								**Belize**
Grants of patents	...	...	...	...	10	28	8	Brevets délivrés
Patents in force	...	...	...	...	102	120	128	Brevets en vigueur
Bhutan								**Bhoutan**
Resident filings (per mil. pop.)	...	...	...	...	4	...	...	Dem. de rés. (par mil. d'hab.)
Patents in force	...	...	...	...	2	...	...	Brevets en vigueur
Bolivia (Plurinational State of)								**Bolivie (État plurinational de)**
Resident filings (per mil. pop.)	1	2	...	...	...	1	...	Dem. de rés. (par mil. d'hab.)
Grants of patents	62	47	...	...	...	97	...	Brevets délivrés
Patents in force	...	...	...	...	...	601	...	Brevets en vigueur
Bosnia and Herzegovina								**Bosnie-Herzégovine**
Resident filings (per mil. pop.)	...	...	17	15	2	11	...	Dem. de rés. (par mil. d'hab.)
Grants of patents	...	...	46	173	31	5	...	Brevets délivrés
Patents in force	...	...	120	716	583	503	...	Brevets en vigueur
Botswana								**Botswana**
Resident filings (per mil. pop.)	...	...	...	...	4	2	...	Dem. de rés. (par mil. d'hab.)
Grants of patents	...	...	...	...	3	...	...	Brevets délivrés
Patents in force	...	...	...	...	...	883	...	Brevets en vigueur
Brazil								**Brésil**
Resident filings (per mil. pop.)	14	17	22	21	24	23	22	Dem. de rés. (par mil. d'hab.)
Grants of patents	3 934	2 659	2 439	3 251	2 972	2 749	3 411	Brevets délivrés
Patents in force	...	...	32 571	40 022	35 517	24 976	23 952	Brevets en vigueur
Brunei Darussalam								**Brunéi Darussalam**
Resident filings (per mil. pop.)	...	...	...	...	49	62	...	Dem. de rés. (par mil. d'hab.)
Grants of patents	...	42	26	40	93	71	...	Brevets délivrés
Patents in force	...	...	...	...	119	...	...	Brevets en vigueur
Bulgaria								**Bulgarie**
Resident filings (per mil. pop.)	...	44	35	34	42	35	44	Dem. de rés. (par mil. d'hab.)
Grants of patents	130	375	313	251	125	72	37	Brevets délivrés
Patents in force	...	...	2 203	6 812	1 431	1 324	1 158	Brevets en vigueur
Burundi								**Burundi**
Grants of patents	...	1	...	...	...	...	...	Brevets délivrés
Cambodia								**Cambodge**
Grants of patents	...	...	...	...	...	...	1	Brevets délivrés
Canada								**Canada**
Resident filings (per mil. pop.)	81	83	160	134	130	118	119	Dem. de rés. (par mil. d'hab.)
Grants of patents	18 697	9 139	15 516	19 120	23 833	23 749	22 201	Brevets délivrés
Patents in force	...	...	125 110	133 355	153 781	161 442	166 771	Brevets en vigueur
Chile								**Chili**
Resident filings (per mil. pop.)	10	12	22	19	19	25	25	Dem. de rés. (par mil. d'hab.)
Grants of patents	448	133	311	1 020	898	1 168	1 058	Brevets délivrés
Patents in force	...	...	...	8 121	9 585	9 987	11 163	Brevets en vigueur
China [1]								**Chine** [1]
Resident filings (per mil. pop.)	4	8	72	219	519	587	706	Dem. de rés. (par mil. d'hab.)
Grants of patents	44	3 393	53 305	135 110	207 688	233 228	359 316	Brevets délivrés
Patents in force	...	...	182 396	564 760	1 033 908	1 196 497	1 472 374	Brevets en vigueur
China, Hong Kong SAR								**Chine, Hong Kong RAS**
Resident filings (per mil. pop.)	3	4	23	19	31	27	33	Dem. de rés. (par mil. d'hab.)
Grants of patents	1 030	1 960	6 518	5 353	6 564	5 932	5 963	Brevets délivrés
Patents in force	...	...	...	33 225	38 858	40 865	42 306	Brevets en vigueur
China, Macao SAR								**Chine, Macao RAS**
Resident filings (per mil. pop.)	...	...	6	7	11	3	5	Dem. de rés. (par mil. d'hab.)
Grants of patents	...	2	5	156	22	16	36	Brevets délivrés
Patents in force	...	...	12	377	442	451	470	Brevets en vigueur
Colombia								**Colombie**
Resident filings (per mil. pop.)	2	4	2	3	5	5	7	Dem. de rés. (par mil. d'hab.)
Grants of patents	169	365	256	639	2 264	1 212	1 003	Brevets délivrés
Patents in force	...	...	...	...	5 967	6 710	7 858	Brevets en vigueur
Congo								**Congo**
Grants of patents	...	15	...	...	...	...	...	Brevets délivrés
Costa Rica								**Costa Rica**
Resident filings (per mil. pop.)	...	...	...	2	4	3	4	Dem. de rés. (par mil. d'hab.)
Grants of patents	...	...	...	45	106	114	130	Brevets délivrés
Patents in force	...	...	...	239	417	518	635	Brevets en vigueur

29 Patents *(continued)*

Resident filings (per million population), grants and patents in force

Brevets *(suite)*

Demandes émanant de résidents (par million d'habitants), délivrances et brevets en vigueur

Region, country or area	1985	1995	2005	2010	2013	2014	2015	Région, pays ou zone
Croatia								**Croatie**
Resident filings (per mil. pop.)	...	57	82	62	56	43	42	Dem. de rés. (par mil. d'hab.)
Grants of patents	...	25	140	82	159	90	45	Brevets délivrés
Patents in force	...	...	1 094	2 134	4 243	4 838	5 621	Brevets en vigueur
Cuba								**Cuba**
Resident filings (per mil. pop.)	...	10	9	...	2	2	...	Dem. de rés. (par mil. d'hab.)
Grants of patents	18	77	64	...	125	94	...	Brevets délivrés
Patents in force	...	...	653	...	972	927	...	Brevets en vigueur
Cyprus								**Chypre**
Resident filings (per mil. pop.)	...	...	53	35	40	44	37	Dem. de rés. (par mil. d'hab.)
Grants of patents	43	...	68	19	1	...	...	Brevets délivrés
Patents in force	...	...	3 521	333	82	149	114	Brevets en vigueur
Czechia								**Tchéquie**
Resident filings (per mil. pop.)	...	61	65	99	108	102	104	Dem. de rés. (par mil. d'hab.)
Grants of patents	...	1 299	1 551	911	611	688	749	Brevets délivrés
Patents in force	...	...	10 165	9 633	7 780	7 157	6 853	Brevets en vigueur
Dem. P. R. Korea								**R. p. dém. de Corée**
Resident filings (per mil. pop.)	...	...	246	327	...	...	...	Dem. de rés. (par mil. d'hab.)
Grants of patents	...	...	3 583	6 290	...	...	...	Brevets délivrés
Denmark								**Danemark**
Resident filings (per mil. pop.)	167	236	523	625	583	595	597	Dem. de rés. (par mil. d'hab.)
Grants of patents	1 054	1 120	389	155	309	292	430	Brevets délivrés
Patents in force	...	...	56 978	47 732	51 277	51 345	52 321	Brevets en vigueur
Djibouti								**Djibouti**
Resident filings (per mil. pop.)	...	...	...	...	1	...	...	Dem. de rés. (par mil. d'hab.)
Dominican Republic								**Rép. dominicaine**
Resident filings (per mil. pop.)	...	...	...	...	1	1	2	Dem. de rés. (par mil. d'hab.)
Grants of patents	...	...	...	...	44	62	24	Brevets délivrés
Patents in force	...	...	...	...	229	294	311	Brevets en vigueur
Ecuador								**Équateur**
Resident filings (per mil. pop.)	...	1	1	...	...	...	...	Dem. de rés. (par mil. d'hab.)
Grants of patents	...	90	38	28	...	...	...	Brevets délivrés
Patents in force	...	...	38	199	...	...	...	Brevets en vigueur
Egypt								**Égypte**
Resident filings (per mil. pop.)	3	7	6	7	7	8	...	Dem. de rés. (par mil. d'hab.)
Grants of patents	298	346	147	321	465	415	...	Brevets délivrés
Patents in force	...	...	...	3 316	3 553	4 012	...	Brevets en vigueur
El Salvador								**El Salvador**
Resident filings (per mil. pop.)	3	1	...	...	...	...	1	Dem. de rés. (par mil. d'hab.)
Grants of patents	70	61	...	...	48	77	35	Brevets délivrés
Patents in force	...	...	...	...	...	1 642	...	Brevets en vigueur
Estonia								**Estonie**
Resident filings (per mil. pop.)	...	11	19	83	50	61	47	Dem. de rés. (par mil. d'hab.)
Grants of patents	...	...	163	120	78	38	24	Brevets délivrés
Patents in force	...	...	1 395	1 320	1 228	1 089	934	Brevets en vigueur
Ethiopia								**Éthiopie**
Grants of patents	...	...	9	...	...	...	...	Brevets délivrés
Fiji								**Fidji**
Grants of patents	15	...	...	...	...	...	...	Brevets délivrés
Finland								**Finlande**
Resident filings (per mil. pop.)	352	403	637	628	642	662	600	Dem. de rés. (par mil. d'hab.)
Grants of patents	2 160	2 347	1 757	923	711	787	931	Brevets délivrés
Patents in force	...	...	39 450	12 221	47 058	47 344	48 242	Brevets en vigueur
France								**France**
Resident filings (per mil. pop.)	212	209	354	373	372	378	375	Dem. de rés. (par mil. d'hab.)
Grants of patents	24 195	17 918	11 473	9 899	11 405	11 889	12 699	Brevets délivrés
Patents in force	...	...	343 568	435 915	500 114	510 490	520 069	Brevets en vigueur
Gambia								**Gambie**
Grants of patents	...	...	2	...	...	...	...	Brevets délivrés
Georgia								**Géorgie**
Resident filings (per mil. pop.)	...	61	54	47	30	30	27	Dem. de rés. (par mil. d'hab.)
Grants of patents	...	133	320	258	286	209	206	Brevets délivrés
Patents in force	...	...	1 040	1 044	2 050	1 486	1 650	Brevets en vigueur

Patents *(continued)*

Resident filings (per million population), grants and patents in force

Brevets *(suite)*

Demandes émanant de résidents (par million d'habitants), délivrances et brevets en vigueur

Region, country or area	1985	1995	2005	2010	2013	2014	2015	Région, pays ou zone
Germany								**Allemagne**
Resident filings (per mil. pop.)	415	467	875	910	900	912	887	Dem. de rés. (par mil. d'hab.)
Grants of patents	19 500	16 000	17 063	13 678	13 858	15 030	14 795	Brevets délivrés
Patents in force	...	...	434 663	514 046	569 340	576 273	602 013	Brevets en vigueur
Greece								**Grèce**
Resident filings (per mil. pop.)	113	25	48	73	70	68	59	Dem. de rés. (par mil. d'hab.)
Grants of patents	3 294	350	320	479	282	316	262	Brevets délivrés
Patents in force	...	...	...	32 120	2 966	3 239	3 172	Brevets en vigueur
Grenada								**Grenade**
Grants of patents	...	...	...	...	...	...	9	Brevets délivrés
Guatemala								**Guatemala**
Resident filings (per mil. pop.)	9	3	1	...	...	1	...	Dem. de rés. (par mil. d'hab.)
Grants of patents	166	22	104	104	65	105	51	Brevets délivrés
Patents in force	...	...	...	590	746	840	867	Brevets en vigueur
Guyana								**Guyana**
Resident filings (per mil. pop.)	1	...	...	...	...	...	...	Dem. de rés. (par mil. d'hab.)
Grants of patents	22	...	...	...	...	...	...	Brevets délivrés
Patents in force	...	...	...	...	...	1 442	...	Brevets en vigueur
Haiti								**Haïti**
Resident filings (per mil. pop.)	1	...	...	...	...	...	...	Dem. de rés. (par mil. d'hab.)
Grants of patents	9	3	11	10	...	...	...	Brevets délivrés
Honduras								**Honduras**
Resident filings (per mil. pop.)	3	1	...	...	1	...	...	Dem. de rés. (par mil. d'hab.)
Grants of patents	19	...	85	81	132	94	69	Brevets délivrés
Hungary								**Hongrie**
Resident filings (per mil. pop.)	273	106	78	75	75	67	68	Dem. de rés. (par mil. d'hab.)
Grants of patents	2 095	1 910	1 126	65	1 351	376	365	Brevets délivrés
Patents in force	...	...	9 125	2 586	5 237	4 695	4 278	Brevets en vigueur
Iceland								**Islande**
Resident filings (per mil. pop.)	87	71	253	343	222	281	257	Dem. de rés. (par mil. d'hab.)
Grants of patents	21	11	101	139	43	54	17	Brevets délivrés
Patents in force	...	...	349	1 892	603	567	502	Brevets en vigueur
India								**Inde**
Resident filings (per mil. pop.)	1	2	4	7	8	9	10	Dem. de rés. (par mil. d'hab.)
Grants of patents	1 814	1 613	4 320	7 138	3 377	6 153	6 022	Brevets délivrés
Patents in force	...	...	16 419	47 224	45 103	49 272	47 113	Brevets en vigueur
Indonesia								**Indonésie**
Resident filings (per mil. pop.)	...	...	1	2	3	3	4	Dem. de rés. (par mil. d'hab.)
Grants of patents	...	...	...	...	...	...	1 911	Brevets délivrés
Patents in force	...	...	...	...	22 564	...	...	Brevets en vigueur
Iran (Islamic Rep. of)								**Iran (Rép. islamique d')**
Resident filings (per mil. pop.)	4	5	58	150	147	175	...	Dem. de rés. (par mil. d'hab.)
Grants of patents	339	166	2 890	5 372	3 476	3 060	2 936	Brevets délivrés
Patents in force	...	...	...	...	3 440	...	...	Brevets en vigueur
Iraq								**Iraq**
Resident filings (per mil. pop.)	19	4	...	...	...	...	9	Dem. de rés. (par mil. d'hab.)
Grants of patents	103	32	...	...	...	...	312	Brevets délivrés
Ireland								**Irlande**
Resident filings (per mil. pop.)	205	233	264	274	192	191	180	Dem. de rés. (par mil. d'hab.)
Grants of patents	1 042	3 525	349	243	214	148	126	Brevets délivrés
Patents in force	...	...	...	79 040	108 218	111 109	118 273	Brevets en vigueur
Israel								**Israël**
Resident filings (per mil. pop.)	187	228	241	190	149	137	153	Dem. de rés. (par mil. d'hab.)
Grants of patents	1 636	2 029	2 269	2 293	3 697	3 984	4 492	Brevets délivrés
Patents in force	...	...	...	26 494	25 372	26 645	28 666	Brevets en vigueur
Italy								**Italie**
Resident filings (per mil. pop.)	35	...	...	219	200	201	...	Dem. de rés. (par mil. d'hab.)
Grants of patents	...	9 164	5 534	16 106	8 114	7 795	7 153	Brevets délivrés
Patents in force	...	...	...	65 417	61 341	63 071	...	Brevets en vigueur
Jamaica								**Jamaïque**
Resident filings (per mil. pop.)	...	3	4	5	8	12	3	Dem. de rés. (par mil. d'hab.)
Grants of patents	...	4	...	...	42	28	74	Brevets délivrés
Patents in force	...	...	527	...	296	324	375	Brevets en vigueur

29 Patents *(continued)*
Resident filings (per million population), grants and patents in force

Brevets *(suite)*
Demandes émanant de résidents (par million d'habitants), délivrances et brevets en vigueur

Region, country or area	1985	1995	2005	2010	2013	2014	2015	Région, pays ou zone
Japan								**Japon**
Resident filings (per mil. pop.)	2 272	2 661	2 880	2 265	2 134	2 092	2 039	Dem. de rés. (par mil. d'hab.)
Grants of patents	50 100	109 100	122 944	222 693	277 079	227 142	189 358	Brevets délivrés
Patents in force	...	...	1 123 055	1 423 432	1 838 177	1 920 490	1 946 568	Brevets en vigueur
Jordan								**Jordanie**
Resident filings (per mil. pop.)	...	...	9	7	5	5	5	Dem. de rés. (par mil. d'hab.)
Grants of patents	...	...	55	64	48	115	83	Brevets délivrés
Patents in force	...	...	...	312	317	377	427	Brevets en vigueur
Kazakhstan								**Kazakhstan**
Resident filings (per mil. pop.)	...	65	101	105	111	105	75	Dem. de rés. (par mil. d'hab.)
Grants of patents	...	1 281	...	1 868	1 500	1 504	1 504	Brevets délivrés
Patents in force	...	...	...	581	377	5 184	3 934	Brevets en vigueur
Kenya								**Kenya**
Resident filings (per mil. pop.)	...	...	1	2	3	3	3	Dem. de rés. (par mil. d'hab.)
Grants of patents	98	...	48	54	71	53	24	Brevets délivrés
Kiribati								**Kiribati**
Resident filings (per mil. pop.)	...	...	...	...	166	...	...	Dem. de rés. (par mil. d'hab.)
Grants of patents	1	...	...	...	...	...	...	Brevets délivrés
Kyrgyzstan								**Kirghizistan**
Resident filings (per mil. pop.)	...	26	...	26	20	23	22	Dem. de rés. (par mil. d'hab.)
Grants of patents	...	133	...	109	88	100	111	Brevets délivrés
Patents in force	...	...	...	112	348	375	347	Brevets en vigueur
Latvia								**Lettonie**
Resident filings (per mil. pop.)	...	85	53	101	152	56	83	Dem. de rés. (par mil. d'hab.)
Grants of patents	...	629	122	184	136	141	147	Brevets délivrés
Patents in force	...	...	4 012	5 680	6 329	6 763	6 938	Brevets en vigueur
Lebanon								**Liban**
Resident filings (per mil. pop.)	...	...	...	...	20	14	19	Dem. de rés. (par mil. d'hab.)
Grants of patents	...	...	...	...	325	316	279	Brevets délivrés
Lesotho								**Lesotho**
Resident filings (per mil. pop.)	...	5	...	...	...	...	...	Dem. de rés. (par mil. d'hab.)
Grants of patents	...	7	...	...	...	...	...	Brevets délivrés
Libya								**Libye**
Resident filings (per mil. pop.)	...	1	...	...	...	...	...	Dem. de rés. (par mil. d'hab.)
Liechtenstein								**Liechtenstein**
Resident filings (per mil. pop.)	...	...	4 355	7 989	6 757	7 453	9 893	Dem. de rés. (par mil. d'hab.)
Lithuania								**Lituanie**
Resident filings (per mil. pop.)	...	29	21	38	47	50	48	Dem. de rés. (par mil. d'hab.)
Grants of patents	...	494	116	84	93	120	133	Brevets délivrés
Patents in force	...	...	768	642	519	520	530	Brevets en vigueur
Luxembourg								**Luxembourg**
Resident filings (per mil. pop.)	221	86	441	990	948	1 053	951	Dem. de rés. (par mil. d'hab.)
Grants of patents	418	...	29	87	...	152	153	Brevets délivrés
Patents in force	...	...	...	21 346	20 421	19 360	19 040	Brevets en vigueur
Madagascar								**Madagascar**
Resident filings (per mil. pop.)	...	2	...	...	...	...	...	Dem. de rés. (par mil. d'hab.)
Grants of patents	...	25	32	55	40	24	23	Brevets délivrés
Patents in force	...	...	249	387	514	390	414	Brevets en vigueur
Malawi								**Malawi**
Grants of patents	43	23	...	...	3	...	1	Brevets délivrés
Malaysia								**Malaisie**
Resident filings (per mil. pop.)	1	7	20	44	41	45	42	Dem. de rés. (par mil. d'hab.)
Grants of patents	1 150	1 753	2 508	2 160	2 660	2 705	2 877	Brevets délivrés
Patents in force	...	...	...	20 908	22 782	21 568	23 538	Brevets en vigueur
Malta								**Malte**
Resident filings (per mil. pop.)	...	30	...	104	132	150	216	Dem. de rés. (par mil. d'hab.)
Grants of patents	20	19	...	4	15	4	10	Brevets délivrés
Patents in force	...	...	...	832	560	490	428	Brevets en vigueur
Mauritius								**Maurice**
Resident filings (per mil. pop.)	4	3	...	...	2	2	1	Dem. de rés. (par mil. d'hab.)
Grants of patents	4	3	...	8	5	9	4	Brevets délivrés
Mexico								**Mexique**
Resident filings (per mil. pop.)	8	5	5	8	10	10	11	Dem. de rés. (par mil. d'hab.)
Grants of patents	977	3 538	8 098	9 399	10 368	9 819	9 338	Brevets délivrés
Patents in force	...	...	48 374	82 017	101 645	106 340	106 648	Brevets en vigueur

29 Patents *(continued)*

Resident filings (per million population), grants and patents in force

Brevets *(suite)*

Demandes émanant de résidents (par million d'habitants), délivrances et brevets en vigueur

Region, country or area	1985	1995	2005	2010	2013	2014	2015	Région, pays ou zone
Monaco								**Monaco**
Resident filings (per mil. pop.)	521	423	503	543	720	745	875	Dem. de rés. (par mil. d'hab.)
Grants of patents	66	36	9	5	5	5	8	Brevets délivrés
Patents in force	...	...	37 483	53 859	41 976	53 893	63 777	Brevets en vigueur
Mongolia								**Mongolie**
Resident filings (per mil. pop.)	...	57	40	41	47	48	37	Dem. de rés. (par mil. d'hab.)
Grants of patents	5	117	197	96	212	216	234	Brevets délivrés
Patents in force	...	...	13 663	2 645	869	...	...	Brevets en vigueur
Montenegro								**Monténégro**
Resident filings (per mil. pop.)	...	...	...	37	37	21	37	Dem. de rés. (par mil. d'hab.)
Grants of patents	...	...	...	264	121	14	10	Brevets délivrés
Patents in force	...	...	...	264	1 448	1 933	2 372	Brevets en vigueur
Morocco								**Maroc**
Resident filings (per mil. pop.)	2	3	5	5	9	10	7	Dem. de rés. (par mil. d'hab.)
Grants of patents	313	354	556	808	937	...	...	Brevets délivrés
Patents in force	...	...	9 872	...	...	...	...	Brevets en vigueur
Mozambique								**Mozambique**
Resident filings (per mil. pop.)	...	...	...	1	...	1	1	Dem. de rés. (par mil. d'hab.)
Grants of patents	...	...	14	...	...	...	...	Brevets délivrés
Nepal								**Népal**
Resident filings (per mil. pop.)	...	...	...	...	1	...	...	Dem. de rés. (par mil. d'hab.)
Grants of patents	1	1	3	...	1	...	74	Brevets délivrés
Patents in force	...	...	...	...	72	72	...	Brevets en vigueur
Netherlands								**Pays-Bas**
Resident filings (per mil. pop.)	134	137	614	511	485	543	549	Dem. de rés. (par mil. d'hab.)
Grants of patents	2 145	673	2 373	1 947	2 029	1 722	1 377	Brevets délivrés
Patents in force	...	...	14 091	...	12 704	12 518	...	Brevets en vigueur
New Zealand								**Nouvelle-Zélande**
Resident filings (per mil. pop.)	310	350	458	364	363	363	258	Dem. de rés. (par mil. d'hab.)
Grants of patents	1 732	2 641	4 189	4 347	4 752	4 677	4 259	Brevets délivrés
Patents in force	...	...	34 182	34 800	28 217	28 854	40 802	Brevets en vigueur
Nicaragua								**Nicaragua**
Resident filings (per mil. pop.)	1	...	...	...	1	...	...	Dem. de rés. (par mil. d'hab.)
Grants of patents	25	1	...	...	72	62	...	Brevets délivrés
Patents in force	...	...	...	...	328	387	...	Brevets en vigueur
Nigeria								**Nigéria**
Grants of patents	...	...	...	...	645	...	...	Brevets délivrés
Norway								**Norvège**
Resident filings (per mil. pop.)	222	259	247	334	317	318	320	Dem. de rés. (par mil. d'hab.)
Grants of patents	2 165	2 014	542	1 631	1 430	1 413	1 446	Brevets délivrés
Patents in force	...	...	...	12 755	19 297	21 882	23 087	Brevets en vigueur
Pakistan								**Pakistan**
Resident filings (per mil. pop.)	...	...	1	1	1	1	1	Dem. de rés. (par mil. d'hab.)
Grants of patents	...	474	393	238	282	185	131	Brevets délivrés
Patents in force	...	...	...	...	...	185	...	Brevets en vigueur
Panama								**Panama**
Resident filings (per mil. pop.)	6	6	...	...	2	3	4	Dem. de rés. (par mil. d'hab.)
Grants of patents	72	80	228	378	266	166	78	Brevets délivrés
Patents in force	...	...	...	378	1 858	1 725	1 684	Brevets en vigueur
Papua New Guinea								**Papouasie-Nvl-Guinée**
Grants of patents	...	...	...	...	57	...	70	Brevets délivrés
Patents in force	...	...	...	...	42	...	71	Brevets en vigueur
Paraguay								**Paraguay**
Resident filings (per mil. pop.)	2	...	4	3	...	...	...	Dem. de rés. (par mil. d'hab.)
Grants of patents	8	...	...	...	...	...	...	Brevets délivrés
Peru								**Pérou**
Resident filings (per mil. pop.)	2	...	1	1	2	3	2	Dem. de rés. (par mil. d'hab.)
Grants of patents	148	...	388	365	287	332	362	Brevets délivrés
Patents in force	...	...	2 252	2 435	2 615	2 651	2 643	Brevets en vigueur
Philippines								**Philippines**
Resident filings (per mil. pop.)	2	2	2	2	2	3	4	Dem. de rés. (par mil. d'hab.)
Grants of patents	1 281	589	1 642	1 153	2 207	2 159	2 200	Brevets délivrés
Patents in force	...	...	...	52 527	...	...	...	Brevets en vigueur

29 Patents (continued)

Resident filings (per million population), grants and patents in force

Brevets (suite)

Demandes émanant de résidents (par million d'habitants), délivrances et brevets en vigueur

Region, country or area	1985	1995	2005	2010	2013	2014	2015	Région, pays ou zone
Poland								**Pologne**
Resident filings (per mil. pop.)	138	67	56	90	121	116	138	Dem. de rés. (par mil. d'hab.)
Grants of patents	4 467	2 608	2 522	3 004	2 804	2 852	2 572	Brevets délivrés
Patents in force	...	...	14 578	30 021	47 610	53 183	57 951	Brevets en vigueur
Portugal								**Portugal**
Resident filings (per mil. pop.)	8	8	19	55	71	80	103	Dem. de rés. (par mil. d'hab.)
Grants of patents	960	960	231	140	130	97	76	Brevets délivrés
Patents in force	...	...	35 871	39 076	36 782	35 561	...	Brevets en vigueur
Qatar								**Qatar**
Resident filings (per mil. pop.)	...	...	...	...	7	4	...	Dem. de rés. (par mil. d'hab.)
Republic of Korea								**République de Corée**
Resident filings (per mil. pop.)	66	1 313	2 538	2 668	3 186	3 254	3 305	Dem. de rés. (par mil. d'hab.)
Grants of patents	2 268	12 512	73 512	68 843	127 330	129 786	101 873	Brevets délivrés
Patents in force	...	...	420 906	640 412	812 595	885 959	912 442	Brevets en vigueur
Republic of Moldova								**République de Moldova**
Resident filings (per mil. pop.)	...	73	105	42	19	19	18	Dem. de rés. (par mil. d'hab.)
Grants of patents	...	227	269	132	61	54	61	Brevets délivrés
Patents in force	...	...	1 108	1 018	471	384	348	Brevets en vigueur
Romania								**Roumanie**
Resident filings (per mil. pop.)	185	80	43	69	51	49	51	Dem. de rés. (par mil. d'hab.)
Grants of patents	2 786	1 860	759	447	451	356	305	Brevets délivrés
Patents in force	...	...	8 627	2 915	17 100	17 268	17 089	Brevets en vigueur
Russian Federation								**Fédération de Russie**
Resident filings (per mil. pop.)	...	118	166	203	203	169	205	Dem. de rés. (par mil. d'hab.)
Grants of patents	...	25 633	23 390	30 322	31 638	33 950	34 706	Brevets délivrés
Patents in force	...	...	123 089	181 904	194 248	208 320	218 974	Brevets en vigueur
Rwanda								**Rwanda**
Grants of patents	1	...	3	...	...	...	...	Brevets délivrés
Patents in force	...	...	...	...	...	135	108	Brevets en vigueur
Saint Vincent-Grenadines								**Saint-Vincent-Grenadines**
Patents in force	...	...	...	...	28	...	...	Brevets en vigueur
Samoa								**Samoa**
Resident filings (per mil. pop.)	...	...	...	...	...	5	5	Dem. de rés. (par mil. d'hab.)
Grants of patents	4	2	...	...	...	...	64	Brevets délivrés
Patents in force	...	...	...	...	...	96	64	Brevets en vigueur
Saudi Arabia								**Arabie saoudite**
Resident filings (per mil. pop.)	...	1	6	12	24	31	29	Dem. de rés. (par mil. d'hab.)
Grants of patents	...	3	225	194	233	561	763	Brevets délivrés
Patents in force	...	...	...	...	1 988	2 338	2 664	Brevets en vigueur
Serbia								**Serbie**
Resident filings (per mil. pop.)	...	...	50	40	29	30	26	Dem. de rés. (par mil. d'hab.)
Grants of patents	...	...	265	427	136	105	86	Brevets délivrés
Patents in force	...	...	...	1 477	2 644	2 964	3 329	Brevets en vigueur
Serbia and Montenegro [former]								**Serbie-et-Monténégro [anc.]**
Grants of patents	1 053	510	...	...	...	...	...	Brevets délivrés
Seychelles								**Seychelles**
Grants of patents	2	1	...	...	...	...	...	Brevets délivrés
Sierra Leone								**Sierra Leone**
Grants of patents	...	5	...	...	...	...	...	Brevets délivrés
Singapore								**Singapour**
Resident filings (per mil. pop.)	1	41	133	176	212	238	265	Dem. de rés. (par mil. d'hab.)
Grants of patents	416	1 750	7 530	4 442	5 575	5 538	7 054	Brevets délivrés
Patents in force	...	...	43 024	43 591	45 999	47 422	46 906	Brevets en vigueur
Slovakia								**Slovaquie**
Resident filings (per mil. pop.)	...	50	32	48	39	44	51	Dem. de rés. (par mil. d'hab.)
Grants of patents	...	381	560	376	115	94	82	Brevets délivrés
Patents in force	...	...	4 033	3 593	2 755	2 357	1 995	Brevets en vigueur
Slovenia								**Slovénie**
Resident filings (per mil. pop.)	...	158	215	282	...	...	...	Dem. de rés. (par mil. d'hab.)
Grants of patents	...	380	285	250	...	...	...	Brevets délivrés
Patents in force	...	...	5 201	1 485	...	...	...	Brevets en vigueur
Solomon Islands								**Îles Salomon**
Grants of patents	4	...	...	...	...	...	...	Brevets délivrés
Somalia								**Somalie**
Grants of patents	7	...	...	...	...	...	...	Brevets délivrés

Patents *(continued)*
Resident filings (per million population), grants and patents in force

Brevets *(suite)*
Demandes émanant de résidents (par million d'habitants), délivrances et brevets en vigueur

Region, country or area	1985	1995	2005	2010	2013	2014	2015	Région, pays ou zone
South Africa								**Afrique du Sud**
Resident filings (per mil. pop.)	129	23	21	16	12	15	16	Dem. de rés. (par mil. d'hab.)
Grants of patents	6 768	5 113	1 831	5 331	4 756	5 065	4 499	Brevets délivrés
Patents in force	...	...	...	...	54 220	55 031	58 624	Brevets en vigueur
Spain								**Espagne**
Resident filings (per mil. pop.)	56	52	92	107	97	95	93	Dem. de rés. (par mil. d'hab.)
Grants of patents	9 115	686	2 769	2 773	3 004	3 235	2 561	Brevets délivrés
Patents in force	...	...	39 297	31 804	36 893	37 581	38 891	Brevets en vigueur
Sri Lanka								**Sri Lanka**
Resident filings (per mil. pop.)	2	4	8	11	16	...	10	Dem. de rés. (par mil. d'hab.)
Grants of patents	112	159	180	504	236	...	262	Brevets délivrés
Sudan								**Soudan**
Resident filings (per mil. pop.)	...	...	...	7	7	...	7	Dem. de rés. (par mil. d'hab.)
Grants of patents	...	...	174	125	216	8	196	Brevets délivrés
Patents in force	...	...	...	...	...	...	196	Brevets en vigueur
Swaziland								**Swaziland**
Grants of patents	30	...	...	...	...	2	2	Brevets délivrés
Patents in force	...	...	...	...	9	...	...	Brevets en vigueur
Sweden								**Suède**
Resident filings (per mil. pop.)	460	446	555	614	625	604	599	Dem. de rés. (par mil. d'hab.)
Grants of patents	5 681	1 541	1 911	1 380	685	588	889	Brevets délivrés
Patents in force	...	...	102 741	96 796	95 695	93 348	92 607	Brevets en vigueur
Switzerland								**Suisse**
Resident filings (per mil. pop.)	493	410	897	1 069	1 012	1 018	1 035	Dem. de rés. (par mil. d'hab.)
Grants of patents	6 421	1 303	...	741	534	677	687	Brevets délivrés
Patents in force	...	...	99 531	123 033	148 759	144 859	162 761	Brevets en vigueur
Syrian Arab Republic								**Rép. arabe syrienne**
Resident filings (per mil. pop.)	...	9	6	...	...	...	11	Dem. de rés. (par mil. d'hab.)
Grants of patents	...	71	72	...	...	...	14	Brevets délivrés
Tajikistan								**Tadjikistan**
Resident filings (per mil. pop.)	...	6	4	1	...	...	...	Dem. de rés. (par mil. d'hab.)
Grants of patents	...	47	...	3	2	...	...	Brevets délivrés
Patents in force	...	...	...	248	256	...	237	Brevets en vigueur
Thailand								**Thaïlande**
Resident filings (per mil. pop.)	1	2	14	18	23	15	...	Dem. de rés. (par mil. d'hab.)
Grants of patents	45	470	553	772	1 149	1 286	1 364	Brevets délivrés
Patents in force	...	...	...	10 201	11 211	11 623	...	Brevets en vigueur
TFYR of Macedonia								**ex-R.Y. de Macédoine**
Resident filings (per mil. pop.)	...	51	26	13	21	...	...	Dem. de rés. (par mil. d'hab.)
Grants of patents	...	163	373	406	378	...	...	Brevets délivrés
Trinidad and Tobago								**Trinité-et-Tobago**
Resident filings (per mil. pop.)	...	19	1	...	...	3	2	Dem. de rés. (par mil. d'hab.)
Grants of patents	...	87	...	...	34	39	33	Brevets délivrés
Tunisia								**Tunisie**
Resident filings (per mil. pop.)	2	3	6	11	10	13	16	Dem. de rés. (par mil. d'hab.)
Grants of patents	...	141	338	620	535	552	589	Brevets délivrés
Patents in force	...	...	...	...	3 685	...	...	Brevets en vigueur
Turkey								**Turquie**
Resident filings (per mil. pop.)	3	3	15	48	63	67	74	Dem. de rés. (par mil. d'hab.)
Grants of patents	385	763	823	...	1 211	1 276	1 723	Brevets délivrés
Patents in force	...	...	...	...	44 867	53 908	54 673	Brevets en vigueur
Uganda								**Ouganda**
Grants of patents	26	...	...	...	3	1	...	Brevets délivrés
Patents in force	...	...	...	...	30	26	...	Brevets en vigueur
Ukraine								**Ukraine**
Resident filings (per mil. pop.)	...	93	75	56	63	54	50	Dem. de rés. (par mil. d'hab.)
Grants of patents	...	1 350	3 719	3 874	3 635	3 319	3 014	Brevets délivrés
Patents in force	...	...	37 336	24 622	26 033	26 183	25 737	Brevets en vigueur
United Arab Emirates								**Émirats arabes unis**
Resident filings (per mil. pop.)	...	...	...	...	3	5	4	Dem. de rés. (par mil. d'hab.)
Grants of patents	...	...	...	...	63	110	177	Brevets délivrés
Patents in force	...	...	...	...	451	561	653	Brevets en vigueur
United Kingdom								**Royaume-Uni**
Resident filings (per mil. pop.)	348	321	372	333	305	308	306	Dem. de rés. (par mil. d'hab.)
Grants of patents	20 880	9 473	10 159	5 594	5 235	4 986	5 464	Brevets délivrés
Patents in force	...	...	377 259	412 519	449 863	491 933	458 422	Brevets en vigueur

29 Patents *(continued)*

Resident filings (per million population), grants and patents in force

Brevets *(suite)*

Demandes émanant de résidents (par million d'habitants), délivrances et brevets en vigueur

Region, country or area	1985	1995	2005	2010	2013	2014	2015	Région, pays ou zone
United Rep. of Tanzania								**Rép.-Unie de Tanzanie**
Grants of patents	30	...	3	1	3	4	1	Brevets délivrés
United States								**États-Unis**
Resident filings (per mil. pop.)	268	466	703	782	910	894	897	Dem. de rés. (par mil. d'hab.)
Grants of patents	71 661	101 419	143 806	219 614	277 835	300 678	298 407	Brevets délivrés
Patents in force	...	...	1 683 968	2 017 318	2 387 502	2 527 750	2 644 697	Brevets en vigueur
Uruguay								**Uruguay**
Resident filings (per mil. pop.)	21	11	7	7	...	11	8	Dem. de rés. (par mil. d'hab.)
Grants of patents	196	36	...	29	...	31	19	Brevets délivrés
Patents in force	...	...	...	877	...	646	606	Brevets en vigueur
Uzbekistan								**Ouzbékistan**
Resident filings (per mil. pop.)	...	46	10	13	10	11	9	Dem. de rés. (par mil. d'hab.)
Grants of patents	...	1 233	407	192	184	179	153	Brevets délivrés
Patents in force	...	...	1 263	1 253	1 155	1 141	1 081	Brevets en vigueur
Venezuela (Boliv. Rep. of)								**Venezuela (Rép. boliv. du)**
Resident filings (per mil. pop.)	13	...	...	...	...	...	...	Dem. de rés. (par mil. d'hab.)
Grants of patents	351	...	...	...	...	...	...	Brevets délivrés
Viet Nam								**Viet Nam**
Resident filings (per mil. pop.)	...	...	2	4	5	5	6	Dem. de rés. (par mil. d'hab.)
Grants of patents	...	56	668	822	1 182	1 397	1 388	Brevets délivrés
Patents in force	...	...	...	9 103	10 615	14 593	16 149	Brevets en vigueur
Yemen								**Yémen**
Resident filings (per mil. pop.)	...	...	1	1	2	1	...	Dem. de rés. (par mil. d'hab.)
Grants of patents	...	...	...	...	62	20	15	Brevets délivrés
Zambia								**Zambie**
Resident filings (per mil. pop.)	...	...	...	...	1	1	...	Dem. de rés. (par mil. d'hab.)
Grants of patents	74	43	14	12	21	23	...	Brevets délivrés
Patents in force	...	...	2 695	3 858	4 122	4 161	...	Brevets en vigueur
Zimbabwe								**Zimbabwe**
Resident filings (per mil. pop.)	4	5	...	...	...	...	1	Dem. de rés. (par mil. d'hab.)
Grants of patents	212	105	...	...	...	...	...	Brevets délivrés
OAPI [2]								**OAPI** [2]
Grants of patents	...	23	374	...	430	550	526	Brevets délivrés
ARIPO [3]								**ARIPO** [3]
Grants of patents	1	64	164	111	271	254	443	Brevets délivrés
Patents in force	...	...	...	...	2 291	2 550	2 964	Brevets en vigueur
EAPO [4]								**EAPO** [4]
Grants of patents	...	...	1 201	1 802	1 581	1 600	1 757	Brevets délivrés
EPO [5]								**OEB** [5]
Grants of patents	15 117	41 609	53 258	58 108	66 696	64 608	68 431	Brevets délivrés
GCC [6]								**CCG** [6]
Grants of patents	...	...	105	362	553	503	662	Brevets délivrés
Patents in force	...	...	...	...	2 510	...	3 242	Brevets en vigueur

Source:

World Intellectual Property Organization (WIPO), Geneva, WIPO statistics database, last accessed March 2017.

Source:

Organisation mondiale de la propriété intellectuelle (OMPI), Genève, la base de données statistiques de l'OMPI, dernier accès mars 2017.

1 For statistical purposes, the data for China do not include those for the Hong Kong Special Administrative Region (Hong Kong SAR) and Macao Special Administrative Region (Macao SAR).

2 Members of the African Intellectual Property Organization (OAPI), which includes Benin, Burkina Faso, Cameroon, Central African Republic, Chad, Congo, Côte d'Ivoire, Equatorial Guinea, Gabon, Guinea, Guinea-Bissau, Mali, Mauritania, Niger, Senegal and Togo.

3 Members of the African Regional Intellectual Property Organization (ARIPO), which includes Botswana, Gambia, Ghana, Kenya, Lesotho, Liberia, Malawi, Mozambique, Namibia, Rwanda, Sao Tome and Principe, Sierra Leone, Somalia, Sudan, Swaziland, Tanzania, Uganda, Zambia and Zimbabwe.

1 Pour la présentation des statistiques, les données pour la Chine ne comprennent pas la Région Administrative Spéciale de Hong Kong (Hong Kong RAS) et la Région Administrative Spéciale de Macao (Macao RAS).

2 Les membres de l'Organisation africaine de la propriété intellectuelle (OAPI) incluent: Bénin, Burkina Faso, Cameroun, Congo, Côte d'Ivoire, Gabon, Guinée, Guinée-Bissau, Guinée équatoriale, Mali, Mauritanie, Niger, République centrafricaine, Sénégal, Tchad et Togo.

3 Les membres de l'Organisation régionale africaine de la propriété intellectuelle (ARIPO) incluent: Botswana, Gambie, Ghana, Kenya, Lesotho, Libéria, Malawi, Mozambique, Namibie, Ouganda, Rwanda, Sao Tomé-et-Principe, Sierra Leone, Somalie, Soudan, Swaziland, Tanzanie, Zambie et Zimbabwe.

4 Members of the Eurasian Patent Organization (EAPO), which includes Armenia, Azerbaijan, Belarus, Kazakhstan, Kyrgyzstan, Moldova, the Russian Federation, Tajikistan and Turkmenistan.

5 Members of the European Patent Organisation (EPO), which includes Albania, Austria, Belgium, Bulgaria, Croatia, Cyprus, Czech Republic, Denmark, Estonia, Finland, France, Germany, Greece, Hungary, Iceland, Ireland, Italy, Latvia, Liechtenstein, Lithuania, Luxembourg, Malta, Monaco, Netherlands, Norway, Poland, Portugal, Romania, San Marino, Serbia, Slovenia, Slovakia, Spain, Sweden, Switzerland, the Former Yugoslav Republic of Macedonia, Turkey and the United Kingdom.

6 Members of the Gulf Cooperation Council (GCC) Patent Office, which includes Bahrain, Kuwait, Oman, Qatar, Saudi Arabia and the United Arab Emirates.

4 Les membres de l'Organisation eurasienne de la propriété intellectuelle (EAPO) incluent: Arménie, Azerbaïdjan, Bélarus, Fédération de Russie, Kazakhstan, Kirghizistan, Moldavie, Tadjikistan et Turkménistan.

5 Les membres de l'Organisation européenne des brevets (OEB) incluent: Albanie, Allemagne, Autriche, Belgique, Bulgarie, Chypre, Croatie, Danemark, Espagne, Estonie, Finlande, France, Grèce, Hongrie, Irlande, Islande, Italie, L'ex-République yougoslave de Macédoine, Lettonie, Liechtenstein, Lituanie, Luxembourg, Malte, Monaco, Norvège, Pays-Bas, Pologne, Portugal, République tchèque, Roumanie, Royaume-Uni, Saint-Marin, Serbie, Slovaquie, Slovénie, Suède, Suisse et Turquie.

6 Les États suivants sont membres de l'Organisation de la propriété intellectuelle pour la Conseil de coopération du Golfe (CCG) incluent: Bahreïn, Arabie saoudite, Émirats arabes unis, Koweït, Oman et Qatar.

30 Tourist/visitor arrivals and tourism expenditure

Thousands arrivals and millions of US dollars

Arrivées de touristes/visiteurs et dépenses touristiques

Milliers d'arrivées et millions de dollars É.-U.

Country or area of destination	Series[&] Série[&]	1995	2005	2010	2013	2014	2015	Pays ou zone de destination
Afghanistan								**Afghanistan**
Tourism expenditure		...	...	169	191	92	92	Dépenses touristiques
Albania								**Albanie**
Tourist/visitor arrivals [1]	TF	...	...	2 191	2 857	3 341	3 784	Arrivées de touristes/visiteurs [1]
Tourism expenditure		70	880	1 780	1 670	1 849	1 614	Dépenses touristiques
Algeria								**Algérie**
Tourist/visitor arrivals [2]	VF	520	1 443	2 070	2 733	2 301	1 710	Arrivées de touristes/visiteurs [2]
Tourism expenditure		...	477	324	326	348	357	Dépenses touristiques
American Samoa								**Samoa américaines**
Tourist/visitor arrivals	TF	34	25	23	21	22	20	Arrivées de touristes/visiteurs
Andorra								**Andorre**
Tourist/visitor arrivals	TF	...	2 418	# 1 808	2 328	2 363	2 670	Arrivées de touristes/visiteurs
Angola								**Angola**
Tourist/visitor arrivals	TF	9[3]	210	425	650	595	592	Arrivées de touristes/visiteurs
Tourism expenditure		27	103	726	1 241	1 597	1 171	Dépenses touristiques
Anguilla								**Anguilla**
Tourist/visitor arrivals [1]	TF	39	62	62	69	71	73	Arrivées de touristes/visiteurs [1]
Tourism expenditure [4]		50	86	99	123	128	128	Dépenses touristiques [4]
Antigua and Barbuda								**Antigua-et-Barbuda**
Tourist/visitor arrivals [1]	TF	220	245[5]	230[5]	243[5]	249[5]	250	Arrivées de touristes/visiteurs [1]
Tourism expenditure [4]		247	309	298	314	316	321	Dépenses touristiques [4]
Argentina								**Argentine**
Tourist/visitor arrivals	TF	2 289	3 823	5 325	# 5 246	5 931	5 736	Arrivées de touristes/visiteurs
Tourism expenditure		2 550	3 209	5 558	4 929	5 235	5 011	Dépenses touristiques
Armenia								**Arménie**
Tourist/visitor arrivals	TF	12	319	684	1 084	1 204	1 192	Arrivées de touristes/visiteurs
Tourism expenditure		14	243	694	905	994	956	Dépenses touristiques
Aruba								**Aruba**
Tourist/visitor arrivals	TF	619	733	824	979	1 072	1 225	Arrivées de touristes/visiteurs
Tourism expenditure		554	...	1 254	1 506	1 625	1 660	Dépenses touristiques
Australia								**Australie**
Tourist/visitor arrivals [6]	VF	3 726	5 499	5 790	6 382	6 868	7 444	Arrivées de touristes/visiteurs [6]
Tourism expenditure		11 915	19 719	31 064	33 576	34 115	31 409	Dépenses touristiques
Austria								**Autriche**
Tourist/visitor arrivals [7]	TCE	17 173	19 952	22 004	24 813	25 291	26 719	Arrivées de touristes/visiteurs [7]
Tourism expenditure [4]		13 435	16 243	18 758	20 220	20 907	18 273	Dépenses touristiques [4]
Azerbaijan								**Azerbaïdjan**
Tourist/visitor arrivals	TF	...	693	1 280	2 130	2 160	1 922	Arrivées de touristes/visiteurs
Tourism expenditure		87	100	792	2 618	2 713	2 535	Dépenses touristiques
Bahamas								**Bahamas**
Tourist/visitor arrivals	TF	1 598	1 608	1 370	1 366	1 427	1 484	Arrivées de touristes/visiteurs
Tourism expenditure		1 356	2 081	2 159	2 305	2 328	2 396	Dépenses touristiques
Bahrain								**Bahreïn**
Tourist/visitor arrivals	VF	2 311	6 313	11 952	9 163	10 452	11 621	Arrivées de touristes/visiteurs
Tourism expenditure		593	1 603	2 163	1 865	1 915	...	Dépenses touristiques
Bangladesh								**Bangladesh**
Tourist/visitor arrivals	TF	156	208	303	148	125	...	Arrivées de touristes/visiteurs
Tourism expenditure		...	82	104	131	154	148	Dépenses touristiques
Barbados								**Barbade**
Tourist/visitor arrivals	TF	442	548	532	509	521	592	Arrivées de touristes/visiteurs
Tourism expenditure		630	1 081	1 074	992	...	...	Dépenses touristiques
Belarus								**Bélarus**
Tourist/visitor arrivals [8]	TF	161	91	119	137	137	102	Arrivées de touristes/visiteurs [8]
Tourism expenditure		28	346	665	1 156	1 230	1 016	Dépenses touristiques
Belgium								**Belgique**
Tourist/visitor arrivals	TCE	5 560	6 747	7 186	7 684	7 887	# 8 355	Arrivées de touristes/visiteurs
Tourism expenditure		...	10 881	...	14 536	15 235	13 084	Dépenses touristiques
Belize								**Belize**
Tourist/visitor arrivals	TF	131	237	242	294	321	341	Arrivées de touristes/visiteurs
Tourism expenditure [4]		78	214	264	351	380	372	Dépenses touristiques [4]
Benin								**Bénin**
Tourist/visitor arrivals	TF	138	176	199	231	242	255	Arrivées de touristes/visiteurs
Tourism expenditure		...	108	149	193	153	160	Dépenses touristiques

30 Tourist/visitor arrivals and tourism expenditure *(continued)*

Thousands arrivals and millions of US dollars

Arrivées de touristes/visiteurs et dépenses touristiques *(suite)*

Milliers d'arrivées et millions de dollars É.-U.

Country or area of destination	Series& Série&	1995	2005	2010	2013	2014	2015	Pays ou zone de destination
Bermuda								**Bermudes**
Tourist/visitor arrivals [5]	TF	387	270	232	236	224	220	Arrivées de touristes/visiteurs [5]
Tourism expenditure		...	...	...	447	419	393	Dépenses touristiques
Bhutan								**Bhoutan**
Tourist/visitor arrivals	TF	5	14	# 41	116	133	155	Arrivées de touristes/visiteurs
Tourism expenditure		5	19	64	116	120	119	Dépenses touristiques
Bolivia (Plurinational State of)								**Bolivie (État plurinational de)**
Tourist/visitor arrivals	TF	284	524	679	798	871	882	Arrivées de touristes/visiteurs
Tourism expenditure		92	345	339	639	736	804	Dépenses touristiques
Bonaire								**Bonaire**
Tourist/visitor arrivals	TF	59	63	71	...	...	...	Arrivées de touristes/visiteurs
Tourism expenditure [4]		37	87	...	...	...	...	Dépenses touristiques [4]
Bosnia and Herzegovina								**Bosnie-Herzégovine**
Tourist/visitor arrivals	TCE	...	217	365	529	536	678	Arrivées de touristes/visiteurs
Tourism expenditure		...	557	662	752	755	702	Dépenses touristiques
Botswana								**Botswana**
Tourist/visitor arrivals	TF	521	1 474	1 973	1 544	1 966	1 528	Arrivées de touristes/visiteurs
Tourism expenditure		176	563	781	888	978	950	Dépenses touristiques
Brazil								**Brésil**
Tourist/visitor arrivals	TF	1 991	5 358	5 161	5 813	6 430	6 306	Arrivées de touristes/visiteurs
Tourism expenditure		1 085	4 168	5 522	6 784	7 405	6 254	Dépenses touristiques
British Virgin Islands								**Îles Vierges britanniques**
Tourist/visitor arrivals	TF	219	337	330	366	386	393	Arrivées de touristes/visiteurs
Tourism expenditure [9]		211	412	389	421	459	484	Dépenses touristiques [9]
Brunei Darussalam								**Brunéi Darussalam**
Tourist/visitor arrivals [5]	TF	...	126	214	225	201	218	Arrivées de touristes/visiteurs [5]
Tourism expenditure [4]		...	191	...	96	79	140	Dépenses touristiques [4]
Bulgaria								**Bulgarie**
Tourist/visitor arrivals	TF	3 466	4 837	6 047	6 898	7 311	7 099	Arrivées de touristes/visiteurs
Tourism expenditure		662	3 063	3 807	4 410	4 518	3 583	Dépenses touristiques
Burkina Faso								**Burkina Faso**
Tourist/visitor arrivals	THS	124	245	274	218	191	163	Arrivées de touristes/visiteurs
Tourism expenditure		...	46	105	200	183	...	Dépenses touristiques
Burundi								**Burundi**
Tourist/visitor arrivals [2]	TF	34	148	# 142	234	235	131	Arrivées de touristes/visiteurs [2]
Tourism expenditure		2	2	2	3	6	3	Dépenses touristiques
Cabo Verde								**Cabo Verde**
Tourist/visitor arrivals	TF	28[5]	198[10]	336[10]	503[10]	494[10]	520[10]	Arrivées de touristes/visiteurs
Tourism expenditure		29	177	387	483	453	396	Dépenses touristiques
Cambodia								**Cambodge**
Tourist/visitor arrivals	TF	220[5]	1 422[11]	2 508[11]	4 210[11]	4 503[11]	4 775[11]	Arrivées de touristes/visiteurs
Tourism expenditure		71	929	1 671	2 895	3 220	3 411	Dépenses touristiques
Cameroon								**Cameroun**
Tourist/visitor arrivals	VF	...	...	573	783	822	...	Arrivées de touristes/visiteurs
Tourism expenditure		75	229	171	607	630	476	Dépenses touristiques
Canada								**Canada**
Tourist/visitor arrivals	TF	16 932	18 771	16 219	16 059	16 537	17 971	Arrivées de touristes/visiteurs
Tourism expenditure		9 176	15 887	18 438	20 941	20 509	...	Dépenses touristiques
Cayman Islands								**Îles Caïmanes**
Tourist/visitor arrivals [5]	TF	361	168	288	345	383	385	Arrivées de touristes/visiteurs [5]
Tourism expenditure [9]		394	356	465	480	541	651	Dépenses touristiques [9]
Central African Rep.								**Rép. centrafricaine**
Tourist/visitor arrivals [12]	TF	26	12	54	84	96	121	Arrivées de touristes/visiteurs [12]
Tourism expenditure		4	7	14	16	...	...	Dépenses touristiques
Chad								**Tchad**
Tourist/visitor arrivals	TF	...	...	71	100	122	120	Arrivées de touristes/visiteurs
Tourism expenditure		43	...	...	...	...	...	Dépenses touristiques
Chile								**Chili**
Tourist/visitor arrivals	TF	1 540	2 027	2 801[2]	3 576[2]	3 674[2]	4 478[2]	Arrivées de touristes/visiteurs
Tourism expenditure		1 186	1 682	2 422	3 144	3 143	3 229	Dépenses touristiques
China [13]								**Chine [13]**
Tourist/visitor arrivals	TF	20 034	46 809	55 664	55 686	55 622	56 886	Arrivées de touristes/visiteurs
Tourism expenditure [4]		8 730	29 296	45 814	51 664	105 380	114 109	Dépenses touristiques [4]

30 Tourist/visitor arrivals and tourism expenditure *(continued)*

Thousands arrivals and millions of US dollars

Arrivées de touristes/visiteurs et dépenses touristiques *(suite)*

Milliers d'arrivées et millions de dollars É.-U.

Country or area of destination	Series& Série&	1995	2005	2010	2013	2014	2015	Pays ou zone de destination
China, Hong Kong SAR								**Chine, Hong Kong RAS**
Tourist/visitor arrivals	TF	...	14 773	20 085	25 661	27 770	26 686	Arrivées de touristes/visiteurs
Tourism expenditure		...	13 588	27 208	42 426	46 079	42 601	Dépenses touristiques
China, Macao SAR								**Chine, Macao RAS**
Tourist/visitor arrivals	TF	* 4 202	* 9 014	* 11 926[14]	* 14 268[14]	* 14 566[14]	* 14 308[14]	Arrivées de touristes/visiteurs
Tourism expenditure		3 233	7 181	22 688	43 665	43 289	31 997	Dépenses touristiques
Colombia								**Colombie**
Tourist/visitor arrivals	TF	1 399	# 933	1 405	2 288	2 565	2 978	Arrivées de touristes/visiteurs
Tourism expenditure		887	1 891	3 441	4 759	4 887	5 251	Dépenses touristiques
Comoros								**Comores**
Tourist/visitor arrivals	TF	23	26	15	22	23	24	Arrivées de touristes/visiteurs
Tourism expenditure		22	24	35	...	...	...	Dépenses touristiques
Congo								**Congo**
Tourist/visitor arrivals	TF	...	35	194[2]	343[2]	227[2]	...	Arrivées de touristes/visiteurs
Tourism expenditure [4]		14	40	63	* 38	...	...	Dépenses touristiques [4]
Cook Islands								**Îles Cook**
Tourist/visitor arrivals	TF	48	88	104	121	121	125	Arrivées de touristes/visiteurs
Tourism expenditure [9]		28	91	111	168	175	...	Dépenses touristiques [9]
Costa Rica								**Costa Rica**
Tourist/visitor arrivals	TF	785	1 679	2 100	2 428	2 527	2 660	Arrivées de touristes/visiteurs
Tourism expenditure		763	1 810	2 179	3 171	3 085	3 396	Dépenses touristiques
Côte d'Ivoire								**Côte d'Ivoire**
Tourist/visitor arrivals	VF	...	...	252	380	471	# 1 441	Arrivées de touristes/visiteurs
Tourism expenditure		103	93	213	191	...	...	Dépenses touristiques
Croatia								**Croatie**
Tourist/visitor arrivals	TCE	1 485	# 7 743[15]	9 111	10 948	11 623	12 683	Arrivées de touristes/visiteurs
Tourism expenditure		...	7 625	8 299	9 715	10 079	9 018	Dépenses touristiques
Cuba								**Cuba**
Tourist/visitor arrivals [5]	TF	742	2 261	2 507	2 829	2 970	3 491	Arrivées de touristes/visiteurs [5]
Tourism expenditure		1 100	2 591	2 396	2 608	2 546	2 819	Dépenses touristiques
Curaçao								**Curaçao**
Tourist/visitor arrivals [5]	TF	224	222	342	441	452	468	Arrivées de touristes/visiteurs [5]
Tourism expenditure		175	244	438	778	820	714	Dépenses touristiques
Cyprus								**Chypre**
Tourist/visitor arrivals	TF	2 100	2 470	2 173	2 405	2 441	2 659	Arrivées de touristes/visiteurs
Tourism expenditure		2 019	2 618	2 424	3 020	2 920	2 489	Dépenses touristiques
Czechia								**Tchéquie**
Tourist/visitor arrivals	TF	...	9 404	8 629	10 300	10 649	11 148	Arrivées de touristes/visiteurs
Tourism expenditure		...	5772	8068	7792	7614	6758	Dépenses touristiques
Dem. Rep. of the Congo								**Rép. dém. du Congo**
Tourist/visitor arrivals	TF	35	61	81[5]	191[16]	...	...	Arrivées de touristes/visiteurs
Tourism expenditure [4]		...	3	11	8[16]	45	~0	Dépenses touristiques [4]
Denmark								**Danemark**
Tourist/visitor arrivals	TCE	...	9 587	9 425	# 8 557	10 267	10 424	Arrivées de touristes/visiteurs
Tourism expenditure [4]		3 691	5 293	5 704	6 490	7 617	6 685	Dépenses touristiques [4]
Djibouti								**Djibouti**
Tourist/visitor arrivals	THS	21	30	51	63	...	...	Arrivées de touristes/visiteurs
Tourism expenditure [4]		5	7	18	22	25	31	Dépenses touristiques [4]
Dominica								**Dominique**
Tourist/visitor arrivals	TF	60	79	77	78	82	75	Arrivées de touristes/visiteurs
Tourism expenditure [4]		42	57	94	103	127	128	Dépenses touristiques [4]
Dominican Republic								**Rép. dominicaine**
Tourist/visitor arrivals [17]	TF	1 776[18]	3 691	4 125	4 690	5 141	5 600	Arrivées de touristes/visiteurs [17]
Tourism expenditure [4]		1 571	3 518	4 163	5 064	5 630	6 118	Dépenses touristiques [4]
Ecuador								**Équateur**
Tourist/visitor arrivals [1]	VF	440	860	1 047	1 364	1 557	1 543	Arrivées de touristes/visiteurs [1]
Tourism expenditure		315	488	786	1 251	1 487	1 557	Dépenses touristiques
Egypt								**Égypte**
Tourist/visitor arrivals	TF	2 871	8 244	14 051	9 174	9 628	9 139	Arrivées de touristes/visiteurs
Tourism expenditure		2 954	7 206	13 633	6 747	7 979	6 897	Dépenses touristiques
El Salvador								**El Salvador**
Tourist/visitor arrivals	TF	235	1 127	1 150	1 283	1 345	1 402	Arrivées de touristes/visiteurs
Tourism expenditure		152	656	646	1 054	1 285	1 203	Dépenses touristiques
Equatorial Guinea								**Guinée équatoriale**
Tourism expenditure		1	...	...	...	...	...	Dépenses touristiques

30 Tourist/visitor arrivals and tourism expenditure *(continued)*
Thousands arrivals and millions of US dollars

Arrivées de touristes/visiteurs et dépenses touristiques *(suite)*
Milliers d'arrivées et millions de dollars É.-U.

Country or area of destination	Series& Série&	1995	2005	2010	2013	2014	2015	Pays ou zone de destination
Eritrea								**Érythrée**
Tourist/visitor arrivals [2]	VF	315	83	84	...	...	...	Arrivées de touristes/visiteurs [2]
Tourism expenditure		58	66	...	...	...	...	Dépenses touristiques
Estonia								**Estonie**
Tourist/visitor arrivals	TF	530	# 1 917[19]	# 2 372[20]	2 873[20]	2 918[20]	2 989[20]	Arrivées de touristes/visiteurs
Tourism expenditure		452	1 229	...	2 022	2 231	1 891	Dépenses touristiques
Ethiopia								**Éthiopie**
Tourist/visitor arrivals	TF	103[21]	227[2,22]	468[2,22]	681[2,22]	770[2,22]	864[2,22]	Arrivées de touristes/visiteurs
Tourism expenditure		177	533	1 434	...	...	...	Dépenses touristiques
Fiji								**Fidji**
Tourist/visitor arrivals [1]	TF	318	545	632	658	693	755	Arrivées de touristes/visiteurs [1]
Tourism expenditure		369	722	825	966	1 034	1 037	Dépenses touristiques
Finland								**Finlande**
Tourist/visitor arrivals	TCE	1 779	# 2 080	2 319	2 797	2 731	2 622	Arrivées de touristes/visiteurs
Tourism expenditure [4]		1 640	2 180	3 040	4 048	3 679	2 560	Dépenses touristiques [4]
France								**France**
Tourist/visitor arrivals	TF	60 033	# 74 988	76 647	83 634	83 701	84 452	Arrivées de touristes/visiteurs
Tourism expenditure		31 295	52 139	56 187	66 049	66 803	54 003	Dépenses touristiques
French Guiana								**Guyane française**
Tourist/visitor arrivals	TF	...	95	189	180	185	199	Arrivées de touristes/visiteurs
Tourism expenditure		...	44	...	...	...	...	Dépenses touristiques
French Polynesia								**Polynésie française**
Tourist/visitor arrivals [1]	TF	172	208	154	164	181	184	Arrivées de touristes/visiteurs [1]
Tourism expenditure [4]		...	530	405	458	510	...	Dépenses touristiques [4]
Gabon								**Gabon**
Tourist/visitor arrivals [23]	TF	125	269	...	...	...	...	Arrivées de touristes/visiteurs [23]
Tourism expenditure		94	13	...	...	...	...	Dépenses touristiques
Gambia								**Gambie**
Tourist/visitor arrivals [24]	TF	45	108	91	171	156	135	Arrivées de touristes/visiteurs [24]
Tourism expenditure		...	59	80	103	127	138	Dépenses touristiques
Georgia								**Géorgie**
Tourist/visitor arrivals	TF	...	...	1 067	2 065	2 229	2 282	Arrivées de touristes/visiteurs
Tourism expenditure		...	287	737	1 916	1 972	2 117	Dépenses touristiques
Germany								**Allemagne**
Tourist/visitor arrivals	TCE	14 847	21 500	26 875	31 545	32 999	34 970	Arrivées de touristes/visiteurs
Tourism expenditure		24 052	40 531	49 128	55 318	55 939	47 393	Dépenses touristiques
Ghana								**Ghana**
Tourist/visitor arrivals [2]	TF	286	429	931	994	825	897	Arrivées de touristes/visiteurs [2]
Tourism expenditure		30	867	706	1 010	1 027	911	Dépenses touristiques
Greece								**Grèce**
Tourist/visitor arrivals	TF	10 130[25]	14 765	15 007	17 920	22 033	23 599	Arrivées de touristes/visiteurs
Tourism expenditure		4 182	13 453	13 858	17 436	19 481	17 260	Dépenses touristiques
Grenada								**Grenade**
Tourist/visitor arrivals	TF	108	99	110	113	134	141	Arrivées de touristes/visiteurs
Tourism expenditure [4]		76	71	112	121	139	147	Dépenses touristiques [4]
Guadeloupe								**Guadeloupe**
Tourist/visitor arrivals [26]	TF	640[27]	372	392	487[28]	486	512	Arrivées de touristes/visiteurs [26]
Tourism expenditure		458	306	510	671	...	614	Dépenses touristiques
Guam								**Guam**
Tourist/visitor arrivals	TF	1 362	1 228	1 197	1 334	1 343	1 409	Arrivées de touristes/visiteurs
Guatemala								**Guatemala**
Tourist/visitor arrivals	TF	...	...	1 119	1 224	1 371	1 473	Arrivées de touristes/visiteurs
Tourism expenditure [4]		213	791	1 378	1 479	1 564	1 580	Dépenses touristiques [4]
Guinea								**Guinée**
Tourist/visitor arrivals [29]	TF	...	45	12	56	33	35	Arrivées de touristes/visiteurs [29]
Tourism expenditure		1	...	2	...	...	...	Dépenses touristiques
Guinea-Bissau								**Guinée-Bissau**
Tourist/visitor arrivals [5]	TF	...	5	22	36	36	44	Arrivées de touristes/visiteurs [5]
Tourism expenditure [4]		...	2	13	17	...	...	Dépenses touristiques [4]
Guyana								**Guyana**
Tourist/visitor arrivals	TF	106	117[30]	152[30]	158[30]	206[30]	207[30]	Arrivées de touristes/visiteurs
Tourism expenditure [4]		33	35	80	77	79	65	Dépenses touristiques [4]
Haiti								**Haïti**
Tourist/visitor arrivals [5]	TF	145	112	255[2]	420[2]	465[2]	516[2]	Arrivées de touristes/visiteurs [5]
Tourism expenditure [4]		90	80	383	546	578	609	Dépenses touristiques [4]

30 Tourist/visitor arrivals and tourism expenditure *(continued)*
Thousands arrivals and millions of US dollars

Arrivées de touristes/visiteurs et dépenses touristiques *(suite)*
Milliers d'arrivées et millions de dollars É.-U.

Country or area of destination	Series& Série&	1995	2005	2010	2013	2014	2015	Pays ou zone de destination
Honduras								**Honduras**
Tourist/visitor arrivals	TF	271	673	863	863	868	880	Arrivées de touristes/visiteurs
Tourism expenditure		85	465	627	618	642	653	Dépenses touristiques
Hungary [31]								**Hongrie** [31]
Tourist/visitor arrivals	TF	...	9 979	9 510	10 624	12 140	14 316	Arrivées de touristes/visiteurs
Tourism expenditure		2 938	4 761	6 595	6 671	7 487	6 944	Dépenses touristiques
Iceland								**Islande**
Tourist/visitor arrivals	TF	190	374	489	807	998	1 289	Arrivées de touristes/visiteurs
Tourism expenditure [4]		186	413	562	1 078	1 375	1 618	Dépenses touristiques [4]
India								**Inde**
Tourist/visitor arrivals [1]	TF	2 124	3 919	5 776	6 968	7679	8027	Arrivées de touristes/visiteurs [1]
Tourism expenditure		...	7 659	...	19 042	20 756	21 472	Dépenses touristiques
Indonesia								**Indonésie**
Tourist/visitor arrivals	VF	4 324	5 002	7 003	8 802	9 435	10 407	Arrivées de touristes/visiteurs
Tourism expenditure		...	5 094	7 618	10 302	11 567	12 054	Dépenses touristiques
Iran (Islamic Rep. of)								**Iran (Rép. islamique d')**
Tourist/visitor arrivals	VF	568	...	2 938	4 769	4 967	5 237	Arrivées de touristes/visiteurs
Tourism expenditure		205	1 025	2 631	3 212	3 676	...	Dépenses touristiques
Iraq								**Iraq**
Tourist/visitor arrivals	VF	61	...	1 518	892	...	...	Arrivées de touristes/visiteurs
Tourism expenditure		...	186	1 736	2 188	2 504	4 076	Dépenses touristiques
Ireland								**Irlande**
Tourist/visitor arrivals [32]	TF	4 818	7 333	# 7 134	8 260	8 813	9 528	Arrivées de touristes/visiteurs [32]
Tourism expenditure		2 698	6 780	8 187	9 538	11 093	10 802	Dépenses touristiques
Israel								**Israël**
Tourist/visitor arrivals [1]	TF	2 215	1 903	2 803	2 962	2 927	2 799	Arrivées de touristes/visiteurs [1]
Tourism expenditure [33]		3 491	3 427	5 824	6 411	6 348	6 061	Dépenses touristiques [33]
Italy								**Italie**
Tourist/visitor arrivals [34]	TF	31 052	36 513	43 626	47 704	48 576	50 732	Arrivées de touristes/visiteurs [34]
Tourism expenditure [4]		28 731	35 319	38 438	43 829	45 547	39 420	Dépenses touristiques [4]
Jamaica								**Jamaïque**
Tourist/visitor arrivals [35]	TF	1 147	1 479	1 922	2 008	2 080	2 123	Arrivées de touristes/visiteurs [35]
Tourism expenditure [4]		1 069	1 545	2 001	2 074	2 255	2 401	Dépenses touristiques [4]
Japan								**Japon**
Tourist/visitor arrivals [36]	VF	3 345	6 728	8 611	10 364	13 413	19 737	Arrivées de touristes/visiteurs [36]
Tourism expenditure		4 894	15 554	15 356	16 865	20 790	27 285	Dépenses touristiques
Jordan								**Jordanie**
Tourist/visitor arrivals [2]	TF	1 075	2 987	4 207	3 945	3 990	3 761	Arrivées de touristes/visiteurs [2]
Tourism expenditure		973	1 759	4 390	5 145	5 518	4 997	Dépenses touristiques
Kazakhstan								**Kazakhstan**
Tourist/visitor arrivals	TF	...	3 143	2 991	4 926	4 560	...	Arrivées de touristes/visiteurs
Tourism expenditure		155	801	1 236	1 779	1 701	1 734	Dépenses touristiques
Kenya								**Kenya**
Tourist/visitor arrivals	TF	918	1 399	1 470	1 434	1 261	1 114	Arrivées de touristes/visiteurs
Tourism expenditure		785	969	1 620	1 829	1 833	...	Dépenses touristiques
Kiribati								**Kiribati**
Tourist/visitor arrivals [37]	TF	4	4	5	6	5	4	Arrivées de touristes/visiteurs [37]
Tourism expenditure		2	3	5	4	4	...	Dépenses touristiques
Kuwait								**Koweït**
Tourist/visitor arrivals	VF	1 443	3 474	5 208	6 217	6 528	6 941	Arrivées de touristes/visiteurs
Tourism expenditure		307	413	574	619	615	931	Dépenses touristiques
Kyrgyzstan								**Kirghizistan**
Tourist/visitor arrivals	VF	...	...	855	3 076	2 849	3 051	Arrivées de touristes/visiteurs
Tourism expenditure		...	94	212	585	468	481	Dépenses touristiques
Lao People's Dem. Rep.								**Rép. dém. pop. lao**
Tourist/visitor arrivals	TF	60	672	1 670	2 700	3 164	3 543	Arrivées de touristes/visiteurs
Tourism expenditure		52	143	385	613	642	680	Dépenses touristiques
Latvia								**Lettonie**
Tourist/visitor arrivals [38]	TF	539	1 116	1 373	1 536	1 843	2 024	Arrivées de touristes/visiteurs [38]
Tourism expenditure		37	446	...	1 190	1 244	1 133	Dépenses touristiques
Lebanon								**Liban**
Tourist/visitor arrivals [39]	TF	450	1 140	2 168	1 274	1 355	1 518	Arrivées de touristes/visiteurs [39]
Tourism expenditure		710	5 969	8 026	7 032	6 835	7 087	Dépenses touristiques

Tourist/visitor arrivals and tourism expenditure *(continued)*
Thousands arrivals and millions of US dollars

Arrivées de touristes/visiteurs et dépenses touristiques *(suite)*
Milliers d'arrivées et millions de dollars É.-U.

Country or area of destination	Series[&] Série[&]	1995	2005	2010	2013	2014	2015	Pays ou zone de destination
Lesotho								**Lesotho**
Tourist/visitor arrivals	VF	209	304	426	433	1 079	1 082	Arrivées de touristes/visiteurs
Tourism expenditure [4]		27	27	23	17	16	34	Dépenses touristiques [4]
Liberia [4]								**Libéria [4]**
Tourism expenditure		...	67	12	...	55	46	Dépenses touristiques
Libya								**Libye**
Tourist/visitor arrivals	THS	...	81	...	...	...	...	Arrivées de touristes/visiteurs
Tourism expenditure		4	301	170	...	...	...	Dépenses touristiques
Liechtenstein								**Liechtenstein**
Tourist/visitor arrivals	TCE	...	...	64	60[40]	61[40]	57[40]	Arrivées de touristes/visiteurs
Lithuania								**Lituanie**
Tourist/visitor arrivals	TF	650	2 000	1 507	2 012	2 063	2 071	Arrivées de touristes/visiteurs
Tourism expenditure [4]		77	920	958	1 374	1 383	1 153	Dépenses touristiques [4]
Luxembourg								**Luxembourg**
Tourist/visitor arrivals	TCE	768	913	805	945	1 038	1 090	Arrivées de touristes/visiteurs
Tourism expenditure		...	3 770	4 519	5 744	6 153	4 875	Dépenses touristiques
Madagascar								**Madagascar**
Tourist/visitor arrivals [41]	TF	75	277	196	196	222	244	Arrivées de touristes/visiteurs [41]
Tourism expenditure		106	190	319	578	...	...	Dépenses touristiques
Malawi								**Malawi**
Tourist/visitor arrivals [42]	TF	192	438	746	795	819	805	Arrivées de touristes/visiteurs [42]
Tourism expenditure		22	48	45	33	36	39	Dépenses touristiques
Malaysia								**Malaisie**
Tourist/visitor arrivals [43]	TF	7 469	16 431	24 577	25 715	27 437	25 721	Arrivées de touristes/visiteurs [43]
Tourism expenditure [4]		3 969	8 846	18 152	21 500	22 600	17 614	Dépenses touristiques [4]
Maldives								**Maldives**
Tourist/visitor arrivals [5]	TF	315	395	792	1 125	1 205	1 234	Arrivées de touristes/visiteurs [5]
Tourism expenditure		...	...	...	2 422	2 811	2 664	Dépenses touristiques
Mali								**Mali**
Tourist/visitor arrivals	TF	...	...	169	142	168	159	Arrivées de touristes/visiteurs
Tourism expenditure		26	149	208	178	214	...	Dépenses touristiques
Malta								**Malte**
Tourist/visitor arrivals	TF	1 116	1 171[44]	1 339[44]	1 582[44]	1 690[44]	1 791[44]	Arrivées de touristes/visiteurs
Tourism expenditure [4]		656	755	1 066	1 402	1 521	1 367	Dépenses touristiques [4]
Marshall Islands								**Îles Marshall**
Tourist/visitor arrivals [5]	TF	6	9[45]	5	...	5	6	Arrivées de touristes/visiteurs [5]
Tourism expenditure		3[46]	4	4	4	5	...	Dépenses touristiques
Martinique								**Martinique**
Tourist/visitor arrivals	TF	457	484	478	490	490	487	Arrivées de touristes/visiteurs
Tourism expenditure		384	280	472	484	483	340	Dépenses touristiques
Mauritania								**Mauritanie**
Tourism expenditure		...	...	...	50	42	31	Dépenses touristiques
Mauritius								**Maurice**
Tourist/visitor arrivals	TF	422	761	935	993	1 039	1 152	Arrivées de touristes/visiteurs
Tourism expenditure		616	1 189	1 585	1 593	1 719	1 679	Dépenses touristiques
Mexico								**Mexique**
Tourist/visitor arrivals [2]	TF	20 241	21 915	23 290	24 151	29 346	32 093	Arrivées de touristes/visiteurs [2]
Tourism expenditure		6 847	12 801	12 628	14 311	16 607	18 451	Dépenses touristiques
Micronesia (Fed. States of)								**Micronésie (États féd. de)**
Tourist/visitor arrivals [47]	TF	...	19	45	42	35	30	Arrivées de touristes/visiteurs [47]
Tourism expenditure [4]		...	...	24	24	25	...	Dépenses touristiques [4]
Monaco								**Monaco**
Tourist/visitor arrivals	THS	233	286	279	328	329	331	Arrivées de touristes/visiteurs
Mongolia								**Mongolie**
Tourist/visitor arrivals [48]	TF	108	338	456	418	393	386	Arrivées de touristes/visiteurs [48]
Tourism expenditure		33	203	288	236	257	279	Dépenses touristiques
Montenegro								**Monténégro**
Tourist/visitor arrivals	TCE	...	272	1 088	1 324	1 350	1 560	Arrivées de touristes/visiteurs
Tourism expenditure		...	...	765	929	959	947	Dépenses touristiques
Montserrat								**Montserrat**
Tourist/visitor arrivals	TF	18	10	6	7	9	9	Arrivées de touristes/visiteurs
Tourism expenditure [4]		17	9	6	8	8	...	Dépenses touristiques [4]
Morocco								**Maroc**
Tourist/visitor arrivals [2]	TF	2 602	5 843	9 288	10 046	10 283	10 177	Arrivées de touristes/visiteurs [2]
Tourism expenditure		1 469	5 426	8 176	8 201	8 747	7 765	Dépenses touristiques

30 Tourist/visitor arrivals and tourism expenditure *(continued)*

Thousands arrivals and millions of US dollars

Arrivées de touristes/visiteurs et dépenses touristiques *(suite)*

Milliers d'arrivées et millions de dollars É.-U.

Country or area of destination	Series[&] Série[&]	1995	2005	2010	2013	2014	2015	Pays ou zone de destination
Mozambique								**Mozambique**
Tourist/visitor arrivals	TF	...	578	# 1 718[49]	1 886[49]	1 661[49]	1 552[49]	Arrivées de touristes/visiteurs
Tourism expenditure		...	138	135	228	225	202	Dépenses touristiques
Myanmar								**Myanmar**
Tourist/visitor arrivals	TF	194	660	792	2 044	3 081	4 681	Arrivées de touristes/visiteurs
Tourism expenditure		169	83	91	964	1 687	2 266	Dépenses touristiques
Namibia								**Namibie**
Tourist/visitor arrivals	TF	272	778	984	1 176	1 320	1 388	Arrivées de touristes/visiteurs
Tourism expenditure		...	363	560	524	522	472	Dépenses touristiques
Nepal								**Népal**
Tourist/visitor arrivals [50]	TF	363	375	603	798	790	539	Arrivées de touristes/visiteurs [50]
Tourism expenditure		232	160	378	460	511	509	Dépenses touristiques
Netherlands								**Pays-Bas**
Tourist/visitor arrivals	TCE	6 574	10 012	10 883	12 783	13 925	15 007	Arrivées de touristes/visiteurs
Tourism expenditure [4]		10 611	...	...	20 910	18 632	19 320	Dépenses touristiques [4]
New Caledonia								**Nouvelle-Calédonie**
Tourist/visitor arrivals [2]	TF	86	101	99	108	107	114	Arrivées de touristes/visiteurs [2]
Tourism expenditure [4]		108	149	129	168	184	...	Dépenses touristiques [4]
New Zealand								**Nouvelle-Zélande**
Tourist/visitor arrivals	TF	...	2 353	2 435	2 629	2 772	3 039	Arrivées de touristes/visiteurs
Tourism expenditure [4]		2 318	6 486	6 523	7 419	8 402	9 410	Dépenses touristiques [4]
Nicaragua								**Nicaragua**
Tourist/visitor arrivals	TF	281	712[2]	1 011[2]	1 229[2]	1 330[2]	1 386[2]	Arrivées de touristes/visiteurs
Tourism expenditure [4]		50	206	313	417	445	529	Dépenses touristiques [4]
Niger								**Niger**
Tourist/visitor arrivals	TF	35	58	74	123	135	135	Arrivées de touristes/visiteurs
Tourism expenditure		...	44	106	59	...	...	Dépenses touristiques
Nigeria								**Nigéria**
Tourist/visitor arrivals	TF	656	1 010	1 555	600	...	1 255	Arrivées de touristes/visiteurs
Tourism expenditure		47	139	736	616	601	470	Dépenses touristiques
Niue								**Nioué**
Tourist/visitor arrivals [51]	TF	2	3	6	7	7	8	Arrivées de touristes/visiteurs [51]
Tourism expenditure		2	1	2	...	...	...	Dépenses touristiques
Northern Mariana Islands								**Îles Mariannes du Nord**
Tourist/visitor arrivals	VF	676[5]	507[5]	379[5]	439	460	479	Arrivées de touristes/visiteurs
Tourism expenditure		655	...	...	...	...	...	Dépenses touristiques
Norway								**Norvège**
Tourist/visitor arrivals	TF	2 880[52]	3 824	4 767[53]	4 778[27]	4 855[27]	5 361[27]	Arrivées de touristes/visiteurs
Tourism expenditure		2 730	4 243	5 299	7 175	7 503	6 385	Dépenses touristiques
Oman								**Oman**
Tourist/visitor arrivals	TF	...	891	1 441	1 392	1 611	1 897	Arrivées de touristes/visiteurs
Tourism expenditure		...	627	1 072	1 888	1 972	2 247	Dépenses touristiques
Other non-specified areas								**Autres zones non-spécifiées**
Tourist/visitor arrivals [2]	VF	2 332	3 378	5 567	8 016	9 910	10 440	Arrivées de touristes/visiteurs [2]
Tourism expenditure		3 985	5 740	10 387	14 782	17 419	17 006	Dépenses touristiques
Pakistan								**Pakistan**
Tourist/visitor arrivals	TF	378	798	907	...	...	...	Arrivées de touristes/visiteurs
Tourism expenditure		582	828	998	938	971	906	Dépenses touristiques
Palau								**Palaos**
Tourist/visitor arrivals [54]	TF	53	81	85	108	140	162	Arrivées de touristes/visiteurs [54]
Tourism expenditure [55]		...	63	76	117	131	156	Dépenses touristiques [55]
Panama								**Panama**
Tourist/visitor arrivals	TF	345	702	1 324	1 658	1 745	2 110	Arrivées de touristes/visiteurs
Tourism expenditure		372	1 108	2 621	5 379	5 750	5 947	Dépenses touristiques
Papua New Guinea								**Papouasie-Nvl-Guinée**
Tourist/visitor arrivals	TF	42	69	140	174	182	184	Arrivées de touristes/visiteurs
Tourism expenditure		...	9	2	4	3	...	Dépenses touristiques
Paraguay								**Paraguay**
Tourist/visitor arrivals [6]	TF	438	341[56]	465[56]	610[56]	649[56]	1 214[56]	Arrivées de touristes/visiteurs [6]
Tourism expenditure		162	96	243	299	314	347	Dépenses touristiques
Peru								**Pérou**
Tourist/visitor arrivals	TF	479	# 1 571[2,57]	2 299[2,57]	3 164[2,57]	3 215[2,57]	* 3 456[2,57]	Arrivées de touristes/visiteurs
Tourism expenditure		521	1 438	2 475	3 925	3 907	4 151	Dépenses touristiques

Country or area of destination	Series& Série&	1995	2005	2010	2013	2014	2015	Pays ou zone de destination
Philippines								**Philippines**
Tourist/visitor arrivals [2]	TF	1 760	2 623	3 520	4 681	4 833	5 361	Arrivées de touristes/visiteurs [2]
Tourism expenditure		1 141	2 863	3 441	5 599	6 059	6 418	Dépenses touristiques
Poland								**Pologne**
Tourist/visitor arrivals	TF	19 215	15 200	12 470	15 800	16 000	16 722	Arrivées de touristes/visiteurs
Tourism expenditure		6 927	7 161	10 037	12 432	12 924	11 354	Dépenses touristiques
Portugal								**Portugal**
Tourist/visitor arrivals	TCE	4 572	5 769	6 756	8 097	9 092	9 957	Arrivées de touristes/visiteurs
Tourism expenditure		5 646	9 042	12 985	16 210	17 723	15 819	Dépenses touristiques
Puerto Rico								**Porto Rico**
Tourist/visitor arrivals [41]	TF	3 131	3 686	3 186	3 172	3 246	3 542	Arrivées de touristes/visiteurs [41]
Tourism expenditure [58]		1 828	3 239	3 211	3 311	3 439	3 825	Dépenses touristiques [58]
Qatar [59]								**Qatar** [59]
Tourist/visitor arrivals	TF	...	...	...	2 611	2 826	2 930	Arrivées de touristes/visiteurs
Tourism expenditure		...	...	...	8 452	10 576	12 131	Dépenses touristiques
Republic of Korea								**République de Corée**
Tourist/visitor arrivals [60]	VF	3 753	6 023	8 798	12 176	14 202	13 232	Arrivées de touristes/visiteurs [60]
Tourism expenditure		6 670	8 290	14 367	19 644	22 704	19 126	Dépenses touristiques
Republic of Moldova								**République de Moldova**
Tourist/visitor arrivals [61,62]	TCE	...	67	64	96	94	94	Arrivées de touristes/visiteurs [61,62]
Tourism expenditure		71	138	222	318	313	291	Dépenses touristiques
Réunion								**Réunion**
Tourist/visitor arrivals	TF	304	409	420	416	406	426	Arrivées de touristes/visiteurs
Tourism expenditure		216	384	392	403	387	339	Dépenses touristiques
Romania								**Roumanie**
Tourist/visitor arrivals	VF	5 445	5 839	7 498	8 019	8 442	9 331	Arrivées de touristes/visiteurs
Tourism expenditure		689	1 324	1 631	2 048	2 225	2 097	Dépenses touristiques
Russian Federation								**Fédération de Russie**
Tourist/visitor arrivals	VF	10 290	22 201	22 281	30 792	32 421	33 729	Arrivées de touristes/visiteurs
Tourism expenditure		...	7 805	13 239	20 198	19 451	13 249	Dépenses touristiques
Rwanda								**Rwanda**
Tourist/visitor arrivals	TF	...	...	504	864	926	987	Arrivées de touristes/visiteurs
Tourism expenditure		4	67	224	351	...	407	Dépenses touristiques
Saba								**Saba**
Tourist/visitor arrivals	TF	10	12	12	...	...	...	Arrivées de touristes/visiteurs
Saint Kitts and Nevis								**Saint-Kitts-et-Nevis**
Tourist/visitor arrivals [41]	TF	79	141	98	107	113	122	Arrivées de touristes/visiteurs [41]
Tourism expenditure [4]		63	121	90	117	126	134	Dépenses touristiques [4]
Saint Lucia								**Sainte-Lucie**
Tourist/visitor arrivals [1]	TF	231	318	306	319	338	345	Arrivées de touristes/visiteurs [1]
Tourism expenditure [4]		230	382	309	354	390	397	Dépenses touristiques [4]
Saint Vincent-Grenadines								**Saint-Vincent-Grenadines**
Tourist/visitor arrivals [41]	TF	60	96	72	72	71	75	Arrivées de touristes/visiteurs [41]
Tourism expenditure [4]		53	104	86	92	93	96	Dépenses touristiques [4]
Samoa								**Samoa**
Tourist/visitor arrivals	TF	68	102	122	116	120	128	Arrivées de touristes/visiteurs
Tourism expenditure		36	74	124	137	147	165	Dépenses touristiques
San Marino [63]								**Saint-Marin** [63]
Tourist/visitor arrivals	THS	28	50	120	71	75	54	Arrivées de touristes/visiteurs
Sao Tome and Principe								**Sao Tomé-et-Principe**
Tourist/visitor arrivals	TF	6	16	8	...	...	...	Arrivées de touristes/visiteurs
Tourism expenditure		...	...	...	31	56	63	Dépenses touristiques
Saudi Arabia								**Arabie saoudite**
Tourist/visitor arrivals	TF	3 325	8 037	10 850	15 772	18 260	17 994	Arrivées de touristes/visiteurs
Tourism expenditure		...	...	7 536	8 690	9 263	11 183	Dépenses touristiques
Senegal								**Sénégal**
Tourist/visitor arrivals	TF	...	769	* 900	* 1 063	* 963	* 1 007	Arrivées de touristes/visiteurs
Tourism expenditure		168	334	464	495	481	...	Dépenses touristiques
Serbia								**Serbie**
Tourist/visitor arrivals	TCE	...	453	683	922	1 029	1 132	Arrivées de touristes/visiteurs
Tourism expenditure		...	308	950	1 221	1 352	1 322	Dépenses touristiques
Seychelles								**Seychelles**
Tourist/visitor arrivals	TF	121	129	175	230	233	276	Arrivées de touristes/visiteurs
Tourism expenditure		224	269	352	484	480	483	Dépenses touristiques

Country or area of destination	Series& Série&	1995	2005	2010	2013	2014	2015	Pays ou zone de destination
Sierra Leone								**Sierra Leone**
Tourist/visitor arrivals [5]	TF	14	40	39	81	44	24	Arrivées de touristes/visiteurs [5]
Tourism expenditure [4]		57	64	26	66	35	23	Dépenses touristiques [4]
Singapore								**Singapour**
Tourist/visitor arrivals	TF	6 070	7 079	9 161	11 899	11 864	12 051	Arrivées de touristes/visiteurs
Tourism expenditure [4]		7 611	6 209	14 178	19 209	19 134	16 743	Dépenses touristiques [4]
Sint Eustatius [64]								**Saint-Eustache [64]**
Tourist/visitor arrivals	TF	9	10	11	…	…	…	Arrivées de touristes/visiteurs
Sint Maarten (Dutch part)								**Saint-Martin (partie néerlandaise)**
Tourist/visitor arrivals [65]	TF	460	468	443	467	500	505	Arrivées de touristes/visiteurs [65]
Tourism expenditure		…	…	681	871	922	951	Dépenses touristiques
Slovakia								**Slovaquie**
Tourist/visitor arrivals	TCE	903	# 1 515	1 327	1 670	1 475	1 721	Arrivées de touristes/visiteurs
Tourism expenditure		630	1 282	2 335	2 633	2 619	2 411	Dépenses touristiques
Slovenia								**Slovénie**
Tourist/visitor arrivals	TCE	732	1 555	1 869	2 259	2 411	2 707	Arrivées de touristes/visiteurs
Tourism expenditure		1 128	1 894	2 721	2 900	2 944	2 697	Dépenses touristiques
Solomon Islands								**Îles Salomon**
Tourist/visitor arrivals	TF	12	9[66]	21	24	20	22	Arrivées de touristes/visiteurs
Tourism expenditure		17	6	51	71	64	56	Dépenses touristiques
South Africa								**Afrique du Sud**
Tourist/visitor arrivals	TF	4 488[67]	7 369[67]	# 8 074	9 537	# 9 549	8 904	Arrivées de touristes/visiteurs
Tourism expenditure		2 654	8 629	10 309	10 468	10 484	9 140	Dépenses touristiques
Spain								**Espagne**
Tourist/visitor arrivals	TF	32 971	# 55 914	52 677	60 675	64 939	68 215	Arrivées de touristes/visiteurs
Tourism expenditure [4]		25 368	49 565	54 305	62 584	65 100	56 426	Dépenses touristiques [4]
Sri Lanka								**Sri Lanka**
Tourist/visitor arrivals [36]	TF	403	549	654	1 275	1 527	1 798	Arrivées de touristes/visiteurs [36]
Tourism expenditure		367	729	1 044	2 506	3 278	3 978	Dépenses touristiques
State of Palestine								**État de Palestine**
Tourist/visitor arrivals	THS	…	88[68]	522[68]	545[69]	556[69]	432[69]	Arrivées de touristes/visiteurs
Tourism expenditure [4]		255	52	409	524	543	452	Dépenses touristiques [4]
Sudan								**Soudan**
Tourist/visitor arrivals [2]	TF	29	246	495	591	684	741	Arrivées de touristes/visiteurs [2]
Tourism expenditure [4]		8	114	82	773	967	949	Dépenses touristiques [4]
Suriname								**Suriname**
Tourist/visitor arrivals	TF	43[70]	161	205	249	252	228	Arrivées de touristes/visiteurs
Tourism expenditure		52	96	69	92	103	99	Dépenses touristiques
Swaziland								**Swaziland**
Tourist/visitor arrivals	TF	300[59]	837	868	968	939	873	Arrivées de touristes/visiteurs
Tourism expenditure		54	77	51	13	16	14	Dépenses touristiques
Sweden								**Suède**
Tourist/visitor arrivals	TF	…	…	…	18 803	19 945	…	Arrivées de touristes/visiteurs
Tourism expenditure [4]		3 471[71]	6 554	8 336	10 857	11 846	11 307	Dépenses touristiques [4]
Switzerland								**Suisse**
Tourist/visitor arrivals [72]	THS	6 946	7 229	8 628	8 967	9 158	9 305	Arrivées de touristes/visiteurs [72]
Tourism expenditure		11 354	11 949	17 617	20 321	21 417	19 588	Dépenses touristiques
Syrian Arab Republic								**Rép. arabe syrienne**
Tourist/visitor arrivals	TCE	815[2]	3 571	8 546[2,73]	…	…	…	Arrivées de touristes/visiteurs
Tourism expenditure		…	2 035	6 308	…	…	…	Dépenses touristiques
Tajikistan								**Tadjikistan**
Tourist/visitor arrivals	VF	…	…	160	208	213	414	Arrivées de touristes/visiteurs
Tourism expenditure		…	9	32	49	220	146	Dépenses touristiques
Thailand								**Thaïlande**
Tourist/visitor arrivals	TF	6 952[2]	11 567[2]	15 936	26 547	24 810	29 923	Arrivées de touristes/visiteurs
Tourism expenditure		9 257	12 102	23 796	45 738	42 047	48 527	Dépenses touristiques
TFYR of Macedonia								**ex-R.Y. de Macédoine**
Tourist/visitor arrivals	TCE	147	197	262	400	425	486	Arrivées de touristes/visiteurs
Tourism expenditure		…	116	199	270	298	270	Dépenses touristiques
Timor-Leste								**Timor-Leste**
Tourist/visitor arrivals [74]	TF	…	…	40	79	60	62	Arrivées de touristes/visiteurs [74]
Tourism expenditure [4]		…	…	24	29	35	51	Dépenses touristiques [4]
Togo								**Togo**
Tourist/visitor arrivals	THS	53	81	202	327	282	273	Arrivées de touristes/visiteurs
Tourism expenditure		…	27	105	233	233	212	Dépenses touristiques

Country or area of destination	Series& Série&	1995	2005	2010	2013	2014	2015	Pays ou zone de destination
Tonga								**Tonga**
Tourist/visitor arrivals [5]	TF	29	42	47	48	50	54	Arrivées de touristes/visiteurs [5]
Tourism expenditure		...	15	28	48	...	...	Dépenses touristiques
Trinidad and Tobago								**Trinité-et-Tobago**
Tourist/visitor arrivals [5]	TF	260	463	388	434	412	440	Arrivées de touristes/visiteurs [5]
Tourism expenditure		232	593	630	...	...	...	Dépenses touristiques
Tunisia								**Tunisie**
Tourist/visitor arrivals	TF	4 120[1]	6 378[1]	7 828	7 352	7 163	5 359	Arrivées de touristes/visiteurs
Tourism expenditure		1 838	2 800	3 477	2 863	3 042	1 869	Dépenses touristiques
Turkey								**Turquie**
Tourist/visitor arrivals	TF	7 083	20 273[75]	31 364[75]	37 795[75]	39 811[75]	39 478[75]	Arrivées de touristes/visiteurs
Tourism expenditure [76]		...	20 760	26 318	36 192	38 766	35 413	Dépenses touristiques [76]
Turkmenistan								**Turkménistan**
Tourist/visitor arrivals	TF	218	12	...	...	...	...	Arrivées de touristes/visiteurs
Turks and Caicos Islands								**Îles Turques-et-Caïques**
Tourist/visitor arrivals	TF	79	176	281	291	357	386	Arrivées de touristes/visiteurs
Tourism expenditure		53	...	...	...	...	...	Dépenses touristiques
Tuvalu								**Tuvalu**
Tourist/visitor arrivals	TF	1	1	2	1	1	2	Arrivées de touristes/visiteurs
Tourism expenditure [4]		...	1	2	2	...	...	Dépenses touristiques [4]
Uganda								**Ouganda**
Tourist/visitor arrivals	TF	160	468	946	1 206	1 266	1 303	Arrivées de touristes/visiteurs
Tourism expenditure		...	382	802	1 355	810	1 171	Dépenses touristiques
Ukraine								**Ukraine**
Tourist/visitor arrivals	TF	3 716	17 631	21 203	24 671	12 712	12 428	Arrivées de touristes/visiteurs
Tourism expenditure		...	3 542	4 696	5 931	2 264	1 656	Dépenses touristiques
United Arab Emirates								**Émirats arabes unis**
Tourist/visitor arrivals [77]	THS	2 315	7 126	...	...	...	...	Arrivées de touristes/visiteurs [77]
Tourism expenditure		632[78,79]	3 218	8 577	12 389	13 969	...	Dépenses touristiques
United Kingdom								**Royaume-Uni**
Tourist/visitor arrivals	TF	21 719	28 039	28 295	31 063	32 613	34 436	Arrivées de touristes/visiteurs
Tourism expenditure		27 577	39 684	40 138	53 052	58 935	60 744	Dépenses touristiques
United Rep. of Tanzania								**Rép.-Unie de Tanzanie**
Tourist/visitor arrivals	TF	285	590	754	1 063	1 113	1 104	Arrivées de touristes/visiteurs
Tourism expenditure		...	835	1 279	1 939	2 047	2 253	Dépenses touristiques
United States								**États-Unis**
Tourist/visitor arrivals	TF	43 318	49 206	60 010	69 995	# 75 022	77 510	Arrivées de touristes/visiteurs
Tourism expenditure		93 743	122 077	167 996	218 496	235 396	246 229	Dépenses touristiques
United States Virgin Is.								**Îles Vierges américaines**
Tourist/visitor arrivals	TF	454	594	572	590	615	637	Arrivées de touristes/visiteurs
Tourism expenditure		822	1 432	1 223	1 168	1 319	1 324	Dépenses touristiques
Uruguay								**Uruguay**
Tourist/visitor arrivals	TF	2 022	1 808	2 353	2 683	2 682	2 773	Arrivées de touristes/visiteurs
Tourism expenditure		725	699	1 669	2 015	1 869	1 880	Dépenses touristiques
Uzbekistan								**Ouzbékistan**
Tourist/visitor arrivals	TF	92	242	975	1 969	...	...	Arrivées de touristes/visiteurs
Tourism expenditure [4]		...	28	121	...	...	...	Dépenses touristiques [4]
Vanuatu								**Vanuatu**
Tourist/visitor arrivals	TF	44	62	97	110	109	90	Arrivées de touristes/visiteurs
Tourism expenditure		...	104	242	314	284	254	Dépenses touristiques
Venezuela (Boliv. Rep. of)								**Venezuela (Rép. boliv. du)**
Tourist/visitor arrivals	TF	700	706	526	986	857	789	Arrivées de touristes/visiteurs
Tourism expenditure		995	722	885	926	707	654	Dépenses touristiques
Viet Nam								**Viet Nam**
Tourist/visitor arrivals	VF	1 351	3 477	5 050	7 572	7 874	7 944	Arrivées de touristes/visiteurs
Tourism expenditure		...	2 300	4 450	7 250	7 410	7 350	Dépenses touristiques
Yemen								**Yémen**
Tourist/visitor arrivals	TF	61	336	1 025[2]	990[2]	1 018[2]	367[2]	Arrivées de touristes/visiteurs
Tourism expenditure		...	...	1 291	1 097	1 199	116	Dépenses touristiques
Zambia								**Zambie**
Tourist/visitor arrivals	TF	163	669	815	915	947	932	Arrivées de touristes/visiteurs
Tourism expenditure [4]		...	447	492	552	642	660	Dépenses touristiques [4]
Zimbabwe								**Zimbabwe**
Tourist/visitor arrivals	VF	1 416	1 559	2 239	1 833	1 880	2 057	Arrivées de touristes/visiteurs
Tourism expenditure		145	99	135	183	186	191	Dépenses touristiques

Source:

World Tourism Organization (WTO), Madrid, the WTO Statistics Database, last accessed December 2016.

The majority of the expenditure data have been provided to the WTO by the International Monetary Fund (IMF). & Series (by order of priority, see Annex II): TF: Arrivals of non-resident tourists at national borders. VF: Arrivals of non-resident visitors at national borders. TCE: Arrivals of non-resident tourists in all types of accommodation establishments. THS: Arrivals of non-resident tourists in hotels and similar establishments.

1 Excluding nationals residing abroad.
2 Including nationals residing abroad.
3 Country data.
4 Excluding passenger transport.
5 Arrivals by air.
6 Excluding nationals residing abroad and crew members.
7 Including leisure and business trips abroad with at least one overnight stay.
8 Package tour only.
9 Fiscal years (October 1 to September 30).
10 Arrivals of non-resident tourists in hotels and similar establishments.
11 Arrivals by all means of transport.
12 Arrivals by air to Bangui only.
13 For statistical purposes, the data for China do not include those for the Hong Kong Special Administrative Region (Hong Kong SAR), Macao Special Administrative Region (Macao SAR) and Taiwan Province of China.
14 Does not include other non-residents namely workers, students, etc.
15 Data from 2005 to 2009 were revised so they can be comparable to 2010 (nautical ports were excluded).
16 The arrivals data relate only to three border posts (N'Djili airport in Kinshasa, the Luano airport in Lubumbashi, and the land border-crossing of Kasumbalesa in Katanga province).
17 Arrivals by air only; including nationals residing abroad.
18 Excluding the passengers at Herrera airport.
19 Calculated on the basis of accommodation statistics and "Foreign Visitor Survey" carried out by the Statistical Office of Estonia. Starting from 2004, border statistics are not collected any more.
20 Based on mobile positioning data by the Bank of Estonia and Positium LBS.
21 Arrivals to Bole airport only.
22 Arrivals through all ports of entry.
23 Arrivals of non-resident tourists at Libreville airport.
24 Charter tourists only.
25 Information based on administrative data.
26 Arrivals by air. Excluding the north islands (Saint Martin and Saint Barthelemy).
27 Non-resident tourists staying in all types of accommodation establishments.
28 Including residents and non-residents.
29 Arrivals by air at Conakry airport.
30 Arrivals to Timehri airport only.
31 New series.
32 Including tourists from Northern Ireland.

Source:

Organisation mondiale du tourisme (OMT), Madrid, la base de données de l'OMT, dernier accés decembre 2016.

La majorité des données sur les dépenses touristiques sont celles que le Fonds monétaire international (FMI) a fournies à l'Organisation mondiale du tourisme (OMT). & Série (par ordre de priorite, voir annexe II): TF: Arrivées de touristes non résidents aux frontières nationales. VF: Arrivées de visiteurs non résidents aux frontières nationales. TCE: Arrivées de touristes non résidents dans tous les types d'établissements d'hébergement touristique. THS: Arrivées de touristes non résidents dans les hôtels et établissements assimilés.

1 A l'exclusion des nationaux résidant à l'étranger.
2 Y compris les nationaux du pays résidant à l'étranger.
3 Données du pays.
4 Non compris le transport de passagers.
5 Arrivées par voie aérienne
6 A l'exclusion des nationaux du pays résidant à l'étranger et des membres des équipages.
7 Y compris les voyages de détente et les voyages d'affaires à l'étranger comportant au moins une nuitée.
8 Tourisme organisé.
9 Années fiscales (du 1er octobre au 30 septembre).
10 Arrivées de touristes non-résidents dans les hôtels et établissements similaires.
11 Arrivées par tous moyens de transport confondus.
12 Arrivées par voie aérienne à Bangui uniquement.
13 Pour la présentation des statistiques, les données pour la Chine ne comprennent pas la Région Administrative Spéciale de Hong Kong (Hong Kong RAS), la Région Administrative Spéciale de Macao (Macao RAS) et la province de Taiwan.
14 Ne comprend pas d'autres catégories de non-résidents tels que les travailleurs, les étudiants, etc.
15 Les données de 2005 à 2009 ont donc été révisées afin qu'ils puissent être comparables à 2010 (les ports nautiques ne sont pas inclus).
16 Les données des entrées ne concernent que 3 postes frontaliers : l'aéroport de N'Djili à Kinshasa, l'aéroport de la Luano à Lubumbashi et le poste frontière terrestre situé à Kasumbalesa dans la province du Katanga.
17 Arrivées par voie aérienne seulement; y compris les nationaux résidant à l'étranger.
18 A l'exclusion des passagers à l'aéroport de Herrera.
19 Calculé sur la base des statistiques d'hébergement et de la "Foreign Visitor Survey" menée par la "Statistical Office of Estonia". À partir de 2004, les statistiques de frontière ne sont plus collectées.
20 Basé sur les données de positionnement mobile par la Banque d'Estonie et Positium LBS.
21 Arrivées à l'aéroport de Bole uniquement.
22 Arrivées à travers tous les ports d'entrée.
23 Arrivées de touristes non résidents à l'aéroport de Libreville.
24 Arrivées en vols à la demande seulement.
25 Information tirée de données administratives.
26 Arrivées par voie aérienne. Les îles du Nord, Saint-Barthélémy et Saint-Martin (partie français), sont exclues.
27 Arrivées de touristes non résidents dans tous les types d'établissements d'hébergement touristique.
28 Y compris les résidents et les non-résidents.
29 Arrivées par voie aérienne à l'aéroport de Conakry.
30 Arrivées à l'aéroport de Timehri seulement.
31 Nouvelle série.
32 Y compris touristes à Irlande du Nord.

30 Tourist/visitor arrivals and tourism expenditure *(continued)*

Thousands arrivals and millions of US dollars

Arrivées de touristes/visiteurs et dépenses touristiques *(suite)*

Milliers d'arrivées et millions de dollars É.-U.

33	Including the expenditures of foreign workers in Israel.	33	Y compris les dépenses des travailleurs étrangers en Israël.
34	Excluding seasonal and border workers.	34	A l'exclusion des travailleurs saisonniers et frontaliers.
35	Arrivals of non-resident tourists by air. Including nationals residing abroad. E/D cards.	35	Arrivées de touristes non résidents par air. Y compris les nationaux qui résident à l'étranger. Cartes d'embarquement et de débarquement.
36	Excluding nationals residing abroad.	36	A l'exclusion des nationaux du pays résidant à l'étranger.
37	Air arrivals. Tarawa and Christmas Island.	37	Arrivées par voie aérienne. Tarawa et Ile Christmas.
38	Non-resident departures. Survey of persons crossing the state border.	38	Départs de non-résidents. Enquête menée auprès de personnes franchissant la frontière de l'État.
39	Excluding nationals residing abroad, Syrian nationals and Palestinians.	39	À l'exclusion des nationaux résidant à l'étranger, Syriens et Palestiniens.
40	Excluding long term tourists on campgrounds and in holiday flats.	40	A l'exclusion des touristes à long terme en camping ou dans des appartements de vacances.
41	Arrivals of non-resident tourists by air.	41	Arrivées de touristes non résidents par voie aérienne.
42	Departures.	42	Départs.
43	Including Singapore residents crossing the frontier by road through Johore Causeway.	43	Y compris les résidents de Singapour traversant la frontière par voie terrestre à travers le Johore Causeway.
44	Departures by air and by sea.	44	Départs par voies aérienne et maritime.
45	Air and sea arrivals.	45	Arrivées par voie aérienne et maritime.
46	Fiscal years (October 1 to September 30).	46	Années fiscales (du 1er octobre au 30 septembre).
47	Arrivals in the States of Kosrae, Chuuk, Pohnpei and Yap; excluding FSM citizens.	47	Arrivées dans les États de Kosrae, Chuuk, Pohnpei et Yap; non compris les citoyens FSM.
48	Excluding diplomats and foreign residents in Mongolia.	48	Sont exclus les diplomates et les étrangers qui résident en Mongolie.
49	The data of all the border posts of the country are used.	49	Les données de l'ensemble des postes frontières du pays sont utilisées.
50	Including arrivals from India.	50	Y compris les arrivées à Inde.
51	Including Niueans residing usually in New Zealand.	51	Y compris les nationaux de Niue résidant habituellement en Nouvelle-Zélande.
52	Non-resident tourists staying in registered hotels.	52	Non résidents touristes dans les hôtels enregistrés.
53	Arrivals of non-resident tourists at national borders.	53	Arrivées de touristes non résidents aux frontières nationales.
54	Air arrivals (Palau International Airport).	54	Arrivées par voie aérienne (Aéroport international de Palau).
55	Fiscal years ending September 30.	55	Exercices terminant le 30 Septembre.
56	E/D cards in the "Silvio Petirossi" airport and passenger counts at the national border crossings - National Police and SENATUR.	56	Cartes d'embarquement et de débarquement à l'aéroport Silvio Petirossi et comptages des passagers lors du franchissement des frontières nationales – Police Nationale et SENATUR.
57	Including tourists with identity document other than a passport.	57	Nouvelle série estimée comprenant les touristes avec une pièce d'identité autre qu'un passeport.
58	Fiscal years (July-June).	58	Années fiscales (juillet-juin).
59	Arrivals in hotels only.	59	Arrivées dans les hôtels uniquement.
60	Including nationals residing abroad and crew members.	60	Y compris les nationaux résidant à l'étranger et membres des équipages.
61	Excluding the left side of the river Nistru and the municipality of Bender.	61	La rive gauche de la rivière Nistru et la municipalité de Bender sont exclues.
62	Visitors who have benefited from tourism services provided by the tourism agencies and tour operators (titular of tourism licences).	62	Visiteurs qui ont bénéficié des services touristiques des agences de tourisme et des voyagistes (titulaires d'une licence touristique).
63	Including Italian tourists.	63	Y compris les touristes italiens.
64	Excluding Netherlands Antillean residents.	64	A l'exclusion des résidents des Antilles Néerlandaises.
65	Arrivals by air. Including arrivals to Saint Maarten (the French side of the island).	65	Arrivées par voie aérienne. Y compris les arrivées à Saint-Martin (la partie française de l'île).
66	Without first quarter.	66	Sans premier trimestre.
67	Excluding arrivals for work and contract workers.	67	À l'exclusion des arrivées par travail et les travailleurs contractuels.
68	West Bank and Gaza.	68	Cisjordanie et Gaza.
69	West Bank only.	69	Cisjordanie seulement.
70	Arrivals at Zanderij Airport.	70	Arrivées à l'aéroport de Zanderij.
71	Camping excluding.	71	Camping exclu.
72	Including health establishments.	72	Y compris les établissements de cure.
73	Including Iraqi nationals.	73	Y compris les nationaux iraquiens.
74	Arrivals by air at Dili Airport.	74	Arrivées par voie aérienne à l'aéroport de Dili.
75	Turkish citizens resident abroad are included.	75	Citoyens turcs résidant à l'étranger sont inclus.
76	Including expenditure of the nationals residing abroad.	76	Y compris dépenses des nationaux résidant à l'étranger.
77	Arrivals in hotels only. Including domestic tourism and nationals of the country residing abroad.	77	Arrivées dans les hôtels uniquement. Y compris le tourisme interne et les nationaux résidant à l'étranger.
78	Hotel revenues.	78	Recettes des hôtels.
79	Including domestic tourism and nationals residing abroad.	79	Y compris le tourisme intérieur et les nationaux du pays résidant à l'étranger.

31 Civil aviation: scheduled airline traffic

Passengers carried (thousands); kilometres, passenger-kilometers and tonne-kilometers (millions)

Aviation civile: trafic aérien régulier

Passagers transportés (milliers); kilomètres, passagers-kilomètres and tonnes-kilomètres (millions)

Country or area and traffic	Total traffic (domestic and international) Trafic total (intérieur et international)			International traffic Trafic international			Pays ou zone et trafic
	2013	2014	2015	2013	2014	2015	
Afghanistan							**Afghanistan**
Km flown	21	20	20	15	12	13	Km parcourus
P'gers carried	2 044	2 209	1 930	979	718	672	P'gers trans.
Passenger-km	2 550	2 344	2 233	1 914	1 499	1 485	Passagers-km
Total tonne-km	85	34	33	76	23	23	Tonnes-km tot.
Albania							**Albanie**
Km flown	10	2	...	10	2	...	Km parcourus
P'gers carried	866	152	...	866	152	...	P'gers trans.
Passenger-km	825	145	...	825	145	...	Passagers-km
Algeria							**Algérie**
Km flown	60	67	73	45	51	53	Km parcourus
P'gers carried	4 492	5 021	5 911	2 949	3 446	3 968	P'gers trans.
Passenger-km	5 452	6 246	7 249	4 592	5 328	6 116	Passagers-km
Total tonne-km	18	22	25	17	21	24	Tonnes-km tot.
Angola							**Angola**
Km flown	25	26	25	20	21	20	Km parcourus
P'gers carried	1 322	1 410	1 244	653	697	636	P'gers trans.
Passenger-km	3 711	4 024	3 535	3 285	3 592	3 179	Passagers-km
Total tonne-km	70	66	46	69	64	45	Tonnes-km tot.
Antigua and Barbuda							**Antigua-et-Barbuda**
Km flown	13	12	10	13	12	10	Km parcourus
P'gers carried	1 218	1 216	1 040	1 218	1 216	1 040	P'gers trans.
Passenger-km	409	408	363	409	408	363	Passagers-km
Total tonne-km	1	1	1	1	1	1	Tonnes-km tot.
Argentina							**Argentine**
Km flown	182	185	201	74	79	83	Km parcourus
P'gers carried	11 951	12 122	14 245	3 296	3 266	3 492	P'gers trans.
Passenger-km	22 103	22 984	26 354	12 385	12 672	14 054	Passagers-km
Total tonne-km	269	262	244	251	243	225	Tonnes-km tot.
Armenia							**Arménie**
Km flown	1	...	...	1	...	...	Km parcourus
P'gers carried	45	...	...	45	...	...	P'gers trans.
Passenger-km	75	...	...	75	...	...	Passagers-km
Total tonne-km	1	...	...	1	...	...	Tonnes-km tot.
Australia							**Australie**
Km flown	861	871	884	323	326	335	Km parcourus
P'gers carried	68 198	67 678	69 294	13 305	13 039	13 859	P'gers trans.
Passenger-km	138 506	139 899	144 361	72 781	73 271	77 599	Passagers-km
Total tonne-km	1 985	1 907	1 887	1 824	1 744	1 752	Tonnes-km tot.
Austria							**Autriche**
Km flown	171	175	172	168	172	168	Km parcourus
P'gers carried	15 037	15 210	14 719	14 459	14 674	14 240	P'gers trans.
Passenger-km	21 433	22 481	22 527	21 275	22 335	22 394	Passagers-km
Total tonne-km	326	370	351	326	370	351	Tonnes-km tot.
Azerbaijan							**Azerbaïdjan**
Km flown	25	31	34	23	28	31	Km parcourus
P'gers carried	1 652	1 770	1 803	1 148	1 221	1 271	P'gers trans.
Passenger-km	2 539	2 889	3 318	2 246	2 561	2 967	Passagers-km
Total tonne-km	18	31	42	17	31	41	Tonnes-km tot.
Bahamas							**Bahamas**
Km flown	8	9	7	4	4	3	Km parcourus
P'gers carried	577	665	588	285	354	313	P'gers trans.
Passenger-km	332	390	306	206	256	190	Passagers-km
Total tonne-km	~0	~0	~0	...	...	...	Tonnes-km tot.
Bahrain							**Bahreïn**
Km flown	73	76	80	73	76	80	Km parcourus
P'gers carried	4 627	5 171	5 314	4 627	5 171	5 314	P'gers trans.
Passenger-km	8 052	8 692	8 908	8 052	8 692	8 908	Passagers-km
Total tonne-km	266	258	240	266	258	240	Tonnes-km tot.

31	Civil aviation: scheduled airline traffic *(continued)*

31 Civil aviation: scheduled airline traffic *(continued)*

Passengers carried (thousands); kilometres, passenger-kilometers and tonne-kilometers (millions)

Aviation civile: trafic aérien régulier *(suite)*

Passagers transportés (milliers); kilomètres, passagers-kilomètres and tonnes-kilomètres (millions)

Country or area and traffic	Total traffic (domestic and international) Trafic total (intérieur et international)			International traffic Trafic international			Pays ou zone et trafic
	2013	2014	2015	2013	2014	2015	
Bangladesh							**Bangladesh**
Km flown	44	43	39	35	34	34	Km parcourus
P'gers carried	2 782	2 762	2 907	2 092	2 023	2 251	P'gers trans.
Passenger-km	6 559	6 322	6 928	6 233	6 005	6 646	Passagers-km
Total tonne-km	225	208	183	211	195	173	Tonnes-km tot.
Belarus							**Bélarus**
Km flown	23	27	28	23	27	28	Km parcourus
P'gers carried	1 160	1 318	1 489	1 160	1 318	1 489	P'gers trans.
Passenger-km	1 624	1 809	1 974	1 624	1 809	1 974	Passagers-km
Total tonne-km	2	2	2	2	2	2	Tonnes-km tot.
Belgium							**Belgique**
Km flown	178	186	191	178	186	191	Km parcourus
P'gers carried	9 521	10 535	11 193	9 514	10 529	11 187	P'gers trans.
Passenger-km	18 789	20 432	21 250	18 788	20 430	21 249	Passagers-km
Total tonne-km	1 561	1 596	1 464	1 561	1 596	1 464	Tonnes-km tot.
Belize							**Belize**
Km flown	3	7	6	1	1	1	Km parcourus
P'gers carried	513	878	936	9	26	30	P'gers trans.
Passenger-km	25	58	47	5	8	9	Passagers-km
Total tonne-km	1	3	2	~0	~0	~0	Tonnes-km tot.
Benin							**Bénin**
Km flown	2	1	1	2	1	1	Km parcourus
P'gers carried	138	60	112	138	60	112	P'gers trans.
Passenger-km	127	55	81	127	55	81	Passagers-km
Total tonne-km	1	1	1	1	1	1	Tonnes-km tot.
Bhutan							**Bhoutan**
Km flown	8	11	6	8	11	6	Km parcourus
P'gers carried	208	302	163	208	302	163	P'gers trans.
Passenger-km	450	654	381	450	654	381	Passagers-km
Total tonne-km	1	1	1	1	1	1	Tonnes-km tot.
Bolivia (Plurin. State of)							**Bolivie (État plurin. de)**
Km flown	20	24	20	5	6	7	Km parcourus
P'gers carried	2 028	2 300	2 579	303	291	365	P'gers trans.
Passenger-km	1 254	1 269	1 425	777	704	826	Passagers-km
Total tonne-km	8	8	9	3	3	4	Tonnes-km tot.
Bosnia and Herzegovina							**Bosnie-Herzégovine**
Km flown	1	~0	~0	1	~0	~0	Km parcourus
P'gers carried	15	37	7	15	37	7	P'gers trans.
Passenger-km	17	13	3	17	13	3	Passagers-km
Total tonne-km	~0	~0	~0	~0	~0	~0	Tonnes-km tot.
Botswana							**Botswana**
Km flown	6	5	5	5	4	4	Km parcourus
P'gers carried	271	206	194	227	172	164	P'gers trans.
Passenger-km	222	169	147	151	115	98	Passagers-km
Total tonne-km	~0	~0	~0	~0	~0	~0	Tonnes-km tot.
Brazil							**Brésil**
Km flown	908	896	925	153	147	171	Km parcourus
P'gers carried	95 592	100 404	102 039	6 103	6 246	7 119	P'gers trans.
Passenger-km	113 188	117 760	122 868	27 304	28 273	32 032	Passagers-km
Total tonne-km	1 637	1 597	1 494	1 047	1 022	982	Tonnes-km tot.
Brunei Darussalam							**Brunéi Darussalam**
Km flown	24	24	25	24	24	25	Km parcourus
P'gers carried	1 140	1 061	1 150	1 140	1 061	1 150	P'gers trans.
Passenger-km	3 872	3 570	3 718	3 872	3 570	3 718	Passagers-km
Total tonne-km	128	115	115	128	115	115	Tonnes-km tot.
Bulgaria							**Bulgarie**
Km flown	15	15	15	14	14	15	Km parcourus
P'gers carried	1 013	1 060	1 119	838	897	952	P'gers trans.
Passenger-km	1 394	1 476	1 545	1 333	1 419	1 487	Passagers-km
Total tonne-km	2	2	2	2	2	2	Tonnes-km tot.

Civil aviation: scheduled airline traffic *(continued)*

Passengers carried (thousands); kilometres, passenger-kilometers and tonne-kilometers (millions)

Aviation civile: trafic aérien régulier *(suite)*

Passagers transportés (milliers); kilomètres, passagers-kilomètres and tonnes-kilomètres (millions)

Country or area and traffic	Total traffic (domestic and international) Trafic total (intérieur et international)			International traffic Trafic international			Pays ou zone et trafic
	2013	2014	2015	2013	2014	2015	
Burkina Faso							**Burkina Faso**
Km flown	3	3	3	3	3	3	Km parcourus
P'gers carried	139	117	123	111	97	98	P'gers trans.
Passenger-km	135	117	122	127	111	115	Passagers-km
Total tonne-km	~0	~0	~0	~0	~0	~0	Tonnes-km tot.
Cabo Verde							**Cabo Verde**
Km flown	8	7	7	6	6	6	Km parcourus
P'gers carried	600	590	567	285	275	276	P'gers trans.
Passenger-km	800	774	711	752	727	666	Passagers-km
Total tonne-km	2	2	2	2	2	2	Tonnes-km tot.
Cambodia							**Cambodge**
Km flown	6	10	11	5	8	10	Km parcourus
P'gers carried	615	1 071	1 104	444	779	809	P'gers trans.
Passenger-km	567	1 029	1 260	525	957	1 187	Passagers-km
Total tonne-km	1	2	2	1	2	2	Tonnes-km tot.
Cameroon							**Cameroun**
Km flown	5	5	5	3	4	4	Km parcourus
P'gers carried	287	276	267	124	125	127	P'gers trans.
Passenger-km	293	291	282	240	243	237	Passagers-km
Canada							**Canada**
Km flown	1 207	1 248	1 313	627	656	710	Km parcourus
P'gers carried	71 527	75 529	80 228	28 215	30 398	33 610	P'gers trans.
Passenger-km	152 627	162 732	177 507	104 475	112 558	124 742	Passagers-km
Total tonne-km	1 946	2 084	2 075	1 591	1 714	1 676	Tonnes-km tot.
Chad							**Tchad**
Km flown	~0	~0	...	~0	~0	...	Km parcourus
P'gers carried	28	28	...	28	28	...	P'gers trans.
Passenger-km	31	31	...	31	31	...	Passagers-km
Total tonne-km	~0	~0	...	~0	~0	...	Tonnes-km tot.
Chile							**Chili**
Km flown	182	184	185	99	104	108	Km parcourus
P'gers carried	13 806	14 348	15 007	4 369	4 599	5 145	P'gers trans.
Passenger-km	25 112	26 331	28 734	14 899	15 807	17 740	Passagers-km
Total tonne-km	1 512	1 553	1 392	1 465	1 505	1 345	Tonnes-km tot.
China [1]							**Chine** [1]
Km flown	4 249	4 699	5 258	729	846	1 088	Km parcourus
P'gers carried	352 795	390 879	436 184	25 523	30 693	42 070	P'gers trans.
Passenger-km	562 748	630 823	725 901	111 918	129 495	169 981	Passagers-km
Total tonne-km	16 054	17 823	19 806	10 416	11 874	13 579	Tonnes-km tot.
China, Hong Kong SAR							**Chine, Hong Kong RAS**
Km flown	572	633	677	572	633	677	Km parcourus
P'gers carried	34 644	37 934	41 867	34 644	37 934	41 867	P'gers trans.
Passenger-km	111 573	122 614	136 156	111 573	122 614	136 156	Passagers-km
Total tonne-km	9 396	10 826	11 294	9 396	10 826	11 294	Tonnes-km tot.
China, Macao SAR							**Chine, Macao RAS**
Km flown	29	33	...	29	33	...	Km parcourus
P'gers carried	1 767	2 079	2 276	1 767	2 079	2 276	P'gers trans.
Passenger-km	2 921	3 442	3 779	2 921	3 442	3 779	Passagers-km
Total tonne-km	20	24	25	20	24	25	Tonnes-km tot.
Colombia							**Colombie**
Km flown	222	233	266	129	134	151	Km parcourus
P'gers carried	26 929	28 789	30 743	5 676	6 029	6 462	P'gers trans.
Passenger-km	23 565	25 168	29 062	14 643	15 519	17 785	Passagers-km
Total tonne-km	1 222	1 320	1 318	1 162	1 252	1 235	Tonnes-km tot.
Congo							**Congo**
Km flown	7	6	7	3	3	3	Km parcourus
P'gers carried	652	554	658	79	81	119	P'gers trans.
Passenger-km	554	486	604	220	227	324	Passagers-km
Total tonne-km	2	2	3	1	1	2	Tonnes-km tot.
Cook Islands							**Îles Cook**
Km flown	2	2	2	...	...	...	Km parcourus
P'gers carried	87	87	87	...	...	...	P'gers trans.
Passenger-km	29	29	29	...	...	...	Passagers-km
Total tonne-km	~0	~0	~0	...	...	...	Tonnes-km tot.

31 Civil aviation: scheduled airline traffic *(continued)*

Passengers carried (thousands); kilometres, passenger-kilometers and tonne-kilometers (millions)

Aviation civile: trafic aérien régulier *(suite)*

Passagers transportés (milliers); kilomètres, passagers-kilomètres and tonnes-kilomètres (millions)

Country or area and traffic	Total traffic (domestic and international) Trafic total (intérieur et international)			International traffic Trafic international			Pays ou zone et trafic
	2013	2014	2015	2013	2014	2015	
Costa Rica							**Costa Rica**
Km flown	28	26	26	24	22	21	Km parcourus
P'gers carried	1 499	1 427	1 617	1 298	1 199	1 261	P'gers trans.
Passenger-km	2 417	2 124	2 282	2 376	2 076	2 198	Passagers-km
Total tonne-km	14	12	9	14	12	9	Tonnes-km tot.
Côte d'Ivoire							**Côte d'Ivoire**
Km flown	4	4	6	4	4	6	Km parcourus
P'gers carried	235	237	359	235	237	359	P'gers trans.
Passenger-km	266	268	405	266	268	405	Passagers-km
Total tonne-km	5	5	5	5	5	5	Tonnes-km tot.
Croatia							**Croatie**
Km flown	15	15	15	13	13	13	Km parcourus
P'gers carried	1 717	1 756	1 783	1 243	1 280	1 312	P'gers trans.
Passenger-km	1 189	1 220	1 248	1 038	1 067	1 097	Passagers-km
Total tonne-km	1	1	1	1	1	1	Tonnes-km tot.
Cuba							**Cuba**
Km flown	22	20	24	15	15	18	Km parcourus
P'gers carried	1 395	1 135	1 294	690	663	802	P'gers trans.
Passenger-km	2 586	2 303	2 734	2 156	1 975	2 392	Passagers-km
Total tonne-km	17	17	21	17	17	21	Tonnes-km tot.
Cyprus							**Chypre**
Km flown	16	9	~0	16	9	~0	Km parcourus
P'gers carried	1 211	688	23	1 211	688	23	P'gers trans.
Passenger-km	1 675	952	33	1 675	952	33	Passagers-km
Total tonne-km	12	7	~0	12	7	~0	Tonnes-km tot.
Czechia							**Tchéquie**
Km flown	70	65	74	70	64	74	Km parcourus
P'gers carried	5 187	5 010	4 972	5 156	4 972	4 938	P'gers trans.
Passenger-km	7 037	6 709	8 077	7 022	6 692	8 054	Passagers-km
Total tonne-km	20	31	27	20	31	27	Tonnes-km tot.
Dem. People's Rep. Korea							**Rép. pop. dém. de Corée**
Km flown	6	4	4	6	4	4	Km parcourus
P'gers carried	371	233	223	371	233	223	P'gers trans.
Passenger-km	854	536	442	854	536	442	Passagers-km
Total tonne-km	3	2	2	3	2	2	Tonnes-km tot.
Dem. Rep. of the Congo							**Rép. dém. du Congo**
Km flown	9	9	10	1	1	1	Km parcourus
P'gers carried	456	456	476	26	26	26	P'gers trans.
Passenger-km	683	684	713	70	70	71	Passagers-km
Total tonne-km	~0	~0	~0	~0	~0	~0	Tonnes-km tot.
Dominican Republic							**République dominicaine**
Km flown	1	~0	~0	1	~0	~0	Km parcourus
P'gers carried	20	16	14	17	16	14	P'gers trans.
Passenger-km	7	6	6	6	6	6	Passagers-km
Ecuador							**Équateur**
Km flown	45	51	62	26	35	45	Km parcourus
P'gers carried	5 158	5 675	5 762	1 077	1 853	2 167	P'gers trans.
Passenger-km	5 284	6 227	6 655	3 644	4 624	5 181	Passagers-km
Total tonne-km	112	82	86	100	75	79	Tonnes-km tot.
Egypt							**Égypte**
Km flown	175	164	165	164	153	154	Km parcourus
P'gers carried	10 594	9 525	10 159	9 158	7 937	8 491	P'gers trans.
Passenger-km	22 125	20 008	20 507	21 482	19 293	19 743	Passagers-km
Total tonne-km	387	419	398	386	419	397	Tonnes-km tot.
El Salvador							**El Salvador**
Km flown	49	54	46	49	54	46	Km parcourus
P'gers carried	2 509	2 817	2 598	2 509	2 817	2 598	P'gers trans.
Passenger-km	5 029	5 656	4 948	5 029	5 656	4 948	Passagers-km
Total tonne-km	16	16	14	16	16	14	Tonnes-km tot.
Equatorial Guinea							**Guinée équatoriale**
Km flown	7	5	9	5	4	8	Km parcourus
P'gers carried	402	303	401	155	145	242	P'gers trans.
Passenger-km	243	199	314	152	148	262	Passagers-km
Total tonne-km	~0	~0	~0	~0	~0	~0	Tonnes-km tot.

31 Civil aviation: scheduled airline traffic *(continued)*

Passengers carried (thousands); kilometres, passenger-kilometers and tonne-kilometers (millions)

Aviation civile: trafic aérien régulier *(suite)*

Passagers transportés (milliers); kilomètres, passagers-kilomètres and tonnes-kilomètres (millions)

Country or area and traffic	Total traffic (domestic and international) Trafic total (intérieur et international)			International traffic Trafic international			Pays ou zone et trafic
	2013	2014	2015	2013	2014	2015	
Eritrea							**Erythrée**
Km flown	...	...	1	...	...	1	Km parcourus
P'gers carried	...	...	53	...	...	53	P'gers trans.
Passenger-km	...	...	69	...	...	69	Passagers-km
Estonia							**Estonie**
Km flown	11	10	10	11	10	10	Km parcourus
P'gers carried	628	603	512	603	570	493	P'gers trans.
Passenger-km	565	524	484	561	519	481	Passagers-km
Total tonne-km	~0	1	1	~0	1	1	Tonnes-km tot.
Ethiopia							**Éthiopie**
Km flown	150	156	179	144	150	171	Km parcourus
P'gers carried	5 672	6 275	7 075	4 934	5 423	5 982	P'gers trans.
Passenger-km	19 970	22 301	25 118	19 646	21 925	24 638	Passagers-km
Total tonne-km	791	950	1 229	791	950	1 229	Tonnes-km tot.
Fiji							**Fidji**
Km flown	11	29	31	10	27	29	Km parcourus
P'gers carried	1 162	1 244	1 337	951	1 034	1 109	P'gers trans.
Passenger-km	3 976	4 328	4 554	3 938	4 290	4 513	Passagers-km
Total tonne-km	69	79	84	69	79	84	Tonnes-km tot.
Finland							**Finlande**
Km flown	170	174	162	154	159	150	Km parcourus
P'gers carried	10 467	10 993	9 972	8 529	9 026	8 158	P'gers trans.
Passenger-km	23 661	24 653	25 655	22 683	23 666	24 744	Passagers-km
Total tonne-km	661	667	713	661	667	713	Tonnes-km tot.
France							**France**
Km flown	901	875	882	666	654	663	Km parcourus
P'gers carried	63 925	63 434	65 040	38 106	38 438	39 967	P'gers trans.
Passenger-km	178 672	178 138	184 146	137 502	137 645	143 494	Passagers-km
Total tonne-km	4 327	4 151	4 098	4 016	3 830	3 637	Tonnes-km tot.
Gabon							**Gabon**
Km flown	...	...	1	...	...	~0	Km parcourus
P'gers carried	...	...	137	...	...	8	P'gers trans.
Passenger-km	...	...	35	...	...	2	Passagers-km
Gambia							**Gambie**
Km flown	3	3	~0	3	3	~0	Km parcourus
P'gers carried	147	152	3	147	152	3	P'gers trans.
Passenger-km	217	225	7	217	225	7	Passagers-km
Total tonne-km	2	2	~0	2	2	~0	Tonnes-km tot.
Georgia							**Géorgie**
Km flown	5	5	6	5	5	6	Km parcourus
P'gers carried	189	197	232	179	181	217	P'gers trans.
Passenger-km	335	355	419	332	350	414	Passagers-km
Total tonne-km	~0	~0	~0	~0	~0	~0	Tonnes-km tot.
Germany							**Allemagne**
Km flown	1 367	1 361	1 390	1 267	1 262	1 294	Km parcourus
P'gers carried	109 062	111 589	115 541	86 224	88 552	92 665	P'gers trans.
Passenger-km	227 528	234 201	244 664	217 455	224 016	234 622	Passagers-km
Total tonne-km	7 336	7 184	6 985	7 330	7 179	6 980	Tonnes-km tot.
Ghana							**Ghana**
Km flown	4	4	5	~0	~0	~0	Km parcourus
P'gers carried	396	408	390	33	34	1	P'gers trans.
Passenger-km	196	201	229	25	25	1	Passagers-km
Total tonne-km	1	1	1	~0	~0	~0	Tonnes-km tot.
Greece							**Grèce**
Km flown	68	84	98	48	58	71	Km parcourus
P'gers carried	8 761	11 152	12 584	3 907	4 701	5 754	P'gers trans.
Passenger-km	7 858	9 652	11 578	6 372	7 641	9 424	Passagers-km
Total tonne-km	1	19	27	~0	17	25	Tonnes-km tot.
Guatemala							**Guatemala**
Km flown	1	1	1	~0	~0	1	Km parcourus
P'gers carried	78	70	93	34	20	41	P'gers trans.
Passenger-km	23	20	38	11	7	24	Passagers-km
Total tonne-km	...	~0	~0	...	~0	~0	Tonnes-km tot.

31 Civil aviation: scheduled airline traffic *(continued)*

Passengers carried (thousands); kilometres, passenger-kilometers and tonne-kilometers (millions)

Aviation civile: trafic aérien régulier *(suite)*

Passagers transportés (milliers); kilomètres, passagers-kilomètres and tonnes-kilomètres (millions)

Country or area and traffic	Total traffic (domestic and international) Trafic total (intérieur et international) 2013	2014	2015	International traffic Trafic international 2013	2014	2015	Pays ou zone et trafic
Honduras							**Honduras**
Km flown	5	5	5	1	1	2	Km parcourus
P'gers carried	373	239	251	12	11	48	P'gers trans.
Passenger-km	101	78	87	21	20	33	Passagers-km
Total tonne-km	2	1	1	~0	~0	~0	Tonnes-km tot.
Hungary							**Hongrie**
Km flown	134	160	188	134	160	188	Km parcourus
P'gers carried	13 927	16 482	20 042	13 927	16 482	20 042	P'gers trans.
Passenger-km	20 867	25 045	29 603	20 867	25 045	29 603	Passagers-km
Iceland							**Islande**
Km flown	52	58	66	49	56	64	Km parcourus
P'gers carried	2 603	2 926	3 414	2 325	2 663	3 143	P'gers trans.
Passenger-km	6 759	7 919	9 394	6 678	7 842	9 315	Passagers-km
Total tonne-km	99	96	102	99	96	102	Tonnes-km tot.
India							**Inde**
Km flown	807	847	1 047	315	333	449	Km parcourus
P'gers carried	75 589	82 719	98 928	15 231	16 812	18 417	P'gers trans.
Passenger-km	112 294	121 040	140 474	53 241	57 323	63 928	Passagers-km
Total tonne-km	1 734	1 851	1 834	1 197	1 231	1 181	Tonnes-km tot.
Indonesia							**Indonésie**
Km flown	542	581	590	148	153	149	Km parcourus
P'gers carried	81 721	87 163	88 686	10 196	10 300	9 919	P'gers trans.
Passenger-km	80 378	84 856	87 569	23 136	23 631	24 678	Passagers-km
Total tonne-km	768	836	747	371	384	315	Tonnes-km tot.
Iran (Islamic Republic of)							**Iran (Rép. islamique d')**
Km flown	145	144	144	44	45	51	Km parcourus
P'gers carried	16 581	16 503	15 004	3 035	2 975	2 853	P'gers trans.
Passenger-km	17 934	17 635	18 169	6 578	6 418	7 287	Passagers-km
Total tonne-km	84	108	107	71	87	88	Tonnes-km tot.
Iraq							**Iraq**
Km flown	5	5	5	5	5	5	Km parcourus
P'gers carried	476	476	485	352	352	357	P'gers trans.
Passenger-km	656	656	665	619	619	627	Passagers-km
Total tonne-km	11	11	11	11	11	11	Tonnes-km tot.
Ireland							**Irlande**
Km flown	771	787	837	770	786	837	Km parcourus
P'gers carried	93 408	98 449	113 145	93 347	98 401	113 145	P'gers trans.
Passenger-km	118 796	125 334	143 527	118 780	125 321	143 527	Passagers-km
Total tonne-km	118	126	139	117	125	139	Tonnes-km tot.
Israel							**Israël**
Km flown	107	112	116	102	107	111	Km parcourus
P'gers carried	5 566	5 887	6 064	4 156	4 517	4 718	P'gers trans.
Passenger-km	18 828	19 677	20 290	18 408	19 264	19 882	Passagers-km
Total tonne-km	802	651	759	802	651	759	Tonnes-km tot.
Italy							**Italie**
Km flown	291	335	328	197	253	257	Km parcourus
P'gers carried	27 846	25 834	26 036	10 827	11 245	12 562	P'gers trans.
Passenger-km	40 279	38 822	38 429	30 364	30 568	31 283	Passagers-km
Total tonne-km	893	992	945	892	991	944	Tonnes-km tot.
Jamaica							**Jamaïque**
Km flown	1	3	3	1	3	3	Km parcourus
P'gers carried	46	76	93	46	76	93	P'gers trans.
Passenger-km	63	228	275	63	228	275	Passagers-km
Japan							**Japon**
Km flown	1 078	1 121	1 186	443	485	541	Km parcourus
P'gers carried	107 573	110 547	113 762	15 085	16 040	17 888	P'gers trans.
Passenger-km	150 774	158 096	167 906	66 630	71 949	79 992	Passagers-km
Total tonne-km	7 716	8 662	8 869	6 749	7 697	7 908	Tonnes-km tot.
Jordan							**Jordanie**
Km flown	72	72	66	72	71	65	Km parcourus
P'gers carried	3 295	3 212	3 065	3 247	3 157	3 013	P'gers trans.
Passenger-km	8 402	8 087	7 322	8 390	8 073	7 308	Passagers-km
Total tonne-km	172	172	169	172	172	169	Tonnes-km tot.

31

Civil aviation: scheduled airline traffic *(continued)*

Passengers carried (thousands); kilometres, passenger-kilometers and tonne-kilometers (millions)

Aviation civile: trafic aérien régulier *(suite)*

Passagers transportés (milliers); kilomètres, passagers-kilomètres and tonnes-kilomètres (millions)

Country or area and traffic	Total traffic (domestic and international) Trafic total (intérieur et international)			International traffic Trafic international			Pays ou zone et trafic
	2013	2014	2015	2013	2014	2015	
Kazakhstan							**Kazakhstan**
Km flown	103	107	109	56	56	57	Km parcourus
P'gers carried	4 786	4 919	5 082	1 804	1 811	1 830	P'gers trans.
Passenger-km	9 352	9 502	9 692	5 462	5 456	5 427	Passagers-km
Total tonne-km	58	45	38	44	34	29	Tonnes-km tot.
Kenya							**Kenya**
Km flown	89	94	91	79	84	83	Km parcourus
P'gers carried	4 517	4 401	4 875	3 219	3 280	4 144	P'gers trans.
Passenger-km	9 793	10 000	10 197	9 300	9 581	9 715	Passagers-km
Total tonne-km	258	269	286	254	266	283	Tonnes-km tot.
Kuwait							**Koweït**
Km flown	54	57	60	54	57	60	Km parcourus
P'gers carried	3 245	3 531	3 655	3 245	3 531	3 655	P'gers trans.
Passenger-km	8 193	8 655	8 950	8 193	8 655	8 950	Passagers-km
Total tonne-km	246	268	276	246	268	276	Tonnes-km tot.
Kyrgyzstan							**Kirghizistan**
Km flown	18	25	23	17	22	21	Km parcourus
P'gers carried	771	712	625	495	409	358	P'gers trans.
Passenger-km	1 098	1 160	1 007	1 022	1 049	909	Passagers-km
Total tonne-km	1	~0	~0	1	~0	~0	Tonnes-km tot.
Lao People's Dem. Rep.							**Rép. dém. populaire lao**
Km flown	13	12	10	10	8	8	Km parcourus
P'gers carried	1 477	1 310	1 181	847	750	739	P'gers trans.
Passenger-km	1 052	885	790	805	674	629	Passagers-km
Total tonne-km	1	1	1	1	1	1	Tonnes-km tot.
Latvia							**Lettonie**
Km flown	39	38	37	39	38	37	Km parcourus
P'gers carried	2 755	2 592	2 527	2 755	2 592	2 527	P'gers trans.
Passenger-km	2 848	2 645	2 559	2 848	2 645	2 559	Passagers-km
Total tonne-km	4	4	2	4	4	2	Tonnes-km tot.
Lebanon							**Liban**
Km flown	40	40	41	40	40	41	Km parcourus
P'gers carried	2 241	2 419	2 583	2 241	2 419	2 583	P'gers trans.
Passenger-km	3 981	4 288	4 544	3 981	4 288	4 544	Passagers-km
Total tonne-km	70	60	54	70	60	54	Tonnes-km tot.
Libya							**Libye**
Km flown	39	41	39	32	34	32	Km parcourus
P'gers carried	2 745	2 677	2 566	2 125	2 131	2 041	P'gers trans.
Passenger-km	3 698	3 789	3 616	3 078	3 193	3 047	Passagers-km
Total tonne-km	4	4	4	4	4	4	Tonnes-km tot.
Lithuania							**Lituanie**
Km flown	15	17	20	14	16	19	Km parcourus
P'gers carried	1 010	1 275	1 364	836	1 033	1 179	P'gers trans.
Passenger-km	1 742	1 763	2 465	1 703	1 637	2 372	Passagers-km
Total tonne-km	5	~0	1	5	~0	1	Tonnes-km tot.
Luxembourg							**Luxembourg**
Km flown	89	97	105	89	97	105	Km parcourus
P'gers carried	1 556	1 711	1 831	1 556	1 711	1 831	P'gers trans.
Passenger-km	1 841	1 977	2 100	1 841	1 977	2 100	Passagers-km
Total tonne-km	5 225	5 753	6 309	5 225	5 753	6 309	Tonnes-km tot.
Madagascar							**Madagascar**
Km flown	10	11	10	7	8	8	Km parcourus
P'gers carried	539	520	547	236	226	222	P'gers trans.
Passenger-km	1 372	1 309	1 302	1 219	1 160	1 137	Passagers-km
Total tonne-km	35	31	31	34	31	30	Tonnes-km tot.
Malawi							**Malawi**
Km flown	~0	~0	~0	~0	~0	~0	Km parcourus
P'gers carried	6	6	6	3	3	3	P'gers trans.
Passenger-km	1	1	1	1	1	1	Passagers-km
Total tonne-km	~0	~0	~0	~0	~0	~0	Tonnes-km tot.

31 Civil aviation: scheduled airline traffic *(continued)*
Passengers carried (thousands); kilometres, passenger-kilometers and tonne-kilometers (millions)

Aviation civile: trafic aérien régulier *(suite)*
Passagers transportés (milliers); kilomètres, passagers-kilomètres and tonnes-kilomètres (millions)

Country or area and traffic	Total traffic (domestic and international) Trafic total (intérieur et international)			International traffic Trafic international			Pays ou zone et trafic
	2013	2014	2015	2013	2014	2015	
Malaysia							**Malaisie**
Km flown	543	595	601	386	429	426	Km parcourus
P'gers carried	47 996	49 674	50 347	25 101	26 673	26 487	P'gers trans.
Passenger-km	92 758	98 880	93 692	74 388	79 817	73 742	Passagers-km
Total tonne-km	2 162	2 193	2 006	2 092	2 097	1 936	Tonnes-km tot.
Mali							**Mali**
Km flown	1	...	...	1	...	...	Km parcourus
P'gers carried	33	...	...	33	...	...	P'gers trans.
Passenger-km	82	...	...	82	...	...	Passagers-km
Total tonne-km	1	...	...	1	...	...	Tonnes-km tot.
Malta							**Malte**
Km flown	21	20	20	21	20	20	Km parcourus
P'gers carried	1 603	1 588	1 583	1 603	1 588	1 583	P'gers trans.
Passenger-km	2 474	2 444	2 410	2 474	2 444	2 410	Passagers-km
Total tonne-km	4	3	3	4	3	3	Tonnes-km tot.
Mauritania							**Mauritanie**
Km flown	4	4	4	3	4	3	Km parcourus
P'gers carried	262	271	248	198	208	185	P'gers trans.
Passenger-km	360	375	338	320	335	298	Passagers-km
Mauritius							**Maurice**
Km flown	41	43	43	40	41	41	Km parcourus
P'gers carried	1 318	1 354	1 467	1 196	1 226	1 312	P'gers trans.
Passenger-km	5 958	6 119	6 497	5 884	6 042	6 403	Passagers-km
Total tonne-km	172	193	169	171	193	169	Tonnes-km tot.
Mexico							**Mexique**
Km flown	494	587	581	175	253	226	Km parcourus
P'gers carried	35 987	39 571	45 560	6 747	7 810	9 828	P'gers trans.
Passenger-km	49 962	55 820	64 923	20 039	23 890	28 897	Passagers-km
Total tonne-km	677	618	714	579	513	601	Tonnes-km tot.
Monaco							**Monaco**
Km flown	1	1	1	1	1	1	Km parcourus
P'gers carried	65	64	60	65	64	60	P'gers trans.
Passenger-km	3	2	2	3	2	2	Passagers-km
Mongolia							**Mongolie**
Km flown	9	11	9	8	8	7	Km parcourus
P'gers carried	586	683	541	429	434	421	P'gers trans.
Passenger-km	1 013	1 180	1 092	976	1 032	994	Passagers-km
Total tonne-km	9	8	7	9	8	7	Tonnes-km tot.
Montenegro							**Monténégro**
Km flown	7	6	6	7	6	6	Km parcourus
P'gers carried	529	503	527	529	503	527	P'gers trans.
Passenger-km	516	491	358	516	491	358	Passagers-km
Morocco							**Maroc**
Km flown	120	128	135	115	123	129	Km parcourus
P'gers carried	6 507	7 018	6 787	5 828	6 175	5 943	P'gers trans.
Passenger-km	13 136	13 399	14 690	12 832	13 019	14 273	Passagers-km
Total tonne-km	43	54	48	43	54	47	Tonnes-km tot.
Mozambique							**Mozambique**
Km flown	17	18	18	6	7	7	Km parcourus
P'gers carried	701	752	687	240	264	241	P'gers trans.
Passenger-km	766	837	787	201	225	211	Passagers-km
Total tonne-km	6	6	5	1	1	1	Tonnes-km tot.
Myanmar							**Myanmar**
Km flown	17	19	21	6	5	4	Km parcourus
P'gers carried	1 572	1 899	2 029	430	390	320	P'gers trans.
Passenger-km	931	1 094	1 058	508	502	404	Passagers-km
Total tonne-km	3	4	3	2	3	2	Tonnes-km tot.
Namibia							**Namibie**
Km flown	13	13	15	11	12	13	Km parcourus
P'gers carried	510	522	553	420	434	462	P'gers trans.
Passenger-km	1 445	1 485	1 402	1 401	1 440	1 355	Passagers-km
Total tonne-km	1	34	30	1	34	30	Tonnes-km tot.

31

Civil aviation: scheduled airline traffic *(continued)*

Passengers carried (thousands); kilometres, passenger-kilometers and tonne-kilometers (millions)

Aviation civile: trafic aérien régulier *(suite)*

Passagers transportés (milliers); kilomètres, passagers-kilomètres and tonnes-kilomètres (millions)

Country or area and traffic	Total traffic (domestic and international) Trafic total (intérieur et international)			International traffic Trafic international			Pays ou zone et trafic
	2013	2014	2015	2013	2014	2015	
Nauru							**Nauru**
Km flown	~0	1	1	~0	1	1	Km parcourus
P'gers carried	16	35	39	16	35	39	P'gers trans.
Passenger-km	66	138	148	66	138	148	Passagers-km
Total tonne-km	7	7	8	7	7	8	Tonnes-km tot.
Nepal							**Népal**
Km flown	10	8	8	5	4	4	Km parcourus
P'gers carried	643	518	510	393	332	327	P'gers trans.
Passenger-km	827	692	681	760	642	632	Passagers-km
Total tonne-km	6	5	5	3	3	3	Tonnes-km tot.
Netherlands							**Pays-Bas**
Km flown	526	522	526	515	517	521	Km parcourus
P'gers carried	33 455	33 956	34 870	32 839	33 683	34 578	P'gers trans.
Passenger-km	100 393	101 424	103 516	98 925	100 605	102 757	Passagers-km
Total tonne-km	5 754	5 726	5 293	5 754	5 726	5 293	Tonnes-km tot.
New Zealand							**Nouvelle-Zélande**
Km flown	193	195	204	129	131	137	Km parcourus
P'gers carried	14 434	14 731	15 304	5 674	5 789	5 985	P'gers trans.
Passenger-km	29 526	30 098	31 776	25 243	25 694	27 103	Passagers-km
Total tonne-km	935	999	999	922	983	983	Tonnes-km tot.
Niger							**Niger**
Km flown	1	~0	~0	1	...	...	Km parcourus
P'gers carried	88	13	15	63	...	...	P'gers trans.
Passenger-km	126	7	9	108	...	...	Passagers-km
Total tonne-km	1	...	...	1	...	...	Tonnes-km tot.
Nigeria							**Nigéria**
Km flown	39	40	36	15	16	15	Km parcourus
P'gers carried	4 210	3 857	3 223	620	535	465	P'gers trans.
Passenger-km	3 281	3 127	2 464	1 618	1 599	1 184	Passagers-km
Total tonne-km	12	12	22	12	12	22	Tonnes-km tot.
Oman							**Oman**
Km flown	89	90	112	84	85	106	Km parcourus
P'gers carried	4 995	5 052	6 366	4 398	4 413	5 707	P'gers trans.
Passenger-km	11 330	11 336	14 709	10 834	10 804	14 151	Passagers-km
Total tonne-km	251	292	412	250	291	411	Tonnes-km tot.
Pakistan							**Pakistan**
Km flown	105	103	116	82	82	92	Km parcourus
P'gers carried	7 834	7 670	8 468	4 789	4 882	5 310	P'gers trans.
Passenger-km	18 115	18 131	19 263	15 325	15 539	16 392	Passagers-km
Total tonne-km	293	205	183	259	183	164	Tonnes-km tot.
Panama							**Panama**
Km flown	228	230	240	215	218	227	Km parcourus
P'gers carried	11 656	11 642	12 018	10 173	10 209	10 561	P'gers trans.
Passenger-km	23 510	25 526	26 216	22 600	24 633	25 311	Passagers-km
Total tonne-km	148	134	122	148	134	122	Tonnes-km tot.
Papua New Guinea							**Papouasie-Nvl-Guinée**
Km flown	24	26	26	10	11	11	Km parcourus
P'gers carried	1 871	2 074	2 063	251	253	274	P'gers trans.
Passenger-km	1 231	1 318	1 295	575	587	614	Passagers-km
Total tonne-km	33	33	35	32	32	34	Tonnes-km tot.
Paraguay							**Paraguay**
Km flown	7	6	5	7	6	5	Km parcourus
P'gers carried	712	609	452	712	609	452	P'gers trans.
Passenger-km	807	706	590	807	706	590	Passagers-km
Total tonne-km	...	2	2	...	2	2	Tonnes-km tot.
Peru							**Pérou**
Km flown	154	155	162	98	98	100	Km parcourus
P'gers carried	12 256	13 063	13 908	4 195	4 482	4 584	P'gers trans.
Passenger-km	19 592	19 600	20 635	14 156	14 123	14 746	Passagers-km
Total tonne-km	335	342	224	304	311	201	Tonnes-km tot.

Civil aviation: scheduled airline traffic *(continued)*

Passengers carried (thousands); kilometres, passenger-kilometers and tonne-kilometers (millions)

Aviation civile: trafic aérien régulier *(suite)*

Passagers transportés (milliers); kilomètres, passagers-kilomètres and tonnes-kilomètres (millions)

Country or area and traffic	Total traffic (domestic and international) Trafic total (intérieur et international)			International traffic Trafic international			Pays ou zone et trafic
	2013	2014	2015	2013	2014	2015	
Philippines							**Philippines**
Km flown	218	280	323	140	194	218	Km parcourus
P'gers carried	25 541	29 667	32 231	9 050	10 562	9 850	P'gers trans.
Passenger-km	35 572	45 769	51 554	25 480	34 781	37 932	Passagers-km
Total tonne-km	326	457	484	278	393	407	Tonnes-km tot.
Poland							**Pologne**
Km flown	75	75	70	67	67	64	Km parcourus
P'gers carried	5 003	5 039	4 841	3 687	3 698	3 632	P'gers trans.
Passenger-km	7 109	7 382	7 580	6 715	6 992	7 234	Passagers-km
Total tonne-km	98	121	120	96	120	120	Tonnes-km tot.
Portugal							**Portugal**
Km flown	244	249	250	222	229	231	Km parcourus
P'gers carried	11 861	12 601	12 635	9 483	10 072	10 058	P'gers trans.
Passenger-km	29 827	31 759	31 295	27 889	29 735	29 365	Passagers-km
Total tonne-km	319	349	344	310	339	334	Tonnes-km tot.
Qatar							**Qatar**
Km flown	457	509	602	457	509	602	Km parcourus
P'gers carried	18 737	21 425	25 263	18 737	21 425	25 263	P'gers trans.
Passenger-km	79 836	91 799	108 311	79 836	91 799	108 311	Passagers-km
Total tonne-km	4 961	5 993	7 563	4 961	5 993	7 563	Tonnes-km tot.
Republic of Korea							**République de Corée**
Km flown	717	703	770	663	643	704	Km parcourus
P'gers carried	54 530	58 289	65 482	37 735	40 394	45 344	P'gers trans.
Passenger-km	109 807	111 594	119 739	103 532	104 959	112 357	Passagers-km
Total tonne-km	11 113	11 125	11 297	11 066	11 072	11 242	Tonnes-km tot.
Republic of Moldova							**République de Moldova**
Km flown	8	11	12	8	11	12	Km parcourus
P'gers carried	558	692	1 006	558	692	1 006	P'gers trans.
Passenger-km	756	1 168	1 448	756	1 168	1 448	Passagers-km
Total tonne-km	1	1	~0	1	1	~0	Tonnes-km tot.
Romania							**Roumanie**
Km flown	45	45	51	41	41	47	Km parcourus
P'gers carried	3 087	3 068	3 637	2 525	2 573	3 150	P'gers trans.
Passenger-km	3 994	4 124	4 986	3 793	3 947	4 813	Passagers-km
Total tonne-km	5	5	5	5	5	5	Tonnes-km tot.
Russian Federation							**Fédération de Russie**
Km flown	1 286	1 379	1 404	606	616	575	Km parcourus
P'gers carried	64 072	72 190	76 846	27 496	27 894	26 147	P'gers trans.
Passenger-km	162 367	176 360	179 680	88 474	90 352	82 983	Passagers-km
Total tonne-km	4 249	4 414	4 761	3 449	3 642	4 129	Tonnes-km tot.
Rwanda							**Rwanda**
Km flown	12	12	13	12	12	13	Km parcourus
P'gers carried	611	627	646	579	599	619	P'gers trans.
Passenger-km	818	847	875	814	843	871	Passagers-km
Total tonne-km	20	21	21	20	21	21	Tonnes-km tot.
Samoa							**Samoa**
Km flown	1	1	2	1	1	2	Km parcourus
P'gers carried	72	77	99	72	77	99	P'gers trans.
Passenger-km	16	17	21	16	17	21	Passagers-km
Total tonne-km	~0	~0	~0	~0	~0	~0	Tonnes-km tot.
Saudi Arabia							**Arabie saoudite**
Km flown	315	350	338	206	236	222	Km parcourus
P'gers carried	28 252	32 269	32 779	11 515	14 332	13 693	P'gers trans.
Passenger-km	49 321	57 092	55 541	35 339	42 023	40 134	Passagers-km
Total tonne-km	1 694	1 600	1 783	1 631	1 547	1 725	Tonnes-km tot.
Scandinavia [2]							**Scandinavie [2]**
Km flown	525	612	619	422	507	516	Km parcourus
P'gers carried	51 926	57 614	58 516	36 443	41 524	42 557	P'gers trans.
Passenger-km	58 310	70 559	74 166	51 265	63 260	67 011	Passagers-km
Total tonne-km	592	563	596	585	555	586	Tonnes-km tot.

31 Civil aviation: scheduled airline traffic *(continued)*

Passengers carried (thousands); kilometres, passenger-kilometers and tonne-kilometers (millions)

Aviation civile: trafic aérien régulier *(suite)*

Passagers transportés (milliers); kilomètres, passagers-kilomètres and tonnes-kilomètres (millions)

Country or area and traffic	Total traffic (domestic and international) Trafic total (intérieur et international)			International traffic Trafic international			Pays ou zone et trafic
	2013	2014	2015	2013	2014	2015	
Senegal							**Sénégal**
Km flown	5	3	3	4	3	2	Km parcourus
P'gers carried	220	132	115	204	116	100	P'gers trans.
Passenger-km	384	222	192	376	214	184	Passagers-km
Total tonne-km	4	4	3	4	3	3	Tonnes-km tot.
Serbia							**Serbie**
Km flown	16	27	28	16	27	28	Km parcourus
P'gers carried	1 241	2 187	2 425	1 241	2 187	2 425	P'gers trans.
Passenger-km	1 250	2 253	2 459	1 250	2 253	2 459	Passagers-km
Total tonne-km	1	3	3	1	3	3	Tonnes-km tot.
Seychelles							**Seychelles**
Km flown	6	7	10	5	7	9	Km parcourus
P'gers carried	344	407	497	188	253	315	P'gers trans.
Passenger-km	685	979	1 157	678	972	1 149	Passagers-km
Total tonne-km	26	32	19	26	32	19	Tonnes-km tot.
Singapore							**Singapour**
Km flown	612	598	601	612	598	601	Km parcourus
P'gers carried	31 729	33 357	33 291	31 729	33 357	33 291	P'gers trans.
Passenger-km	119 102	121 280	123 329	119 102	121 280	123 329	Passagers-km
Total tonne-km	6 360	6 052	6 154	6 360	6 052	6 154	Tonnes-km tot.
Slovakia							**Slovaquie**
Km flown	1	~0	~0	~0	~0	~0	Km parcourus
P'gers carried	64	29	11	32	25	11	P'gers trans.
Passenger-km	44	31	24	31	30	24	Passagers-km
Slovenia							**Slovénie**
Km flown	14	14	17	14	14	17	Km parcourus
P'gers carried	857	917	1 131	857	917	1 131	P'gers trans.
Passenger-km	788	851	1 046	788	851	1 046	Passagers-km
Total tonne-km	1	1	1	1	1	1	Tonnes-km tot.
Solomon Islands							**Îles Salomon**
Km flown	13	13	15	10	9	11	Km parcourus
P'gers carried	302	330	374	24	23	26	P'gers trans.
Passenger-km	283	283	329	179	168	200	Passagers-km
Total tonne-km	3	3	4	1	1	1	Tonnes-km tot.
Somalia							**Somalie**
Km flown	3	3	...	2	2	...	Km parcourus
P'gers carried	258	252	...	146	139	...	P'gers trans.
Passenger-km	219	212	...	144	136	...	Passagers-km
Total tonne-km	1	1	...	1	1	...	Tonnes-km tot.
South Africa							**Afrique du Sud**
Km flown	219	229	224	130	135	129	Km parcourus
P'gers carried	16 311	16 949	17 189	4 508	4 499	4 420	P'gers trans.
Passenger-km	32 259	31 603	31 075	20 885	19 677	18 909	Passagers-km
Total tonne-km	1 123	1 043	885	1 062	978	825	Tonnes-km tot.
Spain							**Espagne**
Km flown	507	558	622	372	418	473	Km parcourus
P'gers carried	48 057	53 069	60 809	24 584	29 366	35 296	P'gers trans.
Passenger-km	82 111	90 949	103 431	66 430	74 616	85 889	Passagers-km
Total tonne-km	958	963	1 041	938	939	1 016	Tonnes-km tot.
Sri Lanka							**Sri Lanka**
Km flown	77	77	79	77	77	79	Km parcourus
P'gers carried	4 793	4 756	4 912	4 789	4 755	4 912	P'gers trans.
Passenger-km	14 517	13 989	14 104	14 516	13 989	14 104	Passagers-km
Total tonne-km	385	385	381	385	385	381	Tonnes-km tot.
Sudan							**Soudan**
Km flown	13	10	9	10	8	8	Km parcourus
P'gers carried	542	502	496	465	446	443	P'gers trans.
Passenger-km	931	888	887	806	781	779	Passagers-km
Total tonne-km	12	12	13	11	11	12	Tonnes-km tot.
Suriname							**Suriname**
Km flown	8	6	6	8	6	6	Km parcourus
P'gers carried	255	269	260	255	269	260	P'gers trans.
Passenger-km	1 095	1 107	1 146	1 095	1 107	1 146	Passagers-km
Total tonne-km	30	29	29	30	29	29	Tonnes-km tot.

Civil aviation: scheduled airline traffic *(continued)*

Passengers carried (thousands); kilometres, passenger-kilometers and tonne-kilometers (millions)

Aviation civile: trafic aérien régulier *(suite)*

Passagers transportés (milliers); kilomètres, passagers-kilomètres and tonnes-kilomètres (millions)

Country or area and traffic	Total traffic (domestic and international) Trafic total (intérieur et international) 2013	2014	2015	International traffic Trafic international 2013	2014	2015	Pays ou zone et trafic
Switzerland							**Suisse**
Km flown	334	345	330	328	340	326	Km parcourus
P'gers carried	27 503	27 923	26 844	26 643	27 198	26 161	P'gers trans.
Passenger-km	49 128	50 292	49 162	48 899	50 096	48 996	Passagers-km
Total tonne-km	1 444	1 509	1 322	1 444	1 508	1 322	Tonnes-km tot.
Syrian Arab Republic							**République arabe syrienne**
Km flown	7	7	...	7	7	...	Km parcourus
P'gers carried	476	476	...	437	437	...	P'gers trans.
Passenger-km	533	533	...	530	530	...	Passagers-km
Total tonne-km	2	2	...	2	2	...	Tonnes-km tot.
Tajikistan							**Tadjikistan**
Km flown	16	19	16	15	19	16	Km parcourus
P'gers carried	683	794	802	625	757	762	P'gers trans.
Passenger-km	1 776	2 146	2 030	1 765	2 138	2 022	Passagers-km
Total tonne-km	~0	~0	~0	~0	~0	~0	Tonnes-km tot.
Thailand							**Thaïlande**
Km flown	415	441	472	313	323	323	Km parcourus
P'gers carried	43 029	45 170	54 260	21 490	21 492	23 694	P'gers trans.
Passenger-km	82 248	80 411	87 124	68 852	65 442	69 473	Passagers-km
Total tonne-km	2 640	2 515	2 134	2 595	2 490	2 108	Tonnes-km tot.
Togo							**Togo**
Km flown	9	8	7	9	8	7	Km parcourus
P'gers carried	841	779	770	841	779	770	P'gers trans.
Passenger-km	696	645	655	696	645	655	Passagers-km
Total tonne-km	32	34	...	32	34	...	Tonnes-km tot.
Trinidad and Tobago							**Trinité-et-Tobago**
Km flown	53	51	51	49	48	47	Km parcourus
P'gers carried	2 866	2 732	2 618	1 997	1 814	1 772	P'gers trans.
Passenger-km	4 672	4 307	4 247	4 600	4 232	4 181	Passagers-km
Total tonne-km	45	44	43	45	44	43	Tonnes-km tot.
Tunisia							**Tunisie**
Km flown	59	45	47	57	44	46	Km parcourus
P'gers carried	4 649	4 629	3 496	4 454	4 436	3 305	P'gers trans.
Passenger-km	5 960	6 055	4 869	5 870	5 976	4 790	Passagers-km
Total tonne-km	15	13	10	15	13	10	Tonnes-km tot.
Turkey							**Turquie**
Km flown	787	999	1 127	618	813	913	Km parcourus
P'gers carried	74 414	84 575	96 605	36 717	42 570	48 246	P'gers trans.
Passenger-km	116 977	137 171	157 419	93 295	110 533	126 684	Passagers-km
Total tonne-km	2 296	2 630	2 882	2 266	2 600	2 857	Tonnes-km tot.
Turkmenistan							**Turkménistan**
Km flown	17	16	16	13	12	13	Km parcourus
P'gers carried	1 801	1 700	2 138	790	746	1 184	P'gers trans.
Passenger-km	3	3	5	3	3	4	Passagers-km
Uganda							**Ouganda**
Km flown	6	4	1	5	4	...	Km parcourus
P'gers carried	199	164	42	150	119	...	P'gers trans.
Passenger-km	125	101	5	119	94	...	Passagers-km
Total tonne-km	1	1	~0	1	1	...	Tonnes-km tot.
Ukraine							**Ukraine**
Km flown	73	71	66	64	66	62	Km parcourus
P'gers carried	5 219	4 527	4 613	4 213	3 923	3 982	P'gers trans.
Passenger-km	7 603	7 643	7 969	7 071	7 350	7 685	Passagers-km
Total tonne-km	14	22	38	14	22	36	Tonnes-km tot.
United Arab Emirates							**Émirats arabes unis**
Km flown	1 202	1 305	1 481	1 202	1 305	1 481	Km parcourus
P'gers carried	68 152	75 608	84 738	68 152	75 608	84 738	P'gers trans.
Passenger-km	283 327	319 148	357 194	283 327	319 148	357 194	Passagers-km
Total tonne-km	14 082	15 527	16 647	14 082	15 527	16 647	Tonnes-km tot.
United Kingdom							**Royaume-Uni**
Km flown	1 521	1 592	1 619	1 410	1 485	1 508	Km parcourus
P'gers carried	118 606	124 873	131 450	99 106	105 221	111 088	P'gers trans.
Passenger-km	259 536	274 966	283 184	251 147	266 563	274 528	Passagers-km
Total tonne-km	6 032	5 917	5 467	6 031	5 917	5 465	Tonnes-km tot.

31 Civil aviation: scheduled airline traffic *(continued)*

Passengers carried (thousands); kilometres, passenger-kilometers and tonne-kilometers (millions)

Aviation civile: trafic aérien régulier *(suite)*

Passagers transportés (milliers); kilomètres, passagers-kilomètres and tonnes-kilomètres (millions)

Country or area and traffic	Total traffic (domestic and international) Trafic total (intérieur et international)			International traffic Trafic international			Pays ou zone et trafic
	2013	2014	2015	2013	2014	2015	
United Rep. of Tanzania							**Rép.-Unie de Tanzanie**
Km flown	22	18	17	5	4	4	Km parcourus
P'gers carried	1 174	1 073	1 240	328	232	279	P'gers trans.
Passenger-km	911	884	964	157	178	220	Passagers-km
Total tonne-km	~0	1	2	~0	~0	~0	Tonnes-km tot.
United States of America							**États-Unis d'Amérique**
Km flown	12 106	12 143	12 338	2 851	2 918	2 926	Km parcourus
P'gers carried	743 171	762 710	798 230	97 491	99 879	102 203	P'gers trans.
Passenger-km	1 352 541	1 387 790	1 451 694	422 522	429 889	436 967	Passagers-km
Total tonne-km	37 114	38 225	37 219	21 786	22 606	21 596	Tonnes-km tot.
Uzbekistan							**Ouzbékistan**
Km flown	51	50	49	46	44	44	Km parcourus
P'gers carried	2 614	2 546	2 487	2 034	1 985	1 886	P'gers trans.
Passenger-km	6 906	6 758	6 464	6 547	6 416	6 095	Passagers-km
Total tonne-km	99	110	114	99	110	114	Tonnes-km tot.
Vanuatu							**Vanuatu**
Km flown	5	4	4	3	3	2	Km parcourus
P'gers carried	327	320	288	165	159	131	P'gers trans.
Passenger-km	365	352	286	331	319	253	Passagers-km
Total tonne-km	2	2	2	2	2	1	Tonnes-km tot.
Venezuela (Boliv. Rep. of)							**Venezuela (Rép. boliv. du)**
Km flown	52	55	49	17	17	19	Km parcourus
P'gers carried	6 867	7 506	6 457	872	859	942	P'gers trans.
Passenger-km	5 495	5 883	5 411	2 016	1 915	2 153	Passagers-km
Total tonne-km	5	6	6	3	4	4	Tonnes-km tot.
Viet Nam							**Viet Nam**
Km flown	224	198	233	165	110	120	Km parcourus
P'gers carried	20 429	23 826	29 945	6 096	6 785	8 150	P'gers trans.
Passenger-km	29 504	33 242	39 402	18 280	19 612	21 783	Passagers-km
Total tonne-km	497	450	384	371	311	222	Tonnes-km tot.
Yemen							**Yémen**
Km flown	16	16	12	13	13	11	Km parcourus
P'gers carried	1 664	1 666	1 388	1 120	1 115	966	P'gers trans.
Passenger-km	2 120	2 116	1 801	1 905	1 897	1 648	Passagers-km
Zambia							**Zambie**
Km flown	5	5	5	2	2	2	Km parcourus
P'gers carried	10	9	12	...	...	...	P'gers trans.
Passenger-km	4	3	4	...	...	...	Passagers-km
Total tonne-km	93	83	79	93	83	79	Tonnes-km tot.
Zimbabwe							**Zimbabwe**
Km flown	21	20	19	9	9	7	Km parcourus
P'gers carried	352	301	370	155	142	157	P'gers trans.
Passenger-km	682	662	808	254	250	270	Passagers-km
Total tonne-km	33	33	1	33	33	1	Tonnes-km tot.

Source:

International Civil Aviation Organization (ICAO), Montreal, ICAO Air Transport Reporting Forms A and A-S plus ICAO estimates, last accessed April 2017.

1 For statistical purposes, the data for China do not include those for the Hong Kong Special Administrative Region (Hong Kong SAR) and Macao Special Administrative Region (Macao SAR).

2 Three States - Denmark, Norway and Sweden.

Source:

Organisation de l'aviation civile internationale (OACI), Montréal, Formulaires A et A-S du transport aérien de l'OACI et estimations de l'OACI, dernier accès avril 2017.

1 Pour la présentation des statistiques, les données pour la Chine ne comprennent pas la Région Administrative Spéciale de Hong Kong (Hong Kong RAS) et la Région Administrative Spéciale de Macao (Macao RAS).

2 Trois états: Danemark, Norvège et la Suède.

32 Net disbursements of official development assistance to recipients

Total, bilateral and multilateral aid (millions of US dollars); and as a percentage of Gross National Income (GNI)

Décaissements nets d'aide publique au développement aux bénéficiaires

Total, bilatérale et multilatérale d'aide (millions de dollars É.-U.); et en pourcentage du Revenu National Brut (RNB)

Region, country or area[&]	1975	1985	1995	2005	2010	2013	2014	2015	Région, pays ou zone[&]
Total, all countries or areas [1]									**Total, tous pays ou zones [1]**
Bilateral	**15 189**	**26 348**	**48 268**	**82 923**	**94 401**	**111 431**	**119 754**	**117 235**	**Bilatérale**
Multilateral	**3 597**	**5 920**	**11 004**	**25 620**	**37 133**	**39 735**	**41 952**	**35 368**	**Multilatérale**
Total	**18 785**	**32 268**	**59 272**	**108 542**	**131 534**	**151 165**	**161 705**	**152 603**	**Total**
% of GNI	**1.7**	**1.3**	**1.0**	**1.2**	**0.7**	**0.6**	**0.6**	**0.7**	**% du RNB**
Africa [1]									**Afrique [1]**
Bilateral	5 671	10 076	16 828	24 081	30 082	38 776	35 143	35 073	Bilatérale
Multilateral	1 105	2 247	5 015	11 740	17 732	18 030	19 156	16 137	Multilatérale
Total	6 775	12 323	21 843	35 821	47 814	56 805	54 299	51 210	Total
% of GNI	4.7	4.1	4.6	3.7	2.6	2.5	2.3	2.4	% du RNB
Northern Africa [1,2]									**Afrique septentrionale [1,2]**
Bilateral	3 062	2 849	2 703	1 705	1 844	7 628	5 584	3 760	Bilatérale
Multilateral	179	142	277	980	823	1 173	1 774	1 294	Multilatérale
Total	3 241	2 991	2 981	2 685	2 667	8 801	7 358	5 054	Total
% of GNI	8.2	2.7	1.9	0.8	0.5	1.3	1.1	0.8	% du RNB
Sub-Saharan Africa [1,3]									**Afrique subsaharienne [1,3]**
Bilateral	2 557	7 017	13 771	21 889	27 167	29 822	27 831	28 583	Bilatérale
Multilateral	926	1 968	4 594	10 532	16 425	16 271	16 614	14 268	Multilatérale
Total	3 483	8 985	18 365	32 420	43 592	46 093	44 445	42 852	Total
% of GNI	3.3	4.7	5.8	5.1	3.4	2.9	2.6	2.9	% du RNB
Americas [1]									**Amériques [1]**
Bilateral	777	3 015	5 484	4 559	8 107	8 029	7 875	8 082	Bilatérale
Multilateral	597	398	935	2 106	2 854	2 263	2 140	2 027	Multilatérale
Total	1 375	3 413	6 418	6 665	10 961	10 292	10 015	10 109	Total
% of GNI	0.4	0.5	0.4	0.3	0.2	0.2	0.2	0.3	% du RNB
North America [1]									**Amérique du Nord [1]**
Bilateral	254	1 989	2 988	2 285	4 938	3 367	3 216	3 604	Bilatérale
Multilateral	280	203	513	1 011	1 886	1 264	1 249	916	Multilatérale
Total	534	2 193	3 501	3 296	6 824	4 631	4 465	4 519	Total
% of GNI	0.4	0.9	0.8	0.3	0.5	0.3	0.3	0.3	% du RNB
South America [1]									**Amérique du Sud [1]**
Bilateral	435	903	2 268	2 038	1 942	3 215	3 541	3 345	Bilatérale
Multilateral	317	150	344	792	858	750	699	928	Multilatérale
Total	752	1 052	2 612	2 829	2 800	3 965	4 240	4 274	Total
% of GNI	0.3	0.2	0.2	0.2	0.1	0.1	0.1	0.2	% du RNB
Asia [1]									**Asie [1]**
Bilateral	6 393	9 033	14 201	39 027	26 899	33 410	42 162	35 835	Bilatérale
Multilateral	1 813	2 747	4 415	7 579	9 896	11 156	11 847	9 737	Multilatérale
Total	8 206	11 780	18 616	46 606	36 795	44 566	54 009	45 572	Total
% of GNI	1.5	0.8	0.6	1.0	0.3	0.3	0.3	0.3	% du RNB
Eastern and South-Eastern Asia [1,4]									**Asie orientale et du Sud-Est [1,4]**
Bilateral	1 495	2 448	7 387	6 613	5 019	3 121	3 483	3 513	Bilatérale
Multilateral	371	498	1 411	1 779	2 515	2 790	2 742	1 901	Multilatérale
Total	1 866	2 946	8 798	8 391	7 534	5 911	6 225	5 414	Total
% of GNI	0.7	0.4	0.4	0.3	0.1	0.1	0.1	~0.0	% du RNB
South-central Asia [1,5]									**Asie centrale et du Sud [1,5]**
Bilateral	2 457	2 678	4 049	7 262	13 216	14 125	12 736	13 626	Bilatérale
Multilateral	1 308	1 998	2 409	4 395	5 499	6 451	7 184	6 155	Multilatérale
Total	3 765	4 676	6 458	11 658	18 715	20 577	19 920	19 781	Total
% of GNI	2.7	1.6	1.2	1.0	0.8	0.7	0.7	0.7	% du RNB
Western Asia [1,6]									**Asie occidentale [1,6]**
Bilateral	2 407	3 856	2 449	24 324	7 766	15 141	23 349	17 621	Bilatérale
Multilateral	134	181	504	1 182	1 709	1 771	1 738	1 530	Multilatérale
Total	2 541	4 037	2 954	25 506	9 475	16 912	25 087	19 151	Total
% of GNI	1.9	0.9	0.7	3.6	1.2	1.9	3.4	7.6	% du RNB
Europe [1,7]									**Europe [1,7]**
Bilateral	96	383	1 753	2 446	3 124	2 780	3 752	2 846	Bilatérale
Multilateral	58	28	534	1 605	2 787	4 676	4 880	4 002	Multilatérale
Total	154	410	2 288	4 051	5 910	7 456	8 632	6 847	Total
% of GNI	0.3	0.6	1.0	0.6	0.6	0.6	0.8	0.7	% du RNB

32

Net disbursements of official development assistance to recipients *(continued)*
Total, bilateral and multilateral aid (millions of US dollars); and as a percentage of Gross National Income (GNI)

Décaissements nets d'aide publique au développement aux bénéficiaires *(suite)*
Total, bilatérale et multilatérale d'aide (millions de dollars É.-U.); et en pourcentage du Revenu National Brut (RNB)

Region, country or area&	1975	1985	1995	2005	2010	2013	2014	2015	Région, pays ou zone&
Oceania [1]									**Océanie** [1]
Bilateral	589	859	1 807	803	1 619	1 843	1 600	1 619	Bilatérale
Multilateral	24	38	62	341	269	322	281	295	Multilatérale
Total	613	897	1 868	1 144	1 888	2 165	1 881	1 914	Total
% of GNI	17.1	14.5	12.3	11.6	12.3	9.4	7.5	28.7	% du RNB
Areas not specified									**Zones non spécifiées**
Bilateral	...	2 982	8 196	12 007	24 571	26 593	29 221	33 780	Bilatérale
Multilateral	...	462	42	2 248	3 595	3 287	3 647	3 171	Multilatérale
Total	1 662	3 445	8 238	14 254	28 166	29 881	32 869	36 951	Total
Afghanistan									**Afghanistan**
Bilateral	41	7	129	2 296	5 759	4 608	4 380	3 873	Bilatérale
Multilateral	29	9	84	542	713	545	565	366	Multilatérale
Total	69	16	213	2 838	6 472	5 153	4 945	4 239	Total
% of GNI	2.9	...	...	45.2	40.5	24.0	23.9	21.4	% du RNB
Albania									**Albanie**
Bilateral	...	...	118	192	253	171	167	232	Bilatérale
Multilateral	...	...	63	123	112	99	114	102	Multilatérale
Total	...	...	181	315	365	270	281	334	Total
% of GNI	...	...	7.3	3.8	3.1	2.1	2.1	3.0	% du RNB
Algeria									**Algérie**
Bilateral	213	161	272	252	131	142	103	37	Bilatérale
Multilateral	23	11	24	96	71	62	58	51	Multilatérale
Total	235	172	296	347	201	203	161	88	Total
% of GNI	1.5	0.3	0.8	0.4	0.1	0.1	0.1	0.1	% du RNB
Angola									**Angola**
Bilateral	4	72	304	217	146	152	100	276	Bilatérale
Multilateral	1	19	113	198	89	134	135	104	Multilatérale
Total	5	90	416	415	235	286	235	380	Total
% of GNI	...	1.4	11.5	1.7	0.3	0.3	0.2	0.4	% du RNB
Anguilla									**Anguilla**
Bilateral	2	2	3	4	-1	4	...	...	Bilatérale
Multilateral	~0	1	1	~0	9	4	...	...	Multilatérale
Total	2	3	3	4	8	8	...	...	Total
Antigua and Barbuda									**Antigua-et-Barbuda**
Bilateral	2	2	2	7	6	~0	1	1	Bilatérale
Multilateral	1	1	~0	1	14	2	2	1	Multilatérale
Total	2	3	2	8	20	2	3	1	Total
% of GNI	...	1.5	0.5	0.8	1.8	0.1	0.2	0.1	% du RNB
Argentina									**Argentine**
Bilateral	3	30	126	62	99	-2	12	-49	Bilatérale
Multilateral	23	9	17	32	30	37	37	26	Multilatérale
Total	26	39	143	94	129	35	49	-23	Total
% of GNI	0.1	0.1	0.1	~0.0	~0.0	~0.0	~0.0	...	% du RNB
Armenia									**Arménie**
Bilateral	...	...	111	105	232	127	130	174	Bilatérale
Multilateral	...	...	107	67	111	154	137	173	Multilatérale
Total	...	...	218	173	343	280	268	348	Total
% of GNI	...	...	14.9	3.4	3.5	2.4	2.2	3.2	% du RNB
Aruba									**Aruba**
Bilateral	...	...	23	...	...	...	...	...	Bilatérale
Multilateral	...	...	3	...	...	...	...	...	Multilatérale
Total	...	12	26	...	...	...	...	...	Total
Azerbaijan									**Azerbaïdjan**
Bilateral	...	...	67	119	82	-183	133	23	Bilatérale
Multilateral	...	...	53	91	80	112	83	47	Multilatérale
Total	...	...	120	211	162	-71	217	70	Total
% of GNI	...	...	3.9	1.8	0.3	-0.1	0.3	0.1	% du RNB
Bahamas									**Bahamas**
Bilateral	~0	~0	3	...	...	...	...	...	Bilatérale
Multilateral	1	1	2	...	...	...	...	...	Multilatérale
Total	1	1	4	...	...	...	...	...	Total
% of GNI	0.1	~0.0	0.1	...	...	...	...	...	% du RNB

32 Net disbursements of official development assistance to recipients *(continued)*

Total, bilateral and multilateral aid (millions of US dollars); and as a percentage of Gross National Income (GNI)

Décaissements nets d'aide publique au développement aux bénéficiaires *(suite)*

Total, bilatérale et multilatérale d'aide (millions de dollars É.-U.); et en pourcentage du Revenu National Brut (RNB)

Region, country or area&	1975	1985	1995	2005	2010	2013	2014	2015	Région, pays ou zone&
Bahrain									**Bahreïn**
Bilateral	25	73	100	...	...	...	...	...	Bilatérale
Multilateral	1	1	~0	...	...	...	...	...	Multilatérale
Total	26	74	100	...	...	...	...	...	Total
% of GNI	...	2.2	1.7	...	...	...	...	...	% du RNB
Bangladesh									**Bangladesh**
Bilateral	777	619	907	590	582	1 402	1 346	1 606	Bilatérale
Multilateral	295	508	375	731	822	1 231	1 077	964	Multilatérale
Total	1 072	1 127	1 282	1 320	1 405	2 634	2 423	2 570	Total
% of GNI	5.5	5.0	3.3	1.8	1.1	1.6	1.3	1.2	% du RNB
Barbados									**Barbade**
Bilateral	3	6	-2	-5	-1	...	...	...	Bilatérale
Multilateral	3	1	1	3	18	...	...	...	Multilatérale
Total	5	7	-1	-2	16	...	...	...	Total
% of GNI	...	0.6	-0.1	-0.1	0.4	...	...	...	% du RNB
Belarus									**Bélarus**
Bilateral	...	...	...	40	94	72	78	71	Bilatérale
Multilateral	...	...	...	18	42	35	43	34	Multilatérale
Total	...	...	...	58	136	107	121	105	Total
% of GNI	...	...	...	0.2	0.3	0.2	0.2	0.2	% du RNB
Belize									**Belize**
Bilateral	8	21	12	6	9	30	12	10	Bilatérale
Multilateral	1	1	7	6	16	21	25	17	Multilatérale
Total	9	22	19	12	25	51	38	27	Total
% of GNI	8.2	11.0	3.1	1.2	2.0	3.4	2.4	1.7	% du RNB
Benin									**Bénin**
Bilateral	36	62	229	175	388	330	311	250	Bilatérale
Multilateral	18	32	52	174	301	331	289	180	Multilatérale
Total	54	94	281	349	689	660	599	430	Total
% of GNI	8.0	9.2	13.2	7.3	10.0	7.3	6.3	5.1	% du RNB
Bermuda									**Bermudes**
Bilateral	...	1	-2	...	...	...	...	...	Bilatérale
Multilateral	...	~0	0	...	...	...	...	...	Multilatérale
Total	~0	1	-2	...	...	...	...	...	Total
% of GNI	~0.0	0.1	-0.1	...	...	...	...	...	% du RNB
Bhutan									**Bhoutan**
Bilateral	~0	9	64	52	87	86	67	59	Bilatérale
Multilateral	2	14	10	38	44	51	63	38	Multilatérale
Total	2	23	73	90	131	137	131	97	Total
% of GNI	...	17.0	27.5	11.2	8.8	8.1	7.2	5.3	% du RNB
Bolivia (Plurin. State of)									**Bolivie (État plurin. de)**
Bilateral	27	166	559	486	569	538	562	584	Bilatérale
Multilateral	29	30	153	157	148	164	113	203	Multilatérale
Total	56	196	712	643	718	702	675	787	Total
% of GNI	2.2	4.0	11.0	7.0	3.8	2.4	2.2	2.4	% du RNB
Bosnia and Herzegovina									**Bosnie-Herzégovine**
Bilateral	...	...	900	309	290	219	278	119	Bilatérale
Multilateral	...	...	66	231	222	302	352	236	Multilatérale
Total	...	...	966	540	511	521	630	355	Total
% of GNI	...	...	59.4	4.6	2.9	2.8	3.4	2.2	% du RNB
Botswana									**Botswana**
Bilateral	39	71	71	8	95	73	51	41	Bilatérale
Multilateral	12	24	19	40	60	35	49	24	Multilatérale
Total	51	96	90	48	155	107	99	66	Total
% of GNI	14.4	9.4	1.9	0.5	1.3	0.7	0.6	0.5	% du RNB
Brazil									**Brésil**
Bilateral	101	91	245	88	361	1 043	832	714	Bilatérale
Multilateral	66	31	34	104	88	113	82	284	Multilatérale
Total	166	122	279	193	449	1 156	914	999	Total
% of GNI	0.1	0.1	~0.0	~0.0	~0.0	0.1	~0.0	0.1	% du RNB
British Virgin Islands									**Îles Vierges britanniques**
Bilateral	2	2	~0	...	...	...	...	...	Bilatérale
Multilateral	~0	~0	1	...	...	...	...	...	Multilatérale
Total	2	2	1	...	...	...	...	...	Total

32

Net disbursements of official development assistance to recipients *(continued)*
Total, bilateral and multilateral aid (millions of US dollars); and as a percentage of Gross National Income (GNI)

Décaissements nets d'aide publique au développement aux bénéficiaires *(suite)*
Total, bilatérale et multilatérale d'aide (millions de dollars É.-U.); et en pourcentage du Revenu National Brut (RNB)

Region, country or area[&]	1975	1985	1995	2005	2010	2013	2014	2015	Région, pays ou zone[&]
Brunei Darussalam									**Brunéi Darussalam**
Bilateral	~0	1	4	...	...	...	...	...	Bilatérale
Multilateral	0	~0	~0	...	...	...	...	...	Multilatérale
Total	~0	1	4	...	...	...	...	...	Total
% of GNI	...	...	0.1	...	...	...	...	...	% du RNB
Burkina Faso									**Burkina Faso**
Bilateral	62	134	350	382	554	618	676	526	Bilatérale
Multilateral	27	54	140	316	491	428	448	471	Multilatérale
Total	89	188	490	698	1 045	1 045	1 124	997	Total
% of GNI	9.5	12.2	20.7	12.8	11.4	8.8	9.2	9.1	% du RNB
Burundi									**Burundi**
Bilateral	33	91	147	163	279	262	263	185	Bilatérale
Multilateral	15	46	140	202	349	297	252	181	Multilatérale
Total	47	137	287	366	628	559	515	367	Total
% of GNI	11.5	12.1	29.0	33.2	31.2	20.6	16.7	11.9	% du RNB
Cabo Verde									**Cabo Verde**
Bilateral	4	42	91	112	248	214	183	111	Bilatérale
Multilateral	5	22	25	51	79	32	48	42	Multilatérale
Total	9	64	116	163	327	245	231	153	Total
% of GNI	...	48.0	23.9	17.4	20.6	13.8	13.0	9.8	% du RNB
Cambodia									**Cambodge**
Bilateral	78	9	434	374	524	584	559	520	Bilatérale
Multilateral	4	5	117	165	210	224	243	157	Multilatérale
Total	82	14	551	539	734	808	803	677	Total
% of GNI	...	...	16.3	9.0	6.8	5.5	5.1	4.0	% du RNB
Cameroon									**Cameroun**
Bilateral	72	134	380	279	303	434	515	434	Bilatérale
Multilateral	37	18	64	138	237	318	342	230	Multilatérale
Total	110	152	444	417	540	752	856	664	Total
% of GNI	4.5	1.9	5.4	2.6	2.3	2.6	2.7	2.3	% du RNB
Cayman Islands									**Îles Caïmanes**
Bilateral	1	-~0	-1	...	...	...	...	...	Bilatérale
Multilateral	1	~0	~0	...	...	...	...	...	Multilatérale
Total	2	~0	-1	...	...	...	...	...	Total
Central African Republic									**République centrafricaine**
Bilateral	39	73	126	37	78	112	290	295	Bilatérale
Multilateral	16	31	42	52	183	91	321	192	Multilatérale
Total	55	104	168	89	261	203	611	487	Total
% of GNI	14.5	12.1	15.3	6.6	13.1	13.5	36.0	32.3	% du RNB
Chad									**Tchad**
Bilateral	33	118	165	166	275	218	168	1	Bilatérale
Multilateral	34	61	70	221	215	242	224	606	Multilatérale
Total	67	179	235	386	490	459	392	607	Total
% of GNI	7.7	17.4	16.3	6.9	4.8	3.7	3.0	5.7	% du RNB
Chile									**Chili**
Bilateral	96	37	147	88	145	55	199	32	Bilatérale
Multilateral	31	3	9	83	44	26	47	18	Multilatérale
Total	127	40	157	170	189	81	246	50	Total
% of GNI	1.8	0.3	0.2	0.2	0.1	~0.0	0.1	~0.0	% du RNB
China [8]									**Chine** [8]
Bilateral	...	697	2 560	1 471	344	-1 007	-1 242	-583	Bilatérale
Multilateral	...	242	921	329	327	350	295	252	Multilatérale
Total	...	939	3 481	1 799	672	-656	-947	-332	Total
% of GNI	...	0.3	0.5	0.1	~0.0	-~0.0	-~0.0	0.0	% du RNB
China, Hong Kong SAR									**Chine, Hong Kong RAS**
Bilateral	-1	18	14	...	...	...	...	...	Bilatérale
Multilateral	~0	2	4	...	...	...	...	...	Multilatérale
Total	-1	20	18	...	...	...	...	...	Total
% of GNI	-~0.0	0.1	~0.0	...	...	...	...	...	% du RNB
China, Macao SAR									**Chine, Macao RAS**
Bilateral	~0	~0	-4	...	...	...	...	...	Bilatérale
Multilateral	0	~0	0	...	...	...	...	...	Multilatérale
Total	~0	~0	-4	...	...	...	...	...	Total
% of GNI	...	~0.0	-0.1	...	...	...	...	...	% du RNB

32 Net disbursements of official development assistance to recipients *(continued)*

Total, bilateral and multilateral aid (millions of US dollars); and as a percentage of Gross National Income (GNI)

Décaissements nets d'aide publique au développement aux bénéficiaires *(suite)*

Total, bilatérale et multilatérale d'aide (millions de dollars É.-U.); et en pourcentage du Revenu National Brut (RNB)

Region, country or area&	1975	1985	1995	2005	2010	2013	2014	2015	Région, pays ou zone&
Colombia									**Colombie**
Bilateral	51	45	158	542	576	768	1 113	1 267	Bilatérale
Multilateral	32	17	12	83	98	89	111	81	Multilatérale
Total	83	61	170	625	674	857	1 224	1 347	Total
% of GNI	0.7	0.2	0.2	0.4	0.2	0.2	0.3	0.5	% du RNB
Comoros									**Comores**
Bilateral	19	32	27	5	21	-25	26	30	Bilatérale
Multilateral	2	15	15	18	47	107	49	36	Multilatérale
Total	22	47	42	23	68	81	75	66	Total
% of GNI	35.9	41.7	17.9	6.1	13.2	13.6	12.1	...	% du RNB
Congo									**Congo**
Bilateral	43	55	117	1 350	1 047	83	48	38	Bilatérale
Multilateral	13	14	10	76	267	68	59	51	Multilatérale
Total	56	69	127	1 426	1 314	151	106	89	Total
% of GNI	7.6	3.4	10.3	35.4	14.6	1.4	0.9	1.1	% du RNB
Cook Islands									**Îles Cook**
Bilateral	5	9	12	7	13	15	23	21	Bilatérale
Multilateral	~0	1	1	1	1	1	4	4	Multilatérale
Total	6	10	13	8	14	16	27	24	Total
Costa Rica									**Costa Rica**
Bilateral	16	265	19	13	79	15	21	84	Bilatérale
Multilateral	14	14	13	13	16	18	33	25	Multilatérale
Total	30	279	32	26	95	33	55	109	Total
% of GNI	1.6	6.2	0.3	0.1	0.3	0.1	0.1	0.2	% du RNB
Côte d'Ivoire									**Côte d'Ivoire**
Bilateral	82	110	949	16	476	846	417	302	Bilatérale
Multilateral	18	7	264	75	368	427	508	351	Multilatérale
Total	100	117	1 212	91	844	1 273	925	653	Total
% of GNI	2.7	1.9	12.1	0.6	3.5	4.3	2.8	2.2	% du RNB
Croatia									**Croatie**
Bilateral	...	...	48	58	11	...	...	...	Bilatérale
Multilateral	...	...	5	65	121	...	...	...	Multilatérale
Total	...	...	53	123	132	...	...	...	Total
% of GNI	...	...	0.2	0.3	0.2	...	...	...	% du RNB
Cuba									**Cuba**
Bilateral	11	31	46	67	82	64	229	527	Bilatérale
Multilateral	9	11	17	23	51	35	33	25	Multilatérale
Total	20	42	64	90	132	99	262	553	Total
% of GNI	0.2	0.2	0.2	0.2	0.2	...	...	...	% du RNB
Cyprus									**Chypre**
Bilateral	18	31	15	...	...	...	...	...	Bilatérale
Multilateral	13	6	7	...	...	...	...	...	Multilatérale
Total	31	37	21	...	...	...	...	...	Total
% of GNI	6.3	1.5	0.2	...	...	...	...	...	% du RNB
Dem. People's Rep. Korea									**Rép. pop. dém. de Corée**
Bilateral	...	...	3	33	28	68	109	104	Bilatérale
Multilateral	...	...	11	54	50	41	45	27	Multilatérale
Total	...	6	13	87	79	109	154	131	Total
Dem. Rep. of the Congo									**Rép. dém. du Congo**
Bilateral	219	223	136	1 094	1 042	1 445	1 315	1 663	Bilatérale
Multilateral	39	83	59	788	2 442	1 139	1 085	936	Multilatérale
Total	258	305	195	1 882	3 484	2 584	2 400	2 599	Total
% of GNI	...	...	4.0	16.4	17.8	9.5	8.1	8.0	% du RNB
Djibouti									**Djibouti**
Bilateral	34	71	94	46	105	103	113	136	Bilatérale
Multilateral	~0	11	12	29	27	47	52	33	Multilatérale
Total	34	81	106	74	132	149	165	170	Total
% of GNI	...	...	20.5	9.6	...	...	...	...	% du RNB
Dominica									**Dominique**
Bilateral	6	13	18	13	3	8	10	4	Bilatérale
Multilateral	2	4	7	8	30	12	6	8	Multilatérale
Total	8	17	25	21	32	20	16	12	Total
% of GNI	...	17.8	11.9	6.2	6.7	4.1	3.2	2.4	% du RNB

32 Net disbursements of official development assistance to recipients *(continued)*

Total, bilateral and multilateral aid (millions of US dollars); and as a percentage of Gross National Income (GNI)

Décaissements nets d'aide publique au développement aux bénéficiaires *(suite)*

Total, bilatérale et multilatérale d'aide (millions de dollars É.-U.); et en pourcentage du Revenu National Brut (RNB)

Region, country or area&	1975	1985	1995	2005	2010	2013	2014	2015	Région, pays ou zone&
Dominican Republic									**République dominicaine**
Bilateral	13	195	107	9	60	78	92	238	Bilatérale
Multilateral	17	12	13	67	116	69	74	39	Multilatérale
Total	30	207	120	76	177	147	166	278	Total
% of GNI	0.8	4.4	0.8	0.2	0.3	0.3	0.3	0.4	% du RNB
Ecuador									**Équateur**
Bilateral	21	116	197	159	102	105	120	165	Bilatérale
Multilateral	49	19	27	74	49	45	43	146	Multilatérale
Total	69	135	224	232	151	151	163	311	Total
% of GNI	0.9	0.8	1.0	0.6	0.2	0.2	0.2	0.3	% du RNB
Egypt									**Égypte**
Bilateral	2 413	1 692	1 873	730	412	5 390	3 224	2 331	Bilatérale
Multilateral	100	82	155	316	187	122	314	184	Multilatérale
Total	2 513	1 774	2 028	1 046	599	5 513	3 538	2 515	Total
% of GNI	22.5	5.7	3.4	1.2	0.3	2.0	1.2	0.8	% du RNB
El Salvador									**El Salvador**
Bilateral	4	327	277	127	203	120	72	65	Bilatérale
Multilateral	34	18	19	72	78	49	26	24	Multilatérale
Total	37	345	296	199	282	169	98	88	Total
% of GNI	2.0	9.4	3.2	1.2	1.4	0.7	0.4	0.4	% du RNB
Equatorial Guinea									**Guinée équatoriale**
Bilateral	1	9	23	18	75	1	-3	3	Bilatérale
Multilateral	1	8	10	20	10	3	4	5	Multilatérale
Total	2	17	33	38	85	5	1	8	Total
% of GNI	2.1	29.5	28.3	0.9	1.4	0.1	~0.0	0.2	% du RNB
Eritrea									**Érythrée**
Bilateral	...	...	119	229	49	9	-1	52	Bilatérale
Multilateral	...	...	29	121	114	72	83	40	Multilatérale
Total	2	...	148	350	162	81	82	92	Total
% of GNI	...	...	25.3	32.1	7.7	...	...	...	% du RNB
Ethiopia									**Éthiopie**
Bilateral	73	541	653	1 205	2 223	2 273	2 194	2 238	Bilatérale
Multilateral	59	177	224	724	1 232	1 613	1 391	996	Multilatérale
Total	132	718	877	1 929	3 455	3 886	3 585	3 234	Total
% of GNI	...	7.6	11.5	15.6	11.6	8.2	6.5	5.3	% du RNB
Fiji									**Fidji**
Bilateral	18	28	41	32	56	69	75	73	Bilatérale
Multilateral	2	3	4	34	19	22	19	30	Multilatérale
Total	19	32	44	66	76	91	94	102	Total
% of GNI	2.9	2.8	2.3	2.2	2.5	2.2	2.2	2.5	% du RNB
French Polynesia									**Polynésie française**
Bilateral	71	171	448	...	...	...	...	...	Bilatérale
Multilateral	~0	1	3	...	...	...	...	...	Multilatérale
Total	72	172	451	...	...	...	...	...	Total
% of GNI	10.4	11.4	11.3	...	...	...	...	...	% du RNB
Gabon									**Gabon**
Bilateral	58	55	140	1	82	66	92	81	Bilatérale
Multilateral	3	6	4	50	24	21	19	17	Multilatérale
Total	60	61	144	50	106	87	111	99	Total
% of GNI	3.0	2.0	3.4	0.6	0.9	0.6	0.7	0.7	% du RNB
Gambia									**Gambie**
Bilateral	4	33	25	7	52	52	30	69	Bilatérale
Multilateral	4	15	20	53	70	64	71	39	Multilatérale
Total	8	48	45	61	121	116	102	108	Total
% of GNI	7.0	19.1	5.9	10.3	12.8	13.1	12.4	...	% du RNB
Georgia									**Géorgie**
Bilateral	...	...	104	183	357	365	307	253	Bilatérale
Multilateral	...	...	106	110	270	281	255	194	Multilatérale
Total	...	...	209	293	627	646	562	448	Total
% of GNI	...	...	8.1	4.5	5.6	4.1	3.4	3.3	% du RNB
Ghana									**Ghana**
Bilateral	99	105	362	660	1 132	797	642	1 022	Bilatérale
Multilateral	25	89	288	493	565	532	482	746	Multilatérale
Total	124	194	650	1 153	1 697	1 329	1 124	1 768	Total
% of GNI	4.5	4.4	10.3	10.9	5.4	2.9	3.0	4.8	% du RNB

32

Net disbursements of official development assistance to recipients *(continued)*
Total, bilateral and multilateral aid (millions of US dollars); and as a percentage of Gross National Income (GNI)

Décaissements nets d'aide publique au développement aux bénéficiaires *(suite)*
Total, bilatérale et multilatérale d'aide (millions de dollars É.-U.); et en pourcentage du Revenu National Brut (RNB)

Region, country or area&	1975	1985	1995	2005	2010	2013	2014	2015	Région, pays ou zone&
Gibraltar									**Gibraltar**
Bilateral	...	...	~0	...	...	...	...	...	Bilatérale
Multilateral	...	...	0	...	...	...	...	...	Multilatérale
Total	3	29	~0	...	...	...	...	...	Total
Grenada									**Grenade**
Bilateral	2	32	8	33	10	3	14	7	Bilatérale
Multilateral	1	2	3	20	24	9	26	17	Multilatérale
Total	3	34	11	53	34	13	40	24	Total
% of GNI	...	...	4.1	7.9	4.6	1.5	4.5	2.6	% du RNB
Guatemala									**Guatemala**
Bilateral	25	71	181	189	322	411	188	329	Bilatérale
Multilateral	15	12	27	65	67	86	92	80	Multilatérale
Total	40	83	208	254	389	497	280	408	Total
% of GNI	1.1	0.9	1.4	1.0	1.0	0.9	0.5	0.7	% du RNB
Guinea									**Guinée**
Bilateral	20	74	305	89	47	187	238	247	Bilatérale
Multilateral	4	39	111	104	174	281	325	292	Multilatérale
Total	24	113	416	193	221	468	563	538	Total
% of GNI	...	...	11.5	7.3	5.1	8.1	9.2	8.7	% du RNB
Guinea-Bissau									**Guinée-Bissau**
Bilateral	17	34	95	8	-33	47	16	29	Bilatérale
Multilateral	4	22	23	59	161	59	94	66	Multilatérale
Total	21	56	118	67	128	106	110	95	Total
% of GNI	18.7	35.3	49.8	11.6	15.1	10.3	10.0	9.0	% du RNB
Guyana									**Guyana**
Bilateral	7	21	59	80	106	53	125	10	Bilatérale
Multilateral	3	6	27	70	62	48	36	20	Multilatérale
Total	10	27	86	150	167	101	161	31	Total
% of GNI	2.1	7.0	15.2	19.3	7.4	3.4	5.3	1.0	% du RNB
Haiti									**Haïti**
Bilateral	18	120	603	260	2 337	903	811	833	Bilatérale
Multilateral	38	29	120	165	700	249	272	209	Multilatérale
Total	56	149	722	426	3 038	1 152	1 082	1 043	Total
% of GNI	...	...	...	9.7	45.7	13.6	12.3	11.7	% du RNB
Honduras									**Honduras**
Bilateral	24	245	301	509	436	425	457	409	Bilatérale
Multilateral	26	25	101	183	198	201	149	128	Multilatérale
Total	51	270	402	692	634	626	606	537	Total
% of GNI	4.6	7.8	11.0	7.5	4.2	3.6	3.4	2.9	% du RNB
India									**Inde**
Bilateral	879	844	876	669	1 639	1 152	1 119	1 800	Bilatérale
Multilateral	726	743	862	1 207	1 192	1 306	1 874	1 373	Multilatérale
Total	1 605	1 587	1 738	1 876	2 831	2 457	2 992	3 173	Total
% of GNI	1.6	0.7	0.5	0.2	0.2	0.1	0.2	0.2	% du RNB
Indonesia									**Indonésie**
Bilateral	455	514	1 252	2 255	967	-169	-569	-167	Bilatérale
Multilateral	232	83	50	281	423	238	187	133	Multilatérale
Total	687	597	1 303	2 537	1 390	70	-382	-33	Total
% of GNI	2.2	0.7	0.7	0.9	0.2	~0.0	-~0.0	0.0	% du RNB
Iran (Islamic Republic of)									**Iran (Rép. islamique d')**
Bilateral	-12	2	162	61	72	105	48	92	Bilatérale
Multilateral	13	9	25	40	40	27	33	19	Multilatérale
Total	2	11	187	101	112	132	81	111	Total
% of GNI	0.0	~0.0	0.2	0.1	~0.0	~0.0	~0.0	...	% du RNB
Iraq									**Iraq**
Bilateral	101	19	273	21 999	2 040	1 406	1 234	1 349	Bilatérale
Multilateral	9	1	60	58	138	136	137	136	Multilatérale
Total	110	20	333	22 057	2 178	1 542	1 371	1 485	Total
% of GNI	...	~0.0	...	43.5	1.6	0.7	0.6	0.9	% du RNB
Israel									**Israël**
Bilateral	466	1 978	334	...	...	...	...	...	Bilatérale
Multilateral	2	~0	2	...	...	...	...	...	Multilatérale
Total	467	1 978	336	...	...	...	...	...	Total
% of GNI	3.9	8.5	0.4	...	...	...	...	...	% du RNB

32 Net disbursements of official development assistance to recipients *(continued)*

Total, bilateral and multilateral aid (millions of US dollars); and as a percentage of Gross National Income (GNI)

Décaissements nets d'aide publique au développement aux bénéficiaires *(suite)*

Total, bilatérale et multilatérale d'aide (millions de dollars É.-U.); et en pourcentage du Revenu National Brut (RNB)

Region, country or area[&]	1975	1985	1995	2005	2010	2013	2014	2015	Région, pays ou zone[&]
Jamaica									**Jamaïque**
Bilateral	16	161	82	-9	-10	-12	25	13	Bilatérale
Multilateral	9	7	27	48	150	84	69	44	Multilatérale
Total	24	169	109	40	139	72	93	57	Total
% of GNI	0.8	9.2	2.0	0.4	1.1	0.5	0.7	0.4	% du RNB
Jordan									**Jordanie**
Bilateral	471	598	462	593	692	1 119	2 450	1 909	Bilatérale
Multilateral	21	9	78	117	263	282	247	241	Multilatérale
Total	492	607	540	710	955	1 400	2 697	2 150	Total
% of GNI	35.0	12.4	8.4	5.5	3.6	4.2	7.6	5.8	% du RNB
Kazakhstan									**Kazakhstan**
Bilateral	...	...	54	194	140	46	51	6	Bilatérale
Multilateral	...	...	11	31	72	45	42	77	Multilatérale
Total	...	...	65	225	212	91	93	83	Total
% of GNI	...	...	0.3	0.4	0.2	~0.0	0.1	0.1	% du RNB
Kenya									**Kenya**
Bilateral	99	366	506	475	1 163	2 178	1 549	1 665	Bilatérale
Multilateral	26	61	227	281	468	1 130	1 112	809	Multilatérale
Total	125	427	733	757	1 631	3 308	2 661	2 474	Total
% of GNI	3.9	7.2	8.4	4.0	4.1	6.0	4.4	3.9	% du RNB
Kiribati									**Kiribati**
Bilateral	6	11	14	20	21	53	61	50	Bilatérale
Multilateral	~0	1	2	8	2	12	20	15	Multilatérale
Total	6	12	15	28	23	65	81	65	Total
% of GNI	...	38.8	16.9	17.5	10.5	22.1	24.8	20.1	% du RNB
Kosovo									**Kosovo**
Bilateral	...	...	...	...	215	377	361	252	Bilatérale
Multilateral	...	...	...	...	312	192	219	186	Multilatérale
Total	...	...	...	...	528	569	580	438	Total
% of GNI	...	...	...	...	8.9	7.9	7.7	6.8	% du RNB
Kuwait									**Koweït**
Bilateral	-2	3	4	...	...	...	...	...	Bilatérale
Multilateral	2	1	~0	...	...	...	...	...	Multilatérale
Total	~0	4	4	...	...	...	...	...	Total
% of GNI	0.0	~0.0	~0.0	...	...	...	...	...	% du RNB
Kyrgyzstan									**Kirghizistan**
Bilateral	...	...	191	176	257	384	457	598	Bilatérale
Multilateral	...	...	94	91	127	156	170	172	Multilatérale
Total	...	...	285	267	384	539	627	770	Total
% of GNI	...	...	17.5	11.3	8.6	7.7	8.7	12.2	% du RNB
Lao People's Dem. Rep.									**Rép. dém. populaire lao**
Bilateral	26	19	253	161	285	286	349	394	Bilatérale
Multilateral	13	21	55	137	128	138	126	77	Multilatérale
Total	38	40	308	297	413	423	474	471	Total
% of GNI	...	1.7	17.5	11.1	6.2	4.0	4.3	4.0	% du RNB
Lebanon									**Liban**
Bilateral	7	65	147	142	319	377	584	789	Bilatérale
Multilateral	7	17	44	89	126	245	237	187	Multilatérale
Total	14	82	191	231	445	622	821	975	Total
% of GNI	...	...	1.6	1.1	1.2	1.4	1.8	2.0	% du RNB
Lesotho									**Lesotho**
Bilateral	12	65	81	26	92	200	52	40	Bilatérale
Multilateral	16	28	31	42	164	121	55	43	Multilatérale
Total	28	92	113	68	256	321	107	83	Total
% of GNI	11.4	19.2	9.4	3.7	9.9	11.2	4.1	...	% du RNB
Liberia									**Libéria**
Bilateral	8	72	51	118	957	319	451	764	Bilatérale
Multilateral	12	19	72	104	457	217	299	330	Multilatérale
Total	20	90	123	222	1 414	536	750	1 094	Total
% of GNI	3.3	11.2	...	56.4	127.1	32.6	44.6	61.7	% du RNB
Libya									**Libye**
Bilateral	-6	3	4	17	1	71	173	132	Bilatérale
Multilateral	8	2	2	6	7	57	38	26	Multilatérale
Total	2	5	6	24	8	129	210	158	Total
% of GNI	...	...	...	0.1	~0.0	0.2	0.5	0.5	% du RNB

32 Net disbursements of official development assistance to recipients *(continued)*

Total, bilateral and multilateral aid (millions of US dollars); and as a percentage of Gross National Income (GNI)

Décaissements nets d'aide publique au développement aux bénéficiaires *(suite)*

Total, bilatérale et multilatérale d'aide (millions de dollars É.-U.); et en pourcentage du Revenu National Brut (RNB)

Region, country or area&	1975	1985	1995	2005	2010	2013	2014	2015	Région, pays ou zone&
Madagascar									**Madagascar**
Bilateral	43	118	192	517	263	257	261	400	Bilatérale
Multilateral	39	67	107	399	214	242	326	277	Multilatérale
Total	82	185	299	916	477	499	586	677	Total
% of GNI	3.6	6.7	10.0	18.5	5.5	4.9	5.5	7.1	% du RNB
Malawi									**Malawi**
Bilateral	43	72	286	301	561	720	534	694	Bilatérale
Multilateral	20	41	149	272	456	413	398	355	Multilatérale
Total	63	112	435	574	1 017	1 133	931	1 049	Total
% of GNI	10.1	10.4	32.2	15.9	14.9	21.1	15.8	16.5	% du RNB
Malaysia									**Malaisie**
Bilateral	88	219	104	17	-33	-131	6	-14	Bilatérale
Multilateral	11	10	5	12	27	18	14	13	Multilatérale
Total	99	229	108	29	-6	-113	20	-1	Total
% of GNI	1.1	0.8	0.1	~0.0	0.0	-~0.0	~0.0	0.0	% du RNB
Maldives									**Maldives**
Bilateral	2	6	51	50	72	8	4	17	Bilatérale
Multilateral	1	3	7	27	40	14	19	10	Multilatérale
Total	3	9	58	77	112	22	23	27	Total
% of GNI	...	7.7	15.3	7.0	5.6	0.9	0.8	1.0	% du RNB
Mali									**Mali**
Bilateral	67	308	401	395	770	871	774	786	Bilatérale
Multilateral	76	70	139	330	322	526	462	414	Multilatérale
Total	144	379	540	725	1 091	1 398	1 236	1 200	Total
% of GNI	17.6	27.7	20.3	12.0	10.6	10.9	8.8	9.5	% du RNB
Malta									**Malte**
Bilateral	33	18	7	...	...	...	...	...	Bilatérale
Multilateral	1	~0	2	...	...	...	...	...	Multilatérale
Total	34	18	9	...	...	...	...	...	Total
% of GNI	6.4	1.5	0.3	...	...	...	...	...	% du RNB
Marshall Islands									**Îles Marshall**
Bilateral	...	...	36	55	26	87	55	56	Bilatérale
Multilateral	...	...	2	2	7	6	1	1	Multilatérale
Total	...	...	39	57	33	94	56	57	Total
% of GNI	...	...	25.4	31.7	16.5	41.5	24.1	...	% du RNB
Mauritania									**Mauritanie**
Bilateral	68	179	163	91	277	183	176	240	Bilatérale
Multilateral	15	28	67	97	97	112	85	78	Multilatérale
Total	83	208	230	189	374	295	261	318	Total
% of GNI	18.7	32.9	17.2	8.4	8.8	5.4	5.0	...	% du RNB
Mauritius									**Maurice**
Bilateral	15	24	16	13	41	66	19	29	Bilatérale
Multilateral	13	3	8	22	84	80	26	48	Multilatérale
Total	28	27	24	34	125	146	45	77	Total
% of GNI	...	2.6	0.6	0.6	1.3	1.2	0.4	0.7	% du RNB
Mayotte									**Mayotte**
Bilateral	...	20	107	201	603	...	...	...	Bilatérale
Multilateral	...	~0	1	~0	1	...	...	...	Multilatérale
Total	...	21	108	201	604	...	...	...	Total
Mexico									**Mexique**
Bilateral	-6	121	367	173	406	491	657	262	Bilatérale
Multilateral	62	23	24	29	56	71	158	51	Multilatérale
Total	56	144	391	202	462	562	815	313	Total
% of GNI	0.1	0.1	0.1	~0.0	~0.0	0.1	0.1	~0.0	% du RNB
Micronesia (Fed. States of)									**Micronésie (États féd. de)**
Bilateral	...	...	74	104	62	141	114	77	Bilatérale
Multilateral	...	...	3	3	1	3	3	4	Multilatérale
Total	...	...	77	106	63	143	117	81	Total
% of GNI	...	...	33.0	41.1	20.8	41.9	34.1	...	% du RNB
Mongolia									**Mongolie**
Bilateral	...	...	184	160	222	362	240	190	Bilatérale
Multilateral	...	...	25	61	81	69	77	45	Multilatérale
Total	...	5	209	221	303	431	317	236	Total
% of GNI	...	0.2	14.7	8.9	4.6	3.6	2.8	2.2	% du RNB

32 Net disbursements of official development assistance to recipients *(continued)*

Total, bilateral and multilateral aid (millions of US dollars); and as a percentage of Gross National Income (GNI)

Décaissements nets d'aide publique au développement aux bénéficiaires *(suite)*

Total, bilatérale et multilatérale d'aide (millions de dollars É.-U.); et en pourcentage du Revenu National Brut (RNB)

Region, country or area[&]	1975	1985	1995	2005	2010	2013	2014	2015	Région, pays ou zone[&]
Montenegro									**Monténégro**
Bilateral	...	...	...	4	54	46	20	27	Bilatérale
Multilateral	...	...	...	0	26	71	80	73	Multilatérale
Total	...	...	...	4	80	117	100	100	Total
% of GNI	...	...	...	0.2	2.0	2.6	2.2	2.4	% du RNB
Montserrat									**Montserrat**
Bilateral	4	2	9	27	16	50	36	...	Bilatérale
Multilateral	~0	~0	1	1	10	5	5	...	Multilatérale
Total	4	2	9	28	26	55	40	52	Total
Morocco									**Maroc**
Bilateral	260	836	447	395	708	1 517	1 332	843	Bilatérale
Multilateral	10	30	54	338	278	492	908	645	Multilatérale
Total	270	866	501	733	986	2 009	2 240	1 488	Total
% of GNI	3.0	6.0	1.3	1.2	1.1	1.9	2.1	1.5	% du RNB
Mozambique									**Mozambique**
Bilateral	14	242	799	806	1 432	1 751	1 484	1 306	Bilatérale
Multilateral	6	54	264	483	512	562	622	509	Multilatérale
Total	20	296	1 063	1 290	1 943	2 313	2 106	1 815	Total
% of GNI	...	6.8	44.1	17.5	19.8	14.5	12.6	12.5	% du RNB
Myanmar									**Myanmar**
Bilateral	17	237	109	34	212	3 125	1 109	927	Bilatérale
Multilateral	40	107	42	111	143	811	275	242	Multilatérale
Total	58	344	150	145	355	3 936	1 385	1 169	Total
% of GNI	...	...	...	...	...	6.9	2.2	...	% du RNB
Namibia									**Namibie**
Bilateral	...	...	170	56	207	187	159	106	Bilatérale
Multilateral	...	...	20	58	55	74	67	37	Multilatérale
Total	...	5	190	113	261	261	226	142	Total
% of GNI	...	0.4	4.6	1.6	2.4	2.1	1.8	1.2	% du RNB
Nauru									**Nauru**
Bilateral	...	...	3	9	27	28	20	30	Bilatérale
Multilateral	...	...	~0	~0	1	1	2	1	Multilatérale
Total	~0	~0	3	9	28	29	23	31	Total
Nepal									**Népal**
Bilateral	14	105	303	284	444	470	503	810	Bilatérale
Multilateral	29	126	126	139	370	404	381	406	Multilatérale
Total	44	231	430	423	814	873	884	1 216	Total
% of GNI	2.8	8.8	9.8	5.2	5.1	4.5	4.4	5.7	% du RNB
Netherlands Antilles [former]									**Antilles néerlandaises [anc.]**
Bilateral	28	64	97	...	...	...	...	...	Bilatérale
Multilateral	5	1	2	...	...	...	...	...	Multilatérale
Total	33	65	98	...	...	...	...	...	Total
New Caledonia									**Nouvelle-Calédonie**
Bilateral	65	145	448	...	...	...	...	...	Bilatérale
Multilateral	~0	~0	3	...	...	...	...	...	Multilatérale
Total	65	145	451	...	...	...	...	...	Total
% of GNI	7.9	17.0	12.4	...	...	...	...	...	% du RNB
Nicaragua									**Nicaragua**
Bilateral	17	91	585	594	539	353	313	338	Bilatérale
Multilateral	25	17	65	171	121	143	118	117	Multilatérale
Total	41	108	649	765	660	496	431	454	Total
% of GNI	2.8	4.3	17.2	12.4	7.8	4.7	3.8	3.7	% du RNB
Niger									**Niger**
Bilateral	106	226	211	270	402	431	399	489	Bilatérale
Multilateral	31	72	61	254	339	367	519	379	Multilatérale
Total	137	298	272	523	741	797	918	868	Total
% of GNI	13.2	21.3	14.9	15.4	13.1	10.7	11.3	12.3	% du RNB
Nigeria									**Nigéria**
Bilateral	65	19	88	5 954	1 072	1 310	1 239	1 493	Bilatérale
Multilateral	16	13	122	448	980	1 206	1 240	939	Multilatérale
Total	81	32	211	6 402	2 052	2 516	2 479	2 432	Total
% of GNI	0.3	0.1	0.8	6.5	0.6	0.5	0.5	0.5	% du RNB
Niue									**Nioué**
Bilateral	...	...	8	19	14	18	13	19	Bilatérale
Multilateral	...	...	~0	2	1	~0	1	~0	Multilatérale
Total	2	4	8	21	15	18	14	20	Total

32 Net disbursements of official development assistance to recipients *(continued)*

Total, bilateral and multilateral aid (millions of US dollars); and as a percentage of Gross National Income (GNI)

Décaissements nets d'aide publique au développement aux bénéficiaires *(suite)*

Total, bilatérale et multilatérale d'aide (millions de dollars É.-U.); et en pourcentage du Revenu National Brut (RNB)

Region, country or area[&]	1975	1985	1995	2005	2010	2013	2014	2015	Région, pays ou zone[&]
Northern Mariana Islands									**Îles Mariannes du Nord**
Bilateral	81	158	~0	...	...	...	...	...	Bilatérale
Multilateral	~0	1	-1	...	...	...	...	...	Multilatérale
Total	81	159	-1	...	...	...	...	...	Total
Oman									**Oman**
Bilateral	138	75	74	15	-24	...	...	...	Bilatérale
Multilateral	2	2	1	4	2	...	...	...	Multilatérale
Total	140	78	75	19	-22	...	...	...	Total
% of GNI	7.8	0.8	0.6	0.1	-~0.0	...	...	...	% du RNB
Other non-specified areas									**Autres zones non-spécifiées**
Total	-20	-10	~0	...	...	...	...	...	Total
% of GNI	-0.1	-~0.0	0.0	...	...	...	...	...	% du RNB
Pakistan									**Pakistan**
Bilateral	628	405	474	886	2 181	1 461	2 005	2 345	Bilatérale
Multilateral	119	363	349	731	840	733	1 610	1 446	Multilatérale
Total	747	767	823	1 617	3 021	2 194	3 615	3 790	Total
% of GNI	6.5	2.3	1.4	1.5	1.6	0.9	1.4	1.3	% du RNB
Palau									**Palaos**
Bilateral	...	...	142	23	28	34	23	13	Bilatérale
Multilateral	...	...	0	~0	1	1	1	1	Multilatérale
Total	...	...	142	24	29	35	23	14	Total
% of GNI	...	...	145.2	12.9	16.3	16.3	9.8	5.1	% du RNB
Panama									**Panama**
Bilateral	18	61	32	-3	114	-7	-212	-3	Bilatérale
Multilateral	15	8	8	23	14	16	18	12	Multilatérale
Total	33	69	40	20	127	9	-193	9	Total
% of GNI	1.6	1.2	0.5	0.1	0.5	~0.0	-0.4	~0.0	% du RNB
Papua New Guinea									**Papouasie-Nvl-Guinée**
Bilateral	294	241	343	212	418	533	469	483	Bilatérale
Multilateral	11	16	28	54	94	125	110	107	Multilatérale
Total	305	257	371	267	512	658	580	590	Total
% of GNI	23.8	11.0	8.5	5.9	5.6	4.5	3.5	...	% du RNB
Paraguay									**Paraguay**
Bilateral	11	42	130	39	70	92	35	26	Bilatérale
Multilateral	26	8	10	13	51	38	27	30	Multilatérale
Total	37	50	139	51	121	131	62	56	Total
% of GNI	...	...	1.7	0.7	0.7	0.5	0.2	0.2	% du RNB
Peru									**Pérou**
Bilateral	52	291	341	366	-365	307	272	292	Bilatérale
Multilateral	24	21	31	89	69	57	57	39	Multilatérale
Total	77	312	372	456	-296	364	328	332	Total
% of GNI	0.5	1.9	0.8	0.7	-0.2	0.2	0.2	0.2	% du RNB
Philippines									**Philippines**
Bilateral	150	422	853	490	390	91	528	409	Bilatérale
Multilateral	27	37	60	77	151	101	149	106	Multilatérale
Total	177	459	912	568	541	192	677	515	Total
% of GNI	1.2	1.6	1.2	0.4	0.2	0.1	0.2	0.2	% du RNB
Qatar									**Qatar**
Bilateral	-1	1	4	...	...	...	...	...	Bilatérale
Multilateral	1	1	-~0	...	...	...	...	...	Multilatérale
Total	1	2	4	...	...	...	...	...	Total
% of GNI	~0.0	~0.0	0.1	...	...	...	...	...	% du RNB
Republic of Korea									**République de Corée**
Bilateral	208	-13	54	...	...	...	...	...	Bilatérale
Multilateral	40	4	3	...	...	...	...	...	Multilatérale
Total	248	-9	57	...	...	...	...	...	Total
% of GNI	1.2	-~0.0	~0.0	...	...	...	...	...	% du RNB
Republic of Moldova									**République de Moldova**
Bilateral	...	...	...	94	213	194	326	204	Bilatérale
Multilateral	...	...	...	75	260	154	192	108	Multilatérale
Total	...	...	...	170	473	349	518	313	Total
% of GNI	...	...	...	5.1	7.5	3.9	5.9	4.5	% du RNB

32 Net disbursements of official development assistance to recipients *(continued)*
Total, bilateral and multilateral aid (millions of US dollars); and as a percentage of Gross National Income (GNI)

Décaissements nets d'aide publique au développement aux bénéficiaires *(suite)*
Total, bilatérale et multilatérale d'aide (millions de dollars É.-U.); et en pourcentage du Revenu National Brut (RNB)

Region, country or area&	1975	1985	1995	2005	2010	2013	2014	2015	Région, pays ou zone&
Rwanda									**Rwanda**
Bilateral	54	123	403	271	602	659	518	709	Bilatérale
Multilateral	36	54	291	302	431	427	517	373	Multilatérale
Total	90	177	695	573	1 033	1 086	1 035	1 082	Total
% of GNI	15.9	10.4	53.5	22.4	18.3	14.7	13.4	13.7	% du RNB
Saint Helena									**Sainte-Hélène**
Bilateral	...	...	12	22	...	133	126	82	Bilatérale
Multilateral	...	...	~0	~0	...	6	5	~0	Multilatérale
Total	3	12	13	23	54	139	131	82	Total
Saint Kitts and Nevis									**Saint-Kitts-et-Nevis**
Bilateral	1	3	2	1	-2	8	...	...	Bilatérale
Multilateral	~0	1	2	2	13	23	...	...	Multilatérale
Total	2	4	4	3	11	30	...	...	Total
% of GNI	...	4.2	1.4	0.5	1.7	3.9	...	...	% du RNB
Saint Lucia									**Sainte-Lucie**
Bilateral	8	4	31	4	~0	4	8	1	Bilatérale
Multilateral	1	3	17	6	41	21	11	13	Multilatérale
Total	9	7	48	11	41	25	19	14	Total
% of GNI	...	3.8	9.3	1.2	3.4	1.9	1.4	1.0	% du RNB
Saint Vincent & Grenadines									**Saint-Vincent-Grenadines**
Bilateral	6	3	32	4	-~0	-1	2	3	Bilatérale
Multilateral	~0	3	15	4	17	9	8	11	Multilatérale
Total	6	5	48	8	17	9	10	14	Total
% of GNI	18.1	3.8	15.6	1.5	2.5	1.2	1.4	1.8	% du RNB
Samoa									**Samoa**
Bilateral	4	14	38	24	98	67	61	63	Bilatérale
Multilateral	9	6	5	20	50	47	30	31	Multilatérale
Total	13	19	43	44	148	113	91	94	Total
% of GNI	...	...	...	9.9	23.2	14.8	11.8	12.8	% du RNB
Sao Tome and Principe									**Sao Tomé-et-Principe**
Bilateral	~0	6	72	10	36	28	18	33	Bilatérale
Multilateral	1	6	12	23	14	26	23	16	Multilatérale
Total	1	12	84	33	50	54	41	49	Total
% of GNI	...	...	...	26.6	25.8	17.7	12.4	...	% du RNB
Saudi Arabia									**Arabie saoudite**
Bilateral	-6	16	17	23	...	...	...	...	Bilatérale
Multilateral	9	12	~0	2	...	...	...	...	Multilatérale
Total	3	27	17	25	...	...	...	...	Total
% of GNI	~0.0	~0.0	~0.0	~0.0	...	...	...	...	% du RNB
Senegal									**Sénégal**
Bilateral	103	249	489	429	654	697	822	628	Bilatérale
Multilateral	36	42	163	272	283	297	287	251	Multilatérale
Total	139	290	652	701	936	994	1 109	879	Total
% of GNI	6.5	10.3	13.8	8.2	7.3	6.8	7.2	6.5	% du RNB
Serbia									**Serbie**
Bilateral	...	...	92	838	300	204	15	-75	Bilatérale
Multilateral	...	...	3	231	361	576	358	387	Multilatérale
Total	...	...	95	1 068	661	780	372	313	Total
% of GNI	...	...	...	4.1	1.7	1.8	0.9	0.9	% du RNB
Seychelles									**Seychelles**
Bilateral	7	19	12	12	43	17	-~0	1	Bilatérale
Multilateral	~0	3	2	6	11	11	12	6	Multilatérale
Total	7	22	13	17	54	27	12	7	Total
% of GNI	15.6	13.5	2.7	1.9	5.9	2.1	0.9	0.5	% du RNB
Sierra Leone									**Sierra Leone**
Bilateral	7	43	136	131	221	258	587	708	Bilatérale
Multilateral	10	20	76	209	237	191	327	239	Multilatérale
Total	17	64	212	340	458	449	914	946	Total
% of GNI	2.5	7.7	26.0	21.4	17.3	9.2	19.0	21.6	% du RNB
Singapore									**Singapour**
Bilateral	8	21	16	...	...	...	...	...	Bilatérale
Multilateral	5	2	1	...	...	...	...	...	Multilatérale
Total	12	23	17	...	...	...	...	...	Total
% of GNI	0.2	0.1	~0.0	...	...	...	...	...	% du RNB

32 Net disbursements of official development assistance to recipients *(continued)*

Total, bilateral and multilateral aid (millions of US dollars); and as a percentage of Gross National Income (GNI)

Décaissements nets d'aide publique au développement aux bénéficiaires *(suite)*

Total, bilatérale et multilatérale d'aide (millions de dollars É.-U.); et en pourcentage du Revenu National Brut (RNB)

Region, country or area&	1975	1985	1995	2005	2010	2013	2014	2015	Région, pays ou zone&
Slovenia									**Slovénie**
Bilateral	...	...	40	...	...	...	...	...	Bilatérale
Multilateral	...	...	12	...	...	...	...	...	Multilatérale
Total	...	...	53	...	...	...	...	...	Total
% of GNI	...	...	0.2	...	...	...	...	...	% du RNB
Solomon Islands									**Îles Salomon**
Bilateral	22	16	42	167	301	264	179	170	Bilatérale
Multilateral	1	5	6	32	40	26	19	21	Multilatérale
Total	22	21	48	198	340	290	199	190	Total
% of GNI	45.5	13.5	14.9	47.7	68.5	27.6	18.1	16.5	% du RNB
Somalia									**Somalie**
Bilateral	110	249	134	117	309	882	906	1 028	Bilatérale
Multilateral	55	102	54	123	197	172	204	225	Multilatérale
Total	165	351	188	240	506	1 055	1 110	1 254	Total
% of GNI	...	...	...	...	...	21.4	21.1	22.9	% du RNB
South Africa									**Afrique du Sud**
Bilateral	...	...	358	423	800	1 043	690	901	Bilatérale
Multilateral	...	...	28	259	236	254	387	519	Multilatérale
Total	...	...	386	681	1 036	1 297	1 077	1 420	Total
% of GNI	...	...	0.3	0.3	0.3	0.4	0.3	0.5	% du RNB
South Sudan									**Soudan du sud**
Bilateral	...	...	...	...	...	1 140	1 676	1 407	Bilatérale
Multilateral	...	...	...	...	...	260	288	267	Multilatérale
Total	...	...	...	...	...	1 399	1 964	1 675	Total
% of GNI	...	...	...	...	...	11.4	16.6	21.1	% du RNB
Sri Lanka									**Sri Lanka**
Bilateral	81	343	412	902	284	161	232	174	Bilatérale
Multilateral	67	125	142	263	296	242	259	254	Multilatérale
Total	148	468	555	1 165	580	403	492	427	Total
% of GNI	4.4	7.9	4.3	4.8	1.0	0.6	0.6	0.5	% du RNB
State of Palestine									**État de Palestine**
Bilateral	...	...	374	640	1 818	2 111	1 978	1 397	Bilatérale
Multilateral	...	...	140	376	695	492	510	477	Multilatérale
Total	...	...	514	1 016	2 513	2 602	2 488	1 873	Total
% of GNI	...	...	13.8	19.6	26.4	19.1	17.5	...	% du RNB
Sudan									**Soudan**
Bilateral	227	972	183	1 450	1 557	1 264	671	752	Bilatérale
Multilateral	67	153	54	376	469	243	204	148	Multilatérale
Total	294	1 125	237	1 826	2 026	1 507	875	900	Total
% of GNI	6.2	9.3	1.8	7.4	3.4	2.4	1.2	1.1	% du RNB
Suriname									**Suriname**
Bilateral	50	9	74	31	79	23	11	10	Bilatérale
Multilateral	3	2	3	13	25	8	2	5	Multilatérale
Total	53	11	77	44	104	31	13	15	Total
% of GNI	11.6	1.2	11.1	2.6	2.4	0.6	0.3	0.3	% du RNB
Swaziland									**Swaziland**
Bilateral	5	18	49	-1	21	49	42	42	Bilatérale
Multilateral	10	6	9	47	70	69	44	51	Multilatérale
Total	14	24	58	47	91	118	86	93	Total
% of GNI	...	...	3.2	1.7	2.8	2.8	2.1	2.4	% du RNB
Syrian Arab Republic									**République arabe syrienne**
Bilateral	803	591	306	-3	-31	3 457	4 016	4 660	Bilatérale
Multilateral	25	19	50	74	162	181	182	222	Multilatérale
Total	827	610	356	71	131	3 638	4 198	4 882	Total
% of GNI	11.7	3.6	3.1	0.3	...	...	...	...	% du RNB
Tajikistan									**Tadjikistan**
Bilateral	...	...	49	143	255	243	227	280	Bilatérale
Multilateral	...	...	16	110	178	148	129	147	Multilatérale
Total	...	...	65	252	433	391	356	426	Total
% of GNI	...	...	5.5	11.3	7.8	4.6	3.1	4.6	% du RNB
Thailand									**Thaïlande**
Bilateral	67	403	814	-239	-132	-53	259	-2	Bilatérale
Multilateral	18	55	25	72	111	82	96	61	Multilatérale
Total	85	457	839	-167	-20	29	355	59	Total
% of GNI	0.6	1.2	0.5	-0.1	-~0.0	~0.0	0.1	~0.0	% du RNB

32 Net disbursements of official development assistance to recipients *(continued)*

Total, bilateral and multilateral aid (millions of US dollars); and as a percentage of Gross National Income (GNI)

Décaissements nets d'aide publique au développement aux bénéficiaires *(suite)*

Total, bilatérale et multilatérale d'aide (millions de dollars É.-U.); et en pourcentage du Revenu National Brut (RNB)

Region, country or area[&]	1975	1985	1995	2005	2010	2013	2014	2015	Région, pays ou zone[&]
TFYR of Macedonia									**ex-R.Y. de Macédoine**
Bilateral	...	...	34	154	127	95	62	55	Bilatérale
Multilateral	...	...	45	74	67	102	150	159	Multilatérale
Total	...	...	79	227	194	197	212	214	Total
% of GNI	...	...	1.8	3.7	2.1	1.9	1.9	2.2	% du RNB
Timor-Leste									**Timor-Leste**
Bilateral	...	...	~0	149	252	215	198	174	Bilatérale
Multilateral	...	...	0	35	40	44	51	39	Multilatérale
Total	~0	...	~0	185	291	259	250	212	Total
% of GNI	...	...	...	22.2	9.6	5.9	7.8	8.9	% du RNB
Togo									**Togo**
Bilateral	31	74	156	42	205	111	81	110	Bilatérale
Multilateral	11	37	35	41	198	115	130	90	Multilatérale
Total	42	111	191	83	403	226	211	200	Total
% of GNI	6.8	15.3	15.1	4.0	14.6	6.6	5.2	5.5	% du RNB
Tokelau									**Tokélaou**
Bilateral	...	2	3	16	14	24	19	...	Bilatérale
Multilateral	...	~0	~0	~0	~0	~0	~0	...	Multilatérale
Total	~0	2	4	16	15	24	19	9	Total
Tonga									**Tonga**
Bilateral	3	11	37	23	59	60	61	52	Bilatérale
Multilateral	1	2	2	9	11	22	19	16	Multilatérale
Total	3	13	39	32	70	81	80	68	Total
% of GNI	...	21.2	18.9	12.4	18.4	18.3	18.3	...	% du RNB
Trinidad and Tobago									**Trinité-et-Tobago**
Bilateral	3	3	14	-11	2	...	...	...	Bilatérale
Multilateral	3	4	11	9	2	...	...	...	Multilatérale
Total	5	7	25	-2	4	...	...	...	Total
% of GNI	0.2	0.1	0.5	-~0.0	~0.0	...	...	...	% du RNB
Tunisia									**Tunisie**
Bilateral	176	144	49	240	426	317	511	144	Bilatérale
Multilateral	38	17	27	128	124	398	412	331	Multilatérale
Total	214	160	75	368	550	715	923	475	Total
% of GNI	5.1	2.0	0.4	1.2	1.3	1.6	2.0	1.1	% du RNB
Turkey									**Turquie**
Bilateral	19	168	297	-57	715	662	997	139	Bilatérale
Multilateral	40	12	16	457	334	2 186	2 450	2 006	Multilatérale
Total	58	180	314	399	1 050	2 848	3 447	2 145	Total
% of GNI	0.1	0.3	0.2	0.1	0.1	0.4	0.4	0.3	% du RNB
Turkmenistan									**Turkménistan**
Bilateral	...	...	27	20	29	26	20	13	Bilatérale
Multilateral	...	...	4	10	15	10	15	11	Multilatérale
Total	...	...	31	29	44	36	34	24	Total
% of GNI	...	...	1.2	0.4	0.2	0.1	0.1	0.1	% du RNB
Turks and Caicos Islands									**Îles Turques-et-Caïques**
Bilateral	3	5	5	3	...	...	...	...	Bilatérale
Multilateral	~0	1	1	2	...	...	...	...	Multilatérale
Total	3	6	6	5	...	...	...	...	Total
Tuvalu									**Tuvalu**
Bilateral	...	3	7	6	14	22	26	42	Bilatérale
Multilateral	...	~0	1	4	~0	5	9	8	Multilatérale
Total	~0	3	8	9	14	28	34	50	Total
% of GNI	...	...	...	24.7	27.5	50.2	63.5	...	% du RNB
Uganda									**Ouganda**
Bilateral	37	84	571	699	1 112	1 054	1 092	1 127	Bilatérale
Multilateral	15	96	263	497	578	646	543	502	Multilatérale
Total	52	179	834	1 195	1 690	1 700	1 635	1 628	Total
% of GNI	2.2	5.2	14.6	13.7	8.5	7.0	6.2	6.4	% du RNB
Ukraine									**Ukraine**
Bilateral	...	...	...	248	442	431	955	1 207	Bilatérale
Multilateral	...	...	...	156	214	360	454	251	Multilatérale
Total	...	...	...	404	657	791	1 409	1 458	Total
% of GNI	...	...	...	0.5	0.5	0.4	1.1	1.6	% du RNB

32 Net disbursements of official development assistance to recipients *(continued)*

Total, bilateral and multilateral aid (millions of US dollars); and as a percentage of Gross National Income (GNI)

Décaissements nets d'aide publique au développement aux bénéficiaires *(suite)*

Total, bilatérale et multilatérale d'aide (millions de dollars É.-U.); et en pourcentage du Revenu National Brut (RNB)

Region, country or area&	1975	1985	1995	2005	2010	2013	2014	2015	Région, pays ou zone&
United Arab Emirates									**Émirats arabes unis**
Bilateral	3	3	6	...	...	...	...	...	Bilatérale
Multilateral	1	1	-~0	...	...	...	...	...	Multilatérale
Total	4	4	5	...	...	...	...	...	Total
United Rep. of Tanzania									**Rép.-Unie de Tanzanie**
Bilateral	237	400	613	823	1 923	2 251	1 570	1 714	Bilatérale
Multilateral	57	77	258	670	1 037	1 182	1 078	866	Multilatérale
Total	293	477	871	1 492	2 960	3 434	2 649	2 580	Total
% of GNI	...	...	17.0	9.0	9.5	7.8	5.6	5.9	% du RNB
Uruguay									**Uruguay**
Bilateral	-1	3	60	1	31	15	76	8	Bilatérale
Multilateral	13	2	6	17	17	21	14	12	Multilatérale
Total	12	5	66	18	48	37	90	19	Total
% of GNI	0.4	0.1	0.4	0.1	0.1	0.1	0.2	~0.0	% du RNB
Uzbekistan									**Ouzbékistan**
Bilateral	...	...	76	128	153	158	156	287	Bilatérale
Multilateral	...	...	8	41	81	137	169	161	Multilatérale
Total	...	...	84	169	234	295	325	448	Total
% of GNI	...	...	0.6	1.2	0.6	0.5	0.5	0.7	% du RNB
Vanuatu									**Vanuatu**
Bilateral	12	20	43	29	104	86	98	169	Bilatérale
Multilateral	~0	2	2	11	3	5	3	18	Multilatérale
Total	12	22	46	40	108	91	100	187	Total
% of GNI	...	17.7	21.0	10.8	16.0	11.5	12.3	...	% du RNB
Venezuela (Boliv. Rep. of)									**Venezuela (Rép. boliv. du)**
Bilateral	-~0	9	35	13	33	25	28	23	Bilatérale
Multilateral	19	2	8	36	20	13	16	15	Multilatérale
Total	18	11	43	49	53	38	43	37	Total
% of GNI	0.1	~0.0	0.1	~0.0	~0.0	~0.0	...	...	% du RNB
Viet Nam									**Viet Nam**
Bilateral	367	115	724	1 386	2 010	2 680	2 829	2 240	Bilatérale
Multilateral	22	38	111	525	938	1 406	1 387	918	Multilatérale
Total	390	153	835	1 911	2 948	4 086	4 216	3 157	Total
% of GNI	...	...	4.1	3.4	2.6	2.5	2.4	1.7	% du RNB
Wallis and Futuna Islands									**Îles Wallis-et-Futuna**
Bilateral	2	~0	1	72	123	103	99	106	Bilatérale
Multilateral	~0	~0	~0	~0	5	2	~0	~0	Multilatérale
Total	2	~0	1	72	127	106	100	106	Total
Yemen									**Yémen**
Bilateral	211	342	109	127	418	734	851	1 385	Bilatérale
Multilateral	40	89	63	169	249	306	313	146	Multilatérale
Total	251	431	172	296	667	1 040	1 163	1 531	Total
% of GNI	...	...	4.2	2.0	2.3	3.0	...	...	% du RNB
Zambia									**Zambie**
Bilateral	68	244	1 765	692	654	777	733	564	Bilatérale
Multilateral	18	75	266	478	266	369	264	234	Multilatérale
Total	86	319	2 031	1 169	919	1 145	998	797	Total
% of GNI	3.8	16.1	57.0	15.2	4.9	4.2	3.8	4.0	% du RNB
Zimbabwe									**Zimbabwe**
Bilateral	4	218	438	162	478	568	499	507	Bilatérale
Multilateral	~0	18	53	211	234	260	262	281	Multilatérale
Total	4	235	492	373	713	828	761	788	Total
% of GNI	0.1	4.3	7.2	6.8	8.0	6.6	5.8	6.0	% du RNB

Source:

Organisation for Economic Co-operation and Development (OECD), Paris, the OECD Development Assistance Committee database, last accessed April 2017.

Official Development Assistance (ODA) is defined as those flows to developing countries and multilateral institutions provided by official

Source:

Organisation de coopération et de développement économiques (OCDE), Paris, la base de données du comité d'aide au développement de l'OCDE, dernier accès avril 2017.

On entend par Aide publique au développement (APD), l'ensemble des flux financiers à destination des pays en développement et des institutions agencies, including state and local governments, or by their executive agencies, each transaction of which meets the following tests: i) it is administered with the promotion of the economic development and welfare of developing countries as its main objective; and ii) it is concessional in character and conveys a grant element of at least 25 per cent.

1 Includes regional aid disbursements in addition to the disbursements made to individual countries and areas.
2 Excludes Sudan.
3 Includes Sudan.
4 Excludes Myanmar.
5 Includes Azerbaijan, Armenia, Georgia and Myanmar. Excludes Iran (Islamic Rep. of).
6 Excludes Azerbaijan, Armenia, Georgia, Turkey and Cyprus. Includes Iran (Islamic Rep. of).
7 Includes Turkey and Cyprus.
8 For statistical purposes, the data for China do not include those for the Hong Kong Special Administrative Region (Hong Kong SAR), Macao Special Administrative Region (Macao SAR) and Taiwan Province of China.

multilatérales par des organismes publics (y compris les autorités étatiques et locales) ou par leurs organes exécutifs satisfaisant les critères suivants: a) elle est administrée dans le but premier de promouvoir le développement économique et social des pays en développement ; b) elle est accordée à des conditions de faveur et comporte une élément de subvention d'au moins 25 pour cent.

1 Comprend les versements d'aides régionales en plus des versements effectués aux aux différents pays et régions.
2 Exclut le Soudan.
3 Comprend le Soudan.
4 Non compris Myanmar.
5 Y compris l'Azerbaïdjan, l'Arménie, la Géorgie et le Myanmar. Non compris la Rép. Islamique d 'Iran.
6 Non compris l'Azerbaïdjan, l'Arménie, la Géorgie, la Turquie et Chypre. Y compris la Rép. Islamique d 'Iran.
7 Y compris la Turquie et Chypre.
8 Pour la présentation des statistiques, les données pour la Chine ne comprennent pas la Région Administrative Spéciale de Hong Kong (Hong Kong RAS), la Région Administrative Spéciale de Macao (Macao RAS) et la province de Taiwan.

33 Net disbursements of official development assistance from donors

Millions of US dollars and as a percentage of gross national income (GNI)

Décaissements nets d'aide publique au développement par des donateurs

Millions de dollares É.-U. et en pourcentage du revenu national brut (RNB)

Country or area	1975	1985	1995	2005	2010	2013	2014	2015	2016	Pays ou zone
Total										**Total**
$ millions	20 183	33 855	65 424	120 771	147 644	167 062	178 595	162 739	* 170 315	$millions
DAC total										**CAD total**
$ millions	13 315	28 858	58 896	108 397	128 484	134 847	137 581	131 555	* 142 619	$millions
% of GNI	0.34	0.33	0.26	0.32	0.31	0.30	0.30	0.30	* 0.32	% du RNB
Australia [1]										**Australie** [1]
$ millions	552	749	1 194	1 680	3 826	4 846	4 382	3 494	* 3 025	$millions
% of GNI	0.65	0.48	0.34	0.25	0.32	0.33	0.31	0.29	* 0.25	% du RNB
Austria [1]										**Autriche** [1]
$ millions	79	248	620	1 573	1 208	1 171	1 235	1 324	* 1 583	$millions
% of GNI	0.21	0.38	0.27	0.52	0.32	0.27	0.28	0.35	* 0.41	% du RNB
Azerbaijan										**Azerbaïdjan**
$ millions	...	...	...	...	...	...	16	13	...	$millions
% of GNI	...	...	...	...	...	...	0.02	0.02	...	% du RNB
Belgium [1]										**Belgique** [1]
$ millions	378	440	1 034	1 963	3 004	2 299	2 446	1 904	* 2 306	$millions
% of GNI	0.60	0.55	0.38	0.53	0.64	0.45	0.46	0.42	* 0.49	% du RNB
Bulgaria										**Bulgarie**
$ millions	...	...	...	...	40	50	49	41	...	$millions
% of GNI	...	...	...	...	0.09	0.10	0.09	0.09	...	% du RNB
Canada [1]										**Canada** [1]
$ millions	880	1 631	2 067	3 756	5 214	4 947	4 240	4 277	* 3 962	$millions
% of GNI	0.54	0.49	0.38	0.34	0.34	0.28	0.24	0.28	* 0.26	% du RNB
Croatia										**Croatie**
$ millions	...	...	...	...	...	45	72	51	* 41	$millions
% of GNI	...	...	...	...	...	0.08	0.13	0.09	* 0.07	% du RNB
Cyprus [2]										**Chypre** [2]
$ millions	...	...	...	15	51	20	19	18	...	$millions
% of GNI	...	...	...	0.09	0.23	0.10	0.09	0.09	...	% du RNB
Czechia [1]										**Tchéquie** [1]
$ millions	...	...	...	135	228	211	212	199	* 261	$millions
% of GNI	...	...	...	0.11	0.13	0.11	0.11	0.12	* 0.14	% du RNB
Denmark [1]										**Danemark** [1]
$ millions	205	440	1 623	2 109	2 871	2 927	3 003	2 566	* 2 372	$millions
% of GNI	0.55	0.80	0.96	0.81	0.91	0.85	0.86	0.85	* 0.75	% du RNB
Estonia										**Estonie**
$ millions	...	...	...	10	19	31	38	34	* 44	$millions
% of GNI	...	...	...	0.08	0.10	0.13	0.15	0.15	* 0.19	% du RNB
Finland [1]										**Finlande** [1]
$ millions	48	211	388	902	1 333	1 435	1 635	1 288	* 1 057	$millions
% of GNI	0.17	0.40	0.31	0.46	0.55	0.54	0.59	0.55	* 0.44	% du RNB
France [1]										**France** [1]
$ millions	1 493	3 134	8 443	10 026	12 915	11 339	10 620	9 039	* 9 501	$millions
% of GNI	0.44	0.61	0.55	0.47	0.50	0.41	0.37	0.37	* 0.38	% du RNB
Germany [1]										**Allemagne** [1]
$ millions	1 689	2 942	7 524	10 082	12 985	14 228	16 566	17 940	* 24 670	$millions
% of GNI	0.40	0.47	0.31	0.36	0.39	0.38	0.42	0.52	* 0.70	% du RNB
Greece [1]										**Grèce** [1]
$ millions	...	...	...	384	508	239	247	239	* 264	$millions
% of GNI	...	...	...	0.17	0.17	0.10	0.11	0.12	* 0.14	% du RNB
Hungary [1]										**Hongrie** [1]
$ millions	29	84	...	100	114	128	144	156	* 155	$millions
% of GNI	...	...	...	0.11	0.09	0.10	0.11	0.13	* 0.13	% du RNB
Iceland [1]										**Islande** [1]
$ millions	...	...	...	27	29	35	37	40	* 50	$millions
% of GNI	...	...	...	0.18	0.26	0.23	0.22	0.24	* 0.25	% du RNB
Ireland [1]										**Irlande** [1]
$ millions	8	39	153	719	895	846	816	718	* 802	$millions
% of GNI	0.09	0.24	0.29	0.42	0.52	0.46	0.38	0.32	* 0.33	% du RNB
Israel										**Israël**
$ millions	...	...	...	95	145	202	200	198	* 220	$millions
% of GNI	...	...	...	0.07	0.07	0.07	0.07	0.07	* 0.07	% du RNB

33 Net disbursements of official development assistance from donors *(continued)*

Millions of US dollars and as a percentage of gross national income (GNI)

Décaissements nets d'aide publique au développement par des donateurs *(suite)*

Millions de dollares É.-U. et en pourcentage du revenu national brut (RNB)

Country or area	1975	1985	1995	2005	2010	2013	2014	2015	2016	Pays ou zone
Italy [1]										**Italie** [1]
$ millions	182	1 098	1 623	5 091	2 996	3 430	4 009	4 003	* 4 856	$millions
% of GNI	0.10	0.26	0.15	0.29	0.15	0.17	0.19	0.22	* 0.26	% du RNB
Japan [1]										**Japon** [1]
$ millions	1 148	3 797	14 489	13 126	11 058	11 469	9 483	9 203	* 10 368	$millions
% of GNI	0.23	0.29	0.27	0.28	0.20	0.22	0.20	0.20	* 0.20	% du RNB
Kazakhstan										**Kazakhstan**
$ millions	...	...	...	...	...	8	33	43	...	$millions
% of GNI	...	...	...	...	...	~0.00	0.02	0.02	...	% du RNB
Kuwait										**Koweït**
$ millions	859	647	384	218	232	231	277	304	...	$millions
Latvia										**Lettonie**
$ millions	...	...	...	11	16	24	25	23	* 28	$millions
% of GNI	...	...	...	0.07	0.06	0.08	0.08	0.09	* 0.10	% du RNB
Liechtenstein										**Liechtenstein**
$ millions	...	...	...	...	27	28	27	24	...	$millions
% of GNI	...	...	...	...	0.62	0.64	0.50	...	...	% du RNB
Lithuania										**Lituanie**
$ millions	...	...	...	16	37	50	46	48	* 58	$millions
% of GNI	...	...	...	0.06	0.10	0.11	0.10	0.12	* 0.14	% du RNB
Luxembourg [1]										**Luxembourg** [1]
$ millions	...	8	65	256	403	429	423	363	* 384	$millions
% of GNI	...	0.17	0.36	0.79	1.05	1.00	1.06	0.95	* 1.00	% du RNB
Malta										**Malte**
$ millions	...	...	...	...	14	18	20	17	* 20	$millions
% of GNI	...	...	...	...	0.18	0.20	0.20	0.17	* 0.20	% du RNB
Netherlands [1]										**Pays-Bas** [1]
$ millions	608	1 136	3 226	5 115	6 357	5 435	5 573	5 726	* 4 988	$millions
% of GNI	0.74	0.91	0.81	0.82	0.81	0.67	0.64	0.75	* 0.65	% du RNB
New Zealand [1]										**Nouvelle-Zélande** [1]
$ millions	66	54	123	274	342	457	506	442	* 438	$millions
% of GNI	0.52	0.25	0.23	0.27	0.26	0.26	0.27	0.27	* 0.25	% du RNB
Norway [1]										**Norvège** [1]
$ millions	184	574	1 244	2 794	4 372	5 581	5 086	4 278	* 4 352	$millions
% of GNI	0.65	1.01	0.86	0.94	1.05	1.07	1.00	1.05	* 1.11	% du RNB
Other non-specified areas										**Autres zones non-spécifiées**
$ millions	...	...	92	483	381	272	274	255	...	$millions
% of GNI	...	...	...	0.14	0.10	0.05	0.05	0.05	...	% du RNB
Poland [1]										**Pologne** [1]
$ millions	32	19	...	205	378	487	452	441	* 603	$millions
% of GNI	...	...	...	0.07	0.08	0.10	0.09	0.10	* 0.13	% du RNB
Portugal [1]										**Portugal** [1]
$ millions	...	10	258	377	649	488	430	308	* 340	$millions
% of GNI	...	0.05	0.25	0.21	0.29	0.23	0.19	0.16	* 0.17	% du RNB
Republic of Korea [1]										**République de Corée** [1]
$ millions	...	...	116	752	1 174	1 755	1 857	1 915	* 1 965	$millions
% of GNI	...	...	0.02	0.10	0.12	0.13	0.13	0.14	* 0.14	% du RNB
Romania										**Roumanie**
$ millions	...	...	...	...	114	134	214	158	* 198	$millions
% of GNI	...	...	...	...	0.07	0.07	0.11	0.09	* 0.11	% du RNB
Russian Federation										**Fédération de Russie**
$ millions	...	...	...	...	472	714	876[3]	1 161[3]	* 1 023[3]	$millions
% of GNI	...	...	...	...	0.03	0.03	0.05[3]	0.09[3]	* 0.08[3]	% du RNB
Saudi Arabia										**Arabie saoudite**
$ millions	2 569[4]	2 443[4]	305[4]	1 026[4]	3 480	5 683[4]	13 634[4]	6 758[4]	...	$millions
Slovakia [1]										**Slovaquie** [1]
$ millions	...	...	...	57	74	86	83	85	* 107	$millions
% of GNI	...	...	...	...	0.09	0.09	0.09	0.10	* 0.12	% du RNB
Slovenia [1]										**Slovénie** [1]
$ millions	...	...	...	35	59	62	62	63	* 80	$millions
% of GNI	...	...	...	0.11	0.13	0.13	0.12	0.15	* 0.18	% du RNB
Spain [1]										**Espagne** [1]
$ millions	...	169	1 348	3 018	5 949	2 348	1 877	1 397	* 4 096	$millions
% of GNI	...	0.10	0.24	0.27	0.43	0.17	0.13	0.12	* 0.33	% du RNB

33 Net disbursements of official development assistance from donors *(continued)*

Millions of US dollars and as a percentage of gross national income (GNI)

Décaissements nets d'aide publique au développement par des donateurs *(suite)*

Millions de dollares É.-U. et en pourcentage du revenu national brut (RNB)

Country or area	1975	1985	1995	2005	2010	2013	2014	2015	2016	Pays ou zone
Sweden [1]										**Suède** [1]
$ millions	566	840	1 704	3 362	4 533	5 827	6 233	7 089	* 4 870	$millions
% of GNI	0.78	0.86	0.77	0.94	0.97	1.01	1.09	1.40	* 0.94	% du RNB
Switzerland [1]										**Suisse** [1]
$ millions	104	303	1 084	1 772	2 300	3 200	3 522	3 529	* 3 563	$millions
% of GNI	0.18	0.31	0.33	0.42	0.39	0.46	0.50	0.51	* 0.54	% du RNB
Thailand										**Thaïlande**
$ millions	...	...	...	...	4	36	69	62	...	$millions
% of GNI	...	...	...	...	~0.00	0.01	0.02	0.02	...	% du RNB
Timor-Leste										**Timor-Leste**
$ millions	...	...	...	...	...	...	3	4	...	$millions
Turkey										**Turquie**
$ millions	...	...	107	601	967	3 308	3 591	3 919	* 6 182	$millions
% of GNI	...	...	0.06	0.17	0.13	0.40	0.45	0.50	* 0.79	% du RNB
United Arab Emirates										**Émirats arabes unis**
$ millions	1 998[5]	366[5]	243[5]	510[5]	414	5 402[5]	5 080[5]	4 381[5]	* 4 146[5]	$millions
% of GNI	...	...	...	...	0.14	1.34	1.26	1.18	* 1.12	% du RNB
United Kingdom [1]										**Royaume-Uni** [1]
$ millions	904	1 530	3 202	10 772	13 053	17 871	19 306	18 545	* 18 013	$millions
% of GNI	0.38	0.33	0.29	0.47	0.57	0.70	0.70	0.70	* 0.70	% du RNB
United States of America [1]										**États-Unis d'Amérique** [1]
$ millions	4 161	9 403	7 367	27 935	29 656	31 267	33 096	30 986	* 33 589	$millions
% of GNI	0.27	0.24	0.10	0.23	0.20	0.18	0.19	0.17	* 0.18	% du RNB
Areas not specified										**Zones non spécifiées**
$ millions	721	32	...	...	...	...	...	...	...	$millions
European Union (EU) [1]										**Union européenne (UE)** [1]
$ millions	722[6]	1 510[6]	5 398[6]	9 390[6]	12 747	15 959[6]	16 451[6]	13 670[6]	* 15 737[6]	$millions

Source:

Organisation for Economic Co-operation and Development (OECD), Paris, the OECD Development Assistance Committee database, last accessed April 2017.

Source:

Organisation de coopération et de développement économiques (OCDE), Paris, la base de données du comité d'aide au développement de l'OCDE, dernier accès avril 2017.

1 Development Assistance Committee member (OECD)
2 Data refer to government controlled areas.
3 Some of the debt relief reported by Russia from 2014 onwards may correspond to the credits included in these estimates. Therefore, the statistics currently published on ODA by Russia and the estimates from the previous Chairman's reports should not be used at the same time.
4 Saudi Arabia's reporting to the OECD on its development co-operation programme consists of aggregate figures on humanitarian and development assistance by region, multilateral aid and loan disbursements and repayments by the Saudi Fund for Development.
5 The United Arab Emirates began to report at activity level in 2009. These data represent flows from all government agencies. Commitments are set equal to disbursements for agencies other than the Abu Dhabi Fund for Development.
6 Refers to European Union institutions.

1 Le Comité d'aide au développement (l'OCDE)
2 Les données se rapportent aux zones contrôlées par le Gouvernement.
3 L'allégement de la dette déclarée par la Russie à partir de 2014 correspond aux crédits inclus dans ces estimations. Les statistiques de la la Russie concernant l'APD et les estimations des rapports précédents du Président ne peuvent donc pas être utilisées conjointement.
4 La déclaration de l'Arabie saoudite auprès de l'OCDE relatif au programme de coopération au développement est constituée de données globales sur l'aide humanitaire, l'aide au développement par région, l'aide multilatérale, et les déboursements et les remboursements de prêts par les Fonds saoudien pour le développement.
5 Les Émirats arabes unis ont commencé à présenter au niveau d"activité en 2009. Ces données représentent les flux de tous les organismes gouvernementaux. Les engagements sont égaux aux décaissements pour les organismes autres que le Fond d'Abu Dhabi pour le développement.
6 Se réfèrent aux institutions de l'Union Européenne.

Annex I - Country and area nomenclature, regional and other groupings

The *Statistical Yearbook* lists countries or areas based on the United Nations Standard Country Codes (Series M, No. 49), prepared by the Statistics Division of the United Nations Secretariat and first issued in 1970[1]. The list of countries or areas; the composition of geographical regions and economic, trade and other groupings used within this yearbook (as at 31 July 2017) are presented in this Annex. The names of countries or areas refer to their short form used in day-to-day operations of the United Nations and not necessarily to their official name as used in formal documents[2]. As an aid to statistical data processing, a unique standard three-digit numerical code is assigned to each country or area and to each geographical region and grouping of countries or areas. For reference, these codes, where applicable, are presented to the left of each country or area listed in this Annex. These codes range from 000 to 899, inclusive.

A. Changes in country or area names (since 31 July 2007)

The geographical extent of a country or area, or the composition of a geographical region, may change over time and users should take such changes into account in interpreting the tables in this Yearbook. A change in the name of a country or area while its geographical coverage remains the same is not usually accompanied by a change in its numerical code. Changes in numerical codes and names in the general period covered by the statistics (since 31 July 2007) in the *Yearbook*, are shown below;

Numerical code	Country or area (added or changed)	Date of change	Numerical code	Country or area (Name changes with no change in code)	Date of change
728	South Sudan	2011	203	Czechia, *previously Czech Republic*	2016
729	Sudan	2011	132	Cabo Verde, *previously Cape Verde*	2013
531	Curaçao	2010	275	State of Palestine, *previously Occupied Palestinian Territory*	2013
534	Sint Maarten (Dutch part)	2010			
535	Bonaire, Sint Eustatius and Saba	2010	434	Libya, *previously Libyan Arab Jamahiriya*	2011
652	Saint Barthélemy	2007	068	Bolivia (Plurinational State of), *previously Bolivia*	2009
663	Saint Martin (French part)	2007			
			498	Republic of Moldova, *previously Moldova (since 2007)*	2008

B. Regional groupings

The scheme of regional groupings given on the next page is based mainly on 6 continents; these continental regions, except Antarctica, are further subdivided into 22 sub-regions and 2 intermediary regions (Sub-Saharan Africa and Latin America and the Caribbean) that are drawn as to obtain greater homogeneity in sizes of population, demographic circumstances and accuracy of demographic statistics. This nomenclature is widely used in international statistics and is followed to the greatest extent possible in the present *Yearbook* in order to promote consistency and facilitate comparability and analysis. However, it is by no means universal in international statistical compilation, even at the level of continental regions, and variations in international statistical sources and methods dictate many unavoidable differences in particular fields in the present *Yearbook*. General differences are indicated in the footnotes to the classification presented below. More detailed differences are given in the footnotes and technical notes to individual tables.

Neither is there international standardization in the use of the terms "developed" and "developing" countries, areas or regions. These terms are used in the present publication to refer to regional groupings generally considered as "developed": these are Northern America (numerical code 021), Europe (150), Japan (392) and Australia and New Zealand (053). These designations are intended for statistical convenience and do not necessarily express a judgement about the stage reached by a particular country or area in the development process. Differences from this usage are indicated in the notes to individual tables.

---

[1] Four revisions of this document were published in 1975, 1982, 1996 and 1999. Further revisions are now published on the United Nations Statistics Division website under the M49 section.

[2] A listing in the 6 official languages of the United Nations is contained in Terminology Bulletin No. 347/Rev.1 or the UNTERM website, prepared by the Department of General Assembly Affairs and Conference Services of the United Nations Secretariat.

001 World

002 Africa

202 Sub-Saharan Africa

014 Eastern Africa

086 British Indian Ocean Territory
108 Burundi
174 Comoros
262 Djibouti
232 Eritrea
231 Ethiopia
260 French Southern Territories
404 Kenya
450 Madagascar
454 Malawi
480 Mauritius
175 Mayotte
508 Mozambique
638 Réunion
646 Rwanda
690 Seychelles
706 Somalia
728 South Sudan note 736
800 Uganda
834 United Republic of Tanzania note /a
894 Zambia
716 Zimbabwe

017 Middle Africa

024 Angola
120 Cameroon
140 Central African Republic
148 Chad
178 Congo
180 Democratic Republic of the Congo
226 Equatorial Guinea
266 Gabon
678 Sao Tome and Principe

018 Southern Africa

072 Botswana
426 Lesotho
516 Namibia
710 South Africa
748 Swaziland

011 Western Africa

204 Benin
854 Burkina Faso
132 Cabo Verde
384 Côte d'Ivoire
270 Gambia
288 Ghana
324 Guinea
624 Guinea-Bissau
430 Liberia
466 Mali
478 Mauritania
562 Niger
566 Nigeria
654 Saint Helena note /b
686 Senegal
694 Sierra Leone
768 Togo

015 Northern Africa

012 Algeria
818 Egypt
434 Libya
504 Morocco
729 Sudan note 736
788 Tunisia
732 Western Sahara

Note **Tables may list**
736 *Sudan [former]*

/a Includes
--- *Zanzibar*

/b Includes
--- *Ascension*
--- *Tristan da Cunha*

019 Americas

419 Latin America and the Caribbean

029 Caribbean

660 Anguilla
028 Antigua and Barbuda
533 Aruba
044 Bahamas
052 Barbados
535 Bonaire, Sint Eustatius and Saba note 530
092 British Virgin Islands
136 Cayman Islands
192 Cuba
531 Curaçao note 530
212 Dominica
214 Dominican Republic
308 Grenada
312 Guadeloupe
332 Haiti
388 Jamaica
474 Martinique
500 Montserrat
630 Puerto Rico
652 Saint Barthélemy
659 Saint Kitts and Nevis
662 Saint Lucia
663 Saint Martin (French part)
670 Saint Vincent and the Grenadines
534 Sint Maarten (Dutch part) note 530
780 Trinidad and Tobago
796 Turks and Caicos Islands
850 United States Virgin Islands

013 Central America

084 Belize
188 Costa Rica
222 El Salvador
320 Guatemala
340 Honduras
484 Mexico
558 Nicaragua
591 Panama

005 South America

032 Argentina
068 Bolivia (Plurinational State of)
074 Bouvet Island
076 Brazil
152 Chile
170 Colombia
218 Ecuador
238 Falkland Islands (Malvinas)
254 French Guiana
328 Guyana
600 Paraguay
604 Peru
740 Suriname
239 South Georgia and the South Sandwich Islands
858 Uruguay
862 Venezuela (Bolivarian Republic of)

021 Northern America note 003

060 Bermuda
124 Canada
304 Greenland
666 Saint Pierre and Miquelon
840 United States of America

Note
003 *The continent of* **North America** *comprises Northern America, Caribbean and Central America.*

Tables may list
530 *Netherlands Antilles [former]*

010 Antarctica

001 World

142 Asia

143 Central Asia

398	Kazakhstan
417	Kyrgyzstan
762	Tajikistan
795	Turkmenistan
860	Uzbekistan

030 Eastern Asia

156	China
344	China, Hong Kong Special Administrative Region
446	China, Macao Special Administrative Region
408	Democratic People's Republic of Korea
392	Japan
496	Mongolia
410	Republic of Korea

035 South-eastern Asia

096	Brunei Darussalam
116	Cambodia
360	Indonesia
418	Lao People's Democratic Republic
458	Malaysia
104	Myanmar
608	Philippines
702	Singapore
764	Thailand
626	Timor-Leste
704	Viet Nam

034 Southern Asia

004	Afghanistan
050	Bangladesh
064	Bhutan
356	India
364	Iran (Islamic Republic of)
462	Maldives
524	Nepal
586	Pakistan
144	Sri Lanka

145 Western Asia

051	Armenia
031	Azerbaijan
048	Bahrain
196	Cyprus
268	Georgia
368	Iraq
376	Israel
400	Jordan
414	Kuwait
422	Lebanon
512	Oman
634	Qatar
682	Saudi Arabia
275	State of Palestine
760	Syrian Arab Republic
792	Turkey
784	United Arab Emirates
887	Yemen

150 Europe

151 Eastern Europe

112	Belarus
100	Bulgaria
203	Czechia
348	Hungary
616	Poland
498	Republic of Moldova
642	Romania
643	Russian Federation
703	Slovakia
804	Ukraine

154 Northern Europe

248	Åland Islands
208	Denmark
233	Estonia
234	Faroe Islands
246	Finland
831	Guernsey note 830
352	Iceland
372	Ireland
833	Isle of Man
832	Jersey note 830
428	Latvia
440	Lithuania
578	Norway
744	Svalbard and Jan Mayen Islands
752	Sweden
826	United Kingdom of Great Britain and Northern Ireland

039 Southern Europe

008	Albania
020	Andorra
070	Bosnia and Herzegovina
191	Croatia
292	Gibraltar
300	Greece
336	Holy See
380	Italy
470	Malta
499	Montenegro note 891
620	Portugal
674	San Marino
688	Serbia note 891 & /c
705	Slovenia
724	Spain
807	The former Yugoslav Republic of Macedonia

155 Western Europe

040	Austria
056	Belgium
250	France
276	Germany
438	Liechtenstein
442	Luxembourg
492	Monaco
528	Netherlands
756	Switzerland

Note	**Tables may list**
830	*Channel Islands*
891	*Serbia and Montenegro [former]*
/c	*Kosovo*

009 Oceania

053 Australia and New Zealand

036	Australia
162	Christmas Island
166	Cocos (Keeling) Islands
334	Heard Island and McDonald Islands
554	New Zealand
574	Norfolk Island

054 Melanesia

242	Fiji
540	New Caledonia
598	Papua New Guinea
090	Solomon Islands
548	Vanuatu

057 Micronesia

316	Guam
296	Kiribati
584	Marshall Islands
583	Micronesia (Federated States of)
520	Nauru
580	Northern Mariana Islands
585	Palau
581	United States minor outlying islands

061 Polynesia

016	American Samoa
184	Cook Islands
258	French Polynesia
570	Niue
612	Pitcairn
882	Samoa
772	Tokelau
776	Tonga
798	Tuvalu
876	Wallis and Futuna Islands

Other groupings

Following is a list of other groupings and their compositions presented in the *Yearbook*. These groupings are organized mainly around economic and trade interests in regional associations.

063	**Andean Common Market (ANCOM)**						
068	Bolivia (Plurinational State of)	170	Colombia	218	Ecuador	604	Peru

066	**Asia-Pacific Economic Cooperation (APEC)**						
036	Australia	344	China, Hong Kong Special Administrative Region	554	New Zealand	702	Singapore
096	Brunei Darussalam			598	Papua New Guinea	158	Taiwan Province of China
		360	Indonesia	604	Peru	764	Thailand
124	Canada	392	Japan	608	Philippines	840	United States of America
152	Chile	458	Malaysia	410	Republic of Korea	704	Viet Nam
156	China	484	Mexico	643	Russian Federation		

073	**Association of Southeast Asian Nations (ASEAN)**								
096	Brunei Darussalam	360	Indonesia	458	Malaysia	608	Philippines	764	Thailand
116	Cambodia	418	Lao PDR	104	Myanmar	702	Singapore	704	Viet Nam

130	**Caribbean Community and Common Market (CARICOM)**						
028	Antigua and Barbuda	084	Belize	332	Haiti	662	Saint Lucia
044	Bahamas (member of the Community only)	212	Dominica	388	Jamaica	670	Saint Vincent and the Grenadines
		308	Grenada	500	Montserrat	740	Suriname
052	Barbados	328	Guyana	659	Saint Kitts and Nevis	780	Trinidad and Tobago

395	**Central American Common Market (CACM)**								
188	Costa Rica	222	El Salvador	320	Guatemala	340	Honduras	558	Nicaragua

171	**Common Market for Eastern and Southern Africa (COMESA)**								
108	Burundi	262	Djibouti	404	Kenya	480	Mauritius	748	Swaziland
174	Comoros	818	Egypt	434	Libya	646	Rwanda	800	Uganda
180	Democratic Republic of the Congo	232	Eritrea	450	Madagascar	690	Seychelles	894	Zambia
		231	Ethiopia	454	Malawi	729	Sudan	716	Zimbabwe

172	**Commonwealth of Independent States (CIS)[3]**						
051	Armenia	398	Kazakhstan	643	Russian Federation	804	Ukraine
031	Azerbaijan	417	Kyrgyzstan	762	Tajikistan	860	Uzbekistan
112	Belarus	498	Republic of Moldova	795	Turkmenistan		

692	**Economic and Monetary Community of Central Africa (EMCCA)**										
120	Cameroon	140	Central African Republic	148	Chad	178	Congo	226	Equatorial Guinea	266	Gabon

892	**Economic Community of West African States (ECOWAS)**								
204	Benin	384	Côte d'Ivoire	324	Guinea	466	Mali	686	Senegal
854	Burkina Faso	270	Gambia	624	Guinea-Bissau	562	Niger	694	Sierra Leone
132	Cabo Verde	288	Ghana	430	Liberia	566	Nigeria	768	Togo

098	**Euro Area**								
040	Austria	246	Finland	372	Ireland	528	Netherlands	724	Spain
056	Belgium	250	France	380	Italy	620	Portugal		
196	Cyprus	276	Germany	442	Luxembourg	703	Slovakia		
233	Estonia	300	Greece	470	Malta	705	Slovenia		

197	**European Free Trade Association (EFTA)**						
352	Iceland	438	Liechtenstein	578	Norway	756	Switzerland

097	**European Union (EU)**								
040	Austria	208	Denmark	348	Hungary	470	Malta	705	Slovenia
056	Belgium	233	Estonia	372	Ireland	528	Netherlands	724	Spain
100	Bulgaria	246	Finland	380	Italy	616	Poland	752	Sweden

[3] Georgia (numerical code 268) can be listed as part of this group; for example, in International Merchandise Trade statistics.

097	European Union (EU) *(Continued)*								
191	Croatia	250	France	428	Latvia	620	Portugal	826	United Kingdom
196	Cyprus	276	Germany	440	Lithuania	642	Romania		
203	Czech Republic	300	Greece	442	Luxembourg	703	Slovakia		

095	Latin American Integration Association (LAIA)							
032	Argentina	170	Colombia	591	Panama	862	Venezuela (Bolivarian Republic of)
068	Bolivia (Plurinational State of)	192	Cuba	600	Paraguay		
076	Brazil	218	Ecuador	604	Peru		
152	Chile	484	Mexico	858	Uruguay		

199	Least developed countries (LDCs)						
004	Afghanistan	262	Djibouti	450	Madagascar	706	Somalia
024	Angola	226	Equatorial Guinea	454	Malawi	728	South Sudan
050	Bangladesh	232	Eritrea	466	Mali	729	Sudan
204	Benin	231	Ethiopia	478	Mauritania	626	Timor-Leste
064	Bhutan	270	Gambia	508	Mozambique	768	Togo
854	Burkina Faso	324	Guinea	104	Myanmar	798	Tuvalu
108	Burundi	624	Guinea-Bissau	524	Nepal	800	Uganda
116	Cambodia	332	Haiti	562	Niger	834	United Republic of Tanzania
140	Central African Republic	296	Kiribati	646	Rwanda		
148	Chad	418	Lao People's Democratic Republic	678	Sao Tome and Principe	548	Vanuatu
174	Comoros			686	Senegal	887	Yemen
180	Democratic Republic of the Congo	426	Lesotho	694	Sierra Leone	894	Zambia
		430	Liberia	090	Solomon Islands		

071	North American Free Trade Agreement (NAFTA)				
124	Canada	484	Mexico	840	United States of America

198	Organisation for Economic Co-operation and Development (OECD)						
036	Australia	250	France	442	Luxembourg	705	Slovenia
040	Austria	276	Germany	484	Mexico	724	Spain
056	Belgium	300	Greece	528	Netherlands	752	Sweden
124	Canada	348	Hungary	554	New Zealand	756	Switzerland
152	Chile	352	Iceland	578	Norway	792	Turkey
203	Czech Republic	372	Ireland	616	Poland	826	United Kingdom of Great Britain and Northern Ireland
208	Denmark	376	Israel	620	Portugal		
233	Estonia	380	Italy	410	Republic of Korea		
246	Finland	392	Japan	703	Slovakia	840	United States of America

399	Organization of the Petroleum Exporting Countries (OPEC)						
012	Algeria	364	Iran (Islamic Republic of)	566	Nigeria	862	Venezuela (Bolivarian Republic of)
024	Angola	368	Iraq	634	Qatar		
218	Ecuador	414	Kuwait	682	Saudi Arabia		
360	Indonesia	434	Libya	784	United Arab Emirates		

711	Southern African Customs Union (SACU)								
072	Botswana	426	Lesotho	516	Namibia	710	South Africa	748	Swaziland

069	Southern Common Market (MERCOSUR)				
032	Argentina	076	Brazil	858	Uruguay
068	Bolivia (Plurinational State of)	600	Paraguay	862	Venezuela (Bolivarian Republic of)

Annexe I - Nomenclature des pays ou zones, groupements régionaux et autres groupements

L'Annuaire statistique répertorie de pays ou de zones sur la base de l'opuscule United Nations Standard Country Codes (Série M, nº 49) rédigée par la Division de statistique du Secrétariat de l'Organisation des Nations Unies et publiée en 1970[1]. La liste des pays ou zones; la composition des régions géographiques et économiques, commerciales et d'autres groupements utilisés dans cet annuaire (au 31 juillet 2017) sont présentées dans la présente annexe. On a eu recours à la forme brève des noms des pays et des zones usitées au cours des activités courantes des Nations Unies, et pas nécessairement aux désignations officielles utilisées dans les documents officiels[2]. Afin de faciliter le traitement des données statistiques, un code numérique unique et standard à trois chiffres est attribué à chaque pays ou zone et à chaque région géographique et groupement de pays ou de zones. Pour référence, ces codes, le cas échéant, sont présentés à la gauche de chaque pays ou zone visées dans cette annexe. Ces codes s'échelonnent entre 000 et 899.

A. Changements dans le nom des pays ou zones (depuis 31 juillet 2007)

L'étendue géographique d'un pays ou d'une zone ou la composition d'une région géographique peuvent varier au fil du temps et les utilisateurs devront tenir compte de telles modifications lorsqu'ils ont recours aux codes indiques dans la présente publication et qu'ils établissent des rapports entre les données portant sur différentes périodes. La modification du nom d'un pays ou d'une zone alors que son espace géographique demeure le même n'est pas habituellement accompagnée d'un changement de son code numérique. Changements dans les codes numériques et noms dans la période générale couverts par les statistiques (depuis le 31 juillet 2007) dans l'Annuaire, sont présentés ci-dessous;

Code numérique	Pays ou region (nouveaux codes et codes modifies)	Date de la modification	Code numérique	Pays ou region (Changements de nom sans modification du code)	Date de la modification
728	Soudan du Sud	2011	203	Tchéquie, *ex-République tchèque*	2016
729	Soudan	2011	132	Cabo Verde, *ex-Cap-Vert*	2013
531	Curaçao	2010	434	État de Palestine, *ex-Territoire palestinien occupé*	2013
534	Saint-Martin (partie néerlandaise)	2010	275	Libye, *ex-Jamahiriya arabe libyenne*	2011
535	Bonaire, Saint-Eustache et Saba	2010	068	Bolivie (État plurinational de), *ex-Bolivie*	2009
652	Saint-Barthélemy	2007	498	République de Moldova, *ex-Moldova (depuis 2007)*	2008
663	Saint-Martin (partie française)	2007			

B. Groupements régionaux

Le système des groupements régionaux à la page suivante est principalement basé sur les 6 continents; ces régions continentales, à l'exception de l'Antarctique, sont subdivisées en 22 sous-régions et 2 régions intermédiaires (Afrique subsaharienne et l'Amérique latine et Caraïbes) afin d'obtenir une homogénéité accrue les effectifs de population, les situations démographiques et la précision des statistiques démographiques. Cette nomenclature est couramment utilisée aux fins des statistiques internationales et a été appliquée autant qu'il a été possible dans le présent *Annuaire* en vue de renforcer la cohérence et de faciliter la comparaison et l'analyse. Son utilisation pour l'établissement des statistiques internationales n'est cependant rien moins qu'universelle, même au niveau des régions continentales, et les variations que présentent les sources et méthodes statistiques internationales entraînent inévitablement de nombreuses différences dans certains domaines de cet *Annuaire*. Les différences d'ordre général sont indiquées dans les notes figurant au bas de la classification présentée ci-dessous. Les différences plus spécifiques sont mentionnées dans les notes techniques et notes de bas de page accompagnant les divers tableaux.

L'application des expressions "développés" et "en développement" aux pays, zones ou régions n'est pas non plus normalisée à l'échelle internationale. Ces expressions sont utilisées dans la présente publication en référence aux groupements régionaux généralement considérés comme "développés", à savoir l'Amérique septentrionale (code numérique 021), l'Europe (150), le Japon (392) et l'Australie et la Nouvelle-Zélande (053). Ces appellations sont employées pour des raisons de commodité statistique et n'expriment pas nécessairement un jugement sur le stade de développement atteint par tel ou tel pays ou zone. Les cas différant de cet usage sont signalés dans les notes accompagnant les tableaux concernés.

[1] Quatre révisions de ce document ont été publiés en 1975, 1982, 1996 et 1999. D'autres révisions sont maintenant publiés sur le site internet de la Division de statistique des Nations Unies.

[2] Le Bulletin terminologique No 347/Rev.1 ou UNTERM website, intitulé "Noms de pays" établi par le Département des affaires de l'Assemblée générale et des services de conférence du Secrétariat de l'Organisation des Nations Unies, répertorie les noms des États Membres dans les six langues de l'Organisation.

001 Monde

002 Afrique

202 Afrique subsaharienne

014 Afrique orientale

108	Burundi	
174	Comores	
262	Djibouti	
232	Érythrée	
231	Éthiopie	
404	Kenya	
450	Madagascar	
454	Malawi	
480	Maurice	
175	Mayotte	
508	Mozambique	
800	Ouganda	
834	République-Unie de Tanzanie	note /a
638	Réunion	
646	Rwanda	
690	Seychelles	
706	Somalie	
728	Soudan du Sud	note 736
260	Terres australes françaises	
086	Territoire britannique de l'océan Indien	
894	Zambie	
716	Zimbabwe	

017 Afrique centrale

024	Angola
120	Cameroun
178	Congo
266	Gabon
226	Guinée équatoriale
140	République centrafricaine
180	République démocratique du Congo
678	Sao Tomé-et-Principe
148	Tchad

018 Afrique australe

710	Afrique du Sud
072	Botswana
426	Lesotho
516	Namibie
748	Swaziland

011 Afrique occidentale

204	Bénin	
854	Burkina Faso	
132	Cabo Verde	
384	Côte d'Ivoire	
270	Gambie	
288	Ghana	
324	Guinée	
624	Guinée-Bissau	
430	Libéria	
466	Mali	
478	Mauritanie	
562	Niger	
566	Nigéria	
654	Sainte-Hélène	note /b
686	Sénégal	
694	Sierra Leone	
768	Togo	

015 Afrique septentrionale

012	Algérie	
818	Égypte	
434	Libye	
504	Maroc	
732	Sahara occidental	
729	Soudan	note 736
788	Tunisie	

Note **Certains tableaux peuvent**

736	*Soudan [anc.]*
/a	Incluent
---	*Zanzibar*
/b	Incluent
---	*Ascension*
---	*Tristan da Cunha*

019 Amériques

419 Amérique latine et Caraïbes

029 Caraïbes

660	Anguilla	
028	Antigua-et-Barbuda	
533	Aruba	
044	Bahamas	
052	Barbade	
535	Bonaire, Saint-Eustache et Saba	note 530
192	Cuba	
531	Curaçao	note 530
212	Dominique	
308	Grenade	
312	Guadeloupe	
332	Haïti	
136	Îles Caïmanes	
796	Îles Turques-et-Caïques	
850	Îles Vierges américaines	
092	Îles Vierges britanniques	
388	Jamaïque	
474	Martinique	
500	Montserrat	
630	Porto Rico	
214	République dominicaine	
652	Saint-Barthélemy	
659	Saint-Kitts-et-Nevis	
662	Sainte-Lucie	
663	Saint-Martin (partie française)	
534	Saint-Martin (partie néerlandaise)	note 530
670	Saint-Vincent-et-les Grenadines	
780	Trinité-et-Tobago	

013 Amérique centrale

084	Belize
188	Costa Rica
222	El Salvador
320	Guatemala
340	Honduras
484	Mexique
558	Nicaragua
591	Panama

005 Amérique du Sud

032	Argentine
068	Bolivie (État plurinational de)
076	Brésil
152	Chili
170	Colombie
218	Équateur
239	Géorgie du Sud-et-les Îles Sandwich du Sud
328	Guyana
254	Guyane française
074	Île Bouvet
238	Îles Falkland (Malvinas)
600	Paraguay
604	Pérou
740	Suriname
858	Uruguay
862	Venezuela (République bolivarienne du)

021 Amérique septentrionale

note 003

060	Bermudes
124	Canada
840	États-Unis d'Amérique
304	Groenland
666	Saint-Pierre-et-Miquelon

Note

003 *Le continent de **l'Amérique du Nord** comprend l'Amérique septentrionale, les Caraïbes et l'Amérique centrale*

Certains tableaux peuvent

530 *Antilles néerlandaises [anc.]*

010 Antarctique

001 Monde

142 Asie

143 Asie centrale

398 Kazakhstan
417 Kirghizistan
860 Ouzbékistan
762 Tadjikistan
795 Turkménistan

030 Asie orientale

156 Chine
344 Chine, région administrative spéciale de Hong Kong
446 Chine, région administrative spéciale de Macao
392 Japon
496 Mongolie
410 République de Corée
408 République populaire démocratique de Corée

035 Asie du Sud-Est

096 Brunéi Darussalam
116 Cambodge
360 Indonésie
458 Malaisie
104 Myanmar
608 Philippines
418 République démocratique populaire lao
702 Singapour
764 Thaïlande
626 Timor-Leste
704 Viet Nam

034 Asie méridionale

004 Afghanistan
050 Bangladesh
064 Bhoutan
356 Inde
364 Iran (République islamique d')
462 Maldives
524 Népal
586 Pakistan
144 Sri Lanka

145 Asie occidentale

682 Arabie saoudite
051 Arménie
031 Azerbaïdjan
048 Bahreïn
196 Chypre
784 Émirats arabes unis
275 État de Palestine
268 Géorgie
368 Iraq
376 Israël
400 Jordanie
414 Koweït
422 Liban
512 Oman
634 Qatar
760 République arabe syrienne
792 Turquie
887 Yémen

150 Europe

151 Europe orientale

112 Bélarus
100 Bulgarie
643 Fédération de Russie
348 Hongrie
616 Pologne
498 République de Moldova
642 Roumanie
703 Slovaquie
203 Tchéquie
804 Ukraine

154 Europe septentrionale

208 Danemark
233 Estonie
246 Finlande
831 Guernesey **note 830**
833 Île de Man
248 Îles d'Åland
234 Îles Féroé
744 Îles Svalbard-et-Jan Mayen
372 Irlande
352 Islande
832 Jersey **note 830**
428 Lettonie
440 Lituanie
578 Norvège
826 Royaume-Uni de Grande-Bretagne et d'Irlande du Nord
752 Suède

039 Europe méridionale

008 Albanie
020 Andorre
070 Bosnie-Herzégovine
191 Croatie
724 Espagne
807 Ex-République yougoslave de Macédoine
292 Gibraltar
300 Grèce
380 Italie
470 Malte
499 Monténégro **note 891**
620 Portugal
674 Saint-Marin
336 Saint-Siège
688 Serbie **note 891 & /c**
705 Slovénie

155 Europe occidentale

276 Allemagne
040 Autriche
056 Belgique
250 France
438 Liechtenstein
442 Luxembourg
492 Monaco
528 Pays-Bas
756 Suisse

Note **Certains tableaux peuvent énumérer**
830 *Îles Anglo-Normandes*
891 *Serbie-et-Monténégro [anc.]*
/c *Kosovo*

009 Océanie

053 Australie et Nouvelle-Zélande

036 Australie
162 Île Christmas
334 Île Heard-et-Îles MacDonald
574 Île Norfolk
166 Îles des Cocos (Keeling)
554 Nouvelle-Zélande

054 Mélanésie

242 Fidji
090 Îles Salomon
540 Nouvelle-Calédonie
598 Papouasie-Nouvelle-Guinée
548 Vanuatu

057 Micronésie

316 Guam
580 Îles Mariannes du Nord
584 Îles Marshall
581 Îles mineures éloignées des États-Unis
296 Kiribati
583 Micronésie (États fédérés de)
520 Nauru
585 Palaos

061 Polynésie

184 Îles Cook
876 Îles Wallis-et-Futuna
570 Nioué
612 Pitcairn
258 Polynésie française
882 Samoa
016 Samoa américaines
772 Tokelau
776 Tonga
798 Tuvalu

C. Autres groupements

On trouvera ci-après une liste des autres groupements et de leur composition, présentée dans l'*Annuaire*. Ces groupements correspondent essentiellement à des intérêts économiques et commerciaux d'après les associations régionales.

071 Accord de libre-échange nord-américain (ALENA)

124	Canada	840	États-Unis d'Amérique	484	Mexique

073 Association des nations de l'Asie du Sud-Est (ANASE)

096	Brunéi Darussalam	360	Indonésie	104	Myanmar	418	République démocratique populaire lao	764	Thaïlande
116	Cambodge	458	Malaisie	608	Philippines	702	Singapour	704	Viet Nam

197 Association européenne de libre-échange (AELE)

352	Islande	438	Liechtenstein	578	Norvège	756	Suisse

095 Association latino-américaine d'intégration (ALAI)

032	Argentine	170	Colombie	591	Panama	862	Venezuela (République bolivarienne du)
068	Bolivie (État plurinational de)	192	Cuba	600	Paraguay		
076	Brésil	218	Équateur	604	Pérou		
152	Chili	484	Mexique	858	Uruguay		

130 Communauté des Caraïbes et Marché commun des Caraïbes (CARICOM)

028	Antigua-et-Barbuda	084	Belize	332	Haïti	662	Sainte-Lucie
044	Bahamas (membre de la communauté seulement)	212	Dominique	388	Jamaïque	670	Saint-Vincent-et-les Grenadines
		308	Grenade	500	Montserrat	740	Suriname
052	Barbade	328	Guyana	659	Saint-Kitts-et-Nevis	780	Trinité-et-Tobago

172 Communauté d'Etats indépendants (CEI)[3]

051	Arménie	643	Fédération de Russie	417	Kirghizistan	762	Tadjikistan
031	Azerbaïdjan	268	Géorgie	860	Ouzbékistan	795	Turkménistan
112	Bélarus	398	Kazakhstan	498	République de Moldova	804	Ukraine

892 Communauté économique des Etats de l'Afrique de l'Ouest (CEDEAO)

204	Bénin	384	Côte d'Ivoire	324	Guinée	466	Mali	686	Sénégal
854	Burkina Faso	270	Gambie	624	Guinée-Bissau	562	Niger	694	Sierra Leone
132	Cabo Verde	288	Ghana	430	Libéria	566	Nigéria	768	Togo

692 Communauté économique et monétaire des Etats de l'Afrique Centrale (CEMAC)

120	Cameroun	178	Congo	266	Gabon	226	Guinée équatoriale	140	République centrafricaine	148	Tchad

066 Coopération économique Asie-Pacifique (CEAP)

036	Australie	840	États-Unis d'Amérique	598	Papouasie-Nouvelle-Guinée	704	Viet Nam
096	Brunéi Darussalam	643	Fédération de Russie	604	Pérou		
124	Canada	360	Indonésie	608	Philippines		
152	Chili	392	Japon	158	Province chinoise de Taïwan		
156	Chine	458	Malaisie	410	République de Corée		
344	Chine, région administrative spéciale de Hong Kong	484	Mexique	702	Singapour		
		554	Nouvelle-Zélande	764	Thaïlande		

063 Marché commun andin (ANCOM)

068	Bolivie (État plurinational de)	170	Colombie	218	Équateur	604	Pérou

395 Marché commun centraméricain (MCCA)

188	Costa Rica	222	El Salvador	320	Guatemala	340	Honduras	558	Nicaragua

171 Marché commun de l'Afrique de l'Est et de l'Afrique australe (COMESA)

108	Burundi	232	Érythrée	450	Madagascar	180	République démocratique du Congo	729	Soudan
174	Comores	231	Éthiopie	454	Malawi			748	Swaziland
262	Djibouti	404	Kenya	480	Maurice	646	Rwanda	894	Zambie
818	Égypte	434	Libye	800	Ouganda	690	Seychelles	716	Zimbabwe

[3] La Géorgie (code numérique 268) peut figurer dans ce groupe; par exemple, dans le cadre des statistiques du commerce international de marchandises.

069 Marché commun du Sud (MERCOSUR)

032	Argentine	076	Brésil	858	Uruguay
068	Bolivie (État plurinational de)	600	Paraguay	862	Venezuela (République bolivarienne du)

198 Organisation de coopération et de développement économiques (OCDE)

276	Allemagne	840	États-Unis d'Amérique	392	Japon	203	République tchèque
036	Australie	246	Finlande	442	Luxembourg	826	Royaume-Uni de Grande-Bretagne et d'Irlande du Nord
040	Autriche	250	France	484	Mexique		
056	Belgique	300	Grèce	578	Norvège		
124	Canada	348	Hongrie	554	Nouvelle-Zélande	703	Slovaquie
152	Chili	372	Irlande	528	Pays-Bas	705	Slovénie
208	Danemark	376	Israël	616	Pologne	752	Suède
724	Espagne	352	Islande	620	Portugal	756	Suisse
233	Estonie	380	Italie	410	République de Corée	792	Turquie

399 Organisation des pays exportateurs de pétrole (OPEP)

012	Algérie	218	Équateur	434	Libye	862	Venezuela (République bolivarienne du)
024	Angola	360	Indonésie	414	Koweït		
682	Arabie saoudite	364	Iran (République islamique d')	566	Nigéria		
784	Émirats arabes unis	368	Iraq	634	Qatar		

199 Pays les moins avancés (PMA)

004	Afghanistan	270	Gambie	478	Mauritanie	686	Sénégal
024	Angola	324	Guinée	508	Mozambique	694	Sierra Leone
050	Bangladesh	226	Guinée équatoriale	104	Myanmar	706	Somalie
204	Bénin	624	Guinée-Bissau	524	Népal	728	Soudan du Sud
064	Bhoutan	332	Haïti	562	Niger	729	Soudan
854	Burkina Faso	090	Îles Salomon	800	Ouganda	148	Tchad
108	Burundi	296	Kiribati	140	République centrafricaine	626	Timor-Leste
116	Cambodge	426	Lesotho	180	République démocratique du Congo	768	Togo
174	Comores	430	Libéria	418	République démocratique populaire lao	798	Tuvalu
262	Djibouti	450	Madagascar	834	République-Unie de Tanzanie	548	Vanuatu
232	Érythrée	454	Malawi	646	Rwanda	887	Yémen
231	Éthiopie	466	Mali	678	Sao Tomé-et-Principe	894	Zambie

711 Union douanière d'Afrique australe

710	Afrique du Sud	072	Botswana	426	Lesotho	516	Namibie	748	Swaziland

097 Union européenne (UE)

276	Allemagne	208	Danemark	348	Hongrie	470	Malte	826	Royaume-Uni de Grande-Bretagne et d'Irlande du Nord
040	Autriche	724	Espagne	372	Irlande	528	Pays-Bas		
056	Belgique	233	Estonie	380	Italie	616	Pologne		
100	Bulgarie	246	Finlande	428	Lettonie	620	Portugal	703	Slovaquie
191	Croatie	250	France	440	Lituanie	203	République tchèque	705	Slovénie
196	Chypre	300	Grèce	442	Luxembourg	642	Roumanie	752	Suède

098 Zone euro

276	Allemagne	724	Espagne	300	Grèce	470	Malte	705	Slovénie
040	Autriche	233	Estonie	372	Irlande	528	Pays-Bas		
056	Belgique	246	Finlande	380	Italie	620	Portugal		
196	Chypre	250	France	442	Luxembourg	703	Slovaquie		

Annex II: Technical notes

Chapter I: World summary

Table 1: World statistics – selected series

These world aggregates are obtained from other tables in this *Yearbook*, where available, and are compiled from statistical publications and databases of the United Nations and the specialized agencies and other institutions. The technical notes of the relevant table in this *Yearbook* should be consulted for detailed information on definition, source, compilation and coverage.

Chapter II: Population and migration

Table 2: Population, surface area and density

The total, male and female population, sex ratio, population age distribution and population density are taken from the estimates and projections prepared by the United Nations Population Division, published in *World Population Prospects: The 2017 Revision.* Surface area are obtained from the *Demographic Yearbook*, through this source only official national data are reported.

Total, male and female population refers to the de facto population in a country, area or region as of 1 July of the year indicated, unless otherwise stated in a footnote. Figures are presented in millions. The total population of a country may comprise either all usual residents of the country (de jure population) or all persons present in the country (de facto population) at the time of the census; for purposes of international comparisons, the de facto definition is used, unless otherwise stated in a footnote.

Population aged 0-14 years / 60 years and over refers to the percentage of the population aged 0-14 years and aged 60 years and older, respectively as of 1 July of the year indicated, unless otherwise stated in a footnote.

Population density refers to the population, as of 1 July of the year indicated, per square kilometre of surface area, unless otherwise stated in a footnote.

Sex ratio is calculated as the ratio of the population of men to that of 100 women as of 1 July of the year indicated, unless otherwise stated in a footnote.

Surface area refers to land area plus inland water, unless otherwise stated in a footnote.

Table 3: Population growth and indicators of fertility and mortality

The population rate of increase, fertility rate, infant mortality rate and life expectancy at birth are taken from the estimates and projections prepared by the United Nations Population Division, published in *World Population Prospects: The 2017 Revision*. The data are an average over five-year ranges; 2000-2005 labelled "2005", 2005-2010 labelled "2010" and 2010-2015 labelled "2015", unless otherwise stated in a footnote. Maternal mortality ratio are estimates developed by the World Health Organization, UNICEF, the United Nations Population Fund, the World Bank and United Nations Population Division and published in Trends in Maternal Mortality: 1990 to 2015.

Population rate of increase (or growth rate) is the average annual percentage change in total population size.

Fertility rate is the total fertility rate, a widely used summary indicator of fertility. It refers to the number of children that would be born per woman, assuming no female mortality at child bearing ages and the age-specific fertility rates of a specified country and reference period.

Infant mortality rate (per 1 000 live births) is the ratio of infant deaths (the deaths of children under one year of age) in a given year to the total number of live births in the same year.

Maternal mortality ratio is the ratio of the number of maternal deaths during a given time period per 100 000 live births during the same time-period. A maternal death refers to a female death from any cause related to or aggravated by pregnancy or its management (excluding accidental or incidental causes) during pregnancy and childbirth or within 42 days of termination of pregnancy, irrespective of the duration and site of the pregnancy.

Life expectancy at birth is the average number of years of life at birth (age 0) for males and females according to the expected mortality rates by age estimated for the reference year and population.

Table 4: International migrants and refugees

International migrant stock are taken from the estimates and projections prepared by the United Nations Population Division, published in *International migrant stock: The 2015 Revision.* "Refugees and others of concern to UNHCR" are obtained from the United Nations High Commissioner for Refugees, published in the Population Statistics database.

International migrant stock represents the number of persons born in a country other than that in which they live. When information on country of birth was not recorded, data on the number of persons having foreign citizenship was used instead. In the absence of any empirical data, estimates were imputed. Data refer to mid-2015. Figures for international migrant stock as a percentage of the population are the outcome of dividing the estimated international migrant stock by the estimated total population and multiplying the result by 100.

Refugees include individuals recognised under the 1951 Convention relating to the Status of Refugees; its 1967 Protocol; the 1969 OAU Convention Governing the Specific Aspects of Refugee Problems in Africa; those recognised in accordance with the UNHCR Statute; individuals granted complementary forms of protection; or those enjoying temporary protection. Since 2007, the refugee population also includes people in a refugee-like situation.

Asylum-seekers are individuals who have sought international protection and whose claims for refugee status have not yet been determined, irrespective of when they may have been lodged.

"Other" represents the following 5 categories:

- Internally displaced persons (IDPs) are people or groups of individuals who have been forced to leave their homes or places of habitual residence, in particular as a result of, or in order to avoid the effects of armed conflict, situations of generalised violence, violations of human rights, or natural or man-made disasters, and who have not crossed an international border. For the purposes of UNHCR's statistics, this population only includes conflict-generated IDPs to whom the Office extends protection and/or assistance. Since 2007, the IDP population also includes people in an IDP-like situation. For global IDP estimates, see www.internal-displacement.org.
- Returned refugees are former refugees who have returned to their country of origin spontaneously or in an organised fashion but are yet to be fully integrated. Such return would normally only take place in conditions of safety and dignity.
- Returned IDPs refer to those IDPs who were beneficiaries of UNHCR's protection and assistance activities and who returned to their areas of origin or habitual residence during the year.
- Stateless persons are defined under international law as persons who are not considered as nationals by any State under the operation of its law. In other words, they do not possess the nationality of any State. UNHCR statistics refer to persons who fall under the agency's statelessness mandate because they are stateless according to this international definition, but data from some countries may also include persons with undetermined nationality.
- Others of concern refers to individuals who do not necessarily fall directly into any of the groups above, but to whom UNHCR extends its protection and/or assistance services, based on humanitarian or other special grounds.

Chapter III: Gender

Table 5: Proportion of seats held by women in national parliament

The table shows the percentage of seats held by women members in single or lower chambers of national parliaments as at January/ February each year (see table footnotes for specific details). National parliaments can be bicameral or unicameral. This table covers the single chamber in unicameral parliaments and the lower chamber in bicameral parliaments. It does not cover the upper chamber of bi-cameral parliaments. Seats are usually won by members in general parliamentary elections. Seats may also be filled by nomination, appointment, indirect election, rotation of members and by-election. The proportion of seats held by women in national parliament is derived by dividing the total number of seats occupied by women by the total number of seats in parliament. There is no weighting or normalising of statistics. The source for this table is the Inter-Parliamentary Union (IPU), see www.ipu.org for further information.

Table 6: Ratio of girls to boys in primary, secondary and tertiary education

The ratio of girls to boys (gender parity index) in primary, secondary and tertiary education is the ratio of the number of female students enrolled at primary, secondary and tertiary levels of education to the number of male students in each level. To standardise the effects of the population structure of the appropriate age groups, the Gender Parity Index (GPI) of the Gross Enrolment Ratio (GER) for each level of education is used. The source for this table is the UNESCO Institute for Statistics (UIS), see www.uis.unesco.org for further information.

Chapter IV: Education

Data in Tables 5 and 6 are presented using the 2011 revision of UNESCO's International Standard Classification of Education (ISCED). Data are presented in the tables based on the three main levels of educations defined as follows;

"Primary education" (ISCED level 1) programmes are typically designed to provide students with fundamental skills in reading, writing and mathematics (i.e. literacy and numeracy) and establish a solid foundation for learning and understanding core areas of knowledge, personal and social development, in preparation for lower secondary education. It focuses on learning at a basic level of complexity with little, if any, specialisation.

"Secondary education" (ISCED level 2 and 3) is divided into two different stages, i.e. lower secondary and upper secondary. Lower secondary education programmes are typically designed to build on the learning outcomes from primary. Usually, they aim to lay the foundation for lifelong learning and human development upon which education systems may then expand further educational opportunities. Upper secondary education programmes are typically designed to complete secondary education in preparation for tertiary education or provide skills relevant to employment, or both. Programmes at this level offer students more varied, specialised and in-depth instruction than programmes at lower secondary. They are more differentiated, with an increased range of options and streams available. Teachers are often highly qualified in the subjects or fields of specialisation they teach, particularly in the higher grades.

Tertiary education (ISCED levels 5-8) builds on secondary education, providing learning activities in specialised fields of education. It aims at learning at a high level of complexity and specialisation. Tertiary education includes what is commonly understood as academic education but also includes advanced vocational or professional education. It comprises ISCED levels 5, 6, 7 and 8, which are labelled as short-cycle tertiary education, Bachelor's or equivalent level, Master's or equivalent level, and doctoral or equivalent level, respectively. The content of programmes at the tertiary level is more complex and advanced than in lower ISCED levels.

For more information about the International Standard Classification of Education (ISCED) 2011 please refer to: http://www.uis.unesco.org/Education/Documents/isced-2011-en.pdf

Table 7: Enrollment in the primary, secondary and tertiary levels

The table shows the number of students enrolled as well as the gross enrolment ratio which is the number of students enrolled, regardless of age, expressed as a percentage of the eligible official school-age population corresponding to the same level of education in a given school year. Enrolment is measured at the beginning of the school or academic year. The gross enrolment ratio at each level will include all pupils whatever their ages, whereas the population is limited to the range of official school ages. Therefore, for countries with almost universal education among the school-age population, the gross enrolment ratio can exceed 100 if the actual age distribution of pupils extends beyond the official school ages.

Table 8: Teaching staff at the primary, secondary and tertiary levels

The table shows the total number of teachers at a given level of education, as well as the proportion of female teachers expressed as a percentage of the total (male and female) at the same level in a given school year. The data sources include school census or surveys and teachers' records. Teachers (or teaching staff) are defined as persons employed full-time or part-time in an official capacity to guide and direct the learning experience of pupils and students, irrespective of their qualifications or the delivery mechanism, i.e. face-to-face and/or at a distance. This definition excludes educational personnel who have no active teaching duties (e.g. headmasters, headmistresses or principals who do not teach) or who work occasionally or in a voluntary capacity in educational institutions.

Table 9: Public expenditure on education

Public expenditure on education consists of current and capital expenditures on education by local, regional and national governments, including municipalities. Household contributions are excluded. Current expenditure on education includes expenditure for goods and services consumed within the current year and which would need to be renewed if needed the following year. It includes expenditure on: staff salaries and benefits; contracted or purchased services; other resources including books and teaching materials; welfare services; and other current expenditure such as subsidies to students and households, furniture and equipment, minor repairs, fuel, telecommunications, travel, insurance and rents. Capital expenditure on education includes expenditure for assets that last longer than one year. It includes expenditure for construction, renovation and major repairs of buildings and the purchase of heavy equipment or vehicles.

Chapter V: Health

Table 10: Health personnel

The table shows four main categories of health personnel (out of 9 categories available in the source); Physicians which includes generalist medical practitioners and specialist medical practitioners; Nursing and midwifery personnel which includes nursing professionals, midwifery professionals, nursing associate professionals and midwifery associate professionals. Traditional midwives are not included here; Dentistry personnel includes dentists, dental assistants, dental technicians and related occupations; and Pharmaceutical personnel which includes pharmacists, pharmaceutical assistants, pharmaceutical technicians and related occupations.

The data are obtained from the World Health Organisation's (WHO) Global Health Workforce Statistics database which are compiled from several sources such as national population censuses, labour force and employment surveys, national statistical products and routine administrative information systems. As a result, considerable variability remains across countries in the coverage, quality and reference year of the original data. In general, the denominator data for health workforce density (i.e. national population estimates) were obtained from the United Nations Population Division's *World Population Prospects* publication. In some cases, the official report provided only workforce density indicators, from which estimates of the stock were then calculated.

The classification of health workers used is based on criteria for vocational education and training, regulation of health professions, and activities and tasks of jobs, i.e. a framework for categorizing key workforce variables according to shared characteristics. The WHO framework largely draws on the latest revisions to the internationally standardized classification systems of the International Labour Organization (International Standard Classification of Occupations), United Nations Educational, Scientific and Cultural Organization (International Standard Classification of Education), and the United Nations Statistics Division (International Standard Industrial Classification of All Economic Activities). Depending on the nature of each country's situation and the means of measurement, data are available for up to 9 categories of health workers in the aggregated set, and up to 18 categories in the disaggregated set. The latter essentially reflects attempts to better distinguish some subgroups of the workforce according to assumed differences in skill level and skill specialization.

Table 11: Expenditure on health

Total expenditure on health is the sum of all outlays for health maintenance, restoration or enhancement paid for in cash or supplied in kind. It is the sum of General Government Expenditure on Health and Private Expenditure on Health. General government expenditure on health is the sum of health outlays paid for in cash or supplied in kind by government entities, such as the Ministry of Health, other ministries, parastatal organizations or social security agencies (without double counting government transfers to social security and extra budgetary funds). It includes all expenditure made by these entities, regardless of the source, so includes any donor funding passing through them. It includes transfer payments to households to offset medical care costs and extra budgetary funds to finance health services and goods. It includes current and capital expenditure. More information on the definition, methodology, sources and limitations of the data can be found on the Global Health Expenditure Database (see http://apps.who.int/nha/database/DocumentationCentre/Index/fr)

Chapter VI: Crime

Table 12: Intentional homicides and other crimes

"Intentional homicides" and "other crimes" are taken from the United Nations Office on Drugs and Crime, published in their statistics database.

"Intentional Homicide" means unlawful death purposefully inflicted on a person by another person. Data on intentional homicide should also include serious assault leading to death and death as a result of a terrorist attack. It should exclude attempted homicide, manslaughter, death due to legal intervention, justifiable homicide in self-defence and death due to armed conflict.

"Assault" means physical attack against the body of another person resulting in serious bodily injury, excluding indecent/sexual assault, threats and slapping/punching. 'Assault' leading to death should also be excluded.

“Kidnapping” means unlawfully detaining a person or persons against their will (including through the use of force, threat, fraud or enticement) for the purpose of demanding for their liberation an illicit gain or any other economic gain or other material benefit, or in order to oblige someone to do or not to do something. “Kidnapping” excludes disputes over child custody.

“Theft” means depriving a person or organisation of property without force with the intent to keep it . “Theft” excludes Burglary, housebreaking, Robbery, and Theft of a Motor Vehicle, which are recorded separately.

Total "Sexual violence” means rape and sexual assault, including Sexual Offences against Children.

Chapter VII: National accounts

The National Accounts Main Aggregates Database (available at http://unstats.un.org/unsd/snaama) presents national accounts data for more than 200 countries and areas of the world. It is the basis for the publication of National Account Statistics: Analysis of Main Aggregates (AMA), a publication prepared by the Statistics Division of the Department for Economic and Social Affairs of the United Nations Secretariat with the generous co-operation of national statistical offices. The database is updated in December of each year with newly available national accounts data for all countries and areas.

The National Accounts Main Aggregates Database is based on the data obtained from the United Nations National Accounts Questionnaire (NAQ) introduced in October 1999, which in turn is based on the System of National Accounts 1993 (1993 SNA). The data are supplemented with estimates prepared by the Statistics Division. The updated SNA, called the System of National Accounts 2008 (2008 SNA) was finalised in September 2009. As of 2015, 63 countries and territories (European Union Member States, Albania, Argentina, Australia, Brazil, Brunei Darussalam, Canada, China, Hong Kong SAR, China, Macao SAR, Dominican Republic, Ecuador, India, Indonesia, Israel, Kenya, Mexico, Mongolia, New Zealand, Nigeria, Pakistan, Peru, Philippines, Republic of Korea, Serbia, Singapore, South Africa, Swaziland, Timor-Leste, Uganda, Ukraine, the United States of America and Zambia) have started submitting data according to the 2008 SNA.

Every effort has been made to present the estimates of the various countries or areas in a form designed to facilitate international comparability. To this end, important differences in concept, scope, coverage and classification have been described in the footnotes for individual countries. Such differences should be taken into account to avoid misleading comparisons. Data contained in the tables relate to the calendar year for which they are shown, except in several cases. These special cases are posted on the National Accounts Main Aggregates Database website (http://unstats.un.org/unsd/snaama/notes.asp). The figures shown are the most recent estimates and revisions available at the time of compilation. In general, figures for the most recent year are to be regarded as provisional. The sums of the components in the tables may not necessarily add up to totals shown because of rounding.

Table 13: Gross domestic product and gross domestic product per capita

This table shows gross domestic product (GDP) and GDP per capita in US dollars at current prices, GDP at constant 2005 prices and the corresponding real rates of growth. The tables are intended to facilitate international comparisons of levels of income generated in production. Official data and estimates of total and per capita GDP at current prices have been converted to US dollars, while total GDP at constant prices are converted to 2005 prices before conversion to US dollars using the 2005 exchange rates. The conversion methodology to US dollars is described in the document on the methodology for the National Accounts Main Aggregates Database (http://unstats.un.org/unsd/snaama/methodology.pdf). For inter-country comparisons over time, it would be more appropriate to use the growth rate in the table based on constant price data, which are more indicative of inter-country and intra-grouping comparisons of trends in total GDP. The growth rate shown in the table is computed as geometric mean of annual growth rates expressed as percentages for the years.

Table 14: Gross value added by kind of economic activity

This table presents the shares of the components of gross value added at current prices by kind of economic activity.

Sector	Comprises of (in terms of ISIC 3):
Agriculture	Agriculture, hunting, forestry and fishing (ISIC A-B)

Industry	Mining and quarrying, Manufacturing, Electricity, gas and water supply (ISIC C-E) Construction (ISIC F)
Services	Wholesale and retail trade; repair of motor vehicles, motorcycles and personal and household goods, Hotels and restaurants (ISIC G-H) Transport, storage and communications (ISIC I) Other activities which includes financial intermediation, real estate, renting and business activities, public administration and defense; compulsory social security, education, health and social work, other community, social and personal service activities, private households with employed persons (ISIC J-P).

Chapter VIII: Finance

Detailed information and current figures relating to table 12 are contained in International Financial Statistics, published by the International Monetary Fund (see also http://elibrary-data.imf.org) and in the United Nations Monthly Bulletin of Statistics.

Table 15: Balance of payments summary

A balance of payments can be broadly described as the record of an economy's international economic transactions. It shows (a) transactions in goods, services and income between an economy and the rest of the world, (b) changes of ownership and other changes in that economy's monetary gold, special drawing rights (SDRs) and claims on and liabilities to the rest of the world, and (c) unrequited transfers and counterpart entries needed to balance in the accounting sense any entries for the foregoing transactions and changes which are not mutually offsetting. The balance of payments data are presented on the basis of the methodology and presentation of the sixth edition of the Balance of Payments Manual (BPM6), published by the International Monetary Fund in November 2013. The BPM6 incorporates several major changes to take account of developments in international trade and finance over the years, and to better harmonize the Fund's balance of payments methodology with the methodology of the 2008 System of National Accounts (SNA). The detailed definitions concerning the content of the basic categories of the balance of payments are given in the Balance of Payments Manual (sixth edition)

Brief explanatory notes are given below to clarify the scope of the major items.

Current account is a record of all transactions in the balance of payments covering the exports and imports of goods and services, payments of income, and current transfers between residents of a country and non-residents.

Capital account, n.i.e. refers mainly to capital transfers linked to the acquisition of a fixed asset other than transactions relating to debt forgiveness plus the disposal of nonproduced, nonfinancial assets, and to capital transfers linked to the disposal of fixed assets by the donor or to the financing of capital formation by the recipient, plus the acquisition of nonproduced, nonfinancial assets.

Financial account, n.i.e. is the net sum of the balance of direct investment, portfolio investment, and other investment transactions.

Reserves and related items is the sum of transactions in reserve assets, LCFARs, exceptional financing, and use of Fund credit and loans.

Table 16: Exchange rates

Foreign exchange rates are shown in units of national currency per US dollar. The exchange rates are classified into three broad categories, reflecting both the role of the authorities in the determination of the exchange and/or the multiplicity of exchange rates in a country. The market rate is used to describe exchange rates determined largely by market forces; the official rate is an exchange rate deter-mined by the authorities, sometimes in a flexible manner. For countries maintaining multiple exchange arrangements, the rates are labelled principal rate, secondary rate, and tertiary rate. Unless otherwise stated, the table refers to end of period and period averages of market exchange rates or official exchange rates.

Chapter IX: Labour market

A comparable and comprehensive collection of data on labour force and related topics are available from the International Labour Organisation's (ILO) *Key Indicators of the Labour Market (KILM)* publication, which is updated every 2 years. More timely information is contained in the ILO's ILOSTAT data repository (see www.ilo.org/ilostat) which publishes data as it is received from the countries either on an annual, quarterly or monthly basis but does not include all the consistency checks nor include all the sources used by KILM. For various reasons, national definitions of employment and unemployment often differ from the recommended international standard definitions and thereby limit international comparability. Inter-country comparisons are also complicated by a variety of types of data collection systems used to obtain information on employed and unemployed persons. The ILOSTAT website provides a comprehensive description of the methodology underlying the labour series.

Table 17: Labour force participation rate and unemployment rate

Labour force participation rate is calculated by expressing the number of persons in the labour force as a percentage of the working-age population. The labour force is the sum of the number of persons employed and the number of unemployed (see ILO's current International Recommendations on Labour Statistics). The working-age population is the population above a certain age, prescribed for the measurement of economic characteristics. The data refer to the age group of 15 years and over and are based on ILO's modelled estimates, unless otherwise stated in a footnote.

Unemployment" is defined to include persons above a certain age who, during a specified period of time were:

(a) "Without work", i.e. were not in paid employment or self-employment;

(b) "Currently available for work", i.e. were available for paid employment or self-employment during the reference period; and

(c) "Seeking work", i.e. had taken specific steps in a specified period to find paid employment or self-employment

Persons not considered to be unemployed include:

(a) Persons intending to establish their own business or farm, but who had not yet arranged to do so and who were not seeking work for pay or profit;

(b) Former unpaid family workers not at work and not seeking work for pay or profit.

The series generally represent the total number of persons wholly unemployed or temporarily laid-off. Percentage figures, where given, are calculated by comparing the number of unemployed to the total members of that group of the labour force on which the unemployment data are based.

Table 18: Employment by economic activity

The employment table presents the percentage distribution of employed persons by economic activity, according to International Standard Industry Classification (ISIC) version 4.

Chapter X: Price and production indices

Table 19: Agricultural production

"Agriculture" relates to the production of all crops and livestock products. The "Food Index" includes those commodities which are considered edible and contain nutrients. The index numbers of agricultural output and food production are calculated by the Laspeyres formula with the base year period 2004-2006. The latter is provided in order to diminish the impact of annual fluctuations in agricultural output during base years on the indices for the period. Production quantities of each commodity are weighted by 2004-2006 average national producer prices and summed for each year. The index numbers are based on production data for a calendar year. These may differ in some instances from those actually produced and published by the individual countries themselves due to variations in concepts, coverage, weights and methods of calculation. Efforts have been made to estimate these methodological differences to achieve a better international comparability of data. Detailed data on agricultural production are published by FAO in its *Statistical Yearbook.*

Chapter XI: International merchandise trade

The *International Trade Statistics Yearbook* (ITSY) provides an overview of the latest trends of trade in goods and services of most countries and areas in the world, a publication prepared by the Statistics Division of the Department for Economic and Social Affairs of the United Nations Secretariat. The yearbook, see http://comtrade.un.org/pb/, is released in two volumes; Volume I is compiled earlier in the year to present an advanced overview of international merchandise trade from the previous year, Volume II, generally released six months later, contains detailed tables showing international trade for individual commodities and 11 world trade tables covering trade values and indices.

Volume II also contains updated versions of world trade tables. The table in this yearbook are also updated monthly in the United Nations Monthly Bulletin of Statistics and on the trade statistics website, see http://unstats.un.org/unsd/trade/data/tables.asp#annual.

The statistics in this Yearbook have been compiled by national statistical authorities largely consistent with the United Nations recommended International Merchandise Trade Statistics, Concepts and Definitions 2010 (IMTS 2010). Depending on what parts of the economic territory are included in the statistical territory, the trade data-compilation system adopted by a country (its trade system) may be referred to as general or special.

General trade system	The statistical territory coincides with the economic territory. Consequently, it is recommended that the statistical territory of a country applying the general trade system comprises all applicable territorial elements. In this case, imports include goods entering the free circulation area, premises for inward processing, industrial free zones, premises for customs warehousing or commercial free zones and exports include goods leaving those territorial elements
Special trade system	(strict definition) The statistical territory comprises only a particular part of the economic territory, so that certain flows of goods which are in the scope of IMTS 2010 are not included in either import or export statistics of the compiling country. The strict definition of the special trade system is in use when the statistical territory comprises only the free circulation area, that is, the part within which goods "may be disposed of without customs restriction". Consequently, in such a case, imports include only goods entering the free circulation area of a compiling country and exports include only goods leaving the free circulation area of a compiling country
	(relaxed definition) (a) goods that enter a country for, or leave it after, inward processing, as well as (b) goods that enter or leave an industrial free zone, are also recorded and included in international merchandise trade statistics

Generally, all countries report their detailed merchandise trade data according to the Harmonized Commodity Description and Coding System (HS) and the data correspond and are then presented by Standard International Trade Classifications (SITC, Rev.3). Data refer to calendar years; however, for those countries which report according to some other reference year, the data are presented in the year which covers the majority of the reference year used by the country.

FOB-type values include the transaction value of the goods and the value of services performed to deliver goods to the border of the exporting country. CIF-type values include the transaction value of the goods, the value of services performed to deliver goods to the border of the exporting country and the value of the services performed to deliver the goods from the border of the exporting country to the border of the importing country. Therefore, data for the statistical value of imported goods are presented as a CIF-type value and the statistical value of exported goods as an FOB-type value.

Conversion of values from national currencies into United States dollars is done by means of currency conversion factors based on official exchange rates. Values in currencies subject to fluctuation are converted into United States dollars using weighted average exchange rates specially calculated for this purpose. The weighted average exchange rate for a given currency for a given year is the component monthly factors, furnished by the International Monetary Fund in its International Financial Statistics publication, weighted by the value of the relevant trade in each month; a monthly factor is the exchange rate (or the simple average rate) in effect during that month. These factors are applied to total imports and exports and to the trade in individual commodities with individual countries.

Table 20: Total imports, exports and balance of trade

Figures on the total imports and exports of countries (or areas) presented in this table are mainly taken from International Financial Statistics published monthly by the International Monetary Fund (IMF) but also from other sources such as national publications and websites and the United Nations *Monthly Bulletin of Statistics* Questionnaire, see the *International Trade Statistics Yearbook* for further details. Estimates for missing data are made in order to arrive to regional totals but are otherwise not shown. The estimation process is automated using quarterly year-on-year growth rates for the extrapolation of missing quarterly data (unless quarterly data can be estimated using available monthly data within the quarter). The conversion factors applied to data in this table are published quarterly in the

United Nations *Monthly Bulletin of Statistics* and are also available on the United Nations trade statistics website: http://unstats.un.org/unsd/trade/data/tables.asp#annual.

Table 21: Major trading partners

Figures on major trading partners show the three largest trade partners (countries of last known destination and origin or consignment) in international merchandise trade transactions. In some cases a special partner is shown (i.e. Areas nes, bunkers, etc.) instead of a country and refers to one of the following special categories. Areas not elsewhere specified (i.e. Areas nes) is used (a) for low value trade, (b) if the partner designation was unknown to the country or if an error was made in the partner assignment and (c) for reasons of confidentiality. If a specific geographical location can be identified within Areas nes, then they are recorded accordingly (i.e. Asia nes). Bunkers are ship stores and aircraft supplies, which consists mostly of fuels and food. Free zones belong to the geographical and economic territory of a country but not to its customs territory. For the purpose of trade statistics the transactions between the customs territory and the free zones are recorded, if the reporting country uses the Special Trade System. Free zones can be commercial free zones (duty free shops) or industrial free zones. Data are expressed as percentages of total exports and of total imports of the country, area or special partner.

Chapter XII: Energy

The Energy Statistics Yearbook (available at http://unstats.un.org/unsd/energy/yearbook) is a comprehensive collection of international energy statistics for over 220 countries and areas. The yearbook is prepared by the Statistics Division of the Department for Economic and Social Affairs of the United Nations Secretariat. The yearbook is produced every year with newly available data on energy production, trade, stock changes, bunkers and consumption for all countries and areas, and a historical series back to 1950 are available. The data are compiled primarily from the annual energy questionnaire distributed by the United Nations Statistics Division and supplemented by official national statistical publications, as well as publications from international and regional organizations. Where official data are not available or are inconsistent, estimates are made by the Statistics Division based on governmental, professional or commercial materials.

The period to which the data refer is the calendar year, with the exception of the data of the following countries which refer to the fiscal year: Afghanistan and Iran (Islamic Rep. of) – beginning 21 March of the year stated; Australia, Bangladesh, Bhutan, Egypt (for the latter two, electricity only), Nepal - ending June of the year stated; Pakistan - starting July of the year stated; India, Myanmar and New Zealand – beginning April of the year stated. Data on a per capita basis use population data from the United Nations Population Division as a denominator.

Table 22: Production, trade and supply of energy

Data are presented in petajoules (gigajoules per capita), to which the individual energy commodities are converted in the interests of international uniformity and comparability. To convert from original units to joules, the data in original units (metric tons, metric tons of oil equivalent, kilowatt hours, cubic metres) are multiplied by conversion factors. For a list of the relevant conversion factors and a detailed description of methods, see the Energy Statistics Yearbook.

Included in the production of commercial primary energy for solids are hard coal, lignite, peat and oil shale; liquids are comprised of crude petroleum, natural gas liquids, other hydrocarbons, additives and oxygenates, and liquid biofuels; gas comprises natural gas and primary steam/heat; and electricity is comprised of primary electricity generation from hydro, nuclear, geothermal, wind, tide, wave and solar sources.

Net imports (imports less exports and bunkers) and changes in stocks, refer to all primary and secondary forms of energy (including feedstocks). Within net imports; bunkers refer to bunkers of aviation gasoline, jet fuel and of hard coal, gas-diesel oil and residual fuel oil. International trade of energy commodities is based on the "general trade" system, that is, all goods entering and leaving the national boundary of a country are recorded as imports and exports.

Included in the consumption of energy are primary forms of solid fuels, net imports and changes in stocks of secondary fuels; liquids which is energy use of oil products includes feedstocks and refinery gas, and direct use of crude petroleum; gases include the consumption of natural gas and primary heat, net imports and changes in stocks of manufactured gases; and electricity which is primary electricity production and net imports of electricity. Consumption for some of the petroleum products is negative due to the exclusion of inter-product transfers from the calculations. Negative consumption of electricity is due to negligible primary electricity production as compared to net exports. More generally, negative consumption can represent a residual or statistical difference between production and exports when a particular product is mainly exported.

Chapter XIII: Environment

Table 23: Land

The data on land are compiled by the Food and Agriculture Organization of the United Nations (FAO). FAO's definitions of the land categories are as follows:

Land area	Total area excluding area under inland water bodies. The definition of inland water bodies generally includes major rivers and lakes
Arable land	Land under temporary crops (multiple cropped areas are counted only once); temporary meadows for mowing or pasture; land under market and kitchen gardens; and land temporarily fallow (less than five years). Abandoned land resulting from shifting cultivation is not included in this category. Data for "arable land" are not meant to indicate the amount of land that is potentially cultivable.
Permanent crops	Land cultivated with crops that occupy the land for long periods and need not be replanted after each harvest, such as cocoa, coffee and rubber. This category includes land under flowering shrubs, fruit trees, nut trees and vines, but excludes land under trees grown for wood or timber
Forest	In the Global Forest Resources Assessment 2010 the following definition is used for forest: Land spanning more than 0.5 hectares with trees higher than 5 metres and a canopy cover of more than 10 percent, or trees able to reach these thresholds in situ. It does not include land that is predominantly under agricultural or urban land use.
Sites protected for terrestrial biodiversity	Land which contributes significantly to the global persistence of biodiversity measured as a proportion of which is wholly covered by a designated protected area. Data are based on spatial overlap between polygons for Key Biodiversity Areas from the World Database of key Biodiversity Areas and polygons for protected areas from the World Database on Protected Areas. Figures for each region are calculated as the proportion of each Key Biodiversity Area covered by protected areas, averaged (i.e. calculated as the mean) across all Key Biodiversity Areas within the region.

Table 24: Threatened species

Data on the number of threatened species in each group of animals and plants are compiled by the World Conservation Union (IUCN)/ Species Survival Commission (SSC) and published in the IUCN Red List of Threatened Species. The list provides a catalogue of those species that are considered globally threatened. The number of threatened species for any particular country will change between years for a number of reasons, including:

- New information being available to refine the assessment (e.g., confirmation that the species occurs or does not occur in a particular country, confirmation that the species is or is not threatened, etc.)
- Taxonomic changes (e.g., what was previously recognised as one species is now split into several separate species, or has now been merged with another species).
- Corrections (e.g., the previous assessment may have missed a particular country out of its country occurrence list or included a specific country by mistake).
- Genuine status changes (e.g., a species may have genuinely deteriorated or improved in status and therefore has moved into or out of the threatened categories).

The categories used in the Red List are as follows; extinct, extinct in the wild, critically endangered; endangered, vulnerable, near threatened and data deficient.

Table 25: CO_2 emissions estimates

The source of the data presented on the emissions of carbon dioxide (CO2) is the Carbon Dioxide Information Analysis Centre (CDIAC) of the Oak Ridge National Laboratory in the USA, see http://cdiac.ornl.gov/. The CDIAC estimates of CO2 emissions are derived primarily from United Nations energy statistics on the consumption of liquid and solid fuels and gas consumption and flaring, and from cement production estimates from the Bureau of Mines of the U.S. Department of Interior. The emissions presented in the table are in units of 1,000 metric tons of CO_2; to convert CO_2 into carbon, divide the data by 3.667. Full details of the procedures for calculating emissions are given in Global, Regional, and National Annual CO_2 Emissions Estimates from Fossil Fuel Burning, Hydraulic Cement Production, and Gas Flaring and on the CDIAC web site. Relative to other industrial sources for which CO2 emissions are estimated, statistics on gas flaring activities are sparse and sporadic. In countries where gas flaring activities account for a considerable proportion of the total CO_2 emissions, the sporadic nature of gas flaring statistics may produce spurious or misleading trends in national CO_2 emissions over the period covered by the table.

Table 26: Water supply and sanitation services

These data are estimated by the WHO/UNICEF Joint Monitoring Programme for Water Supply and Sanitation (JMP) based on available country sources, see www.wssinfo.org for further information. The proportion of the population using safely managed drinking water services is defined as the population using an improved drinking water source (the indicator used for Millennium Development Goals monitoring) which is located on premises, and available when needed, and free of faecal and priority chemical contamination. In order to meet the criteria for a safely managed drinking water service, people must use an improved source meeting three criteria:

- it should be accessible on premises,
- water should be available when needed, and
- the water supplied should be free from contamination.

If the improved source does not meet any one of these criteria but a round trip to collect water takes 30 minutes or less, then it will be classified as a basic drinking water service. If water collection from an improved source exceeds 30 minutes it will be categorised as a limited service. The JMP also differentiates populations using unimproved sources such as unprotected wells or springs, and populations drinking surface water collected directly from a river, dam, lake, stream or irrigation canal.

For the proportion of the population using "safely managed sanitation services", there are three main ways to meet the criteria for having a safely managed sanitation service. People should use improved sanitation facilities which are not shared with other households, and the excreta produced should either be:

- treated and disposed in situ,
- stored temporarily and then emptied and transported to treatment off-site, or
- transported through a sewer with wastewater and then treated off-site.

If the excreta from improved sanitation facilities are not safely managed then people using those facilities will be classed as having a basic sanitation service. People using improved facilities which are shared with other households will be classified as having a limited service.

Chapter XIV: Science and technology

Table 27: Population employed in research and development (R&D)

The data presented on human resources in research and development (R&D) are compiled by the UNESCO Institute for Statistics. Data for certain countries are provided to UNESCO by OECD, Eurostat and the Latin-American Network on Science and Technology Indicators (RICYT). The definitions and classifications applied by UNESCO in the table are based on those set out in the Frascati Manual (OECD, 2002). The three categories of personnel shown are defined as follows:

Researchers	Professionals engaged in the conception or creation of new knowledge, products, processes, methods and systems and also in the management of the projects concerned. Postgraduate students at the PhD level (ISCED level 8) engaged in R&D are considered as researchers.
Technicians and equivalent staff	Persons whose main tasks require technical knowledge and experience in one or more fields of engineering, physical and life sciences (technicians) or social sciences and humanities (equivalent staff). They participate in R&D by performing scientific and technical tasks involving the application of concepts and operational methods, normally under the supervision of researchers.
Other supporting staff	Skilled and unskilled craftsmen, secretarial and clerical staff participating in R&D projects or directly associated with (or providing services to researchers involved in) such projects.

Headcount data reflect the total number of persons employed in R&D, independently from their dedication. Full-time equivalent (FTE) may be thought of as one person-year. Thus, a person who normally spends 30% of his/her time on R&D and the rest on other activities (such as teaching, university administration and student counselling) should be considered as 0.3 FTE. Similarly, if a full-time R&D worker is employed at an R&D unit for only six months, this results in an FTE of 0.5.

Table 28: Gross domestic expenditure on research and development (R&D)

The data presented on gross domestic expenditure on research and development are compiled by the UNESCO Institute for Statistics. Data for certain countries are provided to UNESCO by OECD, EUROSTAT and the Network on Science and Technology Indicators (RICYT). Gross domestic expenditure on R&D (GERD) is total intramural expenditure on R&D performed on the national territory during a given period. It includes R&D performed within a country and funded from abroad but excludes payments made abroad for R&D. The sources of funds for GERD are classified according to the following five categories:

Business enterprise funds	Funds allocated to R&D by all firms, organizations and institutions whose primary activity is the market production of goods and services (other than the higher education sector) for sale to the general public at an economically significant price, and those private non-profit institutes mainly serving these firms, organizations and institutions.
Government funds	Funds allocated to R&D by all departments, offices and other bodies which furnish, but normally do not sell to the community, those common services, other than higher education, which cannot otherwise be conveniently and economically provided, as well as those that administer the state and the economic and social policy of the community. Public enterprises, mainly engaged in market production and sale of goods and services, funds are included in the business enterprise funds sector. Government funds also include private non-profit institutes controlled and mainly financed by government, not administered by the higher education sector.
Higher education funds	Funds allocated to R&D by institutions of higher education comprising all universities, colleges of technology, other institutions providing tertiary education (i.e. ISCED 5, 6, 7 or 8), whatever their source or finance or legal status. They also include all research institutes, experimental stations and clinics operating under the direct control of or administered by or associated with higher education institutions.
Private non-profit funds	Funds allocated to R&D by non-market, private non-profit institutions serving households (i.e. the general public), as well as by private individuals and households.
Funds from abroad	Funds allocated to R&D by all institutions and individuals located outside the political borders of a country; and all international organizations (except business enterprises), including facilities and operations within the country's borders.

The absolute figures for R&D expenditure should not be compared country by country. Such comparisons would require the conversion of national currencies into a common currency by means of special R&D exchange rates. Official exchange rates do not always reflect the real costs of R&D activities and comparisons that are based on such rates can result in misleading conclusions, although they can be used to indicate a gross order of magnitude.

Table 29: Patents

A patent is granted by a national patent office or by a regional office that does the work for a number of countries, such as the European Patent Office and the African Regional Intellectual Property Organisation. Under such regional systems, an applicant requests protection for the invention in one or more countries, and each country decides as to whether to offer patent protection within its borders. The World Intellectual Property Organisation (WIPO) administered Patent Cooperation Treaty (PCT) provides for the filling of a single international patent application which has the same effect as national applications filed in the designated countries. Data include resident intensity, patents granted and patents in force. Patent intensity is presented as the resident patent fillings per million population, where as resident Intellectual Property (IP) filling refers to an application filed by an applicant at its national IP office. IP grant (registration) data are based on the same concept. In force refers to a patent or other form of IP protection that is currently valid. Country of origin is used to catgorise IP data by resident (domestic) and non-resident (foreign). The residence of the first-named applicant (or inventor) recorded in the IP document (e.g. patent or trademark application) is used to classify IP data by country of origin. The data are compiled and published by the WIPO.

Chapter XV: International tourism and transport

The data on international tourism have been supplied by the World Tourism Organization (UNWTO) from detailed tourism information published in either the *Yearbook of Tourism Statistics* or *Compendium of Tourism Statistics,* see www.unwto.org/statistics for further information. For statistical purposes, the term "international visitor" describes "any person who travels to a country other than that in which he/she has his/her usual residence but outside his/her usual environment for a period not exceeding 12 months and whose main purpose of visit is other than the exercise of an activity remunerated from within the country visited". There are four series presented in the UNWTO *yearbook* and *compendium*, but only one series is selected to be presented in this yearbook, generally based on the following priority order to best describe an "international visitor";

Order	Series code	Series name
1	TF	*Arrivals of non-resident tourists at national borders* are visitors who stay at least one night in a collective or private accommodation in the country visited (excludes same-day visitors)
2	VF	*Arrivals of non-resident visitors at national borders* are visitors as defined in series "TF" as well as same-day visitors who do not spend the night in a collective or private accommodation in the country visited
3	TCE	*Arrivals of non-resident tourists in all types of accommodation establishments*
4	THS	*Arrivals of non-resident tourists in hotels and similar establishments*

The figures do not include immigrants, residents in a frontier zone, persons domiciled in one country or area and working in an adjoining country or area, members of the armed forces and diplomats and consular representatives when they travel from their country of origin to the country in which they are stationed and vice-versa. The figures also exclude persons in transit who do not formally enter the country through passport control, such as air transit passengers who remain for a short period in a designated area of the air terminal or ship passengers who are not permitted to disembark. This category includes passengers transferred directly between airports or other terminals. Other passengers in transit through a country are classified as visitors.

Table 30: Tourist/visitor arrivals and tourism expenditure

Data on arrivals of non-resident (or international) visitors may be obtained from different sources. In some cases data are obtained from border statistics derived from administrative records (police, immigration, traffic counts and other types of controls), border surveys and registrations at accommodation establishments. Totals correspond to the total number of arrivals from the regions indicated in the table. When a person visits the same country several times a year, an equal number of arrivals is recorded. Likewise, if a person visits several countries during the course of a single trip, his/her arrival in each country is recorded separately. Consequently, arrivals cannot be assumed to be equal to the number of persons travelling.

Expenditure associated with tourism activity of visitors has been traditionally identified with the travel item of the Balance of Payments (BOP): in the case of inbound tourism, those expenditures in the country of reference associated with non-resident visitors are registered as "credits" in the BOP and refer to "travel receipts". The new conceptual framework approved by the United Nations Statistical Commission in relation to the measurement of tourism macroeconomic activity (the so-called Tourism Satellite Account) considers that "tourism industries and products" includes transport of passengers. Consequently, a better estimate of tourism-related expenditures by resident and non-resident visitors in an international scenario would be, in terms of the BOP, the value of the travel item plus that of the passenger transport item. Nevertheless, users should be aware that BOP estimates include, in addition to expenditures associated with visitors, those related to other types of individuals. The data published should allow international comparability and therefore correspond to those published by the International Monetary Fund and provided by the Central Banks, any exceptions are listed within the *Compendium of Tourism Statistics* and the *Yearbook of Tourism Statistics,* see www.unwto.org/statistics for further information.

Table 31: Civil aviation: scheduled airline traffic

The data on civil aviation are published annually in the Annual Report of the Council of the International Civil Aviation Organisation. The data are based on reported data as well as estimates for the non-reporting airlines. Data for total traffic cover both domestic and international scheduled services operated by airlines registered in each country. Scheduled services include supplementary services occasioned by overflow traffic on regularly scheduled trips and preparatory flights for newly scheduled services. The data are prepared by the International Civil Aviation Organisation (see www.icao.int). The following terms have been used in the table:

- Kilometers flown – aircraft kilometres performed, which is the sum of the products obtained by multiplying the number of revenue flight stages flown by the corresponding stage distance.
- Passengers carried – the number of passengers carried is obtained by counting each passenger on a particular flight (with one flight number) once only and not repeatedly on each individual stage of that flight, with a single exception that a passenger flying on both the international and domestic stages of the same flight should be counted as both a domestic and international passenger.
- Passenger-kilometres performed – a passenger kilometre is performed when a passenger is carried one kilometre. Calculation of passenger-kilometres equals the sum of the products obtained by multiplying the number of revenue passengers carried on each flight stage by the stage distance. The resultant figure is equal to the number of kilometres travelled by all passengers.
- Tonne-kilometres performed – a metric tonne of revenue load carried one kilometre. Tonne-kilomtres performed equals the sum of the product obtained by multiplying the number of total tonnes of revenue load (passengers, freight and mail) carried on each flight stage by the stage distance.

Chapter XVI: Development assistance

Table 32: Net disbursements of official development assistance to recipients

The table presents estimates of flows of financial resources to individual recipients either directly (bilaterally) or through multilateral institutions (multilaterally). The multilateral institutions include the World Bank Group, regional banks, financial institutions of the European Union and a number of United Nations institutions, programmes and trust funds. The source of data is the Development Assistance Committee (DAC) of OECD to which member countries reported data on their flow of resources to developing countries and territories, countries and territories in transition, and multilateral institutions. Additional information on definitions, methods and sources can be found in OECD's *Geographical Distribution of Financial Flows to Developing Countries* publication, also see http://stats.oecd.org/ for further information.

Table 33: Net disbursements of official development assistance from donors

The table presents the development assistance expenditures of donor countries. This table includes donors' contributions to multilateral agencies; therefore, the overall totals differ from those in table 25, which include disbursements by multilateral agencies.

***

Annexe II: Notes techniques

Chapitre I: Aperçu mondial

Tableau 1: Statistiques mondiales – séries principales

Ces séries d'agrégats mondiaux sont obtenues à partir d'autres tableaux figurant dans le présent *Annuaire*, lorsque c'est possible, et sont établies à partir de publications et de bases de données statistiques des Nations Unies et des organismes spécialisés ainsi que d'autres institutions. Pour davantage d'information sur les définitions, les sources, les méthodes de compilation et la couverture des données, il convient de se référer aux notes techniques du tableau correspondant dans le présent *Annuaire*.

Chapitre II: Population et migration

Tableau 2: Population, superficie et densité

Les données concernant la population totale, masculine et féminine, le rapport des sexes, la répartition de la population par âge et la densité de la population proviennent des estimations et des projections préparées par la Division de la population de l'Organisation des Nations Unies, qui sont publiées dans *Perspectives de la population mondiale : Révision de 2017*. Les données concernant la superficie sont extraites de l'*Annuaire démographique*, qui ne contient que les données nationales officielles.

La population totale, masculine et féminine correspond à la population de fait dans un pays, un territoire ou une région à compter du 1er juillet de l'année indiquée, sauf indication contraire dans une note en bas de page. Les chiffres sont présentés en millions. La population totale d'un pays peut consister de tous les résidents habituels (population de droit) ou toutes les personnes présentes dans le pays (population de fait) au moment du recensement ; pour permettre les comparaisons internationales, la population de fait est utilisée, sauf indication contraire dans une note en bas de page.

La population âgée de 0 à 14 ans/ 60 ans et plus correspond au pourcentage de la population âgée de 0 à 14 ans et 60 ans et plus, respectivement à compter du 1er juillet de l'année indiquée, sauf indication contraire dans une note en bas de page.

La densité de la population correspond à la population, à compter du 1er juillet de l'année indiquée, par kilomètre carré de superficie, sauf indication contraire dans une note en bas de page.

Le rapport des sexes est calculé en tant que le rapport de la population des hommes à celui de 100 femmes à compter du 1er juillet de l'année indiquée, sauf indication contraire dans une note en bas de page.

La superficie correspond aux territoires plus eaux intérieures, sauf indication contraire dans une note en bas de page.

Tableau 3: Sélection d'indicateurs de l'espérance de vie, de la maternité, de la dépendance et de la mortalité

L'espérance de vie à la naissance, le taux de fécondité, le taux de mortalité infantile et l'espérance de vie à la naissance proviennent des estimations et projections de la Division de la population de l'ONU, publiées dans World Population Prospects : The 2015 Revision. Les données sont une moyenne sur cinq ans ; 2000-2005 qualifié « 2005 », 2005-2010 qualifie « 2010 » et 2010-2015 qualifié « 2015 », sauf indication contraire dans une note en bas de page. Les ratios de mortalité maternelle sont des estimations de l'Organisation mondiale de la santé, de l'UNICEF, du Fonds des Nations Unies pour la Population, de la Banque mondiale et de la Division de la population de l'ONU publiées dans les Tendances du taux de mortalité maternelle: 1990 à 2015.

Le taux d'accroissement de la population (ou taux de croissance) est Le changement de la croissance annuelle moyenne dans la taille de la population totale.

Le taux de fécondité et le taux de fécondité total, un indicateur synthétique de fécondité largement utilisé. Il correspond au nombre total d'enfants que mettrait au monde une femme, en supposant aucune mortalité féminine en âge de procréation et les taux de fécondité par âge d'un pays désignée et une période de référence.

Le taux de mortalité infantile (pour 1 000 naissances vivantes) est le rapport des morts de nourrissons (les décès des enfants de moins de 1 an) dans une année donnée par le nombre total des naissances vivantes dans la même année.

Le ratio de mortalité maternelle est le ratio du nombre de morts maternelles durant une période donnée pour 100 000 naissances vivantes pendant la même période. Un décès maternel se réfère à une mortalité féminine dus à une cause liée à la grossesse ou aggravée par celle-ci ou dus à sa prise en charge (mais non pour des causes accidentelles ou fortuites) pendant sa grossesse ou son accouchement au maximum 42 jours après l'accouchement, quels que soient la durée et le lieu de la grossesse.

L'espérance de vie à la naissance est la moyenne du nombre d'années de vie depuis la naissance (âge 0) pour les hommes et pour les femmes selon les taux de mortalité attendus par âge estimes pour l'année de référence et la population.

Tableau 4: Migrants internationaux et réfugiés

Le stock international de migrants provient d'estimations et de projections préparées par la Division de la population de l'Organisation des Nations Unies, publiées dans *International migrant stock: The 2015 Revision*. Les données sur les «réfugiés et autres personnes relevant de la compétence du HCR» ont été obtenues auprès du Haut-Commissaire des Nations Unies pour les réfugiés, et sont publiées dans la base de données de statistiques démographiques.

Le stock international de migrants représente le nombre de personnes nées dans un autre pays que celui dans lequel elles vivent. Lorsque les informations concernant le pays d'origine font défaut, on a utilisé les données sur le nombre de personnes de nationalité étrangère. Et à défaut de données empiriques, on a eu recours à des estimations. Les données font référence au milieu de l'année 2015. Le stock international de migrants en pourcentage de la population est obtenu en divisant le stock international de migrants estimé par la population totale estimée et en multipliant le résultat par 100.

Les réfugiés sont les personnes reconnues comme telles au sens de la Convention de 1951 relative au statut des réfugiés, de son protocole de 1967 ou de la Convention de l'OUA de 1969 régissant les aspects propres aux problèmes des réfugiés en Afrique; celles reconnues comme réfugiés conformément au Statut du HCR; les personnes qui bénéficient d'une forme de protection complémentaire ou jouissent d'une protection temporaire. Depuis 2007, la population des réfugiés inclut également les personnes dont la situation est assimilable à celle des réfugiés.

Les demandeurs d'asile sont des personnes qui ont déposé une demande de protection internationale et qui n'ont pas encore obtenu le statut de réfugié, quelle que soit la date à laquelle la demande a été présentée.

Les « autres personnes relevant de la compétence du HCR » se composent des cinq catégories suivantes :

Les personnes déplacées sont des personnes ou groupes de personnes qui ont été forcés ou contraints de fuir ou de quitter leurs foyers ou leur lieu de résidence habituel, notamment en raison d'un conflit armé, de situations de violence généralisée, de violations des droits de l'homme ou de catastrophes naturelles ou provoquées par l'homme, ou pour en éviter les effets, et qui n'ont pas franchi les frontières internationalement reconnues d'un État. Aux fins des statistiques du HCR, cette population ne comprend que les personnes déplacées en raison d'un conflit qui bénéficient de la protection et/ou de l'assistance du HCR. Depuis 2007, la population de personnes déplacées inclut également les personnes dont la situation est assimilable à celle des personnes déplacées. On trouvera des estimations de la population mondiale des personnes déplacées sur le site www.internal-displacement.org.

Les réfugiés de retour sont d'anciens réfugiés rentrés dans leur pays d'origine, soit spontanément, soit de façon organisée, mais qui ne sont pas encore pleinement intégrés. Ces retours ne se font normalement que lorsque leur sécurité et leur dignité peuvent être garanties.

Les déplacés de retour sont des personnes déplacée qui bénéficiaient des activités de protection et d'assistance du HCR et qui sont revenues à leur lieu d'origine ou de résidence habituel au cours de l'année.

Les apatrides sont définis par le droit international comme des personnes qu'aucun État ne considère comme ses ressortissants par application de sa législation. En d'autres termes, les apatrides ne possèdent la nationalité d'aucun État. Les statistiques du HCR incluent les personnes qui relèvent de sa compétence en vertu de cette définition, mais les données de certains pays peuvent aussi inclure des personnes de nationalité indéterminée.

Les autres personnes relevant de la compétence du HCR sont des personnes qui ne relèvent pas directement d'une des catégories ci-dessus, mais auxquelles le HCR assure protection et/ou assistance pour des raisons humanitaires ou d'autre motifs particuliers.

Chapitre III: La situation des femmes

Tableau 5: Proportion de sièges occupés par des femmes au parlement national

Ce tableau indique le pourcentage des sièges des chambres uniques ou basses des parlements nationaux occupés par des femmes, en janvier ou février de chaque année (voir les notes du tableau pour plus de détails). Les parlements nationaux peuvent être bicaméraux ou unicaméraux. Ce tableau porte sur la chambre unique des parlements unicaméraux et sur la chambre basse des parlements bicaméraux. Il ne porte pas sur la chambre haute des parlements bicaméraux. Les sièges sont habituellement attribués aux membres à l'issue d'élections parlementaires générales. Certains sièges peuvent aussi être pourvus à l'issue de nominations, de désignations, d'élections indirectes, de roulement des membres et d'élections partielles. La proportion d'élues est obtenue en divisant le nombre total de sièges occupés par des femmes par le nombre total de sièges que compte le parlement. Les statistiques ne sont ni pondérées ni normalisées. La source de ce tableau est l'Union interparlementaire, voir www.ipu.org pour plus d'informations

Tableau 6: Rapport filles/garçons dans l'enseignement primaire, secondaire et supérieur

Ce tableau indique la proportion de filles par rapport aux garçons (indice de parité des sexes) dans l'enseignement primaire, secondaire et supérieur, à savoir le rapport entre le nombre de filles inscrites dans l'enseignement primaire, secondaire et supérieur et le nombre de garçons à chaque niveau. L'indice de parité des sexes du taux brut de scolarisation pour chaque niveau d'enseignement est utilisé. La source de ce tableau est l'Institut de statistique de l'UNESCO, voir www.uis.unesco.org pour plus d'informations.

Chapitre IV: Éducation

Les données des tableaux 5 et 6 sont présentées conformément à la Classification internationale type de l'éducation de l'UNESCO (CITE, révision de 2011). Les données sont présentées dans les tableaux sur la base des trois principaux niveaux d'éducation, présentés comme suit :

L'enseignement primaire (CITE niveau 1) désigne les programmes éducatifs habituellement conçus pour apporter aux élèves les compétences fondamentales en lecture, écriture et en mathématiques (c'est-à-dire en calcul) afin d'établir une base solide pour la compréhension et l'apprentissage des principaux domaines de la connaissance et favoriser le développement personnel et social dans le but de les préparer à l'entrée dans le premier cycle de l'enseignement secondaire. Il privilégie l'enseignement à un niveau de complexité élémentaire avec peu ou pas de spécialisation.

L'enseignement secondaire (niveaux 2 et 3 de la CITE) est divisé en deux parties : le premier et le second cycles du secondaire. Les programmes du premier cycle de l'enseignement secondaire sont généralement conçus de manière à renforcer les acquis scolaires du primaire. L'objectif consiste habituellement à établir la base d'un apprentissage et d'un développement humain valables pour toute la vie et que les systèmes éducatifs pourront ensuite enrichir par de nouvelles possibilités d'éducation. Les programmes du deuxième cycle de l'enseignement secondaire visent en général à achever l'enseignement secondaire et à préparer à l'entrée dans l'enseignement supérieur et/ou à enseigner des compétences utiles à l'exercice d'un emploi. Les programmes de ce niveau offrent aux élèves un enseignement plus varié, spécialisé et approfondi que les programmes du premier cycle. Ils sont davantage différenciés et proposent un éventail plus large d'options et de filières. Les enseignants sont souvent hautement qualifiés dans les matières ou domaines spécialisés qu'ils enseignent, en particulier dans les classes supérieures.

L'enseignement supérieur (niveaux 5 à 8 de la CITE) se fonde sur les acquis de l'enseignement secondaire et offre des activités d'apprentissage dans des domaines d'éducation spécialisés. Il vise à transmettre des connaissances très spécialisées et d'un niveau de complexité élevé. L'enseignement supérieur inclut ce que l'on qualifie habituellement d'enseignement académique mais il comprend aussi l'enseignement technique ou professionnel avancé. Il comprend les niveaux 5, 6, 7 et 8 de la CITE, appelés respectivement enseignement supérieur de cycle court, enseignement du niveau de la licence ou équivalent, niveau master ou équivalent, et niveau doctorat ou équivalent. Le contenu des programmes de l'enseignement supérieur est plus complexe et plus avancé que celui des niveaux inférieurs de la CITE.

On trouvera davantage d'informations sur la Classification internationale type de l'éducation (CITE) 2011 sur le site : http://www.uis.unesco.org/Education/Documents/isced-2011-fr.pdf.

Tableau 7: Enseignement primaire, secondaire et supérieur

Le tableau montre le nombre d'élèves scolarisés ainsi que le taux de scolarisation brut qui est le nombre d'étudiants inscrits, quel que soit leur âge, exprimé en pourcentage de la population d'âge scolaire officiellement admissible correspondant au même niveau d'enseignement pour une année scolaire donnée. Les inscriptions sont mesurées au début de l'année scolaire ou universitaire. Le taux de scolarisation brut pour chaque niveau comprend tous les élèves, quel que soit leur âge, tandis que la population générale considérée ne comprend que ceux dont l'âge correspond à l'âge scolaire officiel. De ce fait, pour les pays dont la population d'âge scolaire est quasi totalement scolarisée, le taux de scolarisation brut peut dépasser 100 si la répartition des âges effectifs des élèves s'étend au-delà des âges scolaires officiels.

Tableau 8: Personnel enseignant au niveau primaire, secondaire et supérieur

Le tableau montre le nombre total d'enseignants à chaque niveau ainsi que la proportion des enseignantes exprimée en pourcentage du nombre total d'enseignants (hommes et femmes) au même niveau au cours d'une année scolaire donnée. Les données proviennent de recensements ou d'enquêtes dans les écoles et des dossiers des enseignants.

Les enseignants (ou personnel enseignant) sont définis comme des personnes qui, dans l'exercice de leur métier, guident et dirigent le parcours didactique des élèves et étudiants, indépendamment de leurs qualifications et du mécanisme de transmission des connaissances (autrement dit soit face-à-face et/ou à distance). L'enseignement consiste à planifier, organiser, et mener des activités de groupe ou les connaissances, aptitudes et compétences des élèves sont développés comme précisé dans le programme d'éducation. Cette définition exclut le personnel enseignant qui n'a pas de fonctions pédagogiques à la période de référence (par exemple les directeurs ou chefs d'établissements scolaires qui n'enseignent pas) et les personnes qui travaillent ponctuellement ou bénévolement dans des établissements d'enseignement.

Le personnel enseignant universitaire est le personnel employé dont la mission principale est l'enseignement et /ou la recherche. Cela comprend le personnel qui détient un grade universitaire avec des titres tels que professeur, professeur agrégé, professeur adjoint, maitre de conférences ou l'équivalent. Le personnel, comme par exemple doyen, directeur, vice-doyen, doyen adjoint, président ou chef de département, est également inclus si leur activité principale est l'enseignement ou la recherche.

Tableau 9: Dépenses publiques afférentes à l'éducation

Les dépenses publiques afférentes à l'éducation consistent en dépenses courantes et dépenses en capital engagées par l'administration aux niveaux local, régional et national, y compris les municipalités. Les contributions des ménages sont exclues. Les dépenses d'éducation courantes comprennent les dépenses en biens et en services consommés dans l'année en cours et qui devront être renouvelées au besoin l'année suivante. Elles comprennent les dépenses au titre des salaires et avantages du personnel; des services achetés ou obtenus par contrat; d'autres ressources, notamment de manuels et autres matériels d'enseignement; des services sociaux; et d'autres dépenses courantes telles que les subventions aux étudiants et aux ménages, l'ameublement et le matériel, les petites réparations, le combustible, les télécommunications, les voyages, l'assurance et les loyers. Les dépenses en capital pour l'éducation consistent en achats de biens dont la durée dépasse une année. Elles comprennent les dépenses de construction, de rénovation et de grosses réparations de bâtiments ainsi que l'achat de matériel lourd et de véhicules.

Chapitre V: Santé

Tableau 10: Le personnel de santé

Le tableau présente quatre grandes catégories de personnel de santé (sur les 9 catégories disponibles à la source) : la catégorie des médecins, qui comprend les médecins généralistes et les spécialistes; celle des infirmiers et sages-femmes comprend les infirmiers et sages-femmes qualifiés, les infirmiers auxiliaires professionnels et les sages-femmes auxiliaires professionnelles. Les accoucheuses traditionnelles ne sont pas incluses; le personnel de dentisterie comprend les dentistes, les assistants dentaires, les techniciens dentaires et les professions associées; et le personnel du secteur pharmaceutique comprend les pharmaciens, les pharmaciens assistants, les préparateurs en pharmacie et les professions associées.

Les données sont extraites des statistiques mondiales des personnels de santé de la base de données de l'Organisation mondiale de la Santé (OMS), qui sont établies à partir de plusieurs sources comme les recensements de population nationaux, les enquêtes sur la population active et l'emploi, les productions statistiques nationales et les données régulières des administrations. Il existe de ce fait d'un pays à l'autre une variabilité considérable dans la couverture, la qualité et l'année de référence des données. Généralement, les données du dénominateur pour le calcul de la densité du personnel de santé (c'est-à-dire les estimations de la population nationale) sont extraites des *Perspectives de la population mondiale* publiées par la Division de la population de l'Organisation des Nations Unies. Parfois le rapport officiel ne fournit que les indicateurs de la densité du personnel de santé, à partir desquels le stock est ensuite estimé.

La classification des personnels du secteur de la santé utilisée repose sur les critères de l'enseignement et formation techniques et professionnels, la réglementation des professions de santé et les activités et tâches des postes, c'est-à-dire sur un cadre de catégorisation des principales variables des personnels selon des caractéristiques communes. Le cadre de l'OMS repose en grande partie sur les révisions les plus récentes des systèmes de classification internationaux normalisés de l'Organisation internationale du Travail (Classification internationale type des professions), de l'Organisation des Nations Unies pour l'éducation, la science et la culture (Classification internationale type de l'éducation) et de la Division de statistique de l'ONU (Classification internationale type, par industrie, de toutes les branches d'activité économique). En fonction de la situation propre à chaque pays et des moyens de mesure, les données disponibles dans l'ensemble agrégé décrivent jusqu'à 9 catégories de personnels de santé, et jusqu'à 18 catégories dans l'ensemble désagrégé. Ce dernier reflète essentiellement une tentative de mieux distinguer certains sous-groupes des personnels du secteur de la santé en fonction de différences supposées dans les niveaux de compétence et de spécialisation.

Tableau 11: Dépenses de santé

Le montant total des dépenses de santé représente la somme de tous les frais encourus pour maintenir, rétablir ou améliorer l'état de santé, qu'il s'agisse de versements en espèces ou de services fournis en nature. C'est la somme des dépenses de santé des administrations publiques et des dépenses de santé privées. Les dépenses de santé des administrations publiques sont la somme des frais de santé engagés par des organismes publics, comme le Ministère de la santé, d'autres ministères, des organismes parapublics ou les caisses de sécurité sociale (sans double comptabilisation des transferts publics aux administrations de sécurité sociale et aux fonds extrabudgétaires), qu'il s'agisse de versements en espèces ou de services fournis en nature. Elle comprend toutes les dépenses effectuées par ces organismes, quelle qu'en soit la source, y compris donc le financement des bailleurs de fonds canalisé par eux. Elle inclut les paiements de transfert aux ménages en compensation du coût des soins médicaux et le financement des services et produits de santé par des fonds extrabudgétaires. Elle comprend les dépenses courantes et en capital. On trouvera davantage d'informations sur la définition, la méthodologie, les sources et les limitations des données sur le site de la base de données mondiale des dépenses de santé (voir http://apps.who.int/nha/database/DocumentationCentre/Index/fr).

Chapitre VI: Criminalité

Tableau 12: Homicides intentionnels et autres crimes

Les données des «homicides intentionnels» et des «autres crimes» proviennent des données recueillies dans la base de données statistiques de l'Office des Nations Unies contre la drogue et le crime.

L'homicide intentionnel est défini comme la mort illégale d'une personne causée par une autre ayant l'intention de tuer ou de blesser gravement. Les données de l'homicide intentionnel doivent aussi inclure les violences suivies de mort et la mort résultant d'une attaque terroriste. Elles excluent la tentative d'homicide intentionnel, l'homicide involontaire, la mort causée par une intervention légale, l'homicide justifiable en état de légitime défense et la mort causée par un conflit armé.

L'agression est une atteinte à l'intégrité physique d'une autre personne entraînant des dommages corporels graves, à l'exclusion des actes préjudiciables à caractère sexuel, des menaces et des gifles/coups de poing. Les agressions graves ayant entraîné la mort sont également exclues.

L'enlèvement désigne la détention et soustraction illégales d'une ou de plusieurs personnes contre leur volonté (y compris par le recours à la force, aux menaces, à la fraude ou à l'incitation) aux fins d'exiger pour leur libération un gain illicite ou un autre avantage économique ou matériel, ou pour contraindre une personne à suivre ou à ne pas suivre une ligne de conduite. L'enlèvement exclut les différends relatifs à la garde d'un enfant.

Le vol est l'appropriation ou l'obtention illégale d'un bien dans l'intention d'en priver une personne ou une organisation de manière permanente sans son consentement et sans recours à la force. Le vol exclut le cambriolage, l'entrée avec effraction, le vol qualifié et le vol de véhicule motorisé, qui sont comptabilisés séparément.

La violence sexuelle désigne le viol et l'agression sexuelle, y compris les agressions sexuelles contre les enfants.

Chapitre VII: Comptes nationaux

La base de données des principaux agrégats des comptes nationaux (consultable sur le site http://unstats.un.org/unsd/snaama) présente les données des comptes nationaux de plus de 200 pays et régions du monde. Elle constitue la base de l'analyse des principaux agrégats des statistiques de la comptabilité nationale (*National Account Statistics: Analysis of Main Aggregates*), une publication préparée par la Division de statistique du Département des affaires économiques et sociales du Secrétariat des Nations Unies avec le généreux concours des offices nationaux de la statistique. La base de données est mise à jour chaque année au mois de décembre avec les données nouvellement disponibles des comptes nationaux de tous les pays et régions.

La base de données des principaux agrégats des comptes nationaux repose sur les données extraites du Questionnaire sur la comptabilité nationale des Nations Unies (NAQ) introduit en octobre 1999, qui lui-même repose sur le Système de comptes nationaux 1993 (SCN 1993). Les données sont complétées par des estimations préparées par la Division de statistique. Le SCN actualisé, appelé Système de comptes nationaux 2008 (SCN 2008) a été finalisé en septembre 2009. En 2015, 63 pays et territoires (États membres de l'Union européenne, Albanie, Argentine, Australie, Brésil, Brunéi Darussalam, Canada, Chine, RAS de Hong Kong, Chine, RAS de Macao, République dominicaine, Équateur, Inde, Indonésie, Israël, Kenya, Mexique, Mongolie, Nouvelle-Zélande, Nigéria, Pakistan, Pérou, Philippines, République de Corée, Serbie, Singapour, Afrique du Sud, Swaziland, Timor-Leste, Ouganda, Ukraine, États-Unis d'Amérique et Zambie) ont commencé de soumettre des données conformément au SCN 2008.

Tout est mis en œuvre pour présenter les estimations des divers pays ou régions sous une forme conçue pour faciliter la comparabilité internationale. À cette fin, les différences importantes entre les concepts, la portée, la couverture et la classification sont décrites dans les notes de chaque pays. Ces différences doivent être prises en compte afin d'éviter les comparaisons fallacieuses. Les données contenues dans les tableaux se rapportent à l'année civile pour laquelle elles sont présentées, sauf exceptions. Ces exceptions sont affichées sur le site Web de la base de données des principaux agrégats des comptes nationaux (http://unstats.un.org/unsd/snaama/notes.asp). Les chiffres présentés sont les estimations et révisions les plus récentes disponibles au moment de leur établissement. En général, les chiffres de l'année la plus récente doivent être considérés comme provisoires. Les sommes des composantes des tableaux ne correspondent pas nécessairement aux totaux indiqués en raison des arrondis.

Tableau 13: Produit intérieur brut et produit intérieur brut par habitant

Ce tableau présente le produit intérieur brut (PIB) et le PIB par habitant en dollars des États-Unis aux prix courants, le PIB à prix constants de 2005 et les taux de croissance réels correspondants. Les tableaux sont destinés à faciliter les comparaisons internationales des niveaux de revenu générés par la production. Les données et les estimations officielles du PIB total et du PIB par habitant aux prix courants sont converties en dollars des États-Unis, tandis que celles du PIB total à prix constants sont converties aux prix de 2005 avant conversion en dollars aux taux de change en vigueur en 2005. La méthode de conversion en dollars des États-Unis est décrite dans le document sur la méthodologie de la base de données des principaux agrégats des comptes nationaux (http://unstats.un.org/unsd/snaama/methodology.pdf). Pour les comparaisons entre pays sur la durée, il est plus approprié d'utiliser les taux de croissance à prix constants du tableau, qui représentent mieux les tendances du PIB total dans les comparaisons entre pays et entre groupes de pays. Le taux de croissance indiqué dans le tableau est calculé comme la moyenne géométrique des taux de croissance annuelle exprimés en pourcentages pour les années.

Tableau 14: Valeur ajoutée brute par type d'activité économique

Ce tableau présente les parts des composantes de la valeur ajoutée brute aux prix courants par type d'activité économique.

Secteur	Composé de (selon la nomenclature CITI 3)
Agriculture	Agriculture, chasse, sylviculture et pêches (CITI A-B)
Industrie	Activités extractives, activités de fabrication, production et distribution d'électricité, de gaz et d'eau (CITI C-E) Construction (CITI F)
Services	Commerce de gros et de détail; réparation de véhicules automobiles, de motocycles et de biens personnels et domestiques, hôtels et restaurants (CITI G-H) Transports, entreposage et communications (CITI I) Autres activités, y compris intermédiation financière, immobilier, location et activités de services aux entreprises, administration publique et défense, sécurité sociale obligatoire, éducation, santé et action sociale, autres activités de services collectifs, sociaux et personnels, ménages privés employant du personnel domestique (CITI J-P).

Chapitre VIII: Finances

Des informations détaillées et les chiffres courants concernant le tableau 12 figurent dans *Statistiques financières internationales*, une publication du Fonds monétaire international (voir aussi http://elibrary-data.imf.org) et dans le *Bulletin mensuel de statistique des Nations Unies*.

Tableau 15: Résumé de la balance des paiements

La balance des paiements peut être décrite d'une façon générale comme l'enregistrement des transactions économiques internationales d'une économie. Elle présente : a) les transactions en biens, services et revenus entre une économie et le reste du monde, b) les changements de propriété et les autres changements des avoirs de cette économie en or monétaire, droits de tirage spéciaux (DTS) et en créances et engagements envers le reste du monde, et c) les transferts sans contrepartie et les écritures de contrepartie nécessaires pour équilibrer au sens comptable les écritures au titre des transactions et changements susmentionnés qui ne s'annulent pas mutuellement. Les données de la balance des paiements sont présentées sur la base de la méthodologie et de la présentation de la sixième édition du *Manuel de la balance des paiements* (MBP6), publiée par le Fonds monétaire international en novembre 2013. Le MBP6 incorpore plusieurs modifications majeures pour tenir compte des évolutions du commerce international et de la finance internationale au fil des années, et de mieux harmoniser la méthodologie de la balance des paiements du Fonds avec celle du Système de comptes nationaux 2008 (SCN 2008). Les définitions détaillées concernant le contenu des catégories fondamentales de la balance des paiements sont données dans le *Manuel de la balance des paiements* (sixième édition).

De brèves notes explicatives sont données ci-dessous pour clarifier la portée des principaux éléments.

Le compte des transactions courantes enregistre toutes les transactions de la balance des paiements couvrant les exportations et les importations de biens et de services, les revenus et les transferts courants entre les résidents d'un pays et des non-résidents.

Le compte de capital, n.i.a. porte principalement sur les transferts de capital liés à l'acquisition d'un actif fixe autres que les transactions relatives à l'annulation de la dette, plus la cession d'actifs non financiers non produits, et les transferts de capital liés à la cession d'actifs fixes par le donateur ou au financement de la formation de capital par le récipiendaire, plus l'acquisition d'actifs non financiers non produits.

Le compte d'opérations financières, n.i.a. représente le solde net de l'investissement direct, de l'investissement de portefeuille et des autres transactions d'investissement.

Les réserves sont la somme des transactions sur actifs de réserve, les engagements constituant des avoirs de réserve pour les autorités étrangères, le financement exceptionnel et l'utilisation des crédits du FMI.

Tableau 16: Cours des changes

Les taux des changes sont exprimés par le nombre d'unités de monnaie nationale pour un dollar des Etats-Unis. Les taux de change sont classés en deux catégories, qui dénotent le rôle des autorités dans l'établissement des taux de change et/ou la multiplicité des taux de change dans un pays. Par taux du marché, on entend les taux de change déterminés essentiellement par les forces du marché; le taux officiel est un taux de change établi par les autorités, parfois selon des dispositions souples. Pour les pays qui continuent à mettre en œuvre des régimes de taux de change multiples, les taux sont désignés par les appellations suivantes: "taux principal", "taux secondaire" et "taux tertiaire". Sauf indication contraire, le tableau indique des taux de fin de période et les moyennes sur la période, des taux de change du marché ou des taux de change officiels.

Chapitre IX: Marché du travail

Une collection complète de données comparables sur la population active et les sujets connexes est disponible sous la forme des *Indicateurs clé du marché du travail* (KILM) publiés par l'Organisation internationale du Travail (OIT), et mis à jour tous les deux ans. Des données plus contemporaines sont accessibles sur ILOSTAT (www.ilo.org/ilostat), le dépôt de données de l'OIT, qui publie des données annuellement, trimestriellement ou mensuellement à mesure de leur communication par les pays mais sans procéder à toutes les vérifications de leur cohérence ni inclure toutes les sources utilisées par les KILM. Pour diverses raisons, les définitions nationales de l'emploi et du chômage diffèrent souvent des définitions internationales normalisées recommandées, ce qui limite la comparabilité internationale. Les comparaisons entre pays se trouvent en outre compliquées par la diversité des systèmes de collecte de données utilisés pour recueillir des informations sur les personnes employées et les chômeurs. Le site Web d'ILOSTAT offre une description complète de la méthodologie employée pour établir les séries sur la main-d'œuvre.

Tableau 17: Taux d'activité et taux de chômage

Le taux de participation à la population active est calculé en exprimant le nombre de personnes de la population active sous forme de pourcentage de la population en âge de travailler. La population active est la somme du nombre de personnes employées et du nombre de personnes sans emploi (voir les Recommandations internationales en vigueur sur les statistiques du travail de l'OIT). La population en âge de travailler est la population d'âge supérieur à un certain seuil, prescrit pour la mesure des caractéristiques économiques. Les données concernent le groupe des personnes de 15 ans et plus et reposent sur les estimations modélisées de l'OIT, sauf indication contraire en note de bas de page.

La définition du chômage inclut les personnes en âge de travailler qui, au cours d'une certaine période, étaient :

a) « Sans emploi », c'est-à-dire sans emploi rémunéré ou indépendant;

b) « Disponibles », c'est-à-dire libres de contracter un emploi rémunéré ou de pratiquer un emploi indépendant au cours de la période de référence; et

c) « À la recherche d'un emploi », c'est-à-dire qui ont pris des mesures déterminées pour trouver un emploi rémunéré ou indépendant au cours de la période spécifiée

Ne sont pas considérées comme sans emploi :

a) Les personnes qui ont l'intention d'établir leur propre activité ou exploitation agricole, mais n'ont pas encore pris les dispositions nécessaires à cet effet et ne recherchent pas un emploi en vue d'une rémunération ou d'un profit;

b) Les anciens travailleurs familiaux non rémunérés qui n'ont pas d'emploi et ne sont pas à la recherche d'un emploi pour rémunération ou profit.

Les séries représentent généralement le nombre total des personnes au chômage complet ou temporairement mises à pied. Les données exprimées en pourcentages, lorsqu'elles figurent dans le tableau, sont calculées en comparant le nombre des chômeurs au total des membres du groupe de la population active sur lequel les données du chômage sont basées.

Tableau 18: Emploi par activité économique

Le tableau de l'emploi présente, exprimée en pourcentages, la répartition des personnes employées par activité économique, conformément à la Classification internationale type, par industrie, de toutes les branches d'activité économique (CITI) version 4.

Chapitre X: Indices des prix et de la production

Tableau 19: Indices de la production agricole

L'agriculture désigne la production de tous les produits de culture et d'élevage. L'indice des produits alimentaires comprend les produits qui sont considérés comme comestibles et qui contiennent des éléments nutritifs. Les indices de la production agricole et de la production alimentaire sont calculés par la formule de Laspeyres avec comme période de base les années 2004-2006. Le choix d'une période de base de plusieurs années permet de réduire l'incidence des fluctuations annuelles de la production agricole sur les indices de cette période. Les quantités de chaque denrée produites sont pondérées par la moyenne nationale des prix à la production pour la période 2004-2006 et sommées pour chaque année. Les indices reposent sur les données de la production d'une année civile. Ceux-ci peuvent différer dans certains cas de ceux effectivement produits et publiés par les pays eux-mêmes en raison de différences dans les concepts, la couverture, les coefficients de pondération et les méthodes de calcul. On s'efforce d'estimer ces différences méthodologiques pour obtenir une meilleure comparabilité internationale des données. Des données détaillées sur la production agricole sont publiées par la FAO dans son *Annuaire statistique*.

Chapitre XI: Commerce international des marchandises

Préparé par la Division de statistique du Département des affaires économiques et sociales du Secrétariat des Nations Unies, l'*Annuaire statistique du commerce international* (ITSY) offre un aperçu des tendances récentes du commerce de biens et de services de la plupart des pays et régions du monde. L'*Annuaire*, voir http://comtrade.un.org/pb/, est publié en deux volumes; le Volume I est établi plus tôt dans l'année pour présenter un aperçu préliminaire du commerce international de marchandises de l'année précédente; le Volume II, publié généralement six mois plus tard, contient des tableaux détaillés qui présentent le commerce international par produit et 11 tableaux du commerce mondial couvrant les valeurs commerciales et les indices. Le Volume II contient également des versions actualisées des tableaux du commerce mondial. Les tableaux de cet *Annuaire* sont également mis à jour mensuellement dans le Bulletin mensuel de statistique des Nations Unies et sur le site des statistiques du commerce, voir http://unstats.un.org/unsd/trade/data/tables.asp#annual.

Les statistiques présentées dans cet *Annuaire* sont établies par les autorités statistiques nationales de façon largement conforme aux concepts et définitions des statistiques du commerce international de marchandises recommandés par les Nations Unies en 2010 (IMTS 2010). En fonction des parties du territoire économique incluses dans le territoire statistique, le système d'établissement des données du commerce adopté par un pays (son système de commerce) sera appelé général ou spécial.

Système de commerce général	Le territoire statistique coïncide avec le territoire économique. Il est donc recommandé que le territoire statistique d'un pays qui applique le système de commerce général englobe tous les éléments territoriaux applicables. Dans ce cas, les importations comprennent les biens qui entrent dans la zone de libre circulation, les installations de perfectionnement actif, les zones franches industrielles, les entrepôts sous douane ou les zones franches commerciales, et les exportations comprennent les biens qui quittent ces éléments territoriaux.
Système de commerce spécial	(définition stricte) Le territoire statistique ne comprend qu'une partie spécifique du territoire économique, de sorte que certains flux de marchandises auxquels les recommandations IMTS 2010 sont applicables ne sont inclus ni dans les statistiques d'importation ni dans les statistiques d'exportation du pays déclarant. La définition stricte du système de commerce spécial est utilisée lorsque le territoire statistique ne comprend que la zone de libre circulation, c'est-à-dire la partie dans laquelle les marchandises « peuvent être écoulées sans restriction douanière ». Par conséquent, dans ce cas, les importations ne comprennent que les marchandises qui entrent dans la zone de libre circulation du pays déclarant et les exportations ne comprennent que les marchandises qui quittent la zone de libre circulation du pays déclarant .
	(définition assouplie) a) les marchandises qui entrent dans un pays aux fins du perfectionnement actif ou en ressortent après, ainsi que b) les marchandises qui entrent dans une zone franche industrielle ou en sortent, sont aussi enregistrées et incluses dans les statistiques du commerce international de marchandises.

Tous les pays communiquent en général leurs données détaillées du commerce de marchandises conformément au Système harmonisé de désignation et de codification des marchandises (SH) et les données correspondent à la Classification type pour le commerce international (CTCI, rév. 3), dans laquelle elles sont ensuite présentées. Les données se réfèrent à des années civiles; cependant, pour les pays qui communiquent leurs données selon une autre année de référence, les données sont présentées dans l'année qui couvre la plus grande partie de l'année de référence utilisée par le pays.

Les valeurs FOB comprennent la valeur transactionnelle des marchandises et la valeur des services fournis pour livrer les marchandises à la frontière du pays exportateur. Les valeurs CIF comprennent la valeur transactionnelle des marchandises, la valeur des services fournis pour livrer les marchandises à la frontière du pays exportateur et la valeur des services fournis pour livrer les marchandises depuis la frontière du pays exportateur jusqu'à la frontière du pays importateur. De ce fait, les données de la valeur statistique des marchandises importées sont présentées dans le format CIF et celles de la valeur statistique des marchandises exportées dans le format FOB.

La conversion des valeurs libellées en monnaies nationales en dollars des États-Unis s'effectue au moyen de facteurs de conversion de devises fondés sur les taux de change officiels. Les valeurs libellées en monnaies sujettes à des fluctuations sont converties en dollars des États-Unis au moyen de taux de change moyens pondérés calculés spécialement à cette fin. Le taux de change moyen pondéré d'une monnaie donnée pour une année donnée est donné par les facteurs composants mensuels, fournis par le Fonds monétaire international dans sa publication *Statistiques financières internationales*, pondérés par la valeur du commerce concerné pour chaque mois; les facteurs mensuels sont les taux de change (ou les taux moyens simples) en vigueur au cours de ce mois. Ces facteurs sont appliqués aux importations et aux exportations totales et au commerce de chaque produit avec chaque pays.

Tableau 20: Total des importations, des exportations et balance commerciale

Les données des importations totales et des exportations totales des pays (ou régions) présentées dans ce tableau proviennent principalement des *Statistiques financières internationales* publiées mensuellement par le Fonds monétaire international (FMI) mais aussi d'autres sources comme les publications et les sites web nationaux et le Questionnaire du *Bulletin mensuel de statistique* des Nations Unies, voir l'*Annuaire statistique du commerce international* pour plus de détails. Les données manquantes sont estimées afin de parvenir à des totaux régionaux mais ne sont pas présentées. La procédure d'estimation est automatisée au moyen des taux de croissance en glissement annuel trimestriels pour l'extrapolation des données trimestrielles manquantes (sauf si les données trimestrielles peuvent être estimées au moyen des données mensuelles disponibles au cours du trimestre). Les facteurs de conversion appliqués aux données de ce tableau sont publiés trimestriellement dans le *Bulletin mensuel de statistique* des Nations Unies et sont aussi disponibles sur le site Web des statistiques du commerce de l'ONU : http://unstats.un.org/unsd/trade/data/tables.asp#annual.

Table 21: Principaux partenaires commerciaux

Les chiffres sur les principaux partenaires commerciaux montrent les trois plus grands partenaires commerciaux (les pays de dernière destination et d'origine ou de provenance) dans les transactions du commerce international de marchandises. Dans certains cas un partenaire privilégié est présenté (zones nca, abris fortifiés, etc.). Les zones ni compris ailleurs (zones nca) sont utilisées (a) pour le commerce de faible valeur, (b)si le partenaire choisi est inconnu ou si une erreur a été commise en choisissant le partenaire et (c) pour des raisons de confidentialité. Si un emplacement géographique précis peut être identifie dans zones nca, elles sont alors enregistrées en conséquence (par exemple, Asie nca). Les abris fortifiés sont des magasins de navires et d'aéronefs, qui consistent pour la plupart de combustibles et de denrées alimentaires. Les zones franches appartiennent au territoire économique et géographique d'un pays et non à leurs territoires douaniers. Aux fins des statistiques sur le commerce les opérations entre les territoires douaniers et les zones franches sont enregistrées, si le pays déclarant utilise le Système de Commerce Spécial. Les zones franches peuvent être des zones franches commerciales (boutiques hors taxes) ou des zones franches industrielles. Les données sont exprimées en pourcentage des exportations totales et des importations totales d'un pays, zone ou partenaire privilégié.

Chapitre XII: Énergie

L'*Annuaire statistique de l'énergie* (consultable sur le site http://unstats.un.org/unsd/energy/yearbook) est une collection complète de statistiques internationales de l'énergie qui couvre plus de 220 pays et régions. L'*Annuaire* est préparé par la Division de statistique du Département des affaires économiques et sociales du Secrétariat des Nations Unies. L'*Annuaire* est produit chaque année avec les nouvelles données disponibles sur la production d'énergie, le commerce, les variations de stocks, les réserves et la consommation de tous les pays et régions, et une série historique remontant à 1950 est disponible. Les données sont établies essentiellement à partir du questionnaire annuel sur l'énergie diffusé par la Division de statistique des Nations Unies et complétées par des publications statistiques officielles nationales, ainsi que des publications des organisations internationales et régionales. Lorsque les données officielles ne sont pas disponibles ou ne sont pas cohérentes, la Division de statistique établit des estimations en s'appuyant sur des éléments d'origine gouvernementale, professionnelle ou commerciale.

Les données se réfèrent à l'année civile, sauf celles des pays suivants qui se rapportent à l'exercice budgétaire : Afghanistan et Iran (République islamique d') – commençant le 21 mars de l'année indiquée; Australie, Bangladesh, Bhoutan, Égypte (électricité seulement pour ces deux derniers pays), Népal – finissant en juin de l'année indiquée; Pakistan – commençant en juillet de l'année indiquée; Inde, Myanmar et Nouvelle-Zélande – commençant en avril de l'année indiquée. Les données exprimées par habitant utilisent comme dénominateur les données démographiques de la Division de la population de l'Organisation des Nations Unies.

Tableau 22: Production, commerce et fourniture d'énergie

Les données sont présentées en pétajoules (ou en gigajoules par habitant), unités auxquelles chaque produit énergétique est converti afin d'assurer l'uniformité et la comparabilité internationales des données. Pour convertir en joules les unités originelles, celles-ci (tonnes métriques, tonnes métriques d'équivalent pétrole, kilowattheures, mètres cubes) sont multipliées par des facteurs de conversion. Voir l'*Annuaire statistique de l'énergie* pour une liste des facteurs de conversion et une description détaillée des méthodes utilisées.

Les combustibles solides inclus dans la production commerciale d'énergie primaire sont l'anthracite, la lignite, la tourbe et le schiste bitumineux; les liquides comprennent le pétrole brut, les condensats de gaz naturel, les autres hydrocarbures, additifs et oxygénats, et les biocarburants liquides; les gaz comprennent le gaz naturel et la vapeur/chaleur primaire; et l'électricité comprend la production primaire d'électricité d'origine hydraulique, nucléaire, géothermique, éolienne, marémotrice, houlomotrice et solaire.

Les importations nettes (importations moins exportations et bunkers) et les variations des stocks font référence à toutes les formes d'énergie primaire et secondaire (y compris les produits intermédiaires). Dans les importations nettes, les bunkers font référence aux bunkers d'essence aviation, de carburéacteur et d'anthracite, de gazole/carburant diesel et de fiouls résiduels. Le commerce international de produits énergétiques repose sur le système du « commerce général », c'est-à-dire que toutes les marchandises entrant sur le territoire national d'un pays ou en sortant sont enregistrées comme importations ou exportations.

La consommation d'énergie comprend les formes primaires des combustibles solides, les importations nettes et les variations des stocks des combustibles secondaires; les liquides comprennent les produits pétroliers utilisés à des fins de production d'énergie y compris les produits intermédiaires, le gaz de raffinerie et le pétrole brut utilisé directement; les gaz comprennent la consommation de gaz naturel et de chaleur primaire, les importations nettes et les variations des stocks de gaz manufacturés; et l'électricité comprend la production primaire d'électricité et les importations nettes d'électricité. La consommation de certains produits pétroliers est négative en raison de l'exclusion des calculs des transferts entre produits. La consommation négative d'électricité est due à une production d'électricité primaire négligeable par rapport aux exportations nettes. Plus généralement, une consommation négative peut représenter une différence résiduelle ou statistique entre la production et les exportations lorsqu'un produit donné est principalement exporté.

Chapitre XIII: Environnement

Tableau 23: Terres

Les données relatives aux terres sont compilées par l'Organisation des Nations Unies pour l'alimentation et l'agriculture (FAO). Les définitions de la FAO en ce qui concerne les terres sont les suivantes:

Superficie totale des terres	Superficie totale, à l'exception des eaux intérieures. Les eaux intérieures désignent généralement les principaux fleuves et lacs.
Terres arables	Terres affectées aux cultures temporaires (les terres sur lesquelles est pratiquée la double culture ne sont comptabilisées qu'une fois); prairies temporaires à faucher ou à pâturer, jardins maraîchers ou potagers et terres en jachère temporaire (moins de cinq ans). Cette définition ne comprend pas les terres abandonnées du fait de la culture itinérante. Les données relatives aux terres arables ne peuvent être utilisées pour calculer la superficie des terres aptes à l'agriculture.
Cultures permanentes	Superficie des terres avec des cultures qui occupent la terre pour de longues périodes et qui ne nécessitent pas d'être replantées après chaque récolte, comme le cacao, le café et le caoutchouc. Cette catégorie comprend les terres plantées d'arbustes à fleurs, d'arbres fruitiers, d'arbres à noix et de vignes, mais ne comprend pas les terres plantées d'arbres destinés à la coupe.
Superficie forestière	Dans l'Évaluation des ressources forestières mondiales 2010, la FAO a défini les forêts comme suit : Terres occupant une superficie de plus de 0,5 hectares avec des arbres atteignant une hauteur supérieure à cinq mètres et un couvert arboré de plus de dix pour cent, ou avec des arbres capables d'atteindre ces seuils en situ. Sont exclues les terres à vocation agricole ou urbaine prédominante.
Sites importants pour la biodiversité terrestre dans les aires protégées	Les terres contribuant énormément à la persistance globale de la biodiversité mesurées en proportion entièrement couverte par des zones protégées désignées. Les données sont fondées sur un chevauchement entre les polygones pour les zones clés de la biodiversité provenant de la base des données mondiales sur les zones clés pour la biodiversité et les polygones pour les zones protégées provenant de la base des données mondiales sur les zones protégées. Les chiffres pour chaque région sont calculés comme la proportion de chaque zone clé pour la biodiversité couverte par des zones protégées, moyennés (c'est-à-dire, calculés comme la moyenne) à travers toutes les zones clés de la biodiversité dans la région.

Tableau 24: Espèces menacées

Les données relatives au nombre d'espèces menacées dans chaque groupe d'animaux et de plantes sont établies par l'Union internationale pour la conservation de la nature et de ses ressources (UICN)/ Commission de sauvegarde des espèces (CSE) et publiées dans la liste rouge des espèces menacées de l'UICN. Cette liste fournit le catalogue des espèces considérées comme menacées au niveau mondial. Le nombre d'espèces menacées dans un pays donné change au cours des années pour diverses raisons, entre autres :

- La disponibilité d'informations nouvelles permet de raffiner l'évaluation (de confirmer par exemple que l'espèce est ou n'est pas présente dans un pays donné, que l'espèce est ou n'est pas menacée, etc.);
- L'évolution de la taxonomie (par exemple ce qu'on reconnaissait auparavant comme une certaine espèce est à présent réparti entre plusieurs espèces distinctes, ou fusionné avec une autre espèce);
- Les corrections (par exemple l'évaluation précédente peut avoir omis d'inscrire un pays donné dans la liste appropriée ou avoir inclus un pays donné par erreur);
- Changement de statut réel (par exemple la situation d'une espèce peut s'être réellement détériorée ou améliorée et l'espèce avoir par conséquent été incorporée aux catégories menacées ou en avoir été retirée).

Les catégories utilisées dans la Liste rouge sont les suivantes : espèce éteinte, éteinte à l'état sauvage, gravement menacée d'extinction; menacée d'extinction, vulnérable, quasi menacée et données insuffisantes.

Tableau 25: Estimations des émissions de CO2

Les données sur les émissions de dioxyde de carbone (CO_2) proviennent du « Carbon Dioxide Information Analysis Centre » (CDIAC) du laboratoire national d'Oak Ridge aux États-Unis, voir http://cdiac.ornl.gov/. Les estimations des émissions de CO_2 du CDIAC sont calculées essentiellement à partir de statistiques de l'énergie des Nations Unies sur la consommation de combustibles liquides et solides et la consommation et le torchage de gaz, ainsi que des estimations de la production de ciment provenant du Bureau des Mines du Département de l'intérieur des États-Unis. Les émissions sont présentées dans le tableau en unités de 1 000 tonnes métriques de CO_2; pour convertir le CO_2 en carbone, il faut diviser les chiffres par 3,667. Tous les détails des procédures de calcul des émissions sont données dans "Global, Regional, and National Annual CO_2 Emissions Estimates from Fossil Fuel Burning, Hydraulic Cement Production, and Gas Flaring" ainsi que sur le site Web du CDIAC. Par rapport aux autres sources industrielles dont les émissions de CO_2 sont estimées, les données relatives aux activités de torchage des gaz sont rares et sporadiques. Dans les pays où les activités de torchage des gaz représentent une proportion considérable des émissions totales de CO_2, la nature sporadique des données de torchage des gaz peut aboutir à l'apparition de tendances aberrantes ou fallacieuses des émissions nationales de CO_2 sur la période couverte par le tableau.

Table 26: Services d'approvisionnement en eau et d'assainissement

Ces données sont estimées par le Programme commun OMS/UNICEF de suivi de l'approvisionnement en eau et de l'assainissement (JMP) s'appuyant sur les sources de pays disponibles, voir www.wssinfo.org pour en savoir davantage. La proportion de la population utilisant les services d'eau potable gérés de manière sûre est définie comme la population utilisant de meilleures sources d'eau potable (l'indicateur utilise pour le suivi des objectifs du Millénaire pour le développement) qui sont situées sur les locaux, et disponibles en cas de besoin, et libre de toute contamination fécale et chimique prioritaire. Pour remplir les critères nécessaires pour un service d'eau potable gérés de manière sûre, les personnes doivent utiliser une source améliorée satisfaisant trois critères:

- Elle doit être accessible sur les locaux,
- L'eau doit être disponible en cas de besoin, et
- L'eau fournie doit être exempts de contamination.

Si la source améliorée ne répond à aucun de ces critères mais un voyage aller-retour pour chercher l'eau prend 30 minutes ou moins, elle sera alors classifiée comme un service d'eau potable de base. Si la recherche d'eau provenant d'une source améliorée dépasse 30 minutes elle sera catégorisée comme un service limite. Le JMP différencie également les populations utilisant des sources non améliorées comme les puits ou sources non protégés, et les populations qui boivent les eaux de surface recueillies directement d'une cour d'eau, d'un barrage, d'un lac, d'un ruisseau ou d'un canal d'irrigation.

Pour la proportion de la population utilisant « les services d'assainissement gérés de manière sûre », Il existe trois manières principales pour remplir les critères afin d'avoir un service d'assainissement géré de manière sûre. Les personnes devraient utiliser des installations d'assainissement améliorées qui ne sont pas partagées avec d'autres familles, et l'excréta produit doit soit être:

- traité et évacué in situ,
- Entreposé temporairement et ensuite vidé et transporté au traitement hors site, ou
- Transporté par le biais d'un égout a eaux usées et ensuite traite hors site.

Si les excréta provenant des installations d'assainissement améliorées ne sont pas gérés de manière sûre les personnes utilisant ces installations seront considérées comme ayant un service d'assainissement de base. Les personnes utilisant les installations améliorées qui sont partagées avec d'autres familles seront catégorisées comme ayant un service limite.

Chapitre XIV: Science et technologie

La recherche et le développement expérimental (R-D) englobe tous les travaux de création entrepris de façon systématique en vue d'accroître la somme des connaissances, y compris la connaissance de l'homme, de la culture et de la société, ainsi que l'utilisation de cette somme de connaissances pour de nouvelles applications. Pour tout renseignement complémentaire, voir le site Web de l'Institut de statistique de l'UNESCO www.uis.unesco.org.

Tableau 27: Personnel employé dans la recherche et le développement (R–D)

Les données présentées sur le personnel employé dans la recherche et le développement (R-D) sont compilées par l'Institut de statistique de l'UNESCO. Les données de certains pays ont été fournies à l'UNESCO par l'OCDE, EUROSTAT et "la Red de Indicadores de Ciencia y Technología (RICYT)". Les définitions et classifications appliquées par l'UNESCO sont basées sur le Manuel de Frascati (OCDE, 2002).

Les trois catégories du personnel présentées sont définies comme suivant:

Les chercheurs	Les chercheurs sont des spécialistes travaillant à la conception ou à la création de connaissances, de produits, de procédés, de méthodes et de systèmes nouveaux et à la gestion des projets concernés. Les étudiants diplômés au niveau du doctorat (CITE niveau 8) ayant des activités de R-D sont considérés comme des chercheurs.
Techniciens et personnel assimilé	Personnes dont les tâches principales requièrent des connaissances et une expérience technique dans un ou plusieurs domaines de l'ingénierie, des sciences physiques et de la vie ou des sciences sociales et humaines. Ils participent à la R-D en exécutant des tâches scientifiques et techniques faisant intervenir l'application de principes et de méthodes opérationnelles, généralement sous le contrôle de chercheurs.
Autre personnel de soutien	les travailleurs, qualifiés ou non, et le personnel de secrétariat et de bureau participant à l'exécution des projets de R-D ou qui sont directement associés à l'exécution de tels projets.

Personnes physiques est le nombre total de personnes qui sont principalement ou partiellement affectées à la R-D. Ce dénombrement inclut les employés à 'temps plein' et les employés à 'temps partiel'. Équivalent temps plein (ETP) peut être considéré comme une année-personne. Ainsi, une personne qui consacre 30% de son temps en R&D et le reste à d'autres activités (enseignement, administration universitaire ou direction d'étudiants) compte pour 0.3 ETP en R&D. De façon analogue, si un employé travaille à temps plein dans un centre de R&D pendant six mois seulement, il compte pour 0.5 ETP.

Tableau 28: Dépenses intérieures brutes de recherche et développement (R–D)

Les données présentées sur les dépenses intérieures brutes de recherche et développement sont compilées par l'Institut de statistique de l'UNESCO. Les données de certains pays ont été fournies à l'UNESCO par l'OCDE, EUROSTAT et "la Red de Indicadores de Ciencia y Technología (RICYT)". La dépense intérieure brute de R-D (DIRD) est la dépense totale intra-muros afférente aux travaux de R-D exécutés sur le territoire national pendant une période donnée. Elle comprend la R-D exécutée sur le territoire national et financée par l'étranger mais ne tient pas compte des paiements effectués à l'étranger pour des travaux de R-D. Les sources de financement pour la DIRD sont classées selon les cinq catégories suivantes:

Les fonds des entreprises	Les fonds alloués à la R-D par toutes les firmes, organismes et institutions dont l'activité première est la production marchande de biens ou de services (autres que dans le secteur d'enseignement supérieur) en vue de leur vente au public, à un prix qui correspond à la réalité économique, et les institutions privées sans but lucratif principalement au service de ces entreprises, organismes et institutions.
Les fonds de l'Etat	Les fonds fournis à la R-D par le gouvernement central (fédéral), d'état ou par les autorités locales. Ceci inclut tous les ministères, bureaux et autres organismes qui fournissent, sans normalement les vendre, des services collectifs autres que d'enseignement supérieur, qu'il n'est pas possible d'assurer de façon pratique et économique par d'autres moyens et qui, de surcroît, administrent les affaires publiques et appliquent la politique économique et sociale de la collectivité. Les fonds des entreprises publiques sont compris dans ceux du secteur des entreprises. Les fonds de l'Etat incluent également les institutions privées sans but lucratif contrôlées et principalement financées par l'Etat.
Les fonds de l'enseignement supérieur	Les fonds fournis à la R-D par les établissements d'enseignement supérieur tels que toutes les universités, grandes écoles, instituts de technologie et autres établissements postsecondaires, ainsi que tous les instituts de recherche, les stations d'essais et les cliniques qui travaillent sous le contrôle direct des établissements d'enseignement supérieur ou qui sont administrés par ces derniers ou leur sont associés
Les fonds d'institutions privées sans but lucratif	Les fonds destinés à la R-D par les institutions privées sans but lucratif non marchandes au service du public, ainsi que par les simples particuliers ou les ménages.

Les fonds étrangers	Les fonds destinés à la R-D par les institutions et les individus se trouvant en dehors des frontières politiques d'un pays, à l'exception des véhicules, navires, avions et satellites utilisés par des institutions nationales, ainsi que des terrains d'essai acquis par ces institutions, et par toutes les organisations internationales (à l'exception des entreprises), y compris leurs installations et leurs activités à l'intérieur des frontières d'un pays

Il faut éviter de comparer les chiffres absolus concernant les dépenses de R-D d'un pays à l'autre. On ne pourrait procéder à des comparaisons détaillées qu'en convertissant en une même monnaie les sommes libellées en monnaie nationale au moyen de taux de change spécialement applicables aux activités de R-D. Les taux de change officiels ne reflètent pas toujours le coût réel des activités de R-D, et les comparaisons établies sur la base de ces taux peuvent conduire à des conclusions trompeuses; toutefois, elles peuvent être utilisées pour donner une idée de l'ordre de grandeur.

Tableau 29: Brevets

Les brevets sont accordés par un office national des brevets ou un office régional qui accomplit cette tâche pour de nombreux pays, comme l'Office européen des brevets et l'African Regional Intellectual Property Organisation. Dans le cadre de ces systèmes régionaux, le requérant demande que son invention soit protégée dans un ou plusieurs pays, et il appartient à chaque pays d'accorder ou non la protection d'un brevet sur son territoire. Le Traité de coopération en matière de brevets (PCT), administré par l'Organisation mondiale de la propriété intellectuelle (OMPI) prévoit le dépôt d'une demande de brevet international unique dotée de la même validité que des demandes nationales déposées dans les pays désignés. Les données comprennent l'intensité de l'activité des résidents, les brevets délivrés et les brevets en vigueur. L'intensité du dépôt de brevets est présentée comme le nombre de demandes de brevet déposées par des résidents par million d'habitants, tandis que le dépôt d'une demande de propriété intellectuelle (PI) par des résidents fait référence à une demande déposée par un requérant auprès de son office national de la propriété intellectuelle. Les statistiques des droits de propriété intellectuelle (enregistrement) reposent sur le même concept. L'expression « en vigueur » désigne un brevet ou une autre forme de protection de la PI en cours de validité. Le pays d'origine sert à catégoriser les données de PI en PI résidente (intérieure) et non résidente (étrangère). La résidence du premier demandeur cité (ou inventeur) enregistré dans le document de PI (par exemple une demande de brevet ou de dépôt de marque) sert à classer les données de PI par pays d'origine. Les données sont établies et publiées par l'OMPI.

Chapitre XV: Tourisme et transport internationaux

Les données sur le tourisme international sont fournies par l'Organisation mondiale du tourisme (OMT) qui publie des renseignements détaillés sur le tourisme dans l'*Annuaire des statistiques du tourisme* ou le *Compendium des statistiques du tourisme*, voir www.unwto.org/statistics pour des informations plus complètes. Aux fins de l'établissement des statistiques, l'expression «visiteur international» décrit «toute personne qui se rend dans un pays autre que celui dans lequel il ou elle a son lieu de résidence habituelle, mais différent de son environnement habituel, pour une période de 12 mois au maximum, dans un but principal autre que celui d'y exercer une activité rémunérée». L'*Annuaire* et le *Compendium* de l'OMT comportent quatre séries distinctes, mais une seule est retenue pour inclusion dans le présent *Annuaire*, en fonction en général de l'ordre de priorité suivant afin de décrire au mieux le «visiteur international»;

Ordre	Code de la série	Nom de la série
1	TF	*Arrivées de touristes non résidents aux frontières nationales* désigne les visiteurs qui passent au moins une nuit dans un logement collectif ou privé dans le pays visité (exclut les visiteurs d'un jour)
2	VF	*Arrivées de visiteurs non résidents aux frontières nationales* désigne les visiteurs définis dans la série « TF » ainsi que les visiteurs d'un jour qui ne passent pas la nuit dans un logement collectif ou privé dans le pays visité
3	TCE	*Arrivées de touristes non résidents dans tous les types d'établissements d'hébergement*
4	THS	*Arrivées de touristes non résidents dans les hôtels et établissements similaires*

Ces chiffres ne comprennent pas les immigrants, les résidents frontaliers, les personnes domiciliées dans un pays ou une région et qui travaillent dans un pays ou une région limitrophe, les membres des forces armées et les diplomates et les représentants consulaires lorsqu'ils se rendent de leur pays d'origine au pays où ils sont en poste et vice-versa. Ne sont pas inclus non plus les voyageurs en transit qui n'entrent pas formellement dans le pays en faisant viser leur passeport, comme les passagers d'un vol en escale qui demeurent pendant un court laps de temps dans une zone distincte d'une aérogare ou les passagers d'un navire qui ne sont pas autorisés à débarquer. Cette catégorie inclut les passagers transférés directement d'une aérogare à une autre ou à un autre terminal. Les autres passagers en transit dans un pays sont classés comme visiteurs.

Tableau 30: Arrivées de touristes/visiteurs et dépenses touristiques

Les données relatives aux arrivées de visiteurs non résidents (ou internationaux) peuvent être obtenues de différentes sources. Dans certains cas, elles proviennent des statistiques frontalières tirées des registres administratifs (contrôles de police, de l'immigration, comptages du trafic routier et autres types de contrôle), des enquêtes statistiques aux frontières et des enregistrements d'établissements d'hébergement. Les totaux correspondent au nombre total d'arrivées depuis les régions indiquées dans le tableau. Lorsqu'une personne visite le même pays plusieurs fois dans l'année, un même nombre d'arrivées est enregistré. De même, si une personne visite plusieurs pays au cours d'un même voyage, son arrivée dans chaque pays est enregistrée séparément. On ne peut donc pas supposer que le nombre des arrivées soit égal au nombre de personnes qui voyagent.

Les dépenses associées à l'activité touristique des visiteurs sont traditionnellement identifiées au poste «Voyages» de la balance des paiements (BDP): dans le cas du tourisme dans le pays récepteur, les dépenses dans le pays de référence associées aux visiteurs non résidents sont enregistrées comme « crédits » dans la BDP et il s'agit de « recettes au titre des voyages». Le nouveau cadre conceptuel approuvé par la Commission de statistique des Nations Unies concernant la mesure de l'activité touristique à l'échelle macroéconomique (le compte satellite du tourisme) considère que la notion « industries et produits touristiques » inclut le transport de passagers. Par conséquent, une meilleure estimation des dépenses liées au tourisme par des visiteurs résidents et non résidents dans un scénario international serait, du point de vue de la BDP, la somme des valeurs du poste « Voyages » et du poste «Transport de passagers». Néanmoins, les utilisateurs doivent être conscients de ce que les estimations de la BDP comprennent, outre les dépenses associées aux visiteurs, celles liées à d'autres types d'individus. Les données publiées doivent permettre la comparabilité internationale et donc correspondre à celles publiées par le Fonds monétaire international et fournies par les banques centrales, les exceptions sont listées dans le *Compendium des statistiques du tourisme* et l'*Annuaire des statistiques du tourisme*, voir www.unwto.org/statistics pour des informations plus complètes.

Tableau 31: Aviation civile: trafic aérien régulier

Les données relatives au trafic total se rapportent aux services réguliers, intérieurs ou internationaux des compagnies de transport aérien enregistrées dans chaque pays. Les services réguliers comprennent aussi les vols supplémentaires nécessités par un surcroît d'activité des services réguliers et les vols préparatoires en vue de nouveaux services réguliers. Les données sont préparées par l'Organisation de l'aviation civile internationale (voir www.icao.int).

Les termes ci-après ont été utilisés dans le tableau ;

- Kilomètres parcours – le nombre de kilomètres parcours équivalent à la somme des produits du nombre de vols payants effectues sur chaque étape par la longueur de l'étape.
- Passagers transportés – pour calculer le nombre de passagers transportés, on compte chaque passager d'un vol donné (correspondant à un numéro de vol) une seule fois et non pour chacune des étapes de ce vol; toutefois, les passagers qui voyagent sur une étape internationale et sur une étape intérieure d'un même vol doivent être comptés à la fois comme passagers d'un vol intérieur et comme passagers d'un vol international.
- Passager-kilomètre réalisé – un passager-kilomètre est réalisé lorsqu'un passager est transporté sur une distance d'un kilomètre. Le nombre de passagers-kilomètre réalisées équivaut à la somme des produits du nombre de passagers payant transportés sur chaque étape par la longueur de l'étape. Le total obtenu est égal au nombre de kilomètres parcours par l'ensemble de passagers.
- Tonnes-kilomètres réalisées – la tonne-kilomètre est une unité de mesure qui correspond au déplacement d'une tonne métrique de charge payante sur un kilomètre. Les tonnes-kilomètres réalisées sont la somme des produits du nombre de tonnes de charge payante (passagers, fret, envois postaux) transportés sur chaque étape par la longueur de l'étape.

Chapitre XVI: Aide au développement

Tableau 32: Décaissements nets d'aide publique au développement aux bénéficiaires

Le tableau présente des estimations des flux de ressources financières à destination des pays bénéficiaires soit directement (aide bilatérale) soit par l'intermédiaire d'institutions multilatérales (aide multilatérale). Les institutions multilatérales comprennent le Groupe de la Banque mondiale, des banques régionales, les institutions financières de l'Union européenne et un certain nombre d'institutions, de programmes et de fonds d'affectation spéciale des Nations Unies. Les données ont été obtenues auprès du Comité d'aide au développement (CAD) de l'OCDE, auquel les pays membres communiquent des données sur les flux de ressources qu'ils mettent à la disposition de pays et territoires en développement, de pays et territoires en transition, et des institutions multilatérales. On trouvera davantage d'informations sur les définitions, les méthodes et les sources dans la publication de l'OCDE intitulée *Répartition géographique des ressources financières allouées aux pays en développement*, ainsi que sur le site http://stats.oecd.org/.

Tableau 33: Décaissements nets d'aide publique au développement par des donateurs

Le tableau présente les dépenses d'aide au développement des pays donateurs. Ce tableau inclut les contributions des donateurs aux institutions multilatérales; les totaux diffèrent donc de ceux du tableau 25, qui incluent les décaissements des institutions multilatérales.

* * *

Annex III

Conversion coefficients and factors

The metric system of weights and measures is employed in the *Statistical Yearbook.* In this system, the relationship between units of volume and capacity is: 1 litre = 1 cubic decimetre (dm^3) exactly (as decided by the 12th International Conference of Weights and Measures, New Delhi, November 1964).

Section A shows the equivalents of the basic metric, British imperial and United States units of measurements. According to an agreement between the national standards institutions of English-speaking nations, the British and United States units of length, area and volume are now identical, and based on the yard = 0.9144 metre exactly. The weight measures in both systems are based on the pound = 0.45359237 kilogram exactly (Weights and Measures Act 1963 (London), and *Federal Register announcement of 1 July 1959: Refinement of Values for the Yard and Pound* (Washington D.C.)).

Section B shows various derived or conventional conversion coefficients and equivalents.

Section C shows other conversion coefficients or factors which have been utilized in the compilation of certain tables in the *Statistical Yearbook*. Some of these are only of an approximate character and have been employed solely to obtain a reasonable measure of international comparability in the tables.

For a comprehensive survey of international and national systems of weights and measures and of units' weights for a large number of commodities in different countries, see *World Weights and Measures.*

Annexe III

Coefficients et facteurs de conversion

L'*Annuaire statistique* utilise le système métrique pour les poids et mesures. La relation entre unités métriques de volume et de capacité est: 1 litre = 1 décimètre cube (dm^3) exactement (comme fut décidé à la Conférence internationale des poids et mesures, New Delhi, novembre 1964).

La section A fournit les principaux équivalents des systèmes de mesure métrique, britannique et américain. Suivant un accord entre les institutions de normalisation nationales des pays de langue anglaise, les mesures britanniques et américaines de longueur, superficie et volume sont désormais identiques, et sont basées sur le yard = 0.9144 mètre exactement. Les mesures de poids se rapportent, dans les deux systèmes, à la livre (pound) = 0.45359237 kilogramme exactement (*Weights and Measures Act 1963* (Londres), et *Federal Register Announcement of 1 July 1959: Refinement of Values for the Yard and Pound* (Washington, D.C.)).

La section B fournit divers coefficients et facteurs de conversion conventionnels ou dérivés.

La section C fournit d'autres coefficients ou facteurs de conversion utilisés dans l'élaboration de certains tableaux de l'*Annuaire statistique.* Certains coefficients ou facteurs de conversion ne sont que des approximations et ont été utilisés uniquement pour obtenir un degré raisonnable de comparabilité sur le plan international.

Pour une étude d'ensemble des systèmes internationaux et nationaux de poids et mesures, et d'unités de poids pour un grand nombre de produits dans différents pays, voir *World Weights and Measures.*

A. Equivalents of metric, British imperial and United States units of measure

A. Equivalents des unités métriques, britanniques et des Etats-Unis

Metric units Unités métriques	British imperial and US equivalents Equivalents en mesures britanniques et des Etats-Unis		British imperial and US units Unités britanniques et des Etats-Unis	Metric equivalents Equivalents en mesures métriques	
Length — Longueur					
1 centimetre – centimètre (cm)	0.3937008	inch	1 inch	2.540	cm
1 metre – mètre (m)	3.280840	feet	1 foot	30.480	cm
	1.093613	yard	1 yard	0.9144	m
1 kilometre – kilomètre (km)	0.6213712	mile	1 mile	1609.344	m
	0.5399568	international nautical mile	1 international nautical mile	1852.000	m
Area — Superficie					
1 square centimetre – (cm^2)	0.1550003	square inch	1 square inch	6.45160	cm^2
1 square metre – (m^2)	10.763910	square feet	1 square foot	9.290304	dm^2
	1.195990	square yards	1 square yard	0.83612736	m^2
1 hectare – (ha)	2.471054	acres	1 acre	0.4046856	ha
1 square kilometre – (km^2)	0.3861022	square mile	1 square mile	2.589988	km^2
Volume					
1 cubic centimetre – (cm^3)	0.06102374	cubic inch	1 cubic inch	16.38706	cm^3
1 cubic metre – (m^3)	35.31467	cubic feet	1 cubic foot	28.316847	dm^3
	1.307951	cubic yards	1 cubic yard	0.76455486	m^3
Capacity — Capacité					
1 litre (l)	0.8798766	British imperial quart	1 British imperial quart	1.136523	l
	1.056688	U.S. liquid quart	1 U.S. liquid quart	0.9463529	l
	0.908083	U.S. dry quart	1 U.S. dry quart	1.1012208	l
1 hectolitre (hl)	21.99692	British imperial gallons	1 British imperial gallon	4.546092	l
	26.417200	U.S. gallons	1 U.S. gallon	3.785412	l
	2.749614	British imperial bushels	1 imperial bushel	36.368735	l
	2.837760	U.S. bushels	1 U.S. bushel	35.239067	l

Metric units Unités métriques	British imperial and US equivalents Equivalents en mesures britanniques et des Etats-Unis		British imperial and US units Unités britanniques et des Etats-Unis	Metric equivalents Equivalents en mesures métriques	
Weight or mass — Poids					
1 kilogram (kg)	35.27396	av. ounces	1 av. ounce	28.349523	g
	32.15075	troy ounces	1 troy ounce	31.10348	g
	2.204623	av. pounds	1 av. pound	453.59237	g
			1 cental (100 lb.)	45.359237	kg
			1 hundredweight (112 lb.)	50.802345	kg
1 ton – tonne (t)	1.1023113	short tons	1 short ton (2 000 lb.)	0.9071847	t
	0.9842065	long tons	1 long ton (2 240 lb.)	1.0160469	t

B. Various conventional or derived coefficients

Air transport

1 passenger-mile = 1.609344 passenger kilometre
1 short ton-mile = 1.459972 tonne-kilometre
1 long ton-mile = 1.635169 tonne kilometre

Electric energy

1 Kilowatt (kW) = 1.34102 British horsepower (hp)
1.35962 cheval vapeur (cv)

C. Other coefficients or conversion factors employed in *Statistical Yearbook* tables

Roundwood

Equivalent in solid volume without bark.

Sugar

1 metric ton raw sugar = 0.9 metric ton refined sugar

For the United States and its possessions:
1 metric ton refined sugar = 1.07 metric tons raw sugar

Energy

1 metric ton peat = .325 metric ton of coal oil equivalent
1 ton oil equivalent = .4186 GJ or 11.63 MWh

B. Divers coefficients conventionnels ou dérivés

Transport aérien

1 voyageur (passager) – kilomètre = 0.621371 passenger-mile
1 tonne-kilomètre = 0.684945 short ton-mile
0.611558 long ton-mile

Energie électrique

1 British horsepower (hp) = 0.7457 kW
1 cheval vapeur (cv) = 0.735499 kW

C. Autres coefficients ou facteurs de conversion utilisés dans les tableaux de l'*Annuaire statistique*

Bois rond

Equivalences en volume solide sans écorce.

Sucre

1 tonne métrique de sucre brut = 0.9 tonne métrique de sucre raffiné

Pour les États-Unis et leurs possessions:
1 tonne métrique de sucre raffiné = 1.07 tonne métrique de sucre brut

Energie

1 tonne métrique d'équivalent charbon = 3.08 tonnes métrique de tourbe
1 GJ = 2.39 tonne d'équivalent pétrol or 1 MWh = .086 tonne métrique d'équivalent pétrol

Annex IV - Tables added, omitted and discontinued

A. Tables added

The present issue of the *Statistical Yearbook* includes the following tables which were not presented in the previous issue:

Table 3	Population growth and indicators of fertility and mortality (*previously* Selected indicators of life expectancy, childbearing, age dependency ratio and mortality)
Table 6	Ratio of girls to boys in primary, secondary and tertiary levels
Table 8	Teaching staff at the primary, secondary and tertiary levels
Table 16	Exchange rates
Table 20	Total imports, exports and balance of trade (*change of source*)
Table 21	Major Trading Partners
Table 23	Land
Table 26	Water supply and sanitation services (*previously* Water supply and sanitation coverage)
Table 27	Population employed in research and development (R&D)
Table 28	Gross domestic expenditure on research and development (R&D)
Table 31	Civil aviation: scheduled airline traffic

B. Tables omitted

The following tables which were presented in previous issues are not presented in the present issue. They will be updated in future issues of the *Yearbook* when new data become available:

- Cellular mobile telephone subscribers
- Consumer price indices
- Index of industrial production
- Internet usage
- Population in the capital city, urban and rural areas

Annexe IV - Tableaux ajoutés, supprimés et discontinués

A.Tableaux ajoutés
Dans ce numéro de l'Annuaire statistique, les tableaux suivants n'ont pas été présentés dans le numéro antérieur, et ont été ajoutés:

Tableau 3	Croissance démographique et indicateurs de fécondité et mortalité (*précédemment* Sélection d'indicateurs de l'espérance de vie, de la maternité, du ratio de dépendance)
Tableau 6	Personnel enseignant au niveau primaire, secondaire et supérieur
Tableau 8	Rapport filles/garçons dans l'enseignement primaire, secondaire et supérieur
Tableau 16	Cours des changes
Tableau 20	Total des importations, des exportations et balance commerciale (*changement de source*)
Tableau 21	Partenaire commercial principal
Tableau 23	Terres
Tableau 26	Services d'alimentation en eau potable et d'assainissement (*précédemment* Accès à l'eau et à l'assainissement)
Tableau 27	Population employé dans la recherche et le développement (R–D)
Tableau 28	Dépenses intérieures brutes de recherche et développement (R–D)
Tableau 31	Aviation civile: trafic aérien régulier

B. Tableaux supprimés
Les tableaux suivants qui ont été repris dans les éditions antérieures n'ont pas été repris dans la présente édition. Ils seront actualisés dans les futures livraisons de l'Annuaire à mesure que des données nouvelles deviendront disponibles:

- Abonnés au téléphone mobile
- Indices de la production industrielle
- Indices des prix à la consommation
- Population et taux de croissance dans les zones urbaines et capitales
- Utilisation de l'internet